THE NEW
CAVALCADE

The New
CAVALCADE

African American Writing from 1760 to the Present

Volume II

Edited by
ARTHUR P. DAVIS,
J. SAUNDERS REDDING,
and JOYCE ANN JOYCE

HOWARD UNIVERSITY PRESS
Washington, D.C., 1992

Howard University Press, Washington, D.C. 20008

Copyright © 1992 by Arthur P. Davis, J. Saunders Redding, and
Joyce Ann Joyce

Originally published as
Cavalcade: Negro American Writing from 1760 to the Present
Copyright © 1971 by
Arthur P. Davis and Saunders Redding

Manufactured in the United States of America

This book is printed on acid-free paper.

10 9 8 7 6 5 4 3 2 1

Library of Congress Cataloging-in-Publication Data

The New cavalcade : African American writing from 1760 to the present /
edited by Arthur P. Davis, J. Saunders Redding, and Joyce Ann Joyce.
     p.   cm.
     Rev. ed. of : Cavalcade. 1971.
     Includes bibliographical references and indexes.
     1. American literature—Afro-American authors.   2. Afro-Americans—
Literary collections.   I. Davis, Arthur Paul, 1904–   .   II. Redding, J.
Saunders (Jay Saunders), 1906–   .   III. Joyce, Joyce Ann, 1949–
IV. Title: Cavalcade.
PS508.N3N48   1991
810.8′0896073—dc20

Volume II
ISBN 0-88258-131-7, cloth
ISBN 0-88258-134-1, paperback
ISBN 0-88258-132-5, set, hardback
ISBN 0-88258-135-X, set, paperback

                                                     90-29285
                                                        CIP

To

J. SAUNDERS REDDING,

scholar, teacher, critic,

and

highly esteemed fellow-editor

CONTENTS

vii

PART 2
The African American Literary Revival:
The 1970s to the Present

PREFACE

The original *Cavalcade* was published in 1971 and was for a generation of students a popular text. Much has happened, however, in the field of African American literature since 1971. There has been a dramatic upsurge in publications by new authors; there has been a reaction to the black revolution, which climaxed during the late sixties and early seventies; there have been new and important national honors for African American writers; and perhaps most important of all, there has come into prominence a cadre of black female authors—authors who, in some cases, have brought to African American literature a new critical outlook. And there are other factors that make a new edition of *Cavalcade* necessary: the death of certain authors, a new type of critical approach, new works written by authors originally in the text, new sources of bibliography, and several other changes brought about by time. Because of the great number of changes that have occurred and because of the recent proliferation of African-American-related books, the editors felt it necessary to make the edition a two-volume text, which we are certain will make it more convenient for a year course in African American studies.

The purpose of this anthology is to provide a representative selection of as much as possible of the best prose and poetry written by African Americans since 1776. While it has been our primary aim to make these choices on the basis of literary merit, we have also tried to cover as many areas of black life in America as was consistent with our first objective. We believe that this collection gives a fairly comprehensive picture of the black experience in America for the past two hundred years.

In making our selections we have tried within reason to avoid duplicating the material in other anthologies. However, to avoid all of the selections in other works would be unwise; to do so would leave out of our book some of the best work done by black writers in America. Since there is a "classic" African American literature just as there is a classic canon of English or French or any other established literature, we inevitably have some duplications. But we also have included many works not found in other collections.

Whenever feasible, we have given whole works rather than excerpts. A few entries, however, have been far too long to include in their entirety in an anthology of this size, and we have used parts of the works—parts which we believe can stand alone. We have done the same for plays, and naturally we have used chapters from novels and autobiographies. In every case we have seen to it that the selection can stand alone and is fairly representative of the author's general matter and manner. Whenever we left out short sections of a work, we have indicated this omission with the conventional ellipses; for longer omissions, we have used ornaments. When novels or autobiographies have chapter titles, we have used them, noting the work from which the excerpt was taken. When there are no titles, we simply note the work from which the selection was taken.

This anthology is designed for use as a text in African American literature courses or as a supplementary text in American literature courses. The introductions to the six sections in volumes I and II provide, we believe, a background sufficient to give meaning and perspective to the offerings in each section. The bibliographical data at the end of the headnotes and in the "Selected Bibliography" should be helpful to student and teacher alike, serving, we hope, as springboards for additional study.

In preparing this volume, we have examined and consulted practically all of the anthologies, collections, and critical works on African American literature extant, and in some ways we are indebted to all of them. We wish, however, to acknowledge a special indebtedness to the following works: *The Negro in Literature and Art* (third edition) and *Early Negro American Writers* by Benjamin Brawley; *To Make a Poet Black* by J. Saunders Redding; *The Negro Author* by Vernon Loggins; *Dictionary of American Negro Biography*, edited by Rayford W. Logan and Michael R. Winston; *Dictionary of Literary Biography, Volume 33, Afro-American Fiction Writers After 1955*; *Dictionary of Literary Biography, Volume 41, Afro-American Poets Since 1955*; *Dictionary of Literary Biography, Volume 50, Afro-American Writers Before the Harlem Renaissance*; *Dictionary of Literary Biography, Volume 51, Afro-American Writers from the Harlem Renaissance to 1940*, all of which were edited by Trudier Harris and Thadious M. Davis.

An anthology of this size needs so much bibliographical, critical, and other kinds of help, from colleagues, fellow scholars, and friends, it is practically impossible to thank all of them here. We must, therefore, settle for a chosen few, especially those who have helped to bring out *The New Cavalcade*; among them Fay Acker, senior editor of the Howard University Press, who, through her guidance, made our job easier; Cynthia Lewis and Iris Eaton, also of Howard University Press, who handled the numerous permissions requests for both volumes of *The New Cavalcade*; Janell Walden

Agyeman, who researched information for the headnotes; Kamili Anderson, who prepared the bibliographies; Rhonda Williams and Lisa McCullough, who worked on headnotes; Professor Eugene Hammond and Janet Duncan of the University of Maryland; Kathy Johnson and Laurie Wilshusen of the University of Nebraska; and O. Rudolph Aggrey, director of the Howard University Press, who encouraged and supported, in every way possible, this project. We cannot thank individually all of the members of the famous Moorland-Spingarn Research Center who helped us almost daily for a long period. It is a great library with a highly efficient and helpful staff. We are also deeply indebted to Ethelbert E. Miller, supervisor of Howard University's African American Resource Center, for his help in securing source material for our book.

The reader will note that *The New Cavalcade* now has three editors rather than the original two, Arthur P. Davis (a professor of English who came from Virginia Union University to Howard University in 1944) and J. Saunders Redding (Ernest I. White Professor of American Studies and Humane Letters at Cornell University). Professor Redding died in 1988. Prior to his death, however, Professors Davis and Redding had decided to add a third editor, some scholar who had a deep knowledge about contemporary criticism and the recent great upsurge in publications by African American women. The new editor is Dr. Joyce A. Joyce, professor of English at the University of Nebraska. Professor Joyce's work complements the critical outlook of the two original editors, and she brings a contemporary balance to *The New Cavalcade*. Professor Redding's sensibility remains in the headnotes, introductions, and selections he chose. We are proud to have worked with him on this volume.

Arthur P. Davis

Joyce Ann Joyce

GENERAL INTRODUCTION

In this enlarged and updated revision of *Cavalcade* (orginially published in 1971), now *The New Cavalcade*, we have worked with a twofold purpose in mind: to show the evolution of African American writing as literary art and to provide the historical context that gives meaning to this writing as the expression of the black American's special experience in the nation. Our work covers the more than two hundred years of this literature's existence and is designed primarily for the student of African-American literature.

It has been our purpose to give not only a comprehensive account of the development of the literature, but, as far as humanly possible, a balanced and impartial account as well. No author has been left out because we disagree with his critical attitudes, his politics, or his stand on certain issues. By the same token, no author has been included because he happens to think as we do. Our selections, for example, represent practically every major African American critic from Alain Locke to Henry Louis Gates, Jr., and their varying and often strongly conflicting critical stands. *Our* criticism is found in the headnotes and chapter introductions.

The term "African American writing" as used in the title requires an explanation that goes beyond the obvious one of a body of writing by black Americans. Some Negro writers like William Stanley Braithwaite, Anne Spencer, and Frank Yerby "write like whites." The entire stock of their referents is white, Anglo-Saxon American derived. Most black American writers, however, create out of a dual consciousness: African and American. The writers are twin-rooted, and while one root is nourished by the myths, customs, culture, and values traditional in the Western world, the other feeds hungrily on the experiential reality of blackness. These writers have a special vision. They are persuaded by a special mission. In their work they combine the sermon and the liturgy, the reality and the dream, the *is* and the *ought to be*. Their writing is intended to appeal as much to the cognitive as to the affective side of man's being.

The question of what to call ourselves has become an issue for *The New Cavalcade*. Frankly, it has been an issue since Emancipation. The popular name at first was, seemingly, colored (as in NAACP), then came negro (with a lower case "n"), then Negro (with an upper case "N"), then Afro-American, then Black (with a capital "B"), then black (with a small "b"), and now African American.

When *Cavalcade* was originally published, *Negro* was still widely accepted, although after the social and literary changes of the sixties *black* gradually became the popular designation. For some older scholars and laypersons, *black* was an ugly term, and they hung on to *Negro* or used *Afro-American*. The editors of *The New Cavalcade* tended to use the term *African-American*; however, we felt free to use *Negro, black,* and *Afro-American*. In short, we have no desire to enter into any controversy over what to call ourselves. It is a decision that the people will make, as they have always done. We are simply trying, as stated previously, to give a comprehensive view of colored, Negro, black, Afro-American, and African American literature.

Though *The New Cavalcade* is comprehensive, the basis on which works were chosen for inclusion is primarily literary merit. This excluded the work of some writers who have a certain historical importance and who, therefore, are subjects of comment in the introductions. When other than an author's best is included, we do so because it represents a critical phase of his or her development.

For the purposes of a historical survey, it seemed sensible to divide the chronology of African American writing into six periods in two volumes. The periods in Volume I are designated and dated: "Pioneer Writers (1760–1830)"; "Freedom Fighters (1830–1865)"; "Accommodation and Protest (1865–1910)"; and "The New Negro Renaissance and Beyond (1910–1954)." The periods covered in Volume II are "Integration versus Black Nationalism (1954–1970)" and "New Directions (1970 to the Present)." Each period is prefaced by a critical introduction; there is a brief bio-bibliographical headnote for each author and a Selected Bibliography at the end of each volume.

The editors have exercised discretion in matters of spelling, punctuation, and capitalization in those works which were carelessly printed and edited in the eighteenth century and the early decades of the nineteenth. After that time, the editors have generally followed the texts as published.

Though the editors designed *The New Cavalcade* primarily as a book for students and scholars, they hope it is something more. They hope that it is a book that the general public may read with pleasure and profit.

A. P. D.

J. S. R.

J. A. J.

THE NEW
CAVALCADE

PART 1

Integration versus Black Nationalism: 1954 to ca. 1970

IN THE PERIOD beginning in 1954, three startling events set the political tone, established the emotional climate, and influenced the choice and treatment of literary themes. These events freshly emphasized the difference between the idealism expressed in the American creed and the actual practices of the American people. They also intensified and established the polarity that, since at least the beginning of the twentieth century, had seemed to draw many members of the black community into opposing clusters: in one group were the black nationalists, who clamored for complete separation of the races, and in the other group were integrationists and assimilationists, who appeared to favor absorption of the black minority into the value system and culture of the whites.

On May 17, 1954, the Supreme Court handed down a ruling in *Brown vs. Topeka Board of Education* that ultimately intended to do away with segregation in the public schools. The South's reluctance to comply with this decision generated a series of courtroom confrontations between the NAACP and the Department of Justice on the one hand, and local and state public school officials on the other.

On December 5, 1955, Rosa Parks, a black dressmaker and minor official in the local branch of the NAACP, refused to give up her seat to a white man on a crowded bus in Montgomery, Alabama. Since her refusal was contrary not only to custom, but also to law, Mrs. Parks was arrested. Reacting to Mrs. Parks's incarceration, the black community in Montgomery, under the leadership of a young black minister named Martin Luther King, Jr., organized a boycott of the buses. The black community in Montgomery, like black communities across the nation, had long resented legalized racial discrimination. Orchestrated boycotts all over the country lasted for a year and ended only when the Supreme Court ruled that state and local laws requiring racial segregation in public transportation were unconstitutional. The Montgomery bus boycott was the first in a series of activities that came to be called the "nonviolent protest movement."

On February 1, 1960, in Greensboro, North Carolina, four students from the predominantly black North Carolina Agricultural and Technical

3

College walked into the Woolworth store, sat down at the lunch counter, which served only whites, and asked to be waited on. Service was refused, but they stayed until closing time. The next day other students joined them, and the group of young black people occupied all the seats so that no one could be served. "Sit-ins" (as they came to be called), along with organized marches, became major tactics in the nonviolent protest movement.

This intense period of political activity was accompanied by a change in the black literary and cultural movements, referred to as the Black Arts Movement, which thrived between 1966 and 1969. The polarity of thought and mood in the black intellectual community was fixed between the integrationists/assimilationists and the nationalists and militants. The majority of the young black literary figures found the ideas of their older assimilationist peers inappropriate to the times in which they lived. Younger black writers began to redefine themselves outside the context of the traditional Euro-American tradition that they believed described the works of novelists such as Ralph Ellison, James Baldwin, William Melvin Kelley, and Ernest Gaines. Ishmael Reed and Clarence Major emerged as novelists whose first novels, published in the 1960s, defied Euro-American expectations of fiction. Because of the political climate of the times, a new generation of poets was more representative of radical thinking of the 1960s than the novelists who had published their first novels in the 1950s. Not only does the work of these new poets—Amiri Baraka (LeRoi Jones), Sonia Sanchez, Larry Neal, Carolyn Rodgers, Haki Madhubuti (Don L. Lee), Mari Evans, and others—vary politically from that of the novelists, but what was referred to as the new black poetry of the 1960s also differs significantly from the works of such older poets as Margaret Walker, Gwendolyn Brooks, Melvin B. Tolson, Margaret Esse Danner, and Robert Hayden. Influenced by the jazz musicians John Coltrane, Sonny Rollins, Ornette Coleman, Cecil Taylor, Pharaoh Sanders, and Sun Ra, the new black poets of the 1960s—those at the vanguard of what they referred to as the Black Aesthetic—turned inside themselves, to their black experiences, and to their black past for the technical innovations and spiritual awakening they needed to inform their poetry. These young writers, whom many referred to as "militant," consciously merged the political and the aesthetic in their attempt to liberate black Americans psychologically, sociologically, economically, and spiritually. The content and physical form of the black poetry that began to flourish in the 1960s reflect the young poets' use of black music and black speech as a framework for their art. This stylistic defiance enhanced the intensity of their racial themes. The aim of these young writers was to illuminate the uniqueness of the black people's history, to show white Americans that they were not like them, and to impress upon the black community the need to withdraw from what they saw as the malign influences of Euro-American political, social, and aesthetic entrapments. In order to appreciate the works of these new black writers, the reader had to disregard Euro-American, middle-class notions of what can and cannot be said in poetry and even of how a poem should look on the printed page. Although their works reflect the influence of some nontraditional white writers such as e. e. cummings, these young poets shunned the sonnet and other well-known poetic techniques.

In contrast to this new generation of writers, whose works were deliberately stylistically unintellectual and unacademic, writers such as Baldwin, Kelley, and Gaines, as representative of their generation, were far more traditional in the way they shaped their art. James Baldwin's first novel, *Go Tell It on the Mountain* (1953), which predates the black literary revolution, and much of his later work reflect an impressive balance between the Euro-American aesthetic tradition and black cultural themes. His *Tell Me How Long the Train's Been Gone* (1968) shows an even more intense awareness of the search for a cultural identity among the members of the American black community. While John O. Killens's *Youngblood* (1954) predates the new Black Arts Movement (1966–1969) and the black cultural revolution that accompanied this movement, his *And Then We Heard the Thunder* (1963) shares an affinity with some of the predominant themes that concern the young rebels: the frequent social and political emasculation of the black male, the corruptive influence of white value systems, the exhilarating and liberating feeling of black empowerment.

Although the form of their novels shares a strong affinity with the Euro-aesthetic tradition, William Melvin Kelley in *A Different Drummer* (1962) and Ernest Gaines in *The Autobiography of Miss Jane Pittman* (1971) create characters who dare to challenge the racist limitations imposed on African Americans by white society. Gaines's portrait of Miss Jane Pittman boldly drinking from the water fountain that is supposed to be used exclusively for whites emerges as the fictional parallel to Rosa Parks's refusal to give up her seat to a white man on the bus sixteen years earlier. Tucker Caliban, the protagonist of Kelley's *A Different Drummer*, is far more rebellious than Miss Pittman. Caliban, a farmer angered and exhausted by his rural racist environment, kills his fields with a truckload of salt, shoots his animals, burns his house, and moves his wife and baby out of the state that had been their home for years.

Kelley, a New Yorker, and Gaines, a southerner from New Orleans, emphasize the ritualistic customs that describe the interaction between blacks and whites in the South. Gaines, perhaps because he is a native of the environment about which he writes, captures the ambiguity of a racist environment in which blacks and whites in their interaction vacillate among hostility and love and comradeship. Despite the fact that *The Autobiography of Miss Jane Pittman* was published in 1971, two years after the cut off date for this part, its spirit reflects the resistance to racism identified with the civil rights movement and the political activities which gained momentum throughout the 1960s. Gaines, like Ellison in *Invisible Man* (1952) and James Weldon Johnson in *The Autobiography of an Ex-Coloured Man*, uses the oldest of the black literary forms, the autobiography, which has its origins in the slave narrative.

Ellison's unnamed narrator in *Invisible Man* moves from the South to the North through a series of episodes that illuminates his naiveté when faced with racial issues and the alienation that results from that naiveté. Johnson's much earlier narrator in *The Autobiography of an Ex-Coloured Man* analyzes his place in the world of other blacks and willfully chooses to pass for white, to marry a white woman, and to conceal his black identity from his daughter. Both novels along with *The Autobiography of Miss Jane Pittman* have as their predecessor the slave narrative or black autobiography that records the ills of slavery with the aim of hastening its abolition. Such ex-slave autobiographers as Harriet Jacobs and William Wells Brown believed that they were not free of slavery until all were free. Although the twentieth-century autobiographies are fictionalized narrations rather than personal stories (with the exception of works like Claude Brown's *Manchild in the Promised Land*), *Invisible Man* and *The Autobiography of Miss Jane Pittman* explore from dramatically different perspectives the question of black identity and the issue of the individual black person's conscious political activity and relationship to the African American community.

These modern autobiographies function as metaphorical representations of the effect racism has on African American consciousness. Although not as rebellious as Brown's *Manchild in the Promised Land* or *The Autobiography of Malcolm X*, *The Autobiography of Miss Jane Pittman* is more spiritually akin to these works than it is to *Invisible Man* and *The Autobiography of An Ex-Coloured Man*.

Along with James Baldwin's, Harold Cruse's, and Eldridge Cleaver's essays, the autobiographical writings of the 1960s emerge as some of the most widely read works of the period, perhaps because they stimulate the moral indignation in their readers as does their precursor, the slave narrative. Reflecting a time when blacks were quite candid and politically active in their confrontations with racism, both *The Autobiography of Malcolm X* and *Manchild in the Promised Land* are forthright revelations of the hidden life of the black ghetto, of internalized conflict, and of tragic alienation.

Writers such as Amiri Baraka, Larry Neal, and Sonia Sanchez—poets and aestheticians of the Black Arts Movement—welcomed a different kind of alienation from white society. They in no way identified with assimilationists who wanted their works accepted by the mainstream. Larry Neal's "The Black Arts Movement," published in 1968, the year of the assassination of Dr. Martin Luther King, Jr., serves as a manifesto for the young writers, who looked to their African heritage as the source of inspiration needed to eschew white middle-class values, create new themes, and shape new forms. In essence, the goal of the black aesthetic movement was to destroy what Neal and others referred to as the white aesthetic, the "Euro-American cultural sensibility," which had too heavily influenced the psyches of black writers. Rather than an art form reserved for the elite few, as suggested in T. S. Eliot's well-known essay "Tradition and the Individual Talent," poetry (and thus literature) should not be alienated from the community; black art should address the cultural and spiritual needs of the African American community. If the African American writer is going to play a "meaningful role in the transformation of society," Baraka—who was the first to use the term *Black Arts* in a positive sense—believed that the black writer must take his or her art to the masses. Thus in 1964 he, along with Johnny Moore, Clarence Reed, William Patterson, and Charles Patterson, began the Black Arts Repertory Theatre/School, whose participants presented plays, poetry readings, and concerts to black people on the streets of Harlem. Despite the fact that this endeavor lasted only three months, the idea became popular and black arts groups were initiated in various cities on the West Coast, and in New Jersey, in Detroit, in Washington, D.C., in New Orleans, in Philadelphia, and on a number of college campuses.

Two plays imbued with the revolutionary spirit of the Black Arts Theatre are Baraka's *Dutchman* and *The Slave*. Challenging and innovative, Baraka's plays attempt to destroy the middle-class values and psychological brainwashing implicitly applauded in mainstream drama. In both *Dutchman* and *The Slave* Baraka presents black male figures whose lives are shattered by their pursuit of the power associated with white society. Though the relationship between the black man and the white woman is the subject of poems by Sonia Sanchez, Carolyn Rodgers, Haki Madhubuti and others associated with the Black Arts Movement, Baraka's *Dutchman* explosively dramatizes how this relationship affects the black male's quest for social and political power. Two of John A. Williams's earlier novels—*The Angry Ones* (1960) and *The Man Who Cried I Am* (1967)—share this kinship with Baraka's *Dutchman* through Williams's recreation of the black lover/white mistress dramatic situation.

A prolific and eclectic writer, Baraka in all his works merges the political and the literary in such a way that the aesthetic of his works becomes inherently political. His important and well-known "The Myth of a Negro Literature," included in this anthology, makes the point that the African American writer's alienation from the author's African homeland displaces the author both culturally and psychologically. Thus, according to Baraka, the black writer in order to maintain a "deep commitment to cultural relevance and intellectual purity" must be ever mindful of the fact that though the writer has individual experiences that have separated the writer from mainstream society, paradoxically, he or she, at the same time, is an integral part of American life. *Black Fire: An Anthology of Afro-American*

Writing (1968), a collection of essays, poetry, fiction, and drama edited by Baraka and Larry Neal, addresses the ideology, technique, and philosophy of the ideas outlined in Baraka's "The Myth of a Negro Literature" and in Neal's manifesto "The Black Arts Movement." Neal's afterword to *Black Fire*, entitled "And Shine Swam On," serves as a companion piece to his "The Black Arts Movement," both published the same year.

Amiri Baraka and Larry Neal were ten and thirteen years younger respectively than James Baldwin, whose earlier essays in some respects assert views diametrically opposed to the revolutionary spirit of essays such as James T. Stewart's "The Development of the Black Revolutionary Artist," James Boggs's "Black Power—A Scientific Concept Whose Time Has Come," and Kwame Touré's (Stokeley Carmichael) "Toward Black Liberation," all collected in *Black Fire*. Whereas Baldwin in the essays collected in *Notes of a Native Son* (1955) focuses on those aspects of the black psyche that make the African American man an integral part of American life, the young writers associated with the Black Arts Movement stressed the African American's uniqueness or individuality. Yet, Baldwin's works demonstrate, more effectively than any other writer of the older generation, the dangers or pitfalls of generalizations. In contrast to the ideology of the Black Arts Movement, which advocated literary and, in some cases, social separation from the white mainstream, Baldwin, particularly in *The Fire Next Time* (1962), maintains that the black American has no choice but to love his white brother.

Baldwin challenged African Americans to understand that their self-hatred is one of many ramifications of slavery and that the only way for the black American to overcome the effects of racism is to know his or her history and understand that black identity is an integral element of black history. For Baldwin, African Americans must love themselves and consciously help bring about changes in whites. Apart from his idea that African Americans should extend their love beyond the self to whites, Baldwin (in his Western, highly rhetorical style that rivals and possibly surpasses the virtuosity of Macaulay, Ruskin, and Newman), like the younger writers, is concerned with the spiritual awakening of black people. Although he does not stress the black American's separation from his African heritage, he, like Neal, Baraka, and others, attacked the horrible conditions in the African American community which breed pimps, drug addicts, pushers, prostitution, hatred, and blind religious faith. Consequently, essays like "Down at the Cross: Letter from a Region in My Mind," found in *The Fire Next Time*, concentrate on the effect racism has on the black community. A vital part of the Baldwinian aesthetic is the idea that the black writer must not beg for his or her humanity. Hence, rather than ignoring racism in his novels, he uses it as background, while the impact of dread, fear, hatred, love, and sexuality on the psyches of blacks and whites makes up the foreground of a Baldwin novel.

This difference between Baldwin's novels and his essays—a difference found in the works of Ralph Ellison as well—parallels the ambiguity that characterized the political forces of the 1960s. Whereas Dr. Martin Luther King, Jr., continued to lead nonviolent demonstrations, Kwame Touré, at one time Dr. King's colleague and leader of SNCC (Student Non-Violent Coordinating Committee), pulled away from Dr. King and aligned himself with black cultural nationalist groups in reaction to the water hoses used by policemen to disperse demonstrations by blacks. Militant political figures including Malcolm X and Eldridge Cleaver and political groups such as Chicago's Black Stone Rangers and Los Angeles's and Harlem's Black Panthers worked toward the improvement of the African American community at the same time as more conservative organizations like CORE (Congress of Racial Equality), the NAACP, and the Urban League. Analogously, the more rebellious writers like Sonia Sanchez, Haki Madhubuti, Larry Neal, Mari Evans, Carolyn Rodgers, Sarah Webster Fabio, Ed Bullins, Nikki Giovanni, Amiri Baraka and others aesthetically aligned themselves in opposition to Euro-American concepts of art that imbued the works of Ernest Gaines, Ralph Ellison, William Melvin Kelley, James Baldwin, John Oliver Killens, and Gwendolyn Brooks before 1967.

We have tried in our selections for this part to choose works that reflect both the ambiguity and the polarity that describe the political and literary climates of the black community between 1954 and 1970.

James Baldwin

(1924–1987)

ONE OF AMERICA'S most eclectic, sensitive, and articulate literary artists, James Baldwin was born in Harlem in 1924 to Emma Jones, who was unmarried, but later married David Baldwin, a storefront preacher. In "Down at the Cross: A Letter from a Region in My Mind," the last of two essays collected in *The Fire Next Time*, Baldwin openly discusses his childhood experiences and his painful relationship with his troubled stepfather. Despite the demanding responsibility of having to care for his eight younger sisters and brothers, Baldwin read voraciously. Because he had exhausted the books in the two libraries in Harlem by age thirteen, he then began to use the Forty-second Street branch of the New York Public Library. His love of reading naturally led to his passion for writing.

At De Witt Clinton High School, a predominantly white school in the Bronx, which accepted Baldwin soon after his religious conversion, Baldwin experienced the sharp contrast between De Witt's intellectual milieu and the insults hurled at him in his black environment because of his sharp intellectual skills and what was perceived as his unattractive physical appearance. Although the young Baldwin had been a member of his Harlem school's literary club, aided by Countee Cullen, and editor of the school's newspaper the *Douglass Pilot*, his literary productivity increased at De Witt, where he worked with Richard Avedon on the *Magpie*, De Witt's literary magazine. By the time Baldwin graduated from high school, his ambition of being a writer was threatened by his stepfather's first giving up his job because of failing mental health and his subsequent admittance into a mental institution. Before his stepfather's death, Baldwin acquired a job in Belle Mead, New Jersey, on the construction of the Army Quartermaster Depot, where because of racism he was fired and rehired twice. After he was fired a third time, Baldwin returned to Harlem.

Determined not to let the death of his father, the birth of another sister, and increasing financial burdens entrap him in Harlem, Baldwin moved to Greenwich Village and began working on numerous jobs all day, sleeping a maximum of four hours at night, and writing for the rest of the night. During this time he worked on his first novel, initially entitled "Crying Holy," later changed to "In My Father's House," and he met Richard Wright, who suggested that Baldwin let him see some of his work. Wright in turn recommended Baldwin for a Eugene F. Saxton Memorial Trust Award, which Baldwin received. Frustrated by his slow progress at writing novels and questioning his skill, he tried writing essays to improve his crafts-manship. The essay entitled "The Harlem Ghetto," which dealt with black anti-Semitism and which appeared in *Commentary*, the publication of the American Jewish Committee, thrust Baldwin into literary success. The intense response of both blacks and Jews alike to "The Harlem Ghetto" serves as a paradigm for the emotional reactions provoked by many of Baldwin's subsequent novels, essays, and plays.

Although many critics feel that Baldwin is a better essayist than novelist, the power and breadth of his novels are undeniable. Moreover, the same Baldwinian sensibility that distinguishes Baldwin's novels is also charac-teristic of his essays—his exploration of bisexuality, sexual repression, guilt, power, shame, hatred, and the extent to which racism exacerbates these psychological forces. The two essays "Everybody's Protest Novel" and "Many Thousands Gone," because of their denunciation of the protest fiction associated with Richard Wright, have mistakenly given the impres-sion that Baldwin's fiction, particularly his earlier works, do not concern themselves with the issue of racism. It is valid, however, to read Baldwin's novels as fictional representations of the ideas he presents in his essays, especially "My Dungeon Shook: Letter to My Nephew on the One Hun-dredth Anniversary of the Emancipation," found in *The Fire Next Time*. In this essay he challenges black Americans first to recognize the source of the self-hatred that molds their personalities and thus conditions their lives and, second, to destroy that hatred by loving their black selves and ac-cepting whites with love as well. In his novels and plays, Baldwin dram-atizes the hate, shame, repression, and guilt that becloud self-knowledge or self-exploration.

His literary productivity is overwhelming. He is the author of five novels, *Go Tell It on the Mountain* (1953), *Giovanni's Room* (1956), *Another Country* (1962), *If Beale Street Could Talk* (1974), and *Just Above My Head* (1978); a collection of short stories, *Going to Meet the Man* (1965); four plays, *The Amen Corner* (1957), *Giovanni's Room* (1957), *Blues for Mister Charlie* (1964), and *A Deed from the King of Spain* (1974); six books of essays, *Notes of a Native Son* (1955), *Nobody Knows My Name* (1961), *The Fire Next Time* (1963), *No Name in the Street* (1972), *The Devil Finds Work: An Essay* (1976), and *Evidence of Things Unseen* (1985); a photographic essay, *Nothing Personal* (1964); a children's book, *Little Man, Little Man: A Story of Childhood* (1976); two books of dialogue, *A Rap on Race* (1971) and *A Dialogue* (1973); a movie scenario, *One Day When I Was Lost: A Scenario Based on "The Autobiography of Malcolm X"* (1972); and *The Price of the Ticket: Collected Nonfiction, 1948–1985* (1985).

In 1948 Baldwin decided to leave the United States for Paris in order to overcome feelings of entrapment and stagnation in his Greenwich Village environment. Throughout his literary career he indefatigably confronted not only the alienation caused by his homosexuality, but also the conflict between his role as an artist and civil rights spokesperson, his haunting religious background, his comprehensive and personal relationship with Jews, and thirty-eight years of reviews aimed at denying his view of the terror, pain, and fragility of the human heart. Baldwin died on November 30, 1987, in St. Paul de Vence, France.

For further reading, see John W. Roberts's entry in *Dictionary of Literary Biography, Volume 51* and the comprehensive bibliography in Horace A. Porter's *Stealing the Fire: The Art and Protest of James Baldwin* (1989). See also Quincy Troupe, ed., *James Baldwin: The Legacy* (1989) and Fred L. Standley and Louis H. Pratt, eds., *Conversations with James Baldwin* (1989).

"Going to Meet the Man" is the title short story from the 1965 collection.

GOING TO MEET THE MAN

"What's the matter?" she asked.

"I don't know," he said, trying to laugh, "I guess I'm tired."

"You've been working too hard," she said. "I keep telling you."

"Well, goddammit, woman," he said, "it's not my fault!" He tried again; he wretchedly failed again. Then he just lay there, silent, angry, and helpless. Excitement filled him just like a toothache, but it refused to enter his flesh. He stroked her breast. This was his wife. He could not ask her to do just a little thing for him, just to help him out, just for a little while, the way he could ask a nigger girl to do it. He lay there, and he sighed. The image of a black girl caused a distant excitement in him, like a far-away light; but, again, the excitement was more like pain; instead of forcing him to act, it made action impossible.

"Go to sleep," she said, gently, "you got a hard day tomorrow."

"Yeah," he said, and rolled over on his side, facing her, one hand still on one breast. "Goddamn the niggers. The black stinking coons. You'd think they'd learn. Wouldn't you think they'd learn? I mean, *wouldn't* you?"

"They going to be out there tomorrow," she said, and took his hand away, "get some sleep."

He lay there, one hand between his legs, staring at the frail sanctuary of his wife. A faint light came from the shutters; the moon was full. Two dogs, far away, were barking at each other, back and forth,

---

insistently, as though they were agreeing to make an appointment. He heard a car coming north on the road and he half sat up, his hand reaching for his holster, which was on a chair near the bed, on top of his pants. The lights hit the shutters and seemed to travel across the room and then went out. The sound of the car slipped away, he heard it hit gravel, then heard it no more. Some liver-lipped students, probably, heading back to that college—but coming from where? His watch said it was two in the morning. They could be coming from anywhere, from out of state most likely, and they would be at the court-house tomorrow. The niggers were getting ready. Well, they would be ready, too.

He moaned. He wanted to let whatever was in him out; but it wouldn't come out. Goddamn! he said aloud, and turned again, on his side, away from Grace, staring at the shutters. He was a big, healthy man and he had never had any trouble sleeping. And he wasn't old enough yet to have any trouble getting it up—he was only forty-two. And he was a good man, a God-fearing man, he had tried to do his duty all his life, and he had been a deputy sheriff for several years. Nothing had ever bothered him before, certainly not getting it up. Sometimes, sure, like any other man, he knew that he wanted a little more spice than Grace could give him and he would drive over yonder and pick up a black piece or arrest her, it came to the same thing, but he couldn't do that now, no more. There was no telling what might happen once your ass was in the air. And they were low enough to kill a man then, too, everyone of them, or the girl herself might do it, right while she was making believe you made her feel so good. The niggers. What had the good Lord Almighty had in mind when he made the niggers? Well. They were pretty good at that, all right. Damn. Damn. Goddamn.

This wasn't helping him to sleep. He turned again, toward Grace again, and moved close to her warm body. He felt something he had never felt before. He felt that he would like to hold her, hold her, hold her, and be buried in her like a child and never have to get up in the morning again and go downtown to face those faces, good Christ, they were ugly! and never have to enter that jail house again and smell that smell and hear that singing; never again feel that filthy, kinky, greasy hair under his hand, never again watch those black breasts leap against the leaping cattle prod, never hear those moans again or watch that blood run down or the fat lips split or the sealed eyes struggle open. They were animals, they were no better than animals, what could be done with people like that? Here they had been in a civilized country for years and they still lived like animals. Their houses were dark, with oil cloth or cardboard in the windows, the smell was enough to make you puke your guts out, and there they sat, a whole tribe, pumping out kids, it looked like, every damn five minutes, and laughing and talking and playing music like they didn't have a care in the world, and he reckoned they didn't, neither, and coming to the door, into the sunlight, just standing there, just looking foolish, not thinking of anything but just getting back to what they were doing, saying, Yes suh, Mr. Jesse. I surely will, Mr. Jesse. Fine weather, Mr. Jesse. Why, I thank you, Mr. Jesse. He had worked for a mail-order house for a while and it had been his job to collect the payments for the stuff they bought. They were too dumb to know that they were being cheated blind, but that was no skin off his ass—he was just supposed to do his job. They would be late—they didn't have the sense to put money aside; but it was easy to scare them, and he never really had any trouble. Hell, they all liked him, the kids used to smile when he came to the door. He gave them candy, sometimes, or chewing gum, and rubbed their rough bullet heads—maybe the candy should have been poisoned. Those kids were grown now. He had had trouble with one of them today.

"There was this nigger today," he said; and stopped; his voice sounded peculiar. He touched Grace. "You awake?" he asked. She mumbled something, impatiently, she was probably telling him to go to sleep. It was all right. He knew that he was not alone.

"What a funny time," he said, "to be thinking about a thing like that—you listening?" She mumbled something again. He rolled over on his back. "This nigger's one of the ringleaders. We had trouble with him before. We must have had him out there at the work farm three or four times. Well, Big Jim C. and some of the boys really had to whip that nigger's ass today." He looked over at Grace; he could not tell whether she was listening or not; and he was afraid to ask again. "They had this line you know, to register"—he laughed, but she did not—"and they wouldn't stay where Big Jim C. wanted them, no, they had to start blocking traffic all around the court house so couldn't nothing or nobody get through, and Big Jim C. told them to disperse and they wouldn't move, they just kept up that singing, and Big Jim C. figured that the others would move if this nigger would move, him being the ring-leader, but he wouldn't move and he wouldn't let the others move, so they had to beat him and a couple of the others and they threw them in the wagon—but *I* didn't see this nigger till I got to the jail. They were still singing and I was supposed to make them stop. Well, I couldn't make them stop for me but I knew he could make them stop. He was lying on the ground jerking and moaning, they had thrown him in a cell by himself, and blood was coming out of his ears from where Big Jim C. and his boys had whipped him. Wouldn't you think they'd learn? I put the prod to him and he jerked some more and he kind of screamed—but he didn't have much voice left. "You make them stop that singing," I said to him, "you hear me? You make them stop that singing." He acted like he didn't hear me and I put it to him again, under his arms, and he just rolled around on the floor and blood started coming from his mouth. He'd pissed his pants already." He paused. His mouth felt dry and his throat was as rough as sandpaper; as he talked, he began to hurt all over with that peculiar excitement which refused to be released. "You all are going to stop your singing, I said to him, and you are going to stop coming down to the court house and disrupting traffic and molesting the people and keeping us from our duties and keeping doctors from getting to sick white women and getting all them Northerners in this town to give our town a bad name—!" As he said this, he kept prodding the boy, sweat pouring from beneath the helmet he had not yet taken off. The boy rolled around in his own dirt and water and blood and tried to scream again as the prod hit his testicles, but the scream did not come out, only a kind of rattle and a moan. He stopped. He was not supposed to kill the nigger. The cell was filled with a terrible odor. The boy was still. "You hear me?" he called. "You had enough?" The singing went on. "You had enough?" His foot leapt out, he had not known it was going to, and caught the boy flush on the jaw. *Jesus*, he thought, *this ain't no nigger, this is a goddamn bull*, and he screamed again, "You had enough? You going to make them stop that singing now?"

But the boy was out. And now he was shaking worse than the boy had been shaking. He was glad no one could see him. At the same time, he felt very close to a very peculiar, particular joy; something deep in him and deep in his memory was stirred, but whatever was in his memory eluded him. He took off his helmet. He walked to the cell door.

"White man," said the boy, from the floor, behind him.

He stopped. For some reason, he grabbed his privates.

"You remember Old Julia?"

The boy said, from the floor, with his mouth full of blood, and one eye, barely open, glaring like the eye of a cat in the dark, "My grandmother's name was Mrs. Julia Blossom. *Mrs.* Julia Blossom. You going to call our women by their right names yet.—And those kids ain't going to stop singing. We going to keep on singing until every one of you miserable white mothers go stark raving out of your minds." Then he closed the one eye; he spat blood; his head fell back against the floor.

He looked down at the boy, whom he had been seeing, off and on, for more than a year, and suddenly remembered him: Old Julia had been one of his mail-order customers, a nice old woman. He had not seen her for years, he supposed that she must be dead.

He had walked into the yard, the boy had been sitting in a swing. He had smiled at the boy, and asked, "Old Julia home?"

The boy looked at him for a long time before he answered. "Don't no Old Julia live here."

"This is her house. I know her. She's lived here for years."

The boy shook his head. "You might know a Old Julia someplace else, white man. But don't nobody by that name live here."

He watched the boy; the boy watched him. The boy certainly wasn't more than ten. *White man.* He didn't have time to be fooling around with some crazy kid. He yelled, "Hey! Old Julia!"

But only silence answered him. The expression on the boy's face did not change. The sun beat down on them both, still and silent; he had the feeling that he had been caught up in a nightmare, a nightmare dreamed by a child; perhaps one of the nightmares he himself had dreamed as a child. It had that feeling—everything familiar, without undergoing any other change, had been subtly and hideously displaced: the trees, the sun, the patches of grass in the yard, the leaning porch and the weary porch steps and the cardboard in the windows and the black hole of the door which looked like the entrance to a cave, and the eyes of the pickaninny, all, all, were charged with malevolence. *White man.* He looked at the boy. "She's gone out?"

The boy said nothing.

"Well," he said, "tell her I passed by and I'll pass by next week." He started to go; he stopped. "You want some chewing gum?"

The boy got down from the swing and started for the house. He said, "I don't want nothing you got, white man." He walked into the house and closed the door behind him.

Now the boy looked as though he were dead. Jesse wanted to go over to him and pick him up and pistol whip him until the boy's head burst open like a melon. He began to tremble with what he believed was rage, sweat, both cold and hot, raced down his body, the singing filled him as though it were a weird, uncontrollable, monstrous howling rumbling up from the depths of his own belly, he felt an icy fear rise in him and raise him up, and he shouted, he howled, "You lucky we *pump* some white blood into you every once in a while—your women! Here's what I got for all the black bitches in the world—!" Then he was, abruptly, almost too weak to stand; to his bewilderment, his horror, beneath his own fingers, he felt himself violently stiffen—with no warning at all; he dropped his hands and he stared at the boy and he left the cell.

"All that singing they do," he said. "All that singing." He could

not remember the first time he had heard it; he had been hearing it
all his life. It was the sound with which he was most familiar—
though it was also the sound of which he had been least conscious
—and it had always contained an obscure comfort. They were singing to God. They were singing for mercy and they hoped to go to
heaven, and he had even sometimes felt, when looking into the eyes
of some of the old women, a few of the very old men, that they were
singing for mercy for his soul, too. Of course, he had never thought
of their heaven or of what God was, or could be, for them; God was
the same for everyone, he supposed, and heaven was where good
people went—he supposed. He had never thought much about what
it meant to be a good person. He tried to be a good person and treat
everybody right: it wasn't his fault if the niggers had taken it into
their heads to fight against God and go against the rules laid down
in the Bible for everyone to read! Any preacher would tell you that.
He was only doing his duty: protecting white people from the niggers and the niggers from themselves. And there were still lots of
good niggers around—he had to remember that; they weren't all like
that boy this afternoon; and the good niggers must be mighty sad
to see what was happening to their people. They would thank him
when this was over. In that way they had, the best of them, not
quite looking him in the eye, in a low voice, with a little smile: We
surely thanks you, Mr. Jesse. From the bottom of our hearts, we
thanks you. He smiled. They hadn't all gone crazy. This trouble
would pass.—He knew that the young people had changed some of
the words to the songs. He had scarcely listened to the words before
and he did not listen to them now; but he knew that the words were
different; he could hear that much. He did not know if the faces
were different, he had never, before this trouble began, watched
them as they sang, but he certainly did not like what he saw now.
They hated him, and this hatred was blacker than their hearts,
blacker than their skins, redder than their blood, and harder, by far,
than his club. Each day, each night, he felt worn out, aching, with
their smell in his nostrils and filling his lungs, as though he were
drowning—drowning in niggers; and it was all to be done again
when he awoke. It would never end. It would never end. Perhaps
this was what the singing had meant all along. They had not been
singing black folks into heaven, they had been singing white folks
into hell.

Everyone felt this black suspicion in many ways, but no one
knew how to express it. Men much older than he, who had been
responsible for law and order much longer than he, were now much
quieter than they had been, and the tone of their jokes, in a way
that he could not quite put his finger on, had changed. These men

were his models, they had been friends to his father, and they had taught him what it meant to be a man. He looked to them for courage now. It wasn't that he didn't know that what he was doing was right—he knew that, nobody had to tell him that; it was only that he missed the ease of former years. But they didn't have much time to hang out with each other these days. They tended to stay close to their families every free minute because nobody knew what might happen next. Explosions rocked the night of their tranquil town. Each time each man wondered silently if perhaps this time the dynamite had not fallen into the wrong hands. They thought that they knew where all the guns were; but they could not possibly know every move that was made in that secret place where the darkies lived. From time to time it was suggested that they form a posse and search the home of every nigger, but they hadn't done it yet. For one thing, this might have brought the bastards from the North down on their backs; for another, although the niggers were scattered throughout the town—down in the hollow near the railroad tracks, way west near the mills, up on the hill, the well-off ones, and some out near the college—nothing seemed to happen in one part of town without the niggers immediately knowing it in the other. This meant that they could not take them by surprise. They rarely mentioned it, but they *knew* that some of the niggers had guns. It stood to reason, as they said, since, after all, some of them had been in the Army. There were niggers in the Army right now and God knows they wouldn't have had any trouble stealing this half-assed government blind—the whole world was doing it, look at the European countries and all those countries in Africa. They made jokes about it—bitter jokes; and they cursed the government in Washington, which had betrayed them; but they had not yet formed a posse. Now, if their town had been laid out like some towns in the North, where all the niggers lived together in one locality, they could have gone down and set fire to the houses and brought about peace that way. If the niggers had all lived in one place, they could have kept the fire in one place. But the way this town was laid out, the fire could hardly be controlled. It would spread all over town—and the niggers would probably be helping it to spread. Still, from time to time, they spoke of doing it, anyway; so that now there was a real fear among them that somebody might go crazy and light the match.

They rarely mentioned anything not directly related to the war that they were fighting, but this had failed to establish between them the unspoken communications of soldiers during a war. Each man, in the thrilling silence which sped outward from their exchanges, their laughter, and their anecdotes, seemed wrestling, in various degrees of darkness, with a secret which he could not articulate to himself, and which, however directly it related to the war, related yet more surely to his privacy and his past. They could no longer be sure, after all, that they had all done the same things. They had never dreamed that their privacy could contain any element of terror, could threaten, that is, to reveal itself, to the scrutiny of a judgment day, while remaining unreadable and inaccessible to themselves; nor had they dreamed that the past, while certainly refusing to be forgotten, could yet so stubbornly refuse to be remembered. They felt themselves mysteriously set at naught, as no longer entering into the real concerns of other people—while here they were, outnumbered, fighting to save the civilized world. They had thought that people would care—people didn't care; not enough, anyway, to help them. It would have been a help, really, or at least a relief, even to have been forced to surrender. Thus they had lost, probably forever, their old and easy connection with each other. They were forced to depend on each other more and, at the same time, to trust each other less. Who could tell when one of them might not betray them all, for money, or for the ease of confession? But no one dared imagine what there might be to confess. They were soldiers fighting a war, but their relationship to each other was that of accomplices in a crime. They all had to keep their mouths shut.

I stepped in the river at Jordan.

Out of the darkness of the room, out of nowhere, the line came flying up at him, with the melody and the beat. He turned wordlessly toward his sleeping wife. *I stepped in the river at Jordan.* Where had he heard that song?

"Grace," he whispered. "You awake?"

She did not answer. If she was awake, she wanted him to sleep. Her breathing was slow and easy, her body slowly rose and fell.

I stepped in the river at Jordan.
The water came to my knees.

He began to sweat. He felt an overwhelming fear, which yet contained a curious and dreadful pleasure.

I stepped in the river at Jordan.
The water came to my waist.

It had been night, as it was now, he was in the car between his mother and his father, sleepy, his head in his mother's lap, sleepy, and yet full of excitement. The singing came from far away, across the dark fields. There were no lights anywhere. They had said good-bye to all the others and turned off on this dark dirt road. They were almost home.

I stepped in the river at Jordan,
The water came over my head,
I looked way over to the other side,
He was making up my dying bed!

"I guess they singing for him," his father said, seeming very weary and subdued now. "Even when they're sad, they sound like they just about to go and tear off a piece." He yawned and leaned across the boy and slapped his wife lightly on the shoulder, allowing his hand to rest there for a moment. "Don't they?"

"Don't talk that way," she said.

"Well, that's what we going to do," he said, "you can make up your mind to that." He started whistling. "You see? When I begin to feel it, I gets kind of musical, too."

Oh, Lord! Come on and ease my troubling mind!

He had a black friend, his age, eight, who lived nearby. His name was Otis. They wrestled together in the dirt. Now the thought of Otis made him sick. He began to shiver. His mother put her arm around him.

"He's tired," she said.

"We'll be home soon," said his father. He began to whistle again.

"We didn't see Otis this morning," Jesse said. He did not know why he said this. His voice, in the darkness of the car, sounded small and accusing.

"You haven't seen Otis for a couple of mornings," his mother said.

That was true. But he was only concerned about *this* morning.

"No," said his father, "I reckon Otis's folks was afraid to let him show himself this morning."

"But Otis didn't do nothing!" Now his voice sounded questioning.

"Otis *can't* do nothing," said his father, "he's too little." The car lights picked up their wooden house, which now solemnly approached them, the lights falling around it like yellow dust. Their dog, chained to a tree, began to bark.

"We just want to make sure Otis *don't* do nothing," said his father, and stopped the car. He looked down at Jesse. "And you tell him what your Daddy said, you hear?"

"Yes sir," he said.

His father switched off the lights. The dog moaned and pranced, but they ignored him and went inside. He could not sleep. He lay awake, hearing the night sounds, the dog yawning and moaning outside, the sawing of the crickets, the cry of the owl, dogs barking far away, then no sounds at all, just the heavy, endless buzzing of the night. The darkness pressed on his eyelids like a scratchy blanket. He turned, he turned again. He wanted to call his mother, but he knew his father would not like this. He was terribly afraid. Then he heard his father's voice in the other room, low, with a joke in it; but this did not help him, it frightened him more, he knew what was going to happen. He put his head under the blanket, then pushed his head out again, for fear, staring at the dark window. He heard his mother's moan, his father's sigh; he gritted his teeth. Then their bed began to rock. His father's breathing seemed to fill the world.

That morning, before the sun had gathered all its strength, men and women, some flushed and some pale with excitement, came with news. Jesse's father seemed to know what the news was before the first jalopy stopped in the yard, and he ran out, crying, "They got him, then? They got him?"

The first jalopy held eight people, three men and two women and three children. The children were sitting on the laps of the grown-ups. Jesse knew two of them, the two boys; they shyly and uncomfortably greeted each other. He did not know the girl.

"Yes, they got him," said one of the women, the older one, who wore a wide hat and a fancy, faded blue dress. "They found him early this morning."

"How far had he got?" Jesse's father asked.

"He hadn't got no further than Harkness," one of the men said. "Look like he got lost up there in all them trees—or maybe he just got so scared he couldn't move." They all laughed.

"Yes, and you know it's near a graveyard, too," said the younger woman, and they laughed again.

"Is that where they got him now?" asked Jesse's father.

By this time there were three cars piled behind the first one, with everyone looking excited and shining, and Jesse noticed that they were carrying food. It was like a Fourth of July picnic.

"Yeah, that's where he is," said one of the men, "declare, Jesse, you going to keep us here all day long, answering your damn fool questions. Come on, we ain't got no time to waste."

"Don't bother putting up no food," cried a woman from one of the other cars, "we got enough. Just come on."

"Why, thank you," said Jesse's father, "we be right along, then."

"I better get a sweater for the boy," said his mother, "in case it turns cold."

Jesse watched his mother's thin legs cross the yard. He knew that she also wanted to comb her hair a little and maybe put on a better dress, the dress she wore to church. His father guessed this, too, for he yelled behind her, "Now don't you go trying to turn yourself into no movie star. You just come on." But he laughed as he said this, and winked at the men; his wife was younger and prettier than most of the other women. He clapped Jesse on the head and started pulling him toward the car. "You all go on," he said, "I'll be right behind you. Jesse, you go tie up that there dog while I get this car started."

The cars sputtered and coughed and shook; the caravan began to move; bright dust filled the air. As soon as he was tied up, the dog began to bark. Jesse's mother came out of the house, carrying a jacket for his father and a sweater for Jesse. She had put a ribbon in her hair and had an old shawl around her shoulders.

"Put these in the car, son," she said, and handed everything to him. She bent down and stroked the dog, looked to see if there was water in his bowl, then went back up the three porch steps and closed the door.

"Come on," said his father, "ain't nothing in there for nobody to steal." He was sitting in the car, which trembled and belched. The last car of the caravan had disappeared but the sound of singing floated behind them.

Jesse got into the car, sitting close to his father, loving the smell of the car, and the trembling, and the bright day, and the sense of going on a great and unexpected journey. His mother got in and closed the door and the car began to move. Not until then did he ask, "Where are we going? Are we going on a picnic?"

He had a feeling that he knew where they were going, but he was not sure.

"That's right," his father said, "we're going on a picnic. You won't ever forget *this* picnic—!"

"Are we," he asked, after a moment, "going to see the bad nigger —the one that knocked down old Miss Standish?"

"Well, I reckon," said his mother, "that we *might* see him."

He started to ask *Will a lot of niggers be there? Will Otis be there?*—but he did not ask his question, to which, in a strange and uncomfortable way, he already knew the answer. Their friends, in the other cars, stretched up the road as far as he could see; other cars had joined them; there were cars behind them. They were singing. The sun seemed suddenly very hot, and he was at once very happy and a little afraid. He did not quite understand what was happening, and he did not know what to ask—he had no one to ask. He had grown accustomed, for the solution of such mysteries, to go to Otis. He felt that Otis knew everything. But he could not ask Otis about this. Anyway, he had not seen Otis for two days; he had not seen a black face anywhere for more than two days; and he now realized, as they began chugging up the long hill which eventually led to Harkness, that there were no black faces on the road this morning, no black people anywhere. From the houses in which they lived, all along the road, no smoke curled, no life stirred—maybe one or two chickens were to be seen, that was all. There was no one at the windows, no one in the yard, no one sitting on the porches, and the doors were closed. He had come this road many a time and seen women washing in the yard (there were no clothes on the clotheslines), men working in the fields, children playing in the dust; black men passed them on the road other mornings, other days, on foot, or in wagons, sometimes in cars, tipping their hats, smiling, joking, their teeth a solid white against their skin, their eyes as warm as the sun, the blackness of their skin like dull fire against the white or the blue or the grey of their torn clothes. They passed the nigger church—dead-white, desolate, locked up; and the grave-yard, where no one knelt or walked, and he saw no flowers. He wanted to ask, *Where are they? Where are they all?* But he did not dare. As the hill grew steeper, the sun grew colder. He looked at his mother and his father. They looked straight ahead, seeming to be lis-tening to the singing which echoed and echoed in this graveyard si-lence. They were strangers to him now. They were looking at something he could not see. His father's lips had a strange, cruel curve, he wet his lips from time to time, and swallowed. He was ter-ribly aware of his father's tongue, it was as though he had never seen it before. And his father's body suddenly seemed immense, big-ger than a mountain. His eyes, which were grey-green, looked yellow in the sunlight; or at least there was a light in them which he had never seen before. His mother patted her hair and adjusted the rib-bon, leaning forward to look into the car mirror. "You look all right," said his father, and laughed. "When that nigger looks at you, he's going to swear he throwed his life away for nothing. Wouldn't be surprised if he don't come back to haunt you." And he laughed again.

The singing now slowly began to cease; and he realized that they were nearing their destination. They had reached a straight, narrow, pebbly road, with trees on either side. The sunlight filtered down on them from a great height, as though they were under-water; and the branches of the trees scraped against the cars with a tearing sound. To the right of them, and beneath them, invisible now, lay the town; and to the left, miles of trees which led to the high mountain range which his ancestors had crossed in order to settle in this valley. Now, all was silent, except for the bumping of the tires against the rocky road, the sputtering of motors, and the sound of a crying child. And they seemed to move more slowly. They were beginning to climb again. He watched the cars ahead as they toiled patiently upward, disappearing into the sunlight of the clearing. Presently, he felt their vehicle also rise, heard his father's changed breathing, the sunlight hit his face, the trees moved away from them, and they were there. As their car crossed the clearing, he looked around. There seemed to be millions, there were certainly hundreds of people in the clearing, staring toward something he could not see. There was a fire. He could not see the flames, but he smelled the smoke. Then they were on the other side of the clearing, among the trees again. His father drove off the road and parked the car behind a great many other cars. He looked down at Jesse.

"You all right?" he asked.

"Yes sir," he said.

"Well, come on, then," his father said. He reached over and opened the door on his mother's side. His mother stepped out first. They followed her into the clearing. At first he was aware only of confusion, of his mother and father greeting and being greeted, himself being handled, hugged, and patted, and told how much he had grown. The wind blew the smoke from the fire across the clearing into his eyes and nose. He could not see over the backs of the people in front of him. The sounds of laughing and cursing and wrath—and something else—rolled in waves from the front of the mob to the back. Those in front expressed their delight at what they saw, and this delight rolled backward, wave upon wave, across the clearing, more acrid than the smoke. His father reached down suddenly and sat Jesse on his shoulders.

Now he saw the fire—of twigs and boxes, piled high; flames made pale orange and yellow and thin as a veil under the steadier light of the sun; grey-blue smoke rolled upward and poured over their heads. Beyond the shifting curtain of fire and smoke, he made out first only a length of gleaming chain, attached to a great limb of the tree; then he saw that this chain bound two black hands together at the wrist, dirty yellow palm facing dirty yellow palm. The smoke poured up; the hands dropped out of sight; a cry went up from the crowd. Then the hands slowly came into view again, pulled upward by the chain. This time he saw the kinky, sweating, bloody head— he had never before seen a head with so much hair on it, hair so black and so tangled that it seemed like another jungle. The head was hanging. He saw the forehead, flat and high, with a kind of arrow of hair in the center, like he had, like his father had; they called it a widow's peak; and the mangled eye brows, the wide nose, the closed eyes, and the glinting eye lashes and the hanging lips, all streaming with blood and sweat. His hands were straight above his head. All his weight pulled downward from his hands; and he was a big man, a bigger man than his father, and black as an African jungle Cat, and naked. Jesse pulled upward; his father's hands held him firmly by the ankles. He wanted to say something, he did not know what, but nothing he said could have been heard, for now the crowd roared again as a man stepped forward and put more wood on the fire. The flames leapt up. He thought he heard the hanging man scream, but he was not sure. Sweat was pouring from the hair in his armpits, poured down his sides, over his chest, into his navel and his groin. He was lowered again; he was raised again. Now Jesse knew that he heard him scream. The head went back, the mouth wide open, blood bubbling from the mouth; the veins of the neck jumped out; Jesse clung to his father's neck in terror as the cry rolled over the crowd. The cry of all the people rose to answer the dying man's cry. He wanted death to come quickly. They wanted to make death wait: and it was they who held death, now, on a leash which they lengthened little by little. *What did he do?* Jesse wondered. *What did the man do? What did he do?*—but he could not ask his father. He was seated on his father's shoulders, but his father was far away. There were two older men, friends of his father's, raising and lowering the chain; everyone, indiscriminately, seemed to be responsible for the fire. There was no hair left on the nigger's privates, and the eyes, now, were wide open, as white as the eyes of a clown or a doll. The smoke now carried a terrible odor across the clearing, the odor of something burning which was both sweet and rotten.

He turned his head a little and saw the field of faces. He watched his mother's face. Her eyes were very bright, her mouth was open: she was more beautiful than he had ever seen her, and more strange. He began to feel a joy he had never felt before. He watched the hanging, gleaming body, the most beautiful and terrible object he had ever seen till then. One of his father's friends reached up and in his hands he held a knife: and Jesse wished that he had been that man. It was a long, bright knife and the sun seemed to catch it, to play with it, to caress it—it was brighter than the fire. And a wave of laughter swept the crowd. Jesse felt his father's hands on his ankles slip and tighten. The man with the knife walked toward the crowd, smiling slightly; as though this were a signal, silence fell; he heard his mother cough. Then the man with the knife walked up to the hanging body. He turned and smiled again. Now there was a silence all over the field. The hanging head looked up. It seemed fully conscious now, as though the fire had burned out terror and pain. The man with the knife took the nigger's privates in his hand, one hand, still smiling, as though he were weighing them. In the cradle of the one white hand, the nigger's privates seemed as remote as meat being weighed in the scales; but seemed heavier, too, much heavier, and Jesse felt his scrotum tighten; and huge, huge, much bigger than his father's, flaccid, hairless, the largest thing he had ever seen till then, and the blackest. The white hand stretched them, cradled them, caressed them. Then the dying man's eyes looked straight into Jesse's eyes—it could not have been as long as a second, but it seemed longer than a year. Then Jesse screamed, and the crowd screamed as the knife flashed, first up, then down, cutting the dreadful thing away, and the blood came roaring down. Then the crowd rushed forward, tearing at the body with their hands, with knives, with rocks, with stones, howling and cursing. Jesse's head, of its own weight, fell downward toward his father's head. Someone stepped forward and drenched the body with kerosene. Where the man had been, a great sheet of flame appeared. Jesse's father lowered him to the ground.

"Well, I told you," said his father, "you wasn't never going to forget *this* picnic." His father's face was full of sweat, his eyes were very peaceful. At that moment Jesse loved his father more than he had ever loved him. He felt that his father had carried him through a mighty test, had revealed to him a great secret which would be the key to his life forever.

"I reckon," he said, "I reckon."

Jesse's father took him by the hand and, with his mother a little behind them, talking and laughing with the other women, they walked through the crowd, across the clearing. The black body was on the ground, the chain which had held it was being rolled up by one of his father's friends. Whatever the fire had left undone, the hands and the knives and the stones of the people had accomplished. The head was caved in, one eye was torn out, one ear was hanging. But one had to look carefully to realize this, for it was, now, merely a black charred object on the black, charred ground. He lay spread-eagled with what had been a wound between what had been his legs.

"They going to leave him here, then?" Jesse whispered.

"Yeah," said his father, "they'll come and get him by and by. I reckon we better get over there and get some of that food before it's all gone."

"I reckon," he muttered now to himself, "I reckon." Grace stirred and touched him on the thigh: the moonlight covered her like glory. Something bubbled up in him, his nature again returned to him. He thought of the boy in the cell; he thought of the man in the fire; he thought of the knife and grabbed himself and stroked himself and a terrible sound, something between a high laugh and a howl, came out of him and dragged his sleeping wife up on one elbow. She stared at him in a moonlight which had now grown cold as ice. He thought of the morning and grabbed her, laughing and crying, crying and laughing, and he whispered, as he stroked her, as he took her, "Come on, sugar, I'm going to do you like a nigger, just like a nigger, come on, sugar, and love me just like you'd love a nigger." He thought of the morning as he labored and she moaned, thought of morning as he labored harder than he ever had before, and before his labors had ended, he heard the first cock crow and the dogs begin to bark, and the sound of tires on the gravel road.

John Killens

(1916–1987)

JOHN OLIVER KILLENS took seriously his role as a writer, feeling that the writer's duty was "to create a new vision for mankind. [The writer] must be forever asking questions." His sincere dedication to the use of art to challenge the sociological, economic, educational, and political obstacles that stifle human productivity was probably learned in his childhood from his parents. He was introduced to African American literature by his father, who encouraged the young Killens to read Langston Hughes's column in the *Chicago Defender*, and by his mother, who gave him Paul Laurence Dunbar's poetry to read.

Born in Macon, Georgia, in 1916, Killens was subject to the experiences of a Southern childhood which were grist for his later realistic novels like *Youngblood* (1954) and *The Cotillion* (1971). His subsequent education was obtained at Edward Waters College, Morris Brown College, Howard University, Terrell Law School (Washington, D.C.), and finally Columbia and New York universities.

After leaving Macon in 1936, Killens at the age of twenty worked for the National Labor Relations Board (NLRB) in Washington, D.C., until 1942, when he began service with the United States Amphibian Forces in the South Pacific. His second novel, *And Then We Heard the Thunder*, contains thematic elements taken from his experiences in the South Pacific. Honorably discharged from the United States military in 1946, he rejoined the NLRB in Brooklyn, New York. For two years he attempted to organize black and white workers for the Congress of Industrial Organizations (CIO). From 1954 to 1970, Killens worked in the civil rights movement. Not only did he work with the NAACP in Brooklyn, he also participated in the Montgomery bus boycott in 1955. He taught creative writing at the New School for Social Research, served as writer-in-residence first at Fisk University and later at Howard University, and as adjunct professor and chairman of the Black Culture Seminar and Creative Writers' Workshop at Columbia University. Killens is best known in the annals of African American literary history as founder and chair of the Harlem Writers' Guild Workshop, organized in the late 1940s with John Henrik Clarke, Rosa Guy, and Walter Christmas as cofounders. He was a professor at Medgar Evers College in Brooklyn when he died on October 27, 1987.

In addition to five novels—*Youngblood* (1954), *And Then We Heard the Thunder* (1962), *Sippi* (1967), *The Cotillion, or One Good Bull Is Half the*

Herd (1971), and *The Great Black Russian: A Novel on the Life of Alexander Pushkin* (1988)—Killens also wrote a collection of political essays entitled *Black Man's Burden* (1965), a biography entitled *Great Gittin' Up Morning: A Biography of Denmark Vesey* (1972), a children's book called *A Man Ain't Nothin' But a Man: The Adventures of John Henry* (1975) as well as two screenplays, three plays, and numerous stories and essays published in an impressive array of anthologies and journals.

So far, a book-length analysis of Killens's work has not been published. For the most comprehensive look at Killens's career, see William H. Wiggins, Jr.'s essay in *Dictionary of Literary Biography, Volume 51.* Also see Addison Gayle, Jr.'s *The Way of the World: The Black Novel in America* (1975), and William H. Wiggins, Jr.'s "Black Folktales in the Novels of John O. Killens," *Black Scholar* 3 (November 1971). See also Bernard W. Bell's *The Afro-American Novel and Its Tradition* (1987).

The following selection "Yoruba" is chapter 1 of *The Cotillion.*

YORUBA

Hey!

CALL HER YORUBA, RIGHT?

High priestess of the Nation!

You ready for that?

Negritude? Okay?

African queen!

Black and comely was this Harlem princess.

Yoruba, her father named her.

And Yoruba she would always be—praise Allah from whom all blessings flow. Would you believe—GreatGodAlmighty!?

She was Yoruba Evelyn Lovejoy, a working girl that summer, and a queen she was among all working girls. Hell yes! Say it plain—Yoruba! Dig it! And named she was, proudly, from her Georgia father's Black and wondrously angry and terribly frustrated nationalism.

Pure, beautiful, untampered-by-the-white-man Yoruba. Black and princessly Yoruba, as if she'd just got off the boat from Yoruba-land in the western region of the then Nigeria. Sometimes, when her father got into one of his rare and whiskeyed moods, he would trace his father's father back to Ogshogbo, then further eastward, to Benin City, then clear across the mighty Niger, at Asaba and Onitsha, south by southeast, by ferry, foot and mammywagon, all the way to Arachuku, that land of fable of the long juju.

Reprinted by permission of Mrs. Grace Killens.

Now—she—the girl—Yoruba—walked westward through the jungle to Eighth Avenue and went down into Manhattan's man-made earth and took the "A" Train. Her middle name was Evelyn, the first syllable pronounced, Britishly, like the woman made from Adam's ribs and like Christmas Eve and the night before the New Year. Spell it E-V-E-L-Y-N—pronounce it Eve-lyn, was her mother's contribution. Her strong, proud, West Indian mother from the small and windward island of Barbados.

The "A" Train almost leaped the tracks, as it thundered underneath the city, reeling and rocking and screeching, like it had blown its natural stack. Winging nonstop from Fifty-ninth all the way to the main stem at One Hundred and Twenty-fifth. Vacuum-packed with perspiring, dehydrated, Black and white humanity of all sizes and denominations. An air-swindled concoction of sound and sweat and soap and perfume and beaucoup talk, Afro-Americanese, West Indianese, Italianese, Jewishese, Puerto-Ricanese, all screwed up with New Yorkese. Africa—Europe—Caribbean. East to West, the twain was met. And it was a mess to listen to. And hot air, baby, by the ton, hot air was blown, stirred together by the whirligig electric fans overhead and shaken up by this St. Vitus-dancing, boogalooing, epileptic "A" Train. Funky Broadway all the time. Funky! Oooh! Yeah! Dig it! Creating one overwhelming impact which rendered Yoruba's senses numb, and the dear child almost senseless. She felt a total assault upon her mouth, nostrils, eyes, ears, throat. Her Black and brown and righteous body. It happened every week-day that memorable summer, after she finished high school and took a job downtown in the garment wilderness.

FIVE P.M. And people erupted out of the monstrous buildings like missiles catapulted from great guns, onto the streets, and flowed in floodtide through the jungle toward those insatiable subways, which, like great carnivorous beasts, starved, and from another age, swallowed men and women whole; then, belching and breaking wind and regurgitating, threw them up again onto the overflowing streets uptown. Every evening it was—

> TAKE THE "A" TRAIN
> Every day. Every day.
> Hurry—Hurry—Hurry—
> TAKE THE "A" TRAIN

She—the girl—Yoruba closed her eyes, as she held onto the subway strap, closed her large eyes, dark and wide ones, and she could hear the Duke of Ellington's immortal music, feel it pouring through her senses like cascades of clear branch water, ooooweee! Hear it, feel it, in all its varied and varying movements, in a stormy crescendo now, surging ever onward, upward, swelling, gathering its forces as it went, sweeping all and everything before it, even as the train itself went clackety-clack, slapping the rails with its own peculiar Afro rhythm, amassing speed and sound and frenzy, as it moved toward its conclusion. Destination Harlem. It was the Soul Train. Dig it, mother—brother—sister—

TAKE THE "A" TRAIN

It was no accident, the girl, Yoruba, thought, that a Black man had composed this great song, this tribute to New York's regal train. A train whose soul was as Black and beautiful as burnished ebony. It had rhythm. It had heart. It had Negritude. Right? And it was not the "B" or "G" Train, but the "A" Train.

With her left hand Yoruba clung to the subway strap with a kind of final desperation, as the train roared past the local stop at One Hundred and Third Street, wailing, moaning, groaning, making with the beat and the righteous sounds and taking care of business. At the same time the Black girl jabbed, accidentally-on-purpose, her right elbow into a cushiony overstuffed belly of a fortyish-year-old manchild, who stood behind her much too close to her for comfort (Yoruba's blessed comfort), and was trying his best to maneuver himself into an even cozier situation. She had a violent, well-trained right elbow for mashers. Sometimes she carried a hatpin for such overfriendly straphangers.

The famous train was moving now past the local stop at One Hundred and Sixteenth Street, and braking, shaking, screaming, rocking, screeching like a jet airliner coming in for landing. A case of pure and sweet hysteria. The sound, the smell of burning black-eyed peas and fresh coffee cooking, the shakes, the dance, the rock-the-roll, the sweat, the vacuum-packed homo sapiens were too much for Yoruba sometimes, and today, this day, she knew a giddiness in her head and a feeling like seasickness at rock-bottom in her stomach. She thought she might faint standing up, and she panicked for a moment. She would not faint though, she knew she could not faint, for there was no space for such bourgeois self-indulgences here on this jam-packed subway train.

She was Yoruba (sometimes her father called her Ruba, with affection). Eve and Ruby to her mother. Yo-roo-ba to some. She was a burnished-Black-brown slightly burnt toast of a girl; her skin was like it had been scrubbed with fine stones from the River Niger (her father used to say); scrubbed till her dear dark skin cried out in hurt and protest. She had her mother's thin nose; the tip was turned up ever so slightly like her mother's disposition. She had her father's wide thick curving generous lips, sensitive and sensuous. Life—

love—anguish. Her mouth told you so many things. Compassion, tears, laughter. Her mouth was soul music, brothers. Listen to the sounds come out. The bottom lip perhaps slightly smaller than the top. Her eyes were Black on Black. Oooh! so deeply black were they, and wide in the middle and narrow at the outer edges. And slanting like the Orient. The girl thought, here on this train there is no room to faint, as smilingly she remembered an old blues fragment she had heard the great Odetta do the one time Ruba had been down to the Village Gate. She thought:

AIN'T IT HARD TO STUMBLE
WHEN YOU GOT NO PLACE TO FALL?

As the train came reeling squealing screaming to a lurching stop, throwing bodies against bodies, in an orgy of crazy off-time dancing, and various and varied familiarities, Yoruba thought she knew how Jonah must have felt in the belly of Moby Dick's great-great-grand-poppa. She thought, Jonah never had it so good. Grandpop's stomach could not possibly have been as congested as the "A" Train. First and foremost, the great train was Billy Strayhorn and Duke Ellington. So it was Blood. Right? It was sound and frenzy, the thunder and the lightning. The train was folks. Right? The train was also happenings. Always and forever happening. Every day—every day. Hurry! Hurry! Hurry!

Halfway between One Hundred and Sixteenth and One Hundred and Twenty-fifth Street, the people fell away from each other, the waves of people parted like the Red Sea must have parted when old Moses waved his famous rod. This time, instead of Moses, here on this train was a tall, powerfully constructed Black woman, weighing in at about two hundred and twenty pounds and nearing forty years of sojourn on this planet. This time, instead of a rod, it was an umbrella that the lady brandished. And she waved it above her head and brought it down again and again upon the blond head of a sawed-off, undernourished, red-faced white man, as she drove him before her, and beat him out of the train onto the platform. She outweighed the pale-faced culprit by seventy pounds or more. A clear-cut case of overmatching, or undermatching, depending on your point of view or how you placed your bets this evening.

As the dangerous and dastardly molester (you ready?) pulled himself, with difficulty, slowly up from the platform, Miss Heavyweight of Nineteen-Sixty-Something shook her umbrella down at him, and told him, with enormous dignity: "I bet you'll think twice about it the next time you git it into your rotten mind to git fresh with a poor helpless Black lady like me, you goddamn no-good peckerwood trash. It's gittin so it ain't safe for a lady to be by herself in broad open daylight. I don't know what's gonna 'come of us poor defenseless womenfolks. I declare before the Lord I don't."

The four-eyed, bug-eyed, cross-eyed desperado looked like an accident on the lookout for a place to make the scene. He mumbled his apologies and dragged himself away down toward the other end of the platform, limping along pathetically, as if his life depended on it. Miss Poor Defenseless Womanhood brandished her umbrella after the hapless hoodlum. Then she turned and walked proudly, and with righteous indignation, up the stairway to the street.

Some of the Black folk (including Yoruba) cracked up with laughter, when a brother amongst them raised his arm and pumped his right fist up and down, and shouted softly: "Black Power, mother! Black Power! Keep the mammy-hunching faith!"

Up topside on the street it was summertime and the breathing was easier than down there in that underworld underneath the city. Are you ready for Yoruba? Yoruba Evelyn Lovejoy? She, the girl, the princess, felt good walking along her street (One Hundred and Twenty-fifth) in the middle September of her eighteenth year, and the dear fox knew she looked good walking; moreover she was a child who loved to walk. She always walked in a hurry, like she was late for an appointment. Long-legged Black girl, she was aware of the men along the main drag and the eyes they had for her and the shaking of their heads in honest admiration. She strolled like she was used to carrying bundles on her lovely head, as if somehow she conjured up from the depths of some dark mysterious whirlpool of sweet remembrance deep inside of her, she called up memories of the roads her great ancestors used to travel on their way to Lagos and Accra. Enugu, Bamako, Ouaga-dougou. Her distant cousins still strolled down those distant highways. Uhuru! Skin-givers—plank-spankers! Ujamaa!

She was Yoruba and she was pretty poetry set to rhythm. Proud she was and princessly. Her long legs were not skinny, neither were they fat. Slimly round—roundly slim. Her ample hips were built a trifle high up from the sidewalk. That was the only thing. Some of her friends in high school used to call the girl "High Pockets." One old fresh big-head boy always called the child "Long Goodie."

But behind all that and notwithstanding, she was Yoruba of the long strides and the swaying hips and the black heavy hair down to her shoulders, of the dark staring eyes, now laughing, now brimming-full with sorrow. She walked along the street of dreams. Past the Baby Grand Club, where Nipsey Russell used to call the question nightly, before he got "discovered." Walked past Frank's Restaurant, and across Eighth Avenue.

One Hundred and Twenty-fifth Street was also the street of

sounds. Magnificent sounds. Jukeboxes all along the main stem blasting out the classics. Blowing love and hate and sorrow. Black classics. Serious music by serious musicians. Max Roach, Ray Charles, Lou Rawls, Etta Jones, Archie Shepp, John Coltrane, horn-blowing horn-blowers. Abbey Lincoln wailing freedom. Nina's Mississippi Goddamn! And always there was the aristocracy. The Duke of Ellington, the Count of Basie and the Earl of Hines, Lester Young, the late lamented President. Yoruba loved the street of sounds. This child dug the aristocracy. And she was an aristocrat. Dig it! She was clean! Black *and* comely! Understand?

The marquee at the Apollo told her James Brown was holding court. And Pigmeat Markham. George Wiltshire—yeah! All right! Well! Folks were lined up almost half the block. New York's riot squad stood at the everloving ready. Three young jiving signifying cats, standing outside the theater away from the line, eyeballed her as she flowed along the main stem. Amongst all these strolling people, she stood out like Lew Alcindor.

As she passed, she heard one of them say, in a kind of singsong, "Hi do, Miss Foxy Youngblood, please m'am!"

Another said, "Walk pretty for the people!"

The third one said, "Lord, make me truly thankful for what I'm about to perceive!"

Yoruba took it all in stride (and this father's child could truly stride). Her head held aloft, she always walked three inches taller than her actual height. (Did you ever dig Miriam, on stage, Makeba?) Yoruba's face did not give away the fact that she had heard the brothers sounding on her, signifying, but all the same she felt a nervous giggle in the bottom of her stomach.

"Walk that walk, Miss Sweet Chocolate Fox!"

"Miss Fine Brown-Black Frame!"

"Come on home, Miss Youngblood!"

Across the street and down the block was the Black and Beautiful Burlesque (the B.B.B. as it was called with fond affection), a famous girlie house, newly founded, where Afro-naturalized Black beauties did a dignified striptease, by the numbers, every day and thrice on Sundays. Long lines of voyeurs clear around the block. And there were pickets picketing pickets picketing pickets, who were picketing. After a while you had to be some kind of a genius to figure who was picketing whom and how come and what for. There was a Black Nationalist group picketing the theater against the whole idea of Black nudity. "*A pure disgrace!*" There was another group of Black picketeers against the admission of white voyeurs.

"*Keep the Hunkie's eyes off our Beautiful Black women!*"

There was a group of integrated picketeers who came out forthright for integrated burlesque queens. White queens had filed complaints against B.B.B. with the Human Rights Commission. B.B.B. was where the action was, and there were fist fights every other night.

Across Seventh Avenue almost a hundred folks were gathered. In the midst of them a Black man stood on a ladder beside a ragged Star-Spangled Banner, which flapped lifelessly and indifferently in a soft September breeze. A reddish-brown smog hung over the city, ominous and brooding, as if it might fling fire and brimstone down upon the Black and true believers any minute. The man on the ladder was waving his arms back and forth and up and down, as if he were directing traffic. He was working up a perspiration. But Yoruba could not make out what he was saying until she crossed over the beautiful wide parkway of an avenue.

Now she stood on the outskirts of the group of Black folk and half listened to Billy "Bad Mouth" Williams. Self-styled Black nationalist leader. Self-appointed. Self-anointed. Mayor of Black nationalist Harlem. God's and/or Allah's most precious gift to the lucky Harlem masses. Don't take anybody else's word for it. Check it out with Bad Mouth himself. He'd tell you he was the last of the great Black Nationalists. Uncrowned prime minister of the Black government in exile. Hey! There was Garvey, Malcolm, Bad Mouth Williams. After that—well, Armageddon.

Yoruba overheard one man in the crowd running down the action to another. "Bad Mouth's here every damn day the Good Lord sends, running his game, just as often as goose go barefooted. He's the biggest bullshitter on the Avenue."

He was a man of medium height, was Bad Mouth, powerfully gotten together, especially through his massive shoulders. Coal-black was his skin, his eyes aflame like burning coals. And he could talk that talk. He could really blow. He never drew large crowds like Malcolm used to draw. And Yoruba remembered Malcolm. Oh my, yes, yes, yes! Yes! Yes! Yes! Praise Allah—she remembered Malcolm. A Salaam Alaikum! Tall and fire-haired, manhood oozing from every pore of him, fiery in his oratory, lightning fast of wit, uncompromising in his integrity, tough and tender with his people. She remembered Malcolm. She had been helplessly and hopelessly in love with him, like a thousand other girls her age who were of the Black persuasion, and she had cried continuously and for four weeks running after that February Sunday of the fatal infamy.

But like the man said, Bad Mouth was consistent. Every day. Every day. And he was a natural-born champeen at haranguing and cajoling. Yoruba had heard most of his spiel it seemed, a hundred times and more, and in many variations. Bad Mouth could phrase like Louis Armstrong, could orchestrate like Cootie Williams.

"I was born in North Carolina." Bad Mouth paused and let this great revelation sink in. "I lived in a house that I could lay on my pallet and look up through the roof and dig the stars, and look down through the floor and count the chickens. It was built-in ventilation."

Behind this statement came a chuckling kind of laughter from his audience. Yoruba laughed, notwithstanding she had heard it all before. She laughed almost unknowingly.

"We got so damn much fresh air we could hardly catch our breath. Almost choked ourselves to death."

They laughed more loudly now. Warming up. And gathering. "Go on, Bad Mouth."

"Tell it like it i-s is!"

"You oughta be shame of yourself telling them all them bogus lies!"

A four-eyed bearded young man shouted, "Check that shit out, Bad Mouth! Run it down, baby brother! Run it down!"

"Watch your language, young man," another man said to the bearded young man.

"You ain't got nothing to laugh about," Bad Mouth told his audience. "Down home we did at least breathe fresh air, but up here you don't do nothing but fill your lungs with poison. Damn white man so greedy behind them Yankee dollars, he has polluted the air you breathe and poisoned the water you need to drink. Charlie so greedy he'll wipe out his own race including his own self just to make some more of that bread. And you niggers running around here following them hustling preachers teaching you to love the white man. You gon pray for him that spitefully use you."

"Put bad mouth on 'em, Bad Mouth!" one tall, skinny Black cat shouted softly. He sported the baddest Afro-natural hairdo Yoruba had ever seen, standing underneath that wild black bush so thick and so way out the sun could never touch his face, and he was slowly going pale from the lack of sunlight. He wore a truly bad dashiki, long earrings flopping from his hound-dog ears like jingle bells. Everybody on the street knew him to be a plainclothesman in the hire of New York's Finest, even though his clothes were hardly plain. Sometimes he wore a long flowing yellow boubou. He made all the meetings, the greatest shouter in the crowd. Every day. Every day. Old Plainclothes always made the scene.

Bad Mouth continued. "These jackleg preachers telling you when Charlie kick your ass on one cheek, you supposed to turn the other one. You supposed to bend over and to tell him, 'Be my guest.' That's how come some of you walk bent over all the time. You done turned them cheeks so many times you can't hardly sit 'em down to rest."

"Blow, Bad Mouth! Blow, baby! You bad-mouth motherfucker!"

"Rap, brother!"

"Sit down—sit down—you can't sit down—"

Bad Mouth paused and asked his people, "Am I right or wrong?"

"Right!" Plainclothes was jumping up and down. "Rap your Black thing, baby!" He was working himself into a lather. Sometimes he wore a red, black and green African robe, one shoulder bare, the hem of the garment sweeping the street, as if he were from the sanitation department instead of the police.

"Check it, Bad Mouth. Check that shit out!"

"Blow, baby, blow!"

"Do your thing, baby!" The dashiki-ed plainclothesman was screaming now at the top of his voice. Some of the brothers called him Maxwell Smart. Some brothers called him less affectionate names.

"Run it down—run it down!"

"Them hustling preachers telling you to love the man that kicks your Black ass, and you ain't got no better sense than to follow what the hustlers tell you. They the biggest shuckers God ever put breath in."

"Blow, baby, blow!"

"Takes a shucker to know a shucker!" From a lady in the crowd.

"One more time!"

Bad Mouth continued, "I know hustling when I see it. I used to be a hustler my own damn self."

"Used to be?" From a brother in the audience.

"My daddy was a stone hustler. Taught me all the fine points of shucking and hustling. That's right. My daddy was one of them big fat greasy Black and burly chicken-eating Baptist preachers down in Peckerwood, North Carolina."

"Peckerwood, North Carolina? Come on, Bad Mouth!"

One brother in the crowd said, "You a lying ass and a tinkling symbol!"

"That's right," Bad Mouth answered. "That's where my daddy used to preach. That's where I come from. Peckerwood, North Carolina. My daddy was a stone jackleg. Picked cotton all week long and talked shit all day Sunday."

The crowd was laughing now, without restraint. A toothless old lady shouted merrily, "Mind your langwitch, son, else I'll pull you down off that ladder and wash your mouth out with lye soap. Don't think you so big, I won't take you down a peg or two."

"Uh-uh!" From a chuckling brother in the crowd.

"Go on, Mother," Bad Mouth said, good naturedly. "Go sell your papers on another corner."

"I ain't your mother," the old lady fired right back at Bad Mouth. Both of them were speaking louder now, almost shouting, competing with the fire trucks that came clanging down the avenue past the meeting, piercing eardrums with their sirens blasting. Every evening about this time the fire trucks paid their respects to Bad Mouth's meetings, or to any other meeting on this corner of all corners. The speaker's ladder stood in front of Michaux's famous Black and nationalistic bookstore.

Diagonally across the avenue stood the famous Hotel Theresa, where the great Joe Louis used to hang out in the late thirties and early forties, and where history was made in the early sixties, when Fidel took up lodging there and people stood outside in the chilly rain and shouted:

"Viva Castro!"

"Viva Fidel!"

"I ain't your mother," the old lady repeated, shouting even louder this time. "If your mother hadda brung you up right, I wouldn't have to be putting your backside down this late in life."

"OOOoo-weeeee! You ready for that?"

"Grandma putting old Bad Mouth in the natural dozens—damn!"

"Blow, grandma! Blow, baby!"

"Old Bad Mouth do not play the two-time-sixes!"

"Let him pat his big bad feet then. Miles Davis plays it!"

Everybody was laughing now, including Yoruba. And more folks were gathering now, attracted by the laughter. It was as if Bad Mouth and the old lady had learned their lines and rehearsed them well ahead of time.

Well?

Would you believe?

"Go along, old lady," Bad Mouth said tolerantly. "I want to talk to my people about some serious matters. If you can't listen quietly, get yourself your own corner and draw your own crowd. I pay weekly rent for this here corner."

Yoruba walked away from the gathering crowd, away from the scattered laughter. Behind her she could hear Bad Mouth's froggy voice croaking to his people.

"Black brothers and sisters, it's time we chased the Bible-toting money-changers out of the holy places of our worship. Am I right or wrong? It's time we got some healthy-sized buggy whips and kicked some big fat rusty-dusties and took some names. We got to get our own houses clean before we can worry about taking care of Whitey's. Am I right or wrong?"

Yoruba thought, It's preachers today. Yesterday it was "Negro" leaders. The day before that it was the "white Communist liberals." Tomorrow he would be doing a putdown on something else. The labor movement. The NAACP. The President. It was always something, or somebody. Bad Mouth was the World's champeen putdowner. He'd tell anybody: "Not a living ass is sacred, when Bad Mouth begins to blow. The best you can do is batten down the hatches, send out hurricane warnings and pray to Allah for a rainbow."

Behind her, she could hear him carrying on. "Take this city! Take it! Take it! It belongs to you. And it's just right here for the taking. Between the spooks and the spicks, we can take this valuable piece of real estate known as New York City. All we got to do is get together. But you wanna chase the great and glorious white folks all over the mother-loving suburbs!" He paused. "And you don't want no power. You just want to intergrate."

She walked a few blocks up the avenue, as the applause and laughter ebbed behind her, walked past a half dozen bars and liquor stores, and people, and just about as many funeral parlors and store-front churches, and people, and she turned right off Seventh Avenue into the block where she had spent most of the eighteen years of her life. She, the girl, Yoruba, was, at long last, home.

This evening, somehow, when she reached the block, she felt an overwhelming relief coursing through all of her senses, as if she had been on a long long journey into a foreign land, a hostile country, and now she had come home at last. It was not the first time she had had this feeling after she had spent all day downtown in Manhattan in that jungle that some people called the garment center. Today, as she walked toward the other end of the block, warm memories poured over her with the coolness of a sweet summer shower. And she was a little girl again. Romping up and down the teeming block. Playing stick-ball and skipping rope (double dutch) and hopscotch (potsy) and tag and ten-ten-double-ten and follow-the-leader. Tag was a game that went on and on and on and never ended. Playing with Enrique and Ernie and Claudie and Lloyd and Susan and Cheryl and all the rest of that ragtag group (her mother's term for the gone friends of her yesteryears). All of the times that came back to her now from that faraway age were good times to her. It seemed a million years ago. But Yoruba remembered.

Remembered skinny, big-eyed, snotty-nosed Ernie when they were both about six and seven and eight years old (he was always two or three years older), and they were puppy-lovers, and he, her ragged Black prince, would come and sit on her stoop with her for hours and pick his nose and sometimes suck his thumb, and stare at her in a kind of wordless admiration. His father was a seaman and was away from home much of the time. His mother did days work away up somewhere in the Bronx. Remembered the day she invited Ernie to dinner, much to her mother's great annoyance. She had told Yoruba a million times: "I ain't want you playing with them common low-class Southern niggers on this block, and I particularly ain't want them in my house."

But at the dinner table she pumped the boy with questions like she was from the FBI or something.

"How many rooms in your apartment, Ernest?"

"Two rooms and a bath, Miss Daphne."

"Is that exclusive of a kitchen?"

"Exwho-sive?"

Yoruba's father said, "If you're so interested, why don't you pay Mrs. Billings a visit sometimes? You are the nosiest woman God ever made."

Mrs. Lovejoy ignored her husband, as she had a way of doing—sometimes. "You mean your mother has one room, one kitchen and a bath, ain't you, Ernest?"

"Yessum, that's what I meant to say. And the toilet is down on the next floor. We use it with the Williamses. Sometimes we have to stand in line. Sometimes we have to use the pot."

"Where do you sleep, Ernest?"

He picked his nose and stared at his finger. "With my mother most of the time, excepting when my uncle spends the night, he sleep with Mama, and I sleep on the cot in the kitchen. Course when my daddy is home, he sleep with Mama—"

Ernie was usually a quiet boy, but when he got turned on, it was hard to turn him off again.

During those days, Yoruba's folks were more "well-off" than Ernie's. They afforded all of two rooms and a kitchen. All this and a private bath. The girl slept in the living room on a great Bistro convertible. It was after midnight when she was awakened by her parents' voices from the bedroom. She lay there between sleep and wake trying to get herself together.

Her mother with her clipped British-Barbadian accent. She talked twice as fast as her father.

"One of these days you'll listen to me, damn your Black soul. I tell you a million times these damn low-class darkies on this block is no damn good! Nothing but a bunch of wort'less vagabunds. I ain't blame the white man for not wanting to live around them."

"Shut up, woman," Matt Lovejoy harshly whispered. "You wanna wake up Ruba?"

"That's why I try to teach my daughter to stay away from these wort'less pickaninnies on the block. But the more I try to culturize her, the more you pull the other way. You're enough to vex the devil himself."

She—the girl—Yoruba—sitting up in bed and staring through the darkness toward the bedroom. She had been dreaming, and she had trouble now figuring out whether this was part of the dream or not, or was the dream the real thing and was this a nightmare she had stumbled into? Lie back on your bed and close your eyes and try to catch up with your dream again. Shut out the sound of battle from the other room. Put your fingers in your ears. Still you hear the battle raging.

"Quiet, woman, goddammit! Keep your mouth shut and people'll just think you a fool. Keep opening it and there ain't gon be no doubt about it."

Yoruba pulled the sheet up over her head and tried in vain to shut out the sound of her mother's weeping. "You ain't appreciate me!" Crying—sobbing—choking. "You ain't love me!"

Her father's rough and tender voice. "Come on now, Daphne—come on now. You know better than that. Come on now, lil ole crybaby." In the eyes of Yoruba's imagination, she could see her mother, still shaking with sobs, cuddling up to her father now. "You ain't appreciate nothing I try to do." She had seen it happen before —the times they'd fought in front of her. "Crybaby—crybaby—crybaby." Her mother was in her father's arms now, and Yoruba was wide awake, and it would be hours before she fell asleep again. She would never catch up with her dream. She could not even remember what her dream had been about.

Ernie's mother had died a few years back, and Yoruba had no idea where Ernie was now or whether he was living or dead. Maybe he was at sea like his father used to be most of the time. It seemed centuries ago when they romped innocent and heedless up and down these streets, this turf, this block. And ripped their dresses and tore their pants. And laughed just for the sheer joy that came from laughter. It didn't have to be funny, whatever it was they laughed about. Her mother wanted her to be a lady and never run and sweat and play or swear or rassle with the hoi polloi. "Never get your face dirty. Never ever soil your dresses." But her mother fought a losing battle.

She remembered how she would be playing in the streets with her friends and she would look down the street and see her father turn the corner coming home from work, and she would take off down the block like jet propulsion and race toward him and leap into his arms. It was the happiest moment in the day for both of them. Her father would put her on his shoulders with her legs around his neck and ride her all the way up the block and into the house.

Her mother would scold the two of them. "Take that child from around your neck. How can I ever teach her to be a lady? Both of you're just as common as all the other no-good darkies in this ratty neighborhood."

And it was indeed a ratty neighborhood. The rat inhabitants made their presence felt all over. Always they were in evidence. Walked along the streets, worshipped in the churches, dug the movies in the theaters, especially the cowboy pictures. Put up light housekeeping in the tenements. But refused to chip in on the rent. The rat population was ever on the increase. Wherever people of the neighborhood were, rats were always very close by. They had a fond affection for the folks of Harlem. Notwithstanding, it was a case of unrequited love. Loveless love. Yoruba would always remember her father's desperate lifelong battle with the rodent citizenry. Big rats, little rats, in-between. "There gon be more of them than Black folks one of these days. They gon take over Harlem before we do." He would put down big steel traps all over the apartment and bait the traps with bread or cheese. But these rats were city-slick and hip to everything and everybody. Next morning, the food would be gone, the traps sprung, but not a single rat in any of the deadly traps. Her father tried to figure it out, and after months of great puzzling and frustration, he concluded: "These damn rats so hip they put broom straws in their mouths to spring the traps and get the cheese."

Yoruba remembered sleepless nights, with the sound of rats playing in the kitchen, in the oven, and rattling the pots and pans. Some nights she would awaken and hear them scratching and romping around inside the walls. One night about three o'clock in the morning, a trap went off (bang!) and they all jumped out of bed and her father switched on the lights, and before they could get to the place of execution, bread, rat and trap had already split the scene.

A couple of rats got so bold and familiar, the Lovejoys knew them by sight. They would walk out in broad open daylight. And stake their claims. Her father named them Pretty Boy Floyd and John Dillinger. He said they had more sense than their namesakes, seeing as how they never got caught.

One night when Yoruba was about five years old, a great big rat got real affectionate and jumped into her bed and bit her on the jaw. Left a scar on her face that was still with her. Her father said it was her tribal mark. People thought it was a birthmark. Said it was her beauty spot. Her father battled the rat for more than half an hour all over the kitchen. Quietly swearing and swinging the broom, he must have struck the rat more than fifty times, blood splattering all over the place, till the rat ran out of steam and let himself get cornered, and Yoruba's father swung away at him till blood flew all over the kitchen floor and all of the poor rat's insides had come outside.

All in all they were good days though, rats and all, the way the girl remembered them. And some days in this new time, she wished desperately she could turn back the clock and be her father's baby again. Dirty-faced, dress-torn, snotty-nosed tomboy. But she could not turn back the clock. She never really wanted to. And she was Yoruba, gentle Yoruba, and she had grown to be a gentlewoman, despite her mother's dedication and determination that this dear child should achieve ladyship. "Lady Eve-lyn."

In front of her house now, three-storied-and-basement brownstone. They lived on the parlor floor. She hoped her father had come home from work by now. Particularly this night, she hoped Matt Lovejoy was already home. She did not feel like facing her mother alone this evening in the very very middle of her eighteenth September.

She turned and stared back down the street past the children skipping rope, playing potsy, a few of them calling playful pleasant motherfuckers, past the winos on a stoop, and the junkies, past the forever double-parked cars, stared longingly toward the corner at the other end of the block trying to look [for] Matt Lovejoy around the corner coming home from work. She felt that if her father did materialize in the deep glow of the Harlem sunset she would break into a run like in the old days when she was six and seven and eight and believed in a jolly, old, fat white man by the name of Santa Claus, and thought the whole wide world was right there on her block in Harlem, and God was great and God was good and everything was for the best, because He worked mysteriously, the Grand Magician of them all. Cars honking, racing motors, fumes belching, children screaming, cursing, squealing, laughing. She stared past the busy intersection clear across Seventh Avenue all the way west to the river where the sun was a blazing disk of fire and washing the streets with a million colors and descending slowly down between the buildings at the very end of the street, down down it was sinking slowly sinking to set afire the Hudson River. Her eyes filled up and almost overflowed at the beauty of the Harlem sunset. The tenements bathed in soft sweet tender shadows now. She took one long last look down toward the other end of her block. Come around the corner, Daddy! Come around the corner! And I will run again to meet you. She turned toward the house. Maybe he was already home. Silently she prayed he was already in the house.

She was in no mood this day to hear her mother carry on and on about the grandest of all the Grand Cotillions. "You are indeed a lucky one, Eve-lyn. And of all the scrumptious places, it will be held downtown at the Waldorf, where few white folks get a chance to go and decidedly no niggers at all. You'll be one of those selected too. The grand magnificent Cotillion. It's everything I've worked to give you, dearie. The opportunity of a lifetime. My own dear baby is going to be a debutante!"

The girl walked wearily up the steps. Suddenly she was of the aged ones. And heavy-limbed. As if great iron weights hung from her arms, her legs. Her body tired; her soul weary; her mind exhausted.

Be home, Daddy!
Be home, Daddy!
Be home, Daddy!
Please!
Be home.

John Henrik Clarke

(1915–   )

A STRONG ADVOCATE of the need for present-day African Americans to know their African background, not through Euro-American myths, but through an objective study of the history of their homeland, John Henrik Clarke shares a kinship with writer/activists Carter G. Woodson, J. A. Rogers, and Malcolm X. All of them used their writings to address the necessity for African Americans to examine their own history.

Born in 1915, in Union Springs, Alabama, the son of a farmer, Clarke was educated at New York University (1948–1952), the New School for Social Research (1956–1958), the University of Ibadan (Nigeria), and the University of Ghana. His early work experiences presage the nature of his scholarship. While serving as a feature writer for the *Pittsburgh Courier* from 1957 to 1958, he also worked as an occasional teacher of African and African American history for the New School for Social Research in New York City, where he developed the African Studies Center and served as assistant to the director from 1958 to 1960. For one year (1958), he was also feature writer for the *Ghana Evening News*, Accra, Ghana.

Clarke's publishing career began in 1964 with his edition of *Harlem U.S.A.: The Story of a City within a City* (revised edition 1970). He is also editor of eight other works that demonstrate the interrelationship between African Americans' history and their present economic and political status: *Harlem: A Community in Transition* (1965), *American Negro Short Stories* (1966), *William Styron's Nat Turner: Ten Black Writers Respond* (1968, 1987), *Malcolm X: The Man and His Times* (1969), *Harlem* (short stories, 1970), J. A. Rogers's *World's Great Men of Color* (two volumes, 1972), *Black Families in the American Economy* (1975), and *Dimensions of the Struggle against Apartheid: A Tribute to Paul Robeson* (1979). And he is co-editor of three more significant publications, one a historical look at the slave trade and the two others biographical analyses: *Slave Trade and Slavery* (1970), *Black Titan: W. E. B. Du Bois* (1970), and *Marcus Garvey and the Vision of Africa* (1974). His most recent publication is *Africans Away from Home* (1988).

A leading historian of Africa and African America, Dr. Clarke has presented numerous papers at international conferences; his articles have appeared in such journals as *Negro History Bulletin*, *Chicago Defender*, *Journal of Negro Education*, *Phylon*, and *Présence Africaine*. His honors and awards include the Carter G. Woodson Award for creative contribution in editing and for excellence in teaching, the National Association for Television and Radio Announcers citation for meritorious achievement in educational television, and an L.H.D. from the University of Denver.

The following selection, "A Search for Identity," is reprinted from *Social Casework*.

A SEARCH FOR IDENTITY

My own search for an identity began—as I think it begins for all young people—a long time ago when I looked at the world around me and tried to understand what it was all about. My first teacher was my great grandmother whom we called "Mom Mary." She had been a slave first in Georgia and later in Alabama where I was born in Union Springs. It was she who told us the stories about our family and about how it had resisted slavery. More than anything else, she repeatedly told us the story of Buck, her first husband, and how he had been sold to a man who owned a stud farm in Virginia. Stud farms are an aspect of slavery that has been omitted from the record and about which we do not talk any more. We should remember, however, that there were times in this country when owners used slaves to breed stronger slaves in the same way that a special breed of horse is used to breed other horses.

My great grandmother had three children with Buck—my grandfather Jonah, my grandaunt Liza who was a midwife, and another child. With Buck, Mom Mary had as close to a marriage as a slave can have—a marriage with the permission of the respective masters. Mom Mary had a lifelong love affair with Buck, and years later after the emancipation she went to Virginia and searched for him for three years. She never found him, and she came back to Alabama where she spent the last years of her life.

My family

Mom Mary was the historian of our family. Years later when I went to Africa and listened to oral historians, I knew that my great grandmother was not very different from the old men and women who sit around in front of their houses and tell the young children the stories of their people—how they came from one place to an-

"A Search for Identity" by John Henrik Clarke is from *Social Casework*, May 1970, published by Family Service America. Reprinted by permission of Family Service America.

other, how they searched for safety, and how they tried to resist when the Europeans came to their lands.

This great grandmother was so dear to me that I have deified her in almost the same way that many Africans deify their old people. I think that my search for identity, my search for what the world was about, and my relationship to the world began when I listened to the stories of that old woman. I remember that she always ended the stories in the same way that she said "Good-bye" or "Good morning" to people. It was always with the reminder, "Run the race, and run it by faith." She was a deeply religious woman in a highly practical sense. She did not rule out resistance as a form of obedience to God. She thought that the human being should not permit himself to be dehumanized, and her concept of God was so pure and so practical that she could see that resistance to slavery was a form of obedience to God. She did not think that any of us children should be enslaved, and she thought that anyone who had enslaved any one of God's children had violated the very will of God.

I think Buck's pride in his manhood was the major force that always made her revere her relationship with him. He was a proud man and he resisted. One of the main reasons for selling him to a man to use on a stud farm was that he could breed strong slaves whose wills the master would then break. This dehumanizing process was a recurring aspect of slavery.

Growing up in Alabama, my father was a brooding, landless sharecropper, always wanting to own his own land; but on my father's side of the family there had been no ownership of land at all. One day after a storm had damaged our farm and literally blown the roof off our house, he decided to take his family to a mill city—Columbus, Georgia. He had hoped that one day he would make enough money to return to Alabama as an independent farmer. He pursued this dream the rest of his life. Ultimately the pursuit of this dream killed him. Now he has a piece of land, six feet deep and the length of his body; that is as close as he ever came to being an independent owner of land.

In Columbus I went to county schools, and I was the first member of the family of nine children to learn to read. I did so by picking up signs, grocery handbills, and many other things that people threw away into the street, and by studying the signboards. I knew more about the different brands of cigarettes and what they contained than I knew about the history of the country. I would read the labels on tin cans to see where the products were made, and these scattered things were my first books. I remember one day picking up a leaflet advertising that the Ku Klux Klan was riding again.

Because I had learned to read early, great things were expected of me. I was a Sunday school teacher of the junior class before I was ten years old, and I was the one person who would stop at the different homes in the community to read the Bible to the old ladies. In spite of growing up in such abject poverty, I grew up in a very rich cultural environment that had its oral history and with people who not only cared for me but pampered me in many ways. I know that this kind of upbringing negates all the modern sociological explanations of black people that assume that everybody who was poor was without love. I had love aplenty and appreciation aplenty, all of which gave me a sense of self-worth that many young black children never develop.

I began my search for my people first in the Bible. I wondered why all the characters—even those who, like Moses, were born in Africa—were white. Reading the description of Christ as swarthy and with hair like sheep's wool, I wondered why the church depicted him as blond and blue-eyed. Where was the hair like sheep's wool? Where was the swarthy complexion? I looked at the map of Africa and I knew Moses had been born in Africa. How did Moses become so white? If he went down to Ethiopia to marry Zeporah, why was Zeporah so white? Who painted the world white? Then I began to search for the definition of myself and my people in relationship to world history, and I began to wonder how we had become lost from the commentary of world history.

My teachers

In my first years in city schools in Columbus, Georgia, my favorite teacher and the one I best remember was Evelena Taylor, who first taught me to believe in myself. She took my face between her two hands and looking at me straight in the eyes, said, "I believe in you." It meant something for her to tell me that she believed in me, that the color of my skin was not supposed to be a barrier to my aspirations, what education is, and what it is supposed to do for me.

These were lonely years for me. These were the years after the death of my mother—a beautiful woman, a washerwoman—who had been saving fifty cents a week for my education, hoping that eventually she would be able to send her oldest son to college. Her hopes did not materialize; she died long before I was ten. I did, however, go to school earlier than some of the other children. We lived just outside of the city limits. Children living beyond the city limits were supposed to go to county schools because the city schools charged county residents $3.75 each semester for the use of books. This was a monumental sum of money for us because my father made from $10.00 to $14.00 a week as a combination farmer and fire tender at brickyards.

In order to get the $3.75 required each semester, my father made a contribution and my various uncles made contributions. It was a collective thing to raise what was for us a large sum of money not only to send a child to a city school instead of to a county school but also to make certain that the one child in the family attending the city school had slightly better clothing than the other children. So I had a coat that was fairly warm and a pair of shoes that was supposed to be warm but really was not. As I think about the shoes, my feet sometimes get cold even now, but I did not tell my benefactors that the shoes were not keeping me warm.

I grew up in a religious environment after we came to Columbus, Georgia, and after the passing of my mother. The local church became my community center and the place where most of the community activities occurred. It was here that I wondered about my place in history and why I could not find any of my people in any of the books that I read, and my concern began to change to irritation. Where were we in history? Did we just spring as a people from nothing? What were our old roots?

As I approached the end of my last year in grammar school, Evelena Taylor told me that she would not let me use the color of my skin as an excuse for not preparing lessons or an excuse for not aspiring to be true to myself and my greatest potential. She taught me that I must always prepare.

I think my value to the whole field of teaching history is that I have prepared during my lifetime, and I have prepared in the years when no one was thinking anything about black studies, but I kept on preparing until ultimately the door opened. I had to search, however, for some definitions of myself, and during that last year in grammar school, I began to receive some of the privileges in the school that generally went to the light-complected youngsters whom we called "The Light Brigade." They were sons and daughters of the professional blacks—the doctors and the teachers who were usually of light complexion. I was the leader of the group called "The Dark Brigade," the poorest of the children who came from the other side of the railroad tracks. I received that privilege in the school, not just as the leader of the contingent of young people who came from my neighborhood, but because for once the teachers could nominate the best student to ring the bell. Mrs. Taylor, who played no favorites, nominated me.

This privilege gave me my first sense of power—the feeling that I could stand in a window and ring a bell and five hundred children would march out, or I could ring it earlier or later, but they were simply immobile until I rang that bell. After handling my responsibility a little recklessly for a few days by ringing the bell a little early or a little late just to prove my prerogative to do it, I realized that I was not living up to my best potential as Mrs. Taylor meant it. Then I began to exercise this responsibility in the exact manner in which it was supposed to be exercised: to ring the bell for the first recess at exactly 10:15 A.M., to ring the bell for the second recess at noon, to ring for the return of the children into the school at exactly 12:45 P.M., and to ring for dismissal at exactly 3:00 P.M. Thereby, I learned something about the proper use of authority and responsibility.

I wanted to advance the status of my particular little group, the poorest students in the school. They were not the poorest in the way they learned their lessons because they could readily compete with students who came from homes where they had books and some degree of comfort and who wore shoes even in the summertime (which was unthinkable to us because generally we had one pair of shoes and that pair had to last the entire year). I wanted, however, to do something to make my group look exceptionally good. I had been the leader of the current events forum in my school, and because I worked before and after school mostly for white people who had good libraries and children who never read the books, I began to borrow books from their libraries and bring them home. In Columbus, Georgia, where they had Jim Crow libraries and black people could not use the public library, I began to forge the names of well-known white people on notes that instructed the librarian to give me a certain book. I accumulated a great many books that way. This illegitimate book borrowing went on for quite some time until one day the white person whose name I had forged appeared in the library at the same time I did. That put an end to my illegitimate use of the public library of Columbus.

One Friday evening when the teachers let us do whatever we wanted to do, I planned to do something extraordinary in the leadership of the current events forum. My group had always done a few exceptional things because I would take the magazines and newspapers from the homes of the whites, and, rather than throw them into the garbage can, I would distribute them among our group. I also brought copies of the World Almanac once a year. My group, therefore, always had news from Atlanta, news about the Japanese navy, and news about many different things. When they spoke in school about current events, they were able to speak with authority about international news because they had authoritative sources.

I have always had a phenomenal memory. When I was a youngster, I could quote verbatim much of what I had read in almanacs and in small encyclopedias. In trying literally to outdo "The Light Brigade," I decided to prepare something on the role of the black man in ancient history. I went to a lawyer for whom I worked. He was a kind man whose library I had used quite extensively. I asked him for a book on the role that black people had played in ancient history. In a kindly way he told me that I came from a people who had no history but, that if I persevered and obeyed the laws, my people might one day make history. Then he paid me the highest compliment that a white man could pay a black man in the period when I was growing up. He told me that one day I might grow up to be a great Negro like Booker T. Washington.

At that time white people considered that the greatest achievement to which a black man could aspire was to reach the status of the great educator, Booker T. Washington. He *had been* a great educator and he *did* build up Tuskegee Institute, but he consistently cautioned his people to be patient with the Jim Crow system and to learn to be good servants and artisans. He said it was more important to earn a dollar a day (at the turn of the century that was considered good pay for a black man) than to hope or work to sit next to white people in the opera. He was actually telling his people never to seek social equality, and later on he was challenged by W. E. B. Du Bois, who created a whole new school of thought based on the belief that blacks should aspire to anything they wanted, be it streetcleaner or president.

At the time of my conversation with the lawyer I had nothing for or against Booker T. Washington. I really didn't know much about the lawyer, and his philosophy of racial equality didn't mean a great deal to me. What insulted every part of me to the very depth of my being was his assumption that I came from a people without any history. At that point of my life I began a systematic search for my people's role in history.

Other influences

During my first year in high school I was doing chores and, because the new high school did not even have a cloak room, I had to hold the books and papers of a guest lecturer. The speaker had a copy of a book called *The New Negro*. Fortunately I turned to an essay written by a Puerto Rican of African descent with a German-sounding name. It was called "The Negro Digs Up His Past," by Arthur A. Schomburg.[1] I knew then that I came from a people with a history older even than that of Europe. It was a most profound and overwhelming feeling—this great discovery that my people did

---

[1]Arthur A. Schomburg, "The Negro Digs Up His Past," in *The New Negro*, ed. Alain Locke (New York: Albert and Charles Boni, 1925), pp. 231–37.

have a place in history and that, indeed, their history is older than that of their oppressors.

The essay, "The Negro Digs Up His Past," was my introduction to the ancient history of the black people. Years later when I came to New York, I started to search for Arthur A. Schomburg. Finally, one day I went to the 135th Street library and asked a short-tempered clerk to give me a letter to Arthur A. Schomburg. In an abrupt manner she said, "You will have to walk up three flights." I did so, and there I saw Arthur Schomburg taking charge of the office containing the Schomburg collection of books relating to African people the world over, while the other staff members were out to lunch. I told him impatiently that I wanted to know the history of my people, and I wanted to know it right now and in the quickest possible way. His patience more than matched my impatience. He said, "Sit down, son. What you are calling African history and Negro history is nothing but the missing pages of world history. You will have to know general history to understand these specific aspects of history." He continued patiently, "You have to study your oppressor. That's where your history got lost." Then I began to think that at last I will find out how an entire people—my people—disappeared from the respected commentary of human history.

It took time for me to learn that there is no easy way to study history. (There is, in fact, no easy way to study anything.) It is necessary to understand all the components of history in order to recognize its totality. It is similar to knowing where the tributaries of a river are in order to understand the nature of what made the river so big. Mr. Schomburg, therefore, told me to study general history. He said repeatedly, "Study the history of your oppressor."

I began to study the general history of Europe, and I discovered that the first rise of Europe—the Greco-Roman period—was a period when Europe "borrowed" very heavily from Africa. This early civilization depended for its very existence on what was taken from African civilization. At that time I studied Europe more than I studied Africa because I was following Mr. Schomburg's advice, and I found out how and why the slave trade started.

When I returned to Mr. Schomburg, I was ready to start a systematic study of the history of Africa. It was he who is really responsible for what I am and what value I have for the field of African history and the history of black people the world over.

I grew up in Harlem during the depression, having come to New York at the age of seventeen. I was a young depression radical—always studying, always reading; taking advantage of the fact that in New York City I could go into a public library and take out books, read them, bring them back, get some more, and even renew them after six weeks if I hadn't finished them. It was a joyous experience to be exposed to books. Actually, I went through a period of adjustment because my illegitimate borrowing of books from the Jim Crow library of Columbus, Georgia, had not prepared me to walk freely out of a library with a book without feeling like a thief. It took several years before I felt that I had every right to go there.

During my period of growing up in Harlem, many black teachers were begging for black students, but they did not have to beg me. Men like Willis N. Huggins, Charles C. Serfait, and Mr. Schomburg literally trained me not only to study African history and black people the world over but to teach this history.

My teaching

All the training I received from my teachers was really set in motion by my great grandmother's telling me the stories of my family and my early attempts to search first for my identity as a person, then for the definition of my family, and finally for the role of my people in the whole flow of human history.

One thing that I learned very early was that knowing history and teaching it are two different things, and the first does not necessarily prepare one for the second. At first I was an exceptionally poor teacher because I crowded too many of my facts together and they were poorly organized. I was nervous, overanxious, and impatient with my students. I began my teaching career in community centers in Harlem. However, I learned that before I could become an effective teacher, I had to gain better control of myself as a human being. I had to acquire patience with young people who giggled when they were told about African kings. I had to understand that these young people had been so brainwashed by our society that they could see themselves only as depressed beings. I had to realize that they had in many ways adjusted to their oppression and that I needed considerable patience, many teaching skills, and great love for them in order to change their attitudes. I had to learn to be a more patient and understanding human being. I had to take command of myself and understand why I was blaming people for not knowing what I knew, and blaming students for not being so well versed in history. In effect, I was saying to them, "How dare you not know this?"

After learning what I would have to do with myself and my subject matter in order to make it more understandable to people with no prior knowledge, I began to become an effective teacher. I learned that teaching history requires not only patience and love but also the ability to make history interesting to the students. I learned that the good teacher is partly an entertainer, and if he loses the attention of his class, he has lost his lesson. A good teacher, like a good entertainer, first must hold his audience's attention. Then he can teach his lesson.

I taught African history in community centers in the Harlem neighborhood for over twenty years before I had any regular school assignment. My first regular assignment was as director of the Heritage Teaching Program at Haryou-Act, an antipoverty agency in Harlem. Here I had the opportunity after school to train young black persons in how to approach history and how to use history as an instrument of personal liberation. I taught them that taking away a people's history is a way to enslave them. I taught them that history is a two-edged sword to be used for oppression or liberation. The major point that I tried, sometimes successfully, to get across to them is that history is supposed to make one self-assured but not arrogant. It is not supposed to give one any privileges over other people, but it should make one see oneself in a new way in relation to other people.

After five years in the Haryou-Act project, I accepted my first regular assignment at the college at which I still teach. I serve also as visiting professor at another university and as an instructor in black heritage during the summer program conducted for teachers by the history department of a third major university. I also travel to the extent that my classes will permit, training teachers how to teach about black heritage. The black power explosion and the black studies explosion have pushed men like me to the forefront in developing approaches to creative and well-documented black curricula. Forced to be in the center of this arena, I have had to take another inventory of myself and my responsibilities. I have found young black students eager for this history and have found many of them having doubts about whether they really had a history in spite of the fact that they had demanded it. I have had to learn patience all over again with young people on another level.

On the college level I have encountered another kind of young black student—much older than those who giggled—the kind who does not believe in himself, does not believe in history, and who consequently is in revolt. This student says in effect, "Man, you're turning me on. You know that we didn't rule ancient Egypt." I have had to learn patience all over again as I learned to teach on a level where students come from a variety of cultural backgrounds.

In all my teaching, I have used as my guide the following definition of heritage, and I would like to conclude with it.

Heritage, in essence, is the means by which people have used their talents to create a history that gives them memories they can respect and that they can use to command the respect of other people. The ultimate purpose of heritage and heritage teaching is to use people's talents to develop awareness and pride in themselves so that they themselves can achieve good relationships with other people.

Dudley Randall

(1914–   )

POET, LIBRARIAN, AND PUBLISHER, Dudley Randall has the distinction of being noted for his association with and publication of now very noted African American literary figures as well as for seven collections of his own poetry. Born in Washington, D.C., in 1914, Randall had the intellectual and cultural advantages of having had parents who introduced him to the works of African American literary artists at a very young age. Though born in Washington, he has made his adult home in Detroit, Michigan. From 1932 to 1937 he worked in the foundry of the Ford Motor Company and from 1943 to 1946 he was stationed in the South Pacific during his tenure in the United States Signal Corps. After completing his bachelor's degree in English at Wayne State University in 1949, he went on to complete a master's degree in library science at the University of Michigan in 1951. During his matriculation, he worked in the United States Post Office in order to earn money to help with his school expenses; he left the Post Office in 1951 to become a librarian at Lincoln University (Missouri), where he stayed until 1954. In 1954 he moved to Baltimore, Maryland, where he worked again as a librarian at Morgan State College from 1954 to 1956. He ended his library career back in Michigan at the Wayne County Federated Library System, where he worked from 1956 until 1969.

Although Randall began writing poetry at the age of four and despite the fact that he won a Tompkins Award for fiction during his first year at Wayne State and another for poetry in 1966, his career as a poet thrived concomitantly with his role as founder of Broadside Press in 1965. The first major publication of Broadside Press, *Poem Counterpoem* (1966), is a collection of poems written by Randall and Margaret Danner, founder of Boone House, a black cultural center in Detroit where both poets read their poems to audiences on Sundays. As editor of Broadside Press, Randall published the works of many now well-known African American literary figures such as Gwendolyn Brooks, Sonia Sanchez, Naomi Long Madgett, Haki Madhubuti, Nikki Giovanni, James Emanuel, Marvin X, and Keoropetse Kgositsile.

In addition to his work as librarian and publisher, Randall has also served as a visiting lecturer in African American literature at the University of Michigan and as a poet-in-residence at the University of Detroit. He is the author of six collections of poetry: *Poem Counterpoem* (1966), *Cities Burning* (1968), *Love You* (1970), *More to Remember: Poems of Four Decades*

56

(1971), *After the Killing* (1973), *Broadside Memories: Poets I Have Known* (1975), and *A Litany of Friends: New and Selected Poems* (1981). The latest volume bridges the gap aesthetically as well as historically between the Black Renaissance of the 1920s and the revolutionary fervor of the 1960s. Randall is also the editor of several anthologies: *For Malcolm: Poems on the Life and the Death of Malcolm X* (1967), edited with Margaret Burroughs; *Black Poetry: A Supplement to Anthologies Which Exclude Black Poets* (1969); and the still available *Black Poets* (1971). Also see *Homage to Hoyt Fuller* (1984), edited by Dudley Randall and *Golden Song: The Fiftieth Anniversary Anthology of the Poetry Society* (1985), edited by Louis J. Cantuni and Dudley Randall.

For further reading, see Ron Baxter Miller's essay in *Dictionary of Literary Biography, Volume 41*; D. H. Melhem's "Dudley Randall: A Humanist View," *Black American Literature Forum* 4(1983); and Charles Rowell's "In Conversation with Dudley Randall," *Obsidian* 1(1976); Richard Barksdale and Keneth Kinnamon's *Black Writers in America* (1972); and R. Baxter Miller's *Black American Poets between Worlds* (1986).

"Booker T. and W.E.B." is reprinted from *Kaleidoscope*, and "An Answer to Lerone Bennett's Questionnaire on a Name for Black Americans" comes from *More to Remember: Poems of Four Decades*.

BOOKER T. AND W.E.B.

"It seems to me," said Booker T.,
"It shows a mighty lot of cheek
To study chemistry and Greek
When Mister Charlie needs a hand
To hoe the cotton on his land,
And when Miss Ann looks for a cook,
Why stick your nose inside a book?"

"I don't agree," said W.E.B.,
"If I should have the drive to seek
Knowledge of chemistry or Greek,
I'll do it. Charles and Miss can look
Another place for hand or cook.
Some men rejoice in skill of hand,
And some in cultivating land,
But there are others who maintain
The right to cultivate the brain."

"It seems to me," said Booker T.,
"That all you folks have missed the boat
Who shout about the right to vote,
And spend vain days and sleepless nights
In uproar over civil rights.
Just keep your mouths shut, do not grouse,
But work, and save, and buy a house."

"I don't agree," said W.E.B.,
"For what can property avail
If dignity and justice fail.
Unless you help to make the laws,
They'll steal your house with trumped-up clause.
A rope's as tight, a fire as hot,
No matter how much cash you've got.
Speak soft, and try your little plan,
But as for me, I'll be a man."

"It seems to me," said Booker T.—

"I don't agree,"
Said W.E.B.

AN ANSWER TO LERONE BENNETT'S QUESTIONNAIRE ON A NAME FOR BLACK AMERICANS

Discarding the Spanish word for black
and taking the Anglo-Saxon word for Negro,
discarding the names of English slavemasters
and taking the names of Arabian slave-traders
won't put a single
bean in your belly
or an inch of steel
in your spine.

Call a skunk a rose,
and he'll still stink,
and make the name stink too.

From *More to Remember* by Dudley Randall. Reprinted by permission of Third World Press.

Call a rose a skunk,
and it'll still smell sweet,
and even sweeten the name.

The spirit informs the name,
not the name the spirit.

If the white man took the name Negro,
and you took the name Caucasian,
he'd still kick your ass,
as long as you let him.

If you're so insecure
that a word makes you quake,
another word
won't cure you.

Change your mind,
not your name.

Change your life,
not your clothes.

Margaret Danner

(1915–1982)

MARGARET ESSE DANNER, born in 1915, began writing poetry in the early 1930s and was long known as a guardian and celebrant of the African roots of black American culture. Much of her work, including her most famous and widely anthologized poem "The Elevator Man Adheres to Form," speaks in a voice of protest against the plight of black Americans in white society, but the main body of her work focuses on African heritage as the wellspring of black power and beauty. Most critics agree that her African poems represent her most significant contribution to black American literature.

Danner was born in Pryorsburg, Kentucky, and spent her college years in Chicago at Loyola and Northwestern universities. Although she had already been writing poetry for many years, her work was first recognized when she won second place in the Poetry Workshop of the Midwestern Writers' Conference in 1945. From 1951 to 1957 she was an editor of *Poetry: The Magazine of Verse*, which published a series of her poems titled "Far from Africa." For this publication Danner received the first of her literary awards, a John Hay Whitney Fellowship, in 1951. She published her first book of poetry, *Impressions of African Art Forms*, in 1960.

In 1961 Danner left Chicago to take up a poet-in-residenceship at Wayne State University in Detroit. She lived in Detroit for the next several years, opening Boone House, a cultural arts center, in 1962 and publishing her second volume of poetry, *To Flower*, in 1963. These years were important ones in her writing career because they brought her into close association with Dudley Randall, Robert Hayden, Owen Dodson, and others who became known as the Detroit poets. As a member of this group, whose influence helped shape the Black Arts Movement of the 1960s, she developed her reputation as a writer of stature and significance in the black arts community. During this period she also won several grants and awards, including the Harriet Tubman Award in 1965. In 1966 she and Randall published a collaborative volume titled *Poem Counterpoem*.

Danner traveled to Africa in 1966 to read her poetry at the World Exposition of Negro Arts in Dakar, Senegal. On her return she took a position as poet-in-residence at Virginia Union University in Richmond, which she held from 1968 to 1969. While at Virginia Union she published her third volume of poetry, *Iron Lace* (1968), and edited two poetry anthologies, *Brass Horses* (1968) and *Regroup* (1969). *The Down of a Thistle*, her final collection of poems, including prose poems and songs, was published in 1976.

For a closer look at Danner's place in the African American literary tradition, see June M. Aldridge's article on her in *Dictionary of Literary Biography, Volume 41.*

The following poems are all taken from *The Down of a Thistle.*

THE ELEVATOR MAN ADHERES TO FORM

I am reminded, by the tan man who wings
the elevator, of Rococo art. His ways
are undulating waves that shepherd and swing
us cupidlike from floor to floor.

He sweethearts us
with polished pleasantries; gallantly
flourishes us up and up. No casual "hi's" from him.

His greetings, God-speedings, display his Ph.D.
aplomb, and I should feel like a cherub,
be fleur-de-lis and pastel-shell-like, but

instead, I vision other tan and deeper much than tan
early Baroque-like men who (seeing themselves still
strutlessly groping, winding down subterranean

grottoes of injustice, down dark spirals) feel
with such tortuous, smoked-stone grey intensity
that they exhale a hurricane of gargoyles, then reel

into it. I see these others boggling in their misery
and wish this elevator artisan would fill his flourishing
form with warmth for them and turn his lettered zeal
toward lifting them above their crippling storm.

LANGSTON HUGHES MADE IT

He made it.
You should have seen Langston Hughes in the land
of the clean white sands of Senegal.

You should have seen his old-ivory face
blending with the sculptured ivories
contrasting with the ebony carvings.

The gleaming eyes have never been more bright
than they were against the sun
and upon the Festival art.

You should have heard Langston Hughes in Africa
yes, he read his own, but as he was known to do
he kept looking for poets.

And he asked me to be on the lookout for poets too
who could come and read their own
as poets love to do.

And this, too, is the Langston Hughes
that we will remember. The Langston Hughes
who was more than true to his colleagues.

> *to fling my arms wide*
> *in this place of the sun*
> *to whirl and dance . . .*

JUST AS OUR AFRICAN ANCESTORS DID

None have gained a loftier recognition
through the medium of The Arts
from four hundred B.C.
than we chrome tones. We Blacks.

And here in Chicago,
about five blocks from where I was born
we are again creating portraits
of other Blacks that we respect, on a wall
of a building that should, long ago
have experienced rejection.

Finally, Blacks are being reawakened to reclaim
another spark of our incomparable heritage.
We enfold again and hold and enhance
and paint (with all the colors of the rainbow)

to testify to our pride of stance,
and attest our love, on this old brick wall.
Just as our forefathers so superbly did
through carving and molding on wood, on stone,
on iron, bronze, ivory and gold.

to the OBACI wall in the ghetto
Chicago Art Scene 1967

Blyden Jackson

(1910–   )

BORN IN 1910, in Paducah, Kentucky, Blyden Jackson is the son of Julia Estelle and George Washington Jackson, a school teacher. He received his A.B. in 1930 from Wilberforce University and his A.M. in 1938 and his Ph.D. in 1952 from the University of Michigan. From 1934 to 1935, Jackson taught high school in Louisville, Kentucky, before joining the faculty at Fisk University in Nashville, Tennessee, where he remained from 1945 to 1954. In 1954 he accepted the position of professor of English at Southern University in Baton Rouge, Louisiana, where he was head of the department from 1954 to 1963 and dean of the graduate school from 1963 to 1964. He is now professor emeritus of English at the University of North Carolina, Chapel Hill, where he joined the faculty in 1969.

In addition to a distinguished teaching record and administrative responsibilities, Professor Jackson is a contributor to a number of scholarly journals such as the *College Language Association Journal* and the *Southern Literary Journal*. He is also the author of two studies of African American literature: *Black Poetry in America* (co-authored with Louis Rubin, 1974) and *The Waiting Years: Essays on American Negro Literature* (1976). His most recent work is the impressive *A History of Afro-American Literature: Volume I, The Long Beginning, 1746–1895* (1989). He is currently working on volume two.

"An Essay in Criticism" comes from *The Waiting Years*.

AN ESSAY IN CRITICISM

I began writing about Negro literature early in the 1940s. The exact circumstances of my beginning, as I remember them now, tell something, in their way, about Negro life.

There are four Negro college fraternities. The oldest of the four, for obvious reasons, is named Alpha Phi Alpha. It is, incidentally, called Alpha, and its members are known as either "Alphas" or "Apes." But the circumstance about the Alphas which tells something about Negro life (and which would be true about any Negro college fraternity, sororities included) is that the Alphas could not be simply a college fraternity. They had to be a social-action group, doing their bit for the advancement of the race.

Alpha men were, and many still are (even in the changed 1970s), Alpha men for life. The fraternity's so-called graduate chapters outnumber its undergraduate chapters. For years the fraternity vigorously prosecuted its famous (among Negroes) "Go to High School, Go to College" campaign. Its general presidents have tended to be quite eminent men in the national Negro community—men like Charles H. Wesley and Rayford Logan, the historians and champions of Negro rights, or Belford Lawson, a lawyer active in the cause of civil rights, or Frank Stanley, publisher of the Louisville Defender, *who, as president of the national organization of Negro newspaper owners, publishers, and editors, in the 1940s and 1950s played a prominent role in fighting racial discrimination of several kinds, especially in the armed services.*

General presidents of Alpha campaigned for their office almost as if they were running for a high post in the national government. It was incumbent upon them to shout from the housetops their achievements as "race" men. They said very little, though always something, about the "social" side of college life. In view of the conduct of these Alpha general presidents and all aspirants to the Alpha general presidency, as well as the sense of mission that permeated all Alphadom (and, indeed, all of Negro Greekdom), no one should be surprised to learn that The Sphinx, *the official journal of the Alphas, had its sense of mission too. It could not be content merely with circulating amiable gossip about Alphas among the Alpha brotherhood.*

My career, then, as a critic of Negro literature, as I remember it, really started when I became the books editor of The Sphinx. *It would have been impossible for me, in the early 1940s, to have been that kind of editor in a magazine like* The Sphinx *without talking about Negro literature.*

"An Essay in Criticism" appeared in Phylon *in the last quarter of 1950.* Phylon *was a quarterly founded by W. E. B. Du Bois (who happened to be an Alpha) when he went back to the changed Atlanta University after his feud with Walter White—a gentleman who could be, upon occasion, as intractable as Du Bois (and who also happened to be an Alpha)—reached unmanageable proportions. Primarily a learned journal for social scientists,* Phylon *was, nevertheless, in 1950, the leading resource for publication about Negro literature under the control of Negroes.*

Du Bois was no longer associated with Atlanta University in 1950. A sociologist of some distinction, Mozell Hill, was editing Phylon. *Un-*

der Hill's direction, Phylon celebrated the middle year of the twentieth century with a symposium about the American Negro that filled all the pages of a special issue. Contributions for this special issue were solicited. In fact, all of the articles in the special issue were by invitation only. Writers who appeared in this issue included Arna Bontemps, Gwendolyn Brooks, Sterling Brown, G. Lewis Chandler, Nick Aaron Ford, Hugh M. Gloster, Robert Hayden, Langston Hughes, Ulysses Lee, Alain Locke, Charles H. Nichols, L. D. Reddick, Saunders Redding, Ira De A. Reid, George S. Schuyler, William Gardner Smith, Era Bell Thompson, and Margaret Walker.

What I had written about Negro literature in The Sphinx *and one or two other places had apparently caught the eye of Mozell Hill and his fellow editors at* Phylon. *I was very proud on my invitation to appear in this special midcentury issue of* Phylon. *I was also very conscious of art as art. I was working on a doctoral dissertation on irony. And so, when one considers the Alphas and my invitation to be in* Phylon *and the nature of my dissertation, perhaps that I should choose to try to speak as I tried to speak in "An Essay in Criticism" was inevitable.*

I think it is a truism that in every regard the Negro writer has been typically American, except, perhaps, in the amount and quality of his work. Whether in absolute or comparative terms, the Negro has not published much in America. Likewise, whether in absolute or comparative terms, his writing has been too often execrable, although throughout the course of Negro literature constant improvement is readily discernible.

Now the problems of both the quantity and the quality of Negro literature are, it seems to me, inextricably intertwined with the problem of the Negro writer's audience. It is nonsense to say that a writer's audience does not influence him, just as nonsensical as it is to hold that writers write—and permit themselves to be published— merely because there is something in them that must come out. And the Negro writer has lacked a helpful audience in two large ways: viz., sympathetically and critically. The lack of a wide sympathetic audience among the only extensive public available to him has undoubtedly inhibited the Negro writer's effective use of symbols; and, of course, creative writing is nothing if not symbolic. However, eliminating the iniquities of racial stereotypes, the indispensable propaedeutic for easing the Negro writer's problem in the handling of symbols, must continue to wait upon the combined action of many forces—among them, incidentally, the services of a competent and forthright critical audience. On the other hand the lack of critical audience is clearly a reflection on Negro literary scholarship more than on anything else.

For Negroes just have not gotten around to real criticism of their own literature. We have done some good things. But all our accomplishments can quickly be demonstrated to be mere prolegomena for the hard, serious, tedious labor of giving our literature the sort of scholarly and critical framework that adds the needed marginal dimensions to the established European literatures. Let us look at the best we have done in criticism. Saunders Redding's *To Make a Poet Black* is a rapid summary, mainly historical, moving too hastily to develop adequately his thesis that Negro literature is a literature of necessity, though often enough delighting us with such trenchant *obiter dicta* as its characterization of Joel Chandler Harris' dialect. Hugh Gloster's more recent *Negro Voices in American Fiction* is an excellent reference work, with an especially valuable bibliography; but, again, Gloster is limited by intentions that are as patently summary as Redding's. Sterling Brown, who has done yeoman work in the area of his choice, has found himself completely occupied with the job of getting Negro literature into the field of vision of a wide public. Benjamin Brawley was always as timid and platitudinous as a Sunday School pamphlet. James Weldon Johnson was an executive, and his criticism, while often redeemed by his native taste, betrayed that tendency of his disposition as well as his lack of academic scholarship. There is little more to say about Negroes' criticism of their own literature, except that here for Negro students with ability and industry is a veritable green pasture.

Sometimes I have dreamed dreams about what could transpire in the criticism of Negro literature. Dreams can be very magnificent. Du Bois, half a century ago at Atlanta, bursting with the enthusiasm of his youth, laid down, it will be remembered, a program for an integrated sociological study of the Negro problem that was to have carried through a hundred years. Incidentally, during the thirteen years that he then stayed at Atlanta, he maintained his program's operation largely according to plan. And I have wished that those of us working with Negro literature might catch some of the magnificence—foolish, arrogant, but, withal, glorious—of young Du Bois' Atlanta dreaming. I do not begrudge a single one of the buildings I see going up on Negro campuses. God knows when one wanders around the great university campuses of America and then comes South again, he knows all too bitterly how much, in the "segregated but equal" dispensation, we are still on short rations. And if one moves through the parts of Negro ghettos where most Negroes have to live, perceiving unavoidably the squalor and meanness everywhere, scrofulous hovels jammed together, filthy, unkept streets, bad odors and harsh atmospheres, he will give thanks for every bit of clean turf, every piece of modern plumbing, every gracious contour on the Negro college campus. It is, indeed, always a matter of great wonder to me, when I recall where Negroes have been cooped up, that we are not all snarling, venomous beasts. After all, how can any man esteem beauty who knows nothing of it? Let us, then, get what we can of beauty on our physical campuses.

And yet—I would sometimes that our college budgets did occasionally contemplate a series of studies in our literature. I can at least pretend names for them: the Atlanta University Series of American Negro Writers; the James T. Shephard Editions of Slave Narratives; the Tennessee State College Studies in Negro Literary Acculturation. I can think, too, of individual studies prepared, if not issued also, under the aegis of some Negro school that has somehow or other managed to institute a program of research. This business of dialect—we have now reached a state of cultural assurance sufficient for us to put it in its right perspectives, both linguistically and psychologically—I should like to see studied. What we know, or ought to know, about the fictional treatment of the Negro middle class has never been systematically assembled. There are handbooks and anthologies of Negro poetry, but no single intensive studies of separate poems of any Negro poets. And, of course, the possibilities for tracing the relations of Negro literature are, as one would expect, virtually legion. Because Negroes have not written in great volume, or because some people say that Negro art is shallow, a dream like this may seem far-fetched. It is not. One competent and diligent student, Lorenzo Dow Turner, working—one almost wants to say barehanded—in the field of linguistics has shown how rich can be the yield from sources that might appear barren to the superficial eye. Moreover, some of the things I suggest have already been attempted. I know, although I have seen neither of them, that within the last several years at least two problems in research have dealt with the too-long-neglected slave narratives. Some time ago Brawley did for Chapel Hill a life of Paul Laurence Dunbar, the first of a series, never continued, which William Edward Farrison tells me Brawley was to have edited. It is a shockingly inadequate and old-maidish performance, but still it was a start. Certainly the materials to justify a host of enterprises by students of Negro literature do exist. The problem is in getting people who know what to do with these materials, and who, moreover, are prepared to endure the drudgery that sustained scholarship demands.

Indeed our literature is thin, not altogether because of its own inherent limitations, but because we have not enriched it and expanded it with the great accretions of interpretation we are likely to recall every time we read a fairly familiar piece of literature by a white author reputable enough to be in the literary histories. To realize this one need not go to Shakespeare, around whom the critical works are so numerous that they literally do constitute fair-sized libraries. One may select almost at random comparatively minor figures in the kingdom of English letters and still have quite a bit of bibliographical sport with them. But, in terms of the assistance that a good critical audience can provide, Negro literature is starved.

Waiving for the moment the possible contributions of diligent research, consider merely the province of aesthetic judgments. There are so many issues to be noted and discussed and argued about in that area alone that we have not set down as fully as we might. There is, for instance, in *One Way to Heaven* the way that Countee Cullen wrote two novels; the larger one about two "little" people, for all that it simpers occasionally, has much of the charm of a fairy story, but the other—which is not fitted too well into the whole—while worthy of commendation as an attempt healthily to laugh at one's self, is too stilted and self-conscious for good satire. Or, since we have started with *One Way to Heaven*, there is also the trouble generally that Negro writers have in writing good, convincing conversation, a trouble especially distressing in comedy-of-manners work like the satirical episodes in Cullen's novel where he brings people together for drawing-room talk, but gets out of them only a painful burlesque of the brilliant stream of *mots* on which one floats gaily through the ether of William Congreve or Oscar Wilde or George Bernard Shaw. And there are countless other items, each of them conceivably a "rift to be loaded with ore": like the way in which—for all the nobility of her intentions, because she is herself so naively philistine, so breathless with adoration of good-looking people Nordic style (even when they are tinted with the tar brush), good-looking clothes, good-looking homes, and country-club ideas of the *summa bona*—Jessie Fauset's defenses of the Negro middle class backfire into an indictment of her horrid copycatting of the wrong values. Or, to speak again of conversation, consider the verisimilitude (as ordinary Negro speech) of the talk in Zora Neale Hurston's *Moses, Man of the Mountain* and the superb rightness of this assimilation of the Old Testament story to Negro mores when Miss Hurston's retelling of the famous Hebrew legend is diagramed, as it should be, allegorically, so that other beautiful hits—like the equation of Moses, from the house of Pharaoh, to our mulatto leadership, or of the grumbling of the Hebrews in the wilderness to the attitudes that Negro masses take toward Negro leaders—assume their due proportions in this parable about one minority group intimated through the tale of another. Or, for perhaps even better art, reflect upon the life-giving quality of Ann Petry's imagination in *The Street*, an achievement the magnitude of which can be sharply realized by placing beside Miss Petry's Lutie Johnson—a woman warm and vital, whose senses, and will, pulse with a fierce indwelling energy—the stillborn and crudely manipulated Mimi Daquin of Walter White's *Flight*. Or, consider the fairly common tendency, exemplified very well in this same *Flight*, for Negro novelists to have conceptions beyond their capacities. Or, to make an end of this, recall what a gratifying thing can happen when the conception and the capacity go hand-in-glove, as they do in William Gardner Smith's *Last of the Conquerors*, where the particular version of irony conceived by Smith, the irony of a Negro boy finding democratic treatment in an experience of life where he least expected it and which he cannot retrieve, is given just the right pitch by the elegiac tone that Smith gets immediately and sustains admirably in spite of the delicacy of its adjustment.

All around us today the air resounds with calls to integrate the Negro into our national life. Very probably the increasingly favorable reaction to those calls is a sign that both America and its Negroes are reaching a certain maturity. Negro writers are promising to do their bit in keeping pace with the latest trend. Symptomatically, they are losing, as never quite before, their exaggerated self-consciousness. Gwendolyn Brooks's *Satin-Legs Smith* represents without apology the South Side of Chicago, but none of his unabashed local color prevents him from representing very well also the diminution of man as a romantic spirit in the machine-made monotony of the modern metropolis. Redding's *Stranger and Alone* is a study of Uncle Tomism, but a study of Uncle Tomism that illuminates *sub specie aeternitatis* the ubiquitous errand-boys for Caesar. The Negro writer, who has always been very American, even in his failings and despite his handicaps, is still responsive to his environment. But there is still too little evidence that Negro criticism developed by literary scholarship is making strenuous efforts to "integrate" itself with any American pattern. For the pattern of American scholarship requires, if nothing else, some activity. We have sent by now a goodly squadron of students to the great graduate schools of America. We are even opening up now graduate schools of our own. Perhaps it may be argued in extenuation of our inertia as productive scholar-critics that our teaching loads are too great and our facilities for research too meager to permit us to do those things that we are really chagrined to leave undone. The argument is objectively sufficient. It faithfully describes current conditions as they statistically are. It is subjectively specious. For it says nothing about our will to change those conditions. It says nothing about our determination to see that integration in American education will mean not only the one-way traffic of Negroes going to white schools, but also the Americanizing in terms of budgets, curricula, physical plants, labor practices, administrative attitudes, and scholarly proficiency of Negro schools so that we may reasonably cherish the hope of finding, in some not-too-far-distant day, a fair amount of people who will want a two-way pattern of integration that will let whites come to "Negro" schools. And, above all, it says nothing about our resolution to do as much as we can under present conditions to integrate our own literature into the national consciousness.

There is really for us no true absolution. We have shirked overmuch our job. In 1945 *Phylon* published a poem by Robert Hayden called "Middle Passage." It was, I thought, a fine poem. Its infinite riches deserve some extended comment. I have never seen a printed reference to it of any consequence. In *The Craft of Fiction*, Percy Lubbock notices admiringly Leo Tolstoi's handling of time in *War and Peace*. In that novel, Lubbock points out, we feel the passage of time in two ways. We are aware of its flow from day to day and year to year, bearing away, like a conveyor belt, the span of a person's life. But we are also aware of it as a cycle of generations, a wheel ceaselessly revolving, always taking some generation up, some generation down. Langston Hughes's *Not Without Laughter* is much less bulky than *War and Peace*. Yet in *Not Without Laughter* one finds this same double sense of time, just as one finds, virtually wherever one stops to analyze Hughes's performance here, casements opening out upon the expansive world of universal suggestion created by great art.

I have said that Negro literature is often execrable. But it is far from being so execrable as to deserve the extent of neglect in which we have allowed it to languish. Moreover, I have tried to show that it is frequently critically challenging; indeed I have hinted that now and then it may reward even the most demanding critic with a moment of rapture. Finally, I have indicated that in my own thinking about the relation of one thing to another in this complex world, I can plainly see the development of a criticism around Negro literature as an integrative factor of no little value for the growth of democracy in America. Actually I look forward to the day when a book about Negroes, if someone should chance then to isolate such another incidental group in our social order, will have about the same significance as John P. Marquand's *The Late George Apley* or A. B. Guthrie's *The Way West* have now. And I want us, as students and teachers of Negro literature, to have had our share in preparing for that day. I want us to have affected both the quality and the reception of Negro writing in such a way as to hasten that age of felicity. I would have us, indeed, feel toward the development of an energetic scholarly criticism within our own ranks a sense of knightly obligation. And I would add, for all those who see eye-to-eye with me, "a fair promise of better things"—even to an increase in one's own sense of being personally alive.

Lance Jeffers

(1919–1985)

LANCE JEFFERS'S POETRY makes a unique contribution to African American poetry in that it combines a thoroughly individual mode of expression with a passionate devotion to the themes and traditions of black literature. Born in Nebraska in 1919, Jeffers grew up in the care of his grandparents. His grandfather, a strong-willed medical doctor working in an almost exclusively white community, was as powerful an influence on the developing poet's sensibilities as was the vast sweep of the midwestern plains.

Jeffers served in the army during World War II and married his first wife, Camille Jones, in 1946. After the war he attended Columbia University, taking there an A.B. (cum laude) in English and, in 1951, the M.A. in English education. He taught at a number of universities, including Howard, until 1974, when he settled at North Carolina State Univerity as professor of English.

Jeffers's short story "The Dawn Swings In" was published in *The Best American Short Stories, 1948*. He married his second wife, Trellie James, in 1959 and began the most productive period of his career with a proliferation of his poetry. In 1962 his poems began appearing in anthologies, including *Burning Spear* (1963) and *Nine Black Poets* (1968). His first book of poetry, *My Blackness Is the Beauty of This Land*, was published in 1970 and was followed by three other volumes in that decade: *When I Know the Power of My Black Hand* (1974), *O Africa, Where I Baked My Bread* (1977), and *Grandsire* (1979). A novel, *Witherspoon*, was published in 1983. Jeffers died in 1985.

For an insightful analysis of Jeffers's poetry, see the article by David F. Dorsey, Jr., in *Dictionary of Literary Biography, Volume 51*. See also Eugene Redmond's *Drumvoices*.

"My Blackness Is the Beauty of This Land" is reprinted from *My Blackness Is the Beauty of This Land*; "On Listening to the Spirituals" is taken from *Nine Black Poets*.

MY BLACKNESS IS THE BEAUTY OF THIS LAND

My blackness is the beauty of this land,
my blackness,
tender and strong, wounded and wise,
my blackness:
I, drawling black grandmother, smile muscular and sweet,
unstraightened white hair soon to grow in earth,
work-thickened hand thoughtful and gentle on grandson's head,
my heart is bloody-razored by a million memories' thrall:

> remembering the crook-necked cracker who spat
> on my naked body,
> remembering the splintering of my son's spirit
> because he remembered to be proud
> remembering the tragic eyes in my daughter's
> dark face when she learned her color's meaning,

and my own dark rage a rusty knife with teeth to gnaw
my bowels,
my agony ripped loose by anguished shouts in Sunday's
humble church,
my agony rainbowed to ecstasy when my feet oversoared
Montgomery's slime,

ah, this hurt, this hate, this ecstasy before I die,
and all my love a strong cathedral!
My blackness is the beauty of this land!

Lay this against my whiteness, this land!
Lay me, young Brutus stamping hard on the cat's tail,
gutting the Indian, gouging the nigger,
booting Little Rock's Minniejean Brown in the buttocks and boast,
my sharp white teeth derision-bared as I the conqueror crush!
Skyscraper-I, white hands burying God's human clouds beneath
the dust!
Skyscraper-I, slim blond young Empire
thrusting up my loveless bayonet to rape the sky,
then shrink all my long body with filth and in the gutter lie
as lie I will to perfume this armpit garbage,

While I here standing black beside
wrench tears from which the lies would suck the salt
to make me more American than America . . .
But yet my love and yet my hate shall civilize this land,
this land's salvation.

ON LISTENING TO THE SPIRITUALS

When the master lived a king and I a starving hutted slave beneath
    the lash, and

when my five-year-old son was driven at dawn to cotton-field to pick
    until he could no longer see the sun, and

when master called my wife to the big house when mistress was gone,
took her against her will and gave her a dollar to be still, and
when she turned upon her pride and cleavered it, cursed her dignity
and stamped on it, came back to me with his evil on her thighs, hung
her head when I condemned her with my eyes,

what broken mettle of my soul wept steel, cracked teeth in self-
    contempt
upon my flesh, crept underground to seek new roots and secret breath-
    ing place?

When all the hatred of my bones was buried in a forgotten county of
    my soul,
then from beauty muscled from the degradation of my oaken bread,
I stroked on slaverysoil the mighty colors of my song, a passionate
    heaven rose no God in heaven could create!

UNCONSCIOUS AND ALONE
Songs of the Boy and Young Man

When he was 12 he defeated Schein in the
100-yard-dash down Pacific Avenue
running beneath the splintery aristocratic
apartment houses overlooking
San Francisco Bay,
passing Schein at 80 yards before
the little gasping rich girls:
he was conqueror, stepson of the janitor
who this Thursday afternoon stood

"On Listening to the Spirituals" reprinted by permission of Dr. Trellie L. Jeffers.

"Unconscious and Alone" from *Crawfish and Other Poems* by Lance Jeffers to be published Fall 1992 by Black Scholar Press. Reprinted by permission of Dr. Trellie L. Jeffers.

across the street, doorman in knee-length
green uniform watching.
When the winner walked across the
street for a whispered word of praise
the man was silent.

II

Compassionate June
passing through the portals of his childhood at grammar
school
was the slim ideal of his blood-turnings who
three years later pushed a bullet
through her brain:
patrician of Pacific Avenue
whose parents would have sent him to
the back door, dark and angry
inhabitant of their kennel
who had become a frothful mouth shrieking
for his escape from prison:

but when June shot herself,
was she not a prisoner,
was she not then a Negro desperate for love,
was she not the hounded janitor-boy?
were not the syllables of her lifeless breasts
an impassioned sermon to the faltering dry stalks
of Pacific Avenue?

III

Among impoverished blackfolk
he stayed with Reverend Magruder
when he escaped the prison house where
the wealthy white boys called him
"hambone" behind his back,
where a black elder (when they were cleaning cars)
scornfully assured him he would never
run the hundred in ten flat.

what secret notch in his intestine
quivers now as he remembers?
what bloated egg lodges in his throat
as he recalls the passionate soloist
in the Reverend's gospel choir

who regularly ran to the street life
and returned penitent to sing?
What far-off creek of sweetness in his belly
threatens to overflood his urine
as he remembers the Magruders' comforting
a black agony escaped from
Pacific Avenue?

IV

He dived into the ocean of his people,
their arms caught him,
frigid San Francisco clung
to the nostrils of his brain
(he remembered:
he returned from the Williamses in San Mateo
when he was ten, and
grief leaped down upon his head
like an eagle of cast iron as
he strode through the elders' door):

Tragedy tracked the elders' steps,
he glanced fearfully at its visage
sliced and bleeding in their skulls,
and he stole from his mother's pocketbook.

Dark women kissed the harelips in his soul;
loving the lava he discovered in their groins,
he wept in ecstasy and clawed at their acceptance.

This was the tear mounted on his forehead
like a ship's mast in a ravening storm,
this was his bulging scrotum
bursting with runaway sperm,
this was his mind roasting in the
oven of his oppression.

V

Dark women
left heavenly embroidery sewn
to his phallus:
Georgia loved like a worshipful tide in the
unhurried serenity of her pelvis.
The Georgias were his dark-skinned mothers,
mentors to his mind, observers of his wounded stature.

VI

He discovered in his visceral pit
a bloody sea of love—

how astonishing to look down upon
this crimson adoration—

how splendid that
he possessed this ocean,
that he could open his mouth
and spout it out to
any human being who appealed—

"Love, love," he called,
"rise from my visceral pit,
fall in bloody puddles
into the famished stomach
of my lover."

VII

suddenly he saw that a
woman's rejection
cracked his spinal cord
and left him foundering:
suddenly saw that
the clicking of the clock
in her vaginal canal
was a bomb that might launch
him into nothingness:
saw suddenly that a petal
of authentic acceptance
hanging from the daisy of a woman's eye
was love enough to stanch
the leakage from his soul.

VIII

Beauty that cannot survive
in this fell land finds its
relief in cancer.

IX

"It's all yours, Daddy!"
the young woman beneath him in San Angelo
shouted
whose shy-face husband

had gone to war, he
who suffered stomach pangs
each month upon her bleeding time,
young black woman who rose cursing
vividly in the restaurant
against a female adversary—

the fire of a folk in this woman
who didn't care that
the old man in whose home they loved
heard "It's all yours, Daddy!"

X

Whom he held gently at midnight
in the hallway of a Harlem tenement
before embarking for a Scottish port,
ship swerving wildly in the sea
to evade U-boat torpedoes,

Whom he held gently at midnight
in the hallway of a Harlem tenement,
her large brown body grieving for acceptance,

He strove to embrace away her sorrow
in the hallway of a Harlem tenement—
the night they heard at the Apollo
the grandeur of Billie's
stern and pitiless "I Cover the Waterfront."

XI

That cockney girl who loved him—
sweet and beaten who sought rejection,
generous in the giving of her body
and her mind,
cousin perhaps of the workingclass redhead girl
on a train to Newcastle
who gazed up at him as at a god
after he the officer angrily commanded
the white American enlisted men
not to call their hosts in this land
"limeys."

XII

Jamaican sergeant
who flew his fighter plane
against the Nazi squadrons:
in a London bar his brown and wisely

smiling face—
the fair-skinned African-American woman
beside him in the London street violently cursing
the American soldiers who stared at them as if they
were interracial tramplers
on God's commandment:

Her cry beneath him in the
cloak of night: "Oh Jesus, baby!"
Six thousand miles away
a sorrowed brownskin woman waited,
self-destruction stirring in her bowel:

Within the dark privates' tents in Southampton
in the climacteric of night they heard
the lyric tendril of a trumpet's "Taps,"
within their tents he heard the voices
of a prophetic generation
lifting in mighty lungeing laughter:

then the call to the docks,
black privates
carrying stretchers
of fright-faced and wounded
Nazi soldiers.

XIII

How he rode his ghost's
unruly horse as if it were the dark flesh
of his pelvis,
how he, the kind and cruel,
heard bombs obliterate in London
and shivered not,

how he lived in the livid volcano
of his belly, unconscious and alone.

Durham, May, 1982

Charles Davis

(1918–1981)

A DISTINGUISHED SCHOLAR and professor at Yale University, Charles Twitchell Davis chaired and helped to expand Yale's excellent program in African American studies. Born in Hampton, Virginia, Davis earned his A.B. degree at Dartmouth College, where he graduated summa cum laude and was a junior-year Phi Beta Kappa. Although he was denied a Rhodes Scholarship because of race, he won at graduation the Fred D. Baker Graduate Fellowship, which allowed him to take his M.A. at the University of Chicago. After a stint in the United States Army, he received his Ph.D. degree in American studies at New York University in 1951.

In 1955 Davis went to Princeton as an assistant professor of English, the first black to teach at that university. In addition to Princeton, he taught or was visiting lecturer at a large number of prestigious academic centers in America and abroad, some of which are the following: New York University, Rutgers, Bryn Mawr, Pennsylvania State, the University of Iowa (where he inaugurated and developed an innovative and effective program in African American Studies), Harvard, and Yale. He also taught at the Salzburg Seminar in Austria; was scholar-in-residence at the Bellagio Study and Conference Center; and served as a fellow at the Stanford Center for Advanced Study in Behavioral Sciences. In 1969 he went to India to lecture on Walt Whitman, in connection with the celebration of the poet's sesquicentennial. He was elected to or appointed to membership on the boards and committees of many of America's most influential academic policy-making bodies, including the Modern Language Association, the National Council of Teachers of English, and the American Studies Association.

The bulk of Davis's scholarly essays are collected in *Black Is the Color of the Cosmos: Essays on Afro-American Literature and Culture, 1942–1981* (1982), edited by Henry Louis Gates, Jr. The foreword, preface, and introduction to *Black is the Color of the Cosmos* also give biographical information about Davis. Davis is also editor or co-editor of a number of books, some of which are as follows: *Walt Whitman's Poems with Critical Aids* (1955, edited with G. W. Allen); *E. A. Robinson: Selected Early Poems and Letters* (1960); *On Being Black: Writings by Afro-Americans from Frederick Douglass to the Present* (1970); and *The Slave's Narrative* (1982, edited with Henry Louis Gates, Jr.).

For further reading, see Linda Metzger, ed., *Black Writers: A Selection of Sketches from Contemporary Authors* (1989); *Black American Literature Forum* (Winter 1984; Spring 1986); *Yale Review* (Summer 1983); and *World Literature Today* (Summer 1983).

The excerpt that follows comes from *Black is the Color of the Cosmos*, an essay originally written in 1979.

FROM EXPERIENCE TO ELOQUENCE
Richard Wright's Black Boy *as Art*

Native Son[1] is the work for which Richard Wright is best known, but *Black Boy*,[2] an autobiography more or less, may be the achievement that offers the best demonstration of his art as a writer. This idea is not so startling given Wright's special talents—the eye of a skilled reporter, the sensibility of a revolutionary poet, alert to varied forms of injustice, and the sense of symbolic meaning carried by the rituals of ordinary life. The problem up to the present time is not the lack of attention the work has received. Like *Native Son, Black Boy* was selected by the Book-of-the-Month Club and was thus assured a wide distribution and a serious if somewhat skewed reading from many critics. In 1970 Stanley Edgar Hyman, in reviewing Wright's entire career, assigned *Black Boy* to a period in which Wright's "important writing" occurred—according to his definition, Wright's last years as resident in America, from 1940 to 1945.[3] But *Black Boy* by itself failed to acquire as an original work of art the reputation it deserves.

It appears now, from the perspective of a generation, that a measure of distortion was unavoidable, given the political temper of the time. The history of the publication of the manuscript entitled *American Hunger*,[4] of which *Black Boy* was a part, encouraged a violent

---

Reprinted by permission of Garland Publishing.

[1](New York: Harper, 1940). Dorothy Canfield Fisher in the introduction writes that the "novel plumbs blacker depths of human experience than American literature has yet had, comparable only to Dostoievski's revelation of human misery in wrongdoing" (p. x).

[2]The full title is *Black Boy: A Record of Childhood and Youth* (New York: Harper, 1945). Dorothy Fisher in the introductory note calls Wright's work "the honest, dreadful, heartbreaking story of a Negro childhood and youth . . ." (p. vii), without referring to its art or even its place in an American literary tradition.

[3]"Life and Letters: Richard Wright Reappraised," *Atlantic Monthly*, 225 (March 1970), 127–132.

[4]*American Hunger* (New York: Harper & Row, Publishers) was published in 1977. It is not the whole autobiography but the second part, the continuation of *Black Boy*. Michel Fabre in the afterword provides an accurate brief history of the decision to publish only the first section in 1945. See pp. 143–144.

political response. It was well known that "I Tried to Be a Communist," which appeared in the August and September issues of *The Atlantic Monthly* in 1944,[5] were chapters of an autobiographical record to be published the following year, even though they were excluded finally with the rest of the matter dealing with the years in Chicago and New York. When *Black Boy* did appear, knowing critics read the book in light of the much-publicized account of Wright's difficulties with the Communist Party. Baldly put, the situation for the critic encouraged a form of outside intrusion, a case of knowing too much, of supplying a frame of reference which a reading of the basic text does not support. The board of the Book-of-the-Month Club or Edward Aswell or both,[6] in suggesting a restriction of autobiographical matter to the period before migration to Chicago, exercised a judgment that displayed something more than the good sense of successful editors; indeed, that judgment pointed up the artistic integrity of the work. Someone concluded accurately that the intensity of *Black Boy* came from a concentration upon one metaphor of oppression, the South, and prevented the diffusion of power that would be the consequence of the introduction of a second, the Communist Party.

If the political reaction created one kind of distortion in the eye of the examiner, more normal literary expectations created another. *Black Boy* baffled W. E. B. Du Bois, the most impressive black intellectual of his time. His review in the New York *Herald Tribune* states his dilemma: ". . . if the book is meant to be a creative picture and a warning, even then, it misses its possible effectiveness because it is as a work of art so patently and terribly overdrawn."[7] By 1945 Du Bois had published three major works with outstanding autobiographical elements, one of which, *Dusk of Dawn*, was a fully developed autobiography of considerable intellectual distinction,[8] and he could not be accused of responding merely to a sense of affront to his middle-class sensibilities. Du Bois was not prepared to accept Wright's bleak Mississippi; he was appalled not so much by the condition of terror there as by a state of mind that denied the possibility of humanity for blacks and frustrated all black efforts to achieve satisfaction beyond the minimal requirements for life. After all, Du Bois

[5]*Atlantic Monthly*, 174 (August 1944), 61–70; (September 1944), 48–56.

[6]Fabre, "Afterword," *American Hunger*, pp. 143–144.

[7]W. E. B. Du Bois, "Richard Wright Looks Back," *New York Herald Tribune*, March 4, 1945, sec. 5, p. 2.

[8]The three are *The Souls of Black Folk: Essays and Sketches* (Chicago: A.C. McClurg, 1903), *Darkwater: Voices from Within the Veil* (New York: Harcourt, Brace, 1920), and *Dusk of Dawn: An Essay toward an Autobiography of a Race Concept* (New York: Harcourt, Brace, 1940).

had vivid memories of his experience as a young teacher in rural Tennessee, where he encountered aspiring, sensitive pupils who, though often defeated or betrayed by their environment, were not totally crushed by Southern oppression.[9] Moreover, Du Bois joined, no doubt, a group of critics of *Black Boy* best defined by Ralph Ellison as consisting of readers who complained that Wright had "omitted the development of his own sensibility."[10] But this is to define sensibility in a way generally understood by the nineteenth century, which is to hold that sensibility is an orderly accretion of the mind and heart within an environment recognizably human, and not to accept Wright's radical equation of the existence of sensibility with survival.

Du Bois did not doubt that autobiography could be art, though more naive critics might. He could not accept the principles of an art as austere as Wright's was, one in which many of the facts of Southern life, so familiar to him, were excluded and in which generalization had been carried to such extreme lengths. After all, the book's title was *Black Boy*, not "A Black Boy,"[11] with an appropriately limiting modifier. Viewed superficially, Richard's odyssey was unique primarily because it had a happy ending—the escape from the hell of the South, where, apparently, all of his black associates (he had no friends in the narrative) were destined to spend the rest of their days. Wright's generalizations about the dehumanizing relationships between whites and blacks and the almost equally unsatisfying connections between blacks and blacks shaped his South, and these assumptions Du Bois thought to be distorted. One sweeping statement by young Wright in Memphis, where he lived from his seventeenth to his nineteenth year and where he committed himself formally to becoming a writer,[12] would certainly extract from Du Bois an expression of disbelief, if not annoyance: "I knew of no Negroes who read the books I liked and I wondered if any Negroes ever thought of them. I knew that there were Negro doctors, law-

---

[9]Chapter IV, "Of the Meaning of Progress," in Du Bois, *The Souls of Black Folk*, pp. 60–74.

[10]"Richard Wright's Blues," *Antioch Review*, 5 (June 1945), 202. Reprinted in *Shadow and Act* (New York: Random House, 1964).

[11]Wright wrote Edward Aswell, his editor at Harper's, on August 10, 1944, suggesting *Black Boy* as a title for the book. He added, for emphasis, that *Black Boy* was "not only a title but also a kind of heading to the whole general theme" (Fabre, "Afterword," *American Hunger*, p. 144).

[12]Wright comments on this commitment in *Black Boy*: "I had once tried to write, had once reveled in feeling, had let my crude imagination roam, but the impulse to dream had been slowly beaten out of me by experience. Now it surged up again and I hungered for books, new ways of looking and seeing" (p. 218).

yers, newspapermen, but I never saw any of them. When I read a Negro newspaper I never caught the faintest echo of my preoccupation in its pages."[13]

Not only Du Bois, but also other blacks, even those lacking in the knowledge of black life in America which Du Bois had acquired from his surveys and research projects at Atlanta University,[14] would be appalled at Richard's confession of his cultural isolation. This is a moment when generalization approaches fiction, when we must say that a statement may be acceptable within its context, but that it is questionable as a fact standing on its own, as something that might be supported by the confessions of other black boys, especially those emerging from families with middle-class aspirations and pretensions like Wright's.

Editing the raw matter of life is necessary, of course, to write an autobiography with any claim to art. No one has described this activity better than Ellison has in his critical examination of *Black Boy*: "The function, the psychology, of artistic selectivity is to eliminate from an art form all those elements of experience which contain no compelling significance. Life is as the sea, art a ship in which man conquers life's crushing formlessness. . . ."[15] What Ellison did not say is that such editing requires the use of controlling principles that are invariably fictional. This is to say that the organizing ideas are assumptions that are not strictly true according to the most objective criteria. Operating from a strict conception of the truth, we have every right to question the emotional basis for *The Education of Henry Adams*, an especially intense form of self-pity coming from the most widely cultivated American of his time, who, nonetheless, constantly reminds us of his lack of preparation for the nineteenth century, not to mention the twentieth. And in *Black Boy* we are asked to accept Richard's cultural isolation as well as his vulnerability to all forms of deprivation—physical, emotional, social, and intellectual.

Some critics, carried off by the impact of *Black Boy*, tend to treat the autobiography as if it were fiction. They are influenced by the fact that much great modern fiction, Joyce's *Portrait of the Artist as a Young Man*, for example, is very close to life. And the tendency here is reinforced by the fact that the author himself, Wright, is a creator of fictions. Yielding so is a mistake because many of the incidents in *Black Boy* retain the sharp angularity of life, rather than fitting into

---

[13]Ibid., p. 220.

[14]Between 1897 and 1915 Du Bois edited fifteen studies on the condition and status of blacks in America. These volumes represented the Proceedings of the Annual Conference on the Negro Problem, organized by Du Bois and held at Atlanta University.

[15]Ellison, "Richard Wright's Blues."

the dramatic or symbolic patterns of fiction. Richard's setting fire to the "fluffy white curtains" (p. 4), and incidentally the house, is not the announcement of the birth of a pyromaniac or a revolutionary, but testimony primarily to the ingenuity of a small black boy in overcoming mundane tedium. We must say "primarily" because this irresponsible act suggests the profound distress and confusion an older Richard would bring to a family that relied heavily upon rigid attitudes toward religion, expected behavior, and an appropriate adjustment to Southern life. Richard's fire is not Bigger's rat at the beginning of *Native Son*, when the act of killing brings out pent-up violence in the young black man and foreshadows, perhaps, the events of Book Two, "Flight," when Bigger's position becomes that of the cornered rat.[16] Nor does Richard's immodest invitation to his grandmother during his bath (p. 49) offer disturbing witness of the emergence of a pornographer or a connoisseur of the erotic; rather, it points to something more general, the singular perversity in Richard that makes him resist family and the South. In *Black Boy* we exist in a world of limited probability that is not life exactly, because there is an order to be demonstrated, and it does not display the perfect design of a serious fiction. We occupy a gray area in between. The patterns are here on several levels. Though they may not be so clear and tight as to permit the critic to predict, they do govern the selection of materials, the rendering of special emphasis, distortions, and the style.

We seldom raise questions about what is omitted from an autobiography, yet if we wish to discover pattern, we must begin with what we do not find. The seasonal metaphor in *Walden* (we move from spring to spring) becomes all the more important once we realize that Henry Thoreau lived on the shore of Walden Pond more than two years.[17] Franklin's few "errata"[18] point up the strong aridity of an autobiography that touches so little on the traumas of the heart. Franklin's education, his achievements in business and science, and his proposals for the benefit of society seem at times supported by an emotional substructure far too frail. But the purposes of both autobiographies—in *Walden*, to offer the model of a renewed

---

[16]*Native Son*, pp. 4–5.

[17]Thoreau is precise about the length of his actual stay, despite the fact that the events of *Walden* fall within the design of a single year: "The present was my next experiment . . . for convenience, putting the experience of two years into one." Henry David Thoreau, *Walden*, ed. Sherman Paul (Boston: Houghton Mifflin, 1957), p. 58.

[18]Franklin refers in this way to his neglect of Miss Read, to whom he was engaged, during a period spent in London: "This was another of the great errata of my life. . . ." "Autobiography" in Benjamin Franklin, *Autobiography and Other Writings*, ed. R. B. Nye (Boston: Houghton Mifflin, 1958), p. 38.

life; in the *Autobiography of Benjamin Franklin,* to sketch a convincing design of a successful life in the new world, one that emphasizes the practical values that most Americans admired and many Europeans envied—were achieved in part because of the shrewdness in excluding truthful, though extraneous, matter. So, too, *Black Boy* profits from rigorous and inspired editing.

One function of the omissions is to strengthen the impression in our minds of Richard's intense isolation. This is no mean achievement given that Wright was born into a large family (on his mother's side, at least) which, despite differences in personality, cooperated in times of need. The father, because of his desertion of his mother, was early in Richard's mind, perhaps in the sentiments of other family members, too, an object of hate and scorn. There are no names in the early pages of *Black Boy,* not even that of Richard's brother, Leon Allan, just a little more than two years younger than Richard. When the names begin to appear in *Black Boy,* they tend to define the objects of adversary, often violently hostile relationships—Grandmother Wilson, Aunt Addie, Uncle Thomas. Two notable exceptions are Grandfather Wilson, an ineffectual man capable only of reliving his past as a soldier in the Civil War, and Richard's mother, Ella, a pathetically vulnerable woman of some original strength who, because of continuing illness, slipped gradually into a state of helplessness that became for Richard symbolic of his whole life as a black boy in the South.[19]

The admirable biography of Wright by Michel Fabre suggests another dimension for Richard's opponents in his embattled household. The climax of the violence in the family occurred with the confrontation with Uncle Tom, portrayed as a retired and defeated schoolteacher reduced at the time to earning a living by performing odd jobs as a carpenter. Richard resented being the victim of Uncle Tom's frustrations, and he responded to orders from the older man by threatening him with razors in both hands and by spitting out hysterically, "You are not an example to me; you could never be. . . . You're a *warning.* Your life isn't so hot that you can tell me what to do. . . . Do you think that I want to grow up and weave the bottoms of chairs for people to sit in?" (p. 140). A footnote from Fabre adds more information about the humiliated uncle:

> The portrait of Uncle Thomas in *Black Boy* is exaggerated. After living with the Wilsons, he moved next door and became a real-estate broker. In 1938, he was a member of the Executive Committee of the Citizen's

[19]See Michel Fabre, *The Unfinished Quest of Richard Wright* (New York: William Morrow, 1973), pp. 1–7.

Civic League in Jackson and wrote a book on the word *Negro*, discussing the superiority complex of the Whites and its effects on the Blacks. At this time Richard put him in contact with Doubleday publishers and the uncle and the nephew were completely reconciled.[20]

Wright includes in *Black Boy* a touching description of meeting his father again after a quarter-century. As the newly successful author looked at a strange black sharecropper in ragged overalls holding a muddy hoe, the old resentment for past neglect faded: "I forgave him and pitied him as my eyes looked past him to the unpainted wooden shack" (p. 30). But *Black Boy* contains no softening reconsiderations of Uncle Tom, or of Aunt Addie, who, like her brother, seems to have possessed some redeeming qualities,[21] or of Granny Wilson for that matter. Their stark portraits dominate the family and define a living space too narrow, too mean, and too filled with frustration and poverty for an imaginative youngster like Richard.

A growing boy, when denied the satisfactions of a loving home, looks for emotional support at school or at play, and if he is lucky, he finds something that moderates domestic discontent. But there is little compensation of this sort in *Black Boy*. The reality of the life away from the family seems to be less bleak than Wright represents it, though his schooling was retarded by early irregularity because of the family's frequent moves, and his play restricted, perhaps, because of the family's desperate need for money and Granny's Seventh Day Adventist scruples. Once again we are struck by the absence of names—of teachers like Lucy McCranie and Alice Burnett, who taught Richard at the Jim Hill School in Jackson and recognized his lively intelligence,[22] or Mary L. Morrison or the Reverend Otto B. Cobbins, Richard's instructors in the eighth and ninth grades of the Smith-Robinson School,[23] to whose dedication and competence, despite personal limitations, Wright paid tribute elsewhere.[24] There was no question about his marginal status in these institutions, since Richard stood regularly at the head of his class.

Black Boy is singularly devoid of references to rewarding peer associations. There is no mention of Dick Jordan, Joe Brown, Perry

---

[20]Fabre, *Unfinished Quest*, p. 533.

[21]Another footnote by Fabre in *Unfinished Quest* suggests an additional dimension for Addie, who, "too, was not spared in *Black Boy*. She reacted rather well to reading the book—she stated that if Richard wrote in that way, it was to support his family . . ." (p. 533).

[22]Ibid., p. 39.

[23]Ibid., p. 48.

[24]E. R. Embree describes, in *Thirteen Against the Odds* (New York: Viking, 1944), Wright's attitude toward his education in Jackson: "He [Wright] remembers the Smith-Robinson school with some gratitude. The teachers tried their best to pump learning into the pupils" (p. 27).

Booker, or Essie Lee Ward, friends of this period and so valued that Wright was in touch with several of them ten years later when he was living in Chicago.[25] The fact that a few of Wright's childhood associates did succeed in making their way to Chicago has an amount of interest in itself, serving, as well, to break the isolation that Wright has fabricated so well. Among the childhood activities that went unrecorded were the exploits of the Dick Wright clan, made up of a group of neighborhood boys who honored in the name of their society, no doubt, their most imaginative member. The clan included Dick Jordan, Perry Booker, Joe Brown, and also Frank Sims, a descendant of a black senator during the Reconstruction period, Blanche K. Bruce.[26] What is amply clear, then, is that Wright had a childhood more than a little touched by the usual rituals and preoccupations of middle-class boys growing up in America, but what is also apparent is that reference to them would modify our sense of Richard's deprived and disturbed emotional life, a necessity for the art of the autobiography, rather more important than any concern for absolute accuracy.

Wright has little to say directly about sex. Richard's most serious temptation for sexual adventure comes toward the end of *Black Boy* in Memphis, when he is taken in by the Moss family. Richard succeeds in resisting the opportunity to take advantage of a cozy arrangement with Bess, the daughter whom Mrs. Moss seeks to thrust upon him, with marriage as her ultimate objective (p. 185). There are some indirect references to frustrated, sublimated, or distorted forms of sexual energy—in Miss Simon, certainly, the tall, gaunt, mulatto woman who ran the orphan home where Richard was deposited for a period (pp. 25–28). And there were exposures to white women, all calculated to teach Richard the strength of the taboo prohibiting the thought (not to mention the fact) of black-white sexual relations in the South. But Richard never takes an aggressive interest in sex; the adventures that he stumbles into create traumas when they are serious and unavoidable, or are embarrassing when he can resist participation and control his reactions. Wright, indeed, seems to be even more discreet than Franklin was; by comparison, Claude Brown is a raving sensualist in *Manchild in the Promised Land*, though roughly the same period of growth is involved. It is strange that so little space is given to sexual episodes and fantasies in the record of the gradual maturing of an adolescent—unbelievable, given the preoccupations of the twentieth century. We face the problem of omission again. Wright deliberately seeks to deprive his hero, his

---

[25]Fabre, *Unfinished Quest*, p. 39.
[26]Ibid., p. 43.

younger self, of any substantial basis for sensual gratification located outside his developing imagination. The world that *Black Boy* presents is uniformly bleak, always ascetic, and potentially violent, and the posture of the isolated hero, cut off from family, peer, or community support, is rigidly defiant, without the softening effects of interludes of sexual indulgence.

Richard's immediate world, not that foreign country controlled by whites, is overwhelmingly feminine. Male contacts are gone, except for occasional encounters with uncles. The father has deserted his home, and the grandfather is lost in the memories of "The War." The uncles tend to make brief entrances and exits, following the pattern of Hoskins, quickly killed off by envious whites in Arkansas, or the unnamed new uncle, forced to flee because of unstated crimes against whites (pp. 48–49, 57–60). Thomas is the uncle who stays around somewhat longer than the others do, long enough to serve as the convenient object for Richard's mounting rebellion. The encounter with Uncle Tom is the culminating episode marking a defiance expressed earlier against a number of authority figures, all women— Richard's mother, Miss Simon, Grandmother Wilson, Aunt Addie. Women dominate in Richard's world, with the ultimate authority vested in Granny—near-white, uncompromising, unloving, and fanatical, daring Richard to desecrate her Seventh Day Adventist Sabbath. The only relief from feminine piety is the pathetic schoolteacher who, in a happy moment, tells an enraptured Richard about Bluebeard and his wives (p. 34). But even this delight, moved in part, no doubt, by Bluebeard's relentless war against females, is short-lived. Granny puts a stop to such sinning, not recognizing, of course, the working out of the law of compensation.

Richard's odyssey takes him from the black world to the white— from the problems of home and family to new and even more formidable difficulties. The movement is outward into the world, to confront an environment that is not controlled by Granny, though it provides much that contributes to an explanation of Granny's behavior. Richard's life among blacks emphasizes two kinds of struggle. One is simply the battle for physical existence, the need for food, clothing, shelter, and protection that is the overwhelming concern of the early pages of *Black Boy*. The second grows out of Richard's deeply felt desire to acquire his own male identity, a sense of self apart from a family that exerts increasing pressure upon this growing black boy to behave properly, to experience Christian conversion, and to accept guidance from his (mostly female) elders. Survival in two senses, then, is the dominant theme, one which does not change when he leaves the black community. The terms are the same, though the landscape is new. Richard desperately seeks employment in white neighborhoods and in the downtown business districts in order to contribute to the support of his family. He discovers, when he does so, that the demand to accommodate becomes even more insistent and less flexible than that exerted by his own family.

The difference is that the stakes are higher. Richard thinks he must find a job, any job, to earn a living. This awareness represents a step beyond the simple dependence that moves a small boy to complain, "Mama, I'm hungry" (p. 13). If he does not find work, Richard feels that he has failed his family in an essential way and made its survival precarious. Though his independence in the black world leads to harsh sanctions—threats, bed without supper, whippings—he is not prepared for the infinitely greater severity of the white world. It is cruel, calculating, and sadistic. Richard never doubts that he will survive the lashings received from his mother, Granny, and assorted aunts and uncles, but he does question his ability to endure exposure to whites. The ways of white folks are capricious and almost uniformly malignant. Richard understands that the penalty for nonconformity, down to the way a black boy walks or holds his head, is not simply a sore body, but death. When Richard gives up a good job with an optical company, with a chance, according to his boss, to become something more than a menial worker, he does so because of the opposition exhibited by whites who think he aspires to do "*white* man's work." Richard confides to his boss when he leaves the factory: "I'm scared. . . . They would kill me" (p. 68).

From the woman who inquires of Richard, looking for yet another job, "Boy, do you steal?" (p. 128) to the two young men who attempt to arrange for Richard to fight another black boy for the amusement of an assembly of whites (pp. 209–210), we witness an unrelieved set of abuses. Certainly omission of some mitigating circumstances and artful distortion are involved in this bitter report. Richard is gradually introduced to a white world that grows progressively more dominant, divisive, and corrupting concerning the black life that serves it. Richard understands fully what is expected of him:

> I began to marvel at how smoothly the black boys acted out the roles that the white race had mapped out for them. Most of them were not conscious of living a special, separate, stunted way of life. Yet I know that in some period of their growing up—a period that they had no doubt forgotten—there had been developed in them a delicate, sensitive controlling mechanism that shut off their minds and emotions from all that the white race had said was taboo. (p. 172)

In Wright's South it was unthinkable for a black boy to aspire to become a lens-grinder, much less to harbor the ambition to become

a writer. When Richard is thoughtless enough to reveal his true aim
in life to one of his white employers, the response is predictable:
"You'll never be a writer. . . . Who on earth put such ideas into your
nigger head?" (p. 129). Given his difficulties in adjusting to an oppressive Southern system, Richard sustains his interest in writing
through a monumental act of will. We are led to the inevitable conclusion that Richard must flee the South if he is to remain alive, and
the desire to achieve an artistic career seems less important in light
of the more basic concern for life itself.

We have every reason to suspect that the treatment of whites
gains a certain strength from artistic deletion, too. Michel Fabre
points out that Wright's relationship with a white family named Wall
does not fit the pattern of abuse and brutal exploitation that emerges
from the autobiography: "Although *Black Boy* was designed to describe the effects of racism on a black child, which meant omitting
incidents tending to exonerate white persons in any way, there is no
doubt that the Walls were liberal and generous employers. For almost two years Richard worked before and after class, earning three
dollars a week bringing in firewood and doing the heavy cleaning."[27]
Fabre adds, with reference especially to Mrs. Wall and her mother,
"Since they respected his qualities as an individual, he sometimes
submitted his problems and plans to them and soon considered their
house a second home where he met with more understanding than
from his own family."[28] This is not matter that reinforces a design
displaying increasing difficulty for Richard as he moves outward and
into contact with white society. Nor does it support Richard's growing conviction that his survival depends upon his escape from the
South. The design of *Black Boy* offers an accelerating pattern of confrontations, taking into account both an increase in danger for Richard and a mounting seriousness in terms of society's estimate of his
deviations. Like Big Boy, Richard must flee or die.

The narrator of *Black Boy* has three voices. The simplest records
recollected events with clarity and a show of objectivity. We may be
troubled by an insufficient context surrounding or an inadequate
connection linking these episodes until we become aware of the suggestion of a psychological dimension for them. The incidents illustrate basic emotions: the discovery of fear and guilt, first, when fire
destroys Richard's house; the experience of hate, directed this time
toward the father, in killing the kitten; the satisfactions of violence,
in defeating the teenage gang; the dangers of curiosity about the
adult world, in Richard's early addiction to alcohol. The psyche of a

---

[27]Ibid., pp. 46–47.
[28]Ibid., p. 47.

child takes shape through exposure to a set of unusual traumas, and the child goes forth, as we have seen, into a world that becomes progressively more brutal and violent. Style in this way reinforces the first theme of the autobiography, survival.

It is in hearing the more complicated and lyrical second voice of the narrator that we sense for the first time another theme in the autobiography. This is the making of the artist. The world, we have been told, is cold, harsh, and cruel, a fact which makes all the more miraculous the emergence of a literary imagination destined to confront it. The bleak South, by some strange necessity, is forced to permit the blooming of a single rose. Wright expends upon the nourishment of this tender plant the care that he has given to describing the sterile soil from which it springs.

A third, didactic voice offers occasional explanations of the matter recorded by the other two. It comments at times upon the lack of love among blacks in the South, the distortions in human relationships involving blacks and whites, and corruption in the social and economic systems. At other times it advises us of the necessity for secrecy when a black boy harbors the ambition to write, and explains the difficulties which he confronts when he seeks to serve an apprenticeship to his art. Despite formidable opposition and the danger of complete isolation, this ambition lives and forces the growth of Richard's imaginative powers.

We do not begin simply with the statement of the intention to become an artist. We start, rather, as Joyce does in *A Portrait of the Artist*, with the sense experience that rests behind the word. Richard's memory offers rich testimony of the capacity to feel objects of nature, small and large. Not only these. We note that accompanying the record of sensations is the tendency to translate sensation into an appropriate emotion—melancholy, nostalgia, astonishment, disdain. All of the senses achieve recognition in Richard's memory, and all combine to emphasize memories of violent experiences: the killing of the chicken; the shocking movement of the snake; the awesome golden glow on a silent night (pp. 7–8).

Apart from this basic repository of sensation and image, we sense early in Richard two other qualities just as essential to the budding artist. One is detachment, the feeling of being different from others. In two worlds to which he is exposed, that of the family and then the more muddled arena of affairs, he rejects all efforts to moderate his apartness. Though conversion and subsequent baptism apparently point to joining the company of the saved, viewed in the conventional way, damnation is assured by the refusal to deliver the right kind of valedictory at the graduation exercises of his grammar school (p. 153). Barely passing one ritual, he flunks another. He maintains under pressure his status as an alien, so ultimately he will be free to exercise the imagination that faces the cold world.

The second quality is curiosity. His mother tells Richard that he asks too many questions. Our young hero is apparently undaunted by the fact that his insistent prying has led to one of the earliest addictions to alcohol recorded in literature. But another addiction is more serious, to the truth in the appearances about him. "Will you stop asking silly questions!" his mother commands (p. 42)—about names, about color, about the relationship between the two. Curiosity constantly leads Richard to forbidden areas more menacing than the saloon, to the mysterious privileged province of whites in Mississippi and the equally mysterious restriction of the blacks.

A neat form of inversion is involved in the development of Richard's artistic talent. We note that the qualities supporting and sustaining the growing boy's imagination are just those preventing a successful adjustment to life in the South. To achieve a tolerable existence, not even a comfortable one, Richard must have firm relationships with the members of his family and with his neighbors and peers; to survive in the larger, white-dominated society he must accept without questioning the inflexible system of Southern mores and customs. Richard, rejecting these imperatives, responds to the demands of his own imagination.

Richard's sensations in nature anticipate a discovery just as valuable and far reaching. This is literature itself. Of the encounter with *Bluebeard* Richard says, "My sense of life deepened. . . ." He recalls, further, a total emotional response, emphasized, no doubt, by the background of an unresponding family, and he realizes that he stands on the threshold of a "gateway to a forbidden and enchanting land" (p. 36). So, early, the opposition is clear. On the one hand is the bleak environment frowning upon any activity of the imagination, whether passive or active, and on the other a determined Richard who will not be turned aside. His reading would be done in secret, a clandestine activity abetted by delivering racist newspapers and borrowing the library card of a compliant white man. There is no evidence that he discussed his reading with anyone, black or white. In Memphis, when he was able to patronize second-hand bookstores and to buy magazines like *Harper's, Atlantic Monthly*, and *American Mercury*, his tastes reflected the shape of his early conditioning (p. 198). He admired the great liberators, the destroyers of provincial and private worlds like the one that oppressed him; Mencken in a *Book of Prefaces and Prejudices*; Sinclair Lewis in *Main Street* and *Babbitt*; Theodore Dreiser in *Sister Carrie* and *Jennie Gerhardt* (pp. 217–219).

It might be said that Richard has the loneliness of a naturalistic hero, of McTeague or of Carrie Meeber. Theirs are worlds in which no one talks to anyone else, worlds entirely given over to the expression of power—one person's drive pitted against that of another— and the consequence of the struggle has more to do with heredity or chemistry than with persuasion. Richard's behavior, much like that of a character created by Norris or Dreiser, though it is not governed by the tight probability of fiction, carries constantly the solemn and overwhelming weight of the universe. He cannot say "sir" without acquiescing to the everpresent power of the white man, and he cannot read Mencken without the satisfaction that he has triumphed over a hostile white South through subterfuge and trickery.

Richard's commitment to write precipitates confrontations. As we have seen, his honest admission of this aspiration to one white lady employer results in bitter ridicule, and Richard feels, despite the pressures of his situation, that his ego has been assaulted. His first publication, "The Voodoo of Hell's Half-Acre," is little more than the crude rendering of the stuff of *Flynn's Detective Weekly*, but Richard discovers that printing it is an act of defiance, further separating him from the world that surrounds him, both black and white (p. 146).

Richard does not intend to restrict his range to any half-acre, though his first is identified as "Hell." His province would be the real world around him. True, it is sometimes not to be distinguished from the subject area defined by his first literary effort. At a very young age Richard sees "elephants" moving across the land—not real "elephants," but convicts in a chain gang, and the child's awe is prompted by the unfortunate confusion of elephant and zebra (p. 52). An inauspicious beginning, perhaps, but the pattern of applying his imagination to his immediate surroundings is firmly set. Later, Richard says more soberly that he rejects religion because it ignores immediate reality. His faith, predictably, must be wedded to "common realities of life" (p. 100), anchored in the sensations of his body and in what his mind could grasp. This is, we see, an excellent credo for an artist, but a worthless one for a black boy growing to maturity in Mississippi.

Another piece of evidence announcing Richard's talent is the compulsion to make symbols of the details of his everyday experience. This faculty is early demonstrated in his tendency to generalize from sensational experience, to define an appropriate emotion to associate with his feelings. A more highly developed example is Richard's reaction to his mother's illness and sufferings, representative for him in later years of the poverty, the ignorance, the helplessness of black life in Mississippi. And it is based on the generalizing process that Richard is a black boy, any black boy experiencing childhood, adolescence, and early manhood in the South.

Richard leaves the South. He must, to survive as a man and to develop as an artist. By the time we reach the end of the narrative, these two drives have merged. We know, as well, that the South will never leave Richard, never depart from the rich imagination that developed despite monumental opposition. We have only the final promise that Richard will someday understand the region that has indelibly marked him.

Richard's ultimate liberation, and his ultimate triumph, will be the ability to face the dreadful experience in the South and to record it. At the end of *A Portrait of the Artist as a Young Man*, the facts of experience have become journal items for the artist.[29] At the conclusion of *Invisible Man*, Ellison's unnamed narrator can record the blues of his black life, with the accompaniment of extraordinary psychedelic effects. Stephen Dedalus is on his way to becoming an artist: Ellison's hero promises to climb out of his hole, half-prepared, at least, to return to mundane life.[30] The conclusion of *Black Boy* is less positive and more tentative. True, Richard has made it; he has whipped the devils of the South, black and white. But he has left us with a feeling that is less than happy. He has yet to become an artist. Then we realize with a start what we have read is not simply the statement of a promise, its background and its development, but its fulfillment. Wright has succeeded in reconstructing the reality that was for a long time perhaps too painful to order, and that reconstruction may be Wright's supreme artistic achievement, *Black Boy*.

---

[29]See James Joyce, *A Portrait of the Artist as a Young Man* (New York: New American Library, 1955), pp. 195–196.

[30]Ellison's narrator states his final position with some care: "Thus, having tried to give pattern to the chaos which lives within the pattern of your certainties, I must come out, I must emerge." *Invisible Man* (New York: New American Library, 1952), p. 502.

Nathan Scott

(1925–   )

NOW THE WILLIAM R. KENAN Professor Emeritus of Religious Studies and Professor Emeritus of English at the University of Virginia, Nathan Alexander Scott, Jr., has had an incredibly full, varied, and productive career in American colleges and universities, black and white.

Born in 1925, in Cleveland, Ohio, the son of Attorney and Mrs. Nathan A. Scott, he was reared in Detroit, Michigan, and attended the public schools of that city. Scott received his B.A. from the University of Michigan in 1944, his B.D. from Union Theological Seminary in 1946, and his Ph.D. from Columbia University in 1949.

He began his teaching career in 1946 as dean of the chapel at Virginia Union University. Leaving there, he moved to Howard University, where he eventually became director of the General Education Program in the Humanities. In 1955, he left Howard for the University of Chicago to teach theology and literature. At Chicago he became the prestigious Shailer Mathews Professor of Theology and Literature. In 1976 he joined the staff of the University of Virginia, where he is currently. In addition, Scott has been visiting or adjunct professor at Gustavus Adolphus College, the University of Michigan, and John Carroll University.

Highly trained in three disciplines—literature, philosophy, and theology, Scott has written brilliantly and prolifically in all three. He has written or edited twenty-five books, contributed articles to fifty books edited by others, and published essays or articles in more than one hundred journals in the three fields mentioned previously. Although he has written outstanding critical comments on several major African American authors, the bulk of his work concerns writers in the fields of literature, philosophy, and theology, without regard to race, nationality, or time period.

A priest of the Episcopal church and a Fellow of the American Academy of Arts and Sciences, Professor Scott has received fourteen honorary doctorates from some of America's best known centers of learning. He has also been co-editor or member of the board for some of the nation's finest theological and literary journals, among them: *The Journal of Religion, The Virginia Quarterly Review, The Christian Scholar*, and *Callaloo*.

For a critical look at Scott's writings, see D. C. Noel's "Nathan Scott and the Nostalgic Fallacy: A Close Reading of Theological Criticism," *Journal of the American Academy of Religion* (December 1970), and R. F. Terry's "To Stay with the Question of Being: A Consideration of Theological

96

Elements in the Criticism of Nathan A. Scott, Jr.," *Anglican Theological Review* 55 (January 1973).

The following selection, "Ralph Ellison's Vision of *Communitas*," appeared originally in the autumn 1978 issue of the *NICM Journal*, published by the National Institute for Campus Ministries, Newton Centre, Massachusetts.

RALPH ELLISON'S VISION OF *COMMUNITAS*

From the time of its first appearance in the spring of 1952 Ralph Ellison's *Invisible Man* has been thrusting itself forward, ever more insistently with the passage of each year, as the commanding masterpiece in the literature of contemporary American fiction—and, now that it has had a career of more than four decades, its priority of place appears indeed to have been solidly consolidated. For no other text of these past years has so lodged itself in the national imagination as has Ellison's great book: it stands today as the pre-eminent American novel of our period, and all that I want here to try to do is to suggest something of what it is that accounts for the kind of powerful claim it continues to exert upon us.

Ours is, of course, a period marked by an efflorescence of fictional talent on the American scene more notable surely than any comparable British or European insurgency. Yet, in its representative expressions, it is a talent, for all its variety and richness, that—in such writers as William Gass, John Barth, Donald Barthelme, and Ronald Sukenick—often chooses to dwell (as the title of a book on American fiction by the English critic Tony Tanner says) in a "City of Words." Bellow, Styron, Updike, and a few others, in their commitment to the traditional arts of narrative, remain sufficiently unreconstructed as to conceive the novel to be a mode of feigned history, but they, though retaining a large and devoted readership, do not carry the day and do not embody what Matthew Arnold called "the tone of the centre." For those who are advancing the new poetics of fiction take it for granted (as William Gass says) "that literature is language, that stories and the places and the people in them are merely made of words as chairs are made of smoothed sticks and sometimes of cloth or metal tubes," and thus, since "there are no

Reprinted by permission of the author. Four paragraphs of this essay have been drawn from an essay ("Black Literature") prepared for *The Harvard Guide to Contemporary American Writing*, edited by Daniel Hoffman (Cambridge, Massachusetts: Harvard University Press, 1979), and are used with the permission of the Harvard University Press.

events but words in fiction,"[1] they think of the novelistic craft as
simply an affair of putting words together in new and surprising
combinations—which record nothing other than the event of the
writer's having done certain interesting things with language itself.
So charmed is the new literature with its own verbal universe of
metaphor and metonymy that it refuses any deep involvements with
the empirical, verifiable world of actual fact, preferring instead what
Conrad long ago called the "prolonged hovering flight of the subjective over the outstretched ground of the case exposed." And thus it
forswears the kind of intentionality that looks toward finding new
strategems wherewith to give a liberating "shape and . . . significance
to the immense panorama of . . . anarchy which is contemporary history": which is perhaps to say that it does not seek (in Yeats's great
phrase) to hold "reality and justice in a single thought."

The kind of *dandysme* which reigns now has in recent years been
denominated by literary academicians specializing in *Tendenz* as
"post-modernism," but a part of the immense appeal that belongs to
a figure like Ralph Ellison is surely an affair of his fidelity to the
ethic of classic modernism. For the great masters of this century—
Joyce and Lawrence and Mann and Faulkner—were indeed propos-
ing to do what T.S. Eliot in his famous review of *Ulysses* (in the
issue of *The Dial* for November 1923) descried as Joyce's intention:
namely, to give a "shape and . . . significance to the immense panorama of . . . anarchy which is contemporary history." *The Magic
Mountain* and *The Death of Virgil*, *Women in Love* and *The Sun Also
Rises*, *The Sound and the Fury* and *Man's Fate* are books that strike us
today as having a remarkable kind of weight and contemporaneity,
because they are, as it were, taking on the age: with a fierce kind of
audacity, they seem to be intending to *displace* a daunting world, to
clear a space for the human endeavor, and thus to keep open the
door of the future. In short, their rites and ceremonies and plots and
arguments are organized toward the end of envisaging new forms of
life for the soul, and it is just in this that one element of the genius
of 20th-century modernism lies.

Now it is in this line that Ralph Ellison stands. Immediately after
Invisible Man first appeared in 1952, the astonishing authority of its
art quickly brought it to the forefront of the literary scene, and this
at a time when, under the new influence of Henry James, so many
representative American writers of the moment—such as Jean Staf-
ford, Frederick Buechner, Isabel Bolton, Monroe Engel, and Mary
McCarthy—were choosing to seek their effects by the unsaid and

---

[1]William H. Gass, *Fiction and the Figures of Life* (New York: Vintage Books, 1972), pp.
27, 30.

the withheld, by the dryly ironic analogy and the muted voice. In the early 1950s Ellison, like Faulkner and Penn Warren, was particularly notable for being unafraid to make his fiction howl and rage and hoot with laughter over "the complex fate" of the *homo Americanus*: indeed, the uninhibited exhilaration and suppleness of his rhetoric were at once felt to be a main source of the richness of texture distinguishing his extraordinary book. Yet the kind of continuing life that his novel has had is surely to be accounted for in terms not of sheer verbal energy alone, but, more principally, in terms of the cogency of systematic vision that it enunciates. And though something like this has frequently been remarked, what is most essential in the basic stress and emphasis of the novel has just as frequently been misreckoned, no doubt largely because the book has so consistently been construed as having an import related exclusively to the experience of black Americans.

The protagonist of *Invisible Man* is, of course, a young black man (unnamed) who must pick his perilous way through the lunatic world that America has arranged for its Negro minority. In the beginning, he is what the white masters of the Southern world in which he grows up were once in the habit of calling "a good Negro": he has cheerfully accepted all the promises of that Establishment, so much so that the oily tongued and cynical president of his college, Dr. Bledsoe, has singled him out as his special ward. But, unhappily, on a certain day he unintentionally exposes a visiting white trustee from the North to the local Negro gin-mill and to the incestuous entanglements of a Negro farmer's family in the neighborhood—and, as a result, he is ousted from the college, as a punishment for his having allowed a donor of the institution to see what visiting white patrons are not supposed to see.

He then moves on to New York, there to journey through the treacherous byways of an infernally labyrinthine world, as he seeks to make contact with whatever it is that may authenticate his existence. The executive powers ordain that, being black, he shall be "invisible," and thus his great central effort becomes that of wresting an acknowledgment, of *achieving* visibility. He gets a job in a Long Island paint factory, and there he becomes involved—again, inadvertently—as a scab in labor violence. Soon afterward, however, he is taken up by "the Brotherhood" (i.e., the Communist Party), after he is heard to deliver an impassioned and a quite spontaneous speech one winter afternoon as he finds himself part of a crowd watching the eviction of an elderly Negro couple from their Harlem tenement flat. The assignment he is given by his new confreres is that of *organizing* the sullenness of Harlem. But he soon discovers that the Negro's cause is but a pawn being used by "the Brotherhood" to promote its "line." So, after the Brotherhood engineers a furious race riot in the Harlem streets, he in utter disillusionment dives through a manhole, down into a cellar, for a period of "hibernation." He has tried the way of "humility," of being a "good Negro"; he has tried to find room for himself in American industry, to become a good cog in the technological machine; he has attempted to attach himself to leftist politics—he has tried all those things by means of which it would seem that a Negro might achieve visibility in American life. But, since none has offered a way into the culture, he has now chosen to become an underground man. All his reversals have been due to the blackness of his skin: so now, at last, he decides to stay in this cellar where, by way of a tapped line, he will steal the electricity for his 1,369 bulbs from Monopolated Light and Power and dine on sloe gin and vanilla ice cream and *embrace* "The Blackness of Blackness."

Yet Ellison's protagonist, unlike so many of his counterparts in Negro fiction, is in the end by no means one *merely* wounded. True, he twice tells us, in the accent of Eliot's *East Coker*—first in the Prologue, and again at the end of his narrative—that his "end is in . . . [his] beginning." And so it is, for his last state—since it is an underworld, a place of exile, of dislodgment and expatriation—is in a way his first. But it is an underworld that *he* has *illuminated*. "Step outside the narrow borders of what men call reality and you step into chaos . . . or imagination," he says. When, that is, you step outside the domesticated and the routinized, you may step into chaos, since the definition of the world, as he has discovered, is possibility—the very infiniteness of which may be defeating unless by dint of a feat of imagination some transcendence can be realized. And since, as it would seem, the protagonist-narrator conceives art itself to be the definition of such a transcendence, he—amidst the misrule and confusion of a demented world—has undertaken to form the lessons he has learned into a story, to "put it [all] down," and thereby (like another young man who became an artist) to forge in the smithy of his own soul the uncreated conscience of his native land. His story ends in a cellar, because, having constantly been told that it is in some such hovel that he belongs, this *eiron* [ironist] has chosen mockingly to descend, then, into a Harlem basement where, if he cannot have visibility, he can at least have *vision*—and where he can produce out of his abysmal pain a poetry that, as he says, "on the lower frequencies . . . [may] speak for you"—*le lecteur*.

The book presents, as Alfred Kazin has suggested, one of the most engaging studies in recent literature in "the art of survival."[2]

[2]Alfred Kazin, *Bright Book of Life: American Novelists and Storytellers from Hemingway to Mailer* (Boston: Little, Brown and Co., 1973), p. 246.

And in relation to everything with which its young anti-hero must reckon Ellison displays a notable mastery. His reader finds himself, indeed, utterly immersed in all the concrete materialities of black experience: one hears the very buzz and hum of Harlem in the racy, pungent speech of his West Indians and his native hipsters; one sees the fearful nonchalance of the zoot-suiter and hears the terrible anger of the black nationalist on his streetcorner platform; and all the *grotesquerie* in the novel's account of a dreary little backwater of a remote Southern Negro college has in it a certain kind of empirically absolute rightness. The book is packed full of the acutest observations of the manners and idioms and human styles that comprise the ethos of black life in America, and it gives us such a sense of social fact as can be come by nowhere in the manuals of academic sociology—all this being done with the ease that comes from enormous expertness of craft, from deep intimacy of knowledge, and love.

Yet, deeply rooted as the novel is in the circumstances of Negro life and experience, it wants on its "lower frequencies" to speak about a larger condition, and, indeed, when Ellison is taken (as he customarily is) to be a barrister seeking on behalf of the black multitudes to impose a certain radical affidavit on the American conscience, what is most deeply prophetic in the testimony brought forward by his book is by way of being obscured. Nor is it at all inapposite to consider the authorial performance conveyed by *Invisible Man* as reflecting a prophetic intention, at least not if one thinks of prophetism in something like the terms proposed by the anthropologist Victor Turner.

Turner's theory of culture, based in large part on his extensive field-researches amongst the Ndembu people of northwest Zambia, entails an elaborate scheme which he developed in numerous writings but most fully in three notable books, *The Forest of Symbols* (1967), *The Ritual Process* (1969), and *Dramas, Fields, and Metaphors* (1974). His starting point is the concept of the "liminal phase" advanced by the Belgian ethnographer Arnold van Gennep in his classic work of 1909, *Les rites de passage*. Van Gennep, in working out the logic of "transition" rites, remarked three phases into which they invariably fall and which he identified as, first, separation, then margin (or *limen*, the Latin signifying "threshold"), and then reaggregation. That is to say, the neophyte first undergoes some detachment or dislocation from his established role in a social structure or cultural polity—whereupon he finds himself as novice in a "liminal" situation in which he is neither one thing nor another, neither here nor there, neither what he was nor yet what he will become. Then, in the third phase, the passage is completed by his reincorporation into a social or religious structure: no longer is he invisible by reason of his divestment of status and role, for, once again, he finds himself with acknowledged rights and obligations vis-à-vis those others who with him are members one of another in whatever body it is to which they jointly belong.

Now Professor Turner is careful to remark that "liminars" are, in most human communities, by no means the only *déclassés*, for always there are various "outsiders" (shamans, monks, priests, hippies, hoboes, gypsies) who either by ascription or choice stand outside the established order, just as there are also various kinds of "marginals" (migrant foreigners, persons of mixed ethnic origin, the upwardly and downwardly mobile) who may be "simultaneously members . . . of two or more groups whose social definitions and cultural norms are distinct from, and often even opposed to, one another."[3] But, though at many points he is strongly insistent on these distinctions, at many others he seems to be treating "outsiderhood" and "marginality" as merely special modes of "liminality," and it appears for him to be the decisive antipode to "aggregation."

What Victor Turner is most eager to remark, however, is the wrongheadedness of regarding liminality as a merely negative state of privation: on the contrary, as he argues, it can be and often is an enormously fruitful seedbed of spiritual creativity, for it is precisely amidst the troubling ambiguities of the liminar's *déclassement* that there is born in him a profound hunger for *communitas*. And Turner prefers the Latin term, since he feels "community" connotes an ordered, systemized society—whereas the liminar's yearning is not for any simple kind of social structure but rather, as he says, for that spontaneous, immediate flowing from *I* to *Thou* of which Martin Buber is our great modern rhapsode.[4] Which is to say that the liminar thirsts for *communitas*: this is what the naked neophyte in a seclusion lodge yearns for; this is what the dispossessed and the exiled dream of; this is what "dharma bums" and millenarians and holy mendicants and "rock" people are moved by—namely, the vision of an *open* society in which all the impulses and affections that are normally bound by social structure are liberated, so that every barrier between *I* and *Thou* is broken down and the wind of *communitas* may blow where it listeth.

Moreover, Victor Turner conceives it to be the distinctive mission of the prophet to lift *communitas* into the subjunctive mood: he is the liminal man *par excellence* whose special vocation, as a frontiers-

---

[3]Victor Turner, *Dramas, Fields, and Metaphors* (Ithaca, New York: Cornell University Press, 1974), p. 233.

[4]See Victor Turner, *The Ritual Process* (Ithaca, New York: Cornell University Press, 1977 [paperback edition]), p. 127.

man dwelling on the edges of the established order, is to puncture "the clichés associated with status incumbency and role-playing"[5] and to fill for his contemporaries the open space of absolute futurity with a vision of that unanimity, that free unity-in-diversity, which graces the human order when men give their suffrage to the "open morality" (as Bergson would have called it) of *agape*.

Now it is when *Invisible Man* is regarded in its relation to the experiential realities addressed by Victor Turner that its special kind of prophetic discernment may perhaps be most clearly identified. True, its narrator is a young black man encumbered with all the disadvantage that American society has imposed on his kind. But his very last word to the reader—*mon semblable, mon frère!* [my fellow-man, my brother]—records his conviction that, "on the lower frequencies," he, in the story he tells about himself, is speaking about a condition that embraces not just his ancestral kinsmen but the human generality of his age. Which suggests that what is most essentially problematic in his situation is not merely his blackness but, rather, something else, and it is this which needs now to be defined.

One of Ellison's critics speaks of how frequently his novel is by way of coming to an end and then having once more to start itself up again,[6] and something like this is surely the case: at least, it may be said that the persistent rhythm of the novel is an affair of the protagonist's drifting into a relation with one or another of the various trustees of social power and then either digging in his heels or taking flight, when the connection threatens to abrogate his freedom. After he is expelled from his college, he takes to New York the various letters of introduction Dr. Bledsoe has provided, and it is his eventual discovery of the cruel dispraise that these sealed letters from the malignant old man have actually conveyed that leads him to think: "Everyone seemed to have some plan for me, and beneath that some more secret plan." And so indeed it is: wherever he turns, he finds himself dealing with those—whether it be Bledsoe or Mr. Norton or the Reverend Homer A. Barbee or the owner of the Long Island paint factory or Brother Jack—who are eager to map out a design for his life and to convert him into a kind of automaton of their own schemes. They may be agents of religion or education or industry or radical politics, but, at bottom, they are (as Tony Tanner says) "mechanizers of consciousness"[7]—and each is prepared to say

---

[5]Ibid., p. 128.

[6]See Marcus Klein, *After Alienation: American Novels in Mid-Century* (Cleveland and New York: World Publishing Co., 1964), pp. 107–109.

[7]Tony Tanner, *City of Words: American Fiction, 1950–1970* (New York: Harper & Row, 1971), p. 53.

something like what Bledsoe says in reference to his college: "This is a power set-up, son, and I'm at the controls." In fact, this young *picaro* does at last himself realize that all his various proctors and patrons have been "very much the same, each attempting to force his picture of reality upon me and neither giving a hoot in hell for how things looked to me." But he is unflagging in his refusal of obedient service to the organizers and manipulators: he wants to be free of that great alien force that we call Society. So, in the logic of the novel, his exemplary role is related not merely to the disinherited American Negro but, far more basically, to that "disintegrated" or "alienated" consciousness which, as Hegel reminds us in the *Phenomenology of Mind* is distinguished by its antagonism to "the external power of society" and which, in the modern period, is not simply here or there—but everywhere.

Yet, in his liminality, Ellison's young knight does not choose merely to pour scornful laughter on the social establishment, in the manner of Rinehart, for, isolated though he is, he remains totally in earnest. There comes a moment when, though having separated himself from the Brotherhood, he is nevertheless one hunted by the partisans of the West Indian black nationalist, Ras the Exhorter, who conceives the interracialism of the Brotherhood to be a fearfully mischievous confusion of "the blahk mahn" and who is unrelenting in his pursuit of him who has been one of its chief spokesmen in Harlem. So, by way of hurriedly arranging a scanty disguise, our principal purchases some darkly tinted spectacles and a flamboyant hat, and immediately he is mistaken on the streets for a man named Rinehart of whom he has never heard—and whom he never sees. One evening there suddenly emerges from a Lenox Avenue subway exit a large, blowsy prostitute reeking with "Christmas Night perfume" who for a moment takes him to be her Man: "Rinehart, baby, is that you? . . . . Say, you ain't Rinehart, man . . . . git away from here before you get me in trouble." And, as he swings on, a few moments later he is hailed by a couple of hipsters who take him to be Rinehart the numbers man: "Rinehart, poppa, tell us what you putting down." Then a group of zoot-suiters greet him: "Hey now, daddy-o." And again, in an Eighth Avenue tavern he is taken to be Rinehart by the barkeeper: "What brand you drinking tonight, Poppa-stopper?" Some larcenous policemen expecting a pay-off summon him from their patrol car to a curb and, when he denies that he is Rinehart, the response flung back at him is—"Well, you better be by morning." Then, again, outside a storefront church he is greeted by two aging, pious drones as "Rever'n Rinehart," and they offer him assurances about how zealously they are collecting money for his building fund. And, after many such encounters, he begins to marvel at this extraordinary personage—"Rine the runner and Rine the gambler and Rine the briber and Rine the lover and Rinehart the Reverend." Indeed, he is at once fascinated by the virtuosity of this remarkable changeling—and, in a way, unhinged by the abyss of infinite possibility opened up by his glimpse of the "multiple personalities" worn by this black Proteus.

But, no, not for him the way of this wily rascal who deals with the intractabilities of social circumstance by simply mocking them in the cultivation of an extravagant histrionism. No, Ellison's protagonist is a liminar who, though separated from the established orders of the world, is yet not estranged from himself. And thus he yearns for an authentic existence, not for Rinehart's world of no boundaries at all but for something like a New Jerusalem, where no man is an island and where Love is the name behind the design of the human City.

He is unable to descry at any point on the horizon the merest prospect, however, of this Good Place. And so at last he descends into an underground world. He is floundering about one night through Harlem streets inflamed by the savage race riot that has been carefully orchestrated by the Brotherhood itself, and, in his abstracted anguish at the sheer futility of this lunatic paroxysm, he stumbles into some black *enragés* who, being suddenly angered by the sight of his briefcase, are about to set upon him, when he lifts the cover of a manhole and plunges down into a coal cellar below. There he finds a narrow passage that leads into a "dimensionless room," and this he elects to occupy as the site of his "hibernation."

This liminar in his cellar bears no resemblance, however, to that bilious and exacerbated little cipher whose portrayal in Dostoevsky's *Notes from the Underground* has made him one of the great modern archetypes of the Underground Man. Ellison's hero has been "hurt to the point of abysmal pain, hurt to the point of invisibility," not only by American racism but by all those "mechanizers of consciousness" —by Bledsoe as well as by Mr. Norton, by Brother Jack as well as by Ras the Exhorter—whose great "passion [is] to make men conform to a pattern." Yet, in his hibernation, he realizes that, for all the vehemence with which he has taken a stand " 'against' society," he still wants to defend "the principle on which the country was built." As he says, "I defend because in spite of all"—though "I sell you no phony forgiveness"—"I find that I love." He harbors no love for those who are moved by a "passion toward conformity," for, as he insists, "diversity is the word." "Life is to be lived, not controlled . . . ." So the dream by which he is enheartened in his basement room is the dream that we shall "become one, and yet many": it is the dream of *communitas*. And it is in the eloquence with which the novel projects this vision for the human future that it proves (in the terms I have taken over from Victor Turner) its prophetic genius—and its special relevance to the American situation of our own immediate present. For, given the furious assertiveness that distinguishes the various racial and ethnic particularisms making up our national society today, ours (as one thoughtful observer has recently remarked) is a country representing something like "pluralism gone mad." One of our great needs as a people is to recover a sense of common purposes and of a common destiny that overrides our "atomized world of a thousand me-first . . . groupings" of one kind or another.[8] And it is the reminder in this connection that Ellison's novel brings that gives its testimony just now a special poignance.

"Who knows," says the nameless protagonist—"Who knows but that, on the lower frequencies, I speak for you?"

---

[8]Meg Greenfield, "Pluralism Gone Mad," *Newsweek*, 27 August 1979, p. 76.

Alice Childress

(1920–   )

BORN IN CHARLESTON, South Carolina, in 1920, Alice Childress at age five moved to New York where she was educated through high school. A self-educated creative artist, she has distinguished herself as playwright, fiction writer, director, actress, lecturer, and scholar. Trudier Harris gives a thorough review of Childress's life and works in her entry in *Dictionary of Literary Biography, Volume 51*. In this entry, Harris makes the following sobering comment: "For all the pioneering, groundbreaking, excellent work, worthy critical laurels have not yet fallen upon Childress. And the greatest testament to her talent—consistent production of her plays—has not yet been forthcoming."

Childress began her career as an actress in 1940 when she appeared in *On Strivers Row* and in *Natural Man* (1941), both plays performed by the original cast of the American Negro Theatre (ANT) in Harlem. She also appeared in this company's opening production of *Anna Lucasta* in 1944. For eight of the eleven years that Childress was affiliated with the original American Negro Theatre, she took lessons from ANT instructors, worked as drama coach, served as personnel director for a short time, and became a member of the board of directors. As she worked to gain experience as a writer and actress, she held a number of menial jobs such as salesperson, assistant machinist, insurance agent, photo retoucher, and domestic worker, all jobs that kept her in contact with the grassroots population that continued to be the subject of her fiction and drama. *Florence*, Childress's own one-act play that treats the meeting of a black woman domestic and a white woman in the waiting room of a Jim Crow train station, was the first play directed by Childress and was produced by ANT. The plays Childress directed, like *Florence*, manifest the same distinguishing characteristic as all her written work: she challenges the stereotypical roles and societal attitudes toward people of the working class. In addition to giving these characters psychological depth, she also affirms blackness in *Wine in the Wilderness and Trouble in Mind*, which won the first Obie Award in 1956 for best original, off-Broadway play. In *Wedding Band*, she exposes the injustice of humiliating laws such as the miscegenation statutes.

Having seen five of her plays produced and performed in New York, as well as one at the University of Michigan and one on television, by the beginning of the 1970s, Childress published two novels—*A Hero Ain't*

Nothin' But a Sandwich (1973) and *A Short Walk* (1979)—and two children's plays—*When the Rattlesnake Sounds* (1975) and *Let's Hear It for the
Queen* (1976). *A Hero Ain't Nothin'* has been made into a movie with the
screenplay written by Childress, and won the Jane Addams Honor Award
in 1974 and the Paul Robeson Award for Outstanding Contributions to
the Performing Arts in 1977, among others. Childress also received the
1990 City College Langston Hughes Award for Outstanding Contributions
to the Arts and Letters. She is a member of the advisory council of NCAC
(National Coalition Against Censorship).

Childress is also the author of *The African Garden* (1971) and *Those
Other People* (1989). Her work is included in *Nine Plays by Black Women*,
edited and with an introduction by Margaret B. Wilkerson (1986).

For further comment on the life and works of Alice Childress, in
addition to the entry by Trudier Harris mentioned previously, see also the
entry on Childress in *Dictionary of Literary Biography, Volume 7*, and Linda
Metzger, ed., *Black Writers: A Selection of Sketches from Contemporary
Authors* (1979). Critical commentary on the works of Childress include
Janet Brown's *Feminist Drama: Definitions and Critical Analysis* (1979),
Rosemary Curb's "An Unfashionable Tragedy, American Racism: Alice
Childress's *Wedding Band*," *MELUS* 7 (Winter 1980); Trudier Harris's *From
Mammies to Militants: Domestics in Black American Literature* (1982); and
Melissa Walker's *Down from the Mountaintop: Black Women's Novels in the
Wake of the Civil Rights Movement, 1966–1989* (1991).

The selection that follows is a chapter from *A Hero Ain't Nothin' But a
Sandwich*.

NIGERIA GREENE
Teacher

This guy across the hall from me is not to be believed. He is white,
and in this school because the system makes damn sure to have
white representation in every nook and corner of the country, the
world, and, in particular, in every Black community. Look around
your city and let me know if you see coloreds represented fifty-fifty
in the white community. No, it doesn't go down that way. I'm sick
of explainin and talkin race. Race is the story of my life and my
father's life, and I guess, his father and all the other fathers before
that. As a kid, I was in on "race" discussions in school, at home, in
church, everywhere. It's a wonder every Black person in the U. S. of

A. hasn't gone stark, ravin mad from racism . . . and the hurtin it's put on us.

My grandfather was a Garveyite, a dues-payin member of the UNIA—United Negro Improvement Association. He talked my mother into givin me the name Nigeria. People used to call me Gerry to get around the pure African sound, but my name comes on fine these days.

As I said, Bernard Cohen is not to be believed. His whole mission in teaching is to convince Black kids that most whites are great except for a "few" rotten apples in every barrel. It burns me to see white teachers bend kid's ears with the same tune, year in and year out. They'd rather ruin their lives by makin them think they're imaginin the game bein run on them than to save them with truth. You can face hardship if you realize it's not all your fault and you are dealin with some things that have been deliberately dropped on you.

Most of the kids don't talk anything but Harlemese, but have minds as sharp as a double-edge razor. They laugh at textbooks because most invite laughter. "Our" school is fulla white-face books written by white writers. Only two pictures on my wall when I came here . . . George Washington and Abraham Lincoln. Abe was, at least, involved with the Civil War and the Emancipation thing; but George was a slaveholder, and it is impossible to hang George over my front blackboard and not discuss him. When I discuss him, I don't go by what's in these history books or we'd be dealin in lies. George was a slaveholder, and he had it put in his will to free alla his slaves *after* his death. But he owned a slave woman whose cookin was so fine that he freed her while he was livin. She musta really known how to barbecue!

Well, that time slot is over and outta our hands. But now is now, and I don't need a slaveholder lookin down on thirty-seven Black students, while I'm teachin history and civics lessons.

From a kid on up I was good at history. I mean I was good at memorizin what was put before me and was a whiz at recitin it back. If the book said a lie was truth, that lie was the answer I put down on my test paper. I learned that from my father. He was slick as a greasy whistle and yessed his way into the post office. It was hard for a brother to get in durin Papa's early years. You had to know somebody. Fortunately, he knew books were full of lies and never minded tellin me so, but he would also say, "Tell the lie back, tell 'em what they wanta hear, cause it's their book and their school and they will fail you if you don't write it down the way it reads. They'll do you outta the chance to earn yourself a crust of bread." Then he'd tag on the clincher, "Furthermore, if you don't bring me a good report, you gonna get outta here and labor hard because I won't support no full-grown man." He meant it too.

He was sincere in a hemmed-in kinda way and dealt with life exactly the way it was laid out, playin the game according to old, tested rules. He was a trustee of the church and took up collection every Sunday mornin. I can see him now, standin at attention, holdin the mahogany plate, his brown face lit by sunlight shinin through a stained-glass window. One Sunday I noticed the window was a picture of a sword-carryin, golden-haired angel, with snowy, feathery wings. The other windows also showed whites as saints and angels, none looked like my father or any of our people; there and then I began to find Black Nationalism within me, to realize there was no integration in God's heaven, and that I must accept even the Christian rejection of me and mine. I felt hatred for that evil God who made us sing, beg, weep and pray for humble admittance into his white heaven.

I decided to correctly give back all the silly answers required of me. I promised myself to make a day when I'd teach what could not be found in my schoolbook, teach how to search for and find withheld truth. I had to have a piece of paper labeled diploma in order to enter this so-called house of learnin where Black children are shut off, shut out and shut up, forced to study the history of their white conquerors, this peculiar place of white facts, white questions, white answers, and white final exams. I couldn't explain it to my father, because Grandpa's Garveyism had skipped right over his head and landed on me. I left Dad to enjoy what he had, the Saturday night poker game, Sunday mornins with stained-glass angels, lodge meetins, all the rituals which kill time from one holiday to the next. We saw the New Year in by eatin peas and rice for good luck. If peas and rice were lucky, we'd be free! My folks had the Fourth of July at the beach, Thanksgivin Day with my aunt in the country. Misery was almost sweet, plenty of finger-poppin and dancin—in between folks bein killed, chased, shot at, segregated. I finger-popped along with the rest and ate my share of souse and sweet potato pie. But I had me a plan, Nigeria Greene was gonna be the Black Messiah of the classroom, gonna light the way with Blackness. I try to do it. I try, like Nat Turner said, "because it pleases me to try."

But, as I was sayin, Cohen, across the hall from me, is not to be believed. Give him his due, he teaches hard, when kids leave his room, they take somethin with them, even if it's a lie. He has a tough hide to take what some-a these roughs can put on you, but spends mosta his time tryin to undo what I taught the term before. Mainly, he wants to make it clear that he's "not the one" who's doin us in. I've heard him sing that chorus so many times.

"Yes, there were slave masters, but *I'm* not a slave master. Yes, there is exploitation, but *I'm* not an exploiter. There are good and bad in all races. Skin color has nothin to do with social wrongs, all groups have been enslaved. . . ."

I have to get my class strong enough to weather his storm. I've confronted him about this time after time. "Hey," I'd say, "why you messin up minds? What you layin on my people? Sound like you teachin us to sing a new song . . . 'God bless segregation and all that it's done for me.' "

He gave me a lotta sass. "Why do you slang talk?" he says. "Are you trying to prove that you're one of the elite underprivileged?"

"Right on," I said, "I'm one of the underprivileged, and I dig Black talk, I smile Black, think Black, walk Black, and all the Black that's not yet discovered is out there waiting for me to find it. You get off my kids!"

We go on like that sorta half jokin but meaning to draw blood with every dig. The oldest white folks' strategy is to attack a person in a way that looks fair. Dig how the Indians got washed away and labeled "hostile." It shakes Cohen to his boots when he hears me ask, "What time is it?" And the class hollers out, "It's nation time!" I'm teachin that it's high time to straighten up and hold hands because my inner clock is tellin me that now is only half past slavery.

I'm only hopin they can *hear* me. The enemy has turned off so many eardrums till some of us now hear only through the bloodstream. No stuff, brains and ears are turned off for the duration! If somethin *feels* good or puts him to sleep, that's all the turned-off brother needs to keep him quiet as the grave until grave time comes.

When I use this segregation they have laid on us, use it to bring us closer and wiser in Blackness, Cohen screams about "segregation in reverse!" I held a two-period rap session on that accusation. "How come it is," I say, "that when whitey pushes us off to one side through law and mass muscle, that is segregation, but when we get to usin our enforced togetherness, they call it 'segregation in reverse'?" Then I go to cookin on the subject and clarify for them. "What they mean," I say, "is that when segregation works against us, that's what it's suppose to do, so it's in forward, but when it starts to work against *them*, it's in reverse, meanin that it's goin the wrong way. You see, whitey is not ever gonna say *he* is being segregated against, that would be too much like what happens to *me*. That's how come it is he yells that it's goin into 'reverse.' " When the hurtin is on us, it's in forward; on him it's in reverse.

Three teachers, two *Negroes* and one white, made complaints to the principal, the gripe was that I am "creating an atmosphere" which breeds hostility. I told them there would be hostility in this school if I had never been born. Dig?

Cohen wasn't in on the complaint because he tries not to stick his head in an electric fan when it's turned on. He also remembers how we almost went to swingin fists when he complained about my givin spellin lessons instead of stickin to history and civics. I challenged all the "expert" opinion that "inner city" children can't read. I told my class, "Yall can read and write, so don't hand me no jive. When I go in the toilet and note the handwritin on the wall, I have yet to see 'fuck you' and 'shit' spelled wrong, nor have I had any hardship in understandin those lines scrawled bout who did what to who, so if you can read and write dirty words, you damn sure can read and write all the rest."

Cohen's complaint resulted in the principal givin me a talk about "decency and morality in teachin methods due to the vulnerability of the young. . ." and so forth and so on. I wasn't ready for that, not ready for any white principal from a suburban-split-level-livin-segregated-Anglo-Saxon neighborhood to question my morality values, specially when he's makin his daily bread in a dirt-poor, so-called Black Community and spends his pay in West Park Gardens Drive, or wherever the hell else he buses out to when the bell rings at three o'clock. I cooked on him, "It's middle-class suburbanites who have been makin all the immorality news here of late," I say, "the ones playin switch partners with one another's wives. We, in the ghetto, think it's not nice to do that kinda thing. You folks got slum minds."

I give Cohen lots of air and plenty good room except to keep him in line when he needs it. My wife tells me to cool it and don't try to change the world all at once. Maybe I need some criticism, but so in hell does she. Why does she go to fashion shows? The community is fulla these clubwomen givin fashion shows at downtown white hotels. Who cares what kinda lace somebody is wearin with their silver fox jacket? Too many hardworkin chicks spendin bread and time on white satin with ermine linin and all that crap. When I read the Black press, I almost choke. Constantly givin champagne sips and one-hundred-dollar-a-plate dinners and costume balls and comin-out parties. Comin out from where? Our folks holdin meets and dances down at the Bunny Club. Why would a woman wanta look like a fur tail is growin outta her butt?

Oh, so much gets to me! I keep seein this kid, Benjie, noddin over his desk when I pass Cohen's room, justa-sleepin and hangin. I walk in, look him over, and walk out. Cohen is gettin hot under the collar; so am I. Finally I take Cohen to one side and tell him the boy looks stoned. He gives me the TV line. "Kids sit up all night watching late TV, when they get to school they have to rest—"

I cut him off. "Don't run that game on me," I say. "Let's take him downstairs and turn him in."

Cohen pulls stubborn on me. "This [is] a class," he says. "I'm not turning in anybody. The parents get upset, the principal gets upset, the kid feels betrayed."

"Right," I say, "but let all that happen rather than see the boy dead, let's don't kill him outta the kindness of our hearts."

We look Benjie over and spot a couple of needle marks. I say, "You been into anything you shouldn't, little brother?"

Kid says, "I'm cool, Nigeria." But his cool is too stoned. Cohen and I take him down to Principal and request notification of parents. Benjie backs up ugly and says, "You a traitor, man! Yall pickin on me cause I'm Black." He really cut up, called me a Oreo Cookie, that's Black on the outside and white on the inside. I wanta knock him down, cause that's my nature, but instead I take his bad mouthin.

William Demby

(1922–   )

WILLIAM DEMBY was born in Pittsburgh, Pennsylvania, spent his child-hood in Clarksburg, West Virginia, and attended West Virginia State Col-lege until he joined the army. After an overseas military tour in Italy, Demby entered Fisk University in 1947. There he wrote stories and did illustrations for the *Fisk University Herald*. Upon graduation from Fisk, he returned to Italy, where he studied art at the University of Rome, worked as a jazz musician, and wrote screenplays for Roberto Rossellini. A major portion of his work there was translating Italian screenplays into English. From Rome Demby traveled in Europe, Ethiopia, Japan, and Thailand. He lived briefly in the United States in 1963, while working for a New York advertising agency. He then settled in Rome until 1969, when he returned to the United States. Since then he has taught at the College of Staten Island, and he presently lives in Sag Harbor, Long Island.

William Demby is the author of *Beetlecreek* (1950; reprinted in 1967 and 1972, it was also published as *Act of Outrage* in 1955). His other novels are *The Catacombs* (1965; reprinted 1970), and *Love Story Black* (1978; reprinted 1986). John O'Brien calls *The Catacombs* "one of the most original and im-portant novels to come out of the 1960s." In "The Achievement of William Demby" Jay R. Berry lauds Demby as a most effective stylist, "one who is extremely self-conscious in his choice of personae and narrative points of view, and in his use of time, imagery, and language" (*CLA Journal*, June 1983).

For further recent commentary see John O'Brien, *Interviews with Black Writers* (1973); Trudier Harris and Thadious M. Davis, eds., *Dictionary of Literary Biography, Volume 33* (1984); Roger Whitlow's *Black American Literature* (1973); Frances Carol Locher, ed., *Contemporary Authors*, vols. 81–84 (1979); and Bernard W. Bell's *The Afro-American Novel and Its Tradition* (1987).

The following selection comes from *Love Story Black*.

FROM **LOVE STORY BLACK**

My next interview with Miss Pariss took place the following night,
after my spirits had been lifted and the shattering damage to my
fragile ego been repaired by the unexpected arrival of a check from
Gracie's office, which I almost literally raced to the bank to deposit.

Thus, my financial woes momentarily cast aside, I was in a whistling elated mood as, athletically, I skipped up the dark steps and
knocked at Miss Pariss' door.

But instead of Miss Pariss' door opening, the door to Reverend
Grooms' apartment banged open as if there had been a gas explosion
inside. And I turned just in time to find myself face to face with a
drunken enraged apparition wearing torn and faded long woolen underwear, brandishing a knob-headed walking cane at me in one hand
and threatening me with a butcher knife with the other.

More than merely drunk, his bloodshot eyes and twisted facial
muscles left no doubt in my mind that I was about to be attacked,
perhaps even murdered, without the benefit of prayers or the slightest possibility of neighbors rushing to my support. I even read the
tiny four-line report in the next day's *Daily News*: "NEGRO COLLEGE
PROFESSOR AND NOVELIST SLAIN IN MUGGING INCIDENT ON UPPER WEST
SIDE."

"Reverend Grooms!" I said in a tremulous voice, backing to the
fartherest and darkest corner of the odorous landing. "Are you feeling all right?"

"You cheap two-bit pimp!" he shrieked, the butcher knife and
cane slashing the half-darkness of the landing in some intricate para-
bolic pattern as though he were performing a kind of sword dance.

"You iniquitous disciple of the devil! You youngblood Superfly
dude—pimping on a fine Christian woman old enough to be your
grandmother! I ought to cut your evil parts and feed them to the
hogs!"

"Reverend Grooms—calm down—that butcher knife is dangerous!"

"I may be old and feeble but this butcher knife is a powerful
equalizer, you low-down street pimp—calling yourself an educated
colored man and a professor—!"

"Reverend Grooms—!"

"Don't you Reverend Grooms me! You haven't the right to speak
forth my name—!"

From *Love Story Black* by William Demby. Printed with permission of Reed & Cannon, Co.

"Sir, perhaps you've had a bit too much to drink. If you'll just calm down I can explain—"

"Explain what?" a peremptory voice behind me said.

Miss Pariss had come to the rescue, and Reverend Grooms slinked back into his door like a vampire suddenly exposed to cloves of garlic, a crucifix and blinding morning light.

"Good evening, Mr. Edwards," Miss Pariss said as though nothing unusual had transpired. "Won't you come in—the reason I couldn't come right away when I heard you knock was I was in the bathroom performing my absolutions. Come in! Come in!"

I slipped hastily into the sanctuary of her apartment, after casting a glance over my shoulder and catching a fleeting strobe light vision of Reverend Grooms' murderous bloodshot eyes stabbing at me through a crack in his door which he hadn't completely closed, the better to overhear our conversation.

"Reverend Grooms' outrageous behavior," Miss Pariss said, as soon as we were seated with our drinks in hand, "must be interpreted in the light of the fact that the poor old fool is desperately in love with me, and has been in love with me since 1923—at least I think that's the year he proposed marriage on the ferris wheel in Atlantic City were I was appearing in the Boardwalk Frolics—a marriage which for professional reasons and his having been gassed in World War I, I under no circumstances could accept or even contemplate, though there is an enduring bond of affection between us —the old wino bum—and he did make the most fantastic costumes for me, far more original and artistic than those rags Josephine Baker used to wear when she wasn't appearing naked or wearing monkey fruit—So you must not judge Reverend Grooms' expressions of jealous passion too harshly, after all you are a novelist and a man of the world as well as a college professor, and a cute dude yourself with who knows how many women running after you all hours of the night—!"

As soon as we finished the drinks Miss Pariss suggested we go straight to bed and begin our memorializing.

"There's so much to tell. I've been thinking about my life experience all day—and to tell you the truth, I didn't eat a bite all day except two Hershey bars, I was so excited about getting started working on the holy book of my life—"

So in less than twenty minutes after that insane attack on my life I found myself once again stretched out under the covers in the incense-laden darkness of Mona Pariss's futurizing temple, ready to listen and take notes while continuously telling myself all this was reality and I wasn't afloat in some transmigratory nightmare.

"Mr. Edwards," she said, after a scotch-sipping silence that lasted so long I though she had fallen asleep, "you want the story of my life—and I am sure you are aware that the real problem is how to begin—"

"That, I might add, Miss Pariss, is the novelist's problem as well—"

"Yeah, honey, but this ain't no novel—this is my life, the holy book of my life—"

"But suppose this *were* a novel, and not just the story of your life, your career as one of the greatest Black entertainers of our time—Where would *you* begin?"

"I wouldn't begin the day I was born—that's for sure—and I wouldn't begin the day my daddy and my mother did their thing in bed either—that's not when lives begin—lives begin when you wake up out of that sleep world ghosts live in and you start to move with your own mind and not the mind of a ghost, that's when lives begin—"

"Well, I must say that's very interesting, Miss Pariss—and yet, obviously, we have to begin somewhere. To paraphrase your remarks, when did you wake up out of the sleep world where ghosts live and begin to move with a mind of your own and not the mind of a ghost?"

"That's a long story, youngblood—a long story, so if that's where we're going to begin, you better get off your butt and bring that bottle of scotch over here on the table beside the bed, cause we're both going to need it—and while you're at it, pour a few drops on the floor to sweeten my memorizing capacities and appease the ghosts of our ancestors that control what we call our earthly lives . . ."

Astonished and intrigued by this social anthropological offhand reference to appeasing the ghosts of our ancestors, I was nevertheless determined not to be sidetracked into any rash intellectual assumptions. After all, this series of articles on Mona Pariss was, in Gracie's hardheaded business-oriented drive for mass circulation, aimed at a vast audience of upward mobile Black housewives more concerned about finding their Black identity in the rosy consumer-oriented American Dream than in any terrifying reminders of a "barbaric" ritual past; so I decided to begin my interview with the most banal talk-show-type question that popped into my mind:

"Just to get started, Miss Pariss," I said, "Let me ask you the one question that tens of thousands of our readers are eager to know about. Just how did you get into show business?"

"How I got started in showbiz? Well, youngblood, that's a book in itself, and not the holy book I be talking about—"

An she laughed, almost girlishly, her eyes half-closed and flickering:

"You see, youngblood—it ain't how I got into showbiz, it's how showbiz got into me. When I was a teeny little girl, but not so teeny the mens didn't undress me with their sanctimonious lecherous eyes, down home in Orlando County, a little cottonfield town stuck in the middle of a spooky pine woods—peanut country—well I used to sing in the church choir, up front—you know, wearing robes that wouldn't hide a peach from a possum, and knowing I was the prettiest girl not only in the choir but in all Orlando County, even though I was only fifteen going on sixteen. You can tell it to the world, youngblood, in those days when I was living down home, I was the prettiest cuddle-up doll the good Lord ever turned out in His heavenly toyshop. I was a sweet little sugar plum, and I knew it, and all the menfolks knew it, and the womens, they knew it too, but there wasn't a thing they could do about it but smile and scrinch their eyes shut like they was praying instead of cursing me under their breath. . . .

"Well, down home in those days in Orlando County they used to have what was called Christian Gospel Fellowship Week, when all the gospel choirs in the backwoods churches—maybe ten or fifteen from as far as fifty miles around—would all come to town in wagons and trains, and there would be a whole week of gospel singing competition, big chicken and potato salad picnics on a long plank table outdoors, cause it always took place in August just before peanut picking time, and the best choir always got to hang the red and gold Christian Gospel Fellowship Banner behind the pulpit in their church until the next competition the following year. . . .

"Lordy me, I used to love those Fellowship meetings, because you'd get all kinds of people coming back home, from Ohio, even Chicago some of them, and naturally every preacher would be trying to show off his choir the best.

"Well, that year our choir we got all dolled up in gold and white robes—and I tell you, youngblood, I looked like an angel, I felt like an angel, and I was so overflowing with the Holy Spirit, and feeling so tingly and holy you couldn't even call it singing what I was doing, it was more like being a radio for the voice of the Lord—I'm telling you, I *was* an angel, and if it wasn't for those heavy white and gold robes and those clodhopper shoes we country girls wore back in those days down home, I'd be off *flying* like an angel—

"So, as I was saying—sweeten up my drink, youngblood—as I was saying, to make a long story short, there was a nice looking light-skinned fellow with good hair I used to go to school with named Doc cause he always used to wear a cute little goatee and keep it Brilliantined all the time, but Doc he dropped out of school and left town telling everybody he was going North because he didn't want to be stuck in no two-bit peanut growing town for the rest of his nigger days, so he finally ended up getting a job as a pullman porter because of his good looks and his smooth talking and Brilliantined goatee so white folks knew he wasn't no surly trouble-making ugly nigger liable to spit in their food, so to make a long story short, every now and then, maybe twice a year, he'd show up in town togged out in his latest Harlem togs and wearing two or three of those biggy pawn shop rings on his fingers, and he kept his nails long like a Chinaman, like he was always holding a cup of tea in his hand. I mean, he was a smart dresser, elegant like a prince, always talking that latest Harlem jive—and being a pullman porter and all and a natural-born ladies' man, he naturally had nice manners for all the nice old church ladies and, as I said, a crooning kind of sweet talk that would melt butter on the top of an iceberg in the North Pole—

"Well, as I keep saying, to make a long story short, that summer at the Gospel Fellowship Week meeting he showed up all dolled up in a white suit and a white fedora even though it was so hot even the dogs were too suffocating from the heat to do their regular dog day duties. And when the ladies in our choir was on stage, there he was standing there—not sitting on the benches like everybody else, mind you—but standing there in the front row staring at me and smiling and winking and flashing his pawnshop rings and getting me so nervous and my nature up I almost lost my cue when it was time to do my solo. I always did know he had a sweet tooth for me, but right there in front of all those peoples, everybody could tell what was on that sly mind of his, especially those jealous frumpy ladies in the choir who didn't even bother to keep their eyes scrinched shut like they was communicating with the Spirit, but kept watching us like we was desecrating the holiness of the occasion. And finally even the preacher, he stopped thinking about the collection plate long enough to realize that a snake had entered the Garden of Eden and was slinking around plotting to take away one of his angels—

"And so after we was packing up our robes for the night, the preacher—a goodlooking dude hisself, Preacher Gore I think his name was, with a tiny diamond in his middle gold tooth, well, he comes over to me behind the tent and starts warning me of the way the devil appears in strange disguises, and if I had one hundredth the sense and experience I got now I would've known any preacher with a diamond in his middle gold tooth should have first-hand knowledge about the strange disguises the devil appears in, cause all those pious frisky ladies weren't spending all those nights practising in the choir just to be singing a new song unto the Lord, no sacreligion meant—I'll have another little taste if you will be so kind, Mr. Edwards—"

And she wiggled her slight petticoated body into an arc-like position and proceeded to emit a series of sonorous farts, so authoritative and prolonged that one was somehow reminded of the lunch hour whistle of the steel mills in Pittsburgh where I was born.

"Thank you kindly, Mr. Edwards," she continued, a wheezing sign celebrating her intestinal tract's jubilant relief.

"Now what was I memorializing about? Oh, yes—how I got into showbiz.

"Well, when the jackleg preacher with the diamond stuck smack in the middle of his middle gold tooth started breathing on me hard in the darkness back of that gospel tent, telling me that the devil appears in mysterious disguises, I thinks now he's about to play one of his laying on of hands sacraments with me like he do with some of those other ugly ladies in the choir. It just never occurred to me that he was warning me about that beautiful dude, Doc. I never would've associated Doc with no devil anyhow—if anything I would have let him come stealing into my sinful dreams like one of them moviestar princes. . . .

"But that Doc, he was something else—I mean he was *fast!* As it happened that night, all us younger girls, we slept in a peanut warehouse which the Goober Peanut Company let the church committee use as a kind of dormitory, so long about midnight I hear this whistling outside the window and I kind of know even though I'm floating off somewhere in a dream that it was Doc whistling out there under the moon, and anyway I couldn't sleep even though I was dreaming on account of being so young with all that hot blood churning me into buttermilk. So I gets off the cot and goes to the window, and there he is standing out there in his white suit and Brilliantined goatee with the full moon shining down upon him just like he the angel of the Lord, and when he motions for me to come on out, well, I just slipped into my dress like I was a sleepwalker or a zombie and snuck out of that peanut warehouse like it was all a part of the dream. And the first thing you know, there we are loving it up in the bushes down by the river—I don't mean intercoursing, I'll tell you about that later, but just hugging and kissing and loving it up like in a nice clean movie. And that was the first time I'd been with a man, and as far as I was concerned that was what being with a man meant, just lying there in the bull rushes hugging and kissing like Cleopatra and the Prophet Moses. . . .

"Well, sir, toward morning, when those mists was coming over the river and turning all pink and golden with the rising of the sun, I turned over and saw Doc lying there like a sleeping prince and I

woke him up and told him I wanted some more hugging and kissing, that I was now ready for the real nitty-gritty—

"When I said that I could tell he was thinking and meditating
about what I said and staring at me like he was trying to figure me
out, so I just kind of laid there resting and listening to the birds
twittle, waiting until whatever he was thinking about would come
manifest in his mind. So, finally he told me this weird story about
how he never did it with girls, and that a young girl like me would
be better off staying a virgin all her life, that way she would be like
a priestess and have power over men instead of men having power
over her.

"Then after I lay there and let that sink in wondering what he
talking about but believing every word of what he saying because of
him being such a gentleman and a traveling man who knows the
world, he finally turn to me and say: 'Little Angel, you got the sweetest singing voice this side of heaven, and I'm going to take you with
me and be your manager, because I'm tired of being a pullman porter and we both special people with a touch of the ghost world kings
in our veins. Sweet little singing angel you going to come away with
me and leave this peanut plantation forever—

"Now as I tell you, I weren't quite sixteen years old yet, but I had
a feeling about things, I mean I could futurize even then, I had this
gift of visionizing the future, and even though I felt my religion
deep, I know that what I was about to do was the Lord's Will, and
that He had sent Doc as His agent and His instrument of fulfilling
my life's work, and freeing me so I could go about doing it—and, to
make a long story short, I went to the railroad station with him before the sun was fully up so we could catch the morning express
train on its northern run as far as the junction, then he hid me in
the linen room of one of them fancy parlour cars they had back in
those days, and I tell you I traveled on that luxury train North, all
the way to Cincinnati—and those colored porters, they brought me
food, the finest food I ever ate in my life, on a silver tray with linen
napkins just like they served the white folks, and he told all the
other porters that I was his cousin and that he was taking me up
North to school to be educated.

"Now whether they believed him or not I guess really don't make
no difference, I still don't know, but they sure treated me like royalty and I been treated like royalty ever since the rest of my life, and
when the train layed over in one of them soup can towns down in
Georgia, I forget the name, Doc got off the train and bought me
some decent clothes and underwear and stockings, you know—city
folk clothes, and when I put them on after he let me slip into the
white ladies' washroom with his passkey so I could look at myself in

the mirror after everybody else had got off in Cincinnati. Lord, I tell
you I looked like just a beautiful Black princess in one of them Walt
Disney fairytales—

"But that don't tell you how I actually got into the business now
do it? Well, youngblood, I'll get around to that in a minute. But first
let me tell you about pullman porters. In those days—if you'll pardon the digression—pullman porters were smart and sophisticated
like Black movie stars today, you know—like Sidney Portier, for example, or Flip Wilson though I don't like it when he do that Geral-
dine act in front of white folks, my personal preference is for Bill
Cosby.

"So, as I was saying, when Doc he take me to Miss Hendley's
Boarding House and he tell her to give me a fine decent room because I was his cousin and that I was going up North to go to
school in Cincinnati, I'm sure not one of them pullman porters believed a word of it, they just figured Doc was setting himself up to
make a hustle on the side, they just acted like true gentlemen and
played along with the game and no questions asked.

"And the first thing I knew there I was all set up in a fine room
with running water and embroidery on the furniture and a picture of
Booker T. Washington on one wall and a picture of some pretty
cows grazing on the side of a mountain in Switzerland—a room all
to myself, the first time in my life, and the good thing about it was
that most the other guests in the boarding house was pullman porters like Doc, all of them treating me like royalty and always compli-
menting me on my good looks, and no lewd hinting around or
trying to rub up against me in the hall, and I'd sing for them sometimes after dinner, and Mrs. Hendley herself would accompany me
on the piano, she being a church woman and a part-time *chanteuse*
herself. I'm telling you, those were happy days, and I never did regret leaving my family and I didn't even miss singing in the church
choir, mostly because of old Preacher Gore's diamond sticking in the
middle of his gold tooth and him warning me about the ways of the
devil when everybody in the choir knew what he was up to with
some of them frisky choir ladies—

"But in every Garden of Eden there always comes a serpent to
mess up everything, and in this case that old serpent turned out to
be none other than that nice little old yellow lady Mrs. Hendley herself. This is what happened. You see, those Pullman porters would
be in town on every Thursday and every Monday—the other days
they were either on the road or took a day off in New York or Chicago. So naturally I was by myself most of the time with a lot of
time on my hands, though I helped some around the house with the
chores, because that's the way my daddy brought us chilluns up. Be-

sides, I was too scared to go outside much with all the fire wagons and horses and people cutting each other up, so most of the time I just hung around the house helping Mrs. Hendley polish the silver and learning embroidery, things like that, so we came to be pretty good friends. Until one day when I was helping her with the ironing, she just ups and says 'Mona, now you tell me the truth—you ain't no cousin of Doc's is you?'

"Well, the way she ask me, all smiling like the serpent, wearing false eyelashes and lipstick, all winking and crooning like, I figger she must know something, but I just stood there looking down at the double-eagle pattern in her rug. But then she ask me *again*, and when I still don't answer her one way or the other she tell me not to be afraid, that she been around even though she be a church woman herself, and that she could well understand how a young pretty girl like me could be sweet talked into leaving home by a smooth operator like Doc. And she tells me that I don't have nothing to worry about, but that being so good looking and with a sweet singing voice like I got, I could do a lot better for myself than just being the plaything of a common pullman porter. And she says I ought to start thinking bout making a career for myself. . . .

"Well, to make a long story short, she stopped what she was doing right then and there and took me to the piano and taught me a couple of them ragtime tunes, I forget the name of all of them except one called 'The Train Came By But It Didn't Stop,' a number she said was just made to order for me because of Doc and all. And she taught me to sing it and swivel my hips and roll my eyes like the words had double intender meanings, you know what I mean— just a little more scotch, youngblood—You's a real gentleman, kind of remind me of Doc a little bit the way your left eye slants kind of wicked like . . .

"Well anyway, the next day, after I had the song down pat along with five or six other songs, mostly whitefolk songs, she sent for a white foreign gentleman I forget his name, Karias or something like that, a little skinny man with a waxed mustache and a cigar and fluttery hands, and she had him listen to me sing, and she told me that this man and she, Mrs. Hendley, was going to be my managers, and that I could forget all about Doc, and they got me this job singing in a white luncheon club in the financial district where rich businessmen would patronize and do business, peanuts and cotton and farm machinery, big business, you can well imagine, and I tell you I was a hit the first time I opened my mouth, and there was one old white-haired man even gave me a fifty-dollar tip and said he wanted me to go home with him and there were more fifty-dollar bills where that came from, but I told him I was a virgin and that I intended to stay a virgin, and whether you want to believe it or not, I been a virgin my whole life ever since. And that's how I got into show business—"

⟨∾⟩

"I only asked you to accompany me to this book party because you're now supposed to be one of our writers. Pure public relations for the magazine. But don't be surprised if they treat you like Uncle Remus out on a pass from the old folks home. You've lived in Europe too long, and the fact that you're an English professor—"

"Come off it, Gracie—I'm not all that new to this scene . . ."

"First of all, this isn't going to be a scene—it's going to be a race riot between Black men and Black women . . ."

The tense Puerto Rican cab driver obviously was ill at ease overhearing our conversation.

"What you say the address is?" he asked, turning his mustache toward us (and almost running down a bleary-eyed wino who was wildly cursing the occupants of an automobile who had refused him a tip for further dirtying their windshield with the filthy fragment of what looked like a stolen shroud).

Gracie efficiently pulled out her polished leather appointment book.

"Avenue A near the corner of Third Street. It's called Soul Conglomerates, Inc.—and since it's next to a police station, you shouldn't have any trouble recognizing it—"

The cab driver nodded without understanding a word of her directions, but somehow ten minutes later we pulled up in front of a drab graffiti decorated building where a rather large crowd of young Blacks was milling about the entrance.

Gracie was immediately recognized by a committee of tough receptionists, elegantly attired male and female literary militants, and we were ushered like distinguished diplomats to the front row of the cavernous room, transformed into an improvised auditorium for the poetry reading, the debate that would follow and the inevitable autographing and book-buying ritual.

Gracie, well-known for her television appearances on "Soul" and other sundry televised debates having to do with the problems of Black women, was hugged and kissed and sistered beyond all propriety. Occasionally she would introduce me to someone as "one of her writers, the novelist, etc.," but she might as well have been introducing Stepin Fetchit at a Black Panther meeting for all the fishy-eyed looks of bewilderment I received.

On the other hand, being completely ignored, anonymous to all, except for some horn-rimmed albino Black History professor from

New Jersey who mistook me for the librarian at Public School Number 73 in Newark, I was completely free as a mere spectator.

The program was late starting, but finally the lights that glared down over the gathering from the ceiling overhead (faded angels and esoteric religious patterns from the days when the edifice had been an Orthodox Greek church) dimmed and Gracie stepped up to the microphone.

There were cheers, and "go girl," and "let's hear what this heavy shit is all about" audible from the crowd, but Gracie had an air of overpowering authority and hipness about her that soon quieted down the overflowing and exuberant crowd.

"Brothers and sisters," she began, "on behalf of *New Black Woman Magazine* it is my unique pleasure to welcome here tonight one of our most controversial bad and beautiful young Black poets. Sisters, I don't have to mention her name. Anyone who doesn't know who she is and what she stands for has no business being here in the first place—"

Raucous laughter greeted this remark, and I cast a sharp glance at Gracie, paranoid again, to see if she was referring to me—but by then she had continued her introduction.

"We may not all agree with what the sister says in her poems, but *New Black Woman Magazine* believes that any time a poet has a perception as radical as the one our young guest tonight expresses in her work, you better listen or you just might miss the boat, and I'm not referring to Marcus Garvey's boat. After the reading, there will be a short question and answer period—and I mean short. So now let's give a big welcome to one of the baddest, heaviest, most scandalous, sweetest and most beautiful sisters writing the new Black poetry today—"

Given the outrageously radical theme of her poetry, the poet struck me as being as fragile and demure as an apprentice hairdresser. She had a timid smile, an almost apologetic stage presence, and was wearing an unfashionable long plaid skirt which had gone out of style at least seven years before. Her only concession to a Third World look was a loose peasant blouse of virtually transparent handmade linen through which an astonishingly erect pair of jewel-topped breasts were distractingly visible.

The drummers and a duet of flute players from the band behind her on the platform set the mood, obsessive and nostalgically lyrical, the flutists' phrasings and chord constructions attacking the consciousness almost inaudibly like radio signals from a distant planet.

Almost ten minutes passed before the poet began to read her poetry. She stood there almost motionless, as if shrinking herself into a trance-like state.

Then when the audience became so quiet and expectant that it was almost as if she were alone in the room, she began to read in a sometimes strident, sometimes crooning, sometimes Gregorian chant tone of voice.

To be truthful, I was so entranced and hypnotized by her performance, and by the rapt attentiveness of the crowded audience, that the only line I can recall, or *think* I recall, was (and I'm paraphrasing) something to the effect of "*Black woman, you been oppressed so long by the snowman master, let's melt the abominable monster, by glorifying the Pimp, gifting him with gold and diamond trappings, drape him in vestments of precious silk, let our beautiful bodies buy him spears and guns, in the degradation of our long centuries of oppression, let us transmute our oppression into the glorification of Revolution and sacred Liberation—*"

The riot began before I realized what was happening around me. It began when a hefty Welfare Rights Mother shouted "Enough of this filth! Bring our men back home so they can pay the bills and help with the dishes!"

Another voice, loud and slightly hysterical (I looked around and saw that it was the albino Black Studies Professor from New Jersey) screamed above the general shouts and catcalls that were making it by now impossible for the performance to continue: "The pimp, the pusher are the real oppressors of the youth of our Black communities! This isn't poetry—What you are suggesting is nothing but pernicious nonsense!"

A fight broke out near the bar: two demonstrating women were struggling with a policeman who was trying to lead them away.

Two more Black policemen blew their whistles and broke through the crowd swinging their clubs. By now half the audience was standing on chairs watching the other half pushing and shoving and milling about.

From the corner where I was sitting I caught a glimpse of a fire exit and made a quick escape. I reached the street corner just as the light changed to red and hailed a taxi. Just as I was getting in, the strident yelling of the riot inside Soul Conglomerates, Inc., merging with the neighborhood noises, I heard a tremulous voice call my name:

"Mr. Edwards! Can you wait a minute!"

It was Hortense Schiller, and in a matter of seconds she was sitting next to me in the back of the cab.

"Oh, God!" she said as soon as the cab swerved recklessly into the uptown traffic. "What happened in there? It was like the assassination of Malcolm X—!"

"What happened—I think—is that the Organization of Welfare Mothers somehow heard about this Pimp as Revolutionary thing and

showed up to start a riot—! Now that I think of it, wasn't there a
TV camera crew parked across the street?"

"Then you think the whole thing was staged?"

"If it was, Gracie's one hell of a PR genius—"

"It was terribly unfair to the poet, disgusting—even worse, barbaric—"

Hortense moved to the far side of the back seat of the cab and
seemed to be deep in thought, seemed to be waiting for me to make
some preordained move. I decided this was not the time to test her
opinions about writers, about the PR aspects of magazine merchandising, about The Pimp as Revolutionary. As a matter of fact, I
wasn't in very much of a mood to discuss anything heavy. So I
turned to her and asked:

"How about dinner?"

Hortense cheered up immediately.

"I'm starved to tell you the truth—"

"Me too," I lied. My stomach was churning like an ice cream machine without any ingredients except rock salt.

"Where would you like to go?"

"Anywhere you say—just get me away from this depressing
neighborhood—"

"How about Luchows—?" I said, naming the first restaurant that
popped into my mind.

We ordered at random, neither of us wanting to pretend to know
German cuisine (a plus for Hortense, I thought, for I was spared the
terror of being embarrassed in front of her by one of the Hussar
troopers serving as waiters). We ended up eating deer meat and potatoes and a sticky strudel washed down with a bottle of white wine
as thin and tasteless as distilled battery water.

But the atmosphere was quiet and intimate and kitschy and I
could pretend we were in love. But there is a kind of built-in banal-
ity to descriptions of evenings like this. There's not really very much
you can say to make them sound fresh and real—so let me try to
report things straight. Actually, the high point of the meal was when
Hortense accidentally covered the back of my hand with a spoonful
of mustard which, since we had just finished off a second bottle of
wine, set us both to laughing hysterically.

We paid. The bill was over forty-seven dollars and I had to pay
cash since all my credit cards had long since become overloaded.
And we left the restaurant with all the Hussar troopers bowing at us
as a sign of their Germanic appreciation of a budding love affair, and
with the string orchestra playing angelically the love theme from
some German operetta.

Outside there was a fresh breeze and the commercial streets were almost deserted. Impulsively she pulled my arm and then took me by the hand and started running up the street.

"It's a splendid night," she said, as I struggled to lower my heartbeat to keep from puffing from the exertion. "What do you say we walk up town?"

"Well—okay, why not?"

"You're not tired, are you?—I mean, after all the excitement of that wild book party?"

So we walked and walked and walked, cutting over to Fifth Avenue at 34th Street, occasionally holding hands, but mostly maintaining a brisk British army marching pace, complete with synchronized swinging arms. This extraordinary consuming of energy prevented conversation or even window shopping for that matter. But after walking through Central Park in spite of my only half-joking reference to muggers we finally decided to sit on a bench near Central Park West near 72nd Street to catch our breath and talk.

Commenting on her tremendous energy, Hortense confessed that she kept herself in shape by working out in a gym frequented by boxers. I was in such bad shape myself (although it must be admitted as a fact, not necessarily a scientific fact, that falling in love with a young girl magically summons up unsuspected dynamos of energy in an older man), that I quickly changed the subject.

Or, to be honest, I placed my hand around the back of her neck and kissed her gently on the lips. She responded. But since we were still breathing heavily from the exertion of the walk I cannot seriously claim that the kiss worked any magic.

At any rate, we went to my apartment on the 28th floor of a new building between 95th and 96th Street on Amsterdam Avenue. And quite naturally and freely we made love. While she was in the bathroom (I assumed she was inserting some contraceptive device or ingesting a pill), I chose a Vivaldi Concerto and on top of that a Hugh Masekela record and on top of that a Stevie Wonder record and on top of that some obscure early seventeenth century Swedish court music as a musical background. What can I say? It was a soft lovely velveted evening, the lovemaking gentle and intimately comfortable. Hortense had just fallen asleep in my arms when the phone rang and, with that sharp infallible instinct that light sleepers and swindlers share, I knew immediately that it was Gracie.

Her voice boomed so loud over the receiver that I thought she had ordered the telephone company to turn up the volume.

"What the hell happened to you?"

"I got scared of being trampled to death."

"Why does your voice sound so skinny and mysterious? Is there someone there with you? Hortense Schiller, for example?"

"Gracie, you know damn well it's none of your business whether I have company or not—"

"That skinny-assed bitch! No doubt you had a fancy candlelight dinner, then walked uptown, stopped in the park and held hands, kissed—and then went to your apartment. That shrewd lettuce-nibbling bitch. Did she tell you what a great writer you are? That you remind her of her English teacher in high school—?"

"Gracie, are you drunk? I mean, have you been drinking? It's after two o'clock in the morning—"

"I don't give a fuck what time of the night it is, you tell that nigger she better get her skinny ass to the office on time tomorrow morning or she can start looking for a job as a welfare investigator—!"

She hung up. The Swedish court music embroidered the abrupt silence and alleviated the ringing in my ears, but was by no means an adequate antidote to the irrational sense of guilt Gracie's contrived wrath has always instilled in me. I returned to the bedroom and Hortense was still asleep, but she had changed into a fetus-like position and had moved to the opposite side of the bed. . . .

⚬⚬⚬

The question was raised by a tall Black girl in the back row who, from the papers she had turned in, had a remarkable questioning mind.

We had finished our reading and discussion of Richard Wright's *Native Son* and were continuing a final discussion in preparation for the essay examination I usually require at the completion of each book that is read in the Black Lit class.

She was a quiet thoughtful girl from Brooklyn who wore her hair in the currently fashionable "corn-row" style. Timidly, tentatively, she raised her hand and when finally she caught my attention, she asked in a barely audible voice:

"Professor Edwards, why are our Black authors—or at least the ones I've read so far—so negative. For example, how come they're always talking about Black people as though they're some kind of sociological disease. Take Bigger Thomas—I don't find him typical at all. He was just one dumb street nigger whose dumb actions naturally led to his dumb downfall—"

"I think you miss the point," I said, secretly agreeing with her, but for different reasons.

"As I've said many times, Bigger Thomas was meant by Richard Wright to represent a certain type of symbolic contemporary situation—the rootless, alienated derelict floating contemporary man, not necessarily Black since his type is to be found in most highly indus-

trialized societies, giving rise to Fascism and Nazism, who is the urbanized refuse, the garbage, thrown out and abandoned by a ruthless
profit-oriented economy where the Bigger Thomases all over the
world have become all too frequently the metaphor for contemporary man in general—even the affluent white middle classes. At least
I think that was what Richard Wright was trying to say. Writers often begin with a thesis, even a political sociological thesis as in the
case of Richard Wright's *Native Son*—but other more poetic influences and intuitions often take over, and I suppose that is why literature is so fascinating—"

The girl frowned. I knew that I had not answered her question
and that my phrasing was, to say the least, pompous. I sat behind
my desk tapping a ballpoint pen on the attendance record book
waiting for her to continue the question that really was on her mind.

"Well, Professor Edwards," she said finally, glancing around at
her Black nursing student girl friends seated on either side of her in
the back row, all of whom were secretly smiling as though this was
a subject they had discussed amongst themselves before. "You're a
writer, I mean you write books. I've never read any of them—"

"I won't hold that against you as long as you read the books assigned in class—"

There was a rustling of suppressed laughter which the girl ignored, then, impetuously, she asked:

"Why don't Black writers ever write about real people—Why do
they always treat Black people like social problems—for example, of
all the books you've assigned us this semester there isn't even one of
them a love story. I'm sure you don't mean to imply that when Bigger Thomas smothers that white girl to death and then tries to stuff
her in the furnace he is doing that out of a feeling of love—"

"In that particular incident in the novel I think what Richard
Wright is trying to symbolize is the psychological Pavlovian reaction
to fear that derives from psychological entrapment. Remember the
rat trapped in the corner in the opening incident?"

"I understand all that, I mean I understand the psychological and
sociological thesis, but Black people are tired of being studied under
a microscope like they're some kind of social disease. Why don't
Black writers write about love, for example?"

At that Melinda Rodriguez snorted with laughter.

"Who has time for love when you're always being oppressed? Anyway love is nothing but a bourgeois fantasy trip—"

"There have been love stories written by Black writers," I said,
"for example—"

But Melinda Rodriguez' mocking expression created a total blank
in my mind. Instead I said:

"I am sure there will be some most beautiful Black love stories in the future—"

"Written by you, Professor—?"

Whatever my instinctive antagonism to Melinda Rodriguez's doctrinaire politics, I had to admit she was well-informed and sharp.

On the other hand, the unexpected direction the class discussion was taking was making me feel uneasy, and for all too obvious reasons. But after a moment of panic I decided there was no possible way that anyone in the class, especially that silent chorus of nursing students in the back row, could know anything about my private life—one of the major advantages of teaching in an urban commuting college.

So I relaxed, stared thoughtfully out of the window as Dr. Phillips my absent-minded sexless philosophy teacher used to do when I was in college, folded my hands behind my neck, leaned back in my chair and said:

"Perhaps this whole concept of romantic love is essentially a Western European concept, that derives from the Middle Ages— courtly love, the Madonna cult, the feudal system—that sort of thing. Perhaps love for Black people means something else, less fantasy, less individualism, less a property-oriented sense of exclusion possession—"

"Well, I'll buy that—" Melinda Rodriguez broke in. "All this love bullshit is a capitalist invention to sell products and exploit cheap labor—!"

"Well, let's take a quick run-down on the history of love in Western societies—and maybe that way we'll come up with an answer to your question—" I looked at my watch, saw there were about twelve minutes left to the class hour, purged all thoughts of Hortense Schiller from my mind, ignored the restless shuffling of feet and the groans of boredom, and began what was to have been a quick and concise history of love in Western Society, and why Black writers do not find love a particularly congenial theme to write about—even though the juke boxes and pop singers moan about nothing else but "Baby, Baby—I love that man of mine, why you treat me so bad, etc., etc."

"But first let me put a question to the class that I asked another class when we were discussing a story dealing with romantic love— Is there such a thing as 'love at first sight'?"

"Professor Edwards, what kind of jive's this you layin' down?" Baby Blue Hawkins, the tall star basketball player, and boss campus grass dealer, said impatiently, gathering up his books and preparing to leave the classroom as indeed everyone else in the room was except the coterie of nursing students in the back row.

"I thought this class was about Black writers of the twentieth century, heavy cats like Malcolm X, Cleaver, Stokely, heavy cats like that—and here you are running down some jive about romantic love and the Middle Ages. Shit! On my block if a dude digs a chick he does a buck and wing, makes a comment on what nice upholstery she got, and if she digs him and he digs her, that's it—"

The bell rang and I realized I had lost yet another round with my Black Lit class, and the raucous laughter that exploded like the sudden electric crackling of a summer storm made me wish I had one of those enormous beach umbrellas to hide under.

Pinkie Gordon Lane

(1923–   )

THE POET LAUREATE of Louisiana, Pinkie Gordon Lane is a popular writer and frequently appears in journals and anthologies. A many-sided person, she has had a fascinating career in education, in the literary and publishing world, and on the lecture circuit, which has taken her to several countries in Africa and the West Indies.

A Philadelphia native, Lane was born in 1923, the youngest of four children, and was the only one to live past infancy. After graduating from high school, she entered the labor force. In 1945 she went to Spelman College in Atlanta, Georgia, on a four-year academic scholarship and graduated magna cum laude with a bachelor's degree in English and art. Working as an English teacher between 1949 and 1955 in Florida and Georgia, Lane earned her master's degree at Atlanta University in 1956. She and her husband then moved to Baton Rouge, Louisiana, where she still lives. In 1963 her first and only child was born.

A former professor at Leland College, which no longer exists, and Southern University, Lane became the first black woman to receive her Ph.D. degree from Louisiana State College in 1967. Originally dabbling in prose writing, Lane turned to poetry in 1960 after reading Gwendolyn Brooks's *A Street in Bronzeville* (1945). She published her first volume of poetry, *Wind Thoughts*, in 1972.

According to Marilyn B. Craig, Lane has reached out to black authors, such as Alice Walker, Nikki Giovanni, and Margaret Danner, and seeks "to legitimize all forms of Black poetic talent." *The Mystic Female* (1978), her second collection of poetry, was nominated for the Pulitzer Prize in 1979. Honored for this volume at the First Annual Black Poetry Festival at Southern University in 1979, Lane appeared in *Callaloo*'s special issue devoted to black women poets that same year.

Lane is an editor-in-chief and vice-president of South and West, an organization that also publishes an international journal by the same name, and an adviser and contributing editor to *Callaloo* and the *Black Scholar*. On a cultural exchange program sponsored by the United States International Communication Agency, she went to Ghana, Cameroon, Zambia, and South Africa in 1981, to lecture and read poetry. Her most recent volume of poetry, *I Never Scream: New and Selected Poems*, was published in 1985.

For further reading on Pinkie Gordon Lane, see in addition to Craig's

article in *Dictionary of Literary Biography, Volume 41*; Dorothy W. Newman's "Lane's Mystic Female," *Callaloo* 2 (February 1979); and papers in
the James Weldon Johnson Memorial Collection of Negro Arts and Letters
in the Beinecke Rare Book and Manuscript Library at Yale University.

The following selections are taken from *I Never Scream: New and Selected Poems.*

ON BEING HEAD OF THE ENGLISH DEPARTMENT

I will look with detachment
on the signing of contracts,
the ordering of books,
and making of schedules—
will sing hymns of praise
to the negative, when
it is necessary, to survive.

    And if the morning
    light freezes in the east,
    a dawn-covered eye
    will tell me I am cold
    to your pleas, but never whore
    to the spirit. I will
    write poems in the blue-
    frosted lake.

If I disdain poetasters,
announcers, and the gods
of mediocrity, knowing
that they too insist on living,
it is because I hand you
the bread and the knife
but never the music and the art
of my existence.

You will not swallow me or absorb me:
I have grown too lean for that.
I am selfish, I am cruel,

    I am love.

WHEN YOU READ THIS POEM

(For Citizens Opposed to Censorship, Baton Rouge)

The earth turns
like a rainbow
And the smell of autumn
drifts down—yellow
leaf on my arched back

The light touches
I see it with my skin,
feel it lean
That furrow of trees
casts its shadow—long
as the night, the wind,
the river
Truth has many faces
My friends, don't honor me
without passion
I will not be
wheat in the summer's fire
I will not lie fallen
like autumn fruit
or die in the evening sun

Listen,
let us band together
and fight evil   We
cannot let it guide
the sun

The world is a bird
in flight

When you read this poem,
love me

THREE LOVE POEMS

I. Love Poem

Man of mystery, power
ambition-driven
and skin of copper-gold
Some call you "dictator"

One called you "naive"
Many call you "bastard"

I reach for you
weep at night
long for your touch
You are beautiful and bright
Damn you!

You know me too well,
man of my needs
I think you must be a root-
worker, a voo doo man
crazysonofabitch!

Why do I lust for you?

II. Leaving

When I leave you
it will be like
coming into the winter
of warmth   You
have given and taken

I survive
a woman beyond grief
glad of the understanding
that hurts
A counter-sign rises
from you—place of darkness
and of light

The quivering mind thrusts
and cuts through granite
and when Philistines
dominate, let the spirit/
intellect carry its own
shield—a mockery
of the battle royal
falling into
ruin

III. What Matters After All

Smoke lifting from the
chimney and the sky beyond
take on a presence of their
own

Perhaps this is all that
matters, I tell myself—
the image that makes
a view, the earth,
the sky, the smell of autumn,
fire under the sun
and a cold moon
acres of darkness
and miles of crimson light

and the dream of you
outlined like a giant
shadow on the clear
white plane

ME

If I could remember back to when
I was an embryo . . .
I probably wondered even then
what queer sauce went into the making
of me—
an odd bunch of wind and straw,
rose water and crushed ice,
a mite, a worm,
a demon-coated, bright-eyed hawk.

And I scrouged against the brick wall
of Edgely Street
sidling like a crab—
shy with strangers
to whom, when friends,
I in reverse became the tyrant,
issuing directives with a particular skill—
and loved too much for my own good
baring the target of my flesh
like a silly bird too tame to fly
too wild to trust to fondling.

I swept down into cellars of thought
and taxed a throbbing brain,
an electric heart,
bursting and bursting through pink walls
and climbing the dust of earth.

Chilling screams were my lullaby.
But in spite of all,
I elongated like a salt water taffy
and claimed my portion
not understanding
but borne by instinct to the stars,
and holding not unseemly.

Gloria Oden

(1923–   )

BORN IN 1923, in Yonkers, New York, Gloria Catherine Oden is the daughter of a minister about whom she writes in *The Tie That Binds*, one of her best-known works. Differing from most creative literary artists and from most university English professors, Oden did not major in English during her years of training in higher education, for she received her B.A. degree in history in 1944 and a J.D. degree in 1948, both from Howard University.

Although she has been publishing poetry since 1959, she is not a well-known figure in today's mainstream literary circles. Yet, in 1952 poet Mark Van Doren, speaking of five poems of Oden's that he especially liked, said: "There is an honesty about them . . . a fierce controlled desire to say exactly what you think that puts them quite in a class by themselves—different from, and better than Marianne Moore in my opinion. . . . I can't believe you won't be published in God's good time."

It was 1978, however, before Oden published her first collection of poems. Between 1952, the year of Van Doren's comment, and 1978, Oden worked as a lecturer in English at the New School for Social Research in English for one year (1966). In the 1960s she was very active editing and supervising the publication of books in mathematics, physics, engineering, and calculus. From 1969 to 1970 she was visiting lecturer in the English department at State University of New York at Stony Brook. And in 1969 she became a member of the faculty at the University of Maryland, Baltimore County, where she is presently a full professor of English. Since the 1960s she has been reading her poetry in art centers, libraries, museums, public schools, and universities all over the United States.

Her poetry can be found in a number of anthologies, including Stephen Henderson's *Understanding the New Black Poetry* (1973), Frank Brady and Martin Price's *Poetry Past and Present* (1974), and Erlene Stetson's *Black Sister* (1981). She has published poems in well over thirty journals and magazines, such as *The New Laurel Review, Weid, Damascus Road, Lynx,* the *Wormwood Review, Mutiny, Epos, Impetus,* and others. She is the author of two narrative poem collections—*Resurrections* (1978) and *The Tie That Binds* (1980).

Her honors and awards include a Creative Writing Fellowship from the John Hay Whitney Foundation, a National Endowment for the Humanities Grant, and the Distinguished Black Women's Award from Towson

State University. She is listed in *Dictionary of Literary Biography, Volume 41, Personalities in the South, The World Who's Who of Women, Who's Who among Black Americans, Index to Black Poetry, International Who's Who in Poetry, Dictionary of American Poets*, and *Living Black American Authors*.

The following selection is the introductory poem as well as parts one, two, and three of *The Tie That Binds*.

FROM **THE TIE THAT BINDS**

However brief their acquaintance with
my Father, none would be surprised
to hear me say that although dead
—buried 25 years—still
Father monitors me as when
flesh on bone he was ever watchful.
Whether night summons me
to dream or day exacts duty,
Father superintends, glacial in his
                              clergyman's collar,
undiminished in my mind's full recollection.

Minister to a needful congregation (depressed
long before 1929),
Father was their fountaineer of faith,
that well spring in our crannies abiding.
At sixty-eight he died, ten years
to the day his youngest son (senior
to me) had gone before, becoming the first
in a chain of abrupt family departures.

With childhood's eye I see him:
Enthroned upon his pulpit, he sits
between his deacons in Pentecostal trinity;
in the sober elegance of serge.
With childhood's ear I hear him:
Whether resonant with God's message or lining
out the common meter of a hymn, he voices
our resolve to forsake this world
of glittering seduction for the untarnishing treasure
of what is to come.

Father was a hard man. Who
ever denied him truth or obedience?
Yet, caring charged him. Why else
when the country martialed into Coxey's army,
laboring alone rude ends
of material, did he raise
from his church's grassless yard
that summer playground to which youngsters
from black pockets in the city came?
Father built that playground on the riverview
side of the church out of
whose opened, leaded, and stained glass windows
(gift of a Dutch Reform congregation
whose edifice remodeled, subsequently was torn
down and replaced by a movie palace)
I could see across the Hudson
to the softly distant Palisades.
How often, as the sun gave
up its orange ghost behind
those blue barricades and some tug-drawn,
overburdened barge inched upriver,
I would imagine Columbus likewise
adventuring while, unobserved and unsuspected,
                              tip-toeing
their high trails above, Indians
shadowed Death's pale stranger
come to seed their virgin land.

Built to Father's specifications, parsonage
and church rose on a corner plot
at the top of a hill bounded by a street
that ran parallel with the river
while, perpendicular, another ran steeply
down. Both buildings fronted
on the side street. While the playground
                              held
that side nearest the river, the parsonage,
on the upper, hemmed tightly by
a closely tended L-shaped sward,
joined the church between. This wedding
of church and parsonage by a shared wall
served Father well; for his ministry
so engrossed him he inhabited one
as much as he did the other.

One

Every Monday, Father took
the train to New York City.
He spent the day in conference with other
ministers of his denomination. He left
early, and the house, oddly vacant,
like a childless schoolyard, made me
wonder if Mother noticed. I couldn't
tell. Monday was laundry day
and the family—I had three sisters
and two brothers—totalled eight.
One such day when I was
seven or so, fretting some souring
hurt late in the afternoon, I
chose to leave home forever.
Striking out, striding down hill,
unexpectedly I faced into Father ascending.
He assumed I had come to meet him
—an assumption I chose not to disturb—
and turning, convinced of God's grace,
marched back uphill beside him.

No sooner returned to the parsonage,
Father would disappear through a door
to his left and down a dozen steps
into the cellar. There, breaching
the party wall, he entered into
an enclosed area of the church
known as the Primary Room
central to the activities of children
in kindergarten and the lower elementary grades.
Exiting it, he downed a flight
of broader steps bringing him underneath
the sanctuary and onto the empty floor
of the large hall used to sustain
the bustling secular life of the congregation.
Crossing swiftly he departed through
another door and descended into
the sub-basement where he now checked
the fire laid and banked before breakfast
to insure that modicum of heat required
to remove the chill from the hall above.
After shaking down the furnace
shoveling and hauling the ash away,

he returned to the hall overhead.
From stacks of wooden folding chairs
lining lengths of opposite wall
he ordered the half-moon for the Girl Scouts
convening at the fast approaching hour of seven.
Those meetings were exuberant. Still,
girls upward from ten could
be persuaded to periods of quiet
attention by their Leaders handsome
in muted grey-green uniforms.
What pride in mastering knots
and hitches in competitive progression
                    from Brownie
to Eagle Scout; to earn badges
of merit attesting competence at home
or in the woods—an expertise gained
when, by ferry, we crossed to the Jersey Palisades
for distance hikes along the Hudson!
Best of all, how grand
those once-a-month nights of "hot chocolate"
storytelling, when we froze in our seats
                    at the sounds
made by my bedeviling brothers
dragging links of chain down the aisles
of the dark and empty sanctuary overhead
Uncrossing arms, Scouting's circle
of friendship dissolved, the meeting ended.
The clatter raised by my sisters—
added to by me in later years—
journeying the cellar steps upwards
signalled Father's return to duty.
Back into the church he would go
to check and latch outside doors,
to shovel the fire's final ash,
to turn off taps and lights,
to secure the church—his congregation's fortress
against abuse; the fruit of their freedom;
their tithing's cherished usable splendor.

Two

Although he returned to the parsonage for lunch
Father spent Tuesdays and Thursdays visiting
those members aged, ill,
or otherwise restricted in their comings and
                                        goings.
He carried with him a box
—black, small, lined with red
velvet—that cradled glasses, thumb-sized
and flaring. It was his communion kit,
kept ready for family desperations
which, when permanently resolved, were
most often a mixture of relief and hardship:
relief because death, that divine euphoria,
that cherished sweet of the Gospel's persuasion,
ended earthly misery whose burdensome shadow
fretted the pathways most blacks walked;
hardship because death—that satin whore—
demanded money. At life's end
who would deny an elder those
funerary refinements calculated to make
"a good impression" on St. Peter and host?

Tuesday evenings at eight, prayer
meeting. For older parishioners an
                                        exercise
of affection. No matter how harsh
long winter's hold, from
outreaches of the city they would come
down and up hill to enjoy
the fellowship of survival. I was,
of course, in bed, resisting sleep.
Catching their wan tenors, trebles,
leaning on Father's vigorous monotone,
I questioned their words, puzzled as
to why only on Jordan's bank
they would set down whatever
it was, daily, they shouldered by
the smoothly flowing, imperial blue
                                        Hudson.

Three

Wednesdays, Father gave the parsonage
his attention: windows, doors, the gas heater
installed in the icy bathroom to warm
his family of early risers. Cold
was endemic to the house and only
when food was being cooked in the kitchen
had we a warm room. When
whatever the season or necessity required
for upkeep of the two floors of the parsonage
was done, Father set about
a task less impersonal, familial,
seemingly satisfying. He repaired
our shoes. Descending into the cellar
—with me tagging behind—Father
would sit on his work chair—an overturned box
upon which rested the cracked-leather seat
of a defunct, armless, spindle-backed chair—
and assemble to hand the tools needed,
tools inherited from his Father,
a shoemaker during slavery. I would watch,
sitting semi-distant on the cellar steps,
as he lifted and fitted over his thighs
the weighty black iron platform
curved to them. In its center
the square hole in which could
be slotted the tapered stems of metal
moulds shaped to three sizes.
Taking up a form and slipping
a shoe over it, Father would begin
cobbling, silent, self-absorbed. He
was not the artful shoemaker Mother
told me Grandfather had been. I
detested the shiny blisters that blossomed
where my soles had worn. Why
could our shoes not be taken
to a store and half-soled there?
Resentful, still I kept silent,
unperceiving of that brute fist
in whose surly grip we were.

I loved the dark and webby cellar
best of all rooms in the sheltering
                    parsonage.

It fitted its warmth about me
like the undershirt, long-sleeved,
I wore from September through June.
Year round it was a playroom;
my special hideaway when others
found me too much underfoot. Here
I spent long winters riding
my kiddy car, and playing house
with a family of stuffed rabbits, two
caramel-colored dolls, and Raggedy Ann.
Still, as much as I inhabited
the cellar it was not mine
alone. Cemented to its floor
were the two white tubs
in which Mother did the laundry.
Also, the three clotheslines on which,
in winter, it was hung. At a distance
from the steps, the squat furnace
gorged on bootleg coal as eagerly
as it did the more costly
"Blue Coal." Anthracite was preferred
over the quick-firing lumps whose soot
like lichen, darkened the flower-papered
walls and panels of delicately-laced curtains
throughout the many-windowed house.
The cellar was also storehouse and museum.
Steamer trunks used for college
as well as those of leather and canvas,
preserved by silver paint, were kept
beneath the steps and lined its walls.
In them, Mother stored clothes,
shoes, and ancient, roomy handbags
that hoarded a jumble of items from
her southern girlhood: photos, letters,
bits of decrepit jewelry whose future
value would depend, to a great extent,
upon the family's legends of ownership.

Wednesday nights were reserved for the
                              meetings
of clubs. Often sex-segregated, each
specified its devotion in its name
—The Altar Guild, The Daughters of
                              Conference,

The Men's Usher Board—dedicated
to keeping the "Old Ship of Zion"
afloat. It was not uncommon to find
parishioners of one group active
members of another. Father permitted
no one to doubt the church's
need; and everyone was eager, proud
to do his "Christian duty."
These groups, too, met
in the large hall. If several
                          were scheduled
for the same evening, the use of the
                                    sanctuary
was permitted. Then the many-colored
                          windows,
illumined by Father's frugal levels
belied the evening's dedication and,
                          often,
passersby would enter mistakenly
expecting the fraternity of those programs
that were the next night's fare.

Charles Gordone

(1925–   )

WINNER OF THE PULITZER PRIZE in 1970 for his play *No Place to Be Somebody: A Black-Black Comedy*, Charles Gordone is a playwright, an actor, and a director whose works have been compared to those of Edward Albee and Eugene O'Neill. Gordone was born in 1925, in Cleveland, Ohio, and received his B.A. degree in 1952 from Los Angeles State College of Applied Arts and Sciences (now California State University, Los Angeles). He also attended the University of California at Los Angeles.

As an actor Gordone appeared in a number of plays, some of which include *Of Mice and Men* (1953), *The Blacks* (1961–1965), and *The Trials of Brother Jero* (1967). He has directed at least twenty-five plays, including *Rebels and Bugs* (1958), *Peer Gynt* (1959), *Tobacco Road* (1960), *Detective Story* (1960), *No Place to Be Somebody* (1976), *Cures* (1978), and *Under the Boardwalk* (1979).

He is author of almost as many plays as he has appeared in as actor. His own plays include *Little More Light around the Place* (written with Sidney Easton, 1964), *No Place to Be Somebody: A Black-Black Comedy* (1967), *Willy Bignigga* (1970), *Chumpanzee* (1970), *Gordone Is a Muthah* (1970), *Baba-Chops* (1975), and *The Last Chord* (1977). He is also the author of five screenplays: *No Place to Be Somebody*, *The W.A.S.P.* (adapted from the novel by Julius Horwitz), *From These Ashes*, *Under the Boardwalk*, and *Liliom*. His latest play, *Anabiosis*, which means resuscitation, new life, or rebirth, was performed by the City Players in St. Louis, Missouri, and received a standing ovation as well as rave reviews.

In an interview in *Contemporary Authors*, Gordone best describes the nature of his plays when he discusses the experiences that make for what he sees as good, lasting drama. He says, "It has to be human experience, you know. In the front of the Samuel French edition of *No Place to Be Somebody* I think is my philosophy as well as the social scientist's who wrote it. The truth is not merely the truth about Negroes. It reflects the deeper torments and anguish of the total human predicament. . . . Where you find one kind of prejudice, you'll find many others. What about the women in this country? There are those who would not like to include women as part of this whole human rights struggle. In the world we live in today, there can be no seniority or preferential treatment. Everything is part of the whole."

In addition to the Pulitzer Prize, his honors and awards are an Obie

Award for best actor in *Of Mice and Men* (1953), the Los Angeles Critics Circle Award and Drama Desk Award, both for *No Place to Be Somebody* (1970), and a grant from the National Institute of Arts and Letters (1971).

For further reading, see *Dictionary of Literary Biography, Volume 38; Black World* (December 1972); *Journal of Negro Education* (Spring 1971); and Linda Metzger, ed., *Black Writers: A Selection of Sketches from Contemporary Authors* (1989).

The selection below is Act II, Scene I from *No Place to Be Somebody.*

FROM **NO PLACE TO BE SOMEBODY**

Time: Two days later
     Place: The same
     Setting: The same
     At rise: GABE sits at table. Whisky bottle before him.
     He is obviously drunk. He begins to sing an old Protestant
     hymn.

Gabe
"Whiter than snow, yes!
Whiter than snow!
Now, wash me, and I shall be
Whiter than snow!"
     He chants.
We moved out of that dirty-black slum!
Away from those dirty-black people!
Who live in those dirty-black hovels,
Amidst all of that garbage and filth!
Away from those dirty-black people,
Who in every way,
Prove daily
They are what they are!
Just dirty-black people!

We moved to a house with a fenced-in yard!
To a clean-white neighborhood!
It had clean-white sidewalks
And clean-white sheets

That hang from clean-white clotheslines to dry!
They were clean-white people!
Who in every way
Prove daily
They are what they are!
Just clean-white people!

Now those clean-white people thought we were
Dirty-black people!
And they treated us like we were
Dirty-black people!
But we stuck it out!
We weathered the storm!
We cleansed and bathed
And tried to be and probably were
Cleaner than most of those clean-white people!
      He sings.
"Break down every idol, cast out every foe!
Oh, wash me and I shall be whiter than snow!"
      He speaks again.
We went to schools that had clean-white
Rooms with clean-white teachers
Who taught us and all of the clean-white
Children how to be clean and white!
      He laughs.
Now, those dirty-black people across
The tracks became angry, jealous and mean!
When they saw us running or skipping or
Hopping or learning with all of those
Clean-white children!

They would catch us alone
When the clean-white children weren't there!
And kick us or slap us and spit
On our clean-white clothes!
Call us dirty-black names
And say that we wanted to be like our clean-white
Neighbors!

But in spite of the kicking, the slapping
The spitting, we were exceedingly glad!
For we knew we weren't trying to be like
Our clean-white neighbors! Most of all,
We were certain we weren't like those
Dirty-black Niggers,

Who lived in hovels, far away across the tracks!
> *He sings.*
"Whiter than snow! Oh, whiter than snow!
Please wash me, and I shall be whiter than snow!"
> *He speaks again.*
So we grew up clean and keen!
And all of our clean-white neighbors
Said we had earned the right to go
Out into the clean-white world
And be accepted as clean-white people!
But we soon learned,
The world was not clean and white!
With all of its powders and soaps!
And we learned too that no matter how
Much the world scrubbed,
The world was getting no cleaner!

Most of all!
We saw that no matter how much or how
Hard we scrubbed,
It was only making us blacker!
So back we came to that dirty-black slum!
To the hovels, the filth and the garbage!
Came back to those dirty-black people!
Away from those clean-white people!
That clean, white anti-septic world!
That scrubs and scrubs and scrubs!

But those dirty-black people!
Those dirty-black people!
Were still angry, jealous and mean!
They kicked us and slapped us and spit again
On our clothes!
Denied us!
Disowned us
And cast us out!
And we still were exceedingly glad!

For at last they knew
We were not like our clean-white neighbors!
Most of all! We were safe!
Assured at last!
We could never more be
Like those dirty-black Niggers!
Those filthy, dirty-black Niggers!

Who live far away!
Far away, in hovels across the tracks!
          He bursts into song.
"Whiter than snow! Yes! Whiter than snow!
Oh, wash me and I shall be whiter than snow!"
          GABE *is on his knees. Hands stretched up to heaven. Lights*
          slowly dim out on him, and come up on bar. SHANTY *is*
          behind the bar. MIKE MAFFUCCI *stands at center, throw-*
          ing darts into a dartboard. SWEETS CRANE *enters.*

Shanty
Hit the wind, Mac. This ain't the place.

Sweets
Johnny here?

Shanty
What you want with Johnny?

Sweets
I'm a frien'a his.

Shanty
Yeah? Well, he ain't here.

Sweets
Where's me a broom an' a drop pan?

Shanty
What for?

Sweets
Need me a bucket an' some rags too.

Shanty
What do you want all that shit for?

Sweets
The floor, they don't look too good an' the windas, it could
stan' . . . .

Shanty
Eighty-six, ol' timer! We ain't hirin'.

Sweets
Ain't askin' f'no pay.

Shanty
What'a ya? Some kind'a nut? C'mon! Out you go. Eighty-six.

Sweets

Think you better wait till Johnny gets here. Let him put me out.

> SWEETS *pushes* SHANTY *roughly aside and moves to kitchen.*

Think I'll fin' what I need back here.

Shanty   *Looks incredulous. Scratches his head and follows* SWEETS *to kitchen.*

> JOHNNY *enters.* SHANTY *rushes in from kitchen.*

Hey, Johnny! Some ol' timer just came in an'. . . .

Maffucci

How you doin', Johnny Cake?

Johnny   *Stops short.*

Only one cat usta call me that.

Maffucci

Gettin' warm, Johnny Cake.

Johnny   *Moves behind bar.*

Little snotty-nose wop kid, name Mike Maffucci.

Maffucci

On the nose.

> *Sends a dart in* JOHNNY's *direction.* JOHNNY *ducks. The dart buries into the wood of the back bar. Both men laugh. They shake hands.*

Long time no see, eh, Johnny Cake?

Johnny

What you drinkin'?

Maffucci

Little dago red. Gotta take it easy on my stomach with the hard stuff.

> JOHNNY *snaps his fingers.* SHANTY *brings bottle.*

Shanty

Dig, Johnny! Some ol' goat. . . .

Johnny

Cool it, Shanty. Can't you see I'm busy? How's your ol' man, Footch?

Maffucci   *Makes the sign of the cross.*

My ol' man chalked out, Johnny. Heart attack. Right after you went to the nursery. You ain't still sore 'bout what happened, are you, Johnny Cake?

Johnny

Bygones is bygones, Footch!

Maffucci

Glad'a hear ya say that, Johnny. Didn't know what happened to you after that. When they tole me you was runnin' this joint, had'a come over an' see ya.

> *He looks around.* SWEETS *enters with broom and rags. Proceeds to sweep the floor.* JOHNNY *registers surprise and anger.* SHANTY *starts to say something but* JOHNNY *puts his finger to his lips.*

How ya doin' with the place, Johnny?

Johnny

Stabbin' horses to steal blankets. Jay Cee ag'inst the worl'.

Maffucci

Joe Carneri used to say that. You ain't never forgot that huh, Johnny?

> JOHNNY *glances angrily at* SWEETS.

Remember the first time they busted him? There was this pitchure on the front page. Joe's standin' on the courthouse steps. Cops an' reporters all aroun'. Joe's yellin' "Jay Cee ag'inst the worl'! Jay Cee ag'inst the worl'!"

Johnny

He sho' was your hero all right.

Maffucci

Too bad he had'a go an' git hit like that. Sittin' in a barber chair!

Johnny

Better'n the electric chair.

> SWEETS *is now dusting the chairs.*

Maffucci

You know, Johnny Cake, that was a groovy idea for a kid! Coppin' all that scrapiron from ol' Julio an' then sellin' it back to him.

> *He breaks up laughing.*

Johnny

Wasn't so pretty when I tried to tell the fuzz you was in on it with me.

Maffucci

Awful sorry 'bout that, Johnny Cake.

> MAFFUCCI *puts his hand on* JOHNNY's *shoulder.*
> JOHNNY *knocks his hand off.* MAFFUCCI *comes down on* JOHNNY's *shoulder with a karate chop.* JOHNNY *punches*

MAFFUCCI *in the stomach and shoves him away. Comes toward* MAFFUCCI *menacingly.* SWEETS *keeps sweeping.*

Johnny
One thing I gotta give you Ginees credit for. Sho' know how to stick together when you wanna.

Maffucci *Backs away.*
He was my father, Johnny. Any father would'a done the same thing. If he had the connections.

Johnny
Who tole you I was runnin' this joint, Footch?

Maffucci
To give you the works, Johnny, I'm one'a Pete Zerroni's local boys now.
SWEETS *dusts near* MAFFUCCI.

Johnny
No jive! Battin' in the big leagues, ain't you? Your ol' man was a-roun', bet he'd be pretty proud'a you.

Maffucci
Would you believe, my ol' man had ideas 'bout me bein' a lawyer or a doctor?

Johnny
What you doin' for Pete?

Maffucci
Sort'a community relations like, Johnny.

Johnny *Laughs.*
I'm one'a Pete's customers! What kind'a community relashuns you got for me?

Maffucci
Glad you opened that, Johnny Cake. Pete says you got him a little concerned.

Johnny
What is he, crazy? Ain't he got more 'portant things on his min'?

Maffucci
Way we got it, first thing ol' Sweets Crane did when he got out was come see you.

Johnny
So what? Sweets was like'a father to me.

Maffucci

So I hear. But before they shut the gate on him, he let some things drop. Like, he made a few threats. What I hear 'bout him, might be crazy enough to give 'em a try.

> JOHNNY *laughs.*

What, am I throwin' zingers or sump'm? What's the joke?

Johnny

Sweets came 'roun' to tell me he's all caught up.

Maffucci

Wouldn't promote me, would you, Johnny Cake? For ol' time's sake, let's not you an' me go horse-to-horse 'bout nothin'.

Johnny

On the up an' up, Footch. Sweets has wrapped it all up for good. Matter'a fack, right now he's doin' odd gigs an' singin' the straight an' narrow.

Maffucci

Wanna believe you, Johnny. But just in case you an' this Sweets are thinkin' 'bout makin' a little noise, Pete wants me to give you the six-to-five!

> SWEETS *bumps into* MAFFUCCI, *spilling the wine down the front of* MAFFUCCI's *suit.*

Hey! Watch it there, pops!

Sweets

Awful sorry 'bout that, mister!

> *Attemps to wipe* MAFFUCCI's *suit with the rag.* MAF-FUCCI *pushes him aside.*

Maffucci

That's okay, pops!

> SWEETS *continues to wipe* MAFFUCCI's *vest.*

Okay, okay, I said!

> SWEETS *stops, and continues with his work.*

Well, Johnny Cake. Like to stay an' rap with ya a little bit but you know how it is. Community relations.

Johnny

Sho' preshiate you lookin' out for me, Footch!

Maffucci

Think nothin' of it, Johnny Cake. It's Pete. He don't like jigs. Says the minute they git a little somethin', they start actin' cute. You an' me, we was like brothers. Way I see it, was like you took a dive for me once. Figger I owe ya.

Johnny
You don't owe me a dam thing, Footch.

Maffucci *Heads for the street doors. Turns back.*
You know, Johnny Cake, some reason I never been able to git you off my mind. After all these years, I think if you'da been a wop, you'da been a big man in the rackets.
            Exits. SWEETS *holds watch to ear.*

Johnny
All right now, Sweets. Goddamit, wha's this game you playin'?

Shanty
Sweets??? That's Sweets Crane?

Johnny
Shut up, Shanty.
            Snatches the rag out of SWEETS' *hand. Gets broom. Gives*
            both to SHANTY.
Take this crap back to the kitchen.
            SHANTY *takes them to kitchen.*
Man, you either gotta be stir-buggy or you puttin' on one helluva ack.

Sweets *Checks the watch.*
Jus' tryin' to be helpful, Sonny Boy.

Johnny
Don't you be kickin' no more farts at me, man. Wha's with this pil'fin stuff off a people an' makin' like'a dam lackey? You mus' be plumb kinky.

Sweets
Cain't see no point in watchin' George Raff on tee vee ev'a night. All my life I been into things. Always active.

Johnny
This what you call bein' active? An' look at you! Look like you jus' come off the Bow'ry! Ain't they no pride lef' in you?

Sweets
Pride? Sheee. Pride, Sonny Boy, is sump'm I ain't got no mo' use for.

Johnny
For the las' time, ol' man. You better tell me wha's happenin' with you. Don't you make me have to kill you.

Sweets   *Produces an envelope.*
I'm as good as dead right now!
          He hands JOHNNY *the envelope.*

Johnny
What the hell is it?

Sweets
Guess you could call it my will.

Johnny   *Turns it over.*
Yo' will??

Sweets
Open it up.

Johnny
Shanty!

Shanty   *Enters.*
How ya doin', Sweets?

Johnny
Check this out, Shanty. I don't read this jive so good.

Shanty   *Reads will.*
It's legal stuff. Says here you're gonna inherit interest in barbershops,
meat markets, stores an' a whole lotta Harlem real estate. Dam!

Johnny   *Snatches the papers out of* SHANTY's *hands.*
You gotta be jokin'.

Sweets
I'm leavin' it all to you, Sonny Boy. My lawyers will take care
ev'thing.

Johnny
How come you ain't tole me nothin' 'bout this before?

Sweets
Couldn't take no chance it gittin' out. Might'a strung me out on a
tax rap too.

Johnny
You lookin' to take some kind'a back gate commute? Suicide?

Sweets   *Coughs.*
Doctors ain't gimme but six months to ride. Didn't wanna lay it on
you till they made sho'.

Johnny
Six months, huh?

Sweets
Mo' or less.

Johnny
Goddamit, Sweets. What the hell kin I say? I sho' been a real bastard. Guess it don't help none for me to say I'm sorry.

Sweets
Might he'p some if you was to turn all this into sump'm worth while an' good. Maybe the Lawd will f'give me f'the way I got it.
> *Bursts into laughter and coughs.*

Johnny
Git off it, Sweets. Jus' 'cause you s'pose to chalk out on us don't mean you gotta go an' 'brace relijun.

Sweets
Figure it won't hurt none if I do.

Johnny
Shit. That good Lawd you talkin' 'bout is jus' as white as that judge who sent yo' black ass to Fedsville.

Sweets
How you know? You ever seen him? When I was down there in that prison, I reads a lot. Mos'ly the Bible. Bible tells me, the Lawd was hard to look upon. Fack is, he was so hard to look upon that nobody eva looked at him an' lived. Well, I got to figgerin' on that. An' reasons that was so, 'cause he was so black.
> *Goes into loud laughter and coughs again.*
Lawd knows! White's easy nuff to look at!
> JOHNNY *throws the will on the floor.* SWEETS *goes to his knees and clutches the will.*
What you doin', Sonny Boy? My life is in them papers!
> *Hits* JOHNNY *with hat.* JOHNNY *reaches under the bar and comes up with a revolver. Levels it at* SWEETS.

Johnny
See this, Sweets? My firs' an' only pistol. You gave it to me long time ago when I was a lookout for you when you was pullin' them owl jobs in Queens. I worshipped the groun' you walked on. I thought the sun rose an' set in yo' ass. You showed me how to make thirteen straight passes without givin' up the dice. Stood behin' me an' nudged me when to play my ace. Hipped me how to make a gapers cut. How to handle myself in a pill joint. Taught me to trust no

woman over six or under sixty. Turned me on to the best horse players an' number runners. Showed me how to keep my ass-pocket full'a coins without goin' to jail. Said the wors' crime I ever committed was comin' out'a my mama screamin' black. Tole me all about white folks an' what to expect from the best of 'em. You said as long as there was a single white man on this earth, the black man only had one free choice. That was the way he died. When you went to jail for shootin' Cholly you said, "Sonny Boy, git us a plan." Well, I got us a plan. Now, you come back here nutty an' half dead, dancin' all over me about me goin' through a change'a life. An' how you want me to help you git ready to meet yo' Lawd. Well, git ready, mother fucker. Tha's exactly what I'm gon' do. Help you to meet him.

> JOHNNY *pulls back the hammer of the gun.* SWEETS *coughs and looks at the barrel of the gun.*

Sweets

You ain't gon' shoot me, Johnny. You cain't shoot me. They's a whole lotta you I ain't even touched.

> SWEETS *exits. Blackout.*

George Kent

(1920–1982)

A STIMULATING SCHOLAR of African American literature, George E. Kent was among the first black scholars to identify the creative motif inherent in black folk literary history. His essays on James Baldwin, Langston Hughes, Ralph Ellison, Richard Wright, and Gwendolyn Brooks, collected in his well-known *Blackness and the Adventure of Western Culture* (1972), for a time represented the definitive analyses of these writers' works in the African American literary community.

Kent was born in 1920, in Columbus, Georgia. He received his B.S. from Savannah State College in 1941, and both his M.A. and Ph.D. from Boston University, in 1948 and 1953, respectively. From 1949 to 1960 he was chairman of the department of languages and literature as well as professor of English and dean of the college of languages and literature at Delaware State College. From 1960 to 1964 he was chairman of the English department at Delaware. In 1964 he joined the faculty at Quinnipiac College in Hamden, Connecticut, where he was professor and English department chairman again. Staying at Quinnipiac five years, he went in 1969 to the University of Chicago as a visiting professor and in 1970 he became a permanent member of the English department there. He held visiting professorships at Wesleyan University, the University of Connecticut, Florida A & M University, and Grambling College. He also served as panelist at innumerable professional meetings and presented papers at colleges and universities across the United States.

His biography of Gwendolyn Brooks *A Life of Gwendolyn Brooks* was published posthumously in 1990. He is also the author of numerous essays on writers such as George Lamming, William Faulkner, John Galsworthy, Stephen Henderson, and Claude McKay. In characterizing George Kent's criticism, scholar Ron Baxter Miller writes, "Looking at once to the aesthetic and political worlds, George Kent naturally assumes that the one influences the other. He roots the symbolic needs of Western culture and white consciousness in economic motivation as well as exploitation. . . ."

Kent's honors and awards include a fellowship from the National Endowment for the Humanities, Distinguished Lecturer (the National Council of Teachers of English), and College Language Association Distinguished Research Award.

For a look at two overviews of George Kent's criticism and an assessment of his place in the African American critical tradition, see Ron Baxter

Miller's "Double Mirror: George E. Kent and the Scholarly Imagination" and Houston A. Baker, Jr.'s "Unraveling a Western Tale: The Critical Legacy of George Kent," in *Studies in Black American Literature, Volume II: Belief vs. Theory in Black American Literary Criticism*, edited by Joe Weixlmann and Chester J. Fontenot (1986).

"Baldwin and the Problem of Being" is taken from *CLA Journal* 7 (March 1964).

BALDWIN AND THE PROBLEM OF BEING

In a *New York Times Book Review* essay, James Baldwin has stated that the effort to become a great novelist "involves attempting to tell as much of the truth as one can bear, and then a little more."[1] It is likely in our time to mean attacking much that Americans tend to hold sacred, in order that reality be confronted and constructively altered. As stated in "Everybody's Protest Novel," it means devotion to the "human being, his freedom and fulfillment; freedom which cannot be legislated, fulfillment which cannot be charted."[2] Baldwin then wishes to confront and affect the human consciousness and conscience. He rejects the tradition of the protest novel because he feels that it denies life, "the human being . . . his beauty, dread, power," and insists "that it is categorization alone which is real and which cannot be transcended."[3] He tries to write the way jazz musicians sound, to reflect their compassion,[4] and it is noteworthy that Baldwin's tendency in *Go Tell It on the Mountain* and *Another Country* is to focus upon the individual characters' experiences in a way similar to Ralph Ellison's description of jazz:

> For true jazz is an art of individual assertion within and against the group. Each true jazz moment (as distinct from the uninspired commercial performance) springs from a contest in which each artist challenges all the rest; each solo flight or improvisation, represents . . . a definition

---

From *CLA Journal* Volume 7 (March 1964). Reprinted by permission of the College Language Association.

[1]James Baldwin, "As Much Truth As One Can Bear," *The New York Times Book Review* (January 14, 1962), p.1.

[2]*Notes of a Native Son* (Boston, 1955), p. 15.

[3]*Ibid.*, p. 23.

[4]"What's the Reason Why: A Symposium by Best Selling Authors," *The New York Times Book Review* (December 2, 1962), p. 3.

of his identity, as member of the collectivity, and as a link in the chain of tradition.[5]

It should be generally observed that Baldwin's writings owe much to Negro folk tradition (the blues, jazz, spirituals, and folk literature), and to the chief experimental practioneers of modernist fiction, with especial emphasis upon Henry James.

The moral vision that emerges is one primarily concerned with man as he relates to good and evil and to society. For there is evil in human nature and evil abroad in the world to be confronted, not through Christianity whose doctrine tends to be the perverted tool of the ruling classes and groups whose bankruptcy was registered by the slaughter of the Jews during the Third Reich,[6] but through the love and involvement available from those able to eat of the tree of knowledge of good and evil and live. Within the breast of each individual, then, rages a universe of forces with which he must become acquainted, often through the help of an initiated person, in order to direct them for the positive growth of himself and others. The foregoing achievement is what Baldwin means by *identity*. To achieve it, one must not be hindered by the detritus of society and one must learn to know detritus when one sees it.

Perhaps the question which throws the most light upon Baldwin's work is simply: How can one achieve, amid the dislocations and disintegrations of the modern world, true, functional being? For Baldwin, the Western concept of reality, with its naive rationalism, its ignoring of unrational forces that abound within and without man, its reductivist activities wherein it ignores the uniqueness of the individual and sees reality in terms of its simplifications and categorizations is simply impoverishing. He who follows it fails to get into his awareness the richness and complexity of experience—he fails to be. And freedom is unattainable, since paradoxically, freedom is discovery and recognition of limitations, one's own and that of one's society;[7] to deny complexity is to paralyze the ability to get at such knowledge—it is to strangle freedom.

Groping unsteadily amidst the reductivist forces is an America which does not achieve, therefore, its primitive and essential moral identity. For the great vision that motivated the American adventure, there has been substituted a quest for spurious glory in mass production and consumption. And yet, ". . . there is so much more than Cadillacs, Frigidaires, and IBM machines. . . . One of the things

---

[5]Ralph Ellison, "The Charlie Christian Story," *Saturday Review of Literature* (May 17, 1958), p. 42.

[6]James Baldwin, *The Fire Next Time* (New York, 1963), p. 66.

[7]"James Baldwin: An Interview," *WMFT Perspective* (December, 1961), p. 37.

wrong with this country is this notion that IBM machines *prove* something."[8] Still until America achieves its moral identity, its people, whether white or black, can fulfill nothing.

The struggle for identity, i.e., for functional being, is the major issue of Baldwin's first novel, *Go Tell It on the Mountain.* Attempting to tell part of the story found in the Negro's music, which "Americans are able to admire because a protective sentimentality limits their understanding of it,"[9] Baldwin examines three generations of a Negro family whose life span extends from slavery to the present day. The novel investigates, with warmth and perception, the Negro's possibility of achieving identity through the discipline of Christianity. The style is richly evocative, and one hears echoes of Joyce and Faulkner, the rhythms of the old time Negro sermon and the King James Bible. Unfolding in a series of major movements, the story proceeds as follows: the first movement introducing the reach of fourteen year old John Grimes for identity, a fearful, faltering reach, from a boy filled with guilt, hatred, fear, love, amidst the stern, religious frustrations of his elders and the pagan rebelliousness of his brother, Roy; the second presenting the tragedy of Florence, unable to overcome, among other things, the concept of the Negro she has internalized from the dominant culture—and therefore on insecure terms with herself and others; the third presenting Gabriel Grimes, stepfather of John, blocked from complete fulfillment by his attempts to escape his pagan drives in a fierce, frustrated embrace of Christianity; the fourth presenting Elizabeth, Mother of John, who after brief fulfillment in illicit love, retreats, frightened and awe-stricken, into the frustrated and frustrating arms of Gabriel Grimes. The final movement is the questionable flight of John Grimes from the quest for identity into the ostensible safety of religious ecstasy.

Vitally represented through a series of scenes occurring on his fourteenth birthday, reflected through images of poetic intensity, are the conflicts of young John. He stands upon a hill in New York's Central Park and feels "like a giant who might crumble this city with anger . . . like a tyrant who might crush this city with his heel . . . like a long awaited conqueror at whose feet flowers would be strewn, and before whom multitudes cried, Hosanna!"[10] Or concerning the rewards to be inherited from his preacher father: ". . . a house like his father's, a church like his father's and a job like his father's where he would grow old and black with hunger and toil. The way of the cross had given him a belly filled with wind and had

---

[8]*Ibid.*
[9]*Notes of a Native Son*, p. 24.
[10]*Go Tell It on the Mountain* (New York, 1953), p. 35.

bent his mother's back. . . ."[11] Mixed with his vision and perverting it is John's guilt over his sexual drives, the religious concept of the city as evil and the fatal tempter of the soul, and his parents' feeling that the city (New York) is filled with antagonistic whites who will block the worldly aspirations of Negroes. Over such obstacles John peers, enveloped in a solitude that seems well nigh unbreakable.

Part II, containing the stories of the adult members of the family who came to manhood and womanhood at the time of Emancipation, begins powerfully. Passionate scenes reveal the problems with which each character struggles. For Florence, the sister of the minister Gabriel, the central problem is to achieve an identity that excludes the concubinage already offered by her white Southern employer, the general sexual opportunism, or the image of the toil blasted bearer of children with its attendant heritage—a cabin like her mother's. In addition, Florence is one of a long line of Baldwin's characters who have absorbed from the dominant culture the concept of Blackness as low, contemptible, evil. Baldwin has said, "The American image of the Negro lives also in the Negro's heart; and when he has surrendered to this image life has no other possible reality."[12] Controlled by such an image, Florence flounders in a mixture of self-hatred, self-righteousness, sadism, and guilt feelings. Married to a ne'er-do-well, she succeeds merely in outraging herself and him, and in driving him away. She bows to religious ecstasy. Baldwin's point, of course, is that she was unable to achieve a life affirming love or her potential identity, and that her ecstatic surrender to Christianity as she nears the end of life is a gesture of desperation.

A man of titanic drives, Gabriel is a sufficient metaphor for man in a grim struggle with the forces of the universe; he stops just short of evoking the sense of tragedy, since self-recognition is not clearly confessed. What is available for articulating the self amid these forces, however, is a vision of St. Paul's Christianity which assures the self a Pyhrric victory by a repression that carries the mere coloring of a humanistic morality. Since sex, for Baldwin, is obviously a metaphor for the act of breaking one's isolation and, properly experienced, responsibly entering into the complexity of another human being, Gabriel's evasion of it by marrying the sexless Deborah (symbolically enough, mass raped by Southern whites and sterile) is his flight from dealing with his humanity. Baldwin contrasts him well with the pagan Esther, by whom a temporarily backsliding Gabriel begets a child he does not acknowledge. Esther has a firm concept

---

[11]*Ibid.*, p. 37.
[12]*Notes*, p. 38.

of her dignity and humanity, and what is life-affirming and what is life-negating, and some of his fellow ministers, too, show that they do not take their fundamentalist concepts to rigid conclusions. Gabriel's response is to retreat more fiercely into religion, marry, after the death of Deborah the fallen Elizabeth, and harden in his grotesqueness.

Elizabeth is the ethical and moral center of the book. It is through her attachment to her father and reaction against her mother and aunt that she gains a sense of a love that is life giving. She knows that love's imprisonment is not a "bribe, a threat, an indecent will to power"; it is "mysteriously, a freedom for the soul and spirit . . . water in dry places."[13] It seems to me, however, that Baldwin's hand falters in his analysis and presentation of her as a young woman. Her important relationship with her father, to the extent that it is at all rendered, is simply that of the conventional petting and "spoiling" afforded by a loose living man who does not take his fatherhood very seriously. That is to say that the father's free loving nature binds him to nothing, and, after cautioning Elizabeth (as we learn though a summary) never to let the world see her suffering, he returns to his job of running a house of prostitution. Amidst the religious illusions of the other characters, however, she retains a strong, quiet sense of her integrity, despite a relative commitment to religious passion.

Her fall came through her common-law husband, Richard, to whom she gave a self-sacrifical, life creating love. Although the portrayal of Richard as victimized by society and as a man whose being cannot fulfill its hunger is moving, the explanation of his curiosity and hunger seems oversimplified, if not, indeed, dehumanized: ". . . that I was going to get to know everything them white bastards knew . . . so could no white-son-of-bitch nowhere never talk me down, and never make feel like I was dirt . . ."[14] Although the statement well reflects Richard's sensitivity and insecurity under the racial system of America, it hardly explains "his great adoration for things dead."

After the proud young Richard kills himself in reaction to extreme humiliation by the police who have imposed upon his consciousness the image of the low bestial Negro that he has tried to escape, Elizabeth gives birth to the bastard John, whose quest for identity forms the central movement of the book. As the second wife

[13]*Go Tell It on the Mountain*, p. 210.
[14]*Ibid.*, pp. 225–226.

of Gabriel, she emerges as a person of complexity, and is sensitively involved in John's reach for life.

By a series of flashbacks, the author keeps us mindful that the present involves John Grimes's search for identity, the achievement of which is to be understood within the context of the lives of his elders. In the last section of the story, he is in crisis, and with the help of his friend Elisha, in a religious ecstasy, commits himself to the Cross. At various points, Baldwin uses a character by whose views the reality witnessed is to be qualified. In addition to the fore-shadowings scattered throughout the story, there is Gabriel to point out that the ecstatic conversion is still to be tested by the long, complex journey of life. So quite without surprise, we encounter in a later short story, "The Death of the Prophet," an apostate Johnny who returns guiltily from some place of estrangement almost to collapse in the presence of his dying father.

That Baldwin in *Go Tell It on the Mountain* has drawn heavily upon autobiographical experiences is obvious, and those who like the pursuit can make interesting parallels with autobiographical situations reported in the essay collections: *Notes of a Native Son, Nobody Knows My Name,* and *The Fire Next Time.* But, from the artistic point of view, what is more interesting is their transmutation, their representation as organized energies that carry mythic force in their reflection of man attempting to deal with destiny. Much power derives from the confrontation of the ambiguity of life. That ambiguity carries into the various attitudes suggested toward the version of Christianity that his characters relate themselves to. The relatively non-religious characters do not deny the relevance of God but seem to feel as Esther, the spurned mother of Gabriel's illegitimate child, puts it: ". . . that [the Lord's] spirit ain't got to work in everybody the same, seems to me."[15] Of the religiously engrossed characters, only Elizabeth achieves a relatively selfless being. However, the religion sustained the slave mother of Gabriel. Even for the twisted, it is a place of refuge, an articulation of the complexity of the mysterious forces of a demanding universe. But finally, the religious only partially illuminates, and the characters must grope in its light and bump against forces within and without that the religion has merely hidden or dammed.

With some admitted oversimplifications inescapable in tracing thematic lines, it may be said that in his two succeeding novels Baldwin is preoccupied with sex and love as instruments in the achievement of full being. As a novelist still under forty, he is no doubt

---

[15]*Go Tell It on the Mountain,* p. 161.

creating works important to his total development, but in neither of these novels—*Giovanni's Room* and the best seller *Another Country*—does he seem to fully create his fictional worlds and characters; in short, he does not seem to have found characters who release his very real ability to create.

In an essay "Preservation of Innocence," Baldwin explicity makes his criticism of popular concepts of sexuality. His chief point is that our rational classification of sexual characteristics and our efforts to preserve conventional norms tell us little about what it means to be a man or a woman. Our classifications are not definitive, and therefore we panic and set up safeguards that do nothing more than guard against sexual activities between members of the same sex. But such reductive simplicity, he argues, guarantees ignorance merely, or worse the probability that the bride and groom will not be able to add to the sum of love or know each other since they do not know themselves. Whatever position one takes regarding the argument, the following statements shed uncomfortable light upon the relationship between the sexes in much of American fiction:

> In the truly awesome attempt of the American to at once preserve his innocence and arrive at man's estate, that mindless monster, the tough guy, has been created and perfected, whose masculinity is found in the most infantile and elementary externals and whose attitude towards women is the wedding of the most abysmal romanticism and the most implacable distrust.[16]

Further complaint of the reductive approach to sexuality is contained in a review of Andre Gide's *Madeline*, in which he describes the possibility of communing with another sex as "the door to life and air and freedom from the tyranny of one's own personality. . . ."[17] And he describes our present day as one in which communion between the sexes "has become so sorely threatened that we depend more and more on the strident exploitation of externals, as, for example, the breasts of Hollywood glamor girls and the mindless grunting and swaggering of Hollywood he-men."[18] Despite our claim to knowledge, Baldwin implies, sex is a mystery that each person must find a way to live with.

In the light of the foregoing, it seems to me, Baldwin's intention in the novel *Giovanni's Room*, is more easily understood. The main line of the story portrays the way a youth's inherited definitions of sexuality fail him in his attempts to come to terms with his own, and adds to the sum of evil in his relationship with others. The chief

---

[16]"Preservation of Innocence," *Zero* (Summer, 1949), pp. 18–19.
[17]*Nobody Knows My Name* (New York, 1961), p. 161.
[18]*Ibid.*, p. 162.

character David represents the rational Westerner, who has absorbed the simplified, compartmentalized thinking of his background. Falling first in a romantic homosexual experience with a fellow adolescent Joey, he experiences that escape from isolation and the heightened spiritual awareness which love is supposed to bring. However, "A cavern opened in my mind, black, full of rumor, suggestion. . . . I could have cried, cried for shame and terror, cried for not understanding how this could have happened to me, how this could have happened in me."[19] Unresolved oedipal conflicts are hinted, and just when he needs spiritual sustenance from a father, his father, who knows nothing of the son's experience, insists upon retaining the simplified concept of himself as his son's "buddy." In flight from Joey, David repeats the mishap in the army, then takes flight to France to "find himself," but once there tentatively enters into a similar relationship with Giovanni. David expects Giovanni to be but an interval in life, since David has also a girlfriend Hella, a very rational minded girl who has gone to Spain to think out whether she is in love. But, moving just one step ahead of the predatory homosexual underworld, Giovanni's life demands David's love as its only hope for transcendence. Irresponsibly, and in a way that denies their complexity as human beings, David disappoints the hopes of Giovanni and disillusions Hella.

What Baldwin registers well is the desperate need for love that brings transcendence. The homosexual's problem is shown to be the threat of being forced into the underworld where bought love of the body, without transcendence, is simply productive of desperation. The women pictured face a similar problem on a heterosexual level. The world portrayed is nightmarish, but hardly, in any sense, really vital. One of its serious problems though is that the reader is not allowed to escape the feeling, in the bad sense, of staginess and theatricality. The characters are in hell all right, but the reader never is, and I do not think that this is so simply because the approach to sex is unconventional. The characters do not root themselves deeply enough to become momentous in fictional terms, nor do they stand with intensity for elemental forces which we are forced to consider an inescapable part of our lives. So that, despite claims for complexity, the characters are too easily defined with relationship to a thesis.

Before coming to a consideration of *Another Country*, I should point out that Baldwin is the author of several stories of distinction, though there is hardly space for more than a brief mentioning of them. "Previous Condition" is the intense story of a young Negro's

---

[19]*Giovanni's Room* (New York, 1956), p. 12.

attempt to secure his being from its alienated condition within and the forces of prejudice without. It appeared in *Commentary*, October, 1948, as Baldwin's first story. "The Death of the Prophet," *Commentary*, March, 1950, was mentioned in connection with *Go Tell It on the Mountain*. "Come Out the Wilderness," *Mademoiselle*, New York, 1961, explores the lostness of a Negro girl who has been alienated from her original racial environment. "Sonny's Blues," *Partisan Review*, Summer, 1957, reprinted in *Best Short Stories of 1958* and Herbert Gold's *Fiction of the Fifties*, New York, 1959, carries the venture of a Negro boy through narcotics to music where he finally gains a sense of identity expressed. "This Morning, This Evening, So Soon," *The Atlantic Monthly*, September, 1960, reprinted in Martha Foley, *The Best Short Stories of 1961*, New York, 1961, an issue dedicated to Baldwin, explores the necessity of a successful young Negro actor to come to terms with his place in history. Each story shows a sure sense of the short story form, a moment of illumination that has significance for the total life of the character. Baldwin's greatest indebtedness in the short story is to Henry James.

Another Country, New York, 1962, Baldwin's latest novel, is a serious and ambitious attempt, a fact which should be recognized despite the fact that to make it a serious novel of the first rank would demand severe cutting and some intensive re-writing. The problem is still that of arriving at a definition of one's being, which will be adequately sustaining in the face of the evils of life, and to support another's complexity through love. Both heterosexual and homosexual scenes abound, but, as stated in the discussion of *Giovanni's Room*, these are the instruments for the exploration of being, the metaphors for self-definition and for responsibly entering the complexity of another. They have, therefore, a serious purpose, and Baldwin is too concerned about whether the sex experience provides a transcending love to make distinctions between the heterosexual and homosexual experience. Most of the men have engaged in a homosexual act, and have from it defined their sex for the future; that is, they decide whether the homosexual experience is or is not for their being, with most deciding in favor of heterosexuality.

The first story is that of Rufus, the Negro musician, who is fighting within himself both the real and the imaginary aspects of the race problem, and therefore cannot communicate with Leona, the Southern poor white girl that he picks up with the conscious purpose of sexual exploitation and of getting rid of her before she can "bug" him with her story (i.e., involve him in her complexity as a person). Rufus has suffered real racial persecution, so that even harmless remarks by Leona send him into a rage, and he finally drives her into a nervous breakdown and succumbs to his own frustrations by committing suicide. The horror of their experience is communicated with considerable skill. Rufus's failure in *being* is then re-tested in the lives of other characters who were, in varying degrees, associated with him.

Vivaldo Moore, the Irish-Italian, attracted to Rufus's sister, at first, partly through being a "liberal," and partly because of his sense of having failed her brother, must be made to confront her as a complex human conundrum, capable of ruthless exploitation and high level prostitution: that is, he must lose his innocence. Cass and Richard Silenski must abandon their oversimplified classification of each other and achieve a sense of reality in their marriage. Eric, the homosexual, must overthrow his Southern background and come to terms with himself in France. Everybody, indeed, must learn his own name. Thus the lives of successive sets of people must come against the problems of being, love, and involvement.

One trouble with the scheme is that so few of the characters exemplify the complexity contended for them. Rufus, Ida, and Eric are the more adequately developed characters. The rest are not projected far enough beyond the level of nice, erring people. Thus the central problem of the book lacks momentousness. Ralph Ellison has said of the novel that ". . . it operates by amplifying and giving resonance to a specific complex of experience until, through the eloquence of its statement, that specific part of life speaks metaphorically for the whole."[20] It is precisely the foregoing illusion that *Another Country* in its totality is unable to create. The section concerned with the discovery of Rufus's death and the attendance at his funeral is excessive reportorial detail, sometimes theatrical, sometimes written at the level of the women's magazine. And the social criticism is inert, for the most part, a part of the chatty reflections of a particular character or of long clinical discussions.

On the other hand, there are some penetrating scenes that reflect the fine talent of Baldwin. In addition to the story of Rufus, I should cite most of the scenes where Ida is present and some of the scenes between Cass Silenski and Eric. In such scenes, the bold use of naturalistic devices—the sex scenes and four-letter words—project meaning well beyond surface communication. What else could so well convey Rufus's horrified retching at his dilemma or the terrible exasperation of Ida and Vivaldo? Still, scenes abound in which naturalistic detail simply thickens the book and the four-letter words provide a spurious emphasis, galvanizing the reader's attention to no

---

[20]Granville Hicks, ed., *The Living Novel* (New York, 1957), p. 61.

end. And yet *Another Country* is a book that has much to say, and, as I have tried to indicate, sometimes does.

It is not too much to assert then that Baldwin's novels since *Go Tell It on the Mountain*, though fine in segments, tend to reflect a hiatus in his artistic development. In *Go Tell It on the Mountain*, he was working with a body of understood, crystallized, and only partially rejected religious and racial mythology that, therefore, carried coiled within it the wires of communication. It is not to say that the artist's challenge and task were simple to point out that he had primarily to manipulate the myth, to steep it in deliberate ambiguity, in order to reflect its Sphinx-like betrayal of those who uncritically absorbed it. The religious interpretation, after all, is within touching distance of the overall idea of Matthew Arnold's famous essay, "Hebraism and Hellenism." His autobiographical intimacy with such material required and received artistic skill and distance. Creating against such a background Baldwin effected a novel which transcended racial and religious categories—became an evoked image of man facing the mysterious universal forces.

On the other hand, the Baldwin of the last two novels confronts the modern consciousness amidst fluxions more talked about than crystallized, and moving at considerable speed: elements of modern man connoting fragmenting certainties eroded at the base, the succor for which has been sought mainly in the vague horizons of the backward look. The workings of sex amidst those fluxions are certainly, in the modern awareness, one major element in the choppy sea of our minds, in which definable shapes seem to appear for the purpose of disappearing. To define them artistically would seem to demand extraordinary effort indeed, whether in traditional or experimental terms.

The conclusion, therefore, to which a full reading of Baldwin seems inescapably to lead is that since his first novel he has not evolved the artistic form that will fully release and articulate his obviously complex awareness. And that to do so may require an abandonment of safety in the use of form equal to that which he has manifested in approach to subject, an act which may concommitantly involve estranging many of the multitude of readers which he has acquired. For an artist of Baldwin's fictional resources, talent, and courage, of his obvious knowledge of evolved fictional techniques, the challenge should hardly be overwhelming.

Naomi Long Madgett

(1923–   )

NAOMI MADGETT, one of the many overlooked figures in African American literary history, best describes herself in her comments in *Contemporary Authors*: "As a child I was motivated by my father's library and the interests and inspiration of literary parents. I discovered Alfred Lord Tennyson and Langston Hughes at about the same time [while] sitting on the floor of my father's study when I was about seven or eight. I think my poetry represents something of the variety of interest and style that these two widely divergent poets represent. I would rather be a good poet than anything else I can imagine."

She was born in 1923, in Norfolk, Virginia, to a clergyman, Clarence Marcellus Long, and a school teacher, Maude Hilton Long. Her education, which spans most of her life, includes a B.A. degree from Virginia State College in 1945, an M.Ed. degree from Wayne State University in 1956, and a Ph.D. degree from the International Institute for Advanced Studies in 1980.

As is the case with a number of creative writers, she began her writing career as a reporter and copy reader, working for the *Michigan Chronicle* in Detroit. Because very few creative artists, especially black ones, are able to make a living from their art alone, Madgett worked as an English teacher in public high schools from 1955 to 1965 and from 1966 to 1968, and as a research associate at Oakland University in Rochester, Michigan, from 1965 to 1966. In 1968 she joined the faculty in the English department at Eastern Michigan in Ypsilanti, Michigan, where she became professor emeritus in 1984.

Covering a span of thirty-one years, her poems have been published in a number of anthologies, including Langston Hughes and Arna Bontemps's *The Poetry of the Negro, 1746–1949* (1949), Robert Hayden's *Kaleidoscope* (1967), Carol Koner and Dorothy Walters's, *I Hear My Sisters Saying* (1976), and Dexter Fisher's *The Third Woman* (1980). Her first collection of poems, *Songs to a Phantom Nightingale* (1941), appeared under the name Naomi Cornelia Long. Her subsequent collections include *One and the Many* (1956), *Star by Star* (1965; rev. ed. 1970), *Pink Ladies in the Afternoon* (1972, 1990), *Exits and Entrances* (1978), and *Octavia and Other Poems* (1988).

The two collections, *Pink Ladies in the Afternoon* and *Exits and Entrances*, were published by Madgett's own publishing house, Lotus Press, located in Detroit. Her publishing house is of indispensable value because it is one of only a handful of black presses in the entire United States. In addition to her own works, she has published collections of poetry by Pinkie Gordon Lane, Haki Madhubuti, E. Ethelbert Miller, and others. Further demonstrating her commitment to the importance of language, she co-edited a high school textbook entitled *Success in Language and Literature—B* (1967) and wrote *A Student's Guide to Creative Writing* (1980).

She has been contributor of poetry to periodicals such as *Negro Digest, Negro History Bulletin, Poetry Digest, Virginia Statesman, Journal of Black Poetry, Ebony,* and *Great Lakes Review.*

Madgett's honors and awards include a Mott Fellowship in English, 1965–1966; the Esther R. Beer Poetry Award; the Josephine Nevins Development Fund Award, 1979; and the Distinguished Service Award, Chesapeake/Virginia Beach Links, Inc., 1981.

For further reading, see *Black American Literature Forum* (Summer 1980); *Black Books Bulletin* (Spring 1974); and Madgett's papers housed in the Special Collections Library at Fisk University.

"The Race Question" comes from *Star by Star* and "Writing a Poem" and "Black Woman" from *Pink Ladies in the Afternoon.*

THE RACE QUESTION

(For one whose fame depends on keeping The Problem a problem)

Would it please you if I strung my tears
In pearls for you to wear?
Would you like a gift of my hands' endless beating
Against old bars?

This time I can forget my Otherness,
Silence my drums of discontent awhile
And listen to the stars.

Wait in the shadows if you choose.
Stand alert to catch
The thunder and first sprinkle of unrest
Your insufficiency demands.
But you will find no comfort.
I will not feed your hunger with my blood
Nor crown your nakedness
With jewels of my elegant pain.

From *Star by Star* by Naomi Long Madgett (Detroit, Harlo, 1965; Evenill, Inc., 1970). Reprinted by permission of the author.

WRITING A POEM

Writing a poem is trying to catch a fluff of cloud
With open-fingered hands.
Slim ghosts of truths, ethereal in twilight's mist,
Glide and evade and dissipate into enormous air.
Making a poem is trying to capture gold-winged
                                butterflies
With only a net of dreams.

BLACK WOMAN

My hair is springy like the forest grasses
That cushion the feet of squirrels—
Crinkled and blown in a south breeze
Like the small leaves of native bushes.

My black eyes are coals burning
Like a low, full jungle moon
Through the darkness of being.
In a clear pool I see my face,
Knowing my knowing.

My hands move pianissimo
Over the music of the night:
Gentle birds fluttering through leaves and grasses
They have not always loved,
Nesting, finding home.

Where are my lovers?
Where are my tall, my lovely princes
Dancing in slow grace
Toward knowledge of my beauty?
Where
Are my beautiful
Black men?

Stephen Henderson

(1925–   )

AN OUTSTANDING figure in the history of African American literary criticism, Stephen E. Henderson has been consistent in his efforts to bring to African American criticism a black aesthetic. The introduction to his *Understanding the New Black Poetry* is a seminal essay that treats the characteristics of black poetry before and after the 1960s. No study of African American literary critical history would be complete without mentioning the influence of Stephen Henderson.

Born on October 13, 1925, in Key West, Florida, he received his A.B. degree from Morehouse College in 1949 and his M.A. and Ph.D. from the University of Wisconsin in 1950 and 1959, respectively. From 1950 to 1962, he taught at Virginia Union University in Richmond. In 1962 he joined the faculty of Morehouse College as professor and chairman of the English department, where he stayed until 1971. His move to Howard University in 1971 marks the beginning of significant changes in the African American literary community.

As director of the Institute for the Arts and Humanities at Howard (from 1973 to 1985), Henderson sponsored five nationwide writers' conferences and two folklore conferences, helped to establish the Association for Afro-American Folklorists, and sponsored a series of interviews with distinguished professors called "The Culture of Social Struggle: A Profile in the Humanities," which documented conversations with such figures as Rayford Logan, Mercer Cook, and Arthur P. Davis. For a short time, the institute published a newsletter and a journal, called *Sagala: A Journal of Art and Ideas,* which remains an indispensable historical source of African American critical issues as well as a documentation of the interplay of politics and academic life. Although the institute is no longer functioning, it has preserved at least eight hundred hours of videotaped programming and many photographs of writers and artists.

Henderson is the author of approximately forty published and unpublished essays. His published essays have appeared separately and many have been collected in books. His most recent publication, "Worrying the Line: Notes on Black Poetry," appears in *The Line in Post-Modern Poetry* (ed. Robert Frank and Henry Sayre, 1988). The anthology *Understanding the New Black Poetry: Black Speech and Black Music as Poetic References* (1972) and the long essay "Survival Motion: A Study of the Black Writer and the Black Revolution in America," found in *The*

Militant Black Writer in Africa and the United States, remain his best-known publications.

Currently professor of African American studies at Howard University, Henderson recently received the Presentation Award from the Institute for the Preservation and Study of African-American Writing. He is also the recipient of a Danforth Research Grant and a Southern Fellowship Fund Grant.

"The Question of Form and Judgment in Contemporary Black American Poetry: 1962–1977" is an abbreviated version of the longer article which previously appeared in *A Dark and Sudden Beauty: Two Essays in Black American Poetry* (1977), a pamphlet edited by Houston A. Baker, Jr.

THE QUESTION OF FORM AND JUDGEMENT
IN CONTEMPORARY BLACK AMERICAN POETRY
1962–1977

For one reason or another, the question of how to judge a Black poem has been fudged, blurred, evaded, or ignored. Now that the spectacular Black Arts Movement seems to have run its course, the question of evaluation takes on crucial importance. Among the signs that the movement is over, or is entering a new phase, are the demise of *Black World* magazine, the most important cultural periodical of the Black Consciousness Movement: the intensified sniping by scholars, Black and white, who disagreed with the idea of a Black Aesthetic; the systematic efforts by white scholars either to blunt, appropriate, or discredit the artistic achievements of the sixties, and their attendant critical justifications; and the defection of important writers to other camps, both aesthetic and political.

Although sniping at the Black Aesthetic is not new, its critics have not relented. In some instances, the concern is largely scholarly, as in the case of Arthur P. Davis, for example. In others, it is essentially polemical. Whether scholarly or not, reactions to the Black Aesthetic rest overtly or implicitly on a political base. At any rate, no one can accuse Prof. Davis of inconsistency, for throughout his long and distinguished career he has made plain his views on integration, on American literature, and the role which Black writers have played in shaping that literature. Yet the achievement of *From the Dark Tower*, 1974, his recent admirable history, is marred by his failure to grapple with the hard issues raised by the Black Aesthetic.

Reprinted by permission of the author.

He lumps all of the critics together, calls them honorable men, but asserts that to date they have failed either to destroy the white aesthetic or to erect another in its place. So, then, the question remains a matter of ranking authors according to their craftsmanship, their thematic concerns, in historical and social context, or the size of their output. Prof. Davis solves the problem of judgment by avoidance or oversimplification.

Another example of scholarly fudging is found in Roger Rosenblatt's recent book *Black Fiction*. He disposes of the problem of judgment by a retreat into formalism. The social issues are not important—technique is technique and pattern is pattern. Although he discusses fiction, not poetry, many of the issues are the same. Professor Rosenblatt solves the problem of judgment by ignoring it.

In Helen Vendler's review of a series of Broadside books for the *New York Times Book Review*, Sept. 29, 1974, liberal sympathy is tempered by unconscious liberal condescension which reveals an essential ignorance of the issues involved in the Black Aesthetic in general and in the evaluation of Black poetry in particular. After praising the range and variety of Black "verse" and the pioneering role of Dudley Randall, she expresses the fond hope that in the future some single giant Black poet will unite all of those varied threads and themes in one single giant voice—as Whitman did, for example, for the American nation. What she fails to realize is that the Black epic voice is collective and communal, and it has already achieved what she speaks of, though in forms, perhaps, which she doesn't understand or recognize—in the tales and the spirituals especially, but also in the worksongs and the blues. Prof. Vendler also solves the problem of judgment by oversimplification.

Not so the editors of the *Saturday Review*. They solve it by overkill. In their infamous issue of November 15, 1975 devoted to "The Arts in Black America," the intent is clearly political, clearly designed to give a *coup de grace* to the Black Arts Movement. The article, written by Robert F. Moss, describes the state of the arts in Black America in pathological and racist terms. It links the political problems of FESTAC and the Nigerian government with the author's views on Black art in general. Of the Black Aesthetic, he predicts that it seems "destined to produce more heat than light." But one important by-product, he asserts, has been the building of Black audiences, presumably for legitimate art, that by whites or based on white models. Matters of "form and style" in Black art, he states, "have not really been ignored so much as they have been translated into ethnic terms, and in some cases thoroughly politicized. Black verse is perhaps the most obvious example." (p. 15) He continues: "The elder statesmen among black poets—notably Robert Hayden,

Melvin B. Tolson, and Gwendolyn Brooks—achieved recognition
from the literary establishment by adjusting their timbre and
rhythms, their style and vocabulary, to the requirements of mainstream verse, although their subject matter was sometimes racial.
Perhaps the last important 'accommodationist' was Baraka, a competent beat poet who was beached by the receding currents of that
short-lived movement in the early sixties. Taking the techniques of
Ginsberg & Company—a declamatory voice, deliberate formlessness,
street language—and fusing them to virulent outbursts of racial protest, Baraka was able to found a new school of black poetry." (pp.
15, 16)

It should be apparent that Moss would not think very highly of
that poetry. Speaking of technical matters, Moss states:

> Baraka-ites such as Don L. Lee, Nikki Giovanni, Sonia Sanchez, and
> David Henderson profess to have tossed every scrap of whitey's *ars poe-
> tica*—along with his "diseased civilization"—onto the cultural bonfire.
> In its place they have introduced black consciousness, carefully
> equipped with a black literary technique to articulate it correctly. In
> practice this usually means a free use of obscenities (especially the om-
> nipresent m-f), ghetto slang, phonetic spellings, typographical hijhinks *a
> la* Cummings, a striving after oral effects, and a tone of voice pitched at
> megaphone level. (p. 16)

After examining examples of "verse" that he disagrees with from
Carolyn Rodgers, Don Lee, and Baraka, Moss concludes his observations on Black literary technique with the following:

> Beyond this, there is a taste for black word games like "playing the Doz-
> ens" and "Signifying." Such is the route favored by Ishmael Reed,
> though he is better known as a novelist than a poet. A devout follower
> of William Burroughs' comic surrealism with generous helpings of black
> folklore, pop culture, and ghetto sociology. Despite its imitativeness, his
> writing has a creative energy and a stylistic reach that is beyond most
> black writers today. (p. 17)

An analysis of these views and others will be made later in this essay. Suffice it to say at present that Prof. Moss repeats most of the
cliches which critics of Black art, especially of the poetry, have made
for some time. He adds a special virulence couched in the self-satisfaction of one who feels that he has done his homework and who
knows, in addition, that his views have the editorial support of a
powerful and influential periodical. That does not, of course, make
them either accurate or important.

A further sign of reaction to the Black Consciousness Movement
can be seen in another recent book by a white scholar,—*Folklore in
Nigerian Literature*, 1973, by Bernth Lindfors. Lindfors' book is rela-

vant to our discussion for several reasons: (a) the aggressive, defensive tone of the introduction; (b) the rejection of white critics of their literature by both African and Afro-American critics; and (c) the theoretical implications of some of the chapters, especially the two listed under "Critical Perspectives" (p. 6, p. 23) and the one under "Rhetoric," entitled "Characteristics of Yoruba and Ibo Prose Styles in English." (p. 153)

Like numerous other white critics of "black" literature, Lindfors is concerned about the "territorial imperative" which Black critics asserted during the sixties. Lindfors quotes a statement which I made in *The Militant Black Writer*, 1969, that "despite the proliferation of 'experts,' whites are unable to evaluate the Black Experience, and, consequently, any work of art derived from it or addressed to those who live it." He adds: "Whites should therefore abandon the field to blacks, who are innately better qualified to understand and appreciate their own literature." (p. 1)

Lindfors calls attention to a similar rejection of white critics by African writers. Then he proceeds to some tacky logic and linguistic sleight of hand. "While these statements condemning the incompetence of white critics are not as extreme as those heard in America today, they do point in the same racial direction: black critics are acclaimed as the best possible interpreters of their own literature." (p. 1) And Prof. Lindfors gives what he calls the "standard reply" to these views.

> A favorite tactic is to reverse the argument by asking "Should all the black critics—and this includes Africans as well as Afro-Americans and teachers and professors of literature throughout the world—be given a similar 'hands off' ultimatum on non-black writing?"

"An affirmative answer to this question," Lindfors concludes, "would be very hard to justify." And, one might add, hardly worth the time.

The reactions cited above have one important common factor: They substitute for the question "How does one judge a Black poem?" the related question "*Who* is to judge a Black poem?" While the substitution reveals a great deal about those who make it, it nonetheless leaves the prior question unanswered. To repeat, then, How does one judge a Black poem?

Curiously, very few answers were given to that question during the sixties. The responses among Blacks tended to be mystical, ideological, defensive, or hostile. Among whites, they tended and still tend to be condescending, defensive or preemptive, when not narrowly or naively academic. At any rate, there has been poor and uninformed criticism written by Blacks and whites alike. And, conversely, there has been on occasion, some useful criticism by

Blacks, less frequently by whites. (A major exception is the important study of Baraka, *The Renegade and the Mask*, 1976, by Kimberly Benston.) Older Black poets and poets who are not Nationalists have stated that they would rather be reviewed by a good white critic than by a poor Black one. And writers as diverse as Frank Marshall Davis, Robert Hayden, and Clarence Major have said that they were not especially writing for a Black audience.

To begin with, the question of judgment is tied up with the question of definition. What is a Black poem? What is Black poetry? In *Understanding the New Black Poetry*, Morrow, 1973, I made an approach to that question in a series of statements, which I repeat below. These statements may be approached in an historical or empirical manner. In either case, one could say with varying degrees of validity that Black poetry is chiefly:

Any poetry by any person or group of persons of known Black African ancestry, whether the poetry is designated Black or not.

Poetry which is somehow structurally Black, irrespective of authorship.

Poetry by any person or group of known Black African ancestry, which is also identifiably Black, in terms of structure, theme, or other characteristics.

Poetry by any identifiably Black person who can be classed as a "poet" by Black people. Judgment may or may not coincide with judgments of whites.

Poetry by any identifiably Black person whose ideological stance vis-a-vis history and the aspirations of his people since slavery is adjudged by them to be "correct." (p. 7)

Since an empirical approach has the advantage of historical anchorage and verifiability, let us place that perspective on the foregoing statements. Again, since I have discussed the implications of these statements in *Understanding the New Black Poetry*, I shall not pursue them here. Nevertheless, when the statements are examined from this perspective one must consider the following items: (a) What the record or canon says, (b) What the poets say, (c) What the reader/audience/critic says, and (d) The notion of standards and evaluation. In the following pages, I shall address each of these items in some detail.

a. What the record reveals is a rich tradition of both oral and written poetry which is usefully designated the folk and the formal. In the United States the oral traditions go back to the emergence of distinctive Afro-American verbal expression—the field cries and hol-

lers, work songs, ballads, spirituals, sermons, and blues. The size of
this literature though not so complex as that of the West Indies or
Africa is enormous. John Lovell, Jr. estimates the number of spirituals alone at over 10,000, with no way of knowing how many were
not recorded. The tradition continues today in children's songs, in
rapping, the dozens and its contemporary descendants, in the sermon, and in gospel and pop songs at their best. But gospel and pop
songs are individually composed and written down, so here the oral
tradition merges with that of the formal literary tradition. The literary tradition itself dates back to Lucy Terry's *Bars Fight,* 1746, a
long ballad of historical rather than literary merit, and to Jupiter
Hammon and Phillis Wheatley.

The nineteenth century produced dozens of published poets,
some of significant talent. Notable among them were George Moses
Horton, Charles L. Reason, Frances E. W. Harper, and Alberry A.
Whitman. An introduction to these writers can be obtained from
Benjamin Brawley's *Early American Negro Writers;* William H. Robinson's *Early Black American Poets;* Sterling A. Brown's *Negro Poetry
and Drama,* and *The Negro Caravan* edited with Arthur P. Davis and
Ulysses Lee. An important work in this area is Joan Sherman's recent
book *The Invisible Poets.* In addition, there are individual volumes
which are listed in Sherman's bibliographies and in checklists by Arthur Schomburg and Dorothy L. Porter.

Paul Laurence Dunbar, W. E. B. Du Bois, and James Weldon
Johnson open the twentieth century. Their work was followed by
Langston Hughes, Claude McKay, Jean Toomer, Sterling Brown,
Countee Cullen, and the various poets of the New Negro Movement.
The next generation produced Margaret Walker, Owen Dodson,
Gwendolyn Brooks, Robert Hayden, and others. Some of these poets
were active in the fifties and the sixties. And, of course, the 1960's
produced a veritable explosion of Black poetry, with such notable
names as Amiri Baraka, Larry Neal, Sonia Sanchez, Nikki Giovanni,
Don L. Lee (Haki Madhubuti), and others. Much of the work of this
period has probably never been published so no one has a complete
picture of the phenomenon. Notwithstanding, one can easily acquaint himself with this poetry by reading the individual volumes
published by Broadside Press, Paul Bremen Press, and by major publications such as *The Journal of Black Poetry; Liberator; Negro Digest/
Black World; Soul Book; Black Creations;* and *Umbra.* Some journals
had limited, regional circulation, such as college publications like *Ex
Umbra.* Some poets printed their works themselves. Many of these
are listed in *Negro Digest/Black World.* Other sources include useful
anthologies such as *Soul Script,* June Jordan; *Dices and Black Bones,*
Adam David Miller; *Natural Process,* Tom Weatherly and Ted Wil-

lenz; *Understanding the New Black Poetry,* S. E. Henderson; *The Black Poets,* Dudley Randall; *The New Black Poetry,* Clarence Major. Current publishers of Black poetry include *First World, Essence, Black Arts South, Yardbird Reader, Black Books Bulletin,* etc. In addition, Black poetry is being published at workshops, on campuses, etc., as well as by white publishers. At any rate, this brief account merely hints at the corpus of poetry produced by Black Americans. To this (if one were talking about the entire range of modern Black poetry) could be added the poetry published in English by Caribbean and African poets living in the United States. Less tenable, but logical, would be the addition of all poetry in English by Africans on the continent and in the Dispersion. While that could be done and, eventually, must be done, the problem of focus would thereby be greatly increased. Thus for the purpose of this study, Black poetry must be studied in historical context—with Black people in the United States as the focus. The justification for this is simple. Modern Black formal poetry has existed longer in the United States than it has in Africa or the West Indies (cf. Jahn, *Neo-African Literature,* p. 50, Table 1). In addition, the poetry of the Harlem Renaissance helped stimulate the flowering of modern Black Poetry in Africa, Europe, and the West Indies, during the Negritude Movement. With that in mind, one could still benefit from studying work produced in Africa and the West Indies, not only in English, but in Portuguese, French, Dutch, Spanish as well as the various African languages. Conversely, any serious and extended study of the oral tradition of Afro-American poetry must recognize the vast resources of that tradition in Africa and the West Indies. This includes not only traditional materials but popular contemporary expression as well.

b. What the poets say. Historically, the question of what constitutes a Black poem or how to judge one does not really come to a head until the 1960's and the promulgation of the Black Aesthetic in literature and the other arts. In a special sense, then, "Black" poetry was invented in the 1960's along with the radicalization of the word "Black" and the emergence of the Black Power philosophy. From the beginning, however, there were problems of definition, contradiction, ideology, and taste, resulting from differences in personal background and in political and cultural orientation. In the January 1968 issue of *Negro Digest,* Hoyt Fuller, the Executive Editor, conducted a survey of the opinions of 38 Black writers on some 25 questions which included the following:

Do you see any future at all for the school of black writers which seeks to establish "a black aesthetic"?

Do you believe that the black writer's journey toward "Art" should lead consciously and deliberately through exploitation of "the black experience"?

Should black writers direct their work toward black audiences?

Some older writers, like Robert Hayden, felt that a writer's chief concern should be with the truth of all people everywhere. Others stressed craftsmanship and felt that writers should write to be read. Others felt enthusiastically that they should write about what they knew best, themselves and their people. There was, in effect, no simple consensus as to what Black writing was, could be, or should be, though there was fairly general agreement that Black writers should write about Black people, for Black people, and sometimes for sympathetic whites. Some younger writers were immersed in the self-consciousness of other "modern" writers; others still were rigidly nationalistic. The split among the younger writers was best exemplified in an exchange between Ron Karenga, of US and James Cunningham of OBAC. Their views were polar. Karenga set forth his famous and influential dicta that literature must be functional, collective, and committing, and must support the Revolution. Cunningham felt that the writer should be free to express himself.

Perhaps the most insightful statement in the *Negro Digest* survey was made by Larry Neal. On the question of the Black Aesthetic, he said:

> There is no need to establish a "black aesthetic." Rather, it is important to understand that one already exists. The question is: where does it exist? And what do we do with it. Further, there is something distasteful about a formalized aesthetic. This is what the so-called New Critics never understood. Essentially, art is relevant when it makes you stronger. (p. 35)

In that opening statement Neal not only demonstrated an understanding of the aesthetic questions under discussion but also an extensive grasp of the roots of Afro-American art, thereby linking up with a tradition of "criticism" which includes James Weldon Johnson, W. E. B. Du Bois, Alain Locke, and Sterling Brown. That was an important linkage, for it not only insured historical continuity but kept the field of discussion open to a wide range of approaches. At the same time that it claimed for the poet much of the personal freedom which Cunningham advocated, it insisted on the wider dedication advocated by Ron Karenga. But this was done with a greater degree of subtlety, as, for example in his sensitive understanding of the blues and the central importance of the Black Church.

c. The Reader/Critic/Audience. Specifically, the question of the poet's audience was crucial to the sixties. It was encapsulated in the

Negro Digest survey. The response ranged from Karenga's paraphrase of Senghor that art is "functional, collective and committing or committed," to Gwendolyn Brooks' shrewd comment that Black writers "should concern themselves with TRUTH." Truth should be put upon paper. That phrase, 'direct their work,' she said in reference to the questionnaire, "suggests a secret contempt for the intelligence of the black audience." (p. 29) Some other writers hedged their bets, writing for ideal audiences, or for anyone who would buy their books. But the question was not altogether new, nor the consciousness. Langston Hughes had said to a similar question posed in 1927 by *Crisis* magazine, "We younger Negro artists who create now intend to express our individual dark-skinned selves without fear or shame. If white people are pleased we are glad. If they are not, it doesn't matter. We know we are beautiful. And ugly too. The tomtom cries and the tom-tom laughs. If colored people are pleased we are glad. If they are not, their displeasure doesn't matter either. We build our temples for tomorrow, strong as we know how, and we stand on top of the mountain, free within ourselves" ("The Negro Artist and the Racial Mountain"). What is often overlooked in this passage is an individualism that borders on "Art for Art's sake."

But Langston Hughes also pioneered some of the techniques of direct audience communication which were to become popular in the sixties. His readings with jazz accompaniment, his strong sense of the aural tradition, of the preacher and the musician, of the oral tradition of the raconteur and the rapper, provided a strong model. So that Larry Neal was to say in the sixties:

> To explore the black experience means that we do not deny the reality and the power of the slave culture; the culture that produced the blues, spirituals, folk songs, work songs, and "jazz." It means that Afro-American life and its myriad of styles are expressed and examined in the fullest, most truthful manner possible. The models for what Black literature should be are found primarily in our folk culture, especially in the blues and jazz. Further models exist in the word-magic of James Brown, Wilson Pickett, Stevie Wonder, Sam Cooke, and Aretha Franklin. Have you ever heard a Black poet scream like James Brown? I mean, we should want to have that kind of energy in our work. The kind of energy that informs the music of John Coltrane, Cecil Taylor, Albert Ayler, and Sun Ra—the modern equivalent of the ancient ritual energy. An energy that demands to be heard, and which no one can ignore. Energy to shake us out of our lethargy and free our bodies and minds, opening us to unrealized possibilities. (*Negro Digest*, p. 81)

Again at this point one sees Neal's understanding of and linkage to the tradition of W. E. B. Du Bois, James Weldon Johnson, Langston Hughes, Sterling Brown, and Richard Wright. He adds two dimensions: popular music and African ritual. The crucial insight is the realization of Black oral expression as a continuum—in fact, oral expression as part of the larger global continuum of Black expressive culture.

Central to that continuum are music and dance. Small wonder then that when Black poets described what they were trying to do they used the language of these arts. Small wonder still that readers who conceived of poetry in Euro-American terms were unable to come to grips with the new Black poetry. This was true of some older Blacks as well as many white professional critics. Again, that should have surprised no one, for the history of the criticism of Black music and dance is a systematic attempt to deny the original-ity, the power, and the ultimate worth of those forms also. Thus Robert Moss and the others have their tradition too, of denial, pre-sumption, subversion, and neglect.

The beauty and power of Black American poetry, notwithstanding these negative views, have long been recognized. Among the first to bring the oral tradition to national attention was Colonel Thomas Wentworth Higginson, in an article which appeared in the *Atlantic Monthly*, June, 1867, entitled "Negro Spirituals." He points out the verbal as well as the musical beauty of the songs. His reaction to one of the songs has been quoted by W. E. B. Du Bois, James Weldon Johnson, Sterling Brown, and John Lovell, Jr. It is worth quoting again. He stated:

> But of all the "spirituals" that which surprised me the most, I think—perhaps because it was that in which external nature furnished the im-ages most directly—was this. With all my experience of their ideal ways of speech, I was startled when first I came on such a flower of poetry in that dark soil:
>
> XVII. I KNOW MOON-RISE
>
> I know moon-rise, I know star-rise,
>   Lay dis body down.
> I walk in de moonlight, I walk in de starlight,
>   To lay dis body down.
> I'll walk in de graveyard, I'll walk through de graveyard,
>   To lay dis body down.
> I'll lie in de grave and stretch out my arms;
>   Lay dis body down.
> I go to de judgment in de evenin' of de day.
>   When I lay dis body down:
> And my soul and your soul will meet in de day,
>   When I lay dis body down.

"I'll lie in de grave and stretch out my arms." Never, it seems to me, since man first lived and suffered, was his infinite longing for peace uttered more plaintively than in that line.

Note Higginson's expression—"their ideal ways of speech." It not only furnishes a corrective to the stereotypes created by the minstrel tradition, but provides an important literary insight. For speech is a chief element of anybody's poetry. And here the manner of the speech is noted in a useful way. We shall return later to this point.

Frequently the words of these songs are referred to as poems, as they are in this study. Their composers are also referred to as poets, by Blacks and whites alike. This practice is found not only in Higginson and others who appreciated the slaves' "ideal ways of speech," but by those who satirized the songs on the minstrel stage, and even, as John Lovell brings to our attention, on the concert stage.

At any rate, the language posed a challenge to the serious collector and the casual listener alike. There were problems of intelligibility and of transcription. Regarding the latter, Y. S. Nathanson recounts his difficulty in transcribing a refrain which imitates a wild turkey's gobble. He concludes that "I am aware that no words can express the rich, unctuous, gutteral flow of the line, when uttered in perfect time by a full gang at their corn-shucking task."

In "Song of the Slaves," John Mason Brown observes:

> To convey a correct idea of negro pronunciation by ordinary rules of orthography is almost impossible. Combinations that would satisfy the ear would be grotesquely absurd to the eye. The habits of the negro in his pronunciation of English words are not such as minstrelsy would indicate. Just as the French and German characters in our comedies have passed into a conventional form of mispronunciation which the bulk of playgoers firmly believe to be lifelike and true, so have minstrels given permanency to very great mistakes in reproducing negro pronunciation. (*Lippincott's Magazine*, II, Philadelphia, December, 1868, 617–623)

The problem confronted Black scholars and poets also, just as it was to confront poets of the 1960's and the present decade. Paul Laurence Dunbar, for example, wrote in a dialect tradition popularized by whites, although his orthography was more idealized than satirical or fanciful. James Weldon Johnson wrote "coon songs" in the white manner of his time, but later turned to a serious confrontation of the problem of rendering the sounds of Black speech and song. In his two collections of Negro spirituals, *The Book of American Negro Spirituals,* 1925, and *The Second Book of Negro Spirituals,* 1926, he indicated the importance of preserving the original pronunciation of the words, and in the preface to the first volume, he discussed serious questions of dialect, voice timbre, and poetry, with informed sensitivity. Like John Mason Brown before him, he attacks visual grotesqueries masquerading as speech.

> Negro dialect is for many people made unintelligible on the printed page by the absurd practice of devising a clumsy, outlandish, so-called phonetic spelling for words in a dialect story or poem when the regular English spelling represents the very same sound. Paul Laurence Dunbar did a great deal to reform the writing down of dialect, but since it is more a matter of ear than of rules those who are not intimately familiar with the sounds continue to make the same blunders. (*The Book of American Negro Spirituals*, James Weldon Johnson and J. Rosamond Johnson, Viking Press, 1940, p. 38)

Later, Johnson spoke thus of his intent and method in his volume *God's Trombones*, 1927. These poems were sermons in the folk manner. He wanted to go beyond the limitations of dialect with its twin stops of pathos and humor. What he wanted was "a form that will express the racial spirit by symbols from within rather than by symbols from without, such as the mere mutilation of English spelling and pronunciation." The form would be "freer and larger than dialect, but which will still hold the racial flavor; a form expressing the imagery, the idioms, the peculiar turns of thought, and the distinctive humor and pathos, too, of the Negro, but which will also be capable of voicing the deepest and highest emotions and aspirations, and allow of the widest range of subjects and the widest scope of treatment." (*The Book of American Negro Poetry*, pp. 41, 42)

But Johnson, like others, was acutely aware of the difficulties involved in developing this form. Earlier, he had said of the spirituals:

> What can be said about the poetry of the texts of the Spirituals? Naturally, not so much as can be said about the music. In the use of the English language both the bards and the group worked under limitations that might appear to be hopeless. Many of the lines are less than trite, and irrelevant repetition often becomes tiresome. They are often saved alone by their naivete. And yet there is poetry, and a surprising deal of it in the Spirituals. There is more than ought to be reasonably expected from a forcedly ignorant people working in an absolutely alien language. (*The Book of American Negro Spirituals*, p. 38)

And Thomas W. Talley makes the point with a Black anecdote. Speaking of the secular rhymes, he observes:

> When critically measured by the laws and usages governing the best English poetry, Negro Folk Rhymes will probably remind readers of the story of the good brother, who arose solemnly in a Christian praise meeting, and thanked God that he had broken all of the Commandments, but had kept his religion. (*Negro Folk Rhymes*, p. 228)

Note Johnson's use of the terms "racial spirit" and "racial flavor" as well as the more explicit reference to "imagery," "idioms," and "peculiar turns of thought." Note, too, the humorous but meaningful use of the term "religion" by Talley. To this one might add a remark by an experienced preacher from the folk tradition. When his language was questioned by his self-consciously academic brothers in the seminary, he stated: "A verb is like a nut. You got to crack it to get the goodie out of it." And Sterling Brown reports an encounter with a young minister at Virginia Seminary, in 1923, when he took his first job, teaching English. He was so exacting in his grading that the students called him a "red ink man." The exasperated seminarian said to him one day, "Prof., you run them verbs, and I'll drive the thought." And Brown concedes, "He could drive the thought."

And a few years later James Weldon Johnson wrote the preface to Sterling Brown's masterly first volume of poems *Southern Road*. He said:

> He infused his poetry with genuine characteristic flavor by adopting as his medium the common, racy, living speech of the Negro in certain phases of *real* life. For his raw material he dug down into the deep mine of Negro folk poetry. He found the unfailing sources from which sprang the Negro folk epics and ballads such as "Stagolee," "John Henry," "Casey Jones," "Long Gone John" and others.

> But as I said in commenting on his work in *The Book of American Negro Poetry*: he has made more than mere transcriptions of folk poetry, and he has done more than bring to it mere artistry; he has deepened its meanings and multiplied its implications. He has actually absorbed the spirit of his material, made it his own; and without diluting its primitive frankness and raciness, truly re-expressed it with artistry and magnified power. In a word, he has taken this raw material and worked it into original authentic poetry.

In other words, Sterling Brown had achieved the kind of form that Johnson himself had spoken of and had experimented with in *God's Trombones*.

Johnson had singled out other young poets for special mention. Among them were Claude McKay, Jean Toomer, Countee Cullen, and Langston Hughes. Even a cursory examination of their work would reveal a wide range of styles, technique, subject matter, and tone, from the Romantic sonorities of Cullen to the jazzy rhythms of Hughes. Yet they had something in common, their concern with "race" and their response to it. Johnson states, "In their approach to 'race' they are less direct and obvious, less didactic or imploratory; and, too, they are less regardful of the approval or disapprobation of their white environment." ("Preface" to *Southern Road*, p. xxxvi)

These statements of Johnson's, taken together with other observations of his, pose most of the larger critical questions of Black poetry, questions of range, theme, form and structure, and judgment. As far as the theme is concerned, that which makes it Black is "race," in his words, "the principal motive of poetry written by Negroes . . ." (xxvi) As for form and structure, they are found in "the deep mine of Negro folk poetry." (xxxvi) Yet he includes the sonnets of Claude McKay and Countee Cullen and the free verse odes of Jean Toomer, all written in "standard English." And we may recall some of the difficulty which Johnson experienced with the language of the spirituals, a difficulty not really unlike that encountered by the white collector John Mason Brown. Not merely the problem of orthography, but of poetic expression. Notwithstanding the beauty of the music, the difficulty of working in an unfamiliar language caused the slaves to produce many lines which "are less than trite, and irrelevant repetition often becomes tiresome. They are often saved alone by their naivete." Yet Johnson makes critical judgments, both of the spirituals, and, as we have seen, of the formal poets, of whom the "Younger Group" received his special blessings.

On what basis was Johnson able to distinguish the excellent from the trite in this vastly varied body of material? Obviously he had some means, some measure, some touchstone that would allow him to accept both the Keatsean lushness of Cullen, the sonorous language of the sermons, and the transcendent simplicity of the spirituals. Johnson himself suggests something of his mechanism, his method, and his considerations in several places, among them the two works previously cited and in his *Autobiography of an Ex-Coloured Man*. The mechanism included a reliance upon the ear rather than the eye, for example, and he states:

> Paul Laurence Dunbar did a great deal to reform the writing down of dialect, but since it is more a matter of ear than of rules those who are not intimately familiar with the sounds continue to make the same blunders.

This reliance upon the ear includes a deep and sympathetic and sensitive knowledge and love of music, not only that of his own people but of other cultures as well. He could thus say with complete assurance of the motif of the spiritual "Go Down Moses" ("Preface," *The Book of American Negro Spirituals*, p. 13):

> I have termed this music noble, and I do so without qualifications. Take, for example *Go Down Moses*; there is not a nobler theme in the whole musical literature of the world. If the Negro had voiced himself in only that one song, it would have been evidence of his nobility of soul.

And his knowledge of Black music ran the gamut, from the work songs and the spirituals to ragtime and the newly emergent jazz. Black music, he says in effect, is the touchstone of Black art. And the touchstone can be applied also to the creative work of other cultures. This is implicit in the statement above. It is more explicit in his poetic statement in "O Black and Unknown Bards."

But Johnson certainly did not slight the verbal component of the songs. He recognized the poetry in their very titles. Although later scholarship has demonstrated that he overstated his case for the originality of the spirituals, it is still essentially correct.

> The white people among whom the slaves lived did not originate anything comparable even to the mere titles of the Spirituals. In truth, the power to frame the poetic phrases that make the titles of so many of the Spirituals betokens the power to create the songs. Consider the sheer magic of:
>
>> Swing Low Sweet Chariot
>> I've Got to Walk My Lonesome Valley
>> Steal Away to Jesus
>> Singing With a Sword in My Hand
>> Rule Death in His Arms
>> Ride on King Jesus
>> We Shall Walk Through the Valley in Peace
>> The Blood Came Twinklin' Down
>> Deep River
>> Death's Goin' to Lay His Cold, Icy Hand on Me
>
> and confess that none but an artistically endowed people could have evoked it.
>
> No one has even expressed a doubt that the poetry of the titles and text of the Spirituals is Negro in character and origin, no one else has dared to lay claim to it; why then doubt the music? ("Preface," pp. 15, 16)

Of course, even the texts were later disputed by George Pullen Jackson. And Johnson's protege, the young Sterling Brown, was to make the final point with his characteristic wit:

> In bringing forth proof that in words and melody many Negro spirituals are traceable to white songs, southern white scholars have succeeded in disproving the romantic theory of completely African origin for the spirituals. All of those who assiduously collect evidence grant, however, that now the Negro song is definitely the Negro's regardless of ultimate origin, and one of them writes as follows: "The words of the best White Spirituals cannot compare as poetry with the words of the best Negro spirituals." It remains to be said that for the best Negro spirituals, camp-meeting models remain to be discovered. (*Negro Poetry and Drama,* p. 17)

d. The notion of standards and evaluation. I have taken thus long to suggest the outlines of this argument on the originality and the

power of Black folk poetry for two reasons: (1) the poets of the sixties claim a kinship with this poetry and music; and (2) the questions raised cast some light on the latter body of poetry, some of the
disputes, some of the achievement, and some of the promise.

Some of the dispute over recent Black poetry is traceable to the
experimental nature of much of it, and it follows that this dispute is
not necessarily racial in character. For example, Robert F. Moss's reference to the "typographical hijinks" of e. e. cummings, or W. E.
Farrison's peevish dismissal of similar experimentation in his review
of Beatrice Murphy's anthology of young Negro poets. White critics,
of course, have dismissed white writers in much the same manner.
And, of course, one remembers the furor raised over Alan Ginsberg's
"Howl" and, earlier, over Walt Whitman's *Leaves of Grass*, to name
two works at random.

But the reaction goes deeper than mere resistance to change and
experimentation. It seems rooted in white America's perception of
the lives and culture of Black Americans, which has been marked by
distortion, and by a continuing and systematic attempt to ridicule, to
deny, to absorb, or to appropriate that culture. Specifically, both traditions of Afro-American poetry have long been under siege, and just
to mention Black poetry is to evoke a history of white critical condescension and snobbery, and more recently, outright pathological ignorance and fear. The roots of this reaction are deep and pervasive.
They are entwined in nineteenth-century attempts to justify slavery
by proving the innate inferiority of the African slave. They are entwined in the African's supposed inability to master the "difficult"
European languages. They are entwined in the questioning of the
African's very humanity. (Cf. Thomas Jefferson on the African and
Greek verb, or on Benjamin Banneker.) They are likewise entwined
in European conceptions of the poet and poetry—the poet as maker,
or prophet, or divine madman; the poetry as sacred text or as edify-
ing verbal diversion, producing pleasure.

Since a poem is made of words and since the slave was incapable
of mastering the "difficult" English tongue, how could one take seriously the idea of a Black American poet? Most did not. A few did, as
the history of the early poets, Jupiter Hammond [sic], Phillis Wheatley, and George Moses Horton attests. But essentially they were cu-
riosities. Phillis Wheatley was a successful experiment to test the
strength of nurture vs. nature; and Hammond and Horton were
sports of nature (which was, indeed, one eighteenth century definition of genius).

Other early poets took as their central aim the vindication of
their race from calumny and, indeed, the larger task of Liberation
through appealing to the conscience of the ruling whites. This ap-

peal ranged from direct protest to demonstrations of worthiness as evinced by learning and by mastery of the craft of poetry. Thus Albery A. Whitman justifies his use of the difficult Spenserian stanza, the " 'stately verse', mastered only by Spenser, Byron, and a very few other great poets," because, "Some negro is sure to do everything that anyone else has ever done, and as none of that race have ever executed a poem in the 'stately verse,' I simply venture in" (quoted by J. Sherman, p. 12).

This emphasis on craftsmanship is historically quite important. It shows the Black poet reflecting the same kind of concerns as other gifted Black individuals. It also shows a continuing need to test oneself according to white standards, and sometimes to receive white praise. Whitman treasured the praise he received from Bryant, just as Phillis Wheatley had treasured the praise of the literati of her day. And decades later, W. D. Howells was to praise Paul Laurence Dunbar in the same liberal manner. Later still Gwendolyn Brooks was awarded a Pulitzer prize for her technical mastery of the forms of Modernist poetry, and Karl Shapiro and Allen Tate were to praise Melvin B. Tolson for having assimilated the language of the Anglo-Saxon poetic tradition and for writing in "Negro" at the same time.

All of this was the recognition of individuals, not of a tradition. Indeed, the attempt has been from the outset to ignore, absorb, or to destroy the tradition in both its folk and formal dimensions. Despite this, however, the beauty and power of the tradition have been recognized by many, even though grudgingly at times.

As I have suggested, a good deal of the confusion comes from the variety of the poetry itself. Some comes from the desire of certain poets to be free from racial identification which implied inferiority of achievement or judgment by less rigorous standards. Some too comes from certain poets' unwillingness to be limited to writing on racial themes. One certainly thinks of Cullen, Hayden, Oden, Major, and others.

The central concern seems to be the assumption that poetry which can be identified as Black is "racist" or inferior or un-American, so that one pretends that race is unimportant or that Black poetry is merely a fad or a bad imitation of experimental white poetry (as the Robert Moss analysis states). All of this, of course, is nonsense. Black poetry can and should be judged by the same standards that any other poetry is judged by—by those standards which validly arise out of the culture. Some of it is good, some excellent, and some downright bad. Much of this awareness has been expressed by the poets themselves, some of whom are excellent critics, like Lance Jeffers, Ethelbert Miller, Sarah Fabio, June Jordan, Margaret Walker, and Carolyn Rodgers to name but a few.

At any rate, scattered throughout their interviews, their essays, and their conversations, there are many critical pronouncements by Black poets themselves. Similarly, there are the pronouncements and preferences of their readers and their audiences, including professional scholars and critics, white, Black, and other. Whether the poets approve or not is now certainly irrelevant since their work has beome part of the general consciousness. And that consciousness has been formed by the media, both the national institutions and myths, and by the educational system, both public and private. That, of course, is obvious. What is less obvious is the extent to which the Black reader/audience/poet has been shaped by these forces and, further still, and more important, how they have created and synthesized a special consciousness out of their special history and experience.

Thus we have the phenomenon of Tolson out-Pounding Pound and critics and scholars employing constructs derived from English, European, or American literature to evaluate Black literature. There is nothing necessarily wrong with this. Intellectually, we are to a large extent what we read. And we certainly need not ignore non-Black writing and criticism. Indeed, we do so at our own risk.

Nevertheless, the question, in a practical sense is whether Black poetry can most effectively be understood, experienced, explicated, and encouraged by complete or even major reliance upon methodologies and standards that have evolved out of the larger Euro-American Society. To the extent that we share those values and concerns, then perhaps it should be, for the sake of efficiency and simplicity, especially for those readers who are university trained. Yet we all know that even those of us who are so trained and are accustomed to think in certain academic patterns also react in complex ways to the cultural referents and forms which arise from our Black Experience. Since the poetry often consciously or unconsciously draws upon this dual heritage one would expect a useful critical method to do likewise. Accordingly, if one were to approach the work of the past fifteen years one could begin at whatever intellectual locus he may inhabit and push toward the central experience of the poem. Easily a good deal of the work is approachable in this way, much of early Baraka, for example.

Notwithstanding, we are soon confronted with the ambiguities and densities which make up a wide range of the poems, which make up, in effect, the blackness of the poems. Some of these elements can be explicated through historical and cultural study. Others have to be experienced because they are "saturated" in Black Experience and these may include some which are written in so-called "Standard English."

Let us recall that there are two large categories of Black poetry of this period: (a) the political poetry of Black Power, and (b) the cultural poetry of the Black Experience. Although these categories overlap, they are by no means congruent, and writers shift from one to the other, sometimes without much clarity.

At any rate, purpose is important. The object of a Black Power poem is to raise Black people's consciousness. The classic statement is given by Ron Karenga in his paraphrase of Leopold Senghor and in Baraka's "Black Art." These poems were often frankly propagandistic and, technically speaking, quite often not very interesting. They were meant to be "throw-away" poems. Perhaps then, they should be examined in this light—they were raps for the occasion, and the occasion was the Revolution.

But all of these were not raps, and certainly not deficient either in execution or in delivery. Excellent examples can be found in Touré, Baraka, Neal, Lee, Sanchez, the Last Poets, Ahmed A. Alhamisi, and elsewhere. And one needs to observe that many great poems of the West were highly political in their time, among them the *Divine Comedy* and *Paradise Lost*. So it does not follow that Black Power poems had to be shoddy or trite. In fact, there is a "revolutionary obligation" to make the poem as good as one can. Too, many of these poems were written by non-poets, by ordinary people in a state of excitement and fervor which they felt compelled to express. This was not a function of education or class necessarily, though many were obviously written by college students. In a word, then, one should judge these poems in historical context, even that of specific readings and performances where records are available. Did the poet "get over"? That was the criterion. That was all he was trying to do.

The other category of poems was generally more sophisticated and ambitious. They not only wanted to raise consciousness, they also wanted to do it with style, to celebrate Black life and culture, to seek a larger cosmic consciousness, which, at any rate, was black, the Original Blackness.

And they wanted to do this with the energy and subtlety and precision of a John Coltrane or with the people-reaching power of a James Brown. In this regard they were certainly following in a long tradition extending formally back to Dunbar and James Weldon Johnson on one hand and to the spirituals and blues on the other. And behind that to Mother Africa.

The more astute among those poets realized that they were seeking interior models, not archeological revivals of older musical/poetic forms. But what were those forms to be like? How were they to be transmitted, created? They spoke by necessity in metaphoric terms, as Neal's mention of "the modern equivalent of the ancient ritual energy" or "word-magic" or Stanley Crouch's "The Big Feeling." And the object of all of this is, again in Neal's words, "to shake us out of our lethargy and free our bodies and minds, opening us to unrealized possibilities." These "unrealized possibilities," as suggested by the work of Baraka, Damas, June Jordan, Ahlamisi, and many others, go far beyond the narrow political concerns of Black Power to a concern (no less rooted in history) with ultimate philosophical and spiritual questions.

How did the poets approach these problems in terms of craft? How successful have they been? As I have stated in this essay, and at considerable length in others, they employed a wide variety of language, at times drawn from Black speech patterns, at times not. They also through a variety of means—some clever, some clumsy—sought to tap the resources latent in Black music. These are structural considerations, and when they are successful, they form the most striking features of the recent Black poetry.

But again, how successful have these works been? And how do we judge? Essentially on the terms posed by the individual poem. If a love poem is written in blues style, it can be judged against thousands of such poems—from the urban and folk traditions, as well as from the literary versions of Hughes and Sterling Brown. There are individual blues poems which stand up under any critical examination—such as Son House's "Death Letter." For drama, for lyrical intensity and sensual precision it competes favorably with many literary poems. Blues lovers, Black, white, and Japanese, know the traditionally great blues songs—the masterpieces, the legendary sessions, the mind melting lines. Any love poem written in the blues manner has to be measured against the bitter humor of: "I asked her for water and she gave me gasoline." Or the pathos of "I folded my arms, I slowly walked away/She's a good old girl—gotta lay there till judgment day." And the self destructive despair of Tommy Johnson's lines—"Canned heat, canned heat, sure, Lord, killin' me." And the poet's angst has to be measured against "the blues ain't nothin' but a low-down shakey chill." Henry Dumas measured against this standard is successful.

But just as jazz musicians have explored and extended the blues experience through technical means, one must ask whether in an analogous way the poets of the sixties were able to extend the achievement of Langston Hughes and Sterling Brown; or better still, whether they have been able to build on the stylistic dynamics of Black language styles (in speech and song) to create the "word-magic" that they aspired to. Intuitively, I know that some like June Jordan, like Baraka, like Neal, like Jayne Cortez, like Carolyn Rodg-

ers, like Sonia—intuitively, I know that they have. However,
in criticism intuition, though vital, is not enough. The canons, the
categories, the dynamics must be as clear and as reasoned as possible. These must rest on a sound empirical base. Beneath Larry Neal's
"word-magic" lie many subtle and useful linguistic patterns which
merit some critical description and organization, not to restrict the
poet's freedom to invent and to discover, but to serve as a guide, a
framework against which these discoveries may be understood and
appreciated. And in the final analysis, the issue is still the problem
of definition and the problem of control, not only in literature, but
in the life which it refracts and reflects.

Eugenia Collier

(1928–   )

ALTHOUGH SHE is the author of more than thirty-three essays on such noted figures as James Weldon Johnson, Claude McKay, Langston Hughes, Margaret Walker, James Baldwin, Ralph Ellison, Paule Marshall, and Maya Angelou, Eugenia Collier says that she sees herself more as a creative writer than as a critic. Yet, she is so dedicated to the field of African American literature and to teaching that she finds herself unable to turn down offers to write critical essays even though these endeavors distract her from her fiction.

She was born in 1928, in Baltimore, Maryland. Her mother was an elementary school teacher who became principal of her own school, and her father was a physician who left private practice to take a position as the first black director of a health center. While Collier was growing up in Baltimore, her mother commuted to Washington, D.C., where she worked throughout her professional career.

Eugenia Collier received her B.A. in 1948 from Howard University, her M.A. in 1950 from Columbia University, and her Ph.D. in 1976 from the University of Maryland. Her first professional job, interestingly enough, was not in teaching. From 1950–1955 she worked as social worker for the Baltimore City Department of Welfare and for Crownsville State Mental Hospital. From 1955–1967 she was an instructor of English at what was then Morgan State College. In 1967 she left Morgan and joined the faculty at the Community College of Baltimore where she worked until 1974. She has also taught at the University of Maryland in Baltimore County and at Howard University where she stayed ten years before going to Coppin State College. She is presently a full professor of English at Coppin State.

Collier's first published story "Marigolds" appeared in the November 1969 issue of *Negro Digest* and has been anthologized frequently. Her short story "Sweet Potato Pie" has been translated into Russian and French for the Voice of America. She is also co-editor of an anthology of African American literature entitled *Afro-American Writing* (published in 1972, co-edited with Richard Long). Her autobiographical essay "Wanderers in the Wilderness" is forthcoming in *Shooting Star* magazine. And her first novel, tentatively titled "Spread My Wings," based on the true story of an elderly woman held in slavery long after 1865, will be published by Third World Press.

Collier's awards include the Gwendolyn Brooks Fiction Award for "Marigolds" and the Distinguished Writers Award from the Mid-Atlantic Writers Association.

"Marigolds" is reprinted here from the November 1969 issue of *Negro Digest*.

MARIGOLDS

When I think of the home town of my youth, all that I seem to remember is dust—the brown, crumbly dust of late summer—arid, sterile dust that gets into the eyes and makes them water, gets into the throat and between the toes of bare brown feet. I don't know why I should remember only the dust. Surely there must have been lush green lawns and paved streets under leafy shade trees somewhere in town; but memory is an abstract painting—it does not present things as they are but rather as they *feel*. And so, when I think of that time and that place, I remember only the dry September of the dirt roads and grassless yards of the shanty-town where I lived. And one other thing I remember, another incongruency of memory—a brilliant splash of sunny yellow against the dust—Miss Lottie's marigolds.

Whenever the memory of those marigolds flashes across my mind, a strange nostalgia comes with it and remains long after the picture has faded. I feel again the chaotic emotions of adolescence, elusive as smoke, yet as real as the potted geranium before me now. Joy and rage and wild animal gladness and shame become tangled together in the multicolored skein of 14-going-on 15 as I recall that devastating moment when I was suddenly more woman than child, years ago in Miss Lottie's yard. I think of those marigolds at the strangest times; I remember them vividly now as I desperately pass away the time waiting for you, who will not come.

I suppose that futile waiting was the sorrowful background music of our impoverished little community when I was young. The Depression that gripped the nation was no new thing to us, for the black workers of rural Maryland had always been depressed. I don't know what it was that we were waiting for; certainly not for the prosperity that was "just around the corner," for those were white folks' words, which we never believed. Nor did we wait for hard work and thrift to pay off in shining success as the American Dream promised, for we knew better than that, too. Perhaps we waited for a miracle, amorphous in concept but necessary if one were to have the grit to rise before dawn each day and labor in the white man's vineyard until after dark, or to wander about in the September dust offering one's sweat in return for some meager share of bread. But God was chary with miracles in those days, and so we waited—and waited.

We children, of course, were only vaguely aware of the extent of our poverty. Having no radios, few newspapers, and no magazines, we were somewhat unaware of the world outside our community. Nowadays we would be called "culturally deprived" and white people would write books and hold conferences about us. In those days everybody we knew was just as hungry and ill-clad as we were. Poverty was the cage in which we all were trapped, and our hatred of it was still the vague, undirected restlessness of the zoo-bred flamingo who knows instinctively that nature created him to be free.

As I think of those days, I feel most poignantly the tag-end of summer, the bright dry times when we began to have a sense of shortening days and the imminence of the cold.

By the time I was 14 my brother Joey and I were the only children left at our house, the older ones having left home for early marriage or the lure of the city, and the two babies having been sent to relatives who might care for them better than we. Joey was three years younger than I, and a boy, and therefore vastly inferior. Each morning our mother and father trudged wearily down the dirt road and around the bend, she to her domestic job, he to his daily unsuccessful quest for work. After our few chores around the tumbledown shanty, Joey and I were free to run wild in the sun with other children similarly situated.

For the most part, those days are ill-defined in my memory, running together and combining like a fresh water-color painting left out in the rain. I remember squatting in the road drawing a picture in the dust, a picture which Joey gleefully erased with one sweep of his dirty foot. I remember fishing for minnows in a muddy creek and watching sadly as they eluded my cupped hands, while Joey laughed uproariously. And I remember, that year, a strange restlessness of body and of spirit, a feeling that something old and familiar was ending, and something unknown and therefore terrifying was beginning.

One day returns to me with special clarity for some reason, perhaps because it was the beginning of the experience that in some inexplicable way marked the end of innocence. I was loafing under the great oak tree in our yard, deep in some reverie which I have now forgotten except that it involved some secret thoughts of one of the Harris boys across the yard. Joey and a bunch of kids were bored now with the old tire suspended from an oak limb which had kept them entertained for awhile.

"Hey, Lizabeth," Joey yelled. He never talked when he could yell. "Hey, Lizabeth, let's go somewhere."

I came reluctantly from my private world. "Where at, Joey?"

The truth was that we were becoming tired of the formlessness of our summer days. The idleness whose prospect had seemed so beautiful during the busy of spring now had degenerated to an almost desperate effort to fill up the empty midday hours.

"Let's go see can we find us some locusts on the hill," someone suggested.

Joey was scornful. "Ain't no more locusts there. Y'all got 'em all while they was still green."

The argument that followed was brief and not really worth the effort. Hunting locust trees wasn't fun any more by now.

"Tell you what," said Joey finally, his eyes sparkling. "Let's us go over to Miss Lottie's."

The idea caught on at once, for annoying Miss Lottie was always fun. I was still child enough to scamper along with the group over rickety fences and through bushes that tore our already raggedy clothes, back to where Miss Lottie lived. I think now that we must have made a tragicomic spectacle, five or six kids of different ages, each of us clad in only one garment—the girls in faded dresses that were too long or too short, the boys in patchy pants, their sweaty brown chests gleaming in the hot sun. A little cloud of dust followed our thin legs and bare feet as we tramped over the barren land.

When Miss Lottie's house came into view we stopped, ostensibly to plan our strategy but actually to reinforce our courage. Miss Lottie's house was the most ramshackle of all our ramshackle homes. The sun and rain had long since faded its rickety frame siding from white to a sullen gray. The boards themselves seemed to remain upright, not from being nailed together but rather from leaning together like a house that a child might have constructed from cards. A brisk wind might have blown it down, and the fact that it was still standing implied a kind of enchantment that was stronger than the elements. There it stood, and as far as I know is standing yet—a gray rotting thing with no porch, no shutters, no steps, set on a cramped lot with no grass, not even any weeds—a monument to decay.

In front of the house in a squeaky rocking chair sat Miss Lottie's son, John Burke, completing the impression of decay. John Burke was what was known as "queer-headed." Black and ageless, he sat, rocking day in and day out in a mindless stupor, lulled by the monotonous squeak-squawk of the chair. A battered hat atop his shaggy

head shaded him from the sun. Usually John Burke was totally unaware of everything outside his quiet dream world. But if you disturbed him, if you intruded upon his fantasies, he would become
enraged, strike out at you, and curse at you in some strange enchanted language which only he could understand. We children
made a game of thinking of ways to disturb John Burke and then to
elude his violent retribution.

But our real fun and our real fear lay in Miss Lottie herself. Miss
Lottie seemed to be at least a hundred years old. Her big frame still
held traces of the tall, powerful woman she must have been in
youth, although it was now bent and drawn. Her smooth skin was a
dark reddish-brown, and her face had Indian-like features and the
stern stoicism that one associates with Indian faces. Miss Lottie
didn't like intruders either, especially children. She never left her
yard, and nobody ever visited her. We never knew how she managed
those necessities which depend on human interaction—how she ate,
for example, or even whether she ate. When we were tiny children,
we thought Miss Lottie was a witch, and we made up tales, which
we half believed ourselves, about her exploits. We were far too sophisticated now, of course, to believe the witch-nonsense. But old
fears have a way of clinging like cobwebs, and so when we sighted
the tumble-down shack, we had to stop to reinforce our nerves.

"Look, there she," I whispered, forgetting that Miss Lottie could
not possibly have heard me from that distance. "She fooling with
them crazy flowers."

"Yeah, look at 'er."

Miss Lottie's marigolds were perhaps the strangest part of the picture. Certainly they did not fit in with the crumbling decay of the
rest of her yard. Beyond the dusty brown yard, in front of the sorry
gray house, rose suddenly and shockingly a dazzling strip of bright
blossoms, clumped together in enormous mounds, warm and passionate and sun-golden. The old black witch-woman worked on
them all summer, every summer, while the house crumbled and
John Burke rocked. For some perverse reason, we children hated
those marigolds. They interfered with the perfect ugliness of the
place; they were too beautiful; they said too much that we could not
understand; they did not make sense. Something in the vigor with
which the old woman destroyed the weeds intimidated us. It should
have been a comical sight—the old woman with the man's hat on
her cropped white head, leaning over the bright mounds, her big
backside in the air—but it wasn't comical, it was something we
could not name. We had to annoy her by whizzing a pebble into her
flowers or by yelling a dirty word, then dancing away from her rage,
revelling in our youth and mocking her age. Actually, I think it was

the flowers we wanted to destroy, but nobody had the nerve to try it, not even Joey, who was usually fool enough to try anything.

"Y'all git some stones," commanded Joey now, and was met with instant giggling obedience as everyone except me began to gather pebbles from the dusty ground. "Come on, Lizabeth."

I just stood there peering through the bushes, torn between wanting to join the fun and feeling that it was all a bit silly.

"You scared, Lizabeth?"

I cursed and spat on the ground—my favorite gesture of phony bravado. "Y'all children git the stones. I'll show you how to use 'em."

I said before that we children were not really aware of how thick were the bars of our cage. I wonder now, though, whether we were not more aware of it than I thought. Perhaps we had some dim notion of what we were and how little chance we had of being anything else. Otherwise, why would we have been so preoccupied with destruction? Anyway, the pebbles were collected quickly, and everybody looked at me to begin the fun.

"Come on, y'all."

We crept to the edge of the bushes that bordered the narrow road in front of Miss Lottie's place. She was working placidly, kneeling over the flowers, her dark hand plunged into the golden mound. Suddenly "zing"—my expertly-aimed stone cut the head off one of the blossoms.

"Who out there?" Miss Lottie's backside came down and her head came up as her sharp eyes searched the bushes. "You better git!"

We had crouched down out of sight in the bushes, where we stifled the giggles that insisted on coming. Miss Lottie gazed warily across the road for a moment, then cautiously returned to her weeding. "Zing"—Joey sent a pebble into the blooms, and another marigold was beheaded.

Miss Lottie was enraged now. She began struggling to her feet, leaning on a rickety cane and shouting, "Y'all git! Go on home!" Then the rest of the kids let loose with their pebbles, storming the flowers and laughing wildly and senselessly at Miss Lottie's impotent rage. She shook her stick at us and started shakily toward the road crying, "Black bastards, git 'long! John Burke! John Burke, come help!"

Then I lost my head entirely, mad with the power of inciting such rage, and ran out of the bushes in the storm of pebbles, straight toward Miss Lottie, chanting madly, "Old lady witch, fell in a ditch, picked up a penny and thought she was rich!" The children screamed with delight, dropped their pebbles and joined the crazy dance, swarming around Miss Lottie like bees and chanting, "Old lady witch!" while she screamed at us. The madness lasted only a moment, for John Burke, startled at last, lurched out of his chair, and we dashed for the bushes just as Miss Lottie's cane went whizzing at my head.

I did not join the merriment when the kids gathered again under the oak in our bare yard. Suddenly I was ashamed, and I did not like being ashamed. The child in me sulked and said it was all in fun, but the woman in me flinched at the thought of the malicious attack that I had led. The mood lasted all afternoon. When we ate the beans and rice that made supper that night, I did not notice my father's silence, for he was always silent these days, nor did I notice my mother's absence, for she always worked until well into evening. Joey and I had a particularly bitter argument after supper; his exuberance got on my nerves. Finally I stretched out upon the pallet in the room we shared and fell into a fitful doze.

When I awoke, somewhere in the middle of the night, my mother had returned, and I vaguely listened to the conversation that was audible through the thin walls that separated our rooms. At first I heard no words, only voices. My mother's voice was like a cool, dark room in summer—peacefully soothing, quiet. I loved to listen to it; it made things seem all right somehow. But my father's voice cut through hers, shattering the peace.

"Twenty-two years, Maybelle, 22 years," he was saying, "and I ain't got nothing for you, nothing."

"It's all right, honey, you'll git something. Everybody outta work now, you know that."

"It ain't right. Ain't no man oughtta eat his woman's food day in and day out, and see his children running wild. Ain't nothing right about that."

"Honey, you took good care of us when you had it. Ain't nobody got nothing nowadays."

"I ain't talking about nobody else, I'm talking about *me*. God knows I try." My mother said something I could not hear, and my father cried out louder, "What must a man do, tell me that?"

"Look, we ain't starving. I git paid every week, and Miz Ellis is real nice about giving me things. She gonna let me have Mr. Ellis' old coat for you this winter—"

"God damn Mr. Ellis' coat! And God damn his money! You think I want white folks' leavings? God damn, Maybelle"—and suddenly he sobbed, loudly and painfully, and cried helplessly and hopelessly in the dark night. I had never heard a man cry before. I did not know that men ever cried. I covered my ears with my hands but could not cut off the sound of my father's harsh, painful, despairing sobs. My father was a strong man who would whisk a child upon his shoulders and go singing through the house. My father whittled toys for us and laughed so loud that the great oak seemed to laugh with him, and taught us how to fish and hunt rabbits. How could it be that my father was crying? But the sobs went on, unstifled, finally quieting until I could hear my mother's voice, deep and rich, humming softly as she used to hum to a frightened child.

The world had lost its boundary lines. My mother, who was small and soft, was now the strength of the family; my father, who was the rock on which the family had been built, was sobbing like the tiniest child. Everything was suddenly out of tune, like a broken accordion. Where did I fit into this crazy picture? I do not now remember my thoughts, only a feeling of great bewilderment and fear.

Long after the sobbing and the humming had stopped, I lay on the pallet, still as stone with my hands over my ears, wishing that I too could cry and be comforted. The night was silent now except for the sound of the crickets and of Joey's soft breathing. But the room was too crowded with fear to allow me to sleep, and finally, feeling the terrible aloneness of 4 am, I decided to awaken Joey.

"Ouch! What's the matter with you? What you want?" he demanded disagreeably when I had pinched and slapped him awake.

"Come on, wake up."

"What for? Go 'way."

I was lost for a reasonable reply. I could not say, "I'm scared and I don't want to be alone," so I merely said, "I'm going out. If you want to come, come on."

The promise of adventure awoke him. "Going out now? Where at, Lizabeth? What you going to do?"

I was pulling my dress over my head. Until now I had not thought of going out. "Just come on," I replied tersely.

I was out the window and halfway down the road before Joey caught up with me.

"Wait, Lizabeth, where you going?"

I was running as if the furies were after me, as perhaps they were—running silently and furiously until I came to where I had half-known I was headed: to Miss Lottie's yard.

The half-dawn light was more eerie than complete darkness, and in it the old house was like the ruin that my world had become— foul and crumbling, a grotesque caricature. It looked haunted, but I was not afraid because I was haunted, too.

"Lizabeth, you lost your mind?" panted Joey.

I had indeed lost my mind, for all of that summer's smoldering emotions swelled in me and burst—the great need for my mother who was never there, the hopelessness of our poverty and degradation, the bewilderment of being neither child nor woman and yet both at once, the fear unleashed by my father's tears. And these feelings combined in one great impulse toward destruction.

"Lizabeth!"

I leaped furiously into the mounds of marigolds and pulled madly, trampling and pulling and destroying the perfect golden blooms. The fresh smell of early morning and of dew-soaked marigolds spurred me on as I went tearing and mangling and sobbing while Joey tugged my dress or my waist crying, "Lizabeth, stop, please stop!"

And then I was sitting in the ruined little garden among the uprooted flowers, crying and crying, and it was too late to undo what I had done. Joey was sitting beside me, silent and frightened, not knowing what to say. Then, "Lizabeth, look!"

I opened my swollen eyes and saw in front of me a pair of large calloused feet; my gaze lifted to the swollen legs, the age-distorted body clad in a tight cotton night dress, and then the shadowed Indian face surrounded by stubby white hair. And there was no rage in the face now, now that the garden was destroyed and there was nothing any longer to be protected.

"M-miss Lottie!" I scrambled to my feet and just stood there and stared at her.

And that was the moment when childhood faded and womanhood began. That violent, crazy act was the last act of childhood. For as I gazed at the immobile face with the sad, weary eyes, I gazed upon a kind of reality which is hidden to childhood. The witch was no longer a witch but only a broken old woman who had dared to create beauty in the midst of ugliness and sterility. She had been born in squalor and lived in it all her life. Now at the end of that life she had nothing except a falling-down hut, a wrecked body, and John Burke, the mindless son of her passion. Whatever verve there was left in her, whatever there was of love and beauty and joy that had not been squeezed out by life, had been there in the marigolds she had so lovingly tended.

Of course I could not express the things that I knew about Miss Lottie as I stood there awkward and ashamed. The years have put words to the things I knew in that moment, and as I look back upon it, I know that that moment marked the end of innocence. Innocence involves an unseeing acceptance of things at face value, an ignorance of the area below the surface. In that humiliating moment I looked beyond myself and into the depths of another person. This was the beginning of compassion, and one cannot have both compassion and innocence.

The years have taken me worlds away from that time and that place, from the dust and squalor of our lives and from the bright thing that I destroyed in a blind childish striking out at God–knows–what. Miss Lottie died long ago and many years have passed since I last saw her hut, completely barren at last, for despite my wild contrition, she never planted marigolds again. Yet there are times when the image of those passionate yellow mounds returns with a painful poignancy. For one doesn't have to be ignorant and poor to find that life is barren as the dusty roads of our town. And I too have planted marigolds.

Sarah Webster Fabio

(1928–1979)

AN INFLUENTIAL FIGURE in the Black Arts Movement, Sarah Webster Fabio was born in Nashville, Tennessee, in 1928. She received her B.A. in 1946 from Fisk University and her M.A. from San Francisco State College (now University). She taught at Oberlin College, the University of California at Berkeley, and Merritt Junior College in Oakland, California, where Black Panther leader Huey Newton was one of her students.

Poet Sonia Sanchez remembers Sarah Fabio as a very active mother, poet, scholar, teacher, and political activist who invigorated the black community and who organized the first black arts event at Merritt Junior College in Oakland, California. It was at Merritt that she organized the first Black Arts Reading Series in which she invited Ed Bullins, Sonia Sanchez, Haki Madhubuti, and Marvin X to read their poetry. The event was a resounding success. In touch with what was happening with the Black Arts Movement on the East Coast, Fabio was the prime mover in bringing the Black Arts Movement to the people of Oakland and San Francisco. She died an early death from cancer in 1979 at the age of fifty-one.

She is the author of five publications: *Race Results: U.S.A.* (1966), *Black Is a Panther Caged* (1968), *Saga of a Black Man* (1968), *A Mirror: A Soul* (1969), *Black Talk: Soul, Shield, and Sword* (1973). Also included in her canon are two sound recordings: *Boss Soul* and *Soul Ain't, Soul Is*, both recorded by Folkways Records in 1972.

Fabio participated in the First World Festival of Negro Art at Dakar, Senegal, in 1966. Though she lived by today's standards a rather short life and though many writers and scholars who came after the 1960s have heard little of her, her contributions to the Black Arts Movement are important and should never be forgotten. For futher reading, see Eugene Redmond's *Drumvoices* (1976).

The following selection, "Tribute to Duke," is taken from *A Mirror: A Soul*.

TRIBUTE TO DUKE

Rhythm and Blues   *Ohh, Ooh, Oh,*
sired you; gospel's   *moaning low,*
your mother tongue: *I got*
that of a MAN   *the blues.*
praying in the
miraculous language   *Sometimes I'm*
of song—soul   *up; sometimes*
communion with   *I'm down.*
his maker,
a sacred offering   *Sometimes I'm*
from the   *down; sometimes*
God-in-man   *I'm up*
to the
God-of-man.
                                        Oh happy day
                                        *   When Jesus washed*
You reigned King   *   my sin away.*
of Jazz before   *(musical background*
Whiteman imitations   *   with a medly of*
of "Black-Brown and   *   tunes)*
Beige" became the
order of the day.   *Boss, boss*
Here, now, we but add   *   tunes in*
one star more to   *   technicolor*
your two-grand   *SOUL—*
jewel-studded crown   *   Black-*
for that many tunes   *   Brown-*
you turned the world   *   Beige-*
onto in your   *   Creole-*
half-centuried
creative fever riffed   *Black*
in scales of color
from "Black Beauty"   *and*
to "Creole Rhapsody"
and "Black and Tan   *Tan*
    Fantasy."
All praises   *is*
to Duke,
King of Jazz   *the color*

Reprinted from *A Mirror: A Soul* by Sarah Webster Fabio with the permission of Cheryl
Fabio-Bradford.

To run it down
for you. That
fever that came on
with that "Uptown Beat"
caused Cotton when
he came to Harlem
that first time to
do a "Sugar Hill
Shim Sham."

of my fantasy.
When things
got down
and really
funky
fever, fever,
light
my fire.

When things got down
and funky
you bit into the blues
and blew into the air,
"I Got It Bad and
That Ain't Good,"
And from deep
down into your
"Solitude," you
touched both
"Satin Doll" and
"Sophisticated Lady"
wrapped them in
"Mood Indigo" and made
each moment
"A Prelude
to a kiss."

Down,
down
down
Nee-eev-eer
treat me
kind
and gentle—
BLOW
(music in the
background)
the way you
should
BLOW, MAN
Ain't
I
Got
it
Bad.

Way back then, Man,
you were doing
your thing.
Blowing minds with
riffs capping
whimsical whiffs of
lush melody—
changing minds
with moods and
modulations,
changing minds,
changing faces,
changing tunes,

Break it down.
Break
it down
Right on down
to
the
Real
nitty gritty.
("Solitude"
as background
sound)
Blow,
blow,

changing changes,
tripping out with
Billy to "Take the
A Train," making it
your theme—
your heat—
coming on strong
with bold dissonance
and fast, fast, beat
of the early, late
sound of our time.

"Harlem Airshaft"
"Rent Party Blues"
jangling jazzed tone
portraits of life
in the streets.
"Harlem"—a symphony
of cacaphonous sound,
bristling rhythms,
haunting laments
trumpeting into the air
defiant blasts blown solo
to fully orchestrated
folk chorus.
World Ambassador,
translating Life
into lyric; voice
into song; pulse
into beat
the beat, the beat,
a beat, a beat, a beat,
beat, beat, beat, beat
Do it now.
Get down.
"A Drum Is a Woman,"
and what more
language does
a sweetback need
to trip out to
"Mood Indigo,"

Right on, Duke

blow

Do your thing.

Change, change, change
your 'chine
and Take
The
A Train.

Ain't
got no
money
Ain't got no bread.
Ain't got
no place
to lay my Afro head.
I got
those low down
blues.
Chorus: Hot-and-Cold-
Running- Harlem
"Rent Party Blues."

Break it down,
down
down
down
Right on down
to the
Real
nitty gritty.
(drums in the
background become
drum solo)

(Theme song)

Do your thing,
your own thing.
And, Man,   *Take*
the word's out
when you   *The*
get down   *A*
Bad   *Train.*
it's good,
Real good,

                                 Right on.

And as you
go   *Right*
know   *on*
you're tops,   *out*
and whatever   *of*
you do,   *this*
"We love you   *funky*
madly."   *world.*

Paule Marshall

(1929–   )

BORN IN BROOKLYN, New York, in 1929, Paule Marshall grew up in a community strongly flavored by Caribbean culture. Her parents were immigrants from Barbados, and her novels and short stories are vibrant with the images, rituals, and oral traditions of her West Indian heritage. Her meticulous rendering of characters, particularly women, struggling for identity within their Caribbean-American community and within the often hostile white world surrounding it has earned her a special place in African American literature.

Marshall received her B.A. (Phi Beta Kappa) from Brooklyn College in 1953 and, while pursuing graduate studies at Hunter College, worked on the staff of a small black magazine called *Our World* from 1955 to 1956. In 1957 she married her first husband, Kenneth Marshall, and two years later published her first novel, *Brown Girl, Brownstones*. Her second book, *Soul Clap Hands and Sing* (1961), is a collection of four novellas completed with the help of a Guggenheim Fellowship after the birth of her only child. From 1962 to 1968 she worked on her third book, a novel titled *The Chosen Place, the Timeless People* (1969), for which she received a number of grants and awards, including a National Endowment for the Arts Fellowship. During this period she also published a number of short stories, some of which were later collected in a volume titled *Reena and Other Stories* (1983).

In 1970 she married her second husband, Nourry Menard, and spent the next decade at work on her novel, *Praisesong for the Widow* (1983), which won the Before Columbus American Book Award in 1984. Her most recent novel is *Daughters* (1991). She and her husband now divide their time between homes in New York City and the West Indies.

More information about Marshall's themes and influences as well as an analysis of each of her books is provided in Barbara T. Christian's article in *Dictionary of Literary Biography, Volume 33*. See also Linda Metzger, ed., *Black Writers: A Selection of Sketches from Contemporary Authors* (1989) and Valerie Smith, ed., *African American Writers* (1991).

The selection "Brooklyn" comes from *Soul Clap Hands and Sing*.

BROOKLYN

A summer wind, soaring just before it died, blew the dusk and the
first scattered lights of downtown Brooklyn against the shut windows of the classroom, but Professor Max Berman—B.A., 1919,
M.A., 1921, New York; Docteur de l'Université, 1930, Paris—alone
in the room, did not bother to open the windows to the cooling
wind. The heat and airlessness of the room, the perspiration inching
its way like an ant around his starched collar were discomforts he
enjoyed; they obscured his larger discomfort: the anxiety which
chafed his heart and tugged his left eyelid so that he seemed to be
winking, roguishly, behind his glasses.

To steady his eye and ease his heart, to fill the time until his
students arrived and his first class in years began, he reached for his
cigarettes. As always he delayed lighting the cigarette so that his
need for it would be greater and, thus, the relief and pleasure it
would bring, fuller. For some time he fondled it, his fingers shaping
soft, voluptuous gestures, his warped old man's hands looking
strangely abandoned on the bare desk and limp as if the bones had
been crushed, and so white—except for the tobacco burn on the
index and third fingers—it seemed his blood no longer traveled
that far.

He lit the cigarette finally and as the smoke swelled his lungs, his
eyelid stilled and his lined face lifted, the plume of white hair waft-
ing above his narrow brow; his body—short, blunt, the shoulders
slightly bent as if in deference to his sixty-three years—settled back
in the chair. Delicately Max Berman crossed his legs and, looking
down, examined his shoes for dust. (The shoes were a very soft,
fawn-colored leather and somewhat foppishly pointed at the toe.
They had been custom made in France and were his one last indulgence. He wore them in memory of his first wife, a French Jewess
from Alsace-Lorraine whom he had met in Paris while lingering over
his doctorate and married to avoid returning home. She had been
gay, mindless and very excitable—but at night, she had also been
capable of a profound stillness as she lay in bed waiting for him to
turn to her, and this had always awed and delighted him. She had
been a gift—and her death in a car accident had been a judgment on
him for never having loved her, for never, indeed, having even allowed
her to matter.) Fastidiously Max Berman unbuttoned his jacket and
straightened his vest, which had a stain two decades old on the pocket.
Through the smoke his veined eyes contemplated other, more pleasura-

ble scenes. With his neatly shod foot swinging and his cigarette at a rakish tilt, he might have been an old *boulevardier* taking the sun and an absinthe before the afternoon's assignation.

A young face, the forehead shiny with earnestness, hung at the half-opened door. "Is this French Lit, fifty-four? Camus and Sartre?"

Max Berman winced at the rawness of the voice and the flat "a" in Sartre and said formally, "This is Modern French Literature, number fifty-four, yes, but there is some question as to whether we will take up Messieurs Camus and Sartre this session. They might prove hot work for a summer-evening course. We will probably do Gide and Mauriac, who are considerably more temperate. But come in nonetheless. . . ."

He was the gallant, half rising to bow her to a seat. He knew that she would select the one in the front row directly opposite his desk. At the bell her pen would quiver above her blank notebook, ready to commit his first word—indeed, the clearing of his throat—to paper, and her thin buttocks would begin sidling toward the edge of her chair.

His eyelid twitched with solicitude. He wished that he could have drawn the lids over her fitful eyes and pressed a cool hand to her forehead. She reminded him of what he had been several lifetimes ago: a boy with a pale, plump face and harried eyes, running from the occasional taunts at his yarmulke along the shrill streets of Brownsville in Brooklyn, impeded by the heavy satchel of books which he always carried as proof of his scholarship. He had been proud of his brilliance at school and the Yeshiva, but at the same time he had been secretly troubled by it and resentful, for he could never believe that he had come by it naturally or that it belonged to him alone. Rather, it was like a heavy medal his father had hung around his neck—the chain bruising his flesh—and constantly exhorted him to wear proudly and use well.

The girl gave him an eager and ingratiating smile and he looked away. During his thirty years of teaching, a face similar to hers had crowded his vision whenever he had looked up from a desk. Perhaps it was fitting, he thought, and lighted another cigarette from the first, that she should be present as he tried again at life, unaware that behind his rimless glasses and within his ancient suit, he had been gutted.

He thought of those who had taken the last of his substance— and smiled tolerantly. "The boys of summer," he called them, his inquisitors, who had flailed him with a single question: "Are you now or have you ever been a member of the Communist party?" Max Berman had never taken their question seriously—perhaps because he had never taken his membership in the party seriously—and he had refused to answer. What had disturbed him, though, even when the investigation was over, was the feeling that he had really been under investigation for some other offense which did matter and of which he was guilty; that behind their accusations and charges had lurked another which had not been political but personal. For had he been disloyal to the government? His denial was a short, hawking laugh. Simply, he had never ceased being religious. When his father's God had become useless and even a little embarrassing, he had sought others: his work for a time, then the party. But he had been middle-aged when he joined and his faith, which had been so full as a boy, had grown thin. He had come, by then, to distrust all pieties, so that when the purges in Russia during the thirties confirmed his distrust, he had withdrawn into a modest cynicism.

But he had been made to answer for that error. Ten years later his inquisitors had flushed him out from the small community college in upstate New York where he had taught his classes from the same neat pack of notes each semester and had led him bound by subpoena to New York and bandied his name at the hearings until he had been dismissed from his job.

He remembered looking back at the pyres of burning autumn leaves on the campus his last day and feeling that another lifetime had ended—for he had always thought of his life as divided into many small lives, each with its own beginning and end. Like a hired mute, he had been present at each dying and kept the wake and wept professionally as the bier was lowered into the ground. Because of this feeling, he told himself that his final death would be anticlimactic.

After his dismissal he had continued living in the small house he had built near the college, alone except for an occasional visit from a colleague, idle but for some tutoring in French, content with the income he received from the property his parents had left him in Brooklyn—until the visits and tutoring had tapered off and a silence had begun to choke the house, like weeds springing up around a deserted place. He had begun to wonder then if he were still alive. He would wake at night from the recurrent dream of the hearings, where he was being accused of an unstated crime, to listen for his heart, his hand fumbling among the bedclothes to press the place. During the day he would pass repeatedly in front of the mirror with the pretext that he might have forgotten to shave that morning or that something had blown into his eye. Above all, he had begun to think of his inquisitors with affection and to long for the sound of their voices. They, at least, had assured him of being alive.

As if seeking them out, he had returned to Brooklyn and to the house in Brownsville where he had lived as a boy and had boldly applied for a teaching post without mentioning the investigation. He had finally been offered the class which would begin in five minutes. It wasn't much: a six-week course in the summer evening session of a college without a rating, where classes were held in a converted factory building, a college whose campus took in the bargain department stores, the five-and-dime emporiums and neon-spangled movie houses of downtown Brooklyn.

Through the smoke from his cigarette, Max Berman's eyes—a waning blue that never seemed to focus on any one thing—drifted over the students who had gathered meanwhile. Imbuing them with his own disinterest, he believed that even before the class began, most of them were longing for its end and already anticipating the soft drinks at the soda fountain downstairs and the synthetic dramas at the nearby movie.

They made him sad. He would have liked to lead them like a Pied Piper back to the safety of their childhoods—all of them: the loud girl with the formidable calves of an athlete who reminded him uncomfortably, of his second wife (a party member who was always shouting political heresy from some picket line and who had promptly divorced him upon discovering his irreverence); the two sallow-faced young men leaning out the window as if searching for the wind that had died; the slender young woman with crimped black hair who sat very still and apart from the others, her face turned toward the night sky as if to a friend.

Her loneliness interested him. He sensed its depth and his eye paused. He saw then that she was a Negro, a very pale mulatto with skin the color of clear, polished amber and a thin, mild face. She was somewhat older than the others in the room—a schoolteacher from the South, probably, who came north each summer to take courses toward a graduate degree. He felt a fleeting discomfort and irritation; discomfort at the thought that although he had been sinned against as a Jew he still shared in the sin against her and suffered from the same vague guilt, irritation that she recalled his own humiliations: the large ones, such as the fact that despite his brilliance he had been unable to get into a medical school as a young man because of the quota on Jews (not that he had wanted to be a doctor; that had been his father's wish) and had changed his studies from medicine to French; the small ones which had worn him thin: an eye widening imperceptibly as he gave his name, the savage glance which sought the Jewishness in his nose, his chin, in the set of his shoulders, the jokes snuffed into silence at his appearance. . . .

Tired suddenly, his eyelid pulsing, he turned and stared out the window at the gaudy constellation of neon lights. He longed for a drink, a quiet place and then sleep. And to bear him gently into sleep, to stay the terror which bound his heart then reminding him of those oleographs of Christ with the thorns binding his exposed heart—fat drops of blood from one so bloodless—to usher him into sleep, some pleasantly erotic image: a nude in a boudoir scattered with her frilled garments and warmed by her frivolous laugh, with the sun like a voyeur at the half-closed shutters. But this time instead of the usual Rubens nude with thighs like twin portals and a belly like a huge alabaster bowl into which he poured himself, he chose Gauguin's Aita Parari, her languorous form in the straight-back chair, her dark, sloping breasts, her eyes like the sun under shadow.

With the image still on his inner eye, he turned to the Negro girl and appraised her through a blind of cigarette smoke. She was still gazing out at the night sky and something about her fixed stare, her hands stiffly arranged in her lap, the nerve fluttering within the curve of her throat, betrayed a vein of tension within the rock of her calm. It was as if she had fled long ago to a remote region within herself, taking with her all that was most valuable and most vulnerable about herself.

She stirred finally, her slight breasts lifting beneath her flowered summer dress as she breathed deeply—and Max Berman thought again of Gauguin's girl with the dark, sloping breasts. What would this girl with the amber-colored skin be like on a couch in a sunlit room, nude in a straight-back chair? And as the question echoed along each nerve and stilled his breathing, it seemed suddenly that life, which had scorned him for so long, held out her hand again— but still a little beyond his reach. Only the girl, he sensed, could bring him close enough to touch it. She alone was the bridge. So that even while he repeated to himself that he was being presumptuous (for she would surely refuse him) and ridiculous (for even if she did not, what could he do—his performance would be a mere scramble and twitch), he vowed at the same time to have her. The challenge eased the tightness around his heart suddenly; it soothed the damaged muscle of his eye and as the bell rang he rose and said briskly, "Ladies and gentlemen, may I have your attention, please. My name is Max Berman. The course is Modern French Literature, number fifty-four. May I suggest that you check your program cards to see whether you are in the right place at the right time."

Her essay on Gide's The Immoralist lay on his desk and the note from the administration informing him, first, that his past political activities had been brought to their attention and then dismissing him at the end of the session weighed the inside pocket of his jacket. The two, her paper and the note, were linked in his mind. Her paper reminded him that the vow he had taken was still an empty one, for the term was half over and he had never once spoken to her (as if she understood his intention she was always late and disappeared as soon as the closing bell rang, leaving him trapped in a clamorous circle of students around his desk), while the note which wrecked his small attempt to start anew suddenly made that vow more urgent. It gave him the edge of desperation he needed to act finally. So that as soon as the bell rang, he returned all the papers but hers, announced that all questions would have to wait until their next meeting and, waving off the students from his desk, called above their protests, "Miss Williams, if you have a moment, I'd like to speak with you briefly about your paper."

She approached his desk like a child who has been cautioned not to talk to strangers, her fingers touching the backs of the chairs as if for support, her gaze following the departing students as though she longed to accompany them.

Her slight apprehensiveness pleased him. It suggested a submissiveness which gave him, as he rose uncertainly, a feeling of certainty and command. Her hesitancy was somehow in keeping with the color of her skin. She seemed to bring not only herself but the host of black women whose bodies had been despoiled to make her. He would not only possess her but them also, he thought (not really thought, for he scarcely allowed these thoughts to form before he snuffed them out). Through their collective suffering, which she contained, his own personal suffering would be eased; he would be pardoned for whatever sin it was he had committed against life.

"I hope you weren't unduly alarmed when I didn't return your paper along with the others," he said, and had to look up as she reached the desk. She was taller close up and her eyes, which he had thought were black, were a strong, flecked brown with very small pupils which seemed to shrink now from the sight of him. "But I found it so interesting I wanted to give it to you privately."

"I didn't know what to think," she said, and her voice—he heard it for the first time for she never recited or answered in class—was low, cautious, Southern.

"It was, to say the least, refreshing. It not only showed some original and mature thinking on your part, but it also proved that you've been listening in class—and after twenty-five years and more of teaching it's encouraging to find that some students do listen. If you have a little time I'd like to tell you, more specifically, what I liked about it. . . ."

Talking easily, reassuring her with his professional tone and a deft gesture with his cigarette, he led her from the room as the next class filed in, his hand cupped at her elbow but not touching it, his manner urbane, courtly, kind. They paused on the landing at the end of the long corridor with the stairs piled in steel tiers above and plunging below them. An intimate silence swept up the stairwell in a warm gust and Max Berman said, "I'm curious. Why did you choose *The Immoralist?*"

She started suspiciously, afraid, it seemed, that her answer might expose and endanger the self she guarded so closely within.

"Well," she said finally, her glance reaching down the stairs to the door marked EXIT at the bottom, "when you said we could use anything by Gide I decided on *The Immoralist*, since it was the first book I read in the original French when I was in undergraduate school. I didn't understand it then because my French was so weak, I guess, but I always thought about it afterward for some odd reason. I was shocked by what I did understand, of course, but something else about it appealed to me, so when you made the assignment I thought I'd try reading it again. I understood it a little better this time. At least I think so. . . . ."

"Your paper proves you did."

She smiled absently, intent on some other thought. Then she said cautiously, but with unexpected force, "You see, to me, the book seems to say that the only way you begin to know what you are and how much you are capable of is by daring to try something, by doing something which tests you. . . ."

"Something bold," he said.

"Yes."

"Even sinful."

She paused, questioning this, and then said reluctantly, "Yes, perhaps even sinful."

"The salutary effects of sin, you might say." He gave the little bow.

But she had not heard this; her mind had already leaped ahead. "The only trouble, at least with the character in Gide's book, is that what he finds out about himself is so terrible. He is so unhappy. . . ."

"But at least he knows, poor sinner." And his playful tone went unnoticed.

"Yes," she said with the same startling forcefulness. "And another thing, in finding out what he is, he destroys his wife. It was as if she had to die in order for him to live and know himself. Perhaps in order for a person to live and know himself somebody else must die. Maybe there's always a balancing out. . . . In a way"—and he had to lean close now to hear her—"I believe this."

Max Berman edged back as he glimpsed something move within her abstracted gaze. It was like a strong and restless seed that had taken root in the darkness there and was straining now toward the light. He had not expected so subtle and complex a force beneath her mild exterior and he found it disturbing and dangerous, but fascinating.

"Well, it's a most interesting interpretation," he said. "I don't know if M. Gide would have agreed, but then he's not around to give his opinion. Tell me, where did you do your undergraduate work?"

"At Howard University."

"And you majored in French?"

"Yes."

"Why, if I may ask?" he said gently.

"Well, my mother was from New Orleans and could speak a little Creole and I got interested in learning how to speak French through her, I guess. I teach it now at a junior high school in Richmond. Only the beginner courses because I don't have my master's. You know, *je vais, tu vas, il va* and *Frère Jacques*. It's not very inspiring."

"You should do something about that then, my dear Miss Williams. Perhaps it's time for you, like our friend in Gide, to try something new and bold."

"I know," she said, and her pale hand sketched a vague, despairing gesture. "I thought maybe if I got my master's . . . that's why I decided to come north this summer and start taking some courses. . . ."

Max Berman quickly lighted a cigarette to still the flurry inside him, for the moment he had been awaiting had come. He flicked her paper, which he still held. "Well, you've got the makings of a master's thesis right here. If you like I will suggest some ways for you to expand it sometime. A few pointers from an old pro might help."

He had to turn from her astonished and grateful smile—it was like a child's. He said carefully, "The only problem will be to find a place where we can talk quietly. Regrettably, I don't rate an office. . . ."

"Perhaps we could use one of the empty classrooms," she said.

"That would be much too dismal a setting for a pleasant discussion."

He watched the disappointment wilt her smile and when he spoke he made certain that the same disappointment weighed his voice. "Another difficulty is that the term's half over, which gives us little or no time. But let's not give up. Perhaps we can arrange to meet and talk over a weekend. The only hitch there is that I spend weekends at my place in the country. Of course you're perfectly welcome to come up there. It's only about seventy miles from New York, in the heart of what's very appropriately called the Borsch Circuit, even though, thank God, my place is a good distance away from the borsch. That is, it's very quiet and there's never anybody around except with my permission."

She did not move, yet she seemed to start; she made no sound, yet he thought he heard a bewildered cry. And then she did a strange thing, standing there with the breath sucked into the hollow of her throat and her smile, that had opened to him with such trust, dying—her eyes, her hands faltering up begged him to declare himself.

"There's a lake near the house," he said, "so that when you get tired of talking—or better, listening to me talk—you can take a swim, if you like. I would very much enjoy that sight." And as the nerve tugged at his eyelid, he seemed to wink behind his rimless glasses.

Her sudden, blind step back was like a man groping his way through a strange room in the dark, and instinctively Max Berman reached out to break her fall. Her arms, bare to the shoulder because of the heat (he knew the feel of her skin without even touching it—it would be like a rich, fine-textured cloth which would soothe and hide him in its amber warmth), struck out once to drive him off and then fell limp at her side, and her eyes became vivid and convulsive in her numbed face. She strained toward the stairs and the exit door at the bottom, but she could not move. Nor could she speak. She did not even cry. Her eyes remained dry and dull with disbelief. Only her shoulders trembled as though she was silently weeping inside.

It was as though she had never learned the forms and expressions of anger. The outrage of a lifetime, of her history, was trapped inside her. And she stared at Max Berman with this mute, paralyzing rage. Not really at him but to his side, as if she caught sight of others behind him. And remembering how he had imagined a column of dark women trailing her to his desk, he sensed that she glimpsed a legion of old men with sere flesh and lonely eyes flanking him: "old lechers with a love on every wind . . ."

"I'm sorry, Miss Williams," he said, and would have welcomed her insults, for he would have been able, at least, to distill from them some passion and a kind of intimacy. It would have been, in a way, like touching her. "It was only that you are a very attractive young woman and although I'm no longer young"—and he gave the tragic little laugh which sought to dismiss that fact—"I can still appreciate and even desire an attractive woman. But I was wrong. . ." His self-disgust, overwhelming him finally, choked off his voice. "And so very crude. Forgive me. I can offer no excuse for my behavior other than my approaching senility."

He could not even manage the little marionette bow this time. Quickly he shoved the paper on Gide into her lifeless hand, but it fell, the pages separating, and as he hurried past her downstairs and out the door, he heard the pages scattering like dead leaves on the steps.

She remained away until the night of the final examination, which was also the last meeting of the class. By that time Max Berman, believing that she would not return, had almost succeeded in forgetting her. He was no longer even certain of how she looked, for her face had been absorbed into the single, blurred, featureless face of all the women who had ever refused him. So that she startled him as much as a stranger would have when he entered the room that night and found her alone amid a maze of empty chairs, her face turned toward the window as on the first night and her hands serene in her lap. She turned at his footstep and it was if she had also forgotten all that had passed between them. She waited until he said, "I'm glad you decided to take the examination. I'm sure you won't have any difficulty with it"; then she gave him a nod that was somehow reminiscent of his little bow and turned again to the window.

He was relieved yet puzzled by her composure. It was as if during her three-week absence she had waged and won a decisive contest with herself and was ready now to act. He was wary suddenly and all during the examination he tried to discover what lay behind her strange calm, studying her bent head amid the shifting heads of the other students, her slim hand guiding the pen across the page, her legs—the long bone visible, it seemed, beneath the flesh. Desire flared and quickly died.

"Excuse me, Professor Berman, will you take up Camus and Sartre next semester, maybe?" The girl who sat in front of his desk was standing over him with her earnest smile and finished examination folder.

"That might prove somewhat difficult, since I won't be here."

"No more?"

"No."

"I mean, not even next summer?"

"I doubt it."

"Gee, I'm sorry. I mean, I enjoyed the course and everything."

He bowed his thanks and held his head down until she left. Her compliment, so piteous somehow, brought on the despair he had forced to the dim rear of his mind. He could no longer flee the thought of the exile awaiting him when the class tonight ended. He could either remain in the house in Brooklyn, where the memory of his father's face above the radiance of the Sabbath candles haunted him from the shadows, reminding him of the certainty he had lost and never found again, where the mirrors in his father's room were still shrouded with sheets, as on the day he lay dying and moaning into his beard that his only son was a bad Jew; or he could return to the house in the country, to the silence shrill with loneliness.

The cigarette he was smoking burned his fingers, rousing him, and he saw over the pile of examination folders on his desk that the room was empty except for the Negro girl. She had finished—her pen lay aslant the closed folder on her desk—but she had remained in her seat and she was smiling across the room at him—a set, artificial smile that was both cold and threatening. It utterly denuded him and he was wildly angry suddenly that she had seen him give way to despair; he wanted to remind her (he could not stay the thought; it attacked him like an assailant from a dark turn in his mind) that she was only black after all. . . . His head dropped and he almost wept with shame.

The girl stiffened as if she had seen the thought and then the tiny muscles around her mouth quickly arranged the bland smile. She came up to his desk, placed her folder on top of the others and said pleasantly, her eyes like dark, shattered glass that spared Max Berman his reflection, "I've changed my mind. I think I'd like to spend a day at your place in the country if your invitation still holds."

He thought of refusing her, for her voice held neither promise nor passion, but he could not. Her presence, even if it was only for a day, would make his return easier. And there was still the possibility of passion despite her cold manner and the deliberate smile. He thought of how long it had been since he had had someone, of how badly he needed the sleep which followed love and of awakening certain, for the first time in years, of his existence.

"Of course the invitation still holds. I'm driving up tonight."

"I won't be able to come until Sunday," she said firmly. "Is there a train then?"

"Yes, in the morning," he said, and gave her the schedule.

"You'll meet me at the station?"

"Of course. You can't miss my car. It's a very shabby but venerable Chevy."

She smiled stiffly and left, her heels awakening the silence of the empty corridor, the sound reaching back to a tap like a warning finger on Max Berman's temple.

The pale sunlight slanting through the windshield lay like a cat on his knees, and the motor of his old Chevy, turning softly under him could have been the humming of its heart. A little distance from the car a log-cabin station house—the logs blackened by the seasons—stood alone against the hills, and the hills, in turn, lifted softly, still green although the summer was ending, into the vague autumn sky.

The morning mist and pale sun, the green that was still somehow new, made it seem that the season was stirring into life even as it died, and this contradiction pained Max Berman at the same time that it pleased him. For it was his own contradiction after all: his desires which remained those of a young man even as he was dying.

He had been parked for some time in the deserted station, yet his hands were still tensed on the steering wheel and his foot hovered near the accelerator. As soon as he had arrived in the station he had wanted to leave. But like the girl that night on the landing, he was too stiff with tension to move. He could only wait, his eyelid twitching with foreboding, regret, curiosity and hope.

Finally and with no warning the train charged through the fiery green, setting off a tremor underground. Max Berman imagined the girl seated at a window in the train, her hands arranged quietly in her lap and her gaze scanning the hills that were so familiar to him, and yet he could not believe that she was really there. Perhaps her plan had been to disappoint him. She might be in New York or on her way back to Richmond now, laughing at the trick she had played on him. He was convinced of this suddenly, so that even when he saw her walking toward him through the blown steam from under the train, he told himself that she was a mirage created by the steam. Only when she sat beside him in the car, bringing with her, it seemed, an essence she had distilled from the morning air and rubbed into her skin, was he certain of her reality.

"I brought my bathing suit but it's much too cold to swim," she said and gave him the deliberate smile.

He did not see it; he only heard her voice, its warm Southern lilt in the chill, its intimacy in the closed car—and an excitement swept him, cold first and then hot, as if the sun had burst in his blood.

"It's the morning air," he said. "By noon it should be like summer again."

"Is that a promise?"

"Yes."

By noon the cold morning mist had lifted above the hills and below, in the lake valley, the sunlight was a sheer gold net spread out on the grass as if to dry, draped on the trees and flung, glinting, over the lake. Max Berman felt it brush his shoulder gently as he sat by the lake waiting for the girl, who had gone up to the house to change into her swimsuit.

He had spent the morning showing her the fields and small wood near his house. During the long walk he had been careful to keep a little apart from her. He would extend a hand as they climbed a rise or when she stepped uncertainly over a rock, but he would not really touch her. He was afraid that at his touch, no matter how slight and causal, her scream would spiral into the morning calm, or worse, his touch would unleash the threatening thing he sensed behind her even smile.

He had talked of her paper and she had listened politely and occasionally even asked a question or made a comment. But all the while detached, distant, drawn within herself as she had been that first night in the classroom. And then halfway down a slope she had paused and, pointing to the canvas tops of her white sneakers, which had become wet and dark from the dew secreted in the grass, she had laughed. The sound, coming so abruptly in the midst of her tense quiet, joined her, it seemed, to the wood and wide fields, to the hills; she shared their simplicity and held within her the same strong current of life. Max Berman had felt privileged suddenly, and humble. He had stopped questioning her smile. He had told himself then that it would not matter even if she stopped and picking up a rock bludgeoned him from behind.

"There's a lake near my home, but it's not like this," the girl said, coming up behind him. "Yours is so dark and serious-looking."

He nodded and followed her gaze out to the lake, where the ripples were long, smooth welts raised by the wind, and across to the other bank, where a group of birches stepped delicately down to the lake and bending over touched the water with their branches as if testing it before they plunged.

The girl came and stood beside him now—and she was like a pale-gold naiad, the spirit of the lake, her eyes reflecting its somber autumnal tone and her body as supple as the birches. She walked slowly into the water, unaware, it seemed, of the sudden passion in his gaze, or perhaps uncaring; and as she walked she held out her arms in what seemed a gesture of invocation (and Max Berman remembered his father with the fringed shawl draped on his outstretched arms as he invoked their God each Sabbath with the same gesture); her head was bent as if she listened for a voice beneath the water's murmurous surface. When the ground gave way she still seemed to be walking and listening, her arms outstretched. The water reached her waist, her small breasts, her shoulders. She lifted her head once, breathed deeply and disappeared.

She stayed down for a long time and when her white cap finally broke the water some distance out, Max Berman felt strangely stranded and deprived. He understood suddenly the profound cleavage between them and the absurdity of his hope. The water between them became the years which separated them. Her white cap was the sign of her purity, while the silt darkening the lake was the flotsam of his failures. Above all, their color—her arms a pale, flashing gold in the sunlit water and his bled white and flaccid with the veins like angry blue penciling—marked the final barrier.

He was sad as they climbed toward the house late that afternoon and troubled. A crow cawed derisively in the bracken, heralding the dusk which would not only end their strange day but would also, he felt, unveil her smile, so that he would learn the reason for her coming. And because he was sad, he said wryly, "I think I should tell you that you've been spending the day with something of an outcast."

"Oh," she said and waited.

He told her of the dismissal, punctuating his words with the little hoarse, deprecating laugh and waving aside the pain with his cigarette. She listened, polite but neutral, and because she remained unmoved, he wanted to confess all the more. So that during dinner and afterward when they sat outside on the porch, he told her of the investigation.

"It was very funny once you saw it from the proper perspective, which I did, of course," he said. "I mean here they were accusing me of crimes I couldn't remember committing and asking me for the names of people with whom I had never associated. It was pure farce. But I made a mistake. I should have done something dramatic or something just as farcical. Bared my breast in the public market place or written a tome on my apostasy, naming names. It would have been a far different story then. Instead of my present ignominy I would have been offered a chairmanship at Yale. . . No? Well, Brandeis then. I would have been draped in honorary degrees. . . ."

"Well, why didn't you confess?" she said impatiently.

"I've often asked myself the same interesting question, but I haven't come up with a satisfactory answer yet. I suspect, though, that I said nothing because none of it really mattered that much."

"What did matter?" she asked sharply.

He sat back, waiting for the witty answer, but none came, because just then the frame upon which his organs were strung seemed to snap and he felt his heart, his lungs, his vital parts fall in a heap within him. Her question had dealt the severing blow, for it was the same question he understood suddenly that the vague forms in his dream asked repeatedly. It had been the plaintive undercurrent to his father's dying moan, the real accusation behind the charges of his inquisitors at the hearing.

For what had mattered? He gazed through his sudden shock at the night squatting on the porch steps, at the hills asleep like gentle beasts in the darkness, at the black screen of the sky where the events of his life passed in a mute, accusing review—and he saw nothing there to which he had given himself or in which he had truly believed since the belief and dedication of his boyhood.

"Did you hear my question?" she asked, and he was glad that he sat within the shadows clinging to the porch screen and could not be seen.

"Yes, I did," he said faintly, and his eyelid twitched. "But I'm afraid it's another one of those I can't answer satisfactorily." And then he struggled for the old flippancy. "You make an excellent examiner, you know. Far better than my inquisitors."

"What will you do now?" Her voice and cold smile did not spare him.

He shrugged and the motion, a slow, eloquent lifting of the shoulders, brought with it suddenly the weight and memory of his boyhood. It was the familiar gesture of the women hawkers in Belmont Market, of the men standing outside the temple on Saturday mornings, each of them reflecting his image of God in their forbidding black coats and with the black, tumbling beards in which he had always imagined he could hide as in a forest. All this had mattered, he called loudly to himself, and said aloud to the girl, "Let me see if I can answer this one at least. What *will* I do?" He paused and swung his leg so that his foot in the fastidious French shoe caught the light from the house. "Grow flowers and write my memoirs. How's that? That would be the proper way for a gentleman and scholar to retire. Or hire one of those hefty housekeepers who will bully me and when I die in my sleep draw the sheet over my head and call my lawyer. That's somewhat European, but how's that?"

When she said nothing for a long time, he added soberly, "But that's not a fair question for me any more. I leave all such considerations to the young. To you, for that matter. What will you do, my dear Miss Williams?"

It was as if she had been expecting the question and had been readying her answer all the time that he had been talking. She leaned forward eagerly and with her face and part of her body fully in the light, she said, "I will do something. I don't know what yet, but something."

Max Berman started back a little. The answer was so unlike her vague, resigned "I know" on the landing that night when he had admonished her to try something new.

He edged back into the darkness and she leaned further into the light, her eyes overwhelming her face and her mouth set in a thin, determined line. "I will do something," she said, bearing down on each word, "because for the first time in my life I feel almost brave."

He glimpsed this new bravery behind her hard gaze and sensed something vital and purposeful, precious, which she had found and guarded like a prize within her center. He wanted it. He would have liked to snatch it and run like a thief. He no longer desired her but it, and starting forward with a sudden envious cry, he caught her arm and drew her close, seeking it.

But he could not get to it. Although she did not pull away her arm, although she made no protest as his face wavered close to hers, he did not really touch her. She held herself and her prize out of his desperate reach and her smile was a knife she pressed to his throat. He saw himself for what he was in her clear, cold gaze: an old man with skin the color and texture of dough that had been kneaded by the years into tragic folds, with faded eyes adrift behind a pair of rimless glasses and roughened flesh at his throat like a bird's wattles. And as the disgust which he read in her eyes swept him, his hand dropped from her arm. He started to murmur, "Forgive me . . ." when suddenly she caught hold of his wrist, pulling him close again, and he felt the strength which had borne her swiftly through the water earlier hold him now as she said quietly and without passion, "And do you know why, Dr. Berman, I feel almost brave today? Because ever since I can remember my parents were always telling me, 'Stay away from white folks. Just leave them alone. You mind your business and they'll mind theirs. Don't go near them.' And they made sure I didn't. My father, who was the principal of a colored grade school in Richmond, used to drive me to and from school every day. When I needed something from downtown my mother would take me and if the white saleslady asked me anything she would answer. . . .

"And my parents were also always telling me, 'Stay away from niggers,' and that meant anybody darker than we were." She held out her arm in the light and Max Berman saw the skin almost as white as his but for the subtle amber shading. Staring at the arm she said tragically, "I was so confused I never really went near anybody. Even when I went away to college I kept to myself. I didn't marry the man I wanted to because he was dark and I knew my parents would disapprove. . . ." She paused, her wistful gaze searching the darkness for the face of the man she had refused, it seemed, and not finding it she went on sadly, "So after graduation I returned home and started teaching and I was just as confused and frightened and ashamed as always. When my parents died I went on the same way. And I would have gone on like that the rest of my life if it hadn't been for you, Dr. Berman"—and the sarcasm leaped behind her cold smile. "In a way you did me a favor. You let me know how you— and most of the people like you—see me."

"My dear Miss Williams, I assure you I was not attracted to you because you were colored. . . ." And he broke off, remembering just how acutely aware of her color he had been.

"I'm not interested in your reasons!" she said brutally. "What matters is what it meant to me. I thought about this these last three weeks and about my parents—how wrong they had been, how frightened, and the terrible thing they had done to me . . . And I wasn't confused any longer." Her head lifted, tremulous with her new assurance. "I can do something now! I can begin," she said with her head poised. "Look how I came all the way up here to tell you this to your face. Because how could you harm me? You're so old you're like a cup I could break in my hand." And her hand tightened on his wrist, wrenching the last of his frail life from him, it seemed. Through the quick pain he remembered her saying on the landing that night: "Maybe in order for a person to live someone else must die" and her quiet "I believe this" then. Now her sudden laugh, an infinitely cruel sound in the warm night, confirmed her belief.

Suddenly she was the one who seemed old, indeed ageless. Her touch became mortal and Max Berman saw the darkness that would end his life gathered in her eyes. But even as he sprang back, jerking his arm away, a part of him rushed forward to embrace the darkness, and his cry, wounding the night, held both ecstasy and terror.

"That's all I came for," she said, rising. "You can drive me to the station now."

They drove to the station in silence. Then, just as the girl started from the car, she turned with an ironic, pitiless smile and said, "You know, it's been a nice day, all things considered. It really turned summer again as you said it would. And even though your lake isn't anything like the one near my home, it's almost as nice."

Max Berman bowed to her for the last time, accepting with that gesture his responsibility for her rage, which went deeper than his, and for her anger, which would spur her finally to live. And not only for her, but for all those at last whom he had wronged through his indifference: his father lying in the room of shrouded mirrors, the wives he had never loved, his work which he had never believed in enough and, lastly (even though he knew it was too late and he would not be spared), himself.

Too weary to move, he watched the girl cross to the train which would bear her south, her head lifted as though she carried life as lightly there as if it were a hat made of tulle. When the train departed his numbed eyes followed it until its rear light was like a single firefly in the immense night or the last flickering of his life. Then he drove back through the darkness.

John A. Williams

(1925–   )

NOVELIST JOHN A. WILLIAMS has stated that the goal of his work is "to bridge the racial gap by telling the truth about both sides." He accomplishes that goal by shattering the misconceptions and stereotypes of blacks through complex characters struggling against the subtle and overt pressures of daily life. In an incisive style that combines the literary forms of the novel and the biography, and with uncompromising integrity and commitment to the truth, Williams examines the personal and social problems that blacks face in modern society.

Williams was born in 1925 in Jackson, Mississippi, and grew up in Syracuse, New York. He served in the navy during World War II, a harsh experience in racism that was later to form the thematic basis of several of his novels. After the war he returned to New York to attend Syracuse University, receiving the B.A. in English and journalism in 1950. His first marriage, to Carolyn Clopton, ended in 1952. He then began a long and varied career, first in radio and television and then in publishing, which took him to Hollywood and later to New York City. By 1958 he had completed two novels: *The Cool Ones*, which remains unpublished, and *One for New York*, which was published in 1960 under the title *The Angry Ones*. During the late 1950s and early 1960s Williams also traveled extensively throughout Europe as a correspondent for several New York-based magazines.

Night Song, Williams's second novel, was published in 1961. Shortly thereafter he was nominated to receive the Prix de Rome of the American Academy of Arts and Letters, but the nomination was subsequently withdrawn for reasons that the academy refused to explain. Much later, Williams would write a fictional account of the affair in what has been called his greatest novel, *The Man Who Cried I Am*, but at the time he only voiced his opinion that the academy had withdrawn the prize out of disapproval of his upcoming marriage to a white woman.

Williams married his second wife, Lorrain Isaac, in 1965, and in 1968 he began a teaching career that took him to the City College of New York (1968), the College of the Virgin Islands (summer of 1968), the University of California at Santa Barbara (1972), Sarah Lawrence College (guest writer, 1972), LaGuardia Community College (1973–1974), the University of Hawaii (summer of 1974), and Boston University (1978–1979). Since 1979 he has been a professor of English at Rutgers University.

In 1963 Williams's third novel, *Sissie*, and a nonfiction work titled *Africa: Her History, Lands, and People* were published. Like his previous novels, both these works attempt to correct the distorted view of black Americans and their African heritage. His next three novels—*The Man Who Cried I Am* (1967), *Sons of Darkness, Sons of Light* (1969), and *Captain Blackman* (1972)—present a darker vision of the black struggle against the manipulations of institutionalized racism and economic exploitation. Two more works of nonfiction were published in 1970: *The Most Native of Sons: A Biography of Richard Wright* and *The King God Didn't Save*, a controversial study of the life and philosophy of Martin Luther King, Jr. These works are in the same vein as Williams's second three novels, probing the reactions of these two black men to a repressive white society. Williams's last four novels—*Mothersill and the Foxes* (1975), *The Junior Bachelor Society* (1976), *!Click Song* (1982), and *Jacob's Ladder* (1987)—look from the pain and violence of the present toward a future of black unity based on strengthening individual and group values. *The Junior Bachelor Society* became the basis for a 1981 TV movie, "Sophisticated Gents." Williams has also written a screenplay, "Sweet Love, Bitter" (1967), and a play, *Last Flight from Ambo Ber* (produced in Boston in 1981), as well as several other works of nonfiction, and he has edited a number of anthologies, including McGraw-Hill's *Introduction to Literature*. He and his son Dennis A. Williams are the authors of a biography of Richard Pryor entitled *If I Stop I'll Die: The Comedy and Tragedy of Richard Pryor* (1991).

For a detailed analysis of Williams's novels, a survey of his nonfiction, and list of references, see James L. de Jongh's article in *Dictionary of Literary Biography, Volume 33*.

"Son in the Afternoon" is reprinted from Langston Hughes's *The Best Short Stories by Negro Writers* (1967).

SON IN THE AFTERNOON

It was hot. I tend to be a bitch when it's hot. I goosed the little Ford over Sepulveda Boulevard toward Santa Monica until I got stuck in the traffic that pours from L.A. into the surrounding towns. I'd had a very lousy day at the studio.

I was—still am—a writer and this studio had hired me to check scripts and films with Negroes in them to make sure the Negro moviegoer wouldn't be offended. The signs were already clear one day the whole of American industry would be racing pell-mell to get a Ne-

Reprinted by permission of the author.

gro, showcase a spade. I was kind of a pioneer. I'm a *Negro* writer,
you see. The day had been tough because of a couple of verbs—
slink and walk. One of those Hollywood hippies had done a script
calling for a Negro waiter to slink away from the table where a dinner party was glaring at him. I said the waiter should walk, not
slink, because later on he becomes a hero. The Hollywood hippie,
who understood it all because he had some colored friends, said that
it was essential to the plot that the waiter slink. I said you don't
slink one minute and become a hero the next; there has to be some
consistency. The Negro actor I was standing up for said nothing either way. He had played Uncle Tom roles so long that he had become Uncle Tom. But the director agreed with me.

Anyway . . . hear me out now. I was on my way to Santa Monica
to pick up my mother, Nora. It was a long haul for such a hot day. I
had planned a quiet evening: a nice shower, fresh clothes, and then I
would have dinner at the Watkins and talk with some of the musicians on the scene for a quick taste before they cut to their gigs.
After, I was going to the Pigalle down on Figueroa and catch Earl
Grant at the organ, and still later, if nothing exciting happened, I'd
pick up Scottie and make it to the Lighthouse on the Beach or to the
Strollers and listen to some of the white boys play. I liked the long
drive, especially while listening to Sleepy Stein's show on the radio.
Later, much later of course, it would be home, back to Watts.

So you see, this picking up Nora was a little inconvenient. My
mother was a maid for the Couchmans. Ronald Couchman was an
architect, a good one I understood from Nora who has a fine sense
for this sort of thing; you don't work in some hundred-odd houses
during your life without getting some idea of the way a house
should be laid out. Couchman's wife, Kay, was a playgirl who drove
a white Jaguar from one party to another. My mother didn't like her
too much; she didn't seem to care much for her son, Ronald, junior.
There's something wrong with a parent who can't really love her
own child, Nora thought. The Couchmans lived in a real fine residential section, of course. A number of actors lived nearby, character
actors, not really big stars.

Somehow it is very funny. I mean that the maids and butlers
knew everything about these people, and these people knew nothing
at all about the help. Through Nora and her friends I knew who was
laying whose wife; who had money and who *really* had money; I
knew about the wild parties hours before the police, and who
smoked marijuana, when, and where they got it.

To get to Couchman's driveway I had to go three blocks up one
side of a palm-planted center strip and back down the other. The
driveway bent gently, then swept back out of sight of the main road.

The house, sheltered by slim palms, looked like a transplanted New England Colonial. I parked and walked to the kitchen door, skirting the growling Great Dane who was tied to a tree. That was the route to the kitchen door.

I don't like kitchen doors. Entering people's houses by them, I mean. I'd done this thing most of my life when I called at places where Nora worked to pick up the patched or worn sheets or the half-eaten roasts, the battered, tarnished silver—the fringe benefits of a housemaid. As a teen-ager I'd told Nora I was through with that crap; I was not going through anyone's kitchen door. She only laughed and said I'd learn. One day soon after, I called for her and without knocking walked right through the front door of this house and right on through the living room. I was almost out of the room when I saw feet behind the couch. I leaned over and there was Mr. Jorgensen and his wife making out like crazy. I guess they thought Nora had gone and it must have hit them sort of suddenly and they went at it like the hell-bomb was due to drop any minute. I've been that way too, mostly in the spring. Of course, when Mr. Jorgensen looked over his shoulder and saw me, you know what happened. I was thrown out and Nora right behind me. It was the middle of winter, the old man was sick and the coal bill three months overdue. Nora was right about those kitchen doors: I learned.

My mother saw me before I could ring the bell. She opened the door. "Hello," she said. She was breathing hard, like she'd been running or something. "Come in and sit down. I don't know *where* that Kay is. Little Ronald is sick and she's probably out gettin' drunk again." She left me then and trotted back through the house, I guess to be with Ronnie. I hated the combination of her white nylon uniform, her dark brown face and the wide streaks of gray in her hair. Nora had married this guy from Texas a few years after the old man had died. He was all right. He made out okay. Nora didn't have to work, but she just couldn't be still; she always had to be doing something. I suggested she quit work, but I had as much luck as her husband. I used to tease her about liking to be around those white folks. It would have been good for her to take an extended trip around the country visiting my brothers and sisters. Once she got to Philadelphia, she could go right out to the cemetery and sit awhile with the old man.

I walked through the Couchman home. I liked the library. I thought if I knew Couchman I'd like him. The room made me feel like that. I left it and went into the big living room. You could tell that Couchman had let his wife do that. Everything in it was fast, dart-like, with no sense of ease. But on the walls were several of Couchman's conceptions of buildings and homes. I guess he was a disciple of Wright. My mother walked rapidly through the room without looking at me and said, "Just be patient, Wendell. She should be here real soon."

"Yeah," I said, "with a snootful." I had turned back to the drawings when Ronnie scampered into the room, his face twisted with rage.

"Nora!" he tried to roar, perhaps the way he'd seen the parents of some of his friends roar at their maids. I'm quite sure Kay didn't shout at Nora, and I don't think Couchman would. But then no one shouts at Nora. "Nora, you come right back here this minute!" the little bastard shouted and stamped and pointed to a spot on the floor where Nora was supposed to come to roost. I have a nasty temper. Sometimes it lies dormant for ages and at other times, like when the weather is hot and nothing seems to be going right, it's bubbling and ready to explode. "Don't talk to *my* mother like that, you little—!" I said sharply, breaking off just before I cursed. I wanted him to be large enough for me to strike. "How'd you like for me to talk to *your* mother like that?"

The nine-year-old looked up at me in surprise and confusion. He hadn't expected me to say anything. I was just another piece of furniture. Tears rose in his eyes and spilled out onto his pale cheeks. He put his hands behind him, twisted them. He moved backwards, away from me. He looked at my mother with a "Nora, come help me" look. And sure enough, there was Nora, speeding back across the room, gathering the kid in her arms, tucking his robe together. I was too angry to feel hatred for myself.

Ronnie was the Couchman's only kid. Nora loved him. I suppose that was the trouble. Couchman was gone ten, twelve hours a day. Kay didn't stay around the house any longer than she had to. So Ronnie had only my mother. I think kids should have someone to love, and Nora wasn't a bad sort. But somehow when the six of us, her own children, were growing up we never had her. She was gone, out scuffling to get those crumbs to put into our mouths and shoes for our feet and praying for something to happen so that all the space in between would be taken care of. Nora's affection for us took the form of rushing out into the morning's five o'clock blackness to wake some silly bitch and get her coffee; took form in her trudging five miles home every night instead of taking the streetcar to save money to buy tablets for us, to use at school, we said. But the truth was that all of us liked to draw and we went through a writing tablet in a couple of hours every day. Can you imagine? There's not a goddamn artist among us. We never had the physical affection, the pat on the head, the quick, smiling kiss, the "gimmee a hug" routine. All of this Ronnie was getting.

Now he buried his little blond head in Nora's breast and sobbed. "There, there now," Nora said. "Don't you cry, Ronnie. Ol' Wendell is just jealous, and he hasn't much sense either. He didn't mean nuthin'."

I left the room. Nora had hit it of course, hit it and passed on. I looked back. It didn't look so incongruous, the white and black together, I mean. Ronnie was still sobbing. His head bobbed gently on Nora's shoulder. The only time I ever got that close to her was when she trapped me with a bearhug so she could whale the daylights out of me after I put a snowball through Mrs. Grant's window. I walked outside and lit a cigarette. When Ronnie was in the hospital the month before, Nora got me to run her way over to Hollywood every night to see him. I didn't like that worth a damn. All right, I'll admit it: it did upset me. All that affection I didn't get nor my brothers and sisters going to that little white boy who, without a doubt, when away from her called her the names he'd learned from adults. Can you imagine a nine-year-old kid calling Nora a "girl," "our girl?" I spat at the Great Dane. He snarled and then I bounced a rock off his fanny. "Lay down, you bastard," I muttered. It was a good thing he was tied up.

I heard the low cough of the Jaguar slapping against the road. The car was throttled down, and with a muted roar it swung into the driveway. The woman aimed it for me. I was evil enough not to move. I was tired of playing with these people. At the last moment, grinning, she swung the wheel over and braked. She bounded out of the car like a tennis player vaulting over a net.

"Hi," she said, tugging at her shorts.

"Hello."

"You're Nora's boy?"

"I'm Nora's son." Hell, I was as old as she was; besides, I can't stand "boy."

"Nora tells us you're working in Hollywood. Like it?"

"It's all right."

"You must be pretty talented."

We stood looking at each other while the dog whined for her attention. Kay had a nice body and it was well tanned. She was high, boy, was she high. Looking at her, I could feel myself going into my sexy bastard routine; sometimes I can swing it great. Maybe it all had to do with the business inside. Kay took off her sunglasses and took a good look at me. "Do you have a cigarette?"

I gave her one and lit it. "Nice tan," I said. Most white people I know think it's a great big deal if a Negro compliments them on their tans. It's a large laugh. You have all this volleyball about color and come summer you can't hold the white folks back from the beaches, anyplace where they can get some sun. And of course the blacker they get, the more pleased they are. Crazy. If there is ever a Negro revolt, it will come during the summer and Negroes will descend upon the beaches around the nation and paralyze the country. You can't conceal cattle prods and bombs and pistols and police dogs when you're showing your birthday suit to the sun.

"You like it?" she asked. She was pleased. She placed her arm next to mine. "Almost the same color," she said.

"Ronnie isn't feeling well," I said.

"Oh, the poor kid. I'm so glad we have Nora. She's such a charm. I'll run right in and look at him. Do have a drink in the bar. Fix me one too, will you?" Kay skipped inside and I went to the bar and poured out two strong drinks. I made hers stronger than mine. She was back soon. "Nora was trying to put him to sleep and she made me stay out." She giggled. She quickly tossed off her drink. "Another, please?" While I was fixing her drink she was saying how amazing it was for Nora to have such a talented son. What she was really saying was that it was amazing for a servant to have a son who was not also a servant. "Anything can happen in a democracy," I said. "Servants' sons drink with madames and so on."

"Oh, Nora isn't a servant," Kay said. "She's part of the family."

Yeah, I thought. Where and how many times had I heard *that* before?

In the ensuing silence, she started to admire her tan again. "You think it's pretty good, do you? You don't know how hard I worked to get it." I moved close to her and held her arm. I placed my other arm around her. She pretended not to see or feel it, but she wasn't trying to get away either. In fact she was pressing closer and the register in my brain that tells me at the precise moment when I'm in, went off. Kay was very high. I put both arms around her and she put both hers around me. When I kissed her, she responded completely.

"Mom!"

"Ronnie, come back to bed," I heard Nora shout from the other room. We could hear Ronnie running over the rug in the outer room. Kay tried to get away from me, push me to one side, because we could tell that Ronnie knew where to look for his Mom: he was running right for the bar, where we were. "Oh, please," she said, "don't let him see us." I wouldn't let her push me away. "Stop!" she hissed, "He'll *see* us!" We stopped struggling just for an instant, and we listened to the echoes of the word *see*. She gritted her teeth and renewed her efforts to get away.

Me? I had the scene laid right out. The kid breaks into the room, see, and sees his mother in this real wriggly clinch with this colored guy who's just shouted at him, see, and no matter how his mother explains it away, the kid has the image—the colored guy and his mother—for the rest of his life, see?

That's the way it happened. The kid's mother hissed under her breath, "*You're crazy!*" and she looked at me as though she were seeing me or something about me for the very first time. I'd released her as soon as Ronnie, romping into the bar, saw us and came to a full, open-mouthed halt. Kay went to him. He looked at me, then at his mother. Kay turned to me, but she couldn't speak.

Outside in the living room my mother called, "Wendell, where are you? We can go now."

I started to move past Kay and Ronnie. I felt many things, but I made myself think mostly, *There you little bastard, there.*

My mother had thrust her face inside the door and said, "Good-bye, Mrs. Couchman. See you tomorrow, 'Bye, Ronnie."

"Yes," Kay said, sort of stunned. "Tomorrow." She was reaching for Ronnie's hand as we left, but the kid was slapping her hand away. I hurried quickly after Nora, hating the long drive back to Watts.

Lorraine Hansberry

(1930–1965)

LORRAINE HANSBERRY, author and playwright, is best known for her drama *A Raisin in the Sun* (1959). The play not only brought Hansberry recognition as a playwright but earned her praise in the literary arena. It received rave reviews and successfully ran for 538 performances on Broadway at the Ethel Barrymore Theatre.

With *A Raisin in the Sun*, she established several milestones. She became the first black woman to have a play on Broadway and the first black and youngest American to win the New York Drama Critics Circle Award for best play of the year. Hansberry's literary genius, however, was lost when she died at the age of thirty-four, a victim of cancer, leaving much of her work to be finished by her husband Robert B. Nemiroff.

Hansberry was born in Chicago in 1930. She was made aware of black economics and culture at a very young age, because her father was politically active in the Urban League and the NAACP. Paul Robeson, Duke Ellington, and others visited her home; she met African students and exiles; she watched her father go to jail to protest housing discrimination. Through this Hansberry developed a deep sense of black pride and resistance, which is manifested in her writings. She also participated in peace and freedom marches throughout her life.

Breaking family tradition, Hansberry decided to attend the University of Wisconsin instead of Howard University. However, displeased with many of her courses, she left in 1950 and went to New York, where she reviewed books and plays by blacks and wrote several articles for Robeson's radical black newspaper, *Freedom*. She later became an associate editor.

She married Nemiroff in 1953, and, deciding to devote all of her time to writing, she resigned from *Freedom* that same year. Working on several plays, a novel, and an opera all at once, Hansberry funneled her energy specifically into one play originally called "The Crystal Stair," which later was renamed *A Raisin in the Sun*.

Hansberry's second drama, *The Sign in Sidney Brustein's Window*, written in 1964, was criticized for focusing on a Greenwich Village Jewish intellectual and overlooking the social conditions of blacks at that time. Her third major play, *Les Blancs*, dramatized the African struggle and the effects of European colonialism. Hansberry wrote it while receiving radiation treatments and even while she was hospitalized, but was not able to finish it. Following the notes his wife left and drawing on conversations they

239

had had, Nemiroff finished the drama, and it was produced for the stage in 1970.

Other works by Hansberry are a book, *The Movement: Documentary of a Struggle for Equality* (1964), which was retitled *A Matter of Colour: Documentary of the Struggles for Racial Equality in the USA* in 1965; *To Be Young, Gifted, and Black: Lorraine Hansberry in Her Own Words* (1969), an autobiography assembled from her writings, and later adapted for stage and television by Nemiroff; a recording, *Lorraine Hansberry Speaks Out: Art and Black Revolution* (1972), selected and edited by Nemiroff; a collection of plays, *Les Blancs: The Collected Last Plays of Lorraine Hansberry* (1972), which includes *Les Blancs*, *The Drinking Gourd*, and *What Use Are Flowers*, her last written play, all edited by Nemiroff; and a series of stories, speeches, and essays published in periodicals.

For further reading see, in addition to Steven R. Carter's article in *Dictionary of Literary Biography, Volume 38*; Ernest Kaiser and Robert Nemiroff's "A Lorraine Hansberry Bibliography," *Freedomways* 19 (Fourth Quarter 1979); Catherine Scheader's *They Found a Way: Lorraine Hansberry* (1978); C. W. E. Bigsby's *Confrontation and Commitment: A Study of Contemporary American Drama, 1959–1966* (1968); and Doris E. Abramson, *Negro Playwrights in the American Theatre, 1925–1959* (1969). See also Loyle Hairston's "Lorraine Hansberry: Portrait of an Angry Young Writer," *Crisis* 86 (April 1979); and the Hansberry papers, which are currently held by Robert B. Nemiroff.

The following is an excerpt from *A Raisin in the Sun*.

A RAISIN IN THE SUN

Act II, Scene 3

TIME   *Saturday, moving day, one week later.*

Before the curtain rises, RUTH'S *voice, a strident, dramatic church alto, cuts through the silence.*

It is, in the darkness, a triumphant surge, a penetrating statement of

---

expectation: "Oh, Lord, I don't feel no ways tired! Children, oh, glory hallelujah!"

As the curtain rises we see that RUTH *is alone in the living room, finishing up the family's packing. It is moving day. She is nailing crates and tying cartons.* BENEATHA *enters, carrying a guitar case, and watches her exuberant sister-in-law.*

RUTH   Hey!

BENEATHA   *(Putting away the case)*   Hi.

RUTH   *(Pointing at a package)*   Honey—look in that package there and see what I found on sale this morning at the South Center. (RUTH *gets up and moves to the package and draws out some curtains)*   Lookahere—hand-turned hems!

BENEATHA   How do you know the window size out there?

RUTH   *(Who hadn't thought of that)*   Oh—Well, they bound to fit something in the whole house. Anyhow, they was too good a bargain to pass up.   (RUTH *slaps her head, suddenly remembering something)*   Oh, Bennie—I meant to put a special note on that carton over there. That's your mama's good china and she wants 'em to be very careful with it.

BENEATHA   I'll do it.

(BENEATHA *finds a piece of paper and starts to draw large letters on it)*

RUTH   You know what I'm going to do soon as I get in that new house?

BENEATHA   What?

RUTH   Honey—I'm going to run me a tub of water up to here . . . *(With her fingers practically up to her nostrils)*   And I'm going to get in it—and I am going to sit . . . and sit . . . and sit in that hot water and the first person who knocks to tell *me* to hurry up and come out—

BENEATHA   Gets shot at sunrise.

RUTH   *(Laughing happily)*   You said it, sister! *(Noticing how large* BENEATHA *is absent-mindedly making the note)*   Honey, they ain't going to read that from no airplane.

BENEATHA   *(Laughing herself)*   I guess I always think things have more emphasis if they are big, somehow.

RUTH   *(Looking up at her and smiling)*   You and your brother seem to have that as a philosophy of life. Lord, that man—done changed so 'round here. You know—you know what we did last night? Me and Walter Lee?

BENEATHA   What?

RUTH   *(Smiling to herself)*   We went to the movies. *(Looking at* BENEATHA *to see if she understands)*   We went to the movies.

You know the last time me and Walter went to the movies together?

BENEATHA   No.

RUTH   Me neither. That's how long it been. (*Smiling again*)   But we went last night. The picture wasn't much good, but that didn't seem to matter. We went—and we held hands.

BENEATHA   Oh, Lord!

RUTH   We held hands—and you know what?

BENEATHA   What?

RUTH   When we come out of the show it was late and dark and all the stores and things was closed up . . . and it was kind of chilly and there wasn't many people on the streets . . . and we was still holding hands, me and Walter.

BENEATHA   You're killing me.

(WALTER *enters with a large package. His happiness is deep in him; he cannot keep still with his new-found exuberance. He is singing and wiggling and snapping his fingers. He puts his package in a corner and puts a phonographic record, which he has brought in with him, on the record player. As the music comes up he dances over to* RUTH *and tries to get her to dance with him. She gives in at last to his raunchiness and in a fit of giggling allows herself to be drawn into his mood and together they deliberately burlesque an old social dance of their youth*)

BENEATHA   (*Regarding them a long time as they dance, then drawing in her breath for a deeply exaggerated comment which she does not particularly mean*)   Talk about—olddddddddddd-fashionedddddddd—Negroes!

WALTER   (*Stopping momentarily*)   What kind of Negroes?
(*He says this in fun. He is not angry with her today, nor with any-one. He starts to dance with his wife again*)

BENEATHA   Old-fashioned.

WALTER   (*As he dances with* RUTH)   You know, when these *New Negroes* have their convention—(*Pointing at his sister*)—that is going to be the chairman of the Committee on Unending Agitation. (*He goes on dancing, then stops*)   Race, race, race! . . . Girl, I do believe you are the first person in the history of the entire human race to successfully brainwash yourself. (BENEATHA *breaks up and he goes on dancing. He stops again, enjoying his tease*) Damn, even the N double A C P takes a holiday sometimes! (BENEATHA *and* RUTH *laugh. He dances with* RUTH *some more and starts to laugh and stops and pantomimes someone over an operating table*)   I can just see that chick someday looking down at some poor cat on an operating table before she starts to slice him, say-ing . . . (*Pulling his sleeves back maliciously*)   "By the way, what

are your views on civil rights down there? . . ."
(*He laughs at her again and starts to dance happily. The bell
sounds*)

BENEATHA Sticks and stones may break my bones but . . . words will
never hurt me!

(BENEATHA *goes to the door and opens it as* WALTER *and* RUTH *go
on with the clowning.* BENEATHA *is somewhat surprised to see a
quiet-looking middle-aged white man in a business suit holding his
hat and a briefcase in his hand and consulting a small piece of
paper*)

MAN Uh—how do you do, miss. I am looking for a Mrs.—(*He looks
at the slip of paper*) Mrs. Lena Younger?

BENEATHA (*Smoothing her hair with slight embarrassment*) Oh—yes,
that's my mother. Excuse me (*She closes the door and turns to
quiet the other two*) Ruth! Brother! Somebody's here. (*Then she
opens the door. The man casts a curious quick glance at all of them*)
Uh—come in please.

MAN (*Coming in*) Thank you.

BENEATHA My mother isn't here just now. Is it business?

MAN Yes . . . well, of a sort.

WALTER (*Freely, the Man of the House*) Have a seat. I'm Mrs. Younger's son. I look after most of her business matters.

(RUTH *and* BENEATHA *exchange amused glances*)

MAN (*Regarding* WALTER, *and sitting*) Well—My name is Karl Lindner . . .

WALTER (*Stretching out his hand*) Walter Younger. This is my
wife—(RUTH *nods politely*)—and my sister.

LINDER How do you do.

WALTER (*Amiably, as he sits himself easily on a chair, leaning with
interest forward on his knees and looking expectantly into the new-
comer's face*) What can we do for you, Mr. Lindner!

LINDNER (*Some minor shuffling of the hat and briefcase on his knees*)
Well—I am a representative of the Clybourne Park Improvement
Association—

WALTER (*Pointing*) Why don't you sit your things on the floor?

LINDNER Oh—yes. Thank you. (*He slides the briefcase and hat under
the chair*) And as I was saying—I am from the Clybourne Park
Improvement Association and we have had it brought to our attention at the last meeting that you people—or at least your
mother—has bought a piece of residential property at—(*He digs
for the slip of paper again*)—four o six Clybourne Street . . .

WALTER That's right. Care for something to drink? Ruth, get Mr.
Lindner a beer.

LINDNER *(Upset for some reason)* Oh—no, really. I mean thank you very much, but no thank you.

RUTH *(Innocently)* Some coffee?

LINDNER Thank you, nothing at all.

(BENEATHA *is watching the man carefully*)

LINDNER Well, I don't know how much you folks know about our organization. *(He is a gentle man; thoughtful and somewhat labored in his manner)* It is one of these community organizations set up to look after—oh, you know, things like block upkeep and special projects and we also have what we call our New Neighbors Orientation Committee . . .

BENEATHA *(Drily)* Yes—and what do they do?

LINDNER *(Turning a little to her and then returning the main force to* WALTER*)* Well—it's what you might call a sort of welcoming committee, I guess. I mean they, we, I'm the chairman of the committee—go around and see the new people who move into the neighborhood and sort of give them the lowdown on the way we do things out in Clybourne Park.

BENEATHA *(With appreciation of the two meanings, which escape* RUTH *and* WALTER*)* Un-huh.

LINDNER And we also have the category of what the association calls—*(He looks elsewhere)*—uh—special community problems . . .

BENEATHA Yes—and what are some of those?

WALTER Girl, let the man talk.

LINDNER *(With understated relief)* Thank you. I would sort of like to explain this thing in my own way. I mean I want to explain to you in a certain way.

WALTER Go ahead.

LINDNER Yes. Well, I'm going to try to get right to the point. I'm sure we'll all appreciate that in the long run.

BENEATHA Yes.

WALTER Be still now!

LINDNER Well—

RUTH *(Still innocently)* Would you like another chair—you don't look comfortable.

LINDNER *(More frustrated than annoyed)* No, thank you very much. Please. Well—to get right to the point I—*(A great breath, and he is off at last)* I am sure you people must be aware of some of the incidents which have happened in various parts of the city when colored people have moved into certain areas—(BENEATHA *exhales heavily and starts tossing a piece of fruit up and down in the air)* Well—because we have what I think is going to be a unique type of organization in American community life—not only do we deplore that kind of thing—but we are trying to do something about it. (BENEATHA *stops tossing and turns with a new and quizzical interest to the man*) We feel—(*gaining confidence in his mission because of the interest in the faces of the people he is talking to*)—we feel that most of the trouble in this world, when you come right down to it—(*He hits his knee for emphasis*)—most of the trouble exists because people just don't sit down and talk to each other.

RUTH (*Nodding as she might in church, pleased with the remark*) You can say that again, mister.

LINDNER (*More encouraged by such affirmation*) That we don't try hard enough in this world to understand the other fellow's prob- lem. The other guy's point of view.

RUTH Now that's right.

(BENEATHA *and* WALTER *merely watch and listen with genuine in- terest*)

LINDNER Yes—that's the way we feel out in Clybourne Park. And that's why I was elected to come here this afternoon and talk to you people. Friendly like, you know, the way people should talk to each other and see if we couldn't find some way to work this thing out. As I say, the whole business is a matter of *caring* about the other fellow. Anybody can see that you are a nice family of folks, hard working and honest I'm sure. (BENEATHA *frowns slightly, quizzically, her head tilted regarding him*) Today every- body knows what it means to be on the outside of *something*. And of course, there is always somebody who is out to take the advantage of people who don't always understand.

WALTER What do you mean?

LINDNER Well—you see our community is made up of people who've worked hard as the dickens for years to build up that lit- tle community. They're not rich and fancy people; just hard- working, honest people who don't really have much but those lit- tle homes and a dream of the kind of community they want to raise their children in. Now, I don't say we are perfect and there is a lot wrong in some of the things they want. But you've got to admit that a man, right or wrong, has the right to want to have the neighborhood he lives in a certain kind of way. And at the moment the overwhelming majority of our people out there feel that people get along better, take more of a common interest in the life of the community, when they share a common back- ground. I want you to believe me when I tell you that race preju- dice simply doesn't enter into it. It is a matter of the people of Clybourne Park believing, rightly or wrongly, as I say, that for

the happiness of all concerned that our Negro families are happier when they live in their *own* communities.

BENEATHA *(With a grand and bitter gesture)* This, friends, is the
Welcoming Committee!

WALTER *(Dumfounded, looking at* LINDNER*)* Is this what you came
marching all the way over here to tell us?

LINDNER Well, now we've been having a fine conversation. I hope
you'll hear me all the way through.

WALTER *(Tightly)* Go ahead, man.

LINDNER You see—in the face of all things I have said, we are prepared to make your family a very generous offer . . .

BENEATHA Thirty pieces and not a coin less!

WALTER Yeah?

LINDNER *(Putting on his glasses and drawing a form out of the briefcase)* Our association is prepared, through the collective effort
of our people, to buy the house from you at a financial gain to
your family.

RUTH Lord have mercy, ain't this the living gall!

WALTER All right, you through?

LINDNER Well, I want to give you the exact terms of the financial
arrangement—

WALTER We don't want to hear no exact terms of no arrangements.
I want to know if you got any more to tell us 'bout getting together?

LINDNER *(Taking off his glasses)* Well—I don't suppose that you
feel . . .

WALTER Never mind how I feel—you got any more to say 'bout
how people ought to sit down and talk to each other? . . . Get
out of my house, man.

(He turns his back and walks to the door)

LINDNER *(Looking around at the hostile faces and reaching and assembling his hat and briefcase)* Well—I don't understand why you
people are reacting this way. What do you think you are going to
gain by moving into a neighborhood where you just aren't
wanted and where some elements—well—people can get awful
worked up when they feel that their whole way of life and everything they've ever worked for is threatened.

WALTER Get out.

LINDNER *(At the door, holding a small card)* Well—I'm sorry it
went like this.

WALTER Get out.

LINDNER *(Almost sadly regarding* WALTER*)* You just can't force people to change their hearts, son.

(He turns and puts his card on a table and exits. WALTER *pushes*

the door to with stinging hatred, and stands looking at it. RUTH
just sits and BENEATHA *just stands. They say nothing.* MAMA *and*
TRAVIS *enter).*

MAMA Well—this all the packing got done since I left out of here
this morning. I testify before God that my children got all the
energy of the dead. What time the moving men due?

BENEATHA Four o'clock. You had a caller, Mama.
(She is smiling, teasingly)

MAMA Sure enough—who?

BENEATHA *(Her arms folded saucily)* The Welcoming Committee.
(WALTER *and* RUTH *giggle)*

MAMA *(Innocently)* Who?

BENEATHA The Welcoming Committee. They said they're sure going
to be glad to see you when you get there.

WALTER *(Devilishly)* Yeah, they said they can't hardly wait to see
your face.
(Laughter)

MAMA *(Sensing their facetiousness)* What's the matter with you all?

WALTER Ain't nothing the matter with us. We just telling you 'bout
the gentleman who came to see you this afternoon. From the
Clybourne Park Improvement Association.

MAMA What he want?

RUTH *(In the same mood as* BENEATHA *and* WALTER) To welcome
you, honey.

WALTER He said they can't hardly wait. He said the one thing they
don't have, that they just *dying* to have out there is a fine family
of colored people! *(To* RUTH *and* BENEATHA) Ain't that right!

RUTH *and* BENEATHA *(Mockingly)* Yeah! He left his card in case—
(They indicate the card, and MAMA *picks it up and throws it on the*
floor—understanding and looking off as she draws her chair up to
the table on which she has put her plant and some sticks and some
cord)

MAMA Father, give us strength. *(Knowingly—and without fun)* Did
he threaten us?

BENEATHA Oh—Mama—they don't do it like that any more. He
talked Brotherhood. He said everybody ought to learn how to sit
down and hate each other with good Christian fellowship.
(She and WALTER *shake hands to ridicule the remark)*

MAMA *(Sadly)* Lord, protect us . . .

RUTH You should hear the money those folks raised to buy the
house from us. All we paid and then some.

BENEATHA What they think we going to do—eat 'em?

RUTH No, honey, marry 'em.

MAMA *(Shaking her head)* Lord, Lord, Lord . . .

RUTH   Well—that's the way the crackers crumble. Joke.

BENEATHA   *(Laughingly noticing what her mother is doing)*   Mama, what are you doing?

MAMA   Fixing my plant so it won't get hurt none on the way . . .

BENEATHA   Mama, you going to take *that* to the new house?

MAMA   Un-huh—

BENEATHA   That raggedy-looking old thing?

MAMA   *(Stopping and looking at her)*   It expresses *me.*

RUTH   *(With delight, to* BENEATHA*)*   So there, Miss Thing!

(WALTER *comes to* MAMA *suddenly and bends down behind her and squeezes her in his arms with all his strength. She is overwhelmed by the suddenness of it and, though delighted, her manner is like that of* RUTH *with* TRAVIS*)*

MAMA   Look out now, boy! You make me mess up my thing here!

WALTER   *(His face lit, he slips down on his knees beside her, his arms still about her)*   Mama . . . you know what it means to climb up in the chariot?

MAMA   *(Gruffly, very happy)*   Get on away from me now . . .

RUTH   *(Near the gift-wrapped package, trying to catch* WALTER's *eye)* Psst—

WALTER   What the old song say, Mama . . .

RUTH   Walter—Now?

(She is pointing at the package)

WALTER   *(Speaking the lines, sweetly, playfully, in his mother's face)*
I got wings . . . you got wings . . .
All God's Children got wings . . .

MAMA   Boy—get out of my face and do some work . . .

WALTER
When I get to heaven gonna put on my wings,
Gonna fly all over God's heaven . . .

BENEATHA   *(Teasingly, from across the room)*   Everybody talking 'bout heaven ain't going there!

WALTER   *(To* RUTH, *who is carrying the box across to them)*   I don't know, you think we ought to give her that . . . Seems to me she ain't been very appreciative around here.

MAMA   *(Eying the box, which is obviously a gift)*   What is that?

WALTER   *(Taking it from* RUTH *and putting it on the table in front of* MAMA*)*   Well—what you all think? Should we give it to her?

RUTH   Oh—she was pretty good today.

MAMA   I'll good you—

(She turns her eyes to the box again)

BENEATHA   Open it, Mama.

(She stands up, looks at it, turns and looks at all of them, and then presses her hands together and does not open the package)

WALTER *(Sweetly)* Open it, Mama. It's for you. (MAMA *looks in his eyes. It is the first present in her life without its being Christmas. Slowly she opens her package and lifts out, one by one, a brand-new sparkling set of gardening tools.* WALTER *continues, prodding)* Ruth made up the note—read it . . .

MAMA *(Picking up the card and adjusting her glasses)* "To our own Mrs. Miniver—Love from Brother, Ruth and Beneatha." Ain't that lovely . . .

TRAVIS *(Tugging at his father's sleeve)* Daddy, can I give her mine now?

WALTER All right son. (TRAVIS *flies to get his gift)* Travis didn't want to go in with the rest of us, Mama. He got his own. *(Somewhat amused)* We don't know what it is . . .

TRAVIS *(Racing back in the room with a large hatbox and putting it in front of his grandmother)* Here!

MAMA Lord have mercy, baby. You done gone and bought your grandmother a hat?

TRAVIS *(Very proud)* Open it!

(She does and lifts out an elaborate, but very elaborate, wide gardening hat, and all the adults break up at the sight of it)

RUTH Travis, honey, what is that?

TRAVIS *(Who thinks it is beautiful and appropriate)* It's a gardening hat! Like the ladies always have on in the magazines when they work in their gardens.

BENEATHA *(Giggling fiercely)* Travis—we were trying to make Mama Mrs. Miniver—not Scarlett O'Hara!

MAMA *(Indignantly)* What's the matter with you all! This here is a beautiful hat! *(Absurdly)* I always wanted me one just like it!

(She pops it on her head to prove it to her grandson, and the hat is ludicrous and considerably oversized)

RUTH Hot dog! Go, Mama!

WALTER *(Doubled over with laughter)* I'm sorry, Mama—but you look like you ready to go out and chop you some cotton sure enough!

(They all laugh except MAMA, out of deference to TRAVIS' feelings)

MAMA *(Gathering the boy up to her)* Bless your heart—this is the prettiest hat I ever owned— (WALTER, RUTH *and* BENEATHA *chime in—noisily, festively and insincerely congratulating* TRAVIS *on his gift)* What are we all standing around here for? We ain't finished packin' yet. Bennie, you ain't packed one book.

(The bell rings)

BENEATHA That couldn't be the movers . . . it's not hardly two good yet—

*(BENEATHA *goes into her room,* MAMA *starts for door)*

WALTER *(Turning, stiffening)* Wait—wait—I'll get it.
(He stands and looks at the door)
MAMA You expecting company, son?
WALTER *(Just looking at the door)* Yeah—yeah . . .
(MAMA looks at RUTH, and they exchange innocent and unfrightened glances)
MAMA *(Not understanding)* Well, let them in, son.
BENEATHA *(From her room)* We need some more string.
MAMA Travis—you run to the hardware and get me some string cord.
(MAMA goes out and WALTER turns and looks at RUTH. TRAVIS goes to a dish for money)
RUTH Why don't you answer the door, man?
WALTER *(Suddenly bounding across the floor to her)* 'Cause sometimes it hard to let the future begin! *(Stooping down in her face)*
I got wings! You got wings!
All God's children got wings!
(He crosses to the door and throws it open. Standing there is a very slight little man in a not too prosperous business suit and with haunted frightened eyes and a hat pulled down tightly, brim up, around his forehead. TRAVIS passes between the men and exits. WALTER leans deep in the man's face, still in his jubilance)
When I get to heaven gonna put on my wings,
Gonna fly all over God's heaven . . .
(The little man just stares at him)
Heaven—
(Suddenly he stops and looks past the little man into the empty hallway) Where's Willy, man?
BOBO He ain't with me.
WALTER *(Not disturbed)* Oh—come on in. You know my wife.
BOBO *(Dumbly, taking off his hat)* Yes—h'you, Miss Ruth.
RUTH *(Quietly, a mood apart from her husband already, seeing BOBO)* Hello, Bobo.
WALTER You right on time today . . . Right on time. That's the way!
(He slaps BOBO on his back) Sit down . . . lemme hear.
(RUTH stands stiffly and quietly in back of them, as though somehow she senses death, her eyes fixed on her husband)
BOBO *(His frightened eyes on the floor, his hat in his hands)* Could I please get a drink of water, before I tell you about it, Walter Lee?
(WALTER does not take his eyes off the man. RUTH goes blindly to the tap and gets a glass of water and brings it to BOBO)
WALTER There ain't nothing wrong, is there?

BOBO   Lemme tell you—

WALTER   Man—didn't nothing go wrong?

BOBO   Lemme tell you—Walter Lee. (*Looking at* RUTH *and talking to her more than to* WALTER)   You know how it was. I got to tell you how it was. I mean first I got to tell you how it was all the way . . . I mean about the money I put in, Walter Lee . . .

WALTER   (*With taut agitation now*)   What about the money you put in?

BOBO   Well—it wasn't much as we told you—me and Willy—(*He stops*)   I'm sorry, Walter. I got a bad feeling about it. I got a real bad feeling about it . . .

WALTER   Man, what you telling me about all this for? . . . Tell me what happened in Springfield . . .

BOBO   Springfield.

RUTH   (*Like a dead woman*)   What was supposed to happen in Springfield?

BOBO   (*To her*)   This deal that me and Walter went into with Willy—Me and Willy was going to go down to Springfield and spread some money 'round so's we wouldn't have to wait so long for the liquor license . . . That's what we were going to do. Everybody said that was the way you had to do, understand, Miss Ruth?

WALTER   Man—what happened down there?

BOBO   (*A pitiful man, near tears*)   I'm trying to tell you, Walter.

WALTER   (*Screaming at him suddenly*)   THEN TELL ME, GODDAMMIT . . . WHAT'S THE MATTER WITH YOU?

BOBO   Man . . . I didn't go to no Springfield, yesterday.

WALTER   (*Halted, life hanging in the moment*)   Why not?

BOBO   (*The long way, the hard way to tell*)   'Cause I didn't have no reasons to . . .

WALTER   Man, what are you talking about!

BOBO   I'm talking about the fact that when I got to the train station yesterday morning—eight o'clock like we planned . . . Man— *Willy didn't never show up.*

WALTER   Why . . . where was he . . . where is he?

BOBO   That's what I'm trying to tell you . . . I don't know . . . I waited six hours . . . (*Breaking into tears*)   That was all the extra money I had in the world . . . (*Looking up at* WALTER *with the tears running down his face*)   Man, *Willy is gone.*

WALTER   Gone, what you mean Willy is gone? Gone where? You mean he went by himself. You mean he went off to Springfield by himself—to take care of getting the license—(*Turns and looks anxiously at* RUTH)   You mean maybe he didn't want too many people in on the business down there? (*Looks to* RUTH *again, as before*) You know Willy got his own ways. (*Looks back to* BOBO) Maybe you was late yesterday and he just went on down there without you. Maybe—maybe—he's been callin' you at home tryin' to tell you what happened or something. Maybe—maybe—he just got sick. He's somewhere—he's got to be somewhere. We just got to find him—me and you got to find him. (*Grabs* BOBO *senselessly by the collar and starts to shake him*) We got to!

BOBO   (*In sudden angry, frightened agony*) What's the matter with you, Walter! *When a cat take off with your money he don't leave you no maps!*

WALTER   (*Turning madly, as though he is looking for* WILLY *in the very room*) Willy! . . . Willy . . . don't do it . . . Please don't do it . . . Man, not with that money . . . Man, please not with that money . . . Oh, God . . . Don't let it be true . . . (*He is wandering around, crying out for* WILLY *and looking for him or perhaps for help from God*) Man . . . I trusted you . . . Man, I put my life in your hands . . . (*He starts to crumble down on the floor as* RUTH *just covers her face in horror,* MAMA *opens the door and comes into the room, with* BENEATHA *behind her*) Man . . . (*He starts to pound the floor with his fists, sobbing wildly*) That money is made out of my father's flesh . . .

BOBO   (*Standing over him helplessly*) I'm sorry, Walter . . . (*Only* WALTER's *sobs reply.* BOBO *puts on his hat*) I had my life staked on this deal, too . . .

(*He exits*)

MAMA   (*To* WALTER) Son—(*She goes to him, bends down to him, talks to his bent head*) Son . . . Is it gone? Son, I gave you sixty-five hundred dollars. Is it gone? All of it? Beneatha's money too?

WALTER   (*Lifting his head slowly*) Mama . . . I never . . . went to the bank at all . . .

MAMA   (*Not wanting to believe him*) You mean . . . your sister's school money . . . you used that too . . . Walter?

WALTER   Yessss! . . . All of it . . . It's all gone . . .

(*There is total silence,* RUTH *stands with her face covered with her hands;* BENEATHA *leans forlornly against a wall, fingering a piece of red ribbon from the mother's gift.* MAMA *stops and looks at her son without recognition and then, quite without thinking about it, starts to beat him senselessly in the face.* BENEATHA *goes to them and stops it*)

BENEATHA   Mama!

(MAMA *stops and looks at both of her children and rises slowly and wanders vaguely, aimlessly away from them*)

MAMA I seen . . . him . . . night after night . . . come in . . . and look at that rug . . . and then look at me . . . the red showing in his eyes . . . the veins moving in his head . . . I seen him grow thin and old before he was forty . . . working and working and working like somebody's old horse . . . killing himself . . . and you—you give it all away in a day . . .

BENEATHA Mama—

MAMA Oh, God . . . (*She looks up to Him*) Look down here—and show me the strength.

BENEATHA Mama—

MAMA (*Folding over*) Strength . . .

BENEATHA (*Plaintively*) Mama . . .

MAMA Strength!

CURTAIN

Darwin Turner

(1931–1991)

SCHOLAR-CRITIC-TEACHER Darwin Theodore Turner was a man of remarkable talents. Born in 1931, in Cincinnati, Ohio, Turner received his B.A. degree at the age of sixteen and at eighteen his M.A., both in English, from the University of Cincinnati. He graduated with his Ph.D. from the University of Chicago at age twenty-five.

The seriousness and the high intelligence reflected in the rapid pace of Turner's academic career manifest themselves in his numerous teaching experiences, professional responsibilities, and prodigious scholarly record. After his first teaching position as an assistant professor of English at Clark College from 1949 to 1951, Professor Turner later taught at Morgan State College, Florida A & M University, North Carolina A & T College, the University of Wisconsin, the University of Michigan, and the University of Hawaii. At the time of his death, he was full professor of English and chairman of Afro-American studies at the University of Iowa, where he had been since 1971.

He worked with a legion of professional organizations such as the Graduate Record Examination Board, Southern Association of Land-Grant Colleges and State Supported Universities, College Language Association, National Council of Teachers of English, Conference on College Composition and Communication, South Atlantic Modern Language Association, Midwest Modern Language Association, North Carolina–Virginia College English Association, Modern Language Association, Iowa Humanities Board, College English Association, Association for the Study of Afro-American Life and History, National Council of Black Studies, Rockefeller Commission on the Humanities, and the American Association for the Advancement of the Humanities. In addition to fulfilling responsibilities with these various organizations, Professor Turner taught a wide range of courses, including Afro-American literature, American literature, world drama from the Restoration through the nineteenth century, Afro-American culture, eighteenth-century English literature, and literary criticism.

Turner's creative and scholarly productivity was even more impressive. For not only had he written original poems that appeared in various books and journals from 1953 to 1975, he also authored fifty-seven articles in journals such as *English Journal, Black World, Parnassus, Studies in American Fiction, The CEA Critic, The Mississippi Quarterly*, and many others. He is co-author of one book, co-editor of four, editor of ten, and the author of three. His best-known works are *In a Minor Chord: Three Afro-American Writers and Their Search for Identity* (1971), various critical essays on Charles Chesnutt, Jean Toomer, and Zora Neale Hurston; his edition of the unpublished works of Jean Toomer entitled *The Wayward and the Seeking: Selected Writings of Jean Toomer* (1980); and his Norton Critical Edition and introduction to Jean Toomer's *Cane* (1987). Turner also wrote introductions to various African American literary works, contributed articles to many books, and wrote numerous book reviews.

Clearly, Professor Darwin Turner was one of the most prolific and well-respected scholars in the field of African American literature. His indefatigable energy also extended into his efforts to improve the status of the profession. He received a National Defense Education Act Grant to provide fellowships to prepare teachers of elementary education and eight grants from the National Endowment for the Humanities to improve research and teaching in Afro-American studies in colleges and universities. He was selected as a delegate to represent the United States at the Second World Festival of Black and African Arts and Culture in Lagos, Nigeria, in 1977. Professor Turner was a recipient of the University of Chicago's Alumni Association Professional Achievement Award, the Carter G. Woodson Award, Simpson College's George Washington Carver Award, the University of Cincinnati's Distinguished Alumnus Award, and the Distinguished Writer Award of the Middle Atlantic Writers Association.

For further reading, see Linda Metzger, ed., *Black Writers: A Selection of Sketches from Contemporary Authors* (1989).

The selection that follows is one of Turner's seminal essays, "Afro-American Critics: An Introduction," originally published in Addison Gayle's *The Black Aesthetic* (1971).

AFRO-AMERICAN LITERARY CRITICS
An Introduction

Each year, increasing numbers of American readers are becoming familiar with and often enthusiastic about black creative writers. White scholars, critics, and students fret anxiously about the probable date of Ellison's next novel. They debate the value of Gwendolyn Brooks's latest style. They choose sides to support or attack Eldridge Cleaver's repudiation of James Baldwin. Without hesitation, reasonably knowledgeable readers could rattle off names of black writers who have earned national attention and acclaim in various literary

Reprinted by permission of Maggie Jean Lewis-Turner.

genres and fields. If, however, one wanted to silence the chatter, he would need merely to ask for the names of black literary critics; for, even in this decade of discovery of black culture, Afro-American critics remain blackly invisible. Few are known among the general reading public; and perhaps only one—Nathan Scott, Jr.—is judged to be both eminent and influential.

Even when their subject has been literature by Afro-American writers, black critics have failed to make America see them, to say nothing of reading or hearing their words. The best-known critics of Afro-American literature are white. White Vernon Loggins, author of *The Negro Author* (1931); Robert Bone, author of *The Negro Novel in America* (1952, 1965); and Herbert Hill, editor of *Soon, One Morning* (1963) and *Anger and Beyond* (1966), are better known than black Hugh Gloster or Saunders Redding. The fact is ironic and regrettable, since black American critics can offer insights into the language, styles, and meanings intended by black writers, insights frequently denied to those who have not shared the experience of living as black people in the United States of America.

The irony cannot be overemphasized. Many Americans today read black writers with the hope of learning who black people are, what they think, and what they propose to be. These readers, however, seem not to comprehend that they will never understand blacks as long as they seek such understanding *solely* in judgments, evaluations, and interpretations made by others who are equally distant from the black experience. The individual who wishes to understand the literature of black people must know the ablest intepreters of that literature.

Many superficial explanations for the apparent dearth of eminent black critics have been whispered at one time or another: Afro-Americans do not write well; or they cannot write objectively about the work of other blacks; or they cannot think abstractly and formulate critical theories. Since these explanations are illogical and easily disproved, let us consider some of the actual reasons before turning to a history of the Afro-American critics themselves.

An established critic in a field is not necessarily the individual who has written the best work on a particular subject; instead, he is the individual who is most widely known for writing on that subject. This one fact, more than any other, has segregated black critics into the basement of the club of literary criticism: the masses of literate Americans do not read the publications of black critics and, consequently, do not know them.

Where does one look for a literary critic? He reads respected newsstand periodicals: *The Saturday Review, The New York Review of Books*, the New York *Times*, or, in years past, *Dial, The Atlantic*, or

The Nation. He looks in the nationally known "little" magazines, such as *Poetry* or *The Kenyon Review.* He studies the anthologies of literary criticism, and he notes the names of editors of anthologies of literature. He scrutinizes the journals of the professional associations—*PMLA, American Literature, Shakespeare Quarterly,* for example. He attends lectures at the large universities and at the annual meetings of academic societies. In such arenas as these, one would expect to discover more literary critics than he could read or listen to in a lifetime.

But, except for rare individuals, the critics in these sources are white. Few anthologies include criticism by blacks: *The New Negro* (Alain Locke, 1925), *The Negro Caravan* (Sterling Brown *et al.,* 1941), *Soon, One Morning* (Herbert Hill, 1963), *Anger and Beyond* (Hill, 1966), *Images of the Negro in America* (Darwin T. Turner and Jean Bright, 1965), *Black Voices* (Abraham Chapman, 1968), *Images of the Negro in American Literature* (Seymour Gross and John Hardy, 1966), *Black Fire* (LeRoi Jones and Larry Neal, 1968), *Black Expression* (Addison Gayle, Jr., 1969), *Black American Literature: Essays* (Turner, 1969). Most of these anthologies have been published within the past five years; and, significantly, of the eight anthologies during that half decade, four have been edited by white men. Few blacks have been hired into the white world of professional journalism as critics or columnists (the William Stanley Braithwaites and Carl Rowans are rare), and few white readers have searched the back pages of black newspapers for critical reviews. In general, the blacks who are invited to review for nationally known periodicals are those who have distinguished themselves as creative writers rather than as critics. They are such men as Langston Hughes, Ralph Ellison, James Baldwin, and Arna Bontemps. Until recently, few black scholars were hired on the staffs of large universities even as visiting lecturers— the Hugh Glosters, Sterling Browns, and Alain Lockes of previous decades were conspicuous. From 1949 to 1965, no more than two or three black scholars read papers at the annual meeting of the Modern Language Association, and only a few more appeared on programs of the National Council of Teachers of English. In fact, as recently as 1939, black scholars felt that they had so little opportunity to present papers at the regional or national Modern Language Association meetings that they formed an organization for black teachers of language and literature—the College Language Association. In short, black critics have been denied opportunity to present their works in the most respected media—or at least they have not been encouraged to contribute.

These facts, however, do not entirely absolve blacks of the responsibility for failing to produce more critics. Afro-American professional journalism has failed to develop and promote a literary market. *Negro Digest*, now called *The Black World* (1942–51, 1961 to date), has been the most enduring among the commercial magazines that devote significant space to literature, but the Johnson Publishing Company has not given the *Digest* support equal to that for *Ebony* and *Jet*. Black commercial publishers have alleged that they would waste money if they attempted to promote literary culture among the disinterested black masses. (One wonders how these publishers explain the fact that, with little advertising and limited distribution, Broadside Press has managed, in two years, to sell fifty-six thousand copies of the poetry of Don Lee.)

Many white commercial publishers have similar reservations about the cultural interests of Americans, even though their potential market is eight times as large. Among whites, however, a substantial amount of literary criticism is published within the academic world. Here, too, black Americans have failed to promote literary scholarship as effectively as might be expected. Most major universities sponsor publishing companies, which promote the university's reputation within the academic community and simultaneously provide platforms for the university's scholars. In contrast, although many predominantly Negro colleges have offered courses and even majors in printing and in journalism, very few have attempted to publish anything more scholarly than a catalogue and a schedule of classes. Even though any one of these colleges may complain that high costs and a limited market militate against establishing an individual publishing company, it seems feasible for several black colleges to pool their resources to form a combined press.

Equally significant is the failure of black institutions to promote journals. Relatively small white universities have sponsored journals that have gained respect; but, at black colleges, such journals—when attempted—have rarely endured for more than an issue or two: the *Journal of Negro Education* at Howard University, *Phylon* at Atlanta University, and the *Journal of Human Relations* at Central State College in Ohio are perhaps the most successful. And the College Language Association is the only professional association for blacks to give attention primarily to literature. Furthermore, no enduring journal has concentrated on the study and promotion of Afro-American contributions in the arts. *Phylon* probably has achieved more toward this end than any other journal, but *Phylon* has reflected the social-science orientation that might be expected from a periodical established by W. E. B. Du Bois.

Finally, black scholars know how the fifteen-hour teaching schedule has buried research under mounds of freshman composition and how the small pay checks have driven potential critics into administrative positions merely to gain reasonable compensation for their drudgery.

After this pessimistic review of the problems of Afro-American literary critics, it may seem amazing that any have existed. And in limited space, I can do little more than name a few of the more prolific and to consider their practices briefly. I wish to give special attention to the Afro-American critics who have written about literature by blacks, and I shall include both literary historians and critics under the rubric of "critic." For convenience of discussion, I shall over-simplify by categorizing the historians and critics in six groups: (1) Afro-Americans who have become identified primarily with the "mainstream" of American criticism because of their research in the work of white authors; (2) black historians who have described literary achievements merely as a part of their broader study of Afro-American culture; (3) those individuals who have attracted attention because of their pronouncements about one particular black writer or one group of writers; (4) the creative writers, whose fame rests upon their own work rather than upon their criticism; (5) the academic critics, and (6) the new black critics, who argue for a Black Aesthetic. This survey is not definitive but suggestive: it is an introduction to a study that needs to be made.

i.

Some Afro-Americans have earned recognition primarily by writing about literature by whites. Probably the first such successful critic was William Stanley Braithwaite, a Bostonian black man of West Indian ancestry. A professional journalist, Braithwaite from 1913 to 1929 edited an annual anthology of magazine verse. In introductions to these volumes, Braithwaite directed attention to young white poets who had not yet been recognized by American critics. One should not look to Braithwaite for objective criticism, however. Generally, he assumed the role of a sociable master of ceremonies, introducing his protégés, rejoicing in their virtues, and abstaining from caustic condemnation. Although he published only one volume of criticism, *The Poetic Year*, a collection of essays about the poetry of 1916, he wrote a biography of the Brontë sisters, and he edited anthologies of Elizabethan, Georgian, and Restoration verse.

A second critic who published before World War I was Benjamin Brawley. Although his principal reputation today is based on his studies of black cultural history, Brawley, a professor at Morehouse College, Shaw University, and Howard University, also wrote *A Short History of English Literature*, designed for use in college classes. In taste, Brawley was a Victorian, in the conservative and genteel sense in which that term is understood. He preferred writers who wrote of beauty rather than squalor; and in his own biographical work he ignored those activities of his subjects that he could not commend. Although he must be mentioned at this point, Brawley will be considered more fully in a later section of this paper.

Some more-recent scholars have earned wider recognition for their publications about white authors than for their studies of blacks. For example, although Philip Butcher, a professor at Morgan State College, has written articles about young black novelists, he is better known for his two biographies of George Washington Cable, a nineteenth-century white novelist. Similarly, Esther Merle Jackson, recently a Fullbright professor at the University of Berlin and currently a professor at the University of Wisconsin, is better known as the author of a brilliant book-length study of Tennessee Williams than as a critic of black literature.

The contemporary black critic who is most firmly anchored in the mainstream is Nathan A. Scott, professor of theology at the University of Chicago, whose race is unknown to many of his ardent admirers. Scott occasionally has written about Afro-American literature, a field in which he is very knowledgeable. His best piece in black literary criticism is "The Dark and Haunted Tower of Richard Wright" (1964), one of the few articles commending Richard Wright as an existentialist. Nathan Scott's reputation, however, is based on such books as *Rehearsals of Discomposure* (1952) and *Modern Literature and the Religious Frontier* (1958), excellent works in which he examined philosophical and psychological dilemmas as they are revealed in the fiction of such writers as Kafka, Silone, Lawrence, and Eliot.

As was stated earlier, however, most of the attention in this paper will be focused on those black literary historians and critics who have been especially concerned with studies of black literature.

ii.

Criticism of black writers as a group is a relatively new venture. It was necessary, first, for black writers to produce a considerable body of literature and, second, for black and white critics to develop awareness that that work could be examined as literature rather than merely as sociology. As early as 1863, William Wells Brown included Phillis Wheatley among the black heroes whose lives he recorded in *The Black Man: His Antecedents, His Genius, and His Achievements*. Almost one half century later, Benjamin Brawley produced a pioneer work, *The Negro in Literature and Art* (1910). Like Brown, Brawley offered more biography than critical evaluation. Perceiving America's ignorance about black writers, Brawley chiefly assumed the responsibility of familiarizing readers with them; hence, he remained more historian than critic.

By the middle of the 1920s, the two requisite forces—an ample volume of work by black writers, and readers' respect for that work as literature—had coalesced. Therefore, most significant criticism of Afro-American literature dates from that time.

Prominent among the black scholars since 1925 who have earned reputations for knowledge of black literature, have been several whose major interests lay in other disciplines. The first of these was W. E. B. Du Bois, who earned his doctorate from Harvard in history. Although he did not publish any books of criticism, Du Bois, as the first editor of *The Crisis*, regularly commented on the work of black writers. Unfortunately, during the 1920s, one of the most exciting periods in the annals of Afro-American literature, Du Bois proved incapable of shedding the ideals of an earlier generation. Like most black intellectuals of the last decade of the nineteenth century, Du Bois sought to earn equality for black Americans by educating white Americans to awareness of their virtues and their sensitivity to oppression. A talented writer who judged creative literature to be a major vehicle for such education, Du Bois was appalled by some black writers of the twenties who seemed to sully the black man's image by revealing the squalid aspects of Afro-American life and character.

Few men, if any, have had greater success than Alain Locke in familiarizing America with the culture of black people. Although he earned a doctorate from Harvard in philosophy, served for many years as chairman of the Philosophy Department at Howard University, and published studies in philosophy, Locke used his compendious knowledge and his aesthetic sensitivity to art, music, and literature as a basis for many articles and books about black culture. In 1925, he edited *The New Negro*, an anthology that is still respected as the best introduction to the temper and art of the early years of the Negro Awakening. He was the first to edit an anthology of Afro-American drama, *Plays of Negro Life* (1927). He edited one of the earliest critical anthologies of poetry, *Four Negro Poets* (1927). For more than twenty years, he annually reviewed literature of black Americans—first in *Opportunity*, then in *Phylon*. Like Braithwaite, he applauded more than he appraised; for his purpose was to record literary achievement and to encourage additional activity.

More recent historians of Afro-American literature are John Hope Franklin, Margaret Just Butcher, and Ernest Kaiser. In *From Slavery to Freedom* (1948, 1956), Franklin, professor of history at the University of Chicago, commented on Afro-American writers as part of the cultural history of black America. Margaret Butcher, a professor at Federal City College, included appraisals of literary works in *The Negro in American Culture* (1956), which she developed from notes and materials that Alain Locke had compiled. Ernest Kaiser, librarian at the Schomburg Collection in New York City, is best known as the author of brilliant essays on black scholarship in history. In addition, Kaiser, who is incredibly knowledgeable about literature by and about Afro-Americans, has written perceptively about current black writers. His work is frequently published in *Negro Digest* and in *Freedomways*, for which he regularly reviews recent books by and about blacks.

All these cultural historians have played important roles by familiarizing Americans with the names and works of black writers; but, because of their training and their purpose, they had no desire to provide for individual works or individual authors the kind of in-depth examination that is essential to literary criticism.

iii.

A few essayists have become known as critics chiefly because of their evaluation of one writer or one group. It may be unfair to place Harold Cruse in this category, for *The Crisis of the Negro Intellectual* (1967) is now judged on its own merits. Nevertheless, when the book was first published, the criticism Cruse had written for magazines was not known widely; consequently, his name was less familiar than were the names of black writers he attacked and black scholars whose critical theories he denounced. It is probable, therefore, that much of the early reaction to the book was stimulated by general interest in Cruse's assault on such writers as Lorraine Hansberry and John Killens. Similarly, the first international recognition of James Baldwin as a critic came in response to "Everybody's Protest Novel," which seemed to question the artistic competence of Richard Wright, who was then the most famed and respected among Afro-American novelists. As the wheel turns and attacker becomes the attacked, it is fashionable today to quote Eldridge Cleaver's denunciation of Baldwin in *Soul on Ice* (1968).

What is startling about these few instances is the apparent eagerness of the reading public to accept instantly the scathing pronouncements of an individual who had no previous reputation as a critic or who at least lacked a literary reputation comparable to that of the writer he rejected. The reason for this phenomenon, I believe, is that, despite fifty years of criticism of Afro-American literature, criteria for that criticism have not been established. Consequently, some readers judge literature by Afro-Americans according to its moral value, a few for its aesthetic value, most by its social value, and too many according to their responses to the personalities of the black authors. As long as this confusion continues, many readers, lacking confidence in their own ability to distinguish the worthwhile black literature from the inept, echo the most recent voice they hear.

iv.

When a white publisher has wanted a black man to write about Afro-American literature, the publisher generally has turned to a famous creative writer. The reason is obvious. White publishers and readers have not been, and are not, familiar with the names and work of black scholars—the academic critics. Therefore, publishers have called upon the only blacks they have known—the famous writers.

Since all the best-known black writers and many of the less well known have been asked or permitted to serve as historian, critic, or polemicist, only a minimal summary of their work is possible in a paper as brief as this.

In 1922, novelist and poet James Weldon Johnson edited an anthology, *The Book of American Negro Poetry* (revised in 1931), for which he wrote an excellent critical introduction to black poets. From 1926 to 1928, Countee Cullen, best-known Afro-American poet of his day, wrote randomly about literary topics in "The Black Tower," published monthly in *Opportunity*. In 1927, he, too, prepared an anthology of poetry, *Caroling Dusk*, for which he provided an introduction and headnotes. Both Johnson and Cullen, however, are suspect as critics. Like many other authors, they sometimes devised theory to defend their personal practices. Nevertheless, both gave more attention to aesthetic theory than was common among Afro-American critics.

During the twenties, novelist Wallace Thurman received frequent invitations to write articles about fiction. From the thirties until his death in the sixties, Langston Hughes probably received more requests to write about Afro-American authors than any other black writer prior to James Baldwin. Most often, Hughes described personalities rather than works, or he recited the problems of black writers. It is difficult to determine whether Hughes chose to restrict his writing in this manner, or, more probably, whether these were the subjects of prime interest to the soliciting editors. In the forties, Richard Wright was the one whom editors called for articles; and, when he chose, he produced as effectively in literary history as in fiction. One of the most perceptive analyses by an Afro-American writer is

Wright's long essay on black poets, "The Literature of the Negro in the United States," published first in a French journal and later included in Wright's *White Man! Listen* (1957). In the essay, Wright describes the poets since Phillis Wheatley, and scrutinizes their relationships to American society.

The two best-known writer-critics are James Baldwin and Ralph Ellison, who come closer than any others to being the professional critics among black writers. A professional critic, as I use the term, is a man who earns his living primarily by writing about literature; for example, Brooks Atkinson, for years drama critic for the New York *Times*, or Edmund Wilson or George Jean Nathan. To survive, a professional critic normally must be associated with a newspaper or magazine; a free-lance critic risks starvation. (And, as I have said earlier, few blacks have been hired on the staffs of periodicals or dailies.) Nevertheless, Baldwin, in his early years in Paris, gambled at being a free-lance writer on literary subjects even before he became famous as a novelist. He included many of his better essays in *Notes of a Native Son* (1955) and *Nobody Knows My Name* (1961). Ralph Ellison also distinguished himself as a free-lance writer on literary and musical topics. Some of his more significant essays are included in his collection *Shadow and Act* (1964).

A writer-critic in great demand at the moment is Arna Bontemps, one of the last of the talented writers of the Harlem Renaissance. By preference and by invitation, Bontemps most frequently writes nostalgically and illuminatingly about the twenties and thirties. Although he has published many novels and anthologies, Bontemps has published no books of literary history, an oversight one hopes he will correct.

v.

The most significant group of black literary critics should be the academic critics, for these are the individuals trained to study and evaluate literature. They have the breadth of information to facilitate comparison of American writers with foreign ones and comparison of current writers with those of previous centuries. Unfortunately, because they have published most often for small printing houses or in professional journals (often those read by few whites), the academic critics are the least well known of black critics.

The first major academic critic was Benjamin Brawley, whose early efforts were designed to promote appreciation rather than evaluation. For example, in his critical biography of Paul Laurence Dunbar (1936), Brawley deliberately ignored personal failings of the man, and minimized many of Dunbar's weaknesses as a writer.

When the writers of the twenties appeared, Brawley, like Du Bois, revealed himself unable to adapt to the tastes of a new generation: He continued to echo the precepts of Matthew Arnold. Complaining about what he believed to be the young writers' unnecessary interest in the ugliness of life, he argued that they lacked the high moral purpose essential to great literature. Perhaps the most accurate measure of Brawley's literary taste is the fact that he selected as Dunbar's best story a highly sentimental one in which a husband decides to remain with his wife because he is thrilled by the tenderness with which their newly born child clutches his hand.

Despite his deficiencies in criticism, Brawley was the first significant academic critic-historian of Afro-American literature. The next was Sterling Brown, younger than Brawley but his contemporary as a teacher at Howard University. Brown is the dean of black academic critics. No other black critic has inspired as much admiration and respect from his students and his successors in the field. In every stream of creative black literature, Sterling Brown is the source to which critics return. His first published critical books were *The Negro in American Fiction* (1937), a detailed examination of the Afro-American as a character, and *The Negro in Poetry and Drama* (1937). An almost unknown classic is his unpublished study of Afro-American drama, which he undertook as part of the Myrdal-Carnegie research project. Brown was the senior editor of *The Negro Caravan* (1941), the most comprehensive anthology of Afro-American letters that has been published. Unlike Brawley, Brown understood the need to evaluate the image of the black man as character and the achievement of the black man as writer. Brown has published no books since 1941, although he continued until recently to publish infrequent articles on folk tales, folklore, and folk speech. As a critic, Brown benefited from catholic taste and sensitivity, which enabled him to appreciate and applaud the realistic as well as the genteel, the folk as well as the sophisticated.

The best single volume of criticism by a black, I believe, is Saunders Redding's *To Make a Poet Black* (1939). A brilliant writer, the author of history, an autobiography, a novel, and a collection of essays, Redding, now a professor at Georgetown University, studied writers from Jupiter Hammon through those of the twenties. His insights are striking, and his style is admirable. This is a book to read; it is regrettable that Redding has not revised the book to bring it up to the present.

In the 1930s and 1940s, two other academic critics—Nick Ford and Hugh Gloster—published book-length studies of Afro-American literature. Ford examined twentieth-century fiction in *The Contemporary Negro Novel* (1936). Gloster's *Negro Voices in American Fiction*

(1948)—the more detailed of the two—focuses on the Afro-American writers' depiction of the relationship of the black characters to the American scene. Gloster, however, was concerned more with sociological import than with aesthetic quality.

The forties and fifties spawned numerous Afro-American critics who published in *Phylon*, the *College Language Association Journal*, and other professional periodicals. Among the most productive of these were John Lash, Blyden Jackson, and Nick Ford. All three, at various times, prepared the annual review of Negro literature for *Phylon*, but also published frequently in other journals. All three concentrated on fiction. Criticism of poetry is surprisingly sparse during the period, and criticism of drama is almost non-existent.

A characteristic common to all these critics—and one that Harold Cruse denounces—is the tendency to evaluate literature by black writers according to the criteria established and approved for white American writers. In one sense, this standard is justifiable, for most of the black writers, in their effort to earn respect, imitated the styles supposedly approved. But this insistence encouraged excessively enthusiastic praise of writers working within tradition, and suspicion of the few who broke away from tradition.

vi.

For a decade, there was a hiatus in criticism by the academicians. Many of the black scholars drifted into administrative positions to secure financial rewards commensurate with their ability. Others abandoned Afro-American literature because they believed that black writers had finally become part of the mainstream of American literature. During this period—roughly, 1954 to 1965—significant social changes occurred. The Supreme Court desegregation decision of 1954 at first seemed to assure Afro-Americans the equality they had desired. Consequently, many black educators considered it deplorable and un-American to study Negro identity apart from American identity. However, by 1960, only six years later, it was evident that school integration had not produced the anticipated amalgamation. Meanwhile, intensifying insistence from black Americans persuaded blacks and whites to want to learn more about Afro-American culture and history.

This impulse has produced two developments. The first is the emergence of a new generation of academic critics and a return of many who had discontinued their studies about Afro-American literature: James Emanuel, W. Edward Farrison, Addison Gayle, Stephen Henderson, and George Kent are among the currently productive writers. Richard Long, Helen Johnson, and Richard Barksdale are perfecting studies intended for publication. Of these, only Emanuel and Farrison have written books of criticism—Emanuel, a biography of Langston Hughes (1967), and Farrison, a biography of William Wells Brown (1969). Gayle, however, has published two anthologies of criticism by Afro-Americans—*Black Expression* (1969) and this volume on the Black Aesthetic—and a collection of essays *The Black Situation* (1970).

The second development is perhaps more significant. A new group of black critics has developed. These reject the standards previously applied to works by Afro-Americans, and are demanding that that literature be judged according to an aesthetic grounded in Afro-American culture. Many of these new critics insist that, to have value, black literature must contribute to the revolutionary cause of black liberation, not merely in polemics against white oppression but also in reinterpretation of the black experience. All the new critics agree that the literature should not be judged good or bad according to its imitation of the styles and tastes of Europeans, but according to its presentation of the styles and traditions stemming from African and Afro-American culture. For example, they point out the foolishness of expecting iambic meter in work of a poet who moves instead to the rhythms of jazz or be-bop, and they argue that it is supercilious or even racist to complain that literature does not conform to the patterns and tastes of the white literary world if it does suit and meet the needs of black people.

None of these critics has yet produced a book; they were given platforms originally by Hoyt Fuller of *Negro Digest* and John Henrik Clarke of *Freedomways*. More recently, they have been publishing in newer magazines. The best-known are LeRoi Jones and Larry Neal, who coedited *Black Fire* (1968). Jones is known as a writer of the new literature; Neal has been more productive as an exponent of the theories of the new literature. Others of significance are Clarence Major, editor of *New Black Poetry* (1969); Carolyn Rodgers, whose "Black Poetry—Where It's At" (*Negro Digest*, 1969) is the best essay on the work of new black poets; Sarah Fabio; Cecil Brown, author of a recent novel, *The Life and Loves of Mr. Jive-Ass Nigger*; and Ed Bullins, the leading interpreter of current black theater.

It is important that these new critics are explaining theory rather than merely commenting on practice. Previously, as I have said, most Afro-American critics assumed that the desirable standards were necessarily those currently favored by the American literary establishment. This attitude inevitably restricted black writers to imitation rather than innovation: the "good" writer was expected to use the forms and styles that appealed to white readers. And he dared not aspire to the avant-garde, because he needed assurance that the style was approved. In a sense, then, he continued to permit himself to be defined by the white American. Today, however, black critics are postulating theories about what literature is or should be for black people, according to a Black Aesthetic, as was explained in a recent issue of *Negro Digest*.

The writings of these theorists and critics are not hammering at the consciousness of the American literary masses, because most new critics are not attempting to publish in the journals subscribed to predominantly by whites. Most are publishing in *Negro Digest, Journal of Black Poetry, Critique, The Black Scholar, Black Theater*, and other popular publications aimed at a black market. One who wishes to learn what the new black critics are doing and saying must read such journals as these.

At present, the major weakness of the Black Aesthetic critics are their tendencies to denigrate older black writers while lauding the newest. They are further handicapped by the necessity of devising theory prior to the creation of works. That is, Aristotle actually did little more than examine works he and other Greeks admired. He distinguished the elements these works shared. Then he stipulated that great literature must include such elements. Arnold, too, deduced his theories from literature already created. Many new black critics, however, are structuring theories while calling for writers to create the works that are needed to demonstrate the excellence of the theories. It is not accidental, therefore, that most of the new critics are writers. And because their social theories are as revolutionary as their literary theories, few are permanently connected with the well-established academic institutions.

It is always dangerous to predict the future for any group of writers; nevertheless, a few guesses can be made about future directions of black critics. First, as increasing numbers of predominantly white institutions hire black instructors, and as additional money is given to black institutions, black scholars will find the time, the motivation, and the connections for publishing. This means that they will be producing increasing numbers of books about both white and black writers. As their publications increase, more black critics will become recognized and respected.

Second, as some of the present ferment subsides, the new black critics will look more closely at the current black writers. They will begin to evaluate more carefully on aesthetic bases, as Carolyn Rodgers is now doing. Perhaps by that time, or soon afterwards, they will have expanded American critical theory to a degree at which Americans can more fully appreciate poetry that depends on oral presentation and can appreciate drama that involves less physical action than has been the custom in the Anglo-American theatre. In short, the new black critics may develop theory that may become influential in the evaluation of all American literature.

I would like to conclude on this note of optimism. But I cannot. The chances are great that unless America changes drastically within the next few years, most American readers will continue to look at literature through the eyes of the white critics rather than the black. Full awareness of black critics will develop only when publishers make greater effort to look beyond the prestige colleges for authors of scholarly books, and when the literary public learns to look beyond the prestige journals for literary scholarship. And full appreciation of the criticism of Afro-American literature will develop only when all readers perceive that a thorough knowledge and understanding of the Afro-American experience, culture, and literary history is a prerequisite for an individual who wishes to be a critic of that literature.

Adrienne Kennedy

(1931-   )

PLAYWRIGHT ADRIENNE KENNEDY was born Adrienne Lita in 1931 in Pittsburgh, Pennsylvania, and grew up in Cleveland, Ohio. She graduated from The Ohio State University in 1953 and married Joseph Kennedy that same year. In 1954 she and her husband moved to New York City, where she began taking creative writing classes at Columbia University. She wrote her best-known play, *Funnyhouse of a Negro*, while on a trip through Europe and Africa from 1960 to 1961. Returning to the United States, she began studying with Edward Albee in his workshop at Circle-in-the-Square Theater. Her formal career as a playwright began in 1962 when Albee produced *Funnyhouse of a Negro* at Circle-in-the-Square. Two years later he produced it again off-Broadway at the East End Theater, where it ran for forty-six performances and won an Obie Award in 1964.

Kennedy's next play, *The Owl Answers*, was produced in 1963 in Connecticut and later at the Joseph Papp Public Theater in New York, where it ran as part of the New York Shakespeare Festival. In 1969 her third play, *A Rat's Mass*, ran at La Mama Experimental Theater Club. Others of her fifteen plays have been performed at the National Theatre in London, the Petit Odeon in Paris, and various theaters throughout the United States. She is the author of *People Who Led to My Plays* (1987), *Adrienne Kennedy in One Act* (1988), and *Deadly Triplets: A Theatre Mystery and Journal* (1990).

Kennedy has won grants for her work from the Rockefeller Foundation (1969, 1973, and 1976), a Guggenheim Fellowship (1968), a National Endowment for the Arts grant (1977), and other awards. She has taught creative writing at Yale, Harvard, and Princeton universities and at the University of California at Berkeley and at Davis. She has written an unpublished retrospective, "Recollections of Writers and Theater People" and is currently at work on a film project. Her plays are taught throughout the United States, Europe, and Africa.

For further reading, see Margaret B. Wilkerson's essay in *Dictionary of Literary Biography, Volume 38*, and Doris Abramson's *Negro Playwrights in the American Theatre, 1925–59* (1969). See also the interview "A Growth of Images" in *Drama Review* 21 (December 1977) and Kimberly W. Benston, "Cities in Bezique: Adrienne Kennedy's Expressionistic Vision," *CLA Journal* 20 (December 1976).

The following selection is *Funnyhouse of a Negro*.

FUNNYHOUSE OF A NEGRO

CHARACTERS

NEGRO-SARAH
DUCHESS OF HAPSBURG .... *One of herselves*
QUEEN VICTORIA REGINA .... *One of herselves*
JESUS .... *One of herselves*
PATRICE LUMUMBA .... *One of herselves*
SARAH'S LANDLADY .... *Funnyhouse Lady*
RAYMOND .... *Funnyhouse Man*
THE MOTHER

AUTHOR'S NOTE

FUNNYHOUSE OF A NEGRO is perhaps clearest and most explicit when the play is placed in the girl Sarah's room. The center of
the stage works well as her room, allowing the rest of the stage as
the place for herselves. Her room should have a bed, a writing table
and a mirror. Near her bed is the statue of Queen Victoria; other
objects might be her photographs and her books. When she is
placed in her room with her belongings, then the director is free to
let the rest of the play happen around her.

BEGINNING Before the closed curtain a woman dressed in a white
nightgown walks across the stage carrying before her a bald head.
She moves as one in a trance and is mumbling something inaudi-
ble to herself. She appears faceless, wearing a yellow whitish
mask over her face, with no apparent eyes. Her hair is wild,
straight and black and falls to her waist. As she moves, holding
her hands before her, she gives the effect of one in a dream. She
crosses the stage from right to left. Before she has barely vanished, the curtain opens. It is a white satin curtain of a cheap
material and a ghastly white, a material that brings to mind the
interior of a cheap casket; parts of it are frayed and it looks as if
it has been gnawed by rats.

THE SCENE Two women are sitting in what appears to be a queen's
chamber. It is set in the middle of a stage in a strong white light,
while the rest of the stage is in strong unnatural blackness. The
quality of the white light is unreal and ugly. The monumental

bed resembling an ebony tomb, a low dark chandelier with candles and wine-colored walls. Flying about are great black ravens. Queen Victoria is standing before her bed, holding a small mirror in her hand. On the white pillow of her bed is a dark indistinguishable object. The Duchess of Hapsburg is standing at the foot of her bed. Her back is to us as is the Queen's. Throughout the entire scene they do not move. Both women are dressed in royal gowns of white, a white similar to the white of the curtain, the material cheap satin. Their headpieces are white and of a net that falls over their faces. From beneath both their headpieces springs a headful of wild kinky hair. Although in this scene we do not see their faces, they look exactly alike and will wear masks or be made up to appear a whitish yellow. It is an alabaster face, the skin drawn tightly over the high cheekbones, great dark eyes that seem gouged out of the head, a high forehead, a full red mouth and a head of frizzy hair. If the characters do not wear a mask, the face must be highly powdered and possess a hard expressionless quality and a stillness as in the face of death.

(We hear a knocking.)

VICTORIA   *(listening to the knocking).*   It is my father. He is arriving again for the night. *(The* DUCHESS *makes no reply.)*   He comes through the jungle to find me. He never tires of his journey.

DUCHESS   How dare he enter the castle, he who is the darkest of them all, the darkest one. My mother looked like a white woman, hair as straight as any white woman's. And at least I am yellow, but he is black, the blackest one of them all. I hoped he was dead. Yet he still comes through the jungle to find me. *(The knocking is louder.)*

VICTORIA   He never tires of the journey, does he, Duchess? *(Looking at herself in the mirror.)*

DUCHESS   How dare him enter the castle of Queen Victoria Regina, Monarch of England. It is because of him that my mother died. The wild black beast put his hands on her. She died.

VICTORIA   Why does he keep returning? He keeps returning forever, coming back ever and keeps coming back forever. He is my father.

DUCHESS   He is a black Negro.

VICTORIA   He is my father. I am tied to the black Negro. He came when I was a child in the south, before I was born he haunted my conception, diseased my birth.

DUCHESS   Killed my mother.

VICTORIA   My mother was the light. She was the lightest one. She looked like a white woman.

DUCHESS   We are tied to him unless, of course, he should die.

VICTORIA   But he is dead.

DUCHESS   And he keeps returning. (*The knocking is louder, black-out. Onto the stage from the left comes the figure in the white night-gown carrying the bald head. This time we hear her speak.*)

MOTHER   Black man, black man, I never should have let a black man put his hands on me. The wild black beast raped me and now my skull is shining.

(She disappears to the right. Now the light is focused on a single white square wall that is to the left of the stage that is suspended and stands alone, of about five feet in dimension and width. It stands with the narrow part facing the audience. A character steps through. She is a faceless dark character with a hangman's rope about her neck and red blood on the part that would be her face. She is the Negro. On first glance she might be a young person but at a closer look the impression of an ancient character is given. The most noticeable aspect of her looks is her wild kinky hair, part of which is missing. It is a ragged head with a patch of hair missing from the crown which the Negro carries in her hand. She is dressed in black. She steps slowly through the wall, stands still before it and begins her monologue.)

NEGRO   Part of the time I live with Raymond, part of the time with God, Prince Charlies and Albert Saxe Coburg. I live in my room. It is a small room on the top floor of a brownstone in the West Nineties in New York, a room filled with my dark old volumes, a narrow bed and on the wall old photographs, castles and monarchs of England. It is also Victoria's chamber, Queen Victoria Regina's. Partly because it is consumed by a gigantic plaster statue of Queen Victoria, who is my idol, and partly for other reasons; three steps that I contrived out of boards lead to the statue which I have placed opposite the door as I enter the room. It is a sitting figure, a replica of one in London, and a thing of astonishing whiteness. I found it in a dusty shop on Morningside Heights. Raymond says it is a thing of terror, possessing the quality of nightmares, suggesting large and probable deaths. And of course he is right. When I am the Duchess of Hapsburg, I sit opposite Victoria in my headpiece and we talk. The other times I wear the dress of a student, dark clothes and dark stockings. Victoria always wants me to tell her of whiteness. She wants me to tell her of a royal world where everything and everyone is white and there are no unfortunate black ones. For as we of royal blood know, black is evil and has been from the beginning. Even before my mother's hair started to fall out. Before she was raped by a wild black beast. Black was evil.

When I am not the Duchess of Hapsburg I am myself. As for myself, I long to become even a more pallid Negro than I am now, pallid like Negroes on the covers of American Negro magazines; soulless, educated and irreligious. I want to possess no moral value, particularly value as to my being. I want not to be. I ask nothing except anonymity.

I am an English major, as my mother was when she went to school in Atlanta. My father majored in social work. I am graduated from a city college and have occasional work in libraries, but mostly spend my days preoccupied with the placement and geometric position of words on paper. I write poetry, filling white page after white page with imitations of Edith Sitwell. It is my dream to live in rooms with European antiques and my Queen Victoria, photographs of Roman ruins, walls of books, a piano, oriental carpets, and to eat my meals on a white glass table. I will visit my friends' apartments which will contain books, photographs of Roman ruins, pianos, and oriental carpets. My friends will be white. I need them as an embankment to keep me from reflecting too much upon the fact that I am a Negro. For, like all educated Negroes—out of life and death essential—I find it necessary to maintain a stark fortress against recognition of myself. My white friends like myself will be shrewd, intellectual and anxious for death. Anyone's death. I will mistrust them, as I do myself. But if I had not wavered in my opinion of myself then my hair would never have fallen out. And if my hair hadn't fallen out, I wouldn't have bludgeoned my father's head with an ebony mask.

In appearance I am good-looking in a boring way; no glaring Negroid features, medium nose, medium mouth and pale yellow skin. My one defect is that I have a head of frizzy hair, unmistakably Negro kinky hair; and it is indisguisable. I would like to lie and say I love Raymond. But I do not. He is a poet and is Jewish. He is very interested in Negroes.

*(The Negro stands by the wall and throughout her following speech, the following characters come through the wall, disappearing off into the varying directions in the darkened night of the stage—*DUCHESS, QUEEN VICTORIA, JESUS, PATRICE LUMUMBA. JESUS *is a hunchback, yellow-skinned dwarf, dressed in white rags and sandals.* PATRICE LUMUMBA *is a black man. His head appears to be split in two with blood and tissue in eyes. He carries an ebony mask.)*

The characters are myself: the Duchess of Hapsburg, Queen Victoria Regina, Jesus, Patrice Lumumba. The rooms are my rooms; a Hapsburg chamber, a chamber in a Victorian castle, the hotel where I killed my father, the jungle. These are the places myselves exist in. I know no places. That is I cannot believe in places. To believe in places is to know hope and to know the emotion of hope is to know beauty. It links us across a horizon and connects us to the world. I find there are no places, only my funnyhouse. Streets are rooms, cities are rooms, eternal rooms. I try to create a space for myself in cities. New York, the midwest, a southern town but it becomes a lie. I try to give myselves a logical relationship but that too is a lie. For relationships was one of my last religions. I clung loyally to the lie of relationships, again and again seeking to establish a connection between my characters. Jesus is Victoria's son. Mother loved my father before her hair fell out. A loving relationship exists between myself and Jesus but they are lies. You will assume I am trifling with you, teasing your intellect, dealing in subtleties, denying connection then suddenly at a point reveal a startling heartbreaking connection. You are wrong. For the days are past when there are places and characters with connections with themes as in stories you pick up on the shelves of public libraries.

Too, there is no theme. No statements. I might borrow a statement, struggle to fabricate a theme, borrow one from my contemporaries, renew one from the master, hawkishly scan other stories searching for statements, consider the theme then deceive myself that I held such a statement within me, refusing to accept the fact that a statement has to come from an ordered force. I might try to join horizontal elements such as dots on a horizontal line, or create a centrifugal force, or create causes and effects so that they would equal a quantity but it would be a lie. For the statement is the characters and the characters are myself.

(*Blackout—then to the right front of the stage comes the white light. It goes to a suspended stairway. At the foot of it stands the* LANDLADY. *She is a tall, thin woman dressed in a black hat with red and appears to be talking to someone in a suggested open doorway in a corridor of a rooming house. She laughs like a mad character in a funnyhouse throughout her speech.*)

LANDLADY (*looking up the stairway*). Ever since her father hung himself in a Harlem hotel when Patrice Lumumba was murdered, she hides in her room. Each night she repeats; he keeps returning. How dare he enter the castle walls, he who is the darkest of them all, the darkest one. My mother looked like a white woman, hair as straight as any white woman's. And I am yellow but he, he is black, the blackest one of them all. I hoped he was dead. Yet still he comes through the jungle.

I tell her: Sarah, honey, the man hung himself. It's not your blame. But, no, she stares at me: No, Mrs. Conrad, he did not hang himself, that is only the way they understand it, they do, but the truth is that I bludgeoned his head with an ebony skull that he carries about with him. Wherever he goes, he carries out black masks and heads.

She's suffering so till her hair has fallen out. But then she did always hide herself in that room with the walls of books and her statues. I always did know she thought she was somebody else, a Queen or something, somebody else.

(*Blackout.* FUNNYMAN's *place. The next scene is enacted with the* DUCHESS *and* RAYMOND. RAYMOND's *place is suggested as being above the* NEGRO's *room, and is etched in with a prop of blinds and a bed . . . behind the blinds are mirrors and when the blinds are opened and closed by* RAYMOND, *this is revealed.* RAYMOND *turns out to be the* FUNNYMAN *of the funnyhouse. He is tall, white and ghostly thin and dressed in a black shirt and black trousers in attire suggesting an artist. Throughout his dialogue he laughs. The* DUCHESS *is partially disrobed and it is implied from their attitudes of physical intimacy—he is standing and she is sitting before him clinging to his leg. During the scene,* RAYMOND *keeps opening and closing the blinds. His face has black sores on it and he is wearing a black hat. Throughout the scene he strikes her as in affection when he speaks to her.*)

DUCHESS   (*carrying a red paper bag*).   My father is arriving, and what am I to do?

(RAYMOND *walks about the place opening the blinds and laughing.*)

FUNNYMAN   He is arriving from Africa, is he not?

DUCHESS   Yes, yes, he is arriving from Africa.

FUNNYMAN   I always knew your father was African.

DUCHESS   He is an African who lives in the jungle. He is an African who has always lived in the jungle. Yes, he is a nigger who is an African, who is a missionary teacher and is now dedicating his life to the erection of a Christian mission in the middle of the jungle. He is a black man.

FUNNYMAN   He is a black man who shot himself when they murdered Patrice Lumumba.

DUCHESS   (*goes on wildly*).   Yes, my father is a black man who went to Africa years ago as a missionary teacher, got mixed up in politics, was reviled and is now devoting his foolish life to the erection of a Christian mission in the middle of the jungle in one of those newly freed countries. Hide me. (*Clinging to his knees*). Hide me here so the nigger will not find me.

FUNNYMAN (*laughing*). Your father is in the jungle dedicating his life to the erection of a Christian mission.

DUCHESS Hide me here so the jungle will not find me. Hide me.

FUNNYMAN Isn't it cruel of you?

DUCHESS Hide me from the jungle.

FUNNYMAN Isn't it cruel?

DUCHESS No, no.

FUNNYMAN Isn't it cruel of you?

DUCHESS No. (*She screams and opens her red paper bag and draws from it her fallen hair. It is a great mass of dark wild. She holds it up to him. He appears not to understand. He stares at it.*) It is my hair. (*He continues to stare at her.*) When I awakened this morning it had fallen out, not all of it but a mass from the crown of my head that lay on the center of my pillow. I rose and in the greyish winter morning light of my room I stood staring at my hair, dazed by my sleeplessness, still shaken by nightmares of my mother. Was it true, yes, it was my hair. In the mirror I saw that, although my hair remained on both sides, clearly on the crown and at my temples my scalp was bare. (*She removes her black crown and shows him the top of her head.*)

RAYMOND (FUNNYMAN) (*staring at her*). Why would your hair fall out? Is it because you are cruel? How could a black father haunt you so?

DUCHESS He haunted my very conception. He was a black beast who raped my mother.

RAYMOND (FUNNYMAN) He is a black Negro. (*Laughing.*)

DUCHESS Ever since I can remember he's been a nigger pose of agony. He is the wilderness. He speaks niggerly, grovelling about wanting to touch me with his black hand.

FUNNYMAN How tormented and cruel you are.

DUCHESS (*as if not comprehending*). Yes, yes, the man's dark, very dark skinned. He is the darkest, my father is the darkest, my mother is the lightest. I am between. But my father is the darkest. My father is a nigger who drives me to misery. Any time spent with him evolves itself into suffering. He is a black man and the wilderness.

FUNNYMAN How tormented and cruel you are.

DUCHESS He is a nigger.

FUNNYMAN And your mother, where is she?

DUCHESS She is in the asylum. In the asylum bald. Her father was a white man. And she is in the asylum. (*He takes her in his arms. She responds wildly.*)

(Blackout. Knocking is heard, it continues, then somewhere near the center of the stage a figure appears in the darkness, a large dark faceless man carrying a mask in his hand.)

HE SPEAKS   It begins with the disaster of my hair. I awaken. My hair has fallen out, not all of it, but a mass from the crown of my head that lies on the center of my white pillow. I arise and in the greyish winter morning light of my room I stand staring at my hair, dazed by sleeplessness, still shaken by nightmares of my mother. Is it true? Yes. It is my hair. In the mirror I see that although my hair remains on both sides, clearly on the crown and at my temples my scalp is bare. And in my sleep I had been visited by my bald crazy mother who comes to me crying, calling me to her bedside. She lies on the bed watching the strands of her own hair fall out. Her hair fell out after she married and she spent her days lying on the bed watching the strands fall from her scalp, covering the bedspread until she was bald and admitted to the hospital. Black man, black man, my mother says I never should have let a black man put his hands on me. She comes to me, her bald skull shining. Black diseases, Sarah, she says. Black diseases. I run. She follows me, her bald skull shining. That is the beginning.

(Several women with white nightgowns on, waist-length black hair, all identical, emerge from the sides of the stage and run into the darkness, toward him shouting—black man, black man. They are carrying bald heads. Blackout.)

(Queen's Chamber: Her hair is in a small pile on the bed and in a small pile on the floor, several other small piles of hair are scattered about her and her white gown is covered with fallen out hair.)

(QUEEN VICTORIA acts out the following scene: She awakens [in pantomime] and discovers her hair has fallen. It is on her pillow. She arises and stands at the side of the bed with her back toward us staring at her hair. She opens the red paper bag that she is carrying and takes out her hair, attempting to place it back on her head [for unlike VICTORIA, she does not wear her headpiece now]. Suddenly the women in white gowns come carrying their skulls before them screaming.)

(The unidentified MAN returns out of the darkness and speaks. He carries the mask.)

MAN   I am a nigger of two generations. I am Patrice Lumumba.

PATRICE LUMUMBA   I am a nigger of two generations. I am the black shadow that haunted my mother's conception. I belong to the generation born at the turn of the century and the generation born before the depression. At present I reside in New York City in a brownstone in the West Nineties. I am an English major at a city college. My nigger father majored in social work, so did my mother. I am a student and have occasional work in libraries. But mostly I spend my vile days preoccupied with the placement and geometric position of words on paper. I write poetry filling white page after white page with imitations of Sitwell. It is my vile dream to live in rooms with European antiques and my statues of Queen Victoria, photographs of Roman ruins, pianos and oriental carpets. My friends will be white. I need them as an embankment to keep me from reflecting too much upon the fact that I am Patrice Lumumba who haunted my mother's conception. They are necessary for me to maintain recognition against myself. My white friends, like myself, will be shrewd intellectuals and anxious for death. Anyone's death. I will despise them as I do myself. For if I did not despise myself then my hair would not have fallen and if my hair had not fallen then I would not have bludgeoned my father's face with the ebony mask.

(Then another wall is dropped, larger than the first one was.
This one is near the front of the stage facing thus.
Throughout the following monologue the characters DUCHESS, *VICTORIA and* JESUS *go back and forth. As they go in their backs are to us but the* NEGRO *faces us speaking.)*

NEGRO   I always dreamed of a day when my mother would smile at me. My father—his mother wanted him to be Christ. From the beginning in the lamp of their dark room she said—I want you to be Jesus, to walk in Genesis and save the race. You must return to Africa, find revelation in the midst of golden savannas, nim and white frankopenny trees, white stallions roaming under a blue sky, you must walk with a white dove and heal the race, heal the misery, take us off the cross . . . at dawn he watched her rise, kill a hen for him to eat at breakfast, then go to work, down at the big house till dusk, till she died.

His father told him the race was no damn good. He hated his father and adores his mother. His mother didn't want him to marry my mother and sent a dead chicken to the wedding. I *don't* want you marrying that child, she wrote, she's not good enough for you, I want you to go to Africa. When they first married they lived in New York.

Then they went to Africa where my mother fell out of love with my father. She didn't want him to save the black race and spent her days combing her hair. She would not let him touch her in their wedding bed and called him black. He is black of skin with dark eyes and a great dark square brow. Then in Africa he started to drink and came home drunk one night and raped

my mother. The child from the union is me. I clung to my
mother. Long after she went to the asylum I wove long dreams of
her beauty, her straight hair and fair skin and gray eyes, so identical to mine. How it anguished him. I turned from him, nailing
him to the cross, he said, dragging him through grass and nailing
him on a cross until he bled. He pleaded with me to help him
find Genesis, search for Genesis in the minds of golden savannas,
nim and white frankopenny trees and white stallions roaming under a blue sky, help him search for the white dove; he wanted
the black man to make a pure statement, he wanted the black
man to rise from colonialism. But I sat in the room with my
mother, sat by her bedside and helped her comb her straight
black hair and wove long dreams of her beauty. She had long
since begun to curse the place and spoke of herself trapped in
blackness. She preferred the company of night owls. Only at
night did she rise, walking in the garden among the trees with
the owls. When I spoke to her she saw I was a black man's child
and she preferred speaking to owls. Nights my father came from
his school in the village struggling to embrace me. But I fled and
hid under my mother's bed while she screamed of remorse. Her
hair was falling badly and after a while we had to return to this
country.

He tried to hang himself once. After my mother went to the
asylum he had hallucinations, his mother threw a dead chicken
at him, his father laughed and said the race was no damn good,
my mother appeared in her nightgown screaming she had
trapped herself in blackness. No white doves flew. He had left
Africa and was again in New York. We lived in Harlem and no
white doves flew. Sarah, Sarah, he would say to me, the soldiers
are coming and a cross they are placing high on a tree and are
dragging me through the grass and nailing me upon the cross.
My blood is gushing. I wanted to live in Genesis in the midst of
golden savannas, nim and white frankopenny trees and white
stallions roaming under a blue sky. I wanted to walk with a
white dove. I wanted to be a Christian. Now I am Judas, I betrayed my mother. I sent your mother to the asylum. I created a
yellow child who hates me. And he tried to hang himself in a
Harlem hotel.

(*Blackout. A bald head is dropped on a string. We hear laughing.*)

(DUCHESS's *place: The next scene is done in the* DUCHESS *of* HAPS-
BURG's *place which is a chandelier ballroom with snow falling, a
black and white marble floor, a bench decorated with white
flowers, all of this can be made of obviously fake materials as*

they would be in a funnyhouse. The DUCHESS *is wearing a white dress and as in the previous scene a white headpiece with her kinky hair springing out from under it. In the scene are the* DUCHESS *and* JESUS. JESUS *enters the room which is at first dark, then suddenly brilliant, he starts to cry out at the* DUCHESS *who is seated on a bench under the chandelier, and pulls his hair from the red paper bag holding it up for the* DUCHESS *to see.)*

JESUS My hair! (*The* DUCHESS *does not speak,* JESUS *again screams.)* My hair. (*Holding the hair up, waiting for a reaction from the* DUCHESS.)

DUCHESS (*as if oblivious*). I have something I must show you. (*She goes quickly to shutters and darkens the room, returning standing before* JESUS. *She then slowly removes her headpiece and from under it takes a mass of her hair.*) When I awakened I found it fallen out, not all of it but a mass that lay on my white pillow. I could see, although my hair hung down at the sides, clearly on my white scalp it was missing. (*Her baldness is identical to* JESUS'S.)

(*A blackout. Then the light comes back up. They are both sitting on the bench examining each other's hair, running it through their fingers, then slowly the* DUCHESS *disappears behind the shutters and returns with a long red comb. She sits on the bench next to* JESUS *and starts to comb her remaining hair over her baldness. (This is done slowly.)* JESUS *then takes the comb and proceeds to do the same to the* DUCHESS *of* HAPSBURG'S *hair. After they finish they place the* DUCHESS'S *headpiece back on and we can see the strands of their hair falling to the floor.* JESUS *then lies down across the bench while the* DUCHESS *walks back and forth, the knocking does not cease.)*

(*They speak in unison as the* DUCHESS *walks and* JESUS *lies on the bench in the falling snow, staring at the ceiling.)*

DUCHESS and JESUS (*their hair is falling more now, they are both hideous*). My father isn't going to let us alone. (*Knocking.*) Our father isn't going to let us alone, our father is the darkest of us all, my mother was the fairest, I am in between, but my father is the darkest of them all. He is a black man. Our father is the darkest of them all. He is a black man. My father is a dead man. (*Then they suddenly look up at each other and scream, the lights go to their heads and we see that they are totally bald.)*

(*There is a knocking. Lights go to the stairs and the* LANDLADY.)

LANDLADY He wrote to her saying he loved her and asked for forgiveness. He begged her to take him off the cross. (He had dreamed she would.) Stop them for tormenting him, the one with the chicken and his cursing father. Her mother's hair fell

out, the race's hair fell out because he left Africa, he said. He had
tried to save them. She must embrace him. He said his existence
depended on her embrace. He wrote her from Africa where he is
creating his Christian center in the jungle and that is why he
came here. I know that he wanted her to return there with him
and not desert the race. He came to see her once before he tried
to hang himself, appearing in the corridor of my apartment. I had
let him in. I found him sitting on a bench in the hallway. He put
out his hand to her, tried to take her in his arms, crying out—
Forgiveness, Sarah, Is it that you will never forgive me for being
black. I know you were a child of torment. But forgiveness. That
was before his breakdown. Then, he wrote her and repeated that
his mother hoped he would be Christ but he failed. He had married his mother because he could not resist the light. Yet, his
mother from the beginning in the kerosene lamp of their dark
rooms in Georgia said—I want you to be Jesus, to walk in Genesis and save the race, return to Africa, find revelation in the
black. He went away.

But Easter morning, she got to feeling badly and went into
Harlem to see him; the streets were filled with vendors selling
lilies. He had checked out of that hotel. When she arrived back
at my brownstone he was there, dressed badly, rather drunk. I
had let him in again. He sat on a bench in the dark hallway, put
out his hand to her, trying to take her in his arms, crying out—
Forgiveness, Sarah. Forgiveness for my being black, Sarah. I
know you are a child of torment. I know on dark winter afternoons you sat alone, weaving stories of your mother's beauty.
But, Sarah, answer me, don't turn away, Sarah. Forgive my blackness. She would not answer. He put out his hand to her. She ran
past him on the stairs, left him there with his hands out to me,
repeating his past, saying his mother hoped he would be Christ.
From the beginning in the kerosene lamp of their dark room, she
said—Wally, I want you to be Jesus, to walk in Genesis and save
the race. You must return to Africa, Wally, find revelation in the
midst of golden savannas, nim and white frankopenny trees and
white stallions roaming under a blue sky. Wally, you must find
the white dove and heal the pain of the race, heal the misery of
the black man, Wally, take us off the cross, Wally. In the kerosene light she stared at him anguished from her old Negro face
. . . but she ran past him leaving him. And now he is dead, she
says, now he is dead. He left Africa and now Patrice Lumumba is
dead.

(The next scene is enacted back in the DUCHESS of HAPSBURG'S
place. JESUS is still in the DUCHESS'S chamber, apparently he has

fallen asleep and we see him awakening with the DUCHESS *by his side, and then sitting as in a trance. He rises terrified and speaks.)*

JESUS   (*He is awakening*).   Through my apocalypses and my raging sermons I have tried so to escape him, through God Almighty I have tried to escape being black.   (*He then appears to rouse himself from his thoughts and calls.*)   Duchess, Duchess.   (*He looks about for her, there is no answer. He gets up slowly, walks back into the darkness and there we see that she is hanging on the chandelier, her bald head suddenly drops to the floor and she falls upon* JESUS. *He screams.*)   I am going to Africa and kill this black man named Patrice Lumumba. Why? Because all my life I believed my Holy Father to be God, but now I know that my father is a black man. I have no fear for whatever I do I will do in the name of God, I will do in the name of Albert Saxe Godburg, in the name of Victoria, Queen Victoria Regina, the monarch of England, I will.

(Blackout.)

(Next scene. In the jungle, red run, flying things, wild black grass. The effect of the jungle is that it, unlike the other scenes, is over the entire scene. In time this is the longest scene in the play and is played the slowest as the slow, almost standstill, stages of a dream. By lighting the desired effect would be—suddenly the jungle has overgrown the chambers and all the other places with a violence and a dark brightness, a grim yellowness.)

*(*JESUS *is the first to appear in the center of the jungle darkness. Unlike in previous scenes, he has a nimbus above his head. As they each successively appear, they all too have nimbuses atop their heads in a manner to suggest that they are saviours.)*

JESUS   I always believed my father to be God.

(Suddenly they all appear in various parts of the jungle. PATRICE LUMUMBA, *the* DUCHESS, VICTORIA, *wandering about speaking at once. Their speeches are mixed and repeated by one another.)*

He never tires of the journey, he who is the darkest one, the darkest one of them all. My mother looked like a white woman, hair as straight as any white woman's. I am yellow but he is black, the darkest one of us all. How I hoped he was dead, yet he never tired of the journey. It was because of him that my mother died because she let a black man put his hands on her. Why does he keep returning? He keeps returning forever, keeps returning and returning and he is my father. He is a black Negro. They told me my father was God but my father is black. He is my father. I am tied to a black Negro. He returned when I lived in the south back in the twenties, when I was a child, he returned. Before I was born at the turn of the century, he haunted my conception, diseased my birth . . . killed my mother. He killed the light. My mother was the lightest one. I am bound to him unless, of course, he should die.

But he is dead.

And he keeps returning. Then he is not dead.

Then he is not dead.

Yes, he is dead, but dead he comes knocking at my door.

(This is repeated several times, finally reaching a loud pitch and then all rushing about the grass. They stop and stand perfectly still. All speaking tensely at various times in a chant.)

I see him. The black ugly thing is sitting in his hallway, surrounded by his ebony masks, surrounded by the blackness of himself. My mother comes into the room. He is there with his hand out to me, groveling, saying—Forgiveness, Sarah, is it that you will never forgive me for being black.

Forgiveness, Sarah. I know you are a nigger of torment.

Why? Christ would not rape anyone.

You will never forgive me for being black.

Wild beast. Why did you rape my mother?

Black beast, Christ would not rape anyone.

He is in grief from that black anguished face of his.

Then at once the room will grow bright and my mother will come toward me smiling while I stand before his face and bludgeon him with an ebony head.

Forgiveness, Sarah, I know you are a nigger of torment.

(SILENCE—VICTORY: *Then they suddenly begin to laugh and shout as though they are in. They continue for some minutes running about laughing and shouting.)*

(Blackout.)

(Another wall drops. There is a white plaster of QUEEN VICTORIA *which represents the* NEGRO'S *room in the brownstone, the room appears near the staircases highly lit and small. The main prop is the statue but a bed could be suggested. The figure of* VICTORIA *is a sitting figure, one of astonishing repulsive whiteness, possessing the quality of nightmares and terror.* SARAH'S *room could be further suggested by dusty volumes of books and old yellowed walls. The* NEGRO SARAH *is standing perfectly still, we hear the knocking, the lights come on quickly, her father's black figures with bludgeoned hands rush upon her, the lights black and we see her hanging in the room.)*

(Lights come on the laughing LANDLADY. *At the same time remain on the hanging figure of the* NEGRO.)*

LANDLADY   The poor bitch has hung herself.

(FUNNYMAN RAYMOND *appears from his room at the commotion.*)

LANDLADY   The poor bitch has hung herself.

RAYMOND   (*observing her hanging figure*).   She was a funny little liar.

LANDLADY   (*informing him*).   Her father hung himself in a Harlem hotel when Patrice Lumumba died.

RAYMOND   She was a funny little liar.

LANDLADY   Her father hung himself in a Harlem hotel when Patrice Lumumba died.

RAYMOND   Her father never hung himself in a Harlem hotel when Patrice Lumumba was murdered.

I know the man. He is a doctor, married to a white whore. He lives in the city in a room with European antiques, photographs of Roman ruins, walls of books and oriental carpets. Her father is a nigger who eats his meals on a white glass table.

CURTAIN

Kristin Hunter

(1931–   )

KRISTIN HUNTER, author of novels for adults and young adults, was born Kristin Eggleston in Philadelphia, Pennsylvania, in 1931. She graduated from the University of Pennsylvania in 1951 and for a short time taught elementary school. In 1952 she married her first husband, Joseph Hunter, and began working as an advertising copywriter with Lavenson Bureau in Philadelphia. By 1955 she had written a television script, *Minority of One*, which won a national competition sponsored by CBS.

Hunter published her first novel, *God Bless the Child*, in 1964, while she was working as a research assistant at the University of Pennsylvania School of Social Work. This novel was well received by the critics and won the Philadelphia Athenaeum Award in the year of its publication. Her second novel, *The Landlord*, was published in 1966. Soon afterward she wrote the first of her popular novels for young people, *The Soul Brothers and Sister Lou* (1968), which won the Council on Interracial Books for Children prize. In the following years she published *Boss Cat* (1971), a family-oriented novelette, and *Guests in the Promised Land* (1973), a collection of short stories for children. The latter of these won the Chicago Tribune Book World Prize in 1973.

Hunter took a position as adjunct professor of creative writing at the University of Pennsylvania in 1972 and published her third adult novel, *The Survivors*, in 1975. In 1978 she published *The Lakestown Rebellion* and in 1981 *Lou in the Limelight*, which is the latest in her young adult novel series.

For further reading, see Sondra O'Neale's essay in *Dictionary of Literary Biography, Volume 33*. See also Trudier Harris, *From Mammies to Militants: Domestics in Black American Literature* (1982); Melissa Walker's *Down from the Mountaintop: Black Women's Novels in the Wake of the Civil Rights Movement, 1966–1989* (1991); and Maralyn Lois Polak, "Kristin Hunter: A Writer and a Fighter," *Philadelphia Inquirer*, 24 November 1974.

"Debut" is taken from *Negro Digest* 17 (June 1968).

DEBUT

"Hold *still*, Judy," Mrs. Simmons said around the spray of pins that protruded dangerously from her mouth. She gave the thirtieth tug to the tight sash at the waist of the dress. "Now walk over there and turn around slowly."

The dress, Judy's first long one, was white organdy over taffeta, with spaghetti straps that bared her round brown shoulders and a floating skirt and a wide sash that cascaded in a butterfly effect behind. It was a dream, but Judy was sick and tired of the endless fittings she had endured so that she might wear it at the Debutantes' Ball. Her thoughts leaped ahead to the Ball itself . . .

"*Slowly*, I said!" Mrs. Simmons' dark, angular face was always grim, but now it was screwed into an expression resembling a prune. Judy, starting nervously, began to revolve by moving her feet an inch at a time.

Her mother watched her critically. "No, it's still not right. I'll just have to rip out that waistline seam again."

"Oh, Mother!" Judy's impatience slipped out at last. "Nobody's going to notice all those little details."

"They will too. They'll be watching you every minute, hoping to see something wrong. You've got to be the *best*. Can't you get that through your head?" Mrs. Simmons gave a sigh of despair. "You better start noticin' 'all those little details' yourself. I can't do it for you all your life. Now turn around and stand up straight."

"Oh, Mother," Judy said, close to tears from being made to turn and pose while her feet itched to be dancing, "I can't stand it any more!"

"You can't stand it, huh? How do you think *I* feel?" Mrs. Simmons said in her harshest tone.

Judy was immediately ashamed, remembering the weeks her mother had spent at the sewing machine, pricking her already tattered fingers with needles and pins, and the great weight of sacrifice that had been borne on Mrs. Simmons' shoulders for the past two years so that Judy might bare hers at the Ball.

"All right, take it off," her mother said. "I'm going to take it up the street to Mrs. Luby and let her help me. It's got to be right or I won't let you leave the house."

"Can't we just leave it the way it is, Mother?" Judy pleaded without hope of success. "I think it's perfect."

"You would," Mrs. Simmons said tartly as she folded the dress

Reprinted by permission of Don Congdon Associates, Inc. Copyright © 1968 by Kristin Hunter.

and prepared to bear it out of the room. "Sometimes I think I'll
never get it through your head. You got to look just right and act
just right. That Rose Griffin and those other girls can afford to be
careless, maybe, but you can't. You're gonna be the darkest, poorest
one there."

Judy shivered in her new lace strapless bra and her old, childish
knit snuggies. "You make it sound like a battle I'm going to instead
of just a dance."

"It is a battle," her mother said firmly. "It starts tonight and it
goes on for the rest of your life. The battle to hold your head up and
get someplace and be somebody. We've done all we can for you,
your father and I. Now you've got to start fighting some on your
own." She gave Judy a slight smile; her voice softened a little. "You'll
do all right, don't worry. Try and get some rest this afternoon. Just
don't mess up your hair."

"All right, Mother," Judy said listlessly.

She did not really think her father had much to do with anything
that happened to her. It was her mother who had ingratiated her
way into the Gay Charmers two years ago, taking all sorts of humiliation from the better-dressed, better-off, lighter-skinned women,
humbly making and mending their dresses, fixing food for their
meetings, addressing more mail and selling more tickets than anyone
else. The club had put it off as long as they could, but finally they
had to admit Mrs. Simmons to membership because she worked so
hard. And that meant, of course, that Judy would be on the list for
this year's Ball.

Her father, a quiet carpenter who had given up any other ambitions years ago, did not think much of Negro society or his wife's
fierce determination to launch Judy into it. "Just keep clean and be
decent," he would say. "That's all anybody has to do."

Her mother always answered, "If that's all I did we'd still be on
relief," and he would shut up with shame over the years when he
had been laid off repeatedly and her days' work and sewing had kept
them going. Now he had steady work but she refused to quit, as if
she expected it to end at any moment. The intense energy that
burned in Mrs. Simmons' large dark eyes had scorched her features
into permanent irony. She worked day and night and spent her spare
time scheming and planning. Whatever her personal ambitions had
been, Judy knew she blamed Mr. Simmons for their failure; now all
her schemes revolved around their only child.

Judy went to her mother's window and watched her stride down
the street with the dress until she was hidden by the high brick wall
that went around two sides of their house. Then she returned to her
own room. She did not get dressed because she was afraid of pulling a

sweater over her hair—her mother would notice the difference even if it looked all right to Judy—and because she was afraid that doing anything, even getting dressed, might precipitate her into the battle. She drew a stool up to her window and looked out. She had no real view, but she liked her room. The wall hid the crowded tenement houses beyond the alley, and from its cracks and bumps and depressions she could construct any imaginary landscape she chose. It was how she had spent most of the free hours of her dreamy adolescence.

"Hey, can I go?"

It was the voice of an invisible boy in the alley. As another boy chuckled, Judy recognized the familiar ritual; if you said yes, they said, "Can I go with you?" It had been tried on her dozens of times. She always walked past, head in the air, as if she had not heard. Her mother said that was the only thing to do; if they knew she was a lady, they wouldn't dare bother her. But this time a girl's voice, cool and assured, answered.

"If you think you're big enough," it said.

It was Lucy Mae Watkins; Judy could picture her standing there in a tight dress with bright, brazen eyes.

"I'm big enough to give you a baby," the boy answered.

Judy would die if a boy ever spoke to her like that, but she knew Lucy Mae could handle it. Lucy Mae could handle all the boys, even if they ganged up on her, because she had been born knowing something other girls had to learn.

"Aw, you ain't big enough to give me a shoe-shine," she told him.

"Come here and I'll show you how big I am," the boy said.

"Yeah, Lucy Mae, what's happenin'?" another, younger boy said. "Come here and tell us."

Lucy Mae laughed. "What I'm puttin' down is too strong for little boys like you."

"Come here a minute, baby," the first boy said. "I got a cigarette for you."

"Aw, I ain't studyin' your cigarettes," Lucy Mae answered. But her voice was closer, directly below Judy. There were the sounds of a scuffle and Lucy Mae's muffled laughter. When she spoke her voice sounded raw and cross. "Come on now, boy. Cut it out and give me the damn cigarette." There was more scuffling, and the sharp crack of a slap, and then Lucy Mae said, "Cut it out, I said. Just for that I'm gonna take 'em all." The clack of high heels rang down the sidewalk with a boy's clumsy shoes in pursuit.

Judy realized that there were three of them down there. "Let her go, Buster," one said. "You can't catch her now."

"Aw, hell, man, she took the whole damn pack," the one called Buster complained.

"That'll learn you!" Lucy Mae's voice mocked from down the street. "Don't mess with nothin' you can't handle."

"Hey, Lucy Mae. Hey, I heard Rudy Grant already gave you a baby," a second boy called out.

"Yeah. Is that true, Lucy Mae?" the youngest one yelled.

There was no answer. She must be a block away by now.

For a moment the hidden boys were silent; then one of them guffawed directly below Judy, and the other two joined in the secret male laughter that was oddly high-pitched and feminine.

"Aw, man, I don't know what you all laughin' about," Buster finally grumbled. "That girl took all my cigarettes. You got some, Leroy?"

"Naw," the second boy said.

"Me neither," the third one said.

"What we gonna do? I ain't got but fifteen cent. Hell, man, I want more than a feel for a pack of cigarettes." There was an unpleasant whine in Buster's voice. "Hell, for a pack of cigarettes I want a bitch to come across."

"She will next time, man," the boy called Leroy said.

"She better," Buster said. "You know she better. If she pass by here again, we gonna jump her, you hear?"

"Sure, man," Leroy said. "The three of us can grab her easy."

"Then we can all three of us have some fun. Oh, *yeah*, man," the youngest boy said. He sounded as if he might be about 14.

Leroy said, "We oughta get Roland and J. T. too. For a whole pack of cigarettes she oughta treat all five of us."

"Aw, man, why tell Roland and J. T.?" the youngest voice whined. "They ain't in it. Them was *our* cigarettes."

"They was *my* cigarettes, you mean," Buster said with authority. "You guys better quit it before I decide to cut you out."

"Oh, man, don't do that. We with you, you know that."

"Sure, Buster, we your aces, man."

"All right, that's better." There was a minute of silence.

Then, "What we gonna do with the girl, Buster?" the youngest one wanted to know.

"When she come back we gonna jump the bitch, man. We gonna jump her and grab her. Then we gonna turn her every way but loose." He went on, spinning a crude fantasy that got wilder each time he retold it, until it became so secretive that their voices dropped to a low indistinct murmur punctuated by guffaws. Now and then Judy could distinguish the word "girl" or the other word they used for it; these words always produced the loudest guffaws of all. She shook off her fear with the thought that Lucy Mae was too smart to pass there again today. She had heard them at their dirty

talk in the alley before and had always been successful in ignoring it;
it had nothing to do with her, the wall protected her from their
kind. All the ugliness was on their side of it, and this side was hers
to fill with beauty.

She turned on her radio to shut them out completely and began
to weave her tapestry to its music. More for practice than anything
else, she started by picturing the maps of the places to which she
intended to travel, then went on to the faces of her friends. Rose
Griffin's sharp, Indian profile appeared on the wall. Her coloring was
like an Indian's too and her hair was straight and black and glossy.
Judy's hair, naturally none of these things, had been "done" four
days ago so that tonight it would be "old" enough to have a gloss as
natural-looking as Rose's. But Rose, despite her handsome looks, was
silly; her voice broke constantly into high-pitched giggles and she
became even sillier and more nervous around boys.

Judy was not sure that she knew how to act around boys either.
The sisters kept boys and girls apart at the Catholic high school
where her parents sent her to keep her away from low-class kids.
But she felt that she knew a secret; tonight, in that dress, with her
hair in a sophisticated upsweep, she would be transformed into a
poised princess. Tonight all the college boys her mother described so
eagerly would rush to dance with her, and then from somewhere *the
boy* would appear. She did not know his name; she neither knew nor
cared whether he went to college, but she imagined that he would
be as dark as she was, and that there would be awe and diffidence in
his manner as he bent to kiss her hand . . .

A waltz swelled from the radio; the wall, turning blue in deepening twilight, came alive with whirling figures. Judy rose and began to
go through the steps she had rehearsed for so many weeks. She
swirled with a practiced smile on her face, holding an imaginary
skirt at her side; turned, dipped, and flicked on her bedside lamp
without missing a fraction of the beat. Faster and faster she danced
with her imaginary partner, to an inner music that was better than
the sounds on the radio. She was "coming out," and tonight the
world would discover what it had been waiting for all these years.

"Aw, git it, baby." She ignored it as she would ignore the crowds
that lined the streets to watch her pass on her way to the Ball.

"Aw, do your number." She waltzed on, safe and secure on her
side of the wall.

"Can I come up there and do it with you?"

At this she stopped, paralyzed. Somehow they had come over the
wall or around it and into her room.

"Man, I sure like the view from here," the youngest boy said.
"How come we never tried this view before?"

She came to life, ran quickly to the lamp and turned it off, but not before Buster said, "Yeah, and the back view is fine, too."

"Aw, she turned off the light," a voice complained.

"Put it on again, baby, we don't mean no harm."

"Let us see you dance some more. I bet you can really do it."

"Yeah, I bet she can shimmy on down."

"You know it, man."

"Come on down here, baby," Buster's voice urged softly dangerously. "I got a cigarette for you."

"Yeah, and he got something else for you, too."

Judy, flattened against her closet door, gradually lost her urge to scream. She realized that she was shivering in her underwear. Taking a deep breath, she opened the closet door and found her robe. She thought of going to the window and yelling down, "You don't have a thing I want. Do you understand?" But she had more important things to do.

Wrapping her hair in protective plastic, she ran a full steaming tub and dumped in half a bottle of her mother's favorite cologne. At first she scrubbed herself furiously, irritating her skin. But finally she stopped, knowing she would never be able to get cleaner than this again. She could not wash away the thing they considered dirty, the thing that made them pronounce "girl" in the same way as the other four-letter words they wrote on the wall in the alley; it was part of her, just as it was part of her mother and Rose Griffin and Lucy Mae. She relaxed then because it was true that the boys in the alley did not have a thing she wanted. She had what they wanted, and the knowledge replaced her shame with a strange, calm feeling of power.

After her bath she splashed on more cologne and spent 40 minutes on her makeup, erasing and retracing her eyebrows six times until she was satisfied. She went to her mother's room then and found the dress, finished and freshly pressed, on its hanger.

When Mrs. Simmons came upstairs to help her daughter she found her sitting on the bench before the vanity mirror as if it were a throne. She looked young and arrogant and beautiful and perfect and cold.

"Why, you're dressed already," Mrs. Simmons said in surprise. While she stared, Judy rose with perfect, icy grace and glided to the center of the room. She stood there motionless as a mannequin.

"I want you to fix the hem, Mother," she directed. "It's still uneven in back."

Her mother went down obediently on her knees muttering, "It looks all right to me." She put in a couple of pins. "That better?"

"Yes," Judy said with a brief glance at the mirror. "You'll have to sew it on me, Mother. I can't take it off now. I'd ruin my hair."

Mrs. Simmons went to fetch her sewing things, returned, and surveyed her daughter. "You sure did a good job on yourself, I must say," she admitted grudgingly. "Can't find a thing to complain about. You'll look as good as anybody there."

"Of course, Mother," Judy said as Mrs. Simmons knelt and sewed. "I don't know what you were so worried about." Her secret feeling of confidence had returned, stronger than ever, but the evening ahead was no longer the vague girlish fantasy she had pictured on the wall; it had hard, clear outlines leading up to a definite goal. She would be the belle of the Ball because she knew more than Rose Griffin and her silly friends; more than her mother; more, even, than Lucy Mae, because she knew better than to settle for a mere pack of cigarettes.

"There," her mother said, breaking the thread. She got up. "I never expected to get you ready this early. Ernest Lee won't be here for another hour."

"That silly Ernest Lee," Judy said, with a new contempt in her young voice. Until tonight she had been pleased by the thought of going to the dance with Ernest Lee; he was nice, she felt comfortable with him, and he might even be the awe-struck boy of her dream. He was a dark, serious neighborhood boy who could not afford to go to college; Mrs. Simmons had reluctantly selected him to take Judy to the dance because all the Gay Charmers' sons were spoken for. Now, with an undertone of excitement, Judy said, "I'm going to ditch him after the first dance, Mother. You'll see. I'm going to come home with one of the college boys."

"It's very nice, Ernest Lee," she told him an hour later when he handed her the white orchid, "but it's rather small. I'm going to wear it on my wrist, if you don't mind." And then, dazzling him with a smile of sweetest cruelty, she stepped back and waited while he fumbled with the door.

"You know, Edward, I'm not worried about her any more," Mrs. Simmons said to her husband after the children were gone. Her voice became harsh and grating. "Put down that paper and listen to me! Aren't you interested in your child?—That's better," she said as he complied meekly. "I was saying, I do believe she's learned what I've been trying to teach her, after all."

Douglas Turner Ward

(1930–)

AN AWARD-WINNING actor and playwright, Douglas Turner Ward is a significant figure in American theater. His efforts to establish a legitimate theater by, for, and about African Americans finally came to fruition in 1967 with the formation of the Negro Ensemble Company, which since its earliest days has consistently provided a stage on which black playwrights and performers can show their work.

Born in 1930 in Burnside, Louisiana, a small town outside New Orleans, Ward grew up on a plantation and received his early education in a two-room schoolhouse. In 1946 he moved to Xenia, Ohio, and attended Wilberforce University. The next year he transferred to the University of Michigan to play junior varsity football and to study journalism. A knee injury ended his football career, and in 1948 he dropped out of college and moved to New York City.

Ward had become involved in political activities while in college and continued as an activist in New York, writing for the *Daily Worker* and attending rallies and political meetings. At the age of nineteen he wrote a cantata based on the life of Nat Turner, which was performed at a rally to an audience of more than five thousand people. This first taste of stage success led him away from political activism and toward a formal career in the theater. He took acting classes and soon began to understudy, and later to take over, such important roles as Joe Mott in *The Iceman Cometh* (Circle-in-the-Square Theater, 1956) and Lee Younger in *A Raisin in the Sun* (Broadway touring company, 1959). During this period he was also writing his own plays, and in 1965 the first two of these, *Happy Ending* and *Day of Absence*, opened at St. Mark's Playhouse in New York's Lower East Side. These two plays, like all of Ward's work, are comic satires of relationships between blacks and whites. In 1966 Ward won two Obies, one as author of the plays and one for his starring role in *Day of Absence*.

In 1967 Ward wrote an article titled "American Theater: For Whites Only?" that was published in the *New York Times*. In it, he presented the need for a permanent black repertory company to give black playwrights and actors a place to develop and perform their work. Shortly after the article appeared, the Ford Foundation responded with a $434,000 grant to subsidize such a company under the direction of Ward, Robert Hooks, and Gerald Krone, two friends he had made while in the cast of *Raisin in the Sun*. Thus was born the Negro Ensemble Company.

Ward took over administrative duties in the company in addition to producing and directing many of its works. By its third season he had a play of his own ready for production, *The Reckoning* (1970). Two more short plays followed, *Brotherhood* (1970) and *The Redeemer* (1979). Ward continues with the Negro Ensemble Company, but little of his own work has been performed since 1970. His commitment to the fostering of black theater and dramatic arts has taken the form of producer and director over the last years.

For further reading, see Stephen M. Vallillo's article in *Dictionary of Literary Biography, Volume 38*. See also "Douglas Turner Ward" [interview], *Blackstage* (January–February 1974); Trudier Harris, *From Mammies to Militants: Domestics in Black American Literature* (1982); and Loften Mitchell, *Black Drama* (1967).

"Day of Absence" is taken from *Happy Ending and Day of Absence: Two Plays by Douglas Turner Ward*, published by the Dramatists Play Service, Inc.

DAY OF ABSENCE
A Satirical Fantasy

The time is now. Play opens in unnamed Southern town of medium population on a somnolent cracker morning—meaning no matter the early temperature, it's gonna get hot. The hamlet is just beginning to rouse itself from the sleepy lassitude of night.

NOTES ON PRODUCTION

No scenery is necessary—only actors shifting in and out on an almost bare stage and freezing into immobility as focuses change or blackouts occur.

Play is conceived for performance by a Negro cast, a reverse minstrel show done in white-face. Logically, it might also be performed by whites—at their own risk. If any producer is faced with choosing between opposite hues, author strongly suggests: "Go 'long wit' the blacks—besides all else, they need the work more."

If acted by the latter, race members are urged to go for broke, yet cautioned not to ham it up too broadly. In fact—it just might be more effective if they aspire for serious tragedy. Only qualification needed for Caucasian casting is that the company fit a uniform pattern—insipid white; also played in white-face.

Before any horrifying discrimination doubts arise, I hasten to add that a bonafide white actor should be cast as the Announcer in all productions, likewise a Negro thespian in pure native black as Rastus. This will truly subvert any charge that the production is unintegrated.

All props, except essential items (chairs, brooms, rags, mop, debris) should be imaginary (phones, switchboard, mikes, eating utensils, food, etc.). Actors should indicate their presence through mime.

The cast of characters develops as the play progresses. In the interest of economical casting, actors should double or triple in roles wherever possible.

PRODUCTION CONCEPT

This is a red-white-and-blue play—meaning the entire production should be designed around the basic color scheme of our patriotic trinity. LIGHTING should illustrate, highlight and detail time, action and mood. Opening scenes stage-lit with white rays of morning, transforming to panic reds of afternoon, flowing into ominous blues of evening. COSTUMING should be orchestrated around the same color scheme. In addition, subsidiary usage of grays, khakis, yellows, pinks, and combinated patterns of stars-and-bars should be employed. Some actors (Announcer and Rastus excepted, of course) might wear white shoes or sneakers, and some women characters clothed in knee-length frocks might wear white stockings. Blonde wigs, both for males and females, can be used in selected instances. MAKEUP should have uniform consistency, with individual touches thrown in to enhance personal identity.

SAMPLE MODELS OF MAKEUP AND COSTUMING

MARY: Kewpie-doll face, ruby-red lips painted to valentine-pursing, moon-shaped rouge circles implanted on each cheek, blond wig of fat-flowing ringlets, dazzling ankle-length snow-white nightie.

MAYOR: Seersucker white ensemble, ten-gallon hat, red string-tie and blue belt.

CLEM: Khaki pants, bareheaded and blond.

LUKE: Blue work-jeans, strawhatted.

CLUB WOMAN: Yellow dress patterned with symbols of Dixie, gray hat.

CLAN: A veritable, riotous advertisement of red-white-and-blue combinations with stars-and-bars tossed in.

PIOUS: White ministerial garb with *black* cleric's collar topping his snow-white shirt.

OPERATORS: All in red with different color wigs.

All other characters should be carefully defined through costuming which typify their identity.

SCENE   *Street.*

TIME   *Early morning.*

CLEM   (*Sitting under a sign suspended by invisible wires and bold-printed with the lettering: "STORE."*) 'Morning, Luke. . . .

LUKE   (*Sitting a few paces away under an identical sign.*) 'Morning, Clem. . . .

CLEM   Go'n' be a hot day.

LUKE   Looks that way. . . .

CLEM   Might rain though. . . .

LUKE   Might.

CLEM   Hope it does. . . .

LUKE   Me, too. . . .

CLEM   Farmers could use a little wet spell for a change. . . . How's the Missis?

LUKE   Same.

CLEM   'N' the kids?

LUKE   Them, too. . . . How's yourns?

CLEM   Fine, thank you. . . . (*They both lapse into drowsy silence, waving lethargically from time to time at imaginary passersby.*) Hi, Joe. . . .

LUKE   Joe. . . .

CLEM   . . . . How'd it go yesterday, Luke?

LUKE   Fair.

CLEM   Same wit' me. . . . Business don't seem to git no better or no worse. Guess we in a rut, Luke, don't it 'pear that way to you?— Morning, ma'am.

LUKE   Morning. . . .

CLEM   Tried display, sales, advertisement, stamps—everything, yet merchandising stumbles 'round in the same old groove. . . . But— that's better than plunging downwards, I reckon.

LUKE   Guess it is.

CLEM   Morning, Bret. How the family? . . . That's good.

LUKE   Bret—

CLEM   Morning, Sue.

LUKE   How do, Sue.

CLEM   *(Staring after her.)* . . . . Fine hunk of woman.

LUKE   Sure is.

CLEM   Wonder if it's any good?

LUKE   Bet it is.

CLEM   Sure like to find out!

LUKE   So would I.

CLEM   You ever try?

LUKE   Never did. . . .

CLEM   Morning, Gus. . . .

LUKE   Howdy, Gus.

CLEM   Fine, thank you. *(They lapse into silence again. Clem rouses himself slowly, begins to look around quizzically.)* Luke . . . ?

LUKE   Huh?

CLEM   Do you . . . er, er—feel anything—funny . . . ?

LUKE   Like what?

CLEM   Like . . . er—something—strange?

LUKE   I dunno . . . haven't thought about it.

CLEM   I mean . . . like something's wrong—outta place, unusual?

LUKE   I don't know. . . . What you got in mind?

CLEM   Nothing . . . just that—just that—like somp'ums outta kilter. I got a funny feeling somp'ums not up to snuff. Can't figger out what it is . . .

LUKE   Maybe it's in your haid?

CLEM   No, not like that. . . . Like somp'ums happened—or happening—gone haywire, loony.

LUKE   Well, don't worry 'bout it, it'll pass.

CLEM   Guess you right. *(Attempts return to somnolence but doesn't succeed.)* . . . I'm sorry, Luke, but you sure you don't feel nothing peculiar . . . ?

LUKE   *(Slightly irked.)* Toss it out your mind, Clem! We got a long day ahead of us. If something's wrong, you'll know 'bout it in due time. No use worrying about it 'till it comes and if it's coming, it will. Now, relax!

CLEM   All right, you right. . . . Hi, Margie. . . .

LUKE   Marge.

CLEM   *(Unable to control himself.)* Luke, I don't give a damn what you say. Somp'ums topsy-turvy, I just know it!

LUKE   *(Increasingly irritated.)* Now look here, Clem—It's a bright day, it looks like it's go'n' git hotter. You say the wife and kids are fine and the business is no better or no worse? Well, what else could be wrong? . . . If somp'ums go'n' happen, it's go'n' happen anyway and there ain't a damn fool thing you kin do to stop it! So you ain't helping me, yourself or nobody else by thinking 'bout it. It's not go'n' be no better or no worse when it gits here. It'll come to you when it gits ready to come and it's go'n' be the same whether you worry about it or not. So stop letting it upset you! *(Luke settles back in his chair. Clem does likewise. Luke shuts his eyes. After a few moments, they reopen. He forces them shut again. They reopen in greater curiosity. Finally, he rises slowly to an upright position in the chair, looks around frowningly. Turns slowly to Clem.)* ... Clem? ... You know something? ... Somp'um is peculiar ...

CLEM *(Vindicated.)* I knew it, Luke! I just knew it! Ever since we been sitting here, I been having that feeling! *(Scene is blacked out abruptly. Lights rise on another section of the stage where a young couple lie in bed under an invisible-wire-suspension-sign lettered: "HOME." Loud insistent sounds of baby yells are heard. John, the husband, turns over trying to ignore the cries, Mary, the wife, is undisturbed. John's efforts are futile, the cries continue until they cannot be denied. He bolts upright, jumps out of bed and disappears offstage. Returns quickly and tries to rouse Mary.)*

JOHN Mary ... *(Nudges her, pushes her, yells into her ear, but she fails to respond.)* Mary, get up. . . . Get up!

MARY Ummm ... *(Shrugs away, still sleeping.)*

JOHN. GET UP!

MARY UMMMMMMMMMM!

JOHN Don't you hear the baby bawling! ... NOW GET UP!

MARY *(Mumbling drowsily.)* ... What baby ... whose baby ... ?

JOHN Yours!

MARY Mine? That's ridiculous. . . . what'd you say ... ? Somebody's baby bawling? ... How could that be so? *(Hearing screams.)* Who's crying? Somebody's crying! ... What's crying? ... WHERE'S LULA?!

JOHN I don't know. You better get up.

MARY That's outrageous! ... What time is it?

JOHN Late 'nuff! Now rise up!

MARY You must be joking. . . . I'm sure I still have four or five hours sleep in store—even more after that head-splittin' blow-out last night ... *(Tumbles back under covers.)*

JOHN Nobody told you to gulp those last six bourbons—

MARY Don't tell me how many bourbons to swallow, not after you guzzled the whole stinking bar! ... Get up? ... You must be cracked. . . . Where's Lula? She must be here, she always is ...

JOHN Well, she ain't here yet, so get up and muzzle that brat before she does drive me cuckoo!

MARY   (*Springing upright, finally realizing gravity of situation.*) Whaddaya mean Lula's not here? She's always here, she must be here. . . . Where else kin she be? She supposed to be. . . . She just can't *not* be here—CALL HER!   (*Blackout as John rushes offstage. Scene shifts to a trio of Telephone Operators perched on stools before imaginary switchboards. Chaos and bedlam are taking place to the sound of buzzes.* PRODUCTION NOTE: *Effect of following dialogue should simulate rising pandemonium.*)

FIRST OPERATOR   The line is busy—
SECOND OPERATOR   Line is busy—
THIRD OPERATOR   Is busy—
FIRST OPERATOR   Doing best we can—
SECOND OPERATOR   Having difficulty—
THIRD OPERATOR   Soon as possible—
FIRST OPERATOR   Just one moment—
SECOND OPERATOR   Would you hold on—
THIRD OPERATOR   Awful sorry, madam—
FIRST OPERATOR   Would you hold on, please—
SECOND OPERATOR   Just a second, please—
THIRD OPERATOR   Please hold on, please—
FIRST OPERATOR   The line is busy—
SECOND OPERATOR   The line is busy
THIRD OPERATOR   The line is busy—
FIRST OPERATOR   Doing best we can—
SECOND OPERATOR   Hold on please—
THIRD OPERATOR   Can't make connections—
FIRST OPERATOR   Unable to put it in—
SECOND OPERATOR   Won't plug through—
THIRD OPERATOR   Sorry madam—
FIRST OPERATOR   If you'd wait a moment—
SECOND OPERATOR   Doing best we can—
THIRD OPERATOR   Sorry—
FIRST OPERATOR   One moment—
SECOND OPERATOR   Just a second—
THIRD OPERATOR   Hold on—
FIRST OPERATOR   YES—
SECOND OPERATOR   STOP IT!—
THIRD OPERATOR   HOW DO I KNOW—
FIRST OPERATOR   YOU ANOTHER ONE!
SECOND OPERATOR   HOLD ON DAMMIT!
THIRD OPERATOR   UP YOURS, TOO!
FIRST OPERATOR   THE LINE IS BUSY—
SECOND OPERATOR   THE LINE IS BUSY—
THIRD OPERATOR   THE LINE IS BUSY—   (*The switchboard clamors a*

cacophony of buzzes as Operators plug connections with the frenzy of a Chaplin movie. Their replies degenerate into a babble of gibberish. At the height of frenzy, the Supervisor appears.)

SUPERVISOR   WHAT'S THE SNARL-UP???!!!

FIRST OPERATOR   Everybody calling at the same time, ma'am!

SECOND OPERATOR   Board can't handle it!

THIRD OPERATOR   Like everybody in big New York City is trying to squeeze a call through to li'l' ole us!

SUPERVISOR   God! . . . Somp'un terrible musta happened! . . . Buzz the emergency frequency hookup to the Mayor's office and find out what the hell's going on!   *(Scene blacks out quickly to Clem and Luke.)*

CLEM   *(Something slowly dawning on him.)*   Luke . . . ?

LUKE   Yes, Clem?

CLEM   *(Eyes roving around in puzzlement.)*   Luke . . . ?

LUKE   *(Irked.)* I said what, Clem!

CLEM   Luke . . . ? Where—where is—the—the—?

LUKE   THE WHAT?!

CLEM   Nigras . . . ?

LUKE   ?????What . . . ?

CLEM   Nigras. . . . Where is the Nigras, where is they, Luke . . . ? ALL THE NIGRAS! . . . I don't see no Nigras . . . ?!

LUKE   Whatcha mean . . . ?

CLEM   *(Agitatedly.)*   Luke, there ain't a darky in sight. . . . And if you remember, we ain't spied a nappy hair all morning. . . . The Nigras, Luke! We ain't laid eyes on nary a coon this whole morning!!!

LUKE   You must be crazy or something, Clem!

CLEM   Think about it, Luke, we been sitting here for an hour or more—try and recollect if you remember seeing jist *one* go by?!!!

LUKE   *(Confused.)*   . . . I don't recall. . . . But . . . but there musta been some. . . . The heat musta got you, Clem! How in hell could that be so?!!!

CLEM   *(Triumphantly.)*   Just think, Luke! . . . Look around ya. . . . Now, every morning mosta people walkin' 'long this street is colored. They's strolling by going to work, they's waiting for the buses, they's sweeping sidewalks, cleaning stores, starting to shine shoes and wetting the mops—right?! . . . Well, look around you, Luke—where is they? *(Luke paces up and down, checking.)* I told you Luke, they ain't nowheres to be seen.

LUKE   ???? . . . This . . . this . . . some kind of holiday for 'em—or something?

CLEM   I don't know, Luke . . . but . . . but what I do know is they ain't here 'n' we haven't seen a solitary one. . . . It's scaryfying, Luke . . . !

LUKE   Well . . . maybe they's jist standing 'n' walking and shining on
other streets.—Let's go look!   *(Scene blacks out to John and
Mary. Baby cries are as insistent as ever.)*

MARY   *(At end of patience.)*   SMOTHER IT!

JOHN   *(Beyond his.)*   That's a hell of a thing to say 'bout your own
child! You should know what to do to hush her up!

MARY   Why don't you try?!

JOHN   You had her!

MARY   You shared in borning her?!

JOHN   Possibly not!

MARY   Why, you lousy—!

JOHN   What good is a mother who can't shut up her own daughter?!

MARY   I told you she yells louder every time I try to lay hands on
her.—Where's Lula? Didn't you call her?!

JOHN   I told you I can't get the call through!

MARY   Try ag'in—

JOHN   It's no use! I tried numerous times and can't even git through
to the switchboard. You've got to quiet her down yourself.
(Firmly.)   Now, go in there and clam her up 'fore I lose my patience!   *(Mary exits. Soon, we hear the yells increase. She rushes
back in.)*

MARY   She won't let me touch her, just screams louder!

JOHN   Probably wet 'n' soppy!

MARY   Yes! Stinks something awful! Phooooey! I can't stand that
filth and odor!

JOHN   That's why she's screaming! Needs her didee changed.—Go
change it!

MARY   How you 'spect me to when I don't know how?! Suppose I
faint?!

JOHN   Well let her blast away. I'm getting outta here.

MARY   You can't leave me here like this!

JOHN   Just watch me! . . . See this nice split-level cottage, peachy
furniture, multi-colored teevee, hi-fi set 'n' the rest? . . . Well,
how you think I scraped 'em together while you curled up on
your fat li'l' fanny? . . . By gitting outta here—not only *on time*
. . . but EARLIER!—Beating a frantic crew of nice young execu-
tives to the punch—gitting there fustest with the mostest brown-
nosing you ever saw! Now if I goof one day—just ONE DAY!—
You reckon I'd stay ahead? NO! . . . There'd be a wolfpack trampling over my prostrate body, racing to replace my smiling face
against the boss' left rump! . . . NO, MAM! I'm zooming outta
here on time, just as I always have and what's more—you go'n'
fix me some breakfast, I'M HUNGRY!

MARY   But—

JOHN   No buts about it!   *(Flash blackout as he gags on a mouthful of coffee.)*   What you trying to do, STRANGLE ME!!!   *(Jumps up and starts putting on jacket.)*

MARY   *(Sarcastically.)*   What did you expect?

JOHN   *(In biting fury.)*   That you could possibly boil a pot of water, toast a few slices of bread and fry a coupler eggs! . . . It was a mistaken assumption!

MARY   So they aren't as good as Lula's!

JOHN   That is an overstatement. Your efforts don't result in anything that could possibly be digested by man, mammal, or insect! . . . When I married you, I thought I was fairly acquainted with your faults and weaknesses—I chalked 'em up to human imperfection. . . . But now I know I was being extremely generous, over-optimistic and phenomenally deluded!—You have no idea how useless you really are!

MARY   Then why'd you marry me?!

JOHN   Decoration!

MARY   You shoulda married Lula!

JOHN   I might've if it wasn't 'gainst the segregation law! . . . But for the sake of my home, my child and my sanity, I will even take a chance on sacrificing my slippery grip on the status pole and drive by her shanty to find out whether she or someone like her kin come over here and prevent some ultimate disaster.   *(Storms toward door, stopping abruptly at exit.)*   Are you sure you kin make it to the bathroom wit'out Lula backing you up?!!!   *(Blackout. Scene shifts to Mayor's office where a cluttered desk stands c. amid papered debris.)*

MAYOR   *(Striding determinedly toward desk, stopping midways, bellowing.)*   WOODFENCE! . . . WOODFENCE! . . . WOODFENCE! *(Receiving no reply, completes distance to desk.)* JACKSON! . . . JACKSON!

JACKSON   *(Entering worriedly.)*   Yes, sir . . . ?

MAYOR   Where's Vice-Mayor Woodfence, that no-good brother-in-law of mine?!

JACKSON   Hasn't come in yet, sir.

MAYOR   HASN'T COME IN?!!! . . . Damn bastard! Knows we have a crucial conference. Soon as he staggers through that door, tell him to shoot in here!   *(Angrily focusing on his disorderly desk and littered surroundings.)*   And git Mandy here to straighten up this mess—Rufus too! You know he shoulda been waiting to knock dust off my shoes soon as I step in. Get 'em in here! . . . What's the matter wit' them lazy Nigras? . . . Already had to dress myself because of JC, fix my own coffee without MayBelle, drive

myself to work 'counta Bubber, feel my old Hag's tits after Sap-
phi—NEVER MIND!—Git 'em in here—QUICK!

JACKSON   *(Meekly.)*   They aren't . . . they aren't here, sir . . .

MAYOR   Whaddaya mean they aren't here? Find out where they at.
We got important business, man! You can't run a town wit' laxity
like this. Can't allow things to git snafued jist because a bunch of
lazy Nigras been out gitting drunk and living it up all night! Discipline, man, discipline!

JACKSON   That's what I'm trying to tell you, sir . . . they didn't come
in, can't be found . . . none of 'em.

MAYOR   Ridiculous, boy! Scare 'em up and tell 'em scoot here in a
hurry befo' I git mad and fire the whole goddamn lot of 'em!

JACKSON   But we can't find 'em, sir.

MAYOR   Hogwash! Can't nobody in this office do anything right?!
Do I hafta handle every piddling little matter myself?! Git me
their numbers, I'll have 'em here befo' you kin shout to—
(Three men burst into room in various states of undress.)

ONE   Henry—they vanished!

TWO   Disappeared into thin air!

THREE   Gone wit'out a trace!

TWO   Not a one on the street!

THREE   In the house!

ONE   On the job!

MAYOR   Wait a minute!! . . . Hold your water! Calm down—!

ONE   But they've gone, Henry—GONE! All of 'em!

MAYOR   What the hell you talking 'bout? Gone? Who's gone—?

ONE   The Nigras, Henry! They gone!

MAYOR   Gone? . . . Gone where?

TWO   That's what we trying to tell ya—they just disappeared! The
Nigras have disappeared, swallowed up, vanished! All of 'em! Every last one!

MAYOR   Have everybody 'round here gone batty? . . . That's impossible, how could the Nigras vanish?

THREE   Beats me, but it's happened!

MAYOR   You mean a whole town of Nigras just evaporate like this—
poof!—Overnight?

ONE   Right!

MAYOR   Y'all must be drunk! Why, half this town is colored. How
could they just sneak out!

TWO   Don't ask me, but there ain't one in sight!

MAYOR   Simmer down 'n' put it to me easy-like.

ONE   Well . . . I first suspected somp'um smelly when Sarah Jo
didn't show up this morning and I couldn't reach her—

TWO   Dorothy Jane didn't 'rive at my house—

THREE   Georgia Mae wasn't at mine neither—and SHE sleeps in!

ONE   When I reached the office, I realized I hadn't seen nary one Nigra all morning! Nobody else had either—wait a minute—Henry, have you?!

MAYOR   ???Now that you mention it . . . no, I haven't . . .

ONE   They gone, Henry. . . . Not a one on the street, not a one in our homes, not a single, last living one to be found nowheres in town. What we gon' do?!

MAYOR   (*Thinking.*) Keep heads on your shoulders 'n' put clothes on your back. . . . They can't be far. . . . Must be 'round somewheres. . . . Probably playing hide 'n' seek, that's it! . . . JACK-SON!

JACKSON   Yessir?

MAYOR   Immediately mobilize our Citizens Emergency Distress Committee!—Order a fleet of sound trucks to patrol streets urging the population to remain calm—situation's not as bad as it looks—everything's under control! Then, have another squadron of squawk buggies drive slowly through all Nigra alleys, ordering them to come out wherever they are. If that don't git 'em, organize a vigilante search-squad to flush 'em outta hiding! But most important of all, track down that lazy goldbricker, Woodfence and tell him to git on top of the situation! By God, we'll find 'em even if we hafta dig 'em outta the ground! (*Blackout. Scene shifts back to John and Mary a few hours later. A funereal solemnity pervades their mood. John stands behind Mary who sits, in a scene duplicating the famous "American Gothic" painting.*)

JOHN   . . . Walked up to the shack, knocked on door, didn't git no answer. Hollered: "LULA? LULA . . . ?—Not a thing. Went 'round the side, peeped in window—nobody stirred. Next door—nobody there. Crossed other side of street and banged on five or six other doors—not a colored person could be found! Not a man, neither woman or child—not even a little black dog could be seen, smelt or heard for blocks around. . . . They've gone, Mary.

MARY   What does it all mean, John?

JOHN   I don't know, Mary . . .

MARY   I always had Lula, John. She never missed a day at my side. . . . That's why I couldn't accept your wedding proposal until I was sure you'd welcome me and her together as a package. How am I gonna get through the day? My baby don't know *me*, I ain't acquainted wit' *it*. I've never lifted cover off pot, swung a mop or broom, dunked a dish or even pushed a dustrag. I'm lost wit'out Lula, I need her, John, I need her. (*Begins to weep softly. John pats her consolingly.*)

JOHN   Courage, honey. . . . Everybody in town is facing the same dilemma. We mustn't crack up . . . (*Blackout. Scene shifts back to
Mayor's office later in day. Atmosphere and tone resembles a wartime headquarters at the front. Mayor is poring over huge map.*)

INDUSTRIALIST   Half the day is gone already, Henry. On behalf of the
factory owners of this town, you've got to bail us out! Seventy-
five percent of all production is paralyzed. With the Nigra absent,
men are waiting for machines to be cleaned, floors to be swept,
crates lifted, equipment delivered and bathrooms to be deodor-
ized. Why, restrooms and toilets are so filthy until they not only
cannot be sat in, but it's virtually impossible to get within hailing
distance because of the stench!

MAYOR   Keep your shirt on, Jeb—

BUSINESSMAN   Business is even in worse condition, Henry. The volume of goods moving 'cross counters has slowed down to a
trickle—almost negligible. Customers are not only not purchasing—but the absence of handymen, porters, sweepers, stock-
movers, deliverers and miscellaneous dirty-work doers is disrupting the smooth harmony of marketing!

CLUB WOMAN   Food poisoning, severe indigestitis, chronic diarrhea,
advanced diaper chafings and a plethora of unsanitary household
disasters dangerous to life, limb and property! . . . As a representative of the Federation of Ladies' Clubs, I must sadly report that
unless the trend is reversed, a complete breakdown in family unity is imminent. . . . Just as homosexuality and debauchery signalled the fall of Greece and Rome, the downgrading of Southern
Bellesdom might very well prophesy the collapse of our indigenous institutions. . . . Remember—it has always been pure, delicate, lily-white images of Dixie femininity which provided
backbone, inspiration and ideology for our male warriors in their
defense against the on-rushing black horde. If our gallant men
are drained of this worship and idolatry—God knows! The cause
won't be worth a Confederate nickel!

MAYOR   Stop this panicky defeatism, y'all hear me! All machinery at
my disposal is being utilized. I assure you wit' great confidence
the damage will soon repair itself.—Cheerful progress reports are
expected any moment now.—Wait! See, here's Jackson. . . . Well,
Jackson?

JACKSON   (*Entering.*)   As of now, sir, all efforts are fruitless. Neither
hide nor hair of them has been located. We have not unearthed a
single one in our shack-to-shack search. Not a single one has
heeded our appeal. Scoured every crick and cranny inside their
hovels, turning furniture upside down and inside out, breaking
down walls and tearing through ceilings. We made determined

efforts to discover where 'bouts of our faithful uncle Toms and informers—but even they have vanished without a trace. . . . Searching squads are on the verge of panic and hysteria, sir, wit' hotheads among 'em campaigning for scorched earth policies. Nigras on a whole lack cellars, but there's rising sentiment favoring burning to find out whether they're underground—DUG IN!

MAYOR Absolutely counter such foolhardy suggestions! Suppose they are tombed in? We'd only accelerate the gravity of the situation using incendiary tactics! Besides, when they're rounded up where will we put 'em if we've already burned up their shacks— IN OUR OWN BEDROOMS?!!!

JACKSON I agree, sir, but the mood of the crowd is becoming irrational. In anger and frustration, they's forgetting their original purpose was to FIND the Nigras!

MAYOR At all costs! Stamp out all burning proposals! Must prevent extremist notions from gaining ascendancy. Git wit' it. . . . Wait—'n' for Jehovah's sake, find out where the hell is that trifling slacker, WOODFENCE!

COURIER (Rushing in.) Mr. Mayor! Mr. Mayor! . . . We've found some! We've found some!

MAYOR (Excitedly.) Where?!

COURIER In the—in the—(Can't catch breath.)

MAYOR (Impatiently.) Where, man? Where?!!!

COURIER In the colored wing of the city hospital!

MAYOR The hos—? The hospital! I shoulda known! How could those helpless, crippled, cut and shot Nigras disappear from a hospital! Shoulda thought of that! . . . Tell me more, man!

COURIER I—I didn't wait, sir. . . . I—I ran in to report soon as I heard—

MAYOR WELL GIT BACK ON THE PHONE, YOU IDIOT, DON'T YOU KNOW WHAT THIS MEANS!

COURIER Yes, sir. (Races out.)

MAYOR Now we gitting somewhere! . . . Gentlemen, if one sole Nigra is among us, we're well on the road to rehabilitation! Those Nigras in the hospital must know somp'um 'bout the others where'bouts. . . . Scat back to your colleagues, boost up their morale and inform 'em that things will zip back to normal in a jiffy! (They start to file out, then pause to observe the Courier reentering dazedly.) Well . . . ? Well, man . . . ? WHAT'S THE MATTER WIT' YOU, NINNY, TELL ME WHAT ELSE WAS SAID?!

COURIER They all . . . they all . . . they all in a—in a—a coma, sir . . .

MAYOR They all in a what . . . ?

COURIER In a coma, sir . . .

MAYOR Talk sense, man! . . . Whaddaya mean, they all in a coma?

COURIER Doctor says every last one of the Nigras are jist laying in bed . . . STILL . . . not moving . . . neither live or dead . . . laying up there in a coma . . . every last one of 'em . . .

MAYOR *(Sputters, then grabs phone.)* Get me Confederate Memorial. . . . Put me through to the Staff Chief. . . . YES, this is the Mayor. . . . Sam? . . . What's this I hear? . . . But how could they be in a coma, Sam? . . . You don't know! Well, what the hell you think the city's paying you for! . . . You've got 'nuff damn hacks and quacks there to find out! . . . How could it be somp'um unknown? You mean Nigras know somp'um 'bout drugs your damn butchers don't?! . . . Well, what the crap good are they! . . . All right, all right, I'll be calm. . . . Now, tell me. . . . Uh huh, uh huh. . . . Well, can't you give 'em some injections or somp'um . . . ? —You did . . . uh huh . . . DID YOU TRY A LI'L' ROUGH TREATMENT?—that too, huh. . . . All right, Sam, keep trying. . . . *(Puts phone down delicately, continuing absently.)* Can't wake 'em up. Just lay there. Them that's sick won't git no sicker, them that's half-well won't git no better, babies that's due won't be born and them that's come won't show no life. Nigras wit' cuts won't bleed and them which need blood won't be transfused. . . . He say dying Nigras is even refusing to pass away! *(Is silently perplexed for a moment, then suddenly breaks into action.)* JACKSON?! . . . Call the police—THE JAIL! Find out what's going on there! Them Nigras are captives! If there's one place we got darkies under control, it's there! Them sonsabitches too onery to act right either for colored or white! *(Jackson exits. The Courier follows.)* Keep your fingers crossed, citizens, them Nigras in jail are the most important Nigras we got! *(All hands are raised conspicuously aloft, fingers prominently ex-ed. Seconds tick by. Soon Jackson returns crestfallen.)*

JACKSON Sheriff Bull says they don't know whether they still on premises or not. When they went to rouse Nigra jailbirds this morning, cell-block doors refused to swing open. Tried everything—even exploded dynamite charges—but it just wouldn't budge. . . . Then they hoisted guards up to peep through barred windows, but couldn't see good 'nuff to tell whether Nigras was inside or not. Finally, gitting desperate, they power-hosed the cells wit' water but had to cease 'cause Sheriff Bull said he didn't wanta jeopardize drowning the Nigras since it might spoil his chance of shipping a record load of cotton pickers to the State Penitentiary for cotton-snatching jubilee. . . . Anyway—they ain't heard a Nigra-squeak all day.

MAYOR   ???That so . . . ? WHAT 'BOUT TRAINS 'N' BUSSES PASS-
ING THROUGH? There must be some dinges riding through?
JACKSON   We checked . . . not a one on board.
MAYOR   Did you hear whether any other towns lost their Nigras?
JACKSON   Things are status-quo everywhere else.
MAYOR   *(Angrily.)*   Then what the hell they picking on us for!
COURIER   *(Rushing in.)*   MR. MAYOR! Your sister jist called—HYS-
TERICAL! She says Vice-Mayor Woodfence went to bed wit' her
last night, but when she woke up this morning he was gone!
Been missing all day!
MAYOR   ???Could Nigras be holding brother-in-law Woodfence hos-
tage?!
COURIER   No, sir. Besides him—investigations reveal that dozens or
more prominent citizens—two City Council members, the chair-
man of the Junior Chamber of Commerce, our City College All-
Southern half-back, the chairlady of the Daughters of the Confed-
erate Rebellion, Miss Cotton-Sack Festival of the Year and nu-
merous other miscellaneous nobodies—are all absent wit'out
leave. Dangerous evidence points to the conclusion that they
have been infiltrating!
MAYOR   Infiltrating???
COURIER   Passing all along!
MAYOR   ???PASSING ALL ALONG???
COURIER   Secret Nigras all the while!
MAYOR   NAW!   *(Club Woman keels over in faint. Jackson, Business-
man and Industrialist begin to eye each other suspiciously.)*
COURIER   Yessir!
MAYOR   PASSING???
COURIER   Yessir!
MAYOR   SECRET NIG—!???
COURIER   Yessir!
MAYOR   *(Momentarily stunned to silence.)*   The dirty mongrelizers!
. . . Gentlemen, this is a grave predicament indeed. . . . It pains
me to surrender priority of our states' right credo, but it is my
solemn task and frightening duty to inform you that we have no
other recourse but to seek outside help for deliverance. *(Blackout.
Lights re-rise on Huntley-Brinkley-Murrow-Severeid-Cronkite-Rea-
soner-type Announcer grasping a hand-held microphone* [imaginary]
*a few hours later. He is vigorously, excitedly mouthing his commen-
tary, but no sound escapes his lips. . . . During this dumb, wordless
section of his broadcast, a bedraggled assortment of figures marching
with picket signs occupy his attention. On their picket signs are inscribed various appeals and slogans. "CINDY LOU UNFAIR TO
BABY JOE" . . . "CAP'N SAM MISS BIG BOY" . . . "RETURN LI'L'*

BLUE TO MARSE JIM" . . . "INFORMATION REQUESTED 'BOUT MAMMY GAIL" . . . "BOSS NATHAN PROTEST TO FAST LEROY." Trailing behind the marchers, forcibly isolated, is a woman dressed in widow-black holding a placard which reads: "WHY DIDN'T YOU TELL US—YOUR DEFILED WIFE AND TWO ABSENT MONGRELS.")

ANNOUNCER *(Who has been silently mouthing his delivery during the picketing procession, is suddenly heard as if caught in the midst of commentary.)* . . . Factories standing idle from the loss of non-essential workers. Stores shuttered from the absconding of uncrucial personnel. Uncollected garbage threatening pestilence and pollution. . . . Also, each second somewheres in this former utopia below the Mason and Dixon, dozens of decrepit old men and women usually tended by faithful nurses and servants are popping off like flies—abandoned by sons, daughters and grandchildren whose refusal to provide their doddering relatives with bedpans and other soothing necessities result in their hasty, nasty, messy corpus delicties. . . . But most critically affected of all by this complete drought of Afro-American resources are policemen and other public safety guardians denied their daily quota of Negro arrests. One officer known affectionately as "TWO-A-DAY-PETE" because of his unblemished record of TWO Negro headwhippings per day has already been carted off to the County Insane Asylum—straight-jacketed, screaming and biting, unable to withstand the shock of having his spotless slate sullied by interruption. . . . It is feared that similar attacks are soon expected among municipal judges prevented for the first time in years of distinguished bench-sitting from sentencing one single Negro to a hoosegow or pokey. . . . Ladies and gentlemen, as you trudge in from the joys and headaches of workday chores and dusk begins to descend on this sleepy Southern hamlet, we REPEAT—today—before early morning dew had dried upon magnolia blossoms, your comrade citizens of this lovely Dixie village awoke to the realization that some—pardon me! Not some—but ALL OF THEIR NEGROES were missing. . . . Absent, vamoosed, departed, at bay, fugitive, away, gone and so-far unretrieved. . . . In order to dispel your incredulity, gauge the temper of your suffering compatriots and just possibly prepare you for the likelihood of an equally nightmarish eventuality, we have gathered a cross-section of this city's most distinguished leaders for exclusive interviews. . . . First, Mr. Council Clan, grand-dragoon of this area's most active civic organizations and staunch bell-wether of the political opposition. . . . Mr. Clan, how do you ACCOUNT for this incredible disappearance?

CLAN A PLOT, plain and simple, that's what it is, as plain as the corns on your feet!

ANNOUNCER Whom would you consider responsible?

CLAN I could go on all night.

ANNOUNCER Cite a few?

CLAN Too numerous.

ANNOUNCER Just one?

CLAN Name names when time comes.

ANNOUNCER Could you be referring to native Negroes?

CLAN Ever try quaranteening lepers from their spots?

ANNOUNCER Their organizations?

CLAN Could you slice a nose off a mouth and still keep a face?

ANNOUNCER Commies?

CLAN Would you lop off a titty from a chest and still have a breast?

ANNOUNCER Your city government?

CLAN Now you talkin'!

ANNOUNCER State administration?

CLAN Warming up!

ANNOUNCER Federal?

CLAN Kin a blind man see?!

ANNOUNCER The Court?

CLAN Is a pig clean?!

ANNOUNCER Clergy?

CLAN Do a polecat stink?!

ANNOUNCER Well, Mr. Clan, with this massive complicity, how do you think the plot could've been prevented from succeeding?

CLAN If I'da been in office, it never woulda happened.

ANNOUNCER Then you're laying major blame at the doorstep of the present administration?

CLAN Damn tooting!

ANNOUNCER But from your oft-expressed views, Mr. Clan, shouldn't you and your followers be delighted at the turn of events? After all—isn't it one of the main policies of your society to *drive* the Negroes away? *Drive* 'em back where they came from?

CLAN DRIVVVE, BOY! DRIIIIVVVE! That's right! . . . When we say so and not befo'. Ain't supposed to do nothing 'til we tell 'em. Got to stay put until we exercise our God-given right to tell 'em when to git!

ANNOUNCER But why argue if they've merely jumped the gun? Why not rejoice at this premature purging of undesirables?

CLAN The time ain't ripe yet, boy. . . . The time ain't ripe yet.

ANNOUNCER Thank you for being so informative, Mr. Clan—Mrs. Aide? Mrs. Aide? Over here, Mrs. Aide. . . . Ladies and gentlemen, this city's Social Welfare Commissioner, Mrs. Handy Anna

Aide. . . . Mrs. Aide, with all your Negroes *AWOL*, haven't developments alleviated the staggering demands made upon your Welfare Department? Reduction of relief requests, elimination of case loads, removal of chronic welfare dependents, et cetera?

AIDE   Quite the contrary. Disruption of our pilot projects among Nigras saddles our white community with extreme hardship. . . . You see, historically, our agencies have always been foremost contributors to the Nigra Git-A-Job movement. We pioneered in enforcing social welfare theories which oppose coddling the fakers. We strenuously believe in helping Nigras help themselves by participating in meaningful labor. "Relief is Out, Work is In," is our motto. We place them as maids, cooks, butlers, and breast-feeders, cesspool-diggers, wash-basin maintainers, shoe-shine boys, and so on—mostly on a volunteer self-work basis.

ANNOUNCER   Hired at prevailing salaried rates, of course?

AIDE   God forbid! Money is unimportant. Would only make 'em worse. Our main goal is to improve their ethical behavior. "Rehabilitation Through Positive Participation" is another motto of ours. All unwed mothers, loose-living malingering fathers, bastard children and shiftless grandparents are kept occupied through constructive muscle-therapy. This provides the Nigra with less opportunity to indulge his pleasure-loving amoral inclinations.

ANNOUNCER   They volunteer to participate in these pilot projects?

AIDE   Heavens no! They're notorious shirkers. When I said the program is voluntary, I meant white citizens in overwhelming majorities do the volunteering. Placing their homes, offices, appliances and persons at our disposal for use in "Operation Uplift." . . . We would never dare place such a decision in the hands of the Nigra. It would never get off the ground! . . . No, they have no choice in the matter. "Work or Starve" is the slogan we use to stimulate Nigra awareness of what's good for survival.

ANNOUNCER   Thank you, Mrs. Aide, and good luck. . . . Rev? . . . Rev? . . . Ladies and gentlemen, this city's foremost spiritual guidance counselor, Reverend Reb Pious. . . . How does it look to you, Reb Pious?

PIOUS   *(Continuing to gaze skyward.)*   It's in *His* hands, son, it's in *His* hands.

ANNOUNCER   How would you assess the disappearance, from a moral standpoint?

PIOUS   An immoral act, son, morally wrong and ethically indefensible. A perversion of Christian principles to be condemned from every pulpit of this nation.

ANNOUNCER   Can you account for its occurrence after the many decades of the Church's missionary activity among them?

PIOUS   It's basically a reversion of the Nigra to his deep-rooted
primitivism. . . . Now, at last, you can understand the difficulties
of the Church in attempting to anchor God's kingdom among
ungratefuls. It's a constant, unrelenting, no-holds-barred struggle
against Satan to wrestle away souls locked in his possession for
countless centuries! Despite all our aid, guidance, solace and protection, Old BeezleBub still retains tenacious grips upon the Nigras' childish loyalty—comparable to the lure of bright flames to
an infant.

ANNOUNCER   But actual physical departure, Reb Pious? How do you
explain that?

PIOUS   Voodoo, my son, voodoo. . . . With Satan's assist, they have
probably employed some heathen magic which we cultivated, sophisticated Christians know absolutely nothing about. However,
before long we are confident about counteracting this evil witch-
doctory and triumphing in our Holy Savior's name. At this perilous juncture, true believers of all denominations are participating
in joint, 'round-the-clock observances, offering prayers for our
Master's swiftest intercession. I'm optimistic about the outcome
of his intervention. . . . Which prompts me—if I may, sir—to offer these words of counsel to our delinquent Nigras. . . . I say to
you without rancor or vengeance, quoting a phrase of one of
your greatest prophets, Booker T. Washington: "Return your
buckets to where they lay and all will be forgiven."

ANNOUNCER   A very inspirational appeal, Reb Pious. I'm certain they
will find the tug of its magnetic sincerity irresistible. Thank you,
Reb Pious. . . . All in all—as you have witnessed, ladies and gentlemen—this town symbolizes the face of disaster. Suffering as
severe a prostration as any city wrecked, ravaged and devastated
by the holocaust of war. A vital, lively, throbbing organism
brought to a screeching halt by the strange enigma of the missing
Negroes. . . . We take you now to offices of the one man into
whose hands has been thrust the final responsibility of rescuing
this shuddering metropolis from the precipice of destruction. . . .
We give you the honorable Mayor, Henry R. E. Lee. . . . Hello,
Mayor Lee.

MAYOR   (Jovially.)   Hello, Jack.

ANNOUNCER   Mayor Lee, we have just concluded interviews with
some of your city's leading spokesmen. If I may say so, sir, they
don't sound too encouraging about the situation.

MAYOR   Nonsense, Jack! The situation's well-in-hand as it could be
under the circumstances. Couldn't be better in hand. Underneath
every dark cloud, Jack, there's always a ray of sunlight, ha, ha, ha.

ANNOUNCER   Have you discovered one, sir?

MAYOR   Well, Jack, I'll tell you. . . . Of course we've been faced wit' a little crisis, but look at it like this—we've faced 'em befo': Sherman marched through Georgia—ONCE! Lincoln freed the slaves—MOMENTARILY! Carpetbaggers even put Nigras in the Governor's mansion, state legislature, Congress and the Senate of the United States. But what happened?—Ole Dixie bounced right on back up. . . . At this moment the Supreme Court's trying to put Nigras in our schools and the Nigra has got it in his haid to put hisself everywhere. . . . But what you 'spect go'n' happen?— Old Dixie will kangaroo back even higher. Southern courage, fortitude, chivalry and superiority always wins out. . . . SHUCKS! We'll have us some Nigras befo' daylight is gone!

ANNOUNCER   Mr. Mayor, I hate to introduce this note, but in an earlier interview, one of your chief opponents, Mr. Clan, hinted at your own complicity in the affair—

MAYOR   A LOT OF POPPYCOCK! Clan is politicking! I've beaten him four times outta four and I'll beat him four more times outta four! This is no time for partisan politics! What we need now is level-headedness and across-the-board unity. This typical, rash, mealy-mouth, shooting-off-at-the-lip of Clan and his ilk proves their insincerity and voters will remember that in the next election! Won't you, voters?!   *(Has risen to the height of campaign oratory.)*

ANNOUNCER   Mr. Mayor! . . . Mr. Mayor! . . . Please—

MAYOR   . . . I tell you, I promise you—

ANNOUNCER   PLEASE, MR. MAYOR!

MAYOR   Huh? . . . Oh—yes, carry on.

ANNOUNCER   Mr. Mayor, your cheerfulness and infectious good spirits lead me to conclude that startling new developments warrant fresh-found optimism. What concrete, declassified information do you have to support your claim that Negroes will reappear before nightfall?

MAYOR   Because we are presently awaiting the pay-off of a masterful five-point supra-recovery program which can't help but reap us a bonanza of Nigras 'fore sundown! . . . First: Exhaustive efforts to pinpoint the where'bouts of our own missing darkies continue to zero in on the bullseye. . . . Second: The President of the United States, following an emergency cabinet meeting, has designated us the prime disaster area of the century—National Guard is already on the way. . . . Third: In an unusual, but bold maneuver, we have appealed to the NAACP 'n' all other Nigra conspirators to help us git to the bottom of the vanishing act. . . . Fourth: We have exercised our non-reciprocal option and requested that all fraternal southern states express their solidarity by lending us

some of their Nigras temporarily on credit. . . . Fifth and foremost: We have already gotten consent of the Governor to round
up all stray, excess and incorrigible Nigras to be shipped to us
under escort of the State Militia. . . . That's why we've stifled pes-
simism and are brimming wit' confidence that this full-scale con-
certed mobilization will ring down a jackpot of jigaboos 'fore
light vanishes from sky!—

ANNOUNCER   Congratulations! What happens if it fails?

MAYOR   Don't even think THAT! Absolutely no reason to suspect it
will. . . .   (Peers over shoulder, then whispers confidentially while
placing hand over mouth by Announcer's imaginary mike.)   . . . But
speculating on the dark side of your question—if we don't turn
up some by nightfall, it may be all over. The harm has already
been done. You see the South has always been glued together by
the uninterrupted presence of its darkies. No telling how unstuck
we might git if things keep on like they have.—Wait a minute, it
musta paid off already! Mission accomplished 'cause here's Jackson head a time wit' the word. . . . Well, Jackson, what's new?

JACKSON   Situation on the home front remains static, sir—can't uncover scent or shadow. The NAACP and all other Nigra front
groups 'n' plotters deny any knowledge or connection wit' the
missing Nigras. Maintained this even after appearing befo' a Senate Emergency Investigating Committee which subpoenaed 'em to
Washington post haste and threw 'em in jail for contempt. A
handful of Nigras who agreed to make spectacular appeals for
ours to come back to us, have themselves mysteriously disappeared. But, worst news of all, sir, is our sister cities and coun-
ties, inside and outside the state, have changed their minds,
fallen back on their promises and refused to lend us any Nigras,
claiming they don't have 'nuff for themselves.

MAYOR   What 'bout Nigras promised by the Governor?!

JACKSON   Jailbirds and vagrants escorted here from chain-gangs and
other reservations either revolted and escaped enroute or else
vanished mysteriously on approaching our city limits. . . . Deterioration rapidly escalates, sir. Estimates predict we kin hold out
only one more hour before overtaken by anarchistic turmoil. . . .
Some citizens seeking haven elsewheres have already fled, but on
last report were being forcibly turned back by armed sentinels in
other cities who wanted no parts of 'em—claiming they carried a
jinx.

MAYOR   That bad, huh?

JACKSON   Worse, sir . . . we've received at least five reports of plots
on your life.

MAYOR   What?!—We've gotta act quickly then!

JACKSON   Run out of ideas, sir.

MAYOR   Think harder, boy!

JACKSON   Don't have much time, sir. One measly hour, then all hell go'n' break loose.

MAYOR   Gotta think of something drastic, Jackson!

JACKSON   I'm dry, sir.

MAYOR   Jackson! Is there any planes outta here in the next hour?

JACKSON   All transportation's been knocked out, sir.

MAYOR   I thought so!

JACKSON   What were you contemplating, sir?

MAYOR   Don't ask me what I was contemplating! I'm still boss 'round here! Don't forgit it!

JACKSON   Sorry, sir.

MAYOR   . . . Hold the wire! . . .Wait a minute . . . ! Waaaaait a minute—GODAMMIT! All this time crapping 'round, diddling and fotsing wit' puny li'l' solutions—all the while neglecting our ace in the hole, our trump card! Most potent weapon for digging Nigras outta the woodpile!!! All the while right befo' our eyes! . . . Ass! Why didn't you remind me?!!!

JACKSON   What is it, sir?

MAYOR   . . . ME—THAT'S WHAT! ME! A personal appeal from ME! *Directly to them!* . . . Although we wouldn't let 'em march to the polls and express their affection for me through the ballot box, we've always known I'm held highest in their esteem. A direct address from their beloved Mayor! . . . If they's anywheres close within the sound of my voice, they'll shape up! Or let us know by a sign they's ready to!

JACKSON   You sure *that'll* turn the trick, sir?

MAYOR   As sure as my ancestors befo' me who knew that when they puckered their lips to whistle, ole Sambo was gonna come a-lickety-splitting to answer the call! . . . That same chips-down blood courses through these Confederate gray veins of Henry R. E. Lee!!!

ANNOUNCER   I'm delighted to offer our network's facilities for such a crucial public interest address, sir. We'll arrange immediately for your appearance on an international hookup, placing you in the widest proximity to contact them wherever they may be.

MAYOR   Thank you, I'm very grateful. . . . Jackson, re-grease the machinery and set wheels in motion. Inform townspeople what's being done. Tell 'em we're all in this together. The next hour is countdown. I demand absolute cooperation, city-wide silence and inactivity. I don't want the Nigras frightened if they's nearby. This is the most important hour in town's history. Tell 'em if one single Nigra shows up during hour of decision, victory is within sight. I'm gonna git 'em that one—maybe all! Hurry and crack to it! *(Announcer rushes out, followed by Jackson. Blackout. Scene reopens, with Mayor seated, eyes front, spotlight illuminating him in semi-darkness. Shadowy figures stand in the background, prepared to answer phones or aid in any other manner. Mayor waits patiently until "GO!" signal is given. Then begins, his voice combining elements of confidence, tremolo and gravity.)* Good evening. . . . Despite the fact that millions of you wonderful people throughout the nation are viewing and listening to this momentous broadcast—and I thank you for your concern and sympathy in this hour of our peril—I primarily want to concentrate my attention and address these remarks solely for the benefit of our departed Nigra friends who may be listening somewheres in our far-flung land to the sound of my voice. . . . If you are—it is with heartfelt emotion and fond memories of our happy association that I ask—"Where are you . . . ?" Your absence has left a void in the bosom of every single man, woman and child of our great city. I tell you—you don't know what it means for us to wake up in the morning and discover that your cheerful, grinning, happy-go-lucky faces are missing! . . . From the depths of my heart, I can only meekly, humbly suggest what it means to me personally. . . . You see—the one face I will never be able to erase from my memory is the face—not of my Ma, not of Pa, neither wife or child—but the image of the first woman I came to love so well when just a wee lad—the vision of the first human I laid clear sight on at childbirth—the profile—better yet, the full face of my dear old . . . Jemimah—God rest her soul. . . . Yes! My dear ole mammy, wit' her round ebony moonbeam gleaming down upon me in the crib, teeth shining, blood-red bandana standing starched, peaked and proud, gazing down upon me affectionately as she crooned me a Southern lullaby. . . . OH! It's a memorable picture I will eternally cherish in permanent treasure chambers of my heart, now and forever always. . . . Well, if this radiant image can remain so infinitely vivid to me all these many years after her unfortunate demise in the Po' folks home—THINK of the misery the rest of us must be suffering after being *freshly* denied your soothing presence?! We need ya. If you kin hear me, just contact this station 'n' I will welcome you back personally. Let me just tell you that since you eloped, nothing has been the same. How could it? You're part of us, you belong to us. Just give us a sign and we'll be contented that all is well. . . . Now if you've skipped away on a little fun-fest, we understand, ha, ha. We know you like a good time and we don't begrudge it to ya. Hell—er, er, we like a good time ourselves—who doesn't? . . . In fact, think of all the good times we've had together, huh? We've had some real fun, you and us, yesiree! . . . Nobody knows better than you and I what fun we've had together. You singing us those old Southern coon songs and dancing those Nigra jigs and us clapping, prodding 'n' spurring you on! Lots of fun, huh?! . . . OH BOY! The times we've had together. . . . If you've snucked away for a bit of fun by yourself, we'll go 'long wit' ya—long as you let us know where you at so we won't be worried about you. . . . We'll go 'long wit' you long as you don't take the joke too far. I'll admit a joke is a joke and you've played a LULU! . . . I'm warning you, we can't stand much more horsing 'round from you! Business is business 'n' fun is fun! You've had your fun so now let's get down to business! Come on back, YOU HEAR ME!!! . . . . If you been hoodwinked by agents of some foreign government, I've been authorized by the President of these United States to inform you that this liberty-loving Republic is prepared to rescue you from their clutches. Don't pay no 'tention to their sireeen songs and atheistic promises! You better off under our control and you know it! . . . If you been bamboozled by rabble-rousing nonsense of your own so-called leaders, we prepared to offer same protection. Just call us up! Just give us a sign! . . . Come on, give us a sign . . . give us a sign—even a teeny-weeny one . . . ??!! *(Glances around checking on possible communications. A bevy of headshakes indicate no success. Mayor returns to address with desperate fevor.)*   Now look—you don't know what you doing! If you persist in this disobedience, you know all too well the consequences! We'll track you to the end of the earth, beyond the galaxy, across the stars! We'll capture you and chastise you with all the vengeance we command! 'N' you know only too well how stern we kin be when double-crossed! The city, the state and the entire nation will crucify you for this unpardonable defiance! *(Checks again.)*   No call . . . ? No sign . . . ? Time is running out! Deadline slipping past! They gotta respond! They gotta! *(Resuming.)*   Listen to me! I'm begging y'all, you've gotta come back . . . ! LOOK, GEORGE! *(Waves dirty rag aloft.)*   I brought the rag you wax the car wit'. . . . Don't this bring back memories, George, of all the days you spent shining that automobile to shimmering perfection . . . ? And you, Rufus?! . . . Here's the shoe polisher and the brush! . . . 'Member, Rufus? . . . Remember the happy mornings you spent popping this rag and whisking this brush so furiously 'till it created music that was sympho-nee to the ear . . . ? And you—MANDY? . . . Here's the waste-basket you didn't dump this morning. I saved it just for you! . . . LOOK, all y'all out there . . . ? *(Signals and a three-person procession parades one after the other before the imaginary camera.)*

DOLL WOMAN   (*Brandishing a crying baby [doll] as she strolls past and exits.*)   She's been crying ever since you left, Caldonia . . .

MOP MAN   (*Flashing mop.*)   It's been waiting in the same corner, Buster . . .

BRUSH MAN   (*Flagging toilet brush in one hand and toilet plunger in other.*)   It's been dry ever since you left, Washington . . .

MAYOR   (*Jumping in on the heels of the last exit.*)   Don't these things mean anything to y'all? By God! Are your memories so short?! Is there nothing sacred to ya? . . . Please come back, for my sake, please! All of you—even you questionable ones! I promise no harm will be done to you! Revenge is disallowed! We'll forgive everything! Just come on back and I'll git down on my knees— (*Immediately drops to knees.*)   I'll be kneeling in the middle of Dixie Avenue to kiss the first shoe of the first one 'a you to show up. . . . *I'll smooch any other spot you request.* . . . Erase this nightmare 'n' we'll concede any demand you make, just come on back—please???!! . . . PLEEEEEEEZE?!!!

VOICE   (*Shouting.*)   TIME!!!

MAYOR   (*Remaining on knees, frozen in a pose of supplication. After a brief, deadly silence, he whispers almost inaudibly.*)   They wouldn't answer . . . they wouldn't answer . . .   (*Blackout as bedlam erupts offstage. Total blackness holds during a sufficient interval where offstage sound-effects create the illusion of complete pandemonium, followed by a diminution which trails off into an expressionistic simulation of a city coming to a strickened standstill: industrial machinery clanks to halt, traffic blares to silence, etc. . . . The stage remains dark and silent for a long moment, then lights rearise on the Announcer.*)

ANNOUNCER   A pitiful sight, ladies and gentlemen. Soon after his unsuccessful appeal, Mayor Lee suffered a vicious pummeling from the mob and barely escaped with his life. National Guardsmen and State Militia were impotent in quelling the fury of a town venting its frustration in an orgy of destruction—a frenzy of rioting, looting and all other aberrations of a town gone berserk. . . . Then—suddenly—as if a magic wand had been waved, madness evaporated and something more frightening replaced it: Submission. . . . Even whimperings ceased. The city: exhausted, benumbed.—Slowly its occupants slinked off into shadows, and by midnight, the town was occupied exclusively by zombies. The fight and life had been drained out. . . . Pooped. . . . Hope ebbed away as completely as the beloved, absent Negroes. . . . As our crew packed gear and crept away silently, we treaded softly—as if we were stealing away from a mausoleum. . . . The Face Of A Defeated City. (*Blackout. Lights rise slowly at the sound of roos-*

ter-crowing, signalling the approach of a new day, the next morning. Scene is same as opening of play. Clem and Luke are huddled over dazedly, trancelike. They remain so for a long count. Finally, a figure drifts on stage, shuffling slowly.)

LUKE   *(Gazing in silent fascination at the approaching figure.)* . . . Clem . . . ? Do you see what I see or am I dreaming . . . ?

CLEM   It's a . . . a Nigra, ain't it, Luke . . . ?

LUKE   Sure looks like one, Clem—but we better make sure—eyes could be playing tricks on us. . . . Does he still look like one to you, Clem?

CLEM   He still does, Luke—but I'm scared to believe—

LUKE   . . . Why . . . ? It looks like Rastus, Clem!

CLEM   Sure does, Luke . . . but we better not jump to no hasty conclusion . . .

LUKE   *(In timid softness.)*   That you, Rastus . . . ?

RASTUS   *(Stepin Fetchit, Willie Best, Nicodemus, B. McQueen and all the rest rolled into one.)*   Why . . . howdy . . . Mr. Luke . . . Mr. Clem . . .

CLEM   It is him, Luke! It is him!

LUKE   Rastus?

RASTUS   Yas . . . sah?

LUKE   Where was you yesterday?

RASTUS   *(Very, very puzzled.)*   Yes . . . ter . . . day? . . . Yester . . . day . . . ? Why . . . right . . . here . . . Mr. Luke . . .

LUKE   No you warn't, Rastus, don't lie to me! Where was you yestiddy?

RASTUS   Why . . . I'm sure I was . . . Mr. Luke. . . . Remember . . . I made . . . that . . . delivery for you . . .

LUKE   That was MONDAY, Rastus, yestiddy was TUESDAY.

RASTUS   Tues . . . day . . . ? You don't say. . . . Well . . . well . . . well . . .

LUKE   Where was you 'n' all the other Nigras yesterday, Rastus?

RASTUS   I . . . thought . . . yestiddy . . . was . . . Monday, Mr. Luke— I coulda swore it . . . ! . . . See how . . . things . . . kin git all mixed up? . . . I coulda swore it . . .

LUKE   TODAY is WEDNESDAY, Rastus. Where was you TUESDAY?

RASTUS   Tuesday . . . huh? That's somp'um . . . I . . . don't . . . remember . . . missing . . . a day . . . Mr. Luke . . . but I guess you right . . .

LUKE   Then where was you!!!???

RASTUS   Don't rightly know, Mr. Luke. I didn't know I had skipped a day.—But that jist goes to show you how time kin fly, don't it, Mr. Luke. . . . Uuh, uuh, uuh . . . *(He starts shuffling off, scratch-*

ing head, a flicker of a smile playing across his lips. Clem and Luke gaze dumbfoundedly as he disappears.)

LUKE   *(Eyes sweeping around in all directions.)* Well. . . . There's the others, Clem. . . . Back jist like they useta be. . . . Everything's same as always . . .

CLEM   ??? . . . . Is it . . . Luke . . . !   *(Slow fade.)*

CURTAIN

William Melvin Kelley

(1937–   )

THE NOVELS OF WILLIAM MELVIN KELLEY express the efforts of black Americans to define themselves as individuals and as a culture against the hostile backdrop of white society. They also reflect Kelley's personal confrontation with racism and his struggle to understand his responsibilities as a writer and as a human being within an oppressive white environment. His early novels make a quiet demand for individual dignity, and his later ones portray a more violent reaction against racism. This thematic shift recapitulates the change in Kelley's racial politics as the nonviolent civil rights movement gave way to the rage of the black nationalists.

Kelly was born in 1937 in the Bronx and attended a predominantly white private high school in New York. In 1957 he went to Harvard to study law and began to take creative writing courses during his sophomore year. He failed his law classes, but gained the attention of his writing instructors, among them John Hawkes and Archibald MacLeish, for the exceptional quality of his short stories. In 1960 he won the Dana Reed Prize from Harvard, awarded for the best piece of writing published by an undergraduate.

Kelly won a number of other honors and awards during the 1960s, including a grant from the John Hay Whitney Foundation and, in 1963, the Richard and Linda Rosenthal Award from the National Institute of Arts and Letters for his first novel, *A Different Drummer* (1962). He received fellowships to the 1962 Bread Loaf Writers' Conference and to the New York Writers' Conference, and in 1965 he was writer-in-residence at the State University of New York at Geneseo. His second book, a collection of short stories titled *Dancers on the Shore* (1964), won the *Transatlantic Review* award.

In 1965 Kelley traveled to Rome and worked on his second novel, *A Drop of Patience*, which was published that same year. He returned briefly to the United States and in 1967 went back to Europe to travel in France and to work on his third novel, *dem* (1967), and his fourth, *Dunfords Travels Everywheres* (1970). Throughout the 1960s Kelley also published several essays on the state of black culture in America, including "The Ivy League Negro" (*Esquire*, 1963) and "On Africa in the United States" (*Negro Digest*, 1968). After finishing *Dunfords Travels Everywheres*, Kelley returned to the United States and became interested in the racial politics of the Black Power Movement and in the growth of the revolutionary movements in the Third World.

For further reading, see Valerie M. Babb's essay in *Dictionary of Literary Biography, Volume 33*. See also Addison Gayle, *The Way of the New World: The Black Novel in America* (1975); Trudier Harris, *From Mammies to Militants: Domestics in Black American Literature* (1982); Josef Jarab, "The Drop of Patience of the American Negro: W. M. Kelley's *A Different Drummer* (1959), *A Drop of Patience* (1965)," *Philologica Pragensia* 12 (1969); and Phyllis R. Klotman, "The Passive Resistant in *A Different Drummer, Day of Absence,* and *Many Thousands Gone,*" *Studies in Black Literature* 3 (Autumn 1972).

The selection following is from *Dancers on the Shore.*

THE ONLY MAN ON LIBERTY STREET

She was squatting in the front yard, digging with an old brass spoon in the dirt which was an ocean to the islands of short yellow grass. She wore a red and white checkered dress, which hung loosely from her shoulders, and obscured her legs. It was early spring and she was barefoot. Her toes stuck from under the skirt. She could not see the man yet, riding down Liberty Street, his shoulders square, the duster he wore spread back over the horse's rump, a carpetbag tied with a leather strap to his saddle horn and knocking against his leg. She could not see him until he had dismounted and tied his horse to a small, black, iron Negro jockey and unstrapped the bag. She watched now as he opened the wooden gate, came into the yard, and stood, looking down at her, his face stern, almost gray beneath the brim of his wide hat.

She knew him. Her mother called him Mister Herder and had told Jennie that he was Jennie's father. He was one of the men who came riding down Liberty Street in their fine black suits and starched shirts and large, dark ties. Each of these men had a house to go to, into which, in the evening usually, he would disappear. Only women and children lived on Liberty Street. All of them were Negroes. Some of the women were quite dark, but most were coffee-color. They were all very beautiful. Her mother was light. She was tall, had black eyes, and black hair so long she could sit on it.

The man standing over her was the one who came to her house once or twice a week. He was never there in the morning when Jennie got up. He was tall, and thin, and blond. He had a short beard that looked as coarse as the grass beneath her feet. His eyes were blue, like Jennie's. He did not speak English very well. Jennie's mother had told her he came from across the sea and Jennie often wondered if he went there between visits to their house.

"Jennie? Your mother tells me that you ask why I do not stay at night. Is so?"

She looked up at him. "Yes, Mister Herder." The hair under his jaw was darker than the hair on his cheeks.

He nodded. "I stay now. Go bring your mother."

She left the spoon in the dirt, and ran into the house, down the long hall, dark now because she had been sitting in the sun. She found her mother standing over the stove, a great black lid in her left hand, a wooden spoon in her right. There were beads of sweat on her forehead. She wore a full black skirt and a white blouse. Her one waist-length braid hung straight between her shoulder blades. She turned to Jennie's running steps.

"Mama? That man? My father? He in the yard. He brung a carpetbag."

First her mother smiled, then frowned, then looked puzzled. "A carpetbag, darling?"

"Yes, Mama."

She followed her mother through the house, pausing with her at the hall mirror where the woman ran her hand up the back of her neck to smooth stray black hair. Then they went onto the porch, where the man was now seated, surveying the tiny yard and the dark green hedge that enclosed it. The carpetbag rested beside his chair.

Her mother stood with her hands beneath her apron, staring at the bag. "Mister Herder?"

He turned to them. "I will not go back this time. No matter what. Why should I live in that house when I must come here to know what home is?" He nodded sharply as if in answer to a question. "So! I stay. I give her that house. I will send her money, but I stay here."

Her mother stood silently for an instant, then turned to the door. "Dinner'll be on the table in a half hour." She opened the screen door. The spring whined and cracked. "Oh." She let go the door, and picked up the carpetbag. "I'll take this on up." She went inside. As she passed, Jennie could see she was smiling again.

After that, Jennie's mother became a celebrity on Liberty Street. The other women would stop her to ask about the man. "And he staying for good, Josie?"

"Yes."

"You have any trouble yet?"

"Not yet."

"Well, child, you make him put that there house in your name. You don't want to be no Sissie Markham. That white woman come down the same day he died and moved Sissie and her children right into the gutter. You get that house put in your name. You hear?"

"Yes."

"How is it? It different?"

Her mother would look dazed. "Yes, it different. He told me to call him Maynard."

The other women were always very surprised.

At first, Jennie too was surprised. The man was always there in the morning and sometimes even woke her up. Her mother no longer called him Mister Herder, and at odd times, though still quite seldom, said, No. She had never before heard her mother say No to anything the man ever said. It was not long before Jennie was convinced that he actually was her father. She began to call him Papa.

Daily now a white woman had been driving by their house. Jennie did not know who she was or what she wanted, but playing in the yard, would see the white woman's gray buggy turn the corner and come slowly down the block, pulled by a speckled horse that trudged in the dry dust. A Negro driver sat erect in his black uniform, a whip in his fist. The white woman would peer at the house as if looking for an address or something special. She would look at the curtained windows, looking for someone, and sometimes even at Jennie. The look was not kind or tender, but hard and angry as if she knew something bad about the child.

Then one day the buggy stopped, the Negro pulling gently on the reins. The white woman leaned forward, spoke to the driver and handed him a small pink envelope. He jumped down, opened the gate, and without looking at Jennie, his face dark and shining, advanced on the porch, up the three steps, which knocked hollow beneath his boots, opened the screen door and twisted the polished brass bell key in the center of the open, winter door.

Her mother came drying her hands. The Negro reached out the envelope and her mother took it, looking beyond him for an instant at the buggy and the white woman who returned her look coldly. As the Negro turned, her mother opened the letter, and read it, moving her lips slightly. Then Jennie could see the twinkling at the corners of her eyes. Her mother stood framed in the black square of doorway, tall, fair, the black hair swept to hide her ears, her eyes glistening.

Jennie turned back to the white woman now and saw her lean deeper into her seat. Then she pulled forward. "Do you understand what I will have them do?" She was shouting shrilly and spoke like Jennie's father. "You tell him he has got one wife! You are something different!" She leaned back again, waved her gloved hand and the buggy lurched down the street, gained speed, and jangled out of sight around the corner.

Jennie was on her feet and pounding up the stairs. "Mama?"

"Go play, Jennie. Go on now, *play*!" Still her mother stared straight ahead, as if the buggy and the white woman remained in front of the house. She still held the letter as if to read it. The corners of her eyes were wet. Then she turned and went into the house. The screen door clacked behind her.

At nights now Jennie waited by the gate in the yard for her father to turn the corner, walking. In the beginning she had been waiting too for the one day he would not turn the corner. But each night he came, that day seemed less likely to come. Even so, she was always surprised to see him. When she did, she would wave, timidly, raising her hand only to her shoulder, wiggling only her fingers, as if to wave too wildly would somehow cause the entire picture of his advancing to collapse as only a slight wind would be enough to disarrange a design of feathers.

That night too she waved and saw him raise his hand high over his head, greeting her. She backed away when he reached the gate so he might open it, her head thrown way back, looking up at him.

"Well, my Jennie, what kind of day did you have?"

She only smiled, then remembered the white woman. "A woman come to visit Mama. She come in a buggy and give her a letter too. She made Mama cry."

His smile fled. He sucked his tongue, angry now. "We go see what is wrong. Come." He reached for her hand.

Her mother was in the kitchen. She looked as if she did not really care what she was doing or how, walking from pump to stove, stove to cupboard in a deep trance. The pink envelope was on the table.

She turned to them. Her eyes were red. Several strands of hair stuck to her temples. She cleared her nose and pointed to the letter. "She come today."

Her father let go Jennie's hand, picked up the letter and read it. When he was finished he took it to the stove and dropped it into the flame. There was a puff of smoke before he replaced the lid. He shook his head. "She cannot make me go back, Josephine."

Her mother fell heavily into a wooden chair, beginning to cry again. "But she's white, Maynard."

He raised his eyebrows like a priest or a displeased school teacher. "Your skin is whiter."

"My mother was a slave."

He threw up his hands, making fists. "Your mother did not ask to be a slave!" Then he went to her, crouched on his haunches before her, speaking quietly. "No one can make me go back."

"But she can get them to do what she say." She turned her gaze on Jennie, but looked away quickly. "You wasn't here after the war. But I seen things. I seen things happen to field niggers that . . . I was up in the house; they didn't bother me. My own father, General Dewey Willson, he stood on a platform in the center of town and promised to keep the niggers down. I was close by." She took his face in her hands. "Maynard, maybe you better go back, leastways—"

"I go back—dead! You hear? Dead. These children, these cowardly children in their masks will not move me! I go back dead. That is all. We do not discuss it." And he was gone. Jennie heard him thundering down the hall, knocking against the table near the stairs, going up to the second floor.

Her mother was looking at her now, her eyes even more red than before, her lips trembling, her hands active in her lap. "Jennie?"

"Yes, Mama." She took a step toward her, staring into the woman's eyes.

"Jennie, I want you to promise me something and not forget it."

"Yes, Mama." She was between her mother's knees, felt the woman's hands clutching her shoulders.

"Jennie, you'll be right pretty when you get grown. Did you know that? Promise me you'll go up North. Promise me if I'm not here when you get eighteen, you'll go north and get married. You understand?"

Jennie was not sure she did. She could not picture the North, except that she had heard once it was cold and white things fell from the sky. She could not picture being eighteen and her mother not being there. But she knew her mother wanted her to understand and she lied. "Yes, Mama."

"Repeat what I just said."

She did. Her mother kissed her mouth, the first time ever.

From the kitchen below came their voices. Her father's voice sounded hard, cut short; Jennie knew he had made a decision and was sticking to it. Her mother was pleading, trying to change his mind. It was July the Fourth, the day of the shooting match.

She dressed in her Sunday clothes and coming downstairs, heard her mother: "Maynard, please don't take her." She was frantic now. "I'm begging you. Don't take that child with you today."

"I take her. We do not discuss it. I take her. Those sneaking cowards in their masks . . ." Jennie knew now what they were talking about. Her father had promised to take her to the shooting match. For some reason, her mother feared there would be trouble if Jennie went downtown. She did not know why her mother felt that way, except that it might have something to do with the white woman, who continued to ride by their house each morning, after her father had left for the day. Perhaps her mother did not want to be alone in the house when the white woman drove by in her gray buggy, even though she had not stopped the buggy since the day two months ago, when the Negro had given her mother the pink envelope.

But other strange things had happened after that. In the beginning she and her mother, as always before, had gone downtown to the market, to shop amid the bright stalls brimming with green and yellow vegetables and brick-red meats, tended by dark, country Negroes in shabby clothes and large straw hats. It would get very quiet when they passed, and Jennie would see the Negroes look away, fear in their eyes, and knots of white men watching, sometimes giggling. But the white women in fine clothes were the most frightening; sitting on the verandas or passing in carriages, some even coming to their windows, they would stare angrily as if her mother had done something terrible to each one personally, as if all these white women could be the one who drove by each morning. Her mother would walk through it all, her back straight, very like her father's, the bun into which she wove her waist-length braid on market days, gleaming dark.

In the beginning they had gone to the suddenly quiet market. But now her mother hardly set foot from the house, and the food was brought to them in a carton by a crippled Negro boy, who was coming just as Jennie and her father left the house that morning.

Balancing the carton on his left arm, he removed his ragged hat and smiled. "Morning, Mister Herder. Good luck at the shooting match, sir." His left leg was short and he seemed to tilt.

Her father nodded. "Thank you, Felix. I do my best."

"Then you a sure thing, Mister Herder." He replaced his hat and went on around the house.

Walking, her hand in her father's, Jennie could see some of the women of Liberty Street peering out at them through their curtains.

Downtown was not the same. Flags and banners draped the verandas; people wore their best clothes. The Square had been roped off, a platform set up to one side, and New Marsails Avenue, which ran into the Square, had been cleared for two blocks. Far away down the Avenue stood a row of cotton bales onto which had been pinned oilcloth targets. From where they stood, the bull's-eyes looked no bigger than red jawbeakers.

Many men slapped her father on the back, and furtively, looked at her with a kind of clinical interest. But mostly they ignored her. The celebrity of the day was her father, and unlike her mother, he was very popular. Everyone felt sure he would win the match; he was the best shot in the state.

After everyone shot, the judge came running down from the targets, waving his arms. "Maynard Herder. Six shots, and you can cover them all with a good gob of spit!" He grabbed her father's elbow and pulled him toward the platform, where an old man with white hair and beard, wearing a gray uniform trimmed with yellow, waited. She followed them to the platform steps, but was afraid to go any farther because now some women had begun to look at her as they had at her mother.

The old man made a short speech, his voice deep, but coarse, grainy-sounding, and gave her father a silver medal in a blue velvet box. Her father turned and smiled at her. She started up the steps toward him, but just then the old man put his hand on her father's shoulder.

People had begun to walk away down the streets leading out of the Square. There was less noise now, but she could not hear the first words the old man said to her father.

Her father's face tightened into the same look she had seen the day the letter came, the same as this morning in the kitchen. She went halfway up the stairs, stopped.

The old man went on: "You know I'm no meddler. Everybody knows about Liberty Street. I had a woman down there myself . . . before the war."

"I know that." The words came out of her father's face, though his lips did not move.

The old man nodded. "But, Maynard, what you're doing is different."

"She's your own daughter."

"Maybe that's why . . ." The old man looked down the street, toward the cotton bales and the targets. "But she's a nigger. And now the talking is taking an ugly turn and the folks talking are the ones I can't hold."

Her father spoke in an angry whisper. "You see what I do to that target? You tell those children in their masks I do that to the forehead of any man . . . or woman that comes near her or my house. You tell them."

"Maynard, that wouldn't do any real good *after* they'd done something to her." He stopped, looked at Jennie, and smiled. "That's my only granddaughter, you know." His eyes clicked off her. "You're a man who knows firearms. You're a gunsmith. I know firearms too. Pistols and rifles can do lots of things, but they don't make very good doctors. Nobody's asking you to give her up. Just go back home. That's all. Go back to your wife."

Her father turned away, walking fast, came down the stairs and grabbed her hand. His face was red as blood between the white of his collar and the straw yellow of his hair.

They slowed after a block, paused in a small park with green trees shading several benches and a statue of a stern-faced young man in uniform, carrying pack and rifle. "We will sit."

She squirmed up onto the bench beside him. The warm wind smelled of salt from the Gulf of Mexico. The leaves were a dull, low tambourine. Her father was quiet for a long while.

Jennie watched birds bobbing for worms in the grass near them, then looked at the young, stone soldier. Far off, but from where she viewed it, just over the soldier's hat, a gliding sea gull dived suddenly behind the rooftops. That was when she saw the white man, standing across the street from the park, smiling at her. There were other white men with him, some looking at her, others at the man, all laughing. He waved to her. She smiled at him though he was the kind of man her mother told her always to stay away from. He was dressed as poorly as any Negro. From behind his back, he produced a brown rag doll, looked at her again, then grabbed the doll by its legs, and tore it part way up the middle. Then he jammed his finger into the rip between the doll's legs. The other men laughed uproariously.

Jennie pulled her father's sleeve. "Papa? What he doing?"

"Who?" Her father turned. The man repeated the show and her father bolted to his feet, yelling: "I will kill you! You hear? I will kill you for that!"

The men only snickered and ambled away.

Her father was red again. He had clenched his fists; now his hands were white like the bottoms of fishes. He sighed, shook his head and sat down. "I cannot kill everybody." He shook his head again, then leaned forward to get up. But first he thrust the blue velvet medal box into her hand. It was warm from his hand, wet and prickly. "When you grow up, you go to the North like your mother tells you. And you take this with you. It is yours. Always remember I gave it to you." He stood. "Now you must go home alone. Tell your mother I come later."

That night, Jennie tried to stay awake until he came home, until he was there to kiss her good night, his whiskers scratching her cheek. But all at once there was sun at her window and the sound of carts and wagons grating outside in the dirt street. Her mother was quiet while the two of them ate. After breakfast, Jennie went into the yard to wait for the gray buggy to turn the corner, but for the first morning in many months, the white woman did not jounce by, peering at the house, searching for someone or something special.

Lucille Clifton

(1936–   )

BORN IN 1936, IN DEPEW, NEW YORK, Lucille Thelma Clifton is the author of at least six collections of poems for adults and of nineteen books for children. She is indeed one of those rare artists whose imaginative skills are as adept at creating visions for children as for adults.

Her father and mother were both laborers, but she received a good education, attending Howard University from 1953 to 1955 and Fredonia State Teachers College (now State University of New York at Fredonia) in 1955. On May 10, 1958, she married Fred James Clifton, an educator, a writer, and an artist, who died on November 10, 1984. Together they had six children, two daughters and four sons.

Sharing affinities with the works of Walt Whitman, Emily Dickinson, Gwendolyn Brooks, and Langston Hughes, Clifton's poetry has the façade of simplicity. Yet, like her predecessors', her works are technically complex and undeniably thought-provoking. Her six adult collections of poetry are *Good Times: Poems* (1969), *Good News about the Earth: New Poems* (1972), *An Ordinary Woman* (1974), *Two-Headed Woman* (1980), *Good Woman: Poems and a Memoir, 1969–1980* (1987), and *Next: New Poems* (1987). In 1976 she also published *Generations: A Memoir*, an autobiographical piece that was received well by the critics. Reynolds Price, in the *New York Times Book Review*, says that it stands "worthily" among other modern elegies, while another review, in the *Virginia Quarterly Review*, asserts that the book is "more than an elegy or a personal memoir. It is an attempt on the part of one woman to retrieve, and lyrically to celebrate, her Afro-American heritage."

Whether she writes for children or adults, Clifton emphasizes an understanding of the past and present. Her series of books on the young Everett Anderson portray the changes that affect a young child's life. She has published seven collections in the Everett Anderson series: *Some of the Days of Everett Anderson* (1970), *Everett Anderson's Christmas Coming* (1971), *Everett Anderson's Year* (1974), *Everett Anderson's Friend* (1976), *Everett Anderson's 1 2 3* (1977), *Everett Anderson's Nine Month Long* (1978), and *Everett Anderson's Goodbye* (1983).

While Everett Anderson is now a name widely associated with Lucille Clifton, she is also the author of twelve other books written for children: *The Black ABCs* (1970), *Good, Says Jerome* (1973), *All Us Come Cross the Water* (1973), *Don't You Remember?* (1973), *The Boy Who Didn't Believe in Spring* (1973), *The Times They Used to Be* (1974), *My Brother Fine with Me* (1975), *Three Wishes* (1976), *Amifika* (1977), *The Lucky Stone* (1979), *My Friend Jacob* (1980), and *Sonora Beautiful* (1981).

Despite this very productive publication record and her role as wife and mother of six children, Clifton has worked as a claims clerk for the New York State Division of Employment in Buffalo, from 1958 to 1960; as literature assistant in the U.S. Office of Education in Washington, D.C., from 1969 to 1971; as poet-in-residence at Coppin State College in Baltimore, Maryland, from 1971 to 1974; as visiting writer at Columbia University School of Arts; and as Jerry Moore Visiting Writer at George Washington University, from 1982 to 1983. She has also taught literature and creative writing at the University of California at Santa Cruz. She is currently a writer-in-residence at St. Mary's College, St. Mary's, Maryland.

Her awards and honors include honorary degrees from the University of Maryland and Towson State University, the Discovery Award from the New York Young Men's and Young Women's Hebrew Association Poetry Center, a National Endowment for the Arts Award, the Juniper Prize, and the Coretta Scott King Award. Her first collection of poems, *Good Times*, was cited as one of the year's ten best books by the *New York Times* in 1969.

For a look at critical analyses of Clifton's poetry, see Audrey T. McCluskey's "Tell the Good News: A View of the Works of Lucille Clifton" and Haki Madhubuti's "Lucille Clifton: Warm Water, Greased Legs, and Dangerous Poetry," both in Mari Evans's *Black Women Writers 1950–1980: A Critical Evaluation* (1984).

The selections that follow are all taken from *Good Times*.

IN THE INNER CITY

In the inner city
or
like we call it
home
we think a lot about uptown
and the silent nights
and the houses straight as
dead men
and the pastel lights
and we hang on to our no place

happy to be alive
and in the inner city
or
like we call it
home

GOOD TIMES

My Daddy has paid the rent
and the insurance man is gone
and the lights is back on
and my uncle Brud has hit
for one dollar straight
and they is good times
good times
good times

My Mama has made bread
and Grampaw has come
and everybody is drunk
and dancing in the kitchen
and singing in the kitchen
oh these is good times
good times
good times

oh children think about the
good times

THE WAY IT WAS

the way it was
working with the polacks
turning into polacks

walked twelve miles into Buffalo and
bought a dining room suit

Mammy Ca'line
walked from New Orleans
to Virginia
in 1830
seven years old

always said
get what you want
you from Dahomey women

first colored man in town
to own a dining room suit
things was changing
new things was coming

you

FOR DELAWD

people say they have a hard time
understanding how I
go on about my business
playing my Ray Charles
hollering at the kids—
seem like my Afro
cut off in some old image
would show I got a long memory
and I come from a line
of black and going on women
who got used to making it through murdered sons
and who grief kept on pushing
who fried chicken
ironed
swept off the back steps
who grief kept
for their still alive sons
for their sons coming
for their sons gone
just pushing

Al Young

(1939–   )

IN HIS ENTRY in *Dictionary of Literary Biography*, William J. Harris captures the beauty of Albert James Young's creative imagination and his personality. Harris writes, "Al Young is his own man, refusing to go along with anybody's trend or latest survey: he is a black American in the American tradition of the singular individual. His art is dedicated to the destruction of glib stereotypes of black Americans. Not surprisingly, his work illustrates the complexity and richness of contemporary Afro-American life through a cast of highly individualized black characters. Since he is a gifted stylist and a keen observer of the human comedy, he manages to be both a serious and an entertaining author."

Born in Ocean Springs, Mississippi, on May 31, 1939, Albert James Young moved with his parents to Detroit in 1946, but spent many summers of his younger years in Mississippi. He attended the University of Michigan, but completed his B.A. degree in Spanish at the University of California at Berkeley in 1969. He later took courses in advanced fiction writing at Stanford, where in 1972 he taught creative writing. While at Stanford he, along with novelist Ishmael Reed, founded *Yardbird Reader*, a multicultural magazine, which publishes writers from a variety of ethnic backgrounds. Al Young was associate editor of *Yardbird Reader*. He is also the associate editor of *Quilt*, a journal that he and Ishmael Reed founded in 1981. Young now resides in Palo Alto, California.

Screen writer for Hollywood, novelist, poet, and editor, Young has been very productive. He has four collections of poems: *Dancing: Poems* (1969), *The Song Turning Back Into Itself* (1971), *Geography of the Near Past* (1976), and *The Blues Don't Change: New and Selected Poems* (1982). His four novels include *Snakes* (1970), *Who is Angelina?* (1975), *Ask Me Now* (1980), and *Seduction by Light* (1988). He has also made *Bodies and Soul* (1981), a collection of short stories, into a musical memoir. His most recent works are *Kinds of Blue: Musical Memoirs* (1984), *Things Ain't What They Used To Be: Musical Memoirs* (1987), *Heaven: Collected Poems, 1958–1988* (1989), and *Mingus/Mingus: Two Memoirs* (1989), which he co-authored with Janet Coleman.

His honors and awards include the Stegner Fellowship in Creative Writing, the Joseph Henry Jackson Award, the National Arts Council Awards for Poetry and Editing, and the 1980 *New York Times* Outstanding Book of the Year Selection for *Ask Me Now*.

For further reading, see *Dictionary of Literary Biography, Volume 33; Black Writers: A Selection of Sketches from Contemporary Authors* (1989); John O'Brien's *Interviews with Black Writers* (1973); and *Black American Writers Past and Present* (1975). Also see Nathaniel Mackey, "Interview with Al Young," *MELUS* 5 (Winter 1978).

"A Letter from the North, A Lady from the South" is taken from *Who is Angelina?*

A LETTER FROM THE NORTH, A LADY FROM THE SOUTH

dear angelina,

a herd of deer, a pride of lions, a pack of wolves, a lepe of leopards, a sedge of herons, a rafter of turkeys, a nye of pheasants, a flock of pigeons, a school of fish, a gaggle of geese, a nest of ants, a hive of bees, a tribe of indians—what do they all have in common?

even though we only spent a night together, i still find myself thinking of you all the time. i know you were pretty wasted at the time because i was too & you were further out than me, walking around your house naked with the tv on in one room, the record player grinding out marvin gaye in another room, and the radio blowing scott joplin ragtime in the only room left, the bedroom, that cozy little bedroom with the blue light & the posters of ray charles & muhammad ali where we made do so beautifully that my head was permanently taken apart.

you're some lover, ms. angelina green, & i don't only mean this in a gross physical context—i'm saying that the subtlety of your appeal—the secret ways in which we communicated—was enough to make me rush home & write at least a dozen poems in my head. as the days passed, i managed to get a few of them on paper to send to you but my better judgment said no, that i should wait.

i am not a poet, angelina, as much as i would like to be and have tried to be. i am only a poor, lonely dreamer; a thirty-year-old bachelor who by day attends classes at san francisco state with the express purpose of securing a masters degree in business administration. my b.a. which i took at a small black college back home in missouri was in sociology. i've always wanted to be a creative individual & almost majored in english or art history but the pragmatic side of my makeup told me to go into something practical. i still admire creative people, more especially those who perceive that crea-

tivity need not be relegated to mere practice of the arts. you strike
me as being a person who is creative in everything you do.

you may wonder about my writing this letter. i can assure you,
however, that i am not a nut or a chump. i was very much taken
with you that night even though we were only two lonely people
who met at a party. i knew fred, the one who was giving the party,
from my old track-running days in high school back in st. louis,
therefore he invited me. i'm sure glad he did. have you ever seen a
picture called *The Loneliness of the Long-Distance Runner?* well, to me
that was a very moving picture (see, i do keep trying to be a poet in
spite of myself). i was a long-distance runner & even though i'm not
one any longer, i'm still very lonely.

i hope you're having a charming time of it down there in old me-
heeco. i used to go with a puerto rican girl who maintained an intense dislike for mexicans. i never understood it & used to tell her
so. after all, puerto ricans & mexicans speak a mutual language &
have both been exploited by the same oppressor—the blue-eyed
devil, the "gringo" if you will—so why the conflict? what's wrong
with human beings anyway?

i tracked you & your whereabouts down through fred who
knows an honorary soul sister named margo tanaka—a friend of
yours, i believe—& hope that during your broadening travels you
will perhaps find time to respond to my little discursive hello.

reply to my riddle if you can or so wish. i hope you're getting
over your sadness & crying spells & that this awkward missive will
not have annoyed you in any way, shape or manner. don't eat too
much hot, spicey food & watch out for those latin types. i wouldn't
want any of them to steal your sweet little heart.

> yours shyly & respectfully,
> curtis

p.s.: like I say, I think about you all the time & your pretty little
mouth is something more to me than a functional organ designed to
receive food, drink, smoke, or to issue forth words.

It was her fourth day in Mexico, her second visit to American
Express on Calle Niza to ask about mail. The friendly lady had
handed her this envelope sent air mail, special delivery.

At first Curtis's letter annoyed her but more for Margo having
told him where she was than for anything he'd said. In fact, she
rather admired his straightforwardness. She'd felt that way about
more than one man on brief encounter but lacked the nerve to try
and put it into any form as elusive as language. The general tone of
it made her think of all those old records she'd grown up dreaming
by and dancing to as a kid where, in the middle of a song, the band

would relax into a soft background riff for a chorus while the lead
bass singer'd come in with some spoken nitwit soliloquy:

My darlin, I craves you.
If only there was more time
in the day for me to kiss on you
is my one sincere desire, for you see . . .
from the bottom of my deep deep heart
I salute your cold cold eyes and
your bold bold thighs as we pretend
that a youthful young love
like yours and like mine
did not flare up . . . between us . . .
And I know . . . cause you told me so . . .
that in our very souls we connected
(O yes we did)
in that teen-age paradise called eternity.

Jammed between four other passengers in a *pesero*, one of the
jitney-style taxis that shuttle the length of La Reforma, the city's
fashionable main thoroughfare, she read the letter over and over
again, wincing and chuckling.

A Latin-looking lady, a portly beauty-parlor blonde in elegant
middle-aged dress, nudged her and said, "That must be what you
call good reading matter, yes?"

Angelina ignored her.

"I like to see people when they are responding so apparently to a
letter well written, dont you see? It makes me also feel like my day
is made of course." The lady was beaming.

Angelina wasnt sure how she'd handle this. She herself was nosey
to the core but wasnt fond of this quality in others. Should she play
dumb and ignore the woman one more round, do her *no comprendo*
number and play the non-English speaking foreigner, or cop out and
be Latin too? As was often the case in the States, everybody's racism
and her own skin was going in her favor. She could come on anyway she wanted because, no matter what she did, no one would
really take her seriously, the way they would a regular universal individual, a white person.

"*¿Mánde?*" she said, meaning "Beg your pardon?" as she folded
the letter away.

"*Ándele pués*," the lady zipped on, "*usted habla el español. ¿De
dónde es?—¿de Panama, de Costa Rica, de Puerto Rico, de Cuba?*"

Angelina had a good mind to tell Her Nosiness that she was from
Uruguay, descended from a powerful but little-known Afro-Indian
family (her grandmother being of pure Charruan blood) that had
once been the talk of all Montevideo. Instead she decided to put the

lady on with the truth which somehow was always more confusing than sarcasm.

"*Soy de los Estados Unidos,*" she said. Everybody in the taxi, driver included, turned to have a look at her. "*Soy de Michigan y de California.*"

"*¿De qué parte de California es, jovencita?*"

"*Del norte.*"

"*Ah, de San Francisco, ¡no me digas!*"

"*Vivo en un pueblecito muy cerca de allí.*"

"*Ay, eres de Berkeley—eso sí que es, ¿verdad? Debe ser la ciudadita mas bella que visité durante mi breve residencia en su gran país. La conozco bien pues mi hijo mayor es estudiante universitario allí. Dígame, pués, ¿dónde aprendiste el español?*"

"*Lo estudié desde mi niñez . . . en la escuela secundaria, la escuela superior y además fue mi estudio principal en la universidad.*"

"*Ay de mí,*" the lady said, "there's for certain no need of us continuing to do the chitchat in Spanish, yes? You speak it beautifully for a Michigander and a Californian but since you are now from the famous Berkeley then let us why not express ourselves in English. I love the language, the American English, you know. My oldest son is a student of electrical engineering at U.C. Berkeley. I received my doctorate in Education from U.C.L.A."

"What do you teach if I may ask?"

"Certainly you may ask, *jovencita.* I am now professor of Art History at the University of the Republic at Montevideo."

"Are you headed for the Museum of Anthropology too?"

"In fact I am, yes. Have you ever before seen it?"

"Spent all of yesterday here. I love it. Ive never really seen anything like it."

"I am here for a convention of Latin American university professors. This is my one free afternoon to do with myself what I please and I am spending it all touring this remarkable museum which I have already visited four times before. Tell me, what is your occupation?"

Angelina hated that question. "O, I teach—Spanish."

The lady was delighted. "I thought so as much. Spanish, as you must know, is such a universal language. It should be taught everywhere, throughout all the world, yes? We tour the museum together, OK? I show you things. I know it by my heart, OK?"

Angelina felt uneasy but what else was there for her to say except OK? She was growing to like being by herself. Besides, she could always fake a headache if necessary, if Her Nosiness got on her nerves too much, and split to return some other anonymous day.

Ishmael Reed

(1938–   )

ISHMAEL REED'S six satirical novels have earned him the distinction of being one of the most controversial writers in all of black American literature. His work attacks the social evils of racism, sexism, and economic exploitation, but close readers of his fiction have noted that the main target of his satire seems to be literary convention itself. He parodies the formal traditions of Western literature as a whole, but specifically those of such major black American writers as Ralph Ellison, Richard Wright, and James Baldwin. In so doing, he examines the classic themes of black literature with an iconoclastic eye, while expanding the possibilities of the novel as a literary form.

Reed was born in Chattanooga, Tennessee, in 1938 and moved with his mother to Buffalo, New York, in 1942. From 1956 to 1960 he attended the University of Buffalo, first as a night student and later as a full-time undergraduate. In 1960 he left the university and moved into a housing project in rebellion against what he experienced as the racist and elitist environment of American academia.

For the next two years Reed was actively engaged in the civil rights and black power movements while working as a staff reporter with the *Empire Star Weekly* and as co-host of a radio talk show called "Buffalo Community Roundtable." In 1962 he moved to New York City and participated in a number of cultural movements there, including the 1965 American Festival of Negro Art, and was a member of Umbra Workshop, a prominent black writers' group. He was also editor-in-chief of a Newark, New Jersey, weekly called *Advance* and helped plan and organize another newspaper, *East Village Other*. In 1967 his first novel, *The Free-Lance Pallbearers*, was published, receiving wide critical acclaim.

Reed moved from New York to Berkeley, California, in 1967 and took a teaching position at the University of California at Berkeley, where he continues to teach. Since 1967 he has also taught at the University of Washington at Seattle, the State University of New York at Buffalo, Yale University, and Dartmouth College. In 1971 he cofounded the Yardbird Publishing Company and two years later the Reed, Cannon, and Johnson Communications Company, and in 1976 he established the Before Columbus Foundation together with Victor Cruz. Reed was editor-in-chief of *Yardbird Reader*, published by Yardbird Publishing Company. Reed and Al Young also founded the journal *Quilt* in 1981. Reed is editor-in-chief.

340

During the 1970s and early 1980s, Reed published five other novels— *Yellow Back Radio Broke-Down* (1971), *Mumbo Jumbo* (1972), *The Last Days of Louisiana Red* (1974), *Flight to Canada* (1976), and *The Terrible Twos* (1982)—as well as four books of poetry and two collections of essays. During the mid to late 1980s, Reed also published the following books: *Reckless Eyeballing* (1986), a novel; *Writin' is Fightin': Thirty-Seven Years of Boxing on Paper* (1988), a collection of essays; *New and Collected Poems* (1989); and *The Terrible Threes* (1989), a novel. He has also edited and published a number of anthologies. Reed now resides in Oakland, California, with his wife, Carla Blank, whom he married in 1970.

For an examination of Reed's satiric technique and his place in the African American literary tradition, see the article by Henry Louis Gates in *Dictionary of Literary Biography, Volume 33,* and the article in Linda Metzger, ed., *Black Writers: A Selection of Sketches from Contemporary Authors* (1989). Both works include a list of references.

"The Loop Garoo Kid Goes Away Mad" comes from *Yellow Back Radio Broke-Down.*

THE LOOP GAROO KID GOES AWAY MAD

Oh, the hoodoos have chased me and still I am not broke,
I'm going to the mountains and think I am doing well;
I am going to the mountains some cattle for to sell,
And I hope to see the hoodoos dead and damn them all in hell.
        from "The Rustler," an American cowboy song

Folks. This here is the story of the Loop Garoo Kid. A cowboy so bad he made a working posse of spells phone in sick. A bullwhacker so unfeeling he left the print of winged mice on hides of crawling women. A desperado so onery he made the Pope cry and the most powerful of cattlemen shed his head to the Executioner's swine.

A terrible cuss of a thousand shivs he was who wasted whole herds, made the fruit black and wormy, dried up the water holes and caused people's eyes to grow from tiny black dots into slapjacks wherever his feet fell.

Now, he wasn't always bad, trump over hearts diamonds and clubs. Once a wild joker he cut the fool before bemused Egyptians, dressed like Mortimer Snerd and spilled french fries on his lap at Las Vegas' top of the strip.

Booted out of his father's house after a quarrel, whores snapped at his heels and trick dogs did the fandango on his belly. Men called him brother only to cop his coin and tell malicious stories about his cleft foot.

Born with a caul over his face and ghost lobes on his ears, he was a mean night tripper who moved from town to town quoting Thomas Jefferson and allowing bandits to build a flophouse around his genius.

A funny blue hippo who painted himself with water flowers only to be drummed out of each tribe dressed down publicly, his medals ripped off.

⟲⟩⟨⟩⟲

Finally he joined a small circus and happily performed with his fellow 86-D—a Juggler a dancing Bear a fast talking Barker and Zozo Labrique, charter member of the American Hoo-Doo Church.

Their fame spread throughout the frontier and bouquets of flowers greeted them in every town until they moved into that city which seemed a section of Hell chipped off and shipped upstairs, Yellow Back Radio, where even the sun was afraid to show its bottom.

⟲⟩⟨⟩⟲

Some of the wheels of the caravan were stuck in thick red mud formed by a heavy afternoon downpour. The oxen had to be repeatedly whipped. They had become irritable from the rain which splashed against their faces. In the valley below black dust rose in foreboding clouds from herds of wild horses that roamed there. Loop Garoo was driving the horse hitched to Zozo Labrique's covered wagon.

Those were some dangerous stunts you did in the last town, boy, bucking those killer broncos like that. A few more turns with that bull and you would have been really used up. Why you try so hard?

She sent me a letter in the last town, Zozo. She wants me to come to her. The old man spends his time grooming his fur and posing for non-academic painters. He's more wrapped up in himself than ever before and the other one, he's really gone dipso this time. Invites winos up there who pass the bottle and make advances on her. Call her sweet stuff and honey bun—she's really in hard times. She's a constant guest in my dreams Zozo, her face appears the way she looked the night she went uptown on me.

Serves her right Loop, the way she treated you. And that trash she collected around her. They were all butch. As soon as she left, zoom they were gone. And that angel in drag like a john, he gave her the news and showed her her notices—right off it went to her head. When she humiliated you—that emboldened the others to do likewise. Mustache Sal deserted you and Mighty Dike teamed up with that jive fur trapper who's always handing you subpoenas. You know how they are, Loop, you're the original pimp, the royal stud—soon as a bottom trick finds your weakness your whole stable will up and split.

I let her open my nose Zozo. I should have known that if she wasn't loyal to him with as big a reputation as he had—I couldn't expect her to revere me. What a line that guy had. A mitt man from his soul. And her kissing his feet just because those three drunken reporters were there to record it. Ever read their copy on that event Zozo? It's as if they were all witnessing something entirely different. The very next night she was in my bunk gnashing her teeth and uttering obscenities as I climbed into her skull.

She got to your breathing all right Loop. Even the love potions you asked me to mix didn't work, the follow-me-powder. Her connaissance was as strong as mine.

Zozo Labrique lit a corncob pipe. She wore a full skirt and a bandana on her head. Her face was black wrinkled and hard. The sun suddenly appeared, causing the gold hoops on her ears to sparkle.

Jake the Barker rode up alongside the wagon.

Well Loop, Zozo, won't be long now. Maybe thirty minutes before we pull into Yellow Back Radio. We're booked by some guy named Happy Times, who we're to meet at the Hotel.

Jake rode down the mountain's path to advise the rest of the troupe.

This was a pretty good season Loop, what are you going to do with your roll?

O I don't know Zozo, maybe I'll hire some bounty hunters to put a claim on my lost territory.

O Loop quit your joking.

What are you going to do Zozo?

Think the old bag will head back to New Orleans, mecca of Black America. First Doc John kicked out then me—she got her cronies in City Hall to close down my operation. We had to go underground. Things started to disappear from my humfo—even Henry my snake and mummies appeared in the curtains. She warned my clients that if they visited me she'd cross them. Everybody got shook and stayed away. Finally she layed a trick on me so strong that it almost wasted old Zozo, Loop. That Marie is a mess. Seems now though my old arch enemy is about to die. Rumor has it that the daughter is going to take over but I know nothing will come of that fast gal. Nobody but Marie has the type of connaissance to make men get down on their knees and howl like dogs and women to throw back their heads and cackle. Well . . . maybe your old lady, Loop, what's the hussy's name?

Diane, Black Diane, Zozo, you know her name.

Sometimes it's hard to tell, Loop, the bitch has so many aliases.

Before their wagon rounded the mountain curve they heard a gasp go up on the other side. A dead man was hanging upside down from a tree. He had been shot.

He wore a frilled ruffled collar knee britches a fancy shirt and turned up shoes. A cone shaped hat with a carnation on its rim had fallen to the ground.

The two climbed down from the wagon and walked to where Jake the Barker and the Juggler were staring at the hanging man. The dancing Bear watched from his cage, his paws gripping the bars, his head swinging from side to side with curiosity. Handbills which had dropped from the man's pockets littered the ground about the scene.

Plug In Your Head
Look Here Citizens!!
Coming to Yellow Back Radio
Jake the Barker's lecture room
New Orleans Hoodooine Zozo Labrique
Amazing Loop Garoo lariat tricks
Dancing Bear and Juggler too
Free　　　　　　　　　Beer

Above the man's head on the hoodoo rock fat nasty buzzards were arriving. Jake removed his hat and was surrounded by members of the bewildered troupe.

Nearest town Video Junction is about fifty miles away. There's not enough grub in the chuck wagon to supply us for a journey of that length. Besides the horses and oxen have to be bedded down. I wouldn't want any of you to take risks. If this means danger up ahead maybe we should disband here, split the take and put everybody on his own.

We've come this far Jake, may as well go on into Yellow Back Radio, the Juggler said.

Count me in too, Loop said, we're braved alkali, coyotes, wolves, rattlesnakes, catamounts, hunters. Nothing I'm sure could be as fierce down in that town—why it even looks peaceful from here.

I'll go along with the rest, Zozo said. But I have a funny feeling that everything isn't all right down there.

After burying the advance man on a slope they rode farther down the mountain until finally, from a vantage point, they could see the rest of Yellow Back Radio.

The wooden buildings stood in the shadows. The Jail House, the Hat and Boot store the Hardware store the Hotel and Big Lizzy's Rabid Black Cougar Saloon.

Sinister hogs with iron jaws were fenced in behind the scaffold standing in the square. They were the swine of the notorious Hangman, who was such a connoisseur of his trade he kept up with all the latest techniques of murder.

A new device stood on the platform. Imported from France, it was said to be as rational as their recent revolution. The hogs ate the remains of those unfortunate enough to climb the platform. Human heads were particularly delectable to these strange beasts.

The troupe drove through the deserted main street of the town. Suddenly they were surrounded by children dressed in the attire of the Plains Indians. It appeared as if cows had been shucked and their skins passed to the children's nakedness for their shoes and clothes were made of the animals' hides.

Reach for the sky, whiskey drinkers, a little spokesman warned. One hundred flintlocks were aimed at them.

Hey it's a circus, one of the children cried, and some dropped their rifles and began to dance.

A circus? one of the boys who made the warning asked. How do we know this isn't a trap sprung by the cheating old of Yellow Back Radio?

Jake the Barker, holding up his hands, looked around to the other members of the troupe. Amused, Loop, Zozo and the Juggler complied with the little gunmen's request.

What's going on here? Jake asked. We're the circus that travels around this territory each season. We're supposed to end the tour in your town. We're invited by Mister Happy Times. We're to meet him at the Hotel. Where are the adults? The Marshal, the Doctor, the Preacher, or someone in charge?

Some of the children snickered, but became silent when their spokesman called them into a huddle. After some haggling, he stepped towards the lead wagon upon which Jake the Barker rode.

We chased them out of town. We were tired of them ordering us around. They worked us day and night in the mines, made us herd animals harvest the crops and for three hours a day we went to school to hear teachers praise the old. Made us learn facts by rote. Lies really bent upon making us behave. We decided to create our own fiction.

One day we found these pearl-shaped pills in a cave of a mountain. They're what people ages ago called devil's pills. We put them in the streams so that when the grown-ups went to fill their buckets they swallowed some. It confused them more than they were so we moved on them and chased them out of town. Good riddance. They listened to this old Woman on the talk show who filled their heads with rot. She was against joy and life the decrepit bag of sticks, and she put them into the same mood. They always demanded we march and fight heathens.

Where are the old people now? Jake asked.

They're camped out at Drag Gibson's spread. We think they're preparing to launch some kind of invasion but we're ready for them. Drag just sent his herd up the Chisholm to market yesterday but there are enough cowpokes left behind to give us a good fight. Our Indian informant out at Drag's spread tells us the townspeople haven't given in to Drag's conditions yet. He wants them to sign over all of their property in exchange for lending his men to drive us out.

Then he will not only rule his spread which is as large as Venezuela but the whole town as well. He's the richest man in the valley, with prosperous herds, abundant resources and an ego as wide as the Grand Canyon.

This nonsense would never happen in the Seven Cities of Cibola, Jake the Barker said.

The Seven Cities of Cibola? the children asked, moving in closer to Jake's wagon.

Inanimate things, computers do the work, feed the fowl, and programmed cows give cartons of milkshakes in 26 flavors.

Yippppeeeeee, the children yelled. Where is it?

It's as far as you can see from where you're standing now. I'm going to search for it as soon as the show is over here but since there is no sponsor to greet us we may as well disband now, Jake said, looking about at the other members of the troupe.

Why don't you entertain us? the children asked.

It's a plot. We decided that we wouldn't trust anybody greying about the temples anymore!

O don't be paranoid, silly, another child replied to the tiny skeptic. Always trying to be the leader just like those old people we ran into the hills. These aren't ordinary old people they're children like us— look at their costumes and their faces.

Let's have the circus, a cry went up.

Well I don't know—you see we have no leaders holy men or gurus either so I'd have to ask the rest of the troupe.

Loop, Zozo and the Juggler said yes by nodding their heads. The Bear jumped up and down in his chains.

Delighted, the children escorted the small circus group to the outskirts of Yellow Back Radio where they pitched the tents, bedded down the weary horses and oxen and made preparations for the show.

Three horsemen—the Banker, the Marshal and the Doctor—decided to pay a little visit to Drag Gibson's ranch. They had to wait because Drag was at his usual hobby, embracing his property.

A green mustang had been led out of its stall. It served as a symbol for his streams of fish, his herds, his fruit so large they weighed down the mountains, black gold and diamonds which lay in untapped fields, and his barnyard overflowing with robust and erotic fowl.

Holding their Stetsons in their hands the delegation looked on as Drag prepared to kiss his holdings. The ranch hands dragged the animal from his compartment towards the front of the Big Black House where Drag bent over and french kissed the animal between his teeth, licking the slaver from around the horse's gums.

This was one lonely horse. The male horses avoided him because they thought him stuck-up and the females because they thought that since green he was a queer horse. See, he had turned green from old nightmares.

After the ceremony the unfortunate critter was led back to his stall, a hoof covering his eye.

Drag removed a tube from his pocket and applied it to his lips. He then led the men to a table set up in front of the House. Four bottles of whiskey were placed on the table by Drag's faithful Chinese servant, who picked a stray louse from Drag's fur coat only to put it down the cattleman's back. Drag smiled and twitched a bit, slapping his back until his hand found the bullseye. Killing the pest, he and the servant exchanged grins.

Bewildered, the men glanced at each other.

What brings you here? I told you to come only if you were ready for business. Sign the town and your property over to me so that my quest for power will be satisfied. If you do that I'll have my men go in there and wipe them menaces out.

We decided to give in, Drag. Why, we're losing money each day the children hold the town and we have to be around our wives all the time and they call us stupid jerks, buster lamebrain and unpolite things like that. It's a bargain, Drag. What do we do now?

Now you're talking business Doc. Sign this stiffycate which gives me what I asked for and I'll have them scamps out of your hair in no time.

Drag brought forth an official looking document from inside his robe, to which the Banker, Marshal and Doctor affixed their signatures.

It's a good thing we got the people to see it your way, the Banker said, wiping the sweat on his forehead with a crimson handkerchief. Some reinforcements were arriving today. They were in some wagons that was painted real weird and we hanged and shot one who was dressed like a clown. We thought they might be heathens from up North, you dig?

You mulish goofies, that was the circus I ordered to divert the kids so's we could ambush them. Any damned fool knows kids like circuses.

Drag we're confused and nervous. Just today four boxes of drexol were stolen from our already dwindling supply of goods. That's why we didn't think when we killed that man. The old people are wandering around the camp bumping into each other they're so tightened up. All day people are saying hey stupid idiot watch where you're going. It's a mad house.

And the Preacher Rev. Boyd, he's in the dumps in a strong and serious way this time. You know how hard he tried with the kids and the town's heathen, how he'd smoke hookahs with them brats and get stoned with Chief Showcase the only surviving injun and that volume of hip pastorale poetry he's putting together, *Stomp Me O Lord.* He thought that Protestantism would survive at least another month and he's tearing up the Red-Eye and writing more of them poems trying to keep up with the times. Drag you know how out of focus things are around here. After all Drag it's your world completely now.

How can you be so confident your men can take care of them varmits Drag? It takes a trail boss a dozen or so cowboys and a wrangler to get the herd North. You can't have many cowpokes left behind. Don't get me wrong I'm not afraid for myself cause I rode with Doc Holiday and the Dalton Boys before I went peace officer—I have handled a whole slew of punks passing through the hopper in my day . . . why if I hadn't been up the creek at the Law Enforcement Conference it wouldn't have happened anyway.

You always seem to be at some convention when the town needs you Marshal, Drag said, looking into a hand mirror and with a neckerchief wiping the smudges of mascara that showed above his batting lashes.

Drag, the women folk, well you know how women are, what strange creatures they be during menopause. They're against us wiping out the kids. That's one of the reasons we didn't cast lots quicker to give you the hand over of Yellow Back Radio, so that you could adjust all the knobs and turn to whatever station you wished. Anyway we tried to get Big Lizzy to talk to them but they don't recognize her as one of their own.

Pshaw, don't worry about the women Doc, Drag Gibson said, bringing his old fat and ugly frame to its feet. Start appeasing them and pretty soon they'll be trying to run the whole show like that kook back in Wichita who campaigned to cut out likker. Now quit your whining and get back to camp and see after them townsfolk. Leave the job up to me.

The dignitaries rose and tumbled down the hill. The Banker rolled over a couple of times as Drag stood jerking his shoulders and with one finger in his ear as pellet after pellet flew over the Marshal's, Banker's and Doctor's heads. He relaxed, drank a glass of rotgut and gave the appearance of a statesman by returning to his book *The Life of Catherine the Great*. As soon as the delegation disappeared, he slammed the book shut and called his boys.

Get in here cowpokes, we're in business.

Skinny McCullough the foreman followed by some cowhands rushed onto the lawn and surrounded their boss.

Chinaboy! Chinaboy! Bring me that there package.

The Chinese servant rushed into the scene with his arms weighed down with a bundle.

O.K. men, Drag said, this is the opportunity we've been waiting for. They signed the town over to me, the chumps, haw haw.

He opened the package and placed its contents on the table.

This is a brand new revolving cylinder. It has eight chambers. A murderer's dream with a rapid firing breech-loading firearm.

The cowpokes' eyes lit up and foam began to form around their lips.

It was invented by a nice gent lecturer named Dr. Coult of New York London and Calcutta. Just bought it from Royal Flush Goose-man, the shrewd, cunning and wicked fur trapper, the one who sold them injuns those defected flintlocks allowing us to wipe them out.

The kids are down there with a circus I booked under a pseudonym. I been watching them through my long glass. Now get busy and before you know it Drag Gibson will be the big name in Yellow Back Radio then Video Junction then va-va-voom on to the East, heh heh heh.

The cowpokes from Drag Gibson's Purple Bar-B drank some two-bits-a-throw from a common horn and armed with their shiny new weapons headed towards the outskirts of Yellow Back Radio on their nefarious mission.

⟡⟡⟡

The Dancing Bear, the Juggler, Loop and Zozo entertained the children far into the night. The Dancing Bear did acrobatic feats with great deftness, Loop his loco lariat tricks, and Zozo read the children's palms and told their fortunes.

Finally Jake the Barker gathered them near the fire to tell of the Seven Cities of Cibola, magnificent legendary American paradise where tranquilized and smiling machines gladly did all of the work so that man could be free to dream. A paradise whose streets were paved with opals from Idaho, sapphire from Montana, turquoise and silver from the great Southwest:

In the early half of the sixteenth century about 1528 an expedition which included the black slave Estevancio landed at Tampa Bay. He and his companions were lost trapped and enslaved by Indians. Other expeditions also vanished mysteriously. Legend has it that the city can only be found by those of innocent motives, the young without yellow fever in their eyes.

Stupid historians who are hired by the cattlemen to promote reason, law and order—toad men who adore facts—say that such an anarchotechnological paradise where robots feed information into inanimate steer and mechanical fowl where machines do everything from dig irrigation ditches to mine the food of the sea help old ladies across the street and nurture infants is as real as a green horse's nightmare. Shucks I've always been a fool, eros appeals more to me than logos. I'm just silly enough to strike out for it tomorrow as soon as the circus splits up.

A place without gurus monarchs leaders cops tax collectors jails matriarchs patriarchs and all the other galoots who in cahoots have made the earth a pile of human bones under the feet of wolves.

Why don't we all go, the children shrieked.

Wait a minute, Jake said, we don't have enough supplies for the trip. It lies somewhere far to the south.

That's no task, supplies, one of the children said.

After huddling together they all started into the town, leaving the troupe behind. Finally having had a loot-in on the Hat and Boot store, the Feed store and the Bank they returned with enough supplies to make the long journey.

I guess I can't argue against that, Jake said turning to Loop, Zozo and the Juggler. Welcome to my expedition into the unknown.

The children reveled and danced around.

When they finished storing provisions into the wagons the entire party went to sleep. The next morning there would be much work to do. The troupe bedded down in their wagons and the children slept beneath warm buffalo robes.

ᎶᏇᎯ

Loop Garoo was dreaming of bringing down the stars with his tail when all at once he smelled smoke. He awoke to find horsemen surrounding the circle. The children began to scream and some of their clothes caught fire from torches the bandits had tossed into the area. Rapid gunfire started up and the children fell upon each other and ran about in circles as they tried to break the seizure's grip. Zozo Labrique looked out of her wagon and was shot between the eyes. She dropped to the ground next to the wagon. The pitiful moans of the children could be heard above the din of hoofbeats and gunfire as one by one they were picked off by horsemen who fired with amazing accuracy. The Juggler was firing two rifles and before catching a bullet in his throat was able to down two of the horsemen.

Loop crawled to the place where Zozo lay dying. Blood trickled from her nose and mouth.

Zozo let me see if I can get you inside your wagon.

Flee boy, save yourself, I'm done for, the woman murmured pressing something into his hand. It's a mad dog's tooth it'll bring you connaissance and don't forget the gris gris, the mojo, the wangols old Zozo taught you and when you need more power play poker with the dead.

But Zozo I'll try to get you a horse, Loop began—but with a start the woman slumped in his arms.

The grizzly Bear had escaped from the cage and was mangling two horsemen. This allowed an opening in the circle which two children raced through, hanging from the sides of horses. Loop did likewise but so as to divert the men from the children rode in a different direction, towards the desert.

Bullet after bullet zitted above his head. When the burning scene of children and carny freaks was almost out of his sight he looked back. His friends the Juggler, a dancing bear, the fast talking Barker and Zozo Labrique were trapped in a deadly circle. Their figurines were beginning to melt.

Jay Wright

(1935–   )

BORN IN 1935 in Albuquerque, New Mexico, poet Jay Wright graduated from the University of California at Berkeley in 1961. He spent a short period at Union Theological Seminary in New York and in 1962 enrolled in graduate school at Rutgers University, where he earned the M.A. and went on to complete the course work for the doctorate.

Wright's first publication was a poetry chapbook titled *Death as History* (1967). Poems from this volume appeared in his 1971 collection *The Homecoming Singer*. Wright also wrote a one-act play, *Balloons*, which was published in 1968. Between 1968 and 1970 he taught briefly at Tougaloo and Talladega colleges. He has also been a Hodder Fellow at Princeton University and a Fellow in Creative Writing at Dundee University in Scotland (1971–1973). From 1975 to 1979 he taught at Yale University, publishing in 1976 two more volumes of poetry, *Dimensions of History* and *Soothsayers and Omens*. Wright is also the author of *The Double Invention of Komo* (1980), *Explications/Interpolations* (1984), *Selected Poems of Jay Wright* (1987), *Elaine's Book* (1988), and *Boleros* (1991) in the Princeton University Press Series of Contemporary Poets.

For an extensive analysis of Wright's poetry, see Phillip M. Richard's essay in *Dictionary of Literary Biography, Volume 41*. See also Robert B. Stepto, "After Modernism, after Hibernation: Michael Harper, Robert Hayden, and Jay Wright," in *Chant of Saints: A Gathering of Afro-American Literature, Arts, and Scholarship*, edited by Michael S. Harper and Robert B. Stepto (1979). See also brief comments and biographical information in *Black Fire* (1968), edited by Le Roi Jones and Larry Neal, and *The Forerunners* (1975), edited by Woodie King, Jr.

Both "Guadalajara" and "Yemanjá" come from *Elaine's Book*.

GUADALAJARA

Village to village
the spirit seeks its house
—Nochistlán,
    Tonalá,
    Tetlán.
The wind caracols on a bed of stars,
warming itself with the fire that sends
the faithful
        spiraling
                toward that waterless, spiny
moment
        when a river's whisper is enough.
I keep the image of a man walking
in search of a Valley of Stones,
        the mudéjar of this valley,
the Roman aqueduct and foundation,
                the Visigothic spell
pestled by a Spanish horse.
        Godelfare
the Wad-al-hajarah of the Moors
knows the sun here as a bronze cathedral,
the moon as a jade feather crown,
and the whisper of a blue fire dying
raises the sand sound of water again.

These spires above my house are doves,
lifted by grace above the earth's eruption.
Here, we chew the kola nut of lost dreams
and memories of fires we never entered.
It seems now that only the earth moves.
If you tumble from the high air of Tepic,
with its smell of coffee and sunburnt pine,
you fall upon Minerva's foundation
and a stillness that even the father from Dolores
                        couldn't lift.
Cristeros, carrying their sun-drenched blankets
of democratic discontent, may welcome you.
I like to show my sons

—the ones who dress my walls with earth tones,
priestly black and the many colors of blood;
the ones who go searching in angelic prose
for their fathers, or the stability of faith;
the ones who understand life's coursing
in a good name and the well-modulated womb.
I wish you had come in the fall,
when the Virgin takes her great expectations,
through the ribboned streets, from temple to temple,
and returns—only slightly ruffled—
        to the moonlight of Zapopan.

I am a trinity, you see.
Spirits growing out of the fact
that my men shape clay
        as the god shapes spirit.
Yet, in the eucalyptus evening,
light shows me all my failures.
My square is ringed with the names
of those my peace betrayed.
Often, my only song has been
        a denial of prophecies.
And when the night closes
on the redness of my most intense days,
I hear a turtle voice
tolling my sacred impurity.
I should have traveled in the wood smoke
of a burning cross,
or been fettered with birds who would come
to their ends, flinted and bled into earthen bowls.
I should have known the sun in a dawn boat,
with its nets sent deep and filled by simple desire.
I should have heard the crow's song
in my own peasant's pail,
and have eaten the sugared skull
        when the house was done.
I should have been attentive to the moment
when stillness must open another and fiery domain.
I should have given my virginity
to a new hearth, in a new world,
where mercy and rapture rule.

YEMANJÁ

Dawn on a greener earth shapes the woman,
come, with immaculate beads around her neck,
to secure the figure of my infant step.
I ride, in silence, upon her head from water
to water, through the dance in which you hold her.

Where the air is clear they will do even better by you.
Even so, we changed you when we changed your name,
married you to whiteness in a depth of sky quite out of reach
and gave you thunder, arrows and iron for your sons.
Memory tells us you were made water by insult,
the fortunate flicker of wrath that swept you
out of the market and into healing. Or so
these pots reveal our desire for purity.

I hear a toucan over water call me
to my oldest river, the bird's voice filled
with the clamor of cloth and melon seeds.
Weightless now, I climb down from a green
ledge to declare myself your son again.
Near the clearing, where the deer come to nibble
at a late spring, I have your water-worn stones
bathing in the blood of whatever the land gives.

Compassion wears us down like river-worn stones.
I return to your river body.
Your sixteen cowry shells flare in a darker light.
At the river's edge, a young woman bends to bathe
the bite of your porridge from her mouth.
Even in the twilight, I can see her eyes blaze
with the pleasure of having known love alone.

Mari Evans*

AN AUTHOR CONCERNED not only with theme and content but with poetical structure and style, Mari Evans has been praised for poetry which reveals her personal, political, and social beliefs in a concise, clear, and technically precise fashion. Evans is a poet, a dramatist, an essayist, a playwright, a fiction writer, a professor, a community activist, a consultant, a lecturer, a producer, and a director. She is a multitalented artist, whose dedication to her people comes first and foremost.

Born in Toledo, Ohio, Evans attended public school and the University of Toledo. Though originally interested in fashion design, she wrote and printed her first story in fourth grade in the school newspaper. Entering the academic world in 1969, Evans has taught African American literature and been a writer-in-residence at several universities, including Indiana University/Purdue (1969), Indiana University, Bloomington (1972–1973), Washington University, St. Louis (1980), and State University of New York at Albany.

Evans has worked at WTTV, channel 4, in Indianapolis (1968–73), with the National Endowment for the Arts (1969–70), and with the Bobbs-Merrill Publishing Company (1978–83). She has been a director for the Literary Advisory Panel for the Indiana Arts Commission (1976–77) and served on the board of directors of the First World Foundation.

Her poetry mirrors her concern for the state of social affairs. *I Am a Black Woman* (1970) deals primarily with social reality and social relevancy. The opening poem, which takes the name of the collection, relays a sense of black pride and sets the stage for the rest of the book, which addresses serious issues such as the effectiveness of civil rights laws. Evans believes poets have a duty as artists to warn and educate their readers about current social maladies, not just to recount facts and document history.

Evans's works include *Where Is All the Music?* (1968), *I Am a Black Woman* (1970), *Night Star: 1973–1978* (1980), poetry; *J. D.* (1973), *I Look at Me* (1974), *Rap Stories* (1974), *Singing Black* (1976), *Jim Flying High* (1979), juvenile; play productions, *River of My Song* (1977) and *Eyes* (1982), an adaptation of Zora Neale Hurston's *Their Eyes Were Watching God*; and critical essays in *Negro Digest, Black World*, and *Black Enterprise*. Her poems are also reprinted in several anthologies, including Anita Dore's

---

*We have omitted Ms. Evans's birthdate at her request.

357

The Premier Book of Major Poets: An Anthology (1970); Alan Lomax and Raoul Abdul's *3000 Years of Black Poetry: An Anthology* (1970); Arnold Adoff's *Black Out Loud: An Anthology of Modern Poems by Black Americans* (1975); and the anthology Evans edited, *Black Women Writers, 1950–1980: A Critical Evaluation* (1984). Her most recent publication is *Black Women Writers: Arguments and Interviews* (1984).

Evans has received numerous awards and honors, including a John Hay Whitney Fellowship (1965), a Woodrow Wilson Grant (1968), and a National Endowment for the Arts Creative Writing Award (1981–1982).

For commentary on Mari Evans, see David Dorsey's "The Art of Mari Evans" and Solomon Edwards's "Affirmation in the Works of Mari Evans," both in *Black Women Writers*.

"I Am a Black Woman," "Vive Noir," and "The Time Is Now" are taken from the collection *I Am a Black Woman.* "My Father's Passage" is taken from *Black Women Writers, 1950–1980: A Critical Evaluation.*

I AM A BLACK WOMAN

I am a black woman
the music of my song
some sweet arpeggio of tears
is written in a minor key
and I
can be heard humming in the night
Can be heard
                  humming
in the night

I saw my mate leap screaming to the sea
and I/with these hands/cupped the lifebreath
from my issue in the canebrake
I lost Nat's swinging body in a rain of tears
and heard my son scream all the way from Anzio
for Peace he never knew. . . . I
learned Da Nang and Pork Chop Hill
in anguish
Now my nostrils know the gas
and these trigger tire/d fingers
seek the softness in my warrior's beard

All poems from *I Am a Black Woman* published by William Morrow & Co., Inc., 1970. Reprinted by permission of the author.

I
am a black woman
tall as a cypress
strong
beyond all definition still
defying place
and time
and circumstance
  assailed
    impervious
      indestructible
Look
  on me and be
renewed

VIVE NOIR!

i
am going to rise
en masse
from Inner City
        sick
        of newyork ghettos
        chicago tenements
   l
        a's slums
weary
    of exhausted lands
    sagging privies
    saying yessuh yessah
    yesSIR
    in an assortment
    of geographical dialects i
have seen my last
broken down plantation
even from a
distance
    i
will load all my goods
in '50 Chevy pickups '53
Fords fly United and '66
caddys i

have packed in
the old man and the old lady and
wiped the children's noses
    I'm tired
    of hand me downs
    shut me ups
    pin me ins
    keep me outs
    messing me over have
    just had it
    baby
    from
    you . . .
i'm
gonna spread out
over America
    intrude
my proud blackness
all
    over the place
    i have wrested wheat fields
    from the forests

    turned rivers
    from their courses

    leveled mountains
    at a word
    festooned the land with
    bridges
        gemlike
        on filaments of steel
        moved
glistening towersofBabel in place
    like blocks
sweated a whole
civilization

now

        i'm
gonna breathe fire
through flaming nostrils BURN
    a place for

      me

in the skyscrapers and the
schoolrooms on the green
lawns and the white
beaches
       i'm
gonna wear the robes and
sit on the benches
make the rules and make
the arrests say
who can and who
can't
         baby you don't stand
         a
         chance
i'm
    gonna put black angels
in all the books and a black
Christchild in Mary's arms i'm
gonna make black bunnies black
      fairies black santas black
      nursery rhymes and
             black
    ice cream
         i'm
gonna make it a
    crime
      to be anything BUT   black
      pass the coppertone

gonna make white
a twentyfourhour
lifetime
J.O.B.
      an' when all the coppertone's gone . . .?

THE TIME IS NOW

We have screamed
and we have filled our lungs
with revolutionary rhetoric
We sing
the sorrow songs and march
chest tight and elbows
locked
yes
We have learned to mourn
Our martyrs and our children
murdered by our Greater Love
and strewn
like waste before our pious disbelief
What tremors stay our heads?
The monster still contains us!
There is no better time no
Futuretime

if ever we would rise
We could reorder space and time define
the circumstance claim absolutes

If we would rise
Come! Let us Stand
and seize our glorious future
by its beckoning bloodied hand
When our eyes peel the road
Survival stares
and Struggle begs us claim our
own historic role
If we would rise
O brethren
first

we stand!
At one with time.

MY FATHER'S PASSAGE

. . . I cannot imagine a writer who is not continually reaching,
who contains no discontent that what he is producing is not more
than it is. . . .

Who I am is central to how I write and what I write; and I am the
continuation of my father's passage. I have written for as long as I
have been aware of writing as a way of setting down feelings and the
stuff of imaginings.

No single living entity really influenced my life as did my father,
who died two Septembers ago. An oak of a man, his five feet eight
loomed taller than Kilimanjaro. He lived as if he were poured from
iron, and loved his family with a vulnerability that was touching. In-
domitable, to the point that one could not have spent a lifetime in
his presence without absorbing something beautiful and strong and
special.

He saved my first printed story, a fourth-grade effort accepted by
the school paper, and carefully noted on it the date, our home address, and his own proud comment. By this action inscribing on an
impressionable Black youngster both the importance of the printed
word and the accessibility of "reward" for even a slight effort, given
the right circumstances. For I knew from what ease and caprice the
story had come.

Years later, I moved from university journalism to a by-lined column in a Black-owned weekly and, in time, worked variously as an
industrial editor, as a research associate with responsibility for preparing curriculum materials, and as director of publications for the
corporate management of a Job Corps installation.

I have always written, it seems. I have not, however, always been
organized in my approach. Now, I find I am much more productive
when I set aside a specific time and uncompromisingly accept that as
commitment. The ideal, for me, is to be able to write for long periods
of time on an eight-hour-a-day basis. That is, to begin to write—not
to prepare to write, around eight-thirty, stop for lunch, resume writing around twelve-thirty and stop for the day around four-thirty
when I begin to feel both fulfilled and exhausted by the effort. For
most Black writers that kind of leisure is an unaccustomed luxury. I
enjoyed it exactly once, for a two-week period. In that two weeks I

came face to face with myself as a writer and liked what I saw of my productive potential.

When I began to write I concentrated on short stories, but I was soon overwhelmed by the persistency of the rejection slips. Everything I sent out came back, and although many of the comments, when there were comments, were encouraging, the bottom line was that none were accepted.

I drifted into poetry thought by thought; it was never intentional. I had no "dreams of being a poet." I began to write about my environment, a housing project, and to set down my reactions to it—to the physical, the visual aspects of it; to the people I touched in passing, to what I understood of their lives—the "intuited" drama and poignancy a brown paper bag away. It was not from wisdom that I followed that path, it was Langston spoke to me.

When I was about ten I took a copy of his *Weary Blues* from a shelf and, eyes bright with discovery, mouth shaped in astonishment, rhapsodized, "Why he's writing about me!" He was my introduction to a Black literary tradition that began with the inception of writing in the area of Meroe on the African continent many millennia ago.

He was the most generous professional I have ever known. What he gave me was not advice, but his concern, his interest, and, more importantly, he inspired a belief in myself and my ability to produce. With the confidence he instilled, what had been mere exercise, almost caprice—however compulsive—became commitment and I accepted writing as my *direction*. I defined it as craft, and inherent in that definition was the understanding that as craft, it was a rigorous, demanding occupation, to be treated as such. I felt that I should be able to write on demand, that I could not reasonably be worthy of the designation "writer" if my craft depended on dispensations from something uncontrollable, elusive, and unpredictable called "inspiration." I set about learning the profession I had chosen.

A state employment agency referred me to an assistant editor's vacancy at a local chain-manufacturing plant. Watts was already in the air, minority employment quotas were threatening in the background, and the company opted to hire me. In their ninety years of operation I would be the first Black to cross their sacred office threshold for any purpose except to clean. The salary would be almost 50 percent less than what I had previously earned, but I took the job. Writing, as a profession, would start here.

The director of the plant's information system was far from flattered at having as assistant editor the first Black employee to work anywhere in the company other than the foundry or delivery. There was much crude humor at his expense, with me as the butt, and a good deal of it within my hearing. Almost his first act was to call maintenance and have my desk turned away from him, so that I faced the wall. An auspicious beginning.

I am cautious, Cancerian, rarely leaping without the long look, but having looked am inclined to be absolutely without fear or trepidation. It was a gamble, undertaken in the heart of Klan territory; it paid off.

He knew how to write. His first draft was as clean as my final copy, and I resented that so much that even his hassling became a minor annoyance. I revised and revised and revised, and only part of it was voluntary. In time, he began to allow me a certain creative freedom, and I became enthralled with industrial editing.

Time softened the hostility but nothing ever changed the fact that I was a Black woman in a white job.

Those three years, however, underscored for me the principle that writing is a craft, a profession one learns by doing. One must be able to produce on demand, and that requires great personal discipline. I believe that one seldom really perfects. I cannot imagine a writer who is not continually reaching, who contains no discontent that what he is producing is not more than it is. So primarily, I suppose, discipline is the foundation of the profession, and that holds regardless of anything else.

To address specifics: I insist that Black poetry, Black literature if you will, be evaluated stylistically for its imagery, its metaphor, description, onomatopoeia, its polyrhythms, its rhetoric. What is fascinating, however, is that despite the easy application of all these traditional criteria, no allegation of "universality" can be imposed for the simple reason that Black becomes catalyst, and whether one sees it as color, substance, an ancestral bloodstream, or as life-style—historically, when Black is introduced, things change.

And when traditional criteria are refracted by the Black experience they return changed in ways that are unique and specific. Diction becomes unwaveringly precise, arrogantly evocative, knowingly subtle—replete with what one creative Black literary analyst has called "mascon words,"[1] it reconstitutes on paper; "saturation"[2] occurs. Idiom is larger than geography; it is the hot breath of a people—singing, slashing, explorative. Imagery becomes the magic denominator, the language of a passage, saying the ancient unchanging particulars, the connective currents that nod Black heads from Maine to Mississippi to Montana. No there ain't nothin universal about it.

---

[1] Stephen Henderson, *Understanding the New Black Poetry* (New York: William Morrow, 1973), p. 44.

[2] Henderson, *Understanding the New Black Poetry*, p. 10.

So when I write, I write reaching for all that. Reaching for what will nod Black heads over common denominators. The stones thrown that say how it has been/is/must be, for us. If there are those outside the Black experience who hear the music and can catch the beat, that is serendipity; I have no objections. But when I write, I write according to the title of poet Margaret Walker's classic: "for my people."

I originally wrote poems because certain things occurred to me in phrases that I didn't want to lose. The captured phrase is a joyous way to approach the molding and shaping of a poem. More often now, however, because my conscious direction is different, I choose the subject first, then set about the task of creating a work that will please me aesthetically and that will treat the subject with integrity. A work that is imbued with the urgency, the tenderness, the pathos, needed to transmit to readers my sense of why they should involve themselves with what it is I have to say.

I have no favorite themes nor concerns except the overall concern that Black life be experienced throughout the diaspora on the highest, most rewarding, most productive levels. Hardly chauvinistic, for when that is possible for our Black family/nation it will be true and possible for all people.

My primary goal is to command the reader's attention. I understand I have to make the most of the first few seconds his or her eye touches my material. Therefore, for me, the poem is structure and style as well as theme and content; I require something of my poems visually as well as rhetorically. I work as hard at how the poem "looks" as at crafting; indeed, for me the two are synonymous.

I revise endlessly, and am not reluctant to consider a poem "in process" even after it has appeared in print. I am not often completely pleased with any single piece, therefore, I remember with great pleasure those rare "given" poems. "If There Be Sorrow" was such a piece, and there were others, but I remember "Sorrow" because that was the first time I experienced the exquisite joy of having a poem emerge complete, without my conscious intervention.

The title poem for my second volume, *I Am a Black Woman*, on the other hand, required between fifteen and twenty revisions before I felt comfortable that it could stand alone.

My attempt is to be as explicit as possible while maintaining the integrity of the aesthetic; consequently, I work so hard for clarity that I suspect I sometimes run the risk of being, as Ray Durem put it, "not sufficiently obscure." Since the Black creative artist is not required to wait on inspiration nor to rely on imagination—for Black life *is* drama, brutal and compelling—one inescapable reality is that the more explicitly Black writers speak their truths the more difficult it is for them to publish. My writing is pulsed by my understanding of contemporary realities: I am Afrikan first, then woman, then writer, but I have never had a manuscript rejected because I am a woman: I have been rejected more times than I can number because the content of a manuscript was, to the industry-oriented reader, more "Black" ergo "discomforting" than could be accommodated.

Nevertheless, given the crisis nature of the Black position at a time of escalating state-imposed repression and containment, in a country that has a history of blatantly genocidal acts committed against three nonwhite nations (Native Americans, the Japanese of Hiroshima/Nagasaki, the inhabitants of Vietnam), a country that has perfected the systematic destruction of a people, their land, foliage, and food supply; a country that at the stroke of a presidential pen not only revoked the rights and privileges of citizenship for 110,000 American citizens (identifiable, since they were nonwhite) for what they "could" do, but summarily remanded those citizens to American internment camps, I understand that Black writers have a responsibility to use the language in the manner it is and always has been used by non-Black writers and by the state itself: as a political force.

I think of myself as a political writer inasmuch as I am deliberately attempting the delivery of political concepts and premises through the medium of the Black aesthetic, seeing the various art forms as vehicles.

As a Black writer embracing that responsibility, approaching my Black family/nation from within a commonality of experience, I try for a poetic language that says, "This is *who* we are, where we have been, *where* we are. This, is where we must go. And *this*, is what we must do."

Audre Lorde

(1934–   )

A MULTIFACETED and prolific poet, Audre Lorde has had her greatest effect by showing that feminism is an important dimension of the black woman's experience, though as a leading voice in the black poetry movement she has been concerned with the themes of self-love and pride as well. A lesbian, a mother, and a cancer survivor, Lorde expresses her personal, social, and political stances through her poetry.

Born in New York City in 1934, the youngest of three sisters, Audre Lorde attended Catholic school in Manhattan. She received her bachelor's degree in 1959 from Hunter College; attended the National University of Mexico in 1954; and received a master's in library science from Columbia University in 1961. She worked as a young adult librarian at Mount Vernon Public Library from 1961 until 1963 and later became a head librarian at Town School Library in New York City from 1966 to 1968. In 1962 she married Edwin Ashley Rollins, a lawyer, and had two children.

Lorde wrote her first poem in the eighth grade. However, it wasn't until after she stopped working as a librarian after she received a National Endowment for the Arts grant and after she became poet-in-residence at Tougaloo College that her first book of poetry, *The First Cities* (1968), was published.

Lorde received a Creative Artists Public Service grant in 1972, and in 1973 Dudley Randall's Broadside Press, which distributed Lorde's second book of poetry, *Cables to Rage* (1970), published Lorde's third book of poetry, *From a Land Where Other People Live*. Lorde's first published collection of short stories, *The Cancer Journals* (1980), won the American Library Association Gay Caucus Book of the Year Award for 1981.

For a time, she actively promoted a press, of which she is a founding member, that primarily publishes and distributes the works of feminist women of color, the Kitchen Table: Women of Color Press. She also worked as a tenured English professor at two colleges in New York—John Jay College of Criminal Justice and Hunter College.

Lorde has written five other books of poetry: *New York Head Shop and Museum* (1974), *Between Our Selves* (1976), *Coal* (1976), *The Black Unicorn* (1978) and *Our Dead Behind Us* (1986). Her essays include *Use of the Erotic: The Erotic as Power* (1979); a biomythography, *Zami: A New Spelling of My Name* (1982); and two other collections of nonfiction, *Sister Outsider: Essays and Speeches* (1984) and *A Burst of Light* (1988). Her poetry also appears in nine anthologies, including *Black Sister: Poetry by Black American Women* (1981) and *Confirmation: An Anthology of African-American Women* (1983).

For further reading, see in addition to Irma McClaurin-Allen's essay in *Dictionary of Literary Biography, Volume 41*; C. W. E. Bigsby's *The Black American Writer* (1969); Eugene Redmond's *Drumvoices* (1976); Jerome Brooks's "In the Name of the Father: The Poetry of Audre Lorde," in *Black Women Writers (1950–1980): A Critical Evaluation* (1984); and Claudia Tate's *Black Women Writers at Work* (1983).

Both "125th Street and Abomey" and "Power" were first published in the *Village Voice*. The speech, "The Uses of Anger: Women Responding to Racism," is reprinted from *Sister Outsider*.

125TH STREET AND ABOMEY

Head bent, walking through snow
I see you Seboulisa
printed inside the back of my head
like marks of the newly wrapped akai
that kept my sleep fruitful in Dahomey
and I poured on the red earth in your honor
those ancient parts of me
most precious and least needed
my well-guarded past
the energy-eating secrets
I surrender to you as libation
mother, illuminate my offering
of old victories
over men over women over my selves
who has never before dared
to whistle into the night
take my fear of being alone
like my warrior sisters
who rode in defense of your queendom
disguised and apart
give me the woman strength
of tongue in this cold season.

Half earth and time splits us apart

---

like struck rock.
A piece lives elegant stories
too simply put
while a dream on the edge of summer
of brown rain in nim trees
snail shells from the dooryard
of King Toffah
bring me where my blood moves
Seboulisa mother goddess with one breast
eaten away by worms of sorrow and loss
see me now
your severed daughter
laughing our name into echo
all the world shall remember.

POWER

The difference between poetry and rhetoric
is being
ready to kill
yourself
instead of your children.

I am trapped on a desert of raw gunshot wounds
and a dead child dragging his shattered black
face off the edge of my sleep
blood from his punctured cheeks and shoulders
is the only liquid for miles and my stomach
churns at the imagined taste while
my mouth splits into dry lips
without loyalty or reason
thirsting for the wetness of his blood
as it sinks into the whiteness
of the desert where I am lost
without imagery or magic
trying to make power out of hatred and destruction
trying to heal my dying son with kisses
only the sun will bleach his bones quicker.

The policeman who shot down a 10-year-old in Queens

First published by the *Village Voice*. "Power" is reprinted by permission of the Charlotte
Sheedy Agency, Inc.

stood over the boy with his cop shoes in childish blood
and a voice said "Die you little motherfucker" and
there are tapes to prove that. At his trial
this policeman said in his own defense
"I didn't notice the size or nothing else
only the color." and
there are tapes to prove that, too.

Today that 37-year-old white man with 13 years of police forcing
has been set free
by 11 white men who said they were satisfied
justice had been done
and one black woman who said
"They convinced me" meaning
they had dragged her 4'10" black woman's frame
over the hot coals of four centuries of white male approval
until she let go the first real power she ever had
and lined her own womb with cement
to make a graveyard for our children.

I have not been able to touch the destruction within me.
But unless I learn to use
the difference between poetry and rhetoric
my power too will run corrupt as poisonous mold
or lie limp and useless as an unconnected wire
and one day I will take my teenaged plug
and connect it to the nearest socket
raping an 85-year-old white woman
who is somebody's mother
and as I beat her senseless and set a torch to her bed
a greek chorus will be singing in 3/4 time
"Poor thing. She never hurt a soul. What beasts they are."

THE USES OF ANGER
Women Responding to Racism

Racism. The belief in the inherent superiority of one race over all
others and thereby the right to dominance, manifest and implied.

Women respond to racism. My response to racism is anger. I have
lived with that anger, ignoring it, feeding upon it, learning to use it

"The Uses of Anger" was a keynote presentation at the National Women's Studies
Association Conference, Storrs, Connecticut, June 1981. "The Uses of Anger" from *Sister
Outsider* by Audre Lorde. Reprinted by permission of The Crossing Press.

before it laid my visions to waste, for most of my life. Once I did it in silence, afraid of the weight. My fear of anger taught me nothing. Your fear of that anger will teach you nothing, also.

Women responding to racism means women responding to anger; the anger of exclusion, of unquestioned privilege, of racial distortions, of silence, ill-use, stereotyping, defensiveness, misnaming, betrayal, and co-optation.

My anger is a response to racist attitudes and to the actions and presumptions that arise out of those attitudes. If your dealings with other women reflect those attitudes, then my anger and your attendant fears are spotlights that can be used for growth in the same way I have used learning to express anger for my growth. But for corrective surgery, not guilt. Guilt and defensiveness are bricks in a wall against which we all flounder; they serve none of our futures.

Because I do not want this to become a theoretical discussion, I am going to give a few examples of interchanges between women that illustrate these points. In the interest of time, I am going to cut them short. I want you to know there were many more.

For example:

• I speak out of direct and particular anger at an academic conference, and a white woman says, "Tell me how you feel but don't say it too harshly or I cannot hear you." But is it my manner that keeps her from hearing, or the threat of a message that her life may change?

• The Women's Studies Program of a southern university invites a Black woman to read following a week-long forum on Black and white women. "What has this week given to you?" I ask. The most vocal white woman says, "I think I've gotten a lot. I feel Black women really understand me a lot better now; they have a better idea of where I'm coming from." As if understanding her lay at the core of the racist problem.

• After fifteen years of a women's movement which professes to address the life concerns and possible futures of all women, I still hear, on campus after campus, "How can we address the issues of racism? No women of Color attended." Or, the other side of that statement, "We have no one in our department equipped to teach their work." In other words, racism is a Black women's problem, a problem of women of Color, and only we can discuss it.

• After I read from my work entitled "Poems for Women in Rage,"* a white woman asks me: "Are you going to do anything with how we can deal directly with *our* anger? I feel it's so important." I

---

*One poem from this series is included in *Chosen Poems: Old and New* (W. W. Norton and Company, New York, 1978), pp. 105–108.

ask, "How do you use *your* rage?" And then I have to turn away from the blank look in her eyes, before she can invite me to participate in her own annihilation. I do not exist to feel her anger for her.

• White women are beginning to examine their relationships to Black women, yet often I hear them wanting only to deal with little colored children across the roads of childhood, the beloved nurse-maid, the occasional second-grade classmate—those tender memories of what was once mysterious and intriguing or neutral. You avoid the childhood assumptions formed by the raucous laughter at Rastus and Alfalfa, the acute message of your mommy's handkerchief spread upon the park bench because I had just been sitting there, the indelible and dehumanizing portraits of Amos 'n' Andy and your daddy's humorous bedtime stories.

• I wheel my two-year-old daughter in a shopping cart through a supermarket in Eastchester in 1967, and a little white girl riding past in her mother's cart calls out excitedly, "Oh look, Mommy, a baby maid!" And your mother shushes you, but she does not correct you. And so fifteen years later, at a conference on racism, you can still find that story humorous. But I hear your laughter is full of terror and dis-ease.

• A white academic welcomes the appearance of a collection by non-Black women of Color.[†] "It allows me to deal with racism without dealing with the harshness of Black women," she says to me.

• At an international cultural gathering of women, a well-known white american woman poet interrupts the reading of the work of women of Color to read her own poem, and then dashes off to an "important panel."

If women in the academy truly want a dialogue about racism, it will require recognizing the needs and the living contexts of other women. When an academic woman says, "I can't afford it," she may mean she is making a choice about how to spend her available money. But when a woman on welfare says, "I can't afford it," she means she is surviving on an amount of money that was barely subsistence in 1972, and she often does not have enough to eat. Yet the National Women's Studies Association here in 1981 holds a conference in which it commits itself to responding to racism, yet refuses to waive the registration fee for poor women and women of Color who wished to present and conduct workshops. This has made it impossible for many women of Color—for instance, Wilmette Brown, of Black Women for Wages for Housework—to participate in

---

[†] *This Bridge Called My Back: Writings by Radical Women of Color* edited by Cherríe Moraga and Gloria Anzaldua (Kitchen Table: Women of Color Press, New York, 1984), first published in 1981.

this conference. Is this to be merely another case of the academy discussing life within the closed circuits of the academy?

To the white women present who recognize these attitudes as familiar, but most of all, to all my sisters of Color who live and survive thousands of such encounters—to my sisters of Color who like
me still tremble with their rage under harness, or who sometimes
question the expression of our rage as useless and disruptive (the
two most popular accusations)—I want to speak about anger,
my anger, and what I have learned from my travels through its
dominions.

*Everything can be used / except what is wasteful / (you will need /
to remember this when you are accused of destruction.)* ‡

Every woman has a well-stocked arsenal of anger potentially useful against those oppressions, personal and institutional, which
brought that anger into being. Focused with precision it can become
a powerful source of energy serving progress and change. And when
I speak of change, I do not mean a simple switch of positions or a
temporary lessening of tensions, nor the ability to smile or feel good.
I am speaking of a basic and radical alteration in those assumptions
underlining our lives.

I have seen situations where white women hear a racist remark,
resent what has been said, become filled with fury, and remain silent
because they are afraid. That unexpressed anger lies within them like
an undetonated device, usually to be hurled at the first woman of
Color who talks about racism.

But anger expressed and translated into action in the service of
our vision and our future is a liberating and strengthening act of
clarification, for it is in the painful process of this translation that we
identify who are our allies with whom we have grave differences,
and who are our genuine enemies.

Anger is loaded with information and energy. When I speak of
women of Color, I do not only mean Black women. The woman of
Color who is not Black and who charges me with rendering her invisible by assuming that her struggles with racism are identical with
my own has something to tell me that I had better learn from, lest
we both waste ourselves fighting the truths between us. If I participate, knowingly or otherwise, in my sister's oppression and she calls
me on it, to answer her anger with my own only blankets the substance of our exchange with reaction. It wastes energy. And yes, it is
very difficult to stand still and to listen to another woman's voice

---

‡From "For Each of You," first published in *From A Land Where Other People Live*
(Broadside Press, Detroit, 1973), and collected in *Chosen Poems: Old and New* (W. W. Norton
and Company, New York, 1982), p. 42.

delineate an agony I do not share, or one to which I myself have contributed.

In this place we speak removed from the more blatant reminders of our embattlement as women. This need not blind us to the size and complexities of the forces mounting against us and all that is most human within our environment. We are not here as women examining racism in a political and social vacuum. We operate in the teeth of a system for which racism and sexism are primary, established, and necessary props of profit. Women responding to racism is a topic so dangerous that when the local media attempt to discredit this conference they choose to focus upon the provision of lesbian housing as a diversionary device—as if the Hartford *Courant* dare not mention the topic chosen for discussion here, racism, lest it become apparent that women are in fact attempting to examine and to alter all the repressive conditions of our lives.

Mainstream communication does not want women, particularly white women, responding to racism. It wants racism to be accepted as an immutable given in the fabric of your existence, like eveningtime or the common cold.

So we are working in a context of opposition and threat, the cause of which is certainly not the angers which lie between us, but rather that virulent hatred leveled against all women, people of Color, lesbians and gay men, poor people—against all of us who are seeking to examine the particulars of our lives as we resist our oppressions, moving toward coalition and effective action.

Any discussion among women about racism must include the recognition and the use of anger. This discussion must be direct and creative because it is crucial. We cannot allow our fear of anger to deflect us nor seduce us into settling for anything less than the hard work of excavating honesty; we must be quite serious about the choice of this topic and the angers entwined within it because, rest assured, our opponents are quite serious about their hatred of us and of what we are trying to do here.

And while we scrutinize the often painful face of each other's anger, please remember that it is not our anger which makes me caution you to lock your doors at night and not to wander the streets of Hartford alone. It is the hatred which lurks in those streets, that urge to destroy us all if we truly work for change rather than merely indulge in academic rhetoric.

This hatred and our anger are very different. Hatred is the fury of those who do not share our goals, and its object is death and destruction. Anger is a grief of distortions between peers, and its object is change. But our time is getting shorter. We have been raised to view any difference other than sex as a reason for destruction, and for Black women and white women to face each other's angers without denial or immobility or silence or guilt is in itself a heretical and generative idea. It implies peers meeting upon a common basis to examine difference, and to alter those distortions which history has created around our difference. For it is those distortions which separate us. And we must ask ourselves: Who profits from all this?

Women of Color in America have grown up within a symphony of anger, at being silenced, at being unchosen, at knowing that when we survive, it is in spite of a world that takes for granted our lack of humanness, and which hates our very existence outside of its service. And I say *symphony* rather than *cacophony* because we have had to learn to orchestrate those furies so that they do not tear us apart. We have had to learn to move through them and use them for strength and force and insight within our daily lives. Those of us who did not learn this difficult lesson did not survive. And part of my anger is always libation for my fallen sisters.

Anger is an appropriate reaction to racist attitudes, as is fury when the actions arising from those attitudes do not change. To those women here who fear the anger of women of Color more than their own unscrutinized racist attitudes, I ask: Is the anger of women of Color more threatening than the woman-hatred that tinges all aspects of our lives?

It is not the anger of other women that will destroy us but our refusals to stand still, to listen to its rhythms, to learn within it, to move beyond the manner of presentation to the substance, to tap that anger as an important source of empowerment.

I cannot hide my anger to spare you guilt, nor hurt feelings, nor answering anger; for to do so insults and trivializes all our efforts. Guilt is not a response to anger; it is a response to one's own actions or lack of action. If it leads to change then it can be useful, since it is then no longer guilt but the beginning of knowledge. Yet all too often, guilt is just another name for impotence, for defensiveness destructive of communication; it becomes a device to protect ignorance and the continuation of things the way they are, the ultimate protection for changelessness.

Most women have not developed tools for facing anger constructively. CR groups[§] in the past, largely white, dealt with how to express anger, usually at the world of men. And these groups were made up of white women who shared the terms of their oppressions. There was usually little attempt to articulate the genuine differences between women, such as those of race, color, age, class, and sexual

---

[§]"CR groups" are consciousness-raising groups.

identity. There was no apparent need at that time to examine the contradictions of self, woman as oppressor. There was work on expressing anger, but very little on anger directed against each other. No tools were developed to deal with other women's anger except to avoid it, deflect it, or flee from it under a blanket of guilt.

I have no creative use for guilt, yours or my own. Guilt is only another way of avoiding informed action, of buying time out of the pressing need to make clear choices, out of the approaching storm that can feed the earth as well as bend the trees. If I speak to you in anger, at least I have spoken to you: I have not put a gun to your head and shot you down in the street; I have not looked at your bleeding sister's body and asked, "What did she do to deserve it?" This was the reaction of two white women to Mary Church Terrell's telling of the lynching of a pregnant Black woman whose baby was then torn from her body. That was in 1921, and Alice Paul had just refused to publicly endorse the enforcement of the Nineteenth Amendment for all women—by refusing to endorse the inclusion of women of Color, although we had worked to help bring about that amendment.

The angers between women will not kill us if we can articulate them with precision, if we listen to the content of what is said with at least as much intensity as we defend ourselves against the manner of saying. When we turn from anger we turn from insight, saying we will accept only the designs already known, deadly and safely familiar. I have tried to learn my anger's usefulness to me, as well as its limitations.

For women raised to fear, too often anger threatens annihilation. In the male construct of brute force, we were taught that our lives depended upon the good will of patriarchal power. The anger of others was to be avoided at all costs because there was nothing to be learned from it but pain, a judgment that we had been bad girls, come up lacking, not done what we were supposed to do. And if we accept our powerlessness, then of course any anger can destroy us.

But the strength of women lies in recognizing differences between us as creative, and in standing to those distortions which we inherited without blame, but which are now ours to alter. The angers of women can transform difference through insight into power. For anger between peers births change, not destruction, and the discomfort and sense of loss it often causes is not fatal, but a sign of growth.

My response to racism is anger. That anger has eaten clefts into my living only when it remained unspoken, useless to anyone. It has also served me in classrooms without light or learning, where the work and history of Black women was less than a vapor. It has served me as fire in the ice zone of uncomprehending eyes of white women who see in my experience and the experience of my people only new reasons for fear or guilt. And my anger is no excuse for not dealing with your blindness, no reason to withdraw from the results of your own actions.

When women of Color speak out of the anger that laces so many of our contacts with white women, we are often told that we are "creating a mood of hopelessness," "preventing white women from getting past guilt," or "standing in the way of trusting communication and action." All these quotes come directly from letters to me from members of this organization within the last two years. One woman wrote, "Because you are Black and Lesbian, you seem to speak with the moral authority of suffering." Yes, I am Black and Lesbian, and what you hear in my voice is fury, not suffering. Anger, not moral authority. There is a difference.

To turn aside from the anger of Black women with excuses or the pretexts of intimidation is to award no one power—it is merely another way of preserving racial blindness, the power of unaddressed privilege, unbreached, intact. Guilt is only another form of objectification. Oppressed peoples are always being asked to stretch a little more, to bridge the gap between blindness and humanity. Black women are expected to use our anger only in the service of other people's salvation or learning. But that time is over. My anger has meant pain to me, but it has also meant survival, and before I give it up I'm going to be sure that there is something at least as powerful to replace it on the road to clarity.

What woman here is so enamoured of her own oppression that she cannot see her heelprint upon another woman's face? What woman's terms of oppression have become precious and necessary to her as a ticket into the fold of the righteous, away from the cold winds of self-scrutiny?

I am a lesbian woman of Color whose children eat regularly because I work in a university. If their full bellies make me fail to recognize my commonality with a woman of Color whose children do not eat because she cannot find work, or who has no children because her insides are rotted from home abortions and sterilization; if I fail to recognize the lesbian who chooses not to have children, the woman who remains closeted because her homophobic community is her only life support, the woman who chooses silence instead of another death, the woman who is terrified lest my anger trigger the explosion of hers; if I fail to recognize them as other faces of myself, then I am contributing not only to each of their oppressions but also to my own, and the anger which stands between us then must be used for clarity and mutual empowerment, not for evasion by guilt or for further separation. I am not free while any woman is unfree, even when her shackles are very different from my own. And I am not free as long as one person of Color remains chained. Nor is any one of you.

I speak here as a woman of Color who is not bent upon destruction, but upon survival. No woman is responsible for altering the psyche of her oppressor, even when that psyche is embodied in another woman. I have suckled the wolf's lip of anger and I have used it for illumination, laughter, protection, fire in places where there was no light, no food, no sisters, no quarter. We are not goddesses or matriarchs or edifices of divine forgiveness; we are not fiery fingers of judgment or instruments of flagellation; we are women forced back always upon our woman's power. We have learned to use anger as we have learned to use the dead flesh of animals, and bruised, battered, and changing, we have survived and grown and, in Angela Wilson's words, we *are* moving on. With or without uncolored women. We use whatever strengths we have fought for, including anger, to help define and fashion a world where all our sisters can grow, where our children can love, and where the power of touching and meeting another woman's difference and wonder will eventually transcend the need for destruction.

For it is not the anger of Black women which is dripping down over this globe like a diseased liquid. It is not my anger that launches rockets, spends over sixty thousand dollars a second on missiles and other agents of war and death, slaughters children in cities, stockpiles nerve gas and chemical bombs, sodomizes our daughters and our earth. It is not the anger of Black women which corrodes into blind, dehumanizing power, bent upon the annihilation of us all unless we meet it with what we have, our power to examine and to redefine the terms upon which we will live and work; our power to envision and to reconstruct, anger by painful anger, stone upon heavy stone, a future of pollinating difference and the earth to support our choices.

We welcome all women who can meet us, face to face, beyond objectification and beyond guilt.

A. B. Spellman

(1935–   )

A. B. SPELLMAN HAS CREATED a poetic style all his own. He allows his readers to relish the flavor of music and admire the beauty of art by integrating rhythm and imagery into his pieces. Full of life, Spellman's poetry is also personal and political in nature, relaying feelings and making statements about the times.

Spellman was born in Nixonton, North Carolina, in 1935, and grew up with his younger brother in Elizabeth City, North Carolina. His parents were both schoolteachers. He was strongly influenced by this academic background and by his father's painting hobby.

Spellman attended public schools, and went to Howard University in 1952. At Howard, Spellman began to read seriously and to write poetry, and joined an informal writing and support group that included classmates LeRoi Jones (Amiri Baraka) and dramatist Joseph Walker. He also studied under some of the best theatrical and literary personalities of the time, among them Owen Dodson and Sterling Brown. Spellman left Howard in 1958 with a bachelor's degree and credits towards both a master's and a law degree.

He went to New York City that same year. While there his first book of poetry, *The Beautiful Days* (1965), was published. In this collection he writes about love, sexuality, death, and other universal elements.

A year later he published *Four Lives in the Bebop Business* (1966), profiling the lives of jazz greats Herbie Nichols, Jackie McLean, Ornette Coleman, and Cecil Taylor. This book and his other writings on jazz have earned him recognition as one of the best jazz critics in the United States.

A former professor of poetry, black literature, and jazz, Spellman has taught at Atlanta University Center, Rutgers University, Emory University, and Harvard University. In the early 1960s he helped found *Umbra*, a tabloid paper based in New York that was a voice for such black writers as Langston Hughes and Ishmael Reed. In 1969 he founded the Atlanta Center for the Black Arts.

Spellman has conducted policy research for the National Endowment of Arts and Education and has served on a panel studying the arts with the Rockefeller Foundation. Currently, living in Washington, D.C., he works as director of funding for projects with the NEA Expansion Program, which targets minorities and rural people interested in the arts.

Spellman's poetry also appears in several anthologies, including Ansel

Hollo's *Negro Verse* (1964), Clarence Major's *The New Black Poetry* (1969), Dudley Randall's *The Black Poets* (1971), and Arnold Adoff's *The Poetry of Black America* (1972). For further reading see Carmen Subryan's essay in *Dictionary of Literary Biography, Volume 41,* Langston Hughes's *New Negro Poets* (1964) and Stephen Henderson's *Understanding the New Black Poetry* (1973).

"Did John's Music Kill Him?" is reprinted from Stephen Henderson's *Understanding the New Black Poetry.* "When Black People Are" is taken from Dudley Randall's *Black Poets.*

DID JOHN'S MUSIC KILL HIM?

in the morning part
of evening he would stand
before his crowd. the voice
would call his name &
redlight fell around him.
jimmy'd bow a quarter hour
till Mccoy fed block chords
to his stroke. elvin's thunder
roll & eric's scream. then john.

then john. *little old lady*
had a nasty mouth. *summertime*
when the war is. *africa* ululating
a line bunched up like itself
into knots paints beauty black.

trane's horn had words in it
i know when i sleep sober & dream
those dreams i duck in the world
of sun & shadow. yet even in the day john
& a little grass put them on me clear
as tomorrow in a glass enclosure.

kill me john my life eats
life. the thing that beats out of
me happens in a vat enclosed
& fermenting & wanting to explode
like your song.

Both poems are reprinted by permission of the author.

so beat john's death words down
on me in the darker part
of evening. the black light issued
from him in the pit he made
around us. worms came clear
to me where i thought i had been
brilliant. o john death will
not contain you death
will not contain you

WHEN BLACK PEOPLE ARE

when black people are
with each other
we sometimes fear ourselves
whisper over our shoulders
about unmentionable acts
& sometimes we fight & lie.
these are somethings we sometimes do.

& when alone i sometimes walk
from wall to wall fighting visions
of white men fighting me
& black men fighting white men
& fighting me & i lose my
self between walls &
ricocheting shots & can't say
for certain who i have killed
or been killed by.

it is the fear of winter passing
& summer coming & the killing
i have called for coming
to my door saying
hit it a.b., you're in it too.

& the white army moves like thieves
in the night mass producing beautiful
black corpses & then stealing them away
while my frequent death watches me
from orangeburg on cronkite &
i'm oiling my gun & cooking my food
& saying "when the time comes"

to myself, over & over, hopefully.
but i remember driving from atlanta
to the city with stone & featherstone
& cleve & on the way feather talked
about ambushing a pair of klansmen
& cleve told how they hunted
chaney's body in the white night
of the haunted house in the Mississippi
swamp while a runaway survivor
from orangeburg slept between wars
on the back seat.
times like this
are times when black people
are with each other & the strength flows
back & forth between us like
borrowed breath.

Etheridge Knight

(1931–1991)

CONCRETE IMAGES, erratic punctuation, and alternating expressions of love and fear in Etheridge Knight's poetry correspond to the ebb and flow of his own emotional experiences: his ups and downs in marriage, in prison, and with drugs and alcohol. Publishing his first book of poetry, *Poems from Prison* (1968), while still an inmate in Indiana State Prison, Knight stresses the importance of consciousness among black people.

Knight was born in Corinth, Mississippi, in 1931, but grew up in Paducah, Kentucky, with four sisters and two brothers. Quitting school in the eighth grade, he turned to drugs and the seedy side of life after running away from home. He enlisted in the army at age seventeen and served active duty in Korea. During the following years, until 1951, Knight was a medical technician. Still hooked on drugs, he committed a robbery to support his habit. He went to jail in 1960, serving an indeterminate sentence of ten to twenty-five years. In 1963 Knight began to write and to submit his poetry for publication. In 1968 he was granted parole. Knight died in March 1991.

While in prison, Knight corresponded with poets such as Gwendolyn Brooks, Dudley Randall, and Sonia Sanchez, whom he married after his release. This marriage, however, disintegrated, as did his next one, to Mary Ann McAnally. He married a third time to Charlene Blackburn, to whom he dedicated the poem "The Stretching of the Belly," in *Born of a Woman: New and Selected Poems* (1980).

Knight is best known for his "toasts," long narrative poems with rhyming couplets, usually told by men to one another, and for his "belly songs." Writing in the black oral tradition, he incorporates the blues into many of his later poems.

From 1969 to 1972, Knight served as writer-in-residence at the University of Pittsburgh, the University of Hartford, and Lincoln University (Jefferson City, Missouri), respectively. He received several awards, honors, and grants including a Guggenheim Fellowship in 1974. He also served as an editor of poetry for *Motive* magazine. Among his works are *Belly Song and Other Poems* (1973), his third book of published poetry, and the more recent *The Essential Etheridge Knight* (1986).

For further reading, see Shirley Lumpkin's article in *Dictionary of Literary Biography, Volume 41*; H. Bruce Franklin's "The Literature of the American Prison," *Massachusetts Review* 18 (1977); Patrice Liggins

Hill's "Blues for a Mississippi Black Boy: Etheridge Knight's Craft in the Black Oral Tradition," *Mississippi Quarterly* 36 (Winter 1982–1983); Hill's "The New Black Aesthetic as Counterpoetics: The Poetry of Etheridge Knight," Ph.D. dissertation, Stanford University, 1977; Ken McCullough's "Communication and Excommunication: An Interview with Etheridge Knight," *Callaloo* 5 (February–May 1982); and Howard Nelson's "Belly Songs: The Poetry of Etheridge Knight," *Hollins Critic* 18 (December 1981).

The poems that follow are taken from *The Essential Etheridge Knight*.

BELLY SONG

(for the Daytop Family)

"You have made something
Out of the sea that blew
And rolled you on its salt bitter lips.
It nearly swallowed you.
But I hear
You are tough and harder to swallow than most . . ."

—S. Mansfield

1

And I   and I / must admit
that the sea in you
   has sung / to the sea / in me
and I   and I / must admit
that the sea in me
   has fallen / in love
   with the sea in you
because you have made something
out of the sea
   that nearly swallowed you

And this poem
This poem
This poem / I give / to you.
This poem is a song / I sing / I sing / to you

from the bottom
  of the sea
    in my belly

This poem
This poem
This poem / is a song / about FEELINGS
about the Bone of feeling
about the Stone of feeling
  And the Feather of feeling

2

This poem
This poem
This poem / is /
a death / chant
and a grave / stone
and a prayer for the dead:
  for young Jackie Robinson.
a moving Blk / warrior who walked
among us
  with a wide / stride—and heavy heels
moving   moving   moving
thru the blood and mud and shit of Vietnam
moving   moving   moving
thru the blood and mud and dope of America
  for Jackie / who was /

a song
and a stone
and a Feather of feeling
  now dead
and / gone / in this month of love

This poem
This poem / is / a silver feather
and the sun-gold / glinting / green hills
  breathing
river flowing—for Sheryl and David—and
their first / kiss by the river—for Mark and Sue
and a Sunday walk on her grand / father's farm
for Sammy and Marion—love rhythms
for Michael and Jean—love rhythms
love / rhythms—love rhythms—and LIFE.

3

This poem
This poem
This poem
This poem / is / for ME—for me
and the days / that lay / in the back / of my
   mind
when the sea / rose up /
   to swallow me
and the streets I walked
   were lonely streets
   were stone / cold streets

This poem
This poem / is /
for me / and the nights
   when I
wrapped my feelings
   in a sheet of ice
and stared
   at the stars
      thru iron bars
         and cried
in the middle of my eyes . . .

This poem
This poem
This poem / is / for me
   and my woman
   and the yesterdays
when she opened
   to me like a flower
but I fell on her
   like a stone
I fell on her like a stone . . .

4

And now—in my 40th year
   I have come here
to this House of Feelings
to this Singing Sea
and I   and I / must admit
that the sea in me
   has fallen / in love

with the sea in you
because the sea
that now sings / in you
　is the same sea
that nearly swallowed you—
　and me too.

Seymour, Connecticut
June 1971

ILU, THE TALKING DRUM

The deadness was threatening us—15 Nigerians and 1
　Mississippi nigger.
It hung heavily, like stones around our necks, pulling us down
to the ground, black arms and legs outflung
on the wide green lawn of the big white house
The deadness was threatening us, the day
was dying with the sun, the stillness—
unlike the sweet silence after love / making or
the pulsating quietness of a summer night—
the stillness was skinny and brittle and wrinkled
by the precise people sitting on the wide white porch
of the big white house . . .
The darkness was threatening us, menacing . . .
we twisted, turned, shifted positions, picked our noses,
stared at our bare toes, hissed air thru our teeth . . .
Then Tunji, green robes flowing as he rose,
strapped on Ilu, the talking drum,
and began:

kah doom / kah doom-doom / kah doom / kah doom-doom-doom
kah doom / kah doom-doom / kah doom / kah doom-doom-doom
kah doom / kah doom-doom / kah doom / kah doom-doom-doom
kah doom / kah doom-doom / kah doom / kah doom-doom-doom

the heart, the heart beats, the heart, the heart beats slow
the heart beats slowly, the heart beats
the blood flows slowly, the blood flows
the blood, the blood flows, the blood, the blood flows slow
kah doom / kah doom-doom / kah doom / kah doom-doom-doom
and the day opened to the sound

kah doom / kah doom-doom / kah doom / kah doom-doom-doom

and our feet moved to the sound of life
kah doom / kah doom-doom / kah doom / kah doom-doom-doom
and we rode the rhythms as one
from Nigeria to Mississippi
and back
kah doom / kah doom-doom / kah doom / kah doom-doom-doom

Larry Neal

(1937–1981)

LARRY NEAL was one of the central figures of the Black Arts Movement, helping to form and articulate the movement's concerns. His own life served to show how its ideologies could translate into committed action for the sake of black culture. His untimely death of a heart attack in 1981 took from the black community a source of tremendous dynamism and vision, but his contributions to the growth of the black aesthetic endure in his written work and in his influence on the development of such figures as Amiri Baraka, Ishmael Reed, Stanley Crouch, and others with whom he shared close friendships.

Neal was born in 1937 in Atlanta, Georgia, and grew up with his parents and four brothers in Philadelphia, Pennsylvania. In 1961 he graduated from Lincoln University (Pennsylvania), with majors in English literature and history. He received the M.A. from the University of Pennsylvania in 1963, and in 1964 he moved to New York City. His lifelong friendship with Baraka (then LeRoi Jones) dates from this point.

In New York, Neal worked in publishing and wrote on a freelance basis for *Liberator* magazine. His work for *Liberator* exposed him to the major cultural events of the mid-1960s and brought him into contact with writers, artists, and musicians who were rising to prominence in the Black Arts movement at that time. Together with Baraka, Neal became a principal figure in a group that was to become the Black Arts Repertory Theatre in Harlem in 1964. During this period Neal was also engaged in strenuous civil rights activities and was once shot by an individual who disagreed with his politics.

In 1968 Neal co-edited *Black Fire* with Baraka. This book, subtitled *An Anthology of Afro-American Writing*, stands as the seminal anthology of that period, containing as it does works by such major figures as Sonia Sanchez, Stokely Carmichael, and Harold Cruse, among many others. Over the next few years Neal published two books of his own poetry, *Black Boogaloo* (1969) and *Hoodoo Hollerin' Bebop Ghosts* (1971). He also wrote two plays, *The Glorious Monster in the Bell of the Horn* and *In an Upstate Motel*. The former was read in 1976 at Frank Silvera's Writers' Workshop at the Harlem Cultural Council. "New Space: Critical Essays on American Culture" was being prepared for publication when Neal died. *Visions of a Liberated Future* (1989), a collection of Neal's poetry and prose, was published eight years after his death.

Neal held a number of executive and consulting positions from 1976 until his death in 1981. He was the executive director of the Commission on the Arts and Humanities in Washington, D.C., and Andrew W. Mellon Humanist in Residence at Howard University until 1979; later he served as consultant to the Elma Louis School of Arts in Roxbury, Massachusetts, to the Teacher and Writers' Collective of Columbia University, to the American Academy of Dramatic Arts, and to the Gordy Foundation. He also held teaching positions at the City College of New York (1968–1969) and Yale University (1970–1975) and was writer-in-residence at Wesleyan University (1969–1970). He gave readings and lectures at the University of Pennsylvania, New York University, and a host of other institutions.

For further reading, see C. W. E. Bigsby's *The Black American Writer* (1969); *Dictionary of Literary Biography, Volume 38*; and Larry Neal and LeRoi Jones's *Black Fire: An Anthology of Afro-American Writing* (1968).

"The Life: Hoodoo Hollerin' Bebop Ghosts," "Riffin in the Chili House," and "Harlem Gallery" are all taken from *Hoodoo Hollerin' Bebop Ghosts*.

THE LIFE
Hoodoo Hollerin' Bebop Ghosts

We walked the bar
    the neon world of hip players judged us in the after-
      hours
    spot where they busted Booney, and where Leroy was
    blasted in the chest, in the john where we snort
    coke from tips of Broadway polished switchblades,
    talking shit, high on the ego trips.

The fly world in action
    our bitches turning Seventh Avenue tricks;
    whipping her pussy with the coat hanger,
    and saying: stop jiving bitch, get me
    the motherfuckin money now.

We walked the bar
    trying to get it together—
    ghosts of men, but men just the same.
    Yeah . . . this world judging us
    marking our progress from cradle
    to cane, laughing, wishing us luck

All poems are reprinted by permission of Mrs. Evelyn Neal.

while we hover over pits of dry bones
laughing like forgotten pimps—we so hip.

It's all here
all down here in the neon world of flash
and-let-me-fuck-you bullshit.

Even in our weakness here, somewhere we are strong
some snake skinned god hisses here:
hoodoo hollerin' bebop ghosts
some eternal demon squirming
in his head—that's why he be bad
and all them things.

Some of us
teetered on the edge of the Life like peeping
toms; teetered maneuvering for the grand score
that came every night, but every night, came late.
dope pushers
take-off goons
Murphy-working old ladies
one used to dance in the high yaller chorus
of the Cotton Club;
one, a nympho, claimed once to have graduated
from Vassar. (If you can dig it?)
Scenes like that were quite common.

One, a singer, a Chanel No. 5 freak from South Philly
called herself the Duchess, spoke with an English accent.
Lois
the envious one, skinny, frail hunk of bones
and cigarette holder, wraps spider legs around dull
honky sailors; likes going down on Market Street
cowboys.
Up under it all
some ancient memory trying to break through the
perpetual high:
He be hoodoo hollerin' bebop ghosts
some awesome demon twisting close
curling in the smell of beer
and reefer; some dick strong god
hissing softly in his ear
Hey!

And he is mean with his nigger rod
thus note the smell of sen-sen on his breath
but dig how he teeters on the edge of death . . .

Spring, 1969

RIFFIN IN THE CHILI HOUSE

In Memory of Bird

Rim shot, the blue benny hug,
the memories, the hug, chugging
and riffin in the chili house.
I run chords
needing the space
that only the horn provides;
riffin Seventh Avenue blues, the Kansas City
four/four, the women, striding, digging the cool murmur
of morning
a sledgehammer of meaning
balled in sound
slams against the back of my head.

I churn mad
I churn bright bopping colors
I unwind: hoodoo hollering bebop ghosts
blood guts screaming.
I listen for the voice beyond the primary voice
of the horn
I spin cosmic tales
I conjure and work juju with sound.
I knotted deep inside the rocking hull of slaveship
I the castrated darkness
I whisper across seabones and lynched flowers;
there are mysteries and ancestral movements here.
I am the subject of someone's magic;
night sweats
in the steady blow, horns haunt me
the ram of fear tramples me;
I probe, demon touched.
I probe in fear
guts in soul splattering space
flesh explodes

eyes roll
heads roll
meat screams
shit!
fuck it!
shit! meat screams
fuck it!
HOLD ON I'M COMING!!!

Herbie's Coda

The soul in the coil of the ring of the Midnight
Prophets sing for the gods of the Kushites and
the Dahomenians. Sings for the chains, the lynched
flowers and the eternal vision.

HARLEM GALLERY: FROM THE INSIDE

For Melvin Tolson

The bars on Eighth Avenue in Harlem
glow real yellow, hard against formica
tables. They speak of wandering ghosts
and Harlem saints; the words lay slick
on greasy floors: rain-wet butt in the junkie's
mouth, damp notebook in the number runner's hand.
no heads turn as the deal goes down—we wait.

Harlem rain explodes, flooding the avenues
rats float up out of the sewers.
Do we need the Miracles or a miracle?

Listen baby, to the mean scar-faced sister,
between you and her and me and you there are no
distances. short reach of the .38, a sudden
migraine hammering where your brains used to be;
then it's over, no distance between the needle
and the rope, instant time, my man, history as
one quick fuck.

Uptight against these sounds, but everything ain't
all right, the would-be

warriors of the nitty-gritty snap fingers,
ghosts boogaloo against this haze
Malcolm eyes in the yellow glow;
blood on black hands,
compacted rooms of gloom;
Garvey's flesh in the rat's teeth
Lady Day at 100 Centre Street
Charlie Parker dead in the penthouse
of an aristocratic bitch.
Carlos Cook
Ras
Shine and Langston
the Barefoot Prophet
Ira Kemp
the Signifying Monkey
Bud Powell
Trane
Prez
Chano Pozo
Eloise Moore—all
falling faces in the Harlem rain
asphalt memory of blood and pain.

                              Spring, 1966

Ed Bullins

(1935–   )

ED BULLINS is a remarkably prolific dramatist whose more than fifty plays have been produced in prominent New York theaters since the late 1960s. Playwright-in-residence and associate director of the New Lafayette Theatre, which was the most influential force in the black theater during the Black Arts movement, Bullins helped to shape the precepts of black drama from its emergence in the 1960s. He continues to be one of America's important playwrights.

Bullins was born in 1935 and grew up in a north Philadelphia ghetto. In 1952 he joined the navy, and in 1955 he returned to Philadelphia and attended night school. In 1958 he moved to Los Angeles and enrolled in Los Angeles City College. Although he did not do well in his classes there, he began to read extensively and to write poetry and short stories. His time in college contrasted sharply with his earlier years spent on the streets, a time that he has described as "life in the jungle." Although those years were to form the core of his plays' themes, in Los Angeles he came in contact with blacks who were committed to the study and promotion of black culture and arts. In this environment, he received encouragement and support for his artistic pursuits.

Bullins began writing plays in 1964 when he moved to San Francisco and took creative writing classes at San Francisco State College. By 1965 he had completed his first three: *How Do You Do?*, *Dialect Determinism (or The Rally)*, and *Clara's Ole Man*. He produced these plays himself in bars and coffeehouses, until in 1967 he received an invitation from Robert Macbeth, a young black director in New York, to join the newly formed New Lafayette Theater in Harlem. Bullins moved to New York, and in 1968 the company staged a triple-bill production of his plays called collectively *The Electronic Nigger*, which won the Vernon Rice Drama Desk Award that year.

New Lafayette Theater continued to produce many of Bullins's plays until the company folded in 1972 for lack of funds. Among the most notable of these were his first full-length plays, *In the Wine Time* and *Goin' a Buffalo* (both produced in 1968), *The Duplex* (produced in 1970), and *The Fabulous Miss Marie* (produced in 1971). The wide exposure Bullins's work gained from these performances brought him offers from a number of important New York theaters to produce his work, including La Mama Experimental Theater Club, American Place Theatre, and Lincoln Center.

In all, no fewer than twenty-five of his plays were produced by professional companies in New York between 1968 and 1980.

Among the many awards that Bullins has received are the Black Arts Alliance Award (1971) for *In New England Winter*, an Obie (1971) for *The Fabulous Miss Marie*, and the New York Drama Critics' Circle Award (1975) for *The Taking of Miss Janie*. He has also been the recipient of an American Place Theatre grant (1967), Guggenheim fellowships (1971 and 1976), Rockefeller Foundation grants (1968, 1970, and 1972), and a Creative Artists' Public Service Program Award (1973). Columbia College in Chicago bestowed an honorary Doctor of Letters on him in 1976.

Bullins has lectured and taught at various colleges around the country. He has also been playwright-in-residence at the American Place Theatre and a staff member for the New York Shakespeare Festival. Since 1983 he has been living in the San Francisco area, where he teaches and continues work on a long-term theater project called Twentieth-Century Cycle.

For further reading about Bullins's work, see the essay by Leslie Sanders in *Dictionary of Literary Biography, Volume 38*. Also see Jervis Anderson, "Profiles—Dramatist," *New Yorker* 49 (16 June 1973); W. D. E. Andrews, "Theatre of Black Reality: The Blues Drama of Ed Bullins," *Southwest Review* 65 (Spring 1980); Genevieve Fabre, *Drumbeats, Masks, and Metaphor: Contemporary Afro-American Theatre*, translated by Melvin Dixon (Cambridge: Harvard University Press, 1983); and Robert L. Tener, "Pandora's Box— A Study of Ed Bullins's Dramas," *CLA Journal* 19 (June 1976).

Clara's Ole Man is taken from *Five Plays by Ed Bullins*.

CLARA'S OLE MAN

Clara's Ole Man was first performed at the Firehouse Repertory Theatre in San Francisco on August 5, 1965. It was produced by the San Francisco Drama Circle and directed by Robert Hartman. The sets were designed by Louie Gelwicks and Peter Rounds. Lighting by Verne Shreve. In winter, 1968, it was done, along with two other of Mr. Bullins's plays, at the American Place Theatre in New York, and in the Spring the production continued running at the Martinique.

THE PEOPLE

CLARA, *a light brown girl of 18 well-built with long, dark hair. A blond streak runs down the middle of her head, and she affects a pony tail. She is pensive, slow in speech but feline. Her eyes are heavy-lidded and brown; she smiles—rather, blushes—often.*

BIG GIRL, *a stocky woman wearing jeans and tennis shoes and a tight fitting blouse which accents her prominent breasts. She is of an indeterminable age, due partly to her lack of makeup and plain hair style. She is anywhere from 25 to 40, and is loud and jolly, frequently breaking out in laughter from her own jokes.*

JACK, *20 years old, wears a corduroy Ivy League suit and vest. At first, JACK's speech is modulated and too eloquent for the surroundings but as he drinks his words become slurred and mumbled.*

BABY GIRL, BIG GIRL's *mentally retarded teenaged sister. The girl has the same hairdo as CLARA. Her face is made up with mascara, eye shadow, and she has black arching eyebrows penciled darkly, the same as CLARA.*

MISS FAMIE, *a drunken neighbor.*

STOOGIE, *a local street-fighter and gang leader. His hair is processed.*

BAMA, *one of STOOGIE's boys.*

HOSS, *another of STOOGIE's boys.*

C.C., *a young wino.*

TIME   *Early spring, the mid-1950's.*

SCENE   *A slum kitchen on a rainy afternoon in South Philadelphia. The room is very clean, wax glosses the linoleum and old wooden furni-*

*ture; a cheap but clean red checkered oil cloth covers the table. If
the room could speak it would say, "I'm cheap but clean."*
   *A cheap AM radio plays rhythm 'n blues music throughout the
play. The furniture is made up of a wide kitchen table where a gallon jug of red wine sits. Also upon the table is an oatmeal box, cups,
mugs, plates and spoons, ashtrays and packs of cigarettes. Four
chairs circle the table, and two sit against the wall back-stage. An
old fashioned wood and coal burning stove takes up a corner of the
room and a gas range of 1935 vintage is backstage next to the door
to the yard. A large, smoking frying pan is on one of the burners.*
JACK *and* BIG GIRL *are seated at opposite ends of the table;* CLARA *stands
at the stove fanning the fumes toward the door.* BABY GIRL *plays
upon the floor with a homemade toy.*

CLARA, *fans fumes* Uummm uummm . . . well, there goes the lunch.
   I wonder how I was dumb enough to burn the bacon?
BIG GIRL Just comes natural with you, honey, all looks and no
   brains . . . now with me and my looks, anybody in South Philly
   can tell I'm a person that naturally takes care of business . . . hee
   hee . . . ain't that right, Clara?
CLARA Awww girl, go on. You's the worst messer-upper I knows.
   You didn't even go to work this morn'. What kind of business is
   that?
BIG GIRL It's all part of my master plan, baby. Don't you worry none
   . . . Big Girl knows what she's doin'. You better believe that!
CLARA Yeah, you may know what you're doin' but I'm the one
   who's got to call in for you and lie that you're sick.
BIG GIRL Well, it ain't a lie. You know I got this cough and stopped
   up feeling. *Looking at* JACK. You believe that, don't you, young
   blood?
JACK Most certainly. You could very well have a respiratory condition and also have all the appearances of a extremely capable person.

BIG GIRL, *slapping table* HEE HEE ... SEE CLARA? ... SEE? Listen ta that, Clara. I told you anybody could tell it. Even ole hot lips here can tell.

CLARA, *pours out grease and wipes stove* Awww ... he just says that to be nice ... he's always sayin' things like that.

BIG GIRL Is that how he talked when he met you the other day out to your aunt's house?

CLARA, *hesitating* Nawh ... nawh he didn't talk like that.

BIG GIRL Well, how did he talk, huh?

CLARA Awww ... Big Girl. I don't know.

BIG GIRL Well, who else does? You know what kind of a line a guy gives ya. You been pitched at enough times, haven't ya? By the looks of him I bet he gave ya the ole smooth college boy approach ... *To* JACK. C'mon, man, drink up. We got a whole lot mo' ta kill. Don't you know this is my day off and I'm celebratin'?

JACK, *takes a drink* Thanks ... this is certainly nice of you to go to all this trouble for me. I never expected it.

BIG GIRL What did you expect, young blood?

JACK, *takes another sip* Ohhh, well ... I ...

CLARA, *to* BABY GIRL *on floor* Don't put that dirty thing in your mouf, gal! *She walks around the table to* BABY GIRL *and tugs her arm.* Now, keep that out of your mouf!

BABY GIRL, *holds to toy sullenly* NO!

CLARA You keep quiet, you hear, gal!

BABY GIRL NO!

CLARA If you keep tellin' me no I'm goin' ta take you upstairs ta Aunt Toohey.

BABY GIRL, *throws back head and drums feet on floor* NO! NO! SHIT! DAMN! NO! SHIT!

CLARA, *disturbed* NOW STOP THAT! We got company.

BIG GIRL, *laughs hard and leans elbows upon table* HAW HAW HAW ... I guess she told you, Clara. Hee hee ... that little dirty mouf bitch, *pointing to* BABY GIRL *and becoming choked* ... that little ... cough cough ... hooeee boy!

CLARA You shouldn't have taught her all them nasty words, Big Girl. Now we can't do anything with her. *Turns to* JACK. What do you think of that?

JACK Yes, it does seem a problem. But with proper guidance she'll more than likely be conditioned out of it when she gets into a learning situation among her peer group.

BIG GIRL, *takes a drink and scowls* BULLSHIT!

CLARA Aww ... B. G.

JACK I beg your pardon, Miss?

BIG GIRL   I said bullshit! Whatta ya mean with proper guidance . . .
points. I taught that little bitch myself . . . the best cuss words I
know before she ever climbed out of her crib . . . whatta ya mean
when she gets among her "peer" group?
JACK   I didn't exactly say that. I said when . . .
BIG GIRL, *cuts him off*   Don't tell me what you said, boy. I got ears. I
know all them big horseshit doctor words . . . tell him, Clara . . .
tell him what I do. Where do I work. Clara?
CLARA   Awww . . . B.G., please.
BIG GIRL   Do like I say! Do like Big wants you to!
CLARA, *surrenders*   She works out at the state nut farm.
BIG GIRL, *triumphant*   And tell mister smart and proper what I do.
CLARA, *automatically*   She's a technician.
JACK   Oh, that's nice. I didn't mean to suggest there was anything
wrong with how you raised your sister.
BIG GIRL, *jolly again*   Haw haw haw . . . Nawh, ya didn't. I know you
didn't even know what you were sayin', young blood. Do you
know why I taught her to cuss?
JACK   Why no, I have no idea. Why did you?
BIG GIRL   Well, it was to give her freedom, ya know?
    JACK   *shakes his head.*
Ya see, workin' in the hospital with all the nuts and fruits and
crazies and weirdos I get ideas 'bout things. I saw how when they
get these kids in who have cracked up and even with older people who come in out of their skulls they all mostly cuss. Mostly
all of them, all the time they out of their heads, they cuss all the
time and do other wild things, and boy do some of them really
get into it and let out all of that filthy shit that's been stored up
all them years. But when the docs start shockin' them puttin'
them on insulin they quiets down, that's when the docs think
they're gettin' better, but really they ain't. They're just learn'n like
before to hold it in . . . just like before, that's one reason most of
them come back or are always on the verge afterwards of goin'
psycho again.
JACK, *enthusiastic*   Wow, I never thought of that! That ritual action
of purging and catharsis can open up new avenues in therapy
and in learning theory and conditioning subjects . . .
BIG GIRL   Saaay whaaa . . . ? What did you have for breakfast, man?
CLARA, *struck*   That sounds so wonderful . . .
JACK, *still excited*   But I agree with you. You have an intuitive grasp
of very abstract concepts!
BIG GIRL, *beaming*   Yeah, yeah . . . I got a lot of it figured out . . . *To*
JACK. Here, fill up your glass again, man.
JACK, *to* CLARA.   Aren't you drinking with us?

CLARA   Later. Big Girl doesn't allow me to start in drinking too
early.

JACK, *confused*   She doesn't?

BIG GIRL, *cuts in*   Well, in Baby Girl's case I said to myself that I'm
teach'n her how in front and lettin' her use what she knows
whenever it builds up inside. And it's really good for her, gives
her spirit and everything.

CLARA   That's what probably warped her brain.

BIG GIRL   Hush up! You knows it was dat fuckin' disease. All the
doctors said so.

CLARA   You don't believe no doctors 'bout nothin' else!

BIG GIRL, *glares at* CLARA   Are you showin' out, Clara? Are you
showin' out to your little boy friend?

CLARA   He ain't mah boy friend.

JACK, *interrupts*   How do you know she might not have spirit if she
wasn't allowed to curse?

BIG GIRL, *sullen*   I don't know anything, young blood. But I can take
a look at myself and see the two of us. Look at me! *Stares at*
JACK. LOOK AT ME!

JACK   Yes, yes, I'm looking.

BIG GIRL   Well, what do you see?

CLARA   B. G. . . . PLEASE!

BIG GIRL, *ignores*   Well, what do you see?

JACK, *worried*   Well, I don't really know . . . I . . .

BIG GIRL   Well, let me tell you what you see. You see a fat bitch
who's 20 pounds overweight and looks ten years older than she
is. You want to know how I got this way and been this way most
of my life and would be worse off if I didn't let off some steam
drinkin' this rotgut and speakin' my mind?

JACK, *to* BIG GIRL *who doesn't listen but drinks*   Yes, I would like to
hear.

CLARA *finishes the stove and takes seat between the two.* BABY
GIRL *goes to the yard door but does not go out into the rain; she
sits down and looks out through the door at an angle.*

BIG GIRL   Ya see, when I was a little runt of a kid my mother found
out she couldn't keep me or Baby Girl any longer cause she had
T.B., so I got shipped out somewheres and Baby Girl got shipped
out somewheres else. People that Baby Girl went to exposed her
to the disease. She was lucky, I ended up with some fuckin'
Christians . . .

CLARA   Ohhh, B. G., you shouldn't say that!

BIG GIRL   Well, I sho as hell just did! . . . Damned kristers! I spent
12 years with those people, can you imagine? A dozen years in
hell. Christians . . . HAAA . . . always preachin' 'bout some

heaven over yonder and building a bigger hell here den any devil have imagination for.

CLARA You shouldn't go round sayin' things like dat.

BIG GIRL I shouldn't! Well what did you Christian mammy and pot-gutted pappy teach you? When I met you you didn't even know how to take a douche.

CLARA YOU GOT NO RIGHT!!! *She momentarily rises as if she's going to launch herself on* BIG GIRL.

BIG GIRL, *condescending* Awww . . . forget it, sweetie . . . don't make no never mind, but you remember how you us'ta smell when you got ready fo bed . . . like a dead hoss or a baby skunk . . . *To* JACK, *explaining* That damned Christian mamma and pappa of hers didn't tell her a thing 'bout herself . . . ha ha ha . . . thought if she ever found out her little thing was used fo anything else 'cept squattin' she'd fall backwards right up in it . . . ZaaaBOOM . . . STRAIGHT TA HELL . . . ha ha . . . didn't know that lil Clara had already found her heaven and on the same trail.

CLARA, *ashamed* Sometimes . . . sometimes . . . I just want to die for bein' here.

BIG GIRL, *enjoying herself* Ha ha ha . . . that wouldn't do no good. Would it? Just remember what shape you were in when I met you, kid. Ha ha ha. *To* JACK. Hey boy, can you imagine this pretty little trick here had her stomach seven months in the wind, waitin' on a dead baby who died from the same disease that Baby Girl had . . .

CLARA He didn't have any nasty disease like Baby Girl!

BABY GIRL, *hears her name but looks out door* NO! NO! SHIT! DAMN! SHIT! SHIT!

BIG GIRL HAW HAW HAW . . . now we got her started . . .
    She laughs for over a minute; JACK *waits patiently, sipping;*
    CLARA *is grim.* BABY GIRL *has quieted.*

BIG GIRL She . . . she . . . ha ha . . . was walkin' round with a dead baby in her and had no place to go.

CLARA, *fills a glass* I just can't understand you, B. G. You know my baby died after he was born. Somedays you just get besides yourself.

BIG GIRL I'm only helpin' ya entertain your guest.

CLARA Awww . . . B. G. It wasn't his fault. I invited him.

JACK, *dismayed* Well, I asked really. If there's anything wrong I can go.

BIG GIRL Take it easy, young blood. I'm just havin' a little fun. Now let's get back to the Clara Saga . . . ya hear that word, junior? . . . S-A-G-A, SUCKER! You college boys don't know it all. Yeah, her folks had kicked her out and the little punk she was big for what had tried to put her out on the block and when that didn't work

out . . . *mocking and making pretended blushes* . . . because our
sweet little thing here was sooo modest and sedate . . . the nigger
split! . . . HAW HAW HAW . . . HE MADE IT TO NEW YORK!
She goes into a laughing, choking and crying fit. BABY GIRL
rushes over to her and on tip toes pats her back.

BABY GIRL Big Girl! Big Girl! Big Girl! *A knocking sounds and*
CLARA *exits to answer the door.*

BIG GIRL, *catches her breath* Whatcha want, little sister?

BABY GIRL The cat. The cat. Cat got kittens. Cat got kittens.

BIG GIRL, *still coughing and choking* Awww, go on. You know there
ain't no cat under there with no kittens. *To* JACK. She's been
makin' that story up for two months now about how some cat
crawls up under the steps and has kittens. She can't fool me
none. She just wants a cat but I ain't gonna get none.

JACK Why not, cats aren't so bad. My mother has one and he's quite
a pleasure to her.

BIG GIRL For your mammy maybe, but all they mean round here . . .
singsong . . . is fleas and mo mouths to feed. With an invalid
aunt upstairs we don't need anymo expenses.

JACK, *gestures toward* BABY GIRL It shows that she has a very vivid
imagination to make up that story about the kittens.

BIG GIRL Yeah, her big sister ain't the biggest liar in the family.
CLARA *returns with* MISS FAMIE *staggering behind her, a thin*
middle-aged woman in long seamen's raincoat, dripping wet,
and wearing house slippers that are soaked and squish water
about the kitchen floor.

BIG GIRL Hi, Miss Famie. I see you're dressed in your rainy glad rags
today.

MISS FAMIE, *slurred speech of the drunk* Hello, B. G. Yeah, I couldn't
pass up seein' Aunt Toohey, so I put on my weather coat. You
know that don't a day pass that I don't stop up to see her.

BIG GIRL Yeah, I know, Miss Famie. Every day you go up there with
that quart of gin under your dress and you two ole lushes put it
away.

MISS FAMIE Why, B. G. You should know better than that.

CLARA, *re-seated* B. G., you shouldn't say that . . .

BIG GIRL Why shouldn't I? I'm paying' for over half of that juice and
I don't git to see none of it 'cept the empty bottles.

BABY GIRL CAT! CAT! CAT!

MISS FAMIE Oh, the baby still sees them there cats.

CLARA You should be ashamed to talk to Miss Famie like that.

BIG GIRL, *to* JACK Why you so quiet? Can't you speak to folks when
they come in?

JACK I'm sorry. *To* MISS FAMIE Hello, mam.

MISS FAMIE   Why howdie, son.

CLARA   Would you like a glass of wine, Miss Famie?

MISS FAMIE   Don't mind if I do, sister.

BIG GIRL   Better watch it, Miss Famie. Wine and gin will rust your gizzard.

CLARA   Ohh . . . *pours a glass of wine* . . . Here, Miss Famie.

BABY GIRL   CAT! CAT!

BIG GIRL, *singsong, lifting her glass*   Mus' I tell' . . . muscatel . . . jitterbug champagne. *Reminisces.* Remember, Clara, the first time I got you to take a drink? *To* MISS FAMIE. You should of seen her. Some of this same cheap rotgut here. She'd never had a drink before but she wanted to show me how game she was. She was a bright little smart thing, just out of high school and didn't know her butt from a door nob.

MISS FAMIE   Yes, indeed, that was Clara all right.

BIG GIRL   She drank three water glasses down and got so damned sick I had to put my finger down her throat and make her heave it up . . . HAW HAW . . . babbled her fool head off all night . . . said she'd be my friend always . . . that we'd always be together . . .

MISS FAMIE, *gulps down her drink*   Wine will make you do that the first time you get good'n high on it.

JACK, *takes drink*   I don't know. You know . . . I've never really been wasted and I've been drinkin' for quite some time now.

BIG GIRL   Quite some time, huh? Six months?

JACK   Nawh. My mother used to let me drink at home. I've been drinkin' since 15. And I drank all the time I was in the service.

BIG GIRL   Just because you been slippin' some drinks out of ya mammy's bottle and you slipped a few under ya belt with the punks in the barracks don't make ya a drinker, boy!

CLARA   B. G. . . . do you have to?

   MISS FAMIE *finishes her second drink as* BIG GIRL *and* CLARA *stare at each other.*

MISS FAMIE   Well, I guess I better get up and see Aunt Toohey. *She leaves.*

JACK   Nice to have met you, mam.

MISS FAMIE   Well, good-bye, son.

BIG GIRL, *before* MISS FAMIE *reaches top of stairs*   That ole gin-head tracked water all over your floor, Clara.

CLARA   Makes no never mind to me. This place stays so clean I like when someone comes so it gets a little messy so I have somethin' ta do.

BIG GIRL   Is that why Jackie boy is here? So he can do some messin' 'round?

CLARA   Nawh, B. G.

JACK, *stands*   Well, I'll be going. I see that . . .

BIG GIRL, *rises and tugs his sleeve*   Sit down an' drink up, young blood. *Pushes him back into his seat.*   There's wine here . . . *slow and suggestive*   . . . there's a pretty girl here . . . you go for that, don't you?

JACK   It's not that . . .

BIG GIRL   You go for fine little Clara, don't you?

JACK   Well, yes, I do . . .

BIG GIRL   HAW HAW HAW . . .   *slams the table and sloshes wine* . . . HAW HAW HAW . . .   *slow and suggestive*   . . . What I tell ya, Clara? You're a winner. First time I laid eyes on you I said to myself that you's a winner.

CLARA, *takes a drink*   Drink up B. G.

BIG GIRL, *to* JACK   You sho you like what you see, young blood?

JACK, *becomes bold*   Why sure. Do you think I'd come out on a day like this for anybody?

BIG GIRL   HAW HAW HAW . . .   *peals of laughter and more coughs*   . . .

JACK, *to* CLARA   I was going to ask you to go to the matinee 'round Pep's but I guess it's too late now.

CLARA, *hesitates*   I never been.

BIG GIRL, *sobers*   That's right. You never been to Pep's and it's only 'round the corner. What you mean it's too late, young blood? It don't start gettin' good till round four.

JACK   I thought she might have ta start gettin' supper.

BIG GIRL   She'd only burn it the fuck up too if she did.   *To* CLARA. I'm goin' ta take you to Pep's this afternoon.

CLARA   You don't have ta, B. G.

BIG GIRL   It's my day off, ain't it?

CLARA   But it costs so much, don't it?

BIG GIRL   Nawh, not much . . . you'll like it. Soon as C. C. comes over ta watch Baby Girl we can go.

CLARA, *brightens*   O.K.!

JACK   I don't know who's there now, but they always have a good show. Sometimes Ahmad Jamal . . .

BABY GIRL, *cuts speech*   CAT! CAT! CAT!

BIG GIRL   Let's toast to that . . .   *raising her glass*   . . . To Pep's on a rainy day!

JACK   HERE! HERE!   *He drains his glass. A tumbling sound is heard from the backyard as they drink and* BABY GIRL *claps hands as* STOO-GIE, BAMA *and* HOSS *appear in yard doorway. The three boys are no more than 16. They are soaked but wear only thin jackets, caps and pants. Under* STOOGIE'S *cap he wears a bandanna to keep his processed hair dry.*

BIG GIRL   What the hell is this?

STOOGIE,   *goes to* BIG GIRL *and pats her shoulder*   The heat, B. G. The man was on our asses so we had to come on in out of the rain, baby, dig?

BIG GIRL   Well tell me somethin' I don't know, baby. Why you got to pick mah back door? I ain't never ready for any more heat than I gets already.

STOOGIE   It just happened that way, B. G. We didn't have any choice.

BAMA   That's right, Big Girl. You know we ain't lame 'nuf to be usin' yo pad for no highway.

HOSS   Yeah, baby, you know how it is when the man is there.

BIG GIRL   Well, that makes a difference. *Smiles.* Hey, what'cha standin' there with your faces hangin' out for? Get yourselves a drink.

> HOSS *goes to the sink to get glasses for the trio;* STOOGIE *looks* JACK *over and nods to* BAMA, *then turns to* CLARA.

STOOGIE   How ya doin', Clara. Ya lookin' fine as ever.

CLARA   I'm okay, Stoogie. I don't have to ask 'bout you none. Bad news sho travels fast.

STOOGIE, *holds arms apart in innocence*   What'cha mean, baby? What'cha been hearin' 'bout poppa Stoogie?

CLARA   Just the regular. That your gang's fightin' the Peaceful Valley guys up in North Philly.

STOOGIE   Awww . . . dat's old stuff. Sheet . . . you way behind, baby.

BAMA   Yeah sweet cake, dat's over.

CLARA   Already?

HOSS   Yeah, we just finished sign'n a peace treaty with Peaceful Valley.

BAMA   Yeah, we out ta cool the War Lords now from ov'va on Powelton Avenue.

HOSS   Ole Stoogie here is settin' up the war council now; we got a pact with Peaceful Valley and man when we come down on those punk War Lords . . . baby . . . it's just gonna be all ov'va.

BIG GIRL   Yeah, it's always one thing ta another with you punks.

STOOGIE   Hey, B. G., cool it! We can't help it if people always spreadin' rumors 'bout us. Things just happen an' people talk and don' understand and get it all wrong, dat's all.

BIG GIRL   Yeah, all of it just happens, huh? It's just natural . . . you's growin' boys.

STOOGIE   That's what's happen'n baby. Now take for instance Peaceful Valley. Las' week we went up there . . . ya know, only five of us in Crook's Buick.

CLARA   I guess ya was just lookin' at the scenery?

HOSS   Yeah, baby, dat's it. We was lookin' . . . fo' some jive half-ass niggers.

The boys laugh and giggle as STOOGIE *enacts the story.*

STOOGIE   Yeah, we spot Specs from off'a Jefferson and Gratz walkin' with them bad foots down Master . . . ha ha ha . . .

BAMA   Tell them what happened to Specs, man.

HOSS   Awww, man, ya ain't gonna drag mah man Bama again?

They laugh more, slapping and punching each other, taking off their caps and cracking each other with them, gulping their wine and performing for the girls and JACK.

STOOGIE *has his hair exposed.*

STOOGIE   Bama here . . . ha ha ha . . . Bama burnt dat four-eyed mathafukker in the leg.

HOSS   Baby, you should'a seen it!

CLARA   Yeah, that's what I heard.

STOOGIE   Yeah, but listen, baby. *Points to* BAMA.   He was holding the only heat we had . . . ha ho ho . . . and dis jive sucker was aimin' at Spec's bad foots . . . ha ha . . . while that blind mathafukker was blastin' from 'round the corner straight through the car window . . .

They become nearly hysterical with laughter and stagger and stumble around the table.

HOSS   Yeah . . . ha ha . . . mathafukkin' glass was flyin' all over us . . . ha ha . . . we almost got sliced ta death and dis stupid mathafukker was shootin' at the man's bad foots . . . ha ha . . .

BAMA, *scratching his head*   Well, man. Well, man . . . I didn't know what kind of rumble we was in.

CLARA *and* BIG GIRL *laugh as they refill their glasses, nearly emptying the jug.* BIG GIRL *gets up and pulls another gallon out of the refrigerator as laughter subsides . . .*

BIG GIRL, *sits down*   What's the heat doin' after ya?

STOOGIE   Nothin'.

CLARA   I bet!

STOOGIE, *sneer*   That's right, baby. They just singled us out to make examples out of.

This gets a laugh from his friends.

BIG GIRL   What did you get?

HOSS   Get?

BIG GIRL, *turns on him*   You tryin' ta get wise, punk?

STOOGIE, *patronizing*   Awww, B. G. You not goin' ta take us serious, are ya?

Silence.

Well, ya see. We were walking' down Broad Street by the State Store, see? And we see this old rumdum come out and stagger down the street carryin' this heavy package . . .

CLARA And?

STOOGIE And he's stumblin', see. Like he's gonna fall. So good ole Hoss here says, "Why don't we help that pore man out?" So Bama walks up and helps the man carry his package, and do you know what?

BIG GIRL Yeah, the mathafukker "slips" down and screams and some cops think you some wrong doin' studs . . . yeah, I know . . . of course you didn't have time to explain.

STOOGIE That's right, B. G. So to get our breath so we could tell our side of it we just stepped in here, dig?

BIG GIRL Yeah I dig. *Menacing.* Where is it?

HOSS Where's what?

Silence.

STOOGIE If you had just give me another minute, B. G. *Pulls out a quart of vodka.* Well, no use savin' it anyway. Who wants some 100 proof tiger piss?

BAMA, *to* STOOGIE Hey man, how much was in dat mathafukker's wallet?

STOOGIE, *nods toward* JACK Cool it, sucker.

HOSS, *to* STOOGIE But, man, you holdin' the watch and ring too!

STOOGIE, *advancing on them* What's wrong with you jive-ass mathafukkers?

BIG GIRL Okay, cool it? There's only one person gets out of hand 'round here, ya understand?

STOOGIE Okay, B. G. Let it slide . . .

BABY GIRL CAT! CAT! CAT!

BAMA, *to* HOSS Hey man, dis chick's still chasin' dose cats.

STOOGIE, *to* JACK Drink up, man. Not everyday ya get dis stuff. BAMA *picks up the beat of the music and begins a shuffling dance.* BABY GIRL *begins bouncing in time to the music.*

HOSS C'mon, Baby Girl. let me see ya do the slide.

BABY GIRL NO! NO! *She claps and bounces.*

HOSS, *demonstrates his steps, trying to out-dance* BAMA C'mon, Baby Girl, shake that thing!

CLARA No, stop that, Hoss. She don't know what she's doin!

BIG GIRL That's okay Clara. Go on, Baby Girl, do the thing.

STOOGIE *grabs salt from the table and shakes it upon the floor, under the feet of the dancers.*

STOOGIE DO THE SLIDE, MAN! SLIDE!

BABY GIRL *lumbers up and begins a grotesque maneuver while grunting out strained sounds.*

BABY GIRL Uuuhhh . . . sheeeee . . . waaa . . . uuhhh . . .

BIG GIRL, *standing, toasting* DO THE THING, BABY!!!

CLARA Awww . . . B. G. Why don't you stop all dat?

STOOGIE, *to* JACK C'mon, man, git with it.

JACK *shakes his head and* STOOGIE *goes over to* CLARA *and holds out his hand.*

STOOGIE Let's go, Baby.

CLARA Nawh . . . I don't dance no mo . . .

STOOGIE C'mon, pretty mamma . . . watch this step . . . *He cuts a fancy step.*

BIG GIRL Go on and dance, sister.

        STOOGIE *moves off and the three boys dance.*

CLARA Nawh . . . B. G., you know I don't go for that kind of stuff no mo.

BIG GIRL Go on, baby!

CLARA No!

BIG GIRL I want you to dance, Clara.

CLARA Nawh . . . I just can't.

BIG GIRL DO LIKE I SAY! DO LIKE BIG WANTS!

        The dancers stop momentarily but begin again when CLARA *joins them.* BABY GIRL *halts and resumes her place upon the floor, fondling her toy. The others dance until the record stops.*

STOOGIE, *to* JACK Where you from, man?

JACK Oh, I live over in West Philly now, but I come from up around Master.

STOOGIE Oh? Do you know Hector?

JACK, *trying to capture an old voice and mannerism* Yeah, man, I know the cat.

STOOGIE What's your name, man?

JACK Jack man, maybe you know me by Tookie.

STOOGIE, *ritually* Tookie . . . Tookie . . . yeah, man, I think I heard about you. You us'ta be in the ole Jet Cobras!

JACK Well, I us'ta know some of the guys then. I been away for a while.

BAMA, *matter-of-factly* Where you been, man? Jail?

JACK I was in the Marines for three years.

STOOGIE Hey, man. That must'a been a gas.

JACK It was okay. I seen a lot . . . went a lot of places.

BIG GIRL Yeah, you must'a seen it all.

STOOGIE Did you get to go anywhere overseas, man?

JACK Yeah, I was aboard ship most of the time.

HOSS Wow, man. That sounds cool.

BAMA You really was overseas, man?

JACK   Yeah. I went to Europe and North Africa and the Caribbean.

STOOGIE   What kind of a boat were you on, man?

JACK   A ship.

BIG GIRL   A boat!

JACK   No, a ship.

STOOGIE, *rising,* BAMA *and* HOSS *surrounding* JACK   Yeah, man, dat's what she said . . . a boat!

CLARA   STOP IT!!!

BABY GIRL   NO! NO! NO! SHIT! SHIT! SHIT! DAMN! SHIT!

MISS FAMIE'S *voice from upstairs*   Your Aunt don't like all that noise.

BIG GIRL   You and my aunt better mind ya fukkin' ginhead business or I'll come up there and ram those empty bottles up where it counts!

BAMA   *sniggling*   Oh, baby. We forgot your aunt was up dere sick.

STOOGIE   Yeah, baby. Have another drink.

  He fills all glasses except CLARA'S. *She pulls hers away.*

CLARA   Nawh, I don't want any more. Me and Big Girl are goin' out after a while.

BAMA   Can I go too?

BIG GIRL   There's always have to be one wise mathafukker.

BAMA   I didn't mean nuttin', B. G., honest.

STOOGIE, *to* JACK   What did you do in the Army, man?

JACK, *feigns a dialect*   Ohhh, man. I told you already I was in the Marines!

HOSS, *to* CLARA   Where you goin'?

CLARA   B. G.'s takin' me to Pep's.

BAMA   Wow . . . dat's nice, baby.

BIG GIRL, *gesturing toward* JACK   Ole smoothie here suggesting takin' Clara but it seems he backed out, so I thought we might step around there anyway.

JACK, *annoyed*   I didn't back out!

STOOGIE, *to* JACK   Did you screw any of them foreign bitches when you were in Japan, man?

JACK   Yeah, man. I couldn't help it. They was all over, ya know?

BIG GIRL   He couldn't beat them off.

STOOGIE   Yeah, man. I dig.

JACK   Especially in France and Italy. Course, the Spanish girls are the best, but the ones in France and Italy ain't so bad either.

HOSS   You mean those French girls ain't as good as those Spanish girls?

JACK   Nawh, man, the Spanish girls are the best.

BAMA   I never did dig no Mexican nor Rican spic bitches. Too tough, man.

JACK   They ain't Mexican or Puerto Rican. They Spanish . . . from Spain . . . Spanish is different from Mexican. In Spain . . .

STOOGIE   What'cha do now, man?

JACK   Ohhh . . . I'm goin' ta college prep on the G.I. Bill now . . . and workin' a little.

STOOGIE   Is that why you sound like you got a load of shit in your mouth?

JACK   What do you mean!

STOOGIE   I thought you talked like you had shit in your mouth because you had been ta college, man.

JACK   I don't understand what you're tryin' to say, man.

STOOGIE   It's nothin', man. You just talk funny sometimes . . . ya know what I mean. Hey, man, where da you work?

JACK, *visibly feeling his drinks*   Nawh, man, I don't know what ya mean and I don't go to college, man, it's college prep.

STOOGIE   Thanks, man.

JACK   And I work at the P.O.

BAMA   Pee-who?

JACK   The Post Office, man.

BAMA   No shit, baby.

STOOGIE   Thanks, George. I always like know things I don't know anything about. *He turns back on* JACK.

JACK, *to* BIG GIRL   Hey, what time ya goin' round to Pep's?

BIG GIRL   Soon . . . are you in a hurry, young blood? You don't have to wait for us.

JACK, *now drunk*   That's okay . . . it's just gettin' late, ya know, man . . . and I was wonderin' what time Clara's ole man gets home . . .

BIG GIRL   Clara's ole man? . . . Whad do you mean, man? . . . *The trio begins snickering, holding their laughter back;* JACK *is too drunk to notice.*

JACK   Well, Clara said for me to come by today in the afternoon when her ole man would be at work . . . and I was wonderin' what time he got home . . .

        BIG GIRL *stands, tilting over her chair to crash backwards on the floor. Her bust juts out; she is controlled but furious.*

BIG GIRL   Clara's ole man is home now . . .

        A noise is heard outside as C. C. *comes in the front door. The trio are laughing louder but with restraint;* CLARA *looks stunned.*

C.C.   It's just Me . . . just ole C. C.

HOSS   Shsss . . . shut up, man.

JACK, *starts up and feels drunk for the first time*   What . . . you mean he's been upstairs all this time?

BIG GIRL, *staring*   Nawh, man, I don't mean that!

JACK, *looks at* BIG GIRL, *then at the laughing boys and finally to* CLARA

Ohhh . . . jezzus! *He staggers to the backyard door, past* BABY
GIRL, *and becomes sick.*

BIG GIRL, *to* CLARA   Didn't you tell him? Didn't you tell him a fukkin'
thing?

    C. C. *comes in. He is drunk and weaves and says nothing. He
sees the wine, searches for a glass, bumps into one of the boys,
is shoved into another, and gets booted in the rear before he
reaches wine and seat.*

BIG GIRL   Didn't you tell him?

CLARA   I only wanted to talk, B. G. I only wanted to talk to somebody. I don't have anybody to talk to . . . *crying* . . . I don't
have anyone . . .

BIG GIRL   It's time for the matinee. *To* STOOGIE.   Before you go, escort my friend out, will ya?

CLARA   Ohhh . . . B. G. I'll do anything but please . . . ohhh Big . . . I
won't forget my promise.

BIG GIRL   Let's go. We don't want to miss the show, do we?

CLARA   Please, B. G., please. Not that. It's not his fault! Please!

BIG GIRL   DO LIKE I SAY! DO LIKE I WANT YOU TO DO!

    CLARA *drops her head and rises and exits stage right followed
by* BIG GIRL. STOOGIE *and his boys finish their drinks, stalk and
swagger about.* BAMA *opens the refrigerator and* HOSS *takes one
long last guzzle.*

BAMA   Hey, Stoogie babe, what about the split?

STOOGIE, *drunk*   Later, you square-ass, lame-ass mathafukker!

    HOSS *giggles.*

BABY GIRL   CAT! CAT! CAT!

C. C., *seated drinking.*   Shut up, Baby Girl. Ain't no cats out dere.

MISS FAMIE   *staggers from upstairs, calls back*   Good night Toohey.
See ya tomorrow.

    With a nod from STOOGIE, BAMA, *and* HOSS *take* JACK'S *arms
and wrestle him into the yard. The sound of* JACK'S *beating is
heard.* MISS FAMIE *wanders to the yard door, looks out but staggers back from what she sees and continues sprawling toward
the exit, stage right.*

BABY GIRL   CAT! CAT! CAT!

C. C.   SHUT UP! SHUT ON UP, BABY GIRL! I TOLE YA . . . DERE
AIN'T NO CATS OUT DERE!!!

BABY GIRL   NO! DAMN! SHIT! SHIT! DAMN! NO! NO!

    STOOGIE *looks over the scene and downs his drink, then saun-
ters outside. Lights dim out until there is a single soft spot on*
BABY GIRL'S *head, turned wistfully toward the yard, then blackness.*

CURTAIN

Ernest Gaines

(1933–   )

FOCUSING ON THOSE MEMBERS of the African American community who are for the most part ignored in contemporary writings, Ernest J. Gaines centers his plots on black southerners, Cajuns, and Creoles. Gaines depicts the effects of racism on the black community and calls for the reform of society in his writings. He is a master of black dialect, telling his stories in the narrative folk tradition. Probably most widely known for the *Autobiography of Miss Jane Pittman*, (1971) which was made into a television production, Gaines interweaves history in his works to complement his story lines.

Born in 1933 on a plantation in Oscar, Louisiana, Gaines was working by the age of nine, digging potatoes. Because of his early experiences with plantation living, the plantation is a recurring setting in his novels. Another recurring image, the hard-working, self-sacrificing aunt, reflects the reverence with which he holds his Aunt Augusteen Jefferson, who had no legs, but constantly and diligently worked to clothe and feed him.

In 1948, Gaines moved to California with his mother and stepfather. It was there, where he was in a much better educational system, that he began reading, especially Russian novelists, such as Tolstoy and Turgenev, who wrote about the rural community. As early as 1950, he began writing about the rural blacks and their life in the South, publishing his first short story in *Transfer* magazine. Gaines graduated from San Francisco State College in 1957 and studied creative writing at Stanford University from September 1958 to May 1959 on a Wallace Stegner award.

He published his first novel, *Catherine Carmier*, in 1964. Gaines locates most of his novels in Louisiana. *Of Love and Dust* (1967) and *Bloodline* (1968), a collection of stories, follow in this tradition. Employing the storytelling technique of the black folk oral tradition, Gaines discusses social adaptation and survival in the wake of discarding dependency on whites in a period marked by turbulent race relations.

Gaines received a Guggenheim Fellowship (1973–1974), which allowed him to concentrate more on his writing. In 1978 he published *In My Father's House*, a novel revolving around the effects of internalized hatred, which often results in violence. His most current work, *A Gathering of Old Men* (1983), is a novel rooted in the experiences of individual men, their frustrations, and the injustices perpetrated against them.

For further information on Ernest J. Gaines see Keith E. Byerman's article in *Dictionary of Literary Biography, Volume 33*, "An Interview: Ernest J. Gaines," *New Orleans Review* 1 (1969); William L. Andrews's " 'We Ain't Going Back There': The Idea of Progress in *The Autobiography of Miss Jane Pittman*," *Black American Literature Forum* 11 (1977); Jerry Bryant's "From Death to Life: The Fiction of Ernest J. Gaines," *Iowa Review* 3 (1972); William Peden's *The American Short Story: Continuity and Change, 1940–1975* (1975); Frank W. Shelton's "Ambiguous Manhood in Ernest J. Gaines' *Bloodline*," *CLA Journal* 19 (1975); Special Gaines issue, *Callaloo* 1, no. 3 (1978); and Marcia Gaudet and Carl Wooton's *Porch Talk with Ernest Gaines: Conversations on the Writer's Craft* (1990). See also Bernard W. Bell's *The Afro-American Novel and Its Tradition* (1987).

"Just Like a Tree" is taken from *Bloodline*.

JUST LIKE A TREE

I shall not;
  I shall not be moved.
I shall not;
  I shall not be moved.
Just like a tree that's
planted 'side the water.
  Oh, I shall not be moved.

I made my home in glory;
  I shall not be moved.
Made my home in glory;
  I shall not be moved.
Just like a tree that's
planted 'side the water.
  Oh, I shall not be moved.

(*from an old Negro spiritual*)

Chuckkie

Pa hit him on the back and he jeck in them chains like he pulling, but ever'body in the wagon know he ain't, and Pa hit him on the back again. He jeck again like he pulling, but even Big Red know he ain't doing a thing.

"That's why I'm go'n get a horse," Pa say. "He'll kill that other mule. Get up there, Mr. Bascom."

"Oh, let him alone," Gran'mon say. "How would you like it if you was pulling a wagon in all that mud?"

Pa don't answer Gran'mon; he just hit Mr. Bascom on the back again.

"That's right, kill him," Gran'mon say. "See where you get mo' money to buy another one."

"Get up there, Mr. Bascom," Pa say.

"You hear me talking to you, Emile?" Gran'mon say. "You want me hit you with something?"

"Ma, he ain't pulling," Pa say.

"Leave him alone," Gran'mon say.

Pa shake the lines little bit, but Mr. Bascom don't even feel it, and you can see he letting Big Red do all the pulling again. Pa say something kind o' low to hisself, and I can't make out what it is.

I low' my head little bit, 'cause that wind and fine rain was hitting me in the face, and I can feel Mama pressing close to me to keep me warm. She sitting on one side o' me and Pa sitting on the other side o' me, and Gran'mon in the back o' me in her setting chair. Pa didn't want bring the setting chair, telling Gran'mon there was two boards in that wagon already and she could sit on one of 'em all by herself if she wanted to, but Gran'mon say she was taking her setting chair with her if Pa liked it or not. She say she didn't ride in no wagon on nobody board, and if Pa liked it or not, that setting chair was going.

"Let her take her setting chair," Mama say. "What's wrong with taking her setting chair."

"Ehhh, Lord," Pa say, and picked up the setting chair and took it out to the wagon. "I guess I'll have to bring it back in the house, too, when we come back from there."

Gran'mon went and clambed in the wagon and moved her setting chair back little bit and sat down and folded her arms, waiting for us to get in, too. I got in and knelt down 'side her, but Mama told me to come up there and sit on the board 'side her and Pa so I could stay warm. Soon 's I sat down, Pa hit Mr. Bascom on the back, saying what a trifling thing Mr. Bascom was, and soon 's he got some mo' money he was getting rid o' Mr. Bascom and getting him a horse.

I raise my head to look see how far we is.

"That's it, yonder," I say.

"Stop pointing," Mama say, "and keep your hand in your pocket."

"Where?" Gran'mon say, back there in her setting chair.

"'Cross the ditch, yonder," I say.

"Can't see a thing for this rain," Gran'mon say.

"Can't hardly see it," I say. "But you can see the light little bit. That chinaball tree standing in the way."

"Poor soul," Gran'mon say. "Poor soul."

I know Gran'mon was go'n say "poor soul, poor soul," 'cause she had been saying "poor soul, poor soul," ever since she heard Aunt Fe was go'n leave from back there.

Emile

Darn cane crop to finish getting in and only a mule and a half to do it. If I had my way I'd take that shotgun and a load o' buckshots and—but what's the use.

"Get up, Mr. Bascom—please," I say to that little dried-up, long-eared, tobacco-color thing. "Please, come up. Do your share for God sake—if you don't mind. I know it's hard pulling in all that mud, but if you don't do your share, then Big Red'll have to do his and yours, too. So, please, if it ain't asking you too much to—"

"Oh, Emile, shut up," Leola say.

"I can't hit him," I say, "or Mama back there'll hit me. So I have to talk to him. Please, Mr. Bascom, if you don't mind it. For my sake. No, not for mine; for God sake. No, not even for His'n; for Big Red sake. A fellow mule just like yourself is. Please, come up."

"Now, you hear that boy blaspheming God right in front o' me there," Mama say. "Ehhh, Lord—just keep it up. All this bad weather there like this whole world coming apart—a clap o' thunder come there and knock the fool out you. Just keep it up."

Maybe she right, and I stop. I look at Mr. Bascom there doing nothing, and I just give up. That mule know long 's Mama's alive he go'n do just what he want to do. He know when Papa was dying he told Mama to look after him, and he know no matter what he do, no matter what he don't do, Mama ain't go'n never let me do him anything. Sometimes I even feel Mama care mo' for Mr. Bascom 'an she care for me her own son.

We come up to the gate and I pull back on the lines.

"Whoa up, Big Red," I say. "You don't have to stop, Mr. Bascom. You never started."

I can feel Mama looking at me back there in that setting chair, but she don't say nothing.

"Here," I say to Chuckkie.

He take the lines and I jump down on the ground to open the old beat-up gate. I see Etienne's horse in the yard, and I see Chris new red tractor 'side the house, shining in the rain. When Mama die, I say to myself, Mr. Bascom, you going. Ever'body getting tractors and horses and I'm still stuck with you. You going, brother.

"Can you make it through?" I ask Chuckkie. "That gate ain't too wide."

"I can do it," he say.

"Be sure to make Mr. Bascom pull," I say.

"Emile, you better get back up here and drive 'em through," Leola say. "Chuckkie might break up that wagon."

"No, let him stay down there and give orders," Mama say, back there in that setting chair.

"He can do it," I say. "Come on, Chuckkie boy."

"Come up, here, mule," Chuckkie say.

And soon 's he say that, Big Red make a lunge for the yard, and Mr. Bascom don't even move, and 'fore I can bat my eyes I hear *pow-wow; sagg-sagg; pow-wow.* But above all that noise, Leola up there screaming her head off. And Mama—not a word; just sitting in that chair, looking at me with her arms still folded.

"Pull Big Red," I say. "Pull Big Red, Chuckkie."

Poor little Chuckkie up there pulling so hard till one of his little arms straight out in back; and Big Red throwing his shoulders and ever'thing else in it, and Mr. Bascom just walking there just 's loose and free, like he 's suppose to be there just for his good looks. I move out the way just in time to let the wagon go by me, pulling half o' the fence in the yard behind it. I glance up again, and there's Leola still hollering and trying to jump out, but Mama not saying a word—just sitting there in that setting chair with her arms still folded.

"Whoa," I hear little Chuckkie saying. "Whoa up, now."

Somebody open the door and a bunch o' people come out on the gallery.

"What the world—?" Etienne say. "Thought the whole place was coming to pieces there."

"Chuckkie had a little trouble coming in the yard," I say.

"Goodness," Etienne say. "Anybody hurt?"

Mama just sit there about ten seconds, then she say something to herself and start clambing out the wagon.

"Let me help you there, Aunt Lou," Etienne say, coming down the steps.

"I can make it," Mama say. When she get on the ground she look up at Chuckkie. "Hand me my chair there, boy."

Poor little Chuckkie, up there with the lines in one hand, get the chair and hold it to the side, and Etienne catch it just 'fore it hit the ground. Mama start looking at me again, and it look like for at least a' hour she stand there looking at nobody but me. Then she say, "Ehhh, Lord," like that again, and go inside with Leola and the rest o' the people.

I look back at half o' the fence laying there in the yard, and I jump back on the wagon and guide the mules to the side o' the house. After unhitching 'em and tying 'em to the wheels, I look at Chris pretty red tractor again, and me and Chuckkie go inside: I make sure he kick all that mud off his shoes 'fore he go in the house.

Leola

Sitting over there by that fireplace, trying to look joyful when ev-er'body there know she ain't. But she trying, you know; smiling and bowing when people say something to her. How can she be joyful, I ask you; how can she be? Poor thing, she been here all her life—or the most of it, let's say. 'Fore they moved in this house, they lived in one back in the woods 'bout a mile from here. But for the past twenty-five or thirty years, she been right in this one house. I know ever since I been big enough to know people I been seeing her right here.

Aunt Fe, Aunt Fe, Aunt Fe, Aunt Fe; the name's been 'mongst us just like us own family name. Just like the name o' God. Like the name of town—the city. Aunt Fe, Aunt Fe, Aunt Fe, Aunt Fe.

Poor old thing; how many times I done come here and washed clothes for her when she couldn't do it herself. How many times I done hoed in that garden, ironed her clothes, wrung a chicken neck for her. You count the days in the year and you'll be pretty close. And I didn't mind it a bit. No, I didn't mind it a bit. She there trying to pay me. Proud—Lord, talking 'bout pride. "Here." "No, Aunt Fe; no." "Here, here; you got a child there, you can use it." "No, Aunt Fe. No. No. What would Mama think if she knowed I took money from you? Aunt Fe, Mama would never forgive me. No. I love doing these thing for you. I just wish I could do more."

And there, now, trying to make 'tend she don't mind leaving. Ehhh, Lord.

I hear a bunch o' rattling round in the kitchen and I go back there. I see Louise stirring this big pot o' eggnog.

"Louise," I say.

"Leola," she say.

We look at each other and she stir the eggnog again. She know what I'm go'n say next, and she can't even look in my face.

"Louise, I wish there was some other way."

"There's no other way," she say.

"Louise, moving her from here's like moving a tree you been used to in your front yard all your life."

"What else can I do?"

"Oh, Louise, Louise."

"Nothing else but that."

"Louise, what people go'n do without her here?"

She stir the eggnog and don't answer.

"Louise, us'll take her in with us."

"You all no kin to Auntie. She go with me."

"And us'll never see her again."

She stir the eggnog. Her husband come back in the kitchen and kiss her on the back o' the neck and then look at me and grin. Right from the start I can see I ain't go'n like that nigger.

"Almost ready, honey?" he say.

"Almost."

He go to the safe and get one o' them bottles of whiskey he got in there and come back to the stove.

"No," Louise say. "Everybody don't like whiskey in it. Add the whiskey after you've poured it up."

"Okay, hon."

He kiss her on the back o' the neck again. Still don't like that nigger. Something 'bout him ain't right.

"You one o' the family?" he say.

"Same as one," I say. "And you?"

He don't like the way I say it, and I don't care if he like it or not. He look at me there a second, and then he kiss her on the ear.

"Un-unnn," she say, stirring the pot.

"I love your ear, baby," he say.

"Go in the front room and talk with the people," she say.

He kiss her on the other ear. A nigger do all that front o' public got something to hide. He leave the kitchen. I look at Louise.

"Ain't nothing else I can do," she say.

"You sure, Louise? You positive?"

"I'm positive," she say.

The front door open and Emile and Chuckkie come in. A minute later Washington and Adrieu come in, too. Adrieu come back in the kitchen, and I can see she been crying. Aunt Fe is her godmother, you know.

"How you feel, Adrieu?"

"That weather out there," she say.

"Y'all walked?"

"Yes."

"Us here in the wagon. Y'all can go back with us."

"Y'all the one tore the fence down?" she ask.

"Yes, I guess so. That brother-in-law o' yours in there letting Chuckkie drive that wagon."

"Well, I don't guess it'll matter too much. Nobody go'n be here, anyhow."

And she start crying again. I take her in my arms and pat her on the shoulder, and I look at Louise stirring the egg-nog.

"What I'm go'n do and my nan-nane gone? I love her so much."

"Ever'body love her."

"Since my mama died, she been like my mama."

"Shhh," I say. "Don't let her hear you. Make her grieve. You don't want her grieving, now, do you?"

She sniffs there 'gainst my dress few times.

"Oh, Lord," she say. "Lord, have mercy."

"Shhh," I say. "Shhh. That's what life's 'bout."

"That ain't what life's 'bout," she say. "It ain't fair. This been her home all her life. These the people she know. She don't know them people she going to. It ain't fair."

"Shhh, Adrieu," I say. "Now, you saying things that ain't your business."

She cry there some mo'.

"Oh, Lord, Lord," she say.

Louise turn from the stove.

"About ready now," she say, going to the middle door. "James, tell everybody to come back and get some."

James

Let me go on back here and show these country niggers how to have a good time. All they know is talk, talk, talk. Talk so much they make me buggy round here. Damn this weather—wind, rain. Must be a million cracks in this old house.

I go to that old beat-up safe in that corner and get that fifth of Mr. Harper (in the South now; got to say Mister), give the seal one swipe, the stopper one jerk, and head back to that old wood stove. (Man, like, these cats are primitive—goodness. You know what I mean? I mean like wood stoves. Don't mention TV, man, these cats here never heard of that.) I start to dump Mr. Harper in the pot and Baby catches my hand again and say not all of them like it. You ever heard of anything like that? I mean a stud's going to drink eggnog, and he's not going to put whiskey in it. I mean he's going to drink it straight. I mean, you ever heard anything like that? Well, I wasn't pressing none of them on Mr. Harper. I mean, me and Mr. Harper get along too well together for me to go around there pressing.

I hold my cup there and let Baby put a few drops of this egg stuff in it; then I jerk my cup back and let Mr. Harper run a while. Couple of these cats come over (some of them aren't so lame) and set their cups, and I let Mr. Harper run for them. Then this cat says he's got 'nough. I let Mr. Harper run for this other stud, and pretty

soon he says, "Hold it. Good." Country cat, you know. "Hold it.
Good." Real country cat. So I raise the cup to see what Mr. Harper's
doing. He's just right. I raise the cup again. Just right, Mr. Harper;
just right.

I go to the door with Mr. Harper under my arm and the cup in
my hand and I look into the front room where they all are. I mean,
there's about ninety-nine of them in there. Old ones, young ones,
little ones, big ones, yellow ones, black ones, brown ones—you
name them, brother, and they were there. And what for? Brother, I'll
tell you what for. Just because me and Baby are taking this old chick
out of these sticks. Well, I'll tell you where I'd be at this moment if I
was one of them. With that weather out there like it is, I'd be under
about five blankets with some little warm belly pressing against
mine. Brother, you can bet your hat I wouldn't be here. Man, listen
to that thing out there. You can hear the rain beating on that old
house like grains of rice; and that wind coming through them cracks
like it does in those old Charlie Chaplin movies. Man, like you
know—like *whooo-ee; whooo-ee.* Man, you talking about some
weird cats.

I can feel Mr. Harper starting to massage my wig and I bat my
eyes twice and look at the old girl over there. She's still sitting in
that funny-looking little old rocking chair, and not saying a word to
anybody. Just sitting there looking into the fireplace at them two
pieces of wood that aren't giving out enough heat to warm a baby,
let alone ninety-nine grown people. I mean, you know, like that
sleet's falling out there like all get-up-and-go, and them two pieces
of wood are lying there just as dead as the rest of these way-out cats.

One of the old cats—I don't know which one he is—Mose, Sam,
or something like that—leans over and pokes in the fire a minute;
then a little blaze shoots up, and he raises up, too, looking as satisfied as if he'd just sent a rocket into orbit. I mean, these cats are like
that. They do these little bitty things, and they feel like they've really
done something. Well, back in these sticks, I guess there just isn't
nothing big to do.

I feel Mr. Harper touching my skull now—and I notice this little chick passing by me with these two cups of eggnog. She goes
over to the fireplace and gives one to each of these old chicks.
The one sitting in that setting chair she brought with her from
God knows where, and the other cup to the old chick that Baby
and I are going to haul from here sometime tomorrow morning.
Wait, man, I mean like, you ever heard of anybody going to somebody else's house with a chair? I mean, wouldn't you call that an
insult at the basest point? I mean, now, like tell me what you
think of that? I mean—dig—here I am at my pad, and in you

come with your own stool. I mean, now, like man, you know. I
mean that's an insult at the basest point. I mean, you know . . .
you know, like way out. . . .

Mr. Harper, what you trying to do, boy? —I mean, *sir*. (Got to
watch myself, I'm in the South. Got to keep watching myself.)

This stud touches me on the shoulder and raise his cup and say,
"How 'bout a taste?" I know what the stud's talking about, so I let
Mr. Harper run for him. But soon 's I let a drop get in, the stud say,
"'Nough." I mean I let about two drops get in, and already the stud's
got enough. Man, I mean, like you know. I mean these studs are
'way out. I mean like 'way back there.

This stud takes a swig of his eggnog and say, "Ahhh." I mean this
real down-home way of saying "Ahhhh." I mean, man, like these
studs—I notice this little chick passing by me again, and this time
she's crying. I mean weeping, you know. And just because this old
ninety-nine-year-old chick's packing up and leaving. I mean, you
ever heard of anything like that? I mean, here she is pretty as the
day is long and crying because Baby and I are hauling this old chick
away. Well, I'd like to make her cry. And I can assure you, brother,
it wouldn't be from leaving her.

I turn and look at Baby over there by the stove, pouring eggnog
in all these cups. I mean, there're about twenty of these cats lined up
there. And I bet you not half of them will take Mr. Harper along.
Some way-out cats, man. Some way-out cats.

I go up to Baby and kiss her on the back of the neck and give
her a little pat where she likes for me to pat her when we're in the
bed. She say, "Uh-uh," but I know she likes it anyhow.

Ben O

I back under the bed and touch the slop jar, and I pull back my
leg and back somewhere else, and then I get me a good sight on it. I
spin my aggie couple times and sight again and then I shoot. I hit it
right square in the middle and it go flying over the fireplace. I crawl
over there to get it and I see 'em all over there drinking they eggnog
and they didn't even offer me and Chuckkie none. I find my marble
on the bricks, and I go back and tell Chuckkie they over there
drinking eggnog.

"You want some?" I say.

"I want shoot marble," Chuckkie say. "Yo' shot. Shoot up."

"I want some eggnog," I say.

"Shoot up, Ben O," he say. "I'm getting cold staying in one place
so long. You feel that draft?"

"Coming from that crack under that bed," I say.

"Where?" Chuckkie say, looking for the crack.

"Over by that bedpost over there," I say.

"This sure's a beat-up old house," Chuckkie say.

"I want me some eggnog," I say.

"Well, you ain't getting none," Gran'mon say, from the fireplace. "It ain't good for you."

"I can drink eggnog," I say. "How come it ain't good for me? It ain't nothing but eggs and milk. I eat chicken, don't I? I eat beef, don't I?"

Gran'mon don't say nothing.

"I want me some eggnog," I say.

Gran'mon still don't say no more. Nobody else don't say nothing, neither.

"I want me some eggnog," I say.

"You go'n get a eggnog," Gran'mon say. "Just keep that noise up."

"I want me some eggnog," I say; "and I 'tend to get me some eggnog tonight."

Next thing I know, Gran'mon done picked up a chip out o' that corner and done sailed it back there where me and Chuckkie is. I duck just in time, and the chip catch old Chuckkie side the head.

"Hey, who that hitting me?" Chuckkie say.

"Move, and you won't get hit," Gran'mon say.

I laugh at old Chuckkie over there holding his head, and next thing I know here's Chuckkie done haul back there and hit me in my side. I jump up from there and give him two just to show him how it feel, and he jump up and hit me again. Then we grab each other and start tussling on the floor.

"You, Ben O," I hear Gran'mon saying. "You, Ben O, cut that out. Y'all cut that out."

But we don't stop, 'cause neither one o' us want be first. Then I feel somebody pulling us apart.

"What I ought to do is whip both o' you," Mrs. Leola say. "Is that what y'all want?"

"No'm," I say.

"Then shake hand."

Me and Chuckkie shake hand.

"Kiss," Mrs. Leola say.

"No, ma'am," I say. "I ain't kissing no boy. I ain't that crazy."

"Kiss him, Chuckkie," she say.

Old Chuckkie kiss me on the jaw.

"Now, kiss him, Ben O."

"I ain't kissing no Chuckkie," I say. "No'm. Uh-uh. You kiss girls."

And the next thing I know, Mama done tipped up back o' me
and done whop me on the leg with Daddy belt.

"Kiss Chuckkie," she say.

Chuckkie turn his jaw to me and I kiss him. I almost wipe my
mouth. I even feel like spitting.

"Now, come back here and get you some eggnog," Mama say.

"That's right, spoil 'em," Gran'mon say. "Next thing you know,
they be drinking from bottles."

"Little eggnog won't hurt 'em, Mama," Mama say.

"That's right, never listen," Gran'mon say. "It's you go'n suffer for
it. I be dead and gone, me."

Aunt Clo

Be just like wrapping a chain round a tree and jecking and jecking, and then shifting the chain little bit and jecking and jecking
some in that direction, and then shifting it some mo' and jecking
and jecking in that direction. Jecking and jecking till you get it
loose, and then pulling with all your might. Still it might not be
loose enough and you have to back the tractor up some and fix the
chain round the tree again and start jecking all over. Jeck, jeck, jeck.
Then you hear the roots crying, and then you keep on jecking, and
then it give, and you jeck some mo', and then it falls. And not till
then that you see what you done done. Not till then you see the big
hole in the ground and piece of the taproot still way down in it—a
piece you won't never get out no matter if you dig till doomsday.
Yes, you got the tree—least got it down on the ground, but did you
get the taproot? No. No, sir, you didn't get the taproot. You stand
there and look down in this hole at it and you grab yo' axe and
jump down in it and start chopping at the taproot, but do you get
the taproot? No. You don't get the taproot, sir. You never get the
taproot. But, sir, I tell you what you do get. You get a big hole in
the ground, sir; and you get another big hole in the air where the
lovely branches been all these years. Yes, sir, that's what you get.
The holes, sir, the holes. Two holes, sir, you can't never fill no matter how hard you try.

So you wrap yo' chain round yo' tree again, sir, and you start
dragging it. But the dragging ain't so easy, sir, 'cause she's a heavy
old tree—been there a long time, you know—heavy. And you make
yo' tractor strain, sir, and the elements work 'gainst you, too, sir,
'cause the elements, they on her side, too, 'cause she part o' the elements, and the elements, they part o' her. So the elements, they do
they little share to discourage you—yes, sir, they does. But you will
not let the elements stop you. No, sir, you show the elements that

they just elements, and man is stronger than elements, and you jeck
and jeck on the chain, and soon she start to moving with you, sir,
but if you look over yo' shoulder one second you see her leaving a
trail—a trail, sir, that can be seen for miles and miles away. You see
her trying to hook her little fine branches in different little cracks, in
between pickets, round hills o' grass, round anything they might
brush 'gainst. But you is a determined man, sir, and you jeck and
you jeck, and she keep on grabbing and trying to hold, but you
stronger, sir—course you the strongest—and you finally get her out
on the pave road. But what you don't notice, sir, is just 'fore she get
on the pave road she leave couple her little branches to remind the
people that it ain't her that want leave, but you, sir, that think she
ought to. So you just drag her and drag her, sir, and the folks that
live in the houses 'side the pave road, they come out on they gallery
and look at her go by, and then they go back in they house and sit
by the fire and forget her. So you just go on, sir, and you just go
and you go—and for how many days? I don't know. I don't have the
least idea. The North to me, sir, is like the elements. It mystify me.
But never mind, you finally get there, and then you try to find a
place to set her. You look in this corner and you look in that corner,
but no corner is good. She kind o' stand in the way no matter where
you set her. So finally, sir, you say, "I just stand her up here a little
while and see, and if it don't work out, if she keep getting in the
way, I guess we'll just have to take her to the dump."

Chris

    Just like him, though, standing up there telling them lies when
everybody else feeling sad. I don't know what you do without people
like him. And, yet, you see him there, he sad just like the rest. But
he just got to be funny. Crying on the inside, but still got to be
funny.
    He didn't steal it, though; didn't steal it a bit. His grandpa was
just like him. Mat? Mat Jefferson? Just like that. Mat could make
you die laughing. 'Member once at a wake. Who was dead? Yes—
Robert Lewis. Robert Lewis laying up in his coffin dead as a door
nail. Everybody sad and droopy. Mat look at that and start his lying.
Soon, half o' the place laughing. Funniest wake I ever went to,
and yet—
    Just like now. Look at 'em. Look at 'em laughing. Ten minutes
ago you would 'a' thought you was at a funeral. But look at 'em
now. Look at her there in that little old chair. How long she had it?
Fifty years—a hundred? It ain't a chair no mo', it's little bit o' her.
Just like her arm, just like her leg.

You know, I couldn't believe it. I couldn't. Emile passed the house there the other day, right after the bombing, and I was in my yard digging a water drain to let the water run out in the ditch. Emile, he stopped the wagon there 'fore the door. Little Chuckkie, he in there with him with that little rain cap buckled up over his head. I go out to the gate and I say, "Emile, it's the truth?"

"The truth," he say. And just like that he say it. "The truth."

I look at him there, and he looking up the road to keep from looking back at me. You know, they been pretty close to Aunt Fe ever since they was children coming up. His own mon, Aunt Lou, and Aunt Fe, they been like sisters, there, together.

Me and him, we talk there little while 'bout the cane cutting, then he say he got to get on to the back. He shake the lines and drive on.

Inside me, my heart feel like it done swole up ten times the size it ought to be. Water come in my eyes, and I got to 'mit I cried right there. Yes sir, I cried right there by that front gate.

Louise come in the room and whisper something to Leola, and they go back in the kitchen. I can hear 'em moving things round back there, still getting things together they go'n be taking along. If they offer me anything, I'd like that big iron pot out there in the back yard. Good for boiling water when you killing hog, you know.

You can feel the sadness in the room again. Louise brought it in when she come in and whispered to Leola. Only, she didn't take it out when her and Leola left. Every pan they move, every pot they unhook keep telling you she leaving, she leaving.

Etienne turn over one o' them logs to make the fire pick up some, and I see that boy, Lionel, spreading out his hands over the fire. Watch out, I think to myself, here come another lie. People, he just getting started.

Anne-Marie Duvall

"You're not going?"

"I'm not going," he says, turning over the log with the poker. "And if you were in your right mind, you wouldn't go, either."

"You just don't understand, do you?"

"Oh, I understand. She cooked for your daddy. She nursed you when your mama died."

"And I'm trying to pay her back with a seventy-nine-cents scarf. Is that too much?"

He is silent, leaning against the mantel, looking down at the fire. The fire throws strange shadows across the big, old room. Father looks down at me from against the wall. His eyes do not say go nor stay. But I know what he would do.

"Please go with me, Edward."

"You're wasting your breath."

I look at him a long time, then I get the small package from the coffee table.

"You're still going?"

"I am going."

"Don't call for me if you get bogged down anywhere back there."

I look at him and go out to the garage. The sky is black. The clouds are moving fast and low. A fine drizzle is falling, and the wind coming from the swamps blows in my face. I cannot recall a worse night in all my life.

I hurry into the car and drive out of the yard. The house stands big and black in back of me. Am I angry with Edward? No, I'm not angry with Edward. He's right. I should not go out into this kind of weather. But what he does not understand is I must. Father definitely would have gone if he were alive. Grandfather definitely would have gone, also. And, therefore, I must. Why? I cannot answer why. Only, I must go.

As soon as I turn down that old muddy road, I begin to pray. Don't let me go into that ditch, I pray. Don't let me go into that ditch. Please, don't let me go into that ditch.

The lights play on the big old trees along the road. Here and there the lights hit a sagging picket fence. But I know I haven't even started yet. She lives far back into the fields. Why? God, why does she have to live so far back? Why couldn't she have lived closer to the front? But the answer to that is as hard for me as is the answer to everything else. It was ordained before I—before father—was born—that she should live back there. So why should I try to understand it now?

The car slides towards the ditch, and I stop it dead and turn the wheel, and then come back into the road again. Thanks, father. I know you're with me. Because it was you who said that I must look after her, didn't you? No, you did not say it directly, father. You said it only with a glance. As grandfather must have said it to you, and as his father must have said it to him.

But now that she's gone, father, now what? I know. I know. Aunt Lou, Aunt Clo, and the rest.

The lights shine on the dead, wet grass along the road. There's an old pecan tree, looking dead and all alone. I wish I was a little nigger gal so I could pick pecans and eat them under the big old dead tree.

The car hits a rut, but bounces right out of it. I am frightened for a moment, but then I feel better. The windshield wipers are working well, slapping the water away as fast as it hits the glass. If I make the next half mile all right, the rest of the way will be good. It's not much over a mile now.

That was too bad about that bombing—killing that woman and her two children. That poor woman; poor children. What is the answer? What will happen? What do they want? Do they know what they want? Do they really know what they want? Are they positively sure? Have they any idea? Money to buy a car, is that it? If that is all, I pity them. Oh, how I pity them.

Not much farther. Just around that bend and—there's a water hole. Now what?

I stop the car and just stare out at the water a minute; then I get out to see how deep it is. The cold wind shoots through my body like needles. Lightning comes from towards the swamps and lights up the place. For a split second the night is as bright as day. The next second it is blacker than it has ever been.

I look at the water, and I can see that it's too deep for the car to pass through. I must turn back or I must walk the rest of the way. I stand there a while wondering what to do. Is it worth it all? Can't I simply send the gift by someone tomorrow morning? But will there be someone tomorrow morning? Suppose she leaves without getting it, then what? What then? Father would never forgive me. Neither would grandfather or great-grandfather, either. No, they wouldn't.

The lightning flashes again and I look across the field, and I can see the tree in the yard a quarter of a mile away. I have but one choice: I must walk. I get the package out of the car and stuff it in my coat and start out.

I don't make any progress at first, but then I become a little warmer and I find I like walking. The lightning flashes just in time to show up a puddle of water, and I go around it. But there's no light to show up the second puddle, and I fall flat on my face. For a moment I'm completely blind, then I get slowly to my feet and check the package. It's dry, not harmed. I wash the mud off my raincoat, wash my hands, and I start out again.

The house appears in front of me, and as I come into the yard, I can hear the people laughing and talking. Sometimes I think niggers can laugh and joke even if they see somebody beaten to death. I go up on the porch and knock and an old one opens the door for me. I swear, when he sees me he looks as if he's seen a ghost. His mouth drops open, his eyes bulge—I swear.

I go into the old crowded and smelly room, and every one of them looks at me the same way the first one did. All the joking and laughing has ceased. You would think I was the devil in person.

"Done, Lord," I hear her saying over by the fireplace. They move to the side and I can see her sitting in that little rocking chair I bet you she's had since the beginning of time. "Done, Master," she says. "Child, what you doing in weather like this? Y'all move; let her get to that fire. Y'all move. Move, now. Let her warm herself."

They start scattering everywhere.

"I'm not cold, Aunt Fe," I say. "I just brought you something—something small—because you're leaving us. I'm going right back."

"Done, Master," she says. Fussing over me just like she's done all her life. "Done, Master. Child, you ain't got no business in a place like this. Get close to this fire. Get here. Done, Master."

I move closer, and the fire does feel warm and good.

"Done, Lord," she says.

I take out the package and pass it to her. The other niggers gather around with all kinds of smiles on their faces. Just think of it—a white lady coming though all of this for one old darky. It is all right for them to come from all over the plantation, from all over the area, in all kinds of weather: this is to be expected of them. But a white lady, a white lady. They must think we white people don't have their kind of feelings.

She unwraps the package, her bony little fingers working slowly and deliberately. When she sees the scarf—the seventy-nine-cents scarf—she brings it to her mouth and kisses it.

Y'all look," she says. "Y'all look. Ain't it the prettiest little scarf y'all ever did see? Y'all look."

They move around her and look at the scarf. Some of them touch it.

"I go'n put it on right now," she says. "I go'n put it on right now, my lady."

She unfolds it and ties it round her head and looks up at everybody and smiles.

"Thank you, my lady," she says. "Thank you, ma'am, from the bottom of my heart."

"Oh, Aunt Fe," I say, kneeling down beside her. "Oh, Aunt Fe."

But I think about the other niggers there looking down at me, and I get up. But I look into that wrinkled old face again, and I must go back down again. And I lay my head in that bony old lap, and I cry and I cry—I don't know how long. And I feel those old fingers, like death itself, passing over my hair and my neck. I don't know how long I kneel there crying, and when I stop, I get out of there as fast as I can.

Etienne

The boy come in, and soon, right off, they get quiet, blaming the boy. If people could look little farther than the tip of they nose— No, they blame the boy. Not that they ain't behind the boy, what he doing, but they blame him for what she must do. What they don't know is that the boy didn't start it, and the people that bombed the house didn't start it, neither. It started a million years ago. It started when one man envied another man for having a penny mo' 'an he had, and then the man married a woman to help him work the field so he could get much 's the other man, but when the other man saw the man had married a woman to get much 's him, he, himself, he married a woman, too, so he could still have mo'. Then they start having children—not from love; but so the children could help 'em work so they could have mo'. But even with the children one man still had a penny mo' 'an the other, so the other man went and bought him a ox, and the other man did the same—to keep ahead of the other man. And soon the other man had bought him a slave to work the ox so he could get ahead of the other man. But the other man went out and bought him two slaves so he could stay ahead of the other man, and the other man went out and bought him three slaves. And soon they had a thousand slaves apiece, but they still wasn't satified. And one day the slaves all rose and kill the masters, but the masters (knowing slaves was men just like they was, and kind o' expected they might do this) organized theyself a good police force, they come out and killed the two thousand slaves.

So it's not this boy you see standing here 'fore you, 'cause it happened a million years ago. And this boy here's just doing something the slaves done a million years ago. Just that this boy here ain't doing it they way. 'Stead of raising arms 'gainst the masters, he bow his head.

No, I say; don't blame the boy 'cause she must go. 'Cause when she's dead, and that won't be long after they get her up there, this boy's work will still be going on. She's not the only one that's go'n die from this boy's work. Many mo' of 'em go'n die 'fore it's over with. The whole place—everything. A big wind is rising, and when a big wind rise, the sea stirs, and the drop o' water you see laying on top the sea this day won't be there tomorrow. 'Cause that's what wind do, and that's what life is. She ain't nothing but one little drop o' water laying on top the sea, and what this boy's doing is called the wind . . . and she must be moved. No, don't blame the boy. Go out and blame the wind. No, don't blame him, 'cause tomorrow, what he's doing today, somebody go'n say he ain't done a thing. 'Cause tomorrow will be his time to be turned over just like it's hers today. And after that, be somebody else time to turn over. And it keep going like that till it ain't nothing left to turn—and nobody left to turn it.

"Sure, they bombed the house," he say; "because they want us to stop. But if we stopped today, then what good would we have done? What good? Those who have already died for the cause would have just died in vain."

"Maybe if they had bombed your house you wouldn't be so set on keeping this up."

"If they had killed my mother and my brothers and sisters, I'd press just that much harder. I can see you all point. I can see it very well. But I can't agree with you. You blame me for their being bombed. You blame me for Aunt Fe's leaving. They died for you and for your children. And I love Aunt Fe as much as anybody in here does. Nobody in here loves her more than I do. Not one of you." He looks at her. "Don't you believe me, Aunt Fe?"

She nods—that little white scarf still tied round her head.

"How many times have I eaten in your kitchen, Aunt Fe? A thousand times? How many times have I eaten tea cakes and drank milk on the back steps, Aunt Fe? A thousand times? How many times have I sat at this same fireplace with you, just the two of us, Aunt Fe? Another thousand times—two thousand times? How many times have I chopped wood for you, chopped grass for you, ran to the store for you? Five thousand times? How many times have we walked to church together, Aunt Fe? Gone fishing at the river together—how many times? I've spent as much time in this house as I've spent in my own. I know every crack in the wall. I know every corner. With my eyes shut, I can go anywhere in here without bumping into anything. How many of you can do that? Not many of you." He looks at her. "Aunt Fe?"

She looks at him.

"Do you think I love you, Aunt Fe?"

She nods.

"I love you, Aunt Fe, much as I do my own parents. I'm going to miss you much as I'd miss my own mother if she were to leave me now. I'm going to miss you, Aunt Fe, but I'm not going to stop what I've started. You told me a story once, Aunt Fe, about my great-grandpa. Remember? Remember how he died?"

She looks in the fire and nods.

"Remember how they lynched him—chopped him into pieces?"

She nods.

"Just the two of us were sitting here beside the fire when you told me that. I was so angry I felt like killing. But it was you who told me get killing out of my mind. It was you who told me I would only bring harm to myself and sadness to the others if I killed. Do you remember that, Aunt Fe?"

She nods, still looking in the fire.

"You were right. We cannot raise our arms. Because it would mean death for ourselves, as well as for the others. But we will do something else—and that's what we will do." He looks at the people standing round him. "And if they were to bomb my own mother's house tomorrow, I would still go on."

"I'm not saying for you not to go on," Louise says. "That's up to you. I'm just taking Auntie from here before hers is the next house they bomb."

The boy look at Louise, and then at Aunt Fe. He go up to the chair where she sitting.

"Good-bye, Aunt Fe," he say, picking up her hand. The hand done shriveled up to almost nothing. Look like nothing but loose skin's covering the bones. "I'll miss you," he say.

"Good-bye, Emmanuel," she say. She look at him a long time. "God be with you."

He stand there holding the hand a while longer, then he nods his head, and leaves the house. The people stir round little bit, but nobody say anything.

Aunt Lou

They tell her good-bye, and half of 'em leave the house crying, or want cry, but she just sit there 'side the fireplace like she don't mind going at all. When Leola ask me if I'm ready to go, I tell her I'm staying right there till Fe leave that house. I tell her I ain't moving one step till she go out that door. I been knowing her for the past fifty some years now, and I ain't 'bout to leave her on her last night here.

That boy, Chuckkie, want stay with me, but I make him go. He follow his mon and paw out the house and soon I hear that wagon turning round. I hear Emile saying something to Mr. Bascom even 'fore that wagon get out the yard. I tell myself, well, Mr. Bascom, you sure go'n catch it, and me not there to take up for you—and I get up from my chair and go to the door.

"Emile?" I call.

"Whoa," he say.

"You leave that mule 'lone, you hear me?"

"I ain't done Mr. Bascom a thing, Mama," he say.

"Well, you just mind you don't," I say. "I'll sure find out."

"Yes'm," he say. "Come up here, Mr. Bascom."

"Now, you hear that boy. Emile?" I say.

"I'm sorry, Mama," he say. "I didn't mean no harm."

They go out in the road, and I go back to the fireplace and sit down again. Louise stir round in the kitchen a few minutes, then she come in the front where we at. Everybody else gone. That husband o' hers, there, got drunk long 'fore midnight, and Emile and them had to put him to bed in the other room.

She come there and stand by the fire.

"I'm dead on my feet," she say.

"Why don't you go to bed," I say. "I'm go'n be here."

"You all won't need anything?"

"They got wood in that corner?"

"Plenty."

"Then we won't need a thing."

She stand there and warm, and then she say good night and go round the other side.

"Well, Fe?" I say.

"I ain't leaving here tomorrow, Lou," she say.

" 'Course you is," I say. "Up there ain't that bad."

She shake her head. "No, I ain't going nowhere."

I look at her over in her chair, but I don't say nothing. The fire pops in the fireplace, and I look at the fire again. It's a good little fire—not too big, not too little. Just 'nough there to keep the place warm.

"You want sing, Lou?" she say, after a while. "I feel like singing my 'termination song."

"Sure," I say.

She start singing in that little light voice she got there, and I join with her. We sing two choruses, and then she stop.

"My 'termination for Heaven," she say. "Now—now—"

"What's the matter, Fe?" I say.

"Nothing," she say. "I want get in my bed. My gown hanging over there."

I get the gown for her and bring it back to the firehalf. She get out of her dress slowly, like she don't even have 'nough strength to do it. I help her on with her gown, and she kneel down there 'side the bed and say her prayers. I sit in my chair and look at the fire again.

She pray there a long time—half out loud, half to herself. I look at her kneeling down there, little like a little old girl. I see her making some kind o' jecking motion there, but I feel she crying 'cause this her last night here, and 'cause she got to go and leave ever'thing behind. I look at the fire.

She pray there ever so long, and then she start to get up. But she can't make it by herself. I go to help her, and when I put my hand on her shoulder, she say, "Lou? Lou?"

I say, "What's the matter, Fe?"

"Lou?" she say. "Lou?"

I feel her shaking in my hand with all her might. Shaking, shaking, shaking—like a person with the chill. Then I hear her take a long breath, longest I ever heard anybody take before. Then she ease back on the bed—calm, calm, calm.

"Sleep on, Fe," I tell her. "When you get up there, tell 'em all I ain't far behind."

June Jordan

(1936–   )

POWER CHARACTERIZES the writings of June Jordan. In all the genres in which she chooses to write, her mastery of language is evident. Her poetry, which is lyrical, political, and feminist, examines the whites' perceptions of blacks and the blacks' survival in spite of their perception. Even in her children's books, Jordan is frank and open, making sure not to "sugar-coat" her message.

Jordan, whose parents came to New York City from Jamaica, was born in Harlem in 1936. At age five Jordan, an only child, moved to Bedford-Stuyvesant in Brooklyn, where she and her parents lived in a brownstone. The only black in a class of three thousand, she commuted an hour and twenty minutes back and forth to Midwood High School. After high school, she went to prep school at the Northfield School for Girls, which is now a part of Mount Hermon, in Massachusetts. In 1953 she went to Barnard College. It was there that she met and married her husband Michael Meyer, who was a white student at Columbia. While he was in graduate school at the University of Chicago, she attended there for a year before returning to Barnard from 1956 to 1957. Jordan had a son, Christopher David Meyer, in 1958. Her book *Civil Wars* (1981) discusses the difficulties in her marriage, which ended in divorce in 1965.

Prior to the publication of her first book (written for both youth and adults), *Who Look at Me* (1969), Jordan was a research associate and writer for the Technical Housing Department of Mobilization for Youth in New York City, and a professor at City College. She is presently teaching in the Department of African-American Studies at the University of California at Berkeley.

In 1970, Jordan edited two anthologies, *Soulscript: Afro-American Poetry* and *The Voice of the Children*. Jordan's personal life often serves as a basis for her writings: she dedicated her first book and *Civil Wars*, as well as wrote a poem entitled "For Christopher," to her son. In *Some Changes* (1971), she addresses her relationship with her parents.

In some works, such as in the novel *His Own Where* (1971), she uses the black dialect often referred to as black English. Influenced by visiting Rome in 1970 with the help of the Prix de Rome in Environmental Design, she published her second book of poetry, *New Days: Poems of Exile and Return*, in 1974.

Other books by Jordan are *Dry Victories* (1972); *Fannie Lou Hamer*

(1972), a children's novel; *New Life: New Room* (1975); *Things I Do in the Dark: Selected Poetry* (1977), Jordan's major collection of poetry, edited by Toni Morrison; *Passion: New Poems, 1977–1980* (1980); *Kimako's Story* (1981), a children's book dedicated to Alice Walker's daughter; and *Living Room* (1985). Jordan has also written dramatic pieces, including *In the Spirit of Sojourner Truth* (1979) and *For the Arrow That Flies by Day* (1981); released recordings, *Things That I Do in the Dark* (1978) and *For Somebody to Start Singing* (1980); and published essays in periodicals, as well as the collection of political essays *On Call* (1985). Her latest collections are entitled *Naming Our Destiny: New and Selected Poems* (1989), *Moving Towards Home: Political Essays* (1989), and *Lyrical Campaigns: Selected Poems* (1989).

For further reading see in addition to Peter B. Erickson's article in *Dictionary of Literary Biography, Volume 41*; Toni Cade Bambara's "Chosen Weapons," a review of *Civil Wars* in *Ms.* 10 (April 1981); Alexis De Veaux's "Creating Soul Food: June Jordan," *Essence* 11 (April 1981); and Sara Miles's "This Wheel's On Fire," in *Woman Poet: The East* (1982).

"A Song of Sojourner Truth" and "Case in Point" are taken from *Naming Our Destiny, New and Selected Poems*. "Poem About Police Violence" is taken from *Passion: New Poems*. "Independence Day in the U.S.A." comes from *Living Room*.

A SONG OF SOJOURNER TRUTH

Dedicated to Bernice Reagon

The trolley cars was rollin and the passengers all white
when Sojourner just decided it was time to take a seat
The trolley cars was rollin and the passengers all white
When Sojourner decided it was time to take a seat
It was time she felt to rest a while and ease up
on her feet
So Sojourner put her hand out
tried to flag the trolley down
So Sojourner put her hand out
for the trolley crossin town
And the driver did not see her
the conductor would not stop

But Sojourner yelled, "It's me!"
And put her body on the track
"It's me!" she yelled, "And yes,
I walked here but I ain walkin back!"
The trolley car conductor and the driver was afraid
to roll right over her and leave her lying dead
So they opened up the car and Sojourner took a seat
So Sojourner sat to rest a while and eased up on her feet

REFRAIN:

Sojourner had to be just crazy
tellin all that kinda truth
I say she musta been plain crazy
plus they say she was uncouth
talkin loud to any crowd
talkin bad insteada sad
She just had to be plain crazy
talkin all that kinda truth

If she had somewhere to go she said
I'll ride
If she had somewhere to go she said
I'll ride
jim crow or no
she said *I'll go*
just like the lady
that she was in all the knowing darkness
of her pride
she said *I'll ride*
she said *I'll talk*
she said *A Righteous Mouth*
ain nothin you should hide
she said she'd ride
just like the lady
that she was in all the knowing darkness
of her pride
she said *I'll ride*

They said she's Black and ugly and they said she's
really rough
They said if you treat her like a dog
well that'll be plenty good enough
And Sojourner said
I'll ride

And Sojourner said
I'll go
I'm a woman and this hell has made me tough
(Thank God!)
This hell has made me tough
I'm a strong Black woman
and Thank God!

REFRAIN:

Sojourner had to be just crazy
tellin all that kinda truth
I say she musta been plain crazy
plus they say she was uncouth
talkin loud to any crowd
talkin bad insteada sad
She just had to be plain crazy
talkin all that kinda truth

POEM ABOUT POLICE VIOLENCE

Tell me something
what you think would happen if
everytime they kill a black boy
then we kill a cop
everytime they kill a black man
then we kill a cop

you think the accident rate would lower
subsequently?

sometimes the feeling like amaze me baby
comes back to my mouth and I am quiet
like Olympian pools from the running the
mountainous snows under the sun

sometimes thinking about the 12th House of the Cosmos
or the way your ear ensnares the tip
of my tongue or signs that I have never seen
like DANGER WOMEN WORKING

"Poem About Police Violence" from *Passion: New Poems, Nineteen Seventy-Seven to Nineteen Eighty* by June Jordan. Copyright © 1980 by June Jordan. Reprinted by permission of the author.

I lose consciousness of ugly bestial rabid
and repetitive affront as when they tell me
18 cops in order to subdue one man
18 strangled him to death in the ensuing scuffle (don't
you idolize the diction of the powerful: *subdue* and
scuffle my oh my) and that the murder
that the killing of Arthur Miller on a Brooklyn
street was just a "justifiable accident" again
(again)

People been having accidents all over the globe
so long like that I reckon that the only
suitable insurance is a gun
I'm saying war is not to understand or rerun
war is to be fought and won

sometimes the feeling like amaze me baby
blots it out/the bestial but
not too often

tell me something
what you think would happen if
everytime they kill a black boy
then we kill a cop
everytime they kill a black man
then we kill a cop

you think the accident rate would lower
subsequently?

CASE IN POINT

A friend of mine who raised six daughters and
who never wrote what she regards as serious
until she
was fifty-three
tells me there is no silence peculiar
to the female

I have decided I have something to say
about female silence: so to speak
these are my 2¢ on the subject:
2 weeks ago I was raped for the second
time in my life the first occasion
being a whiteman and the most recent

situation being a blackman actually
head of the local NAACP

Today is 2 weeks after the fact
of that man straddling
his knees either side of my chest
his hairy arm and powerful left hand
forcing my arms and my hands over my head
flat to the pillow while he rammed
what he described as his quote big dick
unquote into my mouth
and shouted out: "D'ya want to swallow
my big dick; well, do ya?"

He was being rhetorical.
My silence was peculiar
to the female.

INDEPENDENCE DAY IN THE U.S.A.

I wanted to tell you about July 4th
in northamerica and the lights computerized
shrapnel in white
or red or fast-fuse blue
to celebrate the only revolution
that was legitimate
in human history

I wanted to tell you about the baby
screaming this afternoon where the park
and the music of thousands who eat
food and stay hungry or homicidal
on the subways or the windowsills of the city
came together loud
like the original cannon shots
from that only legitimate revolution
in human history

I wanted to tell you about my Spanish
how it starts like a word aggravating the beat
of my heart then rushes up to my head

where my eyes dream Caribbean
flowers and my mouth waters
around black beans
or coffee that lets me forget
the hours before morning

But I am living inside the outcome
of the only legitimate revolution
in human history
and the operator will not place my call to Cuba
the mailman will not carry my letters to Managua
the State Department will not okay my visa
for a short-wave conversation
and you do not speak English

and I can dig it

Amiri Baraka

(1934–   )

DRAMATIST, POET, NOVELIST, essayist, and political activist, LeRoi Jones changed his name to Ameer Baraka in 1968 and later again changed the "Ameer" to "Amiri." Reflecting his adoption of the Yoruba and Islamic religions, he used the title "Imamu," which means "spiritual leader," a title he later dropped in 1974 upon his return from Africa where people thought he was a priest because of the religious title Imamu. His thirty-one books, twenty-five plays, three screenplays, and four anthologies manifest his adoption of the ideas of bohemian Beat poets of Greenwich Village and Marxist-Leninist socialism to black cultural nationalism. Although the content and form of Baraka's art, his essays, and his political convictions are continually controversial, his place in African American literary history is quite secure.

The son of middle-class parents, Baraka was born in Newark, New Jersey, in 1934. His father was a postal worker, while his mother was a social worker, who earned her degree at Tuskegee Institute. After graduating from Barringer, a predominantly white high school, in 1951, Baraka did undergraduate work at Rutgers for one year and transferred to Howard, where he stayed for two years. Unhappy at Howard because of the elitism and narrow-mindedness of many of his peers and some of his professors, Baraka joined the U.S. Air Force, in whose service he spent three years in Puerto Rico.

In 1958 in Greenwich Village he met Hettie Roberta Cohen, a Jewish American who became his first wife. Together they founded an avant garde magazine, *Yugen*. Although the magazine ran for only eight issues between 1958 and 1962, it served as a forum for an impressive group of Beat writers, among them Allen Ginsberg, William S. Burroughs, Diana DiPrima, Charles Olson, Edward Dahlberg, in addition to black poet A. B. Spellman. During this time Jones entered graduate school at Columbia University. He subsequently broke with the white Bohemian world and, along with Larry Neal, became one of the prime movers of the Black Arts movement. *Blues People, Cuba Libre, Preface to a Twenty Volume Suicide Note, Negro Music in White America, Dutchman, The Slave,* and *The Dead Lecturer* attest to Baraka's separation from the white Bohemian values and his absorption of the black aesthetics of the 1960s.

A prolific and tireless writer, Baraka has almost as many play productions as he does book publications. Along with African American aesth-

443

eticians such as Haki Madhubuti, Sonia Sanchez, Carolyn Rodgers, Sarah Webster Fabio, and Larry Neal, Baraka in his poetry breaks away from Western traditional aesthetics to utilize characteristics of black folk culture, particularly black speech and black music. Similarly in his theater productions of plays like *Dutchman, The Slave, Experimental Death Unit #1, Madheart,* and *Arm Yourself, or Harm Yourself,* among many others, Baraka challenges not only the technical components of Euro-American theater, but also the stereotypical, racist notions that describe the interactions between blacks and whites in America.

Baraka emerges from the pages of African American and American history as a figure with indefatigable energy. He has taught poetry at the New School of Social Research, drama at Columbia University, and literature at the University of Buffalo. He has also served as visiting professor at San Francisco State College. Among other honors and awards, he received a John Hay Whitney Opportunity Fellowship in 1963, a Guggenheim Fellowship in 1965, and an Honorary Doctor of Humane Letters in 1972 from Malcolm X College.

Because of his remarkable productivity, we include here only a few of his works not mentioned previously: *The System of Dante's Hell* (1965), a novel; *Home: Social Essays* (1966); *Black Music* (1967), essay in book form; *Tales* (1967), fiction; *It's Nation Time* (1970), a collection of poetry; *Hard Facts* (1975); *Selected Poetry of Amiri Baraka* (1979); *Selected Plays and Prose of Amiri Baraka* (1979); *Daggers and Javelins: Essays* (1984); and *The Autobiography of LeRoi Jones/Amiri Baraka* (1984). Along with his second wife, Amina Baraka, he also edited *Confirmation: An Anthology of African American Women* (1983). See also *The LeRoi Jones/Amiri Baraka Reader,* edited by William J. Harris (1991).

For bibliographical and critical sources, see Floyd Gaffney's entry in *Dictionary of Literary Biography, Volume 38.* Also see D. H. Melhem's "Revolution: the Constancy of Change—An Interview with Amiri Baraka," *Black America Literature Forum* (Fall 1982); Ikenna Dieke's "Sadeanism: Baraka, Sexuality, and the Perverse Imagination in *The System of Dante's Hell,*" *Black America Literaure Forum* (Winter 1985); and William J. Harris's *The Poetry and Poetics of Amiri Baraka: The Jazz Aesthetic* (1985). Also see Theodore Hudson's *From LeRoi Jones to Amiri Baraka* (1773) and Kimberly Benston's *Imamu Amiri Baraka (LeRoi Jones): A Collection of Critical Essays* (1978).

"Crow Jane in High Society" and "Black Dada Nihilismus" are reprinted from *Selected Poetry of Amiri Baraka/LeRoi Jones.* "The Myth of a 'Negro Literature' " is reprinted from *Home: Social Essays* and was originally presented as an address at the American Society for African Culture, March 14, 1962.

CROW JANE IN HIGH SOCIETY

                          (Wipes
her nose
on the draperies. Spills drinks
fondles another man's
life. She is looking
for alternatives. Openings
where she can lay all
this greasy talk
on somebody. Me, once. Now
I am her teller.
                (And I tell
her symbols, as the gray movement
of clouds. Leave
gray movements
of clouds. Leave, always,
more.

Where is she? That she
moves without light. Even
in our halls. Even with
our laughter, lies, dead drunk
in a slouch hat famous king.
                         Where?

    To come on so.

BLACK DADA NIHILISMUS

                  .Against what light

is false what breath
sucked, for deadness.
              Murder, the cleansed

purpose, frail, against
God, if they bring him

"Crow Jane in High Society," "Black Dada Nihilismus," and "The Myth of a Negro Literature" are reprinted by permission of Sterling Lord Literistic, Inc. Copyright © 1964 by LeRoi Jones (Amiri Baraka).

bleeding, I would not
forgive, or even call him
black dada nihilismus.

The protestant love, wide windows,
color blocked to Mondrian, and the
ugly silent deaths of jews under
the surgeon's knife. (To awake on
69th street with money and a hip
nose. Black dada nihilismus, for

the umbrella'd jesus. Trilby intrigue
movie house presidents sticky the floor.
B.D.N., for the secret men, Hermes, the

blacker art. Thievery (ahh, they return
those secret gold killers. Inquisitors
of the cocktail hour. Trismegistus, have

them, in their transmutation, from stone
to bleeding pearl, from lead to burning
looting, dead Moctezuma, find the West

a gray hideous space.

2.

From Sartre, a white man, it gave
the last breath. And we beg him die,
before he is killed. Plastique, we

do not have, only thin heroic blades.
The razor. Our flail against them, why
you carry knives? Or brutaled lumps of

heart? Why you stay, where they can
reach? Why you sit, or stand, or walk
in this place, a window on a dark

warehouse. Where the minds packed in
straw. New homes, these towers, for those
lacking money or art. A cult of death,

need of the simple striking arm under
the streetlamp. The cutters, from under
their rented earth. Come up, black dada

nihilismus. Rape the white girls. Rape
their fathers. Cut the mother's throats.

Black dada nihilismus, choke my friends
in their bedrooms with their drinks spilling
and restless for tilting hips or dark liver
lips sucking splinters from the master's thigh.

Black scream
and chant, scream,
and dull, un
earthly

hollering. Dada, bilious
what ugliness, learned
in the dome, colored holy
shit (i call them sinned

or lost
    burned masters
           of the lost
                nihil German killers
                    all our learned

art, 'member
what you said
money, God, power,
a moral code, so cruel
it destroyed Byzantium, Tenochtitlan, Commanch
                    (got it, *Baby*!

    For tambo, willie best, dubois, patrice, mantan, the
bronze buckaroos.

           for Jack Johnson, asbestos, tonto, buckwheat,
           billie holiday.

For tom russ, l'ouverture, vesey, beau jack,

(may a lost god damballah, rest or save us
against the murders we intend
against his lost white children
black dada nihilismus

THE MYTH OF A "NEGRO LITERATURE"

The mediocrity of what has been called "Negro Literature" is one of
the most loosely held secrets of American culture. From Phillis
Wheatley to Charles Chesnutt, to the present generation of American
Negro writers, the only recognizable accretion of tradition readily at-

tributable to the black producer of a formal literature in this country, with a few notable exceptions, has been of an almost agonizing mediocrity. In most other fields of "high art" in America, with the same few notable exceptions, the Negro contribution has been, when one existed at all, one of impressive mediocrity. Only in music, and most notably in blues, jazz, and spirituals, *i.e.*, "Negro Music," has there been a significantly profound contribution by American Negroes.

There are a great many reasons for the spectacular vapidity of the American Negro's accomplishment in other formal, serious art forms—social, economic, political, etc.—but one of the most persistent and aggravating reasons for the absence of achievement among serious Negro artists, except in Negro music, is that in most cases the Negroes who found themselves in a position to pursue some art, especially the art of literature, have been members of the Negro middle class, a group that has always gone out of its way to cultivate *any* mediocrity, as long as that mediocrity was guaranteed to prove to America, and recently to the world at large, that they were not really who they were, *i.e.*, Negroes. Negro music alone, because it drew its strengths and beauties out of the depth of the black man's soul, and because to a large extent its traditions could be carried on by the lowest classes of Negroes, has been able to survive the constant and willful dilutions of the black middle class. Blues and jazz have been the only consistent exhibitors of "Negritude" in formal American culture simply because the bearers of its tradition maintained their essential identities as Negroes; in no other art (and I will persist in calling Negro music, Art) has this been possible. Phillis Wheatley and her pleasant imitations of 18th century English poetry are far and, finally, ludicrous departures from the huge black voices that splintered southern nights with their *hollers, chants, arwhoolies,* and *ballits.* The embarrassing and inverted paternalism of Charles Chesnutt and his "refined Afro-American" heroes are far cries from the richness and profundity of the blues. And it is impossible to mention the achievements of the Negro in any area of artistic endeavor with as much significance as in spirituals, blues and jazz. There has never been an equivalent to Duke Ellington or Louis Armstrong in Negro writing, and even the best of contemporary literature written by Negroes cannot yet be compared to the fantastic beauty of the music of Charlie Parker.

American Negro music from its inception moved logically and powerfully out of a fusion between African musical tradition and the American experience. It was, and continues to be, a natural, yet highly stylized and personal version of the Negro's life in America. It is, indeed, a chronicler of the Negro's movement, from African slave to American slave, from Freedman to Citizen. And the literature of the blues is a much more profound contribution to Western culture than any other literary contribution made by American Negroes. Moreover, it is only recently that formal literature written by American Negroes has begun to approach the literary standards of its model, *i.e.*, the literature of the white middle class. And only Jean Toomer, Richard Wright, Ralph Ellison, and James Baldwin have managed to bring off examples of writing, in this genre, that could succeed in passing themselves off as "serious" writing, in the sense that, say, the work of Somerset Maugham is "serious" writing. That is, serious, if one has never read Herman Melville or James Joyce. And it is part of the tragic naïveté of the middle class (brow) writer, that he has not.

Literature, for the Negro writer, was always an example of "culture." Not in the sense of the more impressive philosophical characteristics of a particular social group, but in the narrow sense of "cultivation" or "sophistication" by an individual within that group. The Negro artist, because of his middle-class background, carried the artificial social burden as the "best and most intelligent" of Negroes, and usually entered into the "serious" arts to exhibit his familiarity with the social graces, *i.e.*, as a method or means of displaying his participation in the "serious" aspects of American culture. To be a writer was to be "cultivated," in the stunted bourgeois sense of the word. It was also to be a "quality" black man. It had nothing to do with the investigation of the human soul. It was, and is, a social preoccupation rather than an aesthetic one. A rather daring way of status seeking. The cultivated Negro leaving those ineffectual philanthropies, Negro colleges, looked at literature merely as another way of gaining prestige in the white world for the Negro middle class. And the literary and artistic models were always those that could be socially acceptable to the white middle class, which automatically limited them to the most spiritually debilitated imitations of literature available. Negro music, to the middle class, black and white, was never socially acceptable. It was shunned by blacks ambitious of "waking up white," as low and degrading. It was shunned by their white models simply because it was produced by blacks. As one of my professors at Howard University protested one day, "It's amazing how much bad taste the blues display." Suffice it to say, it is in part exactly this "bad taste" that has continued to keep Negro music as vital as it is. The abandonment of one's local (*i.e.*, place or group) emotional attachments in favor of the abstract emotional response of what is called "the general public" (which is notoriously white and middle class) has always been the great diluter of any Negro culture. "You're acting like a nigger," was the standard disparagement. I remember being chastised severely for daring to eat a piece of watermelon on the Howard campus. "Do you realize you're sitting near the highway?" is what the man said, "This is the capstone of Negro education." And it is too, in the sense that it teaches the Negro how to make out in the white society, using the agonizing overcompensation of pretending he's also white. James Baldwin's play, *The Amen Corner*, when it appeared at the Howard Players theatre, "set the speech department back ten years," an English professor groaned to me. The play depicted the lives of poor Negroes running a store-front church. Any reference to the Negroness of the American Negro has always been frowned upon by the black middle class in their frenzied dash toward the precipice of the American mainstream.

High art, first of all, must reflect the experiences of the human being, the emotional predicament of the man, as he exists, in the defined world of his being. It must be produced from the legitimate emotional resources of the soul in the world. It can *never* be produced by evading these resources or pretending that they do not exist. It can never be produced by appropriating the withered emotional responses of some strictly social idea of humanity. High art, and by this I mean any art that would attempt to describe or characterize some portion of the profound meaningfulness of human life with any finality or truth, cannot be based on the superficialities of human existence. It must issue from *real* categories of human activity, *truthful* accounts of human life, and not fancied accounts of the attainment of cultural privilege by some willingly preposterous apologists for one social "order" or another. Most of the formal literature produced by Negroes in America has never fulfilled these conditions. And aside from Negro music, it is only in the "popular traditions" of the so-called lower class Negro that these conditions are fulfilled as a basis for human life. And it is because of this "separation" between Negro life (as an emotional experience) and Negro art, that, say, Jack Johnson or Ray Robinson is a larger cultural hero than any Negro writer. It is because of this separation, even evasion, of the emotional experience of Negro life, that Jack Johnson is a more modern political symbol than most Negro writers. Johnson's life, as proposed, certainly, by his career, reflects much more accurately the symbolic yearnings for singular values among the great masses of Negroes than any black novelist has yet managed to convey. Where is the Negro-ness of a literature written in imitation of the meanest of social intelligences to be found in American culture, i.e., the white middle class? How can it even begin to express the emotional predicament of black Western man? Such a literature, even if its "characters" *are* black, takes on the emotional barrenness of its model, and the blackness of the characters is like the blackness of Al Jolson, an unconvincing device. It is like using black checkers instead of white. They are still checkers.

The development of the Negro's music was, as I said, direct and instinctive. It was the one vector out of African culture impossible to eradicate completely. The appearance of blues as a native *American* music signified in many ways the appearance of American Negroes where once there were African Negroes. The emotional fabric of the music was colored by the emergence of an American Negro culture. It signified that culture's strength and vitality. In the evolution of form in Negro music it is possible to see not only the evolution of the Negro as a cultural and social element of American culture, but also the evolution of that culture itself. The "Coon Shout" proposed one version of the American Negro—and of America; Ornette Coleman proposes another. But the point is that both these versions are accurate and informed with a legitimacy of emotional concern nowhere available in what is called "Negro Literature," and certainly not in the middlebrow literature of the white American.

The artifacts of African art and sculpture were consciously eradicated by slavery. Any African art that based its validity on the production of an artifact, *i.e.*, some *material* manifestation such as a wooden statue or a woven cloth, had little chance of survival. It was only the more "abstract" aspects of African culture that could continue to exist in slave America. Africanisms still persist in the music, religion, and popular cultural traditions of American Negroes. However, it is not an African art American Negroes are responsible for, but an American one. The traditions of Africa must be utilized within the culture of the American Negro where they *actually* exist, and not because of a defensive rationalization about the *worth* of one's ancestors or an attempt to capitalize on the recent eminence of the "new" African nations. Africanisms do exist in Negro culture, but they have been so translated and transmuted by the American experience that they have become integral parts of that experience.

The American Negro has a definable and legitimate historical tradition, no matter how painful, in America, but it is the only place such a tradition exists, simply because America is the only place the American Negro exists. He is, as William Carlos Williams said, "A pure product of America." The paradox of the Negro experience in America is that it is a separate experience, but inseparable from the complete fabric of American life. The history of Western culture begins for the Negro with the importation of the slaves. It is almost as if all Western history before that must be strictly a learned concept. It is only the American experience that can be a persistent cultural catalyst for the Negro. In a sense, history for the Negro, before America, must remain an emotional abstraction. The cultural mem-

ory of Africa informs the Negro's life in America, but it is impossible
to separate it from its American transformation. Thus, the Negro
writer if he wanted to tap his legitimate cultural tradition should
have done it by utilizing the entire spectrum of the American experience from the point of view of the emotional history of the black
man in this country: as its victim and its chronicler. The soul of
such a man, as it exists outside the boundaries of commercial diversion or artificial social pretense. But without a deep commitment to
cultural relevance and intellectual purity this was impossible. The
Negro as a writer, was always a social object, whether glorifying the
concept of white superiority, as a great many early Negro writers
did, or in crying out against it, as exemplified by the stock "protest"
literature of the thirties. He never moved into the position where he
could propose his own symbols, erect his own personal myths, as
any great literature must. Negro writing was always "after the fact,"
i.e., based on known social concepts within the structure of bourgeois idealistic projections of "their America," and an emotional climate that never really existed.

The most successful fiction of most Negro writing is in its emotional content. The Negro protest novelist postures, and invents a
protest quite amenable with the tradition of bourgeois American life.
He never reaches the central core of the America which *can* cause
such protest. The intellectual traditions of the white middle class
prevent such exposure of reality, and the black imitators reflect this.
The Negro writer on Negro life in America postures, and invents a
Negro life, and an America to contain it. And even most of those
who tried to rebel against the *invented* America were trapped because
they had lost all touch with the reality of their experience within the
real America, either because of the hidden emotional allegiance to
the white middle class, or because they did not realize where the
reality of their experience lay. When the serious Negro writer dis-
dained the "middlebrow" model, as is the case with a few contemporary black American writers, he usually rushed headlong into the
groves of the Academy, perhaps the most insidious and clever dis-
penser of middlebrow standards of excellence under the guise of
"recognizable tradition." That such recognizable tradition is necessary goes without saying, but even from the great philosophies of
Europe a contemporary usage must be established. No poetry has
come out of England of major importance for forty years, yet there
are would-be Negro poets who reject the gaudy excellence of 20th
century American poetry in favor of disembowelled academic models
of second-rate English poetry, with the notion that somehow it is the
only way poetry should be written. It would be better if such a poet
listened to Bessie Smith sing *Gimme a Pigfoot*, or listened to the tragic

verse of a Billie Holiday, than be content to imperfectly imitate the bad poetry of the ruined minds of Europe. And again, it is this striving for *respectability* that has it so. For an American, black or white, to say that some hideous imitation of Alexander Pope means more to him, emotionally, than the blues of Ray Charles or Lightnin' Hopkins, it would be required for him to have completely disappeared into the American Academy's vision of a Europeanized and colonial American culture, or to be lying. In the end, the same emotional sterility results. It is somehow much more tragic for the black man.

A Negro literature, to be a legitimate product of the Negro experience in America, must get at that experience in exactly the terms America has proposed for it, in its most ruthless identity. Negro reaction to America is as deep a part of America as the root causes of that reaction, and it is impossible to accurately describe that reaction in terms of the American middle class; because for them, the Negro has never really existed, never been glimpsed in anything even approaching the complete reality of his humanity. The Negro writer has to go from where he actually is, completely outside of that conscious white myopia. That the Negro does exist is the point, and as an element of American culture he is completely misunderstood by Americans. The middlebrow, commercial Negro writer assures the white American that, in fact, he doesn't exist, and that if he does, he does so within the perfectly predictable finger-painting of white bourgeois sentiment and understanding. Nothing could be further from the truth. The Creoles of New Orleans resisted "Negro" music for a time as raw and raucous, because they thought they had found a place within the white society which would preclude their being Negroes. But they were unsuccessful in their attempts to "disappear" because the whites themselves reminded them that they were still, for all their assimilation, "just coons." And this seems to me an extremely important idea, since it is precisely this bitter insistence that has kept what can be called "Negro Culture" a brilliant amalgam of diverse influences. There was always a border beyond which the Negro could not go, whether musically or socially. There was always a possible limitation to any dilution or excess of cultural or spiritual reference. The Negro could not ever become white and that was his strength; at some point, always, he could not participate in the dominant tenor of the white man's culture, yet he came to understand that culture as well as the white man. It was at this juncture that he had to make use of other resources, whether African, sub-cultural, or hermetic. And it was this boundary, this no-man's-land, that provided the logic and beauty of his music. And this is the only way for the Negro artist to provide his version of America—from that no-man's-land outside the mainstream. A no-man's-land, a black country, completely invisible to white America, but so essentially part of it as to stain its whole being an ominous gray. Were there really a Negro literature, now it could flower. At this point when the whole of Western society might go up in flames, the Negro remains an integral part of that society, but continually outside it, a figure like Melville's Bartleby. He is an American, capable of identifying emotionally with the fantastic cultural ingredients of this society, but he is also, forever, outside that culture, an invisible strength within it, an observer. If there is ever a Negro literature, it must disengage itself from the weak, heinous elements of the culture that spawned it, and use its very existence as evidence of a more profound America. But as long as the Negro writer contents himself with the imitation of the useless ugly inelegance of the stunted middle-class mind, academic or popular, and refuses to look around him and "tell it like it is"—preferring the false prestige of the black bourgeois or the deceitful "acceptance" of *buy and sell* America, something never included in the legitimate cultural tradition of "his people"—he will be a failure, and what is worse, not even a significant failure. Just another dead American.

PART 2

The African American Literary Revival: The 1970s to the Present

In his essay "The Literature of the Negro in the United States," collected in *White Man Listen!* (1957), Richard Wright prophetically describes the state of African American literature in the 1970s and 1980s. In response to the 1954 Supreme Court decision (*Brown v. Board of Education*) to desegregate the schools, Wright says, "The Negro, as he learns to stand on his own feet and expresses himself not in purely racial, but human terms, will launch criticism upon his native land which made him feel a sense of estrangement that he never wanted. This new attitude could have a healthy effect upon the culture of the United States. At long last, maybe a merging of Negro expression with American expression will take place." Both the 1954 Supreme Court decision and the highly diverse black political activity of the 1960s made it possible for many blacks to begin their assimilation into mainstream society. Perhaps no other area manifests signs of this merger more dramatically than the discipline of African American literature and criticism. For, approximately sixteen years after the court's decision and, perhaps, to some degree in reaction to the rebellious black nationalist ideology of the Black Arts movement, African American writers, particularly the women writers, in the 1970s evidenced a move away from their emphasis on what Wright refers to as "purely racial" themes and began to highlight blacks' interaction with each other rather than with whites and to sharpen their aesthetic tools with a precision and an originality that, to paraphrase Wright, thrust them into the forefront of literary expression.

Black drama, perhaps more than any other genre, evinces this dynamic development in African American literature, which brought such playwrights as Douglas Turner Ward, Lorraine Hansberry, Amiri Baraka, Ed Bullins, and Ntozake Shange to the forefront of the American theatrical arena. The 1970s brought a resurgence of black drama with a momentum that began in 1959 with the appearance of Lorraine Hansberry's *A Raisin in the Sun*. Yet, while a black reading audience has been increasingly supportive of black fiction since the 1960s, the black theatrical performances have continued to suffer from the control of whites who attempt to impose their aesthetic standards on black theatre. From the 1920s throughout the 1950s, Harlem was the center of activity for the production of black plays. By the 1960s, however, the black middle class had left Harlem for the suburbs, and Greenwich Village and Broadway began to dominate the black dramatic scene. Companies such as the Harlem Suitcase Theatre and the American Negro Theatre were experiencing difficulties by the 1960s and were being challenged by the revolutionary fervor of a younger generation of black dramatists led by Amiri Baraka, who, through a $40,000 grant from the federal government, opened up the Black Arts Repertoire Theatre School in Harlem in 1965. His plays *The Dutchman* and *The Slave* had already been produced off Broadway, a year earlier. During this time period, Douglas Turner Ward's two most well-known plays, *Happy Ending* (1966) and *Day of Absence* (1966), were produced. Like Baraka, Ward, too, worked toward the goal of a theater by, for, and about blacks.

The history of African American drama from William Wells Brown to contemporary playwrights such as Ntozake Shange demonstrates that black drama has always had a political context, and despite the fact that black drama has historically received little critical attention, black American playwrights are multitalented and their methodologies manifest an impressive diversity. While Adrienne Kennedy's *Funnyhouse of a Negro* (1962) is characterized by surrealism and symbolism, Ntozake Shange's *For Colored Girls* (1975) is a beautiful mixture of poetry, dance, and music. Less innovative than Kennedy's and Shange's works, Joseph Walker's *River Niger* and Charles Fuller's *A Soldier's Story* explore the political and psychological effects of racism on human consciousness. Douglas Turner Ward and Alice Childress write, act, direct, and produce. Loften Mitchell is the scholar among the group. Though he writes drama, he is also a noted historian of black American drama. Two of his books, *Black Drama: The Story of the American Negro in the Theatre* (1967) and *Voices of the Black Theatre* (1975), remain landmark studies indispensable to an investigation of the history of black American drama.

In the midst of this resurgence of black drama in the 1970s, such writers as Margaret Walker and Gwendolyn Brooks, as well as Arthur P. Davis and other critics who began their literary careers in the 1940s, were and still are actively producing. Likewise, the most well known of the young, rebellious poets of the 1960s—Amiri Baraka, Sonia Sanchez, Haki Madhubuti, and Nikki Giovanni—are more productive today than they were in the 1960s. Moreover, their most recent collections of poetry manifest their continued commitment to the aesthetic of the Black Arts movement. The early 1970s showed more influence of the black nationalist ideology than did the late 1970s. Two landmark publications of the early seventies, Addison Gayle, Jr.'s *The Black Aesthetic* (1971) and Stephen Henderson's *Understanding the New Black Poetry* (1972) emerge as necessary resources for anyone studying the contemporary history of African American literature and criticism. *The Black Aesthetic* is a collection of essays by some of the most important writers and scholars of the African American literary tradition, addressing topics on theory, music, poetry, drama, and fiction. Henderson's anthology of African American poetry from its folk origins through the 1960s remains the first source and still the only one that presents a sustained, comprehensive scholarly analysis of the new black poetry of the 1960s. The 1970s and 1980s emerge as periods marked by impressive technical innovations in African American literature and criticism. This period has seen diverse literary productivity for black writers, especially women writers; a decided change in focus in the works of black women; the appearance of new journals and black presses; the appearance of a number of new writers who immediately secured their places in the history of African American literature and criticism; and the merger of African American literary criticism with mainstream theoretical exegesis.

In addition to the rich productivity of black women writers, the 1980s were characterized by prodigious achievements of black male scholars whose literary analyses mark the merger of African American literary criticism with Euro-American criticism and who introduce theoretical models that have left their indelible sign on the history of African American literary history. The appearance of Dexter Fisher and Robert Stepto's edition of *Afro-American Literature: The Reconstruction of Instruction* in 1979 marked the way for the post-structuralist readings by critic Henry Louis Gates, Jr. and others, and the vernacular blues ideology of Houston A. Baker, Jr. Published by the Modern Language Association, the national governing body for American scholars of English and foreign languages, *Reconstruction of Instruction* attempts to correct the problem of an overemphasis on biographical-sociological approaches that dominate analyses of works by black writers. Although the essays collected in this volume are methodologically diverse, the overall, predominant tone reflects the heavy influence of modernist, Euro-American technical innovations in the critical approach. The basic difference, then, between *Reconstruction of Instruction* and the critical analysis of black American literature before 1979 is one of focus. Previously, black literary critics—such as Arthur P. Davis, Saunders Redding, Nick Aaron Ford, George Kent, Richard Barksdale, Eugenia Collier, Therman O'Daniel, and Darwin Turner—frequently challenged historical racial issues in their criticism of African American literary art. It was natural for these black critics to take their cue from the black artists, who, from the slave narratives to the 1960s, had used their art as a means of denouncing slavery and its replacement racism. Nevertheless, the widespread infusion of blacks into mainstream academic circles in the 1970s dramatically affected the focus of black literature and criticism in a profound way. With the exception of Michael Cook's *Afro-American Literature* in the Twentieth Century: The Achievement of Intimacy (1984) and Bernard W. Bell's The Afro-American Novel and Its Tradition (1987), a significant number of the literary analyses written or edited by black American male critics—Chester Fontenot and Joe Weixlmann's Studies in Black American Literature, Volume I: Black American Prose Theory (1984) and Studies in Black American Literature, Volume II: Belief vs. Theory in Black American Literary Criticism (1986); Houston A. Baker, Jr.'s Blues, Ideology, and Afro-American Literature: A Vernacular Theory (1984) and his Modernism and the Harlem Renaissance (1987); and Henry Louis Gates, Jr.'s Black Literature and Literary Theory (1984), his Figures in Black: Words, Signs, and the "Racial" Self (1987), and his The Signifying Monkey: A Theory of Afro-American Literary Criticism (1988)—to varying degrees substantiate the fact that a number of contemporary black male scholars have strayed away from the traditional issues that describe the history of African American literary criticism.

Because of the impressive volume of their publications and the strong support they receive from mainstream publishers, academic institutions, and granting agencies, Baker and Gates emerge as the two most influential African American literary critical voices in the 1980s. Although Baker does not consider himself a post-structuralist per se, his work, particularly his most substantial Blues, Ideology, and Afro-American Literature is suffused with references to semiotic and deconstructionist critics. In essence Baker uses the blues as a trope that illuminates the content and social behavior of African American as well as Euro-American social and literary history. Gates, on the other hand, is the leading practitioner of African American post-structuralist methodology. In The Signifying Monkey: A Theory of Afro-American Literary Criticism, he demonstrates the relationship between the Yoruba trickster figure Esu-Elegbara and the Signifying Monkey, suggesting that contemporary African American literature manifests what he calls a "Talking Book," a trope continually present in African American literature beginning with the slave narrative.

The creative writers of the older generation—Baldwin, Killens, Petry, Marshall, Kelly, Ellison, Gaines, and Demby—all had firmly established their positions in the annals of African American literary history by 1970. Although Larry Neal died an untimely death in 1981, the writers of the younger generation—Sanchez, Madhubuti, Baraka, Evans, and Giovanni, for example—were still at the beginning of their literary careers in 1970, the publication year for Maya Angelou's I know Why the Caged Bird Sings, Alice Walker's The Third Life of Grange Copeland, and Toni Morrison's The Bluest Eye.

The necessity for black Americans to understand how slavery and racism have shaped their consciousness is the thread that connects writers as diverse as James Baldwin, Richard Wright, Toni Cade Bambara, Toni Morrison, Alice Walker, and many others. Although Richard Wright's Na-

tive Son on one level challenges white society to take a look at its role in Bigger Thomas's racial oppression, on a more important level, the novel coerces black Americans to make conscious decisions about their selfhood despite the imposed psychological, sociological, and economical limitations of racism. Of course, the interconnection between identity and a history of racial oppression has its roots in the slave narrative. Consequently, Maya Angelou's five volumes of her autobiography (three of which were published in the 1980s) and Marita Golden's *Migrations of the Heart* (1983) are manifestations of the oldest tradition in African American prose. And interestingly enough, Margaret Walker's *Jubilee* (1966), Morrison's *Song of Solomon* (1977) and *Beloved* (1987), Sherley Anne Williams's *Dessa Rose* (1986), and Alice Walker's *The Temple of My Familiar* (1989) emerge as metaphorical representations of the contemporary African American woman writer's indefatigable interest in the black past and its effect upon character.

Spurred by a sizable black reading audience for the first time in American history, by the support of white feminists, and by endorsements from publishers, contemporary black women writers do not overtly address white audiences. Their novels have black communities that are as self-propelling and separate from the white community as those in Hurston's *Their Eyes Were Watching God*. Quite different from Richard Wright's works and from those of most—if not all—established contemporary black male writers, novels written by black women writers—*Song of Solomon, Beloved,* and *The Salt Eaters*, for example—emphasize the intricate network of a black communal life that functions as setting in the Zora Hurston sense, although the reader must constantly be aware of how the dicta of white society shape black lives. In their attempt to awaken and fortify the historical, political, and psychological consciousness of black people, black women writers technically demonstrate what they see as the inextricable interrelationship between folk myth and reality. Consequently, this focusing inward on the black community and its indigenous traditions has necessitated that the modes of expression (the craft) change. Traditional Euro-American literary tools fall short of unearthing the total craft of these works.

For the first time in African American literary history black women critics in the 1980s responded to the literary call sounded by their creative sisters. Alice Walker's investigative journey to discover Zora Hurston's unmarked grave and her role in resurrecting Hurston's works function as paradigm for the analytical productivity of the black women critics who emerged in the 1980s. Barbara Smith's "Toward a Black Feminist Criticism" (1977), Deborah McDowell's "New Directions for Black Feminist Criticism" (1980), and Mary Helen Washington's introduction to *Midnight Birds: Stories by Contemporary Black Women Writers* (1980) are three of the earliest pieces of criticism written by black women scholars who are not creative artists themselves, and they place these scholars at the forefront of the intense activity in the contemporary African American literary critical community. The term *renaissance* has not yet been used to refer to the current status of black literature and criticism, but the word appropriately describes the diversity and proliferation of works written by and about black women writers. The idea of a revival in the artistic and intellectual achievement of black American literature with emphasis on the imaginative and critical works of black women may be more appropriate today than it was in the 1920s. For the current activity in African American literature and criticism reflects the momentum and variety that began with the Harlem Renaissance. The same kind of diversity that describes the talents of the creative artists from Toni Morrison and Alice Walker to the younger Pulitzer Prize-winning poet Rita Dove and American Book Award winner Gloria Naylor also suggests the range of scholarly analyses by critics as varied as feminists Deborah McDowell, Mary Helen Washington, Gloria Hull, Claudia Tate, Hortense Spillers, Nellie McKay, Cheryl Wall, and Carolivia Herron; lesbian critics Barbara Smith and Barbara Christian; folklorists Daryl Dance and Trudier Harris; socialist Maryemma Graham; traditional critics Thadious Davis, Valerie Smith, Joanne Gabbin, Frances Smith Foster, Sandra O'Neale, Eugenia Collier, Prisilla Ramsey, Sandra Govan, and Jennifer Jordan; literary historians Gloria Wade Gayles and Paula Giddings; and the folk-myth virtuoso Eleanor Traylor.

Far more eclectic than the Harlem Renaissance, the period in African American literary history from 1970 to the present resembles a patchwork quilt whose pieces contain the varying modes of thought, educational background, gender differences, and political allegiances of the writers and critics crisscrossed onto the African American literary framework. This highly productive revival is marked not only by diverse and vehement critical dialogues, new critics, fiction writers, and autobiographers, but also by new poets, presses, and journals as well as the investigative research of Henry Louis Gates, Jr. Although Eugene Redmond, June Jordan, and Audre Lorde wrote some poetry in the 1960s, they began to come into prominence in the 1970s, along with Sonia Sanchez, Haki Madhubuti, and Quincy Troupe. Joining their company are such poets as Sherley Anne Williams, Alexis De Veaux, E. Ethelbert Miller, and Michael Harper, whose works to varying degrees manifest the influence of the black cultural nationalism of the 1960s.

Clearly, a serious imbalance exists between the numbers and diversity of African American writers and their avenues for publication. Hence, the future of what could be called easily a black literary revival depends upon the continued efforts of such scholars as Gates, who is general editor for the Schomburg Library's collection of works by nineteenth-century black women writers, and Deborah McDowell, who is editor for the American Women Writers Series for Rutgers University Press, which has reprinted Nella Larsen's *Quicksand* and *Passing*. Despite the fact that a few trade presses such as Thunder's Mouth demonstrate an interest in publishing works by black writers, not even a handful of presses owned and operated by blacks have existed. Dudley Randall's Broadside Press is no longer functioning, while Haki Madhubuti's Third World Press, Kassahun Checole's Africa World Press, Naomi Madgett's Lotus Press, and Paul Coates's Black Classic Press are forced to operate on rather limited budgets. Widely circulated journals devoted exclusively to black American literature—*Callaloo, Obsidian*, and *Black American Literature Forum*—can in no way carry the weight of the prodigious productivity that characterizes African American literature and criticism in the 1980s and 1990s.

When analyzing this enormous body of work with its complex publication history and with its multifarious components, literary historians and critics must remain ever mindful of the political limitations that have threatened the black writer's productivity. An exploration of stylistic and thematic consistencies will point to and enhance an appreciation of the innovations found in the works of our modern African American literary priests and priestesses, who have surpassed Richard Wright's prediction. Rather than merely merging their expression with that of the mainstream, contemporary African American writers now make up the vanguard of literary activity in the United States.

Sonia Sanchez

(1934–   )

SONIA SANCHEZ, born Wilsonia Driver in 1934, was a shy child who stuttered. Now a dynamic, exuberant, powerful woman, Sanchez is known for her emotional and lively poetry readings. While chanting, she goes into a spell in which she embodies the spirits of Dr. Martin Luther King, Jr., Frederick Douglass, Harriet Tubman, and Malcolm X, and speaks in their voices. A mother, poet, playwright, activist, teacher, and editor, Sanchez is a dynamic spokesperson for those masses who cannot speak for themselves.

Raised in Birmingham, Alabama, by extended family members after her mother died when Sanchez was one, Sanchez moved to Harlem, New York, with her father and sister when she was nine. A stepbrother remained in Alabama. Receiving a bachelor's degree from Hunter College in political science in 1955, Sanchez went to New York University in 1956 to do graduate work in poetry. In the 1960s her works were being published in the *Liberator, Journal of Black Poetry, Negro Digest*, and *Black Dialogue*. She published her first book, *Homecoming*, in 1969.

Employing profanity and the "dozens" (a verbal game in which two or more people use language to outwit each other), Sanchez often reflects militancy and social activism in her works. Sanchez has worked at several universities and colleges, including San Francisco State University, Amherst College, the University of Pittsburgh, and Temple University, where she has been a residential Fellow. She currently teaches African American literature and creative writing and holds the Laura Cornell Chair in English at Temple University. Lecturing at over five hundred universities and colleges in the United States and reading her poetry in Cuba, England, the Caribbean, Australia, Nicaragua, the People's Republic of China, Norway, and Canada, she is one of many black authors and teachers pushing for the initiation of black studies programs in higher education.

Sanchez is the author of thirteen books, three of which are children's books—*It's a New Day* (1971), *The Adventures of Fathead, Smallhead, and Squarehead* (1973), and *A Sound Investment* (1980)—and plays, which are often an extension of her life. Her autobiographical writings, labeled as "neo-slave narratives" by Kalamu ya Salaam in his article in *Dictionary of Literary Biography, Volume 41*, like the slave narratives of the 1800s, seek to free blacks psychologically and physically. She is concerned not only with the meanings of words but their sound as she addresses such themes as alienation and "the ultimate evil" of drug use.

In addition to *Homecoming*, her other collections of poetry and speeches include *Liberation Poem* (1970), *We a BaddDDD People* (1970), *Ima Talken bout the Nation of Islam* (1972), *Love Poems* (1973), *I've Been a Woman: New and Selected Poems* (1981), *Crisis in Culture—Two Speeches by Sonia Sanchez* (1983), *Under a Soprano Sky* (1987); play productions, *The Bronx Is Next* (1970), *Sister Son/jii,* in *Black Visions* (1972), *Uh, Huh; But How Do It Free Us?* (1974), *Malcolm/Man Don't Live Here No Mo'* (1979), *I'm Black When I'm Singing, I'm Blue When I Ain't* (1982); and recordings. Her poetry and plays are reprinted in twenty-two anthologies as well as magazines, such as *Minnesota Review, Black World,* and *Drama Review.* Her most recent publications are *Continuous Fire* (1991), a collection of previously published poetry; *Autumn Blues* (1992), a collection of new poems; and *Shakedown Memory* (1992), a collection of political essays and speeches.

Sanchez has received numerous awards and honors, including an honorary Ph.D. in fine arts from Wilberforce University, the Lucretia Mott Award (1984), an Academy of Arts and Letters Award to continue her work, the P.E.N. Writing Award (1969), an American Book Award (1985) for *homegirls & handgrenades* (1984), and the Peace and Freedom Award from the Women International League for Peace and Freedom for 1988.

For further information on Sonia Sanchez see, in addition to Salaam's article in *Dictionary of Literary Biography, Volume 41,* Sebastian Clarke's "Sonia Sanchez and Her Work," *Black World* 20 (June 1971); Mari Evans's *Black Women Writers, 1950–1980: A Critical Evaluation* (1984); Joyce Joyce's "The Development of Sonia Sanchez: A Continuing Journey," *Indian Journal of American Studies* 13 (July 1983); Raymond Patterson's "What's Happening in Black Poetry?" *Poetry Review* 2 (April 1985); Claudia Tate's *Black Women Writers at Work* (1983); and Barbara Walker's "Sonia Sanchez Creates Poetry for the Stage," *Black Creation* 5 (Fall 1973).

The Bronx Is Next is reprinted from *Drama Review* (Summer 1968). "blk/rhetoric" is taken from *We a BaddDDD People.* "A Poem for Sterling Brown" comes from *I've Been a Woman,* and both "Elegy (for MOVE and Philadelphia)" and "A Poem for My Brother (Reflection on His Death from AIDS: June 8, 1981)" are taken from *Under a Soprano Sky.*

THE BRONX IS NEXT

CHARACTERS

CHARLES

OLD SISTER

LARRY

ROLAND

JIMMY

WHITE COP

BLACK BITCH

The scene is a block in Harlem—a block of tenement houses on either side of a long, narrow, dirty street of full garbage cans. People are moving around in the distance bringing things out of the houses and standing with them in the street. There is activity—but as CHARLES, *a tall, bearded man in his early thirties, and* OLD SISTER *move toward the front, the activity lessens. It is night. The time is now.*

CHARLES   Keep 'em moving Roland. C'mon you mothafuckers. Keep moving. Git you slow asses out of here. We ain't got all night. Into the streets. Oh shit. Look sister. None of that. You can't take those things. Jest important things—things you would grab and carry out in case of a fire. You understand? You wouldn't have time to get all of those things if there was a real fire.

OLD SISTER   Yes son. I knows what you says is true. But you see them things is me. I brought them up with me from Birmingham 40 years ago. I always keeps them right here with me. I jest can't do without them. You know what I mean son? I jest can't leave them you see.

CHARLES   Yes sister. I know what you mean. Look. Someone will help you get back to your apartment. You can stay there. You don't have to come tonight. You can come some other time when we have room for your stuff. OK?

OLD SISTER   Thank you son. Here let me kiss you. Thank the lord there is young men like you who still care about the old people. What is your name son?

CHARLES   My name is Charles, sister. Now I have to get back to work. Hey Roland. Jimmy. Take this one back up to her apartment. Make her comfortable. She ain't coming tonight. She'll come another time.

"The Bronx is Next" by Sonia Sanchez from *The Drama Review*, Volume 12 Number 4 (T40), Summer 1968 by permission of The MIT Press, Cambridge, Massachusetts, and The Drama Review. Copyright © 1968, The Drama Review.

ROLAND   Another time? Man you flipping out? Why don't you realize . . .

CHARLES   I said, Roland, she'll come another time. Now help her up
those fucking stairs. Oh yes. Jimmy, see too that she gets some
hot tea. You dig? Ten o'clock is our time. There ain't no time for
anyone. There ain't no time for nothing 'cept what we came to
do. Understand? Now get your ass stepping.

                    ROLAND *and* JIMMY *exit.*

LARRY   Hey Charles, over here fast. Look what I found coming out
one of the buildings.

CHARLES   What, man? I told you I ain't got no time for nothing 'cept
getting this block cleared out by 10 p.m. What the fuck is it?

LARRY   A white dude. A cop. An almighty fuzz. Look. I thought they
were paid enough to stay out of Harlem tonight. *Turns to* COP.
Man. Now just what you doing here spying on us, huh?

WHITE COP   Spying? What do you mean spying? You see. Well you
know how it is. I have this friend—she lives on this block and
when I got off at 4 p.m., I stopped by. Well. I was just leaving
but this guy and another one taking someone upstairs saw me—
pulled a gun on me and brought me out here.

CHARLES   What building and what apartment were you visiting my
man?

WHITE COP   No. 214—Apt 10—but why are you interested?

CHARLES   Larry, bring the black bitch out fast. Want to get a good
look at her so I'll see jest why we sweating tonight. Yeah. For all
the black bitches like her.

WHITE COP *has turned around and seen the activity.*   Hey. What are all
the people doing out in the middle of the street? What's happening here? There's something going on here I don't know about
and I have a right to know . . .

CHARLES   Right? Man. You ain't got no rights here. Jest shut your
fucking white mouth before you git into something you wish you
wasn't in. Man. I've got to call in about this dude. Is there a
phone in any of these fire traps?

JIMMY   Yeah. I got one in my place during the year I lived here. It's
No. 210—1st floor—1C—back apartment. I'll stay here with this
socializing dude while you call.

                       CHARLES *splits.*

WHITE COP *takes out some cigarettes.*   Want a cigarette?

JIMMY   Thanks man—in fact I'll take the whole pack. It's going to
be a long night.

WHITE COP   What do you mean a long night?

JIMMY, *smiling.*   Jest what I said man—and it might be your longest—*laughs*—maybe the longest of your life.

WHITE COP, *puffing on cigarette—leans against garbage can.* What's your name son?

JIMMY   You don't git nothing out of me 'til Charles returns. You hear me? So stop asking so many damn questions. *Moves to the right. Screams.* Goddamn it Roland. Your building is going too slow. We have only two more hours. Get that shit moving. We have to be finished by 10 p.m.

WHITE COP   Look. What are you people doing? Why are all the people moving out into the street—What's going on here? There's something funny going on here and I want to know what it is. You can't keep me from using my eyes and brains—and pretty soon I'll put two and two together—then you just wait . . . you just wait . . .

> CHARLES *has appeared on stage at this time and has heard what the* COP *has said. Is watchful for a moment—moves forward.*

CHARLES   Wait for what my man? Wait for you to find out what's happening? It's not hard to see. We're moving the people out— out into the cool breezes of the street—is that so difficult to understand?

WHITE COP   No. But why? I mean, yeah I know that the apartments are kinda hot and awful . . .

CHARLES   You right man. Kinda awful. Did you hear that description of these shit houses Jimmy? Kinda awful. I knew we weren't describing this scene right and it took this dude here to finally show us the way. From now on when I talk to people about their places I'll say—I know your places are kinda awful . . .

JIMMY   In fact, Charles, how 'bout—I know your places are maybe kinda awful . . .

CHARLES, *laughing.*   Yeah. That's it. Perhaps. Maybe could there be a slight possibility that your place is kinda—now mind you, we ain't saying for sure—but maybe it's kinda awful—*becomes serious.* Yeah. That's the white man for you man. Always understating things. But since both you and I know that these places are shit-houses that conversation can end now.

JIMMY   What they say 'bout the dude, Charles?

CHARLES, *turns to* WHITE COP.   Oh everything is cool. You can leave man when you want to, but first have a cigarette with us.

WHITE COP, *relaxing.*   I would offer you some of mine but he took them all.

CHARLES   C'mon man. Give them back to the dude. And Jimmy go get Roland. Tell him to come talk a bit. What a night this has been. It's hard working with these people. They like cattle you

know. Don't really understand anything. Being a cop, you probably found that too. Right?

WHITE COP, *lighting a cigarette.* Yeah. I did. A little. But the hardest
thing for me to understand was that all you black people would
even live in these conditions. Well. You know. Everybody has
had ghettos but they built theirs up and there was respect there.
Here. There is none of that.

CHARLES How right you are my man. C'mon in Jimmy and Roland.
We just talking to pass some time. Of course, getting back to
your statement, I think the reason that the black man hasn't
made it—you ain't Irish are you?—is a color thing—I mean even
though the Irish were poor they were still white—but as long as
white people hate because of a difference in color, then they ain't
gonna let the black man do too much. You dig?

WHITE COP But all this hopelessness. Poverty of the mind and spirit.
Why? Things are so much better. All it takes is a little more effort by you people. But these riots. It's making good people have
second thoughts about everything.

ROLAND It's a long time going—man—this hopelessness—and it
ain't no better. Shit. All those good thinking people changing
their minds never believed in the first fucking place.

JIMMY, *stands up.* Man. Do you know that jest yesterday I was running down my ghetto street and these two white dudes stopped
me and asked what I was doing out so early in the morning—
and cuz I was high off some smoke—I said man—it's my
street—I can walk on it any time. And they grabbed me and told
me where everything was.

CHARLES That gives me an idea. Let's change places before this dude
splits. Let him be a black dude walking down a ghetto street and
we'll be three white dudes—white cops on a Harlem street.

WHITE COP Oh c'mon. That's ridiculous. What good would that do.
Why I'd feel silly . . .

CHARLES You mean you'd feel silly being black?

WHITE COP Oh no—not that—I mean what would it prove? How
would it help—what good would it do?

JIMMY But what harm could it do?

WHITE COP None that I could imagine . . . it's just that it's strange
. . . it's like playing games.

ROLAND Oh c'mon. I've always wanted to be a white dude—now's
my chance. It'll be exciting—sure is getting boring handling this
mob of people.

JIMMY If you afraid, man, we don't have to.

WHITE COP Afraid? No. OK. Let's start.

CHARLES, *jumps up—looks elated.* Then we'll jest be standing on the corner talking and you c'mon by. Oh yeah, maybe you should be running. OK?

> CHARLES, ROLAND and JIMMY *move to one side of the stage—the* WHITE COP *moves to the other side and begins to run toward them.*

CHARLES   Hey slow down boy. What's your hurry?

WHITE COP, *stops running.*   Yes. What's wrong officer?

JIMMY   Where you running to so fast?

WHITE COP   I just felt like running officer. I was feeling good so I decided to run.

ROLAND   Oh you were feeling good. So you decided to run. Now ain't that a load of shit if I ever heard one.

WHITE COP   It's true, officer. I was just thinking about the day—it was a great day for me so I felt like running—so I ran.

CHARLES   Boy! Who's chasing you? What did you steal?

WHITE COP   Steal? I haven't stolen anything. I haven't stolen anything. I haven't anything in my pockets. *Goes into his pockets.*

JIMMY *draws gun.*   Get your hands out your pockets boy. Against the wall right now.

WHITE COP   But what have I done? I was just running. This is not legal you know. You have no right to do this . . .

ROLAND   You are perfectly correct. We have no right to do this. Why I even have no right to hit you but I am. *Hits* WHITE COP *with gun.*

WHITE COP, *falls down. Gets up.*   Now wait a minute. That is going just a little too far and . . .

CHARLES   I said why were you running down that street boy?

WHITE COP   Look. Enough is enough. I'm ready to stop—I'm tired.

JIMMY   What's wrong nigger boy—can't you answer simple questions when you're asked them. Oh I know what's wrong. You need me to help you to remember. *Hits* WHITE COP *with gun.*

WHITE COP   Have you gone crazy? Stop this. You stop it now or there will be consequences.

ROLAND   What did you steal black boy—we can't find it on you but we know you got it hidden someplace. *Hits him again.*

WHITE COP   Oh my god. Stop it . . . This can't be happening to me. Look—I'm still me. It was only make believe.

CHARLES   Let's take him in. He won't cooperate. He won't answer the question. Maybe he needs more help than the three of us are giving him.

JIMMY   I don't know. Looks like he's trying to escape to me. Take out your guns. That nigger is trying to run. Look at him. Boy, don't run. Stop. I say if you don't stop I'll have to shoot.

WHITE COP   Are you all mad? I'm not running. I'm on my knees.
Stop it. This can't continue. Why . . .

ROLAND   You ain't shit boy. You black. You a nigger we caught running down the street—running and stealing like all the niggers
around him.

CHARLES   Now you trying to escape—and we warned you three
times already. You only get three warnings then . . .
Noise from off stage—a woman's voice.

LARRY   Man. This bitch ain't cooperating Charles. She said she didn't
have to come. Finally had to slap her around a bit.

CHARLES   Now is that anyway to act bitch? We just want to talk to
you for a minute. Hear you were entertaining this white dude in
your place. Is that so?

BLACK BITCH, *stands defiantly—has a reddish wig on which is slightly
disheveled.*   Who you? Man. I don't owe no black man no explanations 'bout what I do. The last black man I explained to
cleaned me out, so whatever you doing don't concern me 'specially if it has a black man at the head.

JIMMY   Smart—assed—bitch.

BLACK BITCH, *turns to* JIMMY—*walks over to him.*   That's right kid. A
smart—assed—black bitch—that's me. Smart enough to stay
clear of all black bastard men who jump from black pussy to
black pussy like jumping jacks. Yeah, I know all about black
men. The toms and revolutionary ones. I could keep you entertained all night long. But I got to get back. My kids will be coming home.

CHARLES   How many kids you got bitch?

BLACK BITCH   Two. Two boys. Two beautiful black boys. Smart boys
you hear? They read. They know more than me already, but they
still love me. Men. They will know what a woman is for. I'll
teach them. I ain't educated, but I'll say—hold them in your
arms—love them—love your black woman always. I'll say I am a
black woman and I cry in the night. But when you are men you
will never make a black woman cry in the night. You hear. And
they'll promise.

ROLAND   Oh shit. Another black matriarch on our hands—and with
her white boyfriend. How you gonna teach them all this great
stuff when you whoring with some white dude who kills black
men everyday? How you explain that shit to them?
BLACK BITCH, *laughs—high piercing laugh—walks over to*
WHITE COP.   Explain this. *Points to* WHITE COP *on
ground.*

BLACK BITCH   I only explain the important things. He comes once a
week. He fucks me. He puts his grayish white dick in me and

dreams his dreams. They ain't 'bout me. Explain him to my boys. *Laugh*. Man. I am surviving. This dude has been coming regularly for two years—he stays one evening, leaves and then drives on out to Long Island to his white wife and kids and reality. *Laughs*. Explain. I don't explain cuz there ain't nothing to explain.

CHARLES Yeah. But you still a bitch. You know. None of this explaining to us keeps you from being a bitch.

BLACK BITCH Yeah. I know what I am. *Looks around*. But all you revolutionists or nationalists or whatever you call yourselves—do you know where you at? I am a black woman and I've had black men who could not love me or my black boys—where you gonna find black women to love you when all this is over—when you need them? As for me I said no black man would touch me ever again.

CHARLES, *moving toward the* BLACK BITCH. Is that right? You not a bad looking bitch if you take off that fucking wig. *Throws it off*. A good ass. *Touches her face, neck, moves his hands on her body—moves against her until she tries to turn away*. No don't turn away bitch. Kiss me. I said kiss me. *Begins to kiss her face—slowly—sensuously—the* BLACK BITCH *grabs him and kisses him long and hard—moves her body against him*. Yeah. No black man could touch you again, huh? *Laughs and moves away*. I could fuck you right here if I wanted to. You know what a black man is don't you bitch? Is that what happens when you fuck faggoty white men?

> BLACK BITCH *runs across the stage and with that run and cry that comes from her she grabs* CHARLES *and hits him and holds on*. CHARLES *turns and knocks her down. The white dude turns away*. JIMMY *moves toward her*.

BLACK BITCH No. Watch this boy. You still young. Watch me. Don't touch me. Watch me get up. It hurts. But I'll get up. And when I'm up the tears will stop. I don't cry, when I'm standing up. All right. I'm up again. Who else? Here I am, a black bitch, up for grabs. Anyone here for me. Take your choice—your pick—slap me or fuck me—anyway you get the same charge.

JIMMY Here black bitch. Let me help you. Your eye is swollen. *Doesn't look at* CHARLES. Can she go back to her place and get some things out Charles? I'll help her.

CHARLES You have five minutes to help the black bitch then get you black ass back here. We wasted enough time. *Stoops*. Here don't forget her passport to the white world. *Throws wig at her*. And keep your mouth shut black bitch. You hear?

BLACK BITCH, *putting on her wig*. I told you I only explain important things. There ain't nothing happening here yet that's important to me. *Exits with* JIMMY.

CHARLES, *laughs.* That's a woman there. Yeah wig and all. She felt good for awhile. Hey you. Dude. You can get up now. All the unpleasantness is over. Here let me help you get cleaned up. *Begins to brush* WHITE COP *off.* We just got a little carried away with ourselves.

WHITE COP Can I go now? I'm tired. It's been a long night. You said I could go.

CHARLES But don't you want to go and see the bitch—see how she is—make sure she's okay?

WHITE COP No. I don't think so. It's late. My wife will be worrying by now.

CHARLES Isn't there anything else you want to see before you go? Can't I fill you in on anything?

WHITE COP I've seen people moved into the street. That's all. Nothing else. I want to know nothing.

CHARLES Would you believe that it's happening on every street in Harlem?

WHITE COP, *nervously.* I'm not interested. I just want to leave and go home. I'm tired.

CHARLES Yeah man. You look tired. Look. Do me a favor. I want to go to the bitch's place and apologize. You know it wasn't right. Hurting her like that. Come with me. Hey Roland. Shouldn't he come with me?

ROLAND Yeah man. He should. After all, he knows her better than you. He can tell you what approach to use with her.

WHITE COP No. I don't want to go. I don't want to see her again. It's all finished now. I'm tired. You tell her. Just let me go on home.

CHARLES But man. I need you. I need you to help me talk to her. She'll listen to you. Anyway with you there, you'll keep me from getting violent again—c'mon man. Just this one thing then you can go.

LARRY's *voice from off stage.* We ready to light, Charles—should we start now?

CHARLES Yeah. All 'cept No. 214—we have some business there. Give us ten minutes then light it up.

> WHITE COP *tries to run*— CHARLES *and* ROLAND *grab his arm and start walking.*

WHITE COP I don't want to go. I must get home. My wife and two boys are waiting for me. I have never hurt or killed a black person in my life. Yes. I heard talk that some cops did—that they hated black people—but not me. I listened. It made me sick but I never participated in it. I didn't ever do anything to negroes. No. I don't want to go. I haven't done anything. *Begins to cry.*

Holy Mother—you can't do this to me. *Screams.* But, I'm white!
I'm white! No. This can't be happening—I'm white!
    Tries to break away and ROLAND *knocks him out—they*
    pull him off stage. The stage becomes light—buildings are
    burning—people are moving around looking at the blaze.
    JIMMY, ROLAND *and* CHARLES *reappear.*

JIMMY   Well. That's that, man. What a night. Do I still have to write
this up tonight Charles?

CHARLES   Were those your orders?

JIMMY   Yes. Okay. I'll do it while we wait. I'll drop it in the mail box
tonight. See you soon.

CHARLES   A good job, Jimmy. Stay with them. Talk to them. They
need us more than ever now.

ROLAND   We got to split Charles. We got a meeting going tonight.
You know what the meeting is about man? *Takes out a cigarette.*
You think this is the right strategy burning out the ghettoes?
Don't make much sense to me man. But orders is orders. You
know what's going down next?

CHARLES, *lighting a cigarette.*   Yeah. I heard tonight when I called
about that white dude. The Bronx is next—Let's split.

blk / rhetoric

(for Killebrew Keeby, Icewater,
Baker, Gary Adams and
Omar Shabazz)

   who's gonna make all
   that beautiful blk / rhetoric
   mean something.
             like
   i mean
        who's gonna take
   the words
        blk / is / beautiful
   and make more of it
   than blk / capitalism.
             u dig?
       i mean
        like who's gonna

---

take all the young / long / haired
natural / brothers and sisters
and let them
               grow till
                      all that is
impt is them
               selves
                    moving in straight /
revolutionary / lines
                    toward the enemy
(and we know who that is)
                        like. man.
who's gonna give our young
blk / people new heroes
       (instead of catch / phrases)
       (instead of cad / ill / acs)
       (instead of pimps)
       (instead of wite / whores)
       (instead of drugs)
       (instead of new dances)
       (instead of chit / ter / lings)
       (instead of a 35¢ bottle of ripple)
       (instead of quick / fucks in the hall / way
         of wite / america's mind)
like. this. is an S O S
    me. calling. . . . .
                  calling. . . . .
                            some / one
    pleasereplysoon.

ELEGY

(For MOVE* and Philadelphia)

1.

philadelphia
    a disguised southern city
    squatting in the eastern pass of

---

*MOVE: a Philadelphia-based back to nature group whose headquarters was bombed by the police on May 13, 1985, killing men, women, and children. An entire city block was destroyed by fire.

colleges cathedrals and cowboys.
philadelphia. a phalanx of parsons
and auctioneers
   modern gladiators
erasing the delirium of death from their shields
while houses burn out of control.

   2.

c'mon girl hurry on down to osage st
they're roasting in the fire
smell the dreadlocks and blk/skins
roasting in the fire.

c'mon newsmen and tvmen
hurryondown to osage st and
when you have chloroformed the city
and after you have stitched up your words
hurry on downtown for sanctuary
in taverns and corporations

and the blood is not yet dry.

   3.

how does one scream in thunder?

   4.

they are combing the morning for shadows
and screams tongue-tied without faces
look. over there. one eye
escaping from its skin
and our heartbeats slowdown to a drawl
and the kingfisher calls out from his downtown capital
And the pinstriped general reenlists
his tongue for combat
and the police come like twin seasons of drought and flood.
they're combing the city for lifeliberty and
the pursuit of happiness.

   5.

how does one city scream in thunder?

   6.

hide us O lord
deliver us from our nakedness.
exile us from our laughter
give us this day our rest from seduction

peeling us down to our veins.

and the tower was like no other.   amen.
and the streets escaped under the
cover of darkness   amen.
and the voices called out from
their wounds   amen.
and the fire circumsized the city   amen.

    7.

who anointeth this city with napalm?   (i say)
who giveth this city in holy infanticide?

    8.

beyond the mornings and afternoons
and deaths detonating the city.
beyond the tourist roadhouses
trading in lobotomies
there is a glimpse of earth
this prodigal earth.
beyond edicts and commandments
commissioned by puritans
there are people
navigating the breath of hurricanes.
beyond concerts and football
and mummers strutting their
sequined processionals.
there is this earth. this country. this city.
this people.
collecting skeletons from waiting rooms
lying in wait. for honor and peace.
one day.

A POEM FOR MY BROTHER
(Reflections on His Death from AIDS: June 8, 1981)

1. death

The day you died
a fever starched my bones.
within the slurred
sheets, i hoarded my legs
while you rowed out among the boulevards

balancing your veins on sails.
easy the eye of hunger
as i peeled the sharp
sweat and swallowed wholesale molds.

　　2. recovery (a)

What comes after
is consciousness of the morning
of the licensed sun that subdues
immoderate elements.
there is a kindness in illness
the indulgence of discrepancies.

reduced to the ménage of houses
and green drapes that puff their seasons
toward the face.
i wonder what to do now.
i am afraid
i remember a childhood that cried
after extinguished lights
when only the coated banners answered.

　　3. recovery (b)

There is a savior in these buds
look how the phallic stems distend
in welcome.
O copper flowerheads
confine my womb that i may dwell within.

i see these gardens, whom i love
i feel the sky's sweat on my face
now that these robes no longer bark
i praise abandonment.

　　4. wake

i have not come for summary.
must i renounce all babylons?
here, without psalms,
these leaves grow white
and burn the bones with dance.
here, without surfs,
young panicles bloom on the clouds and fly
while myths tick grey as thunder.

5. burial

you in the crow's rain
rusting amid ribs
my mouth spills your birth
i have named you prince of boards
stretching with the tides.

you in the toad's tongue
peeling on nerves
look. look. the earth is running palms.

6. (on) (the) (road). again.

somewhere a flower walks in mass
purchasing wholesale christs
sealing white-willow sacraments.

naked on steeples
where trappist idioms sail
an atom peels the air.

O i will gather my pulse
muffled by sibilants
and follow disposable dreams.

A POEM FOR STERLING BROWN

what song shall i sing you
amid epidemic prophecies
where holy men bleed like water
over the bones of black children?

how shall i call your name
sitting priest/like on mountains
raining incense
scented dancer of the sun?

where shall memory begin you
overturning cradles
rocking cemented eyes
closed flowers
opening like eastern deities under your hand?

From *I've Been A Woman*. Chicago: Third World Press, p. 91. Reprinted by permission
of Third World Press.

and your words.
tall as palm/trees
black with spit
soothing the lacerated mind.

and your words.
scratching the earth
carving dialect men into pyramids
where no minstrel songs
run from their thighs.

your soul. dodging loneliness and
the festivals of Renaissance rhythms
your life
skintight with years
a world created
from love.

you. griot of fire.
harnessing ancient warriors.

                a ye ye ye ye ye ye ye
                a yo yo yo yo yo yo yo
                    da a ye loom boom
                    da a ye loom boom
                    da a ye loom boom
                        boom/boom
                        boom/boom
                        boom/boom
you. griot of the wind
glorifying red gums smiling tom-tom teeth.

Haki Madhubuti

(1942–   )

EMBODYING ALL FACETS of black life, Haki R. Madhubuti's poetry reflects his own coming to grips with his blackness. According to Madhubuti, freedom will come for blacks, as it did for him, only after they begin to understand and learn about their African heritage. For this reason, he consistently stresses through his lyrical, semiautobiographical, and conversational poems how important it is for blacks to have self-pride, self-love, and self-awareness. In 1973 Madhubuti rejected his slave name, Don L. Lee, and all that went with it. His poem "The Self-Hatred of Don L. Lee" mirrors this rejection on a literary level.

Born in Arkansas in 1942 and raised in Detroit, Michigan, Madhubuti endured many hardships growing up. His father deserted the family and his mother, an alcoholic, died when he was only sixteen. Attending Dunbar Vocational High School in Chicago, Madhubuti received his associate's degree from Chicago City College in 1966. He received a master's degree in Fine Arts from the University of Iowa in 1984. After leaving the United States Army (where he served from 1960 to 1963), Madhubuti worked several odd jobs up until 1967 when the publication of his first two books of poetry, *Think Black* (1967) and *Black Pride* (1968), earned him some recognition. Formally withdrawing from the labor force, he decided to dedicate his time to writing.

Though Madhubuti was writer-in-residence at five colleges and universities between 1968 and 1980, his talents stretch far beyond the written word. He is founder and editor of *Black Books Bulletin* and Third World Press, a publishing house that seeks out and prints the writings of black authors. A cofounder and director of the Institute of Positive Education and a founding member of the Organization of Black American Culture Writer's Workshop, Madhubuti is also a critic, essayist, and social activist.

Madhubuti has received several grants and honors, including National Endowment for the Humanities grants in 1969 and 1982 and Dudley Randall's Broadside Press's Outstanding Poet's Award in 1975. He has also served on several committees seeking the liberation and betterment of people of African descent.

Other books by Madhubuti include *Don't Cry, Scream* (1969); *We Walk the Way of the New World* (1970); *Directionscore: Selected and New Poems* (1971); *Dynamite Voices: Black Poets of the 1960s* (1971); *From Plan to Planet; Life Studies: The Need for African Minds and Institutions* (1973); *Book of Life* (1973); *Enemies: The Clash of Races* (1978); *Earthquakes and Sunrise Missions: Poetry and Essays of Black Renewal, 1973–1983* (1984); *Killing Memory, Seeking Ancestors* (1987); and he edited *Say That the River Turns: The Impact of Gwendolyn Brooks* (1987). He also released two recordings, "Rappin' and Readin' by Don L. Lee" (1971) and "Rise Vision Coming," and helped to edit *To Gwen with Love* (1971). He is also the editor of *Confusion by Any Other Name: Essays Exploring the Negative Impact of the Blackman's Guide to Understanding the Blackwoman* (1990) and author of *Black Men: Obsolete, Single, Dangerous?* (1990).

For further reading see Paula Giddings's "From a Black Perspective: The Poetry of Don L. Lee," *Amistad 2* (1971), edited by John A. Williams and Charles F. Harris; Marlene Mosher's *New Directions from Don L. Lee* (1975); Annette Oliver Shands's "The Relevancy of Don L. Lee as a Contemporary Black Poet," *Black World* 21 (June 1972); Darwin T. Turner's Afterword in *Earthquakes and Sunrise Missions* (1984), by Madhubuti; Helen Vendler's *Part of Nature, Part of Us* (1980); Ron Welburn's "Review of *Don't Cry, Scream*," *Negro Digest* (December 1969); Catherine Daniels Hurst's entry in *Dictionary of Literary Biography, Volume 41*; and D. H. Melhem's "Haki R. Madhubuti (Don L. Lee): Prescriptive Revolution" in *Heroism in the New Black Poetry: Introductions and Interviews* (1990).

The poems that follow are the title poems from the collection *Killing Memory, Seeking Ancestors*.

KILLING MEMORY

For Nelson and Winnie Mandela

the soul and fire of windsongs must not be neutral
cannot be void of birth and dying
wasted life
locked
in the path of vicious horrors
masquerading
as progress and spheres of influence

what of mothers
without milk of willing love,
of fathers
whose eyes and vision
have been separated from feelings of earth and growth,

"Killing Memory" and "Seeking Ancestors" from *Killing Memory, Seeking Ancestors* by Haki R. Madhubuti. Chicago: Third World Press, 1987, p. 3 and p. 52.

of children
whose thoughts dwell
on rest and food and
human kindness?

Tomorrow's future rains in
atrocious mediocrity and suffering deaths.

in america's america the excitement is over
a rock singer's glove and burning hair
as serious combat rages over
prayer in schools,
the best diet plan,
and women
learning how to lift weights
to the rhythms of
"what's love got to do with it?"

ask the children,
always the children caught in the
absent spaces of adult juvenility
all
brake dancing and singing to
"everything is everything" while
noise occupies the mind as
garbage feeds the brain.

in el salvador mothers search for their sons
and teach their daughters the way of the knife.

in south afrika mothers bury hearts without bodies
while pursuing the secrets of forgotten foreparents.

in afghanistan mothers claim bones and teeth from
mass graves and curse the silent world.

in lebanon the sons and daughters receive horror hourly
sacrificing childhood for the promise of land.

in ethiopia mothers separate wheat from the desert's dust
while the bones of their children cut through dried skin.

tomorrow's future
may not belong to the people,
may not belong to dance or music
where
getting physical is not an exercise but
simply translates into people working,

people fighting,
people enduring insults and smiles,
enduring crippling histories and black pocket politics
wrapped in diseased blankets
bearing AIDS markings in white,
destined for victims that do not question
gifts from strangers
do not question
love of enemy.

who owns the earth?
most certainly not the people,
not the hands that work the waterways,
nor the backs bending in the sun,
or the boned fingers soldering transistors,
not the legs walking the massive fields,
or the knees glued to pews of storefront or granite
    churches
or the eyes blinded by computer terminals,
not the bloated bellies on toothpick legs
all victims of decisions
made at the washington monument and lenin's tomb
by aged actors viewing
red dawn and the *return of rambo part IX.*

tomorrow
may not belong to the
women and men laboring,
hustling,
determined to avoid contributing
to the wealth
of gravediggers from foreign soil
& soul.
determined to stop the erosion
of indigenous music
of building values
of traditions.

memory is only precious if
you have it.

memory is only functional
if it works for you.

people
of colors and voices

are locked in multi-basement state buildings
stealing memories
more efficient
than vultures tearing flesh
from
decaying bodies.

the order is that the people are to
believe and believe
questioning or contemplating
the direction of the weather is
unpatriotic.

it is not that we distrust poets and politicians.

we fear the disintegration of thought,
we fear the cheapening of language,
we fear the history of victims and the loss of vision,
we fear writers whose answer to
maggots drinking from the open
wounds of babies
is
to cry genocide while demanding
ten cents per word and
university chairs.
we fear politicians
that sell coffins at a discount
and consider ideas blasphemy
as young people world over bleed from the teeth while
aligning themselves with whoever
brings the food.
whoever brings love.

who speaks the language of
bright memory?

who speaks the language of
necessary memory?

the face of poetry must be fire erupting volcanoes,
hot silk forging new histories,
poetry delivering light greater than barricades of silence,
poetry dancing, preparing seers, warriors, healers
and parents beyond the age of babies,
poetry delivering melodies that cure dumbness & stupidity
yes, poets uttering to the intellect and spirit,
screaming to the genes and environments,

revitalizing the primacy of the word and world,
poets must speak the language of the rain,
 decipher the message of the sun,
 play the rhythms of the earth,
 demand the cleaning of the atmosphere,
 carry the will and way of the word,
 feel the heart and questions of the people
 and be conditioned and ready
 to move.

to come
at midnight or noon

to run
against the monied hurricane in this
the hour of forgotten selves.
forgiven promises
and
frightening whispers
of rulers in heat.

SEEKING ANCESTORS

*For the First Annual Egyptian Studies Conference, Los Angeles, California,
February 1984, organized by Maulana Karenga and Jacob Carruthers*

1.

what it was before death traps
before thriller and beat it, beat it
before soaps and reagan being raised to the station
of new redeemer by grandchildren viewing progress as
calvin klein & sonys in the ear.

where are the wise words,
the critical minds,
the questioners of sordid deeds,
the drinkers of pure water,
the doers of large moments?

what it was before emma lou planned her entire life
according to the stars & big sonny wilson hung on to every
syllable spoken by rev. ike, believe in me, and palm readers
from the pentagon?

what it is
is amnesia in america,
is memory the length of private parts,
is junk food masquerading as nutrition,
is projects and tenements replacing pyramids & space,
is fad posing as substance?

what it is
is strength measured by what you drink,
what you drive,
how you dress,
the texture of your hair
and the color of your woman,
"working hard for the money."

in america
working hard for the money
can get you bullets in the spine,
cocaine in the veins or a gold plated watch made in japan.
young death is guaranteed only if you think.
thinking in brazil & uganda,
in pakistan & south afrika is considered
contagious and dangerous.

shame and shock have evaporated,
grown men take their daughters and
boys hump boys and we are told that this
is modern, is normal, is in and in
america
where vacant heads copy & buy and
nourishment is derived from pepsis & cokes,
as vikings suck the blood of black people
draining the vision from the real miracles of the west
as we all approach the time when honor and integrity are obsolete
& preserved only in unread novels, unlistened music
as unattended grandmothers in michigan nursing homes
claim cats as family, friends and lovers.

2.

ever wonder where the circle came from
or who were the first people to use the triangle?
who were the original cultivators of the earth, who used
water of the nile to power minds and machines? what people
created music from instrument and voice and viewed the
building of cities as art and science? who were the

first to love because love contained the secrets of tomorrow?
look at yourselves.

there is magic in colors earthblack & purple issuing in
browns upon greens & oranges & others producing yellows
and ever present blue, skylike rain & water & warm.
today,
it is sure and dangerous to be dark in this universe.
there are secrets in color design,
there are mysteries in the making of the world,
there are complexities in the doings of strangers against the world.
there are clear courses that most minds are not ready for,
will never be able to perceive.
the west does serious damage to the mind.

america is not for sale, it is the buyer.

3.

we need clear language,
able storytellers,
discoverers of crops and seeds.
we need
decipherers and investigators of ideas & promise,
foreparents
screaming music that will arm us
with wisdom of the first,
warnings of
surrogate mothers and gene pool fathers.
we need
memory & moments, melody and song.
expanding vision
in search of winning ways and noble tomorrows.

comin back clearin eyes stompin, steppin, bolder
takin the wind & whispers seriously, takin the
slave beyond copy as cure, coping as necessity,
liftin the self & selves beyond rumor & wigs,
carrying the beauty of thought to completion,
knowing that if we think it,
doin it is only extension and reward
seekin to eclipse the expected to better & best.
if we have to beat it, beat it, try beatin the enemy.
try beatin those who reduced people to excretion & mannequins.

we were once music and might growin steel
we were beauty & find often feeling first drivin fire

we were seer & solution lift on up emma lou.
quiet step step
willinthefire, will in thefire, will in the fire
step step "dance to the music" step "dance to the music" step step
quiet and contemplative,
clearly conscious of wrongness
turn it around big sonny w. believe that
"we are family, my brothers, sisters & me."

4.

we conquered other selves in us
we became before we knew
tradition evaporated as others and many
stole the magic and wealth of millions.
diluting the dark people's walk & way,
cutting out the soul & source extricating the spirit
assassinating the common way.

Conquerors of vastness were
unable to copy lean steam
drumbeat walkers dancers carrying
spirit as gut & drive,
spirit as purpose and future
spirit as loving find,
as will & way
seeking beauty & meaning
in the secrets of ancient wall paintings
& buried souls.

5.

we are here
combat weary and willing
now & singing
looking special devoid of defeat
fired energy & hope imagining the inconceivable
here
urgently seeking lost records
igniting possibilities.

in the light of Amon and ancestors,
in the step of the clear and conscious,
it is beauty most needed in this place
as we recall that
by relinquishing building secrets

we lost clear water & children,
we lost future & wisdom & continuity.
we lost ourselves

demand
that the few & wise of us,
the monk & trane of us,
the careful & intelligent of us,
the hurston and dubois of us,
the silent and enduring of us,
the hansberry and woodson of us,
the conscious and loving of us,
to
recall the memory
to
recall the tradition & meaning
to rename the bringers
genius.
to quietly in the natural light of warm sunrises,
in the arms of loving smiles,
among the care of the consciously certain,
within the circle of the continued questioners,
to remember them ancestors all as
dark & talented.
as
gifted light
bringers of source,
bringers of silence,
bringers of remembrance.

Nikki Giovanni

(1943–   )

AN ACTIVIST and definitely one of the most popular and provocative voices of the black poetry that began to appear in the 1960s, Nikki Giovanni was born Yolande Cornelia Giovanni in Knoxville, Tennessee. Her mother a supervisor for the welfare department and her father a social worker, the young Nikki was heavily influenced by her maternal grandmother, Louvenia Terrell Watson, an assertive, militant black woman who was intolerant of white people. Because of her boldness, Louvenia and her husband, John Brown Watson, had to leave Albany, Georgia, their home, concealed under a blanket in a wagon in order to avoid being lynched. Nikki Giovanni's commitment to black people is a result of the influence of this grandmother, with whom the young poet lived during her sophomore and junior years in high school.

Giovanni attended Fisk University, graduating magna cum laude, with honors in history, in 1967. She pursued graduate study at the University of Pennsylvania School of Social Work and at the School of Fine Arts at Columbia University. She holds an honorary Doctorate of Humanities degree from Wilberforce University. Throughout her entire career as student, mother, and poet, she has continued to be politically active in attempting to improve the quality of lives of blacks across the United States. In 1964 she founded a chapter of the Student Nonviolent Coordinating Committee (SNCC) at Fisk; in 1967 she planned and headed the first Cincinnati Black Arts Festival, hoping to initiate an awareness of arts and culture in the black community; in 1968 she started a black history workshop in the black community in Wilmington, Delaware; in 1970 she founded the publishing cooperative NikTom, Limited and published a number of collections of poetry by such figures as Gwendolyn Brooks, Mari Evans, Jewel C. Latimore (Johari Amini), Carolyn Rodgers, and Margaret Walker; and she has read her poetry and given lectures on college campuses and in black communities not only in this country but in Africa, Europe, and the Caribbean as well.

Giovanni is a prolific writer of essays as well as a poet for both children and adults. A list of her publications include the following: *Black Feeling, Black Talk* (1967), *Black Judgement* (1968), *Black Feeling, Black Talk/Black Judgement* (1970), *Re: Creation* (1970), *Night Comes Softly: Anthology of Black Female Voices* (ed., 1970), *Gemini: An Extended Autobiographical Statement on My First Twenty-Five Years of Being a Black Poet* (1971), *Spin a Soft Black Song: Poems for Children* (1971), *My House: Poems* (1972), *A Dialogue: James Baldwin and Nikki Giovanni* (1973), *Ego-Tripping and Other Poems for Young People* (1973), *A Poetic Equation: Conversations between Nikki Giovanni and Margaret Walker* (1974), *The Women and the Men* (1975), *Cotton Candy on a Rainy Day* (1978), *Vacation Time: Poems for Children* (1980), *Those Who Ride the Night Wind* (1983), and *Sacred Cows and Other Edibles* (1988).

In addition to publishing books, becoming involved in community activities, and teaching at Queens College of the City University of New York and at Livingstone College of Rutgers, Giovanni has also recorded six albums on which she reads her poetry to musical accompaniment: *Truth Is On Its Way* (Right-On Records, 1971), *Like a Ripple on a Pond* (NikTom, 1973), *The Way I Feel* (Atlantic Records, 1974), *Legacies* (Folkways Records, 1976), *The Reason I Like Chocolate* (Folkways Records, 1976), and *Cotton Candy on a Rainy Day* (Folkways Records, 1978).

Her poems have appeared in most of the major African American anthologies and literary journals. A selection of her papers are at the Mugar Memorial Library at Boston University. For the most comprehensive analysis of her work, see Mozella G. Mitchell's entry in *Dictionary of Literary Biography, Volume 41*. Also see A. Russell Brooks, "The Motif of Dynamic Change in Black Revolutionary Poetry," *CLA Journal* 15 (September 1971); Don L. Lee, *Dynamite Voices: Black Poets of the 1960s* (1971); and R. Roderick Palmer, "The Poetry of Three Revolutionists: Don L. Lee, Sonia Sanchez, and Nikki Giovanni," *CLA Journal* 15 (September 1971). See also Mari Evans, ed., *Black Women Writers, 1950–1980: A Critical Evaluation* (1984).

"On Being Asked What It's Like to Be Black" is taken from *Gemini*. "Of Liberation" comes from *Black Feeling, Black Talk*, and "Poetry" is taken from *The Women and the Men*.

ON BEING ASKED WHAT IT'S LIKE TO BE BLACK

I've always known I was colored. When I was a Negro I knew I was colored; now that I'm Black I know which color it is. Any identity crisis I may have had never centered on race. I love those long, involved, big-worded essays on "How I Discovered My Blackness" in twenty-five words more or less which generally appear in some mass magazine—always somehow smelling like Coke or Kellogg's corn flakes—the prize for the best essay being a brass knuckle up your head or behind, if you make any distinction between the two.

It's great when you near your quarter-century mark and someone says, "I want an experience on how you came to grips with being colored." The most logical answer is, "I came to grips with Blackdom when I grabbed my mama"—but I'm told on "Julia" that we don't necessarily know our mothers are colored, and you can win a great big medal if you say it loud. If your parents are colored we have found—statistically—the chances are quite high that so are you. If your parents are mixed the chances are even higher that you'll grow up to be a Nigger. And with the racial situation reaching the proportions that it has, the only people (consistent with history) able to discover anything at all are still honkies. Or if you haven't gotten it together by the time you go to preschool, then you're gonna be left out. Now, that's only on the subconscious level.

My father was a real hip down-home big-time dude from Cincinnati who, through a screw-a-YWCA-lady or kiss-a-nun program, was picked up from the wilds of the West End (pronounced deprived area), where he was wreaking havoc on the girls, and sent to college, mostly I imagine because they recognized him as being so talented. Or if not necessarily talented, then able to communicate well with people. He was sent to Knoxville College in Tennessee. Nestled lovingly in the bosom of the Great Smoky Mountains in the land of Davy Crockett and other heroes of Western civilization is Knoxville, Tennessee. Knoxville, in those times, was noted for *Thunder Road* starring Robert Mitchum and/or Polly Bergen of Helen Morgan fame; but when my father boarded the train to carry him back to his spiritual roots (it was just like my great-grandfather to be the only damned slave in northeastern Tennessee) all he saw were crackers—friendly crackers, mean crackers, liberal crackers, conservative crackers, dumb crackers, smart crackers and just all kinds of crackers, some of whom, much to his surprise, were Black crackers. He hit the campus, "the Nigger the world awaited," shiny head (because Afros were not in vogue), snappy dresser with the one suit he had and a big friendly smile to show them all that just because he was in the South he wasn't going to do like a lot of people and cry all the time and embarrass the school. In walks the fox.

Swishing her behind, most likely carrying a tennis racket and flinging her hair (which at that time hung down to what was swishing) was the woman of the world, the prize of all times—Mommy. Mommy has an illustrious background. Her family, the Mighty Watsons, had moved to Knoxville because my grandmother was going to be lynched. Well, the family never actually said she was going to get lynched. They always stressed the fact that traveling late at night under a blanket in a buggy is fun, and even more fun if a decoy sitting in a buggy is sent off in another direction with Uncle Joe and Uncle Frank carrying guns. They told us the guns were to salute good-bye to Louvenia, my grandmother, and John Brown ("Book") Watson, my grandfather.

If I haven't digressed too much already I want to say something about Grandpapa. He was an extremely handsome man. Grandmother got the hots for him and like any shooting star just fell and hit *splash*. Now, we in the family have always considered it unfortunate that Grandfather was married to another woman at that time. And Grandmother, to make matters even more urgent, would not give him none. Grandfather considered that more unfortunate than his marriage. And since she was the intellectual of the family, hence "Book," he assessed the situation and reached the logical conclusion that he should marry my Grandmother.

The Watsons were quite pleased with Louvenia Terrell because she was so cute and intelligent, but what they didn't know and later learned to their chagrin was that she was terribly intolerant when it came to white people. The Watson clan was the epitome of "Let's get along with the whites"; Grandmother was the height of "We ain't taking no shit, John Brown, off nobody." So the trouble began.

First some white woman wanted to buy some flowers from Grandmother's yard, and as Grandmother told it they were not for sale. She didn't make her living growing flowers for white people. The woman's family came back later to settle it. "John, yo' wife insulted ma wife and we gotta settle this thang." Grandpapa was perfectly willing to make accommodations but when the only satisfactory action was Grandmother's taking twenty-five buggy-whip lashes, he had to draw the line. "Mr. Jenkins, we've known each other a long time. Our families have done business together. But this is too much." "John, we've gotta settle this thang." And about that time Uncle Joe, who always liked to hunt, came out of Grandpapa's house with his gun and powder and asked if he could be of any help. The Jenkinses left. The Watsons stayed up all night with a gun peeking from every window. The guns in those days were not repeaters so the youngsters in the family had been given complete instructions on how to clean and load in the shortest time possible. I'm told by my granduncles there was a general air of disappointment when nobody showed. After almost a week of keeping watch things reverted to normal. Grandpapa says the white dude told him later they didn't need the flowers anyway.

Then one Sunday afternoon Grandmother and Grandpapa were out strolling when a Jewish merchant asked them to come look at his material. He owned one of those old stores with bolts and bolts of material because most clothes were made, not storebought. Well, they looked and looked. Grandmother had him pull bolts from way up high to way down low. Then she got bored and told Grandpapa she was ready to go.

Merchant: You mean you're not going to buy anything?

Grandmother [innocently]: No.

Merchant: you mean you had me pull all this material out and you're not going to buy anything?

Grandmother [a little tired]: My husband and I were walking down the street minding our own business when you asked us to come in. We did not ask you.

Grandfather [wary of the escalation in the exchange]: Let's go, Louvenia.

Grandmother [as she generally did when she was in an argument]: Hell, it's his own fault. [To the merchant] Nah, we don't want none of your material.

Grandfather [pinching and kicking at her]: Let's go, Louvenia.

Merchant [in the background screaming obscenities]: I'll have you horse-whipped for talking to me this way.

Grandmother [really wolfing now]: You and which cavalry troop? My husband will kill you if you come near me!

Grandfather [almost in tears]: Let's go, Louvenia.

They hurried to spread the alarm of impending danger. A woman in the next county had recently been lynched and her womb split open so there was no doubt in Grandfather's mind that the whites might follow through this time. A family meeting was called and all agreed that Grandmother and Grandfather (most especially Grandmother) had to leave Albany, Georgia. The sooner the better. When night came they climbed into a buggy, pulled a blanket over themselves and slept until they reached the Tennessee border. Having no faith in southern Tennessee they began again by public transportation to head North. The intention was to go to Washington, D.C., or Philadelphia, but when they found themselves still in Tennessee they agreed to settle at the first reasonable-sized town they came to— Knoxville. Grandfather settled Grandmother in a good church home and went back to Albany, where he taught school, to finish the term out. Grandfather was like that.

Three lovely daughters were born in four happy years. Grandmother settled down to play house. The girls were all right with Grandpapa but, as Grandmother always said, "John Brown always had plenty of toys," so naturally she had more fun than he did. The oldest child was my mother.

Now, Mommy was an intellectual, aristocratic woman, which in her time was not at all fashionable. She read, liked paintings, played tennis and liked to party a great deal. Had she been rich she would have followed the sun—going places, learning things and being just generally unable to hold a job and be useful. But Mommy made just one bad mistake in the scheme of things—she sashayed across the Knoxville College campus, hair swinging down to her behind, most probably carrying a tennis racket, and ran into a shiny-head Negro with a pretty suit on. He, being warm and friendly and definitely looking for a city girl to roost with, introduced himself. I have always thought that if his name hadn't been exotic she would never have given him a second thought; but Grandfather, whom my mother was so much like, had a weakness for Romance languages and here comes this smiling dude with Giovanni for a name. Mommy decided to take him home.

From the resulting union two girls were born: typical of me, I was the second. Gary, my sister, is what is commonly known to white people as a smart Nigger. In the correct tradition of we-don't-take-no-shit-off-nobody, she could wolf away for hours. I'm still amazed she hasn't risen to national fame for her sheer ability to rap. Me—I'm different. I generally don't like to get into arguments, but I did like to fight. Many's the night if I hadn't remembered my Grandfather's patrician blood I'd have been swinging a blade on the street—that is, until I became a Black and decided Black people should not fight each other under any circumstances. Gary would go out and blow off about what was going to happen if she didn't get what she wanted and, not getting it, would come in and tell me, "You've got to go fight Thelma [or Barbara or Flora] 'cause she's been messing with me." Folks in my home town still have a lot of respect for me dating back to those days.

How and why I became a fighter is still a mystery to me. If you believe in innateness, then I guess the only logical conclusion is that it's in my blood. But most of us have a history of fighting unless you are Whitney Young's daughter or Roy Wilkins's mother. And I'll even bet Roy's mother was a real scrapper. Through a series of discussions I was having with a social worker, I discovered I am not objective. Any feeling I may have for someone or something is based on how he or it relates to me. Like I don't go for people because they are rich or famous or everybody thinks they are so hip. I don't support institutions because they are successful, democratic and said to be the best in the world. If something is good to me I like it; if it hurts me I don't. This feeling is extended to my friends. If someone or something abuses my friends then it has in effect hurt me, and I don't go for that even if *The New York Times* says it is the hippest thing going. Like I wasn't impressed with James Earl Jones as an actor because though he may have done a beautiful job as Jack Johnson, the role is an insult. I'm not impressed with America. It acts well, too. There are no objective standards when it comes to your life; this is crucial. Objective standards and objective feelings always lead to objectionable situations. I'm a revolutionary poet in a pre-revolutionary world.

And dealing with Blackness as a cultural entity can only lead to revolution. America, as Rap Brown pointed out, has always moved militarily because it has no superior culture. We, as beginning revolutionists, ought to understand that. Great cultures have always fallen to great guns. They always will. That's not a subjective thought; it's a fact. Facts are only tools to gain control over yourself and other people. So white folks develop facts about us; we are developing facts about them. In the end it's always a power struggle.

I've been taught all my life that power is an absolute good, not because I'm objectively more fit to wield power but because subjectively if I don't wield it it will be wielded over me. Trade white racism for Black racism? Anytime, since I'm Black. But facts show that Black people by the definition of racism cannot be racist. Racism is the subjugation of one people by another because of their race, and everything I do to white people will be based on what they did to me. Even their Bible, the Christian one, says, "Do unto others as they have done unto you." And Black Christians are becoming more aware of the meaning behind the Golden Rule. It's only logical.

I believe in logic. Logic is not an exercise to prove "*A* implies *B*" but a spiritual understanding of the subjective situation and the physical movement necessary to place life in its natural order. Black people are the natural, hence logical, rulers of the world. This is a fact. And it's illogical for me to assume any other stance or to allow any other possibility. It's self-negating. If you don't love your mama and papa then you don't love yourself. Fathers are very important people.

Black people have been slaves in America and the world. Some slaves cleaned, some cooked, some picked cotton, some oversaw the others, some killed slavemasters, some fucked the slavemaster (and his mama) at their demand. A slave has no control over whom he fucks. Check it. But that's not your father because some beast raped your mother. Neither is it your mother because some beast sneaked down to Uncle Tom's cabin. White folks with degrees in sociology like to make generic judgments about political situations. If your father was drafted and killed in World War I, World War II, the Korean conflict, or the Vietnam advisoryship, they don't tell you he deserted your mother (which he logically did if he went off to fight the enemy's wars). They tell you what a good dude he was and "Ain't you proud of that shiny new medal?" And you are proud of him and say, "My father was a great man," even though he was never around to be anything to you. If the same man had been run out of town or was not allowed to hold a job, or your mother couldn't get relief with him in the household, then you should look upon his leaving home with the same loyalty as if he had gone to fight a war (which he really did). Or look at them both with the same disdain. Neither was there to love you and your mother when you needed to be loved and protected. One of the jobs of a father is to protect and provide, as best he can, for his family. This is related to power.

All Black men in the world today are out of power. Power only means the ability to have control over your life. If you don't have control you cannot take responsibility. That's what makes that latter-generation Irishman's report on the Negro family so ridiculous. How can anyone be responsible without power? Power implies choice. It is not a choice when the options are life or death. It's against the law of nature to choose death. That's why suicides and soldiers make such interesting subjects. They are going against the laws of nature.

If, however, your father is part of the power group and he does not associate with you then he has chosen not to be your father (and the power group does have this choice). It is then up to you, for your own mental health, to put any ideas of generative father out of your mind and function with your father surrogate. That is, if your Uncle Bill is the one who takes you to the zoo, Uncle Jimmy the one who is there at Christmas and Uncle Steve the one who spends your birthdays with you, then you pull from them the composite father—and though Uncle Albert only loves your mother and doesn't pay much attention to you he should be a part of the composite also. Same with mothers.

If people treat you like a child then you pull together the composite feeling of being mothered. It's illogical to hunger after the love of someone who doesn't love you when there are plenty of people who would love you—if you believe in love—because feeling is a tool that can be used to keep you from having the necessary substance for being a healthy person. As long as we as a people must deal with the no-good-man-loses-a-woman syndrome as an objective reality we will never be able to gather unto ourselves the subjective feelings essential for propelling the actions needed to place the world in its natural order. I have learned these things by living in the world for a quarter-century.

Gus, my father, has always been a fascinating man to me. I haven't always liked him, but then I haven't always liked myself. The two are related. Gus just sort of believes in himself and thinks everything he's done has needed to be done so that he could be the really groovy person he is. My mother usually agrees with him about that. He has functioned as a father, which doesn't mean we always had nifty toys or the latest clothes, but to his mind if he couldn't get it for us we didn't need it anyway. There may be more validity to that than meets the eye. Ultimately my mother took a job which led to many quarrels. They still fuss about it now—only because she wants to quit and he won't let her. Gus, being a great believer in Freud, will probably always have some conflict around him. He'd be lost without it. How can you eliminate conflict without changing the system? Most people want to be comfortable, which is illogical if you're not free. Which is maybe why folks still cut each other up. Conflict is active and must be kept near the surface.

Life/personality must be taken as a total entity. All of your life is all of your life, and no one incident stands alone. Most people evolve. The family and how it's conceptualized have a great effect on anyone. No matter what the feelings, the effect is still there. Like James Baldwin in *Tell Me How Long the Train's Been Gone* still has to negate God and the God influence. God still means something to him. The feeling is still there. Base experiences affect people; before they are born, events happen that shape their lives. My family on my grandmother's side are fighters. My family on my father's side are survivors. I'm a revolutionist. It's only logical. There weren't any times I remember wanting to eat in a restaurant or go to a school that I was blocked from because of color. I don't remember anyone getting lynched. And though I had friends who went to jail during the sit-ins, we were committed to action anyway, so there must have been something deeper. Beliefs generally come through training, and training is based on feeling.

I was trained intellectually and spiritually to respect myself and the people who respected me. I was emotionally trained to love those who love me. If such a thing can be, I was trained to be in power—that is, to learn and act upon necessary emotions which will grant me more control over my life. Sometimes it's a painful thing to make decisions based on our training, but if we are properly trained we do. I consider this a good. My life is not all it will be. There is a real possibility that I can be the first person in my family to be free. That would make me happy. I'm twenty-five years old. A revolutionary poet. I love.

OF LIBERATION

Dykes of the world are united
Faggots got their thing together
(Everyone is organized)
Black people these are facts
Where's your power

Honkies rule the world
Where's your power Black people
(There are those who say it's found in the root of all evil)
You are money
You seek property
Own yourself
3/5 of a man
100% whore
Chattel property
All of us
The most vital commodity in america
Is Black people
Ask any circumcised honkie

There are relevant points to be considered, Black People
Honkies tell niggers don't burn
"violence begets you nothing my fellow americans"
But they insist on straightened hair
They insist on bleaching creams
It is only natural that we would escalate
It has been pointed out:
"If we can't out fight them, we can't out vote them"
These are relevant points to consider
If 10% honkies can run south africa
        then
10% Black people (which has nothing to do with negroes)
can run america
These are facts
Deal with them

It has been pointed out:
"The last bastion of white supremacy
is in the Black man's mind"
(Note—this is not a criticism of brothers)

Everything comes in steps
Negative step one: get the white out of your hair
Negative step two: get the white out of your mind
Negative step three: get the white out of your parties
Negative step four: get the white out of your meetings

BLACK STEP ONE:
Get the feeling out (this may be painful—endure)
BLACK STEP TWO:
Outline and implement the program
All honkies and some negroes will have to die
This is unfortunate but necessary

Black law must be implemented
The Black Liberation Front must take responsibility
For Black people
If the choice is between the able and the faithful
The faithful must be chosen
Blackness is its own qualifier
Blackness is its own standard
There are no able negroes
White degrees do not qualify negroes to run
The Black Revolution

The Black Liberation Front must set the standards
These are international rules

Acquaint yourself with the Chinese, The Vietnamese,
The Cubans
And other Black Revolutions
We have tried far too long to ally with whites
Remember the rule of thumb:
WILD ANIMALS CAN BE TRAINED
BUT NEVER TAMED
The honkie is this category
Like any beast he can be trained with varying degrees
of excellence to
1) eat from a table
2) wash his hands
3) drive an automobile or bicycle
4) run a machine
5) And in some rare cases has been known to speak
This is training, Black people
And while it is amusing
It is still a circus we are watching

Barnum and Bailey are the minds
behind president Johnson

You would not trust your life to a wolf or tiger
no matter how many tricks they can learn
You would not turn your back on a cobra
Even if it can dance
Do not trust a honkie
They are all of the same family
The Black Liberation Front has free jobs to offer
for those concerned about the unemployed
The sisters need to make flags
(there are no nations without a flag)
The Red Black and Green must wave from all our
buildings as we build our nation
Even the winos have a part—they empty the bottles
    which the children can collect
Teen-age girls can fill with flammable liquid
and stuff with a rag
Professor Neal says a tampax will do just fine
Ammunition for gun and mind must be smuggled in
Support your local bookstore
Dashikis hide a multitude of Revolution
Support your local dress shop

As all reports have indicated our young men are primary
On the job training is necessary
Support your local rebellion—
send a young man into the streets

Our churches must bless these efforts in the name
of our Black God
Far too long we have been like Jesus
Crucified
It is time for The Resurrection of Blackness
"A little child shall lead them" for the Bible tells me so
And we shall follow our children into battle

Our choice a decade ago was war or dishonor
(another word for integration)
We chose dishonor
We got war

Mistakes are a fact of life
It is the response to error that counts
Erase our errors with the Black Flame

Purify our neighborhoods with the Black Flame
We are the artists of this decade
Draw a new picture with the Black Flame
Live a new life within the Black Flame

Our choice now is war or death
Our option is survival
Listen to your own Black hearts

POETRY

poetry is motion graceful
as a fawn
gentle as a teardrop
strong like the eye
finding peace in a crowded room

we poets tend to think
our words are golden
though emotion speaks too
loudly to be defined
by silence

sometimes after midnight or just before
the dawn
we sit typewriter in hand
pulling loneliness around us
forgetting our lovers or children
who are sleeping
ignoring the weary wariness
of our own logic
to compose a poem
   no one understands it
it never says "love me" for poets are
beyond love
it never says "accept me" for poems seek not
acceptance but controversy
it only says "i am" and therefore
i concede that you are too

Sherley Anne Williams

(1944–   )

WIDELY KNOWN AMONG the Neo-black writers, whose proponents "speak directly *to* Black people *about themselves*," Sherley Anne Williams is a poet and critic whose creative works to date place her among the influential black voices that have sung the blues since the beginnings of black folk culture. Her poetry brings the black oral traditions of the past into the present to create new images of contemporary black culture. Her special interest, the struggles and triumphs of black women, reflects the significant role that the women of her own past and present—her mother, sisters, and close friends—have played in shaping her life and her vision.

Born in Bakersfield, California, in 1944, Williams began writing seriously after receiving her B.A. in history from California State University at Fresno in 1966. She undertook graduate studies at Howard University in Washington, D.C., and later at Brown University in Providence, Rhode Island, where she earned her M.A. in 1972. During this period she published a volume of literary criticism, *Give Birth to Brightness: A Thematic Study in Neo-Black Literature*. After receiving her graduate degree from Brown University, she returned to Fresno and was an associate professor of English at California State University until 1975, when she moved to the University of California at San Diego. She is currently a professor of literature there.

In addition to her critical volume, Williams has published two books of poetry: *The Peacock Poems* (volume 79 in the Wesleyan Poetry Series), which was nominated for the National Book Award in 1976, and *SomeOne Sweet Angel Chile*, which was completed in 1982. Harcourt Brace Jovanovich will publish *Working Cotton*, illustrated by Carole Bayrd, and *Girls Together*, illustrated by Varnette Honeywood, in 1992. Her poetry has been anthologized in *The Third Woman: Minority Women Writers of the United States* and *Black Sister: Poetry by Black American Women*.

For comment on Williams's relation to contemporary black writers and an introduction to her poetry, see Lillie P. Howard's essay in *Dictionary of Literary Biography, Volume 41* and Melissa Walker's *Down from the Mountaintop: Black Women's Novels in the Wake of the Civil Rights Movement, 1966–89* (1991).

Of the following selections, "the earth woman" comes from *SomeOne Sweet Angel Chile*; "Remembering the Prof." originally appeared in a different version in *Black American Literature Forum*; and "Driving Wheel" comes from *The Peacock Poems*.

THE EARTH WOMAN

rap and enter . . .

To sleep again in
some kinhouse on a
floor of double rooms . . .

Blow your horn, baby.

silenced on the first breath

the earth woman

I am always rushed
into their living
rooms; I lie upon
my back This is what
I came for what I
know of love strange
ceilings my own
heavy breathing a
match flaring briefly
some wayward whisper
sounding in this act
I could talk that talk
if they would listen—
I am not an orphan

But these men don't care
a thing about me
Or if they do it's
some paradise behind
my eyes that my body
might be key to They
look up in wonder
from enjoyment of
my twat It is not
what they came to me
    for This eden: too
    much and not enough

    I believe I am
    made to be a full cup

From *SomeOne Sweet Angel Chile* by Sherley Anne Williams. Reprinted by permission of the author.

REMEMBERING THE PROF.
Sterling A. Brown 1901–1989

Professor and Mrs. Brown—it was years before I called them
anything else—had a few students over once or twice a year for
wine and cheese—I think; in those days, I seldom drank. I don't
think I'd ever been inside a professor's house, had little conversation
and no small talk, but such occasions were part of what I'd begun to
dream for myself, so, when asked, I went. And it didn't start out so
bad. There was no need to speak unless spoken to. Sterling, when
his mind was on it, told first rate stories; even the ones delivered
with apparent inattention were worth recording. And some people
did; people came from all over the world to talk to him, published
his comments and became famous or well paid, while he toiled away
at Howard and lived in the cramped little house on Kearney.

I think we were not the brightest group he'd had (by then he'd
been at Howard almost thirty years), and Miss Daisy reminded me of
a robin, the way she chirped right in when Professor Brown's spirits
seem to lag. She was almost bird like beside his great length, her
hair as white as his, her eyes still gypsy dark and glowing. It wasn't
that he'd seen so many like us—he'd never met anyone from
Fresno—and certainly not that he saw in us young negroes (and so
begrudged as did too many of Howard's faculty) the 'somebody' of
his own youthful dreams. I thought the shade of academia hung
over him and pitied his life inside those towers. What could one expect, a lone writer among the scholars?

Books crowded his narrow cubby above Founder's, the spillover,
perhaps, from his house, or vice versa. I realize now they were
mostly dusty, but then I couldn't imagine how he lived with so
many and was afraid to ask. I saw it all as story and itched for a way
to set it down right; he was due at least that much, the gesture of
the present generation to its past. The measure of how much ice this
cut for me with Sterling was the invitation to his house, but Prof
didn't play favorites, treating us all, it seemed to me, like white students for whom Howard was experience, data, proof that they had
known and been accepted by a negro (though by then most of us
said black) and I thirsted for some acknowledgement beyond the
careful criticism of written work he gave any student who asked.

Of course Sterling played the blues. Whatever literature majors
read, I'd learned, they listened to *good* music, the three "B's," my
dear, or at a stretch (and if one were hip), Miles, Mingus, and

Reprinted, with changes, from *Black American Literature Forum*, Volume 23, Number
1 (Spring 1989): 106–108. Copyright © 1989 Indiana State University.

Monk. I cared mainly about rhythm and blues—curiosity and the world had yet to send me farther back—and saw in its twig and root kinship to the blues a metaphor of what I would be to Sterling, though, as the elder, it was on him to proclaim this.

His stories were ritual by then, delivered as performance rather than prayer. He didn't always mention names and not all of those were famous; a lot of what he said was slyly argumentative. There had been no "Harlem" Renassiance; it was the New Negro Movement. Course, he'd been too young to be "New" back then. His first book had not come out until well after the Crash that halted publication of even the handful of books by negroes in the twenties. And no, "An Old Woman Remembers" was not based on his own recollections of the riot that had inspired Du Bois's "Litany of Atlanta." Impatiently, as though we might at least do the simple arithmatic between 1901 and 1905.

Off-hand, and with a deliberate bluing of the beat, Professor Brown spoke of being propositioned by Ma Rainey, Roi's tendency to rap, of listening to the terrible first draft of "Direct Action," his voice rumbling like gravel in honey. Who was the best contemporary blues singer? someone asked in a lull between record and story. Our comments, such as they were, were all of this tenor. The folk blues was dead and he no longer listened to what passed as current, Prof allowed with no trace of embarrassment. Some fellow had come through a few years before raving about some singer, guy by the name of—. Here Sterling fumbled for the name, B. somebody, B—. Oh, I think it was B.F. King.

B.F.? I was chagrined. Of all the Kings my sister listened to, and believe me in those days there were plenty—you know, like all those Smith girls in the twenties—I'd never heard mention of a B.F. and felt a fool when Miss Anne piped up, I have. I should have let it lay, but it shamed me to know so little of our recent history and I began to toll off the Kings I knew; when I got to B.B., Sterling gave a sheepish laugh. "B.B." that long top lip lifted slightly, dawn dark eyes holding mine. "B.B. King, that's who I meant."

DRIVIN WHEEL
Myth Story and Life

I want you to come on, baby
here's where you get
yo steak, potatoes and tea.

first story

The darkened bedroom, the double bed,
the whispers of the city night,
against it her voice, husky, speaking
past the one soft light.

>   I am through you wholly woman. You
>   say I am cold   am hard   am vain. And
>   I know I am fool and bitch. And black.
>   Like my mother before me and my
>   sisters around me. We share the same
>   legacy   are women to the same
>   degree.

And I ain't even touched what's between us.
A sullen, half tearful thought.
Others lay below the surface of her mind,
rushing, gone, finally caught.

>   Not circumstance; history
>   keeps us apart. I'm black. You black. And
>   how have niggas proved they men? Fightin
>   and fuckin as many women as
>   they can. And even when you can do
>   all the things a white man do you may
>   leave fightin behind but fuckin stay
>   the same.

>   For us it's havin babies and how
>   well we treats a man and how long we
>   keep him. And how long don't really have
>   that much to do with how well. I just
>   can't be a woman to yo kinda man.

second song

my man is a fine fine man
the superman of his time

---

the black time   big time
in a mild mannered disguise
revealed only as needed:
    the heart steel   heart stone   heart
and its erratic beating.

        Inner and outer
rine and heart and running.
Running.   Hanging.   Caught by that powerful joint.
But my man can pull his ownself's coat
come at last to see that dick is just the same old rope.

        Yeah.

        A mild mannered
disguise: laughing country boy astride
    a laughing goat.

first fable

We do not tell ourselves all the things we
know or admit, except perhaps in dreams,
oblique reminiscence, in sly yearnings, all
the people we feel ourselves to be.

                    Except
perhaps in dreams   the people we
feel . . .

    Three. A prideful panther who
stalks a white wolf, a goatish rooster who was lured on
by a grey fox and a head, a body
and, lying to one side, a heart.
The head, the heart, the body had always
been apart. The rooster called
them Humpty Dumpty things and urged
the panther to attack. The rooster was accustomed
to command, ruling the panther through
words he had taught the panther to
talk; the words only said what he wanted
the panther to know. He would crow
or blow upon his horn
and the panther would forget
all the questions he had ever known.
And once in a while, just for show,
the rooster would allow the panther
to have his way.
Now, the panther thought it too good

a body to waste, too good a brain to be
forever cut from its source.
     Let's put them together, man,
he called. You begin with the heart.

      But the rooster
knew that rebuilt Humpty Dumpty men have a
way of taking worlds apart, have new ways of
putting them together again. He lived in the world
of putting them together again. He lived in the world
of already was and it was all he ever wanted
to know.
   Not so fast, the rooster cried.

But the panther had already touched the heart
and for the first time he realized
that Not So Fast meant Don't Go. He
could feel something new, something
indefinable pumping through him. The rooster's
words failed to sway him. The rooster, angered,
sank his talons into the panther's shoulder.
The panther turned and, instinctively,
went upside the rooster's head.
The rooster absorbed the first blow;
but he was smart enough to know it was coming.
But the second was a surprise, beyond
his comprehension. He died with a question
Why   still unspoken.

              . . . in glancing asides
we are seen, or in oblique reference. And still
left to answer is how we can pull it all together.

fourth life

They lie up in the darkened bedroom
and listen to the whispers of the city night;
each waits upon the other
to make the final move to the light
or toward the door. They have met
history; it is them. Definitions from the past
—she bitch and fool; he
nigga and therefore jive—seem the last

reality. And, once admitted, mark
the past as them. They are defeated.

She moves to strap on her shoes.

You said,

                and he speaks.

voice and hand holding her seated,
his head moving into the circle of light.

      You said we are more than the
      sum jiveness, the total folishness.
      You are wholly woman, right? Isn't that
      more than bitch?

          What do it matter, huh?

His hand holds her, holds the wary
wearied question. He speaks, slow:
Matter a helluva lot. We can't
get together less we stay together.

His lips brush her cheek; she buries

her fingers in his bush. The question will always
be present, so too the doubt it leaves in its wake.
To question and to answer is to confront. To deal.
History is them; it is also theirs to make.

Sterling D. Plumpp

(1940–   )

STERLING D. PLUMPP'S poetry reflects a history bounded by personal experiences of flight, fear, confusion, growth, perceptiveness, and eventual awareness. He takes the reader on a rollercoaster of disarray, panic, rhythm, and lyricism. Plumpp's works mirror his own growth as a poet and writer who has finally reached artistic maturity.

Plumpp was born in 1940 in Clinton, Mississippi, and brought up primarily by his grandfather in a sharecropping household. In 1956 after his grandfather died, he moved to Jackson, where he attended church schools and converted to Catholicism. He attended St. Benedictine College in Kansas from 1960 to 1962, worked as a clerk in Chicago's main post office, and served as a draftee at the Aberdeen Proving Ground in Maryland. His experiences within these institutions led him to question critically their effect on individuals with no beliefs or practices, and turned him towards writing as a forum for discussing these "effects."

Receiving an undergraduate degree in psychology from Roosevelt University in Chicago, Plumpp's studies helped to lay the foundation for his first full-length book, *Black Rituals* (1972), which dissects and discusses the reasons behind the inescapable cycle of oppression in the black community. It is primarily a social psychological study.

A former editor at the Institute of Positive Education and currently director of African-American studies at the University of Illinois, Chicago, Plumpp published his first book of poetry, *Portable Soul* in 1969. A year later his second book of poetry, *Half Black, Half Blacker*, was published. Humor, narration, and strong characterizations were the tools Plumpp employed in his later pieces, and anguish was often utilized as a theme.

After his next two books of poetry were published, *Steps to Break the Circle* (1974) and *Clinton* (1976), Plumpp's works began to appear in more "mainstream" publications instead of black ones only. In 1981 he won an Illinois Arts Council Award for his poem, "The Mojo Hands Call, I Must Go." He also won the Carl Sandburg Literary Award for Poetry for "Mojo." In 1982, a comprehensive volume entitled after his poem, *The Mojo Hands Call, I Must Go*, was published.

Plumpp's poems appear in the anthology *The Otherwise Room* (1981) and he has written poetry, fiction, and nonfiction articles for several periodicals. He also edited *Somehow We Survive: An Anthology of South African*

Writing (1982), published by Thunder's Mouth Press. His most recent work is *Blues: The Story Always Untold* (1989).

For further reading see James Cunningham's article in *Dictionary of Literary Biography, Volume 41* and Eugene B. Redmond's *Drumvoices: The Mission of Afro-American Poetry, A Critical History* (1976).

"What It Feels Like to Turn Black: An Epilogue" is chapter 10 of *Black Rituals*.

WHAT IT FEELS LIKE TO TURN BLACK
An Epilogue

The problem with psychology is that once you leave averages and mandates concerning human nature and other truisms, that you are finally left with the individual. And what is ultimately passed off as being true of all humans is really something quite true of only a few individuals but should be true of all humans. This is particularly frightening when it comes to Blackness for it means that to understand the phenomena one must come to terms with how different individuals handle the problem, one must come to terms with himself. Blackness is a state of mind. It is a self-image one has of one's self. But before we can discuss Blackness in any detail as a concept we must discuss the Black man's developmental history. For one's history, one's experiences, sets the limits, boundaries, to his actions. This means that if we Africans in America had incorporated various degrees of European brainwashing into our psyches before our discovery of ourselves, our Blackness, then you would expect us to use various methods of coping with the facts of our lives once Blackness becomes an alternative—the only human alternative. It means that initially, before functional ideologies are developed, you would expect as many different shades of Blackness as there were of pre-Blackness. It means that no one man's self-concept will be suitable enough as a model for all other Africans to get Black by. For in the process of becoming Black one man's health may be another one's pathology or vice versa. Blackness is a process of self-discovery, self-assertion, and self-acceptance, and takes some people longer than it does others to become.

I have never been a white man. True, there have been ghostly white periods in my life when I became so thoroughly confused with myself and Black people that I wished that I was white, but it was

From *Black Rituals*. Chicago: Third World Press, 1972:97.

never more than a bad wish. My whole development was among Black people. I only learned the Man's ways at his institutions of greater ignorance. I always find myself eating with the wrong hand, speaking a certain cottonfield rhetoric, and liking cornbread and molasses. Since my home was/is Mississippi, I have always held the picture of the white man as one who will kill you with the least amount of provocation, or with no provocation at all. I was taught from an early age that one must be aware of the white man like one watches for a pit viper in its coils. Black Religion taught me patience, taught me to squeeze out every ounce of goodness from hardships, and it was this worldview that saved me. I became Black the day I decided that I would never again enter another Catholic church unless it was for sightseeing or to cop some of those gold chalices. I didn't know it at the time but the act which meant that I would never again go to Mass was also the act which meant that I would again embrace the onion sensitivity of Black Religion, not that I would again go to church but that I would carry the church within my soul, that I would again let that church within my soul roll like a prancing river. This was not a conscious choice on my part and I thought that I was becoming an atheist.

When the erupting cry for Blackness reached volcanic proportions with the introduction of the Black Power slogan in 1966, I had been trying to become a writer for seven years. My idol was/is James Baldwin because I have always felt and still feel that James Baldwin is the blackest writer I have ever read. The blackest, not the most revolutionary and there is a difference. Baldwin, alone, of all the Black writers is bold enough to parade street niggers, field niggers, society niggers, and white folks in a way that reflects the way people relate to one another in America. Baldwin is the Black church and this saves him from mediocrity. The thing about James Baldwin's work is that though he appreciates and understands jazz, yet what he renders in the form of art is what the Black man lives—blues lives and spiritual lives—and it is his rendering of such that makes him immortal. When I had reached my whitest intellectual hour, it was the work of James Baldwin that re-directed me to the blues, spirituals, the Black church—Black life. I'm not saying that I was aware that I was an African, just that I was aware that I was Black and that the things Black people have done in this country, particularly in song (spirituals and blues), rival the artistic creations of any people, any place in time. Let me be perfectly clear about one thing, a writer cannot write the blues, spirituals, and Black church without writing for Black people. What happened to me when the dynamo of Blackness began to take on a rap and look that differentiated it from Western destruction was that I became very conscious of my need to

use my Blackness in a way that would accelerate the political, economic, and cultural liberation of Black people.

I didn't say that I was always a liberator only that I had always
been Black. Stokely Carmichael, Imamu Baraka, and Malcolm X clarified, articulated the fact that the Black man is in a subordinate position with the white man all over the world, and that made me a
liberator.

But in Black literature Don L. Lee is the most liberating. He is
the most liberating because his work more than any writer in our
history mirrors the changes that he went through and the changes
his people went through, and the terms of his art are such that Black
people respond to it the way they responded to down home revivals.
Don L. Lee is really an old-time preacher using the street symbols,
corner raps and the Black Position as his bibles; when he reads his
poetry, he preaches, he teaches, he condemns, he lauds, he instills
hope, and he warns of damnation. The problem the Black man faces
today is for Don L. Lee to get a church and carry on in the tradition
of a Bishiop Turner. After reading Don L. Lee, and after joining the
Organization of Black American Culture (OBAC), I underwent a
mild form of Blackness; I decided to make Black folklore the foundation for all my later artistic endeavors. I was back home for I had to
deal with the Black church, Black Rituals again.

NEW VALUES
for Don

Nobody wants to see pressures of oppression
see value in values we have
see the need to unpress oppression
to release NEW VALUES

NEW VALUES pop from our actions
pop from people doings
pop from poets and people
popcorning it to artists and
sketches of their positive acts
acts like feeding hungry babies
acts like marrying themselves to sisters
acts like acting like people workers
like establishing schools in their studios

NEW VALUES is magic
only those who act their actions
can make them match their ideas
set fire to their head directions
light up the map of their intentions

with the fuses of their functions
NEW VALUES is the African Revolution
the movement of our minds and actions

We are in REVOLUTION
either we continue to sing
paint poet play and write
to audience of our chains
or we MOVE TO organize
synchronize our TRUTH,
the reality of the MASSES . . .

MASSES are most people
people most oppressed
their acts create NEW VALUES
move them to act
and they act to can their humanity
put away containers to save the world
for they are the TRUTH
and we artists MUST feed
ourselves to people amassed
not tell ourselves to them
show ourselves to them
sing ourselves to them
write ourselves to them
but MUST feed ourselves to them
move ourselves with them

NEW VALUES is revolutionary
BLACK PEOPLE picking up
spades of our collectiveness
to dig the gold of TOMORROWS
we create NEW MAN
when we move OLD MAN
from oppressions of his reactions
to impressions of his actions

I say there is but ONE VALUE
we oppressed should have
and it is our will to crush our walls
knock down valueless institutions
knock down valueless instituted
and this ONE VALUE
leads to NEW VALUES
building ujamaa villages
instilling imani eyes
making ujima hands
teaching kujichagulia feet
transplanting kuumba hearts

cleaning umoja skies
walking on the nia grounds
we black artists must first
teach the ONE VALUE
teach it with our works
and work it in with our actions
and then leafy crops of NEW VALUES
will stand tall, green, defiantly in the sunshine. . . .

* * *

for Murry

There are Deep Pillars
Dropped in Blackmen's steps.

Our fathers' days are pyramids
Under our feet
If we stand naturally.
I never saw my father stride
And my grandfather
Taught me Egyptian climbs
Big steps up calculated slopes
Of peaked Greatness.
My steps were anchors in the wind
Silent drums weeping . . .
But when they dug
For my father
I discovered the Deep Pillars.

There are Deep Pillars
Dropped in Blackmen's steps.

When we dance through
Time our Pharonic Image
Overshadows us
Yet we cannot kneel down
In the shade of our ways.
I know you are stroking
In the cosmic pond of Africa
Making waves wobble minds . . .
As you finger print
In struggles They
Linger as hip Aunt Jemimas.

You are your father
And I am mine
And there are Deep Pillars
Dropped in Blackmen's steps. . . .

Toni Morrison

(1931–   )

WINNER OF THE 1988 PULITZER PRIZE for Fiction for her novel *Beloved* (1987), Toni Morrison has made her presence known in the literary world not only as a writer but as a senior editor for Random House in New York. A prolific author, Morrison draws on her own experiences and travels to the South for her novels. Through complex plots of pathos and violence she emphasizes how self-denial and an incapacity to love can destroy relationships, whether it is with oneself or others.

Born in Lorain, Ohio, in 1931, Toni Morrison, born Chloe Anthony Wofford, was the second of four children. Reading at an early age, she attended public schools in Lorain and went on to become an honors student at Howard University. It was at Howard that she changed her name to Toni because people had a hard time pronouncing Chloe. Having earned a master's degree in 1955 from Cornell University in English, Morrison taught at Texas Southern University for two years before teaching English at Howard in 1957.

At Howard she met and married Harold Morrison, a Jamaican architect, whom she divorced in 1964. She has two children, Harold Ford and Slade Kevin. It was upon returning to Lorain to live with her parents after her divorce that Morrison took a job as an editor with a textbook subsidiary of Random House.

A teacher of Afro-American literature and creative writing at Yale University, Bard College, and State University of New York at Purchase, Morrison has addressed the issues of constraint and freedom in her works. Her first novel, *The Bluest Eye* (1970), written in first-person stream of consciousness, is a critique of white society's values, specifically the idea of beauty as blonde-haired and blue-eyed, and shows the effects this perception has on a little black girl deprived of love. Morrison delves deeper into the issue of love and relationships in *Sula* (1973).

According to Susan L. Blake's article in *Dictionary of Literary Biography, Volume 33*, Morrison is a strong believer in "Black history as the core of Black identity." In 1974, Morrison's "scrapbook project," published as the *Black Book*, by Random House, catalogues over three hundred years of black history. Morrison has also written articles for *Mademoiselle* and the *New York Times Magazine*.

Song of Solomon (1977), a paperback best seller, earned Morrison the National Book Critics' Circle Award for fiction and the American Academy and Institute of Arts and Letters Award. *Tar Baby* (1981), also a best seller, was heralded by a cover story in *Newsweek* magazine.

For further reading, see in addition to Blake's article in *Dictionary of Literary Biography, Volume 33*, Barbara Christian's *Black Women Novelists: The Development of a Tradition, 1892–1976* (1980); Melissa Walker's *Down from the Mountaintop: Black Women's Novels in the Wake of the Civil Rights Movement, 1966–89* (1991); Jacqueline de Weever's "The Inverted World of Toni Morrison's *The Bluest Eye* and *Sula*," *CLA Journal* 22 (June 1979); Robert Fikes, Jr.'s "Echoes from Small Town Ohio: A Toni Morrison Bibliography," *Obsidian* 5 (Spring/Summer 1979); Adam David Miller's "Breedlove, Peace and the Dead: Some Observations on the World of Toni Morrison," *Black Scholar* 9 (March 1978); Chikwenye Okonjo Ogunyemi's "*Sula*: 'A Nigger Joke'," *Black American Literature Forum* 13 (Winter 1979); Jean Strouse's "Toni Morrison's Black Magic," *Newsweek* 97 (30 March 1981); and Joyce A. Joyce's "Structural and Thematic Unity in Toni Morrison's *Song of Solomon*," *CEA Critic* 49 (Winter 1986–Summer 1987). See also Bernard W. Bell's *The Afro-American Novel and Its Tradition* (1987) and Trudier Harris's *Fiction and Folklore: The Novels of Toni Morrison* (1991).

The excerpt that follows is chapter 15 of Morrison's *Song of Solomon*.

FROM **SONG OF SOLOMON**

The fan belt didn't last long enough for him to get to the next gasoline station. It broke on the edge of a little town called Jistann, the needle trembling as H. Milkman sold it to the tow-truck man for twenty dollars and caught the first bus out. It was probably best that way, for over the humming wheels, his legs folded in the little space in front of his seat, he had time to come down from the incredible high that had begun as soon as he slammed the Byrd woman's door.

He couldn't get back to Shalimar fast enough, and when he did get there, dusty and dirty from the run, he leaped into the car and drove to Sweet's house. He almost broke her door down. "I want to swim!" he shouted. "Come on, let's go swimming. I'm dirty and I want waaaaater!"

Sweet smiled and said she'd give him a bath.

"Bath! You think I'd put myself in that tight little porcelain box? I need the sea! The whole goddam sea!" Laughing, hollering, he ran over to her and picked her up at the knees and ran around the room with her over his shoulder. "The sea! I have to swim in the sea.

Don't give me no itty bitty teeny tiny tub, girl. I need the whole entire complete deep blue sea!"

He stood her on her feet. "Don't you all swim around here?"

"Over at the quarry is where the kids go sometimes."

"Quarry? You all don't have no sea? No ocean?"

"Naw; this hill country."

"Hill country. Mountain country. Flying country."

"A man was here to see you."

"Oh, yeah? That would be Mr. Guitar Bains."

"He didn't give his name."

"He don't have to! He's Guitar Bains. *Gitar, Gitar, Gitar* Bains!"
Milkman did a little dance and Sweet covered her mouth, laughing.

"Come on, Sweet, tell me where the sea is."

"They some water comin down below the ridge on the other side.
Real deep; wide too."

"Then let's go! Come on!" He grabbed her arm and pulled her
out to the car. He sang all the way: " 'Solomon 'n Ryna Belali
Shalut . . .' "

"Where you learn that?" she asked him. "That's a game we used
to play when we was little."

"Of course you did. Everybody did. Everybody but me. But I can
play it now. It's my game now."

The river in the valley was wide and green. Milkman took off his
clothes, climbed a tree and dived into the water. He surfaced like a
bullet, iridescent, grinning, splashing water. "Come on. Take them
clothes off and come on in here."

"Naw. I don't wanna swim."

"Come in here, girl!"

"Water moccasins in there."

"Fuck 'em. Get in here. Hurry up!"

She stepped out of her shoes, pulled her dress over her head and
was ready. Milkman reached up for her as she came timidly down
the bank, slipping, stumbling, laughing at her own awkwardness,
then squealing as the cold river water danced up her legs, her hips,
her waist. Milkman pulled her close and kissed her mouth, ending
the kiss with a determined effort to pull her under the water. She
fought him. "Oh, my hair! My hair's gonna get wet."

"No it ain't," he said, and poured a handful right in the middle of
her scalp. Wiping her eyes, spluttering water, she turned to wade
out, shrieking all the way, "Okay, okay," he bellowed. "Leave me.
Leave me in here by myself. I don't care. I'll play with the water
moccasins." And he began to whoop and dive and splash and turn.
"He could fly! You hear me? My great-granddaddy could fly! Goddam!" He whipped the water with his fists, then jumped straight up

as though he too could take off, and landed on his back and sank down, his mouth and eyes full of water. Up again. Still pounding, leaping, diving. "The son of a bitch could fly! You hear me, Sweet? That motherfucker could fly! Could fly! He didn't need no airplane. Didn't need no fuckin tee double you ay. He could fly his own self!"

"Who you talkin 'bout?" Sweet was lying on her side, her cheek cupped in her hand.

"Solomon, that's who."

"Oh, him." She laughed. "You belong to that tribe of niggers?" She thought he was drunk.

"Yeah. That tribe. That flyin motherfuckin tribe. Oh, man! He didn't need no airplane. He just took off; got fed up. *All the way up!* No more cotton! No more bales! No more orders! No more shit! He flew, baby. Lifted his beautiful black ass up in the sky and flew on home. Can you dig it? Jesus God, that must have been something to see. And you know what else? He tried to take his baby boy with him. My grandfather. Wow! Woooee! Guitar! You hear that? Guitar, my great-granddaddy could flyyyyyy and the whole damn town is named after him. Tell him, Sweet. Tell him my great-granddaddy could fly."

"Where'd he go, Macon?"

"Back to Africa. Tell Guitar he went back to Africa."

"Who'd he leave behind?"

"Everybody! He left everybody down on the ground and he sailed on off like a black eagle. 'O-o-o-o-o-o Solomon done fly, Solomon done gone /Solomon cut across the sky, Solomon gone home!' "

He could hardly wait to get home. To tell his father, Pilate; and he would love to see Reverend Cooper and his friends. "You think Macon Dead was something? Huh. Let me tell you about *his* daddy. You ain't heard nothin yet."

Milkman turned in his seat and tried to stretch his legs. It was morning. He'd changed buses three times and was now speeding home on the last leg of his trip. He looked out the window. Far away from Virginia, fall had already come. Ohio, Indiana, Michigan were dressed up like the Indian warriors from whom their names came. Blood red and yellow, ocher and ice blue.

He read the road signs with interest now, wondering what lay beneath the names. The Algonquins had named the territory he lived in Great Water, *michi gami*. How many dead lives and fading memories were buried in and beneath the names of the places in this country. Under the recorded names were other names, just as "Macon Dead," recorded for all time in some dusty file, hid from view the real names of people, places, and things. Names that had mean-

ing. No wonder Pilate put hers in her ear. When you know your
name, you should hang on to it, for unless it is noted down and
remembered, it will die when you do. Like the street he lived on,
recorded as Mains Avenue, but called Not Doctor Street by the Negroes in memory of his grandfather, who was the first colored man
of consequence in that city. Never mind that he probably didn't deserve their honor—they knew what kind of man he was: arrogant,
color-struck, snobbish. They didn't care about that. They were paying their respect to whatever it was that made him *be* a doctor in the
first place, when the odds were that he'd be a yardman all of his life.
So they named a street after him. Pilate had taken a rock from every
state she had lived in—because she *had* lived there. And having
lived there, it was hers—and his, and his father's, his grandfather's,
his grandmother's. Not Doctor Street, Solomon's Leap, Ryna's Gulch,
Shalimar, Virginia.

He closed his eyes and thought of the black men in Shalimar,
Roanoke, Petersburg, Newport News, Danville, in the Blood Bank,
on Darling Street, in the pool halls, the barbershops. Their names.
Names they got from yearnings, gestures, flaws, events, mistakes,
weaknesses. Names that bore witness. Macon Dead, Sing Byrd,
Crowell Byrd, Pilate, Reba, Hagar, Magdalene, First Corinthians,
Milkman, Guitar, Railroad Tommy, Hospital Tommy, Empire State
(he just stood around and swayed), Small Boy, Sweet, Circe, Moon,
Nero, Humpty-Dumpty, Blue Boy, Scandinavia, Quack-Quack, Jeri-
cho, Spoonbread, Ice Man, Dough Belly, Rocky River, Gray Eye,
Cock-a-Doodle-Doo, Cool Breeze, Muddy Waters, Pinetop, Jelly Roll,
Fats, Leadbelly, Bo Diddley, Cat-Iron, Peg-Leg, Son, Shortstuff,
Smoky Babe, Funny Papa, Bukka, Pink, Bull Moose, B.B., T-Bone,
Black Ace, Lemon, Washboard, Gatemouth, Cleanhead, Tampa Red,
Juke Boy, Shine, Staggerlee, Jim the Devil, Fuck-Up, and *Dat* Nigger.

Angling out from these thoughts of names was one more—the
one that whispered in the spinning wheels of the bus: "Guitar is biding his time. Guitar is biding his time. Your day has come. Your day
has come. Guitar is biding his time. Guitar is a very good Day. Guitar is a very good Day. A very good Day, a very good Day, and biding, biding his time."

In the seventy-five-dollar car, and here on the big Greyhound,
Milkman felt safe. But there were days and days ahead. Maybe if
Guitar was back in the city now, among familiar surroundings, Milkman could defuse him. And certainly, in time, he would discover his
foolishness. There was no gold. And although things would never be
the same between them, at least the man-hunt would be over.

Even as he phrased the thought in his mind, Milkman knew it
was not so. Either Guitar's disappointment with the gold that was

not there was so deep it had deranged him, or his "work" had done it. Or maybe he simply allowed himself to feel about Milkman what he had always felt about Macon Dead and the Honoré crowd. In any case, he had snatched the first straw, limp and wet as it was, to prove to himself the need to kill Milkman. The Sunday-school girls deserved better than to be avenged by that hawk-headed raven-skinned Sunday man who included in his blood sweep four innocent white girls and one innocent black man.

Perhaps that's what all human relationships boiled down to: Would you save my life? or would you take it?

"Everybody wants a black man's life."

Yeah. And black men were not excluded. With two exceptions, everybody he was close to seemed to prefer him out of this life. And the two exceptions were both women, both black, both old. From the beginning, his mother and Pilate had fought for his life, and he had never so much as made either of them a cup of tea.

Would you save my life or would you take it? Guitar was exceptional. To both questions he could answer yes.

"Should I go home first, or go to Pilate's first?" Out in the street, late at night with autumn air blowing cold off the lake, he tried to make up his mind. He was so eager for the sight of Pilate's face when he told her what he knew, he decided to see her first. He'd have a long time at his own house. He took a taxi to Darling Street, paid the driver, and bounded up the stairs. He pushed the door open and saw her standing over a tub of water, rinsing out the green bottles she used for her wine.

"Pilate!" he shouted. "Have I got stuff to tell you!"

She turned around. Milkman opened his arms wide so he could hold all of her in a warm embrace. "Come here, sweetheart," he said, grinning. She came and broke a wet green bottle over his head.

When he came to, he was lying on his side in the cellar. He opened one eye and considered the option of not coming to for a little while more. For a long time now he knew that anything could appear to be something else, and probably was. Nothing could be taken for granted. Women who loved you tried to cut your throat, while women who didn't even know your name scrubbed your back. Witches could sound like Katharine Hepburn and your best friend could try to strangle you. Smack in the middle of an orchid there might be a blob of jello and inside a Mickey Mouse doll, a fixed and radiant star.

So he lay on the cool damp floor of the cellar and tried to figure out what he was doing there. What did Pilate knock him out for? About the theft of her sack of bones? No. She'd come to his rescue immediately. What could it be, what else could he have done that would turn her against him? Then he knew. Hagar. Something had happened to Hagar. Where was she? Had she run off? Was she sick or . . . Hagar was dead. The cords of his neck tightened. How? In Guitar's room, did she . . . ?

What difference did it make? He had hurt her, left her, and now she was dead—he was certain of it. He had left her. While he dreamt of flying, Hagar was dying. Sweet's silvery voice came back to him: "Who'd he leave behind?" He left Ryna behind and twenty children. Twenty-one, since he dropped the one he tried to take with him. And Ryna had thrown herself all over the ground, lost her mind, and was still crying in a ditch. Who looked after those twenty children? Jesus Christ, he left twenty-one children! Guitar and the Days chose never to have children. Shalimar left his, but it was the children who sang about it and kept the story of his leaving alive.

Milkman rolled his head back and forth on the cellar floor. It was his fault, and Pilate knew it. She had thrown him in the cellar. What, he wondered, did she plan to do with him? Then he knew that too. Knew what Pilate's version of punishment was when somebody took another person's life. Hagar. Something of Hagar's must be nearby. Pilate would put him someplace near something that remained of the life he had taken, so he could *have* it. She would abide by this commandment from her father herself, and make him do it too. "You just can't fly on off and leave a body."

Suddenly Milkman began to laugh. Curled up like a Polish sausage, a rope cutting his wrists, he laughed.

"Pilate!" he called. "Pilate! That's not what he meant. Pilate! He didn't mean that. He wasn't talking about the man in the cave. Pilate! He was talking about himself. His own father flew away. He was the 'body.' The body you shouldn't fly off and leave. Pilate! Pilate! Come here. Let me tell you what your father said. Pilate, he didn't even tell you to sing, Pilate. He was calling for his wife—your mother. Pilate! Get me out of here!"

Light exploded in his face. The cellar door opened over his head. Pilate's feet appeared on the stone steps, and paused.

"Pilate," said Milkman, softly now, "that's not what he meant. I know what he meant. Come, let me tell you. And Pilate, those bones. They're not that white man's bones. He probably didn't even die. I went there. I saw. He wasn't there and the gold wasn't there either. Somebody found it and found him too. They must have, Pilate. Long before you got there. But, Pilate . . ."

She descended a few steps.

"Pilate?"

She came all the way down and he looked in her eyes and at her still mouth. "Pilate, your father's body floated up out of the grave you all dug for him. One month later it floated up. The Butlers, somebody, put his body in the cave. Wolves didn't drag the white man to the front of the cave and prop him on a rock. That was your father you found. You've been carrying your father's bones—all this time."

"Papa?" she whispered.

"Yes. And, Pilate, you have to bury him. He wants you to bury him. Back where he belongs. On Solomon's Leap."

"Papa?" she asked again.

Milkman did not speak; he watched her long fingers travel up her dress, to rest like the wing of a starling on her face. "I've been carryin Papa?" Pilate moved toward Milkman, stopped and looked at him for a while. Then her eyes turned to a rickety wooden table that stood against the stone wall of the cellar. It was in a part of the room so dark he had not even seen it. She walked over to the table and lifted from it a green-and-white shoe box, its cover held down with a rubber band. "Joyce," it said on the box. "Thank heaven for little Joyce heels."

"If I bury Papa, I guess I ought to bury this too—somewhere." She looked back at Milkman.

"No," he said. "No. Give it here."

When he went home that evening, he walked into the house on Not Doctor Street with almost none of the things he'd taken with him. But he returned with a box of Hagar's hair.

She wouldn't set foot on an airplane, so he drove. She seemed happy now. Her lips mobile again, she sat next to him in Macon's Buick, a mink stole Reba had won wrapped around her shoulders over her old black dress. The knit cap was pulled down on her forehead and her shoes still had no laces. Every now and then she glanced at the back seat to check on the sack. Peace circled her.

Milkman felt it too. His return to Not Doctor Street was not the triumph he'd hoped it would be, but there was relief in his mother's crooked smile. And Lena, though unforgiving as ever, was civil to him, since Corinthians had moved to a small house in Southside, which she shared with Porter. The Seven Days, Milkman guessed, would be looking for a new recruit, as they had to when Robert Smith jumped off the roof of Mercy. But there were long rambling talks with his father, who could not hear it enough—the "boys" who remembered him in Danville; his mother's running off with his father; the story about his father and his grandfather. He wasn't a bit interested in the flying part, but he liked the story and the fact that places were named for his people. Milkman softened his description of Circe, saying simply that she was alive, and taking care of the dogs.

"I ought maybe to take me a trip down there," said Macon.

"Virginia?" Milkman asked him.

"Danville. I ought to go by and see some of those boys before these legs stop moving. Let Freddie pick up the rents, maybe."

It was nice. No reconciliation took place between Pilate and Macon (although he seemed pleased to know that they were going to bury their father in Virginia), and relations between Ruth and Macon were the same and would always be. Just as the consequences of Milkman's own stupidity would remain, and regret would always outweigh the things he was proud of having done. Hagar was dead and he had not loved her one bit. And Guitar was . . . somewhere.

In Shalimar there was general merriment at his quick return, and Pilate blended into the population like a stick of butter in a churn. They stayed with Omar's family, and on the second and last evening, Milkman and Pilate walked up the road to the path that led to Solomon's Leap. It was the higher of two outcroppings of rock. Both flat-headed, both looking over a deep valley. Pilate carried the sack, Milkman a small shovel. It was a long way to the top, but neither stopped for breath. At the very top, on the plateau, the trees that could stand the wind at that height were few. They looked a long time for an area of earth among the rock faces large enough for the interment. When they found one, Pilate squatted down and opened the sack while Milkman dug. A deep sigh escaped from the sack and the wind turned chill. Ginger, a spicy sugared ginger smell, enveloped them. Pilate laid the bones carefully into the small grave. Milkman heaped dirt over them and packed it down with the back of his shovel.

"Should we put a rock or a cross on it?" Milkman asked.

Pilate shook her head. She reached up and yanked her earring from her ear, splitting the lobe. Then she made a little hole with her fingers and placed in it Sing's snuffbox with the single word Jake ever wrote. She stood up then, and it seemed to Milkman that he heard the shot after she fell. He dropped to his knees and cradled her lolling head in the crook of his arm, barking at her, "You hurt? You hurt, Pilate?"

She laughed softly and he knew right away that she was reminded of the day he first met her and said the most stupid thing there was to say.

The twilight had thickened and all around them it was getting dark. Milkman moved his hand over her chest and stomach, trying to find the place where she might be hit. "Pilate? You okay?" He couldn't make out her eyes. His hand under her head was sweating like a fountain. "Pilate?"

She sighed. "Watch Reba for me." And then, "I wish I'd a knowed more people. I would of loved 'em all. If I'd a knowed more, I would a loved more."

Milkman bent low to see her face and saw darkness staining his hand. Not sweat, but blood oozing from her neck down into his cupped hand. He pressed his fingers against the skin as if to force the life back in her, back into the place it was escaping from. But that only made it flow faster. Frantically he thought of tourniquets and could even hear the rip of cloth he should have been tearing. He shifted his weight and was about to lay her down, the better to wrap her wound, when she spoke again.

"Sing," she said. "Sing a little somethin for me."

Milkman knew no songs, and had no singing voice that anybody would want to hear, but he couldn't ignore the urgency in her voice. Speaking the words without the least bit of a tune, he sang for the lady. "Sugargirl don't leave me here/ Cotton balls to choke me/Sugargirl don't leave me here/ Buckra's arms to yoke me." The blood was not pulsing out any longer and there was something black and bubbly in her mouth. Yet when she moved her head a little to gaze at something behind his shoulder, it took a while for him to realize that she was dead. And when he did, he could not stop the worn old words from coming, louder and louder as though sheer volume would wake her. He woke only the birds, who shuddered off into the air. Milkman laid her head down on the rock. Two of the birds circled round them. One dived into the new grave and scooped something shiny in its beak before it flew away.

Now he knew why he loved her so. Without ever leaving the ground, she could fly. "There must be another one like you," he whispered to her. "There's got to be at least one more woman like you."

Even as he knelt over her, he knew there wouldn't be another mistake; that the minute he stood up Guitar would try to blow his head off. He stood up.

"Guitar!" he shouted.

Tar tar tar, said the hills.

"Over here, brother man! Can you see me?" Milkman cupped his mouth with one hand and waved the other over his head. "Here I am!"

Am am am am, said the rocks.

"You want me? Huh? You want my life?"

Life life life life.

Squatting on the edge of the other flat-headed rock with only the night to cover him, Guitar smiled over the barrel of his rifle. "My man," he murmured to himself. "My main man." He put the rifle on the ground and stood up.

Milkman stopped waving and narrowed his eyes. He could just make out Guitar's head and shoulders in the dark. "You want my life?" Milkman was not shouting now. "You need it? Here." Without wiping away the tears, taking a deep breath, or even bending his knees—he leaped. As fleet and bright as a lodestar he wheeled toward Guitar and it did not matter which one of them would give up his ghost in the killing arms of his brother. For now he knew what Shalimar knew: If you surrendered to the air, you could *ride* it.

Carolyn Rodgers

(1945–   )

CAROLYN M. RODGERS was born in Chicago in 1945 and has spent most of her life in that city. She began writing poetry as an undergraduate at the University of Illinois at Chicago (1960 to 1961) and continued writing at Roosevelt University, where she earned the B.A. in 1965. She did social work at the YMCA from 1963 to 1966 and for the Chicago Poverty Program from 1965 to 1968. It was during these years that she became affiliated with the Chicago Organization of Black American Culture, meeting such prominent black writers as Haki Madhubuti, Hoyt Fuller, and Gwendolyn Brooks, who taught a workshop where Rodgers took courses in creative writing and who became Rodger's mentor, helping her to organize her first book of poetry, *Paper Soul*. This book was published in 1968 by Third World Press, which Rodgers had cofounded earlier that year with Johari Amini and Haki Madhubuti, and it won the first Conrad Kent Rivers Memorial Fund Award that same year.

In 1969 Rodgers published her second volume of poems, *Songs of a Blackbird*. She won the Poet Laureate Award of the Society of Midland Authors and a National Endowment for the Arts grant in 1970. Her next book, a collection of new and selected poems titled *how i got ovah*, was published in 1975. She published her most recent volume of poetry, *The Heart As Ever Green*, in 1978.

Rodgers has also written and published a number of short stories, including "Blackbird in a Cage" (*Negro Digest*, 1967), "A Statistic, Trying to Make It Home" (*Negro Digest*, 1969), and "One Time" (*Essence*, 1975). She has taught at Columbia College, Chicago, the University of Washington, and Indiana State University, among other institutions, and has worked on her M.A. at Roosevelt University in Chicago.

For further reading, see Jean Davis's article in *Dictionary of Literary Biography, Volume 41*. Also see Angelene Jamison, "Imagery in the Women Poems: The Art of Carolyn Rodgers," and Bettye J. Parker-Smith, "Running Wild in Her Soul: The Poetry of Carolyn Rodgers," both in *Black Women Writers, 1950–1980: A Critical Evaluation*, edited by Mari Evans (1984).

The following poems are taken from *how i got ovah: new and selected poems*.

U NAME THIS ONE

let uh revolution come. uh
state of peace is not known to me
anyway
since i grew uhround in chi town
where
howlin wolf howled in the tavern on 47th st.
and muddy waters made us cry the salty nigger blues,
    where pee wee cut lonnell fuh messin wid
    his sistuh and blood baptized the street
    at least twice ev'ry week and judy got
    kicked outa grammar school fuh bein pregnant
    and died trying to ungrow the seed
        we was all up in there and
            just living was guerilla warfare, yeah.

let uh revolution come.
couldn't be no action like what
i dun already seen.

I HAVE BEEN HUNGRY

*Preface: This poem was written because I was asked to contribute to an anthology
of black and white women, and the title of the anthology was* I Had Been Hungry
All My Years.

1

and you white girl
shall i call you sister now?
can we share any secrets of sameness,
any singularity of goals. . . .
you, white girl with the head that
perpetually tosses over-rated curls
while i religiously toss my over-rated behind
you white girl
i am yet suspicious of/
for deep inside of me

there is the still belief that
i am
a road
you would travel
to my man.

2

and how could you, any of you
think that a few loud words and years
could erase the tears
blot out the nightmares and knowledge,
smother the breeded mistrust
and how could any of you think that i
after being empty for so long
could fill up on fancy fierce platitudes. . . .

some new/old knowledge has risen in me like yeast
but still old doubts deflate

am i—really—so beautiful
as i sweat and am black and oh so
greasy in the noonday sun

the most beauty that i am i am inside
and so few deign to touch
i am a forest of expectation.
the beauty that i will be is yet
to be defined

what i can be even i can not know.

3

and what does a woman want?
what does any woman want
but a soft man to hold her hard
a sensitive man to help her fight off
the insensitive pangs of living.
and what is living to a woman
without the weight of some man
pulling her down/puffing her out

do not tell me
liberated tales of woman/woeman
who seek only to satisfy them selves
with them selves, all, by them selves
i will not believe you

i will call you a dry canyon
them, a wilderness
of wearying and failures
a fearing of hungerings from
and deep into
the wonderment of loneliness
and what makes any woman so.

4

as for me—
i am simple
a simple foolish woman.
all that i have ever wanted
i have not had
and much of what i have had
i have not wanted.

my father never wanted three girls
and only one son, one sun. . . .
God, how he wished his seeds
had transformed themselves into
three boys and only one girl—
for heaven's sake, only one good for nothing
wanting needing love and approval seeking bleeding
girl.
and so, i have spent my days
so many of my days seeking the approval
which was never there
craving the love
i never got
and what am i now,
no longer a simple girl
bringing lemonade and cookies
begging favor

and what am i now
no longer a world-torn woman
showering my "luck" in a
cold bottle of cold duck

and—who—am i now
but a
saved
sighing
singular thing. a woman. . . .

ah, here i am
and
here have i been
i say,
i
have been hungry,
ravenously hungry,
all
my
years

Eugene B. Redmond

(1937–   )

BORN IN 1937 in St. Louis, Missouri, Eugene B. Redmond grew up in East St. Louis, Illinois, in the care of his grandmother. He served in the Marine Corps from 1958 to 1961, then attended Southern Illinois University, receiving the B.A. in English in 1964. He undertook graduate studies in English at Washington University and earned the M.A. in 1966. During his years as an undergraduate he served as staff writer and then as editor of the school newspaper, and in 1963 he helped found an East St. Louis weekly called *The Monitor*, on which he held various editorial positions until 1970.

Redmond is the literary executor for the estate of the late Henry Dumas, who was his close friend until Dumas's death in 1968. He is guest editor of a special Henry Dumas Issue of *Black American Literature Forum* (Summer 1988), and he succeeded Dumas as director of language workshops and as poet-in-residence at Southern Illinois University's Experiment in Higher Education. Redmond has also served as writer-in-residence at a number of other colleges and universities, including California State University, Oberlin College, and the University of Wisconsin at Madison. From 1967 to 1970 he was senior consultant at Southern Illinois's Performing Arts Training Center. He has written and published many plays, some of which were produced by university theaters during the early 1970s. Among these were *The Face of the Deep* (performed in 1971), *Will I Still Be Here Tomorrow?* (1972), and *There's a Wiretap in My Soup* (1974), the last of which was also performed at Martinique Theater in New York.

Redmond cofounded Black River Writers Publishing Company, which published three volumes of his poetry: *River of Bones and Flesh and Blood* (1971), *Songs from an Afro/Phone* (1972), and *In a Time of Rain and Desire* (1973). Black River Writers also produced a recording of his poems titled *Bloodlinks and Sacred Places* in 1973. Redmond's other books of poetry include *Sentry of the Four Golden Pillars* (1970) and *Consider Loneliness as These Things* (1973). He has also written an important survey of black American poetry from 1746 to 1976 titled *Drumvoices: The Mission of Afro-American Poetry, A Critical History* (1976). Redmond is Poet Laureate of East St. Louis, Illinois, and professor of English at Southern Illinois University at Edwardsville and founding editor of a new journal *Drumvoices Revue*.

For further reading, see Joyce Pettis's essay in *Dictionary of Literary*

Biography, *Volume 41* and Linda Metzger, ed., *Black Writers: A Selection of Sketches from Contemporary Authors* (1989).

The following selections are taken from *River of Bones and Flesh and Blood* and *Amiri Baraka: The Kaleidoscopic Torch.*

EPIGRAMS FOR MY FATHER
(John Henry Redmond, Sr.)

I

Fatherlore: papa-rites, daddyhood;
    Run & trapsong: Search & dodgesong.
Steelhammeringman.
Gunbouter; whiskeywarrior.
Nightgod!
Moonballer/brawler grown old.
Slaughterhouse/river mackman:
Hightale teller & totempoleman.

II

Wanderer across waters:
Folkbrilliance & Geniusgrit;
Railraging railsplitter:
Railrage! Railrage!
IC & BM&O & MoPac & Midnight Special:
Freight train . . . . . . bring my daddy back!

III

Stone-story. The story of stone, brokenbricks—
Rocks hurled in pleasure & rage,
Pebbles soft & silent:
Home-dome is a blues-hard head.

IV

45-degree hat, Bulldurham butt bailing from lips;
Gabardine shining shining shining
Above white silk socks—
    satin man

satin man
silksure & steelstrong
hammerhold on life
hammerhold on life

V

Sun-son. Stonebone. Blackblitz.
Fatherlore. Struggledeep: Afridark, Afrolark,
daddydepth—
Riverbottom song.

THE ARCHED BISHOP OF NEW ART

For Amiri Baraka—In futuriam

I

Proletarian pontif—

His blackfulness
His wholeness

His bopness
His esthetic-efficient exactness

His hipness
His high frequency/fahrenheit coolness

His down/ness   *outlandishness*
His jiveness   *expubidence*

His brashness & his badness, i.e., full-up flame
Buttressed by the quick eyes of the daggerfire

Balancing bloods and Marx   making marks of his own

Lurking for the illusive
The black led-less
The lumpen/humpin bourgeosie

II

Breakpoet of the pivot the pony the shuffle
The bootygreen & the rim shot:

   tack-a-map
   tack-a-map
   tack-a-map

Home-boy & hydra-tongue bard of the Blue Roi

Verb-pugilist in the service of the peoplehood:
When the poem calls
He comes out throwing
Antiphonal combinations
Lyrical lefts & rights
Rhythmical noun-jabs
His lores in the folkweighs
This finesser of rime & mime

III

Retractor of doom   gnome-flirter   dismantler of occults
Divinator:
   'I See Yo Hi C'
   Said the Dark Gree Gree—

Who heals with the uglylanguage;
Unfurls aphorisms and unwigs deceivers

A mass/man prevailing
Arched bishop of his ambivalence:
Worshipping deities of the dirty diction &
Practicing the art of prettyfication:

Wit-conjurer, who wordlessly converts
with the warm arms of consciousness—

Speaking to an anxious & enduring
Moment known as the multitude: a.k.a. people alias worker

Five'll get you some jive
Skin'll get you some kin*

*or: *caint the bishop burn?*

V: 4-14-44

For VALERIE

Awe. It was awe. Awe.
Hey! Choice lady who perplexes
With the walking language: I mean the Right Reverend
Wailwoman of the indelible indigo dark.

With the ambulatory assurance of a seeing-eye:

> Shoo-be-doo
> Bloom-de-bloom
> 4-14-44

Life's oo-la-la ingredient with gravy:
Electric lush smile: unswerved sass;
Plushly ornamental elegance arching
Arching over anatomical swivels: She be's the clean-up woman!

> Uh huh African Prophecy
> Peering thru a hypnotic pelvis uh huh

O ley ley / ley ley: tossing tempest of a mane!
Elliptical bright black laughter   counterpoised
Against the death-serious sabre-stare: The One that
Simultaneously kills and reincarnates you:

> 4-14-44

In-Soul-ated Sway-Sayer: Choice.
Sway-Sayer In-Soul-ated: Choice.
Breath-depth abiding hums   hums   hums:
River-Traverser: Pain-Traverser.
Mama History cuddling, heaving Southend Sighs.

Mural in eminent motion? Or enticing tapestry?
Either way, some part of your prolific
Pulchritude always, always eludes me: you, you
Of that whole and contagious thoughtful joy.

> Yo, now comes a fiendish frown
> Grinding against a gnawing cackle:
>   Choice.

Or Oily bright black laughter

Around emerald-eyes: Rainbowed
By evil eye-brows: <u>Now, Prepare for a Piece of her Mind</u>!

     She, she whose frank rap can create a riot!
     Caw Caw Girl of the Nitty Gritty Gold!

What?
What wonder—WAILER—of-a-Woman!

Toni Cade Bambara

(1939–   )

TONI CADE BAMBARA (born Toni Cade in 1939) grew up in New York City with her mother and brother. She attended Queens College in New York and graduated with the B.A. in theater arts and English in 1959. Also in 1959 she published her first short story in *Vendome* magazine, won the John Golden Award for Fiction from Queens College, and was awarded the *Long Island Star*'s Pauper Press Award for nonfiction. While a graduate student in modern American fiction at City College of New York she did social work for the Harlem Welfare Center from 1959 to 1960 and published her second short story, in *Massachusetts Review*, in 1960. She spent 1961 in Italy, then returned to New York and completed her master's degree at City College in 1965. She taught there until 1969 and then went to Livingston College in New Jersey as an associate professor. During this ten-year period she was active in numerous projects for the black community and took part in workshops and study groups on civil rights and women's liberation. She also published a number of short stories in magazines such as *Redbook* and *Prairie Schooner.*

The City College SEEK program (a New York State school dropout program), for which Bambara served as adviser, sponsored the publication of an anthology titled *The Black Woman* in 1970. Bambara edited this volume of poetry, short stories, and essays by well-known black women writers and students in the SEEK program. She also contributed three essays of her own. In 1971 she edited a second anthology, *Tales and Stories for Black Folks*, a collection of short fiction by prominent black American and African writers and by students in the creative writing course she was teaching at Livingston College. She contributed work to this volume as well.

Fifteen of Bambara's early short stories were collected and published in 1972 as *Gorilla, My Love.* She continued teaching at Livingston College until 1974, when she moved to Atlanta, Georgia, and took a position as writer-in-residence at Spelman College, which she held until 1977. In that year her second collection of ten short stories, titled *The Sea Birds Are Still Alive*, was published. In 1980 she published her first novel, *The Salt Eaters.* When she relocated to Atlanta she became active in filmmaking and producing a number of television scripts. She is currently at work on a movie screenplay and lives in Philadelphia.

For further reading, see Alice A. Deck's article in *Dictionary of Literary*

Biography, Volume 38. Also see Nancy D. Hargrove, "Youth in Toni Cade Bambara's *Gorilla, My Love,*" in *Women Writers of the Contemporary South,* edited by Peggy Whitman Prenshaw (1984), and Mari Evans's *Black Women Writers, 1950–1980: A Critical Evaluation* (1984).

"Gorilla, My Love" is the title story from the 1972 collection.

GORILLA, MY LOVE

That was the year Hunca Bubba changed his name. Not a change up, but a change back, since Jefferson Winston Vale was the name in the first place. Which was news to me cause he'd been my Hunca Bubba my whole lifetime, since I couldn't manage Uncle to save my life. So far as I was concerned it was a change completely to somethin soundin very geographical weatherlike to me, like somethin you'd find in a almanac. Or somethin you'd run across when you sittin in the navigator seat with a wet thumb on the map crinkly in your lap, watchin the roads and signs so when Granddaddy Vale say "Which way, Scout," you got sense enough to say take the next exit or take a left or whatever it is. Not that Scout's my name. Just the name Granddaddy call whoever sittin in the navigator seat. Which is usually me cause I don't feature sittin in the back with the pecans. Now, you figure pecans all right to be sittin with. If you thinks so, that's your business. But they dusty sometime and make you cough. And they got a way of slidin around and dippin down sudden, like maybe a rat in the buckets. So if you scary like me, you sleep with the lights on and blame it on Baby Jason and, so as not to waste good electric, you study the maps. And that's how come I'm in the navigator seat most times and get to be called Scout.

So Hunca Bubba in the back with the pecans and Baby Jason, and he in love. And we got to hear all this stuff about this woman he in love with and all. Which really ain't enough to keep the mind alive, though Baby Jason got no better sense than to give his undivided attention and keep grabbin at the photograph which is just a picture of some skinny woman in a countrified dress with her hand shot up to her face like she shame fore cameras. But there's a movie house in the background which I ax about. Cause I am a movie freak from way back, even though it do get me in trouble sometime.

Like when me and Big Brood and Baby Jason was on our own last Easter and couldn't go to the Dorset cause we'd seen all the

Three Stooges they was. And the RKO Hamilton was closed readying up for the Easter Pageant that night. And the West End, the Regun and the Sunset was too far, less we had grownups with us which we didn't. So we walk up Amsterdam Avenue to the Washington and *Gorilla, My Love* playin, they say, which suit me just fine, though the "my love" part kinda drag Big Brood some. As for Baby Jason, shoot, like Granddaddy say, he'd follow me into the fiery furnace if I say come on. So we go in and get three bags of Havmore potato chips which not only are the best potato chips but the best bags for blowin up and bustin real loud so the matron come trottin down the aisle with her chunky self, flashin that flashlight dead in your eye so you can give her some lip, and if she answer back and you already finish seein the show anyway, why then you just turn the place out. Which I love to do, no lie. With Baby Jason kickin at the seat in front, egging me on, and Big Brood mumblin bout what fiercesome things we goin do. Which means me. Like when the big boys come up on us talkin bout Lemme a nickel. It's me that hide the money. Or when the bad boys in the park take Big Brood's Spaudeen way from him. It's me that jump on they back and fight awhile. And it's me that turns out the show if the matron get too salty.

So the movie come on and right away it's this churchy music and clearly not about no gorilla. Bout Jesus. And I am ready to kill, not cause I got anything gainst Jesus. Just that when you fixed to watch a gorilla picture you don't wanna get messed around with Sunday School stuff. So I am mad. Besides, we see this raggedy old brown film *King of Kings* every year and enough's enough. Grownups figure they can treat you just anyhow. Which burns me up. There I am, my feet up and my Havmore potato chips really salty and crispy and two jawbreakers in my lap and the money safe in my shoe from the big boys, and here comes this Jesus stuff. So we all go wild. Yellin, booin, stompin and carryin on. Really to wake the man in the booth up there who musta went to sleep and put on the wrong reels. But no, cause he holler down to shut up and then he turn the sound up so we really gotta holler like crazy to even hear ourselves good. And the matron ropes off the children section and flashes her light all over the place and we yell some more and some kids slip under the rope and run up and down the aisle just to show it take more than some dusty ole velvet rope to tie us down. And I'm flingin the kid in front of me's popcorn. And Baby Jason kickin seats. And it's really somethin. Then here come the big and bad matron, the one they let out in case of emergency. And she totin that flashlight like she gonna use it on somebody. This here the colored matron Brandy and her friends call Thunderbuns. She do not play. She do not smile. So we shut up and watch the simple ass picture.

Which is not so simple as it is stupid. Cause I realize that just about anybody in my family is better than this god they always talkin about. My daddy wouldn't stand for nobody treatin any of us that way. My mama specially. And I can just see it now, Big Brood up there on the cross talking bout Forgive them Daddy cause they don't know what they doin. And my Mama say Get on down from there you big fool, whatcha think this is, playtime? And my Daddy yellin to Granddaddy to get him a ladder cause Big Brood actin the fool, his mother side of the family showin up. And my mama and her sister Daisy jumpin on them Romans beatin them with they pocketbooks. And Hunca Bubba tellin them folks on they knees they better get out the way and go get some help or they goin to get trampled on. And Granddaddy Vale sayin Leave the boy alone, if that's what he wants to do with his life we ain't got nothin to say about it. Then Aunt Daisy givin him a taste of that pocketbook, fussin bout what a damn fool old man Granddaddy is. Then everybody jumpin in his chest like the time Uncle Clayton went in the army and come back with only one leg and Granddaddy say somethin stupid about that's life. And by this time Big Brood off the cross and in the park playin handball or skully or somethin. And the family in the kitchen throwin dishes at each other, screamin bout if you hadn't done this I wouldn't had to do that. And me in the parlor trying to do my arithmetic yellin Shut it off.

Which is what I was yellin all by myself which make me a sittin target for Thunderbuns. But when I yell We want our money back, that gets everybody in chorus. And the movie windin up with this heavenly cloud music and the smart-ass up there in his hole in the wall turns up the sound again to drown us out. Then there comes Bugs Bunny which we already seen so we know we been had. No gorilla my nuthin. And Big Brood say Awwww sheeet, we goin to see the manager and get our money back. And I know from this we business. So I brush the potato chips out of my hair which is where Baby Jason like to put em, and I march myself up the aisle to deal with the manager who is a crook in the first place for lying out there sayin *Gorilla, My Love* playin. And I never did like the man cause he oily and pasty at the same time like the bad guy in the serial, the one that got a hideout behind a push-button bookcase and play "Moonlight Sonata" with gloves on. I knock on the door and I am furious. And I am alone, too. Cause Big Brood suddenly got to go so bad even though my mama told us bout goin in them nasty bathrooms. And I hear him sigh like he disgusted when he get to the door and see only a little kid there. And now I'm really furious cause I get so tired grownups messin over kids just cause they little and can't take em to court. What is it, he say to me like I lost my mit-tens or wet on myself or am somebody's retarded child. When in reality I am the smartest kid P.S. 186 ever had in its whole lifetime and you can ax anybody. Even them teachers that don't like me cause I won't sing them Southern songs or back off when they tell me my questions are out of order. And cause my Mama come up there in a minute when them teachers start playin the dozens behind colored folks. She stalk in with her hat pulled down bad and that Persian lamb coat draped back over one hip on account of she got her fist planted there so she can talk that talk which gets us all hyp-notized, and teacher be comin undone cause she know this could be her job and her behind cause Mama got pull with the Board and bad by her own self anyhow.

So I kick the door open wider and just walk right by him and sit down and tell the man about himself and that I want my money back and that goes for Baby Jason and Big Brood too. And he still trying to shuffle me out the door even though I'm sittin which shows him for the fool he is. Just like them teachers do fore they realize Mama like a stone on that spot and ain't backin up. So he ain't gettin up off the money. So I was forced to leave, takin the matches from under his ashtray, and set a fire under the candy stand, which closed the raggedy ole Washington down for a week. My Daddy had the suspect it was me cause Big Brood got a big mouth. But I explained right quick what the whole thing was about and I figured it was even-steven. Cause if you say Gorilla, My Love, you suppose to mean it. Just like when you say you goin to give me a party on my birthday, you gotta mean it. And if you say me and Baby Jason can go South pecan haulin with Granddaddy Vale, you better not be comin up with no stuff about the weather look uncer-tain or did you mop the bathroom or any other trickified business. I mean even gangsters in the movies say My word is my bond. So don't nobody get away with nothin far as I'm concerned. So Daddy put his belt back on. Cause that's the way I was raised. Like my Mama say in one of them situations when I won't back down, Okay Badbird, you right. Your point is well-taken. Not that Badbird my name, just what she say when she tired arguin and know I'm right. And Aunt Jo, who is the hardest head in the family and worse even than Aunt Daisy, she say, You absolutely right Miss Muffin, which also ain't my real name but the name she gave me one time when I got some medicine shot in my behind and wouldn't get up off her pillows for nothin. And even Granddaddy Vale—who got no mem-ory to speak of, so sometime you can just plain lie to him, if you want to be like that—he say, Well if that's what I said, then that's it. But this name business was different they said. It wasn't like Hunca Bubba had gone back on his word or anything. Just that he was

thinkin bout gettin married and was usin his real name now. Which
ain't the way I saw it at all.

So there I am in the navigator seat. And I turn to him and just
plain ole ax him. I mean I come right on out with it. No sense goin
all around that barn the old folks talk about. And like my mama say,
Hazel—which is my real name and what she remembers to call me
when she bein serious—when you got somethin on your mind,
speak up and let the chips fall where they may. And if anybody
don't like it, tell em to come see your mama. And Daddy look up
from the paper and say, You hear your mama good, Hazel. And tell
em to come see me first. Like that. That's how I was raised.

So I turn clear round in the navigator seat and say, "Look here,
Hunca Bubba or Jefferson Windsong Vale or whatever your name is,
you gonna marry this girl?"

"Sure am," he say, all grins.

And I say, "Member that time you was baby-sittin me when we
lived at four-o-nine and there was this big snow and Mama and
Daddy got held up in the country so you had to stay for two days?"

And he say, "Sure do."

"Well. You remember how you told me I was the cutest thing
that ever walked the earth?"

"Oh, you were real cute when you were little," he say, which is
suppose to be funny. I am not laughin.

"Well. You remember what you said?"

And Granddaddy Vale squintin over the wheel and axin Which
way, Scout. But Scout is busy and don't care if we all get lost for
days.

"Watcha mean, Peaches?"

"My name is Hazel. And what I mean is you said you were going
to marry *me* when I grew up. You were going to wait. That's what I
mean, my dear Uncle Jefferson." And he don't say nuthin. Just look
at me real strange like he never saw me before in life. Like he lost in
some weird town in the middle of night and looking for directions
and there's no one to ask. Like it was me that messed up the maps
and turned the road posts round. "Well, you said it, didn't you?"
And Baby Jason lookin back and forth like we playin ping-pong.
Only I ain't playin. I'm hurtin and I can hear that I am screamin.
And Granddaddy Vale mumblin how we never gonna get to where
we goin if I don't turn around and take my navigator job serious.

"Well, for cryin out loud, Hazel, you just a little girl. And I was
just teasin."

" 'And I was just teasin,' " I say back just how he said it so he can
hear what a terrible thing it is. Then I don't say nuthin. And he
don't say nuthin. And Baby Jason don't say nuthin nohow. Then

Granddaddy Vale speak up. "Look here, Precious, it was Hunca Bubba what told you them things. This here, Jefferson Winston Vale." And Hunca Bubba say, "That's right. That was somebody else. I'm a new somebody."

"You a lyin dawg," I say, when I meant to say treacherous dog, but just couldn't get hold of the word. It slipped away from me. And I'm crying and crumplin down in the seat and just don't care. And Granddaddy say to hush and steps on the gas. And I'm losin my bearins and don't even know where to look on the map cause I can't see for cryin. And Baby Jason cryin too. Cause he is my blood brother and understands that we must stick together or be forever lost, what with grownups playin change-up and turnin you round every which way so bad. And don't even say they sorry.

Daryl Dance

(1938–   )

WITHOUT A DOUBT, Daryl Cumber Dance is the most noted of contemporary collectors and critics of African American folklore. She is indeed a loyal Virginian: born in Richmond, Virginia, she received her A.B. and M.A. degrees in English at Virginia State College in 1957 and 1963, respectively, and her Ph.D. in English from the University of Virginia in 1971. She is currently a full professor of English at Virginia Commonwealth University, where she has been a member of the faculty since 1972. Before going to Virginia Commonwealth, she taught at Virginia State College from 1962 to 1972.

Dance's many fields of interest—folklore, black American literature, Caribbean literature, southern literature, and the American novel—have given rise to numerous scholarly publications. She is the editor of the important resource guide *Fifty Caribbean Writers: A Bio-Bibliographical and Critical Sourcebook* (1986) and author of *Shuckin' and Jivin': Folklore from Contemporary Black Americans* (1978), *Folklore from Contemporary Jamaicans* (1985), and *Long Gone: The Mecklenburg Six and the Theme of Escape in Black Folklore* (1987). Of her many essays, perhaps the most important is her very thorough, indispensable "Zora Neale Hurston," found in *American Women Writers: Bibliographical Essays*, edited by Maurice Duke, Jackson R. Bryer, and M. Thomas Inge.

In the same tradition as Zora Neale Hurston's *Mules and Men, Shuckin' and Jivin'* is an eclectic collection of tales that address the cruelty of whites, marital infidelity, ethnic jokes, self-degrading tales, tales about religion, conjure tales, tales about women, ghost stories, tales of heaven and hell, and many other types. In her introduction Professor Dance explains the significance of black folk tales: "Forced into a closed society, often largely lacking in literacy, Black Americans developed and maintained an oral tradition probably unmatched, and certainly not surpassed, by that of any other group in America. Their folklore reveals the history of Black people in this country and their psychological reactions to their experience. The similarities of themes appearing throughout their tales, from the slave anecdotes to the contemporary stories, suggest that for Black Americans basically very little has changed."

Professor Dance's most provocative book is *Long Gone: The Mecklenburg Six and the Theme of Escape in Black Folklore*. On one level this very unusual book traces the escape of the Briley brothers and two other death row inmates from the Mecklenburg Correctional Center in Boydton, Virginia, and on another level, *Long Gone* discusses the popularity of the theme of escape in Afro-American history and the historical folk responses to the escapees or fugitives. Among many other points she concludes, "As I met and talked with the condemned men and other inmates, I was amazed at how unlike the stereotype of the hardened, vicious criminal many of them seemed. One cannot interact with and get to know many of these men without feeling a great sense of the loss of human potential and without agonizing over whether a society as great as ours does not have the resources to try to emphasize prevention and rehabilitation and not just punishment."

In addition to being the author of thought-provoking publications, Professor Dance has given more than eighty-one speeches, lectures, and paper presentations across the United States. In 1978 she received a Fulbright research grant to study in Jamaica; she is also the recipient of two National Endowment for the Humanities research grants and a Ford Foundation Fellowship. In April of 1989 she received the College of Humanities and Sciences Distinguished Research Award from Virginia Commonwealth University.

The following selection comes from chapter 1 of *Long Gone*.

"HE'S LONG GONE"
The Theme of Escape in Black Folklore and Literature

> Leader: *It's a Long John.*
> Group: *Long John.*
> Leader: *He's long gone.*
> Group: *Long gone.*
> Leader: *Like a turkey through the corn.*
> Group: *Like a turkey through the corn.*
> Leader: *He's long gone.*
> Group: *Long gone.*
>
> Traditional worksong celebrating Long John's outrunning
> the sheriff and the deputies and their bloodhounds
> in his flight from the chain gang to freedom.

Throughout their experiences in this country, certain segments of the Black population have viewed themselves as enslaved, whether they were chattel owned by slaveowners prior to emancipation, whether they were impressed into peonage and forced to work on white plantations and in chain gangs after slavery, whether they were victims of sharecropping systems that virtually reenslaved them during the twentieth century, whether they were the repressed and disfranchised and persecuted in Southern Jim Crow towns throughout the first half of the twentieth century, whether they are those trapped by unemployment and poverty today, or whether they are among the Blacks who continue to be disproportionately represented in our penal institutions. One has only to talk to contemporary Black slum dwellers, Black prison inmates, and a host of other Blacks as well who may not be ensnared in those situations to have reinforced the observation made by William H. Grier and Price M. Cobbs, "For white America to understand the life of the black man, it must recognize that so much time has passed and so little has changed."[1]

For any individual who is enslaved, incarcerated, constrained, the major goal is freedom. Escape from his or her present entrapment has been the major theme in the Black American's folklore and literature from its beginnings. Slave songs are full of images of escape, some clearly escape from slavery, others apparently escape from this world—which becomes a safe metaphor for expressing the compelling desire for an escape from bondage. The slave sang, "No more hundred lash for me, / No more driver's lash for me, / Many thousand gone." He intoned, "Swing low, sweet chariot, coming for to carry me home." He advised, "Steal away, steal away, steal away to Jesus." He acclaimed, "The gospel train is coming . . . Get on board, children, get on board." He extolled, "Oh, freedom. Oh, freedom. Oh freedom over me, and before I'll be a slave, I'd be buried in my grave and go home to my Lord and be free." He appealed, "Go down, Moses, / Way down in Egypt land, / Tell old Pharoah, / Let my people go / . . . . O, let us all from bondage flee." He taunted, "The devil he thought he had me fast. . . . But I thought I'd break his chains at last." He acclaimed, "I am bound for the land of Canaan." Slave and later tales recount escapes from Ole Master, the paterollers, sheriffs, posses, Ku-Kluxers, bigger and stronger animals, ghosts, the devil, the Lord, or prison. In "Convict's Prayer," the speaker, paraphrasing the twenty-third Psalm, concludes, "Surely goodness and mercy shall find me one of these days in my life / and I will drill away from this house for ever and ever" (*Get Your Ass in the Water*, p. 216). Many is the tale that ends in lines similar to these from *S & J*: "I was

---

[1]William H. Grier and Price M. Cobbs, *Black Rage* (New York: Bantam Books, 1969), p. 31.

makin' *feet* help the *body*! Yes, Lawd, I was gettin' out the way"
(p. 32).

Lacking the political, economic, and military might to win freedom through legal means, through the attainment of economic power, or through revolution,[2] the Black people in this country have found that their best chance for freedom was through running—literally and figuratively. In the Black folk lexicon, noted for its flexibility, its originality, and its vivid metaphors, there is no idea that has so many different words to express it as the idea of leaving, fleeing, running.[3] There is no trait that is regarded as more critical to survival than the ability to run; there is no characteristic more applauded than skill at running:

> You see, the raccoon, you know, he was an engineer
> And the possum, he always tend to the switch,
> Old rabbit didn't have no job at all
> But he was a running son-of-a-bitch.[4]
> > *Negro Tales from Pine Bluff*, p. 24

> [Dis nigger] jumped de fence and run fru de paster,
> White man run, but nigger run faster.
> . . . .
> Dat nigger run, dat nigger flew,
> Dat nigger tore his shirt in two.
> > *Encyclopedia of Black Folklore*, p. 239

> Take dis ole hammer an' carry it
> > to the cap'n
> And tell him I'm gone.

---

[2]This is not to suggest that Blacks have not tried all of these means in their efforts to achieve freedom. From the beginning, individual slaves petitioned in the courts for freedom and other rights, while other slaves organized slave rebellions; and throughout their history in America, Blacks have organized in political, civic, and religious groups that sought redress through the approved channels.

[3]Air out, back off, backtrack, beat it, blow, breeze, brush off, bust out, cop a drill/trot, crash out, cruise, cut, cut out, cut and run, depart, disappear, dodge, drift, duck out, ease on out, ease on down, escape, fade, flake out/off, flee, fly, fly the coop, foot it, freewheel, get on in/off/down/out/back, go, go away, go North, go over the hill/wall, grab a armfull of box-cars/the first thing smoking, hat up, haul ass/it, hightail it, hike, hit the road/street, hoof it, hustle, journey, jump bail, jump a train, lam (or take a lam), leave, light out, make feet help the body, make it, make oneself scarce, make tracks, ooze, percolate, ride, ride the rails, roll out/on, run, scat, scram, sell out, shove, shove off, skip, skivver, slide, space, split, step, take a powder/duck, take off, take to the woods/hills/road, trilly on, trilly walk, trot, truck, truck it, tunnel (go into hiding), vamoose, wheel it, wing it.

[4]In their folklore, Negroes always associate the rabbit with themselves.

If he ask you was I runnin', tell him
no, I was might' near flyin'.
American Negro Folklore, p. 195

Countless tales and songs in the folk tradition have lines that encourage,"Run, nigger, run, or the paterollers will catch you"; "O, run, nigger, run, cause it's almos' day"; or acclaim, "You ought to see that preacher [nigger, man] run"; or brag, "I'm a greasy streak o' lightning" (the last line is from *Negro Workaday Songs*, p. 65). If any conflict comes down to running, there is usually no question that the Negro will win.

So common is the theme of running in Black literature from the slave narratives (whose basic theme is that of the flight from slavery) and the first novel written by a Black American (William Wells Brown's *Clotel*) through the popular works of Richard Wright, Ralph Ellison, and a multitude of others that Phyllis Klotman has entitled her study of Black American literature *Another Man Gone: The Black Runner in Afro-American Literature*. The theme continues with the recently published *Brothers and Keepers* by John Edgar Wideman. As one reads each of the many works that focus on this theme, one witnesses repetition after repetition of the scenarios that involve Ralph Ellison's *Invisible Man*, wherein everyone seems to conspire to "Keep This Nigger-Boy Running."[5] Indeed many of the writers themselves, from Frederick Douglass to Richard Wright, James Baldwin and Eldridge Cleaver, have experienced the dilemma of the man on the run. Several of them fled the American South, and some of them ultimately fled the country.

Thus, as is revealed in both their folklore and their literature, as much pleasure as the Black people might derive from out-smarting white people, there always comes a time when the skill of running is requisite. As the old proverb says, "Whut you don' hab in yo' haid, yuh got ter hab in yo' feet" (*American Negro Folklore*, p. 325). And as a young Black child told Robert Coles in an interview a few years ago: "Legs mean more than hands. So I gives them more attention. If you can run, you're O.K."[6]

---

[5] I do not mean by this discussion to imply that the theme of running, of escape, is unique to Black literature. It may be said to be the common theme in a country founded and populated by a host of peoples running from religious oppression, political oppression, poverty, and imprisonment. The theme laid out in the diaries and travelogues of the Founding Fathers continues as several of our major White writers, such as Irving, Cooper, Melville, Twain, and Faulkner, recorded the journeys of men fleeing everything from domineering wives to the restrictions of organized society. Given the history of Blacks in this country, the theme does, however, have unique implications and variations within the Black tradition.

[6] *The Negro American*, ed. Talcott Parsons and Kenneth B. Clark (Boston: Houghton, 1966), p. 258.

Obviously when the Black man speaks of running, he does not always mean it literally. In addition to "putting on my walkin' shoes," he may find that his flight requires that he "hitch up my buggy," "saddle my ole grey mare," "jump a rail," "get a ole Greyhound bus and ride" (all traditional), or "[cool] 'bout hundred-fifteen miles an hour in my / own limousine" ("The Great MacDaddy," *Deep Down*, p. 163). While his travels might take him many places, most of his songs and tales tell of his traveling some road or highway—"a lonesome road," or "a lonesome highway," the "king's highway," or the "gospel highway." The Black runner most often follows the North Star, traveling from South to North, usually leaving towns in Georgia, Arkansas, Alabama, Mississippi (especially Vicksburg and Clarksdale), and other such "mean ole Jim Crow towns," and setting out for New Orleans, Memphis, Nashville, Chicago, New York, Detroit, and St. Louis. The runner's songs frequently depict the horrors of life in the mean old Southern towns and the anticipation of a better life in the North: he's "*sweet* Chicago bound" or he's headed "up north where money grows on trees." In the Black folk tradition, even snakes get out of Mississippi, and God is afraid to travel any further South than Memphis.

Most of their songs and tales allude to, but generally do not detail, the suffering, hardships, and pain that Blacks are trying to escape. Generally there is enough information (coupled with our own knowledge of the history of race relations) to convince us that escape is requisite for survival, and that it is worth the risk of life and limb that it probably entails. Thus the Black man sings, "I'd rather drink muddy water, sleep in a hollow log, than to stay in this here town, treated like a dirty dog" (traditional). He sings, "The devil he thought he had me fast, but I thought I'd break his chains at last" (*Negro Spirituals*, p. 23). Blind Lemon Jackson sang, "Gettin' tired of sleepin' in this low-down lonesome cell" (*Blues Fell This Morning*, p. 216).

When the Brileys and their cohorts drove out of Mecklenburg prison and entered that long, lonely, dark country road, they triggered on one level the gut reaction that many Blacks have to the archetypal runner.[7] One must remember that the Black runner, whether he or she be Nat Turner or Harriet Tubman or Frederick Douglass or JoAnne Little or Angela Davis or Stagolee or James Briley, is always labeled and regarded by the system as a fugitive, a des-

---

[7]It is interesting to observe that the runner, the legendary hero in Black folklore, and the warrior, the legendary hero in the Western tradition, were ironically counterposed in newspaper accounts of the Great Escape, which shared the headlines from the day the escape was announced (June 1, 1984) and the ensuing days with recollections of D-Day.

perado, a dangerous criminal, a vicious threat to society; and his flight is always in violation of the established law. Whatever one's view of the individuals involved in the Great Escape, whether one reacted fearfully to the threat posed by those convicted felons or whether one harbored suspicions that perhaps they were victims of an unjust legal system more inclined to execute its poor and Black,[8] there was often, before these balanced considerations, a visceral reaction to the *flight* and a recollection of a host of other runners. And those who recognized themselves most susceptible to the possible loss of their own freedom undoubtedly recognized even more keenly that the fugitive who might generally be judged undeserving craved freedom every bit as much as the runner whom some deemed worthy.

> Inside looking out,
> I see the happiness
> and sadness, the hurt
> and pain that everyone feels,
> even while here
> Inside Looking Out . . . .
> James Briley, *Fysk Magazine,*
> Summer 1984, written before the escape

Very likely they recognized as well that while on one level it may seem blasphemous to link the name of so valiant a heroine as Harriet Tubman with that of a cold blooded murderer, that chain was forged by their respective societies who judged them both the same and hunted them in like manner as similarly dangerous threats to the maintenance of order.

RUNAGATE RUNAGATE

I.

Runs falls rises stumbles on from darkness into darkness
and the darkness thicketed with shapes of terror
and the hunters pursuing and the hounds pursuing
and the night cold and the night long and the river
to cross and the jack-muh-lanterns beckoning beckoning
and blackness ahead and when shall I reach that somewhere
morning and keep on going and never turn back and keep on
    going

Runagate

Runagate

---

[8]The blues are full of lines of men being "judged without a trial," and folktales treating the theme of injustice in the courtroom are legion. For additional examples, see Ch. 8.

Runagate

Many thousands rise and go
many thousands crossing over

O mythic North
O star-shaped yonder Bible city

Some go weeping and some rejoicing
some in coffins and some in carriages
some in silks and some in shackles

Rise and go or fare you well

No more auction block for me
no more driver's lash for me
  If you see my Pompey, 30 yrs of age,
  new breeches, plain stockings, negro shoes;
  if you see my Anna, likely young mulatto
  branded E on the right cheek, R on the left,
  catch them if you can and notify subscriber.
  Catch them if you can, but it won't be easy.
  They'll dart underground when you try to catch them,
  plunge into quicksand, whirlpools, mazes,
  turn into scorpions when you try to catch them.

And before I'll be a slave
I'll be buried in my grave

  North star and bonanza gold
  I'm bound for the freedom, freedom-bound
  and oh Susyanna don't you cry for me

Runagate

  Runagate

II.
Rises from their anguish and their power,

          Harriet Tubman,

          woman of earth, whipscarred,
          a summoning, a shining

          Mean to be free

And this was the way of it, brethren brethren,
way we journeyed from Can't to Can.
Moon so bright and no place to hide,
the cry up and the patterollers riding,
hound dogs belling in bladed air.
And fear starts a-murbling, Never make it,
we'll never make it. *Hush that now*,
and she's turned upon us, levelled pistol
glinting in the moonlight:
dead folks can't jaybird-talk, she says;

you keep on going now or die, she says.

Wanted   Harriet Tubman   alias The General
alias Moses   Stealer of Slaves

In league with Garrison   Alcott   Emerson
Garrett   Douglass   Thoreau   John Brown

Armed and known to be Dangerous

Wanted   Reward   Dead or Alive

Tell me, Ezekiel, oh tell me do you see
mailed Jehovah coming to deliver me?

Hoot-owl calling in the ghosted air,
five times calling to the hants in the air.
Shadow of a face in the scary leaves,
shadow of a voice in the talking leaves:

Come ride-a my train

Oh that train, ghost-story train
through swamp and savanna movering movering,
over trestles of dew, through caves of the wish,
Midnight Special on a sabre track movering movering,
first stop Mercy and the last Hallelujah.

Come ride-a my train

Mean mean mean to be free.

"Runagate Runagate" is reprinted from *Angle of Ascent:*
New and Selected Poems by Robert Hayden,
by permission of Liveright Publishing Corporation.
Copyright © 1975, 1972, 1970, 1966 by Robert Hayden.

"It was just like, hey, yawl ain't gon' leave ME in here. You know, if you
got a chance to be free, you aim to take it."   Escapee Derick Peterson
Conversation, June 28, 1985

Eleanor W. Traylor

(1939–   )

BORN IN THOMASVILLE, Eleanor Traylor grew up in Atlanta, Georgia, where her parents were small business merchants on the famed Auburn Avenue. Perhaps the influence of her grandparents in that storyville pear orchard she writes of, the fact that her father played in the Negro Leagues, and her mother being a woman with a secular and sacred spirit are the qualities that influence her creative imagination.

Traylor received her A.B. at Spelman College in her hometown of Atlanta, Georgia, in 1955 and her M.A. at Atlanta University in 1956. Before completing the requirements for her Ph.D. degree at Catholic University in Washington, D.C., she studied as a Merrill Scholar at the University of Stuttgart, Stuttgart, Germany, from 1956 to 1957, as a research fellow at the Institute of African Studies at the University of Ibadan in Nigeria in 1973, and as a research fellow at the Institute of African Studies at the University of Ghana at Legon in the same year.

She worked as an instructor of English at Howard University in Washington, D.C., from 1959 to 1965. In 1965 she became a member of the faculty at Montgomery Junior College in Rockville, Maryland, where she remained until 1990. She is currently a full professor in the English Department at Howard University. She has also worked as visiting lecturer at Georgetown University, Tougaloo College, Cornell University, Hobart College, and William Smith College. Eleanor Traylor is more than a teacher, scholar, and critic, she is a multitalented creative artist. Since 1984 she has been designer and project director of "The Larry Neal Cultural Series" at the Afro-American Historical and Cultural Museum in Philadelphia, Pennsylvania; she is script writer of five historical and biographical dramatic adaptations: "The Musical Ministry of Charles Albert Tindley" (1981); "The Presence of Ancestry: A Three-Part Liturgical Movement in Poetry and Music" (1981); "Langston Hughes: Bluesman" (1981); "Easy Lawd: Death, Afro-American Style" (1982); and "Quilting: A DocuDrama" (1987). She herself has performed as an actress in Douglas Turner Ward's *Happy Ending* with the D.C. Black Repertory Performers and with Avery Brooks and Bernice Reagan in historical and cultural scripts prepared for and presented by the Smithsonian Institution.

Presently she is at work on a book-length manuscript that treats various traditions in recent African American fiction. One of the most sought-after lecturers on African American literature because of her dramatic, oratorical style, Traylor is also the author of numerous essays on African American literature. Three of her most recent are "Henry Dumas and the Discourse of Memory," *Black American Literature Forum* 22 (Summer 1988); "*Bolder Measures* Crashing Through: Margaret Walker's Poem of the Century," *Callaloo* 4 (Fall 1987); and "The Achievement of Larry Neal: A Biobibliography of a Critical Imagination," *Callaloo* 1 (Winter 1985).

The selection that follows, "The Humanities and Afro-American Literary Tradition," was an address presented by Dr. Traylor at the first District of Columbia Public Humanities Lecture sponsored by the D.C. Community Humanities Council in October 1988.

THE HUMANITIES AND AFRO-AMERICAN LITERARY TRADITION

A system of education that fails to nurture memory of the past denies its students the satisfaction of mature thought, an attachment to abiding concerns, a perspective on human existence.
American Memory: A Report on the Humanities
in the Nation's Public Schools by Lynne V. Cheney, Chairman,
National Endowment for the Humanities

. . . they ask me to remember but they want me to remember
their memories and I keep remembering mine.
Lucille Clifton (Afro-American Poet)

There was nothing remarkable about the Saturday afternoon's excursion. We were a small group of friends happy to be gathered at Arundel on the Bay. The heat of the August day had scorched the city, but here, facing the water from a shady porch, we were happy to be cool, to eat our lunches, and to talk about the world which had disappeared beyond the water. "But," said the friend who was a lawyer, in reply to an observation that all had not heard, "Why must it always be fantasy? After all, what are we to make of a ghost—a woman fully clothed who walks from the sea into the lives of people and seems to ruin them?" The world, for a moment, had become a book. We had plunged into the world of Toni Morrison's Beloved (1987). The friend from Trinidad answered her. "Memory," he said, "is sometimes the ghost of a forgotten or unadmitted past, like the stories of the Duennes and La Diablesse." The friend who was a lawyer was annoyed. "There we go again!" she said. But another voice interrupted, "Who are they—the Duennes and La

---

Reprinted by permission of the District of Columbia Community Humanities Council and Eleanor Traylor.

*Diablesse?" "Well," said the friend from Trinidad, "according to the lore
of the island, Duennes are spirits of children who died without the sac-
rament of burial and are fated to roam the forests practicing their repertoire of pranks. Their feet are turned backward, for they belong on
the other side. They wish to be there, but they must be properly buried
before they can go. On the other hand, La Diablesse is really an old
crone whose petticoats rustle like the sound of chains. Sometimes, she
appears as a tall beautiful woman who catches the eye of a man. The
man proceeds to follow her but, never able to catch her, finds himself
bewildered, far from home, and maybe quite mad." "But this is what I
mean," cried the objector. "Why dwell on painful old stories? We live
now, and in a world which requires of us as much reality. . . ." The
friend who had asked to hear the stories interrupted the objector. "It is
what we avoid—what we do not admit—what we impose in its place
that challenges what is real," said the friend. The company of friends
agreed.*

I

The insistence upon a recall of memory, a review of the past, characteristic of Afro-American intellectual and artistic productions, emphasizes the constant humanistic observation that we find living
value in remembering our ancestry: "the sweep of human experience" (Cheney, *American Memory*, 6) which has preceded us. Or as
James Baldwin has put it: "how we may suffer, how we are defeated,
how we may triumph" ("Sonny's Blues," 121) are the great lessons of
the past. Yet when Baldwin, the storefront preacher from Harlem,
the Black writer from America, visits the medieval French town at
Chartres and stands before the great Cathedral there, his response to
what he views as a living text from the past is decidedly different
than that of his countryman, Henry Adams, historian, scholar, man
of letters, who had also read the text of the Cathedral. "We come to
Chartres," said Adams, "for our ideals" (*Chartres*, 9). To the contrary, for Baldwin, the Cathedral becomes not a paragon, but a
speaking subject—a voice from the past. He tells us:

> The Cathedral at Chartres . . . *says* something to the people of this vil-
> lage which it cannot *say* to me; but it is important to understand that
> this Cathedral says something to me which it cannot *say* to them
> ("Stranger in the Village," 88, emphasis added).

The past, for the writer, inspires a conversation between memory
and the moment. It is a call which empowers a creative and recrea-
tive responsive present. He muses:

These [villagers], from the point of view of power, cannot be strangers anywhere in the world . . . even if they do not know it. The most illiterate among them is related, in a way that I am not, to Dante, Shakespeare, Michelangelo, Æschylus, DaVinci, Rembrandt, and Racine; the Cathedral at Chartres says something to them which it cannot say to me . . . Out of their hymns and dances came Beethoven and Bach. Go back a few centuries . . . I am in Africa watching the conquerors arrive ("Stranger," 83).

The dialogue between past and present conjures from the writer a canonical recitation and a review of two histories: in one of these, the Cathedral, the text being read, is representative; the other history is the one by which the reader, speaker, writer views the text. Yet the viewer is participant in both histories and, for that reason, is released to a plenitude unavailable, by exclusion, in one history alone. The viewer, thus enabled, renders a responsible mediation. For in his investigation of the many-layered meanings abiding in the Cathedral, as text of the past, he has also confronted himself in relation to it. The outcome has included us in a drama wherein the Self examines itself in relation to an other. The examination results in "overcoming the other's strangeness without assimilating it wholly to one<u>self</u>" (Bakhtin, 24). Such an examination is the *être de rigueur*, the traditional behavior, of the Afro-American legacy in literature.

In this case, Baldwin concludes his study of the Cathedral by assessing its probable impact upon the villagers and its actual effect upon himself:

Perhaps, they are struck by the power of the spires and the glory of the stained glass windows. . . . I am terrified by the slippery bottomless well to be found in the crypt down which heretics were hurled to death, and by the obscene inescapable gargoyles strutting out of the stone seeming to suggest that God and the devil can never be divorced. . . . Perhaps I have known God in a different way ("Stranger," 89).

II

In a different way. The difference has been the substance and fine tuning of the products shaped by the Afro-American mind. Perhaps the difference becomes apparent in Miz Eva's tale as we visit another village and witness another text. Now, "we have this [little] church in the village," (Lovelace, *Wine*, 32) begins Miz Eva. Miz Eva is a Trinidadian villager who is wife of the Reverend Bee Raymond, pastor of the Spiritualist Baptist Church, in Earl Lovelace's novel *The Wine of Astonishment* published in 1982. Miz Eva is the central vision and narrator of the novel, so, through her eyes, we see the situation surrounding the little church in the village. Indeed, through her sensibility do we apprehend the meaning of "we church" for its members:

> We have this church. The walls make out of mud. The roof covered with carrot leaves; a simple hut with no steeple or cross or acolytes or priests or latin ceremonies. But is our own. Black people own it. Government ain't spent one cent helping us build it or put bench in it or anything; the bell that we ring when we call to the Spirit is our money that pay for it. So we have this church.

> We have this church where we gather to sing hymns and ring the bell and shout hallelujah and speak in tongues when the Spirit come; and we carry the Word to the down-trodden and the forgotten and the lame and the beaten, and we touch black people soul.

> We have this church where in this tribulation country far away from Africa, the home that we don't know, we can come together and be ourselves (*Wine*, 32–33).

By 1903, Dr. W. E. B. Du Bois had inscribed the far reaching implication of "we church" in the development of Black new world literature and art. In his landmark study, *The Souls of Black Folk*, he had written:

> They that walked in darkness sang songs in the olden days. Sorrow songs–for they were weary of heart. And so before each thought that I have written in this book I have set a phrase, a haunting echo of these weird old songs in which the soul of the Black slave spoke to men. Ever since I was a child these songs have stirred me strongly. They come out of the South unknown to me, one by one, and yet at once I knew them [to be] of me and mine (181).

But even before that, in his now classic *Narrative* of 1845 written before the first gun of the Civil War had pronounced the waning of the age of slavery in the United States and, therefore, before the ban prohibiting the literacy of the enslaved had been lifted, Frederick Douglass had written of those songs which we may call the first living monument of "we church." He said:

> . . . they were tones, loud, long and deep . . . revealing at once the highest joy and the deepest sadness . . . they breathed the prayer and complaint of souls boiling over with the bitterest anguish. Every tone was a testimony against slavery and a prayer to God for deliverance . . . to those songs, I trace my first glimmering conception [of humanity] (31).

From then to now, interview a range of artists speaking across the wide diversity of humanistic and aesthetic endeavor. Ask them the inevitable question: Wherein and how from and to what do you attribute your extraordinary and brilliant and powerful and unique expression? From

> Marian Anderson to Leontyne Price
> Paul Robeson to William Warfield
> Ma Rainey to Aretha Franklin
> Ella Fitzgerald to Betty Carter
> Edward Ellington to John Coltrane
> Mahalia Jackson to James Cleveland
> Huddie Leadbetter to Bobby McFerrin
> Hale Woodruff to Romare Bearden and Jacob Lawrence
> Augusta Savage to Valerie Maynard
> Laura Wheeler Waring to Mildred Thompson
> Katherine Dunham to Alvin Ailey
> Rose McClendon to Ruby Dee
> Phillis Wheatley to Gwendolyn Brooks
> Langston Hughes to Sterling Brown
> Claude McKay to Amiri Baraka
> Anna J. Cooper to Maya Angelou
> Zora Neale Hurston to Toni Morrison
> W. E. B. Du Bois to C. L. R. James

(to say nothing of the myraid unnamed of whom those named are representative and to say nothing of the now and emergent present). Ask the question. The answer? Always, "there was this little church."

"We church," say Miz Eva, is a place where "you could hear your own voice . . . feel your own spirit, and catch your own power" (*Wine*, 33). The church, then, is not a land, not an army, not a flag. No, "we church" is the sign of a very different matter. It is a tabernacle of human witness where every voice hears itself speaking; every tear, each acknowledged, fertilizes every shout of joy. It is the place of authentic human feeling—the residence of language which admits the existence of the human heart: that sentient drum beating one insistent message:

> this is your urgency: Live!
> and have your blooming . . .
> (Brooks, "The Second Sermon," 453)

Here at the altar of the little church is the daily round of life whose expression we may call the Humanities. No walls or boundary lines restrict "we church." It is a community of memory and shared experience where all the old stories begin, are recalled, are transformed anew. Here where "the old decapitations and dispossessions" (Brooks, "The Wall," 445) are remembered, where the small and large victories of being are rehearsed, "something profound and unanswerable [stirs] in the consciousness of all . . . " (Baldwin, *The Evidence*, 122). Here, the litany admits no categorical distinction between the Aesthetic and the ethical: "the apostle of Beauty thus becomes the apostle of Truth and Right not by choice but by inner and outer compulsion. Free he is but his freedom is ever bounded by Truth and Justice . . . " (Du Bois, *Criteria*, 258). And here, a common faith abounds: "the world is full of [beauty] . . . its variety is infinite, its possibility endless. In normal life all may have it . . . " (253). Yet, the congregation shares a tacit understanding: "the mass of humanity is locked away from [beauty] and their lives distorted and made ugly . . . " (253). Thus, "we church" intones the common weal: "who shall right this well-nigh universal failing? Who shall let this world be beautiful?" (253). It is here where "our endless connections with and responsibilities for each other" (*The Evidence*, 122) are somehow clarified by the memory of our particular passage through the world: who in the slave ship's pit was the first to lift his head? Who on the southern fields east of Eden was to lift her voice in defiant cry? Who was the first to ratify the daring proclamation: this child shall not be eaten!

> *Jésus, Estrella, Esperanza, Mercy . . .*
> (Hayden, *Ballad*, 48–50)

> *The Nation's hoop was broken, and there was no center any longer . . . and the sacred tree is dead . . . a people's dream died there. It was a beautiful dream . . .* (Black Elk, 182–230).

> *Runs falls rises stumbles on from darkness into darkness and the darkness thicketed with shapes of terror and the hunters pursuing and the hounds pursuing and the night cold and the night long and the river to cross and the jack-muh-lanterns beckoning beckoning and blackness ahead and where shall I reach that somewhere morning and keep on going and never turn back . . .*

> *And this was the way of it, brethren brethren. Way we journeyed from can't to can. Moon so bright and no place to hide, the cry up and the patterollers riding, hound dogs belling in the bladed air. And fear starts a-murbling, Never make it, We'll never make it. Hush that now, and she's turned upon us, levelled pistol glinting in the moon-light: [Hush that now] you keep on going keep on going now, she says* (Hayden, *Ballad*, 59–61).

"We church," say Miz Eva, "*ain't do the white man or his brown tools any wrong . . . We preach the Word and who have ears to hear, hear. And the lost souls scattered in every religion in Babylon was coming home to a Church that is their own, whereafter the service finish the brethren could discuss together how the corn growing, how the children doing, for what price cocoa selling, and the men could know which*

brother they should lend a hand to the coming week, and the sisters
could find out who sick from the congregation so we could go and sit
with her a little and help her out with the cooking for her children or
the washing or the ironing. And it was nice at last to have a place to be
together, where you could hear your own voice shouting hallelujah and
feel the spirit spreading over the Church as the brethren sing and dance
and catch the power" (Wine, 33).

Yet in the world of the novel from which Miz Eva speaks, the
little church is banned. For the novel recreates "the history of a spiritualist Community on the island from the passing of the [British]
Prohibition Ordinance of 1917 until the lifting of the ban in 1951"
(Thorpe, viii). But the beauty of *The Wine of Astonishment* is its or-
chestration of the island's many voices; it choreography of images
painting the epic faces of life; its lyrical evocation of the enduring
spirit of a people whose urgency is the humanistic moment:

Then we was singing a hymn, soft and low, sweet with our rhythm:

The Lion of Judah shall break every chain
And bring us to victory over Satan again.

Then it cool down, die away with sweet, soft humming and low moaning, and a cleanness and a lightness come over the church, and the rain
stop falling, and we was fresh and wash like new grass in the morning
(*Wine*, 62).

III

A rigorous examination of the texts of the past in the present; the
inclusion of two histories in dialectical conversation: one's own history and that of an other; a practical application of the fruit of the
inquiry toward the amelioration of both the individual and society;
the creation of a community of memory where we hear our own
voices, in multiplicity, articulate what we need and what we feel to
be the best in human life—these have been the traditions of the
Afro-American legacy in literature. From the texts arising from "we
church," we receive a vocabulary naming major and broad-reaching
conditions of modern humanity: *the veil* (Du Bois), the distorting,
warping, dwarfing myopia preventing a clear vision of reality; *the*
river (Hughes), the stream of consciousness mapping the journey
back, the journey forward; *the native son* (Wright), the dispossessed
and dispossessing pariah denied the rites of passage essential to self-
knowledge and, therefore, self-fulfillment; *the conjurer*, (Chesnutt-
Bambara), the healing power of insight and imagination; *invisibility*
(Ellison), the denial of authentic being; *the slave* (Baraka), a delusion; *the bluest eye* (Morrison), the dementia of delusion; *Sula* (Mor-

rison), the conundrum of modern woman; *ark of bones* (Dumas), the ship of memory, resisting deluge, conveying "the whole house of thy brothers; (*Ark*, 6).

Nor do the texts which speak from the present of "we church" lack the resonance of the whole humanistic past: the rage of Achilleus, the plight of Andromache, the bold assertion of Antigone, the vengence of Medea, the mission of Moses, the dreams of Joseph, the insistence of Job, the courage of Judith, the quest of Dante, the outrage of Caliban, the arrogance of Prospero, the triumph of Sundiata, the quaking soul of the *Gita*. All these memories are alive in "we church." But memory "involves not just an act of retrieval by the mind of the poet, but simultaneously the perception of what lies before him and her in the present as deficient, as a vice, a lack that memory will fill" (Vance, 382).

Nevertheless, the Prohibition Ordinance is no respecter of virtue beyond its own prescription. The ban of exclusion is, at least, as old as the hemlock and the cross, and, today, it projects its monolithic voice in current policy pronouncements regarding the state of the Humanities and the Nation. Since 1984, when former Chairman of the National Endowment for the Humanities, William Bennett, issued his report, *To Reclaim a Legacy* through the present Chairman, Lynne V. Cheney's 1987 report, *American Memory: A Report on the Humanities in the Nation's Public Schools* to her 1988 *Report to the President, the Congress and the American People: Humanities in America*, the recommendations of the National Endowment have voiced a consensus: to re-erect the great (and phallic) Cathedral of Culture (the great books of the elect of Western tradition) whose seminal flow, by these accounts, is the sure engenderer of "what it means to be human . . . [of] truths that, transcending *accidents* of class, race, and gender, speak to us all" (*Humanities*, 14, emphasis added). Something seems avoided here—something unadmitted. And, once again, the "we churches" in the villages, speaking through the silences of the great cathedral, are the heretics hurled down the slippery bottomless well to be found in the crypt.

At Arundel on the Bay, the evening shadows had deepened, the tide was coming in, and the sound of the water crashing against the rock reminded the company of friends of the world beyond the water. But there was yet a question lurking. The quiet friend who had not spoken all afternoon asked the question: "But, really, who is Beloved?" asked the friend. "Oh!" answered the student, the youngest of the friends, who had charmed the company by speaking of the theory of signs as easily as she had nibbled her papaya. "By its signifying system, the text can't tell us that," said the student. *"It exists to ask us that,"* said the student. *"It works like a praise song,"* she explained. *"The praise song is very old. It is the old griot's song whose job it was to hold in memory the history of the noble houses. It is called by another name in the literary history that we study, but it's the same."* The student said, *"The song must be regularly sung to the young and old, high and low, rich and poor. It tells of the heroic and evil deeds of the past and of the struggles that the tribe has suffered through."* The quiet friend raised a finger to ask another question: *"Is that why they gather around the troubled house to sing?"*

"Well, yes," said the student, *"they sing a song . . ."* the quiet friend finished her query. *"That's the anthem isn't it?"* Sing a song Full of the hope that the dark past has taught us.

"Yes," whispered the student. The company of friends agreed.

REFERENCES

Adams, Henry. *Mont Saint-Michel and Chartres* (1905), Princeton, NJ: Princeton UP, 1981.
Bakhtin, Mikhail. *The Dialogical Principle*. ed. Tzvetan Todorov, *Theory and History of Literature*, 13. Minneapolis: U of Minnesota P, 1984.
Baldwin, James. "Sonny's Blues," *Goin' to Meet the Man*. New York: Dell, 1966.
———. "Stranger in the Village," *Notes of a Native Son* (1955) rpt. *The Price of the Ticket: Collected Non Fiction*. New York: St. Martin's Marek, 1985. Toni Morrison contrasts Adams's and Baldwin's perspectives on Chartres in "City Limits Village Values: Concepts of Urbanism in Black Fiction," *Literature and the Urban Experience*. Michael Jay and Ann Chalmers Watts, eds. New York: Rutgers UP, 1981, 35–43.
———. *The Evidence of Things Not Seen*. New York: Henry Holt, 1985.
Black Elk. *Black Elk Speaks*. ed. John G. Neihardt (1932). New York: Simon and Schuster, 1972.
Brooks, Gwendolyn. "The Second Sermon on the Warpland" (1968) rpt. *Blacks*. Chicago: The David Company, 1987.
———. "The Wall" (1967) rpt. *Blacks*. Chicago: The David Company, 1987.
Cheney, Lynne V. *American Memory: A Report on the Humanities in the Nation's Public Schools*. Washington, DC: The National Endowment for the Humanities, 1987.
———. *Humanities in America: A Report to the President, the Congress, and the American People*. Washington, DC: The National Endowment for the Humanities, 1988.
Douglass, Frederick. *Narrative of the Life of Frederick Douglass, An American Slave: Written by Himself* (1845). New York: New American Library, 1968.
Du Bois, W. E. B. *The Souls of Black Folk* (1903). New York: Fawcett World Library, 1961.
———. "Criteria for Negro Art" (1926), *W. E. B. Du Bois: A Reader*. ed. Meyer Weinberg. New York: Harper and Row, 1970.
Dumas, Henry. *Ark of Bones and Other Stories* (1965–1974) rpt. *Goodbye, Sweetwater: New and Collected Stories*. ed. Eugene B. Redmond. New York: Thunder's Mouth Press, 1988.
Hayden Robert. *A Ballad of Remembrance* (1962–1966) rpt. *Collected Poems*. ed. Frederick Glayser. New York: Liveright, 1985.
Lovelace, Earl. *The Wine of Astonishment*. London: Heinemann P, 1982.
Thorpe, Marjorie. "Introduction," *The Wine of Astonishment*. London: Heinemann P, 1982.
Vance, Eugene. "Roland and the Poetics of Memory," *Textual Strategies: Perspectives in Post Structural Criticism*. ed. Josué Harari. Ithaca, NY: Cornell UP, 1979.

Donald B. Gibson

(1933–   )

DONALD GIBSON is most noted in the African American literary community for his edition of *Five Black Writers: Essays on Wright, Ellison, Baldwin, Hughes and LeRoi Jones* (1970) and for his equally well-known *The Politics of Literary Expression: A Study of Major Black Writers* (1981). Currently a professor in the Department of English at Rutgers University at New Brunswick, he received both his B.A. and M.A. degrees from the University of Kansas City (now University of Missouri at Kansas City) in 1955 and 1957, respectively, and his Ph.D. in 1962 from Brown University where he also taught as an instructor before becoming an assistant professor at Wayne State University from 1962 to 1967. He left Wayne State to take an associate professorship at the University of Connecticut where he was promoted to full professor in 1974, the same year he joined the English Department at Rutgers.

In addition to the publications mentioned previously, he is the author of *The Fiction of Stephen Crane* (1968) and *The Red Badge of Courage: Redefining the Hero* (1988). He has edited *Black and White: Stories of American Life* with Carol Anselment (1971), *Twentieth-Century Interpretations of Modern Black Poets* (1973), and *W. E. B Du Bois, The Souls of Black Folk* (1989). His numerous articles range from subjects such as "Stephen Crane's 'The Blue Hotel'," "Twain's Jim in the Classroom," to "Richard Wright and the Tyranny of Social Convention," and "Text and Countertext in Toni Morrison's *The Bluest Eye*."

In addition to presenting lectures on various African American subjects throughout the United States, Gibson has also lectured in England, Poland, France, and Switzerland. His honors and awards include a study grant from the National Endowment for the Humanities in 1970, an American Philosophical Society award in 1970, a research grant from the American Council of Learned Societies, and a Fulbright to study in Cracow, Poland, from 1964 to 66.

The following selection is an excerpt from a revised version of *Individualism and Community in Black Fiction*, which originally appeared in *Black American Literature Forum*, Volume 11, Number 4 (Winter 1977).

FROM **INDIVIDUALISM AND COMMUNITY IN BLACK FICTION**
Ann Petry

The similarity between Ann Petry's response to the world of black
life as reflected in her novel *The Street* and Richard Wright's as we
see it expressed in *Black Boy* lies in their common understanding of
their situations as Afro-Americans living in their time and place.
Both wrestle mightily with the problem of individualism; both are
people with strong egos who initially believe that they are capable of
directing their own destinies, exclusive of societal and personal influences which militate against such capacities. They are children of
American culture in that sense. In their writing they test the assumption that an American, inheriting the legacy of pilgrim and pioneer, can by dint of the assertion of will carve out his own destiny
in much the same manner that the early inhabitants created a new
world. Such a vision could only belong to these two writers to the
extent that they would have broken away from a system of values
totally inimical to this one. Though that is not what these two writers are writing about directly, it is the source of the tension inherent
within their subjects, the tension between the individual's commitment to, engagement and involvement with a community, and the
individual's inclination to seek out his own destiny alone. *Black Boy*
simply opens up the question, a question Wright pursues throughout
a great part of his career. Ann Petry takes on the whole question at
once. Indeed the main focus of *The Street* is on the issue of whether
a black person, especially a woman, may in fact exist, may lead a
reasonably successful, moral life while following the creed of individualism.

The central character of Ann Petry's *The Street* is Lutie Johnson,
a young black woman, married when we first meet her in the novel,
but soon enough separated from her husband because the family's
need for money, in large part because of the unavailability of a job
for her black husband, forces her to take a job as a live-in domestic
in Westport, Connecticut. The strain of the separation—clearly the
result of racial factors—takes its toll, forcing the couple apart. Prior
to their estrangement Lutie has had no inclination to function in her
world as an individualist; but as she finds herself more and more
dependent upon her own resources, she increasingly attempts to become self-reliant. She attempts to survive in her world alone, not
only shunning the interrelatedness inherent in community relation-

Reprinted by permission of the author. This essay is a revised version of an essay by
the same title which appeared in *Black American Literature Forum*, Volume 11, Number 4
(Winter 1977).

ships but attempting to avoid entirely the least dependence on others
including her husband (who, it is clear, has in many ways failed her)
and her father as well. Her relatedness, or lack thereof, to her immediate family is symptomatic of her relation to community: her thrust
toward autonomy begins with her separation from her immediate
family.

From her Westport, Connecticut employers, the Chandlers, upper middle-class whites, business people, she learns the primary lessons of individualism through observing the relations among
individuals in their family. The first step in her alienation from community is her entanglement in circumstances which initially separate
her from her family. The second step is her observation of the only
alternative she is aware of: the life of a successful, upper middle-
class white family who apparently have all that she, her family, and
most of her race lack. Her employers become for her role models,
and her values from the time she leaves them until the time of the
end of the novel are patterned on theirs. She is specifically aware of
this; she quite consciously attempts to put into operation a plan
which she believes is responsible for the success of the Chandlers'
life. We are told as much.

> After a year of listening to their talk, she absorbed some of the same
> spirit. The belief that anybody could be rich if he wanted to and worked
> hard enough and figured it out carefully enough. . . . She and Jim [her
> husband] could do the same thing, and she thought she saw what had
> been wrong with them before—they hadn't tried hard enough, worked
> long enough, saved enough. There hadn't been any one thing they
> wanted above and beyond everything else. These people had wanted
> only one thing—more and more money—so they got it. Some of this
> new philosophy crept into her letters to Jim. (43)

The flaw of her logic is expressed in the narrative, for though the
Chandlers possess wealth, they are hardly a functioning family unit.
As a matter of fact their wealth permits them an independence an-
tithetical to familial unity and harmony. Their wealth is destructive
to the extent that the question arises finally whether in capitalistic
society any familial life style is viable. Perhaps the point in showing
that the upper-middle class whites' life style is flawed is to show that
the goals of the highest socio-economic group are no different from
the goals of the lowest and hence there is no essential difference between the character of lives of the two. The essential difference between the two groups is in the quality, not the character of their
lives: one group is better off materially but not in any other sense.

The Chandler family is splintered. The mother is estranged from
the husband and her own child, whom "she is always pushing away

from her" (39). She is in love with her husband's brother. Mr. Chandler is likewise estranged, caught up in his affairs to the exclusion of the family, educated at an Ivy League school but concerned with little else than making money. He is a hard and heavy drinker whose hands shake at the breakfast table every morning. The family rarely stays at home, either going out or having guests in most evenings. The family's character and interrelationship is symbolized by the chief action of Lutie's employer's brother who shoots himself to death on Christmas morning in the living room as the family opens gifts around the tree.

When the disintegration of Lutie's domestic life forces her finally to take up residence in Harlem, we then discover that the novel's title *The Street* refers to any street in any ghetto and is syndecdochic for the city as a whole. And surely enough when she first looks for an apartment, she meets the superintendent of the tenement, the devil himself.

> She didn't believe things like that and yet, looking at his tall, gaunt figure going down that last flight of stairs ahead of her, she half expected to see horns sprouting from behind his ears; she wouldn't have been greatly surprised if, in place of one of the heavy work shoes on his feet, there had been a cloven hoof that twitched and jumped as he walked so slowly down the stairs. (20)

The city is indeed hell for her. Before she can get a civil service job she works as a presser in a steam laundry. After she gets the better job she still does not earn enough to provide her and her son a decent living and to protect them both from the evil influences of "the street." During a protracted struggle to do so she finds herself entirely alone despite the fact that there is a community around her. She has no friends in the city, neither her neighbors nor her fellow employees. The environment for her is entirely hostile and threatening, and she feels that she must keep its potentially negative influences at a distance. Out of desperation she finally succumbs only to find herself at last in worse straits than before. Her son ends up headed almost certainly for reform school, innocent though he is; she ends up a murderer and fugitive, finally abandoning her son and fleeing to another hell, Chicago.

> The train crept out of the tunnel, gathered speed as it left the city behind. Snow whispered against the windows. And as the train roared into the darkness, Lutie tried to figure out by what twists and turns of fate she had landed on this train. Her mind balked at the task. All she could think was, it was that street. It was that god-damned street. (436)

Lutie's heading toward Chicago has no historical correlative in

black history. There are no large-scale black migrations from the
northeast westward. The escape to Chicago suggests that she is going
nowhere. She is, in fact, moving backward. There might be more
hope had she moved to California, even in the mid forties. For Richard Wright to have moved from Mississippi to Arkansas to Tennessee to Chicago to New York to Europe makes geo-historical sense.
But Lutie is caught forever in the dilemma which she has defined for
herself: she cannot successfully pursue the path of individualism, for
racism will not allow that; she cannot become a part of any social
group, for her individualistic values set her apart from the black
poor, the have-nots. She has given up racial identity in adapting the
values of the Chandlers, of mainstream upper middle-class Americans. For those values preclude cooperation as a mode of living and
define most people as competitors, not friends.

Where then does Ann Petry stand in this novel in regard to her
commitment to individualistic or communal values? It would not be
correct to say that she is torn, because that suggests a commitment
to both sides of the question. The plot of *The Street* has demonstrated unequivocally that individualism will not work for blacks.
The author can conceive of no place to go, and for that reason her
central character heads off to Chicago. She might have as well
headed off for St. Louis, Detroit, or Santa Fe, not dead end places
for people from the South, but certainly not through streets for any
blacks who have undergone the northern urban experience.

Addison Gayle, Jr.

(1932–1991)

IN THE FIELD OF AFRICAN AMERICAN literary criticism, the name Addison Gayle has become synonymous with the term *black aesthetic*. His 1971 edition of the landmark text *The Black Aesthetic*, a collection of essays on theory, music, poetry, drama, and fiction by prominent black artists and critics, remains the definitive source for a definition of a concept that is, perhaps, the most provocative issue in African American literary history. To a large degree, echoing Larry Neal's ideas in "The Black Arts Movement," Gayle over the last twenty years has been consistent in his contention that Euro-American aesthetics are not appropriate tools with which to judge African American literature. Like Amiri Baraka and Larry Neal, Gayle opposes the idea of art for art's sake and proposes that black art play a role in improving the quality of black people's lives.

Born in 1932 in Newport News, Virginia, Gayle has spent much of his life in New York City. He received his B.A. degree from the City College of New York in 1964 and his M.A. from UCLA in 1965. He taught as a lecturer in English at the City University of New York from 1966 to 1969. In 1969 he joined the faculty at Bernard M. Baruch College, where he held the position of Distinguished Professor of English until his death in October 1991. He has lectured on various subjects in Afro-American literature at various schools across the United States, including Oberlin College, University of Virginia, Yale University, and the University of California, Irvine.

In addition to his edition of *The Black Aesthetic*, which novelist Toni Morrison describes as a "book . . . up to its eyelids in some of the best writing there is on some of the most explosive ideas black people have had since water," Gayle is editor of two other anthologies—*Black Expression: Essays By and About Black Americans in the Creative Arts* (1969) and *Bondage, Freedom, and Beyond: The Prose of Black America* (1970). Gayle has also written three critical analyses—*The Black Situation* (1970), *Claude McKay: The Black Poet at War* (1972), and *The Way of the New World: The Black Novel in America* (1975); an autobiographical sketch—*Wayward Child: A Personal Odyssey* (1977); and two biographies—*Oak and Ivy: A Biography of Paul Laurence Dunbar* (1971) and *Richard Wright: Ordeal of a Native Son* (1980).

A contributor of articles and reviews to numerous anthologies, magazines, and journals, Gayle has been annual donor of the Richard Wright–

Amiri Baraka Award for the best critical essay published in *Black World* and a member of the editorial staff for *Amistad* and Third World Press.

For further reading, see Linda Metzger, ed., *Black Writers: A Selection of Sketches from Contemporary Authors* (1989).

The following selection is taken from *The Black Situation*.

CULTURAL NATIONALISM
The Black Novelist in America

"For the western world holds me in fee
And I can never hope for full release
While to its alien Gods, I bend my knee."
—Claude McKay

We are familiar with the quest for Black Power in the political, social, and educational spheres of American life; however, few of us are familiar with the long struggle for Black Power or black nationalism in Afro-American letters. Yet in one important genre, the novel, cultural nationalism has been explored since Martin Delaney's fragment, *Blake or the Huts of America*, written in 1859. This quest—beginning early in black literature when the majority of black folk inhabited the rural areas of America—reached its apex at the time of the Harlem Renaissance when the greatest immigration in American history transformed a rural folk into an urban folk.

The ramifications of this statement cannot be properly appraised without an understanding of the cultural dichotomy which has existed for so long in the black community; and a brief history of the Afro-American novel prior to the Harlem Renaissance is necessary to bring the novel of the city into sharper focus.

Clotel could have been written by any member of the Plantation School of writers, for in *Clotel*, William Wells Brown does not minimize the debt he owes to this school. His characters are equally romantic, his situations equally improbable, and his attribution of angelic qualities to those Afro-Americans who are white in every essential except color is in the best tradition of the Aryan supremacy mythologists. For Brown, as for his white contemporaries, the standards of beauty and excellence are white in every aspect.

The case is quite different with Martin Delaney. Delaney seeks to turn the black novel inward, to deal with the black experience as distinct, bordering only tangentially on the American experience. And what Frederick Douglass said about Delaney sums up, I believe, Delaney's attitude toward his race and his characters: "I wake up every morning and thank God for making me a man," wrote Douglass, "Delaney thanks God for making him a black man."

What is important here is that these two brother abolitionists viewed the function of black literature in different ways. The novel for Brown was to be at one and the same time a vehicle for protest as well as a vehicle for cataloguing the achievements of the race. Those characters who survived the American racial inferno were rewarded with the artifacts of Western culture. The major thesis of the novel was the Horatio Alger motif done in colors of medium grey.

Delaney too viewed the novel as a vehicle of protest; but even more as a vehicle for affirming the black identity outside of the American context. For Delaney black men were transplanted Africans, brought by misfortune to a strange land to sing their songs before alien Gods. Therefore, these Blacks would have to make the group journey to identity outside the context of the American melting pot theory.

However, the history of the black novel before the Harlem Renaissance is almost a complete negation of Delaney's thesis, and the novel, as seen by Brown, would exist with slight variation for over fifty years. J. McHenry Jones (*Hearts of Gold*, 1898), Pauline Hopkins (*In Contending Forces*, 1900), and Paul Laurence Dunbar (*The Uncalled*, 1901) pay homage to the assimilationist motif. The experiences of their characters are shown to vary little from the experiences of white Americans. They argue, sometimes nauseatingly so, that the only difference between black Americans and white Americans is the accident of color; and they come very close to arguing in fiction, as Phyllis Wheatley does in poetry, that Blacks are little more than reformed savages brought to the altar of Christianity by the grace of Western civilization.

It is not surprising that such novels use as their setting a rural environment. The rural South is the basis of reference and the romantic machinery of Southern life is a necessity for these writers. Mired in the South and steeped in the rural plantation tradition, these early novels were vehicles for the black middle class in the same manner that the novels of Thomas Dixon and Thomas Nelson Page were vehicles for the Southern white aristocracy.

The break with the rural tradition came when the black novel, following the exodus of black people, came to the city. In the nineteenth century, Blacks poured into the nation's urban areas. They went as far west as California, as far north as Canada; and they settled in the Watts', the Houghs, and the Harlems of America. They came, as W. E. B. Du Bois was to note, in search of Canaan, and they were sorely disappointed.

Into urban America, they brought their history, their folklore, their customs, and their anger. They demanded a religion which would suit their needs and their ministers came north to minister to them in a new and different setting. They demanded a social structure based not upon caste and color but upon the brotherhood of one black man with another. The similarities between the injustices, North and South, enabled them to pierce the veil of American mythology; and as a result, they demanded not a literature of manners and gentility, but one which would reflect their hopes, fears and anxieties; a literature which would be as forthright as the Garvey movement in presenting their demands and in helping them to achieve a sense of identity.

Alain Locke best summed up this new mood and its literary implications: "Of all the voluminous literature on the Negro," wrote Professor Locke in the introduction to *The New Negro*, "so much is mere external view and commentary that we may warrantably say that nine-tenths of it is about the Negro rather than of him. . . . We turn, therefore . . . to the elements of truest social portraiture, and discover in the artistic self-expression of the Negro today a new figure on the national canvas. . . ."

The "New Negro" was no longer the stereotype of the Booker T. Washington era; instead he was the new Negro of the cities who, having deserted the farm, was rapidly becoming industrialized and his earliest and most consistent supporter was the poet Langston Hughes.

"To my mind," wrote Hughes in *The Negro Writer and the Racial Mountain*, "it is the duty of the younger Negro artist to change through the force of his art that old whispering 'I want to be white' hidden in the aspirations of his people to 'why should I want to be white? I am a Negro and beautiful.' "

The spirit of Martin Delaney is revived in the Harlem Renaissance; for black was not only beautiful, but also different and distinct. With the acceptance of this fact the black novelist was forced to move away from romanticism and mythology and deal realistically with a people living, dying, hoping, and hating in the ghettoes of America. A cultural renaissance was in its earliest stages and a new cultural awareness was evident in Afro-American life. The pioneers of the Harlem Renaissance did much to bring about this awareness, and in so doing, called for a commitment to reality which would be echoed by the young black writers of the '60s.

The first black writer to affirm this commitment to reality was a young man who, ten years after the Harlem Renaissance, would write in an article, "A Blueprint for Negro Writing": "The Negro writer who seeks to function within his race as a purposeful agent has a serious responsibility. In order to do justice to his subject matter, in order to depict Negro life in all its manifold and intricate relationships, a deep informed and complexed consciousness is necessary; a consciousness which draws its strength upon the fluid lore of a great people, and molds this lore with the concepts that move and direct the forces of history today. The Negro writer is called upon to do no less than create values by which his race is to struggle, live, and die. . . ." The young man was Richard Wright, and four years later he would write *Native Son*, create Bigger Thomas, and move the black novel to a height of realism which, unfortunately, has not been surpassed to this day.

The plot of *Native Son* centers around Bigger Thomas, an uneducated black youngster, born in a Chicago slum, forced to live in a one room hovel with his mother, sister, and brother, and relegated to a life of frustration and futility because of the color of his skin. Given a job as the family chauffeur by Mr. Dalton, a "white liberal" who owns the slums in which he is forced to live, Bigger accidentally murders Mary, the "liberal's" daughter. In addition, Bigger murders his own girl friend, not gratuitously but by design, setting up the interesting angle that he was responsible for only one murder— that of his girl friend—a fact which has no bearing on the outcome of his trial for his life. Caught by the police, Bigger is tried and, despite pleas from his communist lawyer, sentenced to die. He dies without repentance, without atonement for the death of the white girl. The catalyst for the action in *Native Son* is the accidental murder of Mary Dalton.

We should not be swayed by the academic critics who, imbued with the notion that "poetry should not mean but be," have dealt with *Native Son* in terminology more appropriate for dealing with the plastic, not the literary arts. Nor should we be swayed by the psuedo-moralists among us who attempt to find in Bigger Thomas the epitome of man's degradation and inhumanity. Rather, let us put *Native Son* into proper historical perspective, and in so doing, deal with the period of the 1940s when the novel was published.

In Europe, German aggression was well under way. In a short time almost the whole of Europe would come under the sway of a tyranny as vicious as that under which Blacks have lived in this country for over two hundred years. In America, the detention camps which would later house American citizens of Japanese descent would be subjected to persecution and abuse. The paranoiac attacks on the Jewish population of Germany would be reiterated in the propaganda attacks on the Jewish population in America. For

Blacks, the journey from South to North would prove to be no more than a journey from one kind of oppression to another. For any sensitive individual living in this tumultuous period, the symbol of man's reality was not the tragic clown, as Ralph Ellison would have us believe, but rather the concentration camp. It is in this concentration camp environment that Bigger Thomas was born.

The validity of Bigger Thomas and the test of his humanity must be examined in light of the concentration camp metaphor. In so doing we are forced to conclude that the murder of Mary Dalton, at one point so shocking and so senseless, is, when viewed from a different perspective, so cathartic and so necessary. In a world where the concentration camp is man's touchstone for reality, the values by which men live and die are existential ones; and one must create his identity, a sense of his own self-worth, out of the chaos and confusion inherent in living as a victim in a dehumanized world.

We have come a long way from Martin Delaney. Delaney would have settled for black emigration back to Africa, to a place where men, free from arbitrary restrictions, might create their own identities. Richard Wright, on the other hand, would settle for nothing less than a piece of this earth, where men would carve their identity out of violence and despair, thereby transcending the limitations imposed upon them. *Native Son* succeeds in destroying the American myth, in rending to shreds the make-believe world of the romantics, in leaving the American dream in shambles, and, finally, in presenting a portrait of reality which serious black writers who followed would have to confront.

Two of today's most popular black writers have had great difficulty in confronting the reality presented by *Native Son*. Neither has accepted the chaos and violence which the novel presents and neither has accepted Richard Wright's nationalistic formula as the best means for bridging the racial chasm and avoiding racial war.

James Baldwin wavers between the philosophy of assimilationism and that of nationalism unable, until *Blues for Mr. Charlie*, to examine American society in other than personal terms. No writer knows the ghetto or its people better than Baldwin, no one has a clearer insight into the alienation and despair of man in the twentieth century, and yet no writer has failed more miserably in depicting in fiction the plight of urbanized black Americans.

Another Country, his most popular novel, serves as a case in point. The beginning of *Another Country* is to be found in the ending. Here one glimpses the New Society as Baldwin envisions it. At the end of the novel three couples remain: a homosexual couple, a heterosexual couple, and an integrated couple. The emphasis should not be placed upon the makeup of the couples, but instead upon the tolerance each shows toward the differences of the others. In a sense, Baldwin would return us to the Garden of Eden before the fall when Adam and Eve, unconscious of their differences, accepted each other in terms of common humanity.

For Baldwin, however, to tread the road back to innocence entails great difficulty. Man must be created anew, and for the characters of *Another Country*, this implies that one must undergo a fire-baptism in which he either accepts his condition or foregoes it altogether. There is no middle ground. Man accepts himself for what he is and moves forward to reshape the world in his own image or failing to accept himself he attempts self-transcendence which may lead to destruction.

Every man, argues Baldwin, has burdens to bear, and a man is distinguished by how well he stands up under his burden. In *Another Country* the two characters who bear the heaviest burdens are Rufus Scott, black, and Eric Jones, homosexual. Eric survives the end of the novel and emerges as the central figure in the new world. He learns to live with his condition, to accept himself for what he is, and thus he is able to pursue a career, and carry on a meaningful relationship with others. Rufus, on the other hand, cannot rise above his condition. The black skin is, symbolically, his shroud and his inability to shed it subconsciously leads him from poverty to degradation and finally to self-destruction. Unlike Eric, who is free to accept himself as a homosexual, Baldwin implies that Rufus, in accepting himself as a black man, must accept the historical terms of degradation and distortion which circumscribe him: self-hate, self-abnegation, despondency, and frustration leading to vindictive acts toward others. Therefore one is led to believe that, in order to enter paradise, Rufus must discard his blackness altogether. In accepting the myths of American society, Baldwin blames the victim for wearing the Star of David and suggests that for the sake of peace, the victim must thrust aside that which offends the victimizer. What emerges from *Another Country* is a subtle plea for integration which goes far beyond the scope envisioned by the early assimilationists.

Every institution in American society has been designed to substantiate the thesis that to be born black is a sin. This is not so. The sin is not being born black, but being born into a world in which to attain paradise one must pick up the instruments of war. "The symbol of the twentieth century," wrote Richard Wright, "is the man on the corner with a machine gun." In American society, one reaches the Garden of Innocence not through acquiescing in the destruction of his own heritage and identity but by constructing better machine guns than his enemies, or at least, learning to use them more efficiently. To offer black people a Rufus Scott is to offer a Christ in black face, not withstanding the fact that both Christ and Rufus are doomed to die the death of cowards; and that neither the great society nor the Garden of Eden can be built upon a foundation whose chief architects are cowards.

To move from James Baldwin to Ralph Ellison demands that one clarify his own position in regard to the function of the black writer in American society. Mankind exists in a world where injustice is the norm, where persecution is the measure of man's fidelity to his god, where human life is all too often sacrificed on the altar of power politics. Look upon this world of civilized men and your eyes will never fall upon a land where men are not victimized and persecuted by other men whose only claim to power is that they possess an abundance of the instruments of war. Given such conditions, the job of the writer is to wage total war against injustice; in American society this means that the black writer must wage total war against the American system. This does impose a terrible obligation upon the black writer; yet, persecution and oppression are equally terrible. None should argue with the assertion that the writer must be free to utilize his skill in the way he deems best. However, the same scripture holds true for all men, and in a society where some men are not free, freedom for the writer is based upon an absurdity. The black writer in America can never be free until every Black man is free, and the obligation imposed upon the writer is no more severe than that imposed upon any man whose destiny is inextricably bound to that of his brother.

To wage total war against the American system does not mean that the writer will throw a Molotov cocktail or fire a rifle. (Although the time may come when he may have to do just that.) He has far more powerful weapons at his command and these he must use not only to protest the injustices of the present, but also to attempt to bring about those conditions in the future under which peace might prevail.

Such peace can come only when the last tyrant has disappeared from the earth, when the last hydrogen bomb has been dismantled, when the last concentration camp has been razed to the ground, when the last rifle has been broken, when the last man has been lynched because of his color, when the last patriot has died in defense of his Vietnam, and when the last child has gone to bed hungry for the last time in a world rich in natural resources.

Foremost among black writers today, Ralph Ellison is perhaps the best equipped to analyze the precarious peace upon which the American system rests. There is no writer in America who possesses a finer temperament, none with a more thorough knowledge of black history and culture, and none with more devotion to the perfection of the writer's craft. His *Invisible Man* is a masterpiece, unsurpassed by those of his contemporaries, white or black, American or European. Having said this, however, one asks certain questions, and these questions inevitably lead one to the conclusion that masterpieces may sometimes be irrelevant to the lives of men and nations. The portrait of the Mona Lisa belongs in a museum; in a concentration camp it would be out of place. Men who live on the edge of desperation are not likely to be enthusiastic about the Mona Lisa or comparable "works of art."

When one begins to examine the theory of the masterpiece, he finds that it was put forth by men who sought to erect a barrier between themselves and other men. Traditionally, works of art were the private property of the aristocracy, and a Reubens or a first edition of Pope differentiated the haves from the have-nots; in the same manner, poverty and starvation serve a similar function today. The creator of such masterpieces was in turn set off from his brother craftsmen, his nation, and his race, and admitted to the economical, social, and educational elite. However, the black writer can never accept elitism, or a barrier which separates him from other black men. Whether he wills it or not, unless he is very lucky or very white, he is not an individual but part of a group and his fate is mirrored in that of the group's. He is no sophisticated minstrel entertaining the sons and daughters of America's academic establishment, but rather a black artist whose every waking moment is a preparation for war, whose every word is an utterance of defiance, whose every action is calculated to move man towards revolution, and whose every thought centers about the coming conflict. He replaces the formula "art for art's sake," as poet Don L. Lee has written, with the humane formula, "art for people's sake," and instead of entertaining black men, he educates them, instead of appealing to their sense of aesthetics, he appeals to their instinct for survival, instead of reminding them of the rewards of heaven, he warns them of the realities of hell. There is no elite in the concentration camp, and the inmates of the camp demand, not funeral dirges, but martial marches.

In the opening pages of *Invisible Man*, the reader encounters the protagonist in an underground cellar. The protagonist relates the story of his life, taking the reader on a picaresque journey characterized by laughter, tragedy, and pathos. At the conclusion of the final episode, the reader is capable of empathizing with the protagonist's commitment to live the life of an underground man. He is, as he relates, an invisible man, a faceless being in a world where the machine is king. His journey is an attempt to impose his consciousness upon the world, to force the world to acknowledge his existence. In the final episode of the novel, the protagonist is mistaken for a criminal, Rhinehart, who has learned to cope with his invisibility by being all things to all men. A world in which Rhinehart is the symbol for every man is an absurdity, and thus the protagonist returns to his underground retreat.

On a more basic level, Ellison's protagonist seeks to force the American system to validate his existence, to grant him recognition not as a black man nor as a white man, but as an American. The fallacy of the white liberal's theory of integration and the fallacy of the argument of *Invisible Man* are the same: that the black American can find his identity only in a metamorphosed society in which the melting pot, having bubbled over, has fused the disparate cultures within and produced a product labeled American. In this analysis, one does not seek to destroy evil but to join forces with it. Like James Baldwin, Ellison wants racial peace and he is willing to purchase it at the expense of negating race and culture.

But the road to racial peace lies not through the negation of one's race and culture but through the affirmation of it. What black men demand from America is not validation of their identity as Americans, which would only assimilate them into the present society, but freedom and justice which would lead to the creation of a new society. If one accepts the argument offered by white liberals, that the concentration camp metaphor of Richard Wright is no longer valid, one must argue concomitantly that the symbol of a black Rhinehart, he who creates and re-creates his identity with each new experience, is invalid in black America where the individual identity cannot exist apart from that of the group.

It is not too far wrong to suggest that Afro-American literature awaits its Whitman and the chances of this Whitman appearing are better today than at any time before. Young black writers for whom the city is home are attempting to create a revolutionary literature which moves beyond Richard Wright. They accept the basic premises of Black Nationalism—that black people are different from other Americans—and they echo Edward Channing in arguing that such differences mandate a different literature. They are reexamining their own culture and finding it rich and diverse. They do not deny the relevance of American history to their lives, but they would not change their history by merging them into one. Unlike the Ralph Ellisons of the world, these young writers would never trade Frederick Douglass for a Thomas Jefferson for they know that one was a slaveholder and the other a crusader against slavery and that, in such an exchange, they would get the short end of the bargain.

They are such men as Ed Bullins in drama, LeRoi Jones in poetry, and John Williams in fiction; and though I have spoken of them as new, their spirit is not new at all. It is the spirit exemplified by Martin Delaney, Walt Whitman, and Richard Wright. And each has this in common; he realizes with Nietzsche that the old tables of the law have led us to corruption and oppression and must therefore be replaced by new ones. But more important, in adopting the tenets of Black Nationalism, he realizes with James Joyce that the writer can have no greater task than "to forge from the smithy of his soul, the uncreated conscious of the race."

Michael S. Harper

(1938–)

THE POETRY OF MICHAEL S. HARPER is highly esteemed by both black and white writers and critics and is considered of major significance in contemporary American literature. Yet Harper's poetry, which differs from that of many other black poets in that it strives to bridge the gap between black America and white America with a voice that speaks powerfully to both, has also made him a controversial artist among those who advocate a strictly black aesthetic. His work integrates the rich traditions of blues, jazz, and gospel music endemic to black culture with themes and images that bespeak American culture as a whole, creating a vision that is at once black American and American and a style that is uniquely his own.

Born in 1938 in Brooklyn, New York, Harper moved with his family to Los Angeles when he was thirteen. From 1956 to 1961 he attended Los Angeles State College, where for a short time he was enrolled as a premedical student. In 1961 Harper joined the Iowa Writers' Workshop and began serious work as a poet. After a year there he returned to Los Angeles to student teach at Pasadena City College, and in 1963 he went back to Iowa State to fulfill curriculum requirements for the M.A. in English.

For the next several years Harper taught at a number of institutions around the country: Contra Costa College in San Pablo, California (1964–1968), Reed College and Lewis and Clark College (1968–1969), California State College in Hayward (1969–1970), and Brown University (1970 to the present). While an associate professor at Brown he took a one-year leave of absence to undertake postdoctoral work at the University of Illinois Center for Advanced Studies. At Brown Harper was the director of the Graduate Creative Writing Program until 1983, when he received the Israel J. Kapstein Professorship of English. He has also been a visiting professor at Harvard and Yale universities and a Distinguished Professor at Carleton College in Minnesota and at the University of Cincinnati.

Among his grants and awards are a National Institute of Arts and Letters Creative Writing Award (1972), a Guggenheim Fellowship (1976), and a National Endowment for the Arts grant (1977).

Harper's first book of poetry, *Dear John, Dear Coltrane* (1970), was nominated for the National Book Award in 1971. The next seven years were prolific ones, in which he published six more volumes of poetry: *History Is Your Own Heartbeat* (1971); *Photographs: Negatives: History as Apple Tree* (1972, limited edition); *Song: I Want a Witness* (1972); *De-*

bridement (1973); *Nightmare Begins Responsibility* (1975); and *Images of Kin* (1977), which received the Melville-Cane Award and was his second book to be nominated for the National Book Award. His most recent volume, *Healing Song for the Inner Ear*, was published in 1984.

For an examination of Harper's poetic technique and an analysis of his work, see Robert Stepto, "Michael S. Harper, Poet as Kinsman: The Family Sequences," *Massachusetts Review* 17 (Autumn 1976), and Norris B. Clark's article in *Dictionary of Literary Biography, Volume 41*. See also *Callaloo* (Fall 1990), which contains an interview with Harper, conducted by Charles H. Rowell; fourteen poems by Harper; the text of Coe College's citation for Harper's honorary Doctor of Humane Letters (1990); and tributes to Harper.

The following poems come from *Images of Kin: New and Selected Poems*.

LAST AFFAIR: BESSIE'S BLUES SONG

Disarticulated
arm torn out,
large veins cross
her shoulder intact,
her tourniquet
her blood in all-white big bands:

Can't you see
what love and heartache's done to me
I'm not the same as I used to be
this is my last affair

Mail truck or parked car
in the fast lane,
afloat at forty-three
on a Mississippi road,
Two-hundred-pound muscle on her ham bone,
'nother nigger dead 'fore noon:

Can't you see
what love and heartache's done to me
I'm not the same as I used to be
this is my last affair

Fifty-dollar record
cut the vein in her neck,
fool about her money
toll her black train wreck,
white press missed her fun'ral
in the same stacked deck:

Can't you see
what love and heartache's done to me
I'm not the same as I used to be
this is my last affair

Loved a little blackbird
heard she could sing,
Martha in her vineyard
pestle in her spring,
Bessie had a bad mouth
made my chimes ring:

Can't you see
what love and heartache's done to me
I'm not the same as I used to be
this is my last affair

DEAR JOHN, DEAR COLTRANE

a love supreme, a love supreme
a love supreme, a love supreme

Sex fingers toes
in the marketplace
near your father's church
in Hamlet, North Carolina—
witness to this love
in this calm fallow
of these minds,
there is no substitute for pain:
genitals gone or going,
seed burned out,
you tuck the roots in the earth,
turn back, and move
by river through the swamps,
singing: *a love supreme, a love supreme;*
what does it all mean?

Loss, so great each black
woman expects your failure
in mute change, the seed gone.
You plod up into the electric city—
your song now crystal and
the blues. You pick up the horn
with some will and blow
into the freezing night:
a love supreme, a love supreme—

Dawn comes and you cook
up the thick sin 'tween
impotence and death, fuel
the tenor sax cannibal
heart, genitals and sweat
that makes you clean—
a love supreme, a love supreme—
Why you so black?
cause I am
why you so funky?
cause I am
why you so black?
cause I am
why you so sweet?
cause I am
why you so black?
cause I am
a love supreme, a love supreme:

So sick
you couldn't play *Naima,*
so flat we ached
for song you'd concealed
with your own blood,
your diseased liver gave
out its purity,
the inflated heart
pumps out, the tenor kiss,
tenor love:
a love supreme, a love supreme—
a love supreme, a love supreme—

"BIRD LIVES": CHARLES PARKER

Last on legs, last on sax,
last in Indian wars, last on *smack*,
Bird is specious, *Bird* is alive,
horn, unplayable, before, after,
right now: it's heroin time:
smack, in the melody a trip;
smack, in the Mississippi;
smack, in the drug merchant trap;
smack, in St. Louis, Missouri.

We knew you were through—
trying to get out of town,
unpaid bills, connections
unmet, unwanted, unasked,
Bird's in the last arc
of his own light: *blow Bird!*
And you did—
screaming, screaming, baby,
for life, after it, around it,
screaming for life, *blow Bird!*

What is the meaning of music?
What is the meaning of war?
What is the meaning of oppression?
Blow Bird! Ripped up and down
into the interior of life, the pain,
Bird, the embraceable you,
how many brothers gone,
smacked out: blues and racism,
the hardest, longest penis
in the Mississippi urinal:
Blow Bird!

Taught more musicians, then forgot,
space loose, fouling the melodies,
the marching songs, the fine white
geese from the plantations,
syrup in this pork barrel,
Kansas City, the even teeth
of the mafia, the big band:
Blow Bird! Inside out Charlie's
guts, *Blow Bird!* get yourself killed.

In the first wave, the musicians,
out there, alone, in the first wave;
everywhere you went, Massey Hall,
Sweden, New Rochelle, *Birdland*,
nameless bird, Blue Note, Carnegie,
tuxedo junction, out of nowhere,
confirmation, confirmation, confirmation:
Bird Lives! Bird Lives! and you do:
Dead—

Henry Dumas

(1934–1968)

ALTHOUGH HENRY DUMAS was cut down in the prime of his life at age thirty-four by a transit policeman's bullet, his works serve as a memorial to his life and his extraordinary talent. Eugene Redmond, a well-known poet who worked with Dumas at Southern Illinois University, has spent considerable time and energy gathering and editing Dumas's poetry and fiction for posthumous publication.

Born in Sweet Home, Arkansas, in 1934, Dumas moved to Harlem when he was ten and attended public schools there. After graduating from Commerce High School in 1953, he started at City College in New York. That same year, however, he decided to enter the Air Force and did not return to college until after he was married to Loretta Ponton (1955) and their first son, David, was born. Dumas attended Rutgers University full-time from 1958 to 1960, taking etymology and sociology courses before finding his niche in the English department. From 1960 to 1965, he attended school part-time until he left without completing his degree. In 1962 his second son, Michael, was born.

Dumas began to study religion in the 1950s while in the Air Force, where he taught Sunday school classes. He combined his studying with work and writing. Embodying a deep sense of commitment for fellow blacks, Dumas often made trips to tent cities in Mississippi and Tennessee, carrying clothing and supplies to the residents. This concern for communicating with his fellow African Americans as well as for understanding the ways of nature, was the creative source of his work.

Dumas's poetry appears in several anthologies, such as Arnold Adoff's *Black Out Loud: An Anthology of Modern Poems by Black Americans* (1970) and Redmond's *Griefs of Joy: Anthology of Afro-American Poetry for Students* (1971). *Ark of Bones and Other Stories* (1970) is Dumas's first published collection of stories, issued posthumously. His fascination with black music seeps through the verses of his poems and the lines of prose. The blues and theology are also prominent in his writing and make his storytelling style unique. The other posthumous collections are *Poetry for My People* (1970), which was republished in 1974 as *Play Ebony, Play Ivory; Jonoah and the Green Stone* (1976), an unfinished novel; *Rope of Wind and Other Stories* (1979); and *Knees of a Natural Man: The Selected Poetry of Henry Dumas* (1989). All of these collections were edited by Redmond.

Dumas was shot and killed on May 23, 1968, in a case of "mistaken identity." According to Redmond in his introduction to *Goodbye, Sweetwater* (1988), a collection of Dumas's writings, the circumstances of Dumas's violent death are still "unclarified" and "suspicious."

For further reading see Stephen Henderson's *Understanding the New Black Poetry: Black Speech and Black Music as Poetic References* (1973); Clyde Taylor's "Henry Dumas: Legacy of a Longbreath Singer," *Black World* 24 (September 1975); *Black American Literature Forum: Henry Dumas Issue*, guest editor Eugene Redmond, 2 (Summer 1988); and Carolyn A. Mitchell's article in *Dictionary of Literary Biography, Volume 41*.

The following three poems are all taken from *Knees of a Natural Man: The Selected Poetry of Henry Dumas*.

AFRO-AMERICAN

my black mother birthed me
    my white mother girthed me
my black mother suckled me
    my white mother sucked me in
my black mother sang to me
    my white mother sanctified me
    she crucified me

my black mother is a fine beautiful thang
she bathed me and died for me
she stitched me together, took me into her
bosom and mixed her tears with mine
little black baby i was wretched
a shadow without a body, fatherless, sunless
my black mother shook sweet songs and sweat
all over me and her sugar and her salt saved me

    my white mother is a whore
    with the holy white plague
    a hollow cross between Martha and Mary
    she looked at me and screamed bastard!
    she left me light of body and of mind

she took what my black mother gave me
and left me half blind

bone is my black mother
ivory stone
strength is my black mother
my ancient skeletal home
force is my black mother
she maintains and transforms

my black mother is a long-limbed sensuous river
where the Kongo flows into the Mississippi she
is coming where my father's blood rises in jets
and like rain, glows, transformed red, tan, black
I am growing in the bosom and in the loins
of America
born and knitted in the soil, when I finish growing
you can pick me up as you would a rare and fabulous
seed and you can
blow Africa
on me as you would a holy reed.

STANDIN TALL BLUES

Now you say my shoes runover and my hair's long and nappy
Yeah my shoes runover, my hair long and nappy
But you know where your bread and meat comin from baby
             it sure make you happy

Now we walkin down town baby, fightin the mean ole hawk
All bundled up, fightin that mean ole hawk
You lookin in the window, say you need a mink coat

Now that's alright baby, I work hard and my head is nappy
Yeah my shoes runover and my head is nappy
But when you need heat for your cooker
             you come runnin to pappy

So dont worry bout how I look baby
             that aint it at all
Dont worry bout looks pretty baby
             that aint it at all
You cant hide it cause I ride it
             that's me standin tall

I'M YOUR ELECTRIC MAN

Well, baby when I turned you on, I didn't get no juice
I say, when I turned your switch baby, didn't get no juice
Well if you got another meter checker, I guess I have turn you loose

Now I looked in your eyes baby, your eyes just didnt light
Now I looked in your eyes and they wasn't makin they usual light
Think I better check your battery baby, first thing I do tonight

Aint no harm sittin on the couch in the dark
Aint no harm to sit round the house in the dark
But when I come home baby, I like you to generate a spark

Now you sit here baby, get you gas and light free
Now you sit here woman, get your gas and light free
If anybody read your meter, pretty baby its gonna be me

Bernard W. Bell

(1936–)

BORN IN 1936, in Washington, D.C., critic and teacher Bernard Bell was raised in Harlem and South Bronx. Like James Baldwin and Countee Cullen, he graduated from the well-known De Witt Clinton High School. He received both his B.A. and M.A. degrees from Howard University, where Professors Sterling Brown and Arthur P. Davis were his teachers and where he worked as Professor Brown's research assistant for a year (1962–1963). Before graduating with his Ph.D. from the University of Massachusetts in 1970, he taught high school at Calvin Coolidge in Washington, D.C., from 1963 to 1967, worked as a teaching assistant at the University of Massachusetts during the academic year 1967–1968, and held a position in its Upward Bound program. In 1969 he accepted a position as assistant professor in the English department at the University of Massachusetts. He is currently a professor of English and African American Studies at Penn State University.

Presently working on a collection of essays and a book-length manuscript entitled "The Rhetoric of Modernist and Post-Modernist Afro-American Fiction," Bell is the author of an impressive number of essays on African American literature, a monograph entitled *The Folk Roots of Contemporary Afro-American Poetry* (1974), and a much longer study, *The Afro American Novel and Its Tradition* (1987). He is also the editor of *Modern and Contemporary Afro-American Poetry* (1972), one of the few collections of African American poetry.

In addition to having been invited as guest lecturer by the University of Iowa, Smith College, and Williams College, Professor Bell has lectured at the University of Freiburg and at Padagogische Hochschule, both in Germany, and at the University of Coimbra in Coimbra, Portugal, as a Fulbright Scholar. He is listed in the *Dictionary of International Biography*, 13th edition (1976), in *Who's Who in the East*, 16th edition (1976), and in the *Dictionary of American Scholars*, 6th edition (1974).

The selection below, "The Image of Africa in the Afro-American Novel," is reprinted from *Commonwealth: Essays and Studies* 5 (1981–1982).

THE IMAGE OF AFRICA IN THE AFRO-AMERICAN NOVEL

"Conrad," says Chinua Achebe, "was a bloody racist."[1] Neither as injudicious nor as inexplicable as it may seem on the surface, Achebe's indictment was occasioned by Conrad's use of Africa as the psychological and moral antithesis of Europe, of his dehumanization of the African in a novel that critic Albert Guerard considers "among the half-dozen greatest short novels in the English language."[2] For Achebe, the primary question that *Heart of Darkness* raises is "whether a novel which celebrates this dehumanization, which depersonalizes a portion of the human race, can be called a great work of art."[3] Let me leave this question for you to consider for the moment, while I turn from Conrad and the modern British novel to a reviewer's comment on a contemporary American novel by Philip Caputo called *Horn of Africa*, a novel that is already a Book-of-the-Month Club Special Fiction Alternate and Playboy Book Club Main Selection. "Shades of Joseph Conrad and Graham Greene are recalled in Caputo's gripping moral thriller," the reviewer gushes in a full page ad in the *New York Times Book Review* of October 26, " . . . This is a graphic journey into the inner recesses of a man's mind and a startling denunciation of the hollow morality that currently governs international political events." Like the images in the novels of Conrad, Greene, and Caputo, those in Paul Theroux's *Girl at Play*, John Updike's *The Coup*, and William Stevenson's *The Ghosts of Africa* are white images of African culture and character which tell us more about the fantasies and values of the West and the authors than they do about Africa. The topic of my remarks today, however, is not so much the white image of Africa in the modern British and contemporary American novel as it is the black image of Africa in the Afro-American novel. My thesis is that the depiction of Africa in the Afro-American novel reveals more about the struggle for racial equality and personal identity by blacks in the United States and about the moral and political consciousness of the authors than it does about the complex reality of Africa herself. By Afro-American novel I mean any extended prose narrative written by an American of African descent that deals with the experiences of black Americans. In developing this thesis I will begin with an outline of white images of Africa in Western culture, followed by brief surveys of im-

---

Reprinted by permission of the author.
[1] *The Chancellor's Lecture Series, 1974–1975* (Amherst: University of Massachusetts, 1975), p. 38.
[2] *Ibid.*, p. 32.
[3] *Ibid.*, p. 38.

ages of Africa in the early and pre-World War II Afro-American novel, and conclude with images in the novels of Richard Wright, John A. Williams, William M. Kelley, and Frank Yerby.

White Images of Africa in Western Culture

By and large, Afro-Americans did not acquire their knowledge about Africa through direct experience; rather, it was transmitted to them through the eyes and mind of the dominant white social group, which, in satisfying its own psychological, moral, and social needs, spawned many stereotypes of African character and culture. As the studies of Winthrop Jordan, David Brion Davis, George M. Fredrickson, and Thomas Gossett reveal, white images of Africa date back to antiquity, but the most pernicious were developed during the period of European expansion and reinforced in the eighteenth and nineteeth centuries by Europeans and Anglo-Saxons seeking to justify their notions of slavery based on racial and cultural superiority.[4] These stereotypes were rooted in the view of whites that blacks were naturally inferior because they were different in appearance and life-style, differences that were considered in early anthropology as deviations from the Western norm.[5] Christianity and the Bible reinforced Western symbolism that associated the color white with everything good, pure, and beautiful and the color black with everything bad, evil, and ugly. When the skin color of Africans was directly linked to their non-Christian religious customs, the die of racism was cast.

From the Bible, then, came the image of Africans and their descendants as the creatures of Satan, the cursed children of Ham, and the bearers of the curse of Cain. From Montaigne's "Of Cannibals" (1580), Dryden's *The Conquest of Granada* (1671), Rousseau's *Emile* (1672), and Aphra Behn's *Oroonoko* (1688), came the image of Africans as Noble Savages, the embodiment of the theory that men living in harmony with the laws of nature and their own instincts are superior to other men and that whatever evils these natural men develop is the result of civilization. Paradoxically, this benign myth of the Noble Savage was complemented by the more tenacious and malign myth of Africans as Savages and Apes. "It is scarcely surprising,"

---

[4]Winthrop D. Jordan, *White Over Black: American Attitudes Toward the Negro, 1550–1812* (Chapel Hill: The University of North Carolina Press, 1968); David Brion Davis, *The Problem of Slavery in Western Culture* (Ithaca; Cornell Unversity Press, 1966); George W. Fredrickson, *The Black Image in the White Mind: The Debate on Afro-American Character and Destiny, 1817–1914* (New York: Harper Torchbooks, 1972); and Thomas E. Gossett, *Race: The History of an Idea in America* (New York: Schocken, 1965).

[5]Jordan, *White Over Black*, pp. 3–43, 216–265.

Jordan states with obvious irony, "that civilized Englishmen should have taken an interest in reports about cosmetic mutilation, polygamy, infanticide ritual murder and the like—of course *English* men did not really *do* any of these things themselves."[6] Also, given the traditional speculations about anatomical and sexual affinities between apes and men and the tragic coincidence that Englishmen came in contact with apes and Africans at the same time and in the same place, "it was virtually inevitable," says Jordan, "that Englishmen should discern similarity between the man-like beasts and the beast-like men of Africa."[7] These views were embedded in the sixteenth century concept of the universe as "The Great Chain of Being" and reinforced by eighteenth century pseudo-scientific studies that divided mankind into hierarchical systems of ethnic groups with Europeans at the top and Africans on the bottom. Caught in this net of ideological and social forces, Africa and her progeny fell victims to the myth of an ignoble past and were cast by Europeans and Anglo-Americans alike as archetypal scapegoats on a Manichean world stage on which the victims represented evil heathens and savages who were natural slaves.

I will not rehearse here the many indictments of ante-bellum and post-bellum American literature by black critics and literary historians for its creation of a gallery of Buffoons, Sambos, Uncle Toms, Mammies, and Babos, for the following understatement by Sterling Brown, the Dean of Afro-American Letters, aptly sums up the history of the image of blacks in American fiction: "The treatment of the Negro in American fiction, since it parallels his treatment in American life, has naturally been noted for injustice. Like other oppressed and exploited minorites, the Negro has been interpreted in a way to justify his exploiters . . . The African . . . is now receiving substantially the same treatment as the American Negro."[8] From this brief outline of white images of Africa and her sons and daughters in Western culture it can be reasonably inferred that the predominant image transmitted to black Americans of their motherland by the dominant culture was extremely negative. And since their African and slave past was the primary basis for their status and stigma as a discriminated minority, whether they accepted or rejected these white images, Afro-Americans have historically responded with ambivalence to Africa. Marion Berghan's *Images of Africa in Black American Literature* lucidly and persuasively illustrates these attitudes in

---

[6]*Ibid.*, p. 25.
[7]*Ibid.*, p. 30.
[8]Sterling Brown, *The Negro in American Fiction* (New York: Atheneum, 1969), p. 1.

the general literature, especially the poetry, through the 1950s.[9] So I will focus on the Afro-American novel to discover whether and how this ambivalence is expressed in that tradition.

Early Images of Africa in the Afro-American Novel

The attitudes of Afro-American novelists toward Africa are most apparent in their choice of narrative setting, use of color symbolism, delineation of character, and handling of point of view. It is instructive that in the history of the Afro-American novel only three are set in Africa itself: Henry Downing's *The American Cavalryman* (1917), George Schuyler's *Slaves Today* (1931), and Frank Yerby's *The Dahomean* (1971). Before taking a closer look at the pre-World War II novels of Downing and Schuyler, deferring for the moment an analysis of Yerby's novel, let me briefly examine how the use of color symbolism and characterization reveal the mixed attitudes of nineteenth century black novelists toward Africa. In reacting to the grotesque appearance and manners of white stereotypes of blacks and seeking to project their own images of black American identity, both its ugliness and beauty, early black novelists were guided by their struggle for freedom and equality as an ethnic group and as individual artists. Social conditions and cultural exigencies compelled most of them to attempt a synthesis of the contrary narrative tendencies toward social realism and romance. "In giving this little romance expression in print," Pauline Hopkins writes in the preface to *Contending Forces*, "I am not actuated by a desire for notoriety or for profit, but to do all that I can in a humble way to raise the stigma of degradation from my race."[10] Achieving this objective involved adopting, rejecting, or qualifying the black-white symbolism of abolitionist literature, the Bible, and popular fiction of the period. Thus while one novelist wrote: "Surely the Negro race must be productive of some valuable specimens, if only from the infusion which amalgamation with a superior race must eventually bring," another ended his novel with the ominous line: "Woe be unto those devils of whites, I say."[11] These novelists reflect the identity conflict caused by the myth of white supremacy and the rituals and color symbolism that justified and perpetuated it. In many cases white and black characters were idealized, but in the more realistic novels the attitude of the author was ambivalent, and frequently irony was at work.

---

[9] New York: The Macmillan Press Ltd, 1977.

[10] *Contending Forces: A Romance Illustrative of Negro Life North and South* (1900; rpt. Miami: Mnemosyne), p. 272.

[11] *Contending Forces*, p. 87; Martin R. Delany, *Blake; or The Huts of America* (Boston: Beacon Press, 1970), p. 313.

For example, Martin Delany, a black nationalist and abolitionist whose advocacy late in his career of the emigration of blacks to Central America or Africa culminated in his leading an exploration party up the Niger River in 1859, clearly transvaluated traditional Western color symbolism in his novel *Blake*. The beauty and strength of blackness are affirmed in the characterization of servants Ailcey and Sampson, while the discrimination against blacks by mulattoes in the Brown Fellowship Society is condemned. More importantly, a radical consciousness that foreshadows black nationalist sentiments in the United States during the 1960s is apparent in Delany's portrayal of Blake as the archetypal "messenger of light and destruction," the daring black mastermind of an underground organization that plans to liberate slaves in the United States and Cuba. It is also evident in the epithets the protagonist employs for whites—"candle face," "devils," "white oppressor," and "alabasters"—as well as in the depiction of two Africans: Abyssa, a captive Muslim woman trader from the Sudan who becomes a pious Christian convert, and Mendi, a captive Mendi prince who, like Cinque of the *Amistad* revolt in 1839, defies his captors, frees himself, and leads an abortive slave rebellion. Among the psychological and political advantages that Blake and Placido, the rebel Cuban poet and co-leader of the planned revolution, identify for mulattoes to affirm their African heritage are the eventual emergence of a wealthy, powerful new Africa and the political acceptance of African people among the great nations of the world. For Blake and Placido, as for Delany, the attainment of black independence in the Americas and Africa would mean not only the end of white control over the land and lives of non-whites, but also the dawn of a new era of peace and prosperity. Delany's romantic vision was not to become an African reality, as we now know, until after European imperialism, with the support of the United States, reached its peak with the Berlin Conference in 1884, in which the delegates agreed that the Congo should be the personal property of Leopold II, and began its decline in the 1960s.[12]

Images of Africa in the Pre-World War II Novel

Turning from Delany and the nineteenth century to the twentieth century novels of Downing and Schuyler, we discover that both are set in modern Liberia. Both reject direct correlations of evil and good with skin color, both strive for realism in characterization, and

---

[12]Joseph Conrad, *Heart of Darkness*, ed. Robert Kimbrough (New York: W. W. Norton, 1963), pp. 86–98; and Mark Twain, *King Leopold's Soliloquy* (New York: International Publishers, 1961), pp. 77–79.

both are critical of the elitism of Americo-Liberians and the exploitation of the indigenous native populations by the ruling class. On the other hand, whereas Downing's *The American Cavalryman* is a melodramatic love story, Schuyler's *Slaves Today* is a satire; and whereas Downing, a former United States consul in Luanda, Angola, based his romance on the career of Major Charles Young, a black West Pointer,[13] Schuyler, who in 1931 spent three months in West Africa researching his narrative, based his novel on the scandalous contract labor system in which the Liberian government sent thousands of tribesmen on two-year contracts to Fernando Po cacao plantations.[14]

Downing's ambivalence toward Liberia is evident in his depiction of his characters. The African characters are sympathetically yet condescendingly portrayed as superstitious savages. Although Lodango, the paramount chief of the Imbunda, is referred to by the undramatized omniscient narrator as a "savage" and "barbarian," he is described as a "perfectly proportioned bronze statue," and one of the female servants thinks of him as "a perfect specimen of his sex— eloquent, brave, cunning, persuasive, and cruel."[15] Seeing cultural differences through ethnocentric eyes, Downing tacitly imposes negative value judgments on the sketchy descriptions he provides of several "savage rites," including cicatrization and the "sassawood" ordeal in the sacrifice grove. After alluding to "great mounds of human skulls, bleached white," along the sides of the grove, Downing writes: "A witch-doctor, grotesquely decorated with fetiches and charms and carrying two long feathertipped wands, was doing divers terpsichorean gymnastics,—cake-walking, turkey-trotting, sugar-dipping, Halleluiah-jumping,—up and down the path in most wonderful fashion."[16] In contrast to this condescending image, the author intrudes early in the narrative to explain that "no attempt will be made to write the language as it was brokenly spoken by Lupelta, or by any other person, civilized or savage, who appears in these pages, though there are certain peculiarities of speech common among the narratives which must be retained."[17] Even though the most frequent peculiarity of speech that punctuates the dialogue is the exclamation "Wow," the natives in *The American Cavalryman*, unlike those in

---

[13]See George Schuyler, *Black and Conservative* (New York: Arlington House Publishers, 1966), p. 143.

[14]Charles Morrow Wilson, *Liberia: Black Africa in Microcosm* (New York: Harper & Row Publishers, 1971), pp. 115–127.

[15]Henry F. Downing, *The American Cavalryman: A Liberian Romance* (1917; rpt. College Park: McGrath Publishing Company, 1969), pp. 30, 35.

[16]*Ibid.*, p. 281.

[17]*Ibid.*, p. 27.

Heart of Darkness, are nevertheless humanized by their power of speech.

Downing's protagonist, Captain Paul Dale, is portrayed as a fair-skinned West Point graduate and American cavalry officer who rescues and falls in love with Lupelta, who was raised in the bush as a native after being kidnapped as a child from her father, a former trade agent who passes for white and has become an influential New York banker. Captain Dale's view of Liberians is that "because of their ignorance, they have failed to use opportunity wisely. One should not expect children to perform duties such as experienced persons would have found it exceedingly difficult to accomplish. Liberia's present misfortunes are the outcome of the false training of a ruling class lacking in mental and moral virility. The infusion of new life into the country would set things right."[18] Acting on this conviction at the end of the novel, Dale, who has married the President of Liberia's stepdaughter because Lupelta, through an incredible coincidence of plot, is ironically considered to be white, and who has been granted an extended leave from the military, plans to return to Liberia "to develop the agricultural resources" of the country and to help save it "from being absorbed by some European power."[19]

The image of Liberia in Schuyler's *Slaves Today* is more ironic and sympathetic than that in Downing's *The American Cavalryman*. The ironic situation of the novel is that although their forefathers had come to Africa "to found a haven for the oppressed of the black race . . . their descendants were now guilty of the same cruelties from which they had fled. The Americo-Liberians were to rule; the natives to obey."[20] Consistent with his purpose of arousing "enlightened world opinion against this brutalizing of the native population in a Negro republic," Schuyler, a political conservative, acerbic journalist, and racial gadfly, presents ironic descriptions of the Americo-Liberians and sympathetic portrayals of the indigenous peoples, whom the omniscient narrator refers to by their tribal names of Gola, Bassa, Kpwessis, Grebo, and Vai or as natives and aborigines. He not only respects the aborigines as people, but is also sympathetic toward their culture, outlining, for instance, the social advantages of polygyny for the natives. In contrast, he is critical and occasionally satirical in his treatment of the ruling class. Sidney Cooper Johnson, the President of Liberia and a lawyer by training, is

---

[18]*Ibid.*, p. 151.
[19]*Ibid.*, p. 306.
[20]George Schuyler, *Slaves Today: A Story of Liberia* (New York: Brewer, Warren, & Putnam, 1931), pp. 100–101.

described as having "won international fame for saying nothing adroitly."[21] Clearly "not of the material of his pioneer grandparents," he believed that "a ruling class . . . must be supported in leisure by those whom it ruled" and used his office to protect the power and privilege of the Liberian aristocracy and his conservative political party. Commissioner David Jackson, one of his most unscrupulous appointees, used the power of his office to levy exorbitant taxes on the native villages, to take their wives and daughters as concubines, to abuse and kill resisting village leaders, and to kidnap their men for forced domestic and foreign labor. Ironically, Commissioner Jackson and Captain Burns, Schuyler stresses "were but slightly less dark than the natives over whom they ruled but they felt no kinship with the aborigines for that reason. It was no more difficult for them to oppress and exploit fellow black men than it usually is for powerful whites to do the same thing to fellow white men. Color did not enter here—it was class that counted."[22]

Between the publication of *The American Cavalryman* in 1917 and *Slaves Today* in 1931, America experienced the throes of the turbulent twenties, including the resurgence of the Ku Klux Klan. Profoundly disillusioned with American values after World War I, especially with the disparity between industrial wealth and spiritual poverty, many white intellectuals and artists turned for salvation to promoting home-grown urban varieties of the Noble Savage. Carl Van Vechten, a white critic, novelist, and patron of black artists, played a major role in promoting a primitive image of Harlem and blacks in his controversial yet commercially successful *Nigger Heaven* (1926). A transplanted Jamaican and social radical, Claude McKay was ostensibly influenced by Van Vechten's primitivism in his first novel *Home to Harlem* (1928), but moved beyond it in *Banjo* (1929), his second novel to reject white civilization and embrace Africa. Ray, the black protagonist whose education, sensibility, and dreams foster ethnic and cultural ambivalence, feels emotionally and spiritually close to Africans he sees and hears in the old port of Marseilles:

> The Africans gave him a positive feeling of wholesome contact with racial roots. They made him feel that he was not merely an unfortunate accident of birth, but that he belonged definitely to a race weighed, tested and poised in the universal scheme. They inspired him with confidence in them. Short of extermination by the Europeans, they were a safe people, protected by their own indigenous culture. Even though they stood bewildered before the imposing bigness of white things, apparently unaware of the invaluable worth of their own, they were natu-

---

[21] *Ibid.*, p. 11.
[22] *Ibid.*, p. 100.

rally defended by the richness of their fundamental racial values. He did not feel that confidence about Aframericans who, long-deracinated, were still rootless among phantoms and pale shadows and enfeebled by self-effacement before condescending patronage, social negativism, and miscegenation.[23]

Also ambivalent toward his African characters was Rudolph Fisher, the talented M.D. who was one of the most witty and admired of the Harlem Renaissance writers. In his detective novel *The Conjure-Man Dies* (1932) he portrays two idealized modern Africans, N'gana Frimbo and his tribal servant, N'ogo Frimbo. N'gana is an African king, a Harvard graduate, a student of philosophy, and a popular Harlem psychic. Ironically, while the average Harlemite believes Frimbo is a "caster of spells," the erudite Frimbo rejects these beliefs as superstitious nonsense. Characterized by contradictions that suggest the ambivalence of the authors about their self-image, the image of Africa in pre-World War II Afro-American novels thus reflects the efforts of black Americans to define their own personal and ethnic identity by coming to terms with their historical and cultural experience.

Images of Africa in the Post-World War II Novel

Since World War II, the winds of social change have blown through America and Africa with hurricane force, whirling from the integration movement of the forties and fifties to the Black Power movement of the 1960s, and from colonialism to independence and neocolonialism for most of Africa, beginning with Ghana in 1957. In the United States the violent resistance of whites to the Supreme Court school desegregation decision in 1954 and to acknowledging the civil rights of blacks as well as the liberation of African nations and Cuba in the 1960s awakened the dormant political nationalism of many black Americans. Stokely Carmichael and other Black Power advocates redefined the liberation struggle of oppressed people against Western imperialism, revealing both continuity and change in attitudes expressed in the nineteenth century by Delany. Frustrated by the snail's pace of integration efforts and the tactics of passive resistance, they revived indigenous theories of the colonial relationship of blacks to the dominant social group in the United States. Contending with political nationalism in the struggle for black liberation during the period was cultural nationalism. Black was beautiful, and Africa was in vogue. The cry of "We are an Afri-

---

[23]Claude McKay, *Banjo: A Story Without a Plot* (New York: Harvest Book, 1929), p. 320.

can people" was heard from the political platform and the printed page. African art, clothing, names, hair-dos, and foods were the rage, and black intellectuals and artists were going on safari to the motherland in search of their roots. The image of Africa in the novels of Richard Wright, John A. Williams, William Melvin Kelley, and Frank Yerby are representative of this eventful period.

Although Africa and Africans do not play a major role in the novels of Richard Wright, a social radical and the self-exiled grand doyen of the Afro-American novel, and John A. Williams, a longtime journalist, astute critic of American racism, and grossly underrated novelist, their attitudes toward the continent and its politicians in *The Long Dream* (1958) and *The Man Who Cried I Am* (1967) are decidedly negative when not ambivalent. In *The Long Dream*, as in all of his novels and short stories, Wright accepts conventional white-black symbolism and the negative white image of Africa.[24] In a long discussion about Africa with his friends, especially Sam, whose father is a Garveyite, Fish, the protagonist, becomes so consumed by anger and self-hatred at being forced to confront his historical relationship to Africa and his blackness that he attacks Sam and later spits at his own face in the mirror, whispering venomously, "Nigger."[25] In *The Man Who Cried I Am* Williams portrays Jaja Enzkwu, a Nigerian diplomat, as "eagle-faced, hot-eyed Jaja with his sweating pussy-probing fingers and perfumed agbadas."[26] It is Jaja, the Machiavellian African politician with dreams of empire building, who discovers the existence of Alliance Blanc, the confederacy of white Europeans and Americans that plans to subvert potential African unity and terminate the minority threat in the United States. "Any halfway good-looking white woman can make a fool of him," writes Harry Ames, "but he doesn't trust a gathering of more than a single white man."[27] Harry Ames, a fictional treatment of Richard Wright and a major character in the novel, is trapped by his "contempt for everything African," which explains in part why Jaja gave him the key to the safe-deposit box containing the secret information about the Alliance, knowing that if he were killed by agents, Harry probably would also be killed. Although neither Max Reddick, the protagonist, nor apparently the author shares Harry's hatred, they do share his negative image of Jaja, who in pursuit of his objective of ruling all of Africa one day had offered to turn over the secret papers to the Americans if they gave him Nigeria. Instead, they killed him, Harry,

---

[24] Berghahn, *Images of Africa*, pp. 154–167.
[25] Richard Wright, *The Long Dream* (New York: Ace Book, 1958), pp. 29–34.
[26] John A. Williams, *The Man Who Cried I Am* (New York: Signet Book, 1968), p. 299.
[27] *Ibid.*, p. 303.

Max, and every other black who discovered the existence of the Alliance and the King Alfred Plan.

The image of Africa in William Kelley's A Different Drummer (1962) and Dunfords Travels Everywheres (1969) is mythopoeic and evocative of complex racial memories. In Dunfords Travels Everywheres Kelley, a born-again black cultural nationalist and awesomely talented novelist, adapts the characters, structure, and language of Joyce's Finnegan's Wake to express his conviction that Afro-Americans should not subscribe to racial stereotypes about integration nor sacrifice their historical and psychological kinship to Africa and each other for integration with Euro-Americans. He also draws on the poetic and prose Eddas—the mythology, ethical conceptions, and heroic lore of the Norse—to contrast with his reconstruction of African mythology and to "telve int'dRelationship betwine weSelf n d'cold Glareys o'Stunangle." Allusions to the treachery and fratricide of Odin, the father of the gods, and Balder, his son and the most beloved god, who is killed with mistletoe by his brother Hoder in a plot devised by Loki, Odin's foster-brother, link the fall or assassination of a beloved American president to the prophecy of the "Iklander":[28] "the misaltoetumble of the leader of La Colon y de la Thour Yndia Company, Prestodent Eurchill Balderman, preachful as expected, L. Oki to fry."[29] The Northern origins and chilling, life-destroying values of Odin and his descendants are symbolically contrasted with the Equatorial origins and passionate, life-giving values of Africa and her descendants. Africans and their descendants, says the protagonist's dramatized alter ego, should beware that their physical and creative energies not be used for fuel to warm the descendants of "W. Oten Chiltman," whose legends and lives glorify death and destruction: "Almost since the bin of bawn, he lobbed them to lobe a heart for the frigg of it, unrevel a ball for the yarn of it, barn a burn for the beef of it, but a hut for the strut of it, incise a shoe for the sock of it, heat a sheet for the wick of it. That and alotoflikkyr and Heshappy, Mr. Chityle."[30] Unfortunately, readers who resist trends toward modernism in the novel will probably find that it takes too much time and effort to understand Kelley's word-games

---

[28]See C.O.G. Turville-Petrie, Myth and Religion of the North; The Religion of Ancient Scandinavia (New York: Holt, Rinehart and Winston, 1964); The Poetic Edda, 2d rev. ed., trans. Lee M. Hollander (Austin: University of Texas Press, 1964); The Prose Edda of Snorri Sturluson; Tales from Norse Mythology, trans. Jean I. Young (Berkeley: University of California Press, 1973); and Edith Hamilton, Mythology (New York: Mentor Book, 1969), pp. 300–315.

[29]William Melvin Kelley, Dunfords Travels Everywheres (Garden City: Doubleday & Company, Inc., 1970), pp. 49, 89.

[30]Ibid., p. 54.

and multi-level puns, and will not adequately appreciate the richness of his comic imagination and fabulation in projecting an idealized yet positive image of Africa.

More realistic and therefore more accessible, but no less impressive in its fabulation is *A Different Drummer*, which has a double plot and dual protagonists. The first plot concerns the moral awakening and personal revolt of Tucker Caliban against the control of whites over his life, and the second focuses on the education of whites, especially young Harry Leland and Dewey Willson III, about the nature of racism and the meaning of courage and self-reliance. Affirming the principle of self-reliance, *A Different Drummer* is designed to create a transcendental vision of man with historic and mythic dimensions. The legend of the revolutionary heroism of Tucker Caliban's African ancestor and the myth of his blood as the explanation for Tucker's personal courage contrast with the failure of courage of the Willsons, whose name is symbolically ironic, and society in general to affirm the natural rights of man.

It is the world-weary Mr. Harper who passes on to us the local legend of Tucker's great, great grandfather and the continuity of his blood through his infant son down to Tucker, himself. An enlightened white effete who claims to believe in genetics and not in superstition, while simultaneously enjoying his role as oral historian and social analyst, Mr. Harper, and the author himself, disarms us by admitting that his story is not "all truth," justifying half lies and the exaggeration of facts as improving on the truth and the appeal of the story. In describing, for example, the nameless African chief's attack on the slave auctioneer before escaping from De Witt Willson, who had paid a thousand dollars for him, Mr. Harper delights in the hyperbole of the tall-tale: " 'some folks swear, though not all, that using his chains, he sliced his head off—derby and all—and that the head sailed like a cannon ball through the air a quarter mile, bounced another quarter mile and still had up enough steam to cripple a horse some fellow was riding into New Marsails.' "[31] After freeing himself, the African subsequently liberates other slaves in the area, beginning with De Witt Willson's, until he is betrayed by one of his men and shot by Willson before he could take his baby son with him in death. The reader, like the listening men on the porch in the novel, is skeptical of Mr. Harper's story. But Kelley reinforces its validity and Mr. Harper's reliability through the support of the store-owner Mr. Thompson, who tells the skeptics on the porch and the reader: " 'If that's what Mister Harper says, it's got to be part of the answer

---

[31]William Melvin Kelley, *A Different Drummer* (Garden City: Anchor Books, 1969), p. 24.

anyways.' "[32] In other words, recurring images of Africa and Africans in the minds of fictional characters and their authors reveal deeply felt beliefs of not only individuals, but also of a race, a class, and even a nation.

Unquestionably, the most realistic and fascinating images of Africa and Africans are found in Frank Yerby's historical novel, *The Dahomean*. It is the only contemporary Afro-American novel set in Africa. Based principally on Melville J. Herskovits's highly respected two-volume anthropological study, *Dahomey: An Ancient West African Kingdom*, the novel seeks, as a note to the reader states, to entertain and "to correct, so far as it is possible, the Anglo-Saxon reader's historical perspective."[33] For Yerby, a self-exiled debunker of historical myths,[34] "myths solve nothing, arrange nothing"; thus, unlike Kelley and Conrad, he attempts to give us historical truth, no matter how unsettling it is to racists, liberals, black nationalists, and, presumably, Africans themselves.

Introduced by a brief prologue and divided into two major parts, the first showing the ritualistic passage into manhood of the protagonist and the second the precipitous rise and fall of his fortunes among his people, *The Dahomean* opens and closes in Virginia, but its major setting is Dahomey in the late 1830s during the actual reign of His Royal Majesty Gezo, the ninth king of Dahomey.[35] It is the story of "Nyasanu Dosu Agausu Hwesu Gbokau Kesu, son of Gbenu, a great chief, and himself lately governor of the province of Alladah in Dahomey, husband of six wives, one of them the daughter of the king," told by him in retrospective narrative seven months after the murder of his family and his sale to Europeans by black slavers.

As the novel unfolds with the frequent use of Fau words and the occasional use of metaphorical language, all contributing to its verisimilitude, we quickly discover that Yerby is sympathetic toward Africa yet critical of those customs he feels violate a respect for human life, dignity, and freedom, imaginatively but not always convincingly using the Dahomean characters themselves to express the criticisms. Initially, it is Gbenu, a village chief and Nyasanu's father, who educates his son and the reader to the evils of Dahomean culture, particularly the tyranny, extravagance, and human sacrifices of the royal

---

[32]*Ibid.*, p. 33.

[33]Frank Yerby, *The Dahomean* (New York: Dell Book, 1971), p. 5.

[34]See Darwin T. Turner, "Frank Yerby as Debunker", *The Black Novelist*, ed. Robert Hemenway (Columbus: Charles E. Merrill Publishing Company, 1970), pp. 64–71.

[35]*Ibid.*, pp. 14, 133. Yerby states that Gezo was the tenth king, but the chronology of kings in Herskovits indicates that he was the ninth. See Melville J. Herskovits, *Dahomey: An Ancient West African Kingdom* (New York: J. J. Augustin, Publisher, 1938), I, 12–14.

family: "From birth to death we are taxed, taxed, taxed my son—so that the princesses and princes may live in licentious idleness—that is, if even our lives are not required of us for some small fault, or because the king needs a certain kind of worker—a *blacksmith* say, to be sent to the ancestors to make *ase* or hoes for the royal dead!"[36] The only escape from the tyranny of Dahomean life, says Gbenu in fidelity to the thematic and structural design of the novel, is " 'to be sold to the *furtoo*, those hideous creatures who come in high canoes from across the sea.' "[37] Kpadunu, Nyasanu's best friend, is also critical of the moral corruption of the royal family, especially their slave trading:

> We attack the Maxi, *xauntau daxo* mine, so that Dada Gezo can procure a supply of slaves to sell for gold, iron, and gun powder to the *furtoo*, those hideous skinless people from beyond the sea. Thus he adds to the great wealth he has already gained by taxing us nearly to death and enables himself to support his many wives and those puffed-up idlers and eternally rutting she-jackals he *thinks* are his sons and daughters in lascivious idleness. . .[38]

In addition, he is ambivalent about the magic of diviners, priests, and sorcerers, his own guild: " 'I don't believe in it, and I do. The feelings I have alternate—according to the mood I'm in, I suppose. Most of it—nearly all of it—*is* fakery, Brother.' "[39] Since the diviners correctly predicted that Kpadunu would not survive the war campaign for slaves and that Nyasanu's life would end in Dahomey and begin anew in a far off land, Yerby's ambivalence about magic is also apparent.

It is Yerby's emotional and moral identification with his protagonist, however, that most clearly reveals his ambivalence toward Dahomean culture. After having Nyasanu, whose name means "man among men," sympathetically explain early in the novel the religious, economic, and social reasons for polygyny, all of which are related to the importance of having many children, Yerby later has him mentally reject the custom. And then, using the occasion of the jealousy of Nyasanu's principal wife at his imminent marriage to a princess, Yerby editorializes about the custom:

> for the strict truth of the matter was that most West African women, in their heart of hearts, hated it. Even Dahomean custom, rigid enough on most questions of morals, provided two outlets for female rebellion

---

[36] Yerby, *The Dahomean*, p. 31.
[37] *Ibid.*, p. 32.
[38] *Ibid.*, p. 55.
[39] *Ibid.*, p. 153.

against becoming the ninth, the twentieth, or the fortieth wife of some
grizzled old chief their fathers had engaged them to out of policy; *asid-
josi*, in which the girl in question ran off with the younger, handsomer,
simpler man, with fewer wives or none, whom she preferred, whereupon the lover made the relationship legal by paying back the rejected
official suitor's gifts and work; and *xadudo* which was exactly the same
thing except that nothing was paid back, and the marriage rites never
performed so that the couple went on living in sin, as it were.[40]

More sensational than the custom of polygyny, however, were the
atrocities and sadism of war and the custom of human sacrifices. For
brave yet sensitive souls like Nyasanu:

> The tyranny of the Dahomean kings was a soul-crushing thing. How
> many lives did the king take each year in his monstrous 'customs'? More
> than thirty or forty, surely. And if rumors had it right, as rumor often
> did, the king sent a man and a woman of his household *every* morning
> to the ancestors to thank them for allowing him to see a new day.
> Which meant, since the year had three-hundred sixty odd days, that
> Gezo sacrificed over seven hundred human beings a year simply to bid
> the ancestors good morning![41]

In exploding the myths about Africa, Yerby thus points to the absolute power of the king as the greatest evil of Dahomean life and to
the sensitivity of Gbenu, Kpadunu and Nyasanu as the most redeeming trait in the Dahomean man.

In retrospect, then, the image of Africa in the Afro-American
novel reveals changes and continuities in the social arena and tensions in the Afro-American novelist's self-image as he struggles to
become his own mythmaker and to come to terms with the truth of
his African past in defining his personal and ethnic identity in relation to the world. Because their struggle to define themselves in life
and art is waged in a social arena that promotes the myth of white
supremacy, a struggle which has resulted in their socialized ambivalence and double-consciousness, Afro-American novelists have responded with mixed emotions to the question, What is Africa to me?
Unlike Afro-American poets and white American novelists, most
black American novelists avoid treating the question head-on; in
fact, in the history of the Afro-American novel only Downing,
Schuyler, and Yerby use Africa as a setting. Although Martin Delany
displaced the Satanic image with the Messenger of Light and Destruction, neither pre-World War II novelists, despite the Black
Power movement of the 1960s, have broken completely free from

---

[40]*Ibid.*, p. 339–340.
[41]*Ibid.*, p. 55.

white images of the African as Noble Savage and Barbarian. Finally, traditional black-white symbolism is usually transvaluated, with Richard Wright as the most important modern exception, and the criticism of Africa is primarily focused on cultural differences which, even when viewed sympathetically, the novelists generally consider undesirable in modern man when assessed through the prism of Afro-American cultural standards.

In closing, let us return to the question I posed by Achebe at the beginning of these remarks: Can a novel which celebrates the dehumanization of a portion of the human race in the manner of Conrad's *Heart of Darkness* be called a great work of art? Of course, on the face of it this question is aesthetically problematic, but if we assume with Harry Levin that a classic or great work of art is a book that gains a place for itself in our culture by its "precision of style, formality of structure, and, above all, concern for the basic principles that animate and regulate human behavior,"[42] then *Heart of Darkness*, although illuminating and important, is, as Achebe declares, not a great work of art. On the other hand, whereas only Yerby provides a documented, reliable account of West Africa, it seems reasonable to conclude that whether realistic or modernistic, the image of Africa in the Afro-American novel, as in the British and American, generally tells us more about the fantasies and values of the West and the author than it does about Africa.

---

[42]Harry Levin, "Introduction," *The Scarlet Letter*, Nathaniel Hawthorne (Boston: Houghton, Mifflin Company, 1960), p. viii.

Hortense J. Spillers

(1942–   )

BORN IN 1942, in Memphis, Tennessee, critic Hortense Spillers is now in the vanguard of African American feminist literary criticism. After graduating from Melrose High School in Memphis, Tennessee, she began her graduate work at Memphis State University and received her master's degree in May 1966. She receive her doctoral degree from Brandeis University in English and American literature in 1974.

Currently a professor of English and Women's Studies at Emory University in Atlanta, Georgia, Spillers has also taught at Cornell University, Haverford College, the University of Nebraska-Lincoln, Wellesley College, Brandeis University, the University of Massachusetts at Boston, and Kentucky State College. Her professional activities and scholarly work are even more diverse than her teaching career. In addition to co-editing along with Majorie Pryse the well-known collection of essays *Conjuring: Black Women, Fiction, and Literary Tradition*, she is also the author of at least twenty-two critical essays and six reviews.

Spillers also extends the range of her creative abilities by writing fiction. She is the author of "Isom," a short story which appeared in the May 1975 issue of *Essence* and winner of the 1976 Magazine Award for Excellence in Fiction and Belles Lettres. Two other stories, "A Lament" and "A Day in the Life of Civil Rights," appeared in *The Black Scholar*. She is currently at work on a novel tentatively entitled "Sunday of Indulgence." Spillers is also the author of *Comparative American Identities: Race, Sex, and Nationality in the Modern Text*, an edited collection of selected papers from the English Institute, (1991) and *In the Flesh: A Situation for Feminist Inquiry*, (1992).

The titles alone of her published and forthcoming publications illuminate Spiller's commitment to subjects that involve African American women's issues as well as the folk tradition. Her voice is a dominant one among African American feminist scholars. This status is reflected in the number of professional organizations on which she serves an advisory or editorial role. She is currently, or has functioned as, a member of the editorial board of *College English, Black American Literature Forum, American Quarterly,* and the *Norton Anthology of Afro-American Literature,* eds. Henry Louis Gates, Jr., and Nellie McKay.

Her honors and awards include a post-doctoral fellowship from the National Endowment for the Humanities (1976), a Rockefeller Foundation

Grant (1980–81), and a National Research Council for the Ford Foundation Post-Doctoral Fellowship (1985–86).

The following selection "Formalism Comes to Harlem" originally appeared in *Black American Literature Forum*.

FORMALISM COMES TO HARLEM

In attempting to describe the issue through two mutually alien points—Harlem and Formalism—, I think we capture something of the drama that informs the work of Afro-American critics, for it is in the center of antagonisms that they stand, trying to transform an opposition into a dialectical encounter. Du Bois used other words for it—the warring doubles—two striving souls held together by an act of will, one black and African, the other white and European.[1] Fanon saw the same entanglement of opposites, the same endlessly repeating symmetries,[2] which constitute the fabric of images and practice transmitted by mimetic gesture as well as written and oral traditions. One aspect of this perilous adventure, as uncomical now as it was for Du Bois over a half-century ago, is conceivable in the symbolisms of Harlem and Langston Hughes' Simple.[3] This hypothetical confrontation between Simple and a structure of ideas, which, by implication and design, relegates the former and his issue to the backwaters of discourse, is not a well-guarded secret, even when

---

Reprinted from *Black American Literature Forum*, Volume 16, Number 2 (Summer 1982). Copyright © 1982 Indiana State University.

[1]W. E. B. Du Bois, *The Souls of Black Folk* (1903; rpt. New York: Fawcett, 1961), pp. 16–17. This seminal essay on Afro-American life and thought, with its arguments developed through the metaphors and imagery of black spirituals, the "sorrow songs," is a brilliant demonstration for this generation of scholars of the law of mixed styles—lyrical and polemic.

[2]Frantz Fanon, *Black Skin, White Masks* (New York: Grove Press, 1967). I have specific reference here to Fanon's portrayal of the "Negro of the Antilles." This new man's mastery of the symbols of the dominant class worries Fanon's formulations to the point that mastery itself becomes, in Fanon's view, a condition of ambivalence.

[3]Jesse B. Semple, as Hughes explains it, is a composite figure drawn from many. What they all have in common, however, is a complaint about their feet. "Simple" goes back to the Thirties, and Hughes brings the development forward to the period of the Supreme Court's 1954 ruling on the desegregation of public schools and the early years of the King movement. Reflecting the common experiences of the man on the street, "Simple" shows a great deal of sophistication concerning the trickery of words and those who use them unthinkingly. That he realizes that their "polyvalence" often conceals the true political nature of speech suggests Hughes' own unfailing commitment to the rights of the ordinary black man. Hughes' translations of the everyday rhythms of black speech as it occurs in urban life are among the chief interests of his poetry as well. His essay "Who Is Simple?" is the "Foreward" to *The Best of Simple* (New York: Hill & Wang, 1961), pp. vii–viii.

suppressed; nor, probably, is Simple himself the modern personality which elitist Du Bois imaginatively embodied in his "talented tenth," so my appropriation of Hughes' character for the purposes of this essay deliberately intrudes an element of radical waywardness on a discussion otherwise engaged by polite combatants.

Simple in his wisdom of the streets of Harlem, or at least the Harlem that Hughes projected, is not only a contrast to formalism, or the study of art according to its formal properties, but also, we imagine, a detraction from its most eloquent formulations. In his role as debunker, Simple expresses an "attitude" which Afro-American critics might as well elaborate, but precisely what terms are both available and apposite to them in doing so is not a question we have settled overnight; nor are we always sure that the question itself is important. For sure, it recurs, by the decades, and I would pose it again: How does the Afro-American critic preserve the unalterable authenticity of Simple's wisdom, sparing the references to ritual and kinship which Harlem implies, in a conversation which requires the mastery of a technic of ideas and their certain configurations?

In its apparent inclusiveness, in its fertility of vision, the wisdom of Simple never learned to be stunned, or embarrassed, or enraged by alien or borrowed notations, because it is eventually restored to the most intimate self-reference. The world is judged by *it* and is, therefore, disabled of its own capacity to judge. Since this mode of self-knowing expresses the subversive or counter intention, I have no desire to cut it loose. The black critic, then, wants to lose nothing at all, but instead to *attach* the most serviceable of the alien figure-of-thought to his or her efforts to reformulate the propositions that govern the study of literature and critical theory concerning it.

Harlem, to complete the equation, stands here as a common ground of reference for Afro-American cultural experience and, further, we could make it synonymous with "jazz," which even musicians make no effort to define forever; it is something one makes, against the force of his or her own intuitions, or whatever arises freely, spontaneously in the human being's address to his or her environment. There really is no evidence for assuming, however, that Harlem as a universally distributed reference engenders no idioms other than jazz, or that jazz itself is simply generated. Anyone who thought so in the golden age of black American music likely learned very quickly what the true story was. Simple, who embodies the place called Harlem, is systematic in his allegiance to folk utterance, close to jazz idiom in its supreme confidence, and the subtle ways of folk utterance, despite mutations of character which he undergoes over thirty years. But what evades Hughes' straight man is Simple's simple conviction that the most abiding truth is democratic, impressionistic; anybody knows it and can say it in short order. Whatever response Simple might give to Derrida's "Differa / e / nce," for instance, is anybody's guess, but we can rest assured that it would remain loyal to the idiom of comic sabotage. We can already anticipate Simple's overall disposition toward an argument that relies so heavily on the malice of alphabets, on their peculiar adultery. If formalism is to Harlem what cotton is to Harlem, then the realignment of purposes which my title intends is instructive: For Simple and those of a given audience who share his views, the vocation of words talking about other words would very likely take on the status of Broadway entertainment.

But much closer to home (and more troubling) than the intellectual showdown of a hip Frenchman, or even the inflated price of a Broadway show, is this rift of opinion between at least two schools of black critics, both of them straighter, perhaps, than the complicated humor of Simple anticipates. There are those who think that Afro-American literature is the narrative of mute social categories, content determined before particular acts of writing. Then there are those who think this view is one-eyed. On two fairly recent occasions panels of Afro-American critics and scholars called for an end to the study of Afro-American literature as an opportunity for high political polemic, an extension of theories of sociology, a projection of the audience's response to the personality of the writer.[4] At both the 1977 annual meetings of the Midwest Modern Language Association and the parent body, panelists proposed that the methods of formalism be generally applied to the assumptions that cluster about the study of Afro-American literature. Within this inclusive fraternity there are certain decisive emphases—myth, structuralist, phenomenological, etc.—, but the common concern of both panels was differentiation, the wish to distinguish the logics or systems peculiar to literality in the plenitude of cultural modes that define us. One of the terms common to both panels was "criteria": Can anybody judge the literature? Is *any* argument concerning it crucial, or even acceptable? Does the writing itself (critical and creative) mobilize sufficiently certain ideas and displacements so that it gives us the proper

---

[4]The thrust of concern for both panels is briefly captured in remarks by Darwin Turner. I make use of them here: "Despite fifty years of criticism of Afro-American Literature, criteria for the criticism have not been established. Consequently, some readers judge literature by Afro-Americans according to its moral value, a few for its aesthetic value, most by its social value, and too many according to their response to the personalities of the Black authors." Quoted in "Black Critic," by Don L. Lee (Haki R. Madhubuti), in *Jump Bad: A New Chicago Anthology* presented by Gwendolyn Brooks (Detroit: Broadside Press, 1971).

response, or a *response*, to our situation at the moment, to this period of consciousness?

It was obvious to me as a panelist on one occasion and a member of the audience on another that there is some impatience about the issue of terms on both sides (subject to change in a sequence of gestures which often resembles "musical chairs"). Some participants thought, apparently, that *formalism*, by name, by implication, embodies yet another instance of Anglo-American adventurism whose dress conceals at least exclusive aims, at most "genocidal" ones, infinitely more subtle than the arms race because it decides, through intellectual and symbolic sovereignty, precisely what categorical imperatives we will obey. If language is the perfect instrument of empire, then the naming of its formal properties comes to stand for its most privileged manifestation. One part of the audience, for these reasons, which are rarely expressed directly, would, perhaps, prefer to maintain Afro-American literature and theory as a self-generating activity, pure in its aims and directions. On the other side there are those who understand quite well (at least they think they do) how the division came about in the first place, how false it is, and have no interest in choosing between camps of "masters" in the protracted battery of other "enslaved" persons. As far as I can tell, all the principals agree on the essentials: Both the literature and criticism must finally be expressed as counter assumptions, not as moments of negation or absence. In order to enforce the point, are we doomed to repeat and keep on repeating the very clear dilemma of Du Bois' generation of the '20s and Chicago's Obassi Movement of the '60s? From what point can we *move* the discussion right on ahead? If our brilliant political theorists have taught us anything from the Sixties, it is certainly a corrected sense of "heightened contradictions." The cycle of cultural events does repeat, but it also spirals.

There is no more powerful statement of the bases on which the black critic and writer, among others at work, must build than Ellison's germinal essay "Little Man at Chehaw Station."[5] Exploding once again the essentially Manichaean view of American culture, Ellison calibrates his argument along several lines of stress, too numerous and involuted to unravel here, but in readjusting its emphases, I have acquired from his insights another constellation of terms and images which elaborate "the confounding of hierarchal expectations" as the magical truth of black American life. With reference to the scheme I am working out here, such confounding has special mean-

---

[5]"The Little Man at Chehaw Station: The American Artist and His Audience," *The American Scholar*, 47 (1978), 25–48. I am grateful to the late Larry Neal for first calling my attention to this essay.

ing for the critic, for he or she must await from the writer a content
and strategy for its achievement and, in the process, check his or her
own motives of presumption.

My own belief about the relationship between the critical work
and that which it contemplates is this: The literary work describes,
or carves out, an arena of choices, and in doing so, the writer sus-
pends definitive judgment. I think such modification is crucial to
our getting in right perspective the relationship between dynamic social movement and the narrative which locates it. I am not prepared
to argue—primarily because I don't believe it—that the art work is
autonomously derived, that it is isolated in the laws of its being from
the whole circumstances that engender it; but I am fairly certain that
the rather arbitrary movement at which we capture the work (and
vice versa) in its apparent detachment from the historical and most
intimate wishes must be both anticipated and sustained as a necessary act in discrimination. My point is quite simple. The narrative
which the writer offers for consideration operates according to the
logic of literary form. Just as we could not have imagined Martin Luther King or Malcolm X contravening the logic or system of oratory
in making a point, we need not insist that the writer, in turn, preach
to us, or make the very same point in the same way. Certain gestures go along with the "territory," and the critic helps to map it.
Just as the preacher does not say all, even if all his experience is
brought to bear on a performance, the writer also holds something
in abeyance; in other words, the art work for its audience, for the
writer, is an exercise in one system of logic or perception at a time.
Whatever else we bring to it, by grace, by inference, might be considered a bonus. Probably the critic's task, as Northrop Frye observes, is to *speak* or *explain* where the work does not, to supply the
right questions for a proffered riddle, but in any case, I think that it
is necessary for both writer and audience to agree that the process of
writing is a distinctive act of consciousness. It teaches us something
about being alive and asks riddles in a way that is peculiar to itself,
and perhaps that really is enough.

The project of reading work by Afro-American writers in accord
with formalist methods is an approach, not an allegiance. (Black critics are not on the prowl for new religions.) Ultimately, the criticism
seeks to restore a particular point of view to its perspective against
the whole presence of African-American life in this culture, or what
Du Bois called the drama of a "tremendous striving." Any suggestion
that that presence has been delivered into the American kingdom of
God is still a futuristic metaphor. In his four-point program for a
Black Aesthetic criticism, Houston Baker makes several useful suggestions:

. . . first [the critics] must steep themselves in manifold historical evidence that has been too long ignored. The literary text is most revealing to the critic who possesses a high degree of historical knowledge. Second, those who contribute to a just view of Black American literature must be able to move from the broad historical plane to the distinctive Black world. . . .[6]

There is little evidence to suggest to me that the methodology of formalism contravenes historical perspective or deep political commitment when it is clear that formalism itself arises at a particular moment, or series of moments, in the development and advancement of the idea of linguistics. In short, a method is not inherently ahistorical, or endemic to a divine order. Formalism is, I believe, preeminently useful. The attempt, then, to treat a literary text by a black writer as *a text* (a spate of written discourse operating according to certain formal principles) need not exclude the critic's whole consciousness, but, of necessity, draws its plenitude into specific concentration. If there were a better word for saying what I mean, one less riddled by tribalistic implications, I'd say it. *Epistemology* is likely not ideal either, but probably subsumes all other formalists acts—exegesis, hermeneutics, historical method; the near-endless array of etymological activity, which Kenneth Burke summed up under the heading of "logology"—under the broadest of intentions: a method of knowledge, of inquiry, capable of supplying Simple and the straight man (for I'd wish to get them together and keep them together) with certain enabling postulates. I would agree with Geoffrey Hartman's point: "To redeem the word from the superstition of the word is to humanize it, to make it participate once more in a living concert of voices, and to raise exegesis to its former state by confronting art with experience as searchingly as if art were scripture."[7]

In order to nail down my theoretical point and to try to silence the loud, who think that a Daniel Moynihan of Afro-American criticism and letters is a mere figment of a too rich imagination, I would like to offer something of a critical parable. Toni Morrison's *Song of Solomon* was greeted in 1977 with immense critical acclaim, but in several instances, what was said of the novel—its authentic testimony to "Black Experience"—could be applied to a repertoire of

---

[6]Houston A. Baker, Jr., "On the Criticism of Black American Literature: One View of the Black Aesthetic," in *Reading Black: Criticism of African, Caribbean, and Black American Literature*, ed. Houston A. Baker, Jr., Monograph No. 4 (Ithaca, NY: Africana Studies and Research Center, 1976), pp. 48–58.

[7]"Beyond Formalism" in *Beyond Formalism: Literary Essays, 1958–1970* (New Haven, CT: Yale Univ. Press, 1975), p. 57.

black events from Gustavus Vassa's *Narrative* to John Coltrane's "Ascension"; from a night at the concert hall with the Alvin Ailey Dancers to Richard Pryor's short-lived and brilliant career on NBC-TV. To identify the novel in no more differentiated terms than that is to accommodate oneself to the least tense assumptions which suggest that "Black Experience," a monolith down to death, has been exhausted. It is a museum piece, an artifact, something you visit or slum in, and, above all, it has no integrity of its own, no integrity to be regarded against revised patterns of living relationships. Colette Dowling, for example, two years after the publication of *Song of Solomon*, points out that Morrison gives us "exotic stuff" in the novel, from which basis she goes on to itemize exactly what kind of stuff she means: "voodoo dolls, greenish-gray love potions, a sack of daddy's bones hanging from the ceiling." While I concede that the reader of magazines exercises a poetic faith much less compelling than what he or she requires of him- or herself when reading a novel, or the "heavies," what does this same reader think when he or she confronts a similar configuration of intentions from the allegedly more intellectually responsible sources? Dowling goes on to quote from Diane Johnson's *New York Review of Books* assessment of Morrison's and Gayl Jones' novels: "'They *entirely* concern black people who violate, victimize, and kill each other. . . . *No* relationships endure, and *all* are founded on *exploitation.* . . . Are *blacks* really like *this?*'" (emphases mine).[8]

I will not pause (as Dowling's editors clearly did not) to question certain semantically suspect categories from these observations—i.e., "entirely concern," "all are founded," "are blacks" (every one of the thirty or so million souls of them in the continental U.S.A., the question asks!) "like this?"—since I believe that the writer had to have an ending, and these leaping indices give one the sense that *everything* has been accomplished in one bound. Nor will I stop to replay, even if I could and there were time, the level of deception and contempt which guards these precisely segmented portions of American cultural content from profounder inquiry. But I will briefly essay a single symptom of the inevitable: With its intricate network of symbolic supports, the American event of race so thoroughly describes a grammar of negation that those who are subdued by its magic imagine that its traditional sign-vehicles and immanent referential content are not violently arbitrary at all. In short, in some places, there is commentary blissfully, swingingly, unmoved by the

---

[8]"The Song of Toni Morrison," *The New York Times Magazine*, 20 May 1979, p. 56. I am grateful to Ann Leventhal for sharing this long review with me.

course of general linguistics and its aftermath *even* this late in the twentieth century, *even* in the discourse of criticism.

There is, quite legitimately, a category of writing which we designate "black American," but its distinctive traits are not, after all, exhausted by a catalogue of the "exotic," or public memory of Bigger Thomas. I would prefer to begin to talk about Afro-American literature in the following terms: Intent on producing works of filiation, advocacy, preservation, convocation (a literature whose principal movement is informed by an external narrative), black American writers tend to rehearse a metaphorical valuation of human experience. Inspired by an African myth of flying, *Song of Solomon* attempts to elaborate the myth within the local context of a black American family over three generations.[9] That members of the second generation of the Deads appropriate certain attitudes toward ancestry—Dowling's bones hanging from the ceiling—is Morrison's strategy, I believe, for contrasting structures of feeling and belief between old and young. Morrison applies the flying metaphor and its complementary ideas to a problem: What gestures would make possible the total freedom of movement? The meeting place of opposites—control and surrender—identifies the figurative space which the novel would make manifest. When Milkman discovers that he gains control over his life by surrendering it, Morrison has him fly into the arms of his friend-turned-pursuer, Guitar: "Without wiping away the tears, taking a deep breath, or even bending his knees—he leaped. As fleet and bright as a lodestar he wheeled toward Guitar and it did not matter which one of them would give up his ghost in the killing arms of his brother. For now he knew what Shalimar knew: If you surrendered to the air, you could *ride* it."[10] The transformation of the myth to an alien place and its reidentification as a fictional motif form an economy of analogues which render the first, second, and third generations of the Deads synonymous in their

---

[9]During the 1977 Bread Loaf Writers' Conference, Toni Morrison read excerpts from her latest work and lectured on the importance of African and Afro-American myth and symbolism to the novelist. *Song of Solomon* might be considered an investigation into points of contact between history and myth/folklore. I believe that there is a significant philosophical, if not structural, link bwetween her use of the motif of flying in the new work and an earlier novel, *Sula*; in a key passage, the narrator explains that the population of Medallion, Ohio—the scene of Sula's misdeeds and subquent victimization—never learned what to do "with the wings, a way of holding the legs and most of all a full surrender to the downward flight . . ." ([1973; rpt. New York: Bantam Books, 1975], p. 104). In further conversation concerning *Song of Solomon*, Morrison suggested that the crucial moral problem for Milkman was the lesson of surrender, restated in the novel in figurative terms. The African myth of flying seeks a level of displacement and transformation in the novel.

[10]*Song of Solomon* (New York: Knopf, 1977), p. 337.

American destiny. There is essentially no discontinuity now between fathers and sons.

The moral universe from which the work is addressed is based in a perception of restored sympathetic identities. By analogy, juxtaposition, imitation, or a grid of correspondences imposed on disparate conditions, Morrison reconsiders the "impulse of pity," as Wright's protagonist calls such perception in "The Man Who Lived Underground," as a legitimate human response. Through the elaboration of a metaphorical device, Morrison resolves Milkman's state of alienation in relationship to a series of human and social issues—for instance, the outraged fraternity between Guitar and himself is driven to extreme conclusions, but the terms of it appear in a terrible act of irony which releases both from the anguish of their ignorance. At the same time its consequences are both illuminated and borne in a startling moment of mutual revelation—Guitar, the revolutionary of perverted aims, can no more liberate his brother, as he can take life with impunity, while Milkman himself earns the grace of struggle as he has tried to circumvent it in its familial and broader social meanings. That both are brought together in this scene—poised at last against the background of an initial outcome—extends the auspices of the African myth over the tyranny of the particular, of the momentous. In other words, Milkman, in his newfound knowledge, is standing on the Virginia hillside for more than himself. "Leaping" and "wheeling" in the air, actions which replicate the motor behavior of his African ancestor, escaping captivity, and imitate an airborne movement not conventional to human beings, Milkman probably doesn't "fly," but the censure from empirical fact does not interfere with the dream, while the metaphor connotes a heroic act through what is essentially a marvelous, time-honored "lie." In this case, we embrace untruth gladly.

In its passion to resolve contradiction and impose a harmonious order on combative (or simply different) categories of consciousness, the rhetoric of metaphorical discourse achieves its logic by a sort of elliptical subtlety. To connect one human being with another is a vastly more difficult task than fiction itself (or even the Constitution) allows us to know, but to yoke, by analogy, the human and the universal, the momentary and the infinite, is not so much a merciful stroke of heretical arrogance as it is the blind excision of distinctive nominative properties. This tension, however, between the unique and its copulative potential not only gives the sentence and the paragraph their "delegated efficacy," but also helps us imagine that we are locked, ineffably, in an interminable chain of human kinship and, smaller scaled, of consanguineous alignments. The theme of resemblance, of obviously repeating genetic fortune, is not solely the worry or fascination of fathers, but a principle of inclusion that reappears and disperses among vast orders of cultural events.

I think that we could say with a great deal of justification that the thrust of Afro-American writing this century privileges metaphorical truth, or the transcending human possibility. This mode of work, whose demise Ortega y Gasset predicted over a half-century ago, pursues this community of texts throughout a variety of characters, situations, and closures, but variety complicates a fundamental (and apparently shared) structural motive: An allegiance to the linear progression of time, or an insisting that the time of fiction matches at least an illusion which we honor about objective time, places the accent of the works on visible, explicit motivations. The unbroken progression of mimetic gestures moves toward a point of repose for characters *and* readers. It would be pointless, if not wrong, to argue that other American communities of writers do no such thing, when it seems the trend of American writing up to mid-century. I could not claim either that my scheme answers for all black writers in this country for all time; the conclusion is tentative at best. But the suggestion has the virtue of directing one's attention toward tendencies of form rather than laws of tribal behavior. Any literature might eventually reembrace its tribe—and *how* it does so is of no mean interest to me—, but not so fast . . .

Under the requirements of an "objective text," the fictive material appears self-generating through disharmonious voices. The accent here, William Gaddis' *The Recognitions*, for instance, falls on the mental or psychic economy of character rather than on what the characters commonly share, witness, or dispute. In other words, the narration as it modulates and ramifies through central intelligences locates no more common ground between them than the unity of the printed page. Gaddis' characters speak to themselves, apparently, or at least toward that silence not interrupted by a reader's presence. We are there, it seems, by the disgrace of certain social violations—i.e., reading another's letters and diaries—, and the reward is just as disturbing. *Song of Solomon,* by contrast, deploys a concept of character not only around assumptions accessible *among* characters, but also the latter explicitly reenforced by examples borrowed from a common witness. The reader shares the assumptions, in other words, through this imagined concert of being, and that is possible, in turn, by the reappearance of certain public conventions of figurative speech; for instance, "as fleet and bright as a lodestar" has not only unambiguous suggestion, but a comparative reference, which, by precedent, looks beyond the context itself for verification.

At the end of Morrison's novel, we feel that we have come to an end and that there is no very wide disparity between the writer and reader concerning how we got there. The reader feels that various issues of the narrative have been resolved rather than teased or frustrated. The comic closure of *The Recognitions*—with a cathedral destructing in the vibrations of organ music—is, perhaps, a grotesque instance of minor apocalypse or nemesis not unlike Norris' bad guy of *The Octopus*, but, for sure, I am not prepared for it and suspect that the writer and this reader have quite different knowledge concerning the route of escape and how it has been achieved. Gaddis' work appears held together by the logic of association, of obsession; for instance, the recurrence of New England scenery belongs as inescapably to a character as his clothes and indeed constitutes the "tone of voice" by which he is known. Unlike *Song of Solomon*, the characters of *The Recognitions* are not known by name, or more precisely, recognized by name, but, rather, through the repetition of idiomatic gestures and the infinite regression of figurative and scenic details.

It is true that similar structures of imagery, allusion, and syntax are repeated around Morrison's characters, but a crucial difference is that the drama in which they engage is mediated by a narrative intelligence that "explains" the self-sufficient event as it happens. This intercessive token is the voice speaking in the silence which Gaddis' characters in their respective and separate places maintain with brilliant, voracious aptitude. With *The Recognitions* one page succeeds another, but the sense that one anticipates of a progressive unfolding, of a character revealed and changing before the eyes, is neither appropriate to this work, nor rewarded. Gaddis' structure is episodic; but just as importantly, his characters seem to exist as an extension of rhetorical choices, or perhaps it could be said that their narrative dimension is not preeminently decipherable. In this case, we are confronted with uniqueness—the proliferation of difference—untrammeled by a principle of inclusion. Gaddis' irreducible nominative properties, which appear to cling to Jakobson's metonymic pole, are contiguous in avoidance of any obvious transfer of identities and anxieties. On the other hand, Milkman, under other names, in other contexts, is infinitely repeatable. That he insinuates a drama in addition to whatever linguistic vitality Morrison brings to bear on the novel is as sudden and irretrievable an interruption of his unique status as is his mad leap from the hillside.

The sharp disjunctures in narrative time, the intrusion of rhetorical motives as the primary dictate of character, may not be so keen a deviation from the human problematic as Ortega y Gasset anticipated, but for sure they move us toward a program of action which captures the human being in an autonomous frame of reference. Ortega y Gasset called such program "alienation"—"an avoidance of living forms."[11]

Thematic variation from the dynamics of connectedness has become the canon of taste rather than an alternative stylistic route. This practice of influence, in short, the abrogation of statements of transcendence, skepticism of the heroical act or intention, the parodic manipulation of feeling, the detachment of speech from an imagined speaker or human center, which returns the implications of words to a dictionary or thesaurus, seem to be the chief literary dictates of the moment, and writers align themselves with their persuasions by degree. Rather than imagine decisive breaks between the modernist/objective text and the text that contrasts with it, I would prefer to imagine a continuum of responses—from the archetypal to the historical, to the individualistic and momentary, each one increasingly subjective in its human emphasis and reception. Against this continuum of creative activity, black writers tend to stay close to the efficacy of words as an act of reciprocity, an address which anticipates reply. In short, it is not the extension of rhetorical energy alone which inspires *Song of Solomon*, or Ellison's *Invisible Man*, to make a different case; but perhaps the power of language to disclose being, rather than conceal it, is neither moot nor disabled from this angle of vision.

Reciprocity as the expected burden of language is not at this moment a popular idea for fiction, and along with its unpopularity, we have probably lost, again by degree, an interest in narrative, having gained a very high tolerance for the contemplation of smaller and smaller units of verbal and symbolic reference. In light of it, the black American writer's decision to be interested in symbolic behavior whose smallest unit is the narrative, the *story*, may strike some readers as a very strange thing, at least, but one might suppose that their decision has a great deal to do with how these writers understand *speaking* in the first place. Morrison and Ellison, among others, sense too keenly, perhaps, the requirements of their own imposed alienation to raise it to an act of form. For them, language, withheld for so long, by law, from the African/American as the origin of his human power, does *speak*. The suppressed subject now mobilized toward historical movement particular to itself is not, in this case, an optional principle of composition. It matches, again by analogy and sympathetic agreement, an original scene, primal and sacrificial, when living ancestors lost life, lost language. In either

---

[11]"The Dehumanization of Art," in *The Dehumanization of Art and Other Essays*, trans. Alex Brown (New York: Norton, 1972), pp. 65–84.

case, the signifier is not empty. More precisely, it fixes a decisively unambiguous change in the study of nature.

Simple bears the losses from this initial encounter with a kind of terrible finesse and, often enough, in a terrible silence, when in the presence of the many who have forgotten or never knew. And, in effect, his deep knowledge of the implications of violence becomes the crucial aspect of his own private and corporate identity. He cannot forget it, must not abandon it, and goes about saying it through varying degrees of transmutation. To mistake his purposes, however, would be stupid, perhaps ungrateful. For instance, Simple give the straight man a history of the origins of "Be-Bop," and the perception is outrageous enough to be true against the four-square fact and at the level of articulation where only the exaggerated word is uncorrupt:

> "Re-Bop certainly sounds like scat to me," [straight man] insisted.
> "No," said Simple, "Daddy-o, you are wrong. Besides, it was not *Re-Bop*. It is *Be*-Bop."
> "What's the difference," [straight man] asked, "between *Re* and *Be*?"
> "A lot," said Simple. "Re-Bop was an imitation like most of the white boys play. Be-Bop is the real thing like the colored boys play. . . . From the police beating Negroes' heads. . . . Everytime a cop hits a Negro with his billy club, that old club says, 'BOP! BOP! . . . BE-BOP! . . . MOP! . . . BOP!' . . . That's where Be-Bop came from, beaten right out of some Negro's head into them horns and saxophones and piano keys that plays it. Do you call that nonsense?"[12]

Any questions we might entertain about this mode of saying must make their way through layers of American culture as Simple has witnessed it, then toward the metrical near-unity of *re* and *be*. The French school would have field day here. As for me, it is one of those projects which is, as Toni Cade says, brewing under the bed.[13] My simpler wish against it is that Simple speak in as many ways as possible—he's certainly earned that right—and that the criticism pay attention to *that*. In the critical act, there is a man or woman revealed, seeking, like Jesse B. Semple, to retrieve the legitimate name of things lost to the violence, forgetfulness, and contradiction which surround the surrogate name. If I, the black person, can speak freely in my choice of critical and creative forms, then my private and collective suffering is not only mobilized on my own behalf, but also preserves me against the "homicidal" tendencies of strangers.

---

[12]"Bop," in *The Best of Simple*, pp. 117–18.

[13]"Commitment: Toni Cade Bambara Speaks," an interview with Beverly Guy-Sheftall, in *Sturdy Black Bridges*, ed. Roseann P. Bell, Bettye J. Parker, and Beverly Guy-Sheftall (Garden City, NY: Anchor/Doubleday, 1979), pp. 230–49.

Alice Walker

(1944–   )

BEST KNOWN for her highly praised novel *The Color Purple* (1982), which was the basis for the screenplay *The Color Purple*, and her book of womanist essays *In Search of Our Mothers' Gardens* (1983), Alice Walker is one of the most popular black feminist writers of the twentieth century. A victim of the racist system of the South, Walker delves into the experiences of black women and explores their position in a highly discriminatory society.

The last of eight children, Walker was born in Eatonton, Georgia, in 1944. Attending Spelman College on a scholarship from 1961 to 1963, Walker, who was valedictorian of her high school class, later went to Sarah Lawrence College in Bronxville, New York, where she received her B.A. in 1965. Becoming pregnant while at Sarah Lawrence and eventually getting an abortion, Walker discovered what the woman, alone, goes through emotionally, physically, and socially. It is this experience that serves as the basis for her first book, *Once: Poems* (1968).

Most of Walker's fiction revolves around the dual themes of racism and sexism. With the publication of *The Third Life of Grange Copeland* (1970) and *In Love and Trouble: Stories of Black Women* (1973), Walker was one of the first to make it clear that sexism is an additional form of oppression for black women, not just an issue for white women. Walker also funneled some of her creative energies into researching black women writers, such as Zora Neale Hurston. *I Love Myself When I Am Laughing: A Zora Neale Hurston Reader* (1979), a collection of Hurston's writings, and "In Search of Zora Neale Hurston," an article appearing in the March 1975 issue of *Ms.* magazine, are two such works that resulted from that research.

While working in Mississippi from the late 1960s to the mid 1970s, Walker met and married Mel Leventhal, a white civil rights lawyer. Walker's marriage ended in divorce in 1977. She has one daughter. Walker now lives in California, where she owns her own press and devotes most of her time to writing.

Her other works include *Five Poems* (1972); *Revolutionary Petunias and Other Poems* (1973); *Langston Hughes, American Poet* (1974); *Meridian* (1976); *Good Night Willie Lee, I'll See You in the Morning* (1979); *You Can't Keep a Good Woman Down: Stories* (1981, 1982); *Living by the Word*, a collection of essays (1988); *The Temple of My Familiar*, a novel (1989); and *Her Blue Body Everything We Know*, a collection of poetry (1991); as well as other articles in *Ms.* and *Essence*.

For further reading, see Barbara T. Christian's "The Black Woman Writer as Wayward," and Bettye J. Parker-Smith's "Alice Walker's Women: In Search of Some Peace of Mind," both in *Black Women Writers* (1984), edited by Mari Evans; Melissa Walker's *Down from the Mountaintop: Black Women's Novels in the Wake of the Civil Rights Movement, 1966–89* (1991); Christian's article in *Dictionary of Literary Biography, Volume 33*; Peter Erickson's "Cast Out Alone/To Heal/and Re-Create/Ourselves: Family Based Identity in the Work of Alice Walker," *CLA Journal* 23 (September 1979); Trudier Harris's "Folklore in the Fiction of Alice Walker: A Perpetuation of Historical and Literary Traditions," *Black American Literature Forum* (Spring 1977); Deborah McDowell's "The Self in Bloom: Alice Walker's *Meridian*," *CLA Journal* 24 (March 1981); and Mary Helen Washington's "An Essay on Alice Walker," in *Sturdy Black Bridges* (1979), edited by Roseann P. Bell, Bettye J. Parker, and Beverly Guy-Sheftall.

The following selection comes from *You Can't Keep a Good Woman Down*.

NINETEEN FIFTY-FIVE

1955

The car is a brandnew red Thunderbird convertible, and it's passed the house more than once. It slows down real slow now, and stops at the curb. An older gentleman dressed like a Baptist deacon gets out on the side near the house, and a young fellow who looks about sixteen gets out on the driver's side. They are white, and I wonder what in the world they doing in this neighborhood.

Well, I say to J. T., put your shirt on, anyway, and let me clean these glasses offa the table.

We had been watching the ballgame on TV. I wasn't actually watching, I was sort of daydreaming, with my foots up in J. T.'s lap.

I seen 'em coming on up the walk, brisk, like they coming to sell something, and then they rung the bell, and J. T. declined to put on a shirt but instead disappeared into the bedroom where the other television is. I turned down the one in the living room; I figured I'd be rid of these two double quick and J. T. could come back out again.

Are you Gracie Mae Still? asked the old guy, when I opened the door and put my hand on the lock inside the screen.

And I don't need to buy a thing, said I.

What makes you think we're sellin'? he asks, in that hearty Southern way that makes my eyeballs ache.

Well, one way or another and they're inside the house and the first thing the young fellow does is raise the TV a couple of decibels. He's about five feet nine, sort of womanish looking, with real dark white skin and a red pouting mouth. His hair is black and curly and he looks like a Loosianna creole.

About one of your songs, says the deacon. He is maybe sixty, with white hair and beard, white silk shirt, black linen suit, black tie and black shoes. His cold gray eyes look like they're sweating.

One of my songs?

Traynor here just *loves* your songs. Don't you, Traynor? He nudges Traynor with his elbow. Traynor blinks, says something I can't catch in a pitch I don't register.

The boy learned to sing and dance livin' round you people out in the country. Practically cut his teeth on you.

Traynor looks up at me and bites his thumbnail.

I laugh.

Well, one way or another they leave with my agreement that they can record one of my songs. The deacon writes me a check for five hundred dollars, the boy grunts his awareness of the transaction, and I am laughing all over myself by the time I rejoin J. T.

Just as I am snuggling down beside him though I hear the front door bell going off again.

Forgit his hat? asks J. T.

I hope not, I say.

The deacon stands there leaning on the door frame and once again I'm thinking of those sweaty-looking eyeballs of his. I wonder if sweat makes your eyeballs pink because his are sure pink. Pink and gray and it strikes me that nobody I'd care to know is behind them.

I forgot one little thing, he says pleasantly. I forgot to tell you Traynor and I would like to buy up all of those records you made of the song. I tell you we sure do love it.

Well, love it or not, I'm not so stupid as to let them do that without making 'em pay. So I says, Well, that's gonna cost you. Because, really, that song never did sell all that good, so I was glad they was going to buy it up. But on the other hand, them two listening to my song by themselves, and nobody else getting to hear me sing it, give me a pause.

Well, one way or another the deacon showed me where I would come out ahead on any deal he had proposed so far. Didn't I give you five hundred dollars? he asked. What white man—and don't even need to mention colored—would give you more? We buy up all your records of that particular song: first, you git royalties. Let me ask you, how much you sell that song for in the first place? Fifty dollars? A hundred, I say. And no royalties from it yet, right? Right. Well, when we buy up all of them records you gonna git royalties. And that's gonna make all them race record shops sit up and take notice of Gracie Mae Still. And they gonna push all them other records of yourn they got. And you no doubt will become one of the big name colored recording artists. And then we can offer you another five hundred dollars for letting us do all this for you. And by God you'll be sittin' pretty! You can go out and buy you the kind of outfit a star should have. Plenty sequins and yards of red satin.

I had done unlocked the screen when I saw I could get some more money out of him. Now I held it wide open while he squeezed through the opening between me and the door. He whipped out another piece of paper and I signed it.

He sort of trotted out to the car and slid in beside Traynor, whose head was back against the seat. They swung around in a u-turn in front of the house and then they was gone.

J. T. was putting his shirt on when I got back to the bedroom. Yankees beat the Orioles 10–6, he said. I believe I'll drive out to Paschal's pond and go fishing. Wanta go?

While I was putting on my pants J. T. was holding the two checks. I'm real proud of a woman that can make cash money without leavin' home, he said. And I said *Umph*. Because we met on the road with me singing in first one little low-life jook after another, making ten dollars a night for myself if I was lucky, and sometimes bringin' home nothing but my life. And J. T. just loved them times. The way I was fast and flashy and always on the go from one town to another. He loved the way my singin' made the dirt farmers cry like babies and the womens shout Honey, hush! But that's mens. They loves any style to which you can get 'em accustomed.

1956

My little grandbaby called me one night on the phone: Little Mama, Little Mama, there's a white man on the television singing one of your songs! Turn on channel 5.

Lord, if it wasn't Traynor. Still looking half asleep from the neck up, but kind of awake in a nasty way from the waist down. He wasn't doing too bad with my song either, but it wasn't just the song the people in the audience was screeching and screaming over, it was that nasty little jerk he was doing from the waist down.

Well, Lord have mercy, I said, listening to him. If I'da closed my eyes, it could have been me. He had followed every turning of my voice, side streets, avenues, red lights, train crossings and all. It give me a chill.

Everywhere I went I heard Traynor singing my song, and all the little white girls just eating it up. I never had so many ponytails switched across my line of vision in my life. They was so *proud*. He was a *genius*.

Well, all that year I was trying to lose weight anyway and that and high blood pressure and sugar kept me pretty well occupied. Traynor had made a smash from a song of mine, I still had seven hundred dollars of the original one thousand dollars in the bank, and I felt if I could just bring my weight down, life would be sweet.

1957

I lost ten pounds in 1956. That's what I give myself for Christmas. And J. T. and me and the children and their friends and grandkids of all description had just finished dinner—over which I had put on nine and a half of my lost ten—when who would appear at the front door but Traynor. Little Mama, Little Mama! It's that white man who sings —— ——. The children didn't call it my song anymore. Nobody did. It was funny how that happened. Traynor and the deacon had bought up all my records, true, but on his record he had put "written by Gracie Mae Still." But that was just another name on the label, like "produced by Apex Records."

On the TV he was inclined to dress like the deacon told him. But now he looked presentable.

Merry Christmas, said he.

And same to you, Son.

I don't know why I called him Son. Well, one way or another they're all our sons. The only requirement is that they be younger than us. But then again, Traynor seemed to be aging by the minute.

You looks tired, I said. Come on in and have a glass of Christmas cheer.

J. T. ain't never in his life been able to act decent to a white man he wasn't working for, but he poured Traynor a glass of bourbon and water, then he took all the children and grandkids and friends and whatnot out to the den. After while I heard Traynor's voice singing the song, coming from the stereo console. It was just the kind of Christmas present my kids would consider cute.

I looked at Traynor, complicit. But he looked like it was the last thing in the world he wanted to hear. His head was pitched forward over his lap, his hands holding his glass and his elbows on his knees.

I done sung that song seem like a million times this year, he said. I sung it on the Grand Ole Opry, I sung it on the Ed Sullivan show. I

sung it on Mike Douglas, I sung it at the Cotton Bowl, the Orange
Bowl. I sung it at Festivals. I sung it at Fairs. I sung it overseas in
Rome, Italy, and once in a submarine *underseas*. I've sung it and sung
it, and I'm making forty thousand dollars a day offa it, and you know
what, I don't have the faintest notion what that song means.

Whatchumean, what do it mean? It mean what it says. All I
could think was: These suckers is making forty thousand a *day* offa
my song and now they gonna come back and try to swindle me out
of the original thousand.

It's just a song, I said. Cagey. When you fool around with a lot
of no count mens you sing a bunch of 'em. I shrugged.

Oh, he said. Well. He started brightening up. I just come by to
tell you I think you are a great singer.

He didn't blush, saying that. Just said it straight out.

And I brought you a little Christmas present too. Now you take
this little box and you hold it until I drive off. Then you take it outside under that first streetlight back up the street aways in front of
that green house. Then you open the box and see . . . Well, just *see*.

What had come over this boy, I wondered, holding the box. I
looked out the window in time to see another white man come up
and get in the car with him and then two more cars full of white
mens start out behind him. They was all in long black cars that
looked like a funeral procession.

Little Mama, Little Mama, what it is? One of my grandkids come
running up and started pulling at the box. It was wrapped in gay
Christmas paper—the thick, rich kind that it's hard to picture folks
making just to throw away.

J. T. and the rest of the crowd followed me out the house, up the
street to the streetlight and in front of the green house. Nothing was
there but somebody's gold-grilled white Cadillac. Brandnew and most
distracting. We got to looking at it so till I almost forgot the little box in
my hand. While the others were busy making 'miration I carefully took
off the paper and ribbon and folded them up and put them in my pants
pocket. What should I see but a pair of genuine solid gold caddy keys.

Dangling the keys in front of everybody's nose, I unlocked the
caddy, motioned for J. T. to git in on the other side, and us didn't
come back home for two days.

1960
Well, the boy was sure nuff famous by now. He was still a mite shy of
twenty but already they was calling him the Emperor of Rock and Roll.

Then what should happen but the draft.

Well, says J. T. There goes all this Emperor of Rock and Roll
business.

But even in the army the womens was on him like white on rice.
We watched it on the News.

Dear Gracie Mae [he wrote from Germany],

How you? Fine I hope as this leaves me doing real well. Before I come in
the army I was gaining a lot of weight and gitting jittery from making all
them dumb movies. But now I exercise and eat right and get plenty of rest.
I'm more awake than I been in ten years.
I wonder if you are writing any more songs?

Sincerely,
Traynor

I wrote him back:

Dear Son,

We is all fine in the Lord's good grace and hope this finds you the same.
J. T. and me be out all times of the day and night in that car you give
me—which you know you didn't have to do. Oh, and I do appreciate the
mink and the new self-cleaning oven. But if you send anymore stuff to eat
from Germany I'm going to have to open up a store in the neighborhood
just to get rid of it. Really, we have more than enough of everything. The
Lord is good to us and we don't know Want.
Glad to here you is well and gitting your right rest. There ain't nothing
like exercising to help that along. J. T. and me work some part of every day
that we don't go fishing in the garden.
Well, so long Soldier.

Sincerely,
Gracie Mae

He wrote:

Dear Gracie Mae,

I hope you and J. T. like that automatic power tiller I had one of the
stores back home send you. I went through a mountain of catalogs looking
for it—I wanted something that even a woman could use.
I've been thinking about writing some songs of my own but every time I
finish one it don't seem to be about nothing I've actually lived myself. My
agent keeps sending me other people's songs but they just sound mooney. I
can hardly git through 'em without gagging.
Everybody still loves that song of yours. They ask me all the time what
do I think it means, really. I mean, they want to know just what I want to
know. Where out of your life did it come from?

Sincerely,
Traynor

1968

I didn't see the boy for seven years. No. Eight. Because just about everybody was dead when I saw him again. Malcolm X, King, the president and his brother, and even J. T. J. T. died of a head cold. It just settled in his head like a block of ice, he said, and nothing we did moved it until one day he just leaned out the bed and died.

His good friend Horace helped me put him away, and then about a year later Horace and me started going together. We was sitting out on the front porch swing one summer night, dusk-dark, and I saw this great procession of lights winding to a stop.

Holy Toledo! said Horace. (He's got a real sexy voice like Ray Charles.) Look *at* it. He meant the long line of flashy cars and the white men in white summer suits jumping out on the drivers' sides and standing at attention. With wings they could pass for angels, with hoods they could be the Klan.

Traynor comes waddling up the walk.

And suddenly I know what it is he could pass for. An Arab like the ones you see in storybooks. Plump and soft and with never a care about weight. Because with so much money, who cares? Traynor is almost dressed like someone from a storybook too. He has on, I swear, about ten necklaces. Two sets of bracelets on his arms, at least one ring on every finger, and some kind of shining buckles on his shoes, so that when he walks you get quite a few twinkling lights.

Gracie Mae, he says, coming up to give me a hug. J. T.

I explain that J. T. passed. That this is Horace.

Horace, he says, puzzled but polite, sort of rocking back on his heels, Horace.

That's it for Horace. He goes in the house and don't come back.

Looks like you and me is gained a few, I say.

He laughs. The first time I ever heard him laugh. It don't sound much like a laugh and I can't swear that it's better than no laugh a'tall.

He's gitting fat for sure, but he's still slim compared to me. I'll never see three hundred pounds again and I've just about said (excuse me) fuck it. I got to thinking about it one day an' I thought: aside from the fact that they say it's unhealthy, my fat ain't never been no trouble. Mens always have loved me. My kids ain't never complained. Plus they's fat. And fat like I is I looks distinguished. You see me coming and know somebody's *there*.

Gracie Mae, he says, I've come with a personal invitation to you to my house tomorrow for dinner. He laughed. What did it sound like? I couldn't place it. See them men out there? he asked me. I'm sick and tired of eating with them. They don't never have nothing to

talk about. That's why I eat so much. But if you come to dinner tomorrow we can talk about the old days. You can tell me about that
farm I bought you.

I sold it, I said.

You did?

Yeah, I said, I did. Just cause I said I liked to exercise by working
in a garden didn't mean I wanted five hundred acres! Anyhow, I'm a
city girl now. Raised in the country it's true. Dirt poor—the whole
bit—but that's all behind me now.

Oh well, he said, I didn't mean to offend you.

We sat a few minutes listening to the crickets.

Then he said: You wrote that song while you was still on the
farm, didn't you, or was it right after you left?

You had somebody spying on me? I asked.

You and Bessie Smith got into a fight over it once, he said.

You *is* been spying on me!

But I don't know what the fight was about, he said. Just like I
don't know what happened to your second husband. Your first one
died in the Texas electric chair. Did you know that? Your third one
beat you up, stole your touring costumes and your car and retired
with a chorine to Tuskegee. He laughed. He's still there.

I had been mad, but suddenly I calmed down. Traynor was talking very dreamily. It was dark but seems like I could tell his eyes
weren't right. It was like *something* was sitting there talking to me
but not necessarily with a person behind it.

You gave up on marrying and seem happier for it. He laughed
again. I married but it never went like it was supposed to. I never
could squeeze any of my own life either into it or out of it. It was
like singing somebody else's record. I copied the way it was sposed
to be *exactly* but I never had a clue what marriage meant.

I bought her a diamond ring big as your fist. I bought her
clothes. I built her a mansion. But right away she didn't want the
boys to stay there. Said they smoked up the bottom floor. Hell, there
were *five* floors.

No need to grieve, I said. No need to. Plenty more where she
come from.

He perked up. That's part of what that song means, ain't it? No
need to grieve. Whatever it is, there's plenty more down the line.

I never really believed that way back when I wrote that song, I
said. It was all bluffing then. The trick is to live long enough to put
your young bluffs to use. Now if I was to sing that song today I'd
tear it up. 'Cause I done lived long enough to know it's *true*. Them
words could hold me up.

I ain't lived that long, he said.

Look like you on your way, I said. I don't know why, but the
boy seemed to need some encouraging. And I don't know, seem like
one way or another you talk to rich white folks and you end up reassuring *them*. But what the hell, by now I feel something for the
boy. I wouldn't be in his bed all alone in the middle of the night for
nothing. Couldn't be nothing worse than being famous the world
over for something you don't even understand. That's what I tried to
tell Bessie. She wanted that same song. Overheard me practicing it
one day, said, with her hands on her hips: Gracie Mae, I'ma sing
your song tonight. I *likes* it.

Your lips be too swole to sing, I said. She was mean and she was
strong, but I trounced her.

Ain't you famous enough with your own stuff? I said. Leave mine
alone. Later on, she thanked me. By then she was Miss Bessie Smith to
the World, and I was still Miss Gracie Mae Nobody from Notasulga.

The next day all these limousines arrived to pick me up. Five cars
and twelve bodyguards. Horace picked that morning to start painting
the kitchen.

Don't paint the kitchen, fool, I said. The only reason that dumb
boy of ours is going to show me his mansion is because he intends
to present us with a new house.

What you gonna do with it? he asked me, standing there in his
shirtsleeves stirring the paint.

Sell it. Give it to the children. Live in it on weekends. It don't
matter what I do. He sure don't care.

Horace just stood there shaking his head. Mama you sure looks
good, he says. Wake me up when you git back.

Fool, I say, and pat my wig in front of the mirror.

The boy's house is something else. First you come to this mountain,
and then you commence to drive and drive up this road that's lined
with magnolias. Do magnolias grow on mountains? I was wondering.
And you come to lakes and you come to ponds and you come to
deer and you come up on some sheep. And I figure these two is
sposed to represent England and Wales. Or something out of Europe. And you just keep on coming to stuff. And it's all pretty. Only
the man driving my car don't look at nothing but the road. Fool.
And then *finally*, after all this time, you begin to go up the driveway.
And there's more magnolias—only they're not in such good shape.
It's sort of cool up this high and I don't think they're gonna make it.
And then I see this building that looks like if it had a name it would
be The Tara Hotel. Columns and steps and outdoor chandeliers and
rocking chairs. Rocking chairs? Well, and there's the boy on the

steps dressed in a dark green satin jacket like you see folks wearing
on TV late at night, and he looks sort of like a fat dracula with all
that house rising behind him, and standing beside him there's this
little white vision of loveliness that he introduces as his wife.

He's nervous when he introduces us and he says to her: This is
Gracie Mae Still, I want you to know me. I mean . . . and she gives
him a look that would fry meat.

Won't you come in, Gracie Mae, she says, and that's the last I see
of her.

He fishes around for something to say or do and decides to escort me to the kitchen. We go through the entry and the parlor and
the breakfast room and the dining room and the servants' passage
and finally get there. The first thing I notice is that, altogether, there
are five stoves. He looks about to introduce me to one.

Wait a minute, I say. Kitchens don't do nothing for me. Let's go
sit on the front porch.

Well, we hike back and we sit in the rocking chairs rocking until
dinner.

Gracie Mae, he says down the table, taking a piece of fried chicken
from the woman standing over him, I got a little surprise for you.

It's a house, ain't it? I ask, spearing a chitlin.

You're getting *spoiled*, he says. And the way he says *spoiled*
sounds funny. He slurs it. It sounds like his tongue is too thick for
his mouth. Just that quick he's finished the chicken and is now eating chitlins *and* a pork chop. *Me* spoiled, I'm thinking.

I already got a house. Horace is right this minute painting the
kitchen. I bought that house. My kids feel comfortable in that house.

But this one I bought you is just like mine. Only a little smaller.

I still don't need no house. And anyway who would clean it?

He looks surprised.

Really, I think, some peoples advance *so* slowly.

I hadn't thought of that. But what the hell, I'll get you somebody
to live in.

I don't want other folks living 'round me. Makes me nervous.

You *don't?* It *do?*

What I want to wake up and see folks I don't even know for?

He just sits there downtable staring at me. Some of that feeling is
in the song, ain't it? Not the words, the *feeling*. What I want to wake
up and see folks I don't even know for? But I see twenty folks a day
I don't even know, including my wife.

This food wouldn't be bad to wake up to though, I said. The boy
had found the genius of corn bread.

He looked at me real hard. He laughed. Short. They want what

you got but they don't want you. They want what I got only it ain't
mine. That's what makes 'em so hungry for me when I sing. They
getting the flavor of something but they ain't getting the thing itself.
They like a pack of hound dogs trying to gobble up a scent.

You talking 'bout your fans?

Right. Right. He says.

Don't worry 'bout your fans, I say. They don't know their asses
from a hole in the ground. I doubt there's a honest one in the
bunch.

That's the point. Dammit, that's the point! He hits the table
with his fist. It's so solid it don't even quiver. You need a honest
audience! You can't have folks that's just gonna lie right back
to you.

Yeah, I say, it was small compared to yours, but I had one. It
would have been worth my life to try to sing 'em somebody else's
stuff that I didn't know nothing about.

He must have pressed a buzzer under the table. One of his
flunkies zombies up.

Git Johnny Carson, he says.

On the phone? asks the zombie.

On the phone, says Traynor, what you think I mean, git him offa
the front porch? Move your ass.

So two weeks later we's on the Johnny Carson show.

Traynor is all corseted down nice and looks a little bit fat but mostly
good. And all the women that grew up on him and my song squeal
and squeal. Traynor says: The lady who wrote my first hit record is
here with us tonight, and she's agreed to sing it for all of us, just
like she sung it forty-five years ago. Ladies and Gentlemen, the great
Gracie Mae Still!

Well, I had tried to lose a couple of pounds my own self, but
failing that I had me a very big dress made. So I sort of rolls over
next to Traynor, who is dwarfted by me, so that when he puts his
arm around back of me to try to hug me it looks funny to the audience and they laugh.

I can see this pisses him off. But I smile out there at 'em. Imagine squealing for twenty years and not knowing why you're squealing? No more sense of endings and beginnings than hogs.

It don't matter, Son, I say. Don't fret none over me.

I commence to sing. And I sound—wonderful. Being able to sing
good ain't all about having a good singing voice a'tall. A good singing voice helps. But when you come up in the Hard Shell Baptist
church like I did you understand early that the fellow that sings is

the singer. Them that waits for programs and arrangements and letters from home is just good voices occupying body space.

So there I am singing my own song, my own way. And I give it
all I got and enjoy every minute of it. When I finish Traynor is
standing up clapping and clapping and beaming at first me and then
the audience like I'm his mama for true. The audience claps politely
for about two seconds.

Traynor looks disgusted.

He comes over and tries to hug me again. The audience laughs.

Johnny Carson looks at us like we both weird.

Traynor is mad as hell. He's supposed to sing something called a
love ballad. But instead he takes the mike, turns to me and says:
Now see if my imitation still holds up. He goes into the same song,
our song, I think, looking out at his flaky audience. And he sings it
just the way he always did. My voice, my tone, my inflection, everything. But he forgets a couple of lines. Even before he's finished the
matronly squeals begin.

He sits down next to me looking whipped.

It don't matter, Son, I say, patting his hand. You don't even know
those people. Try to make the people you know happy.

Is that in the song? he asks.

Maybe, I say.

1977

For a few years I hear from him, then nothing. But trying to lose
weight takes all the attention I got to spare. I finally faced up to the
fact that my fat is the hurt I don't admit, not even to myself, and that I
been trying to bury it from the day I was born. But also when you git
real old, to tell the truth, it ain't as pleasant. It gits lumpy and slack.
Yuck. So one day I said to Horace, I'ma git this shit offa me.

And he fell in with the program like he always try to do and
Lord such a procession of salads and cottage cheese and fruit juice!

One night I dreamed Traynor had split up with his fifteenth wife.
He said: *You meet 'em for no reason. You date 'em for no reason. You
marry 'em for no reason. I do it all but I swear it's just like somebody
else doing it. I feel like I can't remember Life.*

The boy's in trouble, I said to Horace.

You've always said that, he said.

I have?

Yeah. You always said he looked asleep. You can't sleep through
life if you wants to live it.

You not such a fool after all, I said, pushing myself up with my
cane and hobbling over to where he was. Let me sit down on your
lap, I said, while this salad I ate takes effect.

In the morning we heard Traynor was dead. Some said fat, some said heart, some said alcohol, some said drugs. One of the children called from Detroit. Them dumb fans of his is on a crying rampage, she said. You just ought to turn on the t.v.

But I didn't want to see 'em. They was crying and crying and didn't even know what they was crying for. One day this is going to be a pitiful country, I thought.

Houston Baker, Jr.

(1943–   )

A NOTABLE SCHOLAR-CRITIC in the "new school" of African American literati, Houston A. Baker, Jr., was born in Louisville, Kentucky, in 1943, but spent most of his growing-up years in Washington, D.C. He earned a B.A. degree at Howard University in 1965, an M.A. from the University of California, Los Angeles in 1966. After another year of doctoral study at the University of Edinburgh, he entered Yale, earned a Ph.D., and began his increasingly distinguished career as teacher, scholar, and critic.

He was instructor at Howard University in 1966, and from 1966 to 1968 was an instructor at Yale University. From 1970 to 1974 he taught at the University of Virginia, where he moved up the ranks to professor in four years. In 1974 he was named director of Afro-American Studies at the University of Pennsylvania, and in 1981 he withdrew from the directorship to accept the Albert M. Greenfield Professorship in Human Relations at the same institution.

Since the early 1970s, Professor Baker has been an amazingly prolific scholar. His articles have appeared in *Black American Literature Forum*, *PMLA*, *Critical Inquiry*, and many other journals. He has edited *Black Literature in America* (1971), *Reading Black: Essays in the Criticism of African, Caribbean, and Black American Literature* (1976), *Three American Literatures: Essays in Chicano, Native American, and Asian American Literature* (1976), *A Dark and Sudden Beauty: Two Essays in Black American Poetry* (1977), and a fairly recent edition of *The Narrative of the Life of Frederick Douglass* (1982). He is also the author of five books of criticism: *The Journey Back: Issues in Black Literature and Criticism* (1980), *Singers of Daybreak: Studies in Black American Literature* (1983), *Blues, Ideology, and Afro-American Literature: A Vernacular Theory* (1984), *Modernism and the Harlem Renaissance* (1987), and *Afro-American Poetics: Revision of Harlem and the Black Aesthetic* (1988). Along with Patricia Redmond, Baker is co-editor of *Afro-American Literary Study in the 1990s* (1989). In addition to these scholarly publications, Baker is the author of a collection of poetry entitled *No Matter Where You Travel, You Still Be Black* (1979).

His honors and awards include a Guggenheim Fellowship, the Lindback Teaching Award from the University of Pennsylvania, and grants of $400,000 from the William Penn Foundation and $200,000 from the Rockefeller Foundation to open a national center at the University of Pennsylvania for research on the teaching of black literature.

For further reading, see Linda Metzger, ed., *Black Writers: A Selection of Sketches from Contemporary Authors* (1989).

The selection that follows is the introduction to *Blues, Ideology, and Afro-American Literature*.

FROM **BLUES, IDEOLOGY, AND AFRO-AMERICAN LITERATURE**
A Vernacular Theory

> *Standing at the crossroads, tried to flag a ride,*
> *Standing at the crossroads, tried to flag a ride,*
> *Ain't nobody seem to know me, everybody passed me by.*
> Crossroad Blues

> *In every case the result of an untrue mode of knowledge must not be allowed to run away into an empty nothing, but must necessarily be grasped as the nothing of that from which it results—a result which contains what was true in the preceding knowledge.*
> Hegel, Phenomenology of Spirit

> *So perhaps we shy from confronting our cultural wholeness because it offers no easily recognizable points of rest, no facile certainties as to who, what, or where (culturally or historically) we are. Instead, the whole is always in cacophonic motion.*
> Ralph Ellison, "The Little Man at the Chehaw Station"

> *. . . maybe one day, you'll find they actually do understand exactly what you are talking about, all these fantasy people. All these blues people.*
> Amiri Baraka, Dutchman

From Symbol to Ideology

In my book *The Journey Back: Issues in Black Literature and Criticism* (1980),[1] I envisioned the "speaking subject" creating language (a code) to be deciphered by the present-day commentator. In my current study, I envision language (the code) "speaking" the subject. The subject is "decentered." My quest during the past decade has been for the distinctive, the culturally specific aspects of Afro-American literature and culture. I was convinced that I had found

---

From Blues, Ideology and Afro-American Literature, A Vernacular Theory by Houston A. Baker, Jr., published by the University of Chicago Press. Copyright © 1984 by The University of Chicago.
[1]Chicago: University of Chicago Press, 1980.

such specificity in a peculiar subjectivity, but the objectivity of economics and the sound lessons of poststructuralism arose to reorient
my thinking. I was also convinced that the symbolic, and quite specifically the symbolically anthropological, offered avenues to the
comprehension of Afro-American expressive culture in its plenitude.[2]
I discovered that the symbolic's antithesis—practical reason, or the
material—is as necessary for understanding Afro-American discourse
as the cultural-in-itself.

My shift from a centered to a decentered subject, from an exclusively symbolic to a more inclusively expressive perspective, was
prompted by the curious force of dialectical thought. My access to
the study of such thought came from attentive readings of Fredric
Jameson, Hayden White, Marshall Sahlins, and others. While profit-
ing from observations by these scholars, I also began to attend meetings of a study group devoted to Hegel's *Phenomenology of Spirit.*

Having journeyed with the aid of symbolic anthropology to what
appeared to be the soundest possible observations on Afro-American
art, I found myself confronted suddenly by a figure-to-ground reversal. A fitting image for the effect of my reorientation is the gestalt
illustration of the Greek hydria (a water vase with curved handles)
that transforms itself into two faces in profile. John Keats's "Ode on
a Grecian Urn," with its familiar detailing of the economies of "art"
and human emotion, can be considered one moment in the shift.
Contrasting with Keats's romantic figurations are the emergent faces
of a venerable ancestry. The shift from Greek hydrias to ancestral
faces is a shift from high art to vernacular expression.

The "vernacular" in relation to human beings signals "a slave
born on his master's estate." In expressive terms, vernacular indicates
"arts native or peculiar to a particular country or locale." The material conditions of slavery in the United States and the rhythms of
Afro-American blues combined and emerged from my revised materialistic perspective as an ancestral matrix that has produced a forceful and indigenous American creativity. The moment of emergence
of economic and vernacular concerns left me, as the French say,
entre les deux: suspended somewhere between symbolic anthropology

---

[2]Though a great many sources were involved in my reoriented cultural thinking, certainly
the terminology employed in my discussion at this point derives from Marshall Sahlins's
wonderfully lucid *Culture and Practical Reason* (Chicago: University of Chicago Press, 1976).
Sahlins delineates two modes of thinking that have characterized anthropology from its
inception. These two poles are "symbolic" and "functionalist." He resolves the dichotomy
suggested by these terms through the middle term "cultural proposition," a phrase that he
defines as a cultural mediating ground where the material and symbolic, the useful and the
ineffable, ceaselessly converge and depart.

and analytical strategies that Fredric Jameson calls the "ideology of form."[3]

Ideology, Semiotics, and the Material

In acknowledging a concern for the ideology of form, however, I do not want to imply that my symbolic-anthropological orientation was untrue, in the sense of deluded or deceived.[4] This symbolic orientation was simply one moment in my experiencing of Afro-American culture—a moment superseded now by a prospect that constitutes its determinate negation.[5] What was true in my prior framework remains so in my current concern for the ideology of form. Certainly the mode of ideological investigation proposed by Jameson is an analysis that escapes all hints of "vulgar Marxism" through its studious attention to modern critiques of political economy, and also through its shrewd incorporation of poststructuralist thought.[6]

In chapters that follow, I too attempt to avoid a naive Marxism. I do not believe, for example, that a fruitful correlation exists when one merely claims that certain black folk seculars are determinate re-

---

[3]The "ideology of form" as a description of Jameson's project derives form the essay "The Symbolic Inference; or, Kenneth Burke and Ideological Analysis," *Critical Inquiry* 4 (1978): 507–23. Surely, though, Jameson's most recent study, *The Political Unconscious: Narrative as a Socially Symbolic Act* (Ithaca, N.Y.: Cornell University Press, 1981), offers the fullest description of his views on ways in which cultural texts formally inscribe material/historical conditions of their production, distribution, and consumption.

[4]In *The Journey Back*, I define my project as follows: "The phrase ['the anthropology of art'] expresses for me the notion that art must be studied with an attention to the methods and findings of disciplines which enable one to address such concerns as the status of the artistic object, the relationship of art to other cultural systems, and the nature and function of artistic creation and perception in a given society" (p. xvi). The project's privileging of "symbolic anthropology" and "art" under the sign *interdisciplinary* involved exclusions that were ironical and (I now realize) somewhat disabling where a full description of expressive culture is sought.

[5]The Hegelian epigraph that marks the beginning of these introductory remarks offers the best definition I know of "determinate negation." The epigraph is taken from the *Phenomenology of Spirit*.

[6]I have in mind Louis Althusser and Étienne Balibar, *Reading Capital* (London: New Left Books, 1977), and Jean Baudrillard's *For a Critique of the Political Economy of the Sign* (1972; St. Louis: Telos Press, 1981) and *The Mirror of Production* (1973; St. Louis: Telos Press, 1975). By "poststructuralist" thought, I have in mind the universe of discourse constituted by *deconstruction*. Jacques Derrida's *Of Grammatology* (1967; Baltimore: Johns Hopkins University Press, 1976) is perhaps the locus classicus of the deconstructionist project. One of the more helpful accounts of deconstruction is Christopher Norris's *Deconstruction: Theory and Practice* (London: Methuen, 1982). Of course, there is a certain collapsing of poststructuralism and political economy in the sources cited previously.

sults of agricultural gang labor. Such attributions simply privilege the material as a substrate while failing to provide detailed accounts of processes leading from an apparent substrate to a peculiar expressive form. A faith of enormous magnitude is required to accept such crude formulations as adequate explanations. The "material" is shifty ground, and current critiques of political economy suggest that postulates based on this ground can be understood only in "semiotic" terms. Hence, the employment of ideology as an analytical category begins with the awareness that "production" as well as "modes of production" must be grasped in terms of the sign. An example of a persuasive case for "political economy" as a code existing in a relationship of identity with language can be found in Jean Baudrillard's *For a Critique of the Political Economy of the Sign.*[7] To read economics as a semiotic process leads to the realization that ideological analyses may be as decidedly intertextual as, say, analyses of the relationship between Afro-American vernacular expression and more sophisticated forms of verbal art. If what is normally categorized as *material* (e.g., "raw material," "consumer goods") can be interpreted semiotically, then any collection of such entities and their defining interrelationships may be defined as a *text.*[8]

In the chapters in this book, however, I do not write about or interpret the *material* in exclusively semiotic terms. Although I am fully aware of insights to be gained from semiotics, my analyses focus directly on the living and laboring conditions of people designated as "the desperate class" by James Weldon Johnson's narrator in *The Autobiography of an Ex-Colored Man.* Such people constitute the vernacular in the United States. Their lives have always been sharply conditioned by an "economics of slavery" as they worked the agricultural rows, searing furnaces, rolling levees, bustling roundhouses, and piney-woods logging camps of America. A sense of "production" and "modes of production" that foregrounds such Afro-American labor seems an appropriate inscription of the material.

The Matrix as Blues

The guiding presupposition of the chapters that follow is that Afro-American culture is a complex, reflexive enterprise which finds its proper figuration in blues conceived as a matrix. A matrix is a womb, a network, a fossil-bearing rock, a rocky trace of a gemstone's removal, a principal metal in an alloy, a mat or plate for reproducing

---

[7]For a full citation of Baudrillard, see note 6.
[8]*Ibid.*

print or phonograph records. The matrix is a point of ceaseless input and output, a web of intersecting, crisscrossing impulses always in productive transit. Afro-American blues constitute such a vibrant network. They are what Jacques Derrida might describe as the "always already" of Afro-American culture.[9] They are the multiplex, enabling *script* in which Afro-American cultural discourse is inscribed.

First arranged, scored, and published for commercial distribution early in the twentieth century when Hart Wand, Arthur "Baby" Seals, and W. C. Handy released their first compositions, the blues defy narrow definition. For they exist, not as a function of formal inscription, but as a forceful condition of Afro-American inscription itself. They were for Handy a "found" folk signifier, awakening him from (perhaps) a dream of American form in Tutwiler, Mississippi, in 1903.[10] At a railroad juncture deep in the southern night, Handy dozed restlessly as he waited the arrival of a much-delayed train. A guitar's bottleneck resonance suddenly jolted him to consciousness, as a lean, loose-jointed, shabbily clad black man sang:

> Goin' where the Southern cross the Dog.
> Goin' where the Southern cross the Dog.
> Goin' where the Southern cross the Dog.

This haunting invocation of railroad crossings in bottleneck tones left Handy stupified and inspired. In 1914, he published his own Yellow Dog Blues.

But the autobiographical account of the man who has been called the "Father of the Blues" offers only a simplistic detailing of *a progress*, describing, as it were, the elevation of a "primitive" folk ditty to the status of "art" in America. Handy's rendering leaves unexamined, therefore, myriad corridors, mainroads, and way-stations of an extraordinary and elusive Afro-American cultural phenomenon.

---

[9]In *Of Grammatology*, Derrida defines a problematic in which *writing*, conceived as an iterable *differe(a)nce*, is held to be *always already* instituted (or, in motion) when a traditionally designated *Man* begins to speak. Hence, *script* is anterior to speech, and absence and *differe(a)nce* displace presence and identity (conceived as "Intention") in philosophical discourse.

[10]The story appears in W. C. Handy, *Father of the Blues*, ed. Arna Bontemps (New York: Macmillan Co., 1941), p. 78. Other defining sources of blues include: Paul Oliver, *The Story of the Blues* (London: Chilton, 1969); Samuel B. Charters, *The Country Blues* (New York: Rinehart, 1959); Giles Oakley, *The Devil's Music: A History of the Country Blues* (New York: Harcourt Brace Jovanovich, 1976); Amiri Baraka, *Blues People: Negro Music in White America* (New York: William E. Morrow, 1963); Albert Murray, *Stomping the Blues* (New York: McGraw-Hill Book Co., 1976); and William Ferris, *Blues from the Delta* (New York: Anchor Books, 1979).

Defining Blues

The task of adequately describing the blues is equivalent to the labor of describing a world class athlete's awesome gymnastics. Adequate appreciation demands comprehensive attention. An investigator has to *be* there, to follow a course recommended by one of the African writer Wole Soyinka's ironic narrators to a London landlord: "See for yourself." The elaborations of the blues may begin in an austere self-accusation: "Now this trouble I'm having, I brought it all on myself." But the accusation seamlessly fades into humorous acknowledgment of duplicity's always duplicitous triumph: "You know the woman that I love, I stoled her from my best friend, / But you know that fool done got lucky and stole her back again." Simple provisos for the troubled mind are commonplace, and drear exactions of crushing manual labor are objects of wry, *in situ* commentary. Numinous invocation punctuates a guitar's resonant back beat with: "Lawd, Lawd, Lawd . . . have mercy on me / Please send me someone, to end this misery." Existential declarations of lack combine with lustily macabre prophecies of the subject's demise. If a "matchbox" will hold his clothes, surely the roadside of much-traveled highways will be his memorial plot: "You can bury my body down by the highway side / So my old devil spirit can catch a Greyhound bus and ride." Conative formulations of a brighter future (sun shining in the back door some day, wind rising to blow the blues away) join with a slow-moving *askesis* of present, amorous imprisonment: "You leavin' now, baby, but you hangin' crepe on my door," or "She got a mortgage on my body, and a lien on my soul." Self-deprecating confession and slack-strumming growls of violent solutions combine: "My lead mule's cripple, you know my off mule's blind / You know I can't drive nobody / Bring me a loaded .39 (I'm go'n pop him, pop that mule!)." The wish for a river of whiskey where if a man were a "divin' duck" he would submerge himself and never "come up" is a function of a world in which "when you lose yo' eyesight, yo' best friend's gone / Sometimes yo' own dear people don't want to fool with you long."

Like a streamlined athlete's awesomely dazzling explosions of prowess, the blues song erupts, creating a veritable playful festival of meaning. Rather than a rigidly personalized form, the blues offer a phylogenetic recapitulation—a nonlinear, freely associative, nonsequential meditation—of species experience. What emerges is not a filled subject, but an anonymous (nameless) voice issuing from the black (w)hole.[11] The blues singer's signatory coda is always *atopic*,

---

[11] The description at this point is coextensive with the "decentering" of the subject mentioned at the outset of my introduction. What I wish to effect by noting a "subject"

placeless: "If anybody ask you who sang this song / Tell 'em X done been here and gone." The "signature" is a space already "X"(ed), a trace of the already "gone"—a fissure rejoined. Nevertheless, the "you" (audience) addressed is always free to invoke the X(ed) spot in the body's absence.[12] For the signature comprises a scripted authentication of "your" feelings. Its mark is an invitation to energizing intersubjectivity. Its implied (in)junction reads: Here is my body meant for (a phylogenetically conceived) you.

The blues are a synthesis (albeit one always synthesizing rather than one already hypostatized). Combining work songs, group seculars, field hollers, sacred harmonies, proverbial wisdom, folk philosophy, political commentary, ribald humor, elegiac lament, and much more, they constitute an amalgam that seems always to have been in motion in America—always becoming, shaping, transforming, displacing the peculiar experiences of Africans in the New World.

Blues as Code and Force

One way of describing the blues is to claim their amalgam as a code radically conditioning Afro-America's cultural signifying. Such a description implies a prospect in which any aspect of the blues— a guitar's growling vamp or a stanza's sardonic boast of heroically back-breaking labor—"stands," in Umberto Eco's words, "for something else" in virtue of a systematic set of conventional procedures.[13] The materiality of any blues manifestation, such as a guitar's walking bass or a French harp's "whoop" of motion seen, is, one might say, enciphered in ways that enable the material to escape into a named or coded, blues signification. The material, thus, slips into irreversible difference. And as phenomena named and set in meaningful re-

who is not *filled* is a displacement of the notion that knowledge, or "art," or "song," are manifestations of an ever more clearly defined individual consciousness of *Man*. In accord with Michel Foucault's explorations in his *Archaeology of Knowledge* (1969; New York: Harper & Row, 1972), I want to claim that blues is like a discourse that comprises the "already said" of Afro-America. Blues' governing statements and sites are thus vastly more interesting in the process of cultural investigation than either a history of ideas or a history of individual, subjective consciousness vis-à-vis blues. When I move to the "X" of the trace and the body as host, I am invoking Mark Taylor's formulations in a suggestive deconstructive essay toward radical christology called "The Text as Victim," in *Deconstruction and Theology* (New York: Crossroad, 1982), pp. 58–78.

[12]The terms used in "The Text as Victim," *ibid.*, are "host" and "parasite." The words of the blues are hostlike in the sense of a christological Logos-as-Host. But without the dialogical action of the parasite, of course, there could be no Host. Host is, thus, parasitic on a parasite's citation. Both, in Taylor's statement of the matter, are *para-sites*.

[13]The definition of "code" is drawn from *A Theory of Semiotics* (Bloomington: Indiana University Press, 1976). All references to Eco refer to this work and are hereafter marked by page numbers in parentheses.

lation by a blues code, both the harmonica's whoop and the guitar's bass can recapitulate vast dimensions of experience. For such discrete blues instances are always intertextually related by the blues code as a whole. Moreover, they are involved in the code's manifold interconnections with other codes of Afro-American culture.

A further characterization of blues suggests that they are equivalent to Hegelian "force."[14] In the *Phenomenology*, Hegel speaks of a flux in which there is "only *difference* as a *universal* difference, or as a difference into which the many antitheses have been resolved. This difference, as a *universal* difference, is consequently the *simple element in the play of Force itself* and what is true in it. It is the *law of Force*" (p. 90). Force is thus defined as a relational matrix where *difference* is the law. Finally the blues, employed as an image for the investigation of culture, represents a *force* not unlike electricity. Hegel writes:

> Of course, given *positive* electricity, negative too is given *in principle*; for the positive *is*, only as related to a negative, or, the positive is *in its own self* the difference from itself; and similarly with the negative. But that electricity as such should divide itself in this way is not in itself a necessity. Electricity, as *simple Force*, is indifferent to its law—*to be* positive and negative; and if we call the former its *Notion* but the latter its being, then its Notion is indifferent to its being. It merely *has* this property, which just means that this property is not *in itself* necessary to it. . . . It is only with law as law that we are to compare its *Notion* as Notion, or its necessity. But in all these forms, necessity has shown itself to be only an empty word. [P. 93]

Metaphorically extending Hegel's formulation vis-à-vis electricity, one might say that a traditional property of cultural study may well be the kind of dichotomy inscribed in terms like "culture" and "practical reason." But even if such dichotomies are raised to the status of law, they never constitute the necessity or "determinant instances" of cultural study and explanation conceived in terms of *force*—envisioned, that is, in the analytic notion of a blues matrix as force. The blues, therefore, comprise a mediational site where familiar antinomies are resolved (or dissolved) in the office of adequate cultural understanding.

---

[14]*The Phenomenology of Spirit*, trans. A. V. Miller (New York: Oxford University Press, 1977). While it is true that the material dimensions of the dialectic are of primary importance to my current study, it is also true that the locus classicus of the dialectic, in and for itself, is the *Phenomenology*. Marx may well have stood Hegel on his feet through a materialist inversion of the *Phenomenology*, but subsequent generations have always looked at that uprighted figure—Hegel himself—as an authentic host.

Blues Translation at the Junction

To suggest a trope for the blues as a forceful matrix in cultural understanding is to summon an image of the black blues singer at the railway junction lustily transforming experiences of a durative (unceasingly oppressive) landscape into the energies of rhythmic song. The railway juncture is marked by transience. Its inhabitants are always travelers—a multifarious assembly in transit. The "X" of crossing roadbeds signals the multidirectionality of the juncture and is simply a single instance in a boundless network that redoubles and circles, makes sidings and ladders, forms Y's and branches over the vastness of hundreds of thousands of American miles. Polymorphous and multidirectional, scene of arrivals and departures, place betwixt and between (ever *entres les deux*), the juncture is the way-station of the blues.

The singer and his production are always at this intersection, this crossing, codifying force, providing resonance for experience's multiplicities. Singer and song never arrest transience—fix it in "transcedent form." Instead they provide expressive equivalence for the juncture's ceaseless flux. Hence, they may be conceived as translators.[15]

Like translators of written texts, blues and its sundry performers offer interpretations of the experiencing of experience. To experience the juncture's ever-changing scenes, like successive readings of ever-varying texts by conventional translators, is to produce vibrantly polyvalent interpretations encoded as blues. The singer's product, like the railway juncture itself (or a successful translator's original), constitutes a lively scene, a robust matrix, where endless antinomies are mediated and understanding and explanation find conditions of possibility.

The durative—transliterated as lyrical statements of injustice, despair, loss, absence, denial, and so forth—is complemented in blues performance by an instrumental energy (guitar, harmonica, fiddle, gut-bucket bass, molasses jug, washboard) that employs locomotive

---

[15]Having heard John Felstiner in a session at the 1982 Modern Language Association Convention present a masterful paper defining "translation" as a process of preserving "something of value" by keeping it in motion, I decided that the blues were apt translators of experience. Felstiner, it seemed to me, sought to demonstrate that *translation* was a process equivalent to gift-giving in Mauss's classic definition of that activity. The value of the gift of translation is never fixed because, say, the poem, is always in a transliterational motion, moving from one alphabet to another, always renewing and being *re-newed* in the process. Translation forestalls fixity. It calls attention always to the *translated's* excess—to its complex multivalence.

rhythms, train bells, and whistles as onomatopoeic references. In *A Theory of Semiotics*, Eco writes:

> Music presents, on the one hand, the problem of a semiotic system without a semantic level (or a content plane): on the other hand, however, there are musical "signs" (or syntagms) with an explicit denotative value (trumpet signals in the army) and there are syntagms or entire "texts" possessing pre-culturalized connotative value ("pastoral" or "thrilling" music, etc.). [P. 111]

The absence of a content plane noted by Eco implies what is commonly referred to as the "abstractness" of instrumental music. The "musical sign," on the other hand, suggests cultural signals that function onomatopoeically by calling to mind "natural" sounds or sounds "naturally" associated with common human situations. Surely, though, it would be a mistake to claim that onomatopoeia is in any sense "natural," for different cultures encode even the "same" natural sounds in varying ways. (A rooster onomatopoeically sounded in Puerto Rican Spanish is phonically unrecognizable in United States English, as a classic Puerto Rican short story makes hilariously clear.)

If onomatopoeia is taken as cultural mimesis, however, it is possible to apply the semiotician's observations to blues by pointing out that the dominant blues syntagm in America is an instrumental imitation of *train-wheels-over-track-junctures*. This sound is the "sign," as it were, of the blues, and it combines an intriguing melange of phonics: rattling gondolas, clattering flatbeds, quilling whistles, clanging bells, rumbling boxcars, and other railroad sounds. A blues text may thus announce itself by the onomatopoeia of the train's whistle sounded on the indrawn breath of a harmonica or a train's bell tinkled on the high keys of an upright piano. The blues stanzas may then roll through an extended meditative repertoire with a steady train-wheels-over-track-junctures guitar back beat as a traditional, syntagmatic complement. If desire and absence are driving conditions of blues performance, the amelioration of such conditions is implied by the onomatopoeic *training* of blues voice and instrument. Only a *trained* voice can sing the blues.[16]

At the junctures, the intersections of experience where roads cross and diverge, the blues singer and his performance serve as codifiers, absorbing and transforming discontinuous experience into formal expressive instances that bear only the trace of origins, refusing to be pinned down to any final, dualistic significance. Even as they

---

[16]One of the most inspiring and intriguing descriptions of the relationship between blues voice and sounds of the railroad is Albert Murray's lyrical exposition in *Stomping the Blues*.

speak of paralyzing absence and ineradicable desire, their instrumental rhythms suggest change, movement, action, continuance, unlimited and unending possibility. Like signification itself, blues are always nomadically wandering. Like the freight-hopping hobo, they are ever on the move, ceaselessly summing novel experience.

Antinomies and Blues Mediation

The blues performance is further suggestive if economic conditions of Afro-American existence are brought to mind. Standing at the juncture, or railhead, the singer draws into his repertoire hollers, cries, whoops, and moans of black men and women working in fields without recompense. The performance can be cryptically conceived, therefore, in terms suggested by the bluesman Booker White, who said, "The foundation of the blues is working behind a mule way back in slavery time."[17] As a force, the blues matrix defines itself as a network mediating poverty and abundance in much the same manner that it reconciles durative and kinetic. Many instances of the blues performance contain lyrical inscriptions of both lack and commercial possibility. The performance that sings of abysmal poverty and deprivation may be recompensed by sumptuous food and stimulating beverage at a country picnic, amorous favors from an attentive listener, enhanced Afro-American communality, or Yankee dollars from representatives of record companies traveling the South in search of blues as commodifiable entertainment. The performance, therefore, mediates one of the most prevalent of all antinomies in cultural investigation—creativity and commerce.

As driving force, the blues matrix thus avoids simple dualities. It perpetually achieves its effects as a fluid and multivalent network. It is only when "understanding"—the analytical work of a translator who translates the infinite changes of the blues—converges with such blues "force," however, that adequate explanatory perception (and half-creation) occurs. The matrix effectively functions toward cultural understanding, that is, only when an investigator brings an inventive attention to bear.

The Investigator, Relativity, and Blues Effect

The blues matrix is a "cultural invention": a "negative symbol" that generates (or obliges one to invent) its own referents.[18] As an inventive trope, this matrix provides for my following chapters the type of image or model that is always present in accounts of culture and

---

[17]Quoted in Oakley, *The Devil's Music*, p. 7.
[18]I have appropriated the term "negative symbol" from Roy Wagner's *The Invention of Culture* (Chicago: University of Chicago Press, 1975), p. xvi.

cultural products. If the analyses that I provide are successful, the blues matrix will have *taken effect* (and *affect*) through me.

To "take effect," of course, is not identical with to "come into existence" or to "demonstrate serviceability for the first time." Because what I have defined as a blues matrix is so demonstrably anterior to any single instance of its cultural-explanatory employment, my predecessors as effectors are obviously legion. "Take effect," therefore, does not signify discovery in the traditional sense of that word. Rather, it signals the tropological nature of my uses of an already extant matrix.

Ordinarily, accounts of art, literature, and culture fail to acknowledge their governing theories; further, they invariably conceal the *inventive* character of such theories. Nevertheless, all accounts of art, expressive culture, or culture in general are indisputably functions of their creators' tropological energies. When such creators talk of "art," for example, they are never dealing with existential givens. Rather, they are summoning objects, processes, or events defined by a model that they have created (by and for themselves) as a picture of art. Such models, or tropes, are continually invoked to constitute and explain phenomena inaccessible to the senses. Any single model, or any complementary set of inventive tropes, therefore, will offer only a selective account of experience—a partial reading, as it were, of the world. While the single account temporarily reduces chaos to ordered plan, all such accounts are eternally troubled by "remainders."

Where literary art is concerned, for example, a single, ordering, investigative model or trope will necessarily exclude phenomena that an alternative model or trope privileges as a definitive artistic instance. Recognizing the determinancy of "invention" in cultural explanation entails the acknowledgment of what might be called a normative relativity. To acknowledge relativity in our post-Heisenbergian universe is, of course, far from original. Neither, however, is it an occasion for the skeptics or the conservatives to heroically assume the critical stage.

The assumption of normative relativity, far from being a call to abandonment or retrenchment in the critical arena, constitutes an invitation to speculative explorations that are aware both of their own partiality and their heuristic transitions from suggestive (sometimes dramatic) images to inscribed concepts. The openness implied by relativity enables, say, the literary critic to *re-cognize* his endeavors, presupposing from the outset that such labors are not directed toward independent, observable, empirical phenomena but rather toward processes, objects, and events that he or she half-creates (and privileges as "art") through his or her own speculative, inventive energies and interests.

One axiological extrapolation from these observations on invention and relativity is that no object, process, or single element possesses *intrinsic aesthetic value*. The "art object" as well as its value are selective *constructions* of the critic's tropes and models. A radicalizing uncertainty may thus be said to mark cultural explanation. This uncertainty is similar in kind to the always selective endeavors of, say, the particle physicist.[19]

The physicist is always compelled to choose between velocity and position.[20] Similarly, an investigator of Afro-American expressive culture is ceaselessly compelled to forgo manifold variables in order to apply intensive energy to a selected array.

Continuing the metaphor, one might say that if the investigator's efforts are sufficiently charged with blues energy,[21] he is almost certain to remodel elements and events appearing in traditional, Anglo-American space-time in ways that make them "jump" several rings toward blackness and the vernacular. The blues-oriented observer (the *trained* critic) necessarily "heats up" the observational space by his or her very presence.[22]

An inventive, tropological, investigative model such as that proposed by *Blues, Ideology, and Afro-American Literature* entails not only awareness of the metaphorical nature of the blues matrix, but also a willingness on my own part to do more than merely hear, read, or see the blues. I must also play (with and on) them. Since the explanatory possibilities of a blues matrix—like analytical possibilities of a delimited set of forces in unified field theory—are hypothetically unbounded, the blues challenge investigative *understanding* to an unlimited play.

---

[19]My references to a "post-Heisenbergian universe" and to the "particle physicist" were made possible by a joyful reading of Gary Zukav's *The Dancing Wu Li Masters: An Overview of the New Physics* (New York: William E. Morrow, 1979).

[20]Zukav, *ibid.*, writes: "According to the uncertainty principle, we cannot measure accurately, at the same time, both the position *and* the momentum of a moving particle. The more precisely we determine one of these properties, the less we know about the other. If we precisely determine the position of the particle, then, strange as it sounds, there is *nothing* that we can know about its momentum. If we precisely determine the momentum of the particle, there is no way to determine its position" (p. 111). Briefly, if we bring to bear enough energy actually to "see" the imagined "particle," that energy has always already *moved* the particle from its *position* (which is one of the aspects of its existence that one attempts to *determine*) when we take our measurement. Indeterminacy thus becomes normative.

[21]The "blues force" is my translational equivalent in investigative "energy" for the investigative energy delineated by Heisenberg's formulations. See note 20.

[22]Eco (*A Theory of Semiotics*, p. 29) employs the metaphor of "ecological variation" in his discussions of the semiotic investigation of culture to describe observer effect in the mapping of experience.

Blues and Vernacular Expression in America

The blues should be privileged in the study of American culture to precisely the extent that inventive understanding successfully converges with blues force to yield accounts that persuasively and playfully refigure expressive geographies in the United States. My own ludic uses of the blues are various, and each figuration implies the valorization of vernacular facets of American culture. The Afro-American writer James Alan McPherson is, I think, the commentator who most brilliantly and encouragingly coalesces blues, vernacular, and cultural geographies of the United States in his introduction to *Railroad: Trains and Train People in American Culture.*[23]

Having described a fiduciary reaction to the steam locomotive by nineteenth-century financiers and an adverse artistic response by such traditional American writers as Melville, Hawthorne, and Thoreau, McPherson details the reaction of another sector of the United States population to the railroad:

> To a third group of people, those not bound by the assumptions of either business or classical traditions in art, the shrill whistle might have spoken of new possibilities. These were the backwoodsmen and Africans and recent immigrants—the people who comprised the vernacular level of American society. To them the machine might have been loud and frightening, but its whistle and its wheels promised movement. And since a commitment to both freedom and movement was the basic promise of democracy, it was probable that such people would view the locomotive as a challenge to the integrative powers of their imaginations. [P. 6]

Afro-Americans—at the bottom even of the vernacular ladder in America—responded to the railroad as a "meaningful symbol offering both economic progress and the possibility of aesthetic expression" (p. 9). This possibility came from the locomotive's drive and thrust, its promise of unrestrained mobility and unlimited freedom. The blues musician at the crossing, as I have already suggested, became an expert at reproducing or translating these locomotive energies. With the birth of the blues, the vernacular realm of American culture acquired a music that had "wide appeal because it expressed a toughness of spirit and resilience, a willingness to transcend difficulties which was strikingly familiar to those whites who remembered their own history" (p. 16). The signal expressive achievement of blues, then, lay in their translation of technological innovativeness, unsettling demographic fluidity, and boundless frontier energy

---

[23]New York: Random House, 1976. All citations refer to this edition and are hereafter marked by page numbers in parentheses.

into expression which attracted avid interest from the American masses. By the 1920s, American financiers had become aware of commercial possibilities not only of railroads but also of black music deriving from them.

A "race record" market flourished during the twenties. Major companies issued blues releases under labels such as Columbia, Vocalion, Okeh, Gennett, and Victor. Sometimes as many as ten blues releases appeared in a single week; their sales (aided by radio's dissemination of the music) climbed to hundreds of thousands. The onset of the Great Depression ended this phenomenal boom. During their heyday, however, the blues unequivocally signified a ludic predominance of the vernacular with that sassy, growling, moaning, whooping confidence that marks their finest performances.

McPherson's assessment seems fully justified. It serves, in fact, as a suggestive play in the overall project of refiguring American expressive geographies. Resonantly complementing the insights of such astute commentators as Albert Murray, Paul Oliver, Samuel Charters, Amiri Baraka, and others,[24] McPherson's judgments highlight the value of a blues matrix for cultural analysis in the United States.

In harmony with other brilliant commentators on the blues already noted, Ralph Ellison selects the railroad way-station (the "Chehaw Station") as his topos for the American "little man."[25] In "The Little Man at the Chehaw Station,"[26] he autobiographically details his own confirmation of his Tuskegee music teacher's observation that in the United States

> You must *always* play your best, even if it's only in the waiting room at Chehaw Station, because in this country there'll always be a little man hidden behind the stove . . . and he'll know the *music*, and the *tradition*, and the standards of *musicianship* required for whatever you set out to perform [P. 25].

When Hazel Harrison made this statement to the young Ellison, he felt that she was joking. But as he matured and moved through a diversity of American scenes, Ellison realized that the inhabitants of the "drab, utilitarian structure" of the American vernacular do far more than respond in expressive ways to "blues-echoing, train-whistle rhapsodies blared by fast express trains as they thundered past" the junction. At the vernacular level, according to Ellison, people

---

[24]See note 9 above.

[25]The Chehaw Station is a whistle-stop near Tuskegee, Alabama. It was a feature of the landscape of Tuskegee Institute, where Ellison studied music (and much else).

[26]*American Scholar* 47 (1978): 24–48. All citations refer to this version and are hereafter marked by page numbers in parentheses.

possess a "cultivated taste" that asserts its "authority out of obscurity" (p. 26). The "little man" finally comes to represent, therefore, "that unknown quality which renders the American audience far more than a receptive instrument that may be dominated through a skillful exercise of the sheerly 'rhetorical' elements—the flash and filigree—of the artist's craft" (p. 26).

From Ellison's opening gambit and wonderfully illustrative succeeding examples, I infer that the vernacular (in its expressive adequacy and adept critical facility) always *absorbs* "classical" elements of American life and art. Indeed, Ellison seems to imply that expressive performers in America who ignore the judgments of the vernacular are destined to failure.

Although his injunctions are intended principally to advocate a traditional "melting pot" ideal in American "high art," Ellisons' observations ultimately valorize a comprehensive, vernacular expressiveness in America. Though he seldom loses sight of the possibilities of a classically "transcendent" American high art, he derives his most forceful examples from the vernacular: Blues seem implicitly to comprise the *All* of the American culture.

Blues Moments in Afro-American Expression

In the chapters that follow, I attempt to provide suggestive accounts of moments in Afro-American discourse when personae, protagonists, autobiographical narrators, or literary critics successfully negotiate an obdurate "economics of slavery" and achieve a resonant, improvisational, expressive dignity. Such moments and successful analyses of them provide cogent examples of the blues matrix at work.

The expressive instances that I have in mind occur in passages such as the conclusion of the *Narrative of the Life of Frederick Douglass*. Standing at a Nantucket convention, riffing (in the "break" suddenly confronting him) on the *personal* troubles he has seen and successfully negotiated in a "prisonhouse of American bondage," Douglass achieves a profoundly dignified blues voice. Zora Neale Hurston's protagonist Janie in the novel *Their Eyes Were Watching God*—as she lyrically and idiomatically relates a tale of personal suffering and triumph that begins in the sexual exploitations of slavery—is a blues artist par excellence. Her wisdom might well be joined to that of Amiri Baraka's Walker Vessels (a "locomotive container" of blues?), whose chameleon code-switching from academic philosophy to blues insight makes him a veritable incarnation of the absorptively vernacular. The narrator of Richard Wright's *Black Boy* inscribes a black blues life's lean desire (as I shall demonstrate in chapter 3) and suggests yet a further instance of the blues matrix's expressive energies. Ellison's invisible man and Baraka's narrator in *The System of Dante's Hell* (whose blues book produces dance) provide additional examples. Finally, Toni Morrison's Milkman Dead in *Song of Solomon* discovers through "Sugarman's" song that an awesomely expressive blues response may well consist of improvisational and serendipitous surrender to the air: "As fleet and bright as a lodestar he wheeled toward Guitar and it did not matter which one of them would give up his ghost in the killing arms of his brother. For now he knew what Shalimar knew: If you surrendered to the air, you could *ride* it."[27]

Such blues moments are but random instances of the blues matrix at work in Afro-American cultural expression. In my study as a whole, I attempt persuasively to demonstrate that a blues matrix (as a vernacular trope for American cultural explanation in general) possess enormous force for the study of literature, criticism, and culture. I know that I have appropriated the vastness of the vernacular in the United States to a single matrix. But I trust that my necessary selectivity will be interpreted, not as a sign of myopic exclusiveness, but as an invitation to inventive play. The success of my efforts would be effectively signaled in the following chapters, I think, by the transformation of my "I" into a juncture where readers could freely improvise their own distinctive tropes for cultural explanation. A closing that in fact opened on such inventive possibilities (like the close of these introductory remarks) would be appropriately marked by the crossing sign's inviting "X."

---

[27]*Song of Solomon* (New York: Alfred A. Knopf, 1977), p. 337.

Jayne Cortez

(1936–   )

PERFORMANCE POET Jayne Cortez began writing poetry in the 1960s, and the social and political movements of that period are dominant themes of her early work. In a style that combines elements of black speech and musical traditions ranging from jazz and blues to African praise songs, she continues to be a forceful voice against the injustices perpetrated upon the socially and economically dispossessed: minorities, women, the poor, and the lower classes. At the same time her work pays tribute to the artists and visionaries who have spent their lives in the struggle for cultural and political revolution.

Born in 1936 in Arizona, Cortez grew up in Watts in California, and participated in a number of writing groups during the 1960s. From 1964 to 1970 she was the artistic director of the Watts Repertory Theatre Company, and from 1977 to 1983 she was writer-in-residence at Livingston College of Rutgers University. She currently lives in California.

Although she is best known as a performance poet and has read widely at cultural festivals, universities, and writers' conferences, Cortez has also published a number of books of her poetry, including *Pissstained Stairs and the Monkey Man's Wares* (1969), *Festivals and Funerals* (1971), *Scarifications* (1973), *Mouth on Paper* (1977), *Firespitter* (1982), and *Coagulations: New and Selected Poems* (1984). Her poems have appeared in several anthologies and literary magazines, including the surrealist art journal *Arsenal*. Cortez has also recorded five albums of her poetry, including *Celebrations and Solitudes* (1975), *Unsubmissive Blues* (1980), and *There It Is* (1983). Her most recent book is *Poetic Magnetic* and her latest recording is *Everywhere Drums*. Her work has been published in journals, magazines, and anthologies such as *Women On War*, *Early Ripening*, *Confirmation*, *Black Scholar*, and *UNESCO Courier*.

She is the recipient of several awards: The National Endowment for the Arts, American Book Award, and the New York Artists Foundation Award for poetry. She has lectured and read her poetry with and without music throughout the United States, Africa, Europe, Latin America, and the Caribbean.

An overview of Cortez's work and an examination of her influences is presented in the article by Jon Woodson in *Dictionary of Literary Biography, Volume 41*. See also Eugene B. Redmond, *Drumvoices* (1976) and D. H. Melhem's "Jayne Cortez: Supersurrealist Vision" in *Heroism in the New Black Poetry: Introductions and Interviews* (1990).

The following three poems are all taken from *Confirmation: An Anthology of African American Women.*

RAPE

What was Inez supposed to do for
the man who declared war on her body
the man who carved a combat zone between her breasts
Was she supposed to lick crabs from his hairy ass
kiss every pimple on his butt
blow hot breath on his big toe
draw back the corners of her vagina and
hee haw like a Calif. burro

This being war time for Inez
she stood facing the knife
the insults and
her own smell drying on the penis of
the man who raped her

She stood with a rifle in her hand
doing what a defense department will do in times of war
And when the man started grunting and panting and wobbling
    forward like
a giant hog
She pumped lead into his three hundred pounds of shaking flesh
Sent it flying to the virgin of Guadeloupe
then celebrated day of the dead rapist punk
and just what the fuck else was she supposed to do?

And what was Joanne supposed to do for
the man who declared war on her life
Was she supposed to tongue his encrusted toilet stool lips
suck the numbers off of his tin badge
choke on his clap trap balls
squeeze on his nub of rotten maggots and
sing god bless america thank you for fucking my life away

This being wartime for Joanne
she did what a defense department will do in times of war
and when the piss drinking   shit sniffing guard said

I'm gonna make you wish you were dead black bitch come here
Joanne came down with an ice pick in
the swat freak mother fucker's chest
yes in the fat neck of that racist policeman
Joanne did the dance of the ice picks and once again
from coast to coast
house to house
we celebrated day of the dead rapist punk
and just what the fuck else were we supposed to do

THERE IT IS

My friend
they don't care
if you're an individualist
a leftist   a rightist
a shithead or a snake
They will try to exploit you
absorb you   confine you
disconnect you   isolate you
or kill you

And you will disappear into your own rage
into your own insanity
into your own poverty
into a word a phrase a slogan a cartoon
and then ashes

The ruling class will tell you that
there is no ruling class
as they organize their liberal supporters into
white supremist lynch mobs
organize their children into
ku klux klan gangs
organize their police into
killer cops
organize their propaganda into
a device to ossify us with angel dust
pre-occupy us with western symbols in
african hair styles
inoculate us with hate
institutionalize us with ignorance
hypnotize us with a monotonous sound designed

to make us evade reality and stomp our lives away
And we are programmed to self destruct
to fragment
to get buried under covert intelligence operations of
unintelligent committees impulsed toward death
And there it is

The enemies polishing their penises between
oil wells at the pentagon
the bulldozers leaping into demolition dances
the old folks dying of starvation
the informers wearing out shoes looking for crumbs
the life blood of the earth almost dead in
the greedy mouth of imperialism
And my friend
they don't care
if you're an individualist
a leftist   a rightist
a shithead or a snake

They will spray you with
a virus of legionnaires disease
fill your nostrils with
the swine flu of their arrogance
stuff your body into a tampon of
toxic shock syndrome
try to pump all the resources of the world
into their own veins
and fly off into the wild blue yonder to
pollute another planet
And if we don't fight
if we don't resist
if we don't organize and unify and
get the power to control our own lives
Then we will wear
the exaggerated look of captivity
the stylized look of submission
the bizarre look of suicide
the dehumanized look of fear
and the decomposed look of repression
forever and ever and ever
And there it is

FOR THE BRAVE YOUNG STUDENTS IN SOWETO

Soweto
when i hear your name
I think about you
like the fifth ward in Houston Texas
one roof of crushed oil drums on the other
two black hunters in buckets of blood
walking into the fire of Sharpeville
into the sweat and stink of gold mines
into your childrens eyes suffering from malnutrition
while pellets of uranium are loaded onto boats
headed for France for Israel for Japan
away from the river so full of skulls
and Robben Island so swollen with warriors
and the townships that used to overflow
with such apathy and dreams
and i think about the old Mau Mau
grieving in beer halls
and the corrupt black leaders
singing into police whistles
and i think about the assembly line of dead "Hottentots"
and the jugular veins of Allende
and once again how the coffin is divided into dry ink
how the factory moves like a white cane
like a volley of bullets in the head of Lumumba
and death is a death-life held together by shacks
by widows who cry with their nipples pulled out
by men who shake with electrodes on the tongue
and Soweto
when i hear your name and look at you on the reservation
a Xhosa
in the humid wrinkles of Shreveport Louisiana
walking down fannin street
into the bottom hole in the wall of endurance
i smell the odor of our lives together made of tar paper
the memories opening like stomachs in saw mills
the faces growing old in cigarette burns
and i think about the sacrifices made in Capetown
the sisters being mauled by police dogs
while the minister of justice rides
the tall ship of torture
down the hudson river in New York
while vigilantes under zulu mask

strike through the heartland like robots
in military boots with hatchets made of apartheid lips
and Soweto
when i look at this ugliness
and see once again how we're divided and
forced into fighting each other
over a funky job in the sewers of Johannesburg
divided into labor camps
fighting over damaged meat and stale bread in Harlem
divided into factions fighting to keep from fighting
the ferocious men who are shooting
into the heads of our small children

When i look at this ugliness
and think about the Native Americans pushed
into the famine of tribal reserves
think about the concentration camps full of sad Palestinians
and the slave quarters still existing in Miami
the diamond factories still operating in Amsterdam in Belgium
the gold market still functioning on wall street
and the scar tissues around our necks
swelling with tumors of dead leaves
our bodies exploding like whiskey bottles
as the land shrinks into the bones of ancestor "Bushmen"
and i tell you Soweto
when i see you stand up in the middle of all this
stand up to the exotic white racists
in their armored churches
stand up to these landstealers, infant killers, rapists and rats
to see you stand among the pangas the stones
the war clubs the armadillos dying along this roadside
to see you stand with the ocean the desert
the birthright of red cliffs
to see you stand with your brave young warriors
courageous and strong hearted
looking so confident in battle marks coated
in grief and gunmetal tears
to see you stand up to this epidemic of expansion
and flame passbooks into ashes
fling stones into the mouths of computers
to see you stand on the national bank of america
like monumental sculpture made of stained bullets
to see you stand empty handed
your shoulders open to the world

each day young blood falling on the earth
to see you stand in the armed struggle
next to Mozambique, Angola, Namibia, Zimbabwe
Soweto i tell you Soweto
when i see you standing up like this
I think about all the forces in the world
confronted by the terrifying rhythms of young students
by their sacrifices
and the revelation that it won't be long now
before everything
in this world changes

Charles Johnson

(1948–   )

A CARTOONIST, JOURNALIST, professor, and novelist, Charles R. Johnson not only blends reality with fantasy, but incorporates history in his works as well. His deep concern with the philosophical aspect of life and his projection of varying levels of consciousness give power to his expression of themes that have had or now have social relevance in the lives of African Americans.

Born in 1948 and reared in Evanston, Illinois, Johnson has a love of art and drawing that bloomed, despite his father's dislike of it, under Lawrence Lariar, a cartoonist and writer, by the time Johnson was seventeen. Majoring in journalism at Southern Illinois University in Carbondale, Johnson received his bachelor's degree in 1971. In that same year, he worked for the Public Broadcasting System, hosting, co-producing, and writing a series that ran for fifty-two segments called "Charlie's Pad."

He earned his master's degree in philosophy at the same university in 1973 and worked as a photojournalist in Chicago and Carbondale. Studying under John Gardner, his creative writing teacher at Southern Illinois University, Johnson, who had previously written six novels, showed those to Gardner and wrote a seventh one, *Faith and the Good Thing* (1974). He did graduate work in phenomenology and literary aesthetics at the State University of New York at Stony Brook, but left before finishing his dissertation to teach at the University of Washington in Seattle. While at SUNY, he met and married his classmate Joan New. They now live in Seattle with their two children.

Combining the folk tradition, the African American experience, and philosophy in a literary free-for-all, Johnson published a slave narrative, *Oxherding Tale*, in 1982. He has written several scripts for PBS, such as *Charlie Smith and the Fritter-Tree* (1978), *For Me Myself* (1982), *A Place for Myself* (1982), and *Booker* (1984), which was co-authored with John Allmann. He is currently a professor of creative writing and edits the *Seattle Review*. His other works include *Black Humor* (1970); *Half-Past Nation Time* (1972); *The Sorcerer's Apprentice* (1986); *Being and Race*, a collection of essays (1988); *Middle Passage*, winner of the 1991 National Book Award (1990); *All This and Moonlight* (1990); and fictional and nonfictional publications in magazines such as *Callaloo*, *MSS*, *Intro*, and *Obsidian*.

For further information on Charles R. Johnson see Maryemma Graham's article in *Dictionary of Literary Biography, Volume 33*; Stanley Crouch's

"Charles Johnson, Free at Last," *Village Voice*, 19 July 1983; Raymond Olderman's "American Literature, 1974–1976: The People Fell to the Earth," *Contemporary Literature* 19 (Autumn 1978); Elizabeth Schultz's "The Heirs of Ralph Ellison," *CLA Journal* 22 (December 1978); and interviews, "Writers Should Be Able to Write Everything: Ken McCullough Talks to Charles Johnson," *Coda: Poets and Writers Newsletter* (September/October 1978), and "Reflections on Fiction, Philosophy, and Film: An Interview with Charles Johnson," *Callaloo* 4 (October 1978).

"Exchange Value" comes from the collection *The Sorcerer's Apprentice*.

EXCHANGE VALUE

Me and my brother, Loftis, came in by the old lady's window. There was some kinda boobytrap—boxes of broken glass—that shoulda warned us Miss Bailey wasn't the easy mark we made her to be. She been living alone for twenty years in 4-B down the hall from Loftis and me, long before our folks died—a hincty, halfbald West Indian woman with a craglike face, who kept her door barricaded, shutters closed, and wore the same sorry-looking outfit—black wingtip shoes, cropfingered gloves in winter, and a man's floppy hat—like maybe she dressed half-asleep or in a dark attic. Loftis, he figured Miss Bailey had some grandtheft dough stashed inside, jim, or leastways a shoebox full of money, 'cause she never spent a nickel on herself, not even for food, and only left her place at night.

Anyway, we figured Miss Bailey was gone. Her mailbox be full, and Pookie White, who run the Thirty-ninth Street Creole restaurant, he say she ain't dropped by in days to collect the handouts he give her so she can get by. So here's me and Loftis, tipping around Miss Bailey's blackdark kitchen. The floor be littered with fruitrinds, roaches, old food furred with blue mold. Her dirty dishes be stacked in a sink feathered with cracks, and it looks like the old lady been living, lately, on Ritz crackers and Department of Agriculture (Welfare Office) peanut butter. Her toilet be stopped up, too, and, on the bathroom floor, there's five Maxwell House coffee cans full of shit. Me, I was closing her bathroom door when I whiffed this evil smell so bad, so thick, I could hardly breathe, and what air I breathed was stifling, like solid fluid in my throatpipes, like broth or soup. "Cooter," Loftis whisper, low, across the room, "you smell that?" He went right on sniffing it, like people do for some reason when something be smelling stanky, then took out his headrag and held it over his mouth. "Smells like something crawled up in here and died!" Then, head low, he slipped his long self into the living room. Me, I stayed by the window, gulping for air, and do you know why?

You oughta know, up front, that I ain't too good at this gangster stuff, and I had a real bad feeling about Miss Bailey from the get-go. Mama used to say it was Loftis, not me, who'd go places—I see her standing at the sideboard by the sink now, big as a Frigidaire, white flour to her elbows, a washtowel over her shoulder, while we ate a breakfast of cornbread and syrup. Loftis, he graduated fifth at DuSable High School, had two gigs and, like Papa, he be always wanting the things white people had out in Hyde Park, where Mama did daywork sometimes. Loftis, he be the kind of brother who buys *Esquire*, sews Hart, Schaffner & Marx labels in Robert Hall suits, talks properlike, packs his hair with Murray's; and he took classes in politics and stuff at the Black People's Topographical Library in the late 1960s. At thirty, he make his bed military-style, reads *Black Scholar* on the bus he takes to the plant, and, come hell or high water, plans to make a Big Score. Loftis, he say I'm 'bout as useful on a hustle— or when it comes to getting ahead—as a headcold, and he says he has to count my legs sometimes to make sure I ain't a mule, seeing how, for all my eighteen years, I can't keep no job and sorta stay close to home, watching TV, or reading *World's Finest* comic books, or maybe just laying dead, listening to music, imagining I see faces or foreign places in water stains on the wallpaper, 'cause some days, when I remember Papa, then Mama, killing theyselves for chump change—a pitiful li'l bowl of porridge—I get to thinking that even if I ain't had all I wanted, maybe I've had, you know, all I'm ever gonna get.

"Cooter," Loftis say from the living room. "You best get in here quick."

Loftis, he'd switched on Miss Bailey's bright, overhead living room lights, so for a second I couldn't see and started coughing— the smell be so powerful it hit my nostrils like coke—and when my eyes cleared, shapes come forward in the light, and I thought for an instant like I'd slipped in space. I seen why Loftis called me, and went back two steps. See, 4-B's so small if you ring Miss Bailey's doorbell, the toilet'd flush. But her living room, webbed in dust, be filled to the max with dollars of all denominations, stacks of stock in General Motors, Gulf Oil, and 3M Company in old White Owl cigar boxes, battered purses, or bound in pink rubber bands. It be like the kind of cubby-hole kids play in, but filled with . . . *things*: everything, like a world inside the world, you take it from me, so like picturebook scenes of plentifulness you could seal yourself off in here and settle forever. Loftis and me both drew breath suddenly. There be unopened cases of Jack Daniel's, three safes cemented to the floor, hundreds of matchbooks, unworn clothes, a fuel-burning stove, dozens of wedding rings, rubbish, World War II magazines, a carton of a hundred canned sardines, mink stoles, old rags, a bird-cage, a bucket of silver dollars, thousands of books, paintings, quarters in tobacco cans, two pianos, glass jars of pennies, a set of bagpipes, an almost complete Model A Ford dappled with rust, and, I swear, three sections of a dead tree.

"Damn!" My head be light; I sat on an upended peach crate and picked up a bottle of Jack Daniel's.

"Don't you touch *anything*!" Loftis, he panting a little; he slap both hands on a table. "Not until we inventory this stuff."

"Inventory? Aw, Lord, Loftis," I say, "something ain't *right* about this stash. There could be a curse on it. . . ."

"Boy, sometimes you act weak-minded."

"For real, Loftis, I got a feeling. . . ."

Loftis, he shucked off his shoes, and sat down heavily on the lumpy arm of a stuffed chair. "Don't say *anything*." He chewed his knuckles, and for the first time Loftis looked like he didn't know his next move. "Let me think, okay?" He squeezed his nose in a way he has when thinking hard, sighed, then stood up and say, "There's something you better see in that bedroom yonder. Cover up your mouth."

"Loftis, I ain't going in there."

He look at me right funny then. "She's a miser, that's all. She saves things."

"But a tree?" I say. "Loftis, a *tree* ain't normal!"

"Cooter, I ain't gonna tell you twice."

Like always, I followed Loftis, who swung his flashlight from the plant—he a night watchman—into Miss Bailey's bedroom, but me, I'm thinking how trippy this thing is getting, remembering how, last year, when I had a paper route, the old lady, with her queer, crab-like walk, pulled my coat for some change in the hallway, and when I give her a handful of dimes, she say, like one of them spooks on old-time radio, "Thank you, Co-o-oter," then gulped the coins down like aspirin, no lie, and scurried off like a hunchback. Me, I wanted no parts of this squirrely old broad, but Loftis, he holding my wrist now, beaming his light onto a low bed. The room had a funny, mu-seumlike smell. Real sour. It was full of dirty laundry. And I be sure the old lady's stuff had a terrible string attached when Loftis, looking away, lifted her bedsheets and a knot of black flies rose. I stepped back and held my breath. Miss Bailey be in her long-sleeved flannel nightgown, bloated, like she'd been blown up by a bicycle pump, her old face caved in with rot, flyblown, her fingers big and colored like spoiled bananas. Her wristwatch be ticking softly beside a half-eaten hamburger. Above the bed, her wall had roaches squashed in little swirls of blood-stain. Maggots clustered in her eyes, her ears, and one fist-sized rat hissed inside her flesh. My eyes snapped shut. My knees failed; then I did a Hollywood faint. When I surfaced, Loftis, he be sitting beside me in the living room, where he'd drug me, reading a wrinkled, yellow article from the *Chicago Daily Defender*.

"Listen to this," Loftis say. " 'Elnora Bailey, forty-five, a Negro housemaid in the Highland Park home of Henry Conners, is the beneficiary of her employer's will. An old American family, the Conners arrived in this country on the *Providence* shortly after the voyage of the *Mayflower*. The family flourished in the early days of the 1900s.' . . ." He went on, getting breath: " 'A distinguished and wealthy industrialist, without heirs or a wife, Conners willed his entire estate to Miss Bailey of 3347 North Clark Street for her twenty years of service to his family.' . . ." Loftis, he give that Geoffrey Holder laugh of his, low and deep; then it eased up his throat until it hit a high note and tipped his head back onto his shoulders. "Cooter, that was before we was born! Miss Bailey kept this in the Bible next to her bed."

Standing, I braced myself with one hand against the wall. "She didn't earn it?"

"Naw." Loftis, he folded the paper—"Not one penny"—and stuffed it in his shirt pocket. His jaw looked tight as a horseshoe. "Way *I* see it," he say, "this was her one shot in a lifetime to be rich, but being country, she had backward ways and blew it." Rubbing his hands, he stood up to survey the living room. "Somebody's gonna find Miss Bailey soon, but if we stay on the case—Cooter, don't square up on me now—we can tote everything to our place before daybreak. Best we start with the big stuff."

"But why didn't she *use* it, huh? Tell me that?"

Loftis, he don't pay me no mind. When he gets an idea in his head, you can't dig it out with a chisel. How long it took me and Loftis to inventory, then haul Miss Bailey's queer old stuff to our crib, I can't say, but that cranky old ninnyhammer's hoard come to $879,543 in cash money, thirty-two bank books (some deposits be only $5), and me, I wasn't sure I was dreaming or what, but I suddenly flashed on this feeling, once we left her flat, that all the fears Loftis and me had about the future be gone, 'cause Miss Bailey's property was the past—the power of that fellah Henry Conners trapped like a bottle spirit—which we could live off, so it was the future, too, pure potential: can *do*. Loftis got to talking on about how that piano we pushed home be equal to a thousand bills, jim, which equals, say, a bad TEAC A-3340 tape deck, or a down payment on a deuce-and-a-quarter. Its value be (Loftis say) that of a universal standard of measure, relational, unreal as number, so that tape deck could turn, magically, into two gold lamé suits, a trip to Tijuana, or twenty-five blow jobs from a ho—we had $879,543 worth of wishes, if you can deal with that. Be like Miss Bailey's stuff is raw energy, and Loftis and me, like wizards, could transform her stuff into anything else at will. All we had to do, it seemed to me, was decide exactly what to exchange it for.

While Loftis studied this over (he looked funny, like a potato trying to say something, after the inventory, and sat, real quiet, in the kitchen), I filled my pockets with fifties, grabbed me a cab downtown to grease, yum, at one of them high-hat restaurants in the Loop. . . . But then I thought better of it, you know, like I'd be out of place—just another jig putting on airs—and scarfed instead at a ribjoint till both my eyes bubbled. This fat lady making fishburgers in the back favored an old hardleg baby-sitter I once had, a Mrs. Paine who made me eat ocher, and I wanted so bad to say, "Loftis and me Got Ovuh," but I couldn't put that in the wind, could I, so I hatted up. Then I copped a boss silk necktie, cashmere socks, and a whistle-slick maxi leather jacket on State Street, took cabs *every-where*, but when I got home that evening, a funny, Pandora-like feeling hit me. I took off the jacket, boxed it—it looked trifling in the hallway's weak light—and, tired, turned my key in the door. I couldn't get in. Loftis, he'd changed the lock and, when he finally let me in, looking vaguer, crabby, like something out of the Book of Revelations, I seen this elaborate, booby-trapped tunnel of cardboard and razor blades behind him, with a two-foot space just big enough for him or me to crawl through. That wasn't all. Two bags of trash from the furnace room downstairs be sitting inside the door. Loftis, he give my leather jacket this evil look, hauled me inside, and hit me upside my head.

"How much this thing set us back?"

"Two fifty." My jaws got tight; I toss him my receipt. "You want me to take it back? Maybe I can get something else. . . ."

Loftis, he say, not to me, but to the receipt, "Remember the time Mama give me that ring we had in the family for fifty years? And I took it to Merchandise Mart and sold it for a few pieces of candy?" He hitched his chair forward and sat with his elbows on his knees. "That's what you did, Cooter. You crawled into a Clark bar." He commence to rip up my receipt, then picked up his flashlight and keys. "As soon as you buy something you *lose* the power to buy something." He button up his coat with holes in the elbows, showing his blue shirt, then turned 'round at the tunnel to say, "Don't touch Miss Bailey's money, or drink her splo, or do anything until I get back."

"Where you going?"

"To work. It's Wednesday, ain't it?"

"You going to work?"

"Yeah."

"You got to go really? Loftis," I say, "what you brang them bags of trash in here for?"

"It ain't trash!" He cut his eyes at me. "There's good clothes in there. Mr. Peterson tossed them out, he don't care, but I saw some use in them, that's all."

"Loftis . . ."

"Yeah?"

"What we gonna do with all this money?"

Loftis pressed his fingers to his eyelids, and for a second he looked caged, or like somebody'd kicked him in his stomach. Then he cut me some slack: "Let me think on it tonight—it don't pay to rush—then we can TCB, okay?"

Five hours after Loftis leave for work, that old blister Mr. Peterson, our landlord, he come collecting rent, find Mrs. Bailey's body in apartment 4-B, and phoned the fire department. Me, I be folding my new jacket in tissue paper to keep it fresh, adding the box to Miss Bailey's unsunned treasures when two paramedics squeezed her on a long stretcher through a crowd in the hallway. See, I had to pin her from the stairhead, looking down one last time at this dizzy old lady, and I seen something in her face, like maybe she'd been poor as Job's turkey for thirty years, suffering that special Negro fear of using up what little we get in this life—Loftis, he call that entropy—believing in her belly, and for all her faith, jim, that there just ain't no more coming tomorrow from grace, or the Lord, or from her own labor, like she can't kill nothing, and won't nothing die . . . so when Conners will her his wealth, it put her through changes, she be spellbound, possessed by the promise of life, panicky about depletion, and locked now in the past 'cause every purchase, you know, has to be a poor buy: a loss of life. Me, I wasn't worried none. Loftis, he got a brain trained by years of talking trash with people in Frog Hudson's barbershop on Thirty-fifth Street. By morning, I knew, he'd have some kinda wheeze worked out.

But Loftis, he don't come home. Me, I got kinda worried. I listen to the hi-fi all day Thursday, only pawing outside to peep down the stairs, like that'd make Loftis come sooner. So Thursday go by; and come Friday the head's out of kilter—first there's an ogrelike belch from the toilet bowl, then water bursts from the bathroom into the kitchen—and me, I can't call the super (How do I explain the tunnel?), so I gave up and quit bailing. But on Saturday, I could smell greens cooking next door. Twice I almost opened Miss Bailey's sardines, even though starving be less an evil than eating up our stash, but I waited till it was dark and, with my stomach talking to me, stepped outside to Pookie White's, lay a hard-luck story on him, and Pookie, he give me some jambalaya and gumbo. Back home in the living room, finger-feeding myself, barricaded in by all that hope-made material, the Kid felt like a king in his counting room, and I copped some Zs in an armchair till I heard the door move on its hinges, then bumping in the tunnel, and a heavy-footed walk thumped into the bedroom.

"Loftis?" I rubbed my eyes. "You back?" It be Sunday morning. Six-thirty sharp. Darkness dissolved slowly into the strangeness of twilight, with the rays of sunlight surging at exactly the same angle they fall each evening, as if the hour be an island, a moment outside time. Me, I'm afraid Loftis gonna fuss 'bout my not straightening up, letting things go. I went into the bathroom, poured water in the one-spigot washstand—brown rust come bursting out in flakes—and rinsed my face. "Loftis, you supposed to be home four days ago. Hey," I say, toweling my face, "you okay?" How come he don't answer me? Wiping my hands on the seat on my trousers, I tipped into Loftis's room. He sleeping with his mouth open. His legs be drawn up, both fists clenched between his knees. He'd kicked his blanket on the floor. In his sleep, Loftis laughed, or moaned, it be hard to tell. His eyelids, not quite shut, show slits of white. I decided to wait till Loftis wake up for his decision, but turning, I seen his watch, keys, and what looked in the first stain of sunlight to be a carefully wrapped piece of newspaper on his nightstand. The sunlight swelled to a bright shimmer, focusing the bedroom slowly like solution do a photographic image in the developer. And then something so freakish went down I ain't sure it took place. Fumble-fingered, I unfolded the paper, and inside be a blemished penny. It be like suddenly somebody slapped my head from behind. Taped on the penny be a slip of paper, and on the paper be the note "Found while walking down Devon Avenue." I hear Loftis mumble like he trapped in a nightmare. "Hold tight," I whisper. "It's all right." Me, I wanted to tell Loftis how Miss Bailey looked four days ago, that maybe it didn't have to be like that for us—did it?—because we could change. Couldn't we? Me, I pull his packed sheets over him, wrap up the penny, and, when I locate Miss Bailey's glass jar in the living room, put it away carefully, for now, with the rest of our things.

Gayl Jones

(1949–   )

WORKING IN THE BLACK FOLK TRADITION, Gayl Jones writes intense stories of madness, violence, and sex in the lives of black people. Through the narrative voice, Jones's main characters, primarily black women, reveal their innermost feelings and insecurities dramatizing the constant struggle between the conscious and subconscious mind.

Jones was born in Lexington, Kentucky, in 1949. Following in the footsteps of her grandmother and mother, she began writing as early as age seven or eight. In Lexington, she attended segregated public schools until the tenth grade. Having grown up in a family that kept its heritage alive through discussion and documentation, Jones often draws on familial experiences as well as the dialect of blacks she observed in the streets of her home town.

Jones received her bachelor's degree in English from Connecticut College. While attending graduate school for creative writing at Brown University, she published her first novel, *Corregidora* (1975). A provocative and sexually explicit novel of a black woman who tries to cope with a family history tinged by rape and incest, *Corregidora* delves into the pysche of its main character, Ursa Corregidora, and takes the reader on a journey of suffering and despair. Characterized as a blues narrative (see Keith E. Byerman's article in *Dictionary of Literary Biography, Volume 33*) *Corregidora* "deals with the pains and pleasures of human relationships."

Jones's second novel, *Eva's Man* (1976), goes one step further in complexity than *Corregidora*. Unlike Ursa, who only thinks, Eva actually carries out her sexual frustrations. Jones's narrative voice and use of black oral tradition are strong forces throughout this novel.

Jones has also published a collection of twelve short stores, *White Rat* (1977). As in her first two novels, the characters in *White Rat* vent their frustrations and try to deal with dehumanizing forces in a white racist society. Her most recent publications include *Song for Anninho* (1981), a long narrative poem; *The Hermit Woman* (1983); *Xargue and Other Poems* (1985); and *Liberating Voices: Oral Tradition in African American Literature* (1991). Currently, she is teaching creative writing and Afro-American literature at the University of Michigan.

For further reading on Gayl Jones, see Claudia C. Tate's "Corregidora: Ursa's Blues Medley," *Black American Literature Forum* 13 (Fall 1979); Jerry W. Ward's "Escape from Trublem: The Fiction of Gayl Jones," *Callaloo*

5 (October 1982); and Michael S. Harper's "Gayl Jones: An Interview," in *Chant of Saints: A Gathering of Afro-American Literature, Art, and Scholarship* (1979).

"White Rat" is the title story from the 1977 collection.

WHITE RAT

I learned where she was when Cousin Willie come down home and said Maggie sent for her but told her not to tell nobody where she was, especially me, but Cousin Willie come and told me anyway cause she said I was the lessen two evils and she didn't like to see Maggie stuck up in the room up there like she was. I asked her what she mean like she was. Willie said that she was pregnant by J. T. J. T. the man she run off with because she said I treat her like dirt. And now Willie say J. T. run off and left her after he got her knocked up. I asked Willie where she was. Willie said she was up in that room over Babe Lawson's. She told me not to be surprised when I saw her looking real bad. I said I wouldn't be least surprised. I asked Willie she think Maggie come back. Willie say she better.

The room was dirty and Maggie looked worser than Willie say she going to look. I knocked on the door but there weren't no answer so I just opened the door and went in and saw Maggie laying on the bed turned up against the wall. She turnt around when I come in but she didn't say nothing. I said Maggie we getting out a here. So I got the bag she brung when she run away and put all her loose things in it and just took her by the arm and brung her on home. You couldn't tell nothing was in her belly though.

I been taking care of little Henry since she been gone but he 3½ years old and ain't no trouble since he can play hisself and know what it mean when you hit him on the ass when he do something wrong.

Maggie don't say nothing when we get in the house. She just go over to little Henry. He sleeping in the front room on the couch. She go over to little Henry and bend down an kiss him on the cheek and then she ask me have I had supper and when I say Naw she go back in the kitchen and start fixing it. We sitting at the table and nobody saying nothing but I feel I got to say something.

"You can go ahead and have the baby," I say. "I give him my name."

I say it meaner than I want to. She just look up at me and don't say nothing. Then she say, "He ain't yours."

I say, "I know he ain't mine. But don't nobody else have to know. Even the baby. He don't even never have to know."

She just keep looking at me with her big eyes that don't say nothing, and then she say, "You know. I know."

She look down at her plate and go on eating. We don't say nothing no more and then when she get through she clear up the dishes and I just go round front and sit on the front porch. She don't come out like she used to before she start saying I treat her like dirt, and then when I go on in the house to go to bed, she hunched up on her side, with her back to me, so I just take my clothes off and get on in the bed on my side.

Maggie a light yeller woman with chicken scratch hair. That what my mama used to call it chicken scratch hair cause she say there weren't enough hair for a chicken to scratch around in. If it weren't for her hair she look like she was a white woman, a light yeller white woman though. Anyway, when we was coming up somebody say, "Woman cover you hair if you ain't go'n' straightin' it. Look like chicken scratch." Sometime they say look like chicken shit, but they don't tell them to cover it no more, so they wear it like it is. Maggie wear hers like it is.

Me, I come from a family of white-looking niggers, some of 'em, my mama, my daddy musta been, my half daddy he weren't. Come down from the hills round Hazard, Kentucky most of them and claimed nigger cause somebody grandmammy way back there was. First people I know ever claim nigger, 'cept my mama say my daddy hate hoogies (up North I hear they call em honkies) worser than anybody. She say cause he look like he one hisself and then she laugh. I laugh too but I didn't know why she laugh. She say when I come, I look just like a little white rat, so tha's why some a the people I hang aroun with call me "White Rat." When little Henry come he look just like a little white rabbit, but don't nobody call him "White Rabbit" they just call him little Henry. I guess the other jus' ain't took. I tried to get them to call him little White Rabbit, but Maggie say naw, cause she say when he grow up he develop a complex, what with the problem he got already. I say what you come at me for with this a complex and then she say, Nothin, jus' something I heard on the radio on one of them edgecation morning shows. And then I say Aw. And then she say Anyway by the time he get seven or eight he probably get the pigment and be dark, cause some of her family was. So I say where I heard somewhere where the chil'ren couldn't be no darker'n the darkest of the two parent and bout the

best he could do would be high yeller like she was. And then she
say how her sister Lucky got the pigment when she was bout seven
and come out real dark. I tell her Well y'all's daddy was dark. And
she say, "Yeah." Anyway, I guess well she still think little Henry
gonna get the pigment when he get to be seven or eight, and told
me about all these people come out lighter'n I was and got the pigment fore they growed up.

Like I told you my relatives come down out of the hills and
claimed nigger, but only people that believe 'em is people that got to
know 'em and people that know 'em, so I usually just stay around
with people I know and go in some joint over to Versailles or up to
Lexington or down over in Midway where they know me cause I
don't like to walk in no place where they say, "What's that white
man doing in here." They probably say "yap"—that the Kentucky
word for honky. Or "What that yap doing in here with that nigger
woman." So I jus' keep to the places where they know me. I member
when I was young me and the other niggers used to ride around in
these cars and when we go to some town where they don't know
"White Rat" everybody look at me like I'm some hoogie, but I don't
pay them no mind. 'Cept sometime it hard to pay em no mind cause
I hate the hoogie much as they do, much as my daddy did. I drove
up to this filling station one time and these other niggers drove up
at the same time, they mighta even drove up a little ahead a me, but
this filling station man come up to me first and bent down and said,
"I wait on you first, 'fore I wait on them niggers," and then he laugh.
And then I laugh and say, "You can wait on them first. I'm a nigger
too." He don't say nothing. He just look at me like he thought I was
crazy. I don't remember who he wait on first. But I guess he be careful next time who he say nigger to, even somebody got blonde hair
like me, most which done passed over anyhow. That, or the way
things been go'n, go'n be trying to pass back. I member once all us
was riding around one Saturday night, I must a been bout twenty-
five then, close to forty now, but we was driving around, all us
drunk cause it was Saturday, and Shotgun, he was driving and probably drunker'n a skunk and drunken the rest of us hit up on this
police car and the police got out and by that time Shotgun done
stop, and the police come over and told all us to get out the car, and
he looked us over, he didn't have to do much looking because he
probably smell it before he got there but he looked us all over and
say he gonna haul us all in for being drunk and disord'ly. He say,
"I'm gonna haul all y'all in." And I say, "Haul y'all all." Everybody
laugh, but he don't hear me cause he over to his car ringing up the
police station to have them send the wagon out. He turn his back to
us cause he know we wasn going nowhere. Didn't have to call but

one man cause the only people in the whole Midway police station
is Fat Dick and Skinny Dick, Buster Crab and Mr. Willie. Sometime
we call Buster, Crab Face too, and Mr. Willie is John Willie, but everybody call him Mr. Willie cause the name just took. So Skinny
Dick come out with the wagon and hauled us all in. So they didn't
know me well as I knew them. Thought I was some hoogie jus' run
around with the niggers instead of be one of them. So they put my
cousin Covington, cause he dark, in the cell with Shotgun and the
other niggers and they put me in the cell with the white men. So I'm
drunkern a skunk and I'm yellin' let me outa here I'm a nigger too.
And Crab Face say, "If you a nigger I'm a Chinee." And I keep rattling the bars and saying "Cov', they got me in here with the white
men. Tell 'em I'm a nigger too," and Cov' yell back, "He a nigger
too," and then they all laugh, all the niggers laugh, the hoogies they
laugh too, but for a different reason and Cov' say, "Tha's what you
get for being drunk and orderly." And I say, "Put me in there with
the niggers too, I'm a nigger too." And then one of the white men,
he's sitting over in his corner say, "I ain't never heard of a white
man want to be a nigger. 'Cept maybe for the nigger women." So I
look around at him and haul off cause I'm goin hit him and then
some man grab me and say, "He keep a blade," but that don't make
me no difrent and I say, "A spade don't need a blade." But then he
get his friend to help hole me and then he call Crab Face to come
get me out a the cage. So Crab Face come and get me out a the cage
and put me in a cage by myself and say, "When you get out a here
you can run around with the niggers all you want, but while you in
here you ain't getting no niggers." By now I'm more sober so I jus'
say, "My cousin's a nigger." And he say, "My cousin a monkey's
uncle."

By that time Grandy come. Cause Cov' took his free call but
didn't nobody else. Grandy's Cov's grandmama. She my grandmama
too on my stepdaddy's side. Anyway, Grandy come and she say, "I
want my *two* sons." And he take her over to the nigger cage and say,
"Which two?" and she say, "There one of them," and points to
Cov'ton. "But I don't see t'other one." And Crab Face say, "Well, if
you don't see him I don't see him." Cov'ton just standing there grinning, and don't say nothing. I don't say nothing. I'm just waiting.
Grandy ask, "Cov, where Rat?" Sometime she just call me Rat and
leave the "White" off. Cov' say, "They put him in the cage with the
white men." Crab Face standing there looking funny now. His back
to me, but I figure he looking funny now. Grandy says, "Take me to
my other boy, I want to see my other boy." I don't think Crab Face
want her to know he thought I was white so he don't say nothing.
She just standing there looking up at him cause he tall and fat and

she short and fat. Crab Face finally say, "I put him in a cell by hisself cause he started a rucus." He point over to me, and she turn and
see me and frown. I'm just sitting there. She look back at Crab Face
and say, "I want them both out." "That be about five dollars a piece
for the both of them for disturbing the peace." That what Crab Face
say. I'm sitting there thinking he a poet and don't know it. He a bad
poet and don't know it. Grandy say she pay it if it take all her
money, which it probably did. So the police let Cov' and me out.
And Shotgun waving. Some of the others already settled. Didn't care
if they got out the next day. I wouldn't a cared neither, but Grandy
say she didn like to see nobody in a cage, specially her own. I say I
pay her back. Cov' say he pay her back too. She say we can both pay
her back if we just stay out a trouble. So we got together and pay
her next week's grocery bill.

Well, that was one 'sperience. I had others, but like I said, now I
jus' about keep to the people I know and that know me. The only
other big sperience was when me and Maggie tried to get married.
We went down to the courthouse and fore I even said a word, the
man behind the glass cage look up at us and say, "Round here nigger don't marry white." I don't say nothing just standing up there
looking at him and he looking like a white toad, and I'm wondering
if they call him "white toad" more likely "white turd." But I just
keep looking at him. Then he the one get tired a looking first and he
say, "Next." I'm thinking I want to reach in that little winder and
pull him right out of that little glass cage. But I don't. He say again,
"Around here nigger don't marry white." I say, "I'm a nigger. Nigger
marry nigger, don't they?" He just look at me like he think I'm
crazy. I say, "I got rel'tives blacker'n your shit. Ain't you never heard
a niggers what look like they white." He just look at me like I'm a
nigger too, and tell me where to sign.

Then we get married and I bring her over here to live in this
house in Huntertown ain't got but three rooms and a outhouse that's
where we always lived, seems like to me, all us Hawks, cept the ones
come down from the mountains way back yonder, cept they don't
count no more anyway. I keep telling Maggie it get harder and
harder to be a white nigger now specially since it don't count no
more how much white blood you got in you, in fact, it make you
worser for it. I said nowadays sted a walking around like you something special people look at you, after they find out what you are if
you like me, like you some kind a bad news that you had something
to do with. I tell em I aint had nothing to do with the way I come
out. The ack like they like you better if you go on ahead and try to
pass, cause, least then they know how to feel about you. Cept nowadays everybody want to be a nigger, or it getting that way. I tell

Maggie she got it made, cause at least she got that chicken shit hair, but all she answer is, "That why you treat me like chicken shit." But tha's only since we been having our troubles.

Little Henry the cause a our troubles. I tell Maggie I ain't changed since he was borned, but she say I have. I always say I been a hard man, kind of quick-tempered. A hard man to crack like one of them walnuts. She say all it take to crack a walnut is your teeth. She say she put a walnut between her teeth and it crack not even need a hammer. So I say I'm a nigger toe nut then. I ask her if she ever seen one of them nigger toe nuts they the toughest nuts to crack. She say, "A nigger toe nut is black. A white nigger toe nut be easy to crack." Then I don't say nothing and she keep saying I changed cause I took to drink. I tell her I drink before I married her. She say then I start up again. She say she don't like it when I drink cause I'm quicker tempered than when I ain't drunk. She say I come home drunk and say things and then go to sleep and then the next morning forget what I say. She won't tell me what I say. I say, "You a woman scart of words. Won't do nothing." She say she ain't scart of words. She say one of these times I might not jus' say something. I might *do* something. Short time after she say that was when she run off with J. T.

Reason I took to drink again was because little Henry was borned club-footed. I tell the truth in the beginning I blamed Maggie, cause I herited all those hill man's superstitions and nigger superstitions too, and I said she didn't do something right when she was carrying him or she did something she shouldn't oughta did or looked at something she shouldn't oughta looked at like some cows fucking or something. I'm serious. I blamed her. Little Henry come out looking like a little club-footed rabbit. Or some rabbits being birthed or something. I said there weren't never nothing like that in my family ever since we been living on this earth. And they must have come from her side. And then I said cause she had more of whatever it was in her than I had in me. And then she said that brought it all out. All that stuff I been hiding up inside me cause she said I didn't hated them hoogies like my daddy did and I just been feeling I had to live up to something he set and the onliest reason I married her was because she was the lightest and brightest nigger woman I could get and still be nigger. Once that nigger start to lay it on me she jus' kept it up till I didn't feel nothing but start to feeling what she say, and then I even told her I was leaving and she say, "What about little Henry?" And I say, "He's your nigger." And then it was like I didn't know no other word but nigger when I was going out that door.

I found some joint and went in it and just start pouring the stuff down. It weren't no nigger joint neither, it was a hoogie joint. First

time in my life I ever been in a hoogie joint too, and I kept thinking
a nigger woman did it. I wasn't drunk enough *not* to know what I
was saying neither. I was sitting up to the bar talking to the tender.
He just standing up there, wasn nothing special to him, he probably
weren't even lisen cept but with one ear. I say, "I know this nigger.
You know I know the niggers. (He just nod but don't say nothing.)
Know them close. You know what I mean. Know them like they was
my own. Know them where you s'pose to know them." I grinned at
him like he was s'pose to know them too. "You know my family
came down out of the hills, like they was some kind of rain gods,
you know, miss'ology. What they teached you bout the Juicifer. Anyway, I knew this nigger what made hisself a priest, you know turned
his white color I mean turned his white collar backwards and
dressed up in a monkey suit—you get it?" He didn't get it. "Well, he
made hisself a priest, but after a while he didn't want to be no
priest, so he pronounced hisself." The bartender said, "Renounced."
"So he 'nounced hisself and took off his turned back collar and went
back to just being a plain old every day chi'lins and downhome and
hamhocks and corn pone nigger. And you know what else he did?
He got married. Yeah the nigger what once was a priest got married.
Once took all them vows of cel'bacy come and got married. Got
married so he could come." I laugh. He don't. I got evil. "Well, he
come awright. He come and she come too. She come and had a
baby. And you know what else? The baby come too. Ha. No ha? The
baby come out club-footed. So you know what he did? He didn't
blame his wife he blamed hisself. The nigger blamed hisself cause he
said the God put a curse on him for goin' agin his vows. He said the
God put a curse on him cause he took his vows of cel'bacy, which
mean no fuckin', cept everybody know what *they* do, and went agin
his vows of cel'bacy and married a nigger woman so he could do
what every ord'narry onery person was doing and the Lord didn't
just put a curse on him. He said he could a stood that. But the Lord
carried the curse clear over to the next gen'ration and put a curse on
his little baby boy who didn do nothing in his whole life . . . cept
come." I laugh and laugh. Then when I quit laughing I drink some
more, and then when I quit drinking I talk some more. "And you
know something else?" I say. This time he say, "No." I say, "I knew
another priest what took the vows, only this priest was white. You
wanta know what happen to him. He broke his vows same as the nigger and got married same as the nigger. And they had a baby too.
Want to know what happen to him?" "What?" "He come out a nigger."
  Then I get so drunk I can't go no place but home. I'm thinking
it's the Hawk's house, not hers. If anybody get throwed out it's her.
She the nigger. I'm goin' fool her. Throw her right *out* the bed if she

in it. But then when I get home I'm the one that's fool. Cause she gone *and* little Henry gone. So I guess I just badmouthed the walls like the devil till I jus' layed down and went to sleep. The next morning little Henry come back with a neighbor woman but Maggie don't come. The woman hand over little Henry, and I ask her, "Where Maggie?" She looked at me like she think I'm the devil and say, "I don't know, but she lef' me this note to give to you." So she jus' give me the note and went. I open the note and read. She write like a chicken too, I'm thinking, chicken scratch. I read: "I run off with J. T. cause he been wanting me to run off with him and I ain't been wanting to tell now. I'm send little Henry back cause I just took him away last night cause I didn't want you to be doing nothing you regrit in the morning." So I figured she figured I got to stay sober if I got to take care of myself and little Henry. Little Henry didn't say nothing and I didn't say nothing. I just put him on in the house and let him play with hisself.

That was two months ago. I ain't take a drop since. But last night Cousin Willie come and say where Maggie was and now she moving around in the kitchen and feeding little Henry and I guess when I get up she feed me. I get up and get dressed and go in the kitchen. She say when the new baby come we see whose fault it was. J. T. blacker'n a lump of coal. Maggie keep saying "When the baby come we see who fault it was." It's two more months now that I been look at her, but I still don't see no belly change.

John Edgar Wideman

(1941–   )

ALTHOUGH JOHN WIDEMAN was born in Washington, D.C., he moved during his first year to Pittsburgh, Pennsylvania, whose black communities serve as setting for much of his fiction. His experiences in upper-middle-class primary and secondary schools in Pittsburgh helped to prepare him for his success at the University of Pennsylvania in Philadelphia. Having won a Benjamin Franklin Scholarship to the University of Pennsylvania, Wideman first majored in psychology and later English. The same achievements and popularity he had acquired in high school because of his athletic abilities in basketball also characterize his career at the university. In 1963, he graduated Phi Beta Kappa and won a Rhodes Scholarship to study at Oxford University, where he played on the basketball team and served as captain and coach.

After completing his thesis on four eighteenth-century novels, Wideman graduated from Oxford with a B.A. degree in philosophy in 1966. He received a Kent Fellowship and participated in the Creative Writing Workshop at the University of Iowa from 1966 to 1967. He then spent six years as lecturer and after a short while professor of English at his alma mater, the University of Pennsylvania, where he also instituted and for one year (1972–1973) chaired the Afro-American studies program.

His first novel, *A Glance Away*, was published in 1976, the year he left Iowa. *A Glance Away* and Wideman's second novel, *Hurry Home* (1969), were received extremely well by critics and reviewers. Although both race and class play roles in the lives of the characters in these novels, racial issues receive only covert emphasis in Wideman's novels beginning with *The Lynchers*, published in 1973.

Though *The Lynchers* and Wideman's other works of fiction—*Hiding Place* (1981), *Damballah* (1981), *Sent for You Yesterday* (1983), and *Reuben* (1987)—all manifest the same stylistic precision as his first two novels, they have not yet sparked the same kind of critical enthusiasm. His first nonfiction work, *Brothers and Keepers*, a personal essay about himself and his younger brother, who is serving a life sentence without parole in prison, was published in 1984 during the time Wideman was employed as a professor of English at the University of Wyoming. During the same time, he received the P.E.N./Faulkner Award in 1983 for *Sent for You Yesterday*. Wideman's last two publications to date are *Fever: Twelve Stories* (1989) and *Philadelphia Fire* (1990).

The lack of criticism to date on Wideman's works is one of the greatest oversights in African American literary criticism. So far Wilfred D. Samuels's entry in *Dictionary of Literary Biography, Volume 33* and a few others remain rare scholarly treatments of his art. Also see John O'Brien's *Interviews with Black Writers* (1973) and Bernard W. Bell's *The Afro-American Novel and Its Tradition* (1987).

The following excerpt is reprinted from *The Lynchers.*

FROM **THE LYNCHERS**

Why you think people like it dark when they listen to jazz. Somebody had asked me that in Harold's. In the middle of all the nasty talk they did each morning. Like nobody really ready to git out of bed yet and they are still there dreaming all the pussy they've had or smelling and fingering their bodies or the body they've caught for the night. Coming to Harold's for some extra sleep. Talk and whiskey a woolly gray blanket over their heads. To each his own. But why should it be dark. First of all the dude that said it just knew he was right. People want it dark. Need it dark. And you don't dance either. Almost solemn as a sanctified church. But, hell. That ain't so solemn. Shoutin and signifyin and prayin loud enough to be heard in the street. I would have liked to hear Harold answer. Come up with some of his three years at Morgan State these are the facts of the matter shit. He'd be wrong but at least you have to beat him down and think before you open your mouth or he'll make a fool of you and everybody laughing till you can see somebody getting terrible quiet and tight jawed and then it's time to beat on somebody else. Even in the morning these dudes will fight. Fact is they probably fight sooner in the morning. Everybody still sleepy or sleeping and running down what they want to be not what they are. Like don't rap on my man's new coat if he been working like a dog to get the coins together even if he looks like a damn fool in it. After he starts cursing it himself, talking about how much it cost and wishes he had his coins back then you can beat on him. But these cats still dreaming at Harold's in the morning.

Because maybe jazz dreaming too. Or those listening dreaming of leather coats and big cars and fat thighed sisters. Don't know what a man playing jazz could be thinking. Does he want the lights out? I remember the piano player Childress knew and he came on down to the bar and we all had a drink. Just jiving. The cat was stone folks. Natural and we're rapping like I known him my whole life. Only thing his eyes redder than any eyes I've seen. And he blinks. Take the cover off a skillet with two eggs frying and see them kinda soupy running together before they firm up only these eggs was a pinky red bloodshot and each time he blinks top's off that skillet somebody turned off the fire because they are just sitting there undone and getting no better. He must have seen me looking. Said bitch broke my motherfucking shades. And I understood everything. How jazz men always on the go always moving from town to town and probably have plenty women but keep none of them actually happy so when he calls or knocks on the door the woman feels good but she is mad too because she knows here he is and something real nice is going to happen but sure as morning the nigger will be gone and god knows when he'll be back but sorry assed bitch that I am I'll get up and fix him something to eat and be hurt when he leaves and let him take enough of me with him I'll open the door next time and be opening it for him when others knock or call and them running through me like water because I'm waiting for him and he may not even come back but so good when he does I could kill him. So after he's been good and then getting ready to go she smashes the gold rimmed dark glasses to the floor. Her nail catches in his cheek when she rips them from his face. He knows it has to come to this and no way to change it because this is just the way it has to be if you move from town to town and try to have a little something going each place. But the bitch ain't supposed to fuck with my things. But this is the way it has to be so he doesn't really try to hurt her bad. He blots the sting on his cheek with an open palm and quick like an answer to the trumpet's riff same hand slaps her to the bed. She thinks for a second she is in hell, that the devil is standing over her, eyeless, his stare is so vacant. She thinks he will lean down and scrape his eyes from the back of the broken glasses, and paste them into the rawness above his cheeks. Watching that act worse than the death. But he blinks, doesn't even look down because he knows what he'll see, crumpled on the floor. No sense in saving the jagged pieces. The way it has to be he just walks out saying nothing the way he came.

I am staring at his eyes and he has nothing to say except what he did. After all some things are plainly out of your hands so they are just there and people being what they are can't help noticing. You say a few words and they either understand or no sense in trying to say more. *I coulda killed that silly whore.* And tomorrow you'll find new shades in this city or another city and there will be nothing to say.

Childress said he had met the piano man in a bar one night.

They just started to talk. The cat wasn't jamming just sitting at the bar. Childress didn't know him from Adam but they talked for a long time. Sees him now every time he's in town. The cat's real together. He's been around. One of the best at his trade. Childress didn't know much about music except that some of it got to him especially near the end of the night at the Vets and he thought he was over with some mamma, but since he had talked with the jazz cat Childress say he into his music. Dug the way the piano man played no matter what he played or who he was jamming with. And Childress didn't make a big deal behind knowing the cat. I mean he didn't *I want you to meet my man* loud enough for the whole place to hear and back slapping and tugging at the piano man's elbow like he was some fine bitch Childress was turning out. They both just kind of slid off to the side of the bandstand, at a corner of the bar where the waitress sets her tray and nobody sits. Tight with Childress and Childress say *this is Sweetman my main man*—everything's okay and I'm talking with them.

Cat was from the South. And he laughed about the home folks and country ways. Childress had only been there during the war but they understood one another about how you had to laugh at some of the shit or be dead or crazy. But they didn't talk that much. One would say something and they'd laugh or grunt or make some other noise or repeat a word several times each taking a turn and doing something a little different with how he says it. They didn't want to be in one another's way so lots of space between sounds. Just the bar noise to fill in and little ripples of music from the jukebox somebody had turned on when the set was over. The light wasn't very good anywhere but it was almost black where we stood. Childress and the cat seemed to get far away. Not like they tried to make me feel I shouldn't be with them. It was like I was slipping into a deep thing someplace they might take me but where I'd be alone. I remembered how Childress talked about the cat's music. I thought about moving so fast nobody could see you pass but to you the moving would be very slow, drifting more than anything else, like in water or a scrap of paper sailing. Listening to jazz in the dark. The waitress made her order. Funny stuff like frozen daiquiris, lady fingers, sloe gin fizzes, and it had never seemed so funny until just then. Little kids running to the ice cream truck. Half of them ain't got a damned cent but they's running as fast as the pickaninnies that have dimes in their fists. Candy ice cream cake. And the bell tinkling and some Jew or dago in a frowsy white coat parceling out the goodies. I could see that summer day and me racing with the others and worried somebody would snatch my money or whatever I bought. Right in front of my eyes though I was deep somewhere in the talk of Childress and the jazz man, deep as in a black woods but a summer day I could look at floating like a balloon or closed in a glass ball. The kind you turn upside down and snow falls over the little church and people inside the glass. Snow drifting down lazy. You shake it and down again just as lazy over the house and people.

—She got a nice pair of tits.

—Yeah I was digging.

A small light below the level of the bar haloed the spot where the waitress paid her bills and picked up her orders. I didn't need to look to see her features then her tight white blouse modeled in the glow. His voice made both. Two smoked circles of glass had grown over the jazz man's eyes. They were home again. I did not see them but I knew shades patched the rawness, that he needed them and they slide into place as real as the waitress switching her tail away from the arc of light.

But I be damned if I know. Badass jazz blowing cats travelling from town to town shooting down the locals, doing what they can do best blowing away, gunfighters only not at high noon but doing their fighting in the dark when all the lights out. Time I was in Camden trying to get into something my man Childress and me stopped for a taste in some little hole in the wall. Drinking gin in the middle of the afternoon getting friendly and loud talking with all these strange dudes after a while you get lost could be West Hell or Camden or round the corner from your crib for all you know niggers and gin kind of insinuating wrapping you round till you comfortable and floating with whatever place you be. Sitting there talking away and before you know it you been to New York City and Frisco and Deetroit and Chicago and China and West Hell and back all round the world drinking gin messing with white folks and cutting niggers and somebody smoking a reefer in the toilet good Nam grass a young dude with a black beret slanted on his head and the dude talking a funny game going to change the world you begin to believe his hat is straight and him leaning forty-five degrees he has a purple hand the bones sharp and the skin of his fingers like crusty canvas over tent poles offering you a toke on his shit you take it from him and drag the way it's supposed to be dragged though you don't like tobacco and only smoke once in a great while raggedy weeds like he's offering the dude running down his revolutionary game like you still there when you pull the door closed after you step into the midnight bar everybody bigger than when you left they are moving faster and their voices gathered in a box somewhere near the ceiling that weaves them all together into a riff chasing the juke.

And the riff is people passing me like they going to a fire. Black faces blurring into white. Horns and plate glass windows and sad-eyed mannequins dead for fifty years staring at their own stiff reflections. You thought you were the lizard scuttling fast as four legs could carry you but the others without even trying leave you behind or high heel tramp their way right through you. You are jazz being played in some dark room. In the late afternoon street, sidewalks glinting a shower of golden flecks that swim before your eyes, sin kisses, you are a ghost losing his way. Somebody bumps you and you want to crumple where you are. Be another spot of spit, sweat or wine staining the sidewalk, flat on your back looking up pant legs and mini-skirts. Smell the soft underbellies of the bloodhounds chasing you. A cop is exploding in the middle of an intersection. At any moment the brass and blue and icy leather will tear apart the thick body puffing itself up to hold them together. I can see his belly straining to reach the billows of blue serge.

Because somebody is asking me last week how I am today and they are getting an answer. A lame, wrong answer but the social worker knowingly shakes her head and believes it, and here I am ass over ears bumping along chased by a gorilla riff.

So it must be the dark that does it. Darkness necessary. Like Childress said not so much that the cat was famous or supposed to be the best at what he was doing but that he knew the cat and that's what he heard when he listened.

⟨∞⟩

Outside Harold's, city still dark or at least not light yet. We flowed out into our cars. Fuzzy edges still pretty much like they were when we went in to have our morning drink.

–Later, you badass bunch of sanitary engineers.

You have to go over a bridge to get to the depot. As a matter of fact the depot is kind of under the bridge you go over. Always in the shadow of the bridge so sometimes like you are going into a cave. The crews would be rolling in all at once thirty, thirty-five minutes before the trucks had to go out. Day didn't start till half hour after punch-in time. Union got us thirty minutes for changing, getting the equipment together. A good crew could get a truck ready in ten minutes and most came to work dressed to go so after punching in we had twenty minutes to bullshit and pass around a taste if anybody brought one. You could tell where people was at by the taste they offered around. Like Clarence bring a fifth of Bali Hai once or twice a month and be doing good then one day up he jumps with a pint of Cutty Sark you know he either done left his old lady again or hit the numbers or both if he come along with something top shelf for a couple days in a row.

When is this shit gonna cease. Orin Wilkerson swore softly under his breath. Somebody had killed the pregnant movie star. All that good, white pussy doing nobody any good anymore. A damned shame. Somebody crazy did it. Must of been to look at her fine as she was and in the condition she was and cut her down. Goddamnit. He saw them scurrying around him. The men he saw each morning. He thought he knew them. The way you know Clarence or Clisby who has that Continental he loves and nothing else in the world. But you see them hustling and bustling round here these last ten minutes, cursing, all those raggedy clothes they wear like space suits or second stiff, greasy skins they all look pretty much alike. Then again before the rush they all talk the same shit. Drinking and fucking and how badass they are or whatever team in whatever sport they are following on T.V. Some just sit quiet though. And some only speak when asked but when they put in their two cents you know they're happy to get it out and all they needed was an opening. I think I know them. Can call most names. Then I try to image one of these sorry assed dudes with a knife in his hand going to carve up some white movie star. Standing in her big living room where she paid more for a rug than he can for an automobile, where a picture tacked over the fireplace would buy the whole house in which he's renting three rooms.

I can't figure it out. Had to be somebody just like one of these. Or me. Not that half these niggers ain't stone crazy.

Samuel R. Delany

(1942–   )

ONE OF VERY FEW black science fiction writers, and a very popular science fiction writer and critic, Samuel R. Delany has overcome many obstacles and bad breaks—an unstable family life, dyslexia, mental breakdowns and divorce—in his rise to the top of the literary world. This accounts for the recurring image in his works of the artist who suffers physical and psychological distress. Delany, a mythmaker fascinated with the human language, also tends to explore the relationship between whites and blacks and the way in which their sexual intermixture may affect race relations in future generations.

Delany was born in 1942 and reared in Harlem. His parents were well-to-do, and the benefits he reaped as a consequence—a private school education and summer camps—divided his life into two realms, one in which he saw the violence of poverty in Harlem, and one in which he was able to dally among the privileged at Dalton, a predominantly white upper-class elementary school.

After graduating from Dalton in 1956, he attended the Bronx High School of Science. There Delany, who majored in math and physics, wrote for the school magazine and won several essay contests. By fourteen he had written a complete violin concerto and between 1954 and 1963 wrote several apprentice works, such as *Lost Stars, Those Spared by Fire, Toby, Lovers,* and *Captives of the Flame,* the first book in *The Fall of the Towers* trilogy (1963). By the age of twenty, he had his first book, *The Jewels of Aptor* (1962), which was also his first science fiction novel, published by Ace Books. Marilyn Hacker, who was an assistant editor for Ace Books and who would later become his wife, encouraged him to submit his manuscript to the company.

Delany attended City College of New York but dropped out. By the time he was twenty-two, he had published four more books: *Captives of the Flame* (retitled *Out of the Dead City*), *The Towers of Toron* (1964), and *City of a Thousand Suns* (1965), which make up *The Fall of the Towers* trilogy; and *The Ballad of Beta-2* (1965).

Delany won, consecutively, two Nebula Awards, one for *Babel-17* (1967) and the other for *The Einstein Intersection* (1968). After the publication of six more novels, *Nova* (1968), *The Fall of the Towers* (1970), *Driftglass* (1971), *The Tides of Lust* (1973), *Dhlagren* (1975), and *Triton* (1976), Delany was asked to be Butler Professor of English at the State University of New York. In 1977 he published a book of critical essays, *The Jewel-Hinged Jaw: Notes on the Language of Science Fiction* (1977), and was a senior fellow at the Center for Twentieth Century Studies at the University of Wisconsin-Milwaukee.

His other works include a book of criticism, *The American Shore* (1978), *Empire* (1978), *The Tales of Neveryon* (1979), *Heavenly Breakfast* (1979), *Distant Stars* (1981), and *Neveryona; or The Tales of Signs and Cities* (1983). His most recent works include *Flight From Neveryon* (1985), *The Star Pit* (1986), *The Bridge of Lost Desire* (1987), and *The Straits of Messina* (1989).

For further reading see Sondra Y. Govan's article in *Dictionary of Literary Biography, Volume 33;* Michael W. Peplow and Robert S. Bravard's *Samuel R. Delany: A Primary and Secondary Bibliography, 1962–1979* (1980); Sandra Miesel's "Samuel R. Delany's Use of Myth in *Nova,*" *Extrapolation* 12 (May 1971); Robert Scholes and Eric S. Rabkin's *Science Fiction: History, Science, Vision* (1977); Stephen Scobie's "Different Mazes: Mythology in Samuel R. Delany's *The Einstein Intersection,*" *Riverside Quarterly* 5 (1972); George Edgar Slusser's *The Delany Intersection: Samuel R. Delany Considered as a Writer of Semi-Precious Words* (1977); and collections of Delany's materials, "The Samuel R. Delany Collection," at Boston University's Mugar Memorial Library.

The following selection is *Driftglass*, the short story upon which the novel is based.

DRIFTGLASS

Sometimes I go down to the port, splashing sand with my stiff foot at the end of my stiff leg locked in my stiff hip, with the useless arm a-swinging, to get wet all over again, drink in the dives with cronies ashore, feeling old, broken, sorry for myself, laughing louder and louder. The third of my face that was burned away in the accident was patched with skin-grafts from my chest, so what's left of my mouth distorts all loud sounds; sloppy sartorial reconstruction. Also I have a hairy chest. Chest hair does not look like beard hair, and it grows all up under my right eye. And: my beard is red, my chest hair brown, while the thatch curling down over neck and ears is sun-streaked to white here, darkened to bronze there, 'midst general blondness.

By reason of my being a walking (I suppose my gait could be called headlong limping) horror show, plus a general inclination to

sulk, I spend most of the time up in the wood and glass and alumi-
num house on the surf-sloughed point that the Aquatic Corp ceded
me along with my pension. Rugs from Turkey there, copper pots,
my tenor recorder which I can no longer play, and my books.

But sometimes, when the gold fog blurs the morning, I go down
to the beach and tromp barefoot in the wet edging of the sea,
searching for driftglass.

It was foggy that morning, and the sun across the water moiled
the mists like a brass ladle. I lurched to the top of the rocks, looked
down through the tall grasses into the frothing inlet where she lay,
and blinked.

She sat up, long gills closing down her neck and the secondary
slits along her back just visible at their tips because of much hair,
wet and curling copper, falling there. She saw me. "What are you
doing here, huh?" She narrowed blue eyes.

"Looking for driftglass."

"What?"

"There's a piece." I pointed near her and came down the rocks
like a crab with one stiff leg.

"Where?" She turned over, half in, half out of the water, the
webs of her fingers cupping nodules of black stone.

While the water made cold overtures between my toes, I picked
up the milky fragment by her elbow where she wasn't looking. She
jumped, because she obviously had thought it was somewhere else.

"See?"

"What . . . what is it?" She raised her cool hand to mine. For a
moment the light through the milky gem and the pale film of my
own webs pearled the screen of her palms. (Details like that. Yes,
they are the important things, the points from which we suspend
later pain.) A moment later wet fingers closed to the backs of mine.

"Driftglass," I said. "You know all the Coca-Cola bottles and cut-
crystal punch bowls and industrial silicon slag that goes into the
sea?"

"I know the Coca-Cola bottles."

"They break, and the tide pulls the pieces back and forth over
the sandy bottom, wearing the edges, changing their shape. Sometimes chemicals in the glass react with chemicals in the ocean to
change the color. Sometimes veins work their way through in patterns like snowflakes, regular and geometric; others, irregular and
angled like coral. When the pieces dry, they're milky. Put them in
water and they become transparent again."

"Ohhh!" she breathed as the beauty of the blunted triangular
fragment in my palm assailed her like perfume. Then she looked at

my face, blinking the third, aqueous-filled lid that we use as a cor-
rection lens for underwater vision.

She watched the ruin calmly.

Then her hand went to my foot where the webs had been torn
back in the accident. She began to take in who I was. I looked for
horror, but saw only a little sadness.

The insignia on her buckle—her stomach was making little jerks
the way you always do during the first few minutes when you go
from breathing water to air—told me she was a Biological Technician. (Back up at the house there was a similar uniform of simulated
scales folded in the bottom drawer of the dresser and the belt insignia said Depth Gauger.) I was wearing some very frayed jeans and a
red cotton shirt with no buttons.

She reached for my neck, pushed my collar back from my shoulders and touched the tender slits of my gills, outlining them with
cool fingers. "Who are you?" Finally.

"Cal Svenson."

She slid back down in the water. "You're the one who had the
terrible . . . but that was years ago! They still talk about it, down
. . . " She stopped.

As the sea softens the surface of a piece of glass, so it blurs the
souls and sensibilities of the people who toil beneath her. And according to the last report of the Marine Reclamation Division there
are to date seven hundred and fifty thousand who have been given
gills and webs and sent under the foam where there are no storms,
up and down the American coast.

"You live on shore? I mean around here? But so long ago . . . "

"How old are you?"

"Sixteen."

"I was two years older than you when the accident happened."

"You were eighteen?"

"I'm twice that now. Which means it happened almost twenty
years ago. It is a long time."

"They still talk about it."

"I've almost forgotten," I said. "I really have. Say, do you play the
recorder?"

"I used to."

"Good! Come up to my place and look at my tenor recorder. And
I'll make some tea. Perhaps you can stay for lunch—"

"I have to report back to Marine Headquarters by three. Tork is
going over the briefing to lay the cable for the big dive, with Jonni
and the crew." She paused, smiled. "But I can catch the undertow
and be there in half an hour if I leave by two-thirty."

On the walk up I learned her name was Ariel. She thought the patio was charming, and the mosiac evoked, "Oh, look!" and "Did you do this yourself?" a half-dozen times. (I had done it, in the first lonely years.) She picked out the squid and the whale in battle, the wounded shark and the diver. She told me she didn't get time to read much, but she was impressed by all the books. She listened to me reminisce. She talked a lot to me about her work, husbanding the deep-down creatures they were scaring up. Then she sat on the kitchen stool, playing a Lukas Foss serenade on my recorder, while I put rock salt in the bottom of the broiler tray for two dozen Oysters Rockefeller, and the tea water whistled. I'm a comparatively lonely guy. I like being followed by beautiful young girls.

II

"Hey, Juao!" I bawled across the jetty.

He nodded to me from the center of his nets, sun glistening on polished shoulders, sun lost in rough hair. I walked across to where he sat, sewing like a spider. He pulled another section up over his horny toes, then grinned at me with his mosaic smile: gold, white, black gap below, crooked yellow; white, gold, white. Shoving my bad leg in front I squatted.

"I fished out over the coral where you told me." He filled his cheek with his tongue and nodded. "You come up to the house for a drink, eh?"

"Fine."

"Just—a moment more."

There's a certain sort of Brazilian you find along the shore in the fishing villages, old yet ageless. See one of their men and you think he could be fifty, he could be sixty—will probably look the same when he's eighty-five. Such was Juao. We once figured it out. He's seven hours older than I am.

We became friends some time before the accident when I got tangled in his nets working high lines in the Vorea Current. A lot of guys would have taken their knife and hacked their way out of the situation, ruining fifty-five, sixty dollars' worth of nets. That's an average fisherman's monthly income down here. But I surfaced and sat around in his boat while we untied me. Then we came in and got plastered. Since I cost him a day's fishing, I've been giving him hints on where to fish ever since. He buys me drinks when I come up with something.

This has been going on for twenty years. During that time my life has been smashed up and land-bound. In the same time Juao has married off his five sisters, got married himself and has two children. (Oh, those *bolitos* and *teneros asados* that Amalia—her braids swung out, her brown breasts shook so when she turned to laugh—would make for Sunday dinner/supper/Monday breakfast.) I rode with them in the ambulance 'copter all the way into Brasilia; in the hospital hall Juao and I stood together, both still barefoot, he tattered with fish scales in his hair, me just tattered, and I held him while he cried and I tried to explain to him how a world that could take a pubescent child and with a week of operations make an amphibious creature that can exist for a month on either side of the sea's foam-fraught surface could still be helpless before certain rampant endocrine cancers coupled with massive renal deterioration. Juao and I returned to the village alone, by bus, three days before our birthday—back when I was twenty-three and Juao was twenty-three and seven hours old.

"This morning," Juao said. (The shuttle danced in the web at the end of the orange line.) "I got a letter for you to read me. It's about the children. Come on, we go up and drink." The shuttle paused, backtracked twice, and he yanked the knot tight. We walked along the port toward the square. "Do you think the letter says that the children are accepted?"

"If it's from the Aquatic Corp. They just send postcards when they reject someone. The question is, how do *you* feel about it?"

"You are a good man. If they grow up like you, then it will be fine."

"But you're still worried." I'd been prodding Juao to get the kids into the International Aquatic Corp nigh on since I became their godfather. The operations had to be performed near puberty. It would mean much time away from the village during their training period—and they might eventually be stationed in any ocean in the world. But two motherless children had not been easy on Juao or his sisters. The Corp would mean education, travel, interesting work, the things that make up one kind of good life. They wouldn't look twice their age when they were thirty-five; and not too many amphimen look like me.

"Worry is part of life. But the work is dangerous. Did you know there is an amphiman going to try to lay cable down in the Slash?"

I frowned. "Again?"

"Yes. And that is what you tried to do when the sea broke you to pieces and burned the parts, eh?"

"Must you be so damned picturesque?" I asked. "Who's going to beard the lion this time?"

"A young amphiman named Tork. They speak of him down at the docks as a brave man."

"Why the hell are they still trying to lay the cable there? They've gotten by this long without a line through the Slash."

"Because of the fish," Juao said. "You told me why twenty years ago. The fish are still there, and we fishermen who cannot live below are still here. If the children go for the operations, then there will be less fishermen. But today . . ." He shrugged. "They must either lay the line across the fish paths or down in the Slash." Juao shook his head.

Funny things, the great power cables the Aquatic Corp has been strewing across the ocean floor to bring power to their undersea mines and farms, to run their oil wells—and how many flaming wells have I capped down there—for their herds of whale, and chemical distillation plants. They carry two-hundred-sixty-cycle current. Over certain sections of the ocean floor, or in sections of the water with certain mineral contents, this sets up inductance in the water itself which sometimes—and you will probably get a Nobel prize if you can detail exactly why it isn't always—drives the fish away over areas up to twenty-five and thirty miles, unless the lines are laid in the bottom of those canyons that delve into the ocean floor.

"This Tork thinks of the fishermen. He is a good man too."

I raised my eyebrows—the one that's left, anyway—and tried to remember what my little Undine had said about him that morning. And remembered not much.

"I wish him luck," I said.

"What do you feel about this young man going down into the coral-rimmed jaws to the Slash?"

I thought for a moment. "I think I hate him."

Juao looked up.

"He is an image in a mirror where I look and am forced to regard what I was," I went on. "I envy him the chance to succeed where I failed, and I can come on just as quaint as you can. I hope he makes it."

Juao twisted his shoulders in a complicated shrug (once I could do that) which is coastal Brazilian for, "I didn't know things had progressed to that point, but seeing that they have, there is little to be done."

"The sea is that sort of mirror," I said.

"Yes." Juao nodded.

Behind us I heard the slapping of sandals on concrete. I turned in time to catch my goddaughter in my good arm. My godson had grabbed hold of the bad one and was swinging on it.

"Tio Cal—?"

"Hey, Tio Cal, what did you bring us?"

"You will pull him over," Juao reprimanded them. "Let go."

And, bless them, they ignored their father.

"What did you bring us?"

"What did you bring us, Tio Cal?"

"If you let me, I'll show you." So they stepped back, dark-eyed and quivering. I watched Juao watching: brown pupils on ivory balls, and in the left eye a vein had broken in a jagged smear. He was loving his children, who would soon be as alien to him as the fish he netted. He was also looking at the terrible thing that was me and wondering what would come to his own spawn. And he was watching the world turn and grow older, clocked by the waves, reflected in that mirror.

It's impossible for me to see what the population explosion and the budding colonies on Luna and Mars and the flowering beneath the ocean really look like from the disrupted cultural mélange of a coastal fishing town. But I come closer than many others, and I know what I don't understand.

I pushed around in my pocket and fetched out the milky fragment I had brought from the beach. "Here. Do you like this one?" And they bent above my webbed and alien fingers.

In the supermarket, which is the biggest building in the village, Juao bought a lot of cake mixes. "That moist, delicate texture," whispered the box when you lifted it from the shelf, "with that deep flavor, deeper than chocolate!"

I'd just read an article about the new vocal packaging in a U.S. magazine that had gotten down last week, so I was prepared and stayed in the fresh vegetable section to avoid temptation. Then we went up to Juao's house. The letter proved to be what I'd expected. The kids had to take the bus into Brasilia tomorrow. My godchildren were on their way to becoming fish.

We sat on the front steps and drank and watched the donkeys and the motorbikes and the men in baggy trousers, the women in yellow scarves and bright skirts with wreaths of garlic and sacks of onions. As well, a few people glittered by in the green scales of amphimen uniforms.

Finally Juao got tired and went in to take a nap. Most of my life has been spent on the coast of countries accustomed to siestas, but those first formative ten were passed on a Danish collective farm and the idea never really took. So I stepped over my goddaughter, who had fallen asleep on her fists on the bottom step, and walked back through the town toward the beach.

III

At midnight Ariel came out of the sea, climbed the rocks, and clicked her nails against my glass wall so the droplets ran, pearled by the gibbous moon.

Earlier I had stretched in front of the fireplace on the sheepskin throw to read, then dozed off. The conscientious timer had asked me if there was anything I wanted, and getting no answer had turned off the Dvorak *Cello Concerto* that was on its second time around, extinguished the reading lamp, and stopped dropping logs onto the flame so that now, as I woke, the grate was carpeted with coals.

She clicked again, and I raised my head from the cushion. The green uniform, her amber hair—all color was lost under the silver light outside. I lurched across the rug, touched the button, and the glass slid into the floor. The breeze came to my face, as the barrier fell.

"What do you want?" I asked. "What time is it, anyway?"

"Tork is on the beach, waiting for you."

The night was warm but windy. Below the rocks silver flakes chased each other in to shore. The tide lay full.

I rubbed my face. "The new boss man? Why didn't you bring him up to the house? What does he want to see me about?"

She touched my arm. "Come. They are all down on the beach."

"Who all?"

"Tork and the others."

She led me across the patio and to the path that wound to the sand. The sea roared in the moonlight. Down the beach people stood around a driftwood fire that whipped the night. Ariel walked beside me.

Two of the fishermen from town were crowding each other on the bottom of an overturned washtub, playing guitars. The singing, raucous and rhythmic, jarred across the paled sand. Shark's teeth shook on the necklace of an old woman dancing. Others were sitting on an overturned dinghy, eating.

Over one part of the fire on a skillet two feet across, oil frothed through pink islands of shrimp. One woman ladled them in, another ladled them out.

"Tio Cal!"

"Look, Tio Cal is here!"

"Hey, what are you two doing up?" I asked. "Shouldn't you be home in bed?"

"Poppa Juao said we could come. He'll be here, too, soon."

I turned to Ariel. "Why are they all gathering?"

"Because of the laying of the cable tomorrow at dawn."

Someone was running up the beach, waving a bottle in each hand.

"They didn't want to tell you about the party. They thought that it might hurt your pride."

"My what . . . ?"

"If you knew they were making so big a thing of the job you had failed at—"

"But—"

"—and that had hurt you so in failure. They did not want you to be sad. But Tork wants to see you. I said you would not be sad. So I went to bring you down from the rocks."

"Thanks, I guess."

"Tio Cal?"

But the voice was bigger and deeper than a child's.

He sat on a log back from the fire, eating a sweet potato. The flame flickered on his dark cheekbones, in his hair, wet and black. He stood, came to me, held up his hand. I held up mine and we slapped palms. "Good." He was smiling. "Ariel told me you would come. I will lay the power line down through the Slash tomorrow." His uniform scales glittered down his arms. He was very strong. But standing still, he still moved. The light on the cloth told me that. "I . . ." He paused. I thought of a nervous, happy dancer. "I wanted to talk to you about the cable." I thought of an eagle, I thought of a shark. "And about the . . . accident. If you would."

"Sure," I said. "If there's anything I could tell you that would help."

"See, Tork," Ariel said. "I told you he would talk to you about it."

I could hear his breathing change. "It really doesn't bother you to talk about the accident?"

I shook my head and realized something about that voice. It was a boy's voice that could imitate a man's. Tork was not over nineteen.

"We're going fishing soon," Tork told me. "Will you come?"

"If I'm not in the way."

A bottle went from the woman at the shrimp crate to one of the guitarists, down to Ariel, to me, then to Tork. (The liquor, made in a cave seven miles inland, was almost rum. The too-tight skin across the left side of my mouth makes the manful swig a little difficult to bring off. I got "rum" down my chin.)

He drank, wiped his mouth, passed the bottle on and put his hand on my shoulder. "Come down to the water."

We walked away from the fire. Some of the fishermen stared after us. A few of the amphimen glanced, and glanced away.

"Do all the young people of the village call you Tio Cal?"

"No. Only my godchildren. Their father and I have been friends since I was your age."

"Oh, I thought perhaps it was a nickname. That's why I called you that."

We reached wet sand where orange light cavorted at our feet. The broken shell of a lifeboat rocked in moonlight. Tork sat down on the shell's rim. I sat beside him. The water splashed to our knees.

"There's no other place to lay the power cable?" I asked. "There is no other way to take it except through the Slash?"

"I was going to ask you what you thought of the whole business. But I guess I don't really have to." He shrugged and clapped his hands together a few times. "All the projects this side of the bay have grown huge and cry for power. The new operations tax the old lines unmercifully. There was a power failure last July in Cayine down the shelf below the twilight level. The whole underwater village was without light for two days; and twelve amphimen died of overexposure to the cold currents coming up from the depths. If we laid the cables farther up, we chance disrupting our own fishing operations as well as those of the fishermen on shore."

I nodded.

"Cal, what happened to you in the Slash?"

Eager, scared Tork. I was remembering now, not the accident, but the midnight before, pacing the beach, guts clamped with fists of fear and anticipation. Some of the Indians back where they make the liquor still send messages by tying knots in palm fibers. One could have spread my entrails then, or Tork's tonight, to read our respective horospecs.

Juao's mother knew the knot language, but he and his sisters never bothered to learn because they wanted to be modern, and, as children, still confused with modernity the new ignorances, lacking modern knowledge.

"When I was a boy," Tork said, "we would dare each other to walk the boards along the edge of the ferry slip. The sun would be hot and the boards would rock in the water, and if the boats were in and you fell down between the boats and the piling, you could get killed." He shook his head. "The crazy things kids will do. That was back when I was eight or nine, before I became a waterbaby."

"Where was it?"

Tork looked up. "Oh. Manila. I'm Filipino."

The sea licked our knees, and the gunwale sagged under us.

"What happened in the Slash?"

"There's a volcanic flaw near the base of the Slash."

"I know."

"And the sea is hypersensitive down there. You don't insult her fashion or her figure. We had an avalanche. The cable broke. The sparks were so hot and bright they made gouts of foam fifty feet high on the surface, so they tell me."

"What caused the avalanche?"

I shrugged. "It could have been just a goddamned coincidence. There are rock falls down there all the time. It could have been the noise from the machines—though we masked them pretty well. It

could have been something to do with the inductance from the
smaller power cables. Or maybe somebody just kicked out the wrong
stone that was holding everything up."

One webbed hand became a fist, sank into the other, and hung.
Calling, "Cal!"

I looked up. Juao, pants rolled to his knees, shirt sailing in the
sea wind, stood in the weave of white water. The wind lifted Tork's
hair from his neck; and the fire roared on the beach.

Tork looked up too.

"They're getting ready to catch a big fish!" Juao called.

Men were already pushing their boats out. Tork clapped
my shoulder. "Come, Cal. We fish now." We waded back to
the shore.

Juao caught me as I reached dry sand. "You ride in my boat,
Cal!"

Someone came with the acrid flares that hissed. The water
slapped around the bottom of the boats as we wobbled into the
swell.

Juao vaulted in and took up the oars. Around us green amphimen walked into the sea, struck forward, and were gone.

Juao pulled, leaned, pulled. The moonlight slid down his arms.
The fire diminished on the beach.

Then among the boats, there was a splash, an explosion, and the
red flare bloomed in the sky: the amphimen had sighted a big fish.

The flare hovered, pulsed once, twice, three times, four times
(twenty, forty, sixty, eighty stone they estimated its weight to be),
then fell.

Suddenly I shrugged out of my shirt, pulled at my belt buckle.
"I'm going over the side, Juao!"

He leaned, he pulled, he leaned. "Take the rope."

"Yeah. Sure." It was tied to the back of the boat. I made a loop in
the other end, slipped it around my shoulder. I swung my bad leg
over the side, flung myself on the black water—

—mother-of-pearl shattered over me. That was the moon,
blocked by the shadow of Juao's boat ten feet overhead. I turned below the rippling wounds Juao's oars made stroking the sea.

One hand and one foot with torn webs, I rolled over and looked
down. The rope snaked to its end, and I felt Juao's strokes pulling
me through the water.

They fanned below with underwater flares. Light undulated on
their backs and heels. They circled, they closed, like those deep-sea
fish who carry their own illumination. I saw the prey, glistening as it
neared a flare.

You chase a fish with one spear among you. And that spear

would be Tork's tonight. The rest have ropes to bind him that go up
to the fishermen's boats.

There was a sudden confusion of lights below. The spear had
been shot!

The fish, long as a tall and short man together, rose through the
ropes. He turned out to sea, trailing his pursuers. But others waited
there, tried to loop him. Once I had flung those ropes, treated with
tar and lime to dissolve the slime of the fish's body and hold to the
beast. The looped ropes caught, and by the movement of the flares, I
saw them jerked down their paths. The fish turned, rose again, this
time toward me.

He pulled around when one line ran out (and somewhere on
the surface the prow of a boat doffed deep) but turned back and
came on.

Of a sudden, amphimen were flicking about me as the fray's center drifted by. Tork, his spear dug deep, forward and left of the mar-
lin's dorsal, had hauled himself astride the beast.

The fish tried to shake him, then dropped his tail and rose
straight. Everybody started pulling toward the surface. I broke foam
and grabbed Juao's gunwale.

Tork and the fish exploded up among the boats. They twisted in
air, in moonlight, in froth. The fish danced across the water on its
tail, fell.

Juao stood up in the boat and shouted. The other fishermen
shouted too, and somebody perched on the prow of a boat flung a
rope and someone in the water caught it.

Then fish and Tork and me and a dozen amphimen all went
underwater at once.

They dropped in a corona of bubbles. The fish struck the end of
another line, and shook himself. Tork was thrown free, but he doubled back.

Then the lines began to haul the beast up again, quivering, whipping, quivering again.

Six lines from six boats had him. For one moment he was still in
the submarine moonlight. I could see his wound tossing scarves of
blood.

When he (and we) broke surface, he was thrashing again, near
Juao's boat. I was holding onto the side when suddenly Tork, glistening, came out of the water beside me and went over into the
dinghy.

"Here you go," he said, turning to kneel at the bobbing rim, and
pulled me up while Juao leaned against the far side to keep balance.

Wet rope slopped on the prow. "Hey, Cal!" Tork laughed,
grabbed it up, and began to haul.

The fish prised wave from white wave in the white water.

The boats came together. The amphimen had all climbed up. Ariel was across from us, holding a flare that drooled smoke down her arm. She peered by the hip of the fisherman who was standing in front of her.

Juao and Tork were hauling the rope. Behind them I was coiling it with one hand as it came back to me.

The fish came up and was flopped into Ariel's boat, tail out, head up, chewing air.

I had just finished pulling on my trousers when Tork fell down on the seat behind me and grabbed me around the shoulders with his wet arms. "Look at our fish, Tio Cal! Look!" He gasped air, laughing, his dark face diamonded beside the flares. "Look at our fish there, Cal!"

Juao, grinning white and gold, pulled us back into shore. The fire, the singing, hands beating hands—and my godson had put pebbles in the empty rum bottles and was shaking them to the music— the guitars spiraled around as we carried the fish up the sand and the men brought the spit.

"Watch it!" Tork said, grasping the pointed end of the great stick that was thicker than his wrist.

We turned the fish over.

"Here Cal?"

He prodded two fingers into the white flesh six inches back from the bony lip.

"Fine."

Tork jammed the spit in.

We worked it through the body. By the time we carried it to the fire, they had brought more rum.

"Hey, Tork. Are you going to get some sleep before you go down in the morning?" I asked.

He shook his head. "Slept all afternoon." He pointed toward the roasting fish with his elbow. "That's my breakfast."

But when the dancing grew violent a few hours later, just before the fish was to come off the fire, and the kids were pushing the last of the sweet potatoes from the ashes with sticks, I walked back to the lifeboat shell we had sat on earlier. It was three-quarters flooded.

Curled below still water, Tork slept, fist loose before his mouth, the gills at the back of his neck pulsing rhythmically. Only his shoulder and hip made islands in the floated boat.

"Where's Tork?" Ariel asked me at the fire. They were swinging up the sizzling fish.

"Taking a nap."

"Oh, he wanted to cut the fish!"

"He's got a lot of work coming up. Sure you want to wake him up?"

"No, I'll let him sleep."

But Tork was coming up from the water, brushing his dripping hair back from his forehead.

He grinned at us, then went to carve. I remember him standing on the table, astraddle the meat, arm going up and down with the big knife (details, yes, those are the things you remember), stopping to hand down the portions, then hauling his arm back to cut again.

That night, with music and stomping on the sand and shouting back and forth over the fire, we made more noise than the sea.

IV

The eight-thirty bus was more or less on time.

"I don't think they want to go," Juao's sister said. She was accompanying the children to the Aquatic Corp Headquarters in Brasilia.

"They are just tired," Juao said. "They should not have stayed up so late last night. Get on the bus now. Say good-bye to Tio Cal."

"Good-bye."

"Good-bye."

Kids are never their most creative in that sort of situation. And I suspect that my godchildren may just have been suffering their first (or one of their first) hangovers. They had been very quiet all morning.

I bent down and gave them a clumsy hug. "When you come back on your first weekend off, I'll take you exploring down below at the point. You'll be able to gather your own coral now."

Juao's sister got teary, cuddled the children, cuddled me, Juao, then got on the bus.

Someone was shouting out the bus window for someone at the bus stop not to forget something. They trundled around the square then toward the highway. We walked back across the street where the café owners were putting out canvas chairs.

"I will miss them," he said, like a long-considered admission.

"You and me both." At the docks near the hydrofoil wharf where the submarine launches went out to the undersea cities, we saw a crowd. "I wonder if they had any trouble laying the—"

A woman screamed in the crowd. She pushed from the others, dropping eggs and onions. She began to pull her hair and shriek. (Remember the skillet of shrimp? She had been the woman ladling them out.) A few people moved to help her.

A clutch of men broke off and ran into a side street. I grabbed a running amphiman, who whirled to face me.

"What in hell is going on?"

For a moment his mouth worked on his words for all the trite world like a beached fish.

"From the explosion . . ." he began. "They just brought them back from the explosion at the Slash!"

I grabbed his other shoulder. "What happened!"

"About two hours ago. They were just a quarter of the way through, when the whole fault gave way. They had a goddamn underwater volcano for half an hour. They're still getting seismic disturbances."

Juao was running toward the launch. I pushed the guy away and limped after him, struck the crowd and jostled through calico, canvas, and green scales.

They were carrying the corpses out of the hatch of the submarine and laying them on a canvas spread across the dock. They still return bodies to the countries of birth for the family to decide the method of burial. When the fault had given, the hot slag that had belched into the steaming sea was mostly molten silicon.

Three of the bodies were only slightly burned here and there; from their bloated faces (one still bled from the ear) I guessed they had died from sonic concussion. But several of the bodies were almost totally encased in dull, black glass.

"Tork—" I kept asking. "Is one of them Tork?"

It took me forty-five minutes, asking first the guys who were carrying the bodies, then going into the launch and asking some guy with a clipboard, and then going back on the dock and into the office to find out that one of the more unrecognizable bodies was, yes, Tork.

Juao brought me a glass of buttermilk in a café on the square. He sat still a long time, then finally rubbed away his white moustache, released the chair rung with his toes, put his hands on his knees.

"What are you thinking about?"

"That it's time to go fix nets. Tomorrow morning I will fish." He regarded me a moment. "Where should I fish tomorrow, Cal?"

"Are you wondering about . . . well, sending the kids off today?"

He shrugged. "Fishermen from this village have drowned. Still it is a village of fishermen. Where should I fish?"

I finished my buttermilk. "The mineral content over the Slash should be high as the devil. Lots of algae will gather tonight. Lots of small fish down deep. Big fish hovering over."

He nodded. "Good. I will take the boat out there tomorrow."

We got up.

"See you, Juao."
I limped back to the beach.

V

The fog had unsheathed the sand by ten. I walked around, poking clumps of weeds with a stick, banging the same stick on my numb leg. When I lurched up to the top of the rocks, I stopped in the still grass. "Ariel?"

She was kneeling in the water, head down, red hair breaking over sealed gills. Her shoulder shook, stopped, shook again.

"Ariel?" I came down over the blistered stones.

She turned away to look at the ocean.

The attachments of children are so important and so brittle. "How long have you been sitting here?"

She looked at me now, the varied waters on her face stilled on drawn cheeks. And her face was exhausted. She shook her head.

Sixteen? Seventeen? Who was the psychologist, back in the seventies, who decided that "adolescents" were just physical and mental adults with no useful work? "You want to come up to the house?"

The head shaking got faster, then stopped.

After a while I said, "I guess they'll be sending Tork's body back to Manila."

"He didn't have a family," she explained. "He'll be buried here, at sea."

"Oh," I said.

And the rough volcanic glass, pulled across the ocean's sands, changing shape, dulling—

"You were—you liked Tork a lot, didn't you? You kids looked like you were pretty fond of each other."

"Yes. He was an awfully nice—" Then she caught my meaning and blinked. "No," she said. "Oh, no. I was—I was engaged to Jonni . . . the brown-haired boy from California? Did you meet him at the party last night? We're both from Los Angeles, but we only met down here. And now . . . they're sending his body back this evening." Her eyes got very wide, then closed.

"I'm sorry."

I'm a clumsy cripple, I step all over everybody's emotions. In that mirror I guess I'm too busy looking at what might have been.

"I'm sorry, Ariel."

She opened her eyes and began to look around her.

"Come on up to the house and have an avocado. I mean, they have avocados in now, not at the supermarket. But at the old town market on the other side. And they're better than any they grow in California."

She kept looking around.

"None of the amphimen get over there. It's a shame, because soon the market will probably close, and some of their fresh foods are really great. Oil and vinegar is all you need on them." I leaned back on the rocks. "Or a cup of tea?"

"Okay." She remembered to smile. I know the poor kid didn't feel like it. "Thank you. I won't be able to stay long, though."

We walked back up the rocks toward the house, the sea on our left. Just as we reached the patio, she turned and looked back.

"Cal?"

"Yes? What is it?"

"Those clouds over there, across the water. Those are the only ones in the sky. Are they from the eruption in the Slash?"

I squinted. "I think so. Come on inside."

Quincy Troupe

(1943–   )

QUINCY THOMAS TROUPE, JR. sets the idioms of black American speech to the musical cadences of blues and jazz to create a vibrant, rhythmic poetry whose focus is the lives, life-styles, and daily concerns of black people. Stylistically and thematically, his work is in the mainstream of black American poetry of the 1960s and 1970s. A scholar, teacher, and prolific writer, Troupe has also edited a number of poetry anthologies and magazines and co-authored a book of nonfiction. Together with his wide-ranging teaching career, Troupe's literary achievements make him one of the most active creative forces in the Black Arts movement.

Troupe was born in New York City in 1943 and grew up in St. Louis, Missouri. In 1963 he received the B.A. in history and political science from Grambling College in Louisiana. From Louisiana he moved to Los Angeles and earned the A.A. in journalism at Los Angeles City College in 1967.

During the sixties and early seventies, Troupe was a member of a young black writers' group based in the Los Angeles area and taught creative writing for the Watts Writers' Movement. During the summers of 1969 and 1970 he was director of the Malcolm X Center in Los Angeles and also of the John Coltrane festivals in that city. His activities during this period brought him into close contact with other writers who rose to prominence in the late sixties, including Jayne Cortez and Stanley Crouch. The musical influences on his work sprang from his association with Sly Stone and Maurice White (of Earth, Wind, and Fire), who were also members of the Watts Writers' Movement.

Beginning in 1968 Troupe served as editor of a number of literary journals: *Shrewd, Mundus Artium, American Rag,* and *Confrontation: A Journal of Third World Literature.* He also edited two anthologies: *Watts Poets* (1968) and *Giant Talk: An Anthology of Third World Writings* (1975). His own work began appearing in poetry journals in 1970 and has been widely anthologized since then. Two collections, *Embryo Poems* and *Snake-Back Solos,* were published in 1972 and 1978, respectively. *Snake-Back Solos* won the American Book Award in 1980. *The Inside Story of TV's "Roots,"* which he co-authored with David L. Wolper, was published in 1978. He is also the author of *Skulls Along the River* (1984); *Miles,* an autobiography of Miles Davis (1989); and *Weather Reports: New and Selected Poems* (1991). He has edited *James Baldwin: The Legacy* (1989). Among other awards,

Troupe won a National Endowment for the Arts grant in 1978 and a New York Foundation for the Arts fellowship in poetry in 1987.

Troupe's diverse teaching career, which also began in 1968, has led him from coast to coast and overseas as well. He has taught creative writing and black American, American, and Third World literatures at several California universities and colleges, at Ohio University, at the University of Ghana in Legon, and at the City University of New York's College of Staten Island where he directed the poetry center. At present, he is a professor of literature at the University of California at San Diego. Troupe's poetry readings have included appearances at UCLA, Harvard, Yale, Dartmouth, Howard University, Louisiana State, and Michigan State. More information about Troupe's styles and influences can be found in the article by Horace Coleman in *Dictionary of Literary Biography, Volume 41.*

The following poems are taken from *Weather Reports: New and Selected Poems.*

THE OLD PEOPLE SPEAK OF DEATH

For Leona Smith, my grandmother

the old people speak of death
frequently now
my grandmother speaks of those now
gone to spirit
now less than bone

they speak of shadows
that graced their days made lovelier
by their wings of light speak of years
& corpses of years of darkness
& of relationships buried
deeper even than residue of bone
gone now beyond hardness
gone now beyond form

they smile now from ingrown roots
of beginnings of those who have left us
& climbed back through the holes the old folks
left in their eyes
for them to enter through

eye walk back now with this poem
through the holes the old folks left in their eyes
for me to enter through walk back to where
eye see them there
the ones that have gone beyond hardness
the ones that have gone beyond form
see them there
darker than where roots began
& lighter than where they go
with their spirits
heavier than stone their memories
sometimes brighter than the flash
of sudden lightning

but green branches will grow
from these roots darker than time
& blacker than even the ashes of nations
sweet flowers will sprout
& wave their love-stroked language
in sun-tongued morning's shadow
the spirit in all our eyes

they have gone now back
to shadow as eye climb back out
from the holes of these old folks eyes
those spirits who sing through this poem
gone now back with their spirits
to fuse with greenness
enter stones & glue their invisible
faces upon the transmigration of earth
nailing winds singing guitar blues
voices through the ribcages
of these days
gone now to where the years run
darker than where roots begin
greener than what they bring

the old people speak of death
frequently now
my grandmother speaks of those now
gone to spirit
now less than bone

REFLECTIONS ON GROWING OLDER

eye sit here, now, inside my fast thickening breath
the whites of my catfish eyes, muddy with drink
my roped, rasta hair snaking down in twisted salt & pepper
vines braided from the march of years, pen & ink lines etching
my swollen face, the collected weight of years swelling
around my middle, the fear of it all overloading circuits
here & now with the weariness of tears, coming on in storms
the bounce drained out of my once liquid strut
a stork-like gimpiness there now, stiff as death
my legs climbing steep stairs in protest now, the power gone
slack from when eye once heliocoptered through cheers, hung around rims
threaded rainbowing jumpshots, that ripped, popped cords & envious peers
gone, now the cockiness of that young, firm flesh
perfect as arrogance & the belief that perpetual hard-ons would swell
forever here, smoldering fire in a gristle's desire, drooping limp now
like wet spaghetti, or noodles, the hammer-head that once shot straight in
& ramrod hard into the sucking sweet heat of wondrous women
wears a lugubrious melancholy now, like an old frog wears its knobby head
croaking like a lonely malcontent through midnight hours
eye sit here, now, inside my own gathering flesh
thickening into an image of humpty-dumpty
at the edge of a fall, the white of my hubris gone
muddy as mississippi river water
eye feel now the assault of shotgunned years
shortening breath, charlie horses throbbing through cold
tired muscles, slack & loose as frayed, old ropes
slipping from round the neck of an executed memory
see, now, these signals of irreversible breakdowns—
the ruination of my once, perfect flesh—as medals earned
fighting through the holy wars of passage, see them as miracles
of the glory of living breath, pulsating music through my poetry—
syncopating metaphors turned here inside out—
see it all now as the paths taken, the choices made
the loves lost & broken, the loves retained
& the poems lost & found in the dark
beating like drumbeats through the heart

POEM FOR MY FATHER

For Quincy T. Trouppe Sr.

father, it was an honor to be there, in the dugout
with you, the glory of great black men swinging their lives
as bats, at tiny white balls
burning in at unbelievable speeds, riding up & in & out
a curve breaking down wicked, like a ball falling off a table
moving away, snaking down, screwing its stitched magic
into chitling circuit air, its comma seams spinning
toward breakdown, dipping, like a hipster
bebopping a knee-dip stride, in the charlie parker forties
wrist curling, like a swan's neck
behind a slick black back
cupping an invisible ball of dreams

& you there, father, regal, as an african, obeah man
sculpted out of wood, from a sacred tree, of no name, no place, origin
thick branches branching down, into cherokee & someplace else lost
way back in africa, the sap running dry
crossing from north carolina into georgia, inside grandmother mary's
womb, where your mother had you in the violence of that red soil
ink blotter news, gone now, into blood graves
of american blues, sponging rococo
truth long gone as dinosaurs
the agent-oranged landscape of former names
absent of african polysyllables, dry husk consonants there
now, in their place, names, flat, as polluted rivers
& that guitar string smile always snaking across
some virulent, american, redneck's face
scorching, like atomic heat, mushrooming over nagasaki
& hiroshima, the fever blistered shadows of it all
inked, as etchings, into sizzled concrete

but you, there, father, through it all, a yardbird solo
riffing on bat & ball glory, breaking down the fabricated myths
of white major league legends, of who was better than who
beating them at their own crap game, with killer bats,
as bud powell swung his silence into beauty of a josh
gibson home run, skittering across piano keys of bleachers
shattering all manufactured legends up there in lights
struck out white knights, on the risky edge of amazement
awe, the miraculous truth sluicing through
steeped & disguised in the blues

confluencing, like the point at the cross
when a fastball hides itself up in a slider, curve
breaking down & away in a wicked, sly grin
curved & posed as an ass-scratching uncle tom, who
like old sachel paige delivering his famed hesitation pitch
before coming back with a hard, high, fast one, is slicker
sliding, & quicker than a professional hitman—
the deadliness of it all, the sudden strike
like that of the "brown bomber's" crossing right
of sugar ray robinson's, lightning, cobra bite

& you, there, father, through it all, catching rhythms of chono
pozo balls, drumming, like conga beats into your catcher's mitt
hard & fast as "cool papa" bell jumping into bed
before the lights went out

of the old, negro baseball league, a promise, you were
father, a harbinger, of shock waves, soon come

Arnold Rampersad

(1941–   )

ONE OF THE leading voices in African American literary criticism in the 1980s, Arnold Rampersad is presently Woodrow Wilson Professor of Literature at Princeton University. He graduated *magna cum laude* from Bowling Green State University in 1967, received his M.A. degree from Bowling Green in 1968, and completed the requirements for an A.M. degree from Harvard University in 1969. He also received his Ph.D. degree from Harvard University in 1973.

Professor Rampersad's teaching record has moved with the same pace as the rate with which he received his academic degrees. He has worked as an assistant professor at the University of Virginia and Stanford University where he was promoted to associate and full professor. While a faculty member at Stanford, he served as a visiting associate professor in the Department of Afro-American Studies at Harvard University. He was a full professor in English at Rutgers University from 1983 to 1988 and Zora Neale Hurston Professor of English at Columbia from 1988 to 1990.

Rampersad's scholarly productivity ranges from numerous book reviews on African American literary works, articles on poetry, fiction, biography, autobiography, the Afro-American literary blues tradition, southern literary history, various aspects of the Harlem Renaissance to five books: *Melville's Israel Potter: A Pilgrimage and Progress* (1969); *The Art and Imagination of W. E. B. Du Bois* (1976); *The Life of Langston Hughes. Volume I: 1902–1941: I Too Sing America* (1986); *The Life of Langston Hughes. Volume II: 1941–1967: I Dream a World* (1988); and *Slavery and the Literary Imagination* (1989), which he co-edited with Deborah McDowell. Despite the fact that Rampersad's literary biography of W. E. B. Du Bois is an invaluable source book to anyone teaching Du Bois's works or studying his life, the Du Bois study never became as popular as Rampersad's Hughes biography.

This superb study presents the particular history of Langston Hughes's life so well that the reader not only acquires a feeling of intimacy with Hughes as he lived from day to day, but also with American and world history guided by Langston Hughes between 1902 and 1967. And characteristic of biography at its best, *The Life of Langston Hughes* is not panegyric nor gratuitously condemnatory; it interprets the facts of Langston Hughes's life through his own letters, those who knew him, the diversity of his career, and his works. Though the biography leaves a few issues unresolved, it leaves none unquestioned. As might be expected, Professor

Rampersad has lectured on Langston Hughes throughout the United States—
at UCLA, Atlanta University, the Smithsonian Institution, the University
of Pennsylvania, Chicago, Illinois, Baltimore, Maryland, and the University
of Massachusetts. In addition to serving as consultant to the National
Endowment for the Humanities, the Educational Testing Service, and National Public Radio, he is a recipient of a number of prestigious awards
and honors such as the College Language Association Creative Scholarship
Award, a Guggenheim Fellowship, a Rockefeller Fellowship, Best Books
of 1986 by *Choice* Magazine, and Best Books of 1986 by the *New York
Times Book Review*, and the MacArthur Prize Fellowship (1991).

The following selection comes from *The Life of Langston Hughes. Volume
1: 1902–1941: I Too Sing America.*

THE FALL OF A TITAN

The Big Sea then unfolds as if written by a man completely at ease
with himself. The book covers Hughes's life until 1931, or his departure for Haiti following his break with his wealthy patron Godmother (who is never identified, and who was still alive) and his
controversy with Zora Neale Hurston over their play "Mule Bone."
But apart from his somber words about his break with Godmother, no controversy, whether over race, class, sex, or personality, is allowed to ruffle the smiling surface of Langston's tale. His
leftist opinions and involvements have vanished without a trace.
The poem about the Waldorf-Astoria is presented in excerpts
which criticize the rich without actually asserting any radical sentiment; Hughes carefully omits its last, most radical section ("Hail
Mary, Mother of God!/The new Christ child of the Revolution's
about to be born"). He recalls the poem as his innocent reaction
to the oncoming Depression ("The thought of it made me feel bad,
so I wrote this poem"), and—erroneously—as a cause of his break
with Godmother. While one love affair, with Anne Coussey in Paris
in 1924, is orchestrated into a much more dramatic episode than it
was in reality, it is also finally sacrificed to Langston's life mission
and his greatest love, poetry and the black race.

To a newspaper editor, Hughes described the book as written
with the "pace and incident value of a series of short stories. It is not
'literary' in the highbrow sense." And yet the text remains curiously

poised. The balancing act is forced on Hughes by the double audience that almost any black writer bearing a racial message but dependent on a white publisher has to keep in mind. The smiling poise of *The Big Sea* is, in fact, the poise of the blues, where laughter, art, and the will to survive triumph at last over personal suffering. *The Big Sea* replicates the classic mode of black heroism as exemplified in the blues; it spurns the more violent, cynical, embittered mode, one which Langston, for all his racial radicalism, had never embraced. He wrote very gently, though not unmovingly, about his devastating break with Godmother, and only humorously about Zora Neale Hurston ("a very gay and lively girl") and their controversy. Again, Hughes depends on his black readers to understand at once how the style and substance of his book, and his life, cohere with the style and substance of their lives, as they laughed to keep from crying and, in so doing, endured and even prevailed. The variety of audience and the unusual model of heroism make the depth of *The Big Sea* truly puzzling to both black and white readers. Because it is firmly grounded, however, the narrative eventually succeeds. The powerful ability of the text to convince its readers derives most from its astonishingly simple, water-clear prose, which certifies the integrity of Hughes's narrative. His sentences are utterly devoid of linguistic affectation, as pure and compelling as an innocent child's might be; Hughes wrote a quintessentially American prose. As for the extended section on the Harlem Renaissance, "when the Negro was in vogue," Van Vechten was correct; it would never be surpassed as an original source of insight and information on the age.

With the autobiography virtually set, Langston turned to other projects. He sold two poems to *The New Yorker*, "Hey-Hey Blues" (which appeared in late November) and "Sunday Morning Prophecy." He also sent a revised libretto of *Troubled Island* to William Grant Still, with whom he had worked intermittently on his various trips to Los Angeles. Hughes also pressed on with his García Lorca translations. Typing and binding three private booklets of poems from "Gypsy Ballads," he dedicated one to his old Carmel friend Marie Short, whose mixture of personal sadness and obvious affection for him touched Langston, and who had recently moved to Carmel following a divorce. A fundraising program also kept him busy. In Cleveland, fire had gutted the Karamu theater after a long-envious black newspaper had suggested that the Jelliffes' playhouse needed to be burned down. Appalled, Hughes wrote to a number of his wealthier friends soliciting money on behalf of Karamu, and attacking "the intolerance of many whites and the bigotry and ignorance of many Negroes in the Cleveland community."

In need of cash himself, Langston also began to plan a reading tour for the new year, 1940. But more immediately he needed a vacation, and spent several days in San Francisco. He visited the Golden Gate International Exposition, where Count Basie's orchestra was a sensation; at the city opera house, Hughes heard Kirsten Flagstad in *Tristan und Isolde*. Inside the landmark Coit Tower he proudly inspected his name and Van Vechten's inscribed among others on a mural. He visited Matt and Evelyn "Nebby" Crawford and their little daughter "Nebby Lou," "the prettiest child in the world," nicknamed after her mother and Louise Thompson; and Roy Blackburn, his former secretary at "Ennesfree" in Carmel, now a married man. Then Hughes returned for the Christmas holidays to peaceful Hollow Hills Farm, where the residents hailed the birth of four white lambs and twin black goats on Christmas Eve as a sign from heaven. Under a huge tree in the main house were many gifts for him, including one from Noël Sullivan that was perfect for a restless traveller—an overcoat with a zippered lining. Almost all of Langston's gifts were pieces of clothing; his needs were obvious to his friends.

With *The Big Sea* set for publication, Hughes determined that his next book would be as a lyric and racial poet, an identity generally submerged in the previous decade in favor of fiction and the theater, or altered in the direction of Marxist verse. "I am about to go back to one of my earlier art forms," he wrote Lieber, "having flirted so passionately (but to no purpose) with the theatre. That hussy!" He took yet another step into his past with his choice of poems. Picking through his uncollected pieces, he set aside his radical socialist verse, which Knopf would not have published in any case. Culling about two dozen blues pieces, he added almost a dozen more dialect or ballad poems, including his brilliant "Death in Harlem" about Arabella Johnson and the Texas Kid—"one of the best poems I ever wrote." He then capped them with a sequence of seven poems called "Seven Moments of Love: An Un-Sonnet Sequence in Blues," in which he had tried to merge the blues with a vaguely sonnet-like form. He foresaw "a light and amusing book" just right for an America haunted by fears of war. With the right illustrations, it could make "a marvellous and grand HEY HEY cullud and colorful book" that would be "lots of fun. And ought to sell, too!"

Hughes's judgment of America and the publishing industry seemed on the mark. *Esquire* bought "Seven Moments of Love" for its May, 1940, number for just over $100 (the most ever paid for one of his poems), and *Poetry* accepted two blues poems for its April issue. Robinson Jeffers admired the collection, and Van Vechten was ecstatic. But once again Blanche Knopf was cool to his efforts; she postponed a decision on whether to publish the book. She further

disappointed Langston by declining to bring out a cheap edition of
Not Without Laughter, which he wanted for his coming tour, or to
provide advertising leaflets to give away on the tour. To these rejec-
tions he could say little. After twenty years in the magazines, and
fourteen years with the firm of Alfred A. Knopf, he had still not
brought himself or his publishers anything like financial success. He
was a poor man's literary Titan, without a best-seller.

As in his return to poetry in general and the blues in particular,
and his avoidance of radical writing, Hughes signalled in other ways
his backward turn in life. Once again he published in the *Crisis*,
thus ending the estrangement that had begun with the Scottsboro
controversy, and also in *Opportunity*, the journal of the Urban League. In these magazines he published mostly ballads. Hughes showed
he had not lost the ability to tap the reservoir of hurt, resentment,
and determination in the race, as in his quickly popular "Note on
Commercial Theatre," about the often shameless plundering of black
music and culture by whites:

> You've taken my blues and gone—
> You sing 'em on Broadway
> And you sing 'em in Hollywood Bowl,
> Black and Beautiful—
> And you mixed 'em up with symphonies
> And you fixed 'em
> So they don't sound like me.
> Yep, you done taken my blues and gone.
> . . . .
> But someday somebody'll
> Stand up and talk about me,
> And write about me—
> Black and beautiful—
> And sing about me,
> And put on plays about me!
> I reckon it'll be
> Me myself!
>
> Yes, it'll be me.

Reluctantly on February 10, just after his thirty-eighth birthday,
Langston set out for the East. Ironically, his poetry tour started in
Downington, Pennsylvania, exactly where his epic 1931 to 1932
journey through the South had begun. Then, backed by the Rosenwald Fund but fired by radical zeal, he had taken poetry heroically
to the people. This time, although he was sometimes sponsored by
progressive groups such as the International Workers Order,
Hughes's main interest was in eking out a living. He read his way

south from Downingtown, then turned eastward and north to New York, where he appeared on February 28 at the influential Young Men's Hebrew Association on Lexington Avenue at 92nd Street in Manhattan, brought there by his friend Norman Macleod, the founder of its new Poetry Center. (The previous year, 1939, Macleod had published a novel, *You Get What You Ask For*, in which Langston briefly appeared, thinly disguised as a radical writer named "Larry," just back from the Soviet Union and Japan around 1935, and living first in Carmel, then in New York.) Near mid-March, Hughes spoke to excellent crowds in Lexington and Frankfort, Kentucky; on March 17, over 600 persons turned out for his reading sponsored by the NAACP in Columbus, Ohio. In Dayton two days later to speak to the leftist League for Progressive Action, he eulogized Otto Reeves, a local black youth who had been killed in Spain. He lectured at black Wilberforce University, and in nearby Yellow Springs at the liberal white Antioch College, then went down to Nashville and Chattanooga, Tennessee, the most southern points of the tour. The tour proceeded as planned, except for a quick trip to New York when lawyers at Knopf warned that his portrait of Jean Toomer, especially its mockery of Toomer's flight from the race, was possibly libelous.

Hating the Jim Crow bus above all, he endured the more spacious Jim Crow railroad car, and longed for the luxury of touring in his own automobile as he had in 1931–32. Most of all, he longed to be back in Carmel Valley: "Your farm, Noël, is a little heaven," he had written Sullivan. Hardly an improvement compared to his previous tour, his average fee was around $35, his highest probably $95; his profit would be small. In most places, Hughes simply spun the old scratchy Gramophone disc of his program; he read his poems (more than once Hughes declared that he did not like them enough to memorize them) interspersed with uplifting, gently humorous, only occasionally barbed commentary. He was well aware that this atmosphere of mildness and decorum contrasted sharply with the news from Europe, especially France, where Nazi stormtroopers and the Luftwaffe were inflicting terrible losses on opposing forces and hapless civilian communities. "If Paris is taken I don't know how to stand it," Langston wrote Sullivan in May. Doubtless he had inflated his tone to match his patron's solemnity, but Hughes's feeling was also genuine. When France fell, he agonized about the black writers trapped by the Nazis. "What has become, what will become of them?" he wondered. "The barbarism of the whole thing is more than I can ascribe to human intelligence."

By March 29, he was sick of the road when the toughest part of his schedule began. An eleven-day tour of West Virginia institutions sponsored by the state supervisor of Negro schools led Hughes dizzily through steel and coal towns in "a kind of continual going round the mountain, mighty interesting but tiring, dusty, and dirty." In the Louisville area, dozens of long-lost relatives on his father's side of the family vied with each other to entertain him, with hot toddies for breakfast and so much food that he feared he would soon resemble "Fats" Waller. Near the end of April he reached Cleveland. Then, at long last, the tour ended with a lecture at the University of Chicago on May 8, and another at the inter-racial forum of the Plymouth Congregational Church in Detroit four days later, after which he returned to Chicago and the restful company of Arna and Alberta Bontemps.

As he toiled from town to town, Langston could reflect sorrowfully on how little his financial state had improved since 1931, and how much he still struggled merely to meet his basic expenses. A Titan should not have to go on tour. He had a particular reason now to dwell on this subject of money. On a train north to Cornell University in Ithaca, New York, he finally finished reading a novel he had carried around for some time, Richard Wright's *Native Son*. The previous November, Arna Bontemps had sent the extraordinary news, almost impossible to believe, that the Book of the Month Club had selected the yet unpublished *Native Son* as its offering for January, 1940. As Bontemps wanly observed, Wright's financial problems were solved forever. Langston must have felt at least a twinge of pure envy. After twenty years of publication, he was still poor; with only his second book, Wright now bathed in a shower of gold.

Hughes liked Richard Wright. Their professional relationship was excellent, as when Langston proposed to dramatize a Wright short story for the Suitcase Theatre, or Wright approached Hughes about the magazine *New Challenge*, a revival of Dorothy West's *Challenge*, which Wright had hoped to develop into a significant journal; the men had even collaborated on a song, "Red Clay Blues," published in *New Masses* the previous August. Although some other blacks found Wright ruthlessly self-serving, to Langston the young writer from Chicago out of Mississippi was both charming and highly talented. In any event, the power of *Native Son* could not be denied. "It is a tremendous performance!" Hughes congratulated Wright. "A really great book which sets a new standard for Negro writers from now on. Congratulations and my very best wishes for a great critical and sales success." Langston was doing whatever he could to help Wright: "I've been ballyhooing the book at all my lectures."

Calling *Native Son* a "tremendous performance" did not mean, however, that Hughes liked the book. He did not. And the fact that the novel set new standards for black writers must have brought almost as much pain as pleasure to the most prolific of Negro authors.

The publication of *Native Son* was, moreover, a disheartening challenge to Hughes in that he found the black world it described both familiar and utterly repugnant. The raw, phallic realism and naturalism of Wright's novel, the unrelieved sordidness of his depiction of black life, repelled Langston. Probably the greatest wonder for him, however, was that *Native Son* had succeeded financially and critically in spite of the fact that it bared Wright's almost unrelieved distaste for blacks, on one hand, and his evident love-hatred of whites, on the other. Hughes found almost beyond comprehension the notion that this distaste and love-hatred would yield so compellingly to fictive treatment, and that white America would then embrace such a book and so generously reward its aggressive author. And Langston could hardly forget that he himself had scouted the same South Side of Chicago for his own still-unwritten second novel, intended as a continuation of *Not Without Laughter*.

In three weeks, the story of Bigger Thomas, black rapist and murderer, sold over 200,000 copies, a number far greater than all of Hughes's sales in almost two decades of publishing. Unflattering to Langston, furthermore, Knopf decided to attach *The Big Sea* to the coattails of *Native Son*, hustling for an August publication "to get some benefit out of all that publicity." But whatever Langston's reservations, the brilliant novel opened his eyes. "I keep looking for Bigger running over the roof tops," he wrote to Van Vechten from Chicago. "See plenty of his brothers in the streets." His chance to speak publicly on the novel came on April 28, at a tea sponsored by the Chicago Public Library for hundreds of its employees. Declining, according to one newspaper, to appraise the book as literature, he instead stressed its social import. Bigger Thomas was an exception rather than the rule, he argued, in the reaction by blacks to their suffering; blacks as a whole disapproved of the book because they feared to be identified with a murderer. If Hughes's remarks were accurately reported, they were limp, narrow, and really deprecating, and unworthy of the man who had once excoriated the taste of the black bourgeoisie. Powerfully prophetic, *Native Son* was too divisive, too harsh in its judgment of black and white alike for him to accept Wright's triumph easily.

"The hosannas are all for Dick Wright," Arna Bontemps had comforted him, "from now till *The Big Sea* comes out." Hearing about Hughes's speech, Bontemps sent further encouragement: "Folks think about same concerning Dick's book up here." While he was accurate in his reporting and also loyal to Hughes, Bontemps himself, a far more liberal judge of writing than Langston, had the highest regard for Wright and *Native Son*. Building on their common Seventh Day Adventist background, and as serious readers in a community hardly

devoted to books, Wright and Bontemps had developed a strong affection and respect for one another in Chicago. Disdainful of envy
and somewhat more objective about their race than Langston, Bontemps had no difficulty facing up to the fact, as a black novelist, that
Wright had revolutionized the fictional presentation of Afro-American life with *Native Son*. At the same time, however, Bontemps lost
none of his respect for Hughes, especially as a poet. "According to
my father more than once," one of Bontemps's children later recalled, "almost from the start of their relationship he had recognized
in Langston an original, authentically American artist, a grand creative figure like Mark Twain or Walt Whitman, in spite of his flaws
as a writer, and thus essentially beyond criticism. No new rival, no
matter how accomplished, could diminish Langston's standing in the
national literature. My father admired other black writers, but he
never lost that lofty view of Langston." For one very simple reason,
Bontemps had wanted *The Big Sea* to be "a real titan's book"; he saw
Hughes, with all his shortcomings as a man of literature, as nevertheless a figure of epic proportion.

Hughes's situation, however, left him little opportunity for epic
gestures. While he nervously awaited his share of the hosannas, he
snapped at any offer of work that came his way. Jobs with the radio
networks were so rare for blacks that he jumped at a request from
the Columbia Broadcasting System for scripts for a dramatic series,
"The Pursuit of Happiness." But CBS rejected the first two scripts he
offered. His musical play with James P. Johnson, *The Organizer*, was
"too controversial for us to give it an emotional treatment on an essentially dramatic show." (The play had been performed successfully
at a convention of the progressive International Ladies Garment
Workers Union the previous year.) But a script on the accommodationist educator Booker T. Washington was just right for airing on
April 7, the day the U.S. Post Office released a stamp bearing Washington's likeness—the first time any black American had been so
recognized.

In this crucial period of assessment and reassessment of his life,
Langston drew more and more on his relationship with Arna
Bontemps, whose career as a writer had itself progressed steadily.
With a children's book written with Hughes and two novels, *God
Sends Sunday* and *Black Thunder*, behind him, in 1938 Bontemps had
published another "juvenile," *Sad-Faced Boy*, then brought out his
third novel, *Drums at Dusk*, the following year. After starting graduate work in English at the University of Chicago, he had won a Rosenwald Fellowship to write and travel in the Caribbean. Along with
other writers such as Jack Conroy and Nelson Algren, he had be-

come a recognized part of the younger literary set in Chicago; Bontemps terminated his job with Shiloh Academy and joined Conroy in writing a WPA volume on blacks in Chicago. By this time, his friendship with Langston had become tightly woven by a shuttle of letters, generally circumspect and to the point, but enlivened by an effervescent good humor, that flitted back and forth between them with scarcely a pause. For all their levity, the letters between the men show the high value they both placed on restraint, order, and discipline.

Unquestionably the friendship deepened as Hughes's sense of self as a writer became more materialistic and pragmatic, as his original myth-making power and his radical socialist force became less exuberant. At the base of the relationship was probably Langston's need for a confidant, a shelter on which he could depend in his wanderings, and Bontemps's willingness to fulfill that need in return for a link to someone he saw as both good and great—a spiritual brother and, at the same time, the best of black writers. The cement was their careful integrity in dealing with each other and the world. They trusted one another implicitly; until they died, nothing strained their fraternal relationship. Slowly through the thirties, then accelerating in importance as the decade ended, Arna Bontemps's voice became the sound most trusted by Langston. In some senses, Bontemps was an island Hughes had passed in his wandering, then circled, and finally come back to in a gathering storm.

By 1940, the two men had become, as Alberta Bontemps would remember them, "close, closer than blood brothers." Blood brothers fought or drifted apart; these two men stayed with one another not physically but in their thoughts, expressed in letters. "He was always wherever we were," Alberta Bontemps would recall of Hughes in spite of the infrequency of his visits. "I liked him. I really liked him. I was a little jealous at first because he consumed so much of Arna's time, but that feeling passed. They were different in some ways. You couldn't put either on the best dressed list, but while Langston was only careless, Arna dressed like a gangster; he wore black shirts and white or yellow ties. You see, they were handsome and knew it; they didn't need anything. Langston drank; Arna hardly touched liquor. Langston read very little. Arna read everything, except detective stories. He would drive me crazy—every time he passed a newsstand he picked up a different paper. He always had to have what was current in books and magazines. I used to jump on him about that, when we needed so many things. As for Langston, I think he picked up most of his ideas out of the gutter, if you know what I mean. He had the touch. He could dine with kings and with common people. Arna was not so flexible. But otherwise they were very much alike.

And with all the hard work, Langston was considerate. He was thoughtful about other people. He would always laugh and tell me: 'Alberta, when we come into the money, we are going to buy you a tiara!' "

In Bontemps's children, Hughes clearly vested much of his paternal feeling; to Joan, Paul, Poppy, Camille, and Constance, he was a warm, bubbling presence easily drawn into comradeship. "I have no early memory that doesn't include Langston," Paul Bontemps (Arna's second child) would recall. "His manner with children was wonderful. We loved him. He never patronized us, never descended to baby talk or pats on the head. And he always brought gifts, no matter how small, whenever he visited." Hughes was like Paul's father in "the way he was calm and in control of his emotions. Langston's largest emotion was laughter, or humor. I do not remember him ever being irritable, much less shouting."

Early in 1940, Bontemps accepted the post of cultural director of the state-sponsored American Negro Exposition in Chicago, set to run later that year, from July 4 to Labor Day, in conjunction with the Diamond Jubilee of black emancipation. At once he looked for a place for Hughes, who was paid $140 to confer in New York with Exposition officials about entertainment to be staged in conjunction with the fair. Langston then agreed to write the book for "Jubilee: A Cavalvade of the Negro Theatre," a compendium of scenes from celebrated musicals such as "Shuffle Along." Hughes also was to prepare a smaller, original revue called "The Tropics After Dark." These assignments would keep him in Chicago for some time.

While the now famous Richard Wright (the "sepia Steinbeck") leisurely purchased a house in Chicago for his mother, then prepared to sail for Mexico with his white wife of several months, an elegant ballet dancer named Dhima Meadman (their best man had been young Ralph Ellison), Langston unpacked his belongings in a drab hotel room in Chicago. "The ladies of the race, I presume, are raising hell!" he speculated about the marriage. "Equality, where is thy sting?" As for the Exposition, he began work without a contract. Charmed by the smooth young black men running the fair, he had the promise of generous terms once the shows were launched. Among his co-workers, in addition to Bontemps, was the musician Margaret Bonds; Horace Cayton was director of research, assisted by the scholarly young sociologist St. Clair Drake; the poet Frank Marshall Davis took charge of publicity. The absence of a contract seemed quite unimportant, since Hughes's two projects were prominently featured in advertisements for the fair. Besides, the cause was noble: here were talented young blacks organizing to celebrate the achievement of the race in America. Near the end of March, his book for "The Tropics After Dark" was ready, with music by Margaret Bonds and Zilner Randolph. Then, with the help of W. C. Handy and other veteran black entertainers, the historical "Cavalcade" script was complete. Langston had written two songs for the shows, one set to music by the gospel composer Thomas Dorsey, author of "Precious Lord, Take My Hand," the other by Duke Ellington.

Neither show, however, went into rehearsal as planned. The state grant of $75,000, plus the promise of a matching sum by the federal government, attracted the more brazen elements of Chicago's political and criminal establishments, which were sometimes indistinguishable. One white politician called in his secretary, dictated the History of the Negro Race, and demanded that it be purchased. The carpenters' union insisted that sets built by non-union labor be torn down. The musicians' union set an extortionate scale of payment. For a while, independent financing for "The Tropics After Dark" proved elusive; then, after a skirmish over concession rights, a beer company offered $5000 to launch the show. But the grant was delayed while a fake corporation was established to launder the money. As tempers flared in the summer heat, Hughes began to wonder exactly when he would be paid. Merely to raise the subject of money at the Exposition, he wrote Maxim Lieber, one needed a gun in one hand, a sledgehammer in the other, and a knife between one's teeth.

On July 4, when the Exposition opened at the Chicago Coliseum, neither the "Cavalcade" nor "The Tropics After Dark" was ready. The glories of black achievement proved inadequate as an attraction; without music and dance, the crowds quickly thinned. Hughes, who had warned against expecting people to come simply for information, was fatalistic. "Just how much culture can the masses take," he joked, "unless Little Egypt is around to shake?"

On July 12, the alarmed Exposition leaders stripped "The Tropics After Dark" of Hughes's dialogue and pushed it onto a stage at the beer hall. Rehearsals were a formality: the orchestra itself showed up only four hours before the first performance. The epic "Cavalcade" script remained unused as the Exposition daily fell deeper into debt. When Hughes made a final appeal for payment, the young black lawyer in charge of the Exposition, Truman K. Gibson, meticulously itemized the losses of the fair, then respectfully declined to sign the contracts for Langston's work. When Hughes threatened to sue, Arthur Spingarn sent the names of two eminent black Chicago lawyers, but advised against pressing the case. Disgusted, Hughes saw the entire affair as typical "cullud" mismanagement. The Diamond Jubilee of freedom? "We need twice 75 more years to be ready to celebrate this present period." After visiting the black lawyers named by Spingarn, he gave up all plans to sue. "I think a gangster would have more success collecting our money than a lawyer," he decided, "and would probably ask no higher per centage."

Chicago, he judged sourly, was "certainly one of the chief abodes of the Devil in the Western Hemisphere." His spring and summer, the ill-paying, exhausting tour and the fiasco of an Exposition, had been almost a total loss. One respite had come with a visit to Cleveland to mark both the twentieth anniversary of his high school class and the removal of Central High, now ninety-five percent black, to a new building on 40th Street. Another event of mixed appeal, however, was the appearance of the first book devoted exclusively to him and his work, *Langston Hughes: Un Chant Nouveau*, by the Haitian physician, social scientist, and amateur historian René Piquion, with an introduction by Arna Bontemps. Although Langston was flattered by the attention, Piquion's work was assailed by critics as an unhappy mixture of weak biography and Stalinist propaganda. Hughes had fared better the previous year when the excellent black scholar and critic J. Saunders Redding had praised him as "the most prolific and the most representative of the New Negroes," as well as the finest interpreter of the black masses in their distinctive racial feeling, in Redding's landmark study of black American verse, *To Make A Poet Black*.

In July, Richard Wright was back in town, estranged from his bride but hardly daunted, apparently; within a few months he would marry another bright woman, Ellen Poplar, also white, whom he had known in the party, and whom Bontemps would report as being "perhaps the best bet—if one is to judge by looks." Wright and Hughes were honored at a reception given by Jack Conroy and Nelson Algren for the launching of *New Anvil* (in which the first editorial promised to reveal the Richard Wrights of tomorrow; Langston Hughes, presumably, was passé). Acting more and more with the assurance of a celebrity, like a man who would never again live on the South Side or in any black community, Wright joined Hughes on a tour of the Exposition. Although Langston gave Wright no sign about his reservations concerning the book, he was not happy about the turn of events; a little too gleefully he reported to Noël Sullivan about *Native Son* that "most Negroes hate the book! And lots of left-wingers, too!"

Anxiously awaiting the first copies of *The Big Sea*, he was eager to match Wright's success with a best-seller of his own. At the end of July, when his ten free copies came ("my most handsome jacket so far!"), Langston threw himself into what even for him was a gigantic publicity effort. He stalked the booksellers, checking on their orders; to Knopf in New York went a long list of prospective buyers, including every person mentioned in the book who was still alive.

Concerned with sales overseas, he pressed for a Spanish translation. Portions were sold to *Town and Country* and *Saturday Review of Literature*, and to the *Afro-American* group of newspapers. Blurbs were secured from Erskine Caldwell, Fannie Hurst, Granville Hicks, Janet Flanner, Paul Green, and Louis Adamic; he nudged Mrs. Knopf to try for one from the saintly Eleanor Roosevelt. Appearing on every radio show that would have him, Hughes cocked an ear for the hosannas Bontemps had predicted. The owner of the popular Argus Book Shop in Chicago anticipated "a tremendous sale because it's a terrific book." On August 22, days before the official publication of the book, Blanche Knopf sent him the "really fine" *New York Times* review set to appear the following Sunday. And *Newsweek* magazine called *The Big Sea* perhaps the most readable book of the year.

Still, *Native Son* loomed over Hughes and his autobiography, blocking the sun. "That boy is sure kicking up the dust," Bontemps had written about Wright's latest triumph; *Native Son* was to be made into a play, with Wright collaborating with Paul Green, and Orson Welles, hailed as a genius after *Citizen Kane* the previous year, directing. On September 6, at a dinner in New York, Langston and five thousand others heard Wright tell in great detail exactly how he had come to focus on the extraordinary character of Bigger Thomas. The occasion was a benefit for the Negro Playwrights Company, a group formed earlier in the year to further black drama (it would soon collapse, with a loss of $12,000) and including Hughes in an honorary position, Wright, Theodore "Ted" Ward, and Powell Lindsay.

Given its blend of disingenuousness and complexity, *The Big Sea* not surprisingly drew sometimes contradictory reviews. Alert, the *New York Times Book Review* saw it as "both sensitive and poised, candid and reticent, realistic and embittered." Bitterness, or the lack of bitterness, was a favorite topic with white reviewers. The New York *Sun* noted that Hughes "does not allow much bitterness to creep in"; a syndicated reviewer urged whites to read it "because it is true and honest and not bitter." Where some reviewers found honesty, others saw undue reticence. In the *Nation* Oswald Garrison Villard spoke of initial disappointment, but finally of Hughes's "absolute intellectual honesty and frankness." Alain Locke, however, regretted that Hughes had glossed over important matters (his thanks to Langston, no doubt, for passing over Locke's sexual aggression and his duplicity with Mrs. Mason). Ella Winter, who once had begged Hughes to omit her name from the title page of their radical play, found him "too gentle with us 'white folks.' " Ralph Ellison, by then a Marxist, complaining that "too much attention is apt to be given to the aesthetic aspects of experience at the expense of its deeper mean-

ings," questioned whether the style was appropriate to "the autobiography of a Negro writer of Hughes's importance." Walt Carmon,
with whom Hughes had lived for a while in Moscow, was shocked to
notice "not a single mention of a radical publication you've written
for or a single radical you have met or has meant anything to you."
Several readers linked *Native Son* to *The Big Sea*; one called publicly
for Wright to read Hughes's book before it was too late. In *The New
Republic*, Wright himself, now suddenly the most prestigious voice in
black writing, praised Hughes as "a cultural ambassador" and for
having carried on "a manly tradition" in literature when other writers "have gone to sleep at their posts." But Wright liked the book
much less than he let on. In calling Hughes "a cultural ambassador,"
he invited recollection of a passage in his most important essay,
"Blueprint for Negro Writing." There, he had scorned past black
writers in general as the "prim and decorous ambassadors," the "artistic ambassadors" of the race, "who went a-begging to white America . . . in the knee-pants of servility."

A few days after a reception given for him and Wright by the
New Anvil group in Chicago, Langston left for Carmel Valley. Spending one day in Los Angeles, he conferred with officials of the progressive Hollywood Theatre Alliance about its plan for a socially
conscious "Negro Revue," to include members of the New Negro
Theatre, which Hughes had started there. The Alliance found
Hughes, after his Chicago experience, a tough bargainer. Refusing to
begin work without a signed contract, he declined to manage, direct,
or raise funds for the project. He also declined to wait while the Alliance discussed his terms. Retaining Loren Miller as his local lawyer, he took the noon train to Monterey and Hollow Hills Farm.

To Langston's surprise and delight, he now had a mansion of his
own in Noël Sullivan's "little heaven." On August 1, the Feast of the
Transfiguration, a day considered significant for artists, the devout
Sullivan had started construction of a one-room cottage for Hughes;
a month later, Sullivan and a group of friends, including Robinson
Jeffers, had christened the cottage with champagne. Langston was
touched. Seven years before, he had fled from Carmel in confusion;
now he felt almost at home in Carmel Valley. The autumn rains had
not yet come, the summer hills were brown, the orchards in the valley dark green and heavy with peaches. Comfortable in his little
house, he played with Greta, the aging German Shepherd who had
kept him company in Carmel in 1933, and whose framed portrait he
had carried about with him on his recent travels.

He revised his collection of poems, which Blanche Knopf had finally approved for publication after Van Vechten had sweetly ("Dear

Grand Duchess") petitioned her. On November 2, Hughes sent her the manuscript, now called "Shakespeare in Harlem." He also requested a loan of $50 to pay a dentist to repair his teeth, which were in very bad shape. The money came, but Mrs. Knopf turned down his request for illustrations by Covarrubias of *The Weary Blues* (another glance backwards for Langston), because Covarrubias was never on time with his work. She vetoed Hughes's suggestion of the black *Esquire* cartoonist E. Simms Campbell, the illustrator of *Popo and Fifina*, as inappropriate (perhaps too crude) for Langston's style; she dismissed samples of work by Zell Ingram, Hughes's old friend, as not good enough. She also balked at the title "Shakespeare in Harlem," about which Hughes himself had serious reservations, but Van Vechten rushed to praise it and the entire volume, which had been revised largely according to his advice. "The whole book sings," he assured Hughes, "with that kind of wistful loneliness you have made peculiarly your own."

By this time Langston was back in Los Angeles, staying at the Clark Hotel at the corner of South Central Avenue and Washington Boulevard, lured by an advance of $25 a week against royalties to help Donald Ogden Stewart, the president of the League of American Writers and the husband of Ella Winter, to prepare the "Negro Revue" for the Hollywood Theatre Alliance. Hughes's royalty as sketch "director" would be half of one per cent of the gross, with separate payment for original material.

In Los Angeles, he seized every opportunity that came his way to promote *The Big Sea*. His major chance came on November 15 at the expensive Vista del Arroyo Hotel in the wealthy suburb of Pasadena, when five hundred guests were expected for a "Book and Author" luncheon to be chaired by George Palmer Putnam, the retired publisher and the widower of the aviator Amelia Earhart. Hughes was at the hotel, no doubt anticipating gales of applause and the sale of at least one hundred copies, when a motley caravan of motor vehicles, including a sound-truck blaring a recording of "God Bless America," rumbled up to the elegant entrance. A hundred truculent members and supporters of the Four-Square Gospel Church and the Angelus Bible College had come to protest his appearance by picketing the luncheon. Behind this act was one of the more notorious of American evangelists, Aimee Semple McPherson, who had survived sundry lawsuits, public fights with her mother and her daughter, and a sex scandal involving a cottage in Carmel, to prevail as head of her influential fundamentalist religious group. Just before noon, she telephoned George Palmer Putnam to confirm her leadership of the picketers. McPherson had a specific reason to harass Hughes. She was one of the allegedly fraudulent ministers of religion mentioned by name in his "Goodbye Christ." The entire poem was reprinted on leaflets that denounced Hughes as a communist and challenged the guests: "ATTEND THE LUNCHEON CHRISTIANS . . . and eat, *if you can.*" Hughes and Putnam wanted to press on with the reading, but the manager of the hotel preferred to cancel the lunch rather than have his hotel picketed. The police tried to help by citing two protestors for traffic offences; the group, however, refused to be intimidated. Badly embarrassed, Hughes then offered to withdraw. The Chief of Police of Pasadena and George Palmer Putnam escorted him to an automobile for the ride back to Los Angeles.

That night, he wrote a careful account of the incident to Noël Sullivan, who may not have known about the poem. The next morning, to his relief, the *Los Angeles Times* treated his mishap farcically; Langston Hughes was "Old Satan," wrestled to defeat in a "modern mat encounter" with some local evangelicals. Before a group of black clubwomen, Langston disparaged McPherson's act as a mere publicity stunt, and breezily announced that he would not press a lawsuit against her. But he was frightened by the most formidable personal opposition he had ever encountered, and by the exposure of "Goodbye Christ" after years of silence or inconsequential reprintings. McPherson's followers included some blacks, and certain black ministers had denounced the poem soon after its publication.

Hughes continued work on the revue but did so reluctantly; he longed to be back in his little cottage at Hollow Hills Farm. He was the only black writer on the project, his salary was small, and a long daily commute from the Clark Hotel was necessary because, as he wrote his agent, "in this charming democracy of ours there seems to be no place for Negroes to live in Hollywood even if they do work out there occasionally." And much as he admired fellow writer Charles Leonard, "a swell fellow" who had worked with Wallace Thurman on his Broadway play *Harlem*, and Donald Ogden Stewart, he found the Rodeo Drive radicals in the leftist Hollywood Theatre Alliance exasperating. One day the committee was militant, the next day frivolous, "so the love songs go back in and the lynching numbers come out." He also had trouble convincing "good and clever white writers" that simply transcribing material into black dialect did not necessarily make it genuine black material, or material appealing to blacks. To Maxim Lieber and his wife, Minna, he summed up his trials in dealing with the various Hollywood attitudes and factions: "What would you say is the ratio of *two plus* multiplied by *x-y* over *black z* divided by *liberal q* plus *left a* over the *necessary b* of the unified *zip* desired for a revue? I await your answer for classification."

He stayed in Los Angeles because he needed the money and because he hoped that two or three songs might "click." He hated the thought of going back on tour soon. In addition, songwriting was steadily becoming something of an addiction to him, like gambling, perhaps like the "numbers," where a small investment of time might bring a windfall of reward. Lieber had scolded him the previous year, when he had jumped at Clarence Muse's offer of a long-term contract, that he was more than a lyricist. But if his agent would help him to be a song writer just "one MORE time I will never bother you again," Langston later begged. He sent along an explanatory lyric: "The sweetest words a letter knows / Is *check enclosed*." Two songs, each part of an elaborate skit, with music by the French-trained composer Elliot Carpenter, were promising. One was "Mad Scene From Woolworth's" or "Going Mad With A Dime," in which a woman with only ten cents cavorts against a typical dime store set. The other, even more important to Hughes, was a parody of "Old Black Joe" called "America's Young Black Joe," the climax of a skit about Joe Louis based on an idea by Charles Leonard:

> I'm America's YOUNG BLACK JOE.
> Most times good natured, smiling and gay
> My sky is sometimes cloudy
> But it won't stay that way.
> I'm comin', I'm comin'—
> But my head *ain't* bending low!
> I'm walking proud! I'm speaking loud!—
> I'm America's YOUNG BLACK JOE!

On December 15, when the skit was staged at an NAACP gala, with film clips of black athletes and heroes projected behind the singer, "America's Young Black Joe" created such a stir that Hughes sped it off to Van Vechten, John Hammond of Columbia Records, and Lieber—the song had "a good chance of becoming a kind of Negro GOD BLESS AMERICA, expressing their patriotic and democratic sentiments." Thus Langston began a campaign to counter the charges of un-Americanism made against him, charges especially telling with the surge of patriotism that accompanied the growing expectation that the United States would soon be at war.

One skit that failed to mature showed Hughes's continuing fascination, perhaps obsession, with Richard Wright's success:

> My name's Richard Wright and I try to write
> Like Bigger Thomas talks.
> As a matter of fact for the sake of this act,
> I try to walk like Bigger walks,
> Cause:
> > I'm a boogie woogie man.
> > I'm a native son with a fountain pen gun . . .

The singer is a "great big hairy . . . / Cash and carry, best-selling literary / Boogie, boogie woogie man."

Just after the NAACP gala, and in spite of the success of his patriotic song, Langston slipped out of Los Angeles. He went so quietly that two weeks passed before the Alliance leaders knew that he was gone. Although he was in effect breaking a contract, he was sick of the revue and the factions in the Alliance, tired of the long commute to Hollywood, and anxious to rest at the Farm. But he had barely unpacked in his *retiro* when the *Saturday Evening Post* of December 21 arrived to jolt him. Inside was a reprint of the Aimee McPherson handbill, including the dreaded poem. Like McPherson, the magazine was exacting revenge for having been named in "Goodbye Christ": the *Post* had earned its place in 1932 by curtly refusing to publish "Good Morning Revolution." Langston wrote Blanche Knopf to suggest a lawsuit against the *Post*, which he hoped might deter others from reprinting the poem. But the damage continued. Stanford University, the most fashionable school among the California rich, cancelled a planned appearance there.

The Christmas season, 1940, was haunted by the ghost of "Goodbye Christ" and Hughes's desire to repudiate this extreme evidence of his radical past. In a fateful step, he spent several days laboring on a statement about the poem which he sent to everyone who mattered, including Knopf, the Associated Negro Press, and the Rosenwald Fund, from whom he hoped to win a fellowship soon. Hughes capitulated to his critics. Characterizing himself as "having left the terrain of the 'radical at twenty' to approach the 'conservative at forty,' " he affirmed that he "would not and could not write" such a poem now, "desiring no longer to *épater le bourgeois*." He asserted that the poem had been withdrawn from circulation (but he did not say how or when he had done so). In any case, it had been simply a satire on the exploiters of religion, ironically cast from a Communist point of view that had not been authentically his own. "Lord help me!" Langston sighed to Arna Bontemps about his statement. "Better show it to the Rosenwald Folks so they'll be clarified, too."

The end of the year found him, he confessed, "broke and remorseful as usual," "broke and ruint." Langston was also sick. He told everyone who inquired that he felt vaguely arthritic and influenza-ridden, although he had no clear signs of the flu. Alone in his little cottage, he nursed a deepening sense of depression, of financial and perhaps even artistic failure in his life. He had cleared less than $1200 for the year, or so he reported for his income tax. His long, tiring spring tour had yielded little profit. His trust in the leadership of the Negro Exposition celebrating black emancipation had ended bitterly. "Boy of the Border," the Mexican children's book with Arna Bontemps, had been rejected repeatedly by publishers. And the story of his life, *The Big Sea*, had done poorly, given his high hopes and the grand success of *Native Son*. In spite of decent reviews and Bigger Thomas's bloody coattails, only 2845 copies had been sold so far in the United States. Apparently he was not as popular as he had believed, Hughes might well have thought. From Arna Bontemps he heard that sales of *Native Son* had declined abruptly, once people had discovered that it was not a detective story. But Langston was not much consoled by the news.

Although the Hollywood Theatre Alliance chided him about his sudden, unannounced departure ("a great loss to the project") and pressed for his return, Hughes made no plans to leave the farm. He roused himself on January 10 only to attend a dinner given by Noël Sullivan for Robinson Jeffers on the poet's fifty-fourth birthday. Poet to poet, Hughes praised Jeffers to the skies: "All of human terror and frailty, and all the mud of mankind's earth-rooted feet, and the sea-wind and sky-wind in men's hair, and their hands that would find a star, and the shock of rock here and star there . . . these things come to rest in Jeffers." Robinson Jeffers was so many things that Hughes was not. Settled in a house built virtually with his own hands, protected by a stalwart wife (to whom Langston had just addressed a poem) and handsome sons, Jeffers was a man consistent in his saturnine vision, tenaciously a tragic poet. In Langston's depression, the contrast must have seemed severe; he had described Jeffers in his tribute exactly as one might describe a real Titan.

His illness worsened. Once again, as in the greatest moments of anxiety in his life, he felt his body poisoned, his limbs locking, the bones, especially in his left knee, hurting terribly. To those who sympathized he talked still of sudden arthritis and of a coming cold that never finally came. On January 14, however, he asked Eulah Pharr to drive him to see a local physician, Dr. Russell Williams. The doctor urged his immediate removal to the Peninsula Community Hospital in Carmel.

At half past four that afternoon, Hughes entered the institution as a patient. He was quickly diagnosed as suffering not from influenza or any similar ailment, as he knew well, but from gonorrhea.

By this time, the infection was in an advanced stage. He had picked up the venereal infection about five or six weeks previously, during the first week of December, toward the end of his stay in Los Angeles—under what conditions, it is impossible to say. The length of time before seeking expert treatment suggests strongly that it was his first venereal infection. A Wasserman test for syphilis proved negative. Langston was treated with sulfathiazole, the standard drug in the age before penicillin, but showed only slight response. A course of sulfapyridine brought no response and was stopped. A painful catheter through his penis, applied "with tenderness & caution!!" (as someone teased in his medical record) drained the infection and allowed a gradual clearing of the discharge. His diet of sulfa led to constant grogginess and even delirium, as well as a dramatic loss of appetite and severe constipation. Hughes's temperature remained high for several days, and he was also treated for sinusitis. His bones continued to hurt him, especially in his left leg—a condition he attributed to running down a hill a few weeks before, although the pain was thought to be a side-effect of his infection.

As he lay in the hospital suffering from this unspeakable illness (sciatica, he wrote one friend; arthritis, he assured another), with his medical bills piling up and with no idea of how he might pay them, a succession of lesser blows struck at Langston's crumbling self-esteem. Blanche Knopf advised him that her lawyers could do nothing about "Goodbye Christ," because the poem, published outside the country apparently with his consent, since he had not immediately repudiated it, was in the public domain. His grave doubts about the wisdom of the circulated statement deepened when the tough-minded Carl Van Vechten, who detested the poem, nevertheless questioned whether Hughes should have apologized at all. Perhaps worst of all for Langston, as a symbol of his head-long fall from grace, came the news that he had just been evicted as the tenant of the three-room apartment at 66 St. Nicholas Place in Harlem, after his most recent sub-tenants, including his "brother" Kit, had fallen $98 behind in the rent. Langston's possessions would be removed by Toy Harper.

"Last straw N.Y. eviction," he wrote Arna Bontemps briefly, gasping and in obvious pain. "Guys let their rent get behind—way behind—without my knowing it. And put out. Well, anyhow, here I am moaning and groaning. Fever is down, so can write with effort. . . . More news when able to write. Love to Alberta and kids. I'm weak and groggy."

A newspaper item that must have come to his attention sooner or later brought the chill of public contempt, and the accusation of cowardice and dishonor, to Langston's sick bed. On January 15, the communist *People's World* of San Francisco, long one of his supporters, heaped scorn on his statement about "Goodbye Christ" and his other recent efforts, such as the marching song "America's Young Black Joe," to put as much distance as possible between himself and his old views. "Hughes has been bitten with the war bug," a popular book columnist named Ben Burns judged. "Not only is he primping for ye imperialism but now has renounced all the sentiments expressed in his 'Goodbye Christ.' . . . Instead of defending the poem which appropriately said goodbye to Christ because of all the sins against Negroes committed in His name," Langston Hughes had timidly apologized for having written it. "This Hughes is a long way from the Hughes who not so many years ago wrote:

> 'Put one more 'S' in the USA
> and make it Soviet
>
> 'Put one more 'S' in the USA,
> We'll live to see it yet."

The time had come for the faithful to turn their backs on this traitor. "So goodbye Huges [sic]," the columnist jibed in the *People's World*, mocking the poet with his own reckless phrase from his days of radical glory in 1932 in Moscow. 'This is where you get off."

Gloria T. Hull

(1944–   )

AT THE VANGUARD of the black women's studies movement in the United States, Gloria Hull has since 1972 been teaching, publishing articles, reviews, and books, and editing and lecturing in the field of African American literature with special emphasis on the works of African American women writers. The eldest of three children, Hull was born in Shreveport, Louisiana in 1944. She was reared by her mother, a housewife and domestic, and a stepfather, a carpenter and disabled World War I veteran. She graduated summa cum laude with her B.A. from Southern University at Baton Rouge in 1966 and received her M.A. and Ph.D. in English from Purdue University, in 1968 and 1972, respectively.

Before completing her dissertation, *Women in Byron's Poetry: A Biographical and Critical Study*, Hull accepted a position as instructor in the English department at the University of Delaware. In addition to teaching courses on writing and literary analysis, including African American writing and women's culture, she also worked on numerous university committees, particularly those involving the status or welfare of women and blacks.

The synthesis of women's and racial issues characterizes Hull's prodigious critical output, for which she first received national recognition in 1982 with the publication of the landmark interdisciplinary study *All the Women Are White, All the Blacks Are Men, But Some of Us Are Brave: Black Women's Studies*, which she edited with Patricia Bell Scott and Barbara Smith. Appropriately published by the Feminist Press, this important book is the first of its kind to collect statements by black women feminists who define black feminism and who discuss racism in women's studies and in the feminist movement. It also provides bibliographies, bibliographic essays, and selected course syllabi for black feminist studies.

Hull's other book publications—*Give Us Each Day: The Diary of Alice Dunbar-Nelson* (1986), *Color, Sex, and Poetry: Three Women Writers of the Harlem Renaissance* (1987), and *The Works of Alice Dunbar-Nelson* (1988)— demonstrate her commitment to securing the place of black women writers in the annals of African American literary history and to providing reference and critical tools that greatly aid in the study of these writers. Her book *Color, Sex, and Poetry* in its discussion of the lives and works of Alice Dunbar-Nelson, Angelina Weld Grimké, and Georgia Douglas Johnson is an indispensable work for anyone studying the Harlem Renaissance, particularly black women poets of this time period.

In addition to having published over twenty-three articles that address black women's literary issues in journals as diverse as *The Princeton Encyclopedia of Poetry and Poetics*, *The Radical Teacher*, and *Black American Literature Forum* as well as book reviews of works by women, Professor Hull is also a poet. Her first collection of poetry, *Healing Heart: Poems 1973–1988*, was published by Kitchen Table–Women of Color Press in the winter of 1989. Her long interest in poetry is reflected in her numerous scholarly publications on women poets, in her various lectures across the United States and in Jamaica on women poets, and in the host of journals that have published her own poems such as *Callaloo*, *Women's Studies Newsletter*, *Obsidian*, and *Chrysalis*.

Presently a full professor of women's studies at Kresge College, the University of California, in Santa Cruz, Professor Hull has received an impressive array of awards, honors, and grants, including Who's Who among Black Americans, Outstanding Young Woman of America, National Institute of Women of Color Award, National Endowment for the Humanities Summer Stipend, Rockefeller Foundation Fellowship, Ford Foundation Postdoctoral Fellowship, and a Fulbright Fellowship, which gave her the opportunity to work as a senior lecturer at the University of the West Indies in Kingston, Jamaica.

For further reading, see Linda Metzger, ed., *Black Writers: A Selection of Sketches from Contemporary Authors* (1989).

The following selection is taken from the introduction to *Color, Sex, and Poetry*.

COLOR, SEX, AND POETRY
The Renaissance Legacy

After the Harlem Renaissance, black women writers continued to explore what Gloria Wade-Gayles describes as "the narrow space of race, the dark enclosure of sex."[1] Paralleling Afro-American social, political, and literary history, they have advanced to sharper, more sophisticated racial-sexual self-definitions and a more integrated and provocative handling of these ubiquitous themes. How they treat this material is still an amalgam of personal, racial, sexual, and societal factors impinging upon them as individual creative artists. It proves that, in matters such as this, things change even as they remain the

From *Color, Sex, and Poetry: Three Women Writers of the Harlem Renaissance* by Gloria T. Hull. Published by Indiana University Press. Reported by permission of the publisher.

[1]Gloria Wade-Gayles, *No Crystal Stair: Visions of Race and Sex in Black Women's Fiction* (New York: The Pilgrim Press, 1984).

same. Later writers both echo and extend the issues—personal, thematic, stylistic—of their earlier sisters is an ever-increasing variety of ways. Even a brief look at the poets and writers is revealing.

In the generally depleted 1930s, Zora Neale Hurston's culturally based exploration of black female selfhood in her 1937 novel, *Their Eyes Were Watching God*, was revolutionary. It opened the way for Ann Petry to depict Lutie Johnson entangled in a destructive web of race-sex-class (*The Street*, 1944), and for Dorothy West to evoke the neuroses of Cleo Judson wrought by the same deadly skein (*The Living is Easy*, 1947). Poets, too, were breaking free of limiting notions of poetic femininity and speaking with stronger, surer voices. In her prize-winning 1942 volume, *For My People*, Margaret Walker assumed the griot voice of "her people" to chronicle their defeats and triumphs, celebrate their heroes and heroines, and consider her own specific place in this complex lineage.

Gwendolyn Brooks began presenting the characters from *A Street in Bronzeville* in 1945, often using them as the narrative personae of her poems and ballads. When she wrote *Annie Allen* in 1949, she made explicit her earlier attention to black women by elevating a plain young woman named Annie to the status of an epic hero in "The Anniad." She also embodied a racial-stylistic dilemma reminiscent of the Harlem Renaissance writers when she wrote of Annie in the learned, allusive, and dense academic language of the mainstream poetic elite in order to prove that she, a black woman poet, could also "write well." Brooks's preoccupation with the browns, blacks, tans, chocolates, and yellows of Afro-American color— especially as this schema victimizes her darker-skinned female characters—brings out openly in black women's literature what had been previously submerged or subverted.

Like their earlier counterparts, both Brooks and Walker also wrote novels, the lyrical *Maud Martha* (1953) and the historical *Jubilee* (1966), respectively. Theirs, however, are very successful ones that creatively utilize the autobiographies of their authors. *Jubilee* is based on the life of Walker's great-grandmother during slavery and Reconstruction, while the title character of *Maud Martha* is a fictionalized Gwendolyn Brooks, an ordinary black woman with her own kind of dandelion beauty. It also bears mentioning that Walker spent twenty-seven years writing *Jubilee* because of interruptions resulting from marriage, childbirth, childrearing, scarce money, teaching jobs, and lack of time.

When Afro-American poetry exploded in the 1960s–70s, women were well represented. Mari Evans announced *I Am a Black Woman* (1970) and wrote movingly from that core. Lucille Clifton celebrated husband and children, and her own vaselined legs and nappy hair.

Nikki Giovanni catalogued a long list of black martyrs, then asked her brethren and sistren if they, too, knew how to kill.

Sonia Sanchez suggests the amazing new range of the black female poet. Writing with a harsh, "unfeminine" militancy, she can flatly declare:

> blues ain't culture
> they sounds of
> oppression
> against the white man's
> shit/[2]

In a beautiful, cadenced standard English that contrasts with her rhythmic black street dialect, she eulogizes Malcolm X. However, she also writes of relationships between black men and women, of the problems and possibilities that lie in black children, and, most poignantly, of personal/black female selfhood and pain:

> but i am what i
> am. woman. alone
> amid all this noise.[3]

Throughout, she autobiographically, culturally, and artistically centers herself as

> this honeycoatedalabamianwoman
> raining rhythms of blue/black smiles[4]

Clearly, the Black Power and Black Arts movements provided inspiration and outlet for these new Afro-American women poets as the Harlem Renaissance had for the writers of that era. Interestingly, they, too, found themselves discriminated against because of their sex and gender, so much so that Audre Lorde could protest acidly that "Black is / not beautiful baby."

> not
> being screwed twice
> at the same time

---

[2]Sonia Sanchez, from "liberation/poem," in *We a BadddDDD People* (Detroit: Broadside Press, 1970), p. 54.

[3]Sonia Sanchez, from "personal letter no. 2," in *Home Coming* (Detroit: Broadside Press, 1969), p. 32.

[4]Sonia Sanchez, from *A Blues Book for Blue Black Magical Women* (Detroit: Broadside Press, 1974), p. 41.

from on top
as well as
from my side.[5]

Though these contemporary women poets could not be dismissed for
the araciality of their subjects or the delicacy of their tones or the
anachronism of their style, they could still be relegated to second
place in a movement that was designed, in more than rhetorical
terms, for "the black man."

However, the late 1970s–80s added a new ingredient: The
women's/feminist movement. Black women, who by right of blood
belonged to both the women's and the black movements, found
themselves decrying racism in the one and sexism in the other.
They were also confronted with the falsely dichotomized but still
vexing question of which was paramount—their race or their sex.
Though earlier women sometimes wrote as if they could not make
up their internal minds about this issue (one recalls, for example,
Dunbar-Nelson's many fragmentations and evasions), no one so
directly posed the challenge (sometimes accusation) of choice.
Again, Lorde crystallizes the dilemma in her "Who Said It Was
Simple." This poem features a black woman at a feminist demonstration realizing that she is "bound by my mirror / as well as my
bed" and wondering "which me will survive / all these libera-
tions."[6] Despite apparent contradictions, the women's/feminist
movement—in its critique of patriarchy and raising of female consciousness—contributed significantly to the bold, self-assured
honesty of Afro-American women's work. At the same time, it provided them with another (sometimes alternative) audience and
means of support. Notably, the acceptance of lesbianism and other
heretofore too-personal, too-female themes saved the literary lives
of many women poets, both black and white. Angelina Grimké's
tragedy did not have to be replayed.

The ascendancy of poetry and drama in the 1960s–70s was challenged by the fiction writers of the late 1970s–80s. Unlike the earlier
decades when the post-Harlem Renaissance period of fiction was
dominated by the names of men such as Richard Wright, Ralph Ellison, and James Baldwin, this new age did not witness the disappearance of women. In fact, the primary writers are female—for example, Toni Morrison, Gayle Jones, Alice Walker, Toni Cade Bambara,
Gloria Naylor, and Paule Marshall. Critic Barbara Christian makes a

---

[5]Audre Lorde, from "Hard Love Rock #II," in *The New York Head Shop and Museum*
(Detroit: Broadside Press, 1974), p. 24.
[6]Audre Lorde, from "Who Said It Was Simple," in *From a Land Where Other People Live*
(Detroit: Broadside Press, 1973), p. 39.

statement about these women writers that links them to their pioneering cohorts and simultaneously points out the distance traveled. She posits: "The extent to which Afro-American women writers
in the seventies and eighties have been able to make a commitment
to an exploration of self, as central rather than marginal, is a tribute
to the insights they have culled in a century or so of literary activity."[7] This ability to maintain "an overtly self-centered point of view"
distinguishes modern Afro-American women writers; but it is a
stance made possible by the wobbly steps in that direction of forebears like Alice Dunbar-Nelson, Angelina Grimké, and Georgia
Douglas Johnson.

From this surety of self, black women writers are consciously
exploring their ancient wisdoms and spiritual selves, their relationships with other women (as mothers, sisters, friends, lovers),
their ties to their black communities and culture, their place in
the African diaspora, their multivalent eroticism, their personal relationships to the politics and history of their age, and so on.
More than this, out of their sense of a black female "writerly" self,
they are, like their white contemporaries, devising new, more appropriate forms in which to package their experiences. Walker's
The Color Purple (1982) utilizes the crude but eloquent letters of
uneducated black women. Billie Holiday could sing the lines that
Alexis DeVeaux writes about her in *Don't Explain: A Song of Billie
Holiday* (1980). Paule Marshall chants an African praise poem in
her *Praisesong for the Widow* (1983) and uses the non-naturalistic
techniques of dream and hallucination. Audre Lorde invents a
form, biomythography, in which to tell her story in *Zami: A New
Spelling of My Name* (1982). ntozake shange unifies poetry, drama,
and women's nonliterary expressionistic forms in her "choreopoem," *for colored girls who have considered suicide/when the rainbow is enuf* (1977), while in her more recent *sassafras, cypress, and
indigo* (1982), she incorporates recipes and voodoo charms. Mich-
elle Parkerson combines poetry, fiction, science fiction, and film
in her experimentally effective *Waiting Rooms* (1983). And this already long list could be indefinitely extended.

There is some fear that the current black female literary renaissance may prove to be as much of a "fad" as the New Negro one
of the 1920s. However, whether white people and the literary es-

---

[7]Barbara Christian, "Trajectories of Self-Definition: Placing Contemporary Afro-
American Women's Fiction," in her *Black Feminist Criticism: Perspectives on Black Women
Writers* (New York: Pergamon Press, 1985), p. 172.

tablishment remain thrilled with what black women write should not be the measure of these writers' achievement. Though Afro-American women in general are fighting some of the same old gorgons with fresh-sprung heads, the scribes are depicting this as well as myriad new realities in works that will endure. Some dawns are, in truth, the beginning of a brand-new day.

Robert B. Stepto

(1945–   )

THE 1979 PUBLICATION of Robert B. Stepto's *From Behind the Veil: A Study of Afro-American Narrative, Chant of Saints: A Gathering of Afro-American Literature, Art, and Scholarship* and *Afro-American Literature: The Reconstruction of Instruction* (which he co-edited) signaled the beginning of post-structuralist critical strategies of African American literature. Teaching since 1974 in the English department at Yale University, Professor Stepto has since 1980 been at the forefront of new developments in African American literary criticism.

Born in 1945, in Chicago, Illinois, Stepto received his B.A. degree at Trinity College (Hartford, Conn.) in 1966 and his M.A. and Ph.D. degrees from Stanford University in 1968 and 1974 respectively. Before completing the requirements for the Ph.D., he accepted a position as assistant professor of English and American studies at Williams College from 1971 to 1974. In 1974, he joined the faculty at Yale University, where he is now a full professor of English, Afro-American studies, and American studies. At Yale he served as director of undergraduate studies for Afro-American studies from 1974 to 1977 and as director of graduate studies for Afro-American studies from 1978 to 1981 and again from 1985 to 1989.

In spite of a host of administrative duties, his commitments to professional organizations, his work as consultant for such journals as *American Literature, Callaloo,* and *American Quarterly,* and numerous lectures in this country and abroad, Stepto has also been a very productive scholar. In addition to the works mentioned previously, he is also editor of *The Selected Poems of Jay Wright* (1987) and co-editor of a special edition of *Callaloo* entitled "Recent Essays from Europe: A Special Issue." Selections from his *From Behind the Veil* have been reprinted in eight different literary studies, attesting to the impact the work has had on contemporary African American literary history. His articles include "Afro-American Literature," in Emory Elliott et al., ed., *Columbia History of American Literature* (1978); "After the 1960s: The Boom in Afro-American Fiction," in Malcolm Bradbury and Sigmund Ro, eds., *Contemporary American Fiction,* Stratford-upon-Avon Series (1986); and "I Thought I Knew These People: Richard Wright and the Afro-American Literary Tradition," *Massachusetts Review* 18 (Fall 1977).

His honors and awards include the Trinity College Alumni Medal for Excellence, a National Endowment for the Humanities Fellowship, and a Woodrow Wilson Fellowship.

For further reading, see Linda Metzger, ed., *Black Writers: A Selection of Sketches from Contemporary Authors* (1989).
"Teaching Afro-American Literature: Survey or Tradition" comes from *Afro-American Literature: The Reconstruction of Instruction.*

TEACHING AFRO-AMERICAN LITERATURE: SURVEY OR TRADITION
The Reconstruction of Instruction

1: Survey or Tradition?

Tradition is extradition; art must become transitive vis-à-vis its original site in history.   —Geoffrey Hartman

> *Our mode is our jam session*
> *of tradition,*
> *past in this present moment*
> *articulated, blown through*
> *with endurance*
> *an unreaching extended*
> *improvised love of past masters*
> *instruments technically down*
>   —Michael S. Harper

Survey is the bane of all literary studies, but it has had an especially cursed effect on the study of Afro-American literature. At a time in the academy when most language instruction is being curtailed, Afro-American literature, primarily because it is currently the most visible "minority" literature, has a larger responsibility than ever before in the great enterprise of nurturing young men and women who are literate; who are, regardless of their major discipline, articulate about the myriad cultural metaphors (textual and otherwise) in their world. By and large, however, Afro-American literature is not meeting this educational need and opportunity, primarily because of the antiquated ways in which it is taught and discussed in critical writing. On most campuses, Afro-American literature is still an agreeable entrée to black history, sociology, and politics. Of course, there is both a good side and a bad side to this: Historians and social scientists seem to employ Afro-American literature to illuminate their disciplines; for them, literature is part of a pedagogical strategy. Teachers of literature, however, more often than not attempt to become amateur historians and social scientists in their pursuit of the literature long before they actually get down to the business of teaching literary art. The most infamous proof of this is the rise of what I call the all-purpose Black Studies essay. For some understandable yet lamentable reasons, there are students in the land who have been led to feel that an essay containing an occult potpourri of references to Frederick Douglass, Frantz Fanon, and Richard Wright is acceptable in any Afro-American Studies course taught by any teacher regardless of the discipline in which the course is situated. Insofar as the literature teacher is responsible for this travesty, I would judge that the purveyance of survey approaches to both the taught and written critical discussion of the literature has done the greatest damage. And, really, it is the literature teacher who must make the most dramatic and complete reversal: Above and beyond the issue of extraordinary developments in literary analysis since the nineteenth century (which is where, in terms of sophistication, most criticism of Afro-American literature tends to reside) lies the simple, haunting fact that Afro-American history and social science are being taught while Afro-American language, literature, and literacy are not.

A definition is in order: A survey of literature is a presentation of discrete literary texts for the purposes of (1) explicating and distilling poetic rhetoric in isolatio, or (2) illuminating (however dimly) coded structures (Harlem Renaissance, Black Aesthetic), or (3) reviewing literary chronology (as opposed to literary history), or (4) miraculously, accomplishing all of the above. Lest someone think I am building straw men or tilting at windmills, let me illustrate my definition by constructing a hypothetical but no doubt familiar survey presentation of a popular and often taught black poet, Langston Hughes.

Let us assume that the presentation—to be completed in at most three or four classes—begins with a kind of informal explication de texte of several early Hughes poems, taken most likely from The Weary Blues or Fine Clothes to the Jew or both but certainly not studied within the context of these volumes because the critical and pedagogical tool in hand studies discrete texts; the students are reading the poems in an anthology or perhaps in a sheaf of photocopy material and have not been encouraged to seek out the Hughes volumes in the library; and the instructor, trained as a survey teacher by other survey teachers, has not read the poems—that is, for pedagogical purposes—in their original setting. The explication is informal primarily because of a curious conspiracy between the instructor and

Hughes himself. Consciously or not, and for reasons both textual and atextual, the instructor desires to sustain certain theories (clichés, really) about the "clarity" of Afro-American letters as opposed to the "convolutedness" of "Angry-Saxon" art. In this, the instructor is abetted by Hughes who, as perhaps *the* paradigmatic anti-intellectual among modern Afro-American writers, created poetic surfaces offering collectively what might be termed a quasi-aesthetic of the literal. One result of this conspiracy is what the poet Michael Harper jocularly terms the "explain" approach to literature—the reading of maps as opposed to the reading of landscapes—and the most recent edition of *The Norton Anthology of Poetry* bears him out. There, in the Hughes selections, one can find glosses for "Lenox Avenue" ("A main thoroughfare in the heart of Harlem"), for "W. E. B. Du Bois," for "Sugar Hill" ("a section of Harlem where the more prosperous Negroes once lived"), and for "Virginia Dare" ("A brand of wine"). The classroom equivalent of this sorry map-reading business may take up one class of the three, but usually the count is two. Let us say one class, however, assuming that the survey teacher is "organized."

In phase two of the survey presentation, the instructor employs what Northrop Frye describes as documentary approaches to literature: approaches that attempt to return a text to its place in cultural and literary history without accounting for either the literary form or the poetic and metaphorical language of the literary work. As Frye notes, the most pervasive of the documentary approaches are the biographical, the historical, and the psychological (with some sort of inevitable Freudian base). Most documentary criticism of Afro-American letters concentrates on biographical and historical data and is in this way embarrassingly antiquated. Psychological studies of the literature, at least when pursued by literary scholars, have been viewed traditionally as being suspect, partly because they are rarely done well but mostly because of the somewhat xenophobic and certainly emotional premise that the theories of a fin-de-siècle Austrian Jew cannot possibly illuminate black American art and culture. Despite these disclaimers, one suspects that psychological approaches to Afro-American literature will continue to advance and prosper as younger scholars are exposed to the ideas of established critics (witness the recent "psychobiographical" discussion of black writers such as Ellison, which are clearly indebted to the writings of the anxiety school of romanticists) and are informed also by the more thoughtful critiques of Freudianism and its corollary arguments. Our survey instructor, however, is not about to mystify or convolute the study of Hughes's poetry with psychological speculation (few of the texts can bear that weight anyway); "pure" biographical reference will shade the map outlined before, and not incidentally get instructor and student alike through class number two.

Langston Hughes wrote two autobiographies, *The Big Sea* and *I Wonder as I Wander*, and so our instructor can draw on a veritable wealth of authentic—and authenticating—material while making his or her presentation. Because the course is a survey and there is "no time" for the students themselves to read the autobiographies, the draft is often literally an extraction of pertinent passages from such chapters as "Harlem Literati" in *The Big Sea*, orchestrated agreeably with additional anecdotes, allusions, and cartographical glosses by the instructor. If the instructor is reasonably artful in the creation of documentary mosaics, the students will be entertained (if not exactly enlightened about Hughes's verse) and the class will go down as a good one. Curiously, old but persisting doubts about the efficacy of committing the intentional fallacy will not surface, either because student and teacher alike have tacitly agreed that such ideas do not apply to the study of "minority" literatures or because the business of that particular class never really was the discussion of poetry.

At this point in the presentation—consciously or not, subtly or not—an intellectual and pedagogical crisis occurs, and how the instructor responds to that crisis determines nothing less than whether Hughes's poems will be taught at all. Class one, with its informal (possibly, aformal) explication of texts, timidly began that enterprise, while class two took matters in a far different direction. The crisis is, quite simply, whither does one go? Does one go to the poems, which at this point seems to be a disagreeable form of backtracking, or does one continue with documentation—with the essentially non-literary activity of embellishing the Hughesian map? In most cases, the survey instructor chooses the latter activity, and this choice has both lamentable and alluring dimensions.

What is lamentable of course, is the abandonment of Hughes's texts and, worse, the innocent prostitution of those texts for the sake of potential intimacy with extraliterary concerns. The alluring dimension involves principally the joy of fashioning, albeit with the tools and rules of a false cartography, a reasoned if not envisioned whole. This whole may not be an interpretation of Hughes's verse, and certainly it is not a *reading* of it, but it does have weight and shape; it has presence and is therefore presentable, and this presentability in turn creates the illusion of an accompanying pedagogy. In our hypothetical survey classes one and two, a map—as opposed to both what Octavio Paz, among others, calls a landscape and what Geoffrey Hartman has termed a *genius loci*—has been outlined and, through reference to biographical information, carefully shaded. Although the biographical materials suggest boundaries and even topo-

graphies—of the autobiographies if not the poems—further
embellishment and, more important, contextualization of the map
are required. This, as suggested before, is the seductive, Luciferian
quality of the survey enterprise: The map will not direct one to the
grail, which is the various dimensions of literacy achieved within the
deeper recesses of the art form, but mapmaking in and of itself is an
engaging, self-contained activity. One assumes, in short, that these
satisfactions at least begin to explain why the pursuit of nonreading
is sufficiently resilient to remain au courant.

Contextualizing the map is most frequently the responsibility of
historical documentation. In our hypothetical survey presentation of
Langston Hughes, which is now entering its third and final day, the
informal textual explications, glosses, and mosaic of biographic reference will be conjoined with coded historical reference and structure:
The instructor, in short, will contextualize the map by grounding it
in a somewhat amorphous but nevertheless celebrated historical and
cultural watershed we have come to call the Harlem Renaissance.
References to this Renaissance have no doubt reverberated in parts
one and two of the presentation, but here in class three the subject
becomes a veritable rumble. And with good reason: The presentation
began with the microcosmic—the gloss, the parenthetical reference,
the allusion, and aside—and now it is achieving macrocosmic proportions—Langston Hughes and the Black Map of Modern Western
Civilization. With this level assumed, the last thirty minutes of the
last class on Hughes can be devoted to a breathless sprint through
the Big Questions: Langston Hughes and Black Nationalism; Langston Hughes and Protest; Langston Hughes, Architect of the Black
Aesthetic; and Langston Hughes, Critic of the Bourgeoisie, which is,
or course, a fresh sport of Langston Hughes, Poet of the People. A
first-rate survey instructor might instead devote those final minutes
to an equally breathless discourse on how Hughes's greatness transcends temporal boundaries, how he is representative not merely of
the Harlem Renaissance but also of the entire Modern era. This instructor might even attempt to link Hughes's transtemporal qualities
with his efforts and abilities in several literary genres, the immediate
effect being that the macrocosmic element in the presentation
achieves a truly grand scale. But the final effect of either closure is
regrettably the same: The students will feel that they have "done"
Langston Hughes, and, taking off from any of the topics in either
hypothetical closure, they will write—or warm over—yet another
all-purpose Black Studies essay addressed almost parenthetically to
the art of dear Langston.

Sadly enough, after three organized and possibly charged classes
on Langston Hughes, the students who have received this survey

presentation cannot begin to answer any of the substantial questions concerning Hughes's art. For example, the students ought to be able to discuss intelligently whether Hughes, in writing his "jazz" and "blues" poems, merely duplicates folk forms or achieves what George Kent suggests when he describes the "real opportunity" before the "self-conscious," as opposed to "group-conscious" or "folk," artist: the rendering of new art not by revision but fittingly, as in jazz, by modal improvisation. A good answer to this question will include discussion of both the verbal *and* tonal poetic rhetoric (fulfilled and unfulfilled) in a very few carefully selected Hughes poems, but, of course, the students subjected to the hypothetical presentation just described are totally ill-equipped to pursue this issue. In their first class on Hughes, verbal poetic rhetoric was at best partially explored and tonal poetic rhetoric simply "unheard." What they know of the music in Hughes's verse is most likely anchored in coded cultural/historical referents: cabaret, rent party, Charleston, black bottom, flapper (black, tan, and white), Cotton Club, Jazz Age. And they might not know all of that. The instructor might have been of the multimedia persuasion and played "Take the A Train" and "Creole Love Song" in hopes that a history and culture might be gleaned by a kind of osmosis.

Most certainly, especially if the authors preceding and following Hughes are presented in more or less the same fashion, the students are incapable of placing Hughes in the continuum of Afro-American artists who have wrestled with these very same questions of form, verbal and tonal metaphor, authorial posture, textual control, and shared tradition. They have no basis whatsoever on which to compare Hughes with such early articulators of the musical dimensions to literacy as Frederick Douglass and W. E. B. Du Bois. They are equally incapable of making any comparisons between Hughes and Ralph Ellison or Hughes and LeRoi Jones. The students ought to be able to bring into their discussion of Hughes's persona other personae, including James Weldon Johnson's Ex-Coloured Man and Sterling Brown's Big Boy Davis. But these are leaps that the implicit rhetoric of survey presentations discourages. On the whole, nonreading inaugurates a surprisingly rigid praxis; it encourages ingenious manipulation of nonliterary structures instead of immersion in the multiple images and landscapes of metaphor. In brief, the primacy of the text is obliterated.

Instead of achieving some facility at contextualizing the Hughesian map in nonliterary or, more generally, nonartistic structures, the students should be able to begin to place Hughes in the Afro-American artistic continuum of which literature is but a part, and in doing so, illuminate the text or texts by referring to the artistic whole.

Those students who, as Ralph Ellison reports, persist in the illusion that they possess a "genetic" knowledge of black culture, may very well compose yet another all-purpose "black" essay. Others will take the harder but more rewarding path delineated—and in fact demanded—by the multiple forms of literacy, not "feeling," and draw from *all* their resources the requisite vision and energy to see author, text, and tradition alike.

Of course, the instructor, much more than the students, requires reconstruction. Ironically, the pedagogy he or she has employed is bankrupt because it is self-contained, and self-contained because of some of the procedures used to escape "confinement" in the art form itself. As we observed in the hypothetical classes on Hughes, what passes for pedagogy is an inevitable movement from the text to familiar nonliterary constructs such as the Harlem Renaissance. These constructs in turn become the grand, controlling themes of a survey course; and, when nonliterary structures are both the linchpins and goals of a teaching strategy, the "text" of a course, like a bad poem, yields documentary data stripped of metaphor. For this reason, the students, if asked, might very well explain that in the course they studied slavery times, Reconstruction, the Accommodationist Era, and the Harlem Renaissance, much as they would describe too many Black Studies courses couched in too many disciplines.

The intellectual and pedagogical problems before the survey instructor become manifest when one speculates on what will follow the sessions on Langston Hughes. Moving chronologically, the next good poet is obviously Sterling Brown, whose best volume of verse, *Southern Road*, saw print in 1932. But beyond the all too apparent activities of comparing, say, a Hughes "blues" with a Brown "blues" and glossing "Casey Jones," "Ma Rainey," and "Four and a half and M," our instructor has very little to say about Brown. In contrast to Hughes, Brown has not yet published his autobiography and, for reasons personal as well as historical, is not readily identified with the Harlem Renaissance era. These matters, we have good reason to fear, have far more to do with why Brown is undertaught or considered "difficult" than the more substantial issue of what his poems demand of their readers. In short, our instructor's pedagogy is bankrupt because it neither allows proximity, let alone intimacy, with writers and texts outside the normal boundaries of nonliterary structures nor fosters the literacy required to examine literature without respect to extraliterary concerns. If our instructor were free, in these senses of the term, he or she might be able not only to read and teach both Hughes and Brown but also to judge who is the better poet, even if only along the lines of the aforementioned question of the "real opportunity" before the modern Afro-American writer. But obviously, our instructor and, by extension, our students are not yet free—nor, sadly enough, is the literature that they glimpse but cannot see.

II: Temenos/Notes on a Course

Once a mythology is formed, a temenos or magic circle is drawn around a culture, and literature develops historically within a limited orbit of language, reference, allusion, beliefs, transmitted and shared tradition.   —Northrop Frye

The path to freedom and literacy has many pitfalls, and among the most considerable of these is the trap of bibliography. Let us suppose that our survey instructor senses, despite reassurances to the contrary from questionnaire scores and enrollment figures, that something is mightily wrong with the map-reading system of teaching Afro-American literature. (This in itself is an act of courage; no one relishes altering habits of intellectual discourse that outwardly seem to work.) An initial response might well be to read new texts and to insert them here and there in the old course. No matter how sanctioned this revision might be by the various reading lists compiled by colleagues, committees, or "institutes," the instructor has done little more than perform what one might call a "bibliographical repair": the shuffling of texts like that of cards in hopes of a better "deal." This will not do. What the course needs is not simply new authorial names and textual faces but an aesthetic and rhetorical principle that summons the texts that properly shape a course. A course, as I have suggested before, is a kind of grand text; in its way, a good course assumes a place alongside the great works of a literary tradition because the interdependence of its integral parts (texts) reflects the artistic continuum both celebrated and subsumed in the great works themselves. In order to pursue this ideal of the good course, our instructor must be able to distinguish a literary tradition from a literary survey and an artistic continuum from a bibliography and to see the dialectical relationship between these two distinguishing processes. But before any of this activity is launched, our instructor must discover the Afro-American canonical story or pregeneric myth, the particular historicity of the Afro-American literary tradition, and the Afro-American landscape or *genius loci*.

The Afro-American pregeneric myth is the quest for freedom *and* literacy. Once this is absorbed, our instructor will be able to abandon freely most nonliterary structures because those structures, evolving as they do almost exclusively from freedom myths devoid of linguistic properties, speak rarely to questions of freedom *and* literacy. Because this is so, they are now, if not obsolete, only partially useful to our instructor.

The quest for freedom and literacy is found in every major Afro-American text but is perhaps most accessible in Frederick Douglass's *Narrative of the Life of Frederick Douglass an American Slave Written by Himself* (the last part of the title, as many have remarked, suggests the goal of literacy) and W. E. B. Du Bois's *The Souls of Black Folk*. I mention these works not only because they are familiar and central but also because each yields a remarkable expression of the multiple dimensions to literacy subsumed within a primary Afro-American archetype, the articulate hero. In both works, the hero (that is, a heroic voice created as much by its author's vision as by his condition) discovers the inextricable bonds among study, language, and "the pathway from slavery to freedom" and, in turn, especially with Du Bois, suggests that comprehension of his culture's tongues has led in part to the discovery of his own voice. Thus, the articulate hero achieves the posture of the custodian of the culture—an idea reinforced in other works by less articulate figures such as James Weldon Johnson's Ex-Coloured Man, who seems all too aware that his false mobility (false when compared to that of Douglass's self-become-metaphor and that of Du Bois's truly self-conscious hero-narrator) is a kind of illiteracy. What our instructor learns here is that the pregeneric myth creates both literate and illiterate, free and enclosed, heroes and landscapes, and that both types must be offered in teaching in such a way that what Du Bois termed a "total race consciousness"—as envisioned in art—is presented.

Aware of the quest for freedom and literacy, our instructor may now study how that pregeneric myth and its archetypes generate Afro-American literary forms. As in all literatures, these are bound to specific texts, so that the study of form invariably arrives at some inspection of discrete works. But I am speaking here of another activity as well: What must also be observed is the pregeneric myth *set in motion* in search of its form, and since it is bound to form, its voice. Here, the instructor discovers what is most likely the central intellectual and pedagogical enterprise in the study of Afro-American literary forms: the effort to define and discuss how the pregeneric myth both assumes and does not assume the properties of genre—notably, history, autobiography, fiction, and certain modes of verse. If an Afro-American literary tradition exists, it does so not because there is a sizeable chronology of authors and texts but because those authors and texts seek collectively their own literary forms—their own admixtures of genre—bound historically and linguistically to a shared pregeneric myth.

The historicity of the Afro-American literary tradition is, then, not the chronology of authors and texts but the history of the pre-generic myth in motion through both chronological and linguistic time in search of its form and voice. Thus, the history of tradition differs massively from that of survey in that surveys destroy linguistic time and the continuity of literary history by moving systematically from texts to nonliterary structures and passively allowing those structures to become collectively the "history" of a literature. Once this is absorbed, most of the remaining nonliterary structures impeding the *reading* of the literature will fall away, and, probably for the first time, our instructor will be set in motion, free to learn the rhythm of the history, free to *see* finally what binds, say, *Native Son* to the slave narratives, or a Robert Hayden ballad to a ballad by Sterling Brown or to the "Sorrow Songs," as Du Bois termed them. All this will have pedagogical ramifications. Our instructor's course will still unfold chronologically but will do so for reasons literary, not extraliterary: Literary conventions, archetypes, genres, and pregeneric forms will generate what Northrop Frye describes as "a sense of history within literature to complement the historical criticism that relates literature to a historical background." Obviously, nonliterary structures will still have a place in teaching, but they will no longer define the goals of the pedagogical strategy or control the reading of art. Instead of depicting history, our instructor's course will now illuminate the historical consciousness of an art form.

Once the pregeneric myth has been set in motion, we must concern ourselves not only with the chronicle of that movement, literary history, but also with that movement's direction and shape. In Afro-American letters, the shape of literary history is a circle, a continuum of artistic endeavor; and, like Northrop Frye's *temenos*, it is a magic circle—magical because it is full of resonance generated by artistic acts of modal improvisation upon the pregeneric myth of freedom and literacy. The interior of the Afro-American *temenos* is the culture's landscape or *genius loci* (spirit of place, but also spiritual center), the deeper recesses both attained and realized, as Du Bois instructs us, by penetration of the Veil. Afro-American literature abounds with metaphors for its culture's *genius loci*; the creation of them is indeed one of its major occupations. One of the more apparent is "the black belt," of which Booker T. Washington and Du Bois both write, and it is a good one for our instructor to begin with since it is essentially a geographical metaphor and comprehension of it will yield not only the *temenos* but also the distinction between the reading of maps and that of landscapes.

Put succinctly, Washington, in his public pronouncements if not so much in private exchange, was a mapmaker—a direct result of his great literary offense, the adoption of "the speech and language of triumphant commercialism" (to which, I think, the tongue of non-reading is linked ancestrally). When called upon to define the black belt, Washington wrote in *Up from Slavery*:

> So far as I can learn, the term was first used to designate a part of the country which was distinguished by the colour of the soil. The part of the country possessing this thick, dark, and naturally rich soil was, of course, the part of the south where the slaves were most profitable, and consequently they were taken there in the largest numbers. Later, and especially since the war, the term seems to be used wholly in a political sense—that is, to designate the counties where the black people outnumber the white.

Obviously, Washington carefully avoids any suggestion that the black belt possesses deeper recesses, let alone that it might be the interior of the Afro-American *temenos*. His gloss is that of a map-maker or gazettist. He ventures into politics not as a philosopher but rather as a demographer and creates a linguistic surface that is thin except perhaps in the rather wry phrase, "the part of the south where the slaves were most *profitable*" (italics added). But, of course, Washington had a very specific goal in mind (raising funds for Tuskegee) in thus shaping the rhetoric of his gloss—which parenthetically raises the question of what comparable goals, literary or extraliterary, our instructor had in composing equally thin glosses for the poetry of Langston Hughes.

The wicked subtlety and charm of Washington's description of the black belt are lost unless it is returned to the canon of metaphors for the Afro-American *genius loci*. There, Washington's language enters into dialectical play with Du Bois's portrait of the black belt in *The Souls*: The rhetorical map becomes engaged dynamically with the rhetorical journey into the soul of a race. Our *reading* of this dialectic is what allows us not only to interpret Washington's and Du Bois's language but also to see the black belt whole. This act of reading within tradition affords a pedagogical approximation of artmaking within tradition, and it is reading of this sort that our instructor's new pedagogy should both emulate and promote.

Just as we must learn to pass from metaphor to metaphor and from image to image of the same metaphor in order to locate the Afro-American *genius loci*, we must learn also to move freely throughout the full compass of the Afro-American *temenos*, from the *genius loci* at the center to the outermost reaches of the *temenos* circumference. Geoffrey Hartman speaks of the tension between Genius and *genius loci* and how it takes the form of and also mediates "the conflict between the universal and nationalistic aspirations of art." I would suggest a comparable tension exists in Afro-American letters not only between Genius and *genius loci* but also between the *temenos* (the magical cultural circle that is the most immediate interior region of the Veil) and the *genius loci* (the heart of the interior landscape). In the best Afro-American texts, the nationalistic tendency is not so much a baldly political compulsion as it is a drive to perpetuate the motion of the pregeneric myth of freedom and literacy. Artmaking—craftsmanship—demands a mediation between this nationalistic tendency and Genius. Of course, this produces what is extraordinary about Afro-American art forms: Mediation between the drive to perpetuate the motion of the pregeneric myth and the compulsion to follow Genius is an exquisite definition of modal improvisation; art that does not come from this mediation does not advance, in Octavio Paz's language, the Afro-American's "mode of association" within "the universality of history," and thus does not enter Afro-American literary history even though it does, in some sense, exist.

The reconstruction of an instruction is no simple task: The revised course must attain textual (that is, metaphorical) properties, and the complementing pedagogy must approximate the artistic act itself. This is not as difficult as it sounds once literacy is achieved, because the act of reading is not unlike that of writing. Both require a mediation between Genius and *genius loci* and between *genius loci* and *temenos*, and both require of their practitioners a sense of the counterpoint between texts (or courses) and the rhythm of the artistic continuum subsumed within *temenos*. Our instructor set out in search of a new map but discovered, fortunately, the eternal landscape instead. The new course will, like literary history itself, encompass the landscape, and, more important, the new pedagogy will, like artmaking, mediate between individual talent and the continuity of tradition. But perhaps most important of all will be our instructor's new, reconstructed self: Free to read, free to see; and free to attain that state John Coltrane termed wakefulness.

Wakefulness is not, however, an altogether blissful circumstance. Once sufficiently awake to reconstruct the old Afro-American literature course, the instructor is cognizant also of the other, larger systems and constructs (curricula, departments, schools), which are, like the old course, infested with a kind of intellectual misery. The new course, generated by the artful act of reading, may now enable Afro-American literature to nurture literacy in the academy, but our instructor may ask quite rightfully why does this responsibility exist in the first place, and why must more and more of the burden be assumed by Afro-American letters? The first question will be wrestled with almost endlessly, primarily because it addresses intellectual and pedagogical failures at all levels of instruction; but the answer to the second will, I think, become ringingly clear. The great gift of the best Afro-American literature to its readers is its historical and linguistic portrait of a culture—once imprisoned by an enforced illiteracy—questing for, finding, and relishing the written word. If students can absorb this, they not only will know something important about Afro-American literature but also, quite possibly, will drink of the spirit of the tradition and achieve the discipline required to force a revision of their own verbal inadequacies. It is horrifically ironic that some of our students cannot write as well as Henry Bibb—a fugitive slave with three weeks of schooling—but then, when were they ever imbued with even an ounce of Bibb's motivation? Our mission as teachers is clear: Afro-American literature must be taught, and taught as a literature. Only then will our students learn of a culture's quest for literacy and in turn gain the literacy with which to sustain the tradition.

REFERENCES

Bibb, Henry. *Narrative of the Life and Adventures of Henry Bibb an American Slave Written by Himself.* 1849; rpt. in *Puttin' on Ole Massa.* Ed. Gilbert Osofsky. New York: Harper, 1969.

Brown, Sterling A. *Southern Road.* 1932; rpt. Boston: Beacon, 1974.

Chapman, Abraham. "An Interview with Michael S. Harper." *Arts in Society* pp. 2 (1974), 463–71.

Douglass, Frederick. *Narrative of the Life of Frederick Douglass an American Slave Written by Himself.* 1845; rpt. New York: Signet, 1968.

Du Bois, W. E. B. *The Souls of Black Folk.* Chicago: McClurg, 1903.

———. "The Storm and Stress in the Black World." *Dial*, 16 April 1901, pp. 262–64.

Frye, Northrop. "The Critical Path: An Essay on the Social Context of Literary Criticism." *Daedalus* 99 (1970), pp. 268–342.

Harper, Michael S. *Nightmare Begins Responsibility.* Urbana-Champaign: Univ. of Illinois Press, 1975.

———, and Robert B. Stepto. "Study in Experience: A Conversation with Ralph Ellison." *Massachusetts Review* 18 (1977), pp. 417–35.

Hartman, Geoffrey. "Toward Literary History." In *Beyond Formalism: Literary Essays 1958–1970.* New Haven: Yale Univ. Press, 1970.

Johnson, James Weldon. *The Autobiography of an Ex-Coloured Man.* 1912; rpt. New York: Hill and Wang, 1960.

Kent, George E. *Blackness and the Adventure of Western Culture.* Chicago: Third World Press, 1972.

Paz, Octavio. *The Other Mexico: Critique of the Pyramid.* Trans. Lysander Kemp. New York: Grove, 1972.

Washington, Booker T. *Up from Slavery.* 1901; rpt. in Vol. I of *The Booker T. Washington Papers.* Ed. Louis R. Harlan. Urbana-Champaign: Univ. of Illinois Press, 1972, pp. 211–385.

Claudia Tate

(1946–   )

THE PUBLICATION in 1983 of her *Black Women Writers at Work* almost immediately brought Claudia Tate national recognition. Currently a professor of English at George Washington University in Washington, D.C., Tate received her A.B. from the University of Michigan in 1968 and her A.M. and Ph.D. degrees in English and American literature at Harvard University in 1971 and 1977, respectively. Though she worked as a teaching fellow in the English department and as an instructor in Afro-American studies while at Harvard, her first tenure-track position began in the English department at Howard University, where she taught from 1977 until 1989 and where she was chair of the department from 1988 to 1989.

Although she has published articles on Richard Wright's *Black Boy* and *The Outsider*, Professor Tate is primarily a feminist scholar, having published articles, reviews, and a book on the works of an impressive array of women authors such as Zora Neale Hurston, Nella Larsen, Gwendolyn Brooks, Maya Angelou, Margaret Walker, Audre Lorde, Alice Walker, Gayl Jones, and Toni Morrison. Now available in British, Spanish, and Japanese editions, her *Black Women Writers at Work*, a collection of interviews with fifteen black women writers, is an indispensable research tool for anyone teaching or writing about contemporary black women writers.

Professor Tate has taught as a visiting scholar at the Institute for Research on Women at Rutgers University and as a Distinguished Visiting Minority Professor in the English department at the University of Delaware. Her honors and awards include a Ford Foundation Postdoctoral Fellowship, an Andrew Mellon Incentive Award, and a National Endowment for the Humanities Postdoctoral Fellowship for Independent Study.

The selection that follows, "Laying the Floor, or the History of the Formation of the Afro-American Canon," appeared originally in *Book Research Quarterly*.

LAYING THE FLOOR, OR THE HISTORY OF THE FORMATION OF THE AFRO-AMERICAN CANON

Where do readers get their ideas about Afro-American literature? As an initial answer to this question I offer my own experience as a reader of black literature, as a case study. From 1961–1965, I was a college preparatory student at a public high school that was reputed to be among the best in the Northeast. My high school adhered to the traditional curriculum in English and American literature, which is to say that I did not know that black people wrote books, let alone a substantial amount of literature, until 1968, when I learned in my college Negro literature class, as it was then called, that black literature existed and that it was a largely male enterprise. I was so happy to find black writers that I did not think to ask until much later where the black women writers were. In 1973 I finally learned that black women had also written a large body of literature.

Why were these two facts obscured for so much of my formal education? The answer, I suggest, will explain how the literary accomplishments of black women writers have routinely slipped between the cracks of not only American literary history but Afro-American literary history as well.

Academic scholars and critics set literary curricula for formal education. They inscribe what they value, which usually turns out to be what they were taught and what they understand. In a white male dominated society, the scholars and critics tend to be white men who value and understand white male writers, I suggest, because they share similar concerns. I realize that this is a rather circular and simplistic explanation; nevertheless, it accounts for the traditional literary curriculum in most educational systems from grade school to the university.

When social and political demands of other groups exert sufficient pressure on the dominant group, minority representation appears in direct proportion to that pressure. Thus, when the civil rights and black power movements pressured the academy, it responded by drastically increasing the number of black scholars and

This essay was made possible with support from the Faculty Research Program in the Social Sciences, Humanities, and Education of the Office of the Vice President for Academic Affairs at Howard University, and with the assistance of the staff of the Moorland-Spingarn Research Center at Howard University. This essay is a revised version of a chapter that appeared in *"Of Our Spiritual Strivings": Recent Development in Black Literature and Criticism,* edited by Wilfred Samuels, David Williams, and Richard Yarborough (Urbana: University of Illinois Press, 1988).

From *Book Research Quarterly,* volume 3, number 2 (Summer 1987). Copyright © 1987 by Transaction Publishers. Reprinted by permission of Transaction.

critics and by inscribing black writers (who were usually men) into academic curricula and textbooks. A few years later the pressure from feminist groups led to similar treatment for white women writers and eventually for black women writers.

One particular instance of black feminist vigilance, involved Alice Walker's efforts to rescue Zora Neale Hurston, who published four novels, two collections of folktales, an autobiography and several short stories and plays.[1] Walker was certainly not the only person trying to reinsert Hurston or other black women writers, into American literary history; she was, however, the best known figure to take up Hurston's cause. Hurston waited for more than thirty years for scholars to recognize her as a major American writer. Without the work of Walker (and others), I dare say Hurston would still reside in the cracks of literary history.

Unfortunately, many of the writers who were considered Hurston's peers were either forgotten entirely or relegated to the margins and footnotes of scholarship. Nella Larsen, for instance, who also wrote during the New Negro (or Harlem) Renaissance of the 1920s, published two novels that examine psychological neurosis, racial ambivalence, and sexual repression by focusing on black, female, middle-class characters.[2] During the same period Jessie Fauset published four novels that criticize the institutions of marriage and racial prejudice by using the conventions of both sentimental romance and the novel of racial passing.[3] Georgia Douglas Johnson published three volumes of poetry that focus on personal awareness, human mortality and the relationship between love and beauty.[4] These were not the first black women to pursue literary careers.

Nineteenth-century serials, like *The Colored American, The African Methodist Church Review (The A.M.E. Church Review), The Family Story Paper, The New York Weekly, Our Women and Children,* and *Washington Bee* were filled with fiction, poetry, and feature articles written by black women whose accomplishments have also slipped through the cracks of American as well as Afro-American literary history. Unfortunately, many of these serials are no longer extant; however, those that are record these literary contributions. *The Col-*

---

[1] Hurston's works include two collections of folklore—*Mules and Men* (1935) and *Tell My Horse* (1938); an autobiography—*Dust Tracks on the Road* (1942); and four novels—*Their Eyes Were Watching God* (1937), *Jonah's Gourd Vine* (1934), *Moses, Man of the Mountain* (1939), and *Seraph on the Suwanee* (1948).

[2] Larsen's novels include *Quicksand* (1928) and *Passing* (1929).

[3] Fauset's novels include *There Is Confusion* (1924), *Plum Bum* (1928), *The Chinaberry Tree* (1931), and *Comedy: American Style* (1933).

[4] Johnson's poetry collections include *The Heart of a Woman and Other Poems* (1918), *Bronze* (1922), *Autumn Love Cycle* (1928), and *Share My World: A Book of Poems* (1962).

ored American, for example, contains Pauline Elizabeth Hopkins's (1859–1930) three serial-novels, a dozen short stories, and numerous feature articles.[5] In addition, *The A.M.E. Church Review* preserves much of the fiction of Victoria Earle Matthews (1861–1907) and Katherine Davis Chapman Tillman (1870–?), who were among the most popular black women writers of their day.[6]

My effort to determine why the accomplishments of these and other black women writers were fated either to slip between the cracks of literary history or to be pushed to its margins led me to theoretically construct the surface—or literary floor—in which the cracks appear. I begin by surveying the history of the formation of the Afro-American canon from roughly 1895 to 1968, which I divide into three periods or planks, each with specific criteria for inscription. The first is the Talented-Tenth (1895–1920), using W. E. B. Du Bois's term for designating that portion (10%) of black Americans who had intellectual training. This plank valorized academic educational attainment as the vehicle for securing racial equality. The second plank is the New Negro period (1920–1940), during which time literature that celebrated black cultural values was inscribed into the canon. The final plank is Integrationist Poetics[7] (1940–1968); it argues that black Americans should gain their civil liberties through integration.

Within each period, or plank, I designate three levels of canon-formation: the potential, accessible, and selective canons.[8] The potential canon privileges works that give specific social ideals clear expression. In reference to the potential canon for Afro-American literature, those works that argue for racial pride and equality became precanonical texts. As the political culture for black Americans stabilized, its critics consigned merit to these works, and the works became members of an accessible canon, which scholars, editors, and publishers defined and labeled. They elevated the accessible canon into a canonical discipline (e.g., literature) by selecting mastertexts, or so-called great works, as ideal works for formal classroom instruc-

---

[5]See my "Pauline Elizabeth Hopkins: Our Literary Foremother" in *Conjuring: Black Women, Fiction, and Literary Tradition*. Edited by Marjorie Pryse and Hortense J. Spillers (Bloomington, Indiana, 1985): 53–66.

[6]See I. Garland Penn, *The Afro-American Press, and Its Editors* (Springfield, Massachusetts, 1891): 375–377 and 389–393; Monroe A. Majors, *Noted Negro Women: Their Triumphs and Activities* (Chicago, 1893): 211–213; and Lewis Arthur Scruggs, *Women of Distinction: Remarkable in Works and Invincible in Character* (Raleigh, 1893): 30–32 and 203–207.

[7]Houston A. Baker, Jr. coined the term "Integrationist Poetics" in *Blues, Ideology, and Afro-American Literature* (Chicago, 1984): 66–67.

[8]Alan C. Golding, "A History of American Poetry Anthologies" in *Canons*, ed. Robert von Hallberg (Chicago, 1983): 279.

tion, largely because they inscribe the political and cultural values of the critics. This canon is largely a pedagogic instrument that further institutionalizes and (thereby) obscures the criteria that precipitated the first and second stages of canon-formation. At the last stages scholars frequently evoke so-called objective value criteria, such as universality and aesthetic codes, to validate inscribed texts and to excise the others. All stages are ongoing and can produce either canon-reservation or canon-revision.

Was the neglect of the texts of black female authorship just another example of how the contributions of black people and women of all ethnic backgrounds have been routinely excised or trivialized in American culture history (in which case black women suffer double jeopardy)? Were black women writers relegated to minor status because their work did not meet aesthetic standards? Did women writers tend to address personal issues that scholars (who were almost exclusively men) regarded unworthy of inscription? And lastly, were texts of black female authorship regarded as curiosity pieces for specific literary epochs and as a result considered inherently marginal?

Defining the Potential Afro-American Literary Canon

Literary canons, in general, according to the scholar Charles Altieri, are "simply ideological banners for social groups [who] propose them as forms of self-definition."[9] According to Lillian Robinson, a feminist scholar, a canon is a product of "a gentlemen's agreement," an informal collection of course syllabi, anthologies, and scholarship about so-called "standard" or canonical authors.[10] Paul Lauter defines the American canon as "that set of authors and works generally included in basic American literature college courses and textbooks, and those ordinarily discussed in standard volumes of literary history, bibliography, or criticism."[11] He adds that the canon's power arises from the political influence of its constituency, those members who teach and anthologize literature. Their choices determine the canon and encode "a set of social norms and values; and these . . . help [to] endow [the canon] with force and continuity."[12] Or, as Al-

---

9Charles Altieri, "An Idea and Ideal of a Literary Canon" in *Canons*, ed. Robert von Hallberg (Chicago, 1983): 43.

10Lillian S. Robinson, "Treason Our Text: Feminist Challenges to the Literary Canon" in *Feminist Criticism: Essays on Women, Literature and Theory*, ed. Elaine Showalter (New York, 1985): 106.

11Paul Lauter, "Race and Gender in Shaping of the American Literary Canon: A Case Study from the Twenties" in *Feminist Studies* 9 (Fall, 1983): 436.

12Lauter, 435.

tieri writes, "Once we know the roles a cultural structure [here spe-cifically a canon] plays, or could play, in our lives, we know how to assess any particular claims to be good instances of that structure. Functions establish criteria."[13]

As the political influence of various constituencies change, each stage of canon-formation reflects these changes. Thus, it comes as no surprise to see that canonical authors bear a striking resemblance to those who endorsed (or canonized) them. Like a proper child, the canon reflects its forebears' appearances and values. In contrast to genetic transcription, criteria for canonical inscription, as Robinson further observes, "are nowhere codified."[14] When a canon survives as an unconscious consensus, the criteria for inscription becomes in-creasingly difficult to question, and the canon itself becomes rigid. The first step, then, in examining its formation is understanding its history—that is, its origins and composition—so as to make visible the process by which changing social and aesthetic attitudes, as-sumptions, and expectations inscribe (or excise) texts at particular historical moments. In so doing, I can suggest reasons why scholars routinely accorded minor status to black women writers.

The blueprints of Afro-American canon-formation can be found in its early literary anthologies and scholarship. These documents re-veal the above stages in canon-formation, all of which are subject to on-going revision.

For example, Victoria Earle Matthews in "The Value of Race Lit-erature" (1895) and Daniel W. Culp in his preface to *Twentieth Cen-tury Negro Literature* (1902), as well as Rev. J. Q. Johnson, Walter I. Lewis, and G. M. McClellan (who were contributors to this text), regarded the literature of black authorship as a means of fighting ra-cial prejudice. As Matthews wrote, "The impious wrong [of race prejudice] has made a Race Literature a possibility, even a necessity to dissipate the odium conjured up by the term 'colored person.' "[15] Thus, from the outset, Matthews regarded the writing of race litera-ture as a functional enterprise that would "be a revelation to [black] people, and enlarge [their] scope, make [them] better known wher-ever real lasting culture exists, [and] undermine and utterly drive out the traditional Negro in dialect . . . as the type representing a race whose numbers are now far into the millions."[16] But the litera-

[13]Altieri, 57.

[14]Robinson, 105.

[15]Victoria Earle Matthews, "The Value of Race Literature: An Address, Delivered at the First Congress of Colored Women of the United States, at Boston, Massachusetts," (Occa-sional paper, Boston, 1895): 4.

[16]Matthews, 7–8.

ture's fullest and largest development was not to be circumscribed by the narrow limits of race or creed;[17] instead it was to be a universal literature through which Afro-American writers would "attain and hold imperishable fame."[18]

Although Matthews could not refer to an accessible canon, she did refer to a potential canon that would venerate intellect and high moral standards. Here, she included Phillis Wheatley's poetry, Paul Laurence Dunbar's standard verse, and Frederick Douglass's *Life and Times of Frederick Douglass* (1881). She did not include Douglass's *The Narrative of the Life of Frederick Douglass* (1845), his *My Bondage and My Freedom* (1855), or other slave narratives. Moreover, she did not restrict her listing to literary texts but included "Histor[ies], Biograph[ies], Scientific Treatises, Sermons, Addresses, Novels, Poems, Books of Travel, miscellaneous essays and contributions to magazines and newspapers."[19] These works, in her estimation, would demonstrate "[the Negro's] intrinsic worth, . . . breadth of mind [and] boundless humanity."[20]

Her contemporary, Culp, presented similar objectives in his preface to *Twentieth Century Negro Literature* (1902):

> (1) To enlighten the uninformed white people on the intellectual ability of the Negro. (2) To give . . . a better idea of the extent to which [the Negro] contributed to the promotion of American civilization. . . . (3) To reflect the views of the most scholarly and prominent Negroes of America on those topics, touching the Negro, that are now engaging the attention of the civilized world. (4) To point out . . . those [Negro] men and women . . . who by their scholarship, by their integrity of character, and by their earnest efforts in the work of uplifting their own race, have made themselves illustrious. . . . (5) To enlighten the Negroes on that perplexing problem, commonly called the "Race Problem," that has necessarily grown out of their contact with their ex-masters and their descendants; and also to stimulate them to . . . ascent to that plane of civilization occupied by the other enlightened peoples of the world.[21]

In Chapter XVI "The Negro as a Writer," Johnson corroborated Matthews's selection of texts,[22] and added the work of Charles Chesnutt and Frances W. Harper.[23] Also in this chapter, Lewis contended that Negro folklore should be the foundation for epics of black author-

---

[17]Matthews, 7.
[18]Matthews, 6.
[19]Matthews, 3.
[20]Matthews, 12.
[21]D[aniel] W. Culp. *Twentieth Century Negro Literature* (Toronto: 1902): 5–6.
[22]Culp, 271.
[23]Culp, 271.

ship,[24] and McClellan separated literary writers from those in other disciplines.[25] Moreover, like Lewis, McClellan did not regard dialect verse to be inherently disparaging of the Negro's character and intellect. As a consequence, he reserved his highest esteem for Chesnutt's delineations of Negro life, character, thought, and feeling.[26] In contrast to Matthews, Culp, Johnson, Lewis, and McClellan deleted Wheatley's poetry from their respective potential canons, presumably because her poetry imitated eighteenth-century neo-classical conventions at the expense of protesting racial oppression in clear, emphatic ways. This deletion foreshadowed her problematic relationship to Afro-American canonical literature—which lasted for more than thirty years. However, these critics did corroborate Matthews's position about slave narratives; they held that these texts were inappropriate for inciting feelings of racial equality and therefore deleted them from their discussions.

All of these early critics gave clear expression to the emerging canon's social objectives. This is not to say that they disregarded craft in favor of message; they were, indeed, concerned with adhering to the literary conventions of their day, but they were also pragmatic. They did not focus on the literature's aesthetic value as such but on its dramatization of urgent social imperatives. Moreover, there was little room in this evolving canon for entertaining esoteric arguments about effaced racial consciousness in Wheatley's poetry or the existential polemics of asserting one's humanity in slave narratives. Only those works that directly addressed the injustice of the colorline found a place in early stages of canon-formation for Afro-American literature.

In the late nineteenth-century the growing volume of writing of black authorship was in need of a categorical label, inasmuch as the term "American literature" designated *white* American literary expression. This new label had to indicate whether the racial identity of the author, the subject matter of the text, or both inscribed it into this category. In other words, did inscription depend on black authorship, the depiction of black experience, or both? Answers to this question provided a variety of definitions for Afro-American literature, and each altered the face of the evolving canon.

In 1895 Matthews designated the literary expression of black writers as race literature, which she defined as "all the writings emanating from a distinct class—not necessarily race matter, but a general collection of what has been written by men and women of that

---

[24]Culp, 274.
[25]Culp, 279.
[26]Culp, 284.

Race."[27] She realized that her definition was problematic because she was placing black literary expression within an already ambiguous American context:

[M]any persons may object to the term 'Race Literature', questioning seriously the need, doubting if there be any, or indeed whether there can be a Race Literature in a country like ours apart from the general American Literature. Others may question the correctness of the term American Literature, since our civilization in its essential features is a reproduction of all that is most desirable in the civilizations of the Old World. English being the language of America, they argue in favor of the general term, English Literature.[28]

Although Matthews clearly regarded black culture as fundamentally American in character, she revealed her own as well as her contemporaries' insecurities about measuring American writing against the older and more esteemed tradition of English literature. She argued that American subjects depicted in English language were not regarded as English, inasmuch as the term English did not so much suggest the language of communication as it did a series of cultural expectations associated with Great Britain. Therefore, the literary projections of American life should be labeled American in order to indicate its distinct national character. In addition she used race to designate that writing arising from a specifically Afro-American context, inasmuch as the term American commonly referred to a white American perspective. Given these implications, she and her black contemporaries affirmed their writing with the labels—"race, Negro, and American Negro."

The question of function gained little clarity as time passed. During the decade of the Great War, William E. B. Du Bois wrote about the development of Afro-American literature, and Benjamin Brawley, then the most well-known and productive black literary scholar, criticized the national literature's tendency to depict Negro life as an assortment of negative stereotypes.[29] Du Bois, in "The Negro in Literature and Art" (1913), surveyed black literary expression and explained that it had a consistent development. "As early as the eighteenth-century," Du Bois wrote, "and even before the Revolutionary War the first voices of Negro authorship were heard in the United

---

[27]Matthews, 3.

[28]Matthews, 3.

[29]Brawley wrote several texts on the topic—The Negro in literature and art. They include *The Negro in Literature and Art* (New York, 1910), and *The Negro in Literature and Art in the United States* (New York, 1918).

States."[30] Also during the same period, he observed, national and racial consciousness appeared in Anglo-American literature. Unlike
many of his contemporaries, however, Du Bois did not explicitly
sanction a specific social purpose for black literature; more importantly, he claimed its parity with the dominant literature.

In contrast, Brawley's critical posture was decidedly defensive. In
his 1916 *Dial* essay "The Negro in American Fiction," Brawley criticized white writers for their dependence on the Page-Dixon Negro
stereotypes,[31] and implored them to establish their independence by
presenting both honest and realistic stories about Negro life: "Let
those who mold our ideals and set the standards of our art in fiction
at least be honest with themselves and independent."[32] He concluded
by insisting that authentic treatment of black life would demonstrate
undeniably that "the day of Uncle Remus [and] . . . Uncle Tom
[was] over."[33]

Defining the Accessible Canon
in Anthologies of Afro-American Literature

Defining and labeling those texts that constituted the accessible
canon was equally problematic, especially for those who compiled
anthologies during the first third of the twentieth century. Questions
arose concerning whether critics were to regard Dunbar's novels
about white subjects[34] and the writing about Negro life by white authors as Negro literature. The early anthologists of Negro literature
were inconsistent in making racial designations for this writing. For
most of them, a poem by a black writer about a white subject would
be classified as Negro poetry, but a text about a black subject by a
white writer would not.

White anthologists seemed to have had no problem distinguishing Negro literature from American literature. Robert Kerlin's *Contemporary Poetry of the Negro* (1923), as the title indicates, focused
only on work of Negro authorship without a conscious concern for

---

[30]W[illiam] E. B. Du Bois, "The Negro in Literature and Art" in *Annals of the American
Academy of Political and Social Science* 49 (September, 1913): 233.

[31]Thomas Nelson Page wrote well-known plantation stories in which black people were
depicted as devoted mammies and carefree slaves. These novels include *In Ole Virginia, or
Marse Chan and Other Stories* (1887) and *Red Rock* (1898). Thomas Dixon, in contrast,
portrayed blacks as primitive savages capable of crime and heinous violence. His novels
include *The Leopard's Spots* (1902) and *The Clansman* (1905).

[32]Benjamin Brawley, "The Negro in American Fiction" in *The Dial* 60 (May 11, 1916):
450.

[33]Brawley, "The Negro in American Fiction," 450.

[34]These novels include *The Uncalled* (1898), *The Love of Landry* (1900), and *The Fanatics*
(1901).

placing the work into national consciousness. The editors of *Anthology of Verse by American Negroes* (1924), Newman I. White, Walter C. Jackson, and James H. Dillard, maintained a similar position, although they stated that they "tried to supplant patronage with honest, unbiased appraisal,"[35] a notable ambition that they failed to meet. Regarding Wheatley, they wrote that "Thomas Jefferson . . . was obviously too harsh when he dismissed her poems as 'beneath criticism.' . . . Their claim to literary merit is certainly a very modest one. . ."[36] Moreover, the editors observed that "one must follow [William Lloyd] Garrison's advice in the preface [of *Moses, A Story of the Nile*] and judge [Harper's] volumes [of poetry] by lower standards than those applied to white poets if he is to find much in them worthy of praise."[37] Concerning Claude McKay, they wrote that he "is another poet who may take rank with the two or three really noteworthy poets of the Negro race."[38] Evidently, McKay could not be ranked among American poets in general, and his dilemma was shared by all black writers. Despite its claim of objectivity, the *Anthology of Verse by American Negroes* fell short of its goal by consistently relying on effaced, prejudicial criteria to place all black writers outside a national context and to confine black women writers to a literary ghetto where their work was presumed inherently inferior.

Nevertheless, black anthologists pressed onward in their pursuit to find appropriate labels for this writing in an effort to facilitate its integration into the national canon. For instance, Countee Cullen, a Harvard-educated black poet, characterized black participation in national literature with his subtitle for *Caroling Dusk* (1927):

> I have called this collection an anthology of verse by Negro poets rather than an anthology of Negro verse, since this latter designation would be more confusing than accurate. . . . Moreover, the attempt to corral the outbursts of the ebony muse into some definite model to which all poetry by Negroes will conform seems altogether futile and aside from the facts. . . .[39]

Having only included Dunbar's non-dialect work, Cullen also explained the absence of dialect verse in this anthology, "If dialect is missed in this collection, it is enough to state that the day of dialect

---

[35]Newman Ivey White, Walter Clinton Jackson, and James Hardy Dillard, *An Anthology of Verse by American Negroes* (Durham, 1924): iii.

[36]White, *et. al.*, p. 5.

[37]White, 10.

[38]White, 19.

[39]Countee Cullen, *Caroling Dusk: An Anthology of Verse by Negro Poets* (New York, 1927): xi.

as far as Negro poets are concerned is in the decline."[40] Negro poets, Cullen contended, were moving into the national literary tradition by employing distinctly American literary conventions. Moreover, he looked to the day when Negro poets would be regarded as American poets and contributors to the national canon.[41]

    The Negro Caravan (1941), the most comprehensive and widely used anthology of Afro-American literature from the 1940s to 60s, further delineated these issues.[42] The editors, Sterling Brown, Arthur Davis and Ulysses Lee, who had been educated as traditional literary scholars, placed Negro literature within the stylistic categories frequently found in white American literary anthologies: Puritan didacticism, sentimental humanitarianism, local color, regionalism, realism, naturalism, and experimentalism.[43] Moreover, they placed Negro literature into the national context, as practically every black literary scholar had done for fifty years, by adamantly insisting that "Negro writers [were] . . . American writers, and literature by American Negroes [was] . . . a segment of American literature."[44] The editors also emphatically maintained that the term Negro literature was ambiguous and promoted a critical double standard:

> The chief cause for objection to the term is that "Negro literature" is too easily placed by certain critics, white and Negro, in an alcove apart. The next step is a double standard of judgment, which is dangerous for the future of Negro writers. "Negro novel," thought of as a separate form, is too often condoned as good enough for a Negro.[45]

They contended, on one hand, that white critics either frequently patronized the writing of black authors or they regarded it as inherently inferior and, on the other, that black critics usually subjected every work of black authorship to excessive praise, often finding artistic merit where there was none.[46] Both practices compromised

---

[40]Cullen, xiv.

[41]Cullen, xiv.

[42]John S. Lash, "The Literature of the Negro Colleges" in *Quarterly Review of Higher Education Among Negroes* 16 (April, 1948): 73.

[43]Sterling Brown, Arthur P. Davis, and Ulysees Lee, *The Negro Caravan: Writing by American Negroes* (New York, 1941; rpt. New York, 1970): 5.

[44]Brown, *et. al.*, p. 7. Also see Blyden Jackson's "An Essay on Criticism" in *Phylon* 11 (1950): 342 in which he called for Negro critics to integrate their literary scholarship with American critical patterns. Cullen also discussed the inevitable integration of Negro literature with American literature in his preface to *Caroling Dusk* (1927).

[45]Brown, *et. al.*, 7.

[46]See John S. Lash, "The Literature of the Negro in Negro Colleges: Its Status and Curricular Accommodations" in which he calls the excessive praise of black critics for black writing as "the drool method" of literary criticism. Lash provides an extensive listing of articles by white critics who discuss, in their estimation, the excessive zeal displayed by

efforts to engender objectivity in literary evaluation as well as undermined the canonical status of Afro-American writing.

Fundamental to these scholars' expressed concerns about finding
appropriate labels for this canon and resolving problems arising from
critical double standards was their desire to see this canon integrated
into American literature. This goal, they believed, would eliminate
both problems by placing the literature within national consciousness. Then, there would be one label and one critical standard. Although they acknowledged that black literature was restricted by the
social exigencies of racial separatism, they looked to a brighter day
when Negro literature would be regarded as American literature.

Several Afro-American literary anthologies, periodicals, and critical essays appeared in the 1920s. In 1922 James Weldon Johnson,
best known for *The Autobiography of an Ex-colored Man* (1912), published *The Book of American Negro Poetry*, in which he established
new trends for Afro-American literary scholarship. He argued that
aesthetic values for Negro literature should not imitate Anglo literary
traditions but must arise from Negro cultural history and values.
Thus, literary depictions of slavery and the resulting racial oppression must be endemic to the literature, although that did not mean
that racial oppression qualified the aspirations of black Americans.
Not only did Johnson provide the most substantial critical evaluation
of black literature to date, but more importantly, three years before
the publication of Alain Locke's *The New Negro* (1925), Johnson
shaped critical views that would endure for the remainder of the
twentieth century. He argued that Negro spirituals and dialect literature were high art forms and not stereotypes that denigrated black
Americans.[47] He included Jupiter Hammon in his survey of black authors and gave him the distinction of being the first poet of African
descent in America.[48] Moreover, Johnson insisted that Wheatley had
never been given her rightful place in American (and Afro-American) literature, even though she was among the first American poets

---

black critics in praising Negro literature. He also supplies references to rejoinders written
by black critics.

For discussions about the problem of audience for the black writer see James Weldon
Johnson's "The Dilemma of the Negro Author" in *American Mercury* XV (1928): 477–481;
Saunders Redding's "American Negro Literature" in *The American Scholar* XVIII, 2 (Spring,
1949): 137–48; Carl Van Vechten's "Moanin' Wid a Sword in Ma Han': A Discussion of the
Negro's Reluctance to Develop and Exploit his
Racial Gifts" in *Vanity Fair* 25, 6 (February, 1926): 61, 100, 102, and Carl Van Doren's
"The Roving Critic" in *The Century Magazine* 61 (1926): 635–39.

[47] James Weldon Johnson, *The Book of American Negro Poetry* (New York, 1922): xv and
xi–xii.

[48] Johnson, *The Book of American Negro Poetry*, xxv.

to publish a volume of poems, an accomplishment that merited her inscription in both the American and Afro-American literary canons.[49] In conclusion, he discussed the contributions of four minor poets—George Moses Horton, Frances Harper, Albery Whitman, and James M. Bell—historically situated between Wheatley and Dunbar, and he illuminated a period that both his predecessors and many of his successors insisted was a virtual literary wasteland.[50]

In 1924 William Stanley Braithwaite, poet and editor of the well-known *Poetry, an Anthology of Verse for 1920*, published "The Negro in Literature" in *Crisis*, which was reissued in the most famous literary anthology of the period, Alain Locke's *The New Negro* (1925). In the first essay of *The New Negro* Locke explained this "New Negro's" appearance in art, as one who is "carefully studied, not just talked about and discussed . . . [but one who] is being seriously portrayed and painted."[51] In contrast, Braithwaite's "The Negro in Literature" did not present a bold stand for racial affirmation. Neither did he build upon the critical platforms laid out by Du Bois, Brawley, and Johnson. Instead, Braithwaite referred to Harriet Beecher Stowe's *Uncle Tom's Cabin* (1850) as the original literary text presenting the Negro character, thus contending that "the Negro was projected into literature by his neighbor."[52] In addition, Wheatley is a problem in his list of canonical authors. Although he cited her as "a great tribute to the Race . . . as good, if not a better poetess, than Ann Bradstreet,"[53] he began his survey of poetry of Negro authorship with Dunbar and not with Wheatley, arguing that all the writing between Wheatley and Dunbar, "by critical standards, is negligible, and of historical interests only."[54] Furthermore, he excised slave narratives, Washington's *Up from Slavery* (1900), and Douglass's three autobiographies on aesthetic grounds by claiming, in the latter case, that "Douglass' story . . . [was] eloquent as a human document, but not in the graces of narration and psychologic portraiture which has definitely put this form of literature in the domain of the fine arts."[55] Turning his attention to Dunbar, Braithwaite credited him with cre-

---

[49]Johnson, *The Book of American Negro Poetry*, xxi–xxiv.

[50]Johnson, *The Book of American Negro Poetry*, xxvi. Braithwaite also expressed this viewpoint in "The Negro in Literature" initially published in *Crisis* XXVIII (1924) and reissued in Locke's *The New Negro* (1925), 29–44. Also see Alain Locke's "A Decade of Negro Expression" (1928). Here, Locke discussed a fundamentally different type of Negro literature seen in the work of writers of the New Negro Renaissance.

[51]Alain Locke, *The New Negro* (New York, 1925; rpt. New York, 1969): 9.

[52]Locke, *The New Negro*, 204.

[53]Locke, *The New Negro*, 207.

[54]Locke, *The New Negro*, 207.

[55]Locke, *The New Negro*, 207.

ating "an utterance more authentic . . . for its faithful rendition of Negro life and character than for any rare or subtle artistry of expression."[56] However, Dunbar did not win his unconditional praise. There were, he wrote, "no agitated visions of prophecy . . . in his poems. His dreams were anchored to the minor whimsies, to the ineffectual tears of his people deluded by the Torch of Liberty."[57] Braithwaite surveyed the well-known writers of the New Negro Renaissance and concluded by calling for "a bright morning star of a new day of the Race in literature."[58] Despite this racial exultation, his posture is rather conservative when measured against those of his predecessors.

During the 1920s and 30s Brawley wrote a series of essays that were precursors to his most famous work—*Negro Genius* (1937). In "The Negro Literary Renaissance" (1927), Brawley acknowledged Marcus Garvey as the source of the heightened race consciousness that dominated the literature of the 1920s. "To be black," Brawley wrote, "ceased to be a matter for explanation or apology; instead it became something to be advertised and exploited."[59] In contrast, his full-length study *The Negro in Literature and Art* (1930) was more conservative in its racial affirmation and was merely a collection of rather ordinary literary biographies on Wheatley, Dunbar, Chesnutt, Du Bois, Braithwaite, and Johnson. Brawley regained his posture of staunch racial affirmation with the 1934 publication of "The Promise of Negro Literature" in which he argued that literature of Negro authorship should reclaim the humanity of a people and vindicate the Negro's manhood.[60] Lastly, *Negro Genius*, which appeared three years later, is important because it resolved the problematic status of certain authors and texts, namely Wheatley, the minor poets between her and Dunbar, spirituals, slave narratives and folk literature, biographies, sermons, and social treatises. These authors and works found a definitive place in Brawley's canon and have remained secure in this position.

Whereas Brawley was the most renowned literary critic of the 1930s and 40s, Locke was the Negro cultural spokesman of this period. His work documents changing attitudes toward the Negro and Negro culture. In the title essay of *The New Negro* (1925) Locke

---

[56]Locke, *The New Negro*, 207.
[57]Locke, *The New Negro*, 208.
[58]Locke, *The New Negro*, 210.
[59]Benjamin Brawley, "The Negro Literary Renaissance," in *Southern Workman* 56 (April, 1927): 177.
[60]Benjamin Brawley, "The Promise of Negro Literature," in *The Journal of Negro History* 19 (1934): 53.

characterized the growth of racial pride by describing it as "shedding the old chrysalis of the Negro problem . . . achieving something like a spiritual emancipation . . . producing a fundamentally different Negro from his predecessors," thus the name "the new Negro." Most important, Locke practiced what he preached and included in this anthology the writing that, in his estimation, characterized the new Negro. A year later in 1926 Locke published "American Literary Tradition and the Negro." Here, he demonstrated what we now take for granted, that American literature reflects national attitudes toward the Negro, and in so doing Locke designated the stereotypes that were most frequently attached to black people, "dreaded primitive, a domestic pet, a moral issue, a ward, a scapegoat, a bogey and a pariah."[61] This essay's most significant observation, though, concerned his use of the following historiographic categories for describing racial attitudes in Afro-American literature, "colonial period (1760–1820), pre-abolition period (1820–1845), abolition period (1845–1865), early reconstruction period (1870–1885), the late reconstruction period (1885–1895), the industrial period (1895–1920) and the contemporary period since 1920."[62] In a much later essay, "The Negro in American Literature" (1952), Locke reappraised the development of Afro-American literature and reaffirmed his early contention that the literature had been seriously affected by crippling stereotypes that forced Negro authors either to cater to them, as Dunbar had, or to offset them with unrealistic counter-stereotyping.[63] As a result, Locke explained, Negro writers had a great deal of difficulty convincing the white reading public that black life was a subject for serious artistic treatment, and, hence, vastly more complex than the simple stereotypes indicated.

In summary, these early scholars' expressed purposes for Afro-American literature not only served to elevate the Negro's social and intellectual position but shaped the accessible canonical stage for Afro-American literature as well. Consequently, many texts that currently appear in the contemporary canon did not appear in its early formulation. For example, the contemporary canon begins with the literature written during slavery—the poetry of Jupiter Hammon and Phillis Wheatley, slave narratives, spirituals and folk writing—in order to reflect the literature's historical authenticity.[64] However, early

[61] Alain Locke, "American Literary Tradition and the Negro" in *Modern Quarterly* 3 (1926): 215–216.

[62] Locke, "American Literary Tradition and the Negro," 216.

[63] Alain Locke, "The Negro in American Literature" in *New World Writing* (New York, 1952): 20.

[64] Most of the critical texts mentioned in this essay do not discuss drama as an integral

black literary scholars did not regard these as representative texts of Afro-American literary expression because they did not, at that time, fulfill the canon's prescribed social function. In their estimation these texts did not reveal the Negro's intellectual depth and racial consciousness; nor did these texts explicitly express the Negro's outrage at racial oppression. Although slave narratives did address these concerns, they were deleted, possibly because they arose out of the degradation of slavery, which these early scholars chose not to emphasize. Thus, constant efforts to inscribe social and intellectual parity in Afro-American literature made many black literary scholars extremely conservative, self-conscious, even defensive. Locke noted their conservatism in "Propaganda or Poetry" (1936) in which he explained what he thought to be its origin: "Many forces account for this [conservatism], chief among them is the tendency the world over for the elite of any oppressed minority to aspire to the conventionally established views and court their protection and prestige."[65] Locke's observation recalls Braithwaite's "The Negro in Literature" in particular.

Regardless of whether their critical postures were conservative or radical, early Negro scholars were emphatic in their insistence that "the Negro's values, ideals, and objectives [were] integrally and unreservedly American."[66] Although these scholars may have referred to this body of writing as Negro literature for convenience, that did not mean that it constituted a separate racial canon to be judged by separate criteria. To the contrary, Negro literature, they contended, was as distinctly American as its white counterpart, and together they represented the American literary canon. It is not surprising that they emphatically called for the integration of Negro literature into the national literature. Integration, they contended, would mean the elimination of the double critical standard and would elevate Negro literature to a canonical discipline as it became a segment of the national canon. However, they seemed not to anticipate that the single critical standard would be of white male authorship alone, that it would be particularly inhospitable to texts of black male authorship, and that it would all but eliminate the writing of black female authority from the segregated canon, which meant that black women's writing would have virtually no chance to join the national canon.

part of Negro literature. American drama of both white and black authorship was a very young generic form. Moreover, during the 20s and 30s most plays depicting black culture were written by white playwrights.

[65] Alain Locke, "Propaganda or Poetry?" in *Race* 1 (Summer, 1936): 70.
[66] Locke, "Propaganda or Poetry?" 20.

Afro-American Literature as a Canonical Discipline

Canonical disciplines are central to a society's erection and maintenance of cultural standards. For example, Terry Eagleton observes
that the English literary canon helped to engender values to Victorian British society at a time when religious beliefs were faltering.[67]
The American literary canon has fulfilled similar purposes; it has
historically encoded ideology in support of national consciousness,
heroic destiny, and Anglo-Saxon superiority, as well as disseminated
these values to the public through formal education.[68] Like the British and American canons, the Afro-American canon also has historic
directives, ones that largely concern demands for racial parity and
equal protection under the law. However, these directives have seldom been subtly encoded, but have often been given direct, repetitive, emphatic expression in all types of writing by black authors.

After early black scholars had routinely referred to literature of
black authorship as Negro literature and acclaimed its social merits,
black intellectuals began to speculate about the practical benefits of
this literature for the general Negro population. In "Negro Literature
for Negro Pupils" (1922), Alice Dunbar-Nelson was one of the earliest scholars to suggest that Negro literature could teach racial pride
to Negro children by showing them that they, like other ethnic
groups, were in possession of their own history and literature.[69] Two
college professors followed Dunbar-Nelson's lead. Sterling Brown began teaching Negro literature at Lynchburg Seminary in 1924, and
Arthur P. Davis likewise began at Virginia Union in 1929.[70] Although courses in Negro literature were appearing at black institutions, it was not fully elevated to a canonical discipline until the
early 1940s.[71] During these early years, the significance of this body

---

[67]Terry Eagleton, *Literary Theory* (Minneapolis, 1983): 44–46.

[68]Lauter, 446.

[69]Alice Dunbar-Nelson, "Negro Literature for Negro Pupils" in *Southern Workman* 51
(February, 1922): 63. Also see Alfred Farrell, "Teaching Race Pride Through
Poetry," *The Quarterly Review of Higher Education Among Negroes* 9 (January, 1941): 20–
23, and Nick Aaron Ford's "I Teach Negro Literature," in *College English* 2 (March, 1941):
530–541; and Nick Aaron Ford, "The Negro Novel As a Vehicle of Propaganda" in *The
Quarterly Review of Higher Education Among Negroes* 9 (July, 1941): 135–139.

[70]Taped interview with Arthur P. Davis on June 19, 1985 at his home in Washington,
D.C.

[71]The general anthologies which routinely served as textbooks prior to 1950 were
Brawley's *The Negro in Literature and Art* (1930), *Early Negro American Writers* (1935), and
Negro Genius (1937); Vernon Loggins's *The Negro Author* (1931); Victor E. Calverton's
Anthology of American Negro Literature (1929); *Readings from Negro Authors* (1931), edited
by Otelia Cromwell, Lorenzo Dow Turner, and Eva B. Dykes; *The Negro Caravan* (1941),
edited by Sterling S. Brown, Arthur P. Davis, and Ulysees Lee; and Sylvestre C. Watkins's

of writing was based only partly on its being a collection of master-texts with identifiable aesthetic qualities, and more important was its ability to reflect the American racial climate accurately and to instill black school children with racial pride.

Many national Negro advancement organizations sponsored publications devoted specifically to the study of Negro life and culture, and these publications nurtured Afro-American literature in its early stages as a canonical discipline. Among the better known publications were *The Journal of Negro History* and *The Negro History Bulletin*, with their first issues in 1916 and 1937 respectively, published by the Association for the Study of Negro Life and History; *Opportunity: The Journal of Negro Life*, beginning in 1923, published by the National Urban League; and *The Crisis* in 1910, published by the National Association for the Advancement of Colored People. In 1957 the College Language Association published *College Language Association Journal*, known as *CLA Journal*. Until the 70s, *CLA Journal* and *The Journal of Negro History* were the publications to which editors of *P.M.L.A.* and *American Literature* consistently referred scholars who wrote about black writers.[72] All of these publications provided the means for scholars to valorize and thus canonize texts of black authorship into both accessible and selective canons of Afro-American literature. These publications, in addition to *The Quarterly Review of Higher Education Among Negroes* and *Phylon*, which were first published in 1933 and 1940 respectively, provided actual instances of scholars performing canonical construction.

Anthology of American Negro Literature (1944).

Refer also to the series of articles by Lash who wrote about professionalism and pedagogic practices concerning the teaching of Negro literature in Negro colleges and universities. For a survey of Negro literature courses offered at Negro colleges see "The Literature of the Negro in Negro Colleges" in *Quarterly Review of Higher Education Among Negroes* (April 1948): 66–76. Here he refers to the *College English* publication of Nick Aaron Ford's "I Teach Negro Literature" in 1941 as an indication that Negro literature is recognized as a canonical discipline by a major academic association. "The Study of Negro Literary Expression" published in *Negro History Bulletin* (June 1946): 207–211 provides a summary of the types of scholarship on Negro literature in Negro colleges and black and white graduate schools. This essay also calls for integration of Negro literature but refers to the inhospitality of the current American critical movement—New criticism—as a serious deterrent, "What Is 'Negro Literature'?" published in *College English* (Oct., 1946): 37–42, and "On Negro Literature," in *Phylon* (1945): 240–247, call for the integration of Negro literature within the national canon and for Negro literary scholarship to adhere to the methodology of American literary criticsm. For a bibliography of scholarship about Negro literature from 1900 to the mid-40s, see "The American Negro and American Literature: A Check List of Significant Commentaries," in *Bulletin of Bibliography* IXX 1 (Sept., 1946 to Dec., 1949): 12–36.

[72]Lauter, 445.

Conclusion

By reconstructing the process of canon-formation for Afro-American literature, I can discern specific critical trends regarding the inscription of Phillis Wheatley's poetry, slave narratives, and spirituals and Paul Laurence Dunbar's dialect verse. These trends split over whether Negro literature should be regarded as a collection of mastertexts or a set of texts that depict the social reality of the black American experience. Both trends reflect the changing critical attitudes of dominant scholars during three historical moments, each of which calls attention to the fact that literary scholarship is discursive hindsight.

During the first critical period (1895–1920), early critics (Matthews, Culp, Brawley, and Du Bois) inscribed all texts of black authorship that demonstrated clear intellectual ability and high moral character. As a result, they did not regard Wheatley and Dunbar as problematic, since they met these basic requirements. Matthews, Culp, and Brawley did, however, disregard slave narratives, spirituals, and folk literature, whereas Du Bois inscribed those texts seemingly in the interest of preserving historical authenticity for Afro-American cultural expression.[73] Inasmuch as these early scholars based canonical inscription on the author's demonstration of intellectual talent and moral fiber, I appropriate a modification of Du Bois's term talented-tenth—Talented-Tenth Poetics—to designate this literary period (1895–1920) and its inscribing criteria.

During the New Negro Renaissance, Locke's *The New Negro* (1925) was instrumental in shaping critical values. Affirming racial pride, expressing a renewed, uncompromised sense of self-respect and self-reliance were the artistic mandates for texts of this era that received wide-scale critical acclaim. These texts did not so much address individual concerns as they did the racial consciousness of a people, which was, by and large, construed as masculine. The artistic model for the New Negro, as both writer and subject, was then a young, urban, black male, racially assertive in both tone and subject. Afro-American folk culture, urban and rural, informed this writing, and it embodied the popular vernacular of that day. This model, to the virtual exclusion of others, shaped the contours of literary history for the New Negro or Harlem Renaissance. Consequently, New Negro Poetics is an appropriate label for the scholarly temperament

---

[73]In Brawley's 1910 edition of *The Negro in Literature and Art*, he made nominal reference to folklore. This reference was dropped in the 1918 and 1930 editions, but reinserted in *Negro Genius* (1937).

from roughly 1920–1940 as well as for its corresponding criteria for canonical inscription.[74]

Phillis Wheatley's neoclassical verse and Paul Laurence Dunbar's novels and dialect poetry did not fit the New Negro model. Neither did the middle-class, domestic novels of Jessie Fauset and Nella Larsen, nor the personal lyric poetry of Anne Spenser, Angelina Grimké, and Georgia Douglas Johnson, even though they actually wrote the bulk of their works during the period popularly called the New Negro Renaissance. Under the weight of the New Negro Poetics, scholars maintained that such writers celebrated middle-class pretentiousness or were escapists who chose to write about personal and, therefore, non-racial themes. This critical posture was responsible for relegating them to minor roles, for affixing them with labels like the rear guard,[75] and for pushing them to the margins and footnotes of literary history. Wheatley and Dunbar received similar fates; they too were neglected in the scholarship of this period. None of them could be fashioned as new Negroes; so they were labeled old Negroes and pushed to the background.

With the publication of the anthology *Negro Genius* in 1938 and *The Negro Caravan* in 1941, the accessible and selective canons for Afro-American literature were by and large in place. Both canons included not only Wheatley's poetry, Dunbar's dialect, and standard-English verse, but also slave narratives, spirituals, and folk literature. The later anthology especially called emphatically for the integration of Negro literature into the general American canon. Therefore, the criteria for canonical inscription for this period, from 1940–1968, can be referred to as "Integrationist Poetics."[76]

These two anthologies did not employ the conventional historiographic divisions found in American literature.[77] Such divisions, as

---

[74]This label is mindful of the fact that during this period, inscription for Wheatley's poetry and Dunbar's dialect verse was problematic. Moreover, slave narratives, spirituals, and folk literature were also regarded as inappropriate for canonical inscription.

[75]Robert Bone in *The Negro Novel in America* (New Haven: Yale University Press, 1965), pp. 95–107 uses the label "rear guard" to refer to the novels of Walter White, W. E. B. Du Bois, Jessie Fauset and Nella Larsen. Such terms were often used to criticize these writers' so-called conservative and reactionary posture.

[76]Houston A. Baker, Jr., *Blues, Ideology, and Afro-American Literature: A Vernacular Theory* (Chicago, 1984): 17.

[77]Lauter, 452–457. Anthologies of Negro literature published in the 1920s, 30s and 40s were frequently organized by employing generic categories or by listing authors' names in rough chronological order. Although generic divisions can preclude many literary forms employed by women, such as the sketch, the diary, and the episodic novel, this method was not as restrictive as many common historiographic categories. For example, Arthur Davis's *Calvacade* (1971) contains very few women writers perhaps as a result of its organization. The text is divided into the following historiographic periods, which do not

many scholars have demonstrated, delete the representation of various groups because "historical epochs are experienced differently by
women and men, by whites, and by people of color."[78] Different
group experiences, then, do not lead themselves easily to standard-
ized historiographic divisions. As Elaine Showalter explains,
"[e]vents and periods that are important to the development of male
ideas and institutions may be negligible or irrelevant to women, and
the temporal grid of men's history may filter out women's experiences, values and achievements."[79] Brawley was not concerned with
conceptualizing women's history, and he employed conventional,
white, historical epochs and thematic trends only insofar as they
could be utilized to reflect the black experience (construed, of
course, as masculine). Hence, he outlined his text using general historical and thematic divisions: "The Pioneers; The Era of Effort for
Freedom; Poetry and the Arts, 1830–1865; Literature, 1865–1890;
The Maturing of Negro Literature; Protest and Vindication; The New
Realists; and Drama and Stage, 1916–1936."[80] Brown et al., on the
other hand, employed generic markers: short stories; novels (selections); poetry, folk literature; drama; speeches, pamphlets, and letters; biography and autobiography; and historical, social, cultural,
and personal essays. Although the latter categories do not produce
much historical or cultural cohesion, they do provide a greater opportunity for inscripting those writers who do not fit rigid historical
or thematic structural patterns or critical concepts about mastertexts
and major writers.

Many texts that currently represent each of these three literary
periods—Talented-Tenth Poetics, New Negro Poetics and Integrationist Poetics—were actually absent or marginal during that period.
For example, during the 1920s critics consistently referred to texts
by Hughes, McKay, (James W.) Johnson, and Cullen. Although
Locke and Du Bois mentioned Jean Toomer and Jessie Fauset's noteworthy contributions to the literature of this era, they withheld the
inscription of their work and awaited additional evidence—I suggest,

---

support the ready inclusion of women writers: Pioneer Writers: 1760–1830, Freedom Fighters: 1830–1865, Accommodation and Protest: 1865–1910, The New Negro Renaissance and
Beyond: 1910–1954, Integration versus Black Nationalism: 1954 to the Present. These
categories concern the public sphere of social involvement, and as a result often preclude
the participation of women, who, for the most part, are participants in the private or domestic
sphere.

[78]Lauter, 96.

[79]Elaine Showalter, "Women's Time, Women's Space: Writing in the History of Feminist
Criticism" in *Tulsa Studies in Women's Literature* 3 (Spring/Fall, 1984): 30.

[80]Benjamin Brawley, *The Negro Genius* (New York, 1937): ix–x.

because these writers did not seem to adhere to the paradigm for New Negro Poetics.[81]

During the period of Integrationist Poetics (1940–1968), Toomer and Fauset's work become even more marginal in the canon because Toomer's characterizations were too aberrant to encourage integration and Fauset's domestic novels about so-called tragic mulattoes seem to encode racial insecurities that did not support integrationist polemics. These reasons alone were not entirely responsible for the minor status accorded to both Toomer and Fauset at this time, but they combined with the logistics of course offerings, which usually surveyed texts by major writers or standard texts, to push Toomer and Fauset, as well as others like them (which categorically included black women), to the margins (if not off the pages) of literary history. Only when a large number of scholars who were clearly not governed by these codes focused on the works of Toomer and Fauset did they move up on the canonical ladder.

The intellectual paradigm responsible for elevating Negro literature to a canonical discipline, in historically black institutions during the 1940s and in white institutions during the late 1960s, seems to have been social plurality, specifically racial plurality in the American experience. Currently, however, social plurality includes gender and class diversity as well. This later understanding of plurality has been the major impetus for the current reformation of Afro-American (and American) canonical literature and of canonical disciplines in general.

The process of selecting a specific paradigm or paradigms for canonical inscription is capricious and therefore inherently prejudicial. This can be illustrated by comparing comments about text selection in two well-known Afro-American literary anthologies, *The Negro Caravan* (1941) and *From the Dark Tower* (1974), both edited in part or whole by Arthur P. Davis. The former states that it does not attempt to "maintain an even level of literary excellence [but presents] a balanced picture" of American social reality.[82] The latter selects major authors according to the following criterion, which Davis uses to explain his decision to inscribe Jean Toomer's *Cane* and to delete Frank Yerby's work:

> Yerby's novels, except for the most recent, do not use Negro themes or principal characters; they give little or no interpretation of black life in America; and they add very little to the development of that dual-rooted

---

[81]W[illiam] E. B. Du Bois and Alain Locke "The Younger Literary Movement" in *Crisis* 27 (February, 1924): 161–163.

[82]Brown, *et. al.*, 7.

segment of national writing which we call Negro. Toomer's *Cane*, on the other hand, aside from dealing wholly with Negro material, inaugurated a new approach in black writing . . . and is artistically a brilliant work measured by any standards[83]

A major Negro writer, then, is one whose work deals largely with *the* black experience, measures up to appropriate, though unspecified, aesthetic standards, and influences to some extent his contemporaries or those who come after him.[84] Davis's last criterion is important beyond its designation of major writers; it points to the heart of the process of canon-formation: a writer's status is not so much a product of textuality—of the words printed in the text—but of those individuals he or she influences, a process which Harold Bloom calls the anxiety of influence.[85] Thus, a writer's status is determined not so much by the text itself but by its impact on the literary community and literary history. This impact varies throughout time.

Davis's last criterion and Bloom's anxiety of influence explain, for example, why Zora Neale Hurston, who was regarded as a minor figure from the 1920s to the 70s, is currently considered a major author. Her status as a major figure is dependent on a generation of very prolific black female writers who cited Hurston as an important source of their artistic inspiration. This process also helps to explain why black women writers were categorically regarded as marginal figures for so much of the canonical history of Afro-American literature. For until a substantial number of authors can look backward in time and claim a parent-writer as a major influence, that writer's contribution to the literature remains obscure.

Moreover, this process is double-edged; not only do esteemed writers (in this case, black women) rescue their literary foremothers from obscurity, but they also compel literary scholars to re-examine the past in search of a tradition which accounts for their success. "The authority of any established canon," Annette Kolodny, a feminist theorist, writes, "is reified by our perception that current work seems to grow almost inevitably out of it (even in opposition or rebellion)."[86] Thus, as the critical community attends to the volume of recent, fine literature written by [black] women, it also researches the past in an effort to account for their success. In the process, lit-

---

[83]Arthur P. Davis, *From the Dark Tower: Afro-American Writers 1900–1960* (Washington, 1974): xiv.

[84]Davis, xiv.

[85]Harold Bloom, *The Anxiety of Influence: A Theory of Poetry* (New York, 1973): 5–15.

[86]Annette Kolodny, "Dancing Through the Minefield: Some Observation on the Theory, Practice, and Politics of a Feminist Literary Criticism" in *Feminist Criticism*, ed. Elaine Showalter (New York, 1985): 152.

erary history is modified, as works by black women are retrieved and given "new importance as 'precursors' or as prior influences upon present-day authors."[87]

Male writers wrote the bulk of Afro-American (and American) literature, and their critics, who were also almost exclusively men, wrote its history. Inasmuch as all histories are selective discourses, the literary history that has been inherited by contemporary readers is a consensus of these critics' selection of writers who, in their estimation, have shaped literary tradition. It comes as no surprise, then, that male writers and critics pointed clearly to other men who were their predecessors and who influenced their work, because, I suggest, they were familiar with masculine values and interpretative strategies and, as a result, appreciated texts of male authorship. The converse of this process also helps to explain why many female writers, black and white, may have slipped through the cracks of literary history, as Kolodny further theorizes, "not [because of] any lack of merit in the work but [because of] an incapacity of predominantly male readers to properly interpret and appreciate women's texts—due, in large part, to a lack of prior acquaintance [with female experience, customs, and values]."[88] Therefore, male writers tended to insert their forefathers into the mainstreams of literary tradition.

Only recently has this trend been altered by the substantial increase in the number of writers who happen to be both black and female and of critics (both female and male, black and white) who are currently rescuing black literary foremothers from marginality at best, obscurity at worst. This rescue work explains much of the recent inscription of texts of female authorship into Afro-American and American canonical literatures as well as the gendering of other canonical disciplines.

---

[87]Kolodny, 152.
[88]Kolodny, 155.

Ntozake Shange

(1948–   )

PERHAPS BEST KNOWN for the 1976 Broadway production of her choreopoem *For Colored Girls Who Have Considered Suicide / When the Rainbow
Is Enuf*, Ntozake Shange has been creating her unique blend of poetry,
music, and dance since the early 1970s. Through her plays, poetry, and
novels she pays tribute to black women who have endured physical and
emotional abuse at the hands of white society and insensitive black men.
With compelling, sometimes brutal honesty, Shange portrays the victories
and defeats of these women in their struggle to become self-sufficient.

Born Paulette Williams in 1948 in Trenton, New Jersey, Shange moved
with her parents to St. Louis when she was eight years old. At the age of
thirteen she returned with them to New Jersey, and in 1966 she enrolled
in the American studies program at Barnard College. Although her childhood and youth were materially secure and intellectually stimulating, by
the end of her first year at Barnard she had attempted suicide because of
her intense frustration and rage against the limitations she experienced in
society as a black woman. Her divorce from her first husband not long
before contributed to the bitterness and alienation that culminated in this
attempt to end her life.

For the next several years she grappled with these issues while completing her undergraduate work at Barnard and going on to earn the M.A.
in American studies at the University of Southern California, Los Angeles
in 1973. During the course of her graduate work she took her African
name, perhaps as a reinforcement of her fierce struggle to develop a sense
of self: Ntozake means "she who comes with her own things," and Shange
means "she who walks like a lion."

After leaving USC, Shange taught at a number of California schools
and was also dancing with Raymond Sawyer's Afro-American Dance Company, West Coast Dance Works, and her own company, For Colored Girls
Who Have Considered Suicide. In 1975 she moved to New York City,
where *For Colored Girls* was opening off-Broadway. In 1976 the piece
moved to the Booth Theater on Broadway and in 1977 won Shange an
Obie Award. The play has also won the Outer Critics Circle Award, the
Audelco Award, and the *Mademoiselle* Award and was nominated for a
Tony, a Grammy, and an Emmy.

The late 1970s and early 1980s were productive years for Shange. As
well as giving readings and lectures at Yale, Howard, Southern, and other

universities, she served as a creative writing instructor at the City College
of New York, artist-in-residence for the New Jersey State Council on the
Arts, and assistant professor of English and drama at Douglass College.
During this period she also published poems and short stories in a number
of black arts journals as well as *Sassafrass: A Novella* (1977), *Nappy Edges*,
a volume of poetry (1978), and *Three Pieces* (1981). The last of these
contains three theatre pieces, two of which, *Spell #7* and *A Photograph:
Lovers-in-Motion*, were produced by Joseph Papp's New York Shakespeare
Festival. In 1981 Shange was awarded a Guggenheim Fellowship, the Medal
of Excellence from Columbia University, and her second Obie for her 1980
production of *Mother Courage and Her Children* (an adaptation of Bertolt
Brecht's *Mother Courage*). Her first full-length novel, *Sassafrass, Cypress,
and Indigo*, was published in 1982 and was followed by two more works:
A Daughter's Geography (1983) and *From Okra to Greens* (1984). Shange's
latest works are *See No Evil: Prefaces, Essays and Accounts, 1976–1983*
(1984); *Betsey Brown* (1985), a novel; and *Ridin' the Moon in Texas: Word
Paintings* (1987).

For further reading, see the essay from which some of the information
here is taken, Elizabeth Brown's article in *Dictionary of Literary Biography,
Volume 38*. Also see Martine Latour, "Ntozake Shange: Driven Poet/Play-
wright," *Mademoiselle*, 82 (September 1976): 182, 226.

The first selection, "lady in red" is from *For Colored Girls Who Have
Considered Suicide*; "de poem's gotta come otta my crotch?" is taken from
Nappy Edges.

LADY IN RED

there waz no air / the sheets made ripples under his
body like crumpled paper napkins in a summer park / & lil
specks of somethin from tween his toes or the biscuits
from the day before ran in the sweat that tucked the sheet
into his limbs like he waz an ol frozen bundle of chicken /
& he'd get up to make coffee, drink wine, drink water / he
wished one of his friends who knew where he waz wd come by
with some blow or some shit / anythin / there waz no air /
he'd see the spotlights in the alleyways downstairs movin
in the air / cross his wall over his face / & get under the
covers & wait for an all clear or til he cd hear traffic
again /

there waznt nothin wrong with him / there waznt nothin wrong
with him / he kept tellin crystal /
any niggah wanna kill vietnamese children more n stay home
& raise his own is sicker than a rabid dog /
that's how their thing had been goin since he got back /
crystal just got inta sayin whatta fool niggah beau waz
& always had been / didnt he go all over uptown sayin the
child waznt his / waz some no counts bastard / & any ol city
police cd come & get him if they wanted / cuz as soon as
the blood type & shit waz together / everybody wd know that
crystal waz a no good lyin whore / and this after she'd been
his girl since she waz thirteen / when he caught her
on the stairway /

he came home crazy as hell / he tried to get veterans benefits
to go to school & they kept right on puttin him in
remedial classes / he cdnt read wortha damn / so beau
cused the teachers of holdin him back & got himself
a gypsy cab to drive / but his cab kept breakin
down / & the cops was always messin wit him / plus not
gettin much bread /

& crystal went & got pregnant again / beau most beat
her to death when she tol him / she still gotta scar
under her right tit where he cut her up / still crystal
went right on & had the baby / so now beau willie had
two children / a little girl / naomi kenya & a boy / kwame beau
willie brown / & there waz no air /

how in the hell did he get in this mess anyway / somebody
went & tol crystal that beau waz spendin alla his money
on the bartendin bitch down at the merry-go-round cafe /
beau sat straight up in the bed / wrapped up in the sheets
lookin like john the baptist or a huge baby wit stubble
& nuts / now he hadta get alla that shit outta crystal's
mind / so she wd let him come home / crystal had gone &
got a court order saying beau willie brown had no access
to his children / if he showed his face he waz subject
to arrest / shit / she'd been in his ass to marry her
since she waz 14 years old & here when she 22 / she wanna
throw him out cuz he say he'll marry her / she burst
out laughin / hollerin whatchu wanna marry me for now /
so i can support yr
ass / or come sit wit ya when they lock yr behind
up / cause they gonna come for ya / ya goddamn lunatic /

they gonna come / & i'm not gonna have a thing to do
wit it / o no i wdnt marry yr pitiful black ass for
nothin & she went on to bed /

the next day beau willie came in blasted & got ta swingin
chairs at crystal / who cdnt figure out what the hell
he waz doin / til he got ta shoutin bout how she waz gonna
marry him / & get some more veterans benefits / & he cd
stop drivin them crazy spics round / while they tryin
to kill him for $15 / beau waz sweatin terrible / beatin
on crystal / & he cdnt do no more with the table n chairs /
so he went to get the high chair / & lil kwame waz in it /
& beau waz beatin crystal with the high chair & her son /
& some notion got inta him to stop / and he run out /

crystal most died / that's why the police wdnt low
beau near where she lived / & she'd been tellin the kids
their daddy tried to kill her & kwame / & he just wanted
to marry her / that's what / he wanted to marry her / &
have a family / but the bitch waz crazy / beau willie
waz sittin in this hotel in his drawers drinkin
coffee & wine in the heat of the day spillin shit all
over hisself / laughin / bout how he waz gonna get crystal
to take him back / & let him be a man in the house / & she
wdnt even have to go to work no more / he got dressed
all up in his ivory shirt & checkered pants to go see
crystal & get this mess all cleared up /
he knocked on the door to crystal's rooms / & she
didnt answer / he beat on the door & crystal & naomi
started cryin / beau gotta shoutin again how he wanted
to marry her / & waz she always gonna be a whore / or
did she wanna husband / & crystal just kept on
screamin for him to leave us alone / just leave us
alone / so beau broke the door down / crystal held
the children in fronta her / she picked kwame off the
floor / in her arms / & she held naomi by her shoulders /
& kept on sayin / beau willie brown / get outta here /
the police is gonna come for ya / ya fool / get outta here /
do you want the children to see you act the fool again /
you want kwame to brain damage from you throwin him
round / niggah / get outta here / get out & dont show yr
ass again or i'll kill ya / i swear i'll kill ya /
he reached for naomi / crystal grabbed the lil girl &
stared at beau willie like he waz a leper or somethin /
dont you touch my children / muthafucker / or i'll kill you /

beau willie jumped back all humble & apologetic / i'm
sorry / i dont wanna hurt em / i just wanna hold em &
get on my way / i dont wanna cuz you no more trouble /
i wanted to marry you & give ya things
what you gonna give / a broken jaw / niggah get outta here /
he ignored crystal's outburst & sat down motionin for
naomi to come to him / she smiled back at her daddy /
crystal felt naomi givin in & held her tighter /
naomi / pushed away & ran to her daddy / cryin / daddy, daddy
come back daddy / come back / but be nice to mommy /
cause mommy loves you / and ya gotta be nice /
he sat her on his knee / & played with her ribbons &
they counted fingers & toes / every so often he
looked over to crystal holdin kwame / like a statue /
& he'd say / see crystal / i can be a good father /
now let me see my son / & she didnt move / &
he coaxed her & he coaxed her / tol her she waz
still a hot lil ol thing & pretty & strong / didnt
she get right up after that lil ol fight they had
& go back to work / beau willie oozed kindness &
crystal who had known so lil / let beau hold kwame /

as soon as crystal let the baby outta her arms / beau
jumped up a laughin & a gigglin / a hootin & a hollerin /
awright bitch / awright bitch / you gonna marry me /
you gonna marry me . . .
i aint gonna marry ya / i aint ever gonna marry ya /
for nothin / you gonna be in the jail / you gonna be
under the jail for this / now gimme my kids / ya give
me back my kids /

he kicked the screen outta the window / & held the kids
offa the sill / you gonna marry me / yeh, i'll marry ya /
anything / but bring the children back in the house /
he looked from where the kids were hangin from the
fifth story / at alla the people screamin at him / &
he started sweatin again / say to alla the neighbors /
you gonna marry me /

i stood by beau in the window / with naomi reachin
for me / & kwame screamin mommy mommy from the fifth
story / but i cd only whisper / & he dropped em

DE POEMS GOTTA COME OUTTA MY CROTCH?
(with love to & from ishmael reed)

de kings uv ancient inca-land aztec lakes
& mali bush wuz hi-ho silver / shanghai jack /
garcia gallavante
sometimes shootin sam   dey wuz de empeers
uv de whole civilizations uv de
colored peoples
hi-ho in de cowboy boat
shanghai in de yangtze boat
garcia in a taino roustabout
shootin sam in de slow boat
                    down de nile
de kings uv poesie wid ladies at dey feet /
tween dey thighs a peelin pomegranates
       for our laws uv de given word

diviners n soothsayers outta our archetypal pasts
came to dis heah party de othah nite / met up wid me
n my sierra-brazen colleague uv graceful trapeze lashes
& sequin studded elbows /
                    we weren't claimin to be no queens
                    courtesans uv note or de fianci uv howard hugh
             nicaraguan bastard son or nothin special t'all
       cept i was a tolteca goldsmith's daughter
been mistaken for earth-mama n a particularly pubescent
xhosa sprite
but dis heah king hi-ho he say to me / king hi-ho he say
       i shd make pies n sleep wid
       de consciously fascist man
       cuz he know de way to be
       de same way dey been

50,000 years / uv dese kings uv poesie n de sepia peoples
still aint free n de kings get drunk
try to pull pussy outa linoleum shadows
or de naivete uv would-be geishas
       i says
       hey yr majesty rustler upstart uv de black mountain pass
i handle my liquor / open my own doors / give good head n
       i make poems / jack
             get to dat

my mamma n my daddy wuz craftsmen
in all de places my soul's been nurtured / i come from de workers
uv de ancient worl' / i am de elements

&

de king hi-ho fascist man he say:
  'i'm a man, i can beat em'
  'we men / we can beat em'

& i says
king hi-ho / de fiersomest scout uv scoundrel energies in de west
dis heah a luv-u-bettah-get-yr-stuff-togethah-poem
from de quick hands uv a smart dancin girl
workin dem same saloons u been drinkin
in /

sheriff yo self yo own horizon / toots
          i got too many things to do
        to shoot you rodeo-style from b'hind de knee
      wid a diamond-ringed 45
/lisson here cherokee houngan
              i got my magic covered
        gonna get all up in yr juju-wangol / tear it up n
toss it in some ol cheyenne burial grounds / let yr
inca aztec ibo taino mandarin harlemesque salinas grown
bruised ego get some sun / gotta be healthy on the range /
poem rustlin / be demandin a quik draw /

R. Baxter Miller

(1948–   )

BORN IN ROCKY MOUNT, NORTH CAROLINA, Ron Baxter Miller is the second child and only son of Marcellus C. Miller, a retired high school chemistry teacher, and of the late Elsie B. Miller, an elementary school teacher for more than thirty years. Miller was one of ten blacks to integrate Rocky Mount Senior High School, where he did his best work in French and English. From 1966 to 1970, he attended the predominantly black North Carolina Central University, where he experimented with the publication of poems in *Ex-Libra*, a collegiate magazine, and where he contributed editorial columns to the student newspaper, *Campus Echo*. Entering graduate school at the end of the sixties, the young Miller realized that the decade had had an indelible influence on his cultural consciousness.

Having graduated magna cum laude from North Carolina Central, he was recruited by Brown University, from which he received his A.M. and Ph.D. degrees in 1972 and 1974 respectively. Presently a professor of English and director of the black literature program at the University of Tennessee, Knoxville, Miller has also taught at Haverford College, at State University College of New York at Oneonta, and at Williams College. His teaching experiences range from thematic approaches to freshman English, freshman writing, black American literature, English literature from Chaucer to Shakespeare, and English literature from Samuel Johnson to D. H. Lawrence.

Professor Miller has been active as a scholar in the field of African American literature since the publication of his review "America's First Negro Poet," which appeared in *New York History* in October 1974. He is the editor of the *Reference Guide to Langston Hughes and Gwendolyn Brooks* (1978), of *Black American Literature and Humanism* (1981), and of *Black American Poets between Worlds, 1940–1960* (1986). In addition to being the author of numerous chapters in books and articles in journals such as *Obsidian, Phylon, MELUS, Black American Literature Forum, Southern Literary Journal*, and the *Langston Hughes Review*, he is also the author of the more recent *The Art and Imagination of Langston Hughes* (1989) and editor of the most significant *The Critical Methods of the Black United States, 1865–1988*, a collection of bio-critical essays on African American critics.

The organizer of the division of black American literature for the Modern Language Association in 1983, Miller is president of the Langston Hughes Society. He received the United Negro College Fund Distinguished

Scholar Award from Xavier University in 1988, a National Research Council Fellowship from 1986 to 1987, and a National Endowment for the Humanities Fellowship in 1975. He is listed in *Who's Who among Black Americans, Who's Who in the East, Directory of American Scholars, Who's Who in the South and Southwest, Outstanding Young Men of America, Contemporary Authors,* and *International Authors and Writers Who's Who.*

   " 'Does Man Love Art?': The Humanistic Aesthetic of Gwendolyn Brooks" is taken from *Black American Literature and Humanism.*

"DOES MAN LOVE ART?"
The Humanistic Aesthetic of Gwendolyn Brooks

Humanism has long characterized the poetry of Gwendolyn Brooks. Since *A Street in Bronzeville* (1945) she has varied the forms of Shakespearean and Petrarchan sonnets; especially since *The Bean Eaters* (1960) she has experimented with free verse and social theme. For more than thirty years she has excelled in the skills of alliteration, balance, plosive, and rhetorical question. Against a background of light and dark, her techniques reveal a deeply human struggle. Her world evokes death, history, pain, sickness, identity, and life; her personae seek the grace and vision of personal style. Although her forms vary, her poems generally impose order upon "the flood of chaos."[1] Are the creations ambivalent? Does form sublimate the personality as well as reveal it? Did Keats correctly desire "negative capability" and discern Shakespeare's greatness?

   Appreciation of the paradox gives poetry power and meaning. Humanism is the personally cultural medium for seeking and defining knowledge, ethical value, and aesthetics. Through subjectivity the living writer inspires the inanimate poem. Conversation anthropocentrically signifies the speaker. Written language, rather, implies first an autonomous narrator and second an historical author. Humanism is the instrument for creating and interpreting signs. The method opposes society to self, environment to heredity, death to life, horizontality to verticality, formalism (science) to mythmaking, and barbarism to civilization. By humanism, characters experience choice, empathy, love, style, identity, and need. Humanism represents both the relative and the absolute, and Brooks portrays the ten-

---

   [1]George E. Kent, "Preface: Gwen's Way," in *Report from Part I*, ed. Gwendolyn Brooks (Detroit: Broadside, 1972), p. 31.

sion between the two (her whirlwind) where one struggles for stasis within flux.

Her attempts place Western art forms and artists in a Black folk perspective. At different times her speakers refer to baroque and rococo styles in architecture and to traditional musicians—Saint-Saëns, Brahms, Grieg, or Tschaikovsky. Pablo Picasso appears at least once in her poetry. But these images have counterparts. Satin-Legs Smith and a Black youth rioting in the streets are common people. Even Langston Hughes becomes an ironic means for rehumanizing what F. R. Leavis has called the Great Tradition. By demonstrating the inseparability of objective and subjective art, Brooks frees the tradition from itself. Her formal style creates a poetic world in which a folk view contrasts with an elite one, although class differences obscure a common bond. Here one culture's destruction is another culture's creation, so there is a need to redefine culture itself.

Brooks's personae live somewhere between determinism and personal choice. The artist signifies the reader, his human relative; he represents history and collectivity as well as creative process. Using this framework to portray both narrator and artist as hero and heroine, the poet verifies the importance of his or her personal struggle. Here I describe Brooks's humanistic aesthetic. First, she charts its fall from meaning to meaninglessness in early and more stylized poems such as "The Sundays of Satin-Legs Smith" and "still do I keep my look, my identity . . ." (A Street in Bronzeville); second, she develops the aesthetic through a middle stage characterized by distance, alienation, and continued questioning in the second sonnet of Annie Allen (1949); third, she forcibly reaffirms the principle in freer forms such as "Langston Hughes" (Selected Poems, 1963), or "Boy Breaking Glass" and "The Chicago Picasso" (In the Mecca, 1968).[2]

"Satin-Legs" posed early the existential question which was to concern Brooks for more than thirty years. As with later poems, such as number XV in Annie Allen and "Second Sermon on the Warpland" in Mecca, it sets style and imagination against a deterministic reality and asks if they can prevail. In Annie the answer is maybe; in "Second Sermon," a presupposed yes; in "Satin-Legs," no. "Satin-Legs" can be conveniently divided into three parts. The first (11. 1–42) describes a folk character who rises from bed one morning in Black Chicago and gets dressed. Some sweet scents ironically suggest his royalty and contrast sharply with his impoverished environment. The resulting tensions indirectly show the relative beauty of roses, dandelions, and garbage. The second part (11. 43–74) illus-

---

[2]Unless noted differently, all citations of primary text refer to Gwendolyn Brooks, The World of Gwendolyn Brooks (New York: Harper and Row, 1971).

trates a common journey by narrator and reader into Satin-Legs's closet, a metaphor of man. Here the wide shoulder padding representing Satin-Legs's sculpture and art contrasts with the baroque and rococo styles, European forms of the seventeenth and eighteenth centuries. In the third part (11. 75–158) ear and eye imagery reveal Satin-Legs's unawareness of the world about him, as clothing helps to suggest human deprivation. The narrative movement leads first from the speaker's original antagonism toward her listener ("you") to a light epic concerning Satin-Legs's wardrobe. Following the disappearance of "you" from the poem, the narrator finally views Satin-Legs from a lonely detachment. Ironically this last section juxtaposes blues with the European classics of the late nineteenth century and simultaneously shows that cultural values are relative.[3] In a final irony Satin-Legs ends each Sunday sleeping with a different prostitute.[4]

The human dimension in the first part, more narrowly confined, first depends upon animal imagery (Satin-Legs, the elaborate cat), then upon the metaphor of life's drama (getting dressed), and last upon the irony characterizing social code ("prim precautions"). An oxymoron communicates Satin-Legs's confusion ("clear delirium"), yet the phrase clarifies a double consciousness working in the poem where the narrator's thinking occasionally merges with that of Satin-Legs. Whereas his perspective is generally muddled, hers is usually clear. Applying some theories of Noam Chomsky, Lévi-Strauss, and Jacques Derrida stimulates two questions.[5] First, what unifies Satin-Legs with his narrator? Second, what does the narrator share with the listener whom George Kent (in his essay) calls White? Unconsciously Satin-Legs wants to re-search his limited life and his deferred human potential in order to redefine life's meaning. At first he temporarily succeeds when the narrator's words reveal his consciousness: ". . . life must be aromatic. / There must be scent, somehow there must be some."[6] His clothing style and cologne merely trans-

---

[3]In *Myth and Meaning* (New York: Schocken, 1977), Claude Lévi-Strauss views invariance as being the central unity in structures of human creativity.

[4]For convenience, "prostitute" appears here as a sensible term. "Woman" is inadequate because the poem implies looseness on the woman's part. Yet "looseness" is inexact for the same reason that "whore" would fail. The latter two terms imply the absence of dignity, which Brooks gives to this kind of woman in "a song in the front yard" (*World*, p. 12). Prostitute here is a generic rather than a moral category.

[5]John Lyons, *Noam Chomsky* (New York: Viking, 1970); Claude Lévi-Strauss, *The Savage Mind* (Chicago: Univ. of Chicago Press, 1966); idem, *Myth and Meaning*; Jacques Derrida, *Speech and Phenomena: And Other Essays on Husserl's Theory of Signs* (Evanston, Ill.: Northwestern Univ. Press, 1973).

[6]To observe the way Brooks's speakers function, see R. Baxter Miller, " 'Define . . . the

late beauty into different kinds of imagery, either visual or olfactory. Conceptions of art, ideal in nature, are universal; but their manifestations, their concrete realities, differ. With a playful tone, the narrator begins her journey which leads through aloofness and sarcasm to sympathetic judgment. En route she ironically opposes the cultural transformations of humanity to humanity itself.

The final two stanzas in the first part firmly establish the opposition. Would the "you," the narrator questions, "deny" Satin-Legs his scent of lavender and pine? What substitute would the listener provide? In a recent article on Brooks's *In the Mecca,* I observe that Brooks alludes to the Biblical passage in which God speaks to his afflicted servant Job out of the whirlwind.[7] The observation pertains here because the same chapter ends with God's inquiring, "Who provideth for the raven his food?" (Job 38:41). Whereas in "Satin-Legs" the narrator asks the listener if he can be God, the speaker in "Second Sermon" secularizes God's command: "Live and go out. / Define and / medicate the whirlwind." An overall difference separates Satin-Legs, who needs an external definition for his life, from the speaker who in "Second Sermon" both demonstrates and demands self-definition.

Coming after 1967, "Second Sermon" characterized a later period when Brooks's concern for a White audience lessened and her voice became more definite. "Satin-Legs," in contrast, shows a more introspective and questioning tone. Should Smith have flowers, the speaker asks, good geraniums, formal chrysanthemums, magnificent poinsettias and beautiful roses "in the best / Of taste and straight tradition"? While bolstering the narrator's sensitivity, the images prepare for the inquiry as to whether a common humanity can exist: "But you forget, or did you ever know, / His heritage of cabbage and pigtails. . . ." Here the poem implies some questions. Is oppression both synchronic and diachronic? When does one's perception shift from momentary to universal time? How do race and class transform the perception? For the speaker such unstated queries are secondary because the listener's desire for knowledge must precede their being asked. After the narrator describes Smith as being flowerless, except for a feather in his lapel, she relates dandelions to death. But for whom?

> You [the reader] might as well—
> Unless you care to set the world a-boil

Whirlwind': IN THE MECCA—Urban Setting, Shifting Narrator, and Redemptive Vision," *Obsidian* 4 (Spring 1978): 19–31; and idem, " 'My Hand Is Mode': Gwendolyn Brooks' Speakers and Their Stances," T.V. videotapes for the University of Tennessee Division of Continuing Education, 1978.

[7]Miller, " 'Define . . . the Whirlwind,' " pp. 19, 30.

And do a lot of equalizing things,
Remove a little ermine, say, from kings,
Shake hands with paupers and appoint them men,
For instance—certainly you might as well
Leave him [Smith] his lotion, lavender and oil.

For Brooks's narrator and the reader, to "shake hands with paupers and appoint them men" is to perceive that worth and happiness are human rights, not social privileges. And the poem's listener must accept the responsibility required by the understanding in order to participate fully in the aesthetic experience.

The second part of "Satin-Legs" educates the reader by representing Smith as humanity's icon and its need to create art. Form, as a motif, unifies Smith's clothes style as described in the first part with the literary styles of the sixteenth and seventeenth centuries, as well as with the architectural styles of the seventeenth and eighteenth centuries. "Let us" signals the simultaneous entry by the narrator and the reader into the "innards" of Smith's closet, a journey not into his wardrobe alone but into the human heart. His closet, a vault, lacks those diamonds, pearls, and silver plate which characterize the modern upper class. When addressed earlier to a speaker's coy mistress, Andrew Marvell's lines imply a more genteel tone: "Thy beauty shall no more be found, / Nor, in thy marble vault, shall sound / My echoing song. . . ."[8] Brooks subtly parodies Anglo-American poetry, for to transpose "vault" from the pastoral world to the urban one is to retrace Anglo-American and African literature to their anthropomorphic center. In her only direct intrusion, the narrator interrupts: "People are so in need, in need of help. / People want so much that they do not know." By their directness the lines bridge the aesthetic distance which separates Satin-Legs from his speaker. Yet the closure accentuates human time, the rupture between the flawed medium of language and the mythic ideal which evokes language. Language can only signify myth, and the discrepancy between the two represents the difference between the real and the ideal. Paradoxically the poem becomes a linguistic object which divides Smith from his narrator; its language separates its reader from both, even while simultaneously involving the reader. The aesthetic experience becomes grotesque for the same reason Smith's wardrobe finally does. The weakness of all art forms and styles lies in their absolute objectification, for only humanness can invest art with meaning.

By contrasting Black folk style with traditional style, the last three stanzas of the second part illustrate the theme. Dressed in silk and wool, Smith looks self-lovingly into his mirror, "The neat curve

---

[8]Andrew Marvell, *Selected Poetry* (New York: Signet, 1967), p. 76.

here; the angularity / That is appropriate at just its place; / The technique of a variegated grace." In expanding the range of characterization, Brooks re-searches[9] the tradition of Anglo-American poetry and finds an ontological justification for freeing the tradition from itself. Her means is still parody, but this time the writer parodied is less Marvell than Shakespeare. Written more than three centuries before, the bard's fifty-fifth sonnet associates a lover's affections with marble and stone. By intensity, however, love outshines and outlasts these substances: "When wasteful war shall statues overturn, / And broils root out the work of masonry, / Nor Mars his sword nor war's quick fire shall burn / The living record of your memory." Brooks, by contrast, writes about Smith: "Perhaps you would prefer to this a fine / Value of marble, complicated stone. / Would have him think with horror of baroque, / Rococo. You forget and you forget." The Shakespearean type, literary form here, prepares for Brooks's later description of architectural design. Baroque represents the elaborate and ornate forms of the seventeenth century while rococo signifies the curved, fanciful, and spiralled forms of the eighteenth. Brooks, however, re-places these styles in the wide pattern of human creativity where Smith belongs. For twentieth-century America, her narrator shows, Western humanism's foundation in the Italian and English Renaissance is paradoxical, for even Shakespeare spoke about the "living record," a testimony not of empirical history but of personal engagement. Brooks's Smith is pathetically blameworthy because he has style without the living memory. But a true imagination must fuse the aesthetic object with life.

The third part of the poem, the journey into the world shows that Smith lacks a true imagination. At Joe's Eats he dines with a different prostitute each Sunday.[10] He is not, as George Kent observes, the artist of his existence. Obsessed with sex, he has come to accept the distinction between subjective and objective reality. Having first admired him, the narrator now stands more distantly away. Determinism has overcome the personal flamboyancy which opposed it. Heroic Man, who organizes by art, has deteriorated into Absurd Man, who stands apart from it.[11] Smith and the narrator exchange places; her irony and her judgment become more severe.

---

[9]"Re-search," as used here, linguistically demonstrates the problem of dehumanization. Etymologically the term implies subjective knowing, yet it has been reduced to meaning the verification of scientific data.

[10]Compare the female typology in "a song in the front yard," *World*, p. 12.

[11]This reading expands and applies the idea in Arthur P. Davis, "Gwendolyn Brooks: Poet of the Unheroic," *CLA Journal* 7 (December 1960): 114–25. The unheroism that Davis observes was probably true until 1963.

The dramatic reversal, as Aristotle calls it, is slow. When Smith dances down the steps, his movement, an art form, reminds the reader of Smith's getting dressed earlier. But basking in sunlight and drinking coffee at breakfast merely obscure his lost awareness: "He hears and does not hear / The alarm clock meddling in somebody's sleep; / . . . / An indignant robin's resolute donation. . . . / He sees and does not see the broken windows." The robin unhappily sings its song, as Smith "designed" his "reign" before. Its song symbolically typifies the human assertion which develops first from poem XV in *Annie Allen*, next through the short poems "Langston Hughes" and "Big Bessie throws her son into the street" in *Selected Poems*, finally in "Second Sermon" in *In the Mecca*. In both of the latter volumes, Big Bessie appears at the end because she typologically combines infirmness with endurance.

Smith, however, lacks Big Bessie's complex vision. Although he is the narrator's means for revealing many styles, he cannot recognize that his own flair conceals his sordid environment. He overlooks the wear of a little girl's ribbons and the certain hole that underlies a little boy's neat patch. Socially blind, he ignores the women who return from church to their homes on Sunday. Perceiving them clearly would help him to illuminate his own identity, since their lives illustrate the inseparability of determinism and personal choice. Their social conditions have partially governed whether their service is to God, to those well-off people requiring domestics, or to men's carnality. Verbal play contributes to an overall structure in which music now replaces architecture, although both media demonstrate cultural subjectivity. Smith loiters in the street where he hears "The Lonesome Blues, the Long-lost Blues." In imagining Saint-Saëns, Grieg, Tschaikovsky, and Brahms, the speaker asks, "could he love them?" The four composers represent France (Western Europe), Norway (Northern Europe), Russia (Eastern Europe), and Germany (Central Europe). When considered together they form almost a graphic structure of the continent. All lived in the nineteenth century, and only Grieg (d. 1907) among the three lived into the twentieth. Why does the poem show temporal stasis here when the second part showed a progression from the sixteenth century to the eighteenth? Trying to resolve his historical identity, for Smith, compels first an explanation of his cultural self. His musical aesthetic must include spankings by his mother, forgotten hatreds, devotions, father's dreams, sister's prostitutions, old meals, and deprivations. At the movies Smith boos the hero and heroine because the latter is a blonde. Rehumanizing the movie's iconography means modifying the cultural values which the Renaissance articulated even before the Enlightenment objectified Western culture. By Brooks's standards for a heroine or hero (Langston Hughes, Big Bessie, Pepita, Malcolm X, Medgar Evers, and the narrators in the sermons), Satin-Legs fails, not because of an unwillingness to confront a naturalistic world but in the ignorance which keeps him from defining the world.[12] Understanding must precede confrontation.

When Smith "squires" his "lady" to Joe's Eats his action is just another prelude to sexual intercourse on Sunday. "Squires" evokes the chivalric code of knights, damsels, and jousts, but in the modern world the code lacks meaning. Satin-Legs chooses a different prostitute, an ironic "lady." Each wears Queen Lace stockings and "vivid shoes," without fronts and backs. Thick lipstick characterizes them all, as do Chinese fingernails and earrings. The woman on this particular Sunday has large breasts that comfort Smith in a way that standard morality cannot serve: "He had no education / In quiet arts of compromise. He would / Not understand your counsels on control, nor / Thank you for your late trouble." Here the narrator's consciousness combines with Smith's more closely than anywhere else since the poem's beginning. Why is "education" ambiguous? Does it imply the listener's hidden carnality which equals, possibly even surpasses, Smith's? Does it suggest, as well, the inability of this "you" to distinguish manners, the standardization of values, from the values themselves? As if to suspend her answers, the speaker describes the serving methods at Joe's. Fish and chicken come on meat platters; the coleslaw, macaroni, and candied yams come on the side. Coffee and pie are also available. The yams ("candied sweets") and the possibly sugared coffee foreshadow the sexual act that ends the poem. The scene appears through Satin-Legs's submerging consciousness as the narrator creates a syntactic paradox. Although parentheses usually indicate understatement, dashes generally indicate stress. The speaker comments ironically "(The end is—isn't it?—all that really matters.)" She has shown, rather, that values characterize human life.

"Still do I keep my look, my identity . . ." (*A Street in Bronzeville*), a Petrarchan sonnet, clarifies a humanistic aesthetic by alliteration and plosive, by tension between movement and inertia, and by juxtaposition of heredity with environment. In general the poem associates a soldier's personal or individual style in lovemaking, here ambiguously showing both violence and grace, with the invariant self that appears regardless of social class or life's experiences. Although this self is untranslatable in terms of landscape and finally in

---

[12]See Miller, " 'Define . . . the Whirlwind,' " where I observe this typology in the second half of *In the Mecca*.

terms of this dead soldier's casket, the self does become visible in
forms and situations as different as baseball and school. In the poem,
depicting a soldier who died during World War II, the surviving narrator interprets the man's life, as empathy and love bind the living
with the dead. In thinking highly of her own life-style, the narrator
values his. The particular therefore leads to the general, and the
poem is less about this soldier than about everyone. Two quatrains
and the sestet create the narrator's introspection, as the first lines
emphasize beauty.

With the "p" in "push of pain," the plosives in "precious prescribed pose" suggest harshness and abruptness as well as death. The
timeless narrator portrays a man once alive and transitory. Can form
bridge their two worlds? She recalls his grief, his ambiguous "hatred
hacked." The latter is narrowness, the racial prejudice which he
withstood and overcame. Although the poem states neither race nor
color, he is Black. Like Brooks's persona in "The Mother" (also in
Street), he lives in Bronzeville, a racial section of Chicago; he is at
the same time universal because here too the particular represents
the general. The soldier waltzed—showed grace—when confronting
pain, inertia, and prejudice. As with Brooks's Satin-Legs Smith, his
environment determined his style. So war and dress vary in artistic
mode but not in human desire.

The second quatrain reinforces the dead soldier's "pose," his earlier blending of heredity with environment: "No other stock / That is
irrevocable, perpetual / And its to keep." The off-rhymes imply human indomitability—"irrevocable, perpetual." The archetypal need to
create, to give form, differs as to social class, for the soldier became
his style "In castle or in shack. / With rags or robes. Through good,
nothing, or ill." This last line stands out. Whereas ill is lethargy and
apathy, good is dynamism. As in Brooks's "Sadie and Maud," living
and losing surpasses not living at all. By symbolizing life, style is the
measure of vertical and horizontal space: "And even in death a body,
like no other / On any *hill* or *plain* or crawling cot" (my emphasis).
Height and breadth end in alliteration and perplexity. Does a cot
crawl, or do people? And do people advance, regress? Brooks ended
Street in Bronzeville with "The Progress," a poem that portrays well
civilization's vulnerability. In "still do I keep my look, my identity,"
however, the imaginative mind is invulnerable. Having twisted,
gagged, and died, the soldier shows "the old personal art, the look.
Shows what / It showed at baseball. What it showed in school."

In sonnet 2 of "Children of the Poor" (*Annie Allen*), the narrator
more impersonally desires a humanistic aesthetic. For Brooks the
verse reunited the formal with the emotional and determined her fu-

ture techniques. *Annie Allen* showed her decision to create engaged narrators of the present rather than detached ones of the past.[13] When appearing impersonal ("Bronzeville Mother . . .," "The Chicago *Defender* Sends a Man to Little Rock"), her later speakers mask their actual involvement and sincerity. Here the narrating mother relates directly her children's distressed inquiries. The children request not an easy life but a life with meaning, since they see themselves as dehumanized objects, the heirs of the nineteenth-century slaves who escaped safely to the northern lines. Social reality undermines the children's religious belief, for what God could possibly create such a world? The narrator herself, of course, reflects this powerlessness rooted in social injustice, since she ends by being neither alchemist, magician, nor God. She is only a woman, signifying the writer who creates her, whose planning and love (although great) cannot redeem her children from autumn's cold. Here objectivity, irony, and polish deceive.[14]

The poem opens with the parallelism and balance of a rhetorical question: "What shall I give my children? who are poor, / Who . . . / Who . . . ."[15] Plosives emphasize again the children's plight: "adjudged," "leastwise," "land," "demand," "velvety velour," "begged." Since the narrator's listeners and readers live outside the sonnet, it nearly becomes a monologue written to them. Her children, however, live in the poem's world of suffering, although outside its dramatic action. They speak not through dialogue but through the narrator's memory. Looking for fulfillment rather than for wealth, they are less the individual than the type, and so is she. The second quatrain blends the two viewpoints when her words indirectly recreate theirs. With alliteration and metaphor she questions the fate of those "graven by a hand / Less than angelic, admirable or sure." Does she evoke the myth of Hephaestus-Vulcan, craftsman, symbol of the artist as well as the writer? What were his limitations? What are hers? Must she now rehumanize the metaphor and myth as well as restore it? From "mode, design, device" the narrator advances to grief and love, but her world lacks magic, the alchemical stone. Her poem ends in "autumn freezing" because she has come as far as woman and man can. Having illuminated poverty, she sees her poem

---

[13]See Miller, " 'My Hand Is Mode.' "

[14]Miller, " 'Define . . . the Whirlwind,' " p. 26.

[15]George E. Kent, "The Poetry of Gwendolyn Brooks, Part II," *Black World* 20 (October 1971): 36–48. Kent considers the "Children of the Poor" sequence the most masterful description in poetry of the Black mother's dilemma and one of the most memorable, as well as rhythmical, pieces in English.

end at that magic and divinity which transcend craft. Even the writer and artist finally must speak from a fallen world.

> My hand is stuffed with mode, design, device.
> But I lack access to my proper stone.
> And plenitude of plan shall not suffice
> Nor grief nor love shall be enough alone
> To ratify my little halves who bear
> Across an autumn freezing everywhere.

Brooks explores this idea further in "Langston Hughes" (*Selected Poems*[16]), a short poem that combines cheer and praise with images of speech and muscle. Here the writer's "infirm profession" suggests human life, but Hughes's bond with nature is ambivalent. While opposing its apparent determinism, he demonstrates its aliveness. His name signifies historical Black/Man, Black/Creative Writer, and Humanistic Man-Woman. The poem blends synchrony with diachrony when the narrator's final command "See" compels the reader to share the writer's eternality. Although they are not exclusive, these roles help the student to outline the poem into four parts. The first (11. 1–3) fuses writer, humanist, and historical figure; the second (11. 4–7) emphasizes a quest for meaning; the third (11. 8–15) develops the theme of art; and the fourth (11. 16–18) extends the narrator's invitation to the reader. As the present tense indicates continuity, Hughes synthesizes joy and freedom. He combines integrity with quest (the "long reach"), and his "strong speech" anthropomorphizes language.[17] His "Remedial fears" and "Muscular tears" relate him first to a cultural perception of Black suffering and second to a powerful compassion. His world is an oxymoron, and his patterns of struggle, memory, dramatic action, and celebration suggest Brooks's other writings.

Since 1963 Brooks has portrayed the heroic self as confronting nature's undeniable power. By choice her Langston Hughes timelessly "Holds horticulture / In the eye of the vulture." Having identified with his humanness in sections one and two, the narrator apocalyptically fuses her vision with his in section three. As the storyteller and artist, she represents Gwendolyn Brooks, the creator in the externally historical world. But that parallel (yet real) world can never be identical to the poem's. Brooks has given the speaker autonomy, an eternality like the Hughes in the title when readers re-create the poem. She carefully establishes the bond between narrator

---

[16]*Selected Poems* (New York: Harper and Row, 1963), p. 123.

[17]Compare the theme of reaching (questing) in "Life for my child is simple, and is good," *World*, p. 104.

and persona; between persona, narrator, and reader. All relate to wind imagery which exposes at once man's internal and external worlds. The complementary element of water appears within a framework that implies innovation and illumination. Here alliteration adds fluidity: "In the breath / Of the holocaust he [Hughes] / Is helmsman, hatchet, headlight." The light imagery in the third section blends with the one-word line "See" that begins the last section. The narrator, en route, commands the reader to assume the poet's role, the highest level of possibility. When she calls writing poetry an "infirm profession," her sadness occurs because the limitation (compression) appears within the framing context of style, quest, being, sordidness, and passion. The poem ends by celebrating more than the Harlem Renaissance of the 1920s; it represents more than a writer and a man. It signifies the eternal type which defines itself as freedom, courage, and health: "See / One restless in the exotic time! and ever, / Till the air is cured of its fever."

In "Boy Breaking Glass" (*In the Mecca*), the humanistic aesthetic is social and subjective. The poem presents art, the paradox of beauty, ugliness, destruction, and creation; it fuses desecration with reverence. Complexity grows from allusions to the nineteenth century, as the poem shows that loneliness and neglect reap hardship and revenge. Brooks ironically contrasts the narrator who speaks artificially with the boy who speaks somewhat neurotically. Congress, the Statue of Liberty, the Hawaiian feast, and the Regency Room ironically foreshadow the cliff, the snare, and the "exceeding sun." Mental instability, animal imagery, and social upheaval, in other words, form an unbreakable chain, and Brooks illuminates this continuity against the background of the riots in America during the late 1960s.

The poem has eight stanzas, two having six lines and the remaining six having two. The narrator recognizes both traditional and nontraditional worlds—what W. E. B. Du Bois calls double consciousness.[18] In both instances beauty concerns mythmaking. It approximates Coleridge's primary imagination, the first symbolism and vision of the Western world. But countermythmaking renews the primary myth so as to satisfy contemporary need. When mythmaking declines to science (formalism) the true artist rehumanizes craft; his or her new form changes traditional aesthetics.

The sensitive narrator loves the Black boy because his art suits

---

[18]In "The Achievement of Gwendolyn Brooks," *CLA Journal* 16 (Fall 1972): 23–31, Houston A. Baker, Jr., says well that Brooks's poetry demonstrates White form and Black content. Are these terms difficult to define? Are they mutually exclusive?

his socialization. Temporal and mental space separate him from "us," the listener. His aesthetic, a paradox, is both revolutionary and reactionary, since it resurrects for the future that humanism lost in the past: "I shall create! If not a note, a hole. / If not an overture, a desecretation." Destruction and creation differ in degree rather than in kind, a degree that represents perspective.[19] Within a structure implying racial and literary history, the narrator's kind tone in the first and third stanzas complements the boy's defiant tone in the second. Recalling the cargoes in stanza three, the ship imagery in stanza four alludes by interior monologue to his slave ancestry:

> "Don't go down the plank
> if you see there's no extension.
> Each to his grief, each to
> his loneliness and fidgety revenge.
> Nobody knew where I was and now I am no longer
>   there."

The narrator, however, speaks satirically from the viewpoint of traditional aesthetics: "The only sanity is a cup of tea. / The music is in minors." Her artificiality and delicacy muffle the "cry" of the first stanza as well as the overture of the second. The gentility recalls Brooks's juxtaposition in "The Progress" of Jane Austen's politeness with the carnage of World War II, her masterful incongruity suggesting moral sordidness. In "Boy Breaking Glass," however, politeness facilitates detachment: "Each one other / is having different weather." The narrator indicates that the boy's destruction of a window contrasts with her creation of the poem, even though she understands his need for political power, his expensive food, his lodging, and his freedom; she knows that art explodes as well as beautifies. She appreciates him

> Who has not Congress, lobster, love, luau
> the Regency Room, the Statute of Liberty,
> runs. A sloppy amalgamation.
> A mistake.
> A cliff.
> A hymn, a snare, and an exceeding sun.

because art must reveal the cultural self.

Can understanding the type broaden scholars' readings of Brooks's "The Chicago Picasso"? When reviewing *In the Mecca*, Brian

---

[19]In "'Define ... the Whirlwind,'" my explication of *In the Mecca*, I describe it as a volume that "seeks to balance the sordid realities of urban life with an imaginative process of reconciliation and redemption" (p. 20).

Benson praised the poem's "most starkly beautiful description," and later William Hansell discussed Brooks's self-justification of art in the poem.[20] The piece was written for the occasion of Mayor Richard Daley's dedication of a statue, a bird-woman, to the city on August 15, 1967. By contrasting the willingness to explore life with cowardice and insensitivity, the poem resolves itself in the possibility of human perception. Yet will is necessary to see. The stanzas, nineteen lines altogether, present the nature of creativity (11. 1–7), the paradox of its appreciation (11. 8–15), and the narrator's resulting insight (11. 16–19). First comes the rhetorical question: "Does man love Art?" By exiling one from comfort, home, and beer, aesthetic experience necessitates pain and quest, as balance and personification show: "Art hurts. Art urges voyages—." Both artist and reader transcend animalism ("belch, sniff, or scratch") imperfectly to seek divinity.

Humanism is paradox: ". . . we must cook ourselves and style ourselves for Art, who / is a requiring courtesan." But a courtesan, a prostitute, sells herself to the upper classes. How is Art a prostitute? Does it make one abandon the private self for the public one? Does the creator sacrifice selfhood and humanity? "We do not," the speaker says, "hug the Mona Lisa." "Yes" partially answers the last two questions, although prostitution here implies frailty more than corruption. For the narrator's listeners, artifacts have autonomous meaning. People ("We") admire romantic spectacles ("astounding fountain"), traditional sculpture ("horse and rider"), or standard animal ("lion"). We can bear any burden but our own humanity.

Do the people feel? The poem ends in cold. After the engaged "we," the viewpoint becomes again that of the detached narrator. Her objective poem has been "The Chicago Picasso" because Chicago is American and Picasso is Spanish—even if not parallel—the two representing the impersonalization of art in the Western (modern) world. To the narrator, form should include pain, rawness, and love. Like Brooks's speaker in "Second Sermon on the Warpland," this one shows tension between idealism and realism, Black and White, hatred and love, order and chaos. Resembling a woman and a bird, Picasso's cold steel can only imply flight, but the narrator represents the eternal need to soar, at least to sculpt and to write. Her imperative ending contrasts sharply with her interrogative beginning. Why has a statue now become a blossom to her? Here eternality depends

---

[20]Respectively, "Review of In the Mecca," CLA Journal 13 (December 1969): 203; "Aestheticism versus Political Militancy in Gwendolyn Brooks' 'The Chicago Picasso' and 'The Wall,'" CLA Journal 17 (September 1973): 11–15. See also, R. Baxter Miller, Langston Hughes and Gwendolyn Brooks: A Reference Guide (Boston: G. K. Hall, 1978), p. xxiv.

less upon form (plants are transitory) than upon human perception and sincerity, the necessary qualities for a world facing sunset:

> Observe the tall cold of a Flower
> which is as innocent and as guilty,
> as meaningful and as meaningless as any
> other flower in the western field.

Brooks reaffirms the ontological self. With style and posture her personae withstand the science and barbarism of war or even death. Identity includes vertical and horizontal space as well as time. Living between animalism and divinity, the self seeks resolution; finding grief where magic disappears, it must be content with love. Whether by breaking glass or by creating an overture, separate people diversely experience a common end. To hear Brooks's universal voice, to transcend her form, the reader must ultimately be human.

Alexis De Veaux

(1948–   )

BORN IN 1948, in New York City, Alexis De Veaux is one of African American literary history's unique, multitalented creative artists. Poet, dramatist, political journalist, fiction writer, and sketch artist, she began her professional career at a relatively young age. At age twenty-one, she worked as an assistant instructor in English for the WIN program administered by the New York Urban League; in 1971 she was an instructor in creative writing for the Frederick Douglass Creative Arts Center in New York. Receiving her B.A. degree at the State University of New York, she has also worked as community worker for the Bronx Office of Probations, instructor in reading and creative writing for Project Create in New York City, and as cultural coordinator of the Black Expo for the Black Coalition of Greater New Haven. In 1975 she cofounded the Coeur de l'Unicorne Gallery, where her artwork was among that exhibited.

In her essay on De Veaux in *Dictionary of Literary Biography, Volume 38*, Priscilla R. Ramsey provides a composite analysis of De Veaux's literary art. She says, "In her poetry, drama, political journalism, and fiction, written in the supple rhetoric of nonstandard Black English, Alexis De Veaux has explored the political, economic, and psychological contradictions facing black Americans and Third World peoples. . . . By placing lower-class black people at the center of her artistic world and by forcing her readers to examine not only the characters' anguish but their victories, she creates an art infused with her own version of a black aesthetic, embracing the realities of hope and despair, beauty and pain."

The author of numerous poems that appear in magazines and scholarly journals; of political essays on Zimbabwe and Haiti, which appeared in *Essence* magazine; of two play productions—*Circles*, performed at the Frederick Douglass Creative Arts Center (1973), and *A Season to Unravel*, performed at St. Marks Playhouse (1979)—she has also written *Na-ni* (1973), a juvenile book; *Spirits in the Streets* (1973), a novel; *Li Chen/ Second Daughter First Son* (1975), a prose poem; and *Don't Explain: A Song of Billie Holiday* (1980), a biography. De Veaux's most recent works include *Blue Heat: A Portfolio of Poems and Drawings* (1985) and *An Enchanted Hair Tale* (1987).

For an overview of Alexis De Veaux's work, see the interview with her in Claudia Tate's *Black Women Writers at Work* (1983), in addition to Ramsey's essay in *Dictionary of Literary Biography, Volume 38*.

The following selection is taken from *Don't Explain: A Song of Billie Holiday.*

FROM **DON'T EXPLAIN: A SONG OF BILLIE HOLIDAY**

In July 1953 the first Newport Jazz Festival was held
in Newport Rhode Island.
Loyal fans came by the tribes and
truckloadsful to witness
some of the best known jazz artists
in the world that weekend.
Among them were Ella Fitzgerald
Oscar Peterson
Dizzy Gillespie
Erroll Garner
Billie Holiday and Teddy Wilson.
They had come to hear to blow in the fresh air
they knew their jazz
would dance weightless.
Dizzy's trumpet teased Erroll Garner's piano.
Gerry Mulligan's saxophone cried to Ella's voice.
All day and all night all weekend.
Nothing but sweet music sweet freedom.

Then it was Billie's turn Sunday night.
Onstage to back her were Buck Clayton on
trumpet
drummer Jo Jones
Milt Hinton the bassist
Teddy Wilson on piano and Gerry Mulligan
on baritone saxophone.
Old friends wondered
Will she show up
Will she sing they asked each other
What kind of shape will Billie be in?

With a knack for doing the unexpected
just when folks expected
her to fall apart Billie sang
her most haunting that summer night.

Words of tunes she had made famous soared
and dipped late into
the evening.
Billie was the best she had been in years.
Everyone listening knew it.
Especially Lester Young.

He had been sitting in the audience without
a word.
He walked onstage
Stood behind Billie.

Fingers poised over his saxophone.
Head bent cobalt blue in the sun.
Cheeks puffed.
Singing pretty Lester Young played.
And blew his love through Billie's song.
Jazz healed their broken friendship.
It stitched back together their high laughing
late nights in Harlem
going home.
It stitched back their A flats.
Chicken and cornbread sandwiches.
C sharps.
B blues.
Before the night was over
the Pres and Lady Day were friends
for life again.

Then in October 1953 Billie Holiday's
"Comeback Story" was broadcast
on television.
A musical biography it was a coast to coast show.
Billie was displeased with the suggestion
her career had ever
gone down the drain to come back.
Many of her friends and associates
were invited to attend.
Some came.

Some did not come.
They did not want to be publicly associated
anymore with a well known
drug user so they said the show's producers
are not paying enough money.

Tired and Monkey sick
Billie appeared on the program.
She was glad for the national recognition
she felt she more than
deserved.
Millions of people watched her talk frankly
about her life
in the South
growing up a woman
jazz
light Black skin
no momma no poppa jail
The Chanting Monkey
White laws.

The success of the television show
helped Billie to seek
other possibilities for work.
She did more radio programs
during this time she made many more
recordings.
Went on the road as much as possible.
She hounded anyone and everyone
she knew who could get her
decent work.
And in early 1954 Leonard Feather
the jazz writer offered to star
Billie in a show he had organized to tour Europe.

It was the chance of a lifetime.

Billie had known many other Black artists who had gone
overseas to work.
Those who came back testified:
The Europeans like jazz.
They are more tolerant.
They like musicians no matter what your color.
They are more sophisticated than Americans.
Go to Europe they said.
Go and be recognized.

January 11 1954 Leonard Feather's show
The Jazz Club of America
opened in Stockholm.
Besides Billie it featured folks like Red Norvo's Trio
Carl Drinkard accompanying Billie

Beryl Booker's Trio
and Buddy De Franco's Quintet.

Billie was looking good singing fine
a smashing success.
The Scandinavian audiences loved
her classic renditions
of "Strange Fruit" "Porgy" "Don't Explain"
and "My Man."
They loved her mesmerizing style
and riveting interpretations
her drama
her voice was the bloodline of jazz.

It was the same all over Europe.
Germany.
Switzerland.
Holland.
Paris France.
3 weeks on the road one country after another.
Everywhere she went/no matter what language
people spoke.
Lady Day the gutsy Lady Day dazzled them.
And they loved her full of sass and pain.
And she loved them back.
Especially in London England that February.

The *Jazz Club of America* instrumentalists
were not allowed to play
in England because it was against the English
musicians' union rules.
Billie had no problems entertaining
the English audiences and
carrying the show alone.
Calm and dignified she sparkled
with that impenetrable hip charm.
Gowned down in her lazy finger popping
fuzzy drawl
to the music of "Billie's Blues" "My Man"
"Them There Eyes"
and "Some Other Spring" she delighted crowds
in Manchester
Nottingham and 6000 people
at London's Royal Albert Hall.
There/she was the greatest jazz singer ever.

Not a jailbird.
Or drug addict.
Or freak.

Europe had been the best thing for Billie.
European audiences reassured her
that her music was still important
and still loved.
She was swamped with offers
to work in Paris England and Africa.
She could get work anywhere.
There was no need to worry.

With her spirits lifted
and her voice still powerful Billie
returned home.
Home to fans who loved her even more now.
A changing atmosphere in music.
President Eisenhower.
Offers of more money playing better gigs.
Rock and Roll.
Recognition.
American soldiers across the water in Korea.
Home to Black kids tired of segregated schools.
Tired of segregated public restrooms.
And water fountains.
And restaurants.
And trains and buses.
And you name it
we tired.

Despite her increased popularity
the lack of a cabaret card
forced Billie to accept more and more work
before huge crowds.
A nervous sensitive artist
she was always uneasy facing audiences
like the one in Newport.
She had stage fright and feared
the audience would not like her.

In night clubs and small joints
she felt better singing.
Closer to the audience she could connect
her life with theirs.
That was her style.

Up close where lies are not told.
Eyelids blink together in one rhythm one song.
My face reflects yours reflects the universe here.

But throughout this time
Billie was in need of money.
For The Monkey.
And the expensive image of a Queen
to keep up with.
Her schedule became hectic.
She accepted gigs she wasn't crazy about.
Later in 1954 she began work on an autobiography.
Jotting down thoughts on the road.
Boston.
California.
2 gigs in 1 night.
A concert date and then a night club act
right afterward.
Doing 10 or 15 songs including
"Willow Weep for Me" "Nice Work
If You Can Get It" and "God Bless' the
Child."

No time to catch her breath.
Or 40 winks.
Or 1 good meal.

Working concerts and night clubs back to back
began to unnerve Billie.
The audiences were too different.
One was impersonal/the other intimate.
Billie sang the same songs
to both audiences.
The guttural cadence of tunes like
"Billie's Blues" worked best
in the womb of a night club.
Music critics reviewing her performances
began to question her
judgment.
They said her repertoire had grown stale
the selections too
predictable.
They said Billie's defiance was gone.

Now openly afraid she began to doubt herself
more than ever.

She drank to hide it/she fed The Ridiculous
Chanting Monkey.
Fought stormy battles with Louis.
Got little or no sleep.

Month after month of wear and tear.
The glamorous peach face became puffed
with abuse.
The lips swelled.
The shoulders struggled to be proud.
In the daytime she wore long evening
gloves up the arm
to hide her Monkey scars.
She was tense and nervous.
Her voice still had that cosmic Lady Day
magic filled with
troubles and neglect.

Lord Lord Billie
Was it worth the money and the misery?

The many years of painful living erupted in a
volcano.
What wasn't clear before was clear now.
Billie Holiday was sick.
She went from plump to dreadful thin.
During her performances now she often
needed help getting on
and off stage.
Old fans began to compare a younger Billie
to the older one.
They said her voice lacked vitality.

Where are the stories from your hands?
Bring back the drama they said.
Sing some new tunes Billie.
Don't nod don't give up.
They said how much longer will it be Billie.
How much longer will it be.

So it was no surprise to anyone when
in February 1956
she was arrested again
on a drug charge in South Philadelphia.
Another jail sentence.
Another clinic "cure."

Billie swore this time
she would give up The Monkey.
And she did but it was hard.
She had tried so many times before.
The Monkey's greed had always overcome her.
Determined to win Billie dared The Monkey
once more.
A clean break meant the world to Billie.
Louis McKay meant the rest.
And to prove it after all those years
she married him finally.

Back on the performance circuit
with a fresh start during the summer
of 1956 Billie was again the center
of public attention.
With the help of free-lance writer William Dufty
her autobiography was finished and published.
A melodramatic half true half confusing account
of her life
Lady Sings the Blues helped to keep interest
in Billie's music alive.

However Billie did not like the book's title.
To her it presented a false image.
She frowned at being referred to as a blues singer.
For she had devoted her whole life to jazz.
Jazz/sweet raw elusive it was
the art and essence of her slow time rhythms.
From Baltimore Maryland to New York
all the way halfway round
the world.
Billie suffered for jazz the way
no other singer could.
And that was "Bitter Crop" she said.
That was what *her* book should be called
not *Lady Sings the Blues*.
Nevertheless she wanted her story told.
An example to anybody coming after her
who'd listen.
It was her last song.

Over the next 2 years
she mixed gin and vodka to fill
The Monkey's absence.

With no regard for her weakened health
Billie went on the road
again.
It was a rigorous schedule.
Chicago.
Singing at the House of Jazz in Cleveland.
Las Vegas with 15 tunes in her basic repertoire.
Hollywood California and Jazz City.
Always closing her sets with "Strange Fruit"
she never returned
to the stage after singing it.
On to Honolulu Hawaii.
Miami Florida.
Back to Hollywood.
Billie's voice was failing.
The warm throaty sound became dry brittle.
Central Park in the summer of 1957.
She tried to hide the singing pain.
Because she and Louis had separated.
Because she needed ready money.
Because she was tired and weak.

1958 brought to Billie an opportunity
to tour Europe again.
Billie had always wanted to go back.
She thought now of living and working
there permanently.
Why not?
In Europe she was an *artiste*
not a down and out pop singer.
Well received on her first trip she expected
nothing less
this time.

3 weeks after signing the contract
Billie was singing in Europe.
At the Smeraldo Theatre in Milan Italy.
She appeared in concert with an assortment
of comedians acrobats
impressionists and pop singers.
In that setting Billie's slow tempoed
strained performance
was not appreciated.
She was booed and hissed off the stage.
Her engagement was to last a week.
It lasted one disastrous night.

Heartbroken but not beaten
Billie refused to believe
she had lost her touch with an audience.
Shortly after she accepted an invitation
to sing at La Scala
Milan's famous opera house.
There/in one of the small halls
during a concert organized
by an Italian film producer in love with her music
Billie Holiday proved to herself
she could still mesmerize
an appreciative audience.

But the Parisian audience
at the Olympia Theatre in France
wanted Billie to work for their appreciation.
Arouse us they said.
Sing and be glamorous.
Be legendary.
Haunt us with your painful songs.
Live up to our expectations.
And when she was too weak and could not
they walked out disappointed.
Critics wrote unfavorable reviews.
Soon Billie could not work anywhere decent
in France or Britain.
She was no longer a star.
Unable to support herself in Europe
Billied returned to America.

New York 1959.
There was no Louis around.
No Sadie or Clarence or Lester Young.
For Lester was sensitive original poetic.
He longed for a beautiful world full of love
and beautiful things
but when he realized the world was not
as he wanted it
Lester made it beautiful and precious in his music
everything was C sharp and pungent B flat
tenor beauty.
At jam sessions uptown in basements
night clubs and after hours
joints hotel rooms and ballrooms and theaters
all over the world
Pres blew his sad eyed beautiful song.

But for all his original crescendoes
and iridescent notes
for all his flights into passionate melody
among solos beyond jazz journeys
beyond the ear
the dip shout hoarse glide/of his raucous
tenor laughter
Lester Young/he who had recorded over 40 songs
with the Lady
Lester
in his porkpie hat
with his tenor sax swung to the side
mouthpiece kissing his lips
drank to keep from living
in the world as it was
died at 50
in his room at the Alvin Hotel on Broadway
across from Birdland on 52nd Street
a bottle of gin and his beautiful tenor sax nearby.

Lester Louis Sadie and Clarence.
They were all gone now.
She was lonely and seriously ill.
Once the life of any party
she seldom ventured out now.
At 26 West 87th Street she lived alone
near Central Park.
A handful of friends came to visit.
Others avoided the agony of Billie's solitude.
More than ever she wanted love.
Man love sister mother love/anybody's please.

She was broke.
The thousands of thousands of dollars
she'd made singing
almost 30 years were gone.
Gone to The White Chanting Monkey.
Gone to vodka gin or brandy.
Countless handouts.
Gone to fine clothes for handsome men
given freely.
Dinners for hungry musicians/anyone in need.
Lawyers and court fees.
Clinics and costumes.
Thousands of dollars gone.

A glamorous Billie Holiday began to fade away.
Her health continued to deteriorate.
She drank a river of hard booze.
Once a high paid high class star
she now worked for whatever
she could get.
At cheap low class joints in Massachusetts.
Half filled theaters with no microphones.
Somebody's club dance.
Jobs paying nowhere near her usual concert fee.
A Masonic Lodge affair
as a favor to another musician.
The Phoenix Theatre in Greenwich Village.
She needed money bad now so she agreed
to perform.

It was May and hot.
To see what was left of Lady Day
curiosity seekers packed the theater.
Backstage Billie was weak frail unsteady.
Sick from booze she waited in her dressing room.
No one came to wish her luck.
There was no white gardenia excitement.
Not a soothing word to calm her until.

SHOWTIME
SHOWTIME LADIES AND GENTLEMEN.
Billie pulled herself together and went
onstage.
Leaning against the piano's edge
to hold herself up she sang
only 2 songs then collapsed.
In the arms of friends she insisted
she was all right.

At home friends begged her.
Please Billie
Take care of yourself
You're sick Billie you need help
Go to a hospital
My God
How long you been like this Lady
How long you been skin and bones?

Several days later Billie collapsed into a coma.
On May 31 she was taken to Metropolitan Hospital
In Manhattan.

One more time she rallied to flush
the gin and vodka river swelling
in her body.

Suffering and surely beyond recovery
she laughed and kept her sense
of humor.
Until The Law crawled under her door.
Under her bed.
Between her clothes.
Beneath her sheets.
The unmerciful Law of the United States.
The blank gray face of crawling laws
and restrictions and jails
and convictions.
That same shameless Law
that could not find Southern lynchers in the night
could not find decent jobs for the many up north
found Billie strapped to a hospital bed
and arrested her.
For possession of narcotics The Law said.
For drugs in her coat pocket
who knows how they got there
way across the room.
So the outrageous Law searched and mugged
and fingerprinted Billie
while she was strapped to the metal respiratory
equipment
she depended on to live.
Too sick to resist or get out of bed
she watched them take away
her books flowers records watched them
stand guard outside
her door waiting for who knows.

She talked of club dates.
A new autobiography.
Made jokes with visitors and friends.
She kept smiling no matter what.
Deep down/she was still Lady Day.
She'd lived a defiant life 44 years.
Fought to sing her way the music she loved.
Jazz.
Her life blood.
Jazz was her lover.

It haunted the many songs she wrote.
Inspired her incredible beauty.
Protected her mysterious gift.
Jazz gave Billie the power of flight.
On July 17 1959
her heart began to fail.
Then her liver.
Then her kidneys.
Too weak to fight pain anymore
Lady Day's spirit
went the way of legends.

Robert G. O'Meally

(1948–   )

PERHAPS BEST KNOWN for his analyses of folklore in the works of Ralph Ellison, Robert George O'Meally comes from a long line of Washingtonians. Although his father, a map maker, was by birth a Jamaican, O'Meally's mother and both her parents were born in Washington, D.C. His mother taught at the famous Mott Elementary School for at least thirty years. Having come from a family with a tradition of interest in learning, O'Meally cites his father, a widely read man and a masterful storyteller, as the stimulus for his interest in language and folklore.

After graduating with his A.B. with honors in 1970 from Stanford University, O'Meally went on to receive his A.M. and Ph.D. degrees from Harvard University in 1971 and 1975 respectively. He is one of the very few black scholars after 1969 to receive their degrees in higher education in predominantly white universities and then to accept professorial positions in a predominantly black university. O'Meally's first position was that of assistant professor of English at Howard University in his hometown. While at Howard he served as director of the freshman English program and as chairman of the honors program. He stayed there through the end of the 1978 school term, resigning after he accepted the position of assistant professor of English and Afro-American studies at Wesleyan University. He is currently the Adolph S. and Effie Ochs Professor of English and American Studies at Barnard College. He has also been a visiting professor at Yale University, at École Normale Supérieure, Paris, and at Barnard College.

Much of Professor O'Meally's scholarly activity has focused on critical analyses of Ralph Ellison's *Invisible Man*. He is the author of the invaluable *The Craft of Ralph Ellison* (1980) and the editor of *New Essays on "Invisible Man"* (1988). He is also the editor of *Tales of the Congaree by Edward C. L. Adams* (1987) as well as co-editor of two significant contributions to the field of African American literature and criticism: *The Norton Anthology of Afro-American Literature* and *Critical Essays on Sterling A. Brown*. In addition to his "An Annotated Bibliography of the Works of Sterling A. Brown," which appears in the Winter 1975 issue of the *College Language Association Journal*, O'Meally is also the author of a number of other critiques of Sterling Brown's works. Because of his attraction to folklore, O'Meally's interest in the works of Sterling Brown, a folk poet par excellence, is, perhaps, inevitable. O'Meally is the author of the widely acclaimed *Lady Day: The Many Faces of Billie Holiday* (1991), third prize winner of the 1991 Ralph J. Gleason Music Book Award.

As is customary for the modern-day scholar-teacher-critic, Professor O'Meally delivers lectures and serves as a resource scholar to various groups seeking his expertise. At colleges and universities across the United States and in Europe, Professor O'Meally has lectured on subjects as diverse as "New Perspectives on Black Writing," "The New Black Aesthetic," "Folklore and American Literature," "The Wright-Ellison Debate," "From Theory to Course Design," "Frank Norris's Naturalism," and "Connecticut's Jazz Scene." He also served as associate editor of *Callaloo* and as co-editor of *The Connecticut Scholar*. In addition to serving as reader for a number of university and trade presses, he is a member of the advisory board for Howard University Press. From 1985 to 1986 he was the recipient of a National Research Council Post-doctoral Fellowship.

"Frederick Douglass' 1845 *Narrative*: The Text Was Meant to Be Preached" is from *Afro-American Literature: The Reconstruction of Instruction*, edited by Dexter Fisher and Robert Stepto.

FREDERICK DOUGLASS' 1845 NARRATIVE
The Text Was Meant to Be Preached

Typically, scholars and teachers dealing with Frederick Douglass' *Narrative of the Life of an American Slave* (1845) are concerned with the crucial issue of religion, because the tensions and ironies generated by the sustained contrast between white and black religions constitute a vital "unity" in the work. Slavery sends Old Master to the devil, while the slave's forthright struggle for freedom is a noble, saving quest. Douglass' search for identity—paralleling the search of many and varied American autobiographers before him—is tightly bound with his quest for freedom and for truth. The *Narrative* presents scholars and teachers with a variety of religious questions. How does Douglass reconcile his professed Christianity with his evidently pagan faith in Sandy Jenkins' root? Why does Christian Douglass condone (even applaud!) the slaves' constant "sinning" against (lying to, stealing from, even the threatened killing of) the upholders of slavery? What is suggested by the fact that the most fervently religious whites treat their slaves more barbarously than do even the "unsaved" whites? While such topics are integral to a discussion of Douglass' *Narrative* and its relation to religion, they leave untouched a vital dimension of this broad subject.

The *Narrative* does more than touch upon questions often pondered by black preachers. Its very form and substance are directly influenced by the Afro-American preacher and his vehicle for ritual expression, the sermon. In this sense, Douglass' *Narrative* of 1845 *is* a sermon, and, specifically, it is a black sermon. This is a text meant to be read and pondered; it is also a Clarion call to spiritual affirmation and action: This is a text meant to be preached.

II

The Afro-American sermon is a folkloric process. More than a body of picturesque items for the catalog, the black sermon is a set of oratorical conventions and techniques used by black preachers in the context of the Sunday morning (or weeknight revival) worship service. The black sermon—especially as delivered in churches of independent denominations, which developed in relative isolation from white control—is distinctive in structure, in diction, and in the values it reflects.[1]

Certain aspects of the black sermon's structure vary greatly from preacher to preacher; indeed, the black congregation expects its preacher to have idiosyncrasies in his manner and form of presentation.[2] In keeping with the thinking of the seemingly remote American Puritans, black church men and women view their preacher's personal style and "voice" as bespeaking his discovery of a personal Christian identity and a home in Christiandom; each telling of The Story is as different in detail as each individual teller. In shaping his sermon, a black preacher may follow the American Puritan formula: doctrine, reasons, uses.[3] Or he may use a historical, an analytical, or a narrative scheme for organizing his presentation of the Word. In any case, most Afro-American preachers pace themselves with care, beginning slowly, perhaps with citations from the Bible, or with a prayer, or with a deliberate statement and restatement of the topic for the day.

Most black preachers also build toward at least one ringing crescendo in their sermons, a point when their words are rhythmically sung or chanted in a modified, "ritual" voice. Here the call-response pattern is most marked; the preacher's words are answered by the congregation's phrases, "All right!" "Yes, brother!" "Say *that*!" Sometimes the preacher will rock in rhythm and chant visions of golden heaven and warnings of white-hot hell to his listeners. Sometimes he

---

[1] See Henry Mitchell, *Black Preaching* (Philadelphia: Lippincott, 1970).
[2] Mitchell, pp. 162–63.
[3] Perry Miller, ed. *The American Puritans* (Garden City, N.Y.: Doubleday, 1956), p. 165.

becomes "laughing-happy" as he walks the pulpit, declaring in words half-sung, half-spoken, how glad he is to be saved by the grace of the Lord.[4] In this crescendo section of the sermon, the highly rhythmical language is closer to poetry than it is to prose. Such chanting may occur only at the conclusion of the sermon, or there may be several such poetical sections. In them the preacher seems possessed; the words are not his own, but the Spirit's.

Classic rhetorical and narrative techniques also abound in the Afro-American sermon. One notes the rich use of metaphors and figures of speech, such as repetitions, apostrophes, puns, rhymes, and hyperboles. A good preacher will not just report as a third-person narrator what the Bible says, but he will address the congregation as a first-person observer: "I can see John," the preacher might say, "walking in Jerusalem *early* one Sunday morning."[5] He is a master of rhetorical and narrative devices.

Characteristically, too, Afro-American sermons are replete with stories from the Bible, folklore, current events, and virtually any source whatsoever.[6] Whether or not this storytelling aspect of the black preacher is an African "survival," as some researchers claim, the consistent use of stories determines the black sermon's characteristic structure. Some stories may provide the text for a sermon, while others occur repeatedly as background material.

James Weldon Johnson notes that certain narrative "folk sermons" are repeated in pulpits Sunday after Sunday.[7] Or, a section of one well-known sermon may be affixed to another sermon. Some of these "folk sermons" include "The Valley of Dry Bones," based on Ezekiel's vision; the "Train Sermon," in which God and Satan are portrayed as train conductors transporting saints and sinners to heaven and to hell; and the "Heavenly March," featuring man on his lengthy trek from a fallen world to a heavenly home. Johnson's own famous poem, "The Creation," is based on another "folk sermon" in which the preacher narrates the story of the world from its birth to the day of final judgment.[8]

Black sermons are framed in highly figurative language. Using tropes, particularly from the Bible, spirituals, and other sermons, the black preacher's language—especially in chanted sections of his sermon—is often dramatic and full of imagery. In one transcription of

---

[4]Ralph Ellison, "Hidden Name and Complex Fate," *Shadow and Act* (New York: Random, 1964), p. 158.

[5]Mitchell, p. 172.

[6]Mitchell, p. 98.

[7]James Weldon Johnson, *God's Trombones* (New York: Viking, 1927), p. 1.

[8]Johnson, pp. 1–7.

a black sermon, a preacher speaks in exalted language of the Creator's mightiness:

I vision God wringing
A storm from the heavens
Rocking the world
Like an earthquake;
Blazing the sea
Wid a trail er fire.
His eye the lightening's flash,
His voice the thunder's roll.
Wid one hand He snatched
The sun from its socket,
And the other He clapped across the moon.
I vision God standing
On a mountain
Of burnished gold,
Blowing his breath
Of silver clouds
Over the world,
His eye the lightening's flash,
His voice the thunder's roll.[9]

Like other American preachers, the black preacher speaks to his listeners' hearts as well as to their minds. He persuades his congregation not only through linear, logical argumentation but also through the skillful painting of word pictures and the dramatic telling of stories. His tone is exhortative: He implores his listeners to save themselves from the flaming jaws of hell and to win a resting place in heaven. The black preacher may speak in mild, soothing prose, or he may, filled with the spirit, speak in the fiery, poetical tongue of the Holy Spirit. The black preacher's strongest weapon against the devil has been his inspired use of the highly conventionalized craft of sacred black oratory—a folkloric process.

III

The influences of the black sermon on black literature have been direct and constant. The Afro-American playwright, poet, fiction writer, and essayist have all drawn from the Afro-American sermon. Scenes in black literature occur in church; characters recollect particularly inspiring or oppressive sermons; a character is called upon to speak and falls into the cadences of the black sermon, using the familiar Old Testament black sermonic stories and images. In his

---

[9]Arna Bontemps and Langston Hughes, ed. *Book of Negro Folklore* (New York: Dodd, Mead, 1958), p. 250.

essays, James Baldwin, who preached when he was in his teens, employs the techniques of the sermon as he speaks to his readers' hearts and souls about their sins and their hope for salvation.[10] Just as one finds continuity in tone and purpose from the sermons of the Puritans to the essays of such writers as Emerson and Thoreau, one discovers continuity in the Afro-American literary tradition from the black sermon—still very much alive in the black community—to the Afro-American narrative, essay, novel, story, and poem.

What, then, is *sermonic* about Douglass' *Narrative*? First of all, the introductory notes by William Lloyd Garrison and Wendell Phillips, both fiery orators and spearheads of the abolition movement, prepare the reader for a spiritual message. In his Preface, Garrison recalls Douglass' first speech at an antislavery convention. Thunderous applause follows the ex-slave's words, and Garrison says, "I never hated slavery so intensely as at that moment; certainly my perception of the enormous outrage which is inflicted by it, on the godlike nature of its victims was rendered far more clear." And then, in stormy, revivalist style, Garrison rises and appeals to the convention, "whether they would ever allow him [Douglass] to be carried back into slavery,—law or no law, constitution or no constitution. The response was unanimous and in thunder—tones—'No!' 'Will you succor and protect him as a brother-man—a resident of the old Bay State?' 'Yes!' shouted the whole mass."[11]

As if introducing the preacher of the hour, Garrison says that Douglass "excels in pathos, wit, comparison, imitation, strength of reasoning, and fluency of language" (p. 7). Moreover, in Douglass one finds "that union of head and heart, which is indispensable to an enlightenment of the heads and winning the hearts of others. . . . May he continue to 'grow in grace, and in the knowledge of God' that he may be increasingly serviceable in the cause of bleeding humanity, whether at home or abroad" (p. 7). As for Douglass' present narrative, says Garrison, it grips its readers' hearts:

> He who can peruse it without a tearful eye, a heaving breast, an afflicted spirit,—without being filled with an unutterable abhorrence of slavery and all its abettors, and animated with a determination to seek the immediate overthrow of that execrable system,—without trembling for the fate of this country in the hands of a righteous God, who is ever on the side of the oppressed, and whose arm is not shortened that it cannot

---

[10]For a discussion of this, see David Levin, "Baldwin's Autobiographical Essays: The Problem of Identity," *Massachusetts Review* 5 (1964), pp. 239–47.

[11]Frederick Douglass, *Narrative of the Life of Frederick Douglass an American Slave* (1845; rpt. Cambridge: Harvard Univ. Press, 1848), pp. 4–6. All subsequent references are to this edition.

save,—must have a flinty heart, and be qualified to act the part of a trafficker "in slaves and the souls of men." (p. 9)

The choices, Garrison states, are but two: enrollment in the righteous war against slavery or participation in the infernal traffic in "the souls of men."

In his turn, Wendell Phillips prepares the way for Douglass' "sermon." In his laudatory letter to the author, Phillips speaks of Southern white slave masters as infrequent "converts." Most often, the true freedom fighter detests slavery in his heart even "before he is ready to lay the first stone of his anti-slavery life" (p. 18). Phillips thanks Douglass especially for his testimony about slavery in parts of the country where slaves are supposedly treated most humanely. If things are so abominable in Maryland, says Phillips, think of slave life in "that Valley of the Shadow of Death, where the Mississippi sweeps along" (p. 18).

Douglass' account of his life serves the ritual purpose announced in the prefatory notes: The ex-slave comes before his readers to try to save their souls. His purpose is conversion. In incident upon incident, he shows the slaveholder's vile corruption, his lust and cruelty, his appetite for unchecked power, his vulgarity and drunkenness, his cowardice, and his damning hypocrisy. Slavery, says Douglass, brings sin and death to the slaveholder. Come to the abolition movement, then, and be redeemed. Take, as Douglass has done, the abolitionist paper as a Bible and freedom for all men as your heaven. Addressed to whites, the *Narrative* is a sermon pitting the dismal hell of slavery against the bright heaven of freedom.

Douglass' portrayal of himself and of his fellow slaves is in keeping with the text's ritual function. Like a preacher, he has been touched by God, *called* for a special, holy purpose. Providence protects Douglass from ignorance and despair. Providence selects him to extend his vision of freedom and, concretely, to move to Baltimore. The unexplained selection of Douglass to go to Baltimore he sees as "the first plain manifestation of that kind providence which has ever attended me, and marked my life with so many favors" (p. 56). Of this "providential" removal to Baltimore Douglass further writes:

> I may be deemed superstitious, and even egotistical, in regarding this event as a special interposition of divine Providence in my favor. But I should be false to the earliest sentiments of my soul, if I suppressed the opinion. . . . From my earliest recollection, I date the entertainment of a deep conviction that slavery would not always be able to hold me within its foul embrace; and in the darkest hours of my career in slavery, this living word of faith and spirit of hope departed not from me, but remained like ministering angels to cheer me through the gloom. This

good spirit was from God, and to him I offer thanksgiving and praise. (p. 56)

In his effort to convert white slaveholders and to reassure white abolitionists, Douglass attempts to refute certain racist conceptions about blacks. He presents blacks as a heroic people suffering under the lash of slavery but struggling to stay alive to obtain freedom. To convince whites to aid slaves in their quest for freedom Douglass tackles the crude, prejudiced assumptions—which slavers say are upheld by Scripture—that blacks somehow *deserve* slavery, that they enjoy and feel protected under slavery. Of the notion that blacks are the cursed descendants of Ham, Douglass writes, "if the lineal descendants of Ham are alone to be scripturally enslaved, it is certain that slavery at the south must soon become unscriptural; for thousands are ushered into the world, annually, who, like myself, owe their existence to white fathers, and those fathers most frequently their own masters" (p. 27). Furthermore, if cursed, what of the unshakable conviction of the learned and eloquent Douglass that he is, in fact, chosen by God to help set black people free?

What, then, of the assumption of the plantation novel and the minstrel show that blacks are contented with "their place" as slaves at the crushing bottom of the American social order? Douglass explains that a slave answers affirmatively to a stranger's question, "Do you have a kind master?" because the questioner may be a spy hired by the master. Or the slave on a very large plantation who complains about his master to a white stranger may later learn that the white stranger was, in fact, his master. One slave makes this error with Colonel Lloyd, and, in a few weeks, the complainer is told by his overseer that, for finding fault with his master, he is now being sold into Georgia. Thus, if a slave says his master is kind, it is because he has learned the maxim among his brethren "A still tongue makes a wise head." By suppressing the truth rather than taking the consequences of telling it foolishly, slaves "prove themselves a part of the human family" (p. 43).

At times, slaves from different plantations may argue or even fight over who has the best, the kindest, or the manliest master. "Slaves are like other people and imbibe prejudices quite common to others," explains Douglass. "They think their own better than that of others." Simultaneously, however, slaves who publicly uphold their masters' fairness and goodness, "execrate their masters" privately (p. 43).

Do not the slaves' songs prove their contentedness and joy in bondage? "It is impossible," says Douglass, "to conceive of a greater mistake." Indeed, he says,

> The songs of the slave represent the sorrows of his heart; and he is relieved by them, only as an aching heart is relieved by its tears. At least, such is my experience. I have often sung to drown my sorrow, but seldom to express my happiness. Crying for joy, and singing for joy, were alike uncommon to me while in the jaws of slavery. (p. 38)

Instead of expressing mirth, these songs Douglass heard as a slave "told a tale of woe which was then altogether beyond my feeble comprehension; they were tones loud, long, and deep; they breathed the prayer and complaint of souls boiling over with the bitterest anguish. Every tone was a testimony against slavery, and a prayer to God for deliverance from chains." These songs, Douglass recalls, gave him his "first glimmering conception of the dehumanizing character of slavery" (p. 37). In other words, these songs "prove" the black man's deep, complex humanity. Therefore, whites, come forth, implies Douglass, and join the fight to free these God's children!

The tone of Douglass' *Narrative* is unrelentingly exhortative. Slaveholders are warned that they tread the road toward hell, for even as their crimes subject the slave to misery, they doom the master to destruction. Douglass describes his aged grandmother's abandonment in an isolated cabin in the woods. Then in dramatic, rhythmical language, he warns that,

> My poor old grandmother, the devoted mother of twelve children, is left all alone, in yonder hut, before a few dim embers. She stands—she sits—she staggers—she falls—she groans—she dies—and there are none of her children or grandchildren present, to wipe from her wrinkled brow the cold sweat of death, or to place beneath the sod her fallen remains. Will not a righteous God visit for these things? (p. 78)

Later in the text, Douglass exhorts white readers to sympathize with the escaping slave's plight. To comprehend the escapee's situation, the white sympathizer "must needs experience it, or imagine himself in similar circumstances" (p. 144). In a voice one imagines to be as strong and varied in pitch as a trombone, Douglass reaches a crescendo, in black sermon style, when speaking in highly imagistic language of the white man who would comprehend the escaped slave's feelings:

> Let him be a fugitive slave in a strange land—a land given up to be the hunting ground for slaveholders—whose inhabitants are legalized kidnappers—where he is every moment subjected to the terrible liability of being seized upon by his fellowmen, as the hideous crocodile seizes upon his prey!—I say, let him place himself in my situation—without home or friends—without money or credit—wanting shelter, and no money to buy it,—and at the same time let him feel that he is pursued by merciless menhunters, and in total darkness as to what to do, where

to go, or where to stay,—perfectly helpless both as to the means of defence and means of escape,—in the midst of plenty, yet suffering the terrible gnawings of hunger,—in the midst of houses, yet having no home,—among fellowmen, yet feeling as if in the midst of wild beasts, whose greediness to swallow up the trembling and half-famished fugitive is only equalled by that with which the monsters of the deep swallow up the helpless fish upon which they subsist,—I say, let him be placed in that most trying situation,—the situation in which I was placed,— then, and not till then, will he fully appreciate the hardships of, and know how to sympathize with, the toil-worn and whip-scarred fugitive slave. (p. 144)

In this passage Douglass, like a black preacher, uses a variety of oratorical techniques: alliteration, repetition, parallelism. Also, using conjunctions, commas, and dashes, Douglass indicates the dramatic pauses between phrases and the surging rhythms in the sermon-like prose.

Like a sermon, too, Douglass' *Narrative* argues not only by stern reason but also with tales that may be termed *parables*. One of the most forceful of these parables, one threaded quite successfully into the *Narrative*, is the parable of poor Mrs. Auld. Residing in the border state of Maryland, in the relatively large city of Baltimore, Mrs. Auld, who has never owned a slave before she owns Frederick Douglass, is truly a good woman. Before her marriage, Mrs. Auld worked as a weaver, "dependent upon her own industry for a living." When eight-year-old Douglass is brought into the Auld household, Mrs. Auld is disposed to treat him with human respect and kindness. Indeed, "her face was made of heavenly smiles, and her voice was tranquil music." Douglass obviously presents this woman as a glowing model of Christian charity: "When I went there," he writes, "she was a pious, warm, and tender-hearted woman. There was no sorrow or suffering for which she had not a tear. She had bread for the hungry, clothes for the naked, and comfort for every mourner within her reach" (p. 64). Soon after Douglass arrives in her home, Mrs. Auld begins to do as she has done for her own son; she commences teaching Douglass the alphabet.

Before long, of course, this "kind heart" is blasted by the "fatal poison of irresponsible power" (p. 57). In Douglass' words, Mrs. Auld's "cheerful eye, under the influence of slavery, soon became red with rage; that voice, made all of sweet accord, changed to one of harsh and horrid discord; and that angelic face gave place to that of a demon" (p. 58). In response to her husband's warning that education "would *spoil* the best nigger in the world," she forbids Douglass' further instruction. In fact, she becomes at last "even more violent than her husband himself" in the application of this precept that slave education is a danger (p. 58). Thus, even the mildest forms of slavery—in providential Baltimore—turn the most angelic face to that of a "harsh and horrid" devil.

The central paradox of the story of Mrs. Auld is that Mr. Auld's vitriolic warning against learning actually serves to make Douglass double his efforts to gain literacy. Mr. Auld's words to his wife prove prophetic:

> "Now," said he, "if you teach that nigger . . . how to read, there would be no keeping him. It would forever unfit him to be a slave. He would at once become unmanageable, and of no value to his master. As to himself, it could do him no good, but a great deal of harm. It would make him discontented and unhappy. (p. 58)

Douglass overhears this warning and feels that at last he comprehends the source of the white man's power to enslave blacks. "From that moment," writes Douglass, "I understood the pathway from slavery to freedom." Also, from that moment on, Douglass' holy search for identity and freedom is knotted to his determined quest for literacy and knowledge. For the skill of literacy, "I owe almost as much to the bitter opposition of my master," writes Douglass, "as to the kindly aid of my mistress. I acknowledge the benefit of both" (p. 59). It is as if the providentially guided Douglass receives truth from the mouths of family and friends, and even from the mouths of his most indefatigable enemies. And like a preacher he reports his successes (the Good Word) in exalted prose and in parables.

A second major parable in the *Narrative* concerns the slave-breaker Edward Covey and the wise old slave Sandy Jenkins. Like Mrs. Auld, Covey is a hard worker whose diligence fails to shield him from the blight of slavery. Sent to Covey's plantation to be "broken," Douglass, in a sense, breaks Covey. Douglass leaves the slave-breaker's plantation stronger than ever in his personal resolution to break free. At first, the deceptive Covey, with his killing work schedule and "tiger-like" ferocity, seems to have succeeded in "taming" Douglass. "I was broken," says Douglass, "in body, soul, and spirit. My natural elasticity was crushed, my intellect languished, the disposition to read departed, the cheerful spark that lingered about my eye died; the dark night of slavery closed in upon me; and behold a man transformed into a brute!" (p. 95). On Sundays, his only free day, Douglass would lounge in a "beast-like stupor" under a tree. His thoughts of killing himself and Covey are checked only by fear and dim hope.

Somehow, though, Douglass' spirits are rekindled. First, he observes the white sails of the ships piloting the Chesapeake Bay—through identification with their bold freedom, and through solilo-

quies to them and to God, Douglass finds his hopes revived. He too
will try to sail to freedom. Quoting a line from a spiritual, he says,
"There is a better day coming" (p. 97).

Second, he faces down Covey. "You have seen how a man was
made a slave," writes Douglass. "You shall see how a slave was made
a man" (p. 97). One day he faints and is unable to do his work.
Covey orders him to arise and return to his labor, but Douglass says,
"I made no effort to comply, having now made up my mind to let
him do his worst." Then Douglass runs off to his master, Mr.
Thomas Auld, to express fear that Covey will kill him. But Auld
merely sends Douglass back to the slave-breaker. Back at Covey's,
Douglass is chased into the woods by the slave-breaker, who wields
a cowskin. Ordinarily, running away could only make things worse
for Douglass: "My behavior," he says, "was altogether unaccountable"
(p. 101). Providence seems to be with him though. In the woods,
Douglass meets his old acquaintance Sandy Jenkins, who advises
him to return to Covey. But Jenkins does not send Douglass back to
Covey unarmed. Jenkins directs Douglass to a part of the woods
where he can find a certain root, which, Douglass says, "if I would
take some of it with me, carrying it *always on my right side*, would
render it impossible for Mr. Covey, or any other white man, to whip
me" (p. 102). In the years that he has carried his root, Jenkins says,
he had never been beaten, and he never expects to be again. Douglass seeks relief from Covey by petition to Auld, then by attempted
escape, and then by the spiritual guidance—dependent upon personal fortitude and faith—symbolized by the old slave's root.

Upon his return to Covey's, Douglass is spared an initial attack,
presumably because Covey, a leader in his church, does not want to
work or whip slaves on Sunday. Monday morning, however, Covey
comes forth with a rope and—"from whence came the spirit I don't
know," says Douglass—the slave resolves to fight. They fight for
nearly two hours, Douglass emerging unscarred and Covey bloodied.
This fight marks an important rite of passage for Douglass:

> This battle with Mr. Covey was the turning-point in my career as a
> slave. It rekindled the few expiring embers of freedom, and revived
> within me a sense of my own manhood. It recalled the departed self-
> confidence, and inspired me again with a determination to be free. . . . I
> now resolved that, however long I might remain a slave in form, the day
> had passed forever when I could be a slave in fact. I did not hesitate to
> let it be known of me, that the white man who expected to succeed in
> whipping, must also succeed in killing me.
>
> From this time I was never again what might be called fairly whipped,
> though I remained a slave four years afterwards. I had several fights, but
> was never whipped. (p. 105)

Thus we see Douglass, Providence's hero, maneuvering through deadly dangers. His straightforwardness and courage defeat the serpentine and Pharisee-like Covey. Douglass' hope returns through identification with the white sails on the Bay. He is also given heart by the root, a symbol of spiritual and natural power as well as the supreme power of hope and faith.

As in a successful black sermon, these parables are well woven into the whole cloth of the *Narrative*. They illustrate the corrupting power of slavery upon whites; they illustrate the power of the slave to overcome the slaveowner and to return, mysteriously—and by the power of Providence—to the winding road to freedom. Douglass' *Narrative* is alive with allusions to the Bible. Inevitably, the war waged is between the devil of slavery and the righteous, angry God of freedom. Chapter iii commences with a description of Colonel Lloyd's garden. In its beauty and power to tempt, this "large and finely cultivated garden" recalls the Garden of Eden:

> This garden was probably the greatest attraction of the place. During the summer months, people came from far and near—from Baltimore, Easton, and Annapolis—to see it. It abounded in fruits of almost every description, from the hardy apple of the north to the delicate orange of the south. This garden was not the least source of trouble on the plantation. Its excellent fruit was quite a temptation to the hungry swarms of boys, as well as the older slaves, belonging to the colonel, few of whom had the virtue or the vice to resist it. (p. 39)

This Eden, though carefully tended as God commanded, is vile and corrupt. Colonel Lloyd, merciless owner of the garden and gardeners, forbids the slaves to eat any of its excellent fruits. To enforce his rule he has tarred the garden fence; any slave with tar on his person was deemed guilty of fruit theft and was "severely whipped." This is an Eden controlled not by God but by greedy, selfish, slaveholding man.

Or is this garden under the charge of the devil? As noted, slavery turns the heart of "heavenly" Mrs. Auld to flinty stone. And Mr. Plummer, Douglass' first overseer, is "a miserable drunkard, a profane swearer" known to "cut and slash women's heads so horribly" that even the master becomes enraged. This enraged master, Captain Anthony, *himself* seems "to take great pleasure in whipping a slave." In a grueling scene, he whips Douglass' aunt Hester, a favorite of Anthony's, until only the master's fatigue stops the gory spectacle. "The louder she screamed, the harder he whipped; and where the blood ran fastest, there he whipped longest" (p. 28). Mr. Severe would curse and groan as he whipped the slave women, seeming "to take pleasure in manifesting this fiendish barbarity." Colonel Lloyd renders especially vicious beatings to slaves assigned to the care of his horses. When a horse "did not move fast enough or hold high enough," the slaves were punished. "I have seen Colonel Lloyd make old Barney, a man between fifty and sixty years of age, uncover his bald head, kneel down upon the cold, damp ground, and receive upon his naked and toil-worn shoulders more than thirty lashes at the time" (p. 41). Other slaveowners and overseers, both men and women, kill their slaves in cold blood.

One of the men termed "a good overseer" by the slaves is Mr. Hopkins, who, at least is not quite so profane, noisy, or cruel as his colleagues. "He whipped, but seemed to take no pleasure in it." His tenure as overseer is a short one, conjectures Douglass, because he lacks the brutality and severity demanded by the master.

Covey is the most devil-like slaveholder in the *Narrative*. Hypocritical, masterful at deception, clever, untiring, seemingly omnipresent, Covey is called "The Snake" by the slaves. In one of the *Narrative's* most unforgettable portraits, Douglass tells us that through a cornfield where Covey's slaves work, The Snake would:

> . . . sometimes crawl on his hands and knees to avoid detection, and all at once he would rise nearly in our midst, and scream out, "Ha, ha! Come, come! Dash on, dash on!" This being his mode of attack, it was never safe to stop a single minute. His comings were like a thief in the night. He appeared to us as being ever at hand. He was under every tree, behind every stump, in every bush, and at every window, on the plantation. He would sometimes mount his horse, as if bound to St. Michael's, a distance of seven miles, and in half an hour afterwards you would see him coiled up in the corner of the woodfence, watching every motion of the slaves. (p. 92)

The Snake has built his reputation on being able to reduce spirited men like Douglass to the level of docile, manageable slaves. Under Covey's dominion—before Douglass gains a kind of dominion over Covey—Douglass feels himself "transformed into a brute." In the symbolic geography of his text the Garden is ruled—at least for the moment—by none other than his majesty, the infernal Snake, Satan.

Douglass makes clear that slavery, not the slaveowner, is the supreme Devil in this text: slavery, with its "robes crimsoned with the blood of millions." Mrs. Auld falls from "heavenliness" to the hell of slavery. As a boy Douglass learns from Sheridan's speeches in behalf of Catholic emancipation that "the power of truth [holds sway] over the conscience of even a slaveholder" (p. 66). These white slaveholders, if devil-like, are nonetheless capable of redemption.

Colonel Lloyd, in fact, is described as possessing wealth equal almost to that of Job—the Old Testament's model of supreme faithfulness. Finally, however, the effect of the comparison is ironical, for

Lloyd is a man of increasing cruelty; his very wealth seems to provide his temptation to do evil, and Lloyd yields to temptation with relish.

There are several places in the *Narrative* where American slavery is compared with the holding of the Old Testament Jews in captivity. Douglass points out that, the more he read, the more he viewed his enslavers as "successful robbers, who had left their homes, and gone to Africa, and stolen us from our homes, and *in a strange land* reduced us to slavery" (italics mine). Later in the *Narrative* Douglass describes the fugitive slave in the North as a dweller "in a strange land." The language here and the parallel situations recall the biblical psalm that reads

> By the rivers of Babylon, there we
> sat down, yea, we wept, when
> we remembered Zion
>   we hanged our harps upon the
> willows in the midst thereof.
>   For there they that carried us away
> captive required of us a song; and
> they that wasted us required of us
> mirth, saying, Sing us one of the
> songs of Zion
>   How shall we sing the Lord's
> Song in a strange land?[12]

This allusion is even more suggestive when one considers Douglass' careful explanation of the slaves' songs, demanded, in a sense, and misunderstood by the captors, who, thinking the songs joyous, feel the more justified in their ownership of the black singers.

In the *Narrative*, Douglass calls on the Old Testament God to free His black children. "For what does he hold the thunders in his right hand, if not to smite the oppressor, and deliver the spoiled out of the hand of the spoiler?" (p. 96). Douglass also manifests certain characteristics of an Old Testament hero. He becomes Daniel, blessed with supernatural powers of perception and protected by God's special favor. Like Daniel, thrown into a den of lions for refusing to refrain from praying, Douglass never loses faith while he lives in the very "jaws of slavery." Upon being returned from the Lloyd Plantation to Baltimore, Douglass felt he had "escaped a worse than lion's jaws" (p. 100). Captain Auld in St. Michael's was a vicious, ineffectual master who, Douglass tells us, "Might have passed for a

---

[12]Ps. cxxxvii, King James Version.

lion, but for his ears" (p. 83). Escaping for a brief time from Covey, Douglass, sick and scarred, returns to Auld. The runaway slave supposes himself to have "looked like a man who had escaped a den of wild beasts, and barely escaped them" (p. 100). Unlike Daniel, Douglass actually has to battle with the lions, tigers, and "the Snake" in the den of slavery. Like Daniel, though, he is protected, and once he has Sandy's root on his right side he can never be beaten. Providentially, too, Douglass is eventually rescued from the crushing jaws of slavery.

Douglass' account of his life follows the pattern of the life of a mythic or historic hero—or a hero of Scripture. His birth, if not virginal, as is so often the case with the archetypal hero, is cloaked in mystery. He is never sure who his father is or even when, exactly, he himself was born. Nor does he feel very close to his natural family; slavery kept mother from son, and brother from sister, so that natural familial bonds were felt only remotely. Like Joseph (the biblical son sold into slavery by his brothers) and like Moses, Douglass feels sure he has been selected by heaven for special favor. And like Jesus, he prays for redemption and resurrection from "the coffin of slavery to the heaven of freedom" (p. 105). Christ-like, too, is Douglass' faltering faith at the torturous nadir of his enslavement. Under Covey's lash, Douglass nearly surrenders to the bestial slave system, and to murder and suicide. But Douglass turns from the false religion of such "Pharisees" as Covey; like Jesus, Douglass criticizes white institutionalized worship but clings to his faith in a personal Father.

Douglass' personal sense of ethics contradicts the codes of such men as Covey. For instance, Douglass hails the slave's trickery of the master as wit, if not wisdom. Douglass also approves the attempted assassination of a black informer on runaway slaves; such is justice. Moreover, although Douglass disclaims "ignorant" and "superstitious" belief in the power of the root, his true feeling about root power emerges from the *Narrative*. Clearly, the root, be it pagan or non-pagan, gives Douglass the strength to master Covey. This "superstition" seems no contradiction in Douglass, for he is presented as a hero who transcends strict adherence to existing law. He is the possessor of pure religion; God speaks directly to him. Like a Christ or a Moses, he not only follows God's law, he *gives* the law. Clearly, this pure, felt religion of real experience with Providence is not the religion of the white slaveholding churchmen who merely use Christianity to justify their crimes.

Douglass' rejection of the slaveholder's false religion parallels the rejection of popular conceptions of God by such diverse American writers as Benjamin Franklin, Thomas Paine, and—writing a full century after the *Narrative's* publication—James Baldwin.[13] Like these writers, Douglass replaces the hollow religion of form for a deep, personal religion—in his case, the religion of abolition, which he practices and preaches with fervent passions.

Furthermore, like many black preachers, Douglass' true religion is a practical one that seeks a "heaven" on earth as well as on high. Salvation is not only a personal matter; Douglass labors for the freedom of a *people*. Once free (or at least freer) in Massachusetts, he joins the abolition movement: "It was a severe cross," he writes, "and I took it up reluctantly." His *Narrative* is, then, not only the spiritual journey of one soul but also a testimony and a warning, written with the earnest hope that it "may do something toward throwing light on the American slave system, and hastening the glad day of deliverance to the millions of my brethren" (p. 162). Like a black sermon, it is the story of a people under the guidance of Providence.

Douglass' message is the message of the progressive black preacher: Be hopeful and faithful, but do not fail to fight for the freedom of your brother men. Douglass recognizes that the God of freedom respects the slave who may lie, cheat, steal, or even kill to stay alive and to struggle for freedom. This freedom ethic, "preached" by Douglass, was in the tradition of many militant black preachers, including the black preacher and pamphleteer, Rev. Henry Highland Garnet.[14]

Douglass' *Narrative* is, in its way, a holy book—one full of marvels, demonstrating God's active participation in a vile and fallen world. The *Narrative* is a warning of the terror of God's fury. It is also an account of a black Moses' flight "from slavery to freedom." It is an invitation to join "the church" of abolition, a church that offers freedom not only to the slave and the sympathetic white Northerner but also to the most murderous and bloodthirsty Southern dealers in human flesh. Sinners, Douglass seems to chant, black sermon-style, you are in the hands of an angry God!

Clearly, this is an autobiography, a slave narrative, a fiction-like work shaped by oratory as well as the sentimental romance. But Douglass, who grew up hearing sermons on the plantation and who heard and delivered them throughout his life, produced, in this greatest account of his life, a text shaped by the form and the processes of speaking characteristic of the black sermon. This is a mighty text meant, of course, to be read. But it is also a text meant to be mightily preached.

---

[13]Levin, p. 242.

[14]See Henry Highland Garnet, "An Address to the Slaves of America," *Appeal*, ed. Garnet (1848), 89–96; rpt. in *Negro Caravan*, ed. Sterling A. Brown, Arthur P. Davis, Ulysses Lee (New York: Dryden Press, 1941), pp. 600–06.

Trudier Harris

(1948–   )

BORN IN MANTUA, ALABAMA, in 1948, Professor Trudier Harris graduated magna cum laude from Stillman College at Tuscaloosa, Alabama, in 1969. She later received both her M.A. and Ph.D. degrees from The Ohio State University. While at Ohio State she concentrated on courses not only in Afro-American folklore, but in medieval literature, early American literature, and modern British and American literature.

A prolific author, Harris has written four books—*From Mammies to Militants: Domestics in Black American Literature* (1972), *Exorcising Blackness: Historical and Literary Lynching and Burning Rituals* (1984), *Black Women in the Fiction of James Baldwin* (1985), and *Fiction and Folklore: The Novels of Toni Morrison* (1991); is the co-editor of three volumes of the indispensable *Dictionary of Literary Biography* series—*Afro-American Fiction Writers after 1955* (1984), *Afro-American Writers After 1955: Dramatists and Prose Writers* (1985), and *Afro-American Poets After 1955* (1985); and is the editor of three volumes in this same series—*Afro-American Writers before the Harlem Renaissance* (1986), *Afro-American Writers from the Harlem Renaissance to 1940* (1987), and *Afro-American Writers from 1940 to 1955* (1988).

In addition, Professor Harris is the author of eleven chapters in books, such as her essays "Three Black Women Writers and Humanism: A Folk Perspective," in *Black American Literature and Humanism* (1981), edited by R. Baxter Miller, and "Black Writers in a Changed Landscape, Since 1950," in *The History of Southern Literature* (1985), edited by Louis Rubin, Jr., Blyden Jackson, and others. As is the case with her books and chapters in books, her nineteen articles in such various journals as *Southern Humanities Review, Mississippi Folklore Register, Journal of Popular Culture, College Language Association Journal,* and *Studies in American Fiction* illustrate her impressive ability to integrate folklore and literary analysis, as well as the scope of her scholarly appeal.

Perhaps no other single work demonstrates the peculiarity and value of Harris's craft better than *Exorcising Blackness*. A mixture of history, folklore, politics, sociology, psychology, and literature, this important book begins with a discussion of "Ritual and Ritual Violence in American Life and Culture," delineates the psychological, political, and social motives behind the emasculation associated with lynching, addresses the various offenses that led to the lynching ritual, and ends with several chapters that provide critical analyses of the uses of the lynching ritual in African American literature. Harris concludes, "Of the works in this discussion which actually depict a lynching or burning, in only half of them is the scene of lynching and burning central to the thematic or structural development of the work *as* literature. . . . It is interesting . . . that centralized treatment of lynching and burning scenes grew in inverse proportion to the number of Blacks lynched and burned historically, but in direct proportion to the cruelty with which such acts were carried out and to the increased political significance they served." Professor Harris's study remains the only book-length work in the annals of African American literary history that presents both historical facts about lynching and an exploration of the reasons why black writers have continually pursued this subject in their writing.

Having been a full professor in the English department at the University of Chapel Hill since 1985, Professor Harris now holds an endowed chair as J. Carlyle Sitterson Professor of English. She is the recipient of many awards and honors, among them the Stillman College Distinguished Alumni Award, a National Endowment for the Humanities Fellowship, a South Atlantic Modern Language Association Teaching Award, and a National Research Council/Ford Foundation Fellowship.

The following selection is chapter 7 of *Exorcising Blackness*.

THE MEANING OF A TRADITION

Authors, Issues, Audiences

Of the works in this discussion which actually depict a lynching or burning, in only half of them is the scene of lynching and burning central to the thematic or structural development of the work *as* literature. Works which fit into this category are those by James Weldon Johnson ("Brothers—American Drama"), Claude McKay, Ralph Ellison, Walter White, Langston Hughes, Paul Laurence Dunbar, James Baldwin, and Richard Wright. With these writers, the presentation of lynching and burning scenes is necessary to the development of the poems, stories, and novels in which they appear. In the works by the other writers, these scenes are asides, attempts to paint group character in a traditional way.

For William Wells Brown and Margaret Walker, with the pre-Emancipation settings for their novels, lynching and burning become incidental to the larger question of slavery. Brown's purpose was clearly to influence public opinion in favor of the abolishing of slav-

From *Exorcising Blackness: Historical and Literary Lynching and Burning Rituals* by Trudier Harris. Published by Indiana University Press. Reprinted by permission of the publisher.

ery; thus the horror he presented was yet another evil to be overcome by Emancipation. In *Clotel*, which commentators have
criticized for having enough material and subjects inside its covers
for twelve novels, the burning joins a long list of catalogued evils
and takes up less than two pages in the novel. Similarly, Margaret
Walker's illustration of the lynching of two women becomes a part
of the background of slavery—what the evils were—and is not thematically central to *Jubilee* as literature. Walker is interested in
developing character in a novel which has its context in the ante-
bellum and Reconstruction South; Brown is interested in polemics.

Sutton Griggs's interest in violence is also polemical. He, like
Brown, wants to make a plea for the righting of wrongs. His subplot
of a black man and woman being killed for protecting their property
is designed to strike at the discrepancy in a belief central to American existence. Yet Griggs, like Brown, has too many pieces of stories
straining the novel to be able to make one thematic thrust. Chesnutt
likewise makes lynching subsidiary to other concerns in *The Marrow
of Tradition*, giving the subject even less consideration than does
Griggs. Johnson, too, in *The Autobiography of An Ex-Coloured Man*,
makes the burning incidental. His narrator just happens to be in the
town where the incident occurs, and a decision is made on the basis
of that incident. Johnson uses the scene to effect an epiphanic revelation in his narrator, but given the narrator's basically unstable
character, a slap in the face from a white person might well have
produced a similar reaction.

Toomer's burning scene occurs within a sketch in *Cane*. It is central to that particular sketch, but can only be suggestively connected
with the other over two-hundred pages of the book. Yet Toomer, as
the writers before and after him, felt a need to include this violent
scene in his work. Thus, in addition to their literary purposes, the
abundance with which these scenes appear suggests that they occur
for other reasons as well.

The scenes put these black writers in a traditional vein of portraiture in black American literature, but were they aware of their position as being traditional? Was Baldwin, writing in 1968, aware of
what Sutton Griggs had presented in a ritualized burning in 1905?
To answer this latter question affirmatively is to generalize too
broadly about the process by which writers learn their craft and acquire their sources. Baldwin may never have read Griggs and may or
may not be familiar with his name. To talk about black writers being
conscious of bearing a tradition in the presentation of ritualized violence is perhaps, then, to approach the problem at a slant. Baldwin
may not have been aware of Griggs, but he *is* aware of black history
in this country. Being historically informed about his or her heritage

in blood and violence makes each black writer a member of a club from whose membership he or she cannot be severed.

It is interesting, then, that centralized treatment of lynching and burning scenes grew in inverse proportion to the number of Blacks lynched and burned historically, but in direct proportion to the cruelty with which such acts were carried out and to the increased political significance they served. Brown could mention incidentally a burning in 1853. Dunbar, Wright, and other writers from the turn of the century on had such bestialities stamped on their minds. If Blacks could be burned in 1933, after Emancipation, those famous amendments, and participation in World War I, then the consequences were infinitely more serious than those resulting from the widespread suppression of Blacks during slavery. The more centralized treatments of the theme reflect this.

Still, the question can be asked if black writers are being too propagandistic in their treatment of subjects direct from history, of patterns that retain all aspects of their historical counterparts. Obviously this is not the case; literature, we are taught, approximates life, and if the approximation is authentic enough for the fine line between life and literature to become even more indistinct so much the better. Scenes of ritualized violence do not dominate works until after 1920 or so, and few critics, if any, would gainsay the artistic value of works representative of this period, such as those by Wright and Baldwin. In addition, to dismiss such treatments as mere propaganda is to underestimate the significance of the black experience in America; it is as much a part of the present as it is of the past.

These black authors have shown that black heritage, through black history, is a continuing and integral part of black existence in spite of its brutal and dehumanizing aspects, and frequently because of them. Ensuing generations of Blacks are tied to what has gone before them and should not, even if it were possible, sever the bonds of any part of that heritage. The tie to history, by way of a communal memory, strengthens the roots of continuing generations and allows them to grow from a firmer base. Wright articulated this concern for black writers when he wrote: "Theme for Negro writers will emerge when they have begun to feel the meaning of the history of their race as though they in one lifetime had lived it themselves throughout all the long centuries."[1] Wright worked out the same principle artistically in "Between the World and Me." The speaker, who discovers the lynched/burned man, in turn envisions himself

---

[1]Richard Wright, "Blueprint for Negro Writing," in *Richard Wright Reader*, ed. Ellen Wright and Michael Fabre (New York: Harper and Row, 1978), p. 47.

being lynched and burned. He is a part of a history he cannot escape, and his awareness of his position makes him stronger. His situation can be generalized to all Blacks—the past influences the present; what happened to the slave is as significant to the contemporary suburban black doctor of philosophy as it is to the pullman porter or to the domestic worker. John Wideman echoes the same idea in a discussion of his character Cecil in *Hurry Home*. He suggests that

> what was specifically Cecil's experience becomes conflated with the whole collective history of his race, that there is a thin line between individual and collective experience which permits one to flow into the other. It has to do with imagination. Cecil can suffer because somebody centuries ago suffered on a slave ship. In the novel this happens through an imaginary voyage, but I feel very strongly that people have this capacity to move over time and space in just such an empathetic way.[2]

The roots of black culture, as Jean Toomer so vividly demonstrates in *Cane*, must be embraced, understood, and accepted in all their varying shades of beauty and ugliness before Blacks can grow into a viable future. The heritage of the fathers strengthens the sons to analyze, confront, and overcome the forces that would destroy them. It is by understanding the psychology of the white destroyer, asserts Purlie Victorious, that one can undermine and triumph over him. By presenting such features of white culture in a medium traditionally open to analysis and criticism, these black authors have provided another key with which black people can unlock the myriad complexities of that portion of the white populace which remains a perennial foe.

Obviously the reading of black American literature is not limited to the black population, as the audiences for Brown's, Dunbar's, Grigg's, and Chesnutt's works reveal, but black writers do, within the medium, exhibit a commitment to the role of artist to their people. Interacting with their audience by presenting and keeping before them material of which they are probably aware, but of which they may need occasionally to be reminded, black writers become active tradition-bearers of the uglier phases of black history. As artists, they also become ritual priests ever keeping in sight of their people those mysteries which affect their lives. This kind of education goes far beyond mere didacticism or propaganda and into an awareness which has survival as its basis. By capturing something traditional in history and traditional in literature, black writers fulfill the double

---

[2]John O'Brien, *Interviews With Black Writers* (New York: Liveright, 1973), p. 219.

function of artist and priest for their people.[3] Sir James George Frazer maintains that priests officiated at the carrying out of rituals in ancient societies; they were to assist with the ceremonies and to keep the observances in perspective. They, like their followers, *believed* in the rites. Black writers become officiators of a sort in evoking in their literature the rites whites observe in violently dispensing with Blacks. Priesthood here assumes another dimension, however. Not only do black writers evoke the scene and "assist" in carrying it out for their characters, but they reach outside the work in serving a similar function of evocation. If their audience shares their beliefs, as presumably a black audience would, the ritual of presenting the scene of a ritual would serve to reinforce shared beliefs for writer and audience. In spite of the violence they portray, black writers evince a basic belief in a racial survival. Their ritual of re-creating a ritual keeps that belief alive. They are artists and priests; neither role can be subordinated to the other.

A Male Tradition

The sexual component of the lynching and burning rituals presented in this discussion brings up an issue relating to gender: only black male writers include scenes of castration as a part of lynchings and burnings. Their concerns with the physical presentation of castrations, and with the fear their characters have of that being a consequence of their interaction with white women, are tied again to the history of black males in the United States. From one perspective, black males have felt more acutely the powerless conditions under which black people have been forced to live in this country. Writers among that group, therefore, have been equally conscious of that shared burden and the symbolic emasculation it represents. Their literary creations are thus in general more reactive to the conditions of black people in America than are those of black female writers.

Black males historically, because they could be physically castrated, had a physical part of themselves identified with their powerlessness. Black women, though equally powerless, and equally dehumanized by rape, did not have a part of their anatomy comparable to a penis physically taken away from them. Though they were raped, that act in itself did not immediately conjure up images of death for them; they could envision a future even after such a brutalizing experience, as Alice Walker's Celie does in *The Color Purple*.

---

[3] Ronald Snellings discusses a similar role of priesthood for the black musician. See "We Must Create a National Black Intelligentsia in Order to Survive," in *Black Nationalism in America*, ed. John H. Bracey et al. (New York: Bobbs-Merrill, 1970), pp. 452–62.

After being raped and after twenty years of being beaten by her husband, Celie anticipates the future with peaceful expectation.[4] Black men, on the other hand, knew that castration was almost invariably a prelude to death. Thus black male writers' fascination with that possibility derives from a threat which usually resulted in personal annihilation. It is understandable, therefore, that the male writers are so much more intense in their depictions and so much more unrelenting in their attachments of political significance to the factual history. The personal and communal burden they carried in such depictions highlighted the historical and social condition for Blacks, which, in spite of subtle changes, would continue to be unrelentingly oppressive in its threats of death to black males.

More often than not, when black women were raped, they were psychologically warped, but the violation led to a tainted addition, not to a subtraction from their persons. No matter how perverse we consider such actions today, a black woman in slavery who had several children for her master could feel a degree of pride in her "accomplishments." No matter the father of her children, she still was able to fulfill—in spite of the conditions under which the fulfillment was carried out—her traditional role as woman within the society, that of bearer of children. The black male, on the other hand, could only envision his worth in intangible ways. He may have contributed the sperm which produced the master's children, but the master himself could also, and often did, do that. However, there was no converse situation in which the white woman could be made to bear children who would be sold into slavery. Thus the black male saw his role usurped at will when the white man entered the black woman's bed, and he was powerless to do anything about it. Especially was he forbidden to appropriate the white woman in the way the black woman was appropriated by the white man. Though he may himself have been considered a stud in the breeding of children for sale, he could never really point to any child and be one hundred percent certain that he had indeed fathered it.

If the black man's role could be taken away in these tangible matters of sexuality, and he could be emasculated politically in the symbolic counterpart to the physical emasculation, then he was made to feel in several arenas that he was expendable. How could he assume the role of man when he could not protect his own bed? How could he see himself as a breadwinner when the master provided his food and controlled how much extra money, if any, he could earn by hiring himself out? How, after slavery, could he feel

---

[4]Alice Walker, *The Color Purple* (New York: Harcourt, Brace, Jovanovich, 1982).

himself a man when he was forced, hat in hand, to go to the white boss and ask for a few more beans and fatback to last his family until harvest? How could he find jobs sufficient to support his family during the Depression, or fight his way into unions for better wages? His condition was such that a large portion of the civil rights activity in this country was designed to enhance his status in the hope that such enhancement would benefit the whole race. Ever confronted with the knowledge that he did not matter, the black man cried out again and again against that diminution of his worth. It is not surprising that his fights through marches and verbal protests were designed to emphasize that black men do indeed matter. And it is equally not surprising that black male writers have taken up that cry of demanding to be noticed by calling attention to the things which have historically so pressed them into the ground. What they write about is both a celebration of survival under circumstances which were not designed for their survival, as well as crying out for the rights of manhood which have never been fully granted to them.

Western civilization has unfortunately long identified manhood with primarily one aspect of maleness—that of sexuality. Black male writers who focus upon this in their works on lynchings are reacting to a constraining definition, sometimes simply for the sake of denial, at other times to expose its limitations, and still at other times to demand a redefinition of the concept of manhood. Whenever a black male writer took his pen in hand to depict a lynching for an accusation of rape, he relived for a moment the psychological torment that so many of his brothers lived historically. That vicarious identification is most clearly presented in Richard Wright's "Between the World and Me," but no less is it operating for some of the other writers. James Weldon Johnson, songwriter, lawyer, and diplomat, felt the absolute uselessness of all of those designations when he was almost the victim of a mob attack in Jacksonville, Florida. Whatever separate class distinctions may have been his as a result of education and training were not enough to distinguish him from the masses of raping black males when he was caught alone in a park with a white woman. Johnson's poem, "Brothers—American Drama," written thirty-four years after he barely escaped death, may have been inspired by his personal experience as well as by his general knowledge of the lynching atrocities which were carried out in the United States.[5] Vulnerability defined both Johnson and his black brothers;

---

[5] James Weldon Johnson, *Along This Way* (1933; New York: Viking, 1968), pp. 165–70. Johnson was poignantly aware of lynching through his work with the NAACP, which kept records on lynchings beginning with the inception of the organization, and which used *The Crisis* to print articles and editorials about lynching.

each experienced powerlessness against forces which had taken it upon themselves to determine their fates.

That vulnerability and its accompanying psychological identification served to tie many black male writers to their historically emasculated brothers. James Baldwin, for example, chronicles in many of his essays the difficulties he had in trying to arrive at manhood without getting killed in Harlem, for white policemen there assumed that black males existed for their sadistic pleasure. When Baldwin tried to escape Harlem by going to work for a short time in New Jersey, he experienced even more acutely the denial of his manhood that the whites with whom he worked, especially the Southerners, considered his due by virtue of his black skin. The powerlessness he felt, which produced so much rage in him and contributed to his decision to leave the United States, was equally as restricting as the space in which black sharecroppers were forced to operate and that in which many black migrants from the South had discovered as their lots in Northern ghettos.[6] The accused black man who is brought before the crowd for "knocking down old Miss Standish" in Baldwin's "Going to Meet the Man" is as much the physical plaything of the crowd of whites as Baldwin was to the policemen in his neighborhood and to the whites who would not allow him just to *be* on that job in New Jersey. His situation there can be compared to Richard Wright's in the experience he describes in working for an optical company in Jackson, Mississippi. His white coworkers, insulted and upset by his presence, goad him until he is forced to give up the job. He is caught in a situation in which he must call one white man a liar and run the risk of losing his job and/or suffering physical violence, or he must silently walk away from the job that others have now made it impossible for him to keep.[7] Clearly he cannot win; to be a man by standing up for his rights is to become one more statistic in the racial war. To walk away from the job, as he rather quickly does, is to suppress whatever he has been taught to identify with maleness and therefore to be further emasculated, to be made into a sissy who will not fight back. In life as in literature, then, both Baldwin and Wright knew the consequences of not living the ethics of Jim Crow, just as they knew they had to leave the country to salvage whatever vestiges of manhood they could.

Having his manhood denied at work and being refused the possibility for equal opportunity culminated for Wright in his inability to

---

[6]See especially James Baldwin's *Notes of a Native Son* (1955; New York: Bantam, 1968).

[7]Richard Wright, "The Ethics of Living Jim Crow," in *Dark Symphony: Negro Literature in America*, ed. James A. Emanuel and Theodore Gross (New York: The Free Press, 1968), pp. 240–42.

protect a black woman with whom he worked, an occurrence which made it clear how precarious his manhood was. In a vivid incident in "The Ethics of Living Jim Crow," Wright recounts walking out of the hotel in which he was working with one of the young black women who worked there as a maid. A white doorman, whom they passed on the way out, very casually and proprietarily slapped the black woman on the hip. Wright's objection to the action put his very life in jeopardy, and the woman was forced to pull him away for his own safety.[8] Black men could not play Sir Lancelot to black women in the South, for the white men did not recognize any claims black men made even to black women, and certainly not to white women. Black male writers are almost possessed at times in portraying these matters.

Black women writers, on the other hand, are interested in painting on a different part of the canvas of black American life. In their portrayals of lynchings and of the situations which could possibly lead to lynching, the two black women writers treated in this study are more interested in their characters than in the issues surrounding them. Margaret Walker's intention is to show the growth of Vyry Brown, while Toni Morrison's novel is a study in demythologizing various characters and the ideas held about them. The lynching of the two women accused of poisoning their master in *Jubilee* is important, but it is one incident confined to a few pages of an otherwise rather long novel. Morrison uses the contact between the black man and the "white" woman to focus upon character as it has been formed by culture and education, rather than upon the potential for explosive violence. Both women writers move inward toward their characters instead of outward toward the environments which have shaped them. I am not suggesting that the women here are not concerned with the larger environments, or that the male writers are not concerned with characters; certainly both are, as, for example, Alice Walker in *The Third Life of Grange Copeland* and Richard Wright in *Native Son*. My focus here is upon the *degree* of emphasis as it varies with the gender of the writer.[9]

There is much more of a tendency among black male writers to use their characters in the thematic illustrations of problems in the society. Such a focus gives to their works an intensity of connection to the world beyond that of their poems, short stories, or novels.

[8]Ibid., p. 246. For similar incidents, see Calvin Hernton, *Sex and Racism in America* (New York: Grove Press, 1965), pp. 91–92.

[9]For contrast provided by another black woman writer, see Angelina W. Grimké's *Rachel* (1920; College Park, Maryland: McGrath Publishing Company, 1969), and "The Closing Door," *The Birth Control Review* (September 1919), pp. 10–14; (October 1919), pp. 8–12.

The male writers who perpetuate this tradition of ritualized violence are more directly tied to realistic fiction than are the women writers. Certainly Walker is concerned with portraying the slaveholding world, but not to the minutiae of describing in detail the bodies of the two women as they dangle from the ends of their ropes. Morrison, on the other hand, gives us a world in which some incredible events occur; the circumstances under which Son finds his way to Margaret's bedroom, for example, do not have as many parallels in history as does Wright's lynching and burning in "Big Boy Leaves Home." Nor are the interactions of Margaret, Valerian, Jadine, Sydney, and Ondine as realistic in the historical context of American society; they give none of the sense of being commonplace occurrences such as those that pervade the works of Richard Wright and James Baldwin. The women appear to be more selective in their adherence to history than do the men.

The women writers also seem to be less inclined to present graphic details of violence than do black male writers. Sutton Griggs glues the reader's eyeballs to the corkskew used to bore holes in the flesh of his characters in *The Hindered Hand*, and the pattern of graphic presentation is no less vivid through the works of writers who succeed Griggs and lead up to Baldwin. Action is choreographed in the lynching and burning in "Going to Meet the Man" both to suggest the rising tension of a work of art and to parallel the build-up of tension in the crowd and the ultimate release of that tension. The focus on violence is sustained and unapologetically brutal. It is a rare occasion on which black women writers present violence, either lynchings or otherwise, with the same degree of detail and at the same length. A grisly exception is Alice Walker's depiction of the father cutting off his daughter's breasts in "The Child Who Favored Daughter."[10] Whether the violence is rape or murder, black women writers seem to be less inclined to dwell upon it.

Consider, too, how male and female writers treat the symbolic castration of black males; for example, Alice Walker in *The Third Life of Grange Copeland* as compared with James Baldwin in *Another Country* and with Chester Himes in *If He Hollers Let Him Go*. Walker presents Grange's reaction to the restrictions that are placed upon him in terms of psychological frustration. We know that Grange is made to feel less than a man because of the mask he is forced to adopt whenever he is in the presence of Shipley, his boss. Grange may swing from the rafters like an animal, but that image is superimposed upon his actions. We do not see that Grange's reactions to

---

[10]Alice Walker, *In Love and Trouble: Stories of Black Women* (New York: Harcourt, Brace, Jovanovich, 1973), pp. 35–46.

his circumstances are ever manifested as fear of a threat to his physical person. He never shows concern that Shipley will slap him, or have him horsewhipped, or otherwise treated violently. The tension he feels is tied to being unable to get his family out of debt and to how that reflects upon his economic abilities as a male.

For Walker, symbolic emasculation is a moral and philosophical issue; she believes that the body may be abused through work, but she does not focus upon the body as the potential recipient of the wrath of the white landowner. Ultimately, Grange blames himself and Brownfield for the dehumanization they have allowed others to impose on them. As a human being, Grange maintains, and especially as a black human being, it was his unique responsibility to hold a part of himself inviolable to the poisons which pervaded the air around him. That philosophy may be more exacting than realistic, but it nonetheless shows the distinction to be made between how black female writers such as Walker perceive of oppression for black males as opposed to how they themselves view it.

For both Himes and Baldwin, economic and social restrictions on black males are centered upon the actual bodies of the characters, and it is that focus which consistently ties them to the executions toward which the bulk of this study has been directed. For Bob Jones in Himes's novel, his bulging biceps and well-developed arms are the measure of his manhood. When those are confined by social restrictions, or when he is attacked physically, his frustration becomes one of *feeling* the physical and psychological damage perpetrated against him. That vicarious emotional tie between author and character is never felt in the works by the female writers, while Himes makes the physical body the center of his metaphorical statements about repression of Blacks in the United States. If Bob Jones cannot win the respect of his fellow workers, either black or white, that is in part a measure of the success of his body in performing the jobs he has chosen for it. If he cannot win the hand of the girl he loves, that is another measure of the attractiveness of the body and the physical ability to caress and make love to the woman. By viewing him as the potential rapist, society thus makes Bob's very body his greatest enemy. His emotions and his constant apprehension are both functions of the flesh, not of philosophy.

The same is true of Rufus Scott. The repulsion he is made to feel is not only tied to the blackness of his skin, but to the form of his body as male. In the Army he was literally beaten by the white officer in rejection of his black body. The pain he felt is therefore in some ways more immediate than the mask-wearing pain Grange Copeland must feel before his sharecropping boss. To Rufus, as to Bob, the body becomes the enemy (even as one prizes it). In that

scene on the balcony with Leona, Rufus turns his body into a
weapon against her, because that body is what his oppressors have
used against him. His feelings of persecution are more intense than
are Bob Jones's, for at least Bob can articulate his problem; Rufus is
more consistently left in the realm of emotion, and it is those conflicting emotions which eventually lead to his destruction. Again,
with Baldwin as with Himes, the author has bridged the gap between
his own emotional reaction to oppression and that which he allows
his characters to feel. Rufus never reaches the level of introspection
that Grange Copeland does, for to do so would be to remove himself
from victimization and reaction and to gain control over his life.
Both male writers are less optimistic in their beliefs that black males
can have any control over their lives; consequently, the reactive, feeling stages are viewed as more accurately reflective of their conditions
within the society.

The tendency to focus on issues other than the physical, which was
identified early in the works of black women writers, seems to have
continued into contemporary works. A writer like Alice Walker, for example, has made a conscious effort to move her characters beyond
the realm of physical violence and victimization, such as the incident
in *The Third Life of Grange Copeland* in which Mem is killed by a
shotgun blast in the face, to situations in which they have room to
grow introspectively, such as is the case with Celie in *The Color Purple*. Celie may contemplate committing violence against Albert in re-
taliation for his keeping her sister's letters from her, but she forces
herself to react in other ways until she can control the emotional
response.[11]

Black women writers have been more willing to let some portions
of their history be, and the lynching of black males for sexual crimes
against white women is one of those portions. Black men, less able
and/or willing to let go of something which was such an integral
part of their history, have only in recent years begun to move away
from the graphic depictions of lynchings. Yet the subject pervades
their work in metaphoric ways, such as providing the emotional
touchstone for the characters in John Wideman's *The Lynchers*. The
letting go is primarily a function of changing times, or integrationist
stances, and of black nationalist emphases which suggest that creation is more rewarding than reaction. For the hundred or more years
that reaction did provide a consistent strain of development in black

---

[11]Even Walker's story which treats the rape of a white woman by a black man is done
so from a distance of years; the incident is not dramatized in the work; see "Advancing
Luna—and Ida B. Wells," in *You Can't Keep a Good Woman Down* (New York: Harcourt,
Brace, Jovanovich, 1981).

American literature, the male writers depicted violent scenes with a persistency which suggested that they were involved in their own rite of exorcism.

To exorcise fear from racial memory is as formidable a task as is attempting to obtain equality for black people in the United States. Yet that is the task black male writers seem to have set for themselves in that long history of engagement with lynchings and burnings in their works. Each generation took up the task of convincing the next that black males in particular and black people in general could survive, wholly and with psychological health intact, against the desire of whites to exorcise Blacks from personal interactions with them, and to exorcise them from the earth if they could not. Black male writers, heir to those fears and to that possibility for elimination, took up their own rite of exorcism by emphasizing that, though violence was committed and used to generate fear in other black people, that fear could be overcome by constantly identifying the enemy and perpetuating a tradition of unity to combat him. If those whites who committed acts of violence were presented as monsters, and looked like such to the world, would they not be influenced to change their ways? And if black writers kept accumulating cultural records by painting the true characters of those of their enemies, could not that record itself serve as an indication that all black people were not afraid? Each literary depiction of a lynching or a burning, then, became a loud whistle to sustain a people past the graveyard of white suppression and brutality. From Grigg's polemics, to Chesnutt's bid for equality, to Wright's hammerings, to Baldwin's political essays, the concern with ritualized violence became a baton which each male writer handed to the next in a contest for manhood and civil rights which bound them to history and to literature, and which made their works simultaneously artistic creations and cultural documents.

Paula J. Giddings

(1949–   )

PAULA GIDDINGS, the author of the landmark study *When and Where I Enter: The Impact of Black Women on Race and Sex in America* (1984), is also an editor and a journalist who has written extensively on both international and national issues. A graduate of Howard University (1969), Giddings has worked for Random House and as an editor at Howard University Press.

In addition to lecturing to colleges and universities all over the country, she has also written for *The New York Times Book Review*, *The Nation*, *The Washington Post*, the *International Herald Tribune*, *The Philadelphia Inquirier*, and *Jeune Afrique* (Paris); she has been interviewed on numerous radio and television programs including "All Things Considered" (National Public Radio) and "The Today Show" (NBC).

Her two books, *When and Where I Enter* and *In Search of Sisterhood: Delta Sigma Theta and the Challenge of the Black Sorority Movement* (1988), have been widely reviewed, and *When and Where I Enter* has been translated into Japanese and Dutch. It is an outstanding contribution to American as well as African American social and political history. Her poetry and criticism have appeared in *We Speak as Liberators: Young Black Poets* (1970), edited by Orde Coombs, *Amistad 2* (1971), edited by John A. Williams and Charles F. Harris, *Black Women Writers: A Critical Evaluation* (1984), edited by Mari Evans, and *Contemporary Criticism*.

She has received a Ford Foundation grant and awards from The National Coalition of 100 Black Women, The New York Urban League, the Westchester Black Woman's Political Caucus, and the Howard University Alumni Club. In 1986 she was named the United Negro College Fund Distinguished Scholar and taught at Spelman College in Atlanta, Georgia, for the 1986–1987 academic year. Presently she is contributing and book review editor for *Essence* magazine and serves on the Governor's Advisory Committee on Black Affairs in New York State.

For further reading, see Linda Metzger, ed., *Black Writers: A Selection of Sketches from Contemporary Authors* (1989).

The following selection comes from *When and Where I Enter*.

ENTER MARY McLEOD BETHUNE

In 1927, Mary McLeod Bethune was aboard an ocean liner bound for Europe. At the age of fifty-two she was about to take her first trip outside of the country, and one of the few vacations in her entire life. Friends who felt she needed the well-deserved rest had contributed money toward her expenses. After the excited farewells at the pier, Bethune had little to distract her except the limitless rim of the ocean. For perhaps the first time in her adult life, she had the time to sit down and just think—about the future, about the hard-earned achievements of her past. On the edge of the Depression, Bethune would begin to draw on her own history to outline the future direction of Blacks, and Black women.

Her history was one of almost ceaseless activity—and responsibility—over the last half century. Born in Mayesville, South Carolina, she was the fifteenth of the McLeods' seventeen children to be born and the one chosen to go to school and teach the others the three R's. With the aid of a determined mother, a keen mind, and timely scholarships, Bethune attended Scotia Seminary and the Moody Bible Institute. Subsequently she taught at Kindell Institute, a mission school; Lucy C. Laney's Haines Institute; and the Presbyterian Mission School in Florida, where she served as director. By the time she had moved to Florida she was married and had had a child, Albertus.

The idea of "mission" had imbued Bethune's early thinking. Since leaving school she had professed a desire to do missionary work in Africa. The desire was inspired both by religion and by a special feeling regarding her heritage: She had often expressed pride that pure African blood flowed in her veins and that her mother had come from a matriarchal tribe and royal African ancestry.

After a number of unsuccessful attempts to go to Africa, however, it dawned on Mary McLeod Bethune that her primary mission was in America. Further inspired by the growing number of Blacks going to Florida during the migration, Bethune decided to concentrate her energies on establishing a school for girls in Daytona. Only the sheerest faith could have convinced her that $1.50, the total amount of her investment capital, would suffice to start a school. The money was used as a down payment on a former garbage-dump site; the rest of the money was raised first by selling pies and cakes, and later

From *When and Where I Enter* by Paula Giddings published by William Morrow and Company, Inc. Copyright © 1984 by Paula Giddings. Reprinted by permission of William Morrow and Company, Inc./Publishers, New York.

by pleading her case for the school to philanthropists, industrialists, and the National Association of Colored Women.

It was during one of her fund-raising trips in the Northeast that she decided to make a detour to attend the 1909 NACW conference in Hampton, Virginia. Bethune asked for permission to address the group, and if she felt self-conscious about coming from a less privi-leged background than most of the delegates, or by her dark skin and Negroid features, she certainly didn't show it. Bethune spoke with such impassioned eloquence that at the end of her speech Mar-garet Murray Washington offered to take up a collection for the school. Madame C. J. Walker volunteered to help direct a fund-rais-ing campaign, and Mary Church Terrell prophesied that Bethune would someday head the organization.

By 1924, Terrell's prediction had proven correct. Bethune, who had joined the NACW and subsequently headed the Southeastern Federation of Women's Clubs—one of the most active in the club movement—beat out Ida Wells-Barnett in the election for the NACW presidency. As president, she honed her natural talents for organizational leadership. Bethune knew how to cajole, praise, apply the right pressure here and there, to move toward a group consen-sus. Unlike Wells-Barnett, who would undoubtedly have attempted to push the organization in a more radical direction, Bethune brought to the NACW the same philosophy that had traditionally sparked its activism. "Our field is no longer circumscribed," she an-nounced in one of her first statements as president, "and quality of our service is still distinctly our own." With "minds and souls, chas-tened and refined by a forbearance born of the pain and turmoil which have been the burden and glory of our sex," Bethune be-lieved, Black women were to carry "the steadying, uplifting and cleansing influence" to the struggle.[1]

Under her administration the NACW's programs also reflected the developments of the period: the federal antilynching bill, help for rural women and those in industry, the training of clerks and typists, and the status of women in the Philippines, Puerto Rico, Haiti, and Africa. Bethune's most tangible accomplishment as president was ini-tiating a successful drive for funds to purchase the NACW's first na-tional headquarters in Washington, D.C. Of course the achievement was a high point in the organization's history, but in the long run the NACW would never fully recover from the depletion of energy and resources expended in the campaign.

But in 1927 it was not her tenure as NACW president that was

---

[1]*National Notes* (September 1924), p. 1.

foremost in her mind. Assessing her achievements and those of other Black women, Bethune believed that the founding of schools was the most significant.

In 1915 the first class of five students graduated from Daytona School for Girls, and by the time Bethune was on her way to Europe, the school had merged with a men's college, Cookman Institute—where future Black leaders like A. Philip Randolph had been educated. Despite bitter fights with many of her most influential White board members who wanted the school to maintain a nonacademic curriculum, by 1927 it was on its way to becoming a fully accredited liberal arts college. In relatively few years, the school founded on a garbage dump boasted buildings and property worth over $1 million. Probably due in part to the voyage, Bethune was more philosophical about such things than she ordinarily was. In that year she wrote an unusually revealing letter to Charlotte Hawkins Brown:

> I think of you and Lucy Laney and myself as being in the most sacrificing class in our group of women. I think the work that we have produced will warrant love or consideration or appreciation or confidence that the general public may see fit to bestow on us. I have unselfishly given my best, and I thank God that I have lived long enough to see the fruits from it.[2]

The last sentence of the letter may have been prompted by the recent death of one of her best friends and staunchest supporters, Margaret Murray Washington. On that occasion, Bethune had written to Terrell: "The sad intelligence of Mrs. Washington's death has just reached me. We all bow in submission to God's will. . . . Everytime one of us drops out it seems to me that it is necessary for us to get closer and closer together. . . . I feel very sad . . . I cannot write you much just now."[3]

Something else happened in 1927 that made her reflective. She was invited to a meeting of the National Council of Women as a representative of the NACW—which had been affiliated with the council as early as 1899. This luncheon meeting was held at the home of New York's Governor Franklin D. Roosevelt and was hosted by his wife, Eleanor. When it came time to sit around the table, a perceptible tension filled the room. Who would sit next to Mary Bethune? Before the anxiety could thicken into an embarrassing inci-

---

[2]Mary McLeod Bethune to Charlotte Hawkins Brown, June 12, 1947, Charlotte Hawkins Brown Papers (Schlesinger Library, Radcliffe College, Cambridge, Mass.).

[3]Mary McLeod Bethune to Mary Church Terrell, June 5, 1925, Mary Church Terrell Papers (Library of Congress, Washington, D.C.).

dent, Sara Delano Roosevelt, mother of Franklin, took Bethune by
the arm and beseeched the NACW leader to sit by her. It would be
not unlike Bethune to smile to herself over the incident. When it
came to Whites, it was so much easier to get along with the Sara
Roosevelts of this world, or the Vanderbilts and Rockefellers who
had helped her with the school, or the Gambles (of Procter & Gamble) who had served on the college's board. In any case, Sara Roosevelt's gesture was the beginning of a friendship between the two
women that eventually included her daughter-in-law, who in the
near future would become as important an ally as Bethune ever had.

The following year Mary Bethune was invited to participate in a
White House Conference on Child Welfare. The two experiences
helped shape an idea that Bethune would make public in 1929,
when she announced plans to create a new Black women's organization—a superorganization which, like the National Council of
Women, would act as a cohesive umbrella for women's groups already in existence. As a *New York Age* article quoted her, this wom-
en's group would be "a medium . . . through which women may
make such progress as would be impossible for any national organization working alone." As Bethune may have realized from the
White House Conference, such a superorganization would have
greater access to federal dispensation of funds. About a month after
the *Age* article, Bethune invited a number of leading women to come
to her Florida campus to discuss the organization's formation. In a
letter to Terrell, she explained that she had been thinking about
such an organization for the last three years. The NACW's representation on the National Council of Women was insufficient, Bethune
wrote, to "work out . . . the many problems which face us as a
group."[4] In a subsequent letter to Terrell, Bethune stressed: "The result of such an organization will, I believe, make for unity of opinion among Negro women who must do some thinking on public
questions; it will insure greater cooperation among women in varied
lines of endeavor: and it will lift the ideals not only of the individual
organizations, but of the organizations as a group."[5]

In March 1930, Bethune convened the meeting. Among those
present were such women as Maggie L. Walker, the bank president;
Mrs. George Williams, Republican national committeewoman; and
Mrs. Robert Russa Moton, the wife of Washington's successor at
Tuskegee Institute. All in all, women from twelve national organiza-

[4]Mary McLeod Bethune to Mary Church Terrell, January 29, 1930, Mary Church Terrell
Papers (Library of Congress, Washington, D.C.).

[5]Mary McLeod Bethune to Mary Church Terrell, March 15, 1930, Mary Church Terrell
Papers (Library of Congress, Washington, D.C.).

tions—as well as state, fraternal, and educational leaders—answered
Bethune's call. But several were conspicuously absent, including the
leading lights of the NACW. It soon occurred to Bethune that the
NACW would present the greatest obstacle to her plans.[6] And, in
fact, it would take another five years of lobbying to convince them
of the need for what became the National Council of Negro Women.

It did seem an inauspicious time for a new Black women's organization. The country was in a depression. A number of Black organizations already existed. The Urban League and the NAACP were in
full swing, and many activist women were deeply involved in their
programs. And, largely due to the Depression, there were new indi-
cations of a resuscitated interracial effort which made a new all-
Black organization seem, to some at least, behind the times. Moreover, though it was never stated for the record, one could assume
that the leaders of the NACW may have felt their power threatened
by a new organization, which by its very nature would overshadow
the leaders of other groups.

However, a number of events between 1930 and 1935 would vindicate the idea for an organization like the one Bethune proposed.
There is a story that when Bethune was born, her eyes were wide
open. The midwife who delivered her is said to have told Bethune's
mother that Mary would always see things before they happened.
Whether or not the story, and the prediction, were accurate, events
proved that Bethune did have prophetic tendencies. But before the
National Council of Negro Women became a reality, a number of
scenarios were to be played out.

As a former president of the NACW, Bethune was as aware as
anyone that the organization had by 1930 become an anachronism.
The civil rights and welfare organizations that in some ways it had
helped to spawn were by then doing many of the things that the
NACW had done in the past—and with the financial support of
Whites, were doing them more efficiently. Consequently, the NACW
would make drastic cuts, it announced in 1930. Instead of thirty-
eight departments it would have two, and its focus would be primarily on the home. As "mothers, wives, sisters and daughters of the
men of the race," *National Notes* observed, the NACW "should narrow its functions to combating the source of the evils that give the
race the unenviable place it holds in the United States." This, of
course, was a traditional program of the clubwomen's organization,
but in the light of the new developments of the twenties, a dated one.

How dated was evident in a *National Notes* column written in

---

[6]Bettye Collier-Thomas, *N.C.N.W. 1935–1980* (Washington, D.C.: The National Council
of Negro Women, 1981), p. 1.

1929 by the NACW president, Sallie Stewart. In 1929, when the stock market crashed, making families anxious about their future, Stewart counseled: "We want the mothers to take the children's wearing apparel out of boxes and trunks where they are stored, and allow the children to wear them. We want the families that have table linen to use it. We want those who have silver packed in boxes, saving it for the occasional guest, to get this silver out and use it and give their children the right attitude of life and to help them in the formation of their characters in the formative period of their lives. . . . One general difference between the Negro race and the race with which it is most often compared is the problem of home life and general appearances."[7]

In any case, fewer women saw themselves as only "wives, sisters, and daughters" of the men of the race. They saw themselves as workers—workers who were being laid off and downgraded in increasing numbers. The most poignant symbol of the lowered status of all Black women workers was the phenomenon known as the "slave market" in New York City. Magazines such as *The Crisis* ran articles about how domestic workers lined up on empty lots in the Bronx each day, regardless of the weather, to wait for prospective employers who bargained for their day's services. The Whites, often lower-middle-class women who would not be able to afford domestic help in normal circumstances, would ascertain the lowest wage a woman would accept for that day, thereby forcing the Black women to try to underbid one another. As if that situation wasn't bad enough in itself, horror stories abounded of the hours and kinds of work to which these women were required to acquiesce. Many of them received less than the wage they were promised or did not get paid at all. There were also stories of these Black women workers being asked to sell not only domestic services but their sexual services as well.

Because the downgrading of Black women workers coincided more and more with the unemployment of their men, increasing numbers of these women became by necessity the sole support for themselves and their families. With their men gone or out of work, the situation was perilous. Bethune told an audience of the Chicago Women's Federation in 1933: "In recent years it has become increasingly the case . . . the mother is the sole dependence of the home, while the father submits unwillingly to enforced idleness and unavoidable unemployment."[8] As usual, Nannie Helen Burroughs as-

---

[7] *National Notes*, "Message from the President," 1930.

[8] Mary McLeod Bethune, "A Century of Progress of Negro Women," June 30, 1933, Mary McLeod Bethune Papers (Amistad Research Center, Dillard University, New Orleans, La.).

sessed the situation more graphically: "Black men sing too much 'I Can't Give You Anything But Love, Baby,' " she wrote in the *Louisiana Weekly* in the same year. "The women can't build homes, rear families off love alone. . . . The Negro mother is doing it all."[9]

But as has been true throughout the economic history of Black women, while those with the least resources were sinking lower, those with a foot in the proverbial door were making gains—even during this difficult period. By 1930 four out of every ten graduates from Black colleges were women and their numbers were increasing. Although the number of professional workers was still small in 1930 (63,000), it represented an increase of more than 100 percent since 1910, and similar statistics applied to clerical workers. Though Bethune was aware of the divergent paths that poor and middle-class women were treading, it was the upwardly mobile women who captured her political imagination. By 1930 they were dispersed throughout numerous professional, educational, and social organizations such as the Delta Sigma Theta, Alpha Kappa Alpha, and Sigma Gamma Rho sororities; the National Business and Professional Women's Clubs, and the National Association of Colored Graduate Nurses. Bethune wanted to mobilize their potential power within an all-embracing association. These women, she had said in the 1929 *New York Age* article, were not only "more numerous and diversified and more keenly alive to the group" than Black men on the same level, but were in a "better position to make use of the Negro's purchasing power as an effective instrument to keep open the doors that have remained closed." It was Black women, Bethune contended, who "held the pursestrings."[10]

With such ideas, Bethune belonged to the circle of Black activists who saw racial progress through the lens of newly acquired economic power. Larger numbers of Blacks were earning wages from the industrial sector, giving them discretionary income and potential power as consumers. By the early thirties W. E. B. Du Bois was writing about consumer cooperatives and economic boycotts in the NAACP's *Crisis*, asserting that some 22 million Blacks in the Caribbean and the United States were spending at least $10 million a year as consumers. This perspective, which focused on the collective power of Blacks, would eventually set Bethune and Du Bois against the rising tide of interracialism.

The tide swelled under the gravity of the Depression and the consequent rise of lynching. The lynching of twenty Black men in

[9]Nannie H. Burroughs, *The Louisiana Weekly*, November 23, 1933.
[10]Collier-Thomas, op. cit., p. 2.

1930 amounted to nowhere near the numbers at the turn of the century, or even in the immediate aftermath of World War I. But the news reports of the horrible crimes were made more vivid by the technological advances in communication and photography, and the sensationalism of yellow journalism.

In any case, lynching in 1930 seemed more reprehensible to the White establishment than it had in the past. The reason was, again, economics. The crime was a vivid symbol of the intransigence of a region that threatened the nation's economic survival. The Depression and the problem of national recovery, remarked Ralph Ellison, challenged the assumption of northern capitalists that the social isolation of the South offered "the broadest possibility for business exploitation."[11] Thus, "Northern capital could no longer turn its head while the southern ruling group went its regressive way."[12] As Franklin D. Roosevelt would later remark, the South was the nation's number one economic problem—and this at a time when the southern textile industry was surpassing that of the Northeast, and when southern cities were growing at a faster rate than those in other parts of the country. But lynch law was retarding the South's progress and, as a result, that of the entire nation.

The beginning of the decade was a good time to challenge the "regressive" ways of the southern ruling group. The political force of the KKK was virtually spent. And just as important, southern White women were prepared as never before to confront the sexist notions implicit in the southern lynching mentality. The thirties saw the rise of middle-class urban White women in the South—a group making both economic and educational gains. They were having fewer children. Increasingly sophisticated and independent, they were more aware that southern male chivalry, in its distilled form, was largely a means of control and repression. And they began to realize as well that lynching was an extension of that control, as much over White women as over Blacks. The restiveness of White women was encouraged by the spate of scholarly commentary on the lynching phenomenon. In 1932, Arthur Raper's *The Tragedy of Lynching*, underwritten by the Council of Interracial Cooperation, appeared as one of the earliest scientific analyses of southern mob violence, and other social scientists followed suit. Psychoanalysts like Helene Deutsch also scrutinized the lynching phenomenon. It was Deutsch's opinion that false rape charges reflected the masochistic fantasies of White women. Additionally, the most sophisticated southern White women activists recognized the negative economic impact of violence on the

---

[11]Ralph Ellison, *Shadow and Act* (New York: Signet Books, 1966), p. 297.
[12]Ibid.

region. For these activists, awareness culminated in a new feminist determination. Those in the Council of Interracial Cooperation, for example, were becoming increasingly dissatisfied with their auxiliary roles in the organization and were anxious to strike out on their own. Lynching provided the issue upon which to stake their claims.

Bethune, also a member of the CIC, was always good at recognizing an opening when she saw one. In 1930 she informed Will Alexander, head of the organization, that she intended to issue a press statement demanding that southern White women assume responsibility for halting the rise of racial violence.[13] Whatever Bethune's motives for this move, it was an unmistakable cue to White women activists, particularly to Jessie Daniel Ames, one of the most dynamic of the southern women.

A Texan by birth, Ames had been named the first woman CIC executive director of the state's interracial committee. She also became a CIC salaried field representative for the entire Southwest. A month after Bethune's announcement, Ames issued a call for White women activists to meet in Atlanta to discuss the lynching issue. Born out of that meeting was the Association of Southern Women for the Prevention of Lynching (ASWPL). They were determined that they would "no longer . . . remain silent in the face of this crime done in their name."[14] The ASWPL organizers stumped the South with their message, which was threefold. First, they talked and wrote about lynching as a feminist issue. Behind the guise of chivalry, said Ames, was the axiom "White men hold that White women are their property [and] so are Negro women."[15] Second, they took note of rape's use as an excuse to subordinate Blacks. "Public opinion has accepted too easily the claim of lynchers and mobsters that they were acting *solely in the defense of womanhood*," they declared. As the writer Lillian Smith described the ASWPL stand, women understood that they were being used as a shield for White men's "race-economic exploitation." Smith concluded that they were not afraid of being raped: "As for their sacredness, they could take care of it themselves, they did not need the chivalry of lynching to protect them and they did not want it."[16] For the third part of the message, Ames took Smith's economic analysis a bit further. "For the South to be industrialized," she said, "there was a need to assimilate 'the New

---

[13]Jaquelyn Dowd Hall, *The Revolt Against Chivalry: Jessie Daniel Ames and the Women's Campaign Against Lynching* (New York: Columbia University Press, 1979), p. 161.

[14]Ibid., p. 164.

[15]Ibid., p. 156.

[16]Ibid., p. 196.

Negro,' into the New Southland."[17] Technology, she stated, "had left no room in the economy for twelve million servants."

For the next few years, the ASWPL could claim a number of successes. They galvanized the support, in the form of endorsements, of over 35,000 White southern women by 1936. Their inherent moral authority on the lynching issue had made governors and other officials take note, and even take public stands against mob violence. After 1933, the incidence of mob violence had significantly declined. Black women were enthusiastic about the new political development. They had always held that White women could be the most effective force in putting a stop to lynching—and all that that violent act implied. A Black paper, the Atlanta *World*, observed of the ASWPL: "The greatest gain of the anti-lynching [fight] is to be found in the support now being given by the white women of the South."[18] Even the irrepressible Nannie Helen Burroughs was impressed. The ASWPL was "the most important anti-lynching group in the country," she pronounced in her *Pittsburgh Courier* column.[19]

This was not to say that Black women were unaware of the inherent limitations of the White antilynching organization and its leader. The ASWPL's fundamental philosophy mirrored that of the CIC, which was that racial harmony rather than equality was the primary goal. For example, although one of Ames's most notable accomplishments was helping to achieve better housing conditions for Dallas's Black community, her motivation was not so much racial fairness as it was "to prevent encroachments into White neighborhoods" by middle-class Blacks who were dissatisfied with housing in the Black community. The ASWPL and its leader also exhibited a patronizing attitude toward Blacks who were expected to be passive participants in the interracial process. Only White women were invited into the antilynching organization.

Furthermore, the organization had been painfully silent about the highly publicized Scottsboro case in 1931, when nine Black men were accused of raping several White women on a train. Ames never considered the ASWPL capable of sustaining political battles over such issues. She patronizingly assumed that the women in her organization were not ideologically prepared to deal with politics. They were "sentimental" and "inexperienced," Ames believed, and hence ill-suited to sustained political activism. These shortcomings made the affiliation with the ASWPL untenable for Black women by

---

[17]Ibid., p. 108.
[18]Ibid., p. 164.
[19]Ibid.

1935—the year the Costigan-Wagner Act was introduced in the Congress.

The measure called for federal intervention in lynching cases where local authorities refused to act. Its proposal would reveal within the liberal movement a number of crosscurrents that would tear increasingly uneasy alliances asunder.

The introduction of the Costigan-Wagner Act precipitated a flurry of activity. The NAACP, headed by its executive secretary, Walter White, led an intense lobbying effort for its passage. A close association was established with the CIC, which had unanimously approved active support of the bill. The Southern Methodist Women's Council, whose members made up a major part of the CIC and the ASWPL, also advocated the measure. The First Lady, Eleanor Roosevelt, took a personal interest in passage of the legislation, and of course Black women activists were solidly behind it. However, Jessie Daniel Ames cast a dissenting vote. She felt that federal legislation would do little more in the end than anger Southerners and, rather than ending mob violence, would simply push it underground. Besides, Ames was offended by anything that undermined the sacred southern concept of states' rights, and despite pleas from the other liberals, including Eleanor Roosevelt and a large group within the ASWPL, she stood steadfast in her position. Black women, thoroughly disgusted by Ames's stance, called a meeting with her and some of her supporters, in Atlanta in 1935.

Daisy Lampkin, who had been involved in the confrontation with the National Women's Party and who was now a field secretary for the NAACP, began the discussion. The ASWPL's silence, she said, was strengthening the position of congressional opponents of the bill. They "take new courage and they use it to their advantage when they can stand on the floor and say that the . . . southern white women did not endorse the Costigan-Wagner Bill."[20]

Charlotte Hawkins Brown observed that since Southerners virtually ruled the Congress, southern White women could do more "to bring about . . . freedom for the Negro race than a million from the North." Brown, whose perspective had shifted from the moral to the political, concluded, "I would not have expected you to do it . . . if the South was not in the saddle, but I feel you missed a step."[21]

Poor Lugenia Burns Hope was probably the most emotional about the situation. "My heart is so sick and weak," she said, ". . . that I don't know if I can say anything. . . . You may not think so,

---

[20]Gerda Lerner, ed., *Black Women in White America: A Documentary History* (New York: Pantheon Books, 1972), p. 474.
[21]Ibid.

but it will hold back our interracial work and everything else in the South."[22] If Hope was the most disappointed, Nannie Helen Burroughs was the least surprised about the outcome of it all. "I am sorry," she said, "but I am not disappointed. . . . I did not think this organization was going to endorse the . . . bill. . . . There isn't any use in my telling you in tears that I am so disappointed, because I did not expect you to do it."[23]

Of the entire group, Bethune was the most conciliatory. She would of course have been happy if the ASWPL had endorsed the bill, she told Ames and the others. "But I think you have been cautious and wisely so. . . . My heart is full of appreciation . . . for the step you have taken and the awakening you have given to the courageous because of the daring stand taken by this group of women."[24]

Bethune may have been utterly sincere in her words to Ames, with no ulterior motive whatever. Perhaps she could be sincere because, like Nannie Helen Burroughs, she had understood the political shortcomings of the ASWPL and southern White women from the beginning. As a White delegate to the meeting said, "Our women can go only so far until they have converted the men."[25]

However, Bethune was also capable of suppressing her own personal feelings for political advantage. She admitted this in so many words: "I am diplomatic about certain things," she once said. "I let people infer a great many things, but I am careful about what I say because I want to do certain things."[26] So it may have been no coincidence that in the same year that Bethune expressed patience and understanding of the limitations of an all-White women's group, the all-Black National Council of Negro Women would hold its founding meeting. The failure of the ASWPL served Bethune's own interests.

The year 1935 marked a critical juncture in the direction Black activists would take in the racial struggle. Should their energies be channeled toward interracialism or toward the strengthening of their own institutions? The opposing views among Blacks were dramatically illustrated within the ranks of the NAACP when, in 1935, W. E. B. Du Bois resigned from the organization and from the editorship of *The Crisis*. His repeated confrontations with Walter White, the executive secretary, reflected the debate within the larger Black leadership community. In his *Crisis* editorials Du Bois had counseled

---

[22]Ibid.

[23]Ibid., p. 475.

[24]Hall, op. cit., p. 244.

[25]Lerner, op. cit., p. 477.

[26]Minutes, NCNW meeting, November 26, 1938 (National Archives for Black Women's History, Mary McLeod Bethune Memorial Museum, Washington, D.C.).

that racial segregation and racial discrimination were two different issues. Integration for its own sake was both meaningless and demeaning. "Never in the world should we fight against association with ourselves," he exhorted. Undoubtedly referring to the patronizing nature of interracial cooperation, Du Bois requested that Blacks not "submit to discrimination simply because it does not involve actual and open segregation."[27] He felt that Blacks should be devoting their efforts to building their own institutions instead of integrating White ones. "It must be remembered," Du Bois said, "that in the last quarter of a century, the advance of the colored people has been mainly in the lines where they themselves, working by and for themselves, have accomplished the greater advance."[28]

The implications of Du Bois's position flew in the face of the policies of the NAACP, which throughout the twenties and thirties had fought for integration. Much effort had been directed toward school integration and eliminating restrictive housing covenants, yet here was Du Bois saying there was nothing wrong with living in Black neighborhoods or going to Black schools under the right conditions. Walter White and his high-ranking cohort Roy Wilkins bitterly disagreed with Du Bois. The debate reached its climax when White decided to throw the NAACP's resources behind the interracial effort to lobby for passage of the Costigan-Wagner Act. White had decided to cast his lot with "the rising tide of liberalism in the South and in national politics" in the belief that it "offered an unprecedented opportunity for striking a final blow at terrorism."[29]

Bethune's outlook seemed to fall somewhere between the two camps. Though she publicly supported interracial efforts, many of her actions corresponded to the Du Bois position. For example, Bethune had supported the withdrawal of the NACW from the predominantly White National Council of Women, although a Black clubwoman had recently been named a council vice-president. In July 1935 the NACW president, Mary Waring, criticized Bethune's action before an NACW meeting. She told the membership:

> Affiliation with the National Council of Women means more than you realize. We regret very much the calamity of losing our foothold on that which was gained after much constructive work by our presidents, from Mrs. Mary Church Terrell down to the present, culminating in Mrs. Sallie Stewart being a vice-president. We lost this standing, not by any fault of theirs, but by one of our own women suggesting it go to some

---

[27]W. E. B. Du Bois, "Separation and Self-Respect," *The Crisis* (March 1935), p. 85.

[28]W. E. B. Du Bois, "Segregation," *The Crisis* (January 1934), p. 20.

[29]Harvard Sitkoff, *A New Deal for Blacks*, Vol. I (Oxford and New York: Oxford University Press, 1978), p. 238.

other organization. My dear friends, *now* and *ever* let me admonish you not to burn the bridges over which you pass that those who come after may not cross.[30]

By December, Waring had made her views public, revealing that she opposed not only the withdrawal of the NACW from the National Council of Women, but the idea of forming an all-Black women's organization as well. The debate over interracialism also echoed among the ranks of Black women activists. In a *New York Age* article published in December 1935, Waring's letter to the editor warned that Black women should "beware of forming organizations which discriminated on the basis of race," and that "Negroes should not segregate themselves." She also wrote that there were already enough Black women's organizations, and Black women "should build on what they already had." Waring went on to relate that when, on November 30, Bethune had held a dinner for women to discuss the National Council of Negro Women (NCNW) at the Waldorf-Astoria, the famous hotel had at first refused to serve them. Bethune created a furor, demanding to be served. Waring thought Bethune's demand that the hotel be integrated was inconsistent with plans to form an all-Black organization.[31]

Bethune responded by observing that the National Council of Women had "forty-three organizations with only one Negro organization and we have no specific place on their program." She side-stepped the more controversial implications of her views, simply noting, "We need an organization to open new doors for our young women [which] when [it] speaks, its power will be felt."[32] Whether or not one agreed with Bethune's logic, her growing prestige had become virtually irresistible, at least in political terms. In addition to her stature as a college president and a leader of the CIC, she received the prestigious Spingarn Medal from the NAACP in 1935. In a congratulatory note, Reverend Adam Clayton Powell, Sr., wrote Bethune: "It is a long way from the rice and cotton fields of South Carolina to this distinguished recognition, but you have made it in such a short span of years that I am afraid you are going to be arrested for breaking the speed limit."[33] Also in 1935, after attending a White House meeting Bethune had been asked to become a special consultant to the Advisory Board of the National Youth Administra-

---

[30]Minutes, NCNW meeting, July 1935, loc. cit.

[31]*New York Age* (December 28, 1929), p. 6.

[32]Minutes. NCNW meeting, December 5, 1935, loc. cit.

[33]Adam Clayton Powell, Sr., to Mary McLeod Bethune, June 6, 1935, Mary McLeod Bethune Papers (Amistad Research Center, Dillard University, New Orleans, La.).

tion. As her participation in the Roosevelt administration subsequently revealed, Bethune would use the administration's alleged commitment to civil rights as a means to further her own goals and those of the NCNW.

From the inception of her superorganization idea, Bethune had lobbied the Black women leaders, even sending her own representatives to meetings and asking the various groups to report on their feelings about the proposed organization. By the end of 1935 her entreaties were difficult to deny, Mary Waring notwithstanding. On December 5 she held the founding meeting of the NCNW at the 137th Street branch of the YWCA in Harlem. Not surprisingly, Mary Church Terrell came to the meeting, though she had claimed to be "too busy" to attend the planning conferences. She thought the NCNW "worthwhile," but, she admitted: "Reluctantly, I did not believe in the idea. . . . I can't see how this organization can help. . . . I don't think this Council will be any more successful than other organizations."[34]

Charlotte Hawkins Brown, also in attendance, was another leader hesitant to give full endorsement. There were already too many organizations, she felt. "There is a need for a Council or Conference but none for an organization. Such a council could be used as a clearinghouse for all organizations."[35]

Other women, representing fourteen women's organizations, were fortunately more enthusiastic about Bethune's idea, but the misgivings of her old allies must have been disturbing. Still, a historian of the NCNW observed, one of Bethune's greatest assets was her ability to "neutralize her critics" and get a consensus. Bethune moved to make Terrell and Brown fourth and first vice-presidents respectively, and to incorporate the clearinghouse idea in the NCNW's statement of purpose.* In the end Brown and Terrell not only accepted the idea, but the latter formally moved that a unanimous ballot elect Bethune president.

Her achievement was due to more than Bethune's political acumen, or even her influence. For the most part, Black activist women had always supported one another in the final analysis. This was

[34]Minutes, NCNW meeting, December 5, 1935, loc. cit.
[35]Ibid.
*(1) To unite national organizations into a National Council of Negro Women;

(2) To educate, encourage and effect the participation of Negro women in civic, political, economic and educational activities and institutions;

(3) To serve as a clearing house for the dissemination of activities concerning women;

(4) To plan, initiate and carry out projects which develop, benefit and integrate the Negro and the nation.

particularly true of the early generations in the club movement. Not that they didn't have their differences: A bitter fight over Terrell's quest for a third term as NACW president in 1899 had caused Fannie Barrier Williams to admonish women about potentially destructive battles over leadership. Black women had varying political perspectives (one could hardly imagine Margaret Murry Washington and Ida Wells-Barnett even in the same room), degrees of radicalism, and political loyalties. Terrell was a dyed-in-the-wool Republican, Bethune maintained a close relationship with the Democrats, and others considered neutrality the best means of achieving their goals.

Deep differences existed even in the way they perceived their "Afro-Americanness." Bethune was as proud of her pure African blood as her friend Charlotte Brown was of her English ancestry. Additionally, there were disparities in social background. Still, differences among Black women rarely resulted in the fragmentation or utter alienation of their organizations. William Pickens, field secretary of the NAACP, noticed this, as a letter to Charlotte Hawkins Brown revealed:

> In my own judgment, the colored women are better supplied with eligible leaders than are colored men. And the women are more direct and informal, seemingly more honest than the men, certainly less technical, in carrying out their programs, after choosing their leaders. A woman leader is not so apt to be a "political" choice. I mean a choice of intrigue merely. . . . What a grand line of Negro queens their list of presidents of their national organizations over the last quarter-century makes.[36]

In any case, Black women always found common cause in a vision of the future. And there was no more articulate visionary than Mary McLeod Bethune. "Most people think I am a dreamer," she told the women at the founding meeting of the NCNW. "Through dreams many things have come true. I am interested in women and I believe in their possibilities. . . . We need vision for larger things, for the unfolding and reviewing of worthwhile things."[37] Bethune recognized that the world had widened significantly in the last fifteen years. A growing interest in international affairs had prompted women to see their work in a worldwide context. There was increased awareness that drastic changes had to be made in the political, economic, and social position of Afro-Americans, and that Black intellectuals themselves were capable of drawing up a blueprint for such changes. And yet, as Bethune implied, Black women's organiza-

---

[36] William Pickens to Charlotte Hawkins Brown, 1932, Charlotte Hawkins Brown Papers (Schlesinger Library, Radcliffe College, Cambridge, Mass.).

[37] Minutes, NCNW meeting, December 5, 1935, loc. cit.

tions had become narrower in their concerns, more involved with the singular special interest of their particular group. It was time for a "larger vision." For despite their achievements, the world, Bethune noted, "has not been willing to accept the contributions that women have made." It was time now for them to pool their resources in order to make an impact on the public policies of the nation. Their vehicle was to be the National Council of Negro Women.

Within a year Mary McLeod Bethune, at the age of sixty-one, was wearing three hats. She was the president of the NCNW, the president of Bethune-Cookman College, and an appointee to the National Youth Administration agency. She was in a position to forward her four passions: race, women, education, and youth. It was her deft maneuvering in the FDR administration that helped to place those passions on the national agenda for the first time in the history of Black Americans.

Thulani N. Davis

(1949–   )

FORMERLY A SENIOR EDITOR of *Village Voice*, Thulani N. Davis was born in Hampton, Virginia in 1949, the daughter of Collis H. and Louise Barbour Davis, both professors at Hampton Institute (now University). She was reared on Hampton's campus.

Davis's secondary education was taken at Putney, a progressive school in Vermont. She received her A.B. at Barnard College, winning there the Lenore Marshall Prize for Literature. Davis subsequently studied at the University of Pennsylvania and was chosen during this period by the Academy of American Poets for their 1975 prize. She is married to Joseph Jarman, well-known jazz composer, with whom she occasionally performs, reading her poetry accompanied by his music.

Teacher, reporter, editor, and performer, Davis has had a varied career. As teacher, she worked at Washington, D.C.'s Sidwell Friends School; as a reporter she went to Africa and other places abroad covering the visits of celebrities; as editor, her outstanding abilities took her to the top of the staff of *Village Voice*; and her performing career includes readings at Howard University, the Folger Library, and other schools, libraries, and theaters.

In 1972, her first collection of poems, *All the Renegade Ghosts Rise*, was published. Her most recent collection of poems, *Playing the Changes*, came out in 1985. Davis is also the author of the libretto of an opera on Malcolm X which premiered to rave notices at the New York City Opera, September 28, 1986.

She has written and performed in several works with other actresses or musicians, among them *Where the Mississippi Meets the Amazon* with Ntozake Shange and Jessica Hegedorn at the Public Theater (at the New York Shakespeare Festival). In 1979, Davis wrote and presented *One Day the Dialogue Will Be Endless* with actress Laurie Carlos in Poets at the Public. In 1982, she wrote *Shadow and Veil* for the New Heritage Theater; she also wrote and performed with the Joseph Jarman Sunbound Ensemble *Liberation Suite* at the Public Theater. In addition, she has written and presented many one-woman shows and performed in concert with several well-known musicians, among them Cecil Taylor, Anthony Davis, and Arthur Blythe.

Davis's poems have been published in numerous anthologies and periodicals, including *New American Poetry*, *Third World Women*, *Jambalaya*,

Rolling Stone, *Yardbird Reader*, and *Obsidian*. Davis has completed her first novel, *1959* (1992).

Of the poems that follow, "C.T.'s variation" is from *Playing the Changes*; "Papa Jo Jones" and "baobab" are unpublished works.

C.T.'S VARIATION

some springs the mississippi rose up so high
it drowned the sound of singing and escape
that sound of jazz from back
boarded shanties by railroad tracks
visionary women letting pigeons loose
on unsettled skies
was drowned by the quiet ballad of natural disaster
some springs song was sweeter even so
sudden cracks split the sky/ for only a second
lighting us in a kind of laughter
as we rolled around quilted histories
extended our arms and cries to the rain
that kept us soft together

some springs the mississippi rose up so high
it drowned the sound of singing and escape
church sisters prayed and rinsed
the brown dinge tinting linens
thanked the trees for breeze
and the greenness sticking to the windows
the sound of jazz from back
boarded shanties by railroad tracks
visionary women letting pigeons loose
on unsettled skies
some springs song was sweeter even so

PAPA JO JONES

Everybody knows that
the elder was watching
seen us coming from way far
you could hear his music
over six decades if you lived
that long but you didn't
not then he would say
you wanted him to say
but he wouldn't
he knew what you wanted

I watch the reflection
he said of the bridge
in the painting of the bridge
when the sun sets
his back turned
to the bridge even now

I haven't heard no music
since Kansas City
and I fear no one
cause I fear God
but I have heard 'em cook!
And I am crazy thank God
for that. I am no one
I'm 50 people I once knew

He could see us from way far
he only spoke looking through
your hair past your brain
to your safe zone
where you can be trusted
had no need to talk to you
of time you did not live

I could indulge you
but you can hear me
playing behind Lady Day
I know nothing
bout slavery
I was born free
and heard the blues.

"Papa Jo Jones" and "baobab" reprinted by permission of the author.

When they asked me
was the Count colored
all I could say was very.

You see I played music
with folks who could stand up
with nothing but the rhythm!

BAOBAB

sit by me
tell me a story
how the trees grow
in your part of the land
south of here you say
and in your bag
you carry bronzes
from Benin farther off
twins from Yoruba
faces of Senoufou
slip out your sandals
taking a bench
under a tree

attendez!
permettez moi d'expliquer
and expliquer
in the old way

oh Senegal
I looked down
the passage of no return
onto the sea
rough and gorgeous
love rushed me
and I breathed
into the black stones
through the crumbling walls
into the white light
showing fish swimming gaily
without history
where the sick howled
and were dumped to the sea

beneath my toes
in water like lapis

oh Senegal
I am in hell and heaven
I am in the water
I have seen the net
I am floating
still with the moon
the sunlight on my back

I must partake
drink you in old man
deep cuts in your face
your chapeau just so
robes gathered over
your shoulders
for some talk
he whispered in my ear
just as the ancients said
the gods are born of word
in a woman's ear
I have never been here
it is dry
and I am thirsty

Joyce Ann Joyce

(1949–   )

BORN TO EDNA JOYCE, a cotton mill worker, and Henry Joyce, Jr., a long-distance truck driver, in Valdosta, Georgia, in 1949, Joyce Ann Joyce attended exclusively segregated schools throughout high school. Although she graduated valedictorian with a scholarship to Tuskegee Institute, her mother explained that she saw no reason for her only daughter to go away to college when she was capable of securing a scholarship to Valdosta State College, one of the best liberal arts colleges in the state of Georgia. At that time, Valdosta State College had an enrollment of approximately 4,000 white students and about five blacks. Upon receiving her B.A. in 1970 from Valdosta State College, Joyce then began graduate study at the University of Georgia with a Ford Foundation Fellowship.

After graduating with her Ph.D. in American Literature in 1979, Joyce accepted a position as assistant professor in the English department at the University of Maryland, College Park. There she pursued her interest in the work of Richard Wright and began a career as a critic of African American literature. While at the University of Maryland, she functioned as an affiliate faculty member in the women's studies program, studied post-colonial literature in an NEH Summer Institute at Indiana University, attended a two-week institute on Reconstructing American Literature at Yale University, taught in the University of Maryland's Talented and Gifted Program, served as lecturer at the Smithsonian Institution for three different courses, served on numerous university-wide and departmental committees, delivered papers at various conferences across the country, and completed a book, *Richard Wright's Art of Tragedy*, as well as numerous articles, which appeared in journals as diverse as *New Literary History*, *Black American Literature Forum*, and *CEA Critic*.

Professor Joyce's criticism usually cuts against the mainstream of accepted notions of a particular literary art. For example, defying and transcending the previously accepted ideas that Richard Wright's *Native Son* is naturalistic and existential, Joyce's *Richard Wright's Art of Tragedy* characterizes Bigger Thomas as a hero who transcends the limitations of his environment and grows to self-awareness. Her methodology is as iconoclastic as her thesis. Believing that an inextricable relationship exists between form and content, she views creative art as a laboratory specimen whose every part must be examined and then related to some unifying whole suggested by the individual parts. Her two essays "The Aesthetic of E. Ethelbert Miller" (published by the Institute for the Preservation and Study of African-American Writers in December 1988) and "The Development of Sonia Sanchez: A Continuing Journey" (published in the *Indian Journal of American Studies*, vol. 13, July 1983) provide close examination of the craft that lends power to the subjects these poets address. She holds that the sociological approaches to African American literature have ignored the sublimity of African American literary art and that post-structural analyses with a heavy emphasis on language stripped of meaning undermine the entire tradition of African American literary history. Most of Professor Joyce's criticism addresses these two issues, for she sees African-American literary criticism as an integral aspect of the African-American's political struggle for survival.

Presently a professor of English at the University of Nebraska, Joyce is listed in the *Dictionary of International Biography* (1988), *Who's Who among International Authors and Writers* (1988), *Who's Who among International Women Writers* (1988), *Who's Who in the East* (1984), *Who's Who among Blacks in Urban America* (1983), and *Who's Who in American Colleges and Universities* (1968).

The following selection originally appeared in *A Rainbow Round Her Shoulder: The Zora Neale Hurston Symposium Papers* (1982).

CHANGE, CHANCE, AND GOD IN ZORA NEALE HURSTON'S *THEIR EYES WERE WATCHING GOD*

The criticism written on Zora Neale Hurston's excellent novel *Their Eyes Were Watching God* (1937) serves as a precise example of the literary critics' obsession with categorization and exclusive disciplines. Hurston nicely fits into too many historical categories: she is Black; she is a woman; she is a writer; and she is a writer whose works are atypical of the contemporary Black fiction of her day. Because Hurston and Richard Wright were contemporaries, the differences in their art sharply reflect the diversity of sensibility, philosophy, and craft of the Black American writer. Yet Wright's unfavorable review of *Their Eyes* epitomizes the unfortunate idea that the Black writer only writes about the Black man's reaction to white society.[1] Robert Bone's comments on *Their Eyes* in his *The Negro Novel in America* (1958) and Darwin Turner's analysis in his notable *In a Minor Chord* (1971), like Wright's review, evince these male critics' inability to identify Hurston's unique sensibility and crafts-

---

Reprinted by permission of the author.
[1]Richard Wright, "Between Laughter and Tears," *New Masses*, October 5, 1937.

manship.[2] June Jordan's and Mary Helen Washington's commentaries on the novel exemplify how the changes in the political, social, and literary climate through time enhance our ability to look at works of the past from a more informed and broadened perspective. These Black female critics address the dynamics of stylistic diversity and identity respectively in their analyses of *Their Eyes*, both suggesting that Hurston's love story increases the thematic range of Black fiction and thus moves Black lives beyond stereotype.[3]

So far, the criticism on Hurston's novel remains too lop-sided with its heavy emphasis on theme—Janie's fulfillment of her dream and her concomitant search for identity.[4] When looking at style, critics, for the most part, restrict themselves to a brief comment on Hurston's superb rendering of the dialect of her Eatonville characters. Realistic and scrupulous dialect, however, is not the only or perhaps even the main stylistic characteristic that makes *Their Eyes Were Watching God* a typical reflection of Zora Hurston's unique craftsmanship. It is Hurston's use of organic imagery that exemplifies her ingenious enmeshing of meaning and form. The novel's controlling image is that of the pear tree blossom which symbolizes Janie's emotional growth and her fulfillment of her dream. Moreover, this use of organic imagery to reflect Janie's pursuit of her dream parallels the philosophical premise that underlines Janie's character and her view of life.

Janie Woods, the protagonist of *Their Eyes Were Watching God*, is the creation of Zora Hurston, who is at once a novelist and a behavioral scientist. Literary history refers to Hurston the creative writer, the folklorist, and the anthropologist as if her career reflects the mind of a schizophrenic who had at least three mutually exclusive lives. Of course, this tendency to categorize and to divide knowledge into exclusive disciplines finds its source in our inability to transcend the academic, scholarly evils of typing and stereotyping. In looking at Hurston's novel so far, we have failed to question the influence of Franz Boas and her training as a behavioral scientist on the thought or philosophy that informs her fiction. For Boas' influence and the philosophical concept of pragmatism, akin to Boas' an-

---

[2]Robert Bone, *The Negro Novel in America* (New Haven: Yale University Press, 1958) and Darwin T. Turner, *In a Minor Chord* (Carbondale: Southern Illinois University Press, 1971).

[3]June Jordan, "On Richard Wright and Zora Neale Hurston," *Black World* 23 (August 1974), pp. 4–10 and Mary Helen Washington, "The Black Woman's Search for Identity," *Black World* 21 (August 1972), pp. 68–72.

[4]For an historical preview of the criticism on *Their Eyes Were Watching God*, see Robert E. Hemenway's notes in his *Zora Neale Hurston: A Literary Biography* (Chicago: University of Illinois Press, 1977), pp. 243–45.

thropological view of life, undergird Hurston's representation of Janie and the forces that control Janie's life.

In his book *Anthropology and Modern Life* (1929), Franz Boas presents his views towards the processes of human behavior. He first distinguishes the anthropologist from the sociologist, the anatomist, the physiologist, and the psychologist by explaining that these groups focus more on the individual and his typical form while the anthropologist concerns himself with the behavior of the racial or social group. His central focus is that the idea of proper values is relative to different cultures and that no such thing exists as universal values. He believes that modern civilization could gain a large body of knowledge from studying the customs and habits of so-called primitive cultures. And the differences in the values of primitive cultures and modern civilization evince the cycle of the process of change that governs human behavior. He adds,

> The forces that bring about the changes are active in the individuals composing the social group, not in the abstract culture.
>
> Here, as well as in other social phenomena, accident cannot be eliminated, accident that may depend upon the presence or absence of eminent individuals, upon the favors bestowed by nature, upon chance discoveries or contacts, and therefore prediction is precarious, if not impossible. Laws of development, except in most generalized form, cannot be established and a detailed course of growth cannot be predicted.[5]

Boas' view of the unpredictable and changing cycle of human behavior echoes the philosophical views of William James (1842–1910), the philosopher and brother of the novelist Henry James, and his successor John Dewey (1859–1952) whose goal was to use philosophy as a means of solving man's social problems and improving his daily life. James, who proposed the basic principles of the philosophical concept known as pragmatism, attempts to bring philosophy out of the world of "intellectual abstraction" to the ordinary world in which we live. The world, James believes, is spontaneous, discontinuous and unpredictable. Truth is not inherent in ideas; instead it is subject to the process of change as it relates to varying experiences. He explains, "Since, however, Darwinism has once for all displaced design from the minds of the 'scientific,' theism has lost that foothold; and some kind of an immanent or pantheistic deity working *in* things rather than above them is, if any, the kind recom-

---

[5]Franz Boas, *Anthropology and Modern Life* (London: George Allen & Unwin Ltd, 1929), p. 236.

mended to our contemporary imagination."[6] Thus to James, the universe consists of numerous possibilities with a God that is not in the heavens controlling things. Instead, the universe is governed more by the element of chance than it is by any absolute law or being.

James, the philosopher, and Boas, the anthropologist, assert essentially the same view of the workings of the universe; whereas James addresses ideas and their relationship to human experiences, Boas emphasizes human behavior more directly. The result is the same: mankind is governed by the principle of chance. John Dewey popularizes James' ideas and applies them to education, art, democracy, social doctrine, language, natural science, and metaphysics. He writes, ". . . the outstanding fact in all branches of natural science is that to exist is to be in process, in change."[7] Both Boas and Dewey hold that the cycle of chance and change that controls human experience is reflective of the continuous, unpredictable process that characterizes the world of nature and more importantly they propose that man can learn much about himself from observing the processes of nature.[8]

In Hurston's use of the controlling image of the pear tree blossom to represent Janie's wish for emotional fulfillment and the use of the accompanying motif of the horizon to reflect Janie's persistent ability to give herself up to the processes of change and chance in order to pursue her dreams and thus escape the limitations of her social environment, Hurston echoes the influence of Franz Boas and the philosophical concept of pragmatism still prevalent in intellectual circles during her day. *Their Eyes Were Watching God* begins with the captivating metaphor of the horizon which presents the difference between the life of woman and the life of man which suggests Janie's intuitively philosophical view of life:

> Ships at a distance have every man's wish on board. For some they come in with the tide. For others they sail forever on the horizon, never out of sight, never landing until the Watcher turns his eyes away in resignation, his dreams mocked to death by Time. That is the life of men.
>
> Now, women forget all those things they don't want to remember, and remember everything they don't want to forget. The dream is the truth. Then they act and do things accordingly.[9]

---

[6]Henry James, "What Pragmatism Means," in *Pragmatism and American Culture*, ed. Gail Kennedy (Boston: D.C. Heath and Company, 1950), p. 20.

[7]John Dewey, "What I Believe," in *Pragmatism and American Culture*, p. 26.

[8]*Ibid.* and Franz Boas, *Anthropology*, p. 213.

[9]Zora Neale Hurston, *Their Eyes Were Watching God*, 2nd. ed. (1937; rpt. Chicago: University of Illinois Press, 1978), p. 9. All subsequent references to this work will be cited by page number in the body of the text.

Having married three times and buried her last husband with whom she experienced the fulfillment of her dreams, Janie returns to Eatonville to live out her memories. Thematically the novel ends with its beginning. In this metaphor of the ship and the horizon, we learn that women "remember everything they don't want to forget. The dream is the truth. Then they act and do things accordingly." Hence after Teacake's death, Janie moves out of experience (her life and happiness with Teacake) back to her dream (her memories of Teacake). Hurston sets the novel inside of a frame in which time present begins and ends the novel while time past (Janie's life story that she tells to her friend Pheoby) makes up the middle section which comprises the bulk of the novel. In the beginning and at the end of the novel, we find Janie living inside her dream. She is able to do so at the end because the "self-revelation" that motivates her into telling her story to Pheoby provides her with a knowledge of herself and of her relationship to the cycle of the universe. Embodied in the story Janie tells Pheoby is the principle of change and chance that governed Janie's life.

Fittingly then, Hurston begins the story of Janie's life with an organic simile that uses nature to suggest the transient, temporal cycle of life. The narrator says,

> Janie saw her life like a great tree in leaf with the things suffered, things enjoyed, things done and undone. Dawn and doom was in the branches. (p. 20)

This simile, along with the metaphor of the ship and the pear tree blossom, makes up the novel's three most significant uses of figurative language. As the novel progresses the metaphor of the ship and the horizon merge with the organic imagery to suggest the relationship between time and human experiences. Like the above simile which compares Janie's life to the cycle of a tree, the image of the pear tree blossom narrows its scope to represent first Janie's sexual arousal and later the type of emotional union she wishes to have with Logan Killicks and Jody Starks:

> Janie had spent most of the day under a blossoming pear tree in the back yard. . . . It had called her to come and gaze on a mystery. From barren brown stems to glistening leaf-buds; from the leaf-buds to snowy virginity of bloom. It stirred her tremendously. . . .
>
> She saw a dust-bearing bee sink into the sanctum of a bloom; the thousand sister-calyxes arch to meet the love embrace and the ecstatic shiver of the tree from root to tiniest branch creaming in every blossom and frothing with delight. So this was a marriage! She had been summoned to behold a revelation. (p. 24)

Janie here, barely beyond adolescence, confuses sex with love and marriage.

As the novel progresses through Janie's experiences with her three husbands, this image of the pear tree blossom acquires the status of symbol. In describing Janie's restlessness and boredom with Logan Killicks and the sense of adventure (her search for the horizon) that drives her to Jody Starks, Hurston merges her use of nature to represent change and her use of the horizon to indicate Janie's willingness to let chance control her life. For Hurston demonstrates how the cycle of human existence follows the same pattern of caprice, unpredictability, and transience as the cycle of nature. In explaining Janie's thoughts after Nanny's death, the narrator says, "So Janie waited a bloom time, and a green time and an orange time. But when the pollen again gilded the sun and sifted down on the world she began to stand around the gate and expect things" (p. 43). And later she adds, "She knew the world was a stallion rolling in the blue pasture of ether. She knew that God tore down the old world every evening and built a new one by sun-up. It was wonderful to see it take form with the sun and emerge from the gray dust of its making. The familiar people and things had failed her so she hung over the gate and looked up the road towards way off" (p. 44). As Janie dreams and thinks of a life "towards way off," chance (accident) brings Jody Starks along the road where she lived with Killicks. Although she likes his "big voice" and "his talk about when he would be a big ruler of things," "memories of Nanny held Janie back at first." She "pulled back a long time because he did not represent sun-up and pollen and blooming trees, but he spoke for far horizon. He spoke for *change* and *chance*" [emphasis mine] (p. 50). So finally after a brief argument with Killicks as she prepares his breakfast, "A feeling of sudden newness and change came over her. Janie hurried out of the front gate and turned south. Even if Joe [Jody] was not there waiting for her the change was bound to do her good" (p. 54). Although Janie now realizes that sex and marriage do not bring love or emotional fulfillment and that Jody does not satisfy the image of her dreams, she leaves with him out of a feeling of hope that whatever changes await her will at least approximate her dream.

Janie matures to full womanhood during her marriage to Jody. Her union with him becomes a natural process in the cycle of things. It prepares her for Teacake, the fulfillment of her dream. Her life with Jodie was like a "great tree in leaf with things suffered and undone more than enjoyed or done." Because Jody's idea of the life of man and the life of woman did not differ from Nanny's or Logan Killicks', his aloofness, his alienation, his ignorance of Janie's desires and thoughts, and his middle-class values destroyed the warmth

Janie initially felt for him. Conscious of her extreme unhappiness, Janie resolves to remain with Jody although she at one time contemplates searching for her mother or returning to her childhood environment. After Jody's death she experiences the same feeling of newness, of exhilaration that she felt when she first left Logan Killicks. She feels free. She is calmly enjoying this freedom when chance and change usher Teacake into her store. Reserved at first because of the difference in their ages, she finally surrenders to her love. Teacake becomes the embodiment of the image of the pear tree blossom:

> She couldn't make him look just like any other man to her. He looked like the love thoughts of women. He could be a bee to a blossom—a pear tree blossom in spring. He seemed to be crushing aromatic herbs with every step he took. (p. 161)

Teacake is the man for whom sixteen-year-old Janie was searching when she watched the "dust-bearing bee sink into the sanctum of a bloom."

Experiencing her dream, Janie gives up the security of her home and store to pursue a life with Teacake. Just as her happiness with him is a natural part of the cycle of change and chance, so is Teacake's death. When he successfully saves Janie from a mad dog during a terrible hurricane, he is bitten by the dog and unknowingly contracts rabies. While sick, Teacake himself points out that all of Janie's life before she met him was preparation for their life together. When Janie says that she is too old for any other man and that she harbors no regrets over her life with him, Teacake responds, "Thank yuh, ma'am, but don't say you'se old. You'se uh lil girl baby all de time. God made it so you spent yo' old age first wid somebody else, and saved up yo' young girl days to spend wid me" (p. 268). Janie Woods is not the same woman as was Janie Killicks or Starks; her calmness and awareness of self and her desires grew to maturity during her relationship with Jody and prepared the way for the happiness she experienced with Teacake. Her timely, unpredictable meeting with Teacake is as fortuitous as Motor Boat's escaping death during the hurricane. While Janie and Teacake, as well as many others who died in the storm, ran to save their lives, Motor Boat slept through the hurricane and ironically survives quite peacefully.

As Janie's consciousness matures, she becomes increasingly aware of the caprice, fortuity, and uncertainty that govern her daily life. When she ran away with Jody Starks she was willing to accept the consequences that change brought to her life just as she was willing to accept the unknown effect of change when she left Eatonville with Teacake. And the most important test of her philosophy is Teacake's death. Near the end of her story to Pheoby she proposes that all that can be known through life must come through experience and this experience is relative to the individual. She says:

> It's uh known fact Pheoby, you got tuh *go* there tuh *know* there. Yo' papa and yo' mama and nobody else can't tell yuh and show yuh. Two things everybody's got tuh do fuh theyselves. They got tuh go tuh God, and they got tuh find out about livin' fuh theyselves. (p. 285)

Janie's reference to God is not to be confused with the traditional concept of God and His role in our daily lives. Janie's attitude toward God parallels James' and the pragmatists' who hold that God works more within things than outside of things. Hence our lives are controlled more by the workings of natural processes and forces rather than by a divine Absolute being. The passage which most illuminates this idea is the one which describes Janie's response when she learns that Teacake has rabies. After the doctor leaves, she stands outside their house and questions the relationship between the course of their lives and God:

> She looked hard at the sky for a long time. Somewhere up there beyond blue ether's bosom sat He. Was He noticing what was going on around here? He must be because He knew everything. Did He *mean* to do this thing to Teacake and her? It wasn't anything she could fight. She could only ache and wait. Maybe it was some big tease and when He saw it had gone far enough He'd give her a sign. She looked hard for something up there to move for a sign. . . . Her arms went up in desperate supplication for a minute. It wasn't exactly pleading, it was asking questions. The sky stayed hard looking and quiet so she went inside the house. God would do less than He had in His heart. (p. 264)

Janie resolves that God had already set his processes in motion, and thus she can only acquiesce and endure. For God gives no signs from the skies and her prayers cannot penetrate "blue ether's bosom" to move His heart. Emboldened by a philosophy of life in which she "remembers the things she doesn't want to forget" and maintains a kind of self-satisfaction at having fulfilled her dream and reached the horizon, Janie returns to Eatonville and finds peace and resolution in her memories of her happiness with Teacake. She explains to Pheoby, "Now, dat's how everything wuz, Pheoby, jus' lak Ah told yuh. So Ah'm back home agin and Ah'm satisfied tuh be heah. Ad done been tuh de horizon and back and now Ah kin set heah in mah house and live by comparisons" (p. 284). Thus Janie has learned to reconcile herself to change and chance. The organic imagery in the novel underscores her temporal, transient affinity with the rest of the universe.

According to Janie and her creator Zora Hurston, chance and

change restrict and enrich individual experiences. The beauty of Janie Crawford Killicks Starks Woods is that she is wise and quite self-possessed. She embodies a view of reality that reflects Hurston's personal temperament as well as her educational training. Henry James asserts that a philosopher's way of looking at the world is directed by his temperament and sensibility. Analogously, Zora Hurston's *Their Eyes Were Watching God* exemplifies the affinity between Hurston's sensibility, her attitude toward life and that of her teacher Franz Boas, and the philosophical ideas prevalent during the time she writes her novel. Zora's comments in the section entitled "Religion" in *Dust Tracks on a Road*, her autobiography, serve as a final commentary on the relationship between change, chance, and God in *Their Eyes*. She writes:

> As for me, I do not pretend to read God's mind. If He has a plan of the universe worked out to the smallest detail, it would be folly for me to presume to get down on my knees and attempt to revise it. That, to me, seems the highest form of sacrilege. So I do not pray. I accept the means at my disposal for working out my destiny. . . . I do not choose to admit weakness. I accept the challenge of responsibility. Life, as it is, does not frighten me, since I have made my peace with the universe as I find it, and bow to its laws. . . . I know that nothing is destructible; things merely change forms. When the consciousness we know as life ceases, I know that I shall still be part and parcel of the world. I was part before the sun rolled into shape and burst forth in the glory of change. . . . The stuff of my being is matter ever changing, ever moving, but never lost. . . .[10]

---

[10]Zora Neale Hurston, *Dust Tracks on a Road* (1942; rpt. New York: Arno Press, 1969), pp. 286–87.

Kenneth A. McClane

(1951–   )

THE NATURE OF Kenneth Anderson McClane, Jr.'s poetry is probably best described by the comments he makes in *Contemporary Authors*. He says: "Writing poetry is, I guess, my highest and most fragile pleasure. Words, and you learn to love them, seem to bring everything into question: heaven and hell, the monumental and the commonplace—all want the rigors and excitements of language to occasion them. And I guess that is what I am about, the occasion and its occasion, the world and its greater worlds. And there is a lot that is scary in this: the world does not terribly like one's sense of order—she has her own—and the paths to ruination are most clear. I think (and this is most obvious in my longer poems) that I am losing touch with it all, losing sight of the hill for the valley and yet both exist. The images are most distinct, but the meaning is difficult. And it is in these tough places, these difficult ones, that good writing is found."

Born in 1951, in New York City, McClane received all of his higher education at Cornell University: he completed the requirements for the A.B. with distinction in 1973, the M.A. in 1974, and the M.F.A. in 1976. Before receiving his M.F.A., he worked as an instructor of English at Colby College from 1974 to 1975. In 1976 he became a member of the faculty at Cornell University, where in 1983 he was associate professor of English and director of the creative writing program. In 1984 he was the Luce Visiting Associate Professor of English at Williams College and has given readings and lectures at a number of colleges and universities, including Williams College, Yale University, Wesleyan University, and Bates College. Consultant to educational television in Elmira, New York, from 1977 to 1978, he was also script consultant for the production of Toni Morrison's *The Bluest Eye*.

His poems have appeared in *Nimrod*, *Cornell Review*, *Praxis*, *Vineyard Gazette*, *Beloit Poetry Journal*, *Wind*, *Texas Review*, *Black Scholar*, and *Thoreau Journal Quarterly*. In addition to having contributed poems to several anthologies, he is the author of seven collections of poetry: *Out Beyond the Bay* (1975), *Moons and Low Times* (1978), *To Hear the River* (1981), *At Winter's End* (1982), *A Tree Beyond Telling: Poems, Selected and New* (1983), *These Halves Are Whole* (1983), and *Take Five: Collected Poems, 1972–1986* (1987).

His honors and awards include his nomination for the Lamont Poetry

Prize in 1978 and the Cornell University Clark Distinguished Teaching Award, 1983.

HARLEM

for Gwendolyn Brooks

The wind sings in the slow
trees, while kids swim
in and out of being
like shards of imagination:

The great river muscles, the mythic salmon
gather at insects: the world of living
and plunging out of life
moves in a ceaseless mechanism:

In Harlem they are flung wide
in the streets. One vision
a barren truce, a taut-string, a blue collage; the other,
more beautiful, giddy, a life among ashes.

TO HEAR THE RIVER

for Langston Hughes

To hear
to hear
to hear the
to hear the strong
black song
to hear it—to hear the river
is to know

its ways: to know
the gaunt-thin
source which somehow
like Hughes
becomes long black water, becomes

From *Take Five, Collected Poems 1971–1986* by Kenneth A. McClane (Greenwood Press, 1988). All poems reprinted by permission of the author.

(so that much might come after it)
a handhold, a griot:

And so long black song
comes dark, provident, absolute:

And finally coming to the river, facing
the dogs and white men, facing what is lost
and possible, *we hear the river, we hear
the river, we hear the river*

THE BLACK INTELLECTUAL

for W. E. B. Du Bois

We have shored up so much
to keep from rioting. To keep it down
we move in and out of our skins
in some grotesque obeisance, some wretching of our forms
as if we were addled neon signs.

Indeed we are afraid of ourselves.
Riding in the least seat, in the last car, in the longest
train is still riding; it is safe.
Powers still mightily discipline the universe: and gods
(be they august or sweet) provide a cadence.

Yet when I walk near their big clovered houses,
see their doom-eyed children, watch
their ornamental boats flounder in the river, I
want to save them.

And when they press
me in class, when they want
to know how soil is gathered, how earth
shares so little, I find myself answering:

But sometimes the other voice in me
heaves from the gut.
Cold, defiant, persuasive
it seems to hold everything: Attica
Soweto, Chile, Little Rock, Mozambique:

And now I see nothing in their stunted lives
but death; I see nothing in their hopeless
celebration but blood; I see nothing but the ceaseless waste
of dark bodies, piling up as they ask:

the questions always coming, always coming
as if questions might stop it. Today I have given up
answering: today I no longer look upon or care about the easy
offerings to insatiable gods: today
should a wind swell on the river and wrack their foundering
boat
I might only wish that all were present.

Rita Dove

(1952–   )

WINNER OF THE PULITZER PRIZE for poetry, Rita Dove defines poetry and comments upon the nature of her art in *Contemporary Authors*. She says, "Poetry, for me, must explore the felicities of language; the events of the poem should never be more important than how that event is recreated. This is why the stock question, 'What is your poetry about?,' seems fruitless. In recent work I have been trying to combine historical occurrences with the epiphanal quality of the lyric poem. I find travel to be a good way to gain different perspectives and to avoid becoming complacent."

Born in 1952, in Akron, Ohio, Rita Dove is the daughter of Elvira Hord and Ray Dove, a chemist, who had hoped that his daughter would be a lawyer rather than a poet. Graduating summa cum laude, she received her B.A. from Miami University in Oxford, Ohio, in 1973 and her M.F.A. from the University of Iowa in 1977.

She has traveled to Israel, southern Europe, and West Germany. She spent the years 1981 to 1987 as an assistant professor of creative writing at Arizona State University at Tempe. For one year (1988–1989) she was a fellow at the National Humanities Research Triangle in Durham, North Carolina. Currently, she is professor of English at the University of Virginia.

Though she began her literary career as a poet, Dove has published a collection of short stories entitled *Fifth Sunday* (1985) and is currently at work on a novel. Her poems have appeared in *Callaloo*, *Agni Review*, *Antaeus*, *Georgia Review*, *Nation*, and *Poetry*. She is the author of three poetry chapbooks: *Ten Poems* (1977), *The Only Dark Spot in the Sky* (1980); and *Mandolin* (1982); and three other major collections: *The Yellow House on the Corner* (1980); *Museum* (1983); and *Thomas and Beulah* (1986), which won a Pulitzer Prize for Poetry in 1987. Her most recent poetry collections are *The Other Side of the House* (1988) and *Grace Notes* (1989).

In addition to the Pulitzer Prize, she is recipient of a number of honors and awards: a Fulbright Fellowship, grants from the National Endowment for the Arts and from the Ohio Arts Council, an International Working Period for Authors Fellowship for West Germany, a Portia Pittman Fellowship at Tuskegee Institute from the National Endowment for the Humanities, and a Guggenheim Fellowship.

For a look at critical analyses of her poetry, see Arnold Rampersad's "The Poems of Rita Dove" and Robert McDowell's "The Assembling Vision of Rita Dove" in *Callaloo* 9 (Winter 1986).

For further reading see Linda Metzger, ed., *Black Writers: A Selection of Sketches from Contemporary Authors* (1989).

The poems that follow are taken from *Thomas and Beulah* (1986).

ROAST POSSUM

The possum's a greasy critter
that lives on persimmons and what
the Bible calls carrion.
So much from the 1912 Werner
Encyclopedia, three rows of deep green
along the wall. A granddaughter
propped on each knee,
Thomas went on with his tale—

but it was for Malcolm, little
Red Delicious, that he invented
embellishments: *We shined that possum*
with a torch and I shinnied up,
being the smallest,
to shake him down. He glared at me,
teeth bared like a shark's
in that torpedo snout.
Man he was tough but no match
for old-time know-how.

Malcolm hung back, studying them
with his gold hawk eyes. When the girls
got restless, Thomas talked horses:
Strolling Jim, who could balance
a glass of water on his back
and trot the village square
without spilling a drop. Who put
Wartrace on the map and was buried
under a stone, like a man.

They liked that part.
He could have gone on to tell them
that the Werner admitted Negro children

to be intelligent, though briskness
clouded over at puberty, bringing
indirection and laziness. Instead,
he added: *You got to be careful*
with a possum when he's on the ground;
he'll turn on his back and play dead
till you give up looking. That's
what you'd call sullin'.

Malcom interrupted to ask
who owned Strolling Jim,
and who paid for the tombstone.
They stared each other down
man to man, before Thomas,
as a grandfather, replied:
                          Yessir,
we enjoyed that possum. We ate him
real slow, with sweet potatoes.

THE HOUSE ON BISHOP STREET

No front yard to speak of,
just a porch cantilevered on faith
where she arranged the canary's cage.
The house stayed dark all year
though there was instant light and water.
(No more gas jets hissing,
their flicker glinting off
Anna Rettich's midwife spectacles
as she whispered *think a baby*
and the babies came.) Spring
brought a whiff of cherries, the kind
you boiled for hours in sugar and cloves

from the yard of the Jewish family next door.
Yumanski refused to speak so
she never bought his vegetables
at the Canal Street Market. Gertrude,
his youngest and blondest,
slipped by mornings for bacon and grits.
There were summer floods and mildew

humming through fringe, there was
a picture of a ship she passed
on her way to the porch, strangers calling
from the street *Ma'am, your bird*
shore can sing! If she leaned out she could glimpse
the faintest of mauve—no more than an idea—
growing just behind the last houses.

MOTHERHOOD

She dreams the baby's so small she keeps
misplacing it—it rolls from the hutch
and the mouse carries it home, it disappears
with his shirt in the wash.
Then she drops it and it explodes
like a watermelon, eyes spitting.

Finally they get to the countryside;
Thomas has it in a sling.
He's strewing rice along the road
while the trees chitter with tiny birds.
In the meadow to their right three men
are playing rough with a white wolf. She calls

warning but the wolf breaks free
and she runs, the rattle
rolls into the gully, then she's
there and tossing the baby behind her,
listening for its cry as she straddles
the wolf and circles the throat, counting
until her thumbs push through to the earth.
White fur seeps red. She is hardly breathing.
The small wild eyes
go opaque with confusion and shame, like a child's.

HEADDRESS

The hat on the table
in the dining room
is no pet trained
to sit still. Three

pearl-tipped spears and Beulah
maneuvering her shadow
to the floor. The hat
is cold. The hat
wants more.

(The customer will be
generous when satisfied
beyond belief. Spangled
tulle, then, in green
and gold and sherry.)

Beulah
would have settled
for less. She doesn't
pray when she's
terrified, sometimes, in-
side her skin like
today, humming
through a mouthful of pins.

Finished it's a mountain
on a dish, a capitol
poised on a littered shore.
The brim believes
in itself, its
double rose and feathers
ashiver. Extravagance
redeems. O
intimate parasol
that teaches to walk
with grace along beauty's seam.

E. Ethelbert Miller

(1950–   )

EMBRACING POETRY as a means to encourage cultural exchange and express social and political issues, E. Ethelbert Miller surpasses the notion of art for art's sake. His themes, although ethnic in nature, focus on the human experience as a whole. Figuratively overstepping the color line, Miller's poetry characterizes the emotions and situations in which people of all colors can find themselves. In order to bring poetry to the average person and reflect the average person's concerns, Miller strategically uses "man-on-the-street" language.

A native of the Bronx, New York, and the youngest of three children, Miller was born in 1950. After graduating from Howard University with a bachelor's degree in Afro-American studies in 1972, he became the associate director of Howard University's Afro-American Studies department's Resource Center. Previously an associate editor for *Black Box* magazine and a senior editor for *Washington Review of the Arts*, Miller currently serves as Howard's Resource Center's director.

Andromeda (1974), Miller's second published book of poetry, marks the beginning of a traceable stage of development of self-awareness and sensibility. Miller's poetry is reprinted in several anthologies and magazines, such as *Callaloo*, *Obsidian*, and *Black American Literature Forum*. He has also edited two books, *Synergy: An Anthology of Washington, D.C., Black Poetry* (1975) with Ahmos Zu-Bolton and *Women Surviving Massacres and Men* (1977). Miller also writes nonfiction articles on topics such as the black aesthetic and the survival of black poetry in the District of Columbia.

Miller's other works include his first published book of poetry, *Interface* (1972); *The Land of Smiles and the Land of No Smiles* (1974); *Migrant Worker* (1978); and *Season of Hunger / Cry of Rain: Poems, 1975–1980* (1982). *Where Are the Love Poems for Dictators?* (1986) is Miller's most recent collection of poems.

For further reading see Patrice Gaines-Carter's "Free Verse: E. Ethelbert Miller Is a Poet and a Poem," *Washington Post Magazine*, 3 February 1985; Priscilla Ramsey's "A '60's Harvest: The Poetic Vision of E. Ethelbert Miller," *Freedomways*, 24 (Fourth Quarter 1984); Joyce A. Joyce's "The Aesthetic of E. Ethelbert Miller," Occasional Paper #1, Institute for the Preservation and Study of African-American Writing, 1988, and Priscilla Ramsey's essay in *Dictionary of Literary Biography, Volume 41*.

"Poem for Jomo Kenyatta" and "The Boat People of Haiti" are taken from *Season of Hunger / Cry of Rain*; "When Allende Was Alive" and "Nicaragua" are taken from *Where Are the Love Poems for Dictators?*

POEM FOR JOMO KENYATTA

old man
your eyes now close
your skin greys slowly
becoming the color of your beard

i lift your spear
your name my shield

jomo kenyatta

your name
forever bright
like a red flame across the dawn
one step ahead of tomorrow

old man
the papers
call you moderate and wise
now that you are dead

the papers
call out—HARAMBEE

we will work together
we will work with you

praise kenyatta
praise jomo kenyatta

old man
we are still young

it is only the morning of independence
the air is cold
a thousand skulls guard the borders of angola
a million spirits now arm themselves with flesh
and march towards south africa

All poems are reprinted by permission of E. Ethelbert Miller.

old man
we are still at war
your cry for freedom
must be cried again

only then will flowers live
only then will africa survive

THE BOAT PEOPLE OF HAITI

on the third day
the wind again slapped at the small boat
water came through the cracks
we moved our large bundles of clothes
to the last dry spot beneath our bare feet

the women were hungry
but few things were left in the baskets
i held the hands of my wife
trying my best to comfort her

how far florida—she keeps asking

& it was the fourth day
when i told her
i did not know

the nights are horrible
they are worse than hunger
the cold so near
the stars so far
the water everywhere
rain falling now and then
the children sick with fever

i try to pray
but find myself too weak
i tell myself that death
will come in maybe one or two hours

i try to sleep
i sail this nightmare
to america

WHEN ALLENDE WAS ALIVE

looking through the window of my country
i do not see myself outside
i trace the outline of my breath against glass
the cold enters my fingers

when allende was alive
i could open this window
look out across chile from my home in
santiago

there were no curtains to hide dreams
it was a time of hope

a time to press democracy against my lips
& hold her like a lover

NICARAGUA

what can i give you nicaragua
tears or blood
should i embrace you like i would
another man's wife
the shape of your back curving
against my hands
the brown earth color
of our meeting
on this loveless night

nicaragua
i have known prostitutes
i gave them money
now i look into the eyes of honduras
and costa rica
behind the headlines that hide behind
lies and something called america
a fruit filled with bones

nicaragua
if i never see the sun again
i will count your lovers among the
many that defended you
i will remember you dressing in the morning

near the window
i will remember your voice
and the way the wind carried your song
into the mountains

nicaragua
this poem is for our children
and your friend in managua who asked
me to live with her
whose face i wrapped in tissue
her hair like fine black thread
covering my shirts

this poem is for the poets
who will understand

Gloria Naylor

(1950–   )

GLORIA NAYLOR'S *The Women of Brewster Place* was cited by the American Book Award committee as the best first novel of 1982. The daughter of Mississippi parents who moved north to give their children educational and cultural opportunities not available in their native state, Naylor grew up in the New York City area. As a child, she attended classes for gifted children in the public schools.

Like many others of her generation, she had trouble in "finding herself." After the assassination of Martin Luther King, Jr., which occurred while she was a high school senior. She became a Jehovah's Witness missionary, traveling for seven years through several states. Subsequently, she tried nursing and marriage for very brief periods.

Supporting herself as a switchboard operator, she enrolled in Brooklyn College and received her B.A. in English. She later received the M.A. in Afro-American studies from Yale University. She has taught writing and literature at George Washington University, New York University, and Boston University.

She is author of three impressive publications: *The Women of Brewster Place* (1982), *Linden Hills* (1985), and *Mama Day* (1988). Winner of the 1983 American Book Award, *The Women of Brewster Place*, described as a novel in seven stories, was made into a movie produced for television. Describing the content of her work, a writer for the *Washington Post Book World* says, "Gloria Naylor is not afraid to grapple with life's big subjects: sex, birth, love, death, grief. Her talent glows like beaten copper."

For further reading, see *Contemporary Literary Criticism*, Volume 28 (1984) and Linda Metzger, ed., *Black Writers: A Selection of Sketches from Contemporary Authors* (1989).

The following selection is taken from *The Women of Brewster Place*.

LUCIELIA LOUISE TURNER

The sunlight was still watery as Ben trudged into Brewster Place, and the street had just begun to yawn and stretch itself. He eased himself onto his garbage can, which was pushed against the sagging brick wall that turned Brewster into a dead-end street. The metallic cold of the can's lid seeped into the bottom of his thin trousers. Sucking on a piece of breakfast sausage caught in his back teeth, he began to muse. Mighty cold, these spring mornings. The old days you could build a good trash fire in one of them barrels to keep warm. Well, don't want no summons now, and can't freeze to death. Yup, can't freeze to death.

His daily soliloquy completed, he reached into his coat pocket and pulled out a crumpled brown bag that contained his morning sun. The cheap red liquid moved slowly down his throat, providing immediate justification as the blood began to warm in his body. In the hazy light a lean dark figure began to make its way slowly up the block. It hesitated in front of the stoop at 316, but looking around and seeing Ben, it hurried over.

"Yo, Ben."

"Hey, Eugene, I thought that was you. Ain't seen ya round for a coupla days."

"Yeah." The young man put his hands in his pockets, frowned into the ground, and kicked the edge of Ben's can. "The funeral's today, ya know."

"Yeah."

"You going?" He looked up into Ben's face.

"Naw, I ain't got no clothes for them things. Can't abide 'em no way—too sad—it being a baby and all."

"Yeah. I was going myself, people expect it, ya know?"

"Yeah."

"But, man, the way Ciel's friends look at me and all—like I was filth or something. Hey, I even tried to go see Ciel in the hospital, heard she was freaked out and all."

"Yeah, she took it real bad."

"Yeah, well, damn, I took it bad. It was my kid, too, ya know. But Mattie, that fat, black bitch, just standin' in the hospital hall sayin' to me—to me, now, 'Whatcha want?' Like I was a fuckin' germ or something. Man, I just turned and left. You gotta be treated with respect, ya know?"

"Yeah."

"I mean, I should be there today with my woman in the limo and all, sittin' up there, doin' it right. But how you gonna be a man with them ball-busters tellin' everybody it was my fault and I should be the one dead? Damn!"

"Yeah, a man's gotta be a man." Ben felt the need to wet his reply with another sip. "Have some?"

"Naw, I'm gonna be heading on—Ciel don't need me today. I bet that frig, Mattie, rides in the head limo, wearing the pants. Shit—let 'em." He looked up again. "Ya know?"

"Yup."

"Take it easy, Ben." He turned to go.

"You too, Eugene."

"Hey, you going?"

"Naw."

"Me neither. Later."

"Later, Eugene."

Funny, Ben thought, Eugene ain't stopped to chat like that for a long time—near on a year, yup, a good year. He took another swallow to help him bring back the year-old conversation, but it didn't work; the second and third one didn't either. But he did remember that it had been an early spring morning like this one, and Eugene had been wearing those same tight jeans. He had hesitated outside of 316 then, too. But that time he went in . . .

Lucielia had just run water into the tea kettle and was putting it on the burner when she heard the cylinder turn. He didn't have to knock on the door; his key still fit the lock. Her thin knuckles gripped the handle of the kettle, but she didn't turn around. She knew. The last eleven months of her life hung compressed in the air between the click of the lock and his "Yo, baby."

The vibrations from those words rode like parasites on the air waves and came rushing into her kitchen, smashing the compression into indistinguishable days and hours that swirled dizzily before her. It was all there: the frustration of being left alone, sick, with a month-old baby; her humiliation reflected in the caseworker's blue eyes for the unanswerable "you can find him to have it, but can't find him to take care of it" smile; the raw urges that crept, uninvited, between her thighs on countless nights; the eternal whys all meshed with the explainable hate and unexplainable love. They kept circling in such a confusing pattern before her that she couldn't seem to grab even one to answer him with. So there was nothing in Lucielia's face when she turned it toward Eugene, standing in her kitchen door holding a ridiculously pink Easter bunny, nothing but sheer relief. . . .

"So he's back." Mattie sat at Lucielia's kitchen table, playing with Serena. It was rare that Mattie ever spoke more than two sentences to anybody about anything. She didn't have to. She chose her words with the grinding precision of a diamond cutter's drill.

"You think I'm a fool, don't you?"

"I ain't said that."

"You didn't have to," Ciel snapped.

"Why you mad at me, Ciel? It's your life, honey."

"Oh, Mattie, you don't understand. He's really straightened up this time. He's got a new job on the docks that pays real good, and he was just so depressed before with the new baby and no work. You'll see. He's even gone out now to buy paint and stuff to fix up the apartment. And, and Serena needs a daddy."

"You ain't gotta convince me, Ciel."

No, she wasn't talking to Mattie, she was talking to herself. She was convincing herself it was the new job and the paint and Serena that let him back into her life. Yet, the real truth went beyond her scope of understanding. When she laid her head in the hollow of his neck there was a deep musky scent to his body that brought back the ghosts of the Tennessee soil of her childhood. It reached up and lined the inside of her nostrils so that she inhaled his presence almost every minute of her life. The feel of his sooty flesh penetrated the skin of her fingers and coursed through her blood and became one, somewhere, wherever it was, with her actual being. But how do you tell yourself, let alone this practical old woman who loves you, that he was back because of that. So you don't.

You get up and fix you both another cup of coffee, calm the fretting baby on your lap with her pacifier, and you pray silently—very silently—behind veiled eyes that the man will stay.

Ciel was trying to remember exactly when it had started to go wrong again. Her mind sought for the slender threads of a clue that she could trace back to—perhaps—something she had said or done. Her brow was set tightly in concentration as she folded towels and smoothed the wrinkles over and over, as if the answer lay concealed in the stubborn creases of the terry cloth.

The months since Eugene's return began to tick off slowly before her, and she examined each one to pinpoint when the nagging whispers of trouble had begun in her brain. The friction on the towels increased when she came to the month that she had gotten pregnant again, but it couldn't be that. Things were different now. She wasn't sick as she had been with Serena, he was still working—no it wasn't the baby. It's not the baby, it's not the baby—the rhythm of those words sped up the motion of her hands, and she had almost yanked and folded and pressed them into a reality when, bewildered, she realized that she had run out of towels.

Ciel jumped when the front door slammed shut. She waited tensely for the metallic bang of his keys on the coffee table and the blast of the stereo. Lately that was how Eugene announced his presence home. Ciel walked into the living room with the motion of a swimmer entering a cold lake.

"Eugene, you're home early, huh?"

"You see anybody else sittin' here?" He spoke without looking at her and rose to turn up the stereo.

He wants to pick a fight, she thought, confused and hurt. He knows Serena's taking her nap, and now I'm supposed to say, Eugene, the baby's asleep, please cut the music down. Then he's going to say, you mean a man can't even relax in his own home without being picked on? I'm not picking on you, but you're going to wake up the baby. Which is always supposed to lead to: You don't give a damn about me. Everybody's more important than me—that kid, your friends, everybody. I'm just chickenshit around here, huh?

All this went through Ciel's head as she watched him leave the stereo and drop defiantly back down on the couch. Without saying a word, she turned and went into the bedroom. She looked down on the peaceful face of her daughter and softly caressed her small cheek. Her heart became full as she realized, this is the only thing I have ever loved without pain. She pulled the sheet gently over the tiny shoulders and firmly closed the door, protecting her from the music. She then went into the kitchen and began washing the rice for their dinner.

Eugene, seeing that he had been left alone, turned off the stereo and came and stood in the kitchen door.

"I lost my job today," he shot at her, as if she had been the cause.

The water was turning cloudy in the rice pot, and the force of the stream from the faucet caused scummy bubbles to rise to the surface. These broke and sprayed tiny starchy particles onto the dirty surface. Each bubble that broke seemed to increase the volume of the dogged whispers she had been ignoring for the last few months. She poured the dirty water off the rice to destroy and silence them, then watched with a malicious joy as they disappeared down the drain.

"So now, how in the hell I'm gonna make it with no money, huh? And another brat comin' here, huh?"

The second change of the water was slightly clearer, but the starch-speckled bubbles were still there, and this time there was no way to pretend deafness to their message. She had stood at that sink countless times before, washing rice, and she knew the water was never going to be totally clear. She couldn't stand there forever—her fingers were getting cold, and the rest of the dinner had to be fixed, and Serena would be waking up soon and wanting attention. Feverishly she poured the water off and tried again.

"I'm fuckin' sick of never getting ahead. Babies and bills, that's all you good for."

The bubbles were almost transparent now, but when they broke they left light trails of starch on top of the water that curled around her fingers. She knew it would be useless to try again. Defeated, Ciel placed the wet pot on the burner, and the flames leaped up bright red and orange, turning the water droplets clinging on the outside into steam.

Turning to him, she silently acquiesced. "All right, Eugene, what do you want me to do?"

He wasn't going to let her off so easily. "Hey, baby, look, I don't care what you do. I just can't have all these hassles on me right now, ya know?"

"I'll get a job. I don't mind, but I've got no one to keep Serena, and you don't want Mattie watching her."

"Mattie—no way. That fat bitch'll turn the kid against me. She hates my ass, and you know it."

"No, she doesn't, Eugene." Ciel remembered throwing that at Mattie once. "You hate him, don't you?" "Naw, honey," and she had cupped both hands on Ciel's face. "Maybe I just loves you too much."

"I don't give a damn what you say—she ain't minding my kid."

"Well, look, after the baby comes, they can tie my tubes—I don't care." She swallowed hard to keep down the lie.

"And what the hell we gonna feed it when it gets here, huh—air? With two kids and you on my back, I ain't never gonna have nothin'." He came and grabbed her by the shoulders and was shouting into her face. "Nothin', do you hear me, nothin'!"

"Nothing to it, Mrs. Turner." The face over hers was as calm and antiseptic as the room she lay in. "Please, relax. I'm going to give you a local anesthetic and then perform a simple D&C, or what you'd call a scraping to clean out the uterus. Then you'll rest here for about an hour and be on your way. There won't even be much bleeding." The voice droned on in its practiced monologue, peppered with sterile kindness.

Ciel was not listening. It was important that she keep herself completely isolated from these surroundings. All the activities of the past week of her life were balled up and jammed on the right side of her brain, as if belonging to some other woman. And when she had endured this one last thing for her, she would push it up there, too, and then one day give it all to her—Ciel wanted no part of it.

The next few days Ciel found it difficult to connect herself up again with her own world. Everything seemed to have taken on new textures and colors. When she washed the dishes, the plates felt peculiar in her hands, and she was more conscious of their smoothness and the heat of the water. There was a disturbing split second between someone talking to her and the words penetrating sufficiently to elicit a response. Her neighbors left her presence with slight frowns of puzzlement, and Eugene could be heard mumbling, "Moody bitch."

She became terribly possessive of Serena. She refused to leave her alone, even with Eugene. The little girl went everywhere with Ciel, toddling along on plump uncertain legs. When someone asked to hold or play with her, Ciel sat nearby, watching every move. She found herself walking into the bedroom several times when the child napped to see if she was still breathing. Each time she chided herself for this unreasonable foolishness, but within the next few minutes some strange force still drove her back.

Spring was slowly beginning to announce itself at Brewster Place. The arthritic cold was seeping out of the worn gray bricks, and the tenants with apartment windows facing the street were awakened by six o'clock sunlight. The music no longer blasted inside 3C, and Ciel grew strong with the peacefulness of her household. The playful laughter of her daughter, heard more often now, brought a sort of redemption with it.

"Isn't she marvelous, Mattie? You know she's even trying to make whole sentences. Come on, baby, talk for Auntie Mattie."

Serena, totally uninterested in living up to her mother's proud claims, was trying to tear a gold-toned button off the bosom of Mattie's dress.

"It's so cute. She even knows her father's name. She says, my da da is Gene."

"Better teach her your name," Mattie said, while playing with the baby's hand. "She'll be using it more."

Ciel's mouth flew open to ask her what she meant by that, but she checked herself. It was useless to argue with Mattie. You could take her words however you wanted. The burden of their truth lay with you, not her.

Eugene came through the front door and stopped short when he saw Mattie. He avoided being around her as much as possible. She was always polite to him, but he sensed a silent condemnation behind even her most innocent words. He constantly felt the need to prove himself in front of her. These frustrations often took the form of unwarranted rudeness on his part.

Serena struggled out of Mattie's lap and went toward her father and tugged on his legs to be picked up. Ignoring the child and cutting short the greetings of the two women, he said coldly, "Ciel, I wanna talk to you."

Sensing trouble, Mattie rose to go. "Ciel, why don't you let me take Serena downstairs for a while. I got some ice cream for her."

"She can stay right here," Eugene broke in. "If she needs ice cream, I can buy it for her."

Hastening to soften his abruptness, Ciel said, "That's okay, Mattie, it's almost time for her nap. I'll bring her later—after dinner."

"All right. Now you all keep good." Her voice was warm. "You too, Eugene," she called back from the front door.

The click of the lock restored his balance to him. "Why in the hell is she always up here?"

"You just had your chance—why didn't you ask her yourself? If you don't want her here, tell her to stay out," Ciel snapped back confidently, knowing he never would.

"Look, I ain't got time to argue with you about that old hag. I got big doings in the making, and I need you to help me pack." Without waiting for a response, he hurried into the bedroom and pulled his old leather suitcase from under the bed.

A tight, icy knot formed in the center of Ciel's stomach and began to melt rapidly, watering the blood in her legs so that they almost refused to support her weight. She pulled Serena back from following Eugene and sat her in the middle of the living room floor.

"Here, honey, play with the blocks for Mommy—she has to talk to Daddy." She piled a few plastic alphabet blocks in front of the child, and on her way out of the room, she glanced around quickly and removed the glass ashtrays off the coffee table and put them on a shelf over the stereo.

Then, taking a deep breath to calm her racing heart, she started toward the bedroom.

Serena loved the light colorful cubes and would sometimes sit for an entire half-hour, repeatedly stacking them up and kicking them over with her feet. The hollow sound of their falling fascinated her, and she would often bang two of them together to re-create the magical noise. She was sitting, contentedly engaged in this particular activity, when a slow dark movement along the baseboard caught her eye.

A round black roach was making its way from behind the couch toward the kitchen. Serena threw one of her blocks at the insect, and, feeling the vibrations of the wall above it, the roach sped around the door into the kitchen. Finding a totally new game to amuse herself, Serena took off behind the insect with a block in each hand. Seeing her moving toy trying to bury itself under the linoleum by the garbage pail she threw another block, and the frantic roach now raced along the wall and found security in the electric wall socket under the kitchen table.

Angry at losing her plaything, she banged the block against the socket, attempting to get it to come back out. When that failed, she unsuccessfully tried to poke her chubby finger into the thin horizontal slit. Frustrated, tiring of the game, she sat under the table and realized she had found an entirely new place in the house to play. The shiny chrome of the table and chair legs drew her attention, and she experimented with the sound of the block against their smooth surfaces.

This would have entertained her until Ciel came, but the roach, thinking itself safe, ventured outside of the socket. Serena gave a cry of delight and attempted to catch her lost playmate, but it was too quick and darted back into the wall. She tried once again to poke her finger into the slit. Then a bright slender object, lying dropped and forgotten, came into her view. Picking up the fork, Serena finally managed to fit the thin flattened prongs into the electric socket.

Eugene was avoiding Ciel's eyes as he packed. "You know, baby, this is really a good deal after me bein' out of work for so long." He moved around her still figure to open the drawer that held his T-shirts and shorts. "And hell, Maine ain't far. Once I get settled on the docks up there, I'll be able to come home all the time."

"Why can't you take us with you?" She followed each of his movements with her eyes and saw herself being buried in the case under the growing pile of clothes.

" 'Cause I gotta check out what's happening before I drag you and the kid up there."

"I don't mind. We'll make do. I've learned to live on very little."

"No, it just won't work right now. I gotta see my way clear first."

"Eugene, please." She listened with growing horror to herself quietly begging.

"No, and that's it!" He flung his shoes into the suitcase.

"Well, how far is it? Where did you say you were going?" She moved toward the suitcase.

"I told ya—the docks in Newport."

"That's not in Maine. You said you were going to Maine."

"Well, I made a mistake."

"How could you know about a place so far up? Who got you the job?"

"A friend."

"Who?"

"None of your damned business!" His eyes were flashing with the anger of a caged animal. He slammed down the top of the suitcase and yanked it off the bed.

"You're lying, aren't you? You don't have a job, do you? Do you?"

"Look, Ciel, believe whatever the fuck you want to. I gotta go." He tried to push past her.

She grabbed the handle of the case. "No, you can't go."

"Why?"

Her eyes widened slowly. She realized that to answer that would require that she uncurl that week of her life, pushed safely up into her head, when she had done all those terrible things for that other woman who had wanted an abortion. She and she alone would have to take responsibility for them now. He must understand what those actions had meant to her, but somehow, he had meant even more. She sought desperately for the right words, but it all came out as—

"Because I love you."

"Well, that ain't good enough."

Ciel had let the suitcase go before he jerked it away. She looked at Eugene, and the poison of reality began to spread through her body like gangrene. It drew his scent out of her nostrils and scraped the veil from her eyes, and he stood before her just as he really was—a tall, skinny black man with arrogance and selfishness twisting his mouth into a strange shape. And, she thought, I don't feel anything now. But soon, very soon, I will start to hate you. I promise—I will hate you. And I'll never forgive myself for not having done it sooner—soon enough to have saved my baby. Oh, dear God, my baby.

Eugene thought the tears that began to crowd into her eyes were for him. But she was allowing herself this one last luxury of brief mourning for the loss of something denied to her. It troubled her that she wasn't sure exactly what that something was, or which one of them was to blame for taking it away. Ciel began to feel the over-powering need to be near someone who loved her. I'll get Serena and we'll go visit Mattie now, she thought in a daze.

Then they heard the scream from the kitchen.

The church was small and dark. The air hung about them like a stale blanket. Ciel looked straight ahead, oblivious to the seats filling up behind her. She didn't feel the damp pressure of Mattie's heavy arm or the doubt that invaded the air over Eugene's absence. The plaintive Merciful Jesuses, lightly sprinkled with sobs, were lost on her ears. Her dry eyes were locked on the tiny pearl-gray casket, flanked with oversized arrangements of red-carnationed bleeding hearts and white-lilied eternal circles. The sagging chords that came loping out of the huge organ and mixed with the droning voice of the black-robed old man behind the coffin were also unable to penetrate her.

Ciel's whole universe existed in the seven feet of space between herself and her child's narrow coffin. There was not even room for this comforting God whose melodious virtues floated around her sphere, attempting to get in. Obviously, He had deserted or damned her, it didn't matter which. All Ciel knew was that her prayers had gone unheeded—that afternoon she had lifted her daughter's body off the kitchen floor, those blank days in the hospital, and now. So she was left to do what God had chosen not to.

People had mistaken it for shock when she refused to cry. They thought it some special sort of grief when she stopped eating and even drinking water unless forced to, her hair went uncombed and her body unbathed. But Ciel was not grieving for Serena. She was simply tired of hurting. And she was forced to slowly give up the life that God had refused to take from her.

After the funeral the well-meaning came to console and offer their dog-eared faith in the form of coconut cakes, potato pies, fried chicken, and tears. Ciel sat in the bed with her back resting against the headboard; her long thin fingers, still as midnight frost on a frozen pond, lay on the covers. She acknowledged their kindnesses with nods of her head and slight lip movements, but no sound. It was as if her voice was too tired to make the journey from the diaphragm through the larynx to the mouth.

Her visitors' impotent words flew against the steel edge of her pain, bled slowly, and returned to die in the senders' throats. No one came too near. They stood around the door and the dressing table, or sat on the edges of the two worn chairs that needed upholstering, but they unconsciously pushed themselves back against the wall as if her hurt was contagious.

A neighbor woman entered in studied certainty and stood in the middle of the room. "Child, I know how you feel, but don't do this to yourself. I lost one, too. The Lord will . . ." And she choked, because the words were jammed down into her throat by the naked force of Ciel's eyes. Ciel had opened them fully now to look at the woman, but raw fires had eaten them worse than lifeless—worse

than death. The woman saw in that mute appeal for silence the rag-
ings of a personal hell flowing through Ciel's eyes. And just as she
went to reach for the girl's hand, she stopped as if a muscle spasm
had overtaken her body and, cowardly, shrank back. Reminiscences
of old, dried-over pains were no consolation in the face of this. They
had the effect of cold beads of water on a hot iron—they danced
and fizzled up while the room stank from their steam.

Mattie stood in the doorway, and an involuntary shudder went
through her when she saw Ciel's eyes. Dear God, she thought, she's
dying, and right in front of our faces.

"Merciful Father, no!" she bellowed. There was no prayer, no
bended knee or sackcloth supplication in those words, but a blasphemous fireball that shot forth and went smashing against the gates
of heaven, raging and kicking, demanding to be heard.

"No! No! No!" Like a black Brahman cow, desperate to protect
her young, she surged into the room, pushing the neighbor woman
and the others out of her way. She approached the bed with her lips
clamped shut in such force that the muscles in her jaw and the back
of her neck began to ache.

She sat on the edge of the bed and enfolded the tissue-thin body
in her huge ebony arms. And she rocked. Ciel's body was so hot it
burned Mattie when she first touched her, but she held on and
rocked. Back and forth, back and forth—she had Ciel so tightly she
could feel her young breasts flatten against the buttons of her dress.
The black mammoth gripped so firmly that the slightest increase of
pressure would have cracked the girl's spine. But she rocked.

And somewhere from the bowels of her being came a moan from
Ciel, so high at first it couldn't be heard by anyone there, but the
yard dogs began an unholy howling. And Mattie rocked. And then,
agonizingly slow, it broke its way through the parched lips in a spa-
ghetti-thin column of air that could be faintly heard in the frozen
room.

Ciel moaned. Mattie rocked. Propelled by the sound, Mattie
rocked her out of that bed, out of that room, into a blue vastness
just underneath the sun and above time. She rocked her over Aegean
seas so clean they shone like crystal, so clear the fresh blood of sacrificed babies torn from their mother's arms and given to Neptune
could be seen like pink froth on the water. She rocked her on and
on, past Dachau, where soul-gutted Jewish mothers swept their children's entrails off laboratory floors. They flew past the spilled brains
of Senegalese infants whose mothers had dashed them on the
wooden sides of slave ships. And she rocked on.

She rocked her into her childhood and let her see murdered
dreams. And she rocked her back, back into the womb, to the nadir

of her hurt, and they found it—a slight silver splinter, embedded just below the surface of the skin. And Mattie rocked and pulled—and the splinter gave way, but its roots were deep, gigantic, ragged, and they tore up flesh with bits of fat and muscle tissue clinging to them. They left a huge hole, which was already starting to pus over, but Mattie was satisfied. It would heal.

The bile that had formed a tight knot in Ciel's stomach began to rise and gagged her just as it passed her throat. Mattie put her hand over the girl's mouth and rushed her out the now-empty room to the toilet. Ciel retched yellowish-green phlegm, and she brought up white lumps of slime that hit the seat of the toilet and rolled off, splattering onto the tiles. After a while she heaved only air, but the body did not seem to want to stop. It was exorcising the evilness of pain.

Mattie cupped her hands under the faucet and motioned for Ciel to drink and clean her mouth. When the water left Ciel's mouth, it tasted as if she had been rinsing with a mild acid. Mattie drew a tub of hot water and undressed Ciel. She let the nightgown fall off the narrow shoulders, over the pitifully thin breasts and jutting hip-bones. She slowly helped her into the water, and it was like a dried brown autumn leaf hitting the surface of a puddle.

And slowly she bathed her. She took the soap, and, using only her hands, she washed Ciel's hair and the back of her neck. She raised her arms and cleaned the armpits, soaping well the downy brown hair there. She let the soap slip between the girl's breasts, and she washed each one separately, cupping it in her hands. She took each leg and even cleaned under the toenails. Making Ciel rise and kneel in the tub, she cleaned the crack in her behind, soaped her pubic hair, and gently washed the creases in her vagina—slowly, reverently, as if handling a newborn.

She took her from the tub and toweled her in the same manner she had been bathed—as if too much friction would break the skin tissue. All of this had been done without either woman saying a word. Ciel stood there, naked, and felt the cool air play against the clean surface of her skin. She had the sensation of fresh mint coursing through her pores. She closed her eyes and the fire was gone. Her tears no longer fried within her, killing her internal organs with their steam. So Ciel began to cry—there, naked, in the center of the bathroom floor.

Mattie emptied the tub and rinsed it. She led the still-naked Ciel to a chair in the bedroom. The tears were flowing so freely now Ciel couldn't see, and she allowed herself to be led as if blind. She sat on the chair and cried—head erect. Since she made no effort to wipe them away, the tears dripped down her chin and landed on her chest and rolled down to her stomach and onto her dark pubic hair. Ignoring Ciel, Mattie took away the crumpled linen and made the bed, stretching the sheets tight and fresh. She beat the pillows into a virgin plumpness and dressed them in white cases.

And Ciel sat. And cried. The unmolested tears had rolled down her parted thighs and were beginning to wet the chair. But they were cold and good. She put out her tongue and began to drink in their saltiness, feeding on them. The first tears were gone. Her thin shoulders began to quiver, and spasms circled her body as new tears came—this time, hot and stinging. And she sobbed, the first sound she'd made since the moaning.

Mattie took the edges of the dirty sheet she'd pulled off the bed and wiped the mucus that had been running out of Ciel's nose. She then led her freshly wet, glistening body, baptized now, to the bed. She covered her with one sheet and laid a towel across the pillow—it would help for a while.

And Ciel lay down and cried. But Mattie knew the tears would end. And she would sleep. And morning would come.

Terry McMillan

(1951–   )

THE AUTHOR of two very moving novels, *Mama* (1987) and *Disappearing Acts* (1989), Terry McMillan emerges as one of the newest voices in the African American literary arena. Born in 1951, in Port Huron, Mississippi, she received her B.S. in journalism from University of California at Berkeley in 1978 and attended the Masters of Fine Arts Film Program at Columbia University in 1979. Presently an associate professor in the creative writing department at the University of Arizona at Tucson, she has also held academic appointments in creative writing at Malcolm King College in New York and the University of Wyoming in Laramie.

In addition to teaching and writing two novels, McMillan is quite active contributing stories to literary quarterlies and magazines, writing book reviews, lecturing across the country, appearing on radio and television programs, and writing screenplays of her own fiction. Although she has declined offers to write for "The Cosby Show," "A Different World," "The Robert Guilliume Show," and "Bagdad Cafe," she is presently writing the screenplay of *Disappearing Acts* for Tri-Star Pictures, which will be made into a motion picture. *Disappearing Acts* is a beautiful, sometimes painful, yet optimistic story of a love affair between a black man and woman. Told from the point of view of both its protagonists, the novel gives us an inside look at the individual psyches of two black lovers who learn that in order for them to maintain a healthy relationship with another, they must first fight and conquer their own individual demons that stifle self-assurance and honest introspection.

Although *Mama*, McMillan's first novel, is stylistically and thematically different from *Disappearing Acts*, Mildred, the heroine mother of five children, undergoes a similar transformation when she, at the end of the novel, realizes that she must live for herself and release the interdependent emotional bond she has with her children, now grown-up themselves. Both *Mama* and *Disappearing Acts* are written in fast-moving, humorous, contemporary black speech that makes the reader feel that he or she knows the characters intimately.

McMillan has most recently edited *Breaking Ice: An Anthology of Contemporary African-American Fiction* (1990), the only collection of African American short stories in print to date. She has recently completed a novel entitled *Waiting to Exhale* and is at work on some children's books.

She has been awarded a 1988 National Endowment for the Arts Fellowship in literature, a 1986 New York Foundation for the Arts Fellowship, and the Doubleday/Columbia University Literary Fellowship.

The following selection is chapter 1 from *Disappearing Acts*.

FROM **DISAPPEARING ACTS**

1

I stood outside the apartment I came to look at, and my first impression was that the building was beautiful. That is, until I walked inside and saw that stairwell. Talk about old. The railing looked as rickety as the ones you see in horror movies, and the stairs were so dusty that when I put my foot on the first step, a claylike powder puffed up like a cloud under my dress, and I could've sworn they were going to collapse. I was making a mistake—I knew that already. Something had told me the ad sounded too good to be true: "Large one-bedroom, fully renovated brownstone, 10-foot ceilings, all new appliances, exposed brick, southern exposure, 10 minutes to Wall Street, close to shops, subway: $500."

I heard the sound of hammering from the top of the stairs, so I took my chances and ran up. Sawdust was flying around the white room like gold snow. I looked down, saw a curved red back, then a long arm flying up, thick black fingers grasping a hammer, and when it swung back down, the sound of the impact scared me. I jumped.

He look up, then stood. "What can I do for you?" he asked.

"Lord have mercy," was all I heard inside my head. I couldn't move, let alone speak. I really couldn't believe what I was seeing. This man had to be six foot something, because he was towering over me. His eyes looked like black marbles set in almonds. He wore a Yankees baseball cap, backward, and when he lifted it from his head to shake off the dust, his hair was jet black and wavy. That nose was strong and regal, and beneath it was a thick mustache. His cheeks looked chiseled; his lips succulent. And those shoulders. They were as wide as any linebacker's. His thighs were tight, and his legs went on forever. He was covered with dust, but when he pushed the sleeves of his red sweatshirt up to his elbows, his arms were the color of black grapes.

"Did you come to look at the apartment?" he asked

I cleared my throat and heard a word come out of my mouth. "Yes."

Then he smiled down at me, as if he was thinking about something that had happened to him earlier. "Well, we running behind schedule—as usual—and I don't know when we gon' be finished. I been trying to figure out how all these damn mice been getting in here. Ain't found it yet. And I don't know how the roaches and water bugs getting in here either. Tribes of 'em. We gon' have to fumigate this place good before anybody even *think* about moving in here."

Mice? Water bugs and roaches? This place is brand new. Was he joking? "Are you the owner?"

"I wish I was. He's back there." he said, pointing down a long hallway. "Hey, Vinney!" he yelled. "Somebody's here to see you, man."

Before I started in that direction, I did notice that the living room was big and shaped like an L. Three tall windows extended from the ceiling almost to the floor, which meant sunshine. The kitchen was over in a corner, but I could live with that. Halfway down the hall was the bathroom. I peeked in and turned on the light. I couldn't believe it. A sea-blue bathtub, toilet, and sink! And clean white tile on the floor and walls, and one of those orange lamps in the ceiling to help you dry off. So far so good. When I entered the doorway at the end of the hall, I was standing inside a sunny bedroom, with two more windows.

"Hello, Miss Banks," the owner said, then reached out to shake my hand. I shook his, even though it was filthy.

"Let me say first off that we'll be finished in a day or so. You like what you see?"

"The man up front said he didn't know when you'd be finished. He also said there were problems with bugs and mice."

"That's bullshit. First of all, like I said, we'll be finished in a day or two. And we ain't seen nothing crawling around in here except men. The place has been completely gutted—everything in here is brand-new. Frankie's known for being a jokester, but today he's pushing it."

Frankie? What a stupid name for such a striking man. "What's this little room over here?" I asked.

"Oh, that's just sort of a extra-large closet. It's too small to call it a bedroom, which is why we didn't put it in the ad. Perfect for a kid, though. But you said you didn't have kids. Use it for storage, whatever."

It was a tiny room, but I guessed I could squeeze my piano in. I walked over to the window. At least there were trees back there, even if they were in other people's yards. I looked down at the wooden planks under my feet. "What are you going to do to the floors?"

"We're laying the finest carpet available in every room except the kitchen area and bathroom. Sort of a beigy color—neutral, you know. That suit you?"

"There's no way you could put in hardwood floors?"

"You want the apartment? There's plenty of interest in it already. I coulda rented it this morning, but I knew you were coming, and I wanted to be fair, you know."

"If you can put in hardwood floors and guarantee that the stair-well won't look like it does now for too much longer, I'll take it."

"First off, when you renovate a whole building, you always save stairs till last, or they'd be worse off with all the ripping and running the men do up and down 'em. And hardwood floors? It'll cost you a few dollars extra for the labor, and'll add a few more days to the job."

"How much extra?"

"Not much, if you get pine. Don't worry, we can work something out. You positive you want wood? They collect dust like there ain't no tomorrow."

"I'm positive." I didn't care about the dust. When I first walked in here, I had already pictured shiny wood floors, not some drab carpet. And I hate beige. It's so boring.

"Frankie," he yelled. "Come in here a minute, would you?"

He walked back into the bedroom, ducking his head under the arch. I tried not to look directly at him, because I was thinking that I wished he came with the place. I tried, instead, to look indifferent.

"What's up, boss?" he asked sarcastically.

"Why'd you tell this young lady all those lies?"

He threw his arms up in the air and grinned. And had the nerve to have dimples. "I was just kidding, boss."

"One day all your kidding is gonna cost me money, Frankie. Any-way, she wants wood floors 'steada carpet. I want you to get over to Friendly Freddy's and get a estimate today. Can you have everything finished in four or five days?"

"Maybe," he said, lighting a cigarette. He blew the smoke up-ward, and my eyes watched his lips close around the filter again. I wished I was a cigarette.

"He'll have it done in five days," Vinney said. "If that's soon enough?"

"That's fine."

"Come on down the street to my office, and we can tidy up the particulars. Oh, hell, I ain't got any lease forms. I have to run to the stationery store and pick up some. You can help yourself to a cup of coffee. This won't take but a minute."

"Watch him," Frankie said to me. "He's Italian." I started to follow Vinney down the hall and had to brush past Frankie, because he acted like he didn't have any intention of moving out of my way. My breast wanted to brush against his chest, for the pure warmth alone, but I did just the opposite. When he saw this, he flung his arms up over his head and pressed himself stiffly against the wall. I ignored him and gave the place another once-over. Yep, I thought, I could definitely live here.

"Vinney just sold you a bunch of crap. You the first person to look at this place. This is a racket, they just call it business. See you in three weeks," Frankie said. He was back in the living room, driving more nails in the floor.

When the mover pulled up to my new home, Frankie was sitting out on the stoop in a tight white T-shirt, smoking a cigarette and drinking a Heineken. I swear, he looked like a black Marlboro Man without a hat and horse. Orchards of soft black hair were peeking out from the V, but I didn't want to stare. And muscles? They were everywhere. I wondered if he worked out or just worked hard. His face was drenched with sweat, and it looked like black tears were falling from his temples. I can't lie: I had to stop myself from walking over and patting them dry.

"Your bedroom floor is still wet, so you gon' have to put all this stuff in the living room."

"What? Vinney told me it was finished."

"It is *finished*; it just ain't dry."

Shit. I turned to the driver of the truck and explained the situation to him. He got out to open the back, and I put my hands on my hips and looked up at my windows. "Well, I'm here," I said, to no one in particular.

Frankie just kept on smoking.

When I'd hired the guy to help me move, he'd told me there'd be two of them, but this morning only he showed up. I'd asked some young guy who happened to be passing by if he wanted to make a quick forty dollars, and he jumped at it. Of course I didn't want him to know where I was moving, so I didn't ask him to come to Brooklyn. I had carried enough boxes myself, and now I was tired at the thought of hauling all this stuff upstairs. "Moving sure is hard labor," I sighed.

"Yes, it is," Frankie said, and took a sip from his beer. I thought maybe he'd at least offer to help, but he didn't.

"Would you mind giving me a hand?"

"I don't work for free."

Not only was he a handsome creep, I thought, but he was nasty. Even so, I couldn't carry all those heavy boxes up the stairs. "How much?"

"Not much," he said. He flicked his cigarette about three feet away and at the same time jumped off the stoop. For the next hour, I watched him lift and pull things off the truck. Those muscles kept popping up in his arms and shoulders, and he was sweating like crazy. And every time he walked past me, all I could think about was that I bet some woman loves to roll over into those arms at night.

It took close to two hours for us to get everything except the trunk upstairs. It was full of records, and I knew it was too heavy for one person to carry, so I offered to help, but Frankie refused. He slung it up in the air, balanced it on one shoulder, then walked on up the stairs like it weighed twenty pounds.

I paid the driver and ran upstairs. Frankie was busy pushing the larger things against the living room wall. Boxes were stacked everywhere, including on top of the couch. I walked back to the bedroom and stood in the doorway. Sunlight was streaming through the windows, and the floors looked like strips of gold. When I felt his presence behind me I turned around, and my nose grazed those soft black trees on his chest. My lips felt moist, and my heart was about to jump out of my chest. I inched away from him and almost stepped onto the wet floor, but Frankie grabbed my elbows and pulled me back into the hallway.

"Don't you mess up my floor," he said.

I was nervous, but I willed my mouth to talk. "You did a fantastic job on the floors, Frankie. Really. I didn't expect them to turn out this beautiful."

"Thanks," he said, turning back down the hallway and winking at me. "I try to do everything good."

I guess this was supposed to be his way of flirting. It must've been working, because all the air in the place seemed to be disappearing. I took a deep breath and prayed I could say what was necessary without sounding like I was going through any major changes. "How much do I owe you?"

"How much did you pay the white boy?"

"I gave him a hundred dollars."

Now, why did his eyes light up like that? "Was that too much? All the movers in the *Voice* asked for about the same."

"Naw, that wasn't too much."

"I've only got about thirty dollars in cash left, but if there's a cash machine in the neighborhood, I can go get more. I really appreciated your help."

"Keep your money."

"No, really. You earned it, and you said yourself you didn't work for free."

"I know what I said. A little charity every now and then won't kill me. So tell me, are you a Miss or a Mrs.?"

He sat down on a box and crossed his arms. Before I could tell him it was none of his business, I blurted out, "A Ms."

"Oh, so you one of those feminists?"

"What if I am?"

"I just asked. Does that mean you like women?"

"Give me a break, would you? Do I look like I like women?"

"Looks don't mean nothin' in this day and age. But to answer your question, no."

"Then you've got your answer." I started looking at box labels, to see which one had the dishes in it, not that I really needed a dish right then. He was making me nervous. Shit. Talk about being direct. I had to do something—anything—to keep moving, because he didn't act like he was getting ready to leave, and even though what he just asked me was tacky as hell, I didn't want him to leave yet either. "Can I ask *you* a question?"

"Only if it's personal."

"Is your real name Frankie?"

"No. It's Franklin. Why?"

"You just didn't look like a Frankie to me."

"You can call me Franklin if you want to."

Had I already given him the impression that I planned on seeing him again? Men. Not only are they presumptuous, but this one here can read minds.

"You ain't never been married?" he asked, lighting a cigarette.

"No," I said tartly, and started looking for something he could use for an ashtray.

"Don't get so touchy. I was just curious. What you gon' do with all this space?"

"Put it to good use."

"By yourself?"

He *would* have to make it sound like I'm a damn spinster or something, wouldn't he? "Yes," I said, and handed him a rusty can I found under the sink. It already had ashes in it, which meant it was probably his.

"How?"

"Why?" I asked.

"Because it seems awful funny that a single woman would pay

this much rent with all this space and live here by herself, that's why."

"I sing and play the piano, and I need all the space I can get. And compared to Manhattan, this is cheap. Does that answer your question, Franklin?"

He smiled at me. "A singer, huh?"

"Yes, a singer."

I spotted a box that looked like whatever was in it would look like I needed it. As I went to lift it, Franklin jumped up to help me. Damn, even his funk smelled good.

"What's your name again?" he asked, putting the box on top of the counter.

"Zora. Zora Banks."

"That's a helluva name. Suits you. I know you heard of Zora Neale Hurston, then, right? The writer?"

As much as I hated to admit it, I was becoming more impressed by the minute. "I was named after her."

"You recorded any albums? I'm pretty up on all kinds of music, and your name don't ring no bells."

I knew one thing—his grammar was terrible, but everything else seemed to be compensating for it. "Nope. No albums yet. I'm working on it."

"Well, what kind of music do you sing?"

"All kinds," I said.

"Is that what you gon' tell a record producer? That you sing *all* kinds of music?"

"You know, you sure ask a lot of questions."

He smiled. "How else you suppose to learn things if you don't ask?"

God, his teeth were white. "Well, to be honest, that's exactly what I'm working on, developing my own style."

"I always thought it was about feeling the music. Sing me a few notes."

"Sing you a few notes? Be serious. First of all, I've just barely got inside the door of my new apartment, I don't even know your last name, I'm not in a singing mood, and I'm tired."

"My last name is Swift. I can understand you being tired and everything, but I'd like to hear you sing one day. I don't meet many singers."

Swift was putting it mildly. He stood directly in front of me. He was doing this on purpose, I just knew it. Probably just wanted to see how long it would take me to melt. He was much too good at this. "So you're assuming I'll be seeing you again after today, is that it?"

"I can guarantee it," he said, walking toward the door. "We getting ready to start on the building two doors down."

Then he was gone. I stood there looking at the door like a fool, as if I was in a trance or something. I swear I couldn't move. I felt affected. And that door kept opening and closing, and each time it opened he would just stand there, looking right through me. To snap out of it, I had to shake my head back and forth until the door stayed closed. Then I went over to the sink and dangled my fingers under the water until they could feel that it was too damn hot.

I wanted to unpack my books, but I needed toggle bolts to put the shelves up. I'm terrible when it comes to doing things like that. There are some things I really don't want to learn how to do. I couldn't put my stereo together, because there's too many wires. Which means I'll have to pay somebody to do it, just like I've always done. The phone company was supposed to have been here by now, but of course they're late, so I couldn't call anybody. And last but not least, I was starving.

I walked down the dirty stairs and noticed that the door to the first-floor apartment was cracked open, so I peeked inside. I saw a disgusting shade of yellow tweed shag carpet. I'd been told two women were moving in tomorrow. "Dykes probably," Vinney had said, "Don't bother them, and they won't bother you." I walked out the front door and locked it.

The heat was piercing and the humidity thick. I was trying to decide which way to go. When I looked far to the right, I saw lots of traffic, which meant businesses, so I went that way. At the corner was a fish market, where I bought half a pound of scallops. Right next to it was a produce stand that sold everything from vegetables to Pampers. I bought broccoli, fresh mushrooms, scallions, a large bunch of flowers, paper towels, toilet paper, and white grape juice.

I decided to walk home around the block, to get a better feel for the neighborhood. Some gay guy was standing out in front of this gorgeous little gourmet shop, trying to entice people to come in.

"Free coffee samples to celebrate our grand opening," he said. "You look like a lady with good taste. Come on in, honey. Try some. It's divine."

"Thanks. Maybe another time." I'd only taken a few steps when the rich scent of coffee lured me back. He handed me a finely printed piece of peach-colored paper that described the store's specialties. All kinds of delicacies, imported foods, breads, every kind of cheese you could think of, dried fish, and pickled everything. I went inside, and staring me in the face were samples of white Scandinavian chocolate.

"Go ahead, it's fabulous," he said.

My fingers itched with desire, but I said, "No. I can't."

"Oh, come on. One little piece won't hurt. Go on. Splurge."

The next thing I knew, not only had I eaten a piece, I'd bought a quarter pound (which I vowed to stretch out over a week or two). I also got some dilled Havarti cheese, liver pâté, some kind of crackers I'd never heard of, and a pound of Vienna roast mixed with mocha Java.

"Come back again," he said, and I assured him I would.

Most of the neighborhood was still run down, and even though there were scaffolds everywhere I looked, it would be years before this area was pretty. "You moved here at the right time," Vinney had said. "In a few years everybody and their mother'll be flocking to Brooklyn from Manhattan. Who can afford that rent? This is what you call a changing neighborhood. It's the pits now, but stick around a few years, you won't even recognize it. You're getting this place at a steal, you know."

By the time I got home, I was drenched. I found the box with the towels in it and took a cool shower. Afterwards, I found the box with the cleansers and scrubbed the kitchen shelves inside and out. I didn't care that they were brand-new. I didn't ever want to see another roach. Then I pulled out the pots and pans, cooked dinner, and sat down on top of a box to eat. I sure wished I had some music. I put the flowers in water in my coffeepot and set them next to my plate. Lord only knew when I'd be able to afford a dining room set. The piano comes first.

That night, I slept on the living room floor. The couch was buried in boxes, and my platform bed wouldn't do me much good because I had thrown the mattress out. I made a pallet of three blankets and flipped one of them over me like a sleeping bag. Sometime during the middle of the night, I woke up. I heard a sound, like movement, but I couldn't tell where it was coming from. I was afraid to move, so I just lay there as still as I could. This was the worst part of living alone: when you're scared and don't have anybody to turn to. The noise was coming from the refrigerator. Please, God, don't let it be a mouse. Just the thought of seeing a ball of gray fur made my stomach turn. I got up slowly and went and knocked on the refrigerator door. If it was in there, it could run out the way it came in, and I wouldn't ever have to see it. I waited a few seconds, then opened the door slowly; the only thing inside was my leftover dinner and the things I'd bought. I felt relieved, but to be sure, I opened the freezer. A plastic box was filling up with oval-shaped ice cubes. I had completely forgotten about that damn ice-maker.

I lay back down and stared at the white walls, which now looked blue because of the street light shining through the windows. I closed my eyes, but they wouldn't stay shut. They kept seeing blue. I got up and went over to the counter and broke off a piece of chocolate and lay down again. This is how it always starts, Zora, I thought, then stomped to the bathroom and flushed the entire contents of the bag—including what was in my mouth—down the toilet.

I turned on the fan and stood in the middle of the living room, listening to it oscillate. The blankets felt cool on my bare feet, but it was hot as hell in here. I lay on top of the blankets and tried to go to sleep, but then my breasts started to throb, and I watched them rise and fall. Not tonight, I thought. I don't have the energy. My nipples hardened. This was their way of letting me know they needed to be touched, kissed—something. Without realizing it, I cupped both hands over them and started to massage them, I can't lie: I pretended they were Franklin's hands. Then a heart started beating between my legs. His hands slid down my belly, stroked the inside of my thighs until my body was electric. I couldn't help it when my legs flew open. And by the time his hands found the spot, moved in, and pressed down, I felt like a hot wet sponge being squeezed. My body jerked, and I couldn't stop shivering. I wanted him to kiss me forever, put his arms around me and hold me, keep me warm and safe. I gritted my teeth and squeezed my eyes tighter so I could keep my hands dropped to the floor. "I'm so tired of this," I said out loud. So I wiped my eyes, got under the sheet, and pulled it up to my chin. But I could've sworn Franklin said, "Don't stop now," so I pulled the pillow inside my arms until it felt like a man.

"Come on, baby," I heard him say, "Give it all to *me*." And that's exactly what I did.

In the morning, a knock at the door woke me up. I was lying in front of the stove; the blankets were over by a stack of boxes. I looked at my watch. It wasn't even seven o'clock. I got up from the floor, put on a cotton bathrobe, and opened the door without even thinking to ask who it was. Franklin was standing under the arch. I wiped the sleep from my eyes.

"You drink coffee?" he asked.

"Yes," I said, and let him in.

Henry Louis Gates, Jr.

(1950–   )

IN THE 1980s Henry Louis Gates became one of the most prominent names in American and African American literary circles. Born in 1950, in Keyser, West Virginia, he is the son of Henry Louis and the late Pauline Augusta Coleman Gates. Before completing his educational training, he worked as a general anesthetist in the Anglican Mission Hospital in Kilimatinde, Tanzania, from 1970 to 1971. He graduated summa cum laude with his B.A. from Yale University in 1973 and received his M.A. and Ph.D. degrees from Cambridge in 1974 and 1979 respectively.

Gates's professional career has been impressively diverse. His many articles and reviews have appeared in journals such as *Black World, Critical Inquiry, Yale Review, Black American Literature Forum, Antioch Review, Cultural Critique, New Literary History*, and the *New York Times Book Review*. He is the editor of *Black Is the Color of the Cosmos: Charles T. Davis's Essays on Black Literature and Culture* (1982, 1989); *In the House of Oshugbo: A Collection of Essays on Wole Soyinka* (1989); *The Slave's Narrative: Texts and Contexts* (1983), which he co-edited with Charles T. Davis; and *Black Literature and Literary Theory* (1984). In addition to being the general editor of the *Norton Anthology of Afro-American Literature* and of the Oxford University Press's extremely important thirty-volume series *The Schomburg Library of Nineteenth-Century Black Women Writers*, Gates is the author of two critical texts: *Figures in Black: Words, Signs, and the Racial Self* (1987) and *The Signifying Monkey: A Theory of Afro-American Literary Criticism* (1988). Gates's most recent publication is entitled *Reading Black, Reading Feminist: A Literary Critical Anthology* (1990).

In his attempts to correct the problem of the overabundance of sociological treatises that ignore the artistic beauty of African American literature, Gates uses post-structuralist literary theories to demonstrate the relationship between a black vernacular tradition and an African American literary tradition. As seems natural with criticism, all of his important pieces of criticism from "Preface to Blackness: Text and Pretext," found in Dexter Fisher and Robert Stepto's *Afro-American Literature: The Reconstruction of Instruction* (1979) to *The Signifying Monkey* illustrate a single purpose: the development of Gates's consistent effort to construct an African American literary theory that explores the signs or structures of the black text.

The consistency of Professor Gates's work extends beyond his literary

917

analyses. His discovery of the first published novel by an African American woman writer not only exemplifies his scholarly investigative skills, but also corrects one of the many errors in the annals of African American literary history. His edition of Harriet Wilson's *Our Nig: or, Sketches from the Life of a Free Black* (1983) is now a standard text in many courses in African American literature. In 1982 he created the television series "The Image of the Black in the Western Imagination" for Public Broadcasting Service. He is a member of the editorial boards of *Cultural Critique* and *Critical Inquiry* as well as book review editor of *Black American Literature Forum*. He is currently director of the Afro-American Studies Department at Harvard University.

Gates is a recipient of numerous grants and fellowships, among them, a Carnegie Foundation Fellowship, a Mellon Fellowship, grants from the National Endowment for the Humanities, an A. Whitney Griswold Fellowship, a Rockefeller Foundation Fellowship, and the most prestigious MacArthur Prize Fellowship.

For further reading, see *Dictionary of Literary Biography, Volume 67* and Linda Metzger, ed., *Black Writers: A Selection of Sketches from Contemporary Authors* (1989).

The following section comes from chapter 1 of *Figures in Black*.

LITERARY THEORY AND THE BLACK TRADITION

We have dreamed a dream, and there is no interpreter of it.
Genesis 40:8

Criticism is the habitus *of the contemplative intellect, whereby we try to recognize with probability the genuine quality of a literary work by using appropriate aids and rules.*

. . . The interpreter must know the writer's idiom well, aim at truth without partiality and inquire into the true and false reading.

Note. A painter is known by his painting, a writer by his writing.

The art of interpretation or hermeneutics is the habitus *of the contemplative intellect of probing into the sense of a somewhat special text by using logical rules and suitable means.*

*Note. Hermeneutics differs from criticism as the species does
from the genus and the part does from the whole.
. . . In every interpretation there occur the author, the literary
work, and the interpreter.*

> Antonius Guillelmus Amo, an African from Guinea.
> "On Criticism, Hermeneutics, Method,"
> *Treatise on the Art of Philosophising
> Soberly and Accurately* (1738)

I

The idea of a determining formal relationship between literature and
social institutions does not in itself explain the sense of urgency that
has, at least since the publication in 1760 of *A Narrative of the Uncommon Sufferings and Surprising Deliverance of Briton Hammon, a
Negro Man*, characterized nearly the whole of Afro-American writing.
This idea has often encouraged a posture that belabors the social and
documentary status of black art. Indeed, the earliest discrete examples of written discourse by the slave and ex-slave came under a
scrutiny not primarily literary. Black formal writing, beginning with
the five autobiographical slave narratives published in English between 1760 and 1789, was taken to be collective as well as functional. Because these narratives documented the black's potential for
"culture"—that is, for manners and morals—the command of written English virtually separated the African from the Afro-American,
the slave from the ex-slave, titled property from fledgling human
being. Well-meaning abolitionists cited these texts as proof of the
common humanity of bondsman and lord, yet these same texts also
demonstrated the contrary for slavery's proponents: the African
imagination was merely derivative.

The command of a written language, then, could be no mean
thing in the life of the slave. Learning to read, the slave narratives
repeat again and again, was a decisive political act; learning to write,
as measured against an eighteenth-century scale of culture and society, was an irreversible step away from the cotton field toward a
freedom larger even than physical manumission. What the use of
language entitled for personal social mobility and what it implied
about the public Negro mind made for the onerous burden of literacy, a burden having very little to do with the use of language as
such, a burden so pervasive that the nineteenth-century quest for literacy and the twentieth-century quest for form became the central,
indeed controlling, metaphors (if not mythical matrices) in Afro-
American narrative. Once the private dream fused with a public and
therefore political imperative, the Negro arts were committed; the

pervasive sense of urgency and fundamental unity of the black arts became a millennial, if not precisely apocalyptic, force.

I do not mean to suggest that these ideas were peculiar to eighteenth-century criticism of black texts. For example, William K. Wimsatt argues that we learn from Herder's Prize Essay of 1773 on the *Causes of the Decline of Taste in Different Nations* that in Germany "the appreciation of various folk and Gothic literatures and the comparative study of ancient, eastern, and modern foreign literatures (the criticism of literature by age and race) were strongly established, and these interests profoundly affected theories about the nature of literature as the expression of, or the power that shaped, human cultures or human nature in general." Wimsatt also reminds us that Friedrick Schlegel "only accented an already pervasive view when he called poetry the most specifically human energy, the central document of any culture."[1] It should not surprise us, then, that *Poems on Various Subjects, Religious and Moral, by Phillis Wheatley, Negro Servant to Mr. Wheatley of Boston*, the first book of poems published by an African in English, became almost immediately after its publication in London in 1773 the international antislavery movement's most salient argument of the African's innate mental equality. That the book went to five printings before 1800 testified far more to its acceptance as a "legitimate" product of "the African muse," as Henri Grégoire wrote in 1808, than to the merit of its sometimes vapid elegaic verse.[2] The eighteen signatures, or "certificates of authenticity," that preface the book, including one by John Hancock and another by the governor of Massachusetts, Thomas Hutchinson, meant to "leave no doubt, that [Phillis Wheatley] is its author."[3] Literally scores of public figures—from Voltaire to George Washington, from Benjamin Rush to Benjamin Franklin—reviewed Wheatley's book, yet virtually no one discussed the book as poetry. It was an unequal contest: the documentary status of black art assumed priority over mere literary judgment; criticism rehearsed content to justify one notion of origins or another. Of these discussions, Thomas Jefferson's proved most central to the shaping of the Afro-American critical activity.

Asserted primarily to debunk the exaggerated claims of the aboli-

---

[1] William K. Wimsatt and Cleanth Brooks, *Literary Criticism: A Short History* (New York: Knopf, 1969), p. 360.

[2] *De la littérature des nègres, ou recherches sur leurs facultés intellectuelles, leurs qualités morales, et leur littérature* (Paris: Maradan, 1808), p. 140.

[3] Eugene Parker Chase, *Our Revolutionary Forefathers, The Letters of Francois Marquis de Barbé-Marbois during His Residence in the United States as Secretary of the French Legation, 1779–1884* (New York: Duffield, 1929), pp. 84–85.

tionists, Thomas Jefferson's remarks on Phillis Wheatley's poetry, as well as on Ignatius Sancho's posthumously published *Letters* (1782), exerted a prescriptive influence over the criticism of the writing of blacks for the next 150 years. "Never yet," Jefferson prefaces his discussion of Wheatley, "could I find a Black that had uttered a thought above the level of plain narration; never seen even an elementary trait of painting or sculpture." As a specimen of the human mind, Jefferson continues, Wheatley's poems, as poetry, did not merit discussion. "Religion," he writes, "indeed has produced a Phillis Whately [sic] but it could not produce a poet." "The compositions published under her name," Jefferson concludes, "are below the dignity of criticism. The heroes of the *Dunciad* are to her, as Hercules to the author of the poem." As for Sancho's *Letters*, Jefferson says:

> His imagination is wild and extravagant, escapes incessantly from every restraint of reason and taste, and, in the course of its vagaries, leave a tract of thought as incoherent and eccentric, as is the course of a meteor through the sky. His subjects should have led him to a process of sober reasoning: yet we find him always substituting sentiment for demonstration.[4]

The substitution of sentiment for demonstration is the key opposition in this passage, pitting unreflective emotion against reason. Writing, as I shall argue, was a principle sign of reason, especially since the *spoken* language of black people had become an object of parody at least since 1769 when *The Padlock* appeared on the American stage, including among its cast of characters a West Indian slave called Mungo. We know Mungo's essence by his language, a language represented by a caricature that signifies the difference that separated white from black:

> Me supper ready, and now me go to the
>   cellar—But I
> say, Massa, ax de old man now,
>   what good him watching do, him
> bolts, and him bars, him walls,
> and him padlocks.[5]

No, blacks could not achieve any true presence by speaking, since their "African"-informed English seems to have only underscored their status as *sui generis*, as distinct in spoken language use as in their peculiarly "black" color. If blacks were to signify as full

---

[4]*Notes on the State of Virginia* (London: Stockdale, 1787), book II, p. 196.

[5]These lines, along with an engraving of Ira Aldridge by T. Hollis, were combined to form a popular nineteenth-century broadside. The lines are from Act 2, Scene 1.

members of the Western human community, they would have to do
so in their writings.

Even before Jefferson allowed himself the outrageous remark that
"the improvement of the blacks in body and mind, in the first instance of their mixture with the whites, has been observed by every
one, and provides that their inferiority is not the effect merely of
their condition of life," advocates of the unity of the human species
had forged a union of literary tradition, individual talent, and innate
racial capacity. Phillis Wheatley's "authenticators," for instance, announced:

> We whose Names are under-written, do assure the world, that the
> POEMS specified in the following Page, were (as we verily believe) writ-
> ten by *Phillis*, a young Negro Girl, who was but a few years since,
> brought an uncultured Barbarian from Africa, and has ever since been
> and now is, under the Disadvantage of serving as a Slave of a Family in
> this Town. She has been examined by some of the best judges, and is
> thought qualified to write them.[6]

Further, Wheatley herself asks indulgence of the critic, consider-
ing the occasion of her verse. "As her Attempts in Poetry are now
sent into the World, it is hoped the critic will not severely censure
their Defects; and we presume they have too much Merit to be cast
aside with contempt, as worthless and trifling effusions." Wheatley
clearly could not imagine a critic as harsh as Jefferson. "With all
their Imperfections," she concludes, "the poems are now humbly
submitted to the Perusal of the Public." Other than the tone of the
author's preface, there was little here that was "humbly submitted" to
Wheatley's public. Her volume generated much speculation about
the nature of the "African imagination." So compelling did evidence
of the African's artistic abilities prove to be to Enlightenment speculation on the idea of progress and the precise shape of the *scala na-
turae* that just nine years after Wheatley's *Poems* appeared, more
than one thousand British lords and ladies subscribed to have Ignatius Sancho's collected letters published. Even more pertinent in our
context, Joseph Jekyll, M.P., prefaced the volume with a full biographical account of the colorful Sancho's life, structured curiously
around the received relation between "genius" and "species."

British readers were fascinated by the "African mind" presented
in the collected letters by Ignatius Sancho. Sancho was named "from
a fancied resemblance to the Squire to Don Quixote" and had his
portrait painted by Gainsborough and engraved by Bartolozzi. He
was a correspondent with Garrick and Sterne and, apparently, some-

---

[6]Phillis Wheatley, *Poems* (Philadelphia: A. Bell, 1773), p. vii.

thing of a poet as well. "A commerce with the Muses was supported amid the trivial and momentary interruptions of a shop," Jekyll writes. Indeed, not only were "the Poets studied and even imitated with some success," but "two pieces were constructed for the stage." Moreover, Sancho composed and published musical compositions. In addition to his creative endeavors, Sancho was a critic—perhaps the first African critic of the arts to write in English. His "theory of Music was discussed, published and dedicated to the Princess Royal, and Painting was so much within the circle of Ignatius Sancho's judgment and criticism," Jekyll observes, "that several artists paid great *deference* to his opinion."[7]

Jekyll's rather involved biography is a pretext to display the artifacts of the "sable mind," as was the very publication of the *Letters* themselves. "*Her* motives for laying them before the publick," the publisher admits, "were the desire of showing that an untutored African may possess abilities equal to an European." Sancho was an "extraordinary Negro," his biographer relates, although he was a bit better for being a bit bad. "Freedom, riches, and leisure, naturally led to a disposition of African tendencies into indulgences; and that which dissipated the mind of Ignatius completely drained the purse," Jekyll puns. "In his attachment to women, he displayed a profuseness which not unusually characterizes the excess of the passion." "Cards had formerly seduced him," we are told, "but an unsuccessful contest at cribbage with a jew, who won his cloaths, had determined to abjure the propensity which appears to be innate among his countrymen." Here again we see drawn the thread between phylogeny and ontogeny. "A French writer relates," Jekyll explains, "that in the kingdoms of Ardrah, Whydah, and Benin, a Negro will stake at play his fortune, his children, and his liberty." Thus driven to distraction, Sancho was "induced to consider the stage" since "his complexion suggested an offer to the manager of attempting Othello and Oroonoko; but a defective and incorrigible *articulation* rendered it abortive" (emphasis added).

Colorful though Jekyll's anecdotes are, they are a mere pretext for the crux of his argument: a disquisition on cranial capacity, regional variation, skin color, and intelligence. The example of Sancho, made particularly human by the citation of his foibles, is meant to put to rest any suspicion about the native abilities of the Negro:

> Such was the man whose species philosophers and anatomists have endeavored to degrade as a deterioration of the human; and such was the

---

[7]*Letters of the Late Ignatius Sancho, an African* (London: J. Nichols and C. Dilly, 1783), p. vii.

man whom [Thomas] Fuller, with the benevolence and quaintness of phrase peculiarly his own, accounted "God's Image, though cut in Ebony." To the harsh definition of the naturalist, oppressions political and legislative have added; and such are hourly aggravated towards this unhappy race of men by vulgar prejudice and popular insult. To combat these on commercial principles, has been the labour of [others]—such an effort here [he concludes ironically] would be an impertinent digression.[8]

That Sancho's attainments are not merely isolated exceptions to the general morass is indicated by the state of civilization on the African "slave-coast." Jekyll continues:

Of those who have speculatively visited and described the slave-coast, there are not wanting some who extol the mental abilities of the natives. [Some] speak highly of their mechanical powers and indefatigable industry. [Another] does not scruple to affirm, that their ingenuity rivals the Chinese.

What is more, these marks of culture and capacity signify an even more telling body of data, since the logical extensions of mechanical powers and industry are sublime arts and stable polity:

He who could penetrate the interior of Africa, might not improbably discover negro arts and polity, which could bear little analogy to the ignorance and grossness of slaves in the sugar-islands, expatriated in infamy; and brutalized under the whip and the task-master.

"And he," Jekyll summarizes, "who surveys the extent of intellect to which Ignatius Sancho had attained self-education, will perhaps conclude, that the perfection of the reasoning faculties does not depend on the colour of a common integument."

Jekyll's preface became a touchstone for the literary anthropologists who saw in black art a categorical repository for the African's potential to *deserve* inclusion in the human community. Echoes of Jekyll's language resound throughout the prefaces to slave testimony. Gustavus Vassa's own claim in 1789 that the African's contacts with "liberal sentiments" and "the Christian religion" have "exalted human nature" is vouched for by more than one hundred Irish subscribers. Charles Ball's editor asserts in 1836 that Ball is "embued by nature with a tolerable portion of intellect capacity."[9] Both Garrison's and Phillips's prefaces to *The Narrative of the Life of Frederick Douglass* (1845) and James McCune Smith's introduction to Douglass's *My*

---

[8]Sancho, pp. xiv–xvi.
[9]Charles Ball, *Fifty Years in Chains; Or, The Life of an American Slave* (New York: H. Dayton, 1858), p. 3.

Bondage and My Freedom (1855) attest to Douglass's African heritage, former bestial status, and intellectual abilities. McCune Smith, a black physician, proffers the additional claims for literary excellence demanded by the intensity of doubt toward the black African's mental abilities:

> The Negro, for the first time in the world's history brought in full contact with high civilization, must prove his title first to all that is demanded for him; in the teeth of unequal chances, he must prove himself equal to the mass of those who oppress him—therefore, absolutely superior to his apparent fate, and to their relative ability. And it is most cheering to the friends of freedom, to-day, that evidence of this equality is rapidly accumulating, not from the ranks of the half-breed colored people of the free states, but from the very depths of slavery itself; the indestructible equality of man to man is demonstrated by the ease with which black men, scarce one remove from barbarism—if slavery can be honored with such a distinction—vault into the high places of the most advanced and painfully acquired civilization.[10]

An 1845 review of Douglass's *Narrative* emphasizes the relevance of each "product" of the African mind almost as another primary argument in the abolitionist's brief against slavery:

> Considered merely as a narrative, we have never read one more simple, true, coherent, and warm with genuine feeling. It is an excellent piece of writing, and on that score to be prized as a specimen of the powers of the black race, which prejudice persists in disputing. We prize highly all evidence of this kind, and it is becoming more abundant.[11]

If an abolitionist reviewer in 1845 would admit that "we prize highly all evidence of this kind," he was only summarizing an antislavery emphasis that was at least a century and a half old. Wheatley and Sancho, and much later even the articulate ex-slave Frederick Douglass, commenced their public careers as the result of experiments to ascertain just how much "natural capacity" lay dormant in the "sable mind." Several enlightened aristocrats in the first half of the eighteenth century abstracted individual black children from the daily routine of slavery and educated them with their own children in experiments to ascertain if the "perfectibility of man" applied equally to blacks and to whites. What was at stake in these experiments was nothing less than the determination of the place of the African on the Great Chain of Being, a place that hovered rather precariously well beneath the European (and every other) "race of

---

[10]Introduction, *My Bondage and My Freedom* (New York: Miller, Orton, and Mulligan, 1855), pp. xvii–xxxi.
[11]*New York Tribune*, June 10, 1845, p. 1. Rpt. in *Liberator*, May 30, 1845, p. 97.

man," yet just above—or parallel to—that place reserved for the "orang-outang." As Edward Long put the matter in *The History of Jamaica* (1774), there was a *natural* relation between the ape and the African, and

> If such has been the intention of the Almighty, we are then perhaps to regard the orang-outang as,
> > —the lag of human kind,
> > Nearest to brutes, by God design'd.

For Long, the ape and the African were missing links, sharing "the most intimate connexion and consanguinity," including even "amorous intercourse." While it might sound hyperbolic to state this today, enlightened antislavery advocates turned to writing to determine and to demonstrate in the most public way just how far removed from the ape the African was in fact. Let us examine briefly four instances of blacks whose literacy would serve as an argument against the bestial status of all black people.

Literacy—the literacy of formal writing—was both a technology and a commodity. It was a commodity with which the African's right to be considered a human being could be traded. The slave narratives repeat figures of the complex relationship between freedom and literacy. But well before the first slave narrative was published, the freedom of literacy became inscribed in the curious education of Wilhelm Amo. In 1707, Amo, at the age of four an African slave, was given to the reigning Duke of Brunswick-Wolfenbuttel as a gift. The duke, in turn, gave the slave as a present to his son, Augustus Wilhelm. Augustus Wilhelm ascended the throne in 1714 and became the influential protector and benefactor of the young slave. Amo was christened Anton Wilhelm in 1708 and was educated in the same manner as were the other children of the royal family. Amo matriculated at the Prussian University of Halle on June 9, 1727. In 1732, he defended his thesis, entitled "De jure Maurorum in Europa," and was promoted to the academic degree of a Candidate of the Laws. In 1730, he received the degree of Magister of Philosophy and Liberal Arts at the University of Wittenberg, a degree to be renamed Doctor of Philosophy within a few years. In 1734, Amo published a dissertation entitled *Inaugural philosophical dissertation on the APATHY of the human mind, or the absence of feeling and the faculty of feeling in the human mind and the presence of them in our organic living body*, a thesis on a subject that borders upon psychology and the medical sciences. In 1738, Amo published his treatise on logic, from which the second epigraph of this book is taken, while a university lecturer at Halle. In 1739, Amo assumed a position in the Faculty of Philosophy of Jena. Not much else is known of

Amo's life. Fredrick Blumenbach in 1787 wrote that he had been appointed Councillor at the court of the Prussian king some time between 1740 and 1750. We do know, however, that in 1753 Amo was living back in Africa, near his birthplace on the Gold Coast, known today as Ghana, where he lived as a hermit and was widely known as a magician and a doctor. We also know that Amo returned to Africa willingly.[12]

What is remarkable about Amo's life and writings is that during his lifetime and throughout the Enlightenment they were seized upon by philosophers and critics as proof that the African was innately equal to the European, because this one African had demonstrated mastery of the arts and sciences. His thesis supervisor, for example, wrote that just as Terence, Tertullian, St. Cyprian, and St. Augustine had done for North Africa, Amo proved that those parts of sub-Saharan Africa, populated by beings whose humanity was in doubt, could produce superior intellects. Amo, moreover, demonstrated that from among other "uncivilized" nations outstanding individuals could emerge with the proper formal training.

Let us examine another instance of this curious phenomenon, one that occurred well beyond the confines and luxuries of the palace and the academy. One early eighteenth-century slave's experiences represent the relationship between freedom and literacy dramatically and more directly, indeed, than would seem possible. Job, the son of Solomon (Suleiman), a priest of the Fulani, apparently was a person of some distinction in West Africa, until he was captured by the Mandingos and sold into slavery in 1731. From a plantation in Maryland, Job wrote a letter in Arabic to his father. Mail services between early eighteenth-century Maryland and Senegal, of course, were not quite as direct as they are today. Job, now a slave, had absolutely no chance of seeing a letter written in Arabic reach his African father. This letter, nevertheless, by a remarkable set of accidents eventually came into the possession of James Oglethorpe, one of the founders of the colony of Georgia and then the

---

[12]On Amo, see Wolfram Suchier, "A. W. Amo, Ein Mohr als Student und Privatdozent der Philosophie in Halle, Wittenburg and Iena, 1727–1740," *Akademische Rundschau,* Leipzig (1916) and "Weiteres über den Mohren Amo," *Altsachen Zeitschrift des Altsachenbundes für Heimatschutz und Heimatkunde,* Holminden, Nos. 1–2 (1981); Norbert Lochner, "Anton-Wilhelm Amo," *Transactions of the Historical Society of Ghana,* vol. III (1958); William Abraham, "The Life and Times of Anton-Wilhelm Amo," *Transactions of the Historical Society of Ghana,* vol. VII (1964); and Paulin J. Hountondji, "An African Philosopher in Germany in the Eighteenth Century," in *African Philosophy: Myth and Reality* (Bloomington: Indiana University Press, 1983), chapter V. Amo's work was translated into English in 1968 under the title *Antonius Gulielmus Amo Afer of Axim in Ghana, Translation of His Works* (Martin Luther University: Halle).

deputy governor of the Royal African Company. Oglethorpe sent the Arabic text up to Oxford, where the Huguenot John Gagnier held the Laudian Chair of Arabic. Gagnier's translation so moved Oglethorpe—about whom Pope wrote, "One, driv'n by strong Benevolence of Soul / Shall fly, like Oglethorpe, from Pole to Pole"—and so impressed him with the strength of Job's character that in June 1732 he gave his bond for the payment of this slave at the price of forty-five pounds. Job, I should add, came to London, was the toast of the Duke of Montague (who would soon thereafter repeat the Duke of Brunswick's experiment with Wilhelm Amo and become patron to Francis Williams and Ignatius Sancho) and of the British royal family, and fourteen months later in 1734 returned, as did Amo, to his father's land. Job Ben Solomon literally wrote his way out of slavery; his literacy, translated into forty-five pounds, was the commodity with which he earned his escape price.[13]

Lest we think that Job's was an isolated incident, there were dozens of instances of this use of literacy as a commodity. As late as 1829, in this country, George Moses Horton's master at North Carolina collected his slave's poems, published them as a book, and then falsely advertised widely in Northern black and antislavery newspapers that all proceeds from the book's sales would be used to purchase Horton's freedom! However, royalties of the 1879 edition of Francisco Calcagno's *Poetas de Color*, published at Habana, were used to purchase the freedom of the slave poet, José de Carme Díaz.

There were many other such experiments: "el negro" Juan Latino, who published three books of poems in Latin at Granada between 1573 and 1576; Jacobus Capitein, who graduated from the University of Leyden in 1742 and whose thesis was published in Latin and in Dutch that same year; and Phillis Wheatley, who in 1773 became the first African to publish a book of poems in English. All three, among several others, were the subject of experiments in literature mastery, whose lives and works came to serve as black figures for the idea of progress and the perfectibility of man, as well as human synecdoches for the capacity of the African to assume a parallel rank with the European on the Great Chain of Being.

Amo and his fellow writers, Othello's countrymen, suffered under the sheer burden of literacy: to demonstrate that the person of African descent was indeed a human being. Amo was not competing, as it were, with Newton; he was distinguishing himself from the apes. How curious, how arbitrary that the written word, as early as 1700,

---

[13]On Job-Ben Solomon, see Charles T. Davis and Henry Louis Gates, Jr., *The Slave's Narrative* (New York: Oxford University Press, 1985), pp. 2–3.

signified the presence of a common humanity with the European. Any serious theory of the nature and function of writing in the Western tradition must, to put it bluntly, take the critical reception to this unique genre into full account. What more meaningful example of the eighteenth century's theories of writing can possibly exist? What a profoundly burdensome task to impose upon the philosopher such as Amo—indeed, to impose upon the human being. What an ironic origin of a literary tradition! If Europeans read the individual achievements of blacks in literature and scholarship as discrete commentaries of Africans themselves upon the Western fiction of the "text of blackness," then the figure of blackness as an absence came to occupy an ironic place in the texts of even the most sober European philosophers. In the next section of this chapter, I wish to outline the repetition of the relationship between blackness and writing, so that I may begin to demonstrate how the strategies of negation, so central to Black Aesthetic criticism, were locked in a relation of thesis to antithesis to a racist discourse embedded in Western philosophy.

V

Black literature and its criticism, then, have been put to uses that were not primarily aesthetic; rather, they have formed part of a larger discourse on the nature of the black and his or her role in the order of things. The integral relation between theory and a literary text, therefore, which so often in other traditions has been a sustaining relation, in our tradition has been an extraordinarily problematical one. The relationship among theory, tradition, and integrity within the black literary tradition has not been, and perhaps cannot be, a straightforward matter at all.

Let us consider the etymology of the word *integrity*, which I take to be the keyword in the subject of the relationship between the black tradition and theory. *Integrity* is a curious keyword to address in a period of bold and sometimes exhilarating speculation and experimentation, two other words that aptly characterize literary criticism generally, and Afro-American criticism specifically, at the present time. The Latin origin of the English word, *integritas*, connotes wholeness, entireness, completeness, chastity, and purity, most of which are descriptive terms that made their way frequently into the writings of the American "New Critics," who seem not to have cared particularly for or about the literature of Afro-Americans. Two of the most common definitions of *integrity* elaborate upon the sense of wholeness, derived from the Latin original. Let me cite these here, as taken from the *Oxford English Dictionary:*

1. The condition of having no part or element taken away or wanting; undivided or unbroken state; material wholeness, completeness, entirety; something undivided; an integral whole.
2. The condition of not being marred or violated; unimpaired or uncorrupted condition; original perfect state; soundness.

It is the second definition of *integrity*—that is to say, connoting the absence of violation and corruption, the preservation of an initial wholeness or soundness—which I would like to consider in this deliberation upon theory and the black tradition, or more precisely upon that relationship which ideally should obtain between Afro-American literature and the theories we fabricate to account for its precise nature and shape.

It is probably true that critics of Afro-American literature (which, by the way, I employ as a less ethnocentric designation than "the black American critic") are more concerned with the complex relationship between literature and literary theory than we have ever been before. There are many reasons for this, not the least of which is our increasingly central role in the profession, precisely when our colleagues in other literatures are engulfed in their own extensive debates about the intellectual merit of so very much theorizing. Theory, as a second-order reflection upon a primary gesture such as literature, has always been viewed with deep mistrust and suspicion by those scholars who find it presumptuous and perhaps even decadent when criticism claims the right to stand as discourse on its own, as a parallel textual universe to literature. Theoretical texts breed other, equally decadent theoretical responses, in a creative process that can be remarkably far removed from a poem or a novel.

For the critic of Afro-American literature, this process is even more perilous precisely because the large part of contemporary literary theory derives from critics of Western European languages and literatures. Is the use of theory to write about Afro-American literature, we might ask rhetorically, merely another form of intellectual indenture, a form of servitude of the mind as pernicious in its intellectual implications as any other form of enslavement? This is the issue raised, for me at least, not only by the notion of the word *integrity* in this context but also by my own work in critical theory over the last ten years. Does the propensity to theorize about a text or a literary tradition mar, violate, impair, or corrupt, the soundness of an "original perfect state" of a black text or of the black tradition? This is the implied subject of this book, which I try to address in several ways.

To be sure, this matter of criticism and integrity has a long and ironic history in black letters. It was Hume, we recall, who called the Jamaican poet of Latin verse, Francis Williams, "a parrot who merely speaks a few words plainly"; and Phillis Wheatley has for far too long suffered from the spurious attacks of black and white critics alike for being the original *rara avis* of a school of so-called mockingbird poets, whose use and imitation of received European and American literary conventions has been regarded, simply put, as a corruption itself of a "purer" black expression, privileged somehow in black artistic forms such as the blues, Signifyin(g), the spirituals, and the Afro-American dance. Can we, as critics, escape the mockingbird trap? Can we signify only as critical monkeys?

These are some of the questions that have been debated heatedly by critics of Afro-American literature in the past few years. For example, a conference of twenty-eight college professors, grouped together at Yale for two weeks during the summer of 1977, prefaced their summarizing statement (which outlined the nature and function of black literary criticism) with the premise that "Afro-American literature is, above all, an act of language." The conference itself, funded by the National Endowment for the Humanities, sponsored by the Modern Language Association, and jointly directed by Robert Burns Stepto, Assistant Professor of English at Yale, and Dexter Fisher, then Program Coordinator of the MLA's Commission on Minority Literatures, seemed determined to refute certain received notions of the relationship between black art and black social and political status within American society. Among these presuppositions are the following formulations: that black literature is primarily raw data or cultural artifact for the social scientist determined to explicate the "true nature" of black people; that there is a correlation between a people's artistic excellence and its political authority; and, especially, that the corpus of creative writing by Africans and Afro-Americans, dark and mysterious and foreboding as it might be, is not open to legitimate literary analysis by critics of any "intellectual complexion" employing all of the remarkably sophisticated tools of explication now at their disposal. Further and most crucially, the conference seemed to argue, just as we read and reread Joyce's *Ulysses* more to discover the art of the novel than to remark at the manners and morals of a Dublin Jew, so too must we read the works of black authors as discrete manifestations of form and genre and as implicit commentaries on the white literature of similar structure. The conference itself, in short, represented an attempt to take the "mau-mauing" out of the black literary criticism that defined the "Black Aesthetic Movement" of the sixties and transform it into a valid field of intellectual inquiry once again.

That the conference boldly and successfully addressed these matters is as remarkable as the very need to speak at all. Only ten years
ago, the shared polemic of black criticism was that "blackness" existed as some mythical and mystical absolute, an entity so subtle,
sublime, and unspeakable that only the "very black" racial initiate
could ever begin to trace its contours, let alone force it to utter its
darkest secrets. As I have argued above, our critics' hermeneutical
circle was a mere tautology; only black people could think black
thoughts, and therefore only the black critic could rethink, and
hence criticize, a black text.

Not only the theory but also the practice of black literature has,
for two hundred years, grown stunted within these dubious ideological shadows. The content of a black work of art has, with few but
notable exceptions, assumed primacy in normative analysis, at the
expense of the judgment of form. What's more, many black writers
themselves seem to have conceived their task to be the creation of
an art that reports and directly reflects brute, irreducible, and ineffable "black reality," a reality that in fact was often merely the formu-
laic fictions spawned by social scientists whose work intended to
reveal a black America dehumanized by slavery, segregation, and racial discrimination, in a one-to-one relationship of art to life. Black
literacy, then, became far more preoccupied with the literal representation of social content than with literary form, with ethics and the-
matics rather than poetics and aesthetics. Art, therefore, was argued
implicitly and explicitly to be essentially referential. This theory assumed, first of all, that there existed a common, phenomenal world,
which could be reliably described by the methods of empirical histo-
riography or else by those of empirical social science. It assumed,
second, that the function of the black writer was to testify to the
private world of black pain and degradation, determined by a pervasive white and unblinking racism. Not only would creative writing at
last make visible the face of the victimized and invisible black person, but it would also serve notice to the white world that individual
black people had the requisite imagination to create great art and
therefore to be "equal," an impetus, again, that we have traced to the
eighteenth century.

To signify upon Henry James, the House of Black Fiction has
many windows, but many are cracked and jagged. Haunted by archetypal Running Men who wrestle in dream-and-nightmare sequences
with the unmediated Specter of White Racism, our House of Black
Fiction is strewn with dead rats and cockroaches that feed off the
ashen-pale bodies of dumb and, of course, wealthy white girls. Only
the odor of chittlins and collard greens, steaming on gas burners,
mitigates the certain stench of death. Nowhere can the critic unravel

James's "figure in the carpet," and not only because "the city's" welfare checks are too paltry to afford the luxury. And the kitchen linoleum is worn thin, we fear, from overuse, buried, we suspect,
beneath a growing mound of garbage, and purchased, we assume, on
some usurious Easy Payment Plan. It is a house in tatters, created by
novelists who fail to realize that by the very act of writing—the language of which is not reality but a system of signs—they commit
themselves to the construction of coherent, symbolic worlds related
to but never relegated to be merely plausible reproductions of the
real world, not even the nightmare land of the inner city.

VI

If theories of race and superstructure criticism did not prove to be
fertile grounds in which Afro-American criticism could blossom, it
nevertheless remains incumbent upon critics of black literature to
extend their pioneering search *within the black idiom* for principles of
criticism.

The Afro-American literary tradition has not yet produced a coherent theory of the texts that comprise it. We have benefited little
from this absence of theories that are specific to black texts. What a
fecund field awaits our attention. Perhaps the last black scholar to
write a purely theoretical text was Amo, one of the first persons of
African descent to publish a book in a European language. Amo may
well have been the first, and remains one of the few, writers of African descent to theorize about the integrity of literature as an ideal
institution. Amo was concerned, moreover, with the nature of analysis, of interpretation itself, rather than with containing an ideological
stance about oppression in the guise of criticism. True, there are
ideological presuppositions implicit in any critical judgment; for
Amo, we recognize his explicit formalism as a reaction against
eighteenth-century correlations between the race of an author and
the value of his or her work. The import, if not the stance, of his
work does reflect the world of ideas and economic relations that surround him. Nevertheless, Amo's treatise is a philosophical discourse
upon the role of the reader as he or she interacts with text and author to produce meaning.

To underscore Amo's formalism is not merely to emphasize his
uniqueness in a critical tradition that, consistently since Amo and
until the last half-decade, has privileged the political function of a
work of art at the expense of what it has described as sterile flirta-
tion with "decadent" or "bourgeois" or "white" notions of art for art's
sake. To underscore Amo's concern for the text is to emphasize the
irony of eighteenth-century European theorizing about the nature

and function of writers of African descent publishing texts in European languages. As I hope I have demonstrated above, these Enlightenment theorists privileged the fact of public writing—the literacy of literature, as it were—as the signal criterion for demonstrating the innate mental equality of the African with the European. Contrary to our assumptions that the Western philosophical tradition privileged the spoken over the written text, close readings of the evidence suggest strongly that the written word was privileged, not only above the spoken word but among all of the other representational arts as well. Had polyrhythms in music been privileged, for instance, our history in the West could have been a drastically different one. But is was the literacy of literature that, arbitrarily, was used as a commodity to measure the black's humanity. Amo, we know, was acutely aware of all of this. For Amo, as we have seen, was the very product of one such Enlightenment experiment designed to measure the mental capacity of the African by his ability to master the European arts and letters.

How are we to escape this trap of our own literature mastery, as well as the trap of the mindless imitation of the monkey? Are we doomed as critics of a noncanonical literature merely to cut monkeyshines, or can signifying monkeys decode the signs that comprise our black structures of literature? It seems to me that finding metaphors for black literary relations from within the Afro-American tradition, and combining these with that which is useful in contemporary literary theory, is the challenge of Afro-American literary history. At least two other critics of black literature have developed meaningful metaphors of Afro-American literary history. Houston A. Baker, Jr., and Robert Burns Stepto have defined "repudiation" and "authentication," respectively, as metaphors of literary history.*[30]

Baker's theory of repudiation establishes an inverse relationship between a nonblack text and its black repudiation. This repudiation is essentially thematic, epistemological, and ontological. Baker's metaphor for literary relationships between black and white texts concerns itself with the signified, and not especially with the signifier.

---

*Baker's brilliant theory of the black vernacular, the blues idiom, and its relation to literary structure is fundamentally related to my theory of signifying. Although Baker graciously acknowledges my influence on his work, I would argue that ours is a reciprocal relationship.

[30]Baker's theory of repudiation is found in *Long Black Song*. . . . Stepto's theory of "authentication" is elaborated in *From Behind the Veil: A Study of Afro-American Narrative* (Urbana: University of Illinois Press, 1979).

Stepto's metaphor of authentication draws upon strategies of legitimacy employed by black authors and their white "prefacers," since Phillis Wheatley published her poems in 1773, to attest to the claims of authorship of the black subject. Stepto's work traces this theme of "authorial control," of subject–object dialectics, from its most patent form in the slave narratives to Ralph Ellison's subtle refiguration in *Invisible Man*. Above all else, Stepto is concerned with the capacity of a narrator to tell his or her own tale.

Both Baker and Stepto, curiously enough, have developed metaphors of literary history that are implicitly ideological and antagonistic, turning as they do on notions of power and autonomy, which we may read as themes of racial and individual selfhood. If only in these broad senses, the two metaphors share similar presuppositions about the will to power as the will to write. I have tried to supplement these creative theories by locating a metaphor for literary history that arises from within the black idiom exclusively, that is not dependent upon black–white power or racial relations, and that is essentially rhetorical. I call it critical signification, and I take it from the black rhetorical strategy called Signifyin(g). *Signifyin(g)* is a rhetorical strategy that is indigenously black and that derives from the Signifying Monkey tales. The figure of the Signifying Monkey, in turn, is the profane counterpart of Esu-Elegbara, the Yoruba sacred trickster who is truly Pan-African, manifesting himself among the Cubans, the Haitians, and the Fon as Legba, among the Brazilians as Exu, among the believers of Vodun as Papa Legba, and among the believers of Hoodoo as Papa LaBas. Hermes is his closest Western counterpart. As Hermes is to hermeneutics, so is Esu to the black art of interpretation, *Esu-'tufunaalo.*

I use Esu as the metaphor for the critical activity of interpretation and Signifyin(g) as my metaphor for literary history because these are idiomatically black. I have not had to strain or reinterpret these figures. The discursive, or signifying, structures from which I take them define them in these ways: Esu the Yoruba call the figure of indeterminacy and the figure of interpretation. Signifyin(g) is a uniquely black rhetorical concept, entirely textual or linguistic, by which a second statement or figure repeats, or tropes, or reverses the first. Its use as a figure for intertextuality allows us to understand literary revision without resource to thematic, biographical, or Oedipal slayings at the crossroads; rather, critical signification is tropic and rhetorical. Indeed, the very concept of Signifyin(g) can exist only in the realm of the intertextual relation.

We are able to trace such complex intertextual Signifyin(g) relations by explicating what I like to think of as the Discourse of the Black Other in the eighteenth and early nineteenth centuries. By

"Discourse of the Black" I mean to say the literature that persons of African descent created as well as the nonblack literature that depicts black characters. The phrase, then, suggests both how blacks figured language and how blacks and their blackness were figured in Western languages, especially in English and French. I am speaking here of the black as both subject and object of literature.

Because the discourse of the black occupied a fundamental polemical place in the fight against slavery, literary historians have tended to dismiss or ignore the hundreds of poems, plays, and novels about blacks that Europeans and Americans published between the seventeenth and the mid-nineteenth centuries. This literature contains only a few noble blacks, and even these are rendered ambiguously. Aphra Behn renders Oronooko, for example, as a noble African, but only at the expense of his fellow Africans: they are short, while he is tall; they speak an African language, while he speaks French; they have African features, while his are aquiline; they are weak and cowardly, while he is strong. The "Dying Negro" poems made popular by the English Romantics attempt to elicit pity and sentiment for the insufferable plight of the unfortunate slave. These, too, like the noble Negro tales, draw upon received racist images of the African, even if they intend to arouse the conscience of the European.

We can think of the slave narratives as a reaction to these sentimental figurations. The generic expectations of this aspect of the discourse of the black had a profound effect on the shape of that discourse which we call the slave's narrative, as did the sentimental novel and more especially the particularly American transmutation of the European picaresque. The slave narratives, in turn, spawned their formal antithesis, the Confederate romance. It is useful to think of this curious, dialectical relation of the slave narratives to the confederate romance as that of repetition and reversal. It is as if the figure of the North Star in the slave narratives becomes the figures of moonbeams and magnolia blossoms in the plantation novel. Structurally, the two modes of figuration are opposite, mirror images, in a relation of archetype and stereotype. Furthermore, all of those so-called illegitimate slave narratives, anathema to the historian, are merely novels that refigure tropes and conventions of both genres, often masking themselves as authentic first-person slave narratives, both pro- and anti-slavery, such as Mattie Griffiths's *Autobiography of a Female Slave*, or Richard Hildreth's *Archy Moore* and my absolute favorite, *Peculiar*, published in 1863, the protagonist of which is called Peculiar Institution.

The hundreds of slave narratives and Confederate romances published before 1865 have been documented and analyzed by scholars such as Charles Nichols, Marion Wilson Starling, Margaret Young Jackson, Frances Smith Foster, John W. Blassingame, Vernon Loggins, John Herbert Nelson, Sterling A. Brown, and Jean Fagan Yellin. Moreover, Charles T. Davis, Leslie Fielder, and Harry Levin have explicated the interplay of figures of light and darkness in the works of Hawthorne, Melville, and Poe. No one, to my knowledge, has yet discussed the relationship among the slave narratives, the Confederate romance, and the American Romantics, which we may think of as the three terms of the dialectic—thesis, antithesis, synthesis—wherein the themes of black and white, common to the bipolar moment in which the slave narratives and the plantation novel oscillate, inform the very structuring principles of the great gothic works of Hawthorne, Melville, and Poe. The intertextual relations that obtain here are formal ones; indeed, the use of the power of blackness as a structuring principle in many ways assumes the function of any mythic structure, reconciling the two otherwise irreconcilable forces. Narration here is the trick of mediation.

⚜

In the final chapter of this book [*Figures in Black*], on the Signifying Monkey and on *Mumbo Jumbo*, I supplement my analysis of race and superstructure with an analysis of the idea of a transcendent signified, a belief in an essence called blackness, a presence our tradition has tried of late to will into being, in order to negate two and a half millennia of its figuration as an absence. As healthy politically as such a gesture was, as revealing as it was in this country and abroad of the very arbitrariness of the received sign of blackness itself, we must also criticize the idealism, the notion of essence, implicit in even this important political gesture. To think of oneself as free simply because one can claim—one can utter—the negation of an assertion is not to think deeply enough. *Négritude* already constituted such a claim of blackness as a transcendent signified, of a full and sufficient presence; but to make such a claim, to feel the necessity to make such a claim, is already to reveal too much about perceived absence and desire. It is to take the terms of one's assertion from a discourse whose universe has been determined by an Other. Even the terms of one's so-called spontaneous desire have been presupposed by the Other. I render this critique of blackness as a transcendent signified in order to help break through the enclosure of negation.

The enclosure of negation is only one trap. That sort of intellectual indenture, which we might call, after Jean Price-Mars, "bovarysme collectif," is quite another, and equally deadly, trap. Jules de

Gaultier, expanding upon Price-Mars, defines bovarysme as the phenomenon of being "fated to obey the suggestion of an external millieu, for lack of auto-suggestion from within."[32] The challenge of black literary criticism is to derive principles of literary criticism from the black tradition itself, as defined in the idiom of critical theory but also in the idiom that constitutes the language of blackness, the Signifyin(g) difference that makes the black tradition our very own. To borrow mindlessly, or to vulgarize, a critical theory from another tradition is to satisfy de Gaultier's definition of bovarysme; but is is also to satisfy, in the black idiom, Ishmael Reed's definition of "The Talking Andriod." The sign of the successful negotiation of this precipice of indenture, of slavish imitation, is that the black critical essay refers to two contexts, two traditions, the Western and the Black. Each utterance, then, is "double-voiced."

In a 1925 review of James Weldon Johnson's *The Book of American Negro Spirituals*, W. E. B. Du Bois argued that evidence of critical activity is a sign of a tradition's sophistication, since criticism implies an awareness of the process of art itself and is a second-order reflection upon those primary texts that define a tradition and its canon. Insofar as we, critics of the black tradition, master our craft, we serve both to preserve our own traditions and to shape their direction. All great writers demand great critics. The imperatives of our task are clear. . . .

---

[32]Jules de Gaultier, cited in René Girard, *Deceit, Desire, and the Novel: Self and Other in Literary Structure*, trans. Yvonne Frecerro (Baltimore: Johns Hopkins University Press, 1965), p. 5.

SELECTED BIBLIOGRAPHY

I. ANTHOLOGIES AND COLLECTIONS
(Note: all authors in this section are editors.)

Abrahams, Roger D. *Afro-American Folktales: Stories from Black Traditions in the New World.* Pantheon, 1985.

Andrews, William L. *Six Women's Slave Narratives.* Oxford University Press (The Schomburg Library of Nineteenth-Century Black Women Writers), 1988.

Baker, Houston A., Jr. *A Many-Colored Coat of Dreams: The Poetry of Countee Cullen.* Broadside Press, 1974.

Bambara, Toni Cade.. *The Black Woman: An Anthology.* New American Library, 1970.

————. *Tales and Stories for Black Folks.* Doubleday, 1971.

Baraka, Amiri, and Amina Baraka. *Confirmation: An Anthology of African American Women.* Quill, 1983.

Barksdale, Richard, and Keneth Kinnamon. *Black Writers of America: A Comprehensive Anthology.* Macmillan, 1972.

Barthelemy, Anthony G. *Collected Black Women's Narratives.* Oxford University Press (The Schomburg Library of Nineteenth-Century Black Women Writers), 1988.

Beam, Joseph. *In the Life: A Black Gay Anthology.* Alyson, 1986.

Bell, Bernard W. *Modern and Contemporary Afro-American Poetry.* Allyn & Bacon, 1972.

Berry, Faith. *Good Morning, Revolution: Uncollected Social Protest Writings of Langston Hughes.* Lawrence Hill, 1973.

Bontemps, Arna. *American Negro Poetry.* Hill & Wang, 1963.

————. *Great Slave Narratives.* Beacon Press, 1969.

Brasner, William, and Dominick Consolo. *Black Drama: An Anthology.* Merrill, 1970.

Brawley, Benjamin. *Early Negro American Writers.* University of North Carolina Press, 1935.

Brewer, J. Mason. *American Negro Folklore.* Quadrangle, 1968.

Brooks, Gwendolyn. *Jump Bad, A New Chicago Anthology.* Broadside Press, 1971.

————. *A Broadside Treasury, 1965–1970.* Broadside Press, 1971.

————. *The World of Gwendolyn Brooks.* Harper & Row, 1971.

————. *Blacks/Gwendolyn Brooks.* David, 1987.

Brown, Patricia L., Don L. Lee (a.k.a. Haki R. Madhubuti), and Francis Ward. *To Gwen, with Love: An Anthology Dedicated to Gwendolyn Brooks.* Johnson Publishing Co., 1971.

Brown, Sterling A., Arthur P. Davis, and Ulysses Lee. *The Negro Caravan: Writings by American Negroes.* Dryden, 1941; Arno, 1969.

Chapman, Abraham. *Black Voices: An Anthology of Afro-American Literature.* New American Library, 1968.

————. *Steal Away: Stories of the Runaway Slaves.* Preager, 1971.

————. *New Black Voices: An Anthology of Contemporary Afro-American Literature.* New American Library, 1972.

Clarke, John H. *American Negro Short Stories.* Hill & Wang, 1966.

Cooper, Wayne F. *The Passion of Claude McKay: Selected Prose and Poetry, 1912–1948.* Schocken Books, 1973.

Courlander, Harold. *A Treasury of Afro-American Folklore: The Oral Literature, Traditions, Recollections, Legends, Tales, Songs, Religious Beliefs, Customs, Sayings and Humor of Peoples of African Descent in the Americas.* Crown Publishers, 1976.

Cromwell, Otelia Lorenzo Turner, and Eva B. Dykes. *Readings from Negro Authors.* Harcourt, 1931.

Cullen, Countee. *Caroling Dusk: An Anthology of Verse by Negro Poets.* Harper, 1927.

Dance, Daryl Cumber. *Shuckin' and Jivin': Folklore from Contemporary Black Americans.* Indiana University Press, 1978.

Davis, Angela Y., and Other Political Prisoners. *If They Come in the Morning: Voices of Resistance by Angela Y. Davis and Others.* Third Press, 1971.

Davis, Arthur P., and Saunders Redding. *Cavalcade: Negro American Writing from 1760 to the Present.* Houghton Mifflin, 1971.

Davis, Arthur P., and Michael W. Peplow. *The New Negro Renaissance: An Anthology.* Holt, Rinehart and Winston, 1975.

Emanuel, James A., and Theodore Gross. *Dark Symphony: Negro Literature in America.* Free Press, 1968.

Exum, Pat Crutchfield. *Keeping the Faith: Writings by Contemporary Black American Women.* Fawcett, 1974.

Faggett, Harry Lee, and Nick Aaron Ford. *Best Short Stories by Afro-American Writers (1925–1950).* Meador, 1950; Krause Reprint, 1977.

Ford, Nick Aaron. *Black Insights: Significant Literature by Black Americans, 1760 to the Present.* Ginn, 1971.

Gibson, Donald B. *Black and White: Stories of American Life.* Washington Square Press, 1971.

Giovanni, Nikki. *Night Comes Softly: Anthology of Black Female Voices.* MEDIC Press, 1970.

Glaysher, Frederick. *Collected Prose/Robert Hayden.* University of Michigan Press, 1984.

————. *Collected Poems/Robert Hayden.* Liveright, 1985.

Graham, Maryemma. *The Complete Poems of Frances E. W. Harper.* Oxford University Press (The Schomburg Library of Nineteenth-Century Black Women Writers), 1988.

Greene, J. Lee. *Time's Unfading Garden: Ann Spencer's Life and Poetry.* Louisiana State University Press, 1977.

Hansberry, Lorraine. *To Be Young, Gifted and Black: Lorraine Hansberry in Her Own Words.* New American Library, 1969; Samuel French, 1971.

Harley, Sharon, and Rosalyn Terborg-Penn. *Afro-American Women: Struggles and Images.* Kennikat Press, 1978.

Harper, Michael S. *The Collected Poems of Sterling Brown.* Harper & Row, 1980.

Harper, Michael S., and Robert B. Stepto. *Chant of Saints: A Gathering of Afro-American Literature, Art, and Scholarship.* University of Illinois Press, 1979.

Harrison, Paul Carter. *Kuntu Drama: Plays of the African Continuum.* Grove Press, 1974.

Hayden, Robert E. *Kaleidoscope: Poems by American Negro Poets.* Harcourt, Brace & World, 1967.

————. *Afro-American Literature: An Introduction.* Harcourt, Brace, Jovanovich, 1971.

Hill, Herbert. *Soon, One Morning: New Writings by American Negroes, 1940–1962.* Knopf, 1963.

Himes, Chester. *Black on Black: Baby Sister and Selected Writings.* Doubleday, 1973.

Hopkins, Lee Burnett. *On Our Way: Poems of Pride and Love.* Knopf, 1974.

Houchins, Sue E. *Spiritual Narratives: Maria W. Stewart, Jarena Lee, Julia A. J. Foote, Virginia W. Broughton.* Oxford University Press (The Schomburg Library of Nineteenth-Century Black Women Writers), 1988.

Hudson, Theodore R. *From LeRoi Jones to Amiri Baraka: The Literary Works.* Duke University Press, 1973.

Huggins, Nathan I. *Voices from the Harlem Renaissance.* Oxford University Press, 1976.

Hughes, Langston. *New Negro Poets, U.S.A.* Indiana University Press, 1964.

————. *The Book of Negro Humor.* Dodd, Mead, 1966.

————. *The Best Short Stories by Negro Writers: An Anthology from 1899 to the Present.* Little, Brown, 1967.

Hughes, Langston, and Arna Bontemps. *The Poetry of the Negro.* Doubleday, 1949; rev. ed., *The Poetry of the Negro, 1746–1970,* 1970.

————. *The Book of Negro Folklore.* Dodd, Mead, 1958.

Hull, Gloria T. *The Works of Alice Dunbar-Nelson.* 3 vols. Oxford University Press (The Schomburg Library of Nineteenth-Century Black Women Writers), 1988.

Hurston, Zora Neale. *Spunk: The Selected Stories of Zora Neale Hurston.* Turtle Island Foundation, 1985.

Johnson, Charles S. *Ebony and Topaz: A Collectanea.* National Urban League, 1927.

Johnson, James Weldon. *The Book of American Negro Poetry.* Harcourt, 1922; rev. and enl., 1931.

Jones, LeRoi, and Larry Neal. *Black Fire: An Anthology of Afro-American Writing.* William Morrow, 1968.

Jones, Robert B., and Marjorie Toomer Latimer. *The Collected Poems of Jean Toomer.* University of North Carolina Press, 1988.

Kellner, Bruce. *"Keep A-Inchin Along": Selected Writings of Carl Van Vechten About Black Art and Letters.* Greenwood Press, 1979.

Kerlin, Robert T. *Negro Poets and Their Poems.* Associated Publishers, 1935.

Kinnamon, Keneth. *James Baldwin: A Collection of Critical Essays.* Prentice-Hall, 1974.

King, Woodie. *Black Short Story Anthology.* Columbia University Press, 1972.

————. *The Forerunners: Black Poets in America.* Howard University Press, 1976.

Locke, Alain L. *The New Negro: An Interpretation.* Boni, 1925; Atheneum, 1968.

Long, Richard A., and Eugenia W. Collier. *Afro-American Writing: An Anthology of Prose and Poetry.* 2 vols. New York University Press, 1972.

Major, Clarence. *The New Black Poetry.* International Publications, 1969.

Margolies, Edward. *A Native Sons Reader: Selections by Outstanding Black American Authors of the Twentieth-Century.* Lippincott, 1970.

Mberi, Antar S. K., and Cosmo Pieterse. *Speak Easy, Speak Free.* International Publishers, 1977.

McCluskey, John, Jr. *The City of Refuge: The Collected Stories of Rudolph Fisher.* University of Missouri Press, 1987.

Miller, E. Ethelbert. *Women Surviving Massacres and Men: Nine Women Poets, An Anthology.* Anemone Press, 1977.

Moon, Bucklin. *Primer for White Folks.* Doubleday, 1945.

Murphy, Beatrice M. *Today's Negro Voices: An Anthology by Young Negro Poets.* Messner, 1970.

Osofsky, Gilbert. *Puttin' on Ole Massa: The Slave Narratives of Henry Bibb, William W. Brown, and Solomon Northrop.* Harper, 1969.

Patterson, Lindsay. *A Rock Against the Wind: Black Love Poems, An Anthology.* Dodd, Mead, 1973.

Perry, Margaret. *The Short Fiction of Rudolph Fisher.* Greenwood Press, 1987.

Plato, Ann. *Essays: Including Biographies and Miscellaneous Pieces, in Prose and Poetry.* Introduction by Kenny J. Williams, Oxford University Press (The Schomburg Library of Nineteenth-Century Black Women Writers), 1988.

Plumpp, Sterling D. *Somehow We Survive: An Anthology of South African Writing.* Thunder's Mouth Press, 1982.

Randall, Dudley. *Black Poetry: A Supplement to Anthologies Which Exclude Black Poets.* Broadside Press, 1969.

———. *The Black Poets.* Bantam, 1971.

———. *Homage to Hoyt Fuller.* Broadside Press, 1984.

Randall, Dudley, and Margaret Burroughs. *For Malcolm: Poems on the Life and the Death of Malcolm X.* Broadside Press, 1967.

Redmond, Eugene B. *Rope of Wind and Other Stories/Henry Dumas.* Random House, 1979.

———. *Goodbye, Sweetwater: New and Selected Stories/Henry Dumas.* Thunder's Mouth Press, 1988.

Reed, Ishmael. *Yardbird Lives.* Grove Press, 1978.

Render, Sylvia Lyons. *The Short Fiction of Charles W. Chestnutt.* Howard University Press, 1974.

Robinson, William H. *Early Black American Poets.* Wm. C. Brown, 1969.

Sanchez, Sonia. *We Be Word Sorcerors: 25 Stories by Black Americans.* Bantam, 1973.

Sherman, Joan R. *Invisible Poets: Afro-Americans of the Nineteenth Century.* University of Illinois Press, 1974.

———. *Collected Black Women's Poetry.* 4 vols. Oxford University Press (The Schomburg Library of Nineteenth-Century Black Women Writers), 1988.

Shields, John C. *The Collected Works of Phillis Wheatley.* Oxford University Press (The Schomburg Library of Nineteenth-Century Black Women Writers), 1988.

Shuman, R. Baird. *Nine Black Poets.* Moore, 1968.

———. *A Galaxy of Black Writing.* Moore, 1970.

Smith, Arthur L. *Rhetoric of Black Revolution.* Allyn & Bacon, 1969.

Smith, Barbara. *Home Girls: A Black Feminist Anthology.* Kitchen Table: Women of Color Press, 1983.

Stadler, Quandra P. *Out of Our Lives: A Collection of Contemporary Black Fiction.* Howard University Press, 1975.

Troupe, Quincy, and Rainer Schulte. *Giant Talk: An Anthology of Third World Writers.* Random House, 1975.

Turner, Darwin T. *Black American Literature: Poetry.* Chas. E. Merrill, 1969.

———. *Black Drama in America: An Anthology.* Fawcett, 1971.

———. *The Wayward and the Seeking: A Collection of Writings by Jean Toomer.* Howard University Press, 1980.

Walker, Alice. *I Love Myself When I am Laughing. . . . And Then Again When I am Looking Mean and Impressive: A Zora Neale Hurston Reader.* The Feminist Press, 1979.

Washington, Mary Helen. *Black-Eyed Susans: Classic Stories By and About Black Women.* Anchor Press/Doubleday, 1975.

———. *Midnight Birds: Stories of Contemporary Black Women Writers.* Anchor Press/Doubleday, 1980.

———. *Invented Lives: Narratives of Black Women's Lives, 1860–1960.* Anchor Press/Doubleday, 1987.

Watkins, Sylvester C. *Anthology of American Negro Literature.* Random House, 1944.

Williams, John A., and Charles F. Harris. *Amistad I: Writings on Black History and Culture.* Vintage/Random House, 1970.

———. *Amistad II: Writings on Black History and Culture.* Vintage/Random House, 1971.

Woodson, Carter G. *Negro Orators and Their Orations.* Associated Publishers, 1925.

II. HISTORY, BIBLIOGRAPHY, CRITICISM, AND COMMENT

Allen, William G. *Wheatley, Banneker, and Horton.* Books for Libraries, 1970.

Baker, Houston A., Jr. *Black Literature in America.* McGraw-Hill, 1971.

———. *Long Black Song: Essays in Black American Literature and Culture.* University Press of Virginia, 1972.

———, ed. *Twentieth-Century Interpretations of Native Son: A Collection of Critical Essays.* Prentice-Hall, 1972.

———. *Singers of Daybreak: Studies in Black American Literature.* Howard University Press, 1975, 1983.

———, ed. *A Dark and Sudden Beauty: Two Essays in Black American Poetry by George Kent and Stephen Henderson.* Afro-American Studies Program, University of Pennsylvania, 1977.

———, ed. *Reading Black: Essays in the Criticism of African, Caribbean and Black American Literature.* Cornell University Press, 1978.

———. *The Journey Back: Issues in Black Literature and Criticism.* University of Chicago Press, 1980.

————. *Blues, Ideology, and Afro-American Literature: A Vernacular Theory.* University of Chicago Press, 1984.

————. *Modernism and the Harlem Renaissance.* University of Chicago Press, 1987.

————. *Afro-American Poetics: Revisions of Harlem and the Black Aesthetic.* University of Wisconsin Press, 1988.

Ball, Wendy A., ed. *Rare Afro-Americana: A Reconstruction of the Adger Library.* G. K. Hall, 1981.

Barthold, Bonnie J. *Black Time: Fiction of Africa, the Caribbean, and the United States.* Yale University Press, 1981.

Bell, Bernard W. *The Folk Roots of Contemporary Afro-American Poetry.* Broadside Press, 1974.

————. *The Afro-American Novel and its Traditions.* University of Massachusetts Press, 1987.

Bell, Roseann Pope, Bettye J. Parker, and Beverly Guy-Sheftall. *Sturdy Black Bridges: Visions of Black Women in Literature.* Anchor Press, 1979.

Benston, Kimberly W., ed. *Imamu Amiri Baraka (LeRoi Jones): A Collection of Critical Essays.* Prentice-Hall, 1978.

————, ed. *Speaking for You: The Vision of Ralph Ellison.* Howard University Press, 1987.

Berzon, Judith R. *Neither White Nor Black: The Mulatto Character in American Fiction.* New York University Press, 1978.

Bigsby, C. W. E. *The Second Black Renaissance: Essays in Black Literature.* Greenwood Press, 1980.

Bloom, Harold, ed. *Zora Neale Hurston's "Their Eyes Were Watching God."* Chelsea House, 1987.

Bogle, Donald. *Toms, Coons, Mulattoes, Mammies, and Bucks: An Interpretive History of Blacks in American Films.* Viking Press, 1973; Penguin, 1979; Continuum, 1989.

Bone, Robert A. *The Negro Novel in America.* Yale University Press, 1958, 1965.

Bontemps, Arna, ed. *The Harlem Renaissance Remembered.* Dodd, Mead, 1972.

Brawley, Benjamin. *The Negro in Literature and Art in the United States.* Atlanta, 1910; Duffield, 1918.

Brignano, Russell. *Richard Wright: An Introduction to the Man and His Works.* University of Pittsburgh Press, 1970.

Brown, Sterling A. *The Negro in American Fiction.* Associates in Negro Folk Education, 1937; Atheneum, 1969 (reissued with *Negro Poetry and Drama* in one volume).

————. *Negro Poetry and Drama.* Associates in Negro Folk Education, 1937; Atheneum, 1969 (reissued with *The Negro in American Fiction* in one volume).

Brown, Sterling A., Arthur P. Davis, and Ulysses Lee, eds. *The Negro Caravan: Writings by American Negroes.* Dryden, 1941; Arno, 1969.

Bruce, Dickson D., Jr. *Black American Writing from the Nadir: The Evolution of a Literary Tradition, 1877–1915.* Louisiana State University Press, 1989.

Bruck, Peter, ed. *The Black American Short Story in the 20th Century: A Collection of Critical Essays.* Humanities Press, 1977.

Butcher, Margaret J. *The Negro in American Culture: Based on Materials Left by Alain Locke.* Knopf, 1956, 1972.

Butcher, Philip, ed. *The Minority Presence in American Literature, 1600–1900.* 2 vols. Howard University Press, 1977.

Butler-Evans, Elliott. *Race, Gender, and Desire: Narrative Strategies in the Fiction of Toni Cade Bambara, Toni Morrison, and Alice Walker*. Temple University Press, 1989.

Callahan, John F. *In the Afro-American Grain: The Pursuit of Voice in Twentieth-Century Black Fiction*. University of Illinois Press, 1988.

Christian, Barbara. *Black Women Novelists: The Development of a Tradition, 1892–1976*. Greenwood Press, 1980.

———. *Black Feminist Criticism: Perspectives on Black Women Writers*. Pergamon, 1985.

Cobb, Martha. *Harlem, Haiti, and Havana: A Comparative Critical Study of Langston Hughes, Jacques Romain, and Nicolas Guillen*. Three Continents Press, 1979.

Coleman, James W. *Blackness and Modernism: The Literary Career of John Edgar Wideman*. University Press of Mississippi, 1989.

Cooke, Michael G., ed. *Afro-American Literature in the Twentieth Century: The Achievement of Intimacy*. Yale University Press, 1986.

Dance, Daryl Cumber. *Long Gone: The Mecklenburg Six and the Theme of Escape in Black Folklore*. University of Tennessee Press, 1987.

Davis, Arthur P. *From the Dark Tower: Afro-American Writers, 1900–1960*. Howard University Press, 1974.

Davis, Charles T., and Michel Fabre. *Richard Wright: A Primary Bibliography*. G. K. Hall, 1982.

———. *The Slave's Narrative*. Oxford University Press, 1985.

Deodene, Frank, and William P. French. *Black American Poetry Since 1952: A Preliminary Checklist*. Chatham Bookseller, 1970.

———. *Black American Poetry Since 1944: A Preliminary Checklist*. Chatham Bookseller, 1971.

Dixon, Melvin. *Ride Out the Wilderness: Geography and Identity in Afro-American Literature*. University of Illinois Press, 1987

Dundes, Alan. *Mother Wit from the Laughing Barrel: Readings in the Interpretation of Afro-American Folklore*. Prentice-Hall, 1973.

Evans, Mari. *Black Women Writers, 1950–1980: A Critical Evaluation*. Doubleday, 1984.

Farrison, William E. *William Wells Brown, Author and Reformer*. University of Chicago Press, 1969.

Fisher, Dexter, and Robert B. Stepto, eds. *Afro-American Literature: The Reconstruction of Instruction*. Modern Language Association, 1979.

Fisher, Miles Mark. *Negro Slave Songs in the U.S.* (new edition). Russell and Russell, 1968.

Ford, Nick Aaron. *The Contemporary Negro Novel*. Meador, 1936; McGrath, 1968.

Fox, Robert E. *Conscientious Sorcerors: The Black Post-Modernist Fiction of LeRoi Jones-Amiri Baraka, Ishmael Reed, and Samuel R. Delany*. Greenwood Press, 1987.

French, William P., Michel Fabre, and Amrijit Singh, eds. *Afro-American Poetry and Drama, 1760–1975: A Guide to Information Sources*. Gale, 1979.

Gates, Henry Louis, Jr., ed. *Black Literature and Literary Theory*. Methuen, 1984.

———, ed. *Figures in Black: Words, Signs and the Racial Self*. Oxford University Press, 1987.

———, ed. *The Signifying Monkey: A Theory of Afro-American Literary Criticism*. Oxford University Press, 1988.

Gayle, Addison, Jr., ed. *Black Expression: Essays By and About Black Americans in the Creative Arts.* Weybright and Talley, 1969.

———, ed. *The Black Aesthetic.* Doubleday, 1971.

———. *The Way of the New World: The Black Novel in America.* Doubleday, 1975.

Gibson, Donald B., ed. *Five Black Writers: Essays on Wright, Ellison, Baldwin, Hughes, and LeRoi Jones.* New York University Press, 1970.

———. *The Politics of Literary Expression: A Study of Major Black Writers.* Greenwood Press, 1981.

Gloster, Hugh M. *Negro Voices in American Fiction.* University of North Carolina Press, 1948; Russell, 1965.

Gross, Seymour, and John E. Hardy, eds. *Images of the Negro in American Literature: Essays in Criticism.* University of Chicago Press, 1966.

Gubert, Betty Kaplan. *Early Black Bibliographies, 1863–1918.* Garland, 1982.

Gwaltney, John Langston. *Drylongso: A Self-Portrait of Black America.* Vintage, 1980.

Hansberry, Lorraine. *The Movement: Documentary of a Struggle for Equality.* Simon & Schuster, 1964.

Harris, Norman. *Connecting Times: The Sixties in Afro-American Fiction.* University Press of Mississippi, 1988.

Harris, Trudier. *From Mammies to Militants: Domestics in Black American Literature.* Temple University Press, 1982.

———. *Exorcising Blackness: Historical and Literary Lynching and Burning Rituals.* Indiana University Press, 1985.

Harris, William J. *The Poetry and Poetics of Amiri Baraka: The Jazz Aesthetic.* University of Missouri Press, 1985.

Hatch, James V. *Black Image on the American Stage: A Bibliography of Plays and Musicals, 1770–1970.* Drama Book Specialists, 1970.

Hatch, James V., and Omanii Abdullah, comps. and eds. *Black Playwrights, 1823–1977: An Annotated Bibliography of Plays.* R. R. Bowker, 1977.

Hatcher, John. *From the Auroral Darkness: The Life and Poetry of Robert Hayden.* G. Ronald, 1984.

Hemenway, Robert. *The Black Novelist.* Chas. E. Merrill, 1970.

Henderson, Stephen, ed. *Understanding the New Black Poetry: Black Speech and Black Music as Poetic References.* William Morrow, 1972.

Hernton, Calvin C. *The Sexual Mountain and Black Women Writers: Adventures in Sex, Literature, and Real Life.* Anchor Press/Doubleday, 1987.

Hersey, John, ed. *Ralph Ellison: A Collection of Critical Essays.* Prentice-Hall, 1974.

Hogue, W. Lawrence. *Discourse and the Other: The Production of the Afro-American Text.* Duke University Press, 1986.

Holloway, Karla F. C. *The Character of the Word: The Texts of Zora Neale Hurston.* Greenwood Press, 1987.

Houston, Helen R. *The Afro-American Novel, 1965–1975: A Descriptive Bibliography of Primary and Secondary Materials.* Whitson, 1977.

Howard, Lillie. *Zora Neale Hurston.* Twayne/G. K. Hall, 1980.

Hudson, Theodore R. *From LeRoi Jones to Amiri Baraka: The Literary Works.* Duke University Press, 1973.

Huggins, Nathan I. *Harlem Renaissance.* Oxford University Press, 1971.

Hughes, Carl Milton. *The Negro Novelist: A Discussion of the Writings of American Negro Novelists, 1940–50.* Citadel, 1953.

Jackson, Blyden. *The Waiting Years: Essays on American Negro Literature.* Louisiana State University Press, 1976.

Jackson, Blyden, and Louis D. Rubin, Jr. *Black Poetry in America: Two Essays in Historical Interpretation.* Louisiana State University Press, 1974.

Johnson, Charles. *Being and Race: Black Writing Since 1970.* Indiana University Press, 1988.

Johnson, James Weldon. *Black Manhattan.* Knopf, 1930.

Johnson, Lemuel. *The Devil, the Gargoyle, and the Buffoon: The Negro as Metaphor in Western Literature.* Kennikat Press, 1974.

Joyce, Joyce Ann. *Richard Wright's Art of Tragedy.* University of Iowa Press, 1986.

Kallenbach, Jessamine S. *Index to Black American Literary Anthologies.* G. K. Hall, 1979.

Kent, George E. *Blackness and the Adventure of Western Culture.* Third World Press, 1972.

Kinnamon, Keneth. *The Emergence of Richard Wright: A Study in Literature and Society.* University of Illinois Press, 1972.

Kinnamon, Keneth, Joseph Benson, Michel Fabre, and Craig Werner, eds. *A Richard Wright Bibliography: Fifty Years of Criticism and Commentary, 1933–1982.* Greenwood Press, 1988.

Klotman, Phyllis R. *Another Man Gone: The Black Runner in Contemporary Afro-American Literature.* Kennikat, 1976.

Kramer, Victor A., ed. *The Harlem Renaissance Re-examined.* AMS, 1987.

Lawson, Victor. *Dunbar Critically Examined.* Associated Publishers, 1941.

Locke, Alain L. *The New Negro: An Interpretation.* Boni, 1925; Atheneum, 1968.

Loggins, Vernon. *The Negro Author: His Development in America to 1900.* Columbia University Press, 1931; Kennikat, 1964.

Margolies, Edward. *The Art of Richard Wright.* Southern Illinois University Press, 1969.

———. *Native Sons: A Critical Study of Twentieth-Century Negro American Authors.* Lippincott, 1969.

Martin, Reginald. *Ishmael Reed and the New Black Aesthetic Critics.* St. Martin's Press, 1988.

Mason, Julian D., Jr., ed. *The Poems of Phillis Wheatley.* University of North Carolina Press, 1966, 1989.

McKay, Nellie Y., ed. *Critical Essays on Toni Morrison.* G. K. Hall, 1988.

Miller, R. Baxter. *Black American Literature and Humanism.* University Press of Kentucky, 1981.

———, ed. *Black American Poets Between Worlds, 1940–1960.* University of Tennessee Press, 1986.

Milliken, Stephen F. *Chester Himes: A Critical Appraisal.* University of Missouri Press, 1976.

Mitchell, Loften. *Black Drama: The Story of the American Negro in the Theatre.* Hawthorne Books, 1967.

Mootry, Maria K., and Gary Smith, eds. *A Life Distilled: Gwendolyn Brooks, Her Poetry and Fiction.* University of Illinois Press, 1987, 1989.

Murray, Albert. *The Omni-Americans: New Perspectives on the Black Experience and American Culture.* Outerbridge & Dienstfrey, 1979; rept. as *The Omni-Americans: Some Alterations to the Folklore of White Supremacy,* Vantage, 1983.

———. *The Hero and the Blues.* University of Missouri Press, 1973.

Newson, Adele S. *Zora Neale Hurston*. G. K. Hall, 1987.

Nichols, Charles H. *Many Thousand Gone*. Brill Adler, 1963; Indiana University Press, 1969.

Noble, Peter. *The Negro in Films*. Robinson Ltd. (London), 1948.

———. *The Cinema and the Negro, 1905–1948*. Gordon, 1980.

Null, Gary, *Black Hollywood: The Negro in Motion Pictures*. Citadel, 1977.

O'Daniel, Therman B., ed. *Langston Hughes, Black Genius: A Critical Evaluation*. William Morrow, 1971.

———. ed. *James Baldwin: A Critical Evaluation*. Howard University Press, 1977.

O'Daniel, Therman B., with Cason L. Hill. *Jean Toomer: A Critical Evaluation*. Howard University Press, 1988.

O'Meally, Robert G. *The Craft of Ralph Ellison*. Harvard University Press, 1980.

Peplow, Michael W. *George S. Schuyler*. Twayne/G. K. Hall, 1980.

Peplow, Michael W., and Robert S. Bravard. *Samuel R. Delany: A Primary and Secondary Bibliography, 1962–1979*. G. K. Hall, 1980.

Perry, Margaret. *A Bio-bibliography of Countee P. Cullen (1903–1946)*. Greenwood Press, 1971.

Porter, Dorothy B. *North American Negro Poets: A Bibliographical Checklist of Their Writings (1760–1944)*. The Book Farm, 1945.

———. *The Negro in the United States: A Selected Bibliography*. Library of Congress, 1970.

Pryse, Marjorie, and Hortense Spillers, eds. *Conjuring: Black Women, Fiction, and Literary Tradition*. Indiana University Press, 1985.

Rampersad, Arnold. *The Art and Imagination of W. E. B. DuBois*. Harvard University Press, 1976.

Rampersad, Arnold, and Deborah McDowell, eds. *Slavery and the Literary Imagination*. Johns Hopkins University Press, 1988.

Redding, J. Saunders. *To Make a Poet Black*. University of North Carolina Press, 1939; Core Collection, 1978; Cornell University Press, 1988.

———. *The Lonesome Road: The Story of the Negro in America*. Doubleday, 1958.

Redmond, Eugene B. *Drumvoices: The Mission of Afro-American Poetry, A Critical History*. Doubleday/Anchor Press, 1976.

Richmond, Merle A. *Bid the Vassal Soar: Interpretive Essays on the Life and Poetry of Phillis Wheatley (ca. 1753–1784) and George Moses Horton (ca. 1797–1883)*. Howard University Press, 1974.

Robinson, William H. *Phillis Wheatley: A Bio-Bibliography*. G. K. Hall, 1981.

———, ed. *Critical Essays on Phillis Wheatley*. G. K. Hall, 1982.

Rose, Alan H. *Demonic Vision: Racial Fantasy and Southern Fiction*. Shoe String Press, 1976.

Settle, Elizabeth A., and Thomas A. Settle, eds. *Ishmael Reed: A Primary and Secondary Bibliography*. G. K. Hall, 1982.

Shaw, Harry B., ed. *Gwendolyn Brooks*. Twayne, 1980.

Sheffey, Ruthe T., ed., *A Rainbow Round Her Shoulder: The Zora Neale Hurston Symposium Papers*. Morgan State University Press, 1982.

Sherman, Joan R. *Invisible Poets: Afro-Americans of the Nineteenth Century*. University of Illinois Press, 1974.

Sims, Janet L. *The Progress of Afro-American Women: A Selected Bibliography and Research Guide*. Greenwood Press, 1980.

Sims, Rudine. *Shadow and Substance: Afro-American Experience in Contemporary Children's Fiction*. American Library Association, 1982.

Starling, Marion Wilson. *The Slave Narrative: Its Place in American History*. G. K. Hall, 1981; Howard University Press, 1988.

Stepto, Robert B. *From Behind the Veil: A Study of Afro-American Narrative*. University of Illinois Press, 1979.

Tate, Claudia. *Black Women Writers at Work*. Continuum, 1983.

Turner, Darwin T. *In a Minor Chord: Three Afro-American Writers and Their Search for Identity*. Southern Illinois University Press, 1971.

Tyms, James D. *Spiritual (Religious) Values in the Black Poet*. University Press of America, 1977.

Waldron, Edward E. *Walter White and the Harlem Renaissance*. Kennikat Press, 1978.

Walker, Margaret. *Richard Wright, Daemonic Genius: A Portrait of the Man, A Critical Look at His Work*. Warner Books, 1988.

Walser, Richard, ed. *The Black Poet: Being the Remarkable Story (partly told by himself) of George Moses Horton, a North Carolina Slave*. Philosphical Library, 1966.

Wegelin, Oscar. *Jupiter Hammon, American Negro Poet: Selections from His Writings and a Bibliography*. Heartman, 1915.

Weixlmann, Joe, and Chester Fontenot. *Black American Prose Theory*. Penkevill, 1983.

Weixlmann, Joe, and Houston A. Baker, Jr., eds. *Belief versus Theory in Black American Literary Criticism*. Penkevill, 1985.

Whitlow, Roger. *The Darker Vision: A Socio-Historical Study of Nineteenth-Century Black American Literature*. Gordon Press, 1979.

Williams, George Washington. *The American Negro, from 1776 to 1876*. R. Clarke, 1876.

Williams, Pontheolla T. *Robert Hayden: A Critical Analysis of His Poetry*. University of Illinois Press, 1987.

Williams, Sherley A. *Give Birth to Brightness: A Thematic Study in Neo-Black Literature*. Dial Press, 1972.

Willis, Susan. *Specifying: Black Women Writing the American Experience*. University of Wisconsin Press, 1986.

Yellin, Jean Fagan. *Women and Sisters: The Anti-Slavery Feminists in American Culture*. Yale University Press, 1990.

Young, James O. *Black Writers of the Thirties*. Louisiana State University Press, 1973.

III. POETRY PUBLICATIONS

Allen, Samuel W. (Paul Vesey pseud.) *Elfenbein Zahne (Ivory Tusks)*. Wolfgang Rothe (Heidelberg), 1956.

———. *Ivory Tusks and Other Poems*. Poets Press, 1968.

———. *Paul Vesey's Ledger*. Paul Breman, 1975.

Amini, Johari M. (a.k.a. Jewel C. Latimore). *Images in Black*. Third World Press, 1969.

————. *Let's Go Somewhere.* Third World Press, 1970.

Banks, C. Tillery. *Hello to Me With Love: Poems of Self-Discovery.* William Morrow, 1980.

Baraka, Imamu (a.k.a. LeRoi Jones). *Spirit Reach.* Jihad, 1972.

————. *In the Tradition (For Black Arthur Blythe).* Jihad, 1980.

————. *Reggae or Not: Poems.* Contact II Publications, 1981.

Barrax, Gerald. *Another Kind of Rain: Poems.* University of Pittsburgh Press, 1970.

————. *An Audience of One.* University of Georgia Press, 1980.

Bontemps, Arna. *Personals.* Paul Breman, 1963.

————. *Hold Fast to Dreams: Poems Old and New.* Follet, 1969.

Brooks, Gwendolyn. *Blacks.* David, 1987.

————. *Gottschalk and the Grande Tarantelle/Gwendolyn Brooks.* David, 1988.

————. *Winnie.* David, 1988.

Brown, Sterling A. *Southern Road.* Harcourt, 1932.

————. *The Last Ride of Wild Bill, and Eleven Narrative Poems.* Broadside Press, 1975.

Burroughs, Margaret. *What Shall I Tell My Children Who Are Black?* M.A.A.H. Press, 1968.

————. *Africa, My Africa.* DuSable Museum, 1970.

Campbell, James E. *Echoes from the Cabin and Elsewhere.* Chicago, 1905.

Chase-Riboud, Barbara. *Portrait of a Nude Woman as Cleopatra.* William Morrow, 1987.

Clifton, Lucille. *Good Times.* Random House, 1969.

————. *Good News About the Earth.* Random House, 1972.

————. *An Ordinary Woman.* Random House, 1974.

————. *Two-Headed Woman.* University of Massachusetts, 1980.

————. *Next: New Poems.* BOA Editions, 1987.

————. *Good Woman: Poems and a Memoir, 1969–1980.* BOA Editions, 1987.

Coleman, Wanda. *Mad Dog Black Lady.* Black Sparrow Press, 1979.

————. *Heavy Daughter Blues.* Black Sparrow Press, 1987.

Cortez, Jayne. *Piss-stained Stairs and the Monkey Man's Wares.* Phrase Text, 1969.

————. *Scarifications.* Bola Press, 1973, 1978.

————. *Mouth on Paper.* Bola Press, 1977.

————. *Firespitter.* Bola Press, 1982.

————. *Coagulations.* Thunder's Mouth Press, 1984.

Cullen, Countee. *Color.* Harper, 1925.

————. *The Ballad of the Brown Girl.* Harper, 1927.

————. *Copper Sun.* Harper, 1927.

————. *The Black Christ and Other Poems.* Harper, 1929.

————. *The Medea and Some Poems.* Harper, 1935.

————. *The Lost Zoo.* Harper, 1940.

————. *On These I Stand.* Harper, 1947.

Cuney, Waring. *Puzzles.* Deroos (Utrecht), 1960.

————. *Storefront Church.* Paul Breman, 1973.

Danner, Margaret. *Impressions of African Art Forms.* Broadside Press, 1960.

————. *To Flower.* Hemphill Press, 1963.

————. *Iron Lace.* Kriya Press, 1968.

————. *Down of a Thistle.* Country Beautiful, 1976.

Danner, Margaret, and Dudley Randall. *Poem Counterpoem.* Broadside Press, 1966.

Davis, Frank Marshall. *Black Man's Verse.* Black Cat Press, 1935.

———. *I Am the American Negro.* Black Cat Press, 1937.

———. *47th Street.* Decker Press, 1948.

Davis, Thulani. *All the Renegade Ghosts Rise.* Anemone Press, 1978.

———. *playing the changes.* Wesleyan University Press, 1985.

Dent, Tom. *Magnolia Street.* Published by Author, 1976.

———. *Blue Lights and River Songs.* Lotus Press, 1982.

Derricote, Toi. *The Empress of the Death House.* Lotus Press, 1978.

Deveaux, Alexis. *Li Chen/Second Daughter First Son.* Ba Tone Press, 1975.

———. *Don't Explain: A Song of Billie Holiday.* Harper & Row, 1980; Writers & Readers, 1988.

Dodson, Owen. *Powerful Long Ladder.* Farrar, Straus & Giroux, 1946.

Dove, Rita. *Ten Poems.* Penumbra Press, 1977.

———. *Mandolin.* Ohio Review, 1982.

———. *Museum.* Carnegie-Mellon University Press, 1983.

———. *Thomas and Beulah.* Carnegie-Mellon University Press, 1986.

———. *Grace Notes.* W. W. Norton, 1989.

Dumas, Henry (edited by Eugene B. Redmond). *Play Ebony: Play Ivory.* Random House, 1975; originally published as *Poetry for my People,* Southern Illinois University Press, 1970.

Dunbar, Paul Laurence. *Oak and Ivy.* Dayton, Ohio, 1893.

———. *Majors and Minors.* Toledo, Ohio, 1895.

———. *Lyrics of Lowly Life.* New York, 1896; Citadel Press, 1984.

———. *Lyrics of the Hearthside.* New York, 1899; AMS Press, 1972.

———. *Lyrics of Love and Laughter.* New York, 1903.

———. *Lyrics of Sunshine and Shadow.* New York, 1905; AMS Press, 1972.

———. *The Complete Poems of Paul Laurence Dunbar.* Dodd, Mead, 1913; 1980.

Emanuel, James A. *The Treehouse and Other Poems.* Broadside Press, 1968.

———. *Panther Man.* Broadside Press, 1970.

———. *Black Man Abroad: The Toulouse Poems.* Lotus Press, 1978.

———. *A Chisel in the Dark (Poems, Selected and New).* Lotus Press, 1980.

———. *The Broken Bowl (New and Uncollected Poems).* Lotus Press, 1983.

Evans, Mari. *Where Is All the Music?* Paul Breman, 1968.

———. *I Am a Black Woman.* William Morrow, 1970.

———. *Singing Black.* Reed Visuals, 1976.

———. *Nightstar: 1973–1978.* Center for Afro-American Studies, UCLA, 1981.

Fair, Ronald. *Excerpts.* Paul Breman, 1975.

———. *Rufus.* Lotus Press, 1977.

Fields, Julia. *East of Moonlight.* Chatham Bookseller, 1973.

———. *Slow Coins: Minted by Julia Fields.* Three Continents Press, 1981.

Forbes, Calvin. *From the Book of Shine.* Burning Deck Press, 1979; Razorback Press, 1980.

Giovanni, Nikki. *Black Judgement.* Broadside Press, 1968.

———. *Black Feeling, Black Talk.* Broadside Press, 1970.

———. *Black Feeling Black Talk Black Judgement.* William Morrow, 1970.

———. *Re-Creation.* Broadside Press, 1970.

———. *My House: Poems.* William Morrow, 1972.

————. *The Women and The Men*. William Morrow, 1975, 1979.

————. *Cotton Candy on a Rainy Day*. William Morrow, 1978.

————. *Those Who Ride the Night Wind*. William Morrow, 1983.

Hammon, Jupiter. *An Evening Thought: Salvation by Christ, with Penetential Cries, A Broadside*. Long Island, NY, 1760.

————. *A Poetical Address to Phillis Wheatley, A Broadside*. Long Island, NY, 1779.

Harper, Frances E. W. *Poems on Miscellaneous Subjects*. Boston, 1854.

————. *Moses: A Story of the Nile*. Philadelphia, 1869.

————. *Poems*. Philadelphia, 1871.

————. *Poems*. Philadelphia, 1900.

Harper, Michael S. *Dear John, Dear Coltrane*. University of Pittsburgh Press, 1970; University of Illinois Press, 1985.

————. *History is Your Own Heartbeat*. University of Illinois Press, 1971.

————. *Photographs: Negatives; History As Apple Tree*. Scarab Press, 1972.

————. *Song: I Want a A Witness*. University of Pittsburgh Press, 1972.

————. *Debridement*. Doubleday, 1973.

————. *Nightmare Begins Responsibility*. University of Illinois Press, 1975.

————. *Images of Kin: New and Selected Poems*. University of Illinois Press, 1977.

————. *Rhode Island: Eight Poems*. Pym-Randall Press, 1981.

————. *Healing Song for the Inner Ear: Poems*. University of Illinois Press, 1984.

Hayden, Robert E. *Heart-Shape in the Dust*. Falcon Press, 1940.

————. *Figure of Time: Poems*. Hemphill Press, 1955.

————. *A Ballad of Remembrance*. Paul Breman, 1962.

————. *Selected Poems*. October House, 1966.

————. *Words in the Mourning Time*. October House, 1970.

————. *The Night-Blooming Cereus*. Paul Breman, 1972.

————. *Angle of Ascent: New and Selected Poems*. Liveright, 1975.

————. *American Journal: Poems*. Effendi Press, 1978; Liveright, 1982.

————. *The Legend of John Brown*. Detroit Institute of Art, 1978.

Horton, George Moses. *Hope of Liberty*. Raleigh, N.C., 1829.

————. *Naked Genius*. Raleigh, N.C., 1865; Chapel Hill Historical Society, 1982.

Hughes, Langston. *The Weary Blues*. Knopf, 1926.

————. *Fine Clothes for the Jew*. Knopf, 1927.

————. *Dear Lovely Death*. Troutbeck Press, 1931.

————. *The Dream Keeper*. Knopf, 1932.

————. *A New Song*. International Workers Order, 1938.

————. *Shakespeare in Harlem*. Knopf, 1942.

————. *In Freedom's Plow*. Musette, 1943.

————. *Fields of Wonder*. Knopf, 1947.

————. *One-Way Ticket*. Knopf, 1949.

————. *Montage of a Dream Deferred*. Henry Holt, 1951.

————. *Selected Poems*. Knopf, 1959.

————. *Ask Your Mama: Twelve Moods for Jazz*. Knopf, 1961.

————. *The Panther and the Lash*. Knopf, 1967.

Jeffers, Lance. *When I Know the Power of My Black Hand*. Broadside Press, 1974.

————. *O Africa, Where I Baked My Bread*. Lotus Press, 1977.

————. *Grandsire*. Lotus Press, 1979.

Joans, Ted. *Jazz Poems*. Rhino Review, 1959.

————. *All of Ted Joans and No More.* Excelsior, 1961.

————. *The Hipsters.* Corinth, 1961.

————. *Black Pow-Wow.* Hill & Wang, 1969; Calder & Boyars, 1973.

————. *Afrodisia; New Poems.* Hill & Wang 1970; Calder & Boyars, 1976.

————. *A Black Manifesto in Jazz Poetry and Prose.* Calder & Boyars, 1971.

————. *The Aardvark-Watcher (Der Erdferkelforscher).* Literarisches Colloquium (Berlin), 1980.

Johnson, Fenton. *A Little Dreaming.* Chicago, 1913.

————. *Visions of the Dusk.* New York, 1915.

————. *Songs of the Soil.* New York, 1916.

Johnson, Georgia Douglas. *Autumn Love Cycle.* H. Viral, 1928; Books for Libraries Press, 1971.

————. *Heart of a Woman and Other Poems.* The Cornhill Co., 1918.

Johnson, James Weldon. *Fifty Years, and Other Poems.* The Cornhill Co., 1917.

————. *God's Trombones: Seven Negro Sermons in Verse.* Viking, 1927, 1969.

————. *St. Peter Relates an Incident . . .* Viking, 1935.

Jones, LeRoi (a.k.a. Imamu Baraka). *Preface to a Twenty-Volume Suicide Note.* Totem-Corinth, 1961.

————. *The Dead Lecturer.* Grove, 1964.

————. *Black Arts.* Jihad, 1966.

————. *Black Magic Poetry: 1961–1967.* Bobbs-Merrill, 1969.

Jordan, June. *Who Look at Me.* Crowell, 1969.

————. *His Own Where.* Crowell, 1971.

————. *Some Changes.* Dutton, 1971.

————. *Dry Victories.* Holt, Rinehart and Winston, 1972.

————. *New Days: Poems of Exile and Return.* Emerson Hall, 1974.

————. *Things That I Do in the Dark: Selected Poems.* Random House, 1977.

————. *Passion: New Poems, 1977–1980.* Beacon Press, 1980.

————. *Civil Wars.* Beacon Press, 1981.

————. *Living Room.* Thunder's Mouth Press, 1985.

Knight, Etheridge. *Poems from Prison.* Broadside Press, 1968.

————. *Belly Song and Other Poems.* Broadside Press, 1973.

————. *The Essential Etheridge Knight.* University of Pittsburgh Press, 1986.

Lane, Pinkie Gordon. *Wind Thoughts.* South & West, 1972.

————. *The Mystic Female.* Bailey Press, 1978.

————. *I Never Scream: New and Selected Poems.* Lotus Press, 1985.

Lee, Don L. (a.k.a. Haki R. Madhubuti). *Think Black.* Broadside Press, 1967.

————. *Black Pride.* Broadside Press, 1968.

————. *Don't Cry, Scream.* Broadside Press, 1969.

————. *We Walk the Way of the New World.* Broadside Press, 1970.

Lester, Julius. *Who I Am; Poems.* Dial Press, 1974.

Lorde, Audre. *From a Land Where Other People Live.* Broadside Press, 1973.

————. *The New York Head Shop and Museum.* Broadside Press, 1975.

————. *Coal.* W. W. Norton, 1976.

————. *Between Ourselves.* Eidolon Editions, 1977.

————. *Chosen Poems—Old and New.* W. W. Norton, 1982.

————. *Our Dead Behind Us.* W. W. Norton, 1986.

Madgett, Naomi Long. *One and the Many.* Exposition, 1956.

————. *Star by Star*. Lotus Press, 1965; Evenill, 1970.

————. *Pink Ladies in the Afternoon*. Lotus Press, 1972.

————. *Exits and Entrances*. Lotus Press, 1978.

————. *Phantom Nightingale: Juvenilia: Poems, 1934–1943*. Lotus Press, 1981.

————. *Octavia and Other Poems*. Third World Press, 1988.

Madhubuti, Haki R. (a.k.a. Don L. Lee). *Earthquake & Sunrise Missions*. Third World Press, 1984.

————. *Killing Memory, Seeking Ancestors*. Lotus Press, 1987.

Major, Clarence. *Swallow the Lake*. Wesleyan University Press, 1970.

————. *Symptoms & Madness*. Corinth Books, 1971.

————. *The Cotton Club: New Poems*. Broadside Press, 1972.

————. *The Syncopated Cakewalk*. Barlenmir, 1974.

————. *Inside Diameter: The France Poems*. Permanent Press, 1985.

————. *Painted Turtle: Woman with Guitar*. Sun & Moon, 1988.

————. *Surfaces and Masks: A Poem*. Coffee House Press, 1988.

McClane, Kenneth A. *Out Beyond the Bay*. Ithaca House, 1975.

————. *Moons and Low Times*. Ithaca House, 1978.

————. *To Hear the River*. West End Press, 1981.

————. *These Halves are Whole*. Black Willow Press, 1983.

————. *A Tree Beyond Telling: Poems, Selected and New*. Black Scholar Press, 1983.

————. *Take Five: Collected Poems, 1972–1986*. Greenwood Press, 1987.

McKay, Claude. *Spring in New Hampshire*. Grant Richard (London), 1920.

————. *Harlem Shadows*. Harcourt, 1922.

————. *Selected Poems*. Bookman Associates, 1953.

Miller, E. Ethelbert. *Migrant Worker*. The Washington Writers' Publishing House, 1978.

————. *Season of Hunger—Cry of Rain*. Lotus Press, 1982.

————. *where are the love poems for dictators?* Open Hand, 1986.

Miller, May, *Into the Clearing*. Charioteer Press, 1959.

————. *The Clearing and Beyond*. The Charioteer Press, 1974.

Murray, Pauli. *Dark Testament and Other Poems*. Silvermine, 1970.

Neal, Larry. *Black Boogaloo*. Journal of Black Poetry Press, 1969.

————. *Hoodoo Hollerin' Bebop Ghosts*. Howard University Press, 1974.

Oden, Gloria. *Resurrections*. Olivant Press, 1978.

————. *The Tie That Binds*. Olivant Press, 1980.

Plumpp, Sterling D. *Portable Soul*. Third World Press, 1969.

————. *Half Black, Half Blacker*. Third World Press, 1970.

————. *Clinton*. Broadside Press, 1976.

————.*The Mojo Hands Call, I Must Go*. Thunder's Mouth Press, 1982.

Randall, Dudley. *Cities Burning*. Broadside Press, 1968.

————. *Love You*. Paul Breman, 1970.

————. *More to Remember: Poems for Four Decades*. Third World Press, 1971.

————. *After the Killing*. Third World Press, 1973.

————. *A Litany of Friends: New and Selected Poems*. Lotus Press, 1981, 1983.

————. *Golden Song*. Harlo, 1985.

Redmond, Eugene B. *Sentry of the Four Golden Pillars*. Black River Writers, 1970.

————. *River of Bones and Flesh and Blood: Poems*. Black River Writers, 1971.

————. *Songs from an Afro/Phone*. Black River Writers, 1972.

————. *Consider Loneliness as These Things*. Black River Writers, 1973.

————. *In a Time of Rain and Desire: New Love Poems*. Black River Writers, 1973.

Reed, Ishmael. *Conjure: Selected Poems, 1963–1970*. University of Massachusetts Press, 1973.

————. *Chattanooga: Poems*. Random House, 1974.

————. *A Secretary to the Spirits*. NOK Publishers, 1977.

————. *New and Collected Poems*. Atheneum, 1988.

Rivers, Conrad Kent. *The Black Bodies and This Sunburnt Face*. Free Lance Press, 1962.

Rodgers, Carolyn M. *Songs of a Black Bird*. Third World Press, 1969.

————. *The Heart As Ever Green*. Anchor Press/Doubleday, 1970.

————. *Now Ain't That Love*. Broadside Press, 1970.

————. *How I Got Ovah: New and Selected Poems*. Anchor Press/Doubleday, 1975.

Sanchez, Sonia. *Homecoming*. Broadside Press, 1970.

————. *A Blues Book for Blue Black Magical Women*. Broadside Press, 1973.

————. *Love Poems*. Third World Press, 1973.

————. *I've Been a Woman: New and Selected Poems*. Black Scholar Press, 1979.

————. *homegirls and handgrenades*. Thunder's Mouth Press, 1984.

————. *Under a Soprano Sky*. Africa World Press, 1987.

Scott-Heron, Gil. *Small Talk at 125th Street and Lenox*. World, 1970.

————. *So Far, So Good*. Third World Press, 1990.

Shange, Ntozake. *Melissa & Smith*. Bookslinger Editions, 1976.

————. *Nappy Edges*. St. Martin's Press, 1978.

————. *Three Pieces*. St. Martin's Press, 1981; Penguin, 1982.

————. *A Daughter's Geography*. St. Martin's Press, 1983.

————. *Ridin' the Moon in Texas: Word Paintings*. St. Martin's Press, 1987.

Spellman, A. B. *The Beautiful Days*. Poets Press, 1965.

Stuckey, Elma. *The Big Gate*. Precedent, 1976.

————. *The Collected Poems of Elma Stuckey*. Precedent, 1987.

Tolson, Melvin B. *Rendevous with America*. Dodd, Mead, 1944.

————. *Libretto for the Republic of Liberia*. Twayne, 1953.

————. *Harlem Gallery; Book I: The Curator*. Twayne, 1965.

————. *A Gallery of Harlem Portraits*. University of Missouri Press, 1979.

Troupe, Quincy. *Embryo Poems*. Barlenmir, 1972.

————. *Snake-Back Solos: Selected Poems, 1969–1977*. I. Reed Books, 1978.

————. *Skulls Along the River*. Reed & Cannon, 1984.

Van Der Zee, James (Photography), Owen Dodson (Poetry), and Camille Billops (Text). *The Harlem Book of the Dead*. Morgan & Morgan, 1979.

Walker, Margaret. *For My People*. Yale University Press, 1942; Ayer, 1969.

————. *Prophets for a New Day*. Broadside Press, 1970.

————. *October Journey*. Broadside Press, 1973.

————. *This is My Century: New and Collected Poems/Margaret Walker*. University of Georgia Press, 1989.

Wheatley, Phillis. *An Elegiac Poem, on the Death of the Rev. Mr. George Whitefield*. Boston, 1770.

————. *Poems on Various Subjects, Religious and Moral*. Bell (London), 1773.

Whitfield, James M. *America and Other Poems*. Buffalo, 1853.

————. *Not a Man, and Yet a Man*. Springfield, Ohio, 1877.

———. *The Rape of Florida*. St. Louis, 1884.

———. *Twasinta's Seminoles: or, The Rape of Florida*. St. Louis, 1885.

———. *An Idyl of the South: An Epic in Two Parts*. New York, 1901.

Williams, Sherley Anne. *The Peacock Poems*. Wesleyan University Press, 1978.

———. *Some One Sweet Angel Chile*. William Morrow, 1982.

Wright, Jay. *Death as History*. Kriya Press, 1967.

———. *Dimensions of History*. Kayak, 1976.

———. *Soothsayers and Omens*. Seven Woods Press, 1976.

———. *The Double Invention of Komo*. University of Texas Press, 1980.

———. *Explications/Interpretations*. University of Kentucky Press, 1984.

———. *Selected Poems of Jay Wright*. Princeton University Press, 1987.

———. *Elaine's Book*. University Press of Virginia, 1988.

Young, Al. *Dancing: Poems*. Corinth Books, 1969.

———. *The Song Turning Back into Itself: Poems*. Holt, Rinehart and Winston, 1971.

———. *The Geography of the Near Past*. Holt, Rinehart & Winston, 1976.

———. *The Blues Don't Change: New and Selected Poems*. Louisiana State University Press, 1982.

———. *Heaven: Collected Poems, 1958–1988*. Creative Arts, 1989.

IV. FICTION

Attaway, William. *Let Me Breathe Thunder*. Doubleday, 1939.

———. *Blood on the Forge*. Doubleday, 1941; Macmillan, 1970.

———. *Hear America Singing*. Lion, 1967.

Baldwin, James. *Go Tell It on the Mountain*. Knopf, 1953; Signet, 1954.

———. *Giovanni's Room*. Dial Press, 1956.

———. *Another Country*. Dell, 1960; Dial Press, 1962.

———. *Going to Meet the Man*. Dial Press, 1965.

———. *Tell Me How Long the Train's Been Gone*. Dial Press, 1968.

———. *If Beale Street Could Talk*. Dial Press, 1974.

———. *Just Above My Head*. Dial Press, 1978.

Bambara, Toni Cade. *Gorilla, My Love*. Bantam, 1972; Vintage, 1981.

———. *The Sea Birds are Still Alive*. Random House, 1977; Vintage, 1982.

———. *The Salt Eaters*. Random House, 1980.

Baraka, Imamu (a.k.a. LeRoi Jones) *Three Books*. Grove, 1975.

Barrax, Gerald William. *Another Kind of Rain*. University of Pittsburgh Press, 1970.

Bates, Arthenia J. *Seeds Beneath the Snow: Vignettes from the South*. Greenwich, 1969; Howard University Press, 1975.

Beckham, Barry. *My Main Mother*. Walker, 1969.

———. *Runner Mack*. William Morrow, 1972; Howard University Press, 1984.

———. *Double Dunk*. Holloway House, 1980.

Bontemps, Arna. *God Sends Sunday*. Harcourt, 1931.

———. *Black Thunder*. Macmillan, 1936; Beacon Press, 1968.

———. *Drums at Dusk*. Macmillan, 1939.

Bradley, David. *South Street*. Grossman/Viking, 1975.

———. *The Chaneysville Incident*. Harper and Row, 1981.

Brooks, Gwendolyn. *Maud Martha.* Harper, 1953; Farrar, Straus & Giroux, 1969.

Brown, Cecil. *The Life and Loves of Mr. Jiveass Nigger.* Fawcett World Library, 1969; Farrar, Straus & Giroux, 1970.

———. *Days Without Weather.* Farrar, Straus & Giroux, 1982.

Brown, William Wells. *Clotel; or, The President's Daughter: A Narrative of Slave Life in the United States.* London, 1853; Citadel, 1969; Macmillan, 1970.

Bullins, Ed. *The Reluctant Rapist.* Harper and Row, 1973.

Butler, Octavia. *Kindred.* Doubleday, 1979; Beacon Press, 1988.

———. *Survivor.* New American Library, 1979.

———. *Wild Seed.* Doubleday, 1980; Timescape, 1981.

———. *Dawn.* Warner Books, 1987; Popular Library, 1988.

———. *Adulthood Rites.* Warner Books, 1988.

Cain, George. *Blueschild Baby.* McGraw-Hill, 1971.

Chesnutt, Charles W. *The Conjure Woman.* Houghton Mifflin, 1899.

———. *The Wife of His Youth, and Other Stories of the Color Line.* Houghton Mifflin, 1899.

———. *The House Behind the Cedars.* Houghton Mifflin, 1900.

———. *The Marrow of Tradition.* Houghton Mifflin, 1901.

———. *The Colonel's Dream.* Doubleday, Page, 1905.

Childress, Alice. *Like One of the Family . . . Conversations from a Domestic's Life.* Independence Publishers, 1956; Beacon Press, 1986.

———. *Mojo.* Coward, McCann and Geoghegan, 1972.

———. *A Hero Ain't Nothin' But a Sandwich.* Coward, McCann and Geoghegan, 1973.

———. *A Short Walk.* Coward, McCann and Geoghegan, 1979.

Cooper, J. California. *A Piece of Mine: Short Stories.* Wild Trees Press, 1984.

———. *Homemade Love.* St. Martin's Press, 1987.

———. *Some Soul to Keep.* St. Martin's Press, 1987.

———. *Family.* Doubleday, 1991.

Cullen, Countee. *One Way to Heaven.* Harper, 1932.

Davis, George. *Coming Home.* Random House, 1971; Howard University Press, 1984.

Delany, Martin R. *Blake; or, The Huts of America* (This work originally appeared serially in seven installments of the *Anglo-African* magazine in 1859). Beacon Press, 1970.

Delany, Samuel R. *The Jewels of Aptor.* Ace, 1962; Gregg, 1971, 1972.

———. *Captives of the Flame.* Ace, 1963.

———. *The Towers of Toron.* Ace, 1964, 1977.

———. *The Einstein Intersection.* Ace, 1967; Garland Presss, 1979.

———. *Nova.* Doubleday, 1968; Bantam, 1975.

———. *Driftglass.* Ace, 1971; Gregg, 1977.

———. *Distant Stars.* Ultramarine, 1981.

———. *Neveryona; or The Tales of Signs and Cities.* Bantam, 1983.

Demby, William. *The Catacombs.* Pantheon, 1965.

———. *Love Story Black.* Reed, Cannon & Johnson, 1978; Dutton, 1986.

Deveaux, Alexis. *Spirits in the Streets.* Anchor Press/Doubleday, 1973.

Dodson, Owen. *Boy at the Window.* Farrar, Straus & Giroux, 1951; reissued as *When Trees Were Green,* Popular Library, 1967.

Du Bois, W. E. B., *The Quest of the Silver Fleece*. A. C. McClurg, 1911; Mnemosyne, 1969.

——. *The Dark Princess*. Harcourt, 1928.

——. *The Black Flame: A Trilogy—The Ordeal of Mansart, Mansart Builds a School; Worlds of Color*. Mainstream Publishers, 1957, 1959, 1961.

Dumas, Henry. *Ark of Bones, and Other Stories*. Southern Illinois University Press, 1974.

——. *Jonoah and the Green Stone*. Random House, 1976.

Dunbar, Paul Laurence. *Folks from Dixie*. Dodd, Mead, 1898.

——. *The Uncalled*. Dodd, Mead, 1898; Literature House, 1970; AMS Press, 1972.

——. *The Love of Landry*. Dodd, Mead, 1900; Literature House, 1970.

——. *The Strength of Gideon, and Other Stories*. Dodd, Mead, 1900.

——. *The Fanatics*. Dodd, Mead, 1901; Literature House, 1970.

——. *The Sport of the Gods*. Dodd, Mead, 1902, 1981; Collier, 1970.

——. *In Old Plantation Days*. Dodd, Mead, 1903.

——. *The Heart of Happy Hollow*. Dodd, Mead, 1904; Books for Libraries Press, 1970.

Ellison, Ralph. *Invisible Man*. Random House, 1952.

——. *Going to the Territory*. Vintage Books, 1987.

Fair, Ronald. *Many Thousand Gone*. Harcourt, 1965.

——. *Hog Butcher*. Harcourt, 1966.

——. *World of Nothing: Two Novellas*. Harper and Row, 1970.

——. *We Can't Breathe*. Harper and Row, 1972.

Fauset, Jessie R. *There is Confusion*. Boni & Liveright, 1924.

——. *Plum Bun*. Stokes, 1929.

——. *The Chinaberry Tree*. Stokes, 1931.

——. *Comedy American Style*. Stokes, 1933.

Fisher, Rudolph. *The Walls of Jericho*. Knopf, 1928.

——. *The Conjure Man Dies*. Covici, Friede, 1932.

Forrest, Leon. *There is a Tree More Ancient Than Eden*. Random House, 1973; rev. ed., Another Chicago Press, 1988.

——. *The Bloodworth Orphans*. Random House, 1977; rev. ed., Another Chicago Press, 1987.

——. *Two Wings to Veil My Face*. Random House, 1984.

Gaines, Ernest J. *Catherine Carmier*. Atheneum, 1964; Chatham Booksellers, 1972; North Point Press, 1981.

——. *Of Love and Dust*. Dial Press, 1967; W. W. Norton, 1979.

——. *Bloodline*. Dial Press, 1968; W. W. Norton, 1976.

——. *The Autobiography of Miss Jane Pittman*. Dial Press, 1971; Doubleday, 1987.

——. *A Long Day in November*. Dial Press, 1971.

——. *The Sky is Gray*. Zenith Books, 1971.

——. *In My Father's House*. Knopf, 1978; W. W. Norton, 1983.

——. *A Gathering of Old Men*. Knopf, 1983.

Greenlee, Sam. *The Spook Who Sat by the Door*. R. W. Baron, 1969.

——. *Blues for an African Princess*. Third World Press, 1970.

————. *Bagdad Blues*. Emerson Hall, 1973.
Griggs, Sutton E. *Imperium in Imperio*. Orion, 1899; Arno, 1969.
————. *Overshadowed*. Orion, 1901.
————. *Unfettered*. Orion, 1902.
————. *The Hindered Hand*. Orion, 1905.
————. *Pointing the Way*. Orion, 1908.
Guy, Rosa. *Bird at My Window*. Lippincott, 1966.
————. *Ruby*. Random House, 1976.
————. *Edith Jackson*. Viking, 1978.
————. *The Disappearance*. Delacorte, 1979.
————. *A Measure of Time*. Henry Holt, 1983.
————. *My Love, My Love; or, The Peasant Girl*. Henry Holt, 1985.
Haley, Alex. *Roots*. Doubleday, 1976.
Harper, Frances E. W. *Iola Leroy; or, Shadows Uplifted*. Philadelphia, 1893; Oxford University Press (The Schomburg Library of Nineteenth-Century Black Women Writers), 1988.
Himes, Chester. *If He Hollers Let Him Go*. Doubleday, 1945; Thunder's Mouth Press, 1986.
————. *Lonely Crusade*. Knopf, 1947; Thunder's Mouth Press, 1986.
————. *Cast the First Stone*. Coward-McCann, 1953.
————. *The Real Cool Killers*. Avon, 1959; Berkely Medallion Editions, 1966; Vintage, 1988.
————. *Cotton Comes to Harlem*. Putnam, 1965; Vintage, 1988.
————. *Pinktoes*. Putnam, 1965.
————. *A Rage in Harlem*. Avon, 1965.
————. *Run Man, Run*. Putnam, 1966.
————. *Blind Man with a Pistol*. William Morrow, 1969.
————. *Black on Black: Baby Sister and Selected Writings*. Doubleday, 1973.
————. *A Case of Rape*. Targ Editions, 1980; Howard University Press, 1984.
Hopkins, Pauline. *Contending Forces: A Romance Illustrative of Negro Life North and South*. The Colored Cooperative Publishing Co., 1900; Oxford University Press (The Schomburg Library of Nineteenth-Century Black Women Writers), 1988.
Hughes, Langston. *Not Without Laughter*. Knopf, 1930.
————. *The Ways of White Folks*. Knopf, 1934.
————. *Laughing to Keep from Crying*. Henry Holt, 1952.
————. *Simple Stakes a Claim*. Rinehart, 1957.
————. *Tambourines to Glory*. John Day, 1959.
————. *The Best of Simple*. Hill & Wang, 1961.
————. *Something in Common, and Other Stories*. Hill & Wang, 1963.
————. *Simple's Uncle Sam*. Hill & Wang, 1965.
Hunter, Kristin. *God Bless the Child*. Scribner's, 1964. Howard University Press, 1987.
————. *The Landlord*. Scribner's, 1966.
————. *Boss Cat*. Scribner's Sons, 1971.
————. *The Survivors*. Scribner's Sons, 1975.
————. *The Lakestown Rebellion*. Scribner's Sons, 1978.

Hurston, Zora Neale. *Jonah's Gourd Vine*. Lippincott, 1934, 1971.

———. *Their Eyes Were Watching God*. Lippincott, 1937; University of Illinois Press, 1978.

———. *Moses, Man of the Mountain*. Lippincott, 1939; University of Illinois Press, 1984.

———. *Seraph on the Suwanee*. Scribner's, 1948; AMS Press, 1974.

Jeffers, Lance. *Witherspoon*. Flippin Press, 1983.

Johnson, Charles. *Faith and the Good Thing*. Viking, 1974; Atheneum, 1987.

———. *Oxherding Tale*. Indiana University Press, 1982.

———. *The Sorceror's Apprentice*. Atheneum, 1986.

———. *Middle Passage*. Atheneum, 1990.

Jones, Gayl. *Corregidora: A Novel*. Random House, 1975; Beacon Press, 1986.

———. *Eva's Man*. Random House, 1976; Beacon Press, 1987.

———. *White Rat*. Random House, 1977.

Jones, LeRoi (a.k.a. Imamu Baraka). *The System of Dante's Hell*. Grove, 1965.

———. *Tales*. Grove, 1967.

Kelley, William Melvin. *Different Drummer*. Doubleday, 1962.

———. *Dancers on the Shore*. Doubleday, 1964; Howard University Press, 1984.

———. *A Drop of Patience*. Doubleday, 1965; Chatham Booksellers, 1973.

———. *dem*. Doubleday, 1967.

———. *Dunfords Travels Everywheres*. Doubleday, 1970.

Killens, John O. *Youngblood*. Dial Press, 1956.

———. *And Then We Heard the Thunder*. Knopf, 1963; Howard University Press, 1983.

———. *'Sippi*. Simon & Schuster, 1967; Thunder's Mouth Press, 1988.

———. *Slaves*. Pyramid Press, 1969.

———. *The Great Black Russian: A Novel on the Life and Times of Alexander Pushkin*. Wayne State University Press, 1988.

Larsen, Nella. *Quicksand*. Knopf, 1928; Negro Universities Press, 1969; Collier, 1971; reissued as one volume with *Passing*, Rutgers University Press, 1986.

———. *Passing*. Knopf, 1932; Arno, 1969; Negro Universities Press, 1969; Collier, 1971; reissued as one volume with *Quicksand*, Rutgers University Press, 1986.

Lester, Julius. *This Strange New Feeling*. Dial Press, 1982.

Major, Clarence. *All-Night Visitors*. Olympia, 1969.

———. *Emergency Exit*. Fiction Collective, 1972, 1979.

———. *No*. Emerson Hall, 1973.

———. *Reflex and Bone Structure*. Fiction Collective, 1975; Editions L'Age d'Homme, 1982.

———. *My Amputations: A Novel*. Fiction Collective, 1986.

———. *Such Was the Season*. Mercury House, 1987.

Marshall, Paule. *Brown Girl, Brownstones*. Random House, 1959; The Feminist Press, 1981.

———. *Soul Clap Hands and Sing*. Atheneum, 1961; Howard University Press, 1988.

———. *The Chosen Place, The Timeless People*. Harcourt, 1969.

———. *Praisong for the Widow*. Putnam's Sons, 1983.

———. *Reena and Other Stories*. The Feminist Press, 1983.

Mathis, Sharon Bell. *Teacup Full of Roses.* Viking Press, 1972.

Mayfield, Julian. *The Hit.* Vanguard, 1957.

———. *The Long Night.* Vanguard, 1958.

———. *The Grand Parade.* Vanguard, 1961.

———. *Nowhere Street.* Paper Back Library, 1963.

McKay, Claude. *Home to Harlem.* Harper, 1928.

———. *Banjo.* Harper, 1929.

———. *Gingertown.* Harper, 1932.

———. *Banana Bottom.* Harper, 1933.

McPherson, James Alan. *Hue and Cry.* Atlantic-Little, Brown, 1969; Fawcett, 1979.

———. *Railroad.* Random House, 1976.

———. *Elbow Room.* Little, Brown, 1977; Scribner, 1987.

Meriwether, Louise. *Daddy was a Number Runner.* Prentice-Hall, 1970; Feminist Press, 1986.

Michaux, Oscar. *The Conquest.* Woodruff Press, 1913.

———. *The Forged Note.* Western Book Supply Co., 1915.

———. *The Case of Mrs. Wingate.* Book Supply Co., 1944.

———. *The Story of Dorothy Stanfield.* Book Supply Co., 1946.

———. *The Masquerade: A Historical Novel.* Book Supply Co., 1947.

Morrison, Toni. *The Bluest Eye.* Holt, Rinehart and Winston, 1970.

———. *Sula.* Knopf, 1974.

———. *Song of Solomon.* Knopf, 1977.

———. *Tar Baby.* Knopf, 1981.

———. *Beloved.* Knopf, 1987.

Motley, Willard. *Knock on Any Door.* Appleton-Century, 1947.

———. *We Fished All Night.* Appleton-Century, 1951.

———. *Let No Man Write My Epitaph.* Random House, 1958.

———. *Tourist Town.* Putnam, 1965.

———. *Let Noon Be Fair.* Putnam, 1966.

Murray, Albert. *Train Whistle Guitar.* McGraw-Hill, 1974; Northeastern University Press, 1989.

Naylor, Gloria. *The Women of Brewster Place.* Penguin, 1983.

———. *Linden Hills.* Ticknor and Fields, 1985.

———. *Mama Day.* Ticknor and Fields, 1988.

Petry, Ann. *The Street.* Houghton Mifflin, 1946; Pyramid Books, 1961; Beacon Press, 1985.

———. *Country Place.* Houghton Mifflin, 1947.

———. *The Narrows.* Houghton Mifflin, 1953; Beacon Press, 1988.

———. *Tituba of Salem Village.* Crowell, 1964.

———. *Legend of the Saints.* Crowell, 1972.

———. *Giveadamn Brown.* Doubleday, 1978.

Polite, Carlene Hatcher, (tr. by Pierre Alien). *The Flagellants.* Farrar, Straus & Giroux, 1967; Beacon Press, 1987.

Redding, J. Saunders. *Stranger and Alone.* Harcourt, Brace, 1950.

Reed, Ishmael. *The Free-Lance Pallbearers.* Doubleday, 1967; Chatham Booksellers, 1975; Atheneum, 1988.

———. *Catechism of De Neoamerican Hoodoo Church.* Breman, 1970.

———. *19 Necromancers from Now*. Doubleday, 1970.

———. *Yellow Back Radio Broke-Down*. Doubleday, 1971; Chatham Booksellers, 1975.

———. *Mumbo Jumbo*. Doubleday, 1972; Atheneum, 1989.

———. *The Last Days of Louisiana Red*. Random House, 1974; Atheneum, 1989.

———. *Flight to Canada*. Random House, 1976.

———. *Shrovetide in Old New Orleans*. Doubleday, 1978.

———. *The Terrible Twos*. St. Martin's Press, 1982; Atheneum, 1988.

———. *Reckless Eyeballing*. St. Martin's Press, 1986; Atheneum, 1988.

———. *The Terrible Threes*. Atheneum, 1989.

Schuyler, George. *Black No More*. Macaulay, 1931.

———. *Slaves Today*. Harcourt, 1931.

Scott-Heron, Gil. *The Vulture*. World, 1970.

———. *The Nigger Factory*. Dial Press, 1972.

Shange, Ntozake. *Sassafrass: A Novella*. Shameless Hussy Press, 1977.

———. *Sassafrass, Cypress & Indigo*. St. Martin's Press, 1982.

———. *From Okra to Greens: A Different Love Story*. Coffee House Press, 1984.

Shockley, Ann Allen. *The Black and White of It*. Naiad, 1980, 1987.

Smith, William Gardner. *Last of the Conquerers*. Farrar, Straus & Giroux, 1948.

———. *Anger at Innocence*. Farrar, Straus & Giroux, 1950.

———. *South Street*. Farrar, Straus & Giroux, 1954.

———. *The Stone Face*. Farrar, Straus & Giroux, 1963.

Thurman, Wallace. *The Blacker the Berry*. Macaulay, 1929.

———. *Infants of the Spring*. Macaulay, 1932.

Toomer, Jean. *Cane*. Boni & Liveright, 1923; Harper, 1969.

Turpin, Waters E. *These Low Grounds*. Harper, 1937.

———. *O Canaan!* Doubleday, 1939.

———. *The Rootless*. Vantage, 1957.

Van Dyke, Henry. *Blood of Strawberries*. Farrar, Straus & Giroux, 1968.

———. *Dead Piano*. Farrar, Straus & Giroux, 1971.

Walker, Alice. *The Third Life of Grange Copeland*. Harcourt Brace Jovanovich, 1970.

———. *In Love and Trouble: Stories of Black Women*. Harcourt Brace Jovanovich, 1973.

———. *Meridian*. Harcourt Brace Jovanovich, 1976.

———. *You Can't Keep a Good Woman Down*. Harcourt Brace Jovanovich, 1981.

———. *The Color Purple*. Harcourt Brace Jovanovich, 1982.

———. *The Temple of My Familiar*. Harcourt Brace Jovanovich, 1989.

Walker, Margaret. *Jubilee*. Houghton Mifflin, 1966; Bantam, 1975.

Walrond, Eric. *Tropic Death*. Boni & Liveright, 1926.

Webb, Frank J. *The Garies and Their Friends*. London, 1857; Arno, 1969.

West, Dorothy. *The Living is Easy*. Houghton Mifflin, 1948; Arno, 1969; The Feminist Press, 1982.

West, John B. *Death on the Rocks*. New American Library, 1961.

———. *Never Kill a Cop*. New American Library, 1961.

White, Walter. *The Fire in the Flint*. Knopf, 1924.

———. *Flight*. Knopf, 1926.

Wideman, John Edgar. *A Glance Away*. Harcourt Brace and World, 1967; Chatham Booksellers, 1975; Henry Holt, 1985.

———. *Hurry Home*. Harcourt, 1969; Henry Holt, 1986.
———. *The Lynchers*. Harcourt Brace Jovanovich, 1973; Henry Holt, 1986.
———. *Damballah*. Schocken, 1981; Random House, 1988.
———. *Hiding Place*. Avon Books, 1981; Schocken, 1984; Random House, 1988.
———. *Sent for You Yesterday*. Bard/Avon Books, 1983.
———. *Reuben*. Henry Holt, 1987.
———. *Philadelphia Fire*. Henry Holt, 1990.
Williams, John A. *The Angry Ones*. Ace Books, 1960.
———. *Night Song*. Farrar, Straus & Giroux, 1961.
———. *Sissie*. Farrar, Straus & Giroux, 1963.
———. *The Man Who Cried I Am*. Little, Brown, 1967.
———. *Sons of Darkness, Sons of Light*. Little, Brown, 1969.
———. *Captain Blackman: A Novel*. Doubleday, 1972.
———. *Mothersill and the Foxes*. Doubleday, 1975.
———. *!Clicksong*. Houghton Mifflin, 1982.
———. *Jacob's Ladder*. Thunder's Mouth Press, 1987.
Williams, Sherley Anne. *Dessa Rose*. William Morrow, 1986.
Wilson, Harriet E. *Our Nig*. Rand and Avery, 1859; Vintage Books, 1983.
Wright, Charles, *The Wig, A Mirror Image*. Farrar, Straus & Giroux, 1966.
———. *Absolutely Nothing to Get Alarmed About*. Farrar, Straus & Giroux, 1973.
Wright, Jay. *Homecoming Singer*. Corinth Books, 1971.
Wright, Richard. *Uncle Tom's Children*. Harper, 1938, 1969.
———. *Native Son*. Harper, 1940.
———. *The Outsider*. Harper & Brothers, 1953.
———. *Savage Holiday*. Harper, 1954.
———. *The Long Dream*. Doubleday, 1958.
———. *Eight Men: Stories by Richard Wright*. World, 1961; Thunder's Mouth Press, 1987.
———. *Lawd Today*. Walker, 1963.
Wright, Sara E. *This Child's Gonna Live*. Dell, 1969.
Yerby, Frank. *The Foxes of Harrow*. Dial Press, 1946; Delta Diamond, 1986.
———. *Floodtide*. Dial Press, 1950; Thorndike Press, 1982.
———. *The Old Gods Laugh: A Modern Romance*. Dial Press, 1964.
———. *The Girl From Storyville*. Dial Press, 1972; Heinemann, 1972.
———. *The Voyage Unplanned*. Dial Press, 1974.
———. *Devilseed*. Doubleday, 1984.
———. *McKenzie's Hundred*. Doubleday, 1985.
Young, Al. *Snakes*. Holt, Rinehart & Winston, 1970.
———. *Who Is Angelina?* Holt, Rinehart & Winston, 1975.
———. *Ask Me Now*. McGraw-Hill, 1980.
———. *Seduction by Light*. Delta Fiction, 1988.

V. AUTOBIOGRAPHY

Andrews, William L., ed. *Six Women's Slave Narratives*. Oxford University Press (The Schomburg Library of Nineteenth-Century Black Women Writers), 1988.
Angelou, Maya. *I Know Why the Caged Bird Sings*. Random House, 1969.

————. *Gather Together in My Name*. Random House, 1974; Bantam 1975.

————. *Singin' & Swingin' & Gettin' Merry Like Christmas*. Random House, 1976; Bantam, 1977.

————. *The Heart of a Woman*. Random House, 1981; Bantam 1984.

Baraka, Amiri (a.k.a. LeRoi Jones). *The Autobiography of LeRoi Jones*. Freudlich Books, 1984.

Barthelemy, Anthony G., ed. *Collected Black Women's Narratives*. Oxford University Press (The Schomburg Library of Nineteenth-Century Black Women Writers), 1988.

Barton, Rebecca C. *Witnesses for Freedom: Negro Americans in Autobiography*. Harper, 1948.

Brooks, Gwendolyn Elizabeth. *Report from Part One*. Broadside Press, 1972.

Brown, Claude. *Manchild in the Promised Land*. Macmillan, 1965.

Brown, Hallie Q. *Homespun Heroines and Other Women of Distinction*. Ayer, 1926; Books for Libraries Press, 1971; with introduction by Randall K. Burkett, Oxford University Press (The Schomburg Library of Nineteenth-Century Black Women Writers), 1988.

Brown, Henry Box. *Narrative of Henry Box Brown*. Boston, 1849.

Brown, William Wells. *Narrative of William W. Brown, a Fugitive Slave*. Boston, 1847.

————. *Three Years in Europe: or, Places I Have Seen and People I Have Met*. London, 1852.

Clark, Lewis, and Milton Clark. *Narrative of the Sufferings of Lewis and Milton Clark*. Boston, 1846.

Clifton, Lucille. *Generations: A Memoir*. Random House, 1976.

Craft, William. *Running a Thousand Miles for Freedom; or, The Escape of William and Ellen Craft from Slavery*. London, 1860.

Davis, Angela Y. *Angela Davis: An Autobiography*. Random House, 1974; International Publishers, 1988.

Delany, Samuel R. *Heavenly Breakfast: An Essay on the Winter of Love*. Bantam, 1979.

————. *The Motion of Light in Water: Sex and Science Fiction Writing in the East Village, 1957–1965*. Arbor House, 1988.

Douglass, Frederick. *Narrative of the Life of Frederick Douglass, An American Slave*. Boston, 1845; New American Library and Harvard University Press, 1960.

————. *My Bondage and My Freedom*. New York, 1855.

————. *Life and Times of Frederick Douglass*. Hartford, 1881; Boston, 1892; Pathway Press, 1941; Collier Books, 1962.

Du Bois, W. E. B. *Dusk of Dawn: An Essay Toward an Autobiography of a Race Concept*. Harcourt, 1940; Schocken, 1968.

————. *The Autobiography of W. E. B. Du Bois*. International Publishers, 1968.

Gayle, Addison. *Wayward Child: A Personal Odyssey*. Anchor Press, 1977.

Giovanni, Nikki. *Gemini: An Extended Autobiographical Statement on My First Twenty-Five Years of Being a Black Poet*. Bobbs-Merrill, 1971; Penguin, 1976.

Golden, Marita. *Migrations of the Heart: A Personal Odyssey*. Anchor Press/Doubleday, 1983.

Hammon, Briton. *A Narrative of the Uncommon Sufferings and Surprising Deliverance of Briton Hammon, a Negro Man*. Boston, 1760.

Henson, Josiah. *The Life of Josiah Henson.* Boston, 1849.

———. *Truth Stranger than Fiction: Father Henson's Story of His Own Life.* Boston and Cleveland, 1858.

———. *An Autobiography of Josiah Henson (Mrs. Harriet Beecher Stowe's "Uncle Tom").* London, 1876.

Herndon, Angelo. *Let Me Live.* Arno House, 1937, 1969.

Himes, Chester. *The Quality of Hurt: The Autobiography of Chester Himes* (vol. 1). Doubleday, 1972.

Houchins, Sue E., ed. *Spiritual Narratives: Maria W. Stewart, Jarena Lee, Julia A. J. Foote, Virginia W. Broughton.* Oxford University Press (The Schomburg Library of Nineteenth-Century Black Women Writers), 1988.

Hughes, Langston. *The Big Sea.* Hill & Wang, 1940.

———. *I Wonder as I Wander.* Hill & Wang, 1956.

Hurston, Zora Neale. *Dust Tracks on a Road.* Lippincott, 1942, 1971; University of Illinois Press, 1984.

Jacobs, Harriet (Jean Fagan Yellin, ed.). *Incidents in the Life of a Slave Girl.* Harvard University Press, 1987; Oxford University Press (The Schomburg Library of Nineteenth-Century Black Women Writers), 1988.

Johnson, James Weldon. *Along This Way: The Autobiography of James Weldon Johnson.* Viking, 1933, 1968.

Keckley, Elizabeth. *Behind the Scenes; or, Thirty Years a Slave, and Four Years in the White House.* New York, 1868; Oxford University Press (The Schomburg Library of Nineteenth-Century Black Women Writers), 1988.

Kennedy, Adrienne. *People Who Led to My Plays.* Knopf, 1987.

Lorde, Audre. *The Cancer Journals.* Spinster's Ink, 1980.

———. *Zami: A New Spelling of My Name.* The Crossing Press, 1982.

Marrant, John. *A Narrative of the Lord's Wonderful Dealings with J. Marrant, a Black.* London, 1785.

McKay, Claude. *A Long Way from Home.* Lee Furman, 1937.

Miller, Kelly. *Out of the House of Bondage.* Neale, 1914.

Murray, Pauli. *Proud Shoes.* Harper, 1956.

Nichols, Charles H. *Many Thousand Gone: The Ex-Slaves' Account of Their Bondage and Freedom.* Brill Adler, 1963; Indiana University Press, 1969.

———, comp. *Black Men in Chains: Narratives by Escaped Slaves.* Lawrence Hill, 1972.

Northrup, Solomon (Anonymous). *Twelve Years a Slave: The Narrative of Solomon Northrup.* Auburn, 1853.

Payne, Daniel A. *Recollections of Seventy Years.* Nashville, TN, 1988.

Redding, J. Saunders. *No Day of Triumph.* Harper, 1942.

Robeson, Paul. *Here I Stand.* Othello Associates, 1958.

Roper, Moses. *Narrative of the Adventures and Escapes of Moses Roper, From American Slavery.* London, 1837.

Schuyler, George S. *Black and Conservative.* Arlington House, 1966.

Seacole, Mary. *Wonderful Adventures of Mrs. Seacole in Many Lands.* With introduction by W. L. Andrews, Oxford University Press (The Schomburg Library of Nineteenth-Century Black Women Writers), 1988.

Smith, Amanda. *An Autobiography: The Story of the Lord's Dealings with Mrs. Amanda Smith, the Colored Evangelist.* With introduction by Jualynne E. Dodson, Oxford University Press (The Schomburg Library of Nineteenth-Century Black Women Writers), 1988.

Stevenson, Brenda, ed. *The Journals of Charlotte Forten Grimke.* Oxford University Press (The Schomburg Library of Nineteenth-Century Black Women Writers), 1988.

Truth, Sojourner (Anonymous). *Narrative of Sojourner Truth, Northern Slave.* Boston, 1850.

―――. *Narrative of Sojourner Truth, a Bondswoman of Olden Times.* Boston, 1875.

Vassa, Gustavus. *The Interesting Narrative of the Life of Olaudah Equiano, or Gustavus Vassa, the African.* London, 1789.

Walser, Richard, ed. *The Black Poet; Being the Remarkable Story (partly told by himself) of George Moses Horton, a North Carolina Slave.* Philosophical Library, 1966.

Ward, Samuel Ringgold. *The Autobiography of a Fugitive Negro.* London, 1855.

Washington, Booker Taliaferro. *Up From Slavery; An Autobiography.* New York, 1901.

White, Walter. *A Man Called White.* Viking, 1948.

Wright, Richard. *Black Boy.* Harper, 1945.

X, Malcolm (with Alex Haley). *The Autobiography of Malcolm X.* Grove, 1965.

VI. BIOGRAPHY

Albert, Octavia V. Rogers. *The House of Bondage; or Charlotte Brooks and Other Slaves.* Hunt & Eaton, 1890; Books for Libraries Press, 1972; with introduction by Frances Smith Foster, Oxford University Press (The Schomburg Library of Nineteenth-Century Black Women Writers), 1988.

Benson, Brian Joseph, and Mabel M. Dilliard. *Jean Toomer.* Twayne/G. K. Hall, 1980.

Berry, Faith. *Langston Hughes: Before and Beyond Harlem.* Lawrence Hill & Co., 1983.

Brawley, Benjamin. *Women of Achievement.* Chicago, 1919.

―――. *Paul Laurence Dunbar: Poet of His People.* University of North Carolina Press, 1936; Kennikat Press, 1967.

―――. *Negro Builders and Heroes.* University of North Carolina Press, 1937.

―――. *The Negro Genius.* Dodd, 1937.

Brown, Lloyd W. *Amiri Baraka.* Twayne/G. K. Hall, 1980.

Brown, William Wells. *The Black Man: His Antecedents, His Genius, and His Achievements,* New York and Boston, 1863.

―――. *The Rising Sun; or the Antecedents and Advancement of the Colored Race.* Boston, 1874.

Butcher, Philip. *George W. Cable: The Northampton Years.* Columbia University Press, 1959.

―――. *George W. Cable.* Twayne, 1962.

Cash, E. A. *John A. Williams: The Evolution of a Black Writer.* Okpaku Communications, 1974.

Chesnutt, Charles W. *Frederick Douglass.* Boston, 1899.

Cook, Mercer. *Five French Negro Authors.* Associated Publishers, 1943.

Cooper, Wayne F. *Claude McKay, Rebel Sojourner in the Harlem Renaissance: A Biography*. Louisiana State University Press, 1987.

Cunningham, Virginia. *Paul Laurence Dunbar and His Song*. Dodd, Mead, 1947; Biblo & Tannen, 1969.

Davis, Thadious, and Trudier Harris, eds. *Afro-American Fiction Writers After 1955*. (*Dictionary of Literary Biography*, vol. 33) Gale, 1984.

———. *Afro-American Writers After 1955: Dramatists and Prose Writers* (*Dictionary of Literary Biography*, vol. 38). Gale, 1985.

Dickinson, Donald C. *A Bio-bibliography of Langston Hughes, 1902–1967*. Archon, 1972.

Du Bois, W. E. B. *John Brown*. G. W. Jacobs, 1909; International Publishers, 1962; Metro Books, 1972.

Emanuel, James A. *Langston Hughes*. Twayne, 1967.

Fabre, Michel. *The Unfinished Quest of Richard Wright*. William Morrow, 1973.

Farrison, William E., *William Wells Brown: Author and Reformer*. University of Chicago Press, 1969.

Fauset, Arthur Huff. *Sojourner Truth, God's Faithful Pilgrim*. University of North Carolina Press, 1938.

Ferguson, Blanche E. *Countee Cullen and the Negro Renaissance*. Dodd, Mead, 1966.

Flasch, Joy. *Melvin B. Tolson*. Twayne/G. K. Hall, 1972.

Fleming, Robert E. *Williard Motley*. Twayne/G. K. Hall, 1978.

Franklin, John Hope. *Geroge Washington Williams, A Biography*. University of Chicago Press, 1985.

Gayle, Addison, Jr. *Oak and Ivy: A Biography of Paul Laurence Dunbar*. Doubleday, 1971.

———. *Richard Wright: The Ordeal of a Native Son*. Anchor Press/Doubleday, 1980.

Graham, Shirley. *There Was Once a Slave: The Heroic Story of Frederick Douglass*. Messner, 1947.

———. *Booker T. Washington*. Messner, 1955.

Greene, J. Lee. *Time's Unfading Garden: Ann Spencer's Life and Poetry*. Louisiana State University Press, 1977.

Handy, William C. *Negro Authors and Composers of the United States*. AMS Press, 1976.

Harris, Trudier, ed. *Afro-American Writers, 1940–1955* (*Dictionary of Literary Biography*, vol. 76). Gale, 1988.

Harris, Trudier, and Thadious Davis, eds. *Afro-American Poets Since 1955* (*Dictionary of Literary Biography*, vol. 41). Gale, 1985.

———. *Afro-American Writers Before the Harlem Renaissance* (*Dictionary of Literary Biography*, vol. 50). Gale, 1986.

———. *Afro-American Writers from the Harlem Renaissance to 1940* (*Dictionary of Literary Biography*, vol. 51). Gale, 1987.

Haskins, James. *Always Movin' On: The Life of Langston Hughes*. Watts, 1976.

Hatcher, John. *From the Auroral Darkness: The Life and Poetry of Robert Hayden*. G. Ronald, 1984.

Hemenway, Robert. *Zora Neale Hurston: A Literary Biography*. University of Illinois Press, 1980.

Hughes, Langston. *Famous American Negroes*. Dodd, Mead, 1954.

Hull, Gloria T. *Color, Sex and Poetry: Three Women Writers and the Harlem Renaissance.* Indiana University Press, 1987.

Keller, Frances Richardson. *An American Crusade: The Life of Charles Waddell Chesnutt.* Brigham, 1978.

Kent, George E. *A Life of Gwendolyn Brooks.* University Press of Kentucky, 1990.

Levy, Eugene. *James Weldon Johnson: Black Leader, Black Voice.* University of Chicago Press, 1973.

Linneman, Russell J., ed. *Alain Locke: Reflections on a Modern Renaissance Man.* Louisiana State University Press, 1983.

Longsworth, Polly. *I, Charlotte Forten, Black and Free.* Crowell, 1970.

McKay, Nellie Y. *Jean Toomer, Artist: A Study of His Literary Life and Work, 1894–1936.* University of North Carolina Press, 1984.

Melhem, D. H. *Gwendolyn Brooks: Poetry and the Heroic Voice.* University of Kentucky Press, 1987.

Moore, Jack B. *W. E. B. Du Bois.* Twayne/G. K. Hall, 1981.

Ofari, Earl. *Let Your Motto Be Resistance: The Life and Thought of Henry Highland Garnet.* Beacon Press, 1972.

Ottley, Roi. *The Lonely Warrior: The Life and Times of Robert S. Abbott.* Henry Regnery, 1955.

Peplow, Michael W. *George S. Schuyler.* Twayne/G. K. Hall, 1980.

Perry, Margaret. *A Bio-bibliography of Countee P. Cullen (1903–1946).* Greenwood Press, 1971.

Quarles, Benjamin. *Frederick Douglass.* Associated Publishers, 1948.

Rampersad, Arnold. *The Life of Langston Hughes, Volume I: I, Too, Sing America.* Oxford University Press, 1986.

————. *The Life of Langston Hughes, Volume II: I Dream a World.* Oxford University Press, 1988.

Reddick, Lawrence D. *Crusader Without Violence: A Biography of Martin Luther King, Jr.* Harper, 1959.

Redding, J. Saunders. *The Lonesome Road: The Story of the Negro's Part in America.* Doubleday, 1958.

Render, Sylvia Lyons. *Charles W. Chestnutt.* Twayne/G. K. Hall, 1980.

Robeson, Eslanda Goode. *Paul Robeson, Negro.* Harper, 1930.

Robinson, William H. *Phillis Wheatley in the Black American Beginnings.* Broadside Press, 1975.

Sheppard, Gladys B. *Mary Church Terrell, Respectable Person.* Human Relations Press, 1959.

Shockley, Ann Allen, and Sue P. Chandler. *Living Black American Authors: A Biographical Directory.* R. R. Bowker, 1973.

Simmons, William J. *Men of Mark: Eminent, Progressive & Rising.* Cleveland, 1887; Arno, 1968.

Still, William. *The Underground Rail Road: A Record of Facts, Authentic Narratives, Letters.* Philadelphia, 1872.

Sylvander, Carolyn W. *Jesse Redmon Fauset: Black American Writer.* Whitson, 1980.

Terry, Ellen. *Young Jim: The Early Years of James Weldon Johnson.* Dodd, Mead, 1967.

Troupe, Quincy, ed. *James Baldwin: The Legacy.* Simon & Schuster, 1989.

Turner, Darwin T. *Afro-American Writers.* Appleton-Century-Crofts, 1970.

Wagner, Jean. *Black Poets of the United States: From Paul Laurence Dunbar to Langston Hughes.* University of Illinois Press, 1973.

Walker, Alice. *Langston Hughes, American Poet.* Harper & Row, 1974.

Walker, Margaret. *Richard Wright, Daemonic Genius.* Warner/Amistad, 1988.

Washington, Booker T. *Frederick Douglass.* Philadelphia and London, 1907.

Wegelin, Oscar. *Jupiter Hammon, American Negro Poet: Selections from His Writings and a Bibliography.* Heartman, 1915.

Wideman, John Edgar. *Brothers and Keepers.* Holt, Rinehart & Winston, 1984; Penguin, 1985.

Wiggins, Lida Keck. *The Life and Works of Paul Laurence Dunbar.* Nichols, 1907.

Williams, John A. *The Most Native of Sons: A Biography of Richard Wright.* Doubleday, 1970.

Wright, Richard. *American Hunger.* Harper & Row, 1944, 1977; Thunder's Mouth Press, 1988.

Young, James O. *Black Writers of the Thirties.* Louisiana State University Press, 1973.

VII. ESSAYS

(Note: Book Publications only; for other essays see collections in I and II.)

Baker, Houston, ed. *Reading Black: Essays in the Criticism of African, Caribbean and Black American Literature.* Cornell University Press, 1978.

Baldwin, James. *The Fire Next Time.* Dial, 1955.

————. *Notes of a Native Son.* Beacon Press, 1955.

————. *Nobody Knows My Name.* Dial, 1961; Dell, 1963.

————. *No Name in the Street.* Dial, 1972.

————. *The Devil Finds Work: An Essay.* Dial, 1976.

Baraka, Imamu Amiri (a.k.a. LeRoi Jones). *Daggers and Javelins: Essays, 1974–1979.* William Morrow, 1984.

Benston, Kimberly W., ed. *Imamu Amiri Baraka (LeRoi Jones): A Collection of Critical Essays.* Prentice-Hall, 1978.

Bigsby, C. W. E. *The Second Black Renaissance: Essays in Black Literature.* Greenwood Press, 1980.

————. *The Negro Genius.* Dodd, 1937.

Brown, William Wells. *Three Years in Europe.* London, 1852.

————. *The American Fugitive in Europe.* Boston, Cleveland, and New York, 1855.

————. *My Southern Home; or, the South and Its People.* Boston, 1880.

Bruck, Peter, and Wolfgang Karrer, eds. *The Afro-American Novel Since 1960: A Collection of Critical Essays.* Benjamins North America, 1982.

Butcher, Margaret J. *The Negro in American Culture; Based on Materials Left by Alain Locke.* Knopf, 1956, 1972.

Clarke, John Henrik, ed. *William Styron's "Nat Turner": Ten Black Writers Respond.* Beacon Press, 1968.

Cleaver, Eldridge. *Soul on Ice.* McGraw-Hill, 1968.

Cooke, Michael G., ed. *Modern Black Novelists: A Collection of Critical Essays.* Prentice-Hall, 1971.

Cruse, Harold. *The Crisis of the Negro Intellectual.* William Morrow, 1967.

Davis, Charles T., and Henry Louis Gates, Jr., eds. *Black is the Color of the Cosmos: Essays on Afro-American Literature and Culture, 1942–1981.* Garland, 1982; Howard University Press, 1989.

Du Bois, W. E. B. *The Souls of Black Folk.* A. C. McClurg, 1903.

———. *Darkwater.* Harcourt, 1920.

———. *The Gifts of Black Folk.* Associated Publishers, 1924.

Ellison, Ralph. *Shadow and Act.* Random House, 1964.

Garnet, Henry Highland. *The Past and Present Condition and Destiny of the Colored Race, A Discourse Delivered at the Fifteenth Anniversary of the Female Benevolent Society of Troy, New York, February 14, 1848.* Mnemosyne, 1969.

Gayle, Addison, Jr., ed. *Black Expression: Essays By and About Black Americans in the Creative Arts.* Weybright and Talley, 1969.

———. *The Black Situation.* Horizon, 1970.

———, ed. *Modern Black Poets: A Collection of Critical Essays.* Prentice-Hall, 1973.

Giovanni, Nikki. *Sacred Cows and Other Edibles.* William Morrow, 1988.

Giovanni, Nikki, and Margaret Walker. *A Poetic Equation: Conversations Between Nikki Giovanni and Margaret Walker.* Howard University Press, 1974, 1983.

Goldwin, Robert A., ed. *Civil Disobedience: Five Essays by Martin Luther King, Jr., and Others.* Public Affairs Conference Center, Kenyon College, 1968.

Gross, Seymour, and John E. Hardy, eds. *Images of the Negro in American Literature: Essays in Criticism.* University of Chicago Press, 1966.

Hurston, Zora Neale. *Mules and Men.* Lippincott, 1935; Indiana University Press, 1978.

———. *Tell My Horse.* Lippincott, 1938.

———. *The Sanctified Church.* Turtle Island Foundation, 1983.

Inge, M. Thomas, Maurice Duke, and Jackson R. Bryer, eds. *Black American Writers: Bibliographical Essays.* 2 vols. St. Martin's Press, 1976.

Jackson, Blyden. *The Waiting Years: Essays on American Negro Literature.* Louisiana State University Press, 1976.

Jackson, Blyden, and Louis D. Rubin, Jr. *Black Poetry in America: Two Essays in Historical Interpretation.* Louisiana State University Press, 1974.

Jones, LeRoi (a.k.a. Amiri Baraka). *Home: Social Essays.* William Morrow, 1966.

———. *Raise, Race, Rays, Raze: Essays Since 1965.* Random House, 1971.

———, ed. *The Moderns: New Fiction in America.* Corinth, 1966.

Kaiser, Ernest. *Freedomways Reader: Afro-Americans in the Seventies.* International Publishers, 1977.

Killens, John Oliver. *Black Man's Burden.* Simon & Schuster, 1965.

King, Martin Luther, Jr. *Stride Toward Freedom: The Montgomery Story.* Harper & Row, 1958.

———. *Strength to Love.* Harper & Row, 1963; Fortress Press, 1981.

———. *Why We Can't Wait.* Harper & Row, 1964.

———. *Nobel Lecture by the Reverend Dr. Martin Luther King, Jr.* Harper & Row, 1965; Clarke & Way, 1965.

———. *Conscience for Change.* Canadian Broadcasting Company, 1967.

———. *The Measure of a Man.* Pilgrim Press, 1968; Fortress Press, 1988.

———. *The Trumpet of Conscience.* Harper & Row, 1968.

———. *Where Do We Go From Here?: Chaos or Community?* Hodder & Stoughton, 1968.

Lee, Don L. (a.k.a. Haki R. Madhubuti). *From Plan to Planet.* Broadside Press, 1973.

Lester, Julius. *Search for the New Land.* Dial, 1970.

———. *Look Out, Whitey! Black Power's Gonna Git Your Mama!* Dial, 1968.

———. *Lovesong: Becoming a Jew.* Henry Holt, 1988.

Lorde, Audre. *Sister Outsider: Essays and Speeches.* The Crossing Press, 1984.

———. *A Burst of Light.* Firebrand Books, 1988.

Madhubuti, Haki R. (a.k.a. Don L. Lee). *Black Men: Obsolete, Single, Dangerous?* Third World Press, 1989.

Miller, Kelly. *Race Adjustment.* Neal, 1908.

———. *The Everlasting Stain.* Associated Publishers, 1924.

Nichols, Charles, ed. *Arna Bontemps/Langston Hughes: Letters, 1925–1967.* Dodd, Mead, 1980.

O'Daniel, Therman B., ed. *Langston Hughes, Black Genius: A Critical Evaluation.* William Morrow, 1971.

Plato, Ann. *Essays: Including Biographies and Miscellaneous Pieces, in Prose and Poetry.* With introduction by Kenny J. Williams, Oxford University Press (The Schomburg Library of Nineteenth-Century Black Women Writers), 1988.

Pratt, Louis H., and Fred L. Standley, eds. *Conversation with James Baldwin.* University Press of Mississippi, 1989.

Redding, J. Saunders. *On Being Negro in America.* Bobbs-Merrill, 1951, 1962.

Reed, Ishmael. *Shrovetide in Old New Orleans.* Doubleday, 1978; Avon Books, 1979.

———. *God Made Alaska for the Indians: Selected Essays.* Garland, 1982.

———. *Writin' is Fightin': 37 Years of Boxing on Paper.* Atheneum, 1988.

Ro, Sigmund. *Rage and Celebration: Essays on Contemporary Afro-American Writing.* Humanities Press, 1984.

Robinson, William H., ed. *Critical Essays on Phillis Wheatley.* G. K. Hall, 1982.

Scott, Nathan A., Jr. *Modern Literature and the Religious Frontier.* Harper, 1958.

———. *The Broken Center: Studies in the Theological Horizon of Modern Literature.* Yale University Press, 1966.

———. *Craters of the Spirit: Studies in the Modern Novel.* Corpus, 1968.

———. *Negative Capability: Studies in the New Literature and the Religious Situation.* Yale University Press, 1969.

Shange, Ntozake. *See No Evil: Prefaces, Essays, & Accounts, 1976–1983.* Momo's Press, 1984.

Sheffey, Ruthe T. *Trajectory: Fueling the Future and Preserving the Black Literary Past, Essays in Criticism.* Morgan State University Press, 1986.

Turner, Darwin T., ed. *Black American Literature: Essays.* Charles E. Merrill, 1969.

Walker, Alice. *In Search of Our Mothers' Gardens: Womanist Prose.* Harcourt Brace Jovanovich, 1983.

———. *Living by the Word: Selected Writings, 1973–1987.* Harcourt Brace Jovanovich, 1988.

Walker, Margaret. *How I Wrote Jubilee.* Third World Press, 1977; reissued as *How I Wrote Jubilee, and Other Essays on Life and Literature,* The Feminist Press, 1989.

Washington, Booker T. *The Future of the American Negro.* New York, 1899.

———. (with W. E. B. Du Bois) *The Negro in the South.* G. W. Jacobs, 1907.

Williams, John A. *This Is My Country, Too.* New American Library, 1965; Signet, 1966.

Wright, Richard. *Black Power.* Harper, 1954.
———. *Pagan Spain.* Harper, 1957.
———. *White Man, Listen!* Doubleday, 1957.

VIII. DRAMA
(book publication only)

ANTHOLOGIES, COLLECTIONS, AND CRITICAL COMMENTARY

Abramson, Dorothy. *Negro Playwrights in the American Theatre: 1925–59.* Columbia University Press, 1969.
Adams, William et al., eds. *Afro-American Literature: Drama.* Houghton Mifflin, 1979.
Arata, Esther S. *More Black American Playwrights: A Bibliography.* Scarecrow, 1978.
Arata, Esther S., and Nicholas J. Rotoli. *Black American Playwrights, 1800 to Present: A Bibliography.* Scarecrow, 1976.
Archer, Leonard C. *Black Images in the American Theatre.* Pageant-Poseidon, 1973.
Benston, Kimberly. *Baraka: The Renegade and the Mask.* Yale University Press, 1976.
Bond, Frederick W. *The Negro and the Drama.* Associated Publishers, 1940; McGrath, 1969.
Brown, Sterling A. *Negro Poetry and Drama.* Associates in Negro Folk Education, 1937; Atheneum, 1969.
Brown-Guillory, Elizabeth. *Their Place on the Stage: Black Women Playwrights in America.* Greenwood Press, 1988.
Childress, Alice, ed. *Black Scenes.* Doubleday, 1971.
Couch, William, Jr., ed. *New Black Playwrights: An Anthology.* Louisiana State University Press, 1968; Avon, 1970.
Craig, E. Quita. *Black Drama of the Federal Theatre Era: Beyond the Formal Horizons.* University of Massachusetts Press, 1980.
Davis, Thadious M. and Trudier Harris, eds. *Afro-American Writers After 1955: Dramatists and Prose Writers* (*Dictionary of Literary Biography*, vol. 38). Gale Research, 1985.
Dent, Thomas, C., Gilbert Moses, and Richard Schechner. *The Free Southern Theatre by the Free Southern Theatre.* Bobbs-Merrill, 1969.
Fabre, Genevieve (Melvin Dixon, trans.). *Drumbeats, Masks, and Metaphor: Contemporary Afro-American Theatre.* Harvard University Press, 1983.
Fletcher, Tom. *100 Years of the Negro in Show Business.* Burdge, 1954.
French, William P., Michel J. Fabre, and Amritjit Singh. *Afro-American Poetry and Drama, 1760–1975.* Gale Research, 1979.
Harrison, Paul Carter. *The Drama of Nommo.* Grove, 1972.
Hatch, James V. *Black Image on the American Stage: A Bibliography of Plays and Musicals, 1770–1970.* Drama Book Specialists, 1970.
Hatch, James, and Ted Shine, eds. *Black Theatre, U.S.A.: Forty-five Plays by Black Americans, 1847–1974.* The Free Press, 1974.
Hatch, James, and Omanii Abdullah, comps. and eds. *Black Playwrights 1823–1977: An Annotated Bibliography of Plays.* R. R. Bowker, 1977.
Hill, Errol, ed. *The Theatre of Black Americans.* 2 vols. Prentice-Hall, 1980.
Isaacs, Edith. *The Negro in the American Theatre.* Theatre Arts, 1947.

Jerome, V. J. *The Negro in Hollywood Films*. Masses & Mainstream, 1950.

Kennedy, Adrienne. *People Who Lead to My Plays*. Knopf, 1987.

Keyssar, Helene. *The Curtain and the Veil: Strategies in Black Drama*. Franklin, 1980.

King, Woodie. *Black Theatre, Present Condition*. National Black Theatre Touring Circuit, 1981.

Locke, Alain LeRoy, and Montgomery Gregory, eds. *Plays of Negro Life*. Harper, 1927; Negro Universities Press, 1970.

Mitchell, Loften. *Black Drama: The Story of the American Negro in the Theatre*. Hawthorne Books, 1967.

Noble, Peter. *The Cinema and the Negro, 1905–1948*. Gordon, 1980.

Null, Gary. *Black Hollywood: The Negro in Motion Pictures*. Citadel, 1977.

Oliver, Clinton F., and Stephanie Sills, eds. *Contemporary Black Drama: From A Raisin in the Sun to No Place to Be Somebody*. Scribners, 1971.

Ostrow, Eileen Joyce, ed. *Center Stage: An Anthology of 21 Contemporary Black American Plays*. Sea Urchin, 1981.

Patterson, Lindsay, ed. *Anthology of the American Negro in the Theatre: A Critical Approach*. Publishers Co., 1967.

———, ed. *Black Theatre: A Twentieth-Century Collection of the Works of its Best Playwrights*. Dodd, Mead, 1971; New American Library, 1973.

TDR. *Black Theatre Issue: T-40, Summer*. TDR, 1968.

Turner, Darwin T., ed. *Black Drama in America: An Anthology*. Fawcett, 1971.

Wittke, Carl. *Tambo and Bones: A History of the American Minstrel Stage*. Duke University Press, 1930.

Woll, Allen. *Dictionary of the Black Theatre: Broadway, Off-Broadway, and Selected Harlem Theatre*. Greenwood Press, 1983.

PLAYS IN PRINT

Amis, Lola Jones. *Three Plays*. Exposition, 1965.

Baldwin, James. *Blues for Mr. Charlie*. Dial, 1964.

———. *The Amen Corner*. Dial, 1968.

———. *One Day When I Was Lost: A Scenario Based on The Autobiography of Malcolm X*. Michael Joseph, 1972.

Baraka, Amiri (a.k.a. LeRoi Jones). *Selected Plays and Prose of Amiri Baraka/LeRoi Jones*. William Morrow, 1979.

Brown, William Wells. *The Escape; or A Leap for Freedon—A Drama in Five Acts*. Boston, 1858; Historic Publications, 1969.

Bullins, Ed. *How Do You Do: A Nonsense Drama*. Illuminations Press, 1967.

———. *Five Plays by Ed Bullins*. Bobbs-Merrill, 1969; revised as *The Electronic Nigger and Other Plays*, Faber & Faber, 1970.

———. *The Duplex: A Black Love Fable in Four Movements*. William Morrow, 1971.

———. *Four Dynamite Plays*. William Morrow, 1972.

———. *The Theme is Blackness: The Corner and Other Plays*. William Morrow, 1972.

———, ed. *New Plays from the Black Theatre*. Bantam, 1969.

———, ed. *The New Lafayette Theatre Presents: Plays with Aesthetic Comments by Six Black Playwrights*. Doubleday, 1974.

Caldwell, Ben. *Prayer Meeting (Or, The First Militant Minister)*. Jihad, 1967.

Carter, Steve. *Nevis Mountain Dew*. Dramatists Play Service, 1980.

Childress, Alice. *Wine in the Wilderness: A Comedy-Drama*. Dramatists Play Service, 1969.

———. *Mojo and String*. Dramatists Play Service, 1971.

———. *Wedding Band: A Love/Hate Story in Black and White*. Samuel French, 1973.

———. *Where the Rattlesnake Sounds: A Play about Harriet Tubman*. Coward, McCann & Geoghegan, 1975.

———. *Let's Hear It for the Queen*. Coward, 1976.

Cotter, Joseph Seamon, Sr. *Caleb, the Degenerate: A Play in Four Acts*. Bradley & Gilbert, 1903; New York, 1940.

Davis, Ossie. *Purlie Victorious: A Comedy in Three Acts*. Samuel French, 1961, 1971.

———. *Escape to Freedom: A Play About Young Frederick Douglass*. Viking, 1978.

———. *Langston: A Play*. Delacorte, 1982.

Dean, Darryl. *Family Reunion*. The Dramatic Publishing Co., 1979.

Dean, Phillip Hayes. *This Bird of Dawning Singeth All Night Long*. Dramatists Play Service, 1971.

———. *American Night Cry*. Dramatists Play Service, 1972.

———. *The Sty of the Blind Pig*. Dramatists Play Service, 1972.

———. *Freeman*. Dramatists Play Service, 1973.

———. *Every Night When the Sun Goes Down*. Dramatists Play Service, 1976.

———. *Paul Robeson*. Nelson Doubleday, 1978.

Edmonds, Randolph. *Shades and Shadows*. Meador, 1930.

———. *Six Plays for a Negro Theatre*. W. H. Baker, 1934.

———. *Land of Cotton and Other Plays*. Associated Publishers, 1942.

———. *Earth and Stars*. Florida A & M University, 1961.

Edwards, Gus. *The Offering*. Dramatists Play Service, 1978.

———. *Old Phantoms*. Dramatists Play Service, 1979.

Elder, Lonnie III. *Ceremonies in Dark Old Men*. Farrar, Straus & Giroux, 1969.

Evans, Don. *The Prodigals*. Dramatists Play Service, 1977.

Franklin, J. E. *Black Girl: From Genesis to Revelations*. Howard University Press, 1977.

Fuller, Charles. *A Soldier's Play*. Nelson Doubleday, 1982; Hill & Wang, 1982.

———. *Zooman and the Sign*. Nelson Doubleday, 1982; Samuel French, 1982.

Gordone, Charles. *No Place to Be Somebody*. Bobbs-Merrill, 1969.

Goss, Clay. *Homecookin': Five Plays*. Howard University Press, 1974.

Graham, Arthur. *The Nationals: A Black Happening of Many Minds*. Black Book Production, 1968.

Grimke, Angelina. *Rachel*. Cornhill, 1920.

Gunn, Bill. *Black Picture Show*. Reed, Cannon & Johnson, 1975.

Hansberry, Lorraine. *A Raisin in the Sun*. Signet/New American Library, 1959.

———. *The Sign in Sidney Brustein's Window*. Random House, 1965.

———. *Les Blancs and the Last Plays of Lorraine Hansberry*. Random House, 1972.

———. (Robert Nemiroff, ed.). *The Collected Last Plays of Lorraine Hansberry*. Random House, 1972; New American Library, 1983.

Harrison, Paul Carter, ed. *Kuntu Drama: Plays of the African Continuum*. Grove Press, 1974.

Hill, Leslie Pinckney. *Toussaint L'Ouverture*. Christopher, 1928.

Hughes, Langston. *Tambourines to Glory*. Day, 1958.

————. (W. Smalley, ed.). *Five Plays.* University of Indiana Press, 1963.

Johnson, Georgia Douglas. *Plumes.* Samuel French, 1927.

Jones, LeRoi (a.k.a. Imamu Baraka). *Dutchman; and the Slave.* William Morrow, 1964; Faber & Faber, 1965.

————. *The Baptism and The Toilet.* Grove, 1967.

————. *Four Black Revolutionary Plays.* Bobbs-Merrill, 1969.

————. *Slave Ship.* Jihad, 1969.

————. *J-E-L-L-O.* Third World Press, 1970.

————. *The Motion of History and Other Plays.* William Morrow, 1978.

————. *The Sidney Poet Heroical.* I. Reed Books, 1979.

Kennedy, Adrienne. *Cities in Bezique.* Samuel French, 1969.

————. *Funnyhouse of a Negro.* Samuel French, 1969.

King, Woodie, ed. *A Black Quartet: Four Plays by Amiri Baraka, Ed Bullins, Ben Caldwell, and Ron Milner.* New American Library, 1970.

Lee, Leslie. *The First Breeze of Summer.* Samuel French, 1975.

Mackey, William Wellington. *Behold: Cometh the Vanderkellans!* Azazel Books, 1966; Azakiel Press, 1967.

Milner, Ron. *What the Winesellers Buy.* Samuel French, 1974.

Mitchell, Loften. *A Land Beyond the River.* Pioneer Drama Service, 1963.

————. *Tell Pharaoh.* Negro Universities Press, 1970.

Molette, Carlton, and Barbara Molette. *Rosalee Prichett.* Dramatists Play Service, 1972.

O'Neal, Regina. *Three Television Plays.* Broadside Press, 1974.

Peterson, Louis S. *Take a Giant Step.* Samuel French, 1954.

Richardson, Willis. *Plays and Pageants from the Life of the Negro.* Associated Publishers, 1930.

Richardson, Willis, and May Miller. *Negro History in Thirteen Plays.* Associated Publishers, 1935.

Russell, Charles. *Five on the Black Hand Side.* Samuel French, 1970.

Shange, Ntozake. *For Colored Girls Who Have Considered Suicide When the Rainbow is Enuf: A Choreopoem.* Macmillan, 1977.

————. *From Okra to Greens: A Different Love Story.* Coffee House Press, 1984.

Shears, Carl S. (a.k.a Sagitarius). *I Am Ishmael, Son of Blackamoor.* Nuclassics and Science, 1975.

Shine, Ted. *Contributions.* Dramatists Play Service, 1970.

Spence, Eulalie. *Fool's Errand.* Samuel French, 1927.

————. *Foreign Mail.* Samuel French, 1927.

Stuart, Nuba-Harold. *Hunter!* (revised and rewritten). Samuel French, 1980.

Van Peebles, Melvin. *Sweet Sweetback's Baadasss Song.* Lancer Books, 1971.

————. *Don't Play Us Cheap.* Bantam Books, 1973.

Van Peebles, Melvin, in Collaboration with Paul Carter Harrison. *Ain't Supposed to Die a Natural Death.* Bantam Books, 1973.

Wadud, Ali. *Companions of the Fire.* Dramatists Play Service, 1980.

Walker, Joseph A. *The River Niger.* Hill & Wang, 1973.

Ward, Douglass Turner. *Happy Ending and Day of Absence: Two Plays.* Dramatists Play Service, 1966; Joseph Okpaku, 1966.

————. *The Reckoning.* Dramatists Play Service, 1970.

Wesley, Richard. *The Sirens.* Dramatists Play Service, 1975.

———. *The Mighty Gents.* Dramatists Play Service, 1979.

———. *The Past is the Past and Gettin' It Together.* Dramatists Play Service, 1979.

White, Edgar B. *Underground: Four Plays.* William Morrow, 1970.

———. *The Crucificado: Two Plays.* William Morrow, 1973.

———. *Lament for Rastafari and Other Plays.* Boyars, 1983.

Williams, Samm-Art. *Home.* Nelson Doubleday, 1978; Dramatists Play Service, 1980.

Wilson, August. *Fences.* New American Library/Plume, 1986.

———. *Ma Rainey's Black Bottom.* New American Library/Plume, 1985.

Wright, Jay. *Balloons: A Comedy in One Act.* Baker's Plays, 1968.

Wright, Richard (with Paul Green). *Native Son: A Play in Ten Scenes.* Harper, 1941; Samuel French, 1980.

INDEX